S0-AUP-443

12TH EDITION
REVIEW

The only study guide with more than 800 past GMAT® questions—and their answers—by the creators of the test.

~The~
OFFICIAL
Guide

THE OFFICIAL GUIDE FOR GMAT® REVIEW, 12TH EDITION

- Actual questions from past GMAT tests
- Diagnostic section helps you assess where to focus your test-prep efforts
- Insights into the GMAT exam that debunk test-taking myths

From the Graduate Management Admission Council®

THE OFFICIAL GUIDE FOR GMAT® REVIEW, 12TH EDITION

This edition published by John Wiley & Sons Ltd, The Atrium, Southern Gate, Chichester, West Sussex, PO19 8SQ, United Kingdom.

For details of our global editorial offices, for customer services and for information about how to apply for permission to reuse the copyright material in this book please see our website at www.wiley.com.

Wiley also publishes its books in a variety of electronic formats. Some content that appears in print may not be available in electronic books.

Library of Congress Control Number: 2008940699

A catalogue record for this book is available from the British Library.

ISBN: 978-0-470-74451-2

Printed in Asia

10 9 8 7 6 5 4 3 2

Book production by Wiley Publishing, Inc. Composition Services
Charles Forster, Designer
Mike Wilson, Production Designer

Table of Contents

Dear Future Business Leader,

By using this book to prepare for the GMAT® test, you are taking a very important step toward gaining admission to a high-quality business or management program and achieving a rewarding career in management. I applaud your decision.

The Graduate Management Admission Council® developed the GMAT test more than 50 years ago to help leading graduate schools of business and management choose the applicants who best suit their programs. Today, the test is used by more than 1,800 graduate programs and is given to test takers daily in more than 110 countries around the world. Programs that use GMAT scores in selective admissions have helped establish the MBA degree as a hallmark of excellence worldwide.

Why do GMAT scores matter so much? Other admissions factors—such as work experience, grades, admissions essays, and interviews—can say something about who you are and what you have done in your career, but only your GMAT scores can tell schools how you are likely to perform academically in the business school courses that are fundamental to the MBA degree. In fact, the test has been proven reliable as a predictor of academic performance for more than half a century.

In other words, business schools that require you to take the GMAT really care about the quality of their student body. And excellent MBA students mean a stronger MBA program, a more enriching learning environment, and a more valuable degree for you to take into the business world. By enrolling in a school that uses the GMAT test for your graduate business degree, you will maximize the value of your degree, and that value will pay off in many ways, throughout your career.

I wish you great success in preparing for this important next step in your professional education, and I wish you a very rewarding management career.

Sincerely

David A. Wilson
President and CEO
Graduate Management Admission Council®

1.0   What Is the GMAT®?

1.0 What Is the GMAT®?

The Graduate Management Admission Test® (GMAT®) is a standardized, three-part test delivered in English. The test was designed to help admissions officers evaluate how suitable individual applicants are for their graduate business and management programs. It measures basic verbal, mathematical, and analytical writing skills that a test taker has developed over a long period of time through education and work.

The GMAT test does not measure a person's knowledge of specific fields of study. Graduate business and management programs enroll people from many different undergraduate and work backgrounds, so rather than test your mastery of any particular subject area, the GMAT test will assess your acquired skills. Your GMAT score will give admissions officers a statistically reliable measure of how well you are likely to perform academically in the core curriculum of a graduate business program.

Of course, there are many other qualifications that can help people succeed in business school and in their careers—for instance, job experience, leadership ability, motivation, and interpersonal skills. The GMAT test does not gauge these qualities. That is why your GMAT score is intended to be used as one standard admissions criterion among other, more subjective, criteria, such as admissions essays and interviews.

1.1 Why Take the GMAT® Test?

GMAT scores are used by admissions officers in roughly 1,800 graduate business and management programs worldwide. Schools that require prospective students to submit GMAT scores in the application process are generally interested in admitting the best-qualified applicants for their programs, which means that you may find a more beneficial learning environment at schools that require GMAT scores as part of your application.

Because the GMAT test gauges skills that are important to successful study of business and management at the graduate level, your scores will give you a good indication of how well prepared you are to succeed academically in a graduate management program; how well you do on the test may also help you choose the business schools to which you apply. Furthermore, the percentile table you receive with your scores will tell you how your performance on the test compares to the performance of other test takers, giving you one way to gauge your competition for admission to business school.

Myth -vs- **FACT**

M – **If I don't score in the 90th percentile, I won't get into any school I choose.**

F – **Very few people get very high scores.**

Fewer than 50 of the more than 200,000 people taking the GMAT test each year get a perfect score of 800. Thus, while you may be exceptionally capable, the odds are against your achieving a perfect score. Also, the GMAT test is just one piece of your application packet. Admissions officers use GMAT scores in conjunction with undergraduate records, application essays, interviews, letters of recommendation, and other information when deciding whom to accept into their programs.

Schools consider many different aspects of an application before making an admissions decision, so even if you score well on the GMAT test, you should contact the schools that interest you to learn more about them and to ask about how they use GMAT scores and other admissions criteria (such as your undergraduate grades, essays, and letters of recommendation) to evaluate candidates for admission. School admissions offices, school Web sites, and materials published by the school are the best sources for you to tap when you are doing research about where you might want to go to business school.

For more information about how schools should use GMAT scores in admissions decisions, please read Appendix A of this book. For more information on the GMAT, registering to take the test, sending your scores to schools, and applying to business school, please visit our Web site at www.mba.com.

1.2 GMAT® Test Format

The GMAT test consists of four separately timed sections (see the table on the next page). You start the test with two 30-minute Analytical Writing Assessment (AWA) questions that require you to type your responses using the computer keyboard. The writing section is followed by two 75-minute, multiple-choice sections: the Quantitative and Verbal sections of the test.

The GMAT is a computer-adaptive test (CAT), which means that in the multiple-choice sections of the test, the computer constantly gauges how well you are doing on the test and presents you with questions that are appropriate to your ability level. These questions are drawn from a huge pool of possible test questions. So, although we talk about the GMAT as one test, the GMAT test you take may be completely different from the test of the person sitting next to you.

Here's how it works. At the start of each GMAT multiple-choice section (Verbal and Quantitative), you will be presented with a question of moderate difficulty. The computer uses your response to that first question to determine which question to present next. If you respond correctly, the test usually will give you questions of increasing difficulty. If you respond incorrectly, the next question you see usually will be easier than the one you answered incorrectly. As you continue to respond to the questions presented, the computer will narrow your score to the number that best characterizes your ability. When you complete each section, the computer will have an accurate assessment of your ability.

Myth -vs- FACT

M – Getting an easier question means I answered the last one wrong.

F – Getting an easier question does not necessarily mean you got the previous question wrong.

To ensure that everyone receives the same content, the test selects a specific number of questions of each type. The test may call for your next question to be a relatively hard problem-solving item involving arithmetic operations. But, if there are no more relatively difficult problem-solving items involving arithmetic, you might be given an easier item.

Most people are not skilled at estimating item difficulty, so don't worry when taking the test or waste valuable time trying to determine the difficulty of the questions you are answering.

Because each question is presented on the basis of your answers to all previous questions, you must answer each question as it appears. You may not skip, return to, or change your responses to previous questions. Random guessing can significantly lower your scores. If you do not know the answer to a question, you should try to eliminate as many choices as possible, then select the answer you think is best. If you answer a question incorrectly by mistake—or correctly by lucky guess— your answers to subsequent questions will lead you back to questions that are at the appropriate level of difficulty for you.

Each multiple-choice question used in the GMAT test has been thoroughly reviewed by professional test developers. New multiple-choice questions are tested each time the test is administered. Answers to trial questions are not counted in the scoring of your test, but the trial questions are not identified and could appear anywhere in the test. Therefore, you should try to do your best on every question.

The test includes the types of questions found in this guide, but the format and presentation of the questions are different on the computer. When you take the test:

- Only one question at a time is presented on the computer screen.

- The answer choices for the multiple-choice questions will be preceded by circles, rather than by letters.

- Different question types appear in random order in the multiple-choice sections of the test.

- You must select your answer using the computer.

- You must choose an answer and confirm your choice before moving on to the next question.

- You may not go back to change answers to previous questions.

Format of the GMAT®		
	Questions	Timing

Analytical Writing
    Analysis of an Argument
    Analysis of an Issue
	
	1
	1
		
		30 min.
		30 min.

Optional break		

Quantitative
    Problem Solving
    Data Sufficiency
	37	75 min.

Optional break		

Verbal
    Reading Comprehension
    Critical Reasoning
    Sentence Correction
	41	75 min.

	Total Time:	210 min.

1.3 What Is the Content of the Test Like?

It is important to recognize that the GMAT test evaluates skills and abilities developed over a relatively long period of time. Although the sections contain questions that are basically verbal and mathematical, the complete test provides one method of measuring overall ability.

Keep in mind that although the questions in this guide are arranged by question type and ordered from easy to difficult, the test is organized differently. When you take the test, you may see different types of questions in any order.

1.4 Quantitative Section

The GMAT Quantitative section measures your ability to reason quantitatively, solve quantitative problems, and interpret graphic data.

Two types of multiple-choice questions are used in the Quantitative section:

- Problem solving
- Data sufficiency

Problem solving and data sufficiency questions are intermingled throughout the Quantitative section. Both types of questions require basic knowledge of:

- Arithmetic
- Elementary algebra
- Commonly known concepts of geometry

To review the basic mathematical concepts that will be tested in the GMAT Quantitative questions, see the math review in chapter 4. For test-taking tips specific to the question types in the Quantitative section of the GMAT test, sample questions, and answer explanations, see chapters 5 and 6.

1.5 Verbal Section

The GMAT Verbal section measures your ability to read and comprehend written material, to reason and evaluate arguments, and to correct written material to conform to standard written English. Because the Verbal section includes reading sections from several different content areas, you may be generally familiar with some of the material; however, neither the reading passages nor the questions assume detailed knowledge of the topics discussed.

Three types of multiple-choice questions are used in the Verbal section:

- Reading comprehension
- Critical reasoning
- Sentence correction

These question types are intermingled throughout the Verbal section.

For test-taking tips specific to each question type in the Verbal section, sample questions, and answer explanations, see chapters 7 through 9.

1.6 What Computer Skills Will I Need?

You only need minimal computer skills to take the GMAT Computer-Adaptive Test (CAT). You will be required to type your essays on the computer keyboard using standard word-processing keystrokes. In the multiple-choice sections, you will select your responses using either your mouse or the keyboard.

To learn more about the specific skills required to take the GMAT CAT, download the free test-preparation software available at www.mba.com.

1.7 What Are the Test Centers Like?

The GMAT test is administered at a test center providing the quiet and privacy of individual computer workstations. You will have the opportunity to take two optional breaks—one after completing the essays and another between the Quantitative and Verbal sections. An erasable notepad will be provided for your use during the test.

1.8 How Are Scores Calculated?

Your GMAT scores are determined by:

- The number of questions you answer
- Whether you answer correctly or incorrectly
- The level of difficulty and other statistical characteristics of each question

Your Verbal, Quantitative, and Total GMAT scores are determined by a complex mathematical procedure that takes into account the difficulty of the questions that were presented to you and how you answered them. When you answer the easier questions correctly, you get a chance to answer harder questions—making it possible to earn a higher score. After you have completed all the questions on the test—or when your time is up—the computer will calculate your scores. Your scores on the Verbal and Quantitative sections are combined to produce your Total score. If you have not responded to all the questions in a section (37 Quantitative questions or 41 Verbal questions), your score is adjusted, using the proportion of questions answered.

Appendix A contains the 2007 percentile ranking tables that explain how your GMAT scores compare with scores of other 2007 GMAT test takers.

1.9 Analytical Writing Assessment Scores

The Analytical Writing Assessment consists of two writing tasks: Analysis of an Issue and Analysis of an Argument. The responses to each of these tasks are scored on a 6-point scale, with 6 being the highest score and 1, the lowest. A score of zero (0) is given to responses that are off-topic, are in a foreign language, merely attempt to copy the topic, consist only of keystroke characters, or are blank.

The readers who evaluate the responses are college and university faculty members from various subject matter areas, including management education. These readers read holistically—that is, they respond to the overall quality of your critical thinking and writing. (For details on how readers are qualified, visit www.mba.com.) In addition, responses may be scored by an automated scoring program designed to reflect the judgment of expert readers.

Each response is given two independent ratings. If the ratings differ by more than a point, a third reader adjudicates. (Because of ongoing training and monitoring, discrepant ratings are rare.)

Your final score is the average (rounded to the nearest half point) of the four scores independently assigned to your responses—two scores for the Analysis of an Issue and two for the Analysis of an Argument. For example, if you earned scores of 6 and 5 on the Analysis of an Issue and 4 and 4 on the Analysis of an Argument, your final score would be 5: $(6 + 5 + 4 + 4) \div 4 = 4.75$, which rounds up to 5.

Your Analytical Writing Assessment scores are computed and reported separately from the multiple-choice sections of the test and have no effect on your Verbal, Quantitative, or Total scores. The schools that you have designated to receive your scores may receive your responses to the Analytical Writing Assessment with your score report. Your own copy of your score report will not include copies of your responses.

1.10 Test Development Process

The GMAT test is developed by experts who use standardized procedures to ensure high-quality, widely appropriate test material. All questions are subjected to independent reviews and are revised or discarded as necessary. Multiple-choice questions are tested during GMAT test administrations. Analytical Writing Assessment tasks are tried out on first-year business school students and then assessed for their fairness and reliability. For more information on test development, see www. mba.com.

2.0   How to Prepare

2.0 How to Prepare

2.1 How Can I Best Prepare to Take the Test?

We at the Graduate Management Admission Council® (GMAC®) firmly believe that the test-taking skills you can develop by using this guide—and the Verbal and Quantitative guides, if you want additional practice—are all you need to perform your best when you take the GMAT® test. By answering questions that have appeared on the GMAT test before, you will gain experience with the types of questions you may see on the test when you take it. As you practice with this guide, you will develop confidence in your ability to reason through the test questions. No additional techniques or strategies are needed to do well on the standardized test if you develop a practical familiarity with the abilities it requires. Simply by practicing and understanding the concepts that are assessed on the test, you will learn what you need to know to answer the questions correctly.

2.2 What About Practice Tests?

Because a computer-adaptive test cannot be presented in paper form, we have created GMATPrep® software to help you prepare for the test. The software is available for download at no charge for those who have created a user profile on www.mba.com. It is also provided on a disk, by request, to anyone who has registered for the GMAT test. The software includes two practice GMAT tests plus additional practice questions, information about the test, and tutorials to help you become familiar with how the GMAT test will appear on the computer screen at the test center.

We recommend that you download the software as you start to prepare for the test. Take one practice test to familiarize yourself with the test and to get an idea of how you might score. After you have studied using this book, and as your test date approaches, take the second practice test to determine whether you need to shift your focus to other areas you need to strengthen.

If you complete all the questions in this guide and think you would like additional practice, you may purchase *The Official Guide for GMAT® Verbal Review* or *The Official Guide for GMAT® Quantitative Review* at www.mba.com.

Note: There may be some overlap between this book and the review sections of the GMATPrep software.

Myth -vs- **FACT**

M – **You need very advanced math skills to get a high GMAT score.**

F – **The math skills tested on the GMAT test are quite basic.**

The GMAT test only requires basic quantitative analytic skills. You should review the math skills (algebra, geometry, basic arithmetic) presented in this book, but the required skill level is low. The difficulty of GMAT Quantitative questions stems from the logic and analysis used to solve the problems and not the underlying math skills.

2.3 How Should I Use the Diagnostic Test?

This book contains a Diagnostic Test to help you determine the types of questions that you need to practice most. You should take the Diagnostic Test around the same time that you take the first electronic sample test (using the test-preparation software). The Diagnostic Test will give you a rating—*below average*, *average*, *above average*, or *excellent*—of your skills in each type of GMAT test question. These ratings will help you identify areas to focus on as you prepare for the GMAT test.

Use the results of the Diagnostic Test to help you select the right chapter of this book to start with. Next, read the introductory material carefully, and answer the sample questions in that chapter. Make sure you follow the directions for each type of question and try to work as quickly and as efficiently as possible. Then review the explanations for the correct answers, spending as much time as necessary to familiarize yourself with the range of questions or problems presented.

2.4 Where Can I Get Additional Practice?

If you find you would like additional practice with the Verbal section of the test, *The Official Guide for GMAT® Verbal Review* is available for purchase at www.mba.com. If you want more practice with the Quantitative section, *The Official Guide for GMAT® Quantitative Review* is also available for purchase at www.mba.com.

2.5 General Test-Taking Suggestions

Specific test-taking strategies for individual question types are presented later in this book. The following are general suggestions to help you perform your best on the test.

1. Use your time wisely.

Although the GMAT test stresses accuracy more than speed, it is important to use your time wisely. On average, you will have about 1¾ minutes for each verbal question and about 2 minutes for each quantitative question. Once you start the test, an onscreen clock will continuously count the time you have left. You can hide this display if you want, but it is a good idea to check the clock periodically to monitor your progress. The clock will automatically alert you when 5 minutes remain in the allotted time for the section you are working on.

2. Answer practice questions ahead of time.

After you become generally familiar with all question types, use the sample questions in this book to prepare for the actual test. It may be useful to time yourself as you answer the practice questions to get an idea of how long you will have for each question during the actual GMAT test as well as to determine whether you are answering quickly enough to complete the test in the time allotted.

3. Read all test directions carefully.

The directions explain exactly what is required to answer each question type. If you read hastily, you may miss important instructions and lower your scores. To review directions during the test, click on the Help icon. But be aware that the time you spend reviewing directions will count against the time allotted for that section of the test.

4. Read each question carefully and thoroughly.

Before you answer a multiple-choice question, determine exactly what is being asked, then eliminate the wrong answers and select the best choice. Never skim a question or the possible answers; skimming may cause you to miss important information or nuances.

5. Do not spend too much time on any one question.

If you do not know the correct answer, or if the question is too time-consuming, try to eliminate choices you know are wrong, select the best of the remaining answer choices, and move on to the next question. Try not to worry about the impact on your score—guessing may lower your score, but not finishing the section will lower your score more.

Bear in mind that if you do not finish a section in the allotted time, you will still receive a score.

6. Confirm your answers ONLY when you are ready to move on.

Once you have selected your answer to a multiple-choice question, you will be asked to confirm it. Once you confirm your response, you cannot go back and change it. You may not skip questions, because the computer selects each question on the basis of your responses to preceding questions.

7. Plan your essay answers before you begin to write.

The best way to approach the two writing tasks that comprise the Analytical Writing Assessment is to read the directions carefully, take a few minutes to think about the question, and plan a response before you begin writing. Take care to organize your ideas and develop them fully, but leave time to reread your response and make any revisions that you think would improve it.

Myth -vs- **FACT**

𝓜 – **It is more important to respond correctly to the test questions than it is to finish the test.**

F – **There is a severe penalty for not completing the GMAT test.**

If you are stumped by a question, give it your best guess and move on. If you guess incorrectly, the computer program will likely give you an easier question, which you are likely to answer correctly, and the computer will rapidly return to giving you questions matched to your ability. If you don't finish the test, your score will be reduced greatly. Failing to answer five verbal questions, for example, could reduce your score from the 91st percentile to the 77th percentile. Pacing is important.

Myth -vs- **FACT**

𝓜 – **The first 10 questions are critical and you should invest the most time on those.**

F – **All questions count.**

It is true that the computer-adaptive testing algorithm uses the first 10 questions to obtain an initial estimate of your ability; however, that is only an *initial* estimate. As you continue to answer questions, the algorithm self-corrects by computing an updated estimate on the basis of all the questions you have answered, and then administers items that are closely matched to this new estimate of your ability. Your final score is based on all your responses and considers the difficulty of all the questions you answered. Taking additional time on the first 10 questions will not game the system and can hurt your ability to finish the test.

3.0   Diagnostic Test

3.0 Diagnostic Test

Like the practice sections later in the book, the Diagnostic Test uses questions from real GMAT® tests. The purpose of the Diagnostic Test is to help you determine how skilled you are in answering each of the five types of questions on the GMAT test: data sufficiency, problem solving, reading comprehension, critical reasoning, and sentence correction.

Scores on the Diagnostic Test are designed to help you answer the question, "If all the questions on the GMAT test were like the questions in this section, how well would I do?" Your scores are classified as being *excellent, above average, average,* or *below average,* relative to the scores of other test takers. You can use this information to focus your test-preparation activities.

Instructions

1. Take your time answering these questions. The Diagnostic Test is not timed.

2. If you are stumped by a question, you should guess and move on, just like you should do on the real GMAT test.

3. You can take one segment at a time, if you want. It is better to finish an entire section (Quantitative or Verbal) in one sitting, but this is not a requirement.

4. You can go back and change your answers in the Diagnostic Test.

5. After you take the test, check your answers using the answer key that follows the test. The number of correct answers is your raw score.

6. Convert your raw score, using the table provided.

Note: The Diagnostic Test is designed to give you guidance on how to prepare for the GMAT test; however, a strong score on one type of question does not guarantee that you will perform as well on the real GMAT test. The statistical reliability of scores on the Diagnostic Test ranges from 0.75 to 0.89, and the subscale classification is about 85%–90% accurate, meaning that your scores on the Diagnostic Test are a good, but not perfect, measure of how you are likely to perform on the real test. Use the tests on the free online software to obtain a good estimate of your expected GMAT Verbal, Quantitative, and Total scores.

You should not compare the number of questions you got right in each section. Instead, you should compare how your responses are rated in each section.

3.1 Quantitative Sample Questions

Problem Solving

Solve the problem and indicate the best of the answer choices given.

<u>Numbers:</u> All numbers used are real numbers.

<u>Figures:</u> All figures accompanying problem solving questions are intended to provide information useful in solving the problems. Figures are drawn as accurately as possible. Exceptions will be clearly noted. Lines shown as straight are straight, and lines that appear jagged are also straight. The positions of points, angles, regions, etc., exist in the order shown, and angle measures are greater than zero. All figures lie in a plane unless otherwise indicated.

1. Last month a certain music club offered a discount to preferred customers. After the first compact disc purchased, preferred customers paid $3.99 for each additional compact disc purchased. If a preferred customer purchased a total of 6 compact discs and paid $15.95 for the first compact disc, then the dollar amount that the customer paid for the 6 compact discs is equivalent to which of the following?

   (A) 5(4.00) + 15.90
   (B) 5(4.00) + 15.95
   (C) 5(4.00) + 16.00
   (D) 5(4.00 – 0.01) + 15.90
   (E) 5(4.00 – 0.05) + 15.95

2. The average (arithmetic mean) of the integers from 200 to 400, inclusive, is how much greater than the average of the integers from 50 to 100, inclusive?

   (A) 150
   (B) 175
   (C) 200
   (D) 225
   (E) 300

3. The sequence $a_1, a_2, a_3, ..., a_n, ...$ is such that $a_n = \dfrac{a_{n-1} + a_{n-2}}{2}$ for all $n \geq 3$. If $a_3 = 4$ and $a_5 = 20$, what is the value of a_6?

   (A) 12
   (B) 16
   (C) 20
   (D) 24
   (E) 28

4. Among a group of 2,500 people, 35 percent invest in municipal bonds, 18 percent invest in oil stocks, and 7 percent invest in both municipal bonds and oil stocks. If 1 person is to be randomly selected from the 2,500 people, what is the probability that the person selected will be one who invests in municipal bonds but NOT in oil stocks?

   (A) $\dfrac{9}{50}$
   (B) $\dfrac{7}{25}$
   (C) $\dfrac{7}{20}$
   (D) $\dfrac{21}{50}$
   (E) $\dfrac{27}{50}$

5. A closed cylindrical tank contains 36π cubic feet of water and is filled to half its capacity. When the tank is placed upright on its circular base on level ground, the height of the water in the tank is 4 feet. When the tank is placed on its side on level ground, what is the height, in feet, of the surface of the water above the ground?

   (A) 2
   (B) 3
   (C) 4
   (D) 6
   (E) 9

6. A marketing firm determined that, of 200 households surveyed, 80 used neither Brand A nor Brand B soap, 60 used only Brand A soap, and for every household that used both brands of soap, 3 used only Brand B soap. How many of the 200 households surveyed used both brands of soap?

    (A) 15
    (B) 20
    (C) 30
    (D) 40
    (E) 45

7. A certain club has 10 members, including Harry. One of the 10 members is to be chosen at random to be the president, one of the remaining 9 members is to be chosen at random to be the secretary, and one of the remaining 8 members is to be chosen at random to be the treasurer. What is the probability that Harry will be either the member chosen to be the secretary or the member chosen to be the treasurer?

    (A) $\dfrac{1}{720}$

    (B) $\dfrac{1}{80}$

    (C) $\dfrac{1}{10}$

    (D) $\dfrac{1}{9}$

    (E) $\dfrac{1}{5}$

8. If a certain toy store's revenue in November was $\dfrac{2}{5}$ of its revenue in December and its revenue in January was $\dfrac{1}{4}$ of its revenue in November, then the store's revenue in December was how many times the average (arithmetic mean) of its revenues in November and January?

    (A) $\dfrac{1}{4}$

    (B) $\dfrac{1}{2}$

    (C) $\dfrac{2}{3}$

    (D) 2

    (E) 4

9. A researcher computed the mean, the median, and the standard deviation for a set of performance scores. If 5 were to be added to each score, which of these three statistics would change?

    (A) The mean only
    (B) The median only
    (C) The standard deviation only
    (D) The mean and the median
    (E) The mean and the standard deviation

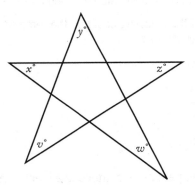

10. In the figure shown, what is the value of $v + x + y + z + w$?

    (A) 45
    (B) 90
    (C) 180
    (D) 270
    (E) 360

11. Of the three-digit integers greater than 700, how many have two digits that are equal to each other and the remaining digit different from the other two?

    (A) 90
    (B) 82
    (C) 80
    (D) 45
    (E) 36

12. Positive integer y is 50 percent of 50 percent of positive integer x, and y percent of x equals 100. What is the value of x ?

    (A) 50
    (B) 100
    (C) 200
    (D) 1,000
    (E) 2,000

13. If s and t are positive integers such that $\frac{s}{t} = 64.12$, which of the following could be the remainder when s is divided by t ?

    (A) 2
    (B) 4
    (C) 8
    (D) 20
    (E) 45

14. Of the 84 parents who attended a meeting at a school, 35 volunteered to supervise children during the school picnic and 11 volunteered both to supervise children during the picnic and to bring refreshments to the picnic. If the number of parents who volunteered to bring refreshments was 1.5 times the number of parents who neither volunteered to supervise children during the picnic nor volunteered to bring refreshments, how many of the parents volunteered to bring refreshments?

    (A) 25
    (B) 36
    (C) 38
    (D) 42
    (E) 45

15. The product of all the prime numbers less than 20 is closest to which of the following powers of 10 ?

    (A) 10^9
    (B) 10^8
    (C) 10^7
    (D) 10^6
    (E) 10^5

16. If $\sqrt{3-2x} = \sqrt{2x}+1$, then $4x^2 =$

    (A) 1
    (B) 4
    (C) $2 - 2x$
    (D) $4x - 2$
    (E) $6x - 1$

17. If $n = \sqrt{\frac{16}{81}}$, what is the value of $\sqrt{n}$?

    (A) $\frac{1}{9}$
    (B) $\frac{1}{4}$
    (C) $\frac{4}{9}$
    (D) $\frac{2}{3}$
    (E) $\frac{9}{2}$

18. If n is the product of the integers from 1 to 8, inclusive, how many different prime factors greater than 1 does n have?

    (A) Four
    (B) Five
    (C) Six
    (D) Seven
    (E) Eight

19. If k is an integer and $2 < k < 7$, for how many different values of k is there a triangle with sides of lengths 2, 7, and k ?

    (A) One
    (B) Two
    (C) Three
    (D) Four
    (E) Five

20. A right circular cone is inscribed in a hemisphere so that the base of the cone coincides with the base of the hemisphere. What is the ratio of the height of the cone to the radius of the hemisphere?

    (A) $\sqrt{3}:1$
    (B) $1:1$
    (C) $\frac{1}{2}:1$
    (D) $\sqrt{2}:1$
    (E) $2:1$

21. John deposited $10,000 to open a new savings account that earned 4 percent annual interest, compounded quarterly. If there were no other transactions in the account, what was the amount of money in John's account 6 months after the account was opened?

    (A) $10,100
    (B) $10,101
    (C) $10,200
    (D) $10,201
    (E) $10,400

22. A container in the shape of a right circular cylinder is $\frac{1}{2}$ full of water. If the volume of water in the container is 36 cubic inches and the height of the container is 9 inches, what is the diameter of the base of the cylinder, in inches?

    (A) $\dfrac{16}{9\pi}$

    (B) $\dfrac{4}{\sqrt{\pi}}$

    (C) $\dfrac{12}{\sqrt{\pi}}$

    (D) $\sqrt{\dfrac{2}{\pi}}$

    (E) $4\sqrt{\dfrac{2}{\pi}}$

23. If the positive integer x is a multiple of 4 and the positive integer y is a multiple of 6, then xy must be a multiple of which of the following?

    I. 8
    II. 12
    III. 18

    (A) II only
    (B) I and II only
    (C) I and III only
    (D) II and III only
    (E) I, II, and III

24. Aaron will jog from home at x miles per hour and then walk back home by the same route at y miles per hour. How many miles from home can Aaron jog so that he spends a total of t hours jogging and walking?

    (A) $\dfrac{xt}{y}$

    (B) $\dfrac{x + t}{xy}$

    (C) $\dfrac{xyt}{x + y}$

    (D) $\dfrac{x + y + t}{xy}$

    (E) $\dfrac{y + t}{x} - \dfrac{t}{y}$

Data Sufficiency

Each <u>data sufficiency</u> problem consists of a question and two statements, labeled (1) and (2), which contain certain data. Using these data and your knowledge of mathematics and everyday facts (such as the number of days in July or the meaning of the word *counterclockwise*), decide whether the data given are sufficient for answering the question and then indicate one of the following answer choices:

A   Statement (1) ALONE is sufficient, but statement (2) alone is not sufficient.
B   Statement (2) ALONE is sufficient, but statement (1) alone is not sufficient.
C   BOTH statements TOGETHER are sufficient, but NEITHER statement ALONE is sufficient.
D   EACH statement ALONE is sufficient.
E   Statements (1) and (2) TOGETHER are not sufficient.

<u>Note:</u> In data sufficiency problems that ask for the value of a quantity, the data given in the statements are sufficient only when it is possible to determine exactly one numerical value for the quantity.

<u>Example:</u>

In $\triangle PQR$, what is the value of x ?

(1) $PQ = PR$
(2) $y = 40$

Explanation: According to statement (1) $PQ = PR$; therefore, $\triangle PQR$ is isosceles and $y = z$. Since $x + y + z = 180$, it follows that $x + 2y = 180$. Since statement (1) does not give a value for y, you cannot answer the question using statement (1) alone. According to statement (2), $y = 40$; therefore, $x + z = 140$. Since statement (2) does not give a value for z, you cannot answer the question using statement (2) alone. Using both statements together, since $x + 2y = 180$ and the value of y is given, you can find the value of x. Therefore, BOTH statements (1) and (2) TOGETHER are sufficient to answer the question, but NEITHER statement ALONE is sufficient.

<u>Numbers:</u> All numbers used are real numbers.

<u>Figures:</u>
- Figures conform to the information given in the question, but will not necessarily conform to the additional information given in statements (1) and (2).
- Lines shown as straight are straight, and lines that appear jagged are also straight.
- The positions of points, angles, regions, etc., exist in the order shown, and angle measures are greater than zero.
- All figures lie in a plane unless otherwise indicated.

25. If the units digit of integer n is greater than 2, what is the units digit of n ?

    (1) The units digit of n is the same as the units digit of n^2.
    (2) The units digit of n is the same as the units digit of n^3.

26. What is the value of the integer p ?

    (1) Each of the integers 2, 3, and 5 is a factor of p.
    (2) Each of the integers 2, 5, and 7 is a factor of p.

27. If the length of Wanda's telephone call was rounded up to the nearest whole minute by her telephone company, then Wanda was charged for how many minutes for her telephone call?

    (1) The total charge for Wanda's telephone call was $6.50.
    (2) Wanda was charged $0.50 more for the first minute of the telephone call than for each minute after the first.

28. What is the perimeter of isosceles triangle MNP ?

    (1) $MN = 16$
    (2) $NP = 20$

29. In a survey of retailers, what percent had purchased computers for business purposes?

    (1) 85 percent of the retailers surveyed who owned their own store had purchased computers for business purposes.
    (2) 40 percent of the retailers surveyed owned their own store.

30. The only gift certificates that a certain store sold yesterday were worth either $100 each or $10 each. If the store sold a total of 20 gift certificates yesterday, how many gift certificates worth $10 each did the store sell yesterday?

    (1) The gift certificates sold by the store yesterday were worth a total of between $1,650 and $1,800.
    (2) Yesterday the store sold more than 15 gift certificates worth $100 each.

31. Is the standard deviation of the set of measurements $x_1, x_2, x_3, x_4, \ldots, x_{20}$ less than 3 ?

    (1) The variance for the set of measurements is 4.
    (2) For each measurement, the difference between the mean and that measurement is 2.

32. Is the range of the integers 6, 3, y, 4, 5, and x greater than 9 ?

    (1) $y > 3x$
    (2) $y > x > 3$

33. Is $\frac{5^{x+2}}{25} < 1$?

    (1) $5^x < 1$
    (2) $x < 0$

34. Of the companies surveyed about the skills they required in prospective employees, 20 percent required both computer skills and writing skills. What percent of the companies surveyed required neither computer skills nor writing skills?

    (1) Of those companies surveyed that required computer skills, half required writing skills.
    (2) 45 percent of the companies surveyed required writing skills but not computer skills.

35. What is the value of $w + q$?

    (1) $3w = 3 - 3q$
    (2) $5w + 5q = 5$

36. If X and Y are points in a plane and X lies inside the circle C with center O and radius 2, does Y lie inside circle C ?

    (1) The length of line segment XY is 3.
    (2) The length of line segment OY is 1.5.

37. Is $x > y$?

    (1) $x = y + 2$
    (2) $\frac{x}{2} = y - 1$

38. If Paula drove the distance from her home to her college at an average speed that was greater than 70 kilometers per hour, did it take her less than 3 hours to drive this distance?

    (1) The distance that Paula drove from her home to her college was greater than 200 kilometers.

    (2) The distance that Paula drove from her home to her college was less than 205 kilometers.

39. In the xy-plane, if line k has negative slope and passes through the point $(-5,r)$, is the x-intercept of line k positive?

    (1) The slope of line k is -5.

    (2) $r > 0$

40. If $5,000 invested for one year at p percent simple annual interest yields $500, what amount must be invested at k percent simple annual interest for one year to yield the same number of dollars?

    (1) $k = 0.8p$

    (2) $k = 8$

41. If $\frac{x+y}{z} > 0$, is $x < 0$?

    (1) $x < y$

    (2) $z < 0$

42. Does the integer k have at least three different positive prime factors?

    (1) $\frac{k}{15}$ is an integer.

    (2) $\frac{k}{10}$ is an integer.

43. In City X last April, was the average (arithmetic mean) daily high temperature greater than the median daily high temperature?

    (1) In City X last April, the sum of the 30 daily high temperatures was 2,160°.

    (2) In City X last April, 60 percent of the daily high temperatures were less than the average daily high temperature.

44. If m and n are positive integers, is $\left(\sqrt{m}\right)^n$ an integer?

    (1) $\left(\sqrt{m}\right)$ is an integer.

    (2) $\left(\sqrt{n}\right)$ is an integer.

45. Of the 66 people in a certain auditorium, at most 6 people have their birthdays in any one given month. Does at least one person in the auditorium have a birthday in January?

    (1) More of the people in the auditorium have their birthday in February than in March.

    (2) Five of the people in the auditorium have their birthday in March.

46. Last year the average (arithmetic mean) salary of the 10 employees of Company X was $42,800. What is the average salary of the same 10 employees this year?

    (1) For 8 of the 10 employees, this year's salary is 15 percent greater than last year's salary.

    (2) For 2 of the 10 employees, this year's salary is the same as last year's salary.

47. In a certain classroom, there are 80 books, of which 24 are fiction and 23 are written in Spanish. How many of the fiction books are written in Spanish?

    (1) Of the fiction books, there are 6 more that are not written in Spanish than are written in Spanish.

    (2) Of the books written in Spanish, there are 5 more nonfiction books than fiction books.

48. If p is the perimeter of rectangle Q, what is the value of p?

    (1) Each diagonal of rectangle Q has length 10.

    (2) The area of rectangle Q is 48.

3.2 Verbal Sample Questions

Reading Comprehension

Each of the <u>reading comprehension</u> questions is based on the content of a passage. After reading the passage, answer all questions pertaining to it on the basis of what is <u>stated</u> or <u>implied</u> in the passage. For each question, select the best answer of the choices given.

Line   According to economic signaling theory, consumers may perceive the frequency with which an unfamiliar brand is advertised as a cue that the brand is of high quality. The notion that
(5)   highly advertised brands are associated with high-quality products does have some empirical support. Marquardt and McGann found that heavily advertised products did indeed rank high on certain measures of product quality. Because
(10)   large advertising expenditures represent a significant investment on the part of a manufacturer, only companies that expect to recoup these costs in the long run, through consumers' repeat purchases of the product,
(15)   can afford to spend such amounts.
    However, two studies by Kirmani have found that although consumers initially perceive expensive advertising as a signal of high brand quality, at some level of spending the manufacturer's
(20)   advertising effort may be perceived as unreasonably high, implying low manufacturer confidence in product quality. If consumers perceive excessive advertising effort as a sign of a manufacturer's desperation, the result may be less favorable
(25)   brand perceptions. In addition, a third study by Kirmani, of print advertisements, found that the use of color affected consumer perception of brand quality. Because consumers recognize that color advertisements are more expensive than
(30)   black and white, the point at which repetition of an advertisement is perceived as excessive comes sooner for a color advertisement than for a black-and-white advertisement.

1.   Which of the following best describes the purpose of the sentence in lines 10–15 ?

   (A)   To show that economic signaling theory fails to explain a finding

   (B)   To introduce a distinction not accounted for by economic signaling theory

   (C)   To account for an exception to a generalization suggested by Marquardt and McGann

   (D)   To explain why Marquardt and McGann's research was conducted

   (E)   To offer an explanation for an observation reported by Marquardt and McGann

2.   The primary purpose of the passage is to

   (A)   present findings that contradict one explanation for the effects of a particular advertising practice

   (B)   argue that theoretical explanations about the effects of a particular advertising practice are of limited value without empirical evidence

   (C)   discuss how and why particular advertising practices may affect consumers' perceptions

   (D)   contrast the research methods used in two different studies of a particular advertising practice

   (E)   explain why a finding about consumer responses to a particular advertising practice was unexpected

3. Kirmani's research, as described in the passage, suggests which of the following regarding consumers' expectations about the quality of advertised products?

    (A) Those expectations are likely to be highest if a manufacturer runs both black-and-white and color advertisements for the same product.

    (B) Those expectations can be shaped by the presence of color in an advertisement as well as by the frequency with which an advertisement appears.

    (C) Those expectations are usually high for frequently advertised new brands but not for frequently advertised familiar brands.

    (D) Those expectations are likely to be higher for products whose black-and-white advertisements are often repeated than for those whose color advertisements are less often repeated.

    (E) Those expectations are less definitively shaped by the manufacturer's advertisements than by information that consumers gather from other sources.

4. Kirmani's third study, as described in the passage, suggests which of the following conclusions about a black-and-white advertisement?

    (A) It can be repeated more frequently than a comparable color advertisement could before consumers begin to suspect low manufacturer confidence in the quality of the advertised product.

    (B) It will have the greatest impact on consumers' perceptions of the quality of the advertised product if it appears during periods when a color version of the same advertisement is also being used.

    (C) It will attract more attention from readers of the print publication in which it appears if it is used only a few times.

    (D) It may be perceived by some consumers as more expensive than a comparable color advertisement.

    (E) It is likely to be perceived by consumers as a sign of higher manufacturer confidence in the quality of the advertised product than a comparable color advertisement would be.

5. The passage suggests that Kirmani would be most likely to agree with which of the following statements about consumers' perceptions of the relationship between the frequency with which a product is advertised and the product's quality?

    (A) Consumers' perceptions about the frequency with which an advertisement appears are their primary consideration when evaluating an advertisement's claims about product quality.

    (B) Because most consumers do not notice the frequency of advertisement, it has little impact on most consumers' expectations regarding product quality.

    (C) Consumers perceive frequency of advertisement as a signal about product quality only when the advertisement is for a product that is newly on the market.

    (D) The frequency of advertisement is not always perceived by consumers to indicate that manufacturers are highly confident about their products' quality.

    (E) Consumers who try a new product that has been frequently advertised are likely to perceive the advertisement's frequency as having been an accurate indicator of the product's quality.

Line   The idea of the brain as an information
processor—a machine manipulating blips of energy
according to fathomable rules—has come to
dominate neuroscience. However, one enemy of
(5)   the brain-as-computer metaphor is John R. Searle,
a philosopher who argues that since computers
simply follow algorithms, they cannot deal with
important aspects of human thought such as
meaning and content. Computers are syntactic,
(10)   rather than semantic, creatures. People, on the
other hand, understand meaning because they have
something Searle obscurely calls the causal powers
of the brain.

Yet how would a brain work if not by reducing
(15)   what it learns about the world to information—some
kind of code that can be transmitted from neuron
to neuron? What else could meaning and content
be? If the code can be cracked, a computer should
be able to simulate it, at least in principle. But
(20)   even if a computer could simulate the workings
of the mind, Searle would claim that the machine
would not really be thinking; it would just be acting
as if it were. His argument proceeds thus: if a
computer were used to simulate a stomach, with
(25)   the stomach's churnings faithfully reproduced on a
video screen, the machine would not be digesting
real food. It would just be blindly manipulating the
symbols that generate the visual display.

Suppose, though, that a stomach were simulated
(30)   using plastic tubes, a motor to do the churning, a
supply of digestive juices, and a timing mechanism.
If food went in one end of the device, what came out
the other end would surely be digested food. Brains,
unlike stomachs, are information processors, and if
(35)   one information processor were made to simulate
another information processor, it is hard to see
how one and not the other could be said to think.
Simulated thoughts and real thoughts are made of
the same element: information. The representations
(40)   of the world that humans carry around in their heads
are already simulations. To accept Searle's argument,
one would have to deny the most fundamental notion
in psychology and neuroscience: that brains work
by processing information.

6.   The main purpose of the passage is to

(A)   propose an experiment

(B)   analyze a function

(C)   refute an argument

(D)   explain a contradiction

(E)   simulate a process

7.   Which of the following is most consistent with Searle's
reasoning as presented in the passage?

(A)   Meaning and content cannot be reduced to
algorithms.

(B)   The process of digestion can be simulated
mechanically, but not on a computer.

(C)   Simulated thoughts and real thoughts are
essentially similar because they are composed
primarily of information.

(D)   A computer can use "causal powers" similar to
those of the human brain when processing
information.

(E)   Computer simulations of the world can achieve
the complexity of the brain's representations of
the world.

8.   The author of the passage would be most likely to
agree with which of the following statements about the
simulation of organ functions?

(A)   An artificial device that achieves the functions of
the stomach could be considered a valid model
of the stomach.

(B)   Computer simulations of the brain are best used
to crack the brain's codes of meaning and
content.

(C)   Computer simulations of the brain challenge
ideas that are fundamental to psychology and
neuroscience.

(D)   Because the brain and the stomach both act as
processors, they can best be simulated by
mechanical devices.

(E)   The computer's limitations in simulating
digestion suggest equal limitations in computer-
simulated thinking.

9.   It can be inferred that the author of the passage believes that Searle's argument is flawed by its failure to

   (A)   distinguish between syntactic and semantic operations
   (B)   explain adequately how people, unlike computers, are able to understand meaning
   (C)   provide concrete examples illustrating its claims about thinking
   (D)   understand how computers use algorithms to process information
   (E)   decipher the code that is transmitted from neuron to neuron in the brain

10.   From the passage, it can be inferred that the author would agree with Searle on which of the following points?

   (A)   Computers operate by following algorithms.
   (B)   The human brain can never fully understand its own functions.
   (C)   The comparison of the brain to a machine is overly simplistic.
   (D)   The most accurate models of physical processes are computer simulations.
   (E)   Human thought and computer-simulated thought involve similar processes of representation.

11.   Which of the following most accurately represents Searle's criticism of the brain-as-computer metaphor, as that criticism is described in the passage?

   (A)   The metaphor is not experimentally verifiable.
   (B)   The metaphor does not take into account the unique powers of the brain.
   (C)   The metaphor suggests that a brain's functions can be simulated as easily as those of a stomach.
   (D)   The metaphor suggests that a computer can simulate the workings of the mind by using the codes of neural transmission.
   (E)   The metaphor is unhelpful because both the brain and the computer process information.

Line   Women's grassroots activism and their vision
        of a new civic consciousness lay at the heart of
        social reform in the United States throughout the
        Progressive Era, the period between the depression
(5)   of 1893 and America's entry into the Second
        World War. Though largely disenfranchised except
        for school elections, white middle-class women
        reformers won a variety of victories, notably in
        the improvement of working conditions, especially
(10)   for women and children. Ironically, though,
        child labor legislation pitted women of different
        classes against one another. To the reformers,
        child labor and industrial home work were equally
        inhumane practices that should be outlawed, but,
(15)   as a number of women historians have recently
        observed, working-class mothers did not always
        share this view. Given the precarious finances of
        working-class families and the necessity of pooling
        the wages of as many family members as possible,
(20)   working-class families viewed the passage and
        enforcement of stringent child labor statutes as a
        personal economic disaster and made strenuous
        efforts to circumvent child labor laws. Yet
        reformers rarely understood this resistance in terms
(25)   of the desperate economic situation of working-
        class families, interpreting it instead as evidence
        of poor parenting. This is not to dispute women
        reformers' perception of child labor as a terribly
        exploitative practice, but their understanding of
(30)   child labor and their legislative solutions for ending
        it failed to take account of the economic needs of
        working-class families.

12. The primary purpose of the passage is to

    (A) explain why women reformers of the Progressive
         Era failed to achieve their goals

    (B) discuss the origins of child labor laws in the late
         nineteenth and early twentieth centuries

    (C) compare the living conditions of working-class
         and middle-class women in the Progressive Era

    (D) discuss an oversight on the part of women
         reformers of the Progressive Era

    (E) revise a traditional view of the role played by
         women reformers in enacting Progressive Era
         reforms

13. The *view* mentioned in line 17 of the passage refers to
    which of the following?

    (A) Some working-class mothers' resistance to the
         enforcement of child labor laws

    (B) Reformers' belief that child labor and industrial
         home work should be abolished

    (C) Reformers' opinions about how working-class
         families raised their children

    (D) Certain women historians' observation that there
         was a lack of consensus between women of
         different classes on the issue of child labor and
         industrial home work

    (E) Working-class families' fears about the adverse
         consequences that child labor laws would have
         on their ability to earn an adequate living

14. The author of the passage mentions the observations
    of women historians (lines 15–17) most probably in
    order to

    (A) provide support for an assertion made in the
         preceding sentence (lines 10–12)

    (B) raise a question that is answered in the last
         sentence of the passage (lines 27–32)

    (C) introduce an opinion that challenges a statement
         made in the first sentence of the passage

    (D) offer an alternative view to the one attributed in
         the passage to working-class mothers

    (E) point out a contradiction inherent in the
         traditional view of child labor reform as it is
         presented in the passage

15. The passage suggests that which of the following was a reason for the difference of opinion between working-class mothers and women reformers on the issue of child labor?

    (A) Reformers' belief that industrial home work was preferable to child labor outside the home
    (B) Reformers' belief that child labor laws should pertain to working conditions but not to pay
    (C) Working-class mothers' resentment at reformers' attempts to interfere with their parenting
    (D) Working-class mothers' belief that child labor was an inhumane practice
    (E) Working-class families' need for every employable member of their families to earn money

16. The author of the passage asserts which of the following about women reformers who tried to abolish child labor?

    (A) They alienated working-class mothers by attempting to enlist them in agitating for progressive causes.
    (B) They underestimated the prevalence of child labor among the working classes.
    (C) They were correct in their conviction that child labor was deplorable but shortsighted about the impact of child labor legislation on working-class families.
    (D) They were aggressive in their attempts to enforce child labor legislation, but were unable to prevent working-class families from circumventing them.
    (E) They were prevented by their nearly total disenfranchisement from making significant progress in child labor reform.

17. According to the passage, one of the most striking achievements of white middle-class women reformers during the Progressive Era was

    (A) gaining the right to vote in school elections
    (B) mobilizing working-class women in the fight against child labor
    (C) uniting women of different classes in grassroots activism
    (D) improving the economic conditions of working-class families
    (E) improving women's and children's working conditions

Critical Reasoning

Each of the <u>critical reasoning</u> questions is based on a short argument, a set of statements, or a plan of action. For each question, select the best answer of the choices given.

18. Vasquez-Morrell Assurance specializes in insuring manufacturers. Whenever a policyholder makes a claim, a claims adjuster determines the amount that Vasquez-Morrell is obligated to pay. Vasquez-Morrell is cutting its staff of claims adjusters by 15 percent. To ensure that the company's ability to handle claims promptly is affected as little as possible by the staff cuts, consultants recommend that Vasquez-Morrell lay off those adjusters who now take longest, on average, to complete work on claims assigned to them.

    Which of the following, if true, most seriously calls into question the consultants' criterion for selecting the staff to be laid off?

    (A) If the time that Vasquez-Morrell takes to settle claims increases significantly, it could lose business to other insurers.

    (B) Supervisors at Vasquez-Morrell tend to assign the most complex claims to the most capable adjusters.

    (C) At Vasquez-Morrell, no insurance payments are made until a claims adjuster has reached a final determination on the claim.

    (D) There are no positions at Vasquez-Morrell to which staff currently employed as claims adjusters could be reassigned.

    (E) The premiums that Vasquez-Morrell currently charges are no higher than those charged for similar coverage by competitors.

19. Prolonged spells of hot, dry weather at the end of the grape-growing season typically reduce a vineyard's yield, because the grapes stay relatively small. In years with such weather, wine producers can make only a relatively small quantity of wine from a given area of vineyards. Nonetheless, in regions where wine producers generally grow their own grapes, analysts typically expect a long, hot, dry spell late in the growing season to result in increased revenues for local wine producers.

    Which of the following, if true, does most to justify the analysts' expectation?

    (A) The lower a vineyard's yield, the less labor is required to harvest the grapes.

    (B) Long, hot, dry spells at the beginning of the grape-growing season are rare, but they can have a devastating effect on a vineyard's yield.

    (C) Grapes grown for wine production are typically made into wine at or near the vineyard in which they were grown.

    (D) When hot, dry spells are followed by heavy rains, the rains frequently destroy grape crops.

    (E) Grapes that have matured in hot, dry weather make significantly better wine than ordinary grapes.

20. In the past, most children who went sledding in the winter snow in Verland used wooden sleds with runners and steering bars. Ten years ago, smooth plastic sleds became popular; they go faster than wooden sleds but are harder to steer and slow. The concern that plastic sleds are more dangerous is clearly borne out by the fact that the number of children injured while sledding was much higher last winter than it was 10 years ago.

    Which of the following, if true in Verland, most seriously undermines the force of the evidence cited?

(A)   A few children still use traditional wooden sleds.

(B)   Very few children wear any kind of protective gear, such as helmets, while sledding.

(C)   Plastic sleds can be used in a much wider variety of snow conditions than wooden sleds can.

(D)   Most sledding injuries occur when a sled collides with a tree, a rock, or another sled.

(E)   Because the traditional wooden sleds can carry more than one rider, an accident involving a wooden sled can result in several children being injured.

21.   Metal rings recently excavated from seventh-century settlements in the western part of Mexico were made using the same metallurgical techniques as those used by Ecuadorian artisans before and during that period. These techniques are sufficiently complex to make their independent development in both areas unlikely. Since the people of these two areas were in cultural contact, archaeologists hypothesize that the metallurgical techniques used to make the rings found in Mexico were learned by Mexican artisans from Ecuadorian counterparts.

Which of the following would it be most useful to establish in order to evaluate the archaeologists' hypothesis?

(A)   Whether metal objects were traded from Ecuador to western Mexico during the seventh century

(B)   Whether travel between western Mexico and Ecuador in the seventh century would have been primarily by land or by sea

(C)   Whether artisans from western Mexico could have learned complex metallurgical techniques from their Ecuadorian counterparts without actually leaving western Mexico

(D)   Whether metal tools were used in the seventh-century settlements in western Mexico

(E)   Whether any of the techniques used in the manufacture of the metal rings found in western Mexico are still practiced among artisans in Ecuador today

22.   Following several years of declining advertising sales, the *Greenville Times* reorganized its advertising sales force. Before reorganization, the sales force was organized geographically, with some sales representatives concentrating on city-center businesses and others concentrating on different outlying regions. The reorganization attempted to increase the sales representatives' knowledge of clients' businesses by having each sales representative deal with only one type of industry or of retailing. After the reorganization, revenue from advertising sales increased.

In assessing whether the improvement in advertising sales can properly be attributed to the reorganization, it would be most helpful to find out which of the following?

(A)   What proportion of the total revenue of the *Greenville Times* is generated by advertising sales?

(B)   Has the circulation of the *Greenville Times* increased substantially in the last two years?

(C)   Among all the types of industry and retailing that use the *Greenville Times* as an advertising vehicle, which type accounts for the largest proportion of the newspaper's advertising sales?

(D)   Do any clients of the sales representatives of the *Greenville Times* have a standing order with the *Times* for a fixed amount of advertising per month?

(E)   Among the advertisers in the *Greenville Times*, are there more types of retail business or more types of industrial business?

23. Motorists in a certain country frequently complain that traffic congestion is much worse now than it was 20 years ago. No real measure of how much traffic congestion there was 20 years ago exists, but the motorists' complaints are almost certainly unwarranted. The country's highway capacity has tripled in the last twenty years, thanks to a vigorous highway construction program, whereas the number of automobiles registered in the country has increased by only 75 percent.

    Which of the following, if true, most seriously weakens the argument?

    (A)   Most automobile travel is local, and the networks of roads and streets in the country's settled areas have changed little over the last 20 years.

    (B)   Gasoline prices are high, and miles traveled per car per year have not changed much over the last 20 years.

    (C)   The country's urban centers have well-developed public transit systems that carry most of the people who commute into those centers.

    (D)   The average age of automobiles registered in the country is lower now than it was 20 years ago.

    (E)   Radio stations have long been broadcasting regular traffic reports that inform motorists about traffic congestion.

24. The percentage of households with an annual income of more than $40,000 is higher in Merton County than in any other county. However, the percentage of households with an annual income of $60,000 or more is higher in Sommer County.

    If the statements above are true, which of the following must also be true?

    (A)   The percentage of households with an annual income of $80,000 is higher in Sommer County than in Merton County.

    (B)   Merton County has the second highest percentage of households with an annual income of $60,000 or more.

    (C)   Some households in Merton County have an annual income between $40,000 and $60,000.

    (D)   The number of households with an annual income of more than $40,000 is greater in Merton County than in Sommer County.

    (E)   Average annual household income is higher in Sommer County than in Merton County.

25. Tiger beetles are such fast runners that they can capture virtually any nonflying insect. However, when running toward an insect, a tiger beetle will intermittently stop and then, a moment later, resume its attack. Perhaps the beetles cannot maintain their pace and must pause for a moment's rest; but an alternative hypothesis is that while running, tiger beetles are unable to adequately process the resulting rapidly changing visual information and so quickly go blind and stop.

Which of the following, if discovered in experiments using artificially moved prey insects, would support one of the two hypotheses and undermine the other?

(A) When a prey insect is moved directly toward a beetle that has been chasing it, the beetle immediately stops and runs away without its usual intermittent stopping.

(B) In pursuing a swerving insect, a beetle alters its course while running and its pauses become more frequent as the chase progresses.

(C) In pursuing a moving insect, a beetle usually responds immediately to changes in the insect's direction, and it pauses equally frequently whether the chase is up or down an incline.

(D) If, when a beetle pauses, it has not gained on the insect it is pursuing, the beetle generally ends its pursuit.

(E) The faster a beetle pursues an insect fleeing directly away from it, the more frequently the beetle stops.

26. Guillemots are birds of Arctic regions. They feed on fish that gather beneath thin sheets of floating ice, and they nest on nearby land. Guillemots need 80 consecutive snow-free days in a year to raise their chicks, so until average temperatures in the Arctic began to rise recently, the guillemots' range was limited to the southernmost Arctic coast. Therefore, if the warming continues, the guillemots' range will probably be enlarged by being extended northward along the coast.

Which of the following, if true, most seriously weakens the argument?

(A) Even if the warming trend continues, there will still be years in which guillemot chicks are killed by an unusually early snow.

(B) If the Arctic warming continues, guillemots' current predators are likely to succeed in extending their own range farther north.

(C) Guillemots nest in coastal areas, where temperatures are generally higher than in inland areas.

(D) If the Arctic warming continues, much of the thin ice in the southern Arctic will disappear.

(E) The fish that guillemots eat are currently preyed on by a wider variety of predators in the southernmost Arctic regions than they are farther north.

27. Some batches of polio vaccine used around 1960 were contaminated with SV40, a virus that in monkeys causes various cancers. Some researchers now claim that this contamination caused some cases of a certain cancer in humans, mesothelioma. This claim is not undercut by the fact that a very careful survey made in the 1960s of people who had received the contaminated vaccine found no elevated incidence of any cancer, since _____.

(A) most cases of mesothelioma are caused by exposure to asbestos

(B) in some countries, there was no contamination of the vaccine

(C) SV40 is widely used in laboratories to produce cancers in animals

(D) mesotheliomas take several decades to develop

(E) mesothelioma was somewhat less common in 1960 than it is now

28. Gortland has long been narrowly self-sufficient in both grain and meat. However, as per capita income in Gortland has risen toward the world average, per capita consumption of meat has also risen toward the world average, and it takes several pounds of grain to produce one pound of meat. Therefore, since per capita income continues to rise, whereas domestic grain production will not increase, Gortland will soon have to import either grain or meat or both.

Which of the following is an assumption on which the argument depends?

(A) The total acreage devoted to grain production in Gortland will soon decrease.

(B) Importing either grain or meat will not result in a significantly higher percentage of Gortlanders' incomes being spent on food than is currently the case.

(C) The per capita consumption of meat in Gortland is increasing at roughly the same rate across all income levels.

(D) The per capita income of meat producers in Gortland is rising faster than the per capita income of grain producers.

(E) People in Gortland who increase their consumption of meat will not radically decrease their consumption of grain.

29. The Hazelton coal-processing plant is a major employer in the Hazelton area, but national environmental regulations will force it to close if it continues to use old, polluting processing methods. However, to update the plant to use newer, cleaner methods would be so expensive that the plant will close unless it receives the tax break it has requested. In order to prevent a major increase in local unemployment, the Hazelton government is considering granting the plant's request.

Which of the following would be most important for the Hazelton government to determine before deciding whether to grant the plant's request?

(A) Whether the company that owns the plant would open a new plant in another area if the present plant were closed

(B) Whether the plant would employ far fewer workers when updated than it does now

(C) Whether the level of pollutants presently being emitted by the plant is high enough to constitute a health hazard for local residents

(D) Whether the majority of the coal processed by the plant is sold outside the Hazelton area

(E) Whether the plant would be able to process more coal when updated than it does now

30. A physically active lifestyle has been shown to help increase longevity. In the Wistar region of Bellaria, the average age at death is considerably higher than in any other part of the country. Wistar is the only mountainous part of Bellaria. A mountainous terrain makes even such basic activities as walking relatively strenuous; it essentially imposes a physically active lifestyle on people. Clearly, this circumstance explains the long lives of people in Wistar.

Which of the following, if true, most seriously weakens the argument?

(A) In Bellaria all medical expenses are paid by the government, so that personal income does not affect the quality of health care a person receives.

(B) The Wistar region is one of Bellaria's least populated regions.

(C) Many people who live in the Wistar region have moved there in middle age or upon retirement.

(D) The many opportunities for hiking, skiing, and other outdoor activities that Wistar's mountains offer make it a favorite destination for vacationing Bellarians.

(E) Per capita spending on recreational activities is no higher in Wistar than it is in other regions of Bellaria.

31. Cheever College offers several online courses via remote computer connection, in addition to traditional classroom-based courses. A study of student performance at Cheever found that, overall, the average student grade for online courses matched that for classroom-based courses. In this calculation of the average grade, course withdrawals were weighted as equivalent to a course failure, and the rate of withdrawal was much lower for students enrolled in classroom-based courses than for students enrolled in online courses.

    If the statements above are true, which of the following must also be true of Cheever College?

    (A) Among students who did not withdraw, students enrolled in online courses got higher grades, on average, than students enrolled in classroom-based courses.

    (B) The number of students enrolled per course at the start of the school term is much higher, on average, for the online courses than for the classroom-based courses.

    (C) There are no students who take both an online and a classroom-based course in the same school term.

    (D) Among Cheever College students with the best grades, a significant majority take online, rather than classroom-based, courses.

    (E) Courses offered online tend to deal with subject matter that is less challenging than that of classroom-based courses.

32. For years the beautiful Renaissance buildings in Palitito have been damaged by exhaust from the many tour buses that come to the city. There has been little parking space, so most buses have idled at the curb during each stop on their tour, and idling produces as much exhaust as driving. The city has now provided parking that accommodates a third of the tour buses, so damage to Palitito's buildings from the buses' exhaust will diminish significantly.

    Which of the following, if true, most strongly supports the argument?

    (A) The exhaust from Palitito's few automobiles is not a significant threat to Palitito's buildings.

    (B) Palitito's Renaissance buildings are not threatened by pollution other than engine exhaust.

    (C) Tour buses typically spend less than one-quarter of the time they are in Palitito transporting passengers from one site to another.

    (D) More tourists come to Palitito by tour bus than by any other single means of transportation.

    (E) Some of the tour buses that are unable to find parking drive around Palitito while their passengers are visiting a site.

33. During the 1980s and 1990s, the annual number of people who visited the Sordellian Mountains increased continually, and many new ski resorts were built. Over the same period, however, the number of visitors to ski resorts who were caught in avalanches decreased, even though there was no reduction in the annual number of avalanches in the Sordellian Mountains.

Which of the following, if true in the Sordellian Mountains during the 1980s and 1990s, most helps to explain the decrease?

(A) Avalanches were most likely to happen when a large new snowfall covered an older layer of snow.

(B) Avalanches destroyed at least some buildings in the Sordellian Mountains in every year.

(C) People planning new ski slopes and other resort facilities used increasingly accurate information about which locations are likely to be in the path of avalanches.

(D) The average length of stay for people visiting the Sordellian Mountains increased slightly.

(E) Construction of new ski resorts often led to the clearing of wooded areas that had helped to prevent avalanches.

34. A year ago, Dietz Foods launched a yearlong advertising campaign for its canned tuna. Last year Dietz sold 12 million cans of tuna compared to the 10 million sold during the previous year, an increase directly attributable to new customers brought in by the campaign. Profits from the additional sales, however, were substantially less than the cost of the advertising campaign. Clearly, therefore, the campaign did nothing to further Dietz's economic interests.

Which of the following, if true, most seriously weakens the argument?

(A) Sales of canned tuna account for a relatively small percentage of Dietz Foods' profits.

(B) Most of the people who bought Dietz's canned tuna for the first time as a result of the campaign were already loyal customers of other Dietz products.

(C) A less expensive advertising campaign would have brought in significantly fewer new customers for Dietz's canned tuna than did the campaign Dietz Foods launched last year.

(D) Dietz made money on sales of canned tuna last year.

(E) In each of the past five years, there was a steep, industry-wide decline in sales of canned tuna.

Sentence Correction

Each of the <u>sentence correction</u> questions presents a sentence, part or all of which is underlined. Beneath the sentence you will find five ways of phrasing the underlined part. The first of these repeats the original; the other four are different. Follow the requirements of standard written English to choose your answer, paying attention to grammar, word choice, and sentence construction. Select the answer that produces the most effective sentence; your answer should make the sentence clear, exact, and free of grammatical error. It should also minimize awkwardness, ambiguity, and redundancy.

35. Unlike <u>the buildings in Mesopotamian cities, which were arranged haphazardly, the same basic plan was followed for all cities of the Indus Valley: with</u> houses laid out on a north-south, east-west grid, and houses and walls were built of standard-size bricks.

(A) the buildings in Mesopotamian cities, which were arranged haphazardly, the same basic plan was followed for all cities of the Indus Valley: with houses

(B) the buildings in Mesopotamian cities, which were haphazard in arrangement, the same basic plan was used in all cities of the Indus Valley: houses were

(C) the arrangement of buildings in Mesopotamian cities, which were haphazard, the cities of the Indus Valley all followed the same basic plan: houses

(D) Mesopotamian cities, in which buildings were arranged haphazardly, the cities of the Indus Valley all followed the same basic plan: houses were

(E) Mesopotamian cities, which had buildings that were arranged haphazardly, the same basic plan was used for all cities in the Indus Valley: houses that were

36. New data from United States Forest Service ecologists show <u>that for every dollar spent on controlled small-scale burning, forest thinning, and the training of fire-management personnel, it saves seven dollars that would not be spent on having to extinguish</u> big fires.

(A) that for every dollar spent on controlled small-scale burning, forest thinning, and the training of fire-management personnel, it saves seven dollars that would not be spent on having to extinguish

(B) that for every dollar spent on controlled small-scale burning, forest thinning, and the training of fire-management personnel, seven dollars are saved that would have been spent on extinguishing

(C) that for every dollar spent on controlled small-scale burning, forest thinning, and the training of fire-management personnel saves seven dollars on not having to extinguish

(D) for every dollar spent on controlled small-scale burning, forest thinning, and the training of fire-management personnel, that it saves seven dollars on not having to extinguish

(E) for every dollar spent on controlled small-scale burning, forest thinning, and the training of fire-management personnel, that seven dollars are saved that would not have been spent on extinguishing

37. Like the grassy fields and old pastures that the upland sandpiper needs for feeding and nesting when it returns in May after wintering in the Argentine Pampas, the sandpipers vanishing in the northeastern United States is a result of residential and industrial development and of changes in farming practices.

    (A) the sandpipers vanishing in the northeastern United States is a result of residential and industrial development and of changes in

    (B) the bird itself is vanishing in the northeastern United States as a result of residential and industrial development and of changes in

    (C) that the birds themselves are vanishing in the northeastern United States is due to residential and industrial development and changes to

    (D) in the northeastern United States, sandpipers' vanishing due to residential and industrial development and to changes in

    (E) in the northeastern United States, the sandpipers' vanishing, a result of residential and industrial development and changing

38. The results of two recent unrelated studies support the idea that dolphins may share certain cognitive abilities with humans and great apes; the studies indicate dolphins as capable of recognizing themselves in mirrors—an ability that is often considered a sign of self-awareness—and to grasp spontaneously the mood or intention of humans.

    (A) dolphins as capable of recognizing themselves in mirrors—an ability that is often considered a sign of self-awareness—and to grasp spontaneously

    (B) dolphins' ability to recognize themselves in mirrors—an ability that is often considered as a sign of self-awareness—and of spontaneously grasping

    (C) dolphins to be capable of recognizing themselves in mirrors—an ability that is often considered a sign of self-awareness—and to grasp spontaneously

    (D) that dolphins have the ability of recognizing themselves in mirrors—an ability that is often considered as a sign of self-awareness—and spontaneously grasping

    (E) that dolphins are capable of recognizing themselves in mirrors—an ability that is often considered a sign of self-awareness—and of spontaneously grasping

39. According to scholars, the earliest writing was probably not a direct rendering of speech, but was more likely to begin as a separate and distinct symbolic system of communication, and only later merged with spoken language.

    (A) was more likely to begin as
    (B) more than likely began as
    (C) more than likely beginning from
    (D) it was more than likely begun from
    (E) it was more likely that it began

40. In 1995 Richard Stallman, a well-known critic of the patent system, testified in Patent Office hearings that, to test the system, a colleague of his had managed to win a patent for one of Kirchhoff's laws, an observation about electric current first made in 1845 and now included in virtually every textbook of elementary physics.

    (A) laws, an observation about electric current first made in 1845 and

    (B) laws, which was an observation about electric current first made in 1845 and it is

    (C) laws, namely, it was an observation about electric current first made in 1845 and

    (D) laws, an observation about electric current first made in 1845, it is

    (E) laws that was an observation about electric current, first made in 1845, and is

41. Excavators at the Indus Valley site of Harappa in eastern Pakistan say the discovery of inscribed shards dating to circa 2800–2600 B.C. indicate their development of a Harappan writing system, the use of inscribed seals impressed into clay for marking ownership, and the standardization of weights for trade or taxation occurred many decades, if not centuries, earlier than was previously believed.

    (A) indicate their development of a Harappan writing system, the use of

    (B) indicate that the development of a Harappan writing system, using

    (C) indicates that their development of a Harappan writing system, using

    (D) indicates the development of a Harappan writing system, their use of

    (E) indicates that the development of a Harappan writing system, the use of

42. The Supreme Court has ruled that public universities may collect student activity fees even with students' objections to particular activities, so long as the groups they give money to will be chosen without regard to their views.

    (A) with students' objections to particular activities, so long as the groups they give money to will be

    (B) if they have objections to particular activities and the groups that are given the money are

    (C) if they object to particular activities, but the groups that the money is given to have to be

    (D) from students who object to particular activities, so long as the groups given money are

    (E) though students have an objection to particular activities, but the groups that are given the money be

43. Despite the increasing number of women graduating from law school and passing bar examinations, the proportion of judges and partners at major law firms who are women have not risen to a comparable extent.

    (A) the proportion of judges and partners at major law firms who are women have not risen to a comparable extent

    (B) the proportion of women judges and partners at major law firms have not risen comparably

    (C) the proportion of judges and partners at major law firms who are women has not risen comparably

    (D) yet the proportion of women judges and partners at major law firms has not risen to a comparable extent

    (E) yet the proportion of judges and partners at major law firms who are women has not risen comparably

44. Seldom more than 40 feet wide and 12 feet deep, but it ran 363 miles across the rugged wilderness of upstate New York, the Erie Canal connected the Hudson River at Albany to the Great Lakes at Buffalo, providing the port of New York City with a direct water link to the heartland of the North American continent.

    (A) Seldom more than 40 feet wide and 12 feet deep, but it ran 363 miles across the rugged wilderness of upstate New York, the Erie Canal connected

    (B) Seldom more than 40 feet wide or 12 feet deep but running 363 miles across the rugged wilderness of upstate New York, the Erie Canal connected

    (C) It was seldom more than 40 feet wide and 12 feet deep, and ran 363 miles across the rugged wilderness of upstate New York, but the Erie Canal, connecting

    (D) The Erie Canal was seldom more than 40 feet wide or 12 feet deep and it ran 363 miles across the rugged wilderness of upstate New York, which connected

    (E) The Erie Canal, seldom more than 40 feet wide and 12 feet deep, but running 363 miles across the rugged wilderness of upstate New York, connecting

45. In 1923, <u>the Supreme Court declared a minimum wage for women and children in the District of Columbia as unconstitutional, and</u> ruling that it was a form of price-fixing and, as such, an abridgment of the right of contract.

    (A) the Supreme Court declared a minimum wage for women and children in the District of Columbia as unconstitutional, and

    (B) the Supreme Court declared as unconstitutional a minimum wage for women and children in the District of Columbia, and

    (C) the Supreme Court declared unconstitutional a minimum wage for women and children in the District of Columbia,

    (D) a minimum wage for women and children in the District of Columbia was declared unconstitutional by the Supreme Court,

    (E) when the Supreme Court declared a minimum wage for women and children in the District of Columbia as unconstitutional,

46. Researchers have found that individuals who have been blind from birth, and <u>who thus have never seen anyone gesture, nevertheless make hand motions when speaking just as frequently and in virtually the same way as sighted people do, and that they will gesture</u> even when conversing with another blind person.

    (A) who thus have never seen anyone gesture, nevertheless make hand motions when speaking just as frequently and in virtually the same way as sighted people do, and that they will gesture

    (B) who thus never saw anyone gesturing, nevertheless make hand motions when speaking just as frequent and in virtually the same way as sighted people did, and that they will gesture

    (C) who thus have never seen anyone gesture, nevertheless made hand motions when speaking just as frequently and in virtually the same way as sighted people do, as well as gesturing

    (D) thus never having seen anyone gesture, nevertheless made hand motions when speaking just as frequent and in virtually the same way as sighted people did, as well as gesturing

    (E) thus never having seen anyone gesture, nevertheless to make hand motions when speaking just as frequently and in virtually the same way as sighted people do, and to gesture

47. Like embryonic germ cells, which are cells that develop early in the formation of the fetus and that later generate eggs or sperm, <u>embryonic stem cells have the ability of developing themselves into different kinds of body tissue</u>.

    (A) embryonic stem cells have the ability of developing themselves into different kinds of body tissue

    (B) embryonic stem cells have the ability to develop into different kinds of body tissue

    (C) in embryonic stem cells there is the ability to develop into different kinds of body tissue

    (D) the ability to develop themselves into different kinds of body tissue characterizes embryonic stem cells

    (E) the ability of developing into different kinds of body tissue characterizes embryonic stem cells

48. Critics contend that the new missile is a weapon whose importance is largely symbolic, more a tool <u>for manipulating people's perceptions than to fulfill</u> a real military need.

    (A) for manipulating people's perceptions than to fulfill

    (B) for manipulating people's perceptions than for fulfilling

    (C) to manipulate people's perceptions rather than that it fulfills

    (D) to manipulate people's perceptions rather than fulfilling

    (E) to manipulate people's perceptions than for fulfilling

49. As an actress and, more importantly, as a teacher of acting, <u>Stella Adler was one of the most influential artists in the American theater, who trained several generations of actors including</u> Marlon Brando and Robert De Niro.

   (A) Stella Adler was one of the most influential artists in the American theater, who trained several generations of actors including

   (B) Stella Adler, one of the most influential artists in the American theater, trained several generations of actors who include

   (C) Stella Adler was one of the most influential artists in the American theater, training several generations of actors whose ranks included

   (D) one of the most influential artists in the American theater was Stella Adler, who trained several generations of actors including

   (E) one of the most influential artists in the American theater, Stella Adler, trained several generations of actors whose ranks included

50. By developing the Secure Digital Music Initiative, the recording industry associations of North America, Japan, and Europe hope to create a standardized way <u>of distributing songs and full-length recordings on the Internet that will protect copyright holders and foil the many audio pirates who copy and distribute</u> digital music illegally.

   (A) of distributing songs and full-length recordings on the Internet that will protect copyright holders and foil the many audio pirates who copy and distribute

   (B) of distributing songs and full-length recordings on the Internet and to protect copyright holders and foiling the many audio pirates copying and distributing

   (C) for distributing songs and full-length recordings on the Internet while it protects copyright holders and foils the many audio pirates who copy and distribute

   (D) to distribute songs and full-length recordings on the Internet while they will protect copyright holders and foil the many audio pirates copying and distributing

   (E) to distribute songs and full-length recordings on the Internet and it will protect copyright holders and foiling the many audio pirates who copy and distribute

51. Whereas a ramjet generally cannot achieve high speeds without the initial assistance of a rocket, <u>high speeds can be attained by scramjets, or supersonic combustion ramjets, in that they reduce</u> airflow compression at the entrance of the engine and letting air pass through at supersonic speeds.

   (A) high speeds can be attained by scramjets, or supersonic combustion ramjets, in that they reduce

   (B) that high speeds can be attained by scramjets, or supersonic combustion ramjets, is a result of their reducing

   (C) the ability of scramjets, or supersonic combustion ramjets, to achieve high speeds is because they reduce

   (D) scramjets, or supersonic combustion ramjets, have the ability of attaining high speeds when reducing

   (E) scramjets, or supersonic combustion ramjets, can attain high speeds by reducing

52. It will not be possible to implicate melting sea ice in the coastal flooding that many global warming models have projected: just <u>like a glass of water that will not overflow due to melting ice cubes,</u> so melting sea ice does not increase oceanic volume.

   (A) like a glass of water that will not overflow due to melting ice cubes,

   (B) like melting ice cubes that do not cause a glass of water to overflow,

   (C) a glass of water will not overflow because of melting ice cubes,

   (D) as melting ice cubes that do not cause a glass of water to overflow,

   (E) as melting ice cubes do not cause a glass of water to overflow,

3.3 Quantitative and Verbal Answer Keys

Quantitative

1. A	17. D	33. D
2. D	18. A	34. C
3. E	19. A	35. D
4. B	20. B	36. B
5. B	21. D	37. A
6. A	22. E	38. B
7. E	23. B	39. E
8. E	24. C	40. D
9. D	25. E	41. C
10. C	26. E	42. C
11. C	27. E	43. B
12. C	28. E	44. A
13. E	29. E	45. D
14. B	30. A	46. E
15. C	31. D	47. D
16. E	32. C	48. C

Verbal

1. E	19. E	37. B
2. C	20. C	38. E
3. B	21. A	39. B
4. A	22. B	40. A
5. D	23. A	41. E
6. C	24. C	42. D
7. A	25. B	43. C
8. A	26. D	44. B
9. B	27. D	45. C
10. A	28. E	46. A
11. B	29. B	47. B
12. D	30. C	48. B
13. B	31. A	49. C
14. A	32. C	50. A
15. E	33. C	51. E
16. C	34. E	52. E
17. E	35. D	
18. B	36. B	

3.4 Interpretive Guide

The following table provides a guide for interpreting your score, on the basis of the number of questions you got right.

Interpretive Guide				
	Excellent	Above Average	Average	Below Average
Problem Solving	19–24	16–18	10–15	0–9
Data Sufficiency	19–24	16–18	10–15	0–9
Reading Comprehension	16–17	14–15	9–13	0–8
Critical Reasoning	14–17	9–13	6–8	0–5
Sentence Correction	16–18	11–15	8–10	0–7

Remember, you should not compare the number of questions you got right in each section. Instead, you should compare how your response rated in each section.

3.5 Quantitative Answer Explanations

Problem Solving

The following discussion is intended to familiarize you with the most efficient and effective approaches to the kinds of problems common to problem solving questions. The particular questions in this chapter are generally representative of the kinds of quantitative questions you will encounter on the GMAT. Remember that it is the problem solving strategy that is important, not the specific details of a particular question.

1. Last month a certain music club offered a discount to preferred customers. After the first compact disc purchased, preferred customers paid $3.99 for each additional compact disc purchased. If a preferred customer purchased a total of 6 compact discs and paid $15.95 for the first compact disc, then the dollar amount that the customer paid for the 6 compact discs is equivalent to which of the following?

   (A)   5(4.00) + 15.90
   (B)   5(4.00) + 15.95
   (C)   5(4.00) + 16.00
   (D)   5(4.00 – 0.01) + 15.90
   (E)   5(4.00 – 0.05) + 15.95

   Arithmetic Operations on rational numbers

   The cost of the 6 compact discs, with $15.95 for the first one and $3.99 for the other 5 discs, can be expressed as 5(3.99) + 15.95. It is clear from looking at the answer choices that some regrouping of the values is needed because none of the answer choices uses $3.99 in the calculation.

   If $4.00 is used instead of $3.99, each one of the 5 additional compact discs is calculated at $0.01 too much, and the total cost is 5(0.01) = $0.05 too high. There is an overage of $0.05 that must be subtracted from the $15.95, or thus $15.95 – $0.05 = $15.90. Therefore, the cost can be expressed as 5(4.00) + 15.90.

   The correct answer is A.

2. The average (arithmetic mean) of the integers from 200 to 400, inclusive, is how much greater than the average of the integers from 50 to 100, inclusive?

   (A)   150
   (B)   175
   (C)   200
   (D)   225
   (E)   300

   Arithmetic Statistics

   In the list of integers from 200 to 400 inclusive, the middle value is 300. For every integer above 300, there exists an integer below 300 that is the same distance away from 300; thus the average of the integers from 200 to 400, inclusive, will be kept at 300. In the same manner, the average of the integers from 50 to 100, inclusive, is 75.

   The difference is 300 – 75 = 225.

   The correct answer is D.

3. The sequence a_1, a_2, a_3,...,a_n,... is such that
   $a_n = \dfrac{a_{n-1} + a_{n-2}}{2}$ for all $n \geq 3$. If $a_3 = 4$ and $a_5 = 20$, what is the value of a_6 ?

   (A)   12
   (B)   16
   (C)   20
   (D)   24
   (E)   28

Algebra Applied problems

According to this formula, it is necessary to know the two prior terms in the sequence to determine the value of a term; that is, it is necessary to know both a_{n-1} and a_{n-2} to find a_n. Therefore, to find a_6, the values of a_5 and a_4 must be determined. To find a_4, let $a_n = a_5$, which makes $a_{n-1} = a_4$ and $a_{n-2} = a_3$. Then, by substituting the given values into the formula

$$a_n = \frac{a_{n-1} + a_{n-2}}{2}$$

$$a_5 = \frac{a_4 + a_3}{2}$$

$$20 = \frac{a_4 + 4}{2} \quad \text{substitute known values}$$

$$40 = a_4 + 4 \quad \text{multiply both sides}$$

$$36 = a_4 \quad \text{subtract 4 from both sides}$$

Then, letting $a_n = a_6$, substitute the known values:

$$a_6 = \frac{a_5 + a_4}{2}$$

$$a_6 = \frac{20 + 36}{2} \quad \text{substitute known values}$$

$$a_6 = \frac{56}{2} \quad \text{simplify}$$

$$a_6 = 28$$

The correct answer is E.

4. Among a group of 2,500 people, 35 percent invest in municipal bonds, 18 percent invest in oil stocks, and 7 percent invest in both municipal bonds and oil stocks. If 1 person is to be randomly selected from the 2,500 people, what is the probability that the person selected will be one who invests in municipal bonds but NOT in oil stocks?

(A) $\dfrac{9}{50}$

(B) $\dfrac{7}{25}$

(C) $\dfrac{7}{20}$

(D) $\dfrac{21}{50}$

(E) $\dfrac{27}{50}$

Arithmetic Probability

Since there are 2,500 people, 2,500(0.35) = 875 people invest in municipal bonds, and 2,500(0.07) = 175 of those people invest in both municipal bonds and oil stocks. Therefore, there are 875 − 175 = 700 people who invest in municipal bonds but not in oil stocks. Probability of an event =

$$\frac{\text{Number of desired outcomes}}{\text{Total number of outcomes that can occur}}.$$

Probability of investing in municipal bonds but not in oil stocks = $\dfrac{700}{2,500} = \dfrac{7}{25}$.

The correct answer is B.

5. A closed cylindrical tank contains 36π cubic feet of water and is filled to half its capacity. When the tank is placed upright on its circular base on level ground, the height of the water in the tank is 4 feet. When the tank is placed on its side on level ground, what is the height, in feet, of the surface of the water above the ground?

(A) 2
(B) 3
(C) 4
(D) 6
(E) 9

Geometry Volume

Since the cylinder is half full, it will be filled to half its height, whether it is upright or on its side. When the cylinder is on its side, half its height is equal to its radius.

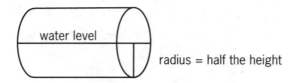

radius = half the height

Using the information about the volume of water in the upright cylinder, solve for this radius to determine the height of the water when the cylinder is on its side.

$V = \pi r^2 h$	volume = (π)(radius²)(height)
$36\pi = \pi r^2 h$	known volume of water is 36π
$36 = r^2(4)$	substitute 4 for h; divide both sides by π
$9 = r^2$	solve for r
$3 = r$	radius = height of the water in the cylinder on its side

The correct answer is B.

6. A marketing firm determined that, of 200 households surveyed, 80 used neither Brand A nor Brand B soap, 60 used only Brand A soap, and for every household that used both brands of soap, 3 used only Brand B soap. How many of the 200 households surveyed used both brands of soap?

(A)   15
(B)   20
(C)   30
(D)   40
(E)   45

Arithmetic Operations on rational numbers

Since it is given that 80 households use neither Brand A nor Brand B, then $200 - 80 = 120$ must use Brand A, Brand B, or both. It is also given that 60 households use only Brand A and that three times as many households use Brand B exclusively as use both brands. If x is the number of households that use both Brand A and Brand B, then $3x$ use Brand B alone. A Venn diagram can be helpful for visualizing the logic of the given information for this item:

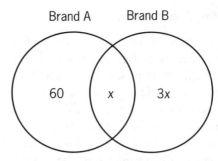

All the sections in the circles can be added up and set equal to 120, and then the equation can be solved for x:

$60 + x + 3x = 120$	
$60 + 4x = 120$	combine like terms
$4x = 60$	subtract 60 from both sides
$x = 15$	divide both sides by 4

The correct answer is A.

7. A certain club has 10 members, including Harry. One of the 10 members is to be chosen at random to be the president, one of the remaining 9 members is to be chosen at random to be the secretary, and one of the remaining 8 members is to be chosen at random to be the treasurer. What is the probability that Harry will be either the member chosen to be the secretary or the member chosen to be the treasurer?

(A) $\dfrac{1}{720}$

(B) $\dfrac{1}{80}$

(C) $\dfrac{1}{10}$

(D) $\dfrac{1}{9}$

(E) $\dfrac{1}{5}$

Arithmetic Probability

Two probabilities must be calculated here: (1) the probability of Harry's being chosen for secretary and (2) the probability of Harry's being chosen for treasurer. For any probability, the probability of an event's occurring =

$$\frac{\text{number of desired outcomes}}{\text{total number of outcomes that can occur}}.$$

(1) If Harry is to be secretary, he first CANNOT have been chosen for president, and then he must be chosen for secretary. The probability that he will be chosen for president is $\frac{1}{10}$, so the probability of his NOT being chosen for president is $1 - \frac{1}{10} = \frac{9}{10}$. Then, the probability of his being chosen for secretary is $\frac{1}{9}$.

Once he is chosen, the probability that he will be selected for treasurer is 0, so the probability that he will NOT be selected for treasurer is $1 - 0 = 1$. Thus, the probability that Harry will be chosen for secretary is $\left(\frac{9}{10}\right)\left(\frac{1}{9}\right)(1) = \frac{1}{10}$.

(2) If Harry is to be treasurer, he needs to be NOT chosen for president, then NOT chosen for secretary, and then finally chosen for treasurer.

The probability that he will NOT be chosen for president is again $1 - \frac{1}{10} = \frac{9}{10}$. The probability of his NOT being chosen for secretary is $1 - \frac{1}{9} = \frac{8}{9}$. The probability of his being chosen for treasurer is $\frac{1}{8}$, so the probability that Harry will be chosen for treasurer is $\left(\frac{9}{10}\right)\left(\frac{8}{9}\right)\left(\frac{1}{8}\right) = \frac{1}{10}$.

(3) So, finally, the probability of Harry's being chosen as either secretary or treasurer is thus $\frac{1}{10} + \frac{1}{10} = \frac{2}{10} = \frac{1}{5}$.

The correct answer is E.

8. If a certain toy store's revenue in November was $\frac{2}{5}$ of its revenue in December and its revenue in January was $\frac{1}{4}$ of its revenue in November, then the store's revenue in December was how many times the average (arithmetic mean) of its revenues in November and January?

(A) $\frac{1}{4}$

(B) $\frac{1}{2}$

(C) $\frac{2}{3}$

(D) 2

(E) 4

Arithmetic Statistics

Let n be the store's revenue in November, d be the store's revenue in December, and j be the store's revenue in January. The information from the problem can be expressed as $n = \frac{2}{5}d$ and $j = \frac{1}{4}n$. Substituting $\frac{2}{5}d$ for n in the second equation gives $j = \frac{1}{4}\left(\frac{2}{5}d\right) = \frac{1}{10}d$. Then, the average of the revenues in November and January can be found by using these values in the formula

$$\text{average} = \frac{\text{sum of values}}{\text{number of values}}, \text{ as follows:}$$

$$\text{average} = \frac{\frac{2}{5}d + \frac{1}{10}d}{2} = \frac{\frac{4}{10}d + \frac{1}{10}d}{2} = \frac{\frac{5}{10}d}{2} = \frac{1}{2}d\left(\frac{1}{2}\right) = \frac{1}{4}d$$

Solve for the store's revenue in December by multiplying both sides of this equation by 4:

$$\text{average} = \frac{1}{4}d$$

$$4(\text{average}) = d$$

Thus, the store's revenue in December was 4 times its average revenue in November and January.

The correct answer is E.

9. A researcher computed the mean, the median, and the standard deviation for a set of performance scores. If 5 were to be added to each score, which of these three statistics would change?

    (A) The mean only
    (B) The median only
    (C) The standard deviation only
    (D) The mean and the median
    (E) The mean and the standard deviation

Arithmetic Statistics

If 5 were added to each score, the mean would go up by 5, as would the median. However, the spread of the values would remain the same, simply centered around a new value. So, the standard deviation would **NOT** change.

The correct answer is D.

10. In the figure shown, what is the value of $v + x + y + z + w$?

    (A) 45
    (B) 90
    (C) 180
    (D) 270
    (E) 360

Geometry Angles and their measure

In the following figure, the center section of the star is a pentagon.

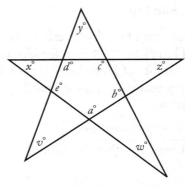

The sum of the interior angles of any polygon is $180(n - 2)$, where n is the number of sides. Thus, $a + b + c + d + e = 180(5 - 2) = 180(3) = 540$.

Each of the interior angles of the pentagon defines a triangle with two of the angles at the points of the star. This gives the following five equations:

$a + x + z = 180$
$b + v + y = 180$
$c + x + w = 180$
$d + v + z = 180$
$e + y + w = 180$

Summing these 5 equations gives:

$a + b + c + d + e + 2v + 2x + 2y + 2z + 2w = 900$.

Substituting 540 for $a + b + c + d + e$ gives:

$540 + 2v + 2x + 2y + 2z + 2w = 900$.

From this:

$2v + 2x + 2y + 2z + 2w = 360$	subtract 540 from both sides
$2(v + x + y + z + w) = 360$	factor out 2 on the left side
$v + x + y + z + w = 180$	divide both sides by 2

The correct answer is C.

11. Of the three-digit integers greater than 700, how many have two digits that are equal to each other and the remaining digit different from the other two?

    (A) 90
    (B) 82
    (C) 80
    (D) 45
    (E) 36

Arithmetic Properties of numbers

In three-digit integers, there are three pairs of digits that can be the same while the other digit is different: tens and ones, hundreds and tens, and hundreds and ones. In each of these pairs, there are 9 options for having the third digit be different from the other two. The single exception to this is in the 700–799 set, where the number 700 cannot be included because the problem calls for integers "greater than 700." So, in the 700–799 set, there are only 8 options for when the tens and ones are the same. This is shown in the table below.

Number of digits available for the third digit when two given digits are the same			
Same	701–799	800–899	900–999
tens and ones	8	9	9
hundreds and tens	9	9	9
hundreds and ones	9	9	9

Thus, of the three-digit integers greater than 700, there are $9(9) - 1 = 80$ numbers that have two digits that are equal to each other when the remaining digit is different from these two.

The correct answer is C.

12. Positive integer y is 50 percent of 50 percent of positive integer x, and y percent of x equals 100. What is the value of x ?

(A)   50
(B)   100
(C)   200
(D)   1,000
(E)   2,000

Arithmetic; Algebra Percents; Simultaneous equations

Because y is a positive integer, y percent is notated as $\frac{y}{100}$. According to the problem, $y = 0.50(0.50x)$ and $\left(\frac{y}{100}\right)x = 100$.

The first equation simplifies to $y = 0.25x$, and multiplying the second equation by 100 gives $xy = 10{,}000$.

Substituting the simplified first equation into this second equation gives:

$x(0.25x) = 10{,}000$

$0.25x^2 = 10{,}000$ simplify left side

$x^2 = 40{,}000$ divide both sides by 0.25

$x = 200$ solve for the value of x

The correct answer is C.

13. If s and t are positive integers such that $\frac{s}{t} = 64.12$, which of the following could be the remainder when s is divided by t ?

(A)   2
(B)   4
(C)   8
(D)   20
(E)   45

Arithmetic Operations on rational numbers

By using a long division model, it can be seen that the remainder after dividing s by t is $s - 64t$:

$$
\begin{array}{r}
64 \\
t{\overline{)\,s}} \\
-64t \\
\hline
s - 64t
\end{array}
$$

Then, the given equation can be written as $64.12t = s$. By splitting portions of t into its integer multiple and its decimal multiple, this becomes $64t + 0.12t = s$, or $0.12t = s - 64t$, which is the remainder. So, $0.12t$ = remainder. Test the answer choices to find the situation in which t is an integer.

A	$0.12t = 2$ or $t = 16.67$	NOT an integer
B	$0.12t = 4$ or $t = 33.33$	NOT an integer
C	$0.12t = 8$ or $t = 66.67$	NOT an integer
D	$0.12t = 20$ or $t = 166.67$	NOT an integer
E	$0.12t = 45$ or $t = 375$	INTEGER

The correct answer is E.

14. Of the 84 parents who attended a meeting at a school, 35 volunteered to supervise children during the school picnic and 11 volunteered both to supervise children during the picnic and to bring refreshments to the picnic. If the number of parents who volunteered to bring refreshments was 1.5 times the number of parents who neither volunteered to supervise children during the picnic nor volunteered to bring refreshments, how many of the parents volunteered to bring refreshments?

(A) 25
(B) 36
(C) 38
(D) 42
(E) 45

Arithmetic Operations on rational numbers

Out of the 35 parents who agreed to supervise children during the school picnic, 11 parents are also bringing refreshments, so 35 − 11 = 24 parents are only supervising children. Let x be the number of parents who volunteered to bring refreshments, and let y be the number of parents who declined to supervise or to bring refreshments. The fact that the number of parents who volunteered to bring refreshments is 1.5 times the number who did not volunteer at all can then be expressed as $x = 1.5y$. A Venn diagram, such as the one below, can be helpful in answering problems of this kind.

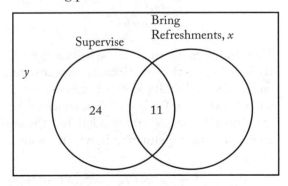

Then, the sum of the sections can be set equal to the total number of parents at the picnic, and the equation can be solved for y:

$y + 24 + x = 84$	sum of sections = total parents at picnic
$y + x = 60$	subtract 24 from each side
$y = 60 - x$	subtract x from each side

Then, substituting the value $60 - x$ for y in the equation $x = 1.5y$ gives the following:

$x = 1.5(60 - x)$	
$x = 90 - 1.5x$	distribute the 1.5
$2.5x = 90$	add $1.5x$ to both sides
$x = 36$	divide both sides by 2.5

The correct answer is B.

15. The product of all the prime numbers less than 20 is closest to which of the following powers of 10 ?

(A) 10^9
(B) 10^8
(C) 10^7
(D) 10^6
(E) 10^5

Arithmetic Properties of numbers

The prime numbers less than 20 are 2, 3, 5, 7, 11, 13, 17, and 19. Their product is 9,699,690 (arrived at as follows: $2 \times 3 \times 5 \times 7 \times 11 \times 13 \times 17 \times 19 = 9{,}699{,}690$). This is closest to $10{,}000{,}000 = 10^7$ ($10 \times 10 \times 10 \times 10 \times 10 \times 10 \times 10 = 10{,}000{,}000$).

The correct answer is C.

16. If $\sqrt{3 - 2x} = \sqrt{2x} + 1$ then, $4x^2 =$

(A) 1
(B) 4
(C) $2 - 2x$
(D) $4x - 2$
(E) $6x - 1$

Algebra Second-degree equations

Work with the equation to create $4x^2$ on one side.

$$\sqrt{3-2x}=\sqrt{2x}+1$$

$$\left(\sqrt{3-2x}\right)^2=\left(\sqrt{2x}+1\right)^2 \quad \text{square both sides}$$

$$3-2x=2x+2\sqrt{2x}+1$$

$$2-4x=2\sqrt{2x} \quad \begin{array}{l}\text{move all non–}\\ \text{square-root terms to}\\ \text{one side (i.e.,}\\ \text{subtract } 2x \text{ and 1)}\end{array}$$

$$1-2x=\sqrt{2x} \quad \text{divide both sides by 2}$$

$$(1-2x)^2=\left(\sqrt{2x}\right)^2 \quad \text{square both sides}$$

$$1-4x+4x^2=2x$$

$$4x^2=6x-1 \quad \begin{array}{l}\text{isolate the } 4x^2 \text{(add}\\ 4x \text{ and subtract 1}\\ \text{from both sides)}\end{array}$$

The correct answer is E.

17. If $n=\sqrt{\dfrac{16}{81}}$, what is the value of $\sqrt{n}$?

(A) $\dfrac{1}{9}$

(B) $\dfrac{1}{4}$

(C) $\dfrac{4}{9}$

(D) $\dfrac{2}{3}$

(E) $\dfrac{9}{2}$

Arithmetic Operations on radical expressions

Work the problem.

Since $n=\sqrt{\dfrac{16}{81}}=\dfrac{4}{9}$, then $\sqrt{n}=\sqrt{\dfrac{4}{9}}=\dfrac{2}{3}$.

The correct answer is D.

18. If n is the product of the integers from 1 to 8, inclusive, how many different prime factors greater than 1 does n have?

(A) Four
(B) Five
(C) Six
(D) Seven
(E) Eight

Arithmetic Properties of numbers

If n is the product of the integers from 1 to 8, then its prime factors will be the prime numbers from 1 to 8. There are four prime numbers between 1 and 8: 2, 3, 5, and 7.

The correct answer is A.

19. If k is an integer and $2 < k < 7$, for how many different values of k is there a triangle with sides of lengths 2, 7, and k ?

(A) One
(B) Two
(C) Three
(D) Four
(E) Five

Geometry Triangles

In a triangle, the sum of the smaller two sides must be larger than the largest side.

For k values 3, 4, 5, and 6, the only triangle possible is 2, 7, and k = 6 because only 2 + 6 > 7. For k values 3, 4, and 5, the sum of the smaller two sides is not larger than the third side; thus, 6 is the only possible value of k that satisfies the conditions.

The correct answer is A.

20. A right circular cone is inscribed in a hemisphere so that the base of the cone coincides with the base of the hemisphere. What is the ratio of the height of the cone to the radius of the hemisphere?

    (A) $\sqrt{3}:1$

    (B) 1:1

    (C) $\frac{1}{2}:1$

    (D) $\sqrt{2}:1$

    (E) 2:1

Geometry Volume

As the diagram below shows, the height of the cone will be the radius of the hemisphere, so the ratio is 1:1.

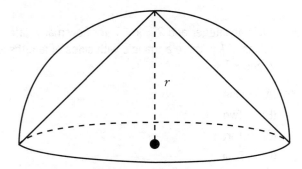

The correct answer is B.

21. John deposited $10,000 to open a new savings account that earned 4 percent annual interest, compounded quarterly. If there were no other transactions in the account, what was the amount of money in John's account 6 months after the account was opened?

    (A) $10,100
    (B) $10,101
    (C) $10,200
    (D) $10,201
    (E) $10,400

Arithmetic Operations on rational numbers

Since John's account is compounded quarterly, he receives $\frac{1}{4}$ of his annual interest, or 1%, every three months. This is added to the amount already in the account to accrue interest for the next quarter. After 6 months, this process will have occurred twice, so the amount in John's account will then be

$$(\$10{,}000)(1.01)(1.01) = \$10{,}000(1.01)^2 = \$10{,}201$$

The correct answer is D.

22. A container in the shape of a right circular cylinder is $\frac{1}{2}$ full of water. If the volume of water in the container is 36 cubic inches and the height of the container is 9 inches, what is the diameter of the base of the cylinder, in inches?

    (A) $\dfrac{16}{9\pi}$

    (B) $\dfrac{4}{\sqrt{\pi}}$

    (C) $\dfrac{12}{\sqrt{\pi}}$

    (D) $\sqrt{\dfrac{2}{\pi}}$

    (E) $4\sqrt{\dfrac{2}{\pi}}$

Geometry Volume

For a right cylinder, volume = π (radius)^2(height). Since the volume of water is 36 cubic inches and since this represents $\frac{1}{2}$ the container, the water is occupying $\frac{1}{2}$ the container's height, or $9\left(\frac{1}{2}\right) = 4.5$ inches. Let r be the radius of the cylinder.

$36 = \pi r^2(4.5)$	
$8 = \pi r^2$	divide both sides by 4.5
$\dfrac{8}{\pi} = r^2$	divide both sides by π
$\sqrt{\dfrac{8}{\pi}} = r$	take the square root of both sides
$\dfrac{2\sqrt{2}}{\sqrt{\pi}} = r$	simplify the $\sqrt{8}$ to get the radius

Then, since the diameter is twice the length of the radius, the diameter equals

$$2\left(\frac{2\sqrt{2}}{\sqrt{\pi}}\right) = 4\frac{\sqrt{2}}{\sqrt{\pi}} = 4\sqrt{\frac{2}{\pi}} \cdot$$

The correct answer is E.

23. If the positive integer x is a multiple of 4 and the positive integer y is a multiple of 6, then xy must be a multiple of which of the following?

  I. 8
  II. 12
  III. 18

  (A) II only
  (B) I and II only
  (C) I and III only
  (D) II and III only
  (E) I, II, and III

Arithmetic Properties of numbers

The product xy must be a multiple of $4(6) = 24$ and any of its factors. Test each alternative.

  I. $\dfrac{24}{8} = 3$ 8 is a factor of 24
                      MUST be a multiple of 8

  II. $\dfrac{24}{12} = 2$ 12 is a factor of 24
                      MUST be a multiple of 12

  III. $\dfrac{24}{18} = 1\frac{1}{3}$ 18 is NOT a factor of 24
                      NEED NOT be a multiple of 18

The correct answer is B.

24. Aaron will jog from home at x miles per hour and then walk back home by the same route at y miles per hour. How many miles from home can Aaron jog so that he spends a total of t hours jogging and walking?

  (A) $\dfrac{xt}{y}$

  (B) $\dfrac{x + t}{xy}$

  (C) $\dfrac{xyt}{x + y}$

  (D) $\dfrac{x + y + t}{xy}$

  (E) $\dfrac{y + t}{x} - \dfrac{t}{y}$

Algebra Simplifying algebraic expressions

Let j be the number of hours Aaron spends jogging; then let $t - j$ be the total number of hours he spends walking. It can be stated that Aaron jogs a distance of xj miles and walks a distance of $y(t - j)$ miles. Because Aaron travels the same route, the miles jogged must equal the miles walked, and they can be set equal.

$xj = y(t - j)$ set number of miles equal to each other

$xj = yt - jy$ distribute the y

$xj + jy = yt$ add jy to both sides to get all terms with j to one side

$j(x + y) = yt$ factor out the j

$j = \dfrac{yt}{x + y}$ divide both sides by $x + y$

So, the number of hours Aaron spends jogging is

$j = \dfrac{yt}{x + y}.$

The number of miles he can jog is xj or, by substitution of this value of j, $x\left(\dfrac{yt}{x + y}\right) = \dfrac{xyt}{x + y}.$

The correct answer is C.

Data Sufficiency

The following section on data sufficiency is intended to familiarize you with the most efficient and effective approaches to the kinds of problems common to data sufficiency. The particular questions in this chapter are generally representative of the kinds of data sufficiency questions you will encounter on the GMAT. Remember that it is the problem solving strategy that is important, not the specific details of a particular question.

25. If the units digit of integer n is greater than 2, what is the units digit of n ?

  (1) The units digit of n is the same as the units digit of n^2.
  (2) The units digit of n is the same as the units digit of n^3.

Arithmetic Arithmetic operations

If the units digit of n is greater than 2, then it can only be the digits 3, 4, 5, 6, 7, 8, or 9.

(1) To solve this problem, it is necessary to find a digit that is the same as the units digit of its square. For example, both 43 squared (1,849) and 303 squared (91,809) have a units digit of 9, which is different from the units digit of 43 and 303. However, 25 squared (625) and 385 squared (148,225) both have a units digit of 5, and 16 and 226 both have a units digit of 6 and their squares (256 and 51,076, respectively) do, too. However, there is no further information to choose between 5 or 6; NOT sufficient.

(2) Once again, 5 and 6 are the only numbers which, when cubed, will both have a 5 or 6 respectively in their units digits. However, the information given does not distinguish between them; NOT sufficient.

Since (1) and (2) together yield the same information but with no direction as to which to choose, there is not enough information to determine the answer.

The correct answer is E;
both statements together are still not sufficient.

26. What is the value of the integer p ?

  (1) Each of the integers 2, 3, and 5 is a factor of p.
  (2) Each of the integers 2, 5, and 7 is a factor of p.

Arithmetic Properties of numbers

(1) These are factors of p, but it is not clear that they are the only factors of p; NOT sufficient.

(2) These are factors of p, but it is not clear that they are the only factors of p; NOT sufficient.

Taken together, (1) and (2) overlap, but again there is no clear indication that these are the only factors of p.

The correct answer is E;
both statements together are still not sufficient.

27. If the length of Wanda's telephone call was rounded up to the nearest whole minute by her telephone company, then Wanda was charged for how many minutes for her telephone call?

  (1) The total charge for Wanda's telephone call was $6.50.
  (2) Wanda was charged $0.50 more for the first minute of the telephone call than for each minute after the first.

Arithmetic Arithmetic operations

(1) This does not give any information as to the call's cost per minute; NOT sufficient.

(2) From this, it can be determined only that the call was longer than one minute and that the charge for the first minute was $0.50 more than the charge for each succeeding minute; NOT sufficient.

Taking (1) and (2) together, the number of minutes cannot be determined as long as the cost of each minute after the first is unknown. For example, if the cost of each minute after the first minute were $0.40, then the cost of the first minute would be $0.90. Then the total cost of the other minutes would be $6.50 – $0.90 = $5.60, and $5.60 ÷ $0.40 would yield 14. In this case, the time of the call would be 1 + 14 = 15 minutes. If, however, the cost of each minute after the first minute were $0.15, then the cost of the first minute would be $0.65. Then $6.50 – $0.65 would be $5.85, and this in turn, when divided by $0.15, would yield 39 minutes, for a total call length of 40 minutes. More information on the cost of each minute after the first minute is still needed.

**The correct answer is E;
both statements together are still not sufficient.**

28. What is the perimeter of isosceles triangle *MNP* ?

    (1) *MN* = 16
    (2) *NP* = 20

Geometry Triangles

The perimeter of a triangle is the sum of all three sides. In the case of an isosceles triangle, two of the sides are equal. To determine the perimeter of this triangle, it is necessary to know both the length of an equal side and the length of the base of the triangle.

(1) Only gives the length of one side; NOT sufficient.

(2) Only gives the length of one side; NOT sufficient.

Since it is unclear whether *MN* or *NP* is one of the equal sides, it is not possible to determine the length of the third side or the perimeter of the triangle. The perimeter could be either $((2)(16)) + 20 = 52$ or $((2)(20)) + 16 = 56$.

**The correct answer is E;
both statements together are still not sufficient.**

29. In a survey of retailers, what percent had purchased computers for business purposes?

    (1) 85 percent of the retailers surveyed who owned their own store had purchased computers for business purposes.
    (2) 40 percent of the retailers surveyed owned their own store.

Arithmetic Percents

(1) With only this, it cannot be known what percent of the retailers not owning their own store had purchased computers, and so it cannot be known how many retailers purchased computers overall; NOT sufficient.

(2) While this permits the percent of owners and nonowners in the survey to be deduced, the overall percent of retailers who had purchased computers cannot be determined; NOT sufficient.

Using the information from both (1) and (2), the percent of surveyed owner-retailers who had purchased computers can be deduced, and the percent of nonowner-retailers can also be deduced. However, the information that would permit a determination of either the percent of nonowner-retailers who had purchased computers or the overall percent of all retailers (both owners and nonowners) who had purchased computers is still not provided.

**The correct answer is E;
both statements together are still not sufficient.**

30. The only gift certificates that a certain store sold yesterday were worth either $100 each or $10 each. If the store sold a total of 20 gift certificates yesterday, how many gift certificates worth $10 each did the store sell yesterday?

    (1) The gift certificates sold by the store yesterday were worth a total of between $1,650 and $1,800.
    (2) Yesterday the store sold more than 15 gift certificates worth $100 each.

Algebra Applied problems; Simultaneous equations; Inequalities

Let *x* represent the number of $100 certificates sold, and let *y* represent the number of $10 certificates sold. Then the given information can be expressed as $x + y = 20$ or thus $y = 20 - x$. The value of the $100 certificates sold is $100x$, and the value of the $10 certificates sold is $10y$.

(1) From this, it is known that $100x + 10y > 1,650$. Since $y = 20 - x$, this value can be substituted for y, and the inequality can be solved for x:

$$100x + 10y > 1,650$$
$$100x + 10(20 - x) > 1,650 \quad \text{substitute for } y$$
$$100x + 200 - 10x > 1,650 \quad \text{distribute}$$
$$90x + 200 > 1,650 \quad \text{simplify}$$
$$90x > 1,450 \quad \text{subtract 200 from both sides}$$
$$x > 16.1$$

Thus, more than 16 of the $100 certificates were sold. If 17 $100 certificates were sold, then it must be that 3 $10 certificates were also sold for a total of $1,730, which satisfies the condition of being between $1,650 and $1,800. If, however, 18 $100 certificates were sold, then it must be that 2 $10 certificates were sold, and this totals $1,820, which is more than $1,800 and fails to satisfy the condition. Therefore, 3 of the $10 certificates were sold; SUFFICIENT.

(2) From this it can be known only that the number of $10 certificates sold was 4 or fewer; NOT sufficient.

The correct answer is A;
statement 1 alone is sufficient.

31. Is the standard deviation of the set of measurements $x_1, x_2, x_3, x_4, ..., x_{20}$ less than 3 ?

    (1) The variance for the set of measurements is 4.
    (2) For each measurement, the difference between the mean and that measurement is 2.

Arithmetic Statistics

In determining the standard deviation, the difference between each measurement and the mean is squared, and then the squared differences are added and divided by the number of measurements. The quotient is the variance and the positive square root of the variance is the standard deviation.

(1) If the variance is 4, then the standard deviation = $\sqrt{4}$ = 2, which is less than 3; SUFFICIENT.

(2) For each measurement, the difference between the mean and that measurement is 2. Therefore, the square of each difference is 4, and the sum of all the squares is $4 \times 20 = 80$. The standard deviation is $\sqrt{\dfrac{80}{20}} = \sqrt{4} = 2$, which is less than 3; SUFFICIENT.

The correct answer is D;
each statement alone is sufficient.

32. Is the range of the integers 6, 3, y, 4, 5, and x greater than 9 ?

    (1) $y > 3x$
    (2) $y > x > 3$

Arithmetic Statistics

The range of a set of integers is equal to the difference between the largest integer and the smallest integer. The range of the set of integers 3, 4, 5, and 6 is 3, which is derived from $6 - 3$.

(1) Although it is known that $y > 3x$, the value of x is unknown. If, for example, $x = 1$, then the value of y would be greater than 3. However, if $x = 2$, then the value of y would be greater than 6, and, since 6 would no longer be the largest integer, the range would be affected. Because the actual values of x and y are unknown, the value of the range is also unknown; NOT sufficient.

(2) If $x > 3$, and $y > x$, then x could be 4 and y could be 5. Then the range of the 6 integers would still be $6 - 3$ or 3. However, if x were 4 and y were 15, then the range of the 6 integers would be $15 - 3$, or 12. There is no means to establish the values of x and y, beyond the fact that they both are greater than 3; NOT sufficient.

Taking (1) and (2) together, it is known that $x > 3$ and that $y > 3x$. Since the smallest integer that x could be is thus 4, then $y > 3(4)$ or $y > 12$. Therefore, the integer y must be 13 or larger. When y is equal to 13, the range of the 6 integers is $13 - 3 = 10$, which is larger than 9. As y increases in value, the value of the range will also increase.

The correct answer is C;
both statements together are sufficient.

33. Is $\dfrac{5^{x+2}}{25} < 1$?

    (1) $5^x < 1$
    (2) $x < 0$

    Algebra Inequalities

    Note that $x^{r+s} = (x^r)(x^s)$.

    If $5^x < 1$, then $\dfrac{5^{x+2}}{25} < 1$ since

    $\dfrac{5^{x+2}}{25} = \dfrac{5^x \cdot 5^2}{25} = 5^x$; SUFFICIENT.

    (2) If $x < 0$, then

    $\quad x + 2 < 2$ add 2 to both sides

    $\quad 5^{x+2} < 5^2$ because $a < b$ implies $5^a < 5^b$

    $\quad \dfrac{5^{x+2}}{25} < 1$ divide both sides by $5^2 = 25$;

    SUFFICIENT.

    **The correct answer is D;
    each statement alone is sufficient.**

34. Of the companies surveyed about the skills they required in prospective employees, 20 percent required both computer skills and writing skills. What percent of the companies surveyed required neither computer skills nor writing skills?

    (1) Of those companies surveyed that required computer skills, half required writing skills.

    (2) 45 percent of the companies surveyed required writing skills but not computer skills.

    Arithmetic Percents

    The surveyed companies could be placed into one of the following four categories:

    1. Requiring computer skills and requiring writing skills

    2. Requiring computer skills but not requiring writing skills

    3. Not requiring computer skills but requiring writing skills

    4. Not requiring either computer skills or writing skills

    It is given that 20 percent of the surveyed companies fell into category 1. It is necessary to determine what percent of the surveyed companies fell into category 4.

    (1) This helps identify the percentage in category 2. Since $\dfrac{1}{2}$ the companies that required computer skills also required writing skills (i.e., those in category 1), then the other $\dfrac{1}{2}$ of the companies that required computer skills did not require writing skills (thus category 2 = category 1). However, this information only establishes that 20 percent required computer skills, but not writing skills; NOT sufficient.

    (2) While this establishes category 3, that is, that 45 percent required writing skills but not computer skills, no further information is available; NOT sufficient.

    Taking (1) and (2) together, the first three categories add up to 85 percent (20 + 20 + 45). Therefore, category 4 would be equal to $100 - 85 = 15$ percent of the surveyed companies required neither computer skills nor writing skills.

    **The correct answer is C;
    both statements together are sufficient.**

35. What is the value of $w + q$?

    (1) $3w = 3 - 3q$
    (2) $5w + 5q = 5$

    Algebra First- and second-degree equations

    (1) If $3q$ is added to both sides of this equation, it can be rewritten as $3w + 3q = 3$. When each term is then divided by 3, it yields $w + q = 1$; SUFFICIENT.

    (2) When each term in this equation is divided by 5, it becomes $w + q = 1$; SUFFICIENT.

    **The correct answer is D;
    each statement alone is sufficient.**

36. If X and Y are points in a plane and X lies inside the circle C with center O and radius 2, does Y lie inside circle C ?

  (1) The length of line segment XY is 3.

  (2) The length of line segment OY is 1.5.

Geometry Circles

(1) The maximum distance between two points that lie on a circle is equal to the diameter, or 2 times the radius. Since the radius of circle C is 2, the diameter in this case is 4. It cannot be assumed, however, that X and Y are points on the diameter; X can lie anywhere within the circle. When the distance between X and Y is 3, it is still possible either that Y is within the circle or that Y is outside the circle; NOT sufficient.

(2) If the length of the line segment OY is 1.5 and the circle has a radius of 2, then the distance from the center O to point Y is less than the radius, and point Y must therefore lie within the circle; SUFFICIENT.

The correct answer is B; statement 2 alone is sufficient.

37. Is x > y ?

  (1) x = y + 2

  (2) $\dfrac{x}{2} = y - 1$

Algebra First- and second-degree equations

(1) Since 2 has to be added to y in order to make it equal to x, it can be reasoned that x > y; SUFFICIENT.

(2) Multiplying both sides of this equation by 2 results in $x = 2(y - 1)$ or $x = 2y - 2$. If y were 0, then x would be −2, and y would be greater than x. If y were a negative number like −2, then $x = 2(-2) - 2 = -6$, and again y would be greater than x. However, if y were a positive number such as 4, then $x = 2(4) - 2 = 6$, and x > y. Since there is no other information concerning the value of y, it cannot be determined if x > y; NOT sufficient.

The correct answer is A; statement 1 alone is sufficient.

38. If Paula drove the distance from her home to her college at an average speed that was greater than 70 kilometers per hour, did it take her less than 3 hours to drive this distance?

  (1) The distance that Paula drove from her home to her college was greater than 200 kilometers.

  (2) The distance that Paula drove from her home to her college was less than 205 kilometers.

Arithmetic Distance problem

A distance problem uses the formula distance = rate × time. To find the time, the formula would be rearranged as time = $\dfrac{\text{distance}}{\text{rate}}$. To solve this problem, it is necessary to know the rate (given here as 70 kilometers per hour) and the distance.

(1) If D is the distance Paula drove then $D > 200$ and $\dfrac{D}{70} > \dfrac{200}{70} = 2\dfrac{6}{7}$ so $t > 2\dfrac{6}{7}$ and t may or may not be less than 3; NOT sufficient.

(2) If D is the distance Paula drove then $D < 205$ and $\dfrac{D}{70} < \dfrac{205}{70} = 2\dfrac{13}{14}$ so $t < 2\dfrac{13}{14} < 3$; SUFFICIENT.

The correct answer is B; statement 2 alone is sufficient.

39. In the xy-plane, if line k has negative slope and passes through the point (−5,r), is the x-intercept of line k positive?

  (1) The slope of line k is −5.

  (2) r > 0

Geometry Coordinate geometry

The x-intercept is the x-coordinate of the point in which the line k crosses the x-axis and would have the coordinates $(x,0)$.

(1) Knowing the slope of the line does not help in determining the x-intercept, since from point $(-5,r)$ the line k extends in both directions. Without knowing the value of r, the x-intercept could be -5 if r were 0, or it could be other numbers, both positive and negative, depending on the value of r; NOT sufficient.

(2) Knowing that $r > 0$, suggests that the x-intercept is not -5; the point $(-5,r)$, where r is a positive number, does lie in quadrant II. It could, however, be any point with an x-coordinate of -5 in that quadrant and line k could have any negative slope, and so the line k would vary with the value of r. Therefore, the x-intercept of line k cannot be determined; NOT sufficient.

Using (1) and (2) together does not help in the determination of the x-intercept, since the point $(-5,r)$ could have any positive y-coordinate and thus line k could cross the x-axis at many different places.

**The correct answer is E;
both statements together are still not sufficient.**

40. If \$5,000 invested for one year at p percent simple annual interest yields \$500, what amount must be invested at k percent simple annual interest for one year to yield the same number of dollars?

(1) $k = 0.8p$
(2) $k = 8$

Arithmetic Interest problem

With simple annual interest, the formula to use is interest = principal × rate × time. It is given that $\$500 = \$5,000 \times \frac{p}{100} \times 1$ (year), so $p = 10$ percent interest.

(1) If p is 10 percent, then $k = 0.8p$ is 0.08. Using the same formula, the time is again 1 year; the interest is the same amount; and the rate is 0.08, or 8 percent. Thus, $\$500 = $ principal $\times 0.08 \times 1$, or principal $= \$6,250$; SUFFICIENT.

(2) If $k = 8$, then the rate is 8 percent, and the same formula and procedure as above are employed again; SUFFICIENT.

**The correct answer is D;
each statement alone is sufficient.**

41. If $\frac{x+y}{z} > 0$, is $x < 0$?

(1) $x < y$
(2) $z < 0$

Algebra Inequalities

If $\frac{x+y}{z} > 0$, then either one of two cases holds true. Either $(x + y) > 0$ **and** $z > 0$, or $(x + y) < 0$ **and** $z < 0$. In other words, in order for the term to be greater than zero, it must be true that either 1) both the numerator and denominator are greater than 0 or 2) both the numerator and denominator are less than 0.

(1) Regardless of whether $(x + y)$ is positive or negative, the positive or negative value of z must be in agreement with the sign of $(x + y)$ in order for $\frac{x+y}{z} > 0$. However, there is no information about z here; NOT sufficient.

(2) If $z < 0$, then $(x + y)$ must be less than 0. However, this statement gives no information about $(x + y)$; NOT sufficient.

This can be solved using (1) and (2) together. From (2), it is known that $z < 0$, and, going back to the original analysis, for the term to be greater than zero, $(x + y)$ must also be less than 0. If $x + y < 0$ then $x < -y$. But $x < y$ from (1) so

$$x + x < -y + y$$
$$2x < 0$$
$$x < 0.$$

**The correct answer is C;
both statements together are sufficient.**

42. Does the integer k have at least three different positive prime factors?

    (1) $\frac{k}{15}$ is an integer.

    (2) $\frac{k}{10}$ is an integer.

Arithmetic Properties of numbers

(1) The prime factors of 15 are 3 and 5. So in this case, k has at least 2 different positive prime factors, but it is unknown if there are more positive prime factors; NOT sufficient.

(2) The prime factors of 10 are 2 and 5, showing that k has at least these 2 different positive prime factors, but k might or might not have more; NOT sufficient.

Taking (1) and (2) together, since k is divisible by both 10 and 15, it must be divisible by their different positive prime factors of 2, 3, and 5. Thus k has at least 3 different positive prime factors.

The correct answer is C; both statements together are sufficient.

43. In City X last April, was the average (arithmetic mean) daily high temperature greater than the median daily high temperature?

    (1) In City X last April, the sum of the 30 daily high temperatures was 2,160°.

    (2) In City X last April, 60 percent of the daily high temperatures were less than the average daily high temperature.

Arithmetic Statistics

The formula for calculating the arithmetic mean, or the average, is as follows:

$$\text{Average} = \frac{\text{sum of } v \text{ values}}{v}$$

(1) These data will produce an average of $\frac{2160}{30} = 72°$ for last April in City X. However, there is no information regarding the median for comparison; NOT sufficient.

(2) The median is the middle temperature of the data. As such, 50 percent of the daily high temperatures will be at or above the median, and 50 percent will be at or below the median. If 60 percent of the daily high temperatures were less than the average daily high temperature, then the average of the daily highs must be greater than the median; SUFFICIENT.

The correct answer is B; statement 2 alone is sufficient.

44. If m and n are positive integers, is $\left(\sqrt{m}\right)^n$ an integer?

    (1) $\left(\sqrt{m}\right)$ is an integer.

    (2) $\left(\sqrt{n}\right)$ is an integer.

Arithmetic Properties of numbers

(1) If $\left(\sqrt{m}\right)$ is an integer and n is a positive integer, then $\left(\sqrt{m}\right)^n$ is an integer because an integer raised to a positive integer is an integer; SUFFICIENT.

(2) The information that $\left(\sqrt{n}\right)$ is an integer is not helpful in answering the question. For example, if $m = 2$ and $n = 9$, $\sqrt{9} = 3$, which is an integer, but $\left(\sqrt{2}\right)^9 = \left(16\sqrt{2}\right)$, which is not an integer. But if $m = 4$ and $n = 9$, then $\sqrt{9} = 3$, which is an integer, and $\left(\sqrt{4}\right)^9 = 2^9 = 512$ is an integer; NOT sufficient.

The correct answer is A; statement 1 alone is sufficient.

45. Of the 66 people in a certain auditorium, at most 6 people have birthdays in any one given month. Does at least one person in the auditorium have a birthday in January?

(1) More of the people in the auditorium have birthdays in February than in March.

(2) Five of the people in the auditorium have birthdays in March.

Algebra Sets and functions

Because it is given that 6 is the greatest number of individuals who can have birthdays in any particular month, these 66 people could be evenly distributed across 11 of the 12 months of the year. That is to say, it could be possible for the distribution to be 11 × 6 = 66, and thus any given month, such as January, would not have a person with a birthday. Assume that January has no people with birthdays, and see if this assumption is disproved.

(1) The information that more people have February birthdays than March birthdays indicates that the distribution is not even. Therefore, March is underrepresented and must thus have fewer than 6 birthdays. Since no month can have more than 6 people with birthdays, and every month but January already has as many people with birthdays as it can have, January has to have at least 1 person with a birthday; SUFFICIENT.

(2) Again, March is underrepresented with only 5 birthdays, and none of the other months can have more than 6 birthdays. Therefore, the extra birthday (from March) must occur in January; SUFFICIENT.

**The correct answer is D;
each statement alone is sufficient.**

46. Last year the average (arithmetic mean) salary of the 10 employees of Company X was $42,800. What is the average salary of the same 10 employees this year?

(1) For 8 of the 10 employees, this year's salary is 15 percent greater than last year's salary.

(2) For 2 of the 10 employees, this year's salary is the same as last year's salary.

Arithmetic Statistics

(1) Since all 10 employees did not receive the same 15 percent increase, it cannot be assumed that the mean this year is 15 percent higher than last year. It remains unknown whether these 8 salaries were the top 8 salaries, the bottom 8 salaries, or somewhere in-between. Without this type of information from last year, the mean for this year cannot be determined; NOT sufficient.

(2) If 2 salaries remained the same as last year, then 8 salaries changed. Without further information about the changes, the mean for this year cannot be determined; NOT sufficient.

Even taking (1) and (2) together, it remains impossible to tell the mean salary for this year without additional data.

**The correct answer is E;
both statements together are still not sufficient.**

47. In a certain classroom, there are 80 books, of which 24 are fiction and 23 are written in Spanish. How many of the fiction books are written in Spanish?

(1) Of the fiction books, there are 6 more that are not written in Spanish than are written in Spanish.

(2) Of the books written in Spanish, there are 5 more nonfiction books than fiction books.

Algebra Sets and functions

Let x represent the fiction books that are written in Spanish. A table could be set up like the one below, filling in the information that is known or able to be known:

	Spanish	Non-Spanish	Total
Fiction	x		24
Nonfiction			56
Total	23	57	80

(1) If x represents the fiction books written in Spanish, then $x + 6$ can now be used to represent the fiction books that are not written in Spanish. From the table above, it can be seen then that $x + x + 6 = 24$, or $2x = 18$. Therefore, x, or the number of fiction books written in Spanish, is 9; SUFFICIENT.

(2)   If x represents the fiction books written in Spanish, then $x + 5$ can now be used to represent the nonfiction books written in Spanish. From the table, it can be said that $x + x + 5 = 23$, or $2x = 18$. Therefore, x, or the number of fiction books written in Spanish, is 9; SUFFICIENT.

**The correct answer is D;
each statement alone is sufficient.**

48.   If p is the perimeter of rectangle Q, what is the value of p ?

(1)   Each diagonal of rectangle Q has length 10.

(2)   The area of rectangle Q is 48.

Geometry Rectangles; Perimeter; Area

The perimeter of a rectangle is equal to 2 times the rectangle's length plus 2 times the rectangle's width, or $p = 2l + 2w$. The diagonals of a rectangle are equal. In a rectangle, because a diagonal forms a right triangle, the length of a diagonal is equal to the square root of the length squared plus the width squared, or $d = \sqrt{l^2 + w^2}$.

(1)   If a diagonal = 10, then $10 = \sqrt{l^2 + w^2}$, or, by squaring both sides, $100 = l^2 + w^2$. Without knowing the value or the relationship between the other two sides of the right triangle, it is impossible to solve for l or w, and thus for the perimeter of the rectangle; NOT sufficient.

(2)   If the area of the rectangle is 48, then it can be stated that $lw = 48$. However, without further information, the perimeter cannot be determined. For example, l could be 6 and w could be 8, and the perimeter would then be $12 + 16 = 28$. However, it could also be that l is 4 and w is 12, and in that case the perimeter would be $8 + 24 = 32$; NOT sufficient.

Using (1) and (2) together, it is possible to solve this problem. Since from (2) $lw = 48$, then $w = \dfrac{48}{l}$. Substituting this into $100 = l^2 + w^2$ from (1) the equation can be solved as follows:

$100 = l^2 + \left(\dfrac{48}{l}\right)^2$ substitution

$100l^2 = l^4 + 2{,}304$ multiply both sides by l^2

$l^4 - 100l^2 + 2{,}304 = 0$ move all terms to one side

$(l^2 - 64)(l^2 - 36) = 0$ factor like a quadratic

$l^2 = 64, \ l^2 = 36$ solve for l^2

Since l is a length, it must be positive, so l is either 8 or 6. When $l = 8$, $w = \dfrac{48}{6} = 6$, and when $l = 6$, $w = \dfrac{48}{6} = 8$, both of which give the same perimeter.

**The correct answer is C;
both statements together are sufficient.**

3.6 Verbal Answer Explanations

Reading Comprehension

The following discussion is intended to familiarize you with the most efficient and effective approaches to the kinds of problems common to reading comprehension. The particular questions in this chapter are generally representative of the kinds of reading comprehension questions you will encounter on the GMAT. Remember that it is the problem solving strategy that is important, not the specific details of a particular question.

Questions 1–5 refer to the passage on page 27.

1. Which of the following best describes the purpose of the sentence in lines 10–15?

   (A) To show that economic signaling theory fails to explain a finding

   (B) To introduce a distinction not accounted for by economic signaling theory

   (C) To account for an exception to a generalization suggested by Marquardt and McGann

   (D) To explain why Marquardt and McGann's research was conducted

   (E) To offer an explanation for an observation reported by Marquardt and McGann

Logical structure

Marquardt and McGann found a correlation between highly advertised products and high-quality products. The connection can be explained by understanding that companies may invest heavily in such advertising, anticipating that recurring purchases of high-quality products will eventually recover these advertising costs. The consumers will continue to buy these products over time because of loyalty to their high quality. The statement in bold provides this explanation for the correlation noted by Marquardt and McGann.

A   The shaded sentence does not explain a failure of the economic signaling theory.

B   Economic signaling theory is about perceptions of quality, but this explanation is about actual quality and its correlation with advertising.

C   No exception is mentioned in Marquardt and McGann's work.

D   The statement does not examine why or how the research was undertaken.

E   **Correct.** This statement provides an explanation of why highly advertised products *did indeed rank high on certain measures of product quality.*

The correct answer is E.

2. The primary purpose of the passage is to

   (A) present findings that contradict one explanation for the effects of a particular advertising practice

   (B) argue that theoretical explanations about the effects of a particular advertising practice are of limited value without empirical evidence

   (C) discuss how and why particular advertising practices may affect consumers' perceptions

   (D) contrast the research methods used in two different studies of a particular advertising practice

   (E) explain why a finding about consumer responses to a particular advertising practice was unexpected

Main idea

The primary purpose can be determined only by evaluating the whole passage. The first paragraph discusses consumers' perceptions of quality based on frequency of advertising. The second paragraph discusses three studies that show how consumers base their evaluations of products on the kinds of advertising they see. Therefore, the purpose of the whole passage is to show how consumers' perceptions of products are shaped by certain advertising practices.

A   The passage shows that expensive advertising works to a certain point, but not after it; this method examines a continuum, not a contradiction.

B   Most of the passage is devoted to empirical evidence.

C   **Correct.** The passage shows how the frequency and the kind of advertising influence consumers' perceptions about the quality of the products advertised.

D   The passage reports the findings of four studies but does not mention research methods.

E   The passage does not indicate that any of the findings were unexpected.

The correct answer is C.

3.   Kirmani's research, as described in the passage, suggests which of the following regarding consumers' expectations about the quality of advertised products?

(A)   Those expectations are likely to be highest if a manufacturer runs both black-and-white and color advertisements for the same product.

(B)   Those expectations can be shaped by the presence of color in an advertisement as well as by the frequency with which an advertisement appears.

(C)   Those expectations are usually high for frequently advertised new brands but not for frequently advertised familiar brands.

(D)   Those expectations are likely to be higher for products whose black-and-white advertisements are often repeated than for those whose color advertisements are less often repeated.

(E)   Those expectations are less definitively shaped by the manufacturer's advertisements than by information that consumers gather from other sources.

Inference

The question's use of the word *suggests* means that the answer depends on making an inference. This research is discussed in the second paragraph. Kirmani found that too much advertising tended to make the consumers believe that manufacturers were desperate. The use of color was also found to affect consumers' perceptions of brand quality. Realizing that color advertising is more expensive than black-and-white, consumers react more quickly to what they perceive to be its overuse than they do to a repetition of black-and-white advertisements.

A   This situation is not discussed in the research, at least as it is reported in this passage.

B   Correct. It can be inferred that consumers' perceptions of product quality are influenced by the use of color in an advertisement and by the frequency of the advertisement's appearance.

C   The research does not make a distinction between new and familiar brands.

D   The research indicates only that consumers can tolerate black-and-white advertisements for a longer time than color advertisements before dismissing them as excessive.

E   There is no discussion of what consumers learn from other sources.

The correct answer is B.

4.   Kirmani's third study, as described in the passage, suggests which of the following conclusions about a black-and-white advertisement?

(A)   It can be repeated more frequently than a comparable color advertisement could before consumers begin to suspect low manufacturer confidence in the quality of the advertised product.

(B)   It will have the greatest impact on consumers' perceptions of the quality of the advertised product if it appears during periods when a color version of the same advertisement is also being used.

(C)   It will attract more attention from readers of the print publication in which it appears if it is used only a few times.

(D)   It may be perceived by some consumers as more expensive than a comparable color advertisement.

(E)   It is likely to be perceived by consumers as a sign of higher manufacturer confidence in the quality of the advertised product than a comparable color advertisement would be.

Inference

Kirmani's third study is discussed in the final two sentences. Consumers suspect expensive advertising results from a manufacturer's lack of confidence in the quality of the product. Consumers reach the point at which they find advertising *excessive* more quickly with color advertising than with black-and-white advertising because they understand that the addition of color increases advertising expenses. It is reasonable to infer that the reverse is also true and thus that consumers will tolerate lengthier repetitions of black-and-white advertising without becoming suspicious of product quality.

A   Correct. Consumers find color advertising excessive more quickly and thus can be expected to find black-and-white advertising excessive less quickly.

B   The study does not discuss concurrent appearances of color and black-and-white advertisements for the same product.

C   The sole conclusion about frequency is that consumers can tolerate a greater frequency of black-and-white advertisements than color advertisements.

D   It is stated that consumers understand that color advertisements are more expensive.

E   The research certainly does not report this finding.

The correct answer is A.

5.   The passage suggests that Kirmani would be most likely to agree with which of the following statements about consumers' perceptions of the relationship between the frequency with which a product is advertised and the product's quality?

(A)   Consumers' perceptions about the frequency with which an advertisement appears are their primary consideration when evaluating an advertisement's claims about product quality.

(B)   Because most consumers do not notice the frequency of advertisement, it has little impact on most consumers' expectations regarding product quality.

(C)   Consumers perceive frequency of advertisement as a signal about product quality only when the advertisement is for a product that is newly on the market.

(D)   The frequency of advertisement is not always perceived by consumers to indicate that manufacturers are highly confident about their products' quality.

(E)   Consumers who try a new product that has been frequently advertised are likely to perceive the advertisement's frequency as having been an accurate indicator of the product's quality.

Inference

The first sentence of the second paragraph provides the answer to this question: *at some level of spending the manufacturer's advertising effort may be perceived as unreasonably high, implying low manufacturer confidence in product quality.* Thus, it is logical to assume that if a product is advertised too frequently, consumers may believe that the manufacturer is spending excessive amounts on advertising because that manufacturer is not confident of the product's quality.

A   Kirmani's research, as reported here, does not support this claim.

B   Kirmani's research examines how consumers respond to the frequency of advertising; the research does not indicate that consumers do not notice frequency.

C   The research does not distinguish between new and familiar products.

D   Correct. Excessive advertising may lead consumers to believe that the manufacturer lacks confidence in the quality of the product.

E   Kirmani's research does not specifically address new products.

The correct answer is D.

Questions 6–11 refer to the passage on page 29.

6.   The main purpose of the passage is to

(A)   propose an experiment

(B)   analyze a function

(C)   refute an argument

(D)   explain a contradiction

(E)   simulate a process

Main idea

Determining the main purpose comes from considering the passage as a whole. The first paragraph begins by noting that *the idea of the brain as an information processor* is generally accepted by neuroscientists. The author then presents Searle as an *enemy* of this position and explains Searle's belief that human thought is more than information processing. The second paragraph questions Searle's position, and the third asserts that the brain is an information processor, refuting Searle's argument.

A   The author uses the idea of a mechanical simulation of a stomach as a metaphor for a computer's simulation of thought; this is not a proposal for an experiment.

B   The author analyzes Searle's position, but no function is analyzed.

C   Correct. The author explains Searle's argument in order to refute it.

D   The author points out a weakness in Searle's thinking, but not a contradiction.

E   The simulation of a process is included as a metaphor, but it is not essential to the passage.

The correct answer is C.

7.   Which of the following is most consistent with Searle's reasoning as presented in the passage?

(A)   Meaning and content cannot be reduced to algorithms.

(B)   The process of digestion can be simulated mechanically, but not on a computer.

(C)   Simulated thoughts and real thoughts are essentially similar because they are composed primarily of information.

(D)   A computer can use "causal powers" similar to those of the human brain when processing information.

(E)   Computer simulations of the world can achieve the complexity of the brain's representations of the world.

Evaluation

Searle's position is stated in the first paragraph: because computers merely follow algorithms, *they cannot deal with important aspects of human thought such as meaning and content.* Thus, Searle believes that meaning and content cannot be reduced to algorithms.

A   Correct. Searle believes that meaning and content cannot be reduced to algorithms.

B   The author argues for the mechanical simulation, but offers no evidence that Searle would agree.

C   This statement reflects the author's position, but it is the opposite of Searle's.

D   Searle asserts that only people, not computers, have *the causal powers of the brain.*

E   The passage does not discuss computer simulations of the world.

The correct answer is A.

8.   The author of the passage would be most likely to agree with which of the following statements about the simulation of organ functions?

(A)   An artificial device that achieves the functions of the stomach could be considered a valid model of the stomach.

(B)   Computer simulations of the brain are best used to crack the brain's codes of meaning and content.

(C)   Computer simulations of the brain challenge ideas that are fundamental to psychology and neuroscience.

(D)   Because the brain and the stomach both act as processors, they can best be simulated by mechanical devices.

(E)   The computer's limitations in simulating digestion suggest equal limitations in computer-simulated thinking.

Application

To answer this question, think about how the author would respond to each statement. Anticipating the author's response depends on understanding the author's point of view. In this passage, the author is arguing against Searle's view of the brain and in favor of the brain as information processor. The author believes that the computer can be a model of the brain and uses the example of the mechanical stomach to support his position on simulations.

A **Correct.** The first two sentences of the third paragraph imply that a mechanical device is a valid model.

B The author believes a computer can simulate the brain but does not comment on how these simulations should be used. There is no way to predict the author's reaction to this statement.

C The author would reject this statement since neuroscience and psychology do in fact see the brain as an information processor.

D The author agrees that both the brain and the stomach act as processors; believes that the computer, a nonmechanical device, can simulate the brain; and offers a way that a mechanical device could simulate the stomach. The author does not suggest that mechanical devices are the best way to simulate both their processes.

E This statement reflects Searle's viewpoint, which the author rejects.

The correct answer is A.

9. It can be inferred that the author of the passage believes that Searle's argument is flawed by its failure to

(A) distinguish between syntactic and semantic operations

(B) explain adequately how people, unlike computers, are able to understand meaning

(C) provide concrete examples illustrating its claims about thinking

(D) understand how computers use algorithms to process information

(E) decipher the code that is transmitted from neuron to neuron in the brain

Inference

The author's attitude toward Searle's argument is apparent in the first paragraph, which ends with the author's summary of what Searle is saying. Computers understand structures, Searle argues, but only people understand meaning. How do people understand meaning? The author notes that Searle is not able to answer this question and is able only to assert that people have *causal powers of the brain*.

A The author makes it clear in the first paragraph that Searle does distinguish between the two. In Searle's view computers are syntactic, interpreting structure or arrangement, rather than semantic, understanding meaning.

B **Correct.** The first paragraph ends with the contrast between people and computers: *People, on the other hand, understand meaning because they have something Searle obscurely calls the causal powers of the brain.* By calling Searle's explanation obscure, the author implies that Searle has not adequately clarified how people understand meaning.

C Nothing in the passage criticizes Searle for not providing concrete examples. Indeed, in the second paragraph, the author anticipates how Searle would react to one concrete example, the computer simulation of the stomach.

D In the first paragraph, the author says that Searle argues that *computers simply follow algorithms*; whether or not Searle understands how they use algorithms is irrelevant.

E Since, as the author suggests in the first paragraph, Searle does not believe information could be a code transmitted from neuron to neuron, he cannot be expected to decipher that code.

The correct answer is B.

10. From the passage, it can be inferred that the author would agree with Searle on which of the following points?

    (A) Computers operate by following algorithms.
    (B) The human brain can never fully understand its own functions.
    (C) The comparison of the brain to a machine is overly simplistic.
    (D) The most accurate models of physical processes are computer simulations.
    (E) Human thought and computer-simulated thought involve similar processes of representation.

Inference

An inference requires going beyond the material explicitly stated in the passage to the author's ideas that underlie that material. The author and Searle take opposite points of view on the brain as information processor. Their area of agreement is narrow. However, they do both agree that computers work by following algorithms.

A **Correct.** The first paragraph explains that Searle dismisses computers because they *simply follow algorithms*; while the author disagrees with Searle on virtually every other point, no disagreement is voiced here.

B The first paragraph shows this to be Searle's position, but not the author's.

C The first paragraph shows this to be Searle's position, but not the author's.

D The second paragraph explains Searle's rejection of this position.

E The final paragraph establishes this as the author's position, but not Searle's.

The correct answer is A.

11. Which of the following most accurately represents Searle's criticism of the brain-as-computer metaphor, as that criticism is described in the passage?

    (A) The metaphor is not experimentally verifiable.
    (B) The metaphor does not take into account the unique powers of the brain.
    (C) The metaphor suggests that a brain's functions can be simulated as easily as those of a stomach.
    (D) The metaphor suggests that a computer can simulate the workings of the mind by using the codes of neural transmission.
    (E) The metaphor is unhelpful because both the brain and the computer process information.

Inference

Searle's criticism of the brain-as-computer metaphor is discussed in the first paragraph. Computers are merely machines; only people are endowed with *causal powers of the brain* that allow them to understand meaning and content.

A Searle does not believe in the value of the metaphor, so its verification is beside the point.

B **Correct.** Searle believes that people have something computers do not, *causal powers of the brain* for understanding *important aspects of human thought*.

C Comparing the brain to a computer, the metaphor does not make this suggestion.

D In the second paragraph, the author says, *but even if a computer could simulate the workings of the mind,* making it clear that presently it cannot; this statement does not reflect why Searle rejects the metaphor.

E This is not the basis of Searle's objection since he does not accept the premise that the brain is an information processor.

The correct answer is B.

Questions 12–17 refer to the passage on page 31.

12. The primary purpose of the passage is to

   (A) explain why women reformers of the Progressive Era failed to achieve their goals

   (B) discuss the origins of child labor laws in the late nineteenth and early twentieth centuries

   (C) compare the living conditions of working-class and middle-class women in the Progressive Era

   (D) discuss an oversight on the part of women reformers of the Progressive Era

   (E) revise a traditional view of the role played by women reformers in enacting Progressive Era reforms

Main idea

Understanding the author's purpose comes only from reflecting on the passage as a whole. The beginning of the passage notes the success of middle-class women reformers in improving working conditions for women and children. The middle discusses the position of working-class mothers, who were more concerned with the economic survival of their families than with labor reform and consequently tried to circumvent the laws. The close of the passage observes that, although middle-class reformers were right to point out exploitation of children, they failed to understand the economic plight of working-class families, who needed the income earned by every possible member. The purpose of this passage is to show the failure of middle-class reformers to understand the economic position of working-class families.

A Lines 6–10 emphasize the victories of the reformers.

B The passage discusses the effects, rather than the origins, of child labor laws.

C Living conditions of middle-class and working-class women are not compared.

D Correct. As is made clear, especially in the final sentence of the passage, women reformers failed to understand the economic needs of working-class families.

E A traditional view is not compared with a newer, revised view of the reformers.

The correct answer is D.

13. The *view* mentioned in line 17 of the passage refers to which of the following?

   (A) Some working-class mothers' resistance to the enforcement of child labor laws

   (B) Reformers' belief that child labor and industrial home work should be abolished

   (C) Reformers' opinions about how working-class families raised their children

   (D) Certain women historians' observation that there was a lack of consensus between women of different classes on the issue of child labor and industrial home work

   (E) Working-class families' fears about the adverse consequences that child labor laws would have on their ability to earn an adequate living

Inference

To find what this appearance of *view* refers to, it is necessary to look back to the beginning of the sentence. *This view*, not shared by working-class mothers, refers to the reformers' conviction that *child labor and industrial home work were equally inhumane practices that should be outlawed.*

A   *This view* must refer back to a point already stated; resistance to child labor laws is not discussed until the following sentence.

B   **Correct.** *This view* refers to the position of reformers stated earlier in the same sentence: that *child labor and industrial home work...should be outlawed.*

C   *This view* must refer back to a point already stated; the reformers' belief that resistance to child labor laws was due to poor parenting is discussed later in the passage.

D   A number of women historians have said that working-class mothers did not always share the *view* of middle-class women reformers about child labor.

E   *This view* must refer back to a point already stated; the fears of working-class families are examined in the following sentence.

The correct answer is B.

14. The author of the passage mentions the observations of women historians (lines 15–17) most probably in order to

(A) provide support for an assertion made in the preceding sentence (lines 10–12)

(B) raise a question that is answered in the last sentence of the passage (lines 27–32)

(C) introduce an opinion that challenges a statement made in the first sentence of the passage

(D) offer an alternative view to the one attributed in the passage to working-class mothers

(E) point out a contradiction inherent in the traditional view of child labor reform as it is presented in the passage

Evaluation

In lines 10–12, the author asserts that child labor laws *pitted women of different classes against one another.* The view of the middle-class women reformers is stated, and then, to show that working-class mothers did not hold the same opinion, the author turns to the recent work of women historians to support this statement.

A   **Correct.** The author uses the recent work of women historians to support the statement that women of different social classes were pitted against one another.

B   The women historians *have recently observed*; the verb *observed* introduces a statement rather than a question.

C   The reference to women historians has to do with working-class mothers; it does not challenge women's activism and role in social reform.

D   The passage supports what the women historians say about working-class mothers.

E   The author does not define or present the *traditional* view of child labor reform, nor is any inherent contradiction pointed out.

The correct answer is A.

15. The passage suggests that which of the following was a reason for the difference of opinion between working-class mothers and women reformers on the issue of child labor?

(A) Reformers' belief that industrial home work was preferable to child labor outside the home

(B) Reformers' belief that child labor laws should pertain to working conditions but not to pay

(C) Working-class mothers' resentment at reformers' attempts to interfere with their parenting

(D) Working-class mothers' belief that child labor was an inhumane practice

(E) Working-class families' need for every employable member of their families to earn money

Inference

The question's use of the word *suggests* means that the answer depends on making an inference. Lines 12–23 examine the different views of middle-class reformers and working-class mothers on child labor laws. While the reformers saw child labor as an *inhumane* practice that should be *outlawed*, working class mothers understood *the necessity of pooling the wages of as many family members as possible* and viewed child labor legislation as *a personal economic disaster.*

A   Lines 12–14 show that reformers regarded both kinds of work as *equally inhumane practices that should be outlawed.*

B   Pay is not specifically discussed in the passage.

C   Lines 24–27 indicate that the reformers believed working-class resistance to child labor laws was a sign of poor parenting, but nothing is said about the working-class response to this view.

D   Lines 12–17 say that the reformers held this position, but *working class mothers did not always share this view.*

E   **Correct.** Lines 17–23 explain that working-class families needed *the wages of as many family members as possible.*

The correct answer is E.

16.   The author of the passage asserts which of the following about women reformers who tried to abolish child labor?

(A)   They alienated working-class mothers by attempting to enlist them in agitating for progressive causes.

(B)   They underestimated the prevalence of child labor among the working classes.

(C)   They were correct in their conviction that child labor was deplorable but shortsighted about the impact of child labor legislation on working-class families.

(D)   They were aggressive in their attempts to enforce child labor legislation, but were unable to prevent working-class families from circumventing them.

(E)   They were prevented by their nearly total disenfranchisement from making significant progress in child labor reform.

Supporting ideas

This question is based on information explicitly stated in the final sentence of the passage. Women reformers viewed *child labor as a terribly exploitative practice* but they *failed to take account of the economic needs of working-class families.*

A   The passage does not say that reformers tried to enlist working-class mothers in progressive causes.

B   No evidence is offered to support such a statement.

C   **Correct.** The final sentence makes clear that the reformers recognized child labor as *exploitative* but did not understand *the economic needs of working-class families.*

D   The reformers' activities involved promoting legislation; there is no evidence in the passage that the reformers themselves attempted to enforce these laws.

E   Lines 6–10 show that the reformers improved working conditions for women and children, despite their disenfranchisement.

The correct answer is C.

17. According to the passage, one of the most striking achievements of white middle-class women reformers during the Progressive Era was

    (A) gaining the right to vote in school elections
    (B) mobilizing working-class women in the fight against child labor
    (C) uniting women of different classes in grassroots activism
    (D) improving the economic conditions of working-class families
    (E) improving women's and children's working conditions

Supporting ideas

The question's use of the phrase *according to the passage* indicates that the answer can be found through careful reading of the passage. This question is based on information explicitly stated in lines 7–10, which state that *white middle-class women reformers won a variety of victories, notably in the improvement of working conditions, especially for women and children.*

A   Lines 6–7 show that women already had the right to vote in school elections.

B   Lines 20–24 show that working-class families *tried to circumvent child labor laws.*

C   Lines 11–12 say that one product of grassroots activism, child labor legislation, *pitted women of different classes against one another.*

D   Lines 31–32 say that the reformers *failed to take account of the economic needs of working-class families.*

E   **Correct.** The passage states that reformers improved the working conditions of women and children.

The correct answer is E.

Critical Reasoning

The following discussion is intended to familiarize you with the most efficient and effective approaches to critical reasoning questions. The particular questions in this chapter are generally representative of the kinds of critical reasoning questions you will encounter on the GMAT. Remember that it is the problem solving strategy that is important, not the specific details of a particular question.

18. Vasquez-Morrell Assurance specializes in insuring manufacturers. Whenever a policyholder makes a claim, a claims adjuster determines the amount that Vasquez-Morrell is obligated to pay. Vasquez-Morrell is cutting its staff of claims adjusters by 15 percent. To ensure that the company's ability to handle claims promptly is affected as little as possible by the staff cuts, consultants recommend that Vasquez-Morrell lay off those adjusters who now take longest, on average, to complete work on claims assigned to them.

    Which of the following, if true, most seriously calls into question the consultants' criterion for selecting the staff to be laid off?

    (A) If the time that Vasquez-Morrell takes to settle claims increases significantly, it could lose business to other insurers.
    (B) Supervisors at Vasquez-Morrell tend to assign the most complex claims to the most capable adjusters.
    (C) At Vasquez-Morrell, no insurance payments are made until a claims adjuster has reached a final determination on the claim.
    (D) There are no positions at Vasquez-Morrell to which staff currently employed as claims adjusters could be reassigned.
    (E) The premiums that Vasquez-Morrell currently charges are no higher than those charged for similar coverage by competitors.

Evaluation of a Plan

Situation   An insurance company must reduce its staff of claims adjusters. To ensure continuing promptness in handling claims, consultants advise the company to lay off those adjusters who take the longest to complete claims.

Reasoning   *What problem could there be with the criterion?* The consultants' criterion is the time an adjuster takes to settle a claim. However, some claims are naturally more complicated and require more time. If it is true that the company now assigns these time-consuming cases to its most capable adjusters, then these adjusters would be likely to be the ones who take longest to complete their cases. Laying off the adjusters who take the longest would thus mean laying off the company's most capable staff, which could very well decrease its ability to handle claims promptly.

A   The consultants' advice makes sense if increased time to handle claims causes the company to lose business.

B   **Correct.** This statement properly identifies the problem with the consultants' criterion.

C   This statement merely describes the process of handling a claim; it does not provide any information about the criterion for layoffs.

D   The consultants make no recommendations for reassigning staff, so indicating that there are no positions available does not call their advice into question.

E   The consultants do not recommend a change in premiums; noting that they are similar to competitors' premiums does not undermine the plan that the consultants recommend.

The correct answer is B.

19. Prolonged spells of hot, dry weather at the end of the grape-growing season typically reduce a vineyard's yield, because the grapes stay relatively small. In years with such weather, wine producers can make only a relatively small quantity of wine from a given area of vineyards. Nonetheless, in regions where wine producers generally grow their own grapes, analysts typically expect a long, hot, dry spell late in the growing season to result in increased revenues for local wine producers.

Which of the following, if true, does most to justify the analysts' expectation?

(A) The lower a vineyard's yield, the less labor is required to harvest the grapes.

(B) Long, hot, dry spells at the beginning of the grape-growing season are rare, but they can have a devastating effect on a vineyard's yield.

(C) Grapes grown for wine production are typically made into wine at or near the vineyard in which they were grown.

(D) When hot, dry spells are followed by heavy rains, the rains frequently destroy grape crops.

(E) Grapes that have matured in hot, dry weather make significantly better wine than ordinary grapes.

Argument Construction

Situation   Hot, dry weather at the end of the grape-growing season reduces yield, so winemakers can only produce a small quantity of wine. However, analysts expect that this weather will increase winemakers' revenues.

Reasoning   *What additional piece of information explains the analysts' expectations?* The same conditions that lead to low quantity also lead to something that increases revenues. What could this be? If these weather conditions lead to higher-quality wine that will sell for higher prices, the analysts' expectations for increased revenues are justified.

A   Lower labor costs mean less expenditure for the winemakers; this does not explain how revenues would increase.

B   This statement about low yields does not explain an increase in revenues.

C   The proximity of production to the vineyard is irrelevant to the question of how hot, dry weather can be responsible for decreased yield and increased revenues.

D   This statement gives another example of weather's effect on grape crops, but it does not explain how revenues are increased.

E   **Correct.** This statement properly provides the explanation that the weather conditions will lead to better wines. With better wines typically commanding higher prices, the winemakers will gain the increased revenues that the analysts anticipate.

The correct answer is E.

20. In the past, most children who went sledding in the winter snow in Verland used wooden sleds with runners and steering bars. Ten years ago, smooth plastic sleds became popular; they go faster than wooden sleds but are harder to steer and slow. The concern that plastic sleds are more dangerous is clearly borne out by the fact that the number of children injured while sledding was much higher last winter than it was 10 years ago.

Which of the following, if true in Verland, most seriously undermines the force of the evidence cited?

(A) A few children still use traditional wooden sleds.

(B) Very few children wear any kind of protective gear, such as helmets, while sledding.

(C) Plastic sleds can be used in a much wider variety of snow conditions than wooden sleds can.

(D) Most sledding injuries occur when a sled collides with a tree, a rock, or another sled.

(E) Because the traditional wooden sleds can carry more than one rider, an accident involving a wooden sled can result in several children being injured.

Argument Evaluation

Situation   Ten years ago, wooden sleds began to be replaced by plastic sleds that go faster but are harder to control. Plastic sleds are more dangerous than wooden sleds because more children suffered injuries last year than they did 10 years ago.

Reasoning   *What weakens this argument?* This argument depends on a comparison of two kinds of sleds. Any evidence that would either strengthen or weaken the argument must indicate a comparison. Evidence that applies only to one kind of sled or to both kinds of sleds equally cannot weaken this argument. Consider the implications of the evidence presented in the answer choices. If plastic sleds can be used in a wider variety of conditions than wooden sleds can, then plastic sleds can be used more frequently. It is possible that more frequent use, rather than the sleds themselves, has led to more accidents.

A   The limited use of some wooden sleds does not weaken the argument.

B   The absence of protective gear would affect accidents with both kinds of sleds.

C   **Correct.** This statement weakens the argument by providing an alternate explanation for the increased accidents.

D   This statement is true of accidents with both kinds of sleds.

E   This explains why wooden sleds may be dangerous but does not weaken the argument that plastic sleds are even more dangerous.

The correct answer is C.

21. Metal rings recently excavated from seventh-century settlements in the western part of Mexico were made using the same metallurgical techniques as those used by Ecuadorian artisans before and during that period. These techniques are sufficiently complex to make their independent development in both areas unlikely. Since the people of these two areas were in cultural contact, archaeologists hypothesize that the metallurgical techniques used to make the rings found in Mexico were learned by Mexican artisans from Ecuadorian counterparts.

Which of the following would it be most useful to establish in order to evaluate the archaeologists' hypothesis?

(A) Whether metal objects were traded from Ecuador to western Mexico during the seventh century

(B) Whether travel between western Mexico and Ecuador in the seventh century would have been primarily by land or by sea

(C) Whether artisans from western Mexico could have learned complex metallurgical techniques from their Ecuadorian counterparts without actually leaving western Mexico

(D) Whether metal tools were used in the seventh-century settlements in western Mexico

(E) Whether any of the techniques used in the manufacture of the metal rings found in western Mexico are still practiced among artisans in Ecuador today

Argument Evaluation

Situation   Metal rings excavated from seventh-century settlements in western Mexico were made with the same complex techniques used in Ecuador before and during a period when the two cultures were known to be in contact. Mexican artisans are thought to have learned the techniques from Ecuadorian artisans.

Reasoning   *What point could best be applied in evaluating this hypothesis?* Consider what specific information would help to assess the archaeologists' theory. It is given that the two areas had some cultural contact. If it were determined that metal objects were traded from one culture to the other, it could be possible that the metalworking techniques were passed along as well. Such evidence would be relevant to the hypothesis that Mexican artisans saw the work of their Ecuadorian counterparts and, from this exchange, learned the techniques to make the metal rings.

A   **Correct.** This statement properly identifies information that would be useful in the evaluation of the archaeologists' hypothesis.

B   The means of travel is irrelevant to the hypothesis about the source of the techniques.

C   The hypothesis is not about where Mexican artisans learned the techniques, but whether they learned them from the Ecuadorians.

D   The existence of metal tools provides no helpful information in establishing whether the Ecuadorians were the source of the metallurgical techniques.

E   The comparison to the present day is irrelevant to the hypothesis.

The correct answer is A.

22. Following several years of declining advertising sales, the *Greenville Times* reorganized its advertising sales force. Before reorganization, the sales force was organized geographically, with some sales representatives concentrating on city-center businesses and others concentrating on different outlying regions. The reorganization attempted to increase the sales representatives' knowledge of clients' businesses by having each sales representative deal with only one type of industry or of retailing. After the reorganization, revenue from advertising sales increased.

In assessing whether the improvement in advertising sales can properly be attributed to the reorganization, it would be most helpful to find out which of the following?

(A) What proportion of the total revenue of the *Greenville Times* is generated by advertising sales?

(B) Has the circulation of the *Greenville Times* increased substantially in the last two years?

(C) Among all the types of industry and retailing that use the *Greenville Times* as an advertising vehicle, which type accounts for the largest proportion of the newspaper's advertising sales?

(D) Do any clients of the sales representatives of the *Greenville Times* have a standing order with the *Times* for a fixed amount of advertising per month?

(E) Among the advertisers in the *Greenville Times*, are there more types of retail business or more types of industrial business?

Evaluation of a Plan

Situation In the face of declining advertising sales, a newspaper reorganizes its sales force so that sales representatives have a better understanding of businesses. Revenue from advertising sales increased after the reorganization.

Reasoning *What additional evidence would help determine the source of the increased revenue?* In order to attribute the increased revenue to the reorganization of the sales force, other possible causes must be eliminated. Newspaper advertising rates are linked to circulation; when circulation increases, higher rates can be charged and revenues will increase. An alternate explanation might be a significant rise in circulation, so it would be particularly helpful to know if circulation had increased.

A The question concerns only increased revenue from advertising sales; the proportion of advertising revenue to total revenue is outside the scope of the question.

B **Correct.** This statement provides another possible explanation for increased revenue of advertising sales, and so the answer to this question would help to clarify the reason for the increased revenue.

C Knowing how the advertising sales break down by type of business might be useful for other purposes, but it does not help to show the cause of the increase.

D A fixed amount of advertising would not explain increased revenue, so the answer to this question would be irrelevant.

E Distinguishing between the types of businesses will not contribute to determining whether the reorganization was responsible for the increased revenue.

The correct answer is B.

23. Motorists in a certain country frequently complain that traffic congestion is much worse now than it was 20 years ago. No real measure of how much traffic congestion there was 20 years ago exists, but the motorists' complaints are almost certainly unwarranted. The country's highway capacity has tripled in the last twenty years, thanks to a vigorous highway construction program, whereas the number of automobiles registered in the country has increased by only 75 percent.

Which of the following, if true, most seriously weakens the argument?

(A) Most automobile travel is local, and the networks of roads and streets in the country's settled areas have changed little over the last twenty years.

(B) Gasoline prices are high, and miles traveled per car per year have not changed much over the last 20 years.

(C) The country's urban centers have well-developed public transit systems that carry most of the people who commute into those centers.

(D) The average age of automobiles registered in the country is lower now than it was 20 years ago.

(E) Radio stations have long been broadcasting regular traffic reports that inform motorists about traffic congestion.

Argument Evaluation

Situation   Motorists complain that traffic congestion in their country is much worse than it was twenty years ago. But these complaints have no basis since the highway capacity in this country has tripled in the same period, whereas the number of cars registered has risen by only 75 percent.

Reasoning   *Which point most undermines the argument that the complaints are unwarranted?* Consider that the response to the generalized complaints about congestion discusses only the topic of highway capacity. What if the congestion that motorists are complaining about is not on highways but on local roads? Discovering that travel tends to be local in this country and that the local roads have not been improved in the last twenty years would seriously weaken the argument.

A   **Correct.** This statement properly identifies a weakness in the argument: the response to the broad complaint addresses a different subject, highway capacity, not the issue of traffic congestion encountered by most motorists.

B   If high gas prices actually prevented motorists from driving, and if motorists' driving habits were the same as they were twenty years ago, then these points should strengthen the argument that there is no basis for their complaints.

C   The number of commuters who use public transit does not affect the argument that the motorists' complaints have no basis.

D   The age of registered cars is irrelevant to the argument.

E   The radio broadcasts attest to the existence of traffic, but not to its increase, so they do not affect the argument.

The correct answer is A.

24. The percentage of households with an annual income of more than $40,000 is higher in Merton County than in any other county. However, the percentage of households with an annual income of $60,000 or more is higher in Sommer County.

   If the statements above are true, which of the following must also be true?

   (A) The percentage of households with an annual income of $80,000 is higher in Sommer County than in Merton County.
   (B) Merton County has the second highest percentage of households with an annual income of $60,000 or more.
   (C) Some households in Merton County have an annual income between $40,000 and $60,000.
   (D) The number of households with an annual income of more than $40,000 is greater in Merton County than in Sommer County.
   (E) Average annual household income is higher in Sommer County than in Merton County.

Argument Construction

Situation   The percentage of households with annual incomes of more than $40,000 is higher in Merton County than in any other county; the percentage of households with annual incomes of $60,000 or more is higher in Sommer County.

Reasoning   *On the basis of this information, what point must be true?* The given information makes clear that Merton County has some households that exceed $40,000 in annual income. Sommer County has a higher percentage of households with annual incomes at or above $60,000. A higher percentage of the Merton County households must in turn have annual incomes of $60,000 or less. Thus, the annual income of some households in Merton County is between $40,000 and $60,000.

A   Since it is possible that there are no households with an annual income of $80,000 in Sommer County, this statement does not follow from the situation.

B   It is not possible to make this determination on the basis of the available evidence; Merton County may have no households at all with an income of more than $60,000.

C   **Correct.** This statement properly identifies a conclusion that can be drawn from the given information: in order for the percentage of $40,000-plus incomes to be higher in Merton county than any other county while Sommer has the highest percentage of $60,000-plus incomes, there must be some households in Merton County that bring in between $40,000 and $60,000 annually.

D   On the basis of information about the *percentages* of households, it is not possible to arrive at this conclusion about the *number* of households.

E   From the given information, it is not possible to determine where the average income is greater. It is entirely possible that the number of $60,000-plus incomes in Sommer County is quite small and that the number of $40,000-plus incomes in Merton County is substantial.

The correct answer is C.

25. Tiger beetles are such fast runners that they can capture virtually any nonflying insect. However, when running toward an insect, a tiger beetle will intermittently stop and then, a moment later, resume its attack. Perhaps the beetles cannot maintain their pace and must pause for a moment's rest; but an alternative hypothesis is that while running, tiger beetles are unable to adequately process the resulting rapidly changing visual information and so quickly go blind and stop.

    Which of the following, if discovered in experiments using artificially moved prey insects, would support one of the two hypotheses and undermine the other?

    (A) When a prey insect is moved directly toward a beetle that has been chasing it, the beetle immediately stops and runs away without its usual intermittent stopping.
    (B) In pursuing a swerving insect, a beetle alters its course while running and its pauses become more frequent as the chase progresses.
    (C) In pursuing a moving insect, a beetle usually responds immediately to changes in the insect's direction, and it pauses equally frequently whether the chase is up or down an incline.
    (D) If, when a beetle pauses, it has not gained on the insect it is pursuing, the beetle generally ends its pursuit.
    (E) The faster a beetle pursues an insect fleeing directly away from it, the more frequently the beetle stops.

Argument Evaluation

Situation   Two hypotheses are offered to explain the sudden stop that tiger beetles make while pursuing their prey: (1) they cannot maintain the rapid pace and must rest, and (2) they run too quickly to process visual information and so temporarily go blind.

Reasoning   *What point would strengthen one of the two hypotheses and weaken the other?* Consider the information provided in each answer choice, remembering that information that supports one hypothesis must necessarily detract from the other. Any information that is not about pursuit or that affects the two hypotheses equally may be dismissed from consideration. If the frequency of stopping increases when the beetle follows a swerving insect and must constantly change its course, then the second hypothesis is strengthened; the beetle's pauses increase as the variety of visual information that it needs to deal with increases.

A   The hypotheses concern ongoing pursuit; since this information is not about the beetle's continuing pursuit of prey, it neither strengthens nor weakens either hypothesis.

B   **Correct.** This statement provides information that strengthens the second hypothesis: the swerving pursuit and the resulting continual course adjustments appear to be forcing the beetle to stop with increasing frequency to sort out the erratic visual information.

C   In this experiment, since neither vision nor tiredness appears to be problematic, the beetle could be stopping for either reason; this information neither strengthens nor weakens either hypothesis.

D   This information is irrelevant since both the hypotheses are about mid-pursuit behaviors.

E   The correlation of frequency of stops with speed affects both hypotheses equally; the pauses could be equally due to an inability to maintain the pace or due to a need to process the visual information.

The correct answer is B.

26. Guillemots are birds of Arctic regions. They feed on fish that gather beneath thin sheets of floating ice, and they nest on nearby land. Guillemots need 80 consecutive snow-free days in a year to raise their chicks, so until average temperatures in the Arctic began to rise recently, the guillemots' range was limited to the southernmost Arctic coast. Therefore, if the warming continues, the guillemots' range will probably be enlarged by being extended northward along the coast.

Which of the following, if true, most seriously weakens the argument?

(A) Even if the warming trend continues, there will still be years in which guillemot chicks are killed by an unusually early snow.

(B) If the Arctic warming continues, guillemots' current predators are likely to succeed in extending their own range farther north.

(C) Guillemots nest in coastal areas, where temperatures are generally higher than in inland areas.

(D) If the Arctic warming continues, much of the thin ice in the southern Arctic will disappear.

(E) The fish that guillemots eat are currently preyed on by a wider variety of predators in the southernmost Arctic regions than they are farther north.

Argument Evaluation

Situation   In the southern Arctic, guillemots find their prey beneath thin sheets of ice, nest nearby, and require 80 snow-free days to raise their young. A warming trend means that their range may be enlarged by extending northward along the coast.

Reasoning   *Which point weakens the argument about the enlargement of the guillemots' range?* How could the birds move northward and simultaneously not enlarge their range? Consider the assumption implied by the idea of *enlargement*. If the guillemots lost their southern habitat, then their northward move would be a displacement rather than an enlargement. If their source of food was no longer available to them in the southern Arctic, then they would abandon that area as part of their range.

A   An exceptional year is not an argument against an enlarged range because *an unusually early snow* could happen in the southern Arctic as well.

B   If their current predators also migrate northward, then the guillemots' situation has not changed, so this is not an argument against their enlarged range.

C   The argument suggests that they will move not inland, but *northward along the coast.*

D   **Correct.** This statement properly identifies a factor that weakens the argument: the guillemots' move northward would not enlarge their range if they lost their food source, fish found under thin ice, in the southern Arctic.

E   The possibility that they may find prey more easily in the north does not mean that they would abandon the southern Arctic, and so this point does not weaken the argument.

The correct answer is D.

27. Some batches of polio vaccine used around 1960 were contaminated with SV40, a virus that in monkeys causes various cancers. Some researchers now claim that this contamination caused some cases of a certain cancer in humans, mesothelioma. This claim is not undercut by the fact that a very careful survey made in the 1960s of people who had received the contaminated vaccine found no elevated incidence of any cancer, since _____.

   (A) most cases of mesothelioma are caused by exposure to asbestos

   (B) in some countries, there was no contamination of the vaccine

   (C) SV40 is widely used in laboratories to produce cancers in animals

   (D) mesotheliomas take several decades to develop

   (E) mesothelioma was somewhat less common in 1960 than it is now

Argument Construction

Situation   Researchers claim that contaminated polio vaccine administered in 1960 caused some cases of mesothelioma, a type of cancer. Their claim is not undermined by the results of a 1960s survey showing that those who received the contaminated vaccine had no elevated incidence of cancer.

Reasoning   *Why did the survey results not challenge the researchers' claim?* The survey did not reveal a higher incidence of mesothelioma. This question then requires completing a sentence that establishes cause. What could be the reason that the people surveyed in the 1960s showed no signs of the disease? If the disease takes decades to develop, then those people surveyed would not yet have shown any signs of it; less than a decade had passed between their exposure to the vaccine and the survey.

A   The contaminated vaccine is said to have caused *some* cases, not *most*; the question remains why the survey results pose no obstacle to the researchers' claim.

B   The claim is only about contaminated vaccine, not uncontaminated vaccine.

C   That the virus can cause cancers in laboratory animals had already been provided as a given; this additional information is irrelevant to the survey of people who received contaminated vaccine.

D   **Correct.** This statement properly identifies the reason that the survey does not call into question the researchers' claim: the people surveyed in the 1960s showed no signs of disease because the cancer takes decades to develop.

E   The frequency of mesothelioma in the general population is not related to the claim that contaminated vaccine caused the disease in a specific population.

The correct answer is D.

28. Gortland has long been narrowly self-sufficient in both grain and meat. However, as per capita income in Gortland has risen toward the world average, per capita consumption of meat has also risen toward the world average, and it takes several pounds of grain to produce one pound of meat. Therefore, since per capita income continues to rise, whereas domestic grain production will not increase, Gortland will soon have to import either grain or meat or both.

Which of the following is an assumption on which the argument depends?

(A) The total acreage devoted to grain production in Gortland will soon decrease.

(B) Importing either grain or meat will not result in a significantly higher percentage of Gortlanders' incomes being spent on food than is currently the case.

(C) The per capita consumption of meat in Gortland is increasing at roughly the same rate across all income levels.

(D) The per capita income of meat producers in Gortland is rising faster than the per capita income of grain producers.

(E) People in Gortland who increase their consumption of meat will not radically decrease their consumption of grain.

Argument Construction

Situation   A country previously self-sufficient in grain and meat will soon have to import one or the other or both. Consumption of meat has risen as per capita income has risen, and it takes several pounds of grain to produce one pound of meat.

Reasoning   *What conditions must be true for the conclusion to be true?* Meat consumption is rising. What about grain consumption? A sharp reduction in the amount of grain consumed could compensate for increased meat consumption, making the conclusion false. If people did radically decrease their grain consumption, it might not be necessary to import grain or meat or both. Since the argument concludes that the imports are necessary, it assumes grain consumption will not plunge.

A   The argument makes no assumptions about the acreage devoted to grain; it assumes only that the demand for grain will rise.

B   The argument does not discuss the percentage of their income that Gortlanders spend on food, so an assumption about this topic is not needed.

C   The argument involves only meat consumption in general, not its distribution by income level.

D   Since the argument does not refer to the incomes of meat producers and grain producers, it cannot depend on an assumption about them.

E   **Correct.** This statement properly identifies the assumption that there will be no great decrease in grain consumption.

The correct answer is E.

29. The Hazelton coal-processing plant is a major employer in the Hazelton area, but national environmental regulations will force it to close if it continues to use old, polluting processing methods. However, to update the plant to use newer, cleaner methods would be so expensive that the plant will close unless it receives the tax break it has requested. In order to prevent a major increase in local unemployment, the Hazelton government is considering granting the plant's request.

   Which of the following would be most important for the Hazelton government to determine before deciding whether to grant the plant's request?

   (A) Whether the company that owns the plant would open a new plant in another area if the present plant were closed
   (B) Whether the plant would employ far fewer workers when updated than it does now
   (C) Whether the level of pollutants presently being emitted by the plant is high enough to constitute a health hazard for local residents
   (D) Whether the majority of the coal processed by the plant is sold outside the Hazelton area
   (E) Whether the plant would be able to process more coal when updated than it does now

Evaluation of a Plan

Situation   Because of the expenses of mandatory updating, a plant that is a major employer in the local area will close unless it receives the tax break it has requested from the local government.

Reasoning   *What point is most critical to the evaluation of the request?* Consider the information provided in the answer choices. The plant is important to the local government primarily because it is a major employer of local residents. What if updating the plant significantly reduced the number of employees needed? It is crucial for the local government to determine whether the plant will continue to employ the same number of people once it has updated.

A   The local government is concerned only with the local area, so a new site outside that area is irrelevant.

B   **Correct.** This statement properly identifies a factor that is critical to the plant's argument and the local government's decision.

C   Updating is mandatory under national environmental regulations, whether the local residents are affected by the plant's pollutants or not.

D   At issue is the plant's role as a major employer; where its product is sold is irrelevant.

E   The amount of coal processed by the updated plant is irrelevant to the critical issue of the number of people employed to process that coal.

The correct answer is B.

30. A physically active lifestyle has been shown to help increase longevity. In the Wistar region of Bellaria, the average age at death is considerably higher than in any other part of the country. Wistar is the only mountainous part of Bellaria. A mountainous terrain makes even such basic activities as walking relatively strenuous; it essentially imposes a physically active lifestyle on people. Clearly, this circumstance explains the long lives of people in Wistar.

Which of the following, if true, most seriously weakens the argument?

(A) In Bellaria all medical expenses are paid by the government, so that personal income does not affect the quality of health care a person receives.

(B) The Wistar region is one of Bellaria's least populated regions.

(C) Many people who live in the Wistar region have moved there in middle age or upon retirement.

(D) The many opportunities for hiking, skiing, and other outdoor activities that Wistar's mountains offer make it a favorite destination for vacationing Bellarians.

(E) Per capita spending on recreational activities is no higher in Wistar than it is in other regions of Bellaria.

Argument Evaluation

Situation   People in one region of a country live longer than people in other areas. The higher average age at time of death is attributed to the healthy lifestyle of the people in this region, where the mountainous terrain demands a physically active life.

Reasoning   *What point weakens the argument?* Consider what assumption underlies the argument that the physically active lifestyle required of living in Wistar is responsible for its residents' relative longevity. The mountainous environment necessitates lifelong levels of rigorous physical activity that build a more robust population. What if a significant portion of the population has not been conditioned since childhood to the demands of the terrain? It is assumed here that the healthy lifestyle imposed by the terrain has shaped residents from birth and accounts for their longer life span. If many residents only moved there later in life, the argument is weakened.

A   The argument is not about the quality of health care throughout the country, but the length of the residents' lives in a particular region.

B   The rate of population density does not affect the argument.

C   **Correct.** This statement properly identifies a point that weakens the argument.

D   The area's popularity as a vacation destination does not affect the longevity of the local residents.

E   The argument establishes that merely living in the region is strenuous; the spending on recreational activities is irrelevant.

The correct answer is C.

31.   Cheever College offers several online courses via remote computer connection, in addition to traditional classroom-based courses. A study of student performance at Cheever found that, overall, the average student grade for online courses matched that for classroom-based courses. In this calculation of the average grade, course withdrawals were weighted as equivalent to a course failure, and the rate of withdrawal was much lower for students enrolled in classroom-based courses than for students enrolled in online courses.

If the statements above are true, which of the following must also be true of Cheever College?

(A)   Among students who did not withdraw, students enrolled in online courses got higher grades, on average, than students enrolled in classroom-based courses.

(B)   The number of students enrolled per course at the start of the school term is much higher, on average, for the online courses than for the classroom-based courses.

(C)   There are no students who take both an online and a classroom-based course in the same school term.

(D)   Among Cheever College students with the best grades, a significant majority take online, rather than classroom-based, courses.

(E)   Courses offered online tend to deal with subject matter that is less challenging than that of classroom-based courses.

Argument Construction

Situation   A comparison of online and classroom courses showed similar average grades. In determining average grades, a course withdrawal was weighted as a course failure. The rate of withdrawal was higher from online than from classroom courses.

Reasoning   *What conclusion about the courses can be derived from this comparison?* Consider the ramifications of the methodology used to calculate the grade averages for the two types of courses. Because of course withdrawals, the online courses experienced a higher rate of failure, but the average grade for these courses still matched the average grade for classroom courses. From this it is logical to conclude that, for the two averages to match, the students who remained in the online courses must have had higher initial average grades than those in classroom courses.

A   **Correct.** This statement properly identifies the logical conclusion that the higher percentage of withdrawals from online classes requires higher grades, on average, to compensate for the higher rate of failure.

B   A number of students cannot be derived from a discussion of average grades and rates of withdrawal.

C   This conclusion cannot be determined on the basis of the information provided.

D   The information is about average grades; the argument does not provide any basis for a conclusion about best grades.

E   It is impossible to determine the difficulty of subject matter from this information.

The correct answer is A.

32. For years the beautiful Renaissance buildings in Palitito have been damaged by exhaust from the many tour buses that come to the city. There has been little parking space, so most buses have idled at the curb during each stop on their tour, and idling produces as much exhaust as driving. The city has now provided parking that accommodates a third of the tour buses, so damage to Palitito's buildings from the buses' exhaust will diminish significantly.

Which of the following, if true, most strongly supports the argument?

(A) The exhaust from Palitito's few automobiles is not a significant threat to Palitito's buildings.

(B) Palitito's Renaissance buildings are not threatened by pollution other than engine exhaust.

(C) Tour buses typically spend less than one-quarter of the time they are in Palitito transporting passengers from one site to another.

(D) More tourists come to Palitito by tour bus than by any other single means of transportation.

(E) Some of the tour buses that are unable to find parking drive around Palitito while their passengers are visiting a site.

Argument Evaluation

Situation   Tour buses have damaged Renaissance buildings with their exhaust fumes because lack of parking has kept the buses idling at curbs. Providing new parking for a third of the buses should significantly reduce the damage caused by the exhaust.

Reasoning   *What point strengthens the argument?* The argument for reduced damage relies on the reduction of the vehicles' exhaust fumes. Any additional evidence regarding the extent to which the vehicular emissions are likely to be reduced also supports the argument for the benefits of the new parking spaces. Learning that tour buses spend not just a few minutes but most of their time idling at the curb strengthens the argument. The new parking spaces will allow a third of the tour buses to spend 75 percent of their time with their engines off, causing no damage at all.

A   If automobile exhaust is not a threat, the argument is not affected.

B   This statement does not address the question of whether the new parking will reduce the damage caused by engine exhaust from the buses.

C   **Correct.** This statement properly cites a factor that supports the argument: since most of the buses' time has been spent producing damaging exhaust, the new parking should reduce the damage significantly.

D   This statement about tourists' chosen means of transportation is irrelevant to the issue of what the buses do while in the city.

E   It is given that the new parking will only provide space for a third of the buses, and thus some buses will continue to idle and some to drive around, continuing to contribute equally to the building damage. This statement does not strengthen the argument.

The correct answer is C.

33. During the 1980s and 1990s, the annual number of people who visited the Sordellian Mountains increased continually, and many new ski resorts were built. Over the same period, however, the number of visitors to ski resorts who were caught in avalanches decreased, even though there was no reduction in the annual number of avalanches in the Sordellian Mountains.

Which of the following, if true in the Sordellian Mountains during the 1980s and 1990s, most helps to explain the decrease?

(A) Avalanches were most likely to happen when a large new snowfall covered an older layer of snow.

(B) Avalanches destroyed at least some buildings in the Sordellian Mountains in every year.

(C) People planning new ski slopes and other resort facilities used increasingly accurate information about which locations are likely to be in the path of avalanches.

(D) The average length of stay for people visiting the Sordellian Mountains increased slightly.

(E) Construction of new ski resorts often led to the clearing of wooded areas that had helped prevent avalanches.

Argument Construction

Situation   Over a certain period, new ski resorts accommodated an increasing number of visitors at the same time that fewer visitors were caught in avalanches. Yet there were no fewer avalanches than usual during this period.

Reasoning   *What explains the apparent contradiction of increased visitors but fewer visitors caught in avalanches?* More resort visitors would imply more avalanche-related accidents, but the average has shifted so that fewer visitors are being caught in the avalanches. It must be that fewer visitors are exposed to this danger; consider the answer choices to identify a logical reason for this improvement in their exposure. If the likely paths of avalanches had become better understood, that information would have been applied to identify safer locations for new ski slopes and ski resorts. The facilities would thus have been built well out of the way of avalanches, resulting in fewer visitors trapped in avalanches.

A   This likelihood would remain true from year to year; it does not explain the decrease.

B   This point does not explain why fewer visitors were caught in these avalanches.

C   **Correct.** This statement properly identifies a factor that explains the decreased number of accidents.

D   The greater length of stay would seem to expose visitors to greater danger.

E   This information points to an expected increase, rather than decrease, in visitors who might be caught by avalanches.

The correct answer is C.

34. A year ago, Dietz Foods launched a yearlong advertising campaign for its canned tuna. Last year Dietz sold 12 million cans of tuna compared to the 10 million sold during the previous year, an increase directly attributable to new customers brought in by the campaign. Profits from the additional sales, however, were substantially less than the cost of the advertising campaign. Clearly, therefore, the campaign did nothing to further Dietz's economic interests.

Which of the following, if true, most seriously weakens the argument?

(A) Sales of canned tuna account for a relatively small percentage of Dietz Foods' profits.

(B) Most of the people who bought Dietz's canned tuna for the first time as a result of the campaign were already loyal customers of other Dietz products.

(C) A less expensive advertising campaign would have brought in significantly fewer new customers for Dietz's canned tuna than did the campaign Dietz Foods launched last year.

(D) Dietz made money on sales of canned tuna last year.

(E) In each of the past five years, there was a steep, industry-wide decline in sales of canned tuna.

Argument Evaluation

Situation   An advertising campaign was responsible for increased sales of canned tuna. Since the profits from the increased sales were less than the costs of the campaign, the campaign did not contribute to the company's economic interests.

Reasoning   *Which point weakens the argument?* Consider the basis of the argument: if profits are lower than costs, the campaign made no contribution to the company's financial well-being. In what case might this be untrue? What if the advertising campaign reversed an industry-wide trend of declining sales? If Dietz experienced increasing sales, while other companies experienced decreased sales, then the campaign did contribute to the economic interests of the company, and the argument is considerably weakened.

A   The issue is not the percentage of profits that canned tuna contributes, but the success of the advertising campaign.

B   If the customers bought the tuna because of the campaign, it is irrelevant to the argument that they also bought other Dietz products.

C   This information neither strengthens nor weakens the argument.

D   The argument is not about profits only, but about whether the advertising campaign contributed to the economic interests of the company.

E   **Correct.** This statement properly identifies a factor that weakens the argument: the campaign secured the benefits of increased sales at a time when the entire industry was experiencing a decline in sales.

The correct answer is E.

Sentence Correction

The following discussion is intended to familiarize you with the most efficient and effective approaches to sentence correction questions. The particular questions in this chapter are generally representative of the kinds of sentence correction questions you will encounter on the GMAT. Remember that it is the problem solving strategy that is important, not the specific details of a particular question.

35. Unlike <u>the buildings in Mesopotamian cities, which were arranged haphazardly, the same basic plan was followed for all cities of the Indus Valley: with houses</u> laid out on a north-south, east-west grid, and houses and walls were built of standard-size bricks.

    (A) the buildings in Mesopotamian cities, which were arranged haphazardly, the same basic plan was followed for all cities of the Indus Valley: with houses

    (B) the buildings in Mesopotamian cities, which were haphazard in arrangement, the same basic plan was used in all cities of the Indus Valley: houses were

    (C) the arrangement of buildings in Mesopotamian cities, which were haphazard, the cities of the Indus Valley all followed the same basic plan: houses

    (D) Mesopotamian cities, in which buildings were arranged haphazardly, the cities of the Indus Valley all followed the same basic plan: houses were

    (E) Mesopotamian cities, which had buildings that were arranged haphazardly, the same basic plan was used for all cities in the Indus Valley: houses that were

Comparison-contrast; Modifying clause

The contrast introduced by *unlike* must be logical and clear. Contrasting *the buildings in Mesopotamian cities* with *the same basic plan* does not make sense; *Mesopotamian cities* should be contrasted with *the cities of the Indus Valley*. Also, it needs to be clear that it was the *buildings* in the cities that *were arranged haphazardly* rather than the *cities*. The second half of the sentence needs *houses were laid out* to be parallel in structure to *and houses and walls were built*.

A   Illogically contrasts *the buildings in Mesopotamian cities* with *the same basic plan*; not clear whether *which were arranged haphazardly* modifies *cities* or *buildings*; *with houses* lacks parallelism and is confusing.

B   Illogically contrasts *the buildings in Mesopotamian cities* with *the same basic plan*; does not clarify what *which were haphazard in arrangement* modifies.

C   Illogically contrasts *the arrangement of buildings* with *the cities of the Indus Valley*; not clear whether *which were haphazard* modifies *buildings* or *cities*; *houses* not followed by a verb.

D   Correct. In this sentence, *Mesopotamian cities* are properly contrasted with *the cities of the Indus Valley*; *in which buildings were arranged haphazardly* expresses the idea clearly; and *houses* is followed by *were* as required.

E   Illogically contrasts *Mesopotamian cities* with *the same basic plan*; *houses that were* lacks parallelism and is confusing.

The correct answer is D.

36. New data from United States Forest Service ecologists show <u>that for every dollar spent on controlled small-scale burning, forest thinning, and the training of fire-management personnel, it saves seven dollars that would not be spent on having to extinguish</u> big fires.

    (A) that for every dollar spent on controlled small-scale burning, forest thinning, and the training of fire-management personnel, it saves seven dollars that would not be spent on having to extinguish

(B)   that for every dollar spent on controlled small-scale burning, forest thinning, and the training of fire-management personnel, seven dollars are saved that would have been spent on extinguishing

(C)   that for every dollar spent on controlled small-scale burning, forest thinning, and the training of fire-management personnel saves seven dollars on not having to extinguish

(D)   for every dollar spent on controlled small-scale burning, forest thinning, and the training of fire-management personnel, that it saves seven dollars on not having to extinguish

(E)   for every dollar spent on controlled small-scale burning, forest thinning, and the training of fire-management personnel, that seven dollars are saved that would not have been spent on extinguishing

Logical predication; Rhetorical construction

The pronoun *it* (*it saves seven dollars*) has no referent. Making *seven dollars* the subject of the clause eliminates this problem, and it also fulfills a reader's expectation that after the phrase beginning *for every dollar* another specific amount will be given to balance it. This change in structure also allows the awkward and wordy clause *that would not be spent on having to extinguish* to be rewritten so that *spent* balances *saved*: *seven dollars are saved that would have been spent on extinguishing*, and the unnecessary *having to* is omitted.

A   *It* has no referent; *not be spent* is awkward; *on having to extinguish* is wordy.

B   **Correct.** This sentence properly uses *seven dollars* as the subject of the clause to balance *every dollar* in the introductory phrase; the phrasing is concise and parallel.

C   *Saves* does not have a subject; construction is not a complete sentence; *not having to extinguish* is wordy and awkward.

D   *That* introduces a subordinate rather than main clause, making a sentence fragment; *it* has no referent; *not having to extinguish* is wordy and awkward.

E   Introductory *that* makes a sentence fragment; *that would not have been spent on extinguishing* is awkward and illogical.

The correct answer is B.

37.   Like the grassy fields and old pastures that the upland sandpiper needs for feeding and nesting when it returns in May after wintering in the Argentine Pampas, the sandpipers vanishing in the northeastern United States is a result of residential and industrial development and of changes in farming practices.

(A)   the sandpipers vanishing in the northeastern United States is a result of residential and industrial development and of changes in

(B)   the bird itself is vanishing in the northeastern United States as a result of residential and industrial development and of changes in

(C)   that the birds themselves are vanishing in the northeastern United States is due to residential and industrial development and changes to

(D)   in the northeastern United States, sandpipers' vanishing due to residential and industrial development and to changes in

(E)   in the northeastern United States, the sandpipers' vanishing, a result of residential and industrial development and changing

Comparison; Sentence structure

The comparison introduced by *like* must be logical and clear; the point of this comparison is that both the habitat and the bird are disappearing for similar reasons. The comparison must use comparable grammatical components; *the bird itself* is a noun phrase and matches the noun phrases *grassy fields* and *old pastures*.

A   Illogically compares *the sandpipers vanishing* to *grassy fields and old pastures*; omits apostrophe in *sandpipers' vanishing*; wordy.

B   **Correct.** This sentence properly compares *the bird itself* to *grassy fields and old pastures*; *is vanishing* as the verb strengthens the sentence by making the comparison clearer.

C   Does not finish the comparison begun with *like* but instead substitutes a clause (*that the birds themselves are vanishing*).

D   Illogically compares *the sandpipers' vanishing* to *grassy fields and old pastures*; creates a sentence fragment.

E   Illogically compares *the sandpipers' vanishing* to *grassy fields and old pastures*; creates a sentence fragment.

The correct answer is B.

38.   The results of two recent unrelated studies support the idea that dolphins may share certain cognitive abilities with humans and great apes; the studies indicate dolphins as capable of recognizing themselves in mirrors—an ability that is often considered a sign of self-awareness—and to grasp spontaneously the mood or intention of humans.

(A)   dolphins as capable of recognizing themselves in mirrors—an ability that is often considered a sign of self-awareness—and to grasp spontaneously

(B)   dolphins' ability to recognize themselves in mirrors—an ability that is often considered as a sign of self-awareness—and of spontaneously grasping

(C)   dolphins to be capable of recognizing themselves in mirrors—an ability that is often considered a sign of self-awareness—and to grasp spontaneously

(D)   that dolphins have the ability of recognizing themselves in mirrors—an ability that is often considered as a sign of self-awareness—and spontaneously grasping

(E)   that dolphins are capable of recognizing themselves in mirrors—an ability that is often considered a sign of self-awareness—and of spontaneously grasping

Grammatical construction; Parallelism

In the context of this sentence, *the studies indicate* must introduce a clause; the clause must begin with *that* and have a subject, *dolphins*, and a verb, *are* (the complete verb phrase would be *are capable of*). The two capabilities should be parallel: *capable of recognizing...and of spontaneously grasping*.

A   Context requires a clause, but this construction is not a clause; *capable of recognizing* is not parallel to *to grasp spontaneously*.

B   Construction is not a clause, and a clause is required; *dolphins' ability to recognize* is not parallel to *of spontaneously grasping*.

C   A clause is required following *the studies indicate*; *to be capable of recognizing* is not parallel to *to grasp spontaneously*.

D   *Have the ability of* is wordy and unidiomatic; *of recognizing* and *spontaneously grasping* are not parallel.

E   **Correct.** *That* introduces the subordinate clause necessary to complete this sentence properly; *of recognizing* and *of spontaneously grasping* are parallel.

The correct answer is E.

39.   According to scholars, the earliest writing was probably not a direct rendering of speech, but was more likely to begin as a separate and distinct symbolic system of communication, and only later merged with spoken language.

(A)   was more likely to begin as

(B)   more than likely began as

(C)   more than likely beginning from

(D)   it was more than likely begun from

(E)   it was more likely that it began

Idiom; Verb form

This sentence is a comparison in which *probably not x* is balanced by *but more than likely y*. When *more* is used in the comparative form of an adjective (*more difficult*) or adverb (*more likely*), it is followed by *than*. The words used to show the comparison between *x* and *y*, *but more than likely*, must also introduce the correct verb form, allowing *y* to fit grammatically into the rest of the sentence. The subject of the sentence has three verbs, all of which should be parallel: *the earliest writing was...began...merged. Was...to begin* is not parallel and results in a construction that is not grammatically correct.

A In this context, *more likely* is not a complete idiomatic expression; *was...to begin* is not parallel to *was* and *merged*.

B Correct. In this sentence, *more than likely* is the correct comparative construction; the simple past tense *began*, parallel to *was* and *merged*, fits grammatically into the sentence.

C Subject should be followed by three verbs; *beginning from* is not a verb.

D Use of the pronoun *it* makes this construction a main clause, in which case the comma after *communication* must be omitted and *began* must be used to be parallel to *merged*; *was...begun* is not the correct tense.

E In this awkward, unclear, and wordy construction, the first *it* must be followed by *is*, not *was*, because the theory is current; the second *it* acts as the subject of the subordinate clause, and this usage requires the omission of the comma after *communication*.

The correct answer is B.

40. In 1995 Richard Stallman, a well-known critic of the patent system, testified in Patent Office hearings that, to test the system, a colleague of his had managed to win a patent for one of Kirchhoff's laws, an observation about electric current first made in 1845 and now included in virtually every textbook of elementary physics.

(A) laws, an observation about electric current first made in 1845 and

(B) laws, which was an observation about electric current first made in 1845 and it is

(C) laws, namely, it was an observation about electric current first made in 1845 and

(D) laws, an observation about electric current first made in 1845, it is

(E) laws that was an observation about electric current, first made in 1845, and is

Logical predication; Parallelism

The function of the entire long phrase (*observation...physics*) that follows *one of Kirchhoff's laws* is to describe that law. It is a noun phrase in apposition, which means that it has the same syntactic relation to all the other parts of the sentence that the noun phrase *one of Kirchhoff's laws* does. Within the long modifying phrase, parallelism is maintained by balancing *an observation...first made* with *and now included*.

A Correct. In this sentence, the noun phrase in apposition properly identifies and explains the law, using parallel structure and concise expression.

B *Which* is ambiguous because it could refer to *one* or to *laws*; *it is* violates the parallelism of *first made* and *now included*.

C *It* is ambiguous; the introduction of *it was* does not allow this construction to fit grammatically into the sentence.

D The referent of *it* is unclear; *it is* creates a run-on sentence and violates the parallelism of *first made* and *now included*.

E *That* appears to refer to *laws* rather than *one*, but the verb is singular; setting off the phrase *first made in 1845* in commas distorts meaning; *is* violates parallelism.

The correct answer is A.

41. Excavators at the Indus Valley site of Harappa in eastern Pakistan say the discovery of inscribed shards dating to circa 2800–2600 B.C. <u>indicate their development of a Harappan writing system, the use of</u> inscribed seals impressed into clay for marking ownership, and the standardization of weights for trade or taxation occurred many decades, if not centuries, earlier than was previously believed.

    (A) indicate their development of a Harappan writing system, the use of

    (B) indicate that the development of a Harappan writing system, using

    (C) indicates that their development of a Harappan writing system, using

    (D) indicates the development of a Harappan writing system, their use of

    (E) indicates that the development of a Harappan writing system, the use of

Agreement; Idiom; Parallelism

In long sentences such as this one, the relationship between parts of the sentence may be difficult to see. Here, the main clause of the sentence is *excavators…say* and the logical sequence that follows is *the discovery…indicates that*. The subject of this first subordinate clause is the singular noun *discovery*, which should be followed by the singular verb *indicates* rather than by the plural *indicate*, as is done in the original sentence. *Their*, used with either *development* or *use*, has no clear or logical referent in any of the alternatives. The subject of the following subordinate (*that*) clause, which has *occurred* as its verb, is a series of three phrases, which must be parallel, especially in a sentence of this length and complexity: *the development of…, the use of…, and the standardization of….*

A *Indicate* does not agree with *discovery*; the pronoun *their* has no logical referent, and *their development* is not parallel to *the use* and *the standardization*.

B *Indicate* does not agree with *discovery*; *using* is not parallel to *the development* and *the standardization*.

C *Their* has no logical referent; the series of three elements should be parallel, but here all are different.

D The pronoun *their* has no logical referent, and *their use* is not parallel to *the development* and *the standardization*; the preferred sentence structure would have *indicates* followed by *that* when introducing a clause.

E **Correct.** In this sentence, *indicates* agrees with *discovery* and is followed by *that* to introduce a clause; the three parallel phrases begin with an article (*the*), a noun, and the preposition *of*.

The correct answer is E.

42. The Supreme Court has ruled that public universities can collect student activity fees even <u>with students' objections to particular activities, so long as the groups they give money to will be</u> chosen without regard to their views.

    (A) with students' objections to particular activities, so long as the groups they give money to will be

    (B) if they have objections to particular activities and the groups that are given the money are

    (C) if they object to particular activities, but the groups that the money is given to have to be

    (D) from students who object to particular activities, so long as the groups given money are

    (E) though students have an objection to particular activities, but the groups that are given the money be

Logical predication; Rhetorical construction

The underlined portion of the sentence fails to establish a clear relationship among *universities*, *students*, and *groups*. To which of these three does *they* refer? It would appear that the *universities* must give the money, but *they* does not have a referent. Furthermore, *they* is followed by *their views*, and in this case *their* must refer to *groups*. Wordy and awkward phrasing as well as an unnecessary shift in verb tense (*will be chosen*) compound the difficulty of understanding this sentence in its original form.

A *With students' objections…*is awkward and dense; *they* does not have a referent; the future *will be* is incorrect since the Supreme Court *has* already *ruled*.

B   Referent for *they* is *student activity fees*, which cannot possibly *have objections…*; the use of *and* is illogical.

C   *They* refers to student *activity fees* rather than *students*; *but* does not have the requisite sense of *with the provision that*; *have to be* is wordy.

D   **Correct.** In this sentence, *from students who object* is clear and idiomatic; *so long as* is used appropriately; *groups given money* eliminates the problem of a pronoun without a referent; *are* is the proper tense.

E   *Have an objection* is an unnecessarily wordy way to say *object*; the verb *be* does not complete the latter part of the sentence.

The correct answer is D.

43. Despite the increasing number of women graduating from law school and passing bar examinations, <u>the proportion of judges and partners at major law firms who are women have not risen to a comparable extent</u>.

(A) the proportion of judges and partners at major law firms who are women have not risen to a comparable extent

(B) the proportion of women judges and partners at major law firms have not risen comparably

(C) the proportion of judges and partners at major law firms who are women has not risen comparably

(D) yet the proportion of women judges and partners at major law firms has not risen to a comparable extent

(E) yet the proportion of judges and partners at major law firms who are women has not risen comparably

Agreement; Rhetorical construction

When a number of plural nouns appear in phrases between a singular subject and the verb, it can be easy to overlook the true subject of the verb. Here, *judges, partners, firms,* and *women* all occur between the singular subject, *proportion,* and the verb, which should also be singular, *has risen.* Concise expression is particularly important in a long construction; *to a comparable extent* may be more concisely expressed as *comparably.*

A   Plural verb, *have risen,* does not agree with the singular subject, *proportion.*

B   *Have risen* does not agree with *proportion*; here, *women* applies only to *judges,* not to *partners at major law firms.*

C   **Correct.** In this sentence, *has risen* agrees with *proportion,* and *comparably* is more concise than *to a comparable extent.* The modifying clause *who are women* follows (1) *judges* and (2) *partners at major law firms* as closely as is possible given the content of the sentence; this positioning has the virtue of being clear in its meaning.

D   The contrast has already been introduced by *despite,* so the addition of *yet* is illogical and ungrammatical; *to a comparable extent* is wordy.

E   *Despite* introduces the contrast; adding *yet* is illogical and results in an ungrammatical construction.

The correct answer is C.

44. <u>Seldom more than 40 feet wide and 12 feet deep, but it ran 363 miles across the rugged wilderness of upstate New York, the Erie Canal connected</u> the Hudson River at Albany to the Great Lakes at Buffalo, providing the port of New York City with a direct water link to the heartland of the North American continent.

(A) Seldom more than 40 feet wide and 12 feet deep, but it ran 363 miles across the rugged wilderness of upstate New York, the Erie Canal connected

(B) Seldom more than 40 feet wide and 12 feet deep but running 363 miles across the rugged wilderness of upstate New York, the Erie Canal connected

(C) It was seldom more than 40 feet wide and 12 feet deep, and ran 363 miles across the rugged wilderness of upstate New York, but the Erie Canal, connecting

(D) The Erie Canal was seldom more than 40 feet wide or 12 feet deep and it ran 363 miles across the rugged wilderness of upstate New York, which connected

(E) The Erie Canal, seldom more than 40 feet wide and 12 feet deep, but running 363 miles across the rugged wilderness of upstate New York, connecting

Logical predication; Grammatical construction

The phrase *seldom…deep* is the first half of a modifier that describes *the Erie Canal*. However, because a comma incorrectly follows *deep*, this phrase appears to be the entire modifier, which must agree with the noun or pronoun that immediately follows it. This phrase cannot modify the conjunction *but*, and *it* has no referent; *but it ran* is not a logical or grammatical construction following the modifying phrase. Substituting *running* for *it ran* creates an adjective phrase parallel to the first adjective phrase (*seldom…deep*). To contrast the small size reported in the first phrase with the great distance reported in the second, the two phrases may be joined with *but*; together they create a single modifier correctly modifying *the Erie Canal*. *The Erie Canal* is then the subject of the sentence and requires the verb *connected* to provide a logical statement.

A *But it ran* cannot logically or grammatically follow the modifying phrase.

B **Correct.** This sentence properly has the single modifier consisting of two contrasting parts.

C Neither *and* nor *but* acts as a logical connector; the use of *connecting* results in a sentence fragment.

D The paired concepts of width and depth should be joined by *and*, not *or*; this construction calls for two main clauses to be separated by a comma after *deep*; *which* is ambiguous.

E The two halves of the modifier should not be separated by a comma after *deep*; the subject is awkwardly and confusingly placed at a great distance from the predicate; the use of *connecting* rather than *connected* creates a sentence fragment.

The correct answer is B.

45. In 1923, the Supreme Court declared a minimum wage for women and children in the District of Columbia as unconstitutional, and ruling that it was a form of price-fixing and, as such, an abridgment of the right of contract.

(A) the Supreme Court declared a minimum wage for women and children in the District of Columbia as unconstitutional, and

(B) the Supreme Court declared as unconstitutional a minimum wage for women and children in the District of Columbia, and

(C) the Supreme Court declared unconstitutional a minimum wage for women and children in the District of Columbia,

(D) a minimum wage for women and children in the District of Columbia was declared unconstitutional by the Supreme Court,

(E) when the Supreme Court declared a minimum wage for women and children in the District of Columbia as unconstitutional,

Idiom; Grammatical construction

This sentence depends on the correct use of an idiom: *the court declares x unconstitutional*. The inverted form should be used here because of the long phrases involved: *the court declares unconstitutional x*. *The Supreme Court* is the subject of the sentence; *declared* is the verb. *Ruling…contract* acts a modifier describing the action of the main clause; because the modifier is subordinate to the main clause, the conjunction *and* must be omitted. *And* is used to join two independent clauses, not a clause and its modifier.

A *Declared…as unconstitutional* is not the correct idiom; the use of *and* creates an ungrammatical construction.

B *Declared as unconstitutional* is not the correct idiom; the use of *and* creates an ungrammatical construction.

C   **Correct.** In this sentence, the correct idiom is used, and the modifier is grammatically and logically attached to the main clause.

D   Passive voice construction is weak and wordy; its use causes the modifier to be misplaced and ambiguous.

E   *Declared…as unconstitutional* is not the correct idiom; *when* transforms the main clause into a subordinate clause, resulting in a sentence fragment.

The correct answer is C.

46.   Researchers have found that individuals who have been blind from birth, and <u>who thus have never seen anyone gesture, nevertheless make hand motions when speaking just as frequently and in virtually the same way as sighted people do, and that they will gesture</u> even when conversing with another blind person.

(A)   who thus have never seen anyone gesture, nevertheless make hand motions when speaking just as frequently and in virtually the same way as sighted people do, and that they will gesture

(B)   who thus never saw anyone gesturing, nevertheless make hand motions when speaking just as frequent and in virtually the same way as sighted people did, and that they will gesture

(C)   who thus have never seen anyone gesture, nevertheless made hand motions when speaking just as frequently and in virtually the same way as sighted people do, as well as gesturing

(D)   thus never having seen anyone gesture, nevertheless made hand motions when speaking just as frequent and in virtually the same way as sighted people did, as well as gesturing

(E)   thus never having seen anyone gesture, nevertheless to make hand motions when speaking just as frequently and in virtually the same way as sighted people do, and to gesture

Parallelism; Verb form; Diction

The researchers have found (1) *that individuals… make hand motions…as sighted people do* and (2) *that they will gesture…with another blind person.* In the original sentence, the two findings are reported in two parallel subordinate clauses introduced by *that.* The verb tenses are logical and parallel: *who have been blind* and *who have never seen* indicate a condition that began in the past and continues in the present; *make* and *do* refer to present actions. The verb *make* (*hand motions*) is correctly modified by the adverb *frequently* to show how the action of the verb is carried out. The emphatic future *will gesture* is properly used here with *even* to emphasize the extreme or the unexpected.

A   **Correct.** Although the original sentence is complicated, the parallelism of its structure and phrasing allows its meaning to be clear and its expression effective.

B   Verbs *saw* and *did* indicate action completed in the past; the simple past tense is not appropriate in either case; the adjective *frequent* cannot modify the verb; awkward and muddy.

C   *Made* indicates past action, but the present tense is logically required; *as well as gesturing* violates the parallelism of the two subordinate (*that*) clauses; choppy and unclear.

D   *Having seen* is not parallel to *have been*; *made* and *did* do not show ongoing action; *frequent* incorrectly modifies the verb; *as well as gesturing* destroys the parallelism of the two subordinate (*that*) clauses; awkward and unclear.

E   Replacing the verb *make* with the infinitive *to make* results in an ungrammatical construction that fails to complete the sentence.

The correct answer is A.

47. Like embryonic germ cells, which are cells that develop early in the formation of the fetus and that later generate eggs or sperm, <u>embryonic stem cells have the ability of developing themselves into different kinds of body tissue.</u>

(A) embryonic stem cells have the ability of developing themselves into different kinds of body tissue

(B) embryonic stem cells have the ability to develop into different kinds of body tissue

(C) in embryonic stem cells there is the ability to develop into different kinds of body tissue

(D) the ability to develop themselves into different kinds of body tissue characterizes embryonic stem cells

(E) the ability of developing into different kinds of body tissue characterizes embryonic stem cells

Idiom; Grammatical construction

Two constructions create problems in the original sentence. The first is the unidiomatic construction *have the ability of developing*; *ability* must be followed by an infinitive, *to develop*, not a phrase. The second problematic construction is *to develop themselves into*. In this biological context, the verb *develop* means to progress from an earlier to a later stage; it is used intransitively, which means that it cannot take an object. The pronoun *themselves* acts as an object, creating a construction that is not grammatical or logical. Omitting the pronoun removes the problem.

A *Ability* is incorrectly followed by *of developing*; a pronoun cannot follow *develop*, when it is used, as it is here, in its intransitive sense.

B **Correct.** *Ability* is properly followed by the infinitive in this sentence, and the pronoun *themselves* is omitted.

C This awkward and wordy construction violates the parallelism of *like embryonic germ cells…embryonic stem cells….*

D The two parts of the comparison must be parallel; *like embryonic germ cells* must be followed by *embryonic stem cells*, not *the ability to develop*.

E *Ability* is followed by the unidiomatic *of developing* rather than *to develop*; the main clause must begin with *embryonic stem cells* to balance and complete *like embryonic germ cells*.

The correct answer is B.

48. Critics contend that the new missile is a weapon whose importance is largely symbolic, more a tool <u>for manipulating people's perceptions than to fulfill</u> a real military need.

(A) for manipulating people's perceptions than to fulfill

(B) for manipulating people's perceptions than for fulfilling

(C) to manipulate people's perceptions rather than that it fulfills

(D) to manipulate people's perceptions rather than fulfilling

(E) to manipulate people's perceptions than for fulfilling

Parallelism

This sentence uses the comparative construction *more x than y* where *x* and *y* must be parallel. Here, *x* is *a tool for manipulating people's perceptions*, and *y* is *to fulfill a real military need*. *A tool* does not need to be repeated in the second half of the comparison because it is understood, but the wording of the two phrases does need to match. There are two acceptable solutions: (1) *for manipulating* can be followed by *for fulfilling* or (2) *to manipulate* can be followed by *to fulfill*.

A *For manipulating* is not parallel to *to fulfill*.

B **Correct.** *For manipulating* and *for fulfilling* are parallel in this sentence.

C *To manipulate* is not parallel to *that it fulfills*.

D *To manipulate* is not parallel to *fulfilling*.

E *To manipulate* is not parallel to *for fulfilling*.

The correct answer is B.

49. As an actress and, more importantly, as a teacher of acting, Stella Adler was one of the most influential artists in the American theater, who trained several generations of actors including Marlon Brando and Robert De Niro.

    (A) Stella Adler was one of the most influential artists in the American theater, who trained several generations of actors including

    (B) Stella Adler, one of the most influential artists in the American theater, trained several generations of actors who include

    (C) Stella Adler was one of the most influential artists in the American theater, training several generations of actors whose ranks included

    (D) one of the most influential artists in the American theater was Stella Adler, who trained several generations of actors including

    (E) one of the most influential artists in the American theater, Stella Adler, trained several generations of actors whose ranks included

Logical predication

The original sentence contains a number of modifiers, but not all of them are correctly expressed. The clause *who trained…* describes *Stella Adler*, yet a relative clause such as this one must be placed immediately after the noun or pronoun it modifies, and this clause follows *theater* rather than *Adler*. Replacing *who trained* with *training* corrects the error because the phrase *training…* modifies the whole preceding clause rather than the single preceding noun. *Several generations of actors including* shows the same error in reverse; *including* modifies the whole phrase, but the two actors named are not *generations of actors*. The more limiting clause *whose ranks included* (referring to *actors*) is appropriate here.

A   Relative (*who*) clause follows *theater* rather than *Adler*; *including* refers to *generations of actors*, when the reference should be to *actors* only.

B   This construction, in which the subject is both preceded and followed by modifiers, is awkward; the verbs should be consistently in the past tense, but *include* is present tense.

C   **Correct.** In this sentence, substituting *training* for *who trained* and *whose ranks included* for *including* eliminates the modification errors.

D   Introductory modifier must be immediately followed by *Stella Adler*, not *one…*; *including* refers to *generations of actors* rather than to *actors* only.

E   Introductory modifier must be immediately followed by *Stella Adler*, not *one*.

The correct answer is C.

50. By developing the Secure Digital Music Initiative, the recording industry associations of North America, Japan, and Europe hope to create a standardized way of distributing songs and full-length recordings on the Internet that will protect copyright holders and foil the many audio pirates who copy and distribute digital music illegally.

    (A) of distributing songs and full-length recordings on the Internet that will protect copyright holders and foil the many audio pirates who copy and distribute

    (B) of distributing songs and full-length recordings on the Internet and to protect copyright holders and foiling the many audio pirates copying and distributing

    (C) for distributing songs and full-length recordings on the Internet while it protects copyright holders and foils the many audio pirates who copy and distribute

    (D) to distribute songs and full-length recordings on the Internet while they will protect copyright holders and foil the many audio pirates copying and distributing

    (E) to distribute songs and full-length recordings on the Internet and it will protect copyright holders and foiling the many audio pirates who copy and distribute

Parallelism

The original sentence depends on the parallelism of its verbs to make its point clearly and effectively. *A standardized way…will protect* and (*will* understood) *foil*; *pirates…copy and distribute*. In the first pair of parallel verbs, *will* does not need to be repeated because it is understood.

A **Correct.** The verbs *will protect* and (*will*) *foil* are parallel in this sentence, as are the verbs *copy* and *distribute*.

B *And to protect* distorts meaning, suggesting that protection comes in addition to *the standardized way*; *foiling* is not parallel to *to protect*.

C *Way for* should instead be *way of*; the pronoun reference in *while it protects* is ambiguous; construction suggests that protection comes from something other than the *standardized way*.

D Pronoun *they* has no referent; use of *while* suggests that protection comes from something other than the *standardized way* of distribution.

E *And it will protect* distorts meaning, suggesting that protection comes in addition to *the standardized way*; *will protect* and *foiling* are not parallel.

The correct answer is A.

51. Whereas a ramjet generally cannot achieve high speeds without the initial assistance of a rocket, high speeds can be attained by scramjets, or supersonic combustion ramjets, in that they reduce airflow compression at the entrance of the engine and letting air pass through at supersonic speeds.

(A) high speeds can be attained by scramjets, or supersonic combustion ramjets, in that they reduce

(B) that high speeds can be attained by scramjets, or supersonic combustion ramjets, is a result of their reducing

(C) the ability of scramjets, or supersonic combustion ramjets, to achieve high speeds is because they reduce

(D) scramjets, or supersonic combustion ramjets, have the ability of attaining high speeds when reducing

(E) scramjets, or supersonic combustion ramjets, can attain high speeds by reducing

Rhetorical construction

The underlined portion of the original sentence is wordy and ineffective. Transforming it from passive (*high speeds can be attained by scramjets*) to active voice (*scramjets can attain high speeds*) eliminates much of the problem. As the subject of the main clause, *scramjets* correctly parallels *a ramjet*, the subject of the subordinate clause; the contrast is thus clearly and effectively drawn. *In that they reduce* is wordy and awkward; it can be replaced by the more concise phrase *by reducing*.

A Passive voice contributes to a wordy, awkward, and ineffective construction; *in that they reduce* is also wordy and awkward.

B Passive voice and subordinate (*that*) clause constructions are wordy, awkward, and ineffective.

C *The ability…is because* is not a grammatical construction; *scramjets*, not *the ability*, should be parallel to *a ramjet*.

D *Have the ability of attaining* is wordy; *when* does not indicate the cause-and-effect relationship.

E **Correct.** *Scramjets* parallels *a ramjet* for an effective contrast in this sentence; the active voice is clear and concise; *by reducing* shows how scramjets attain high speeds.

The correct answer is E.

52. It will not be possible to implicate melting sea ice in the coastal flooding that many global warming models have projected: just <u>like a glass of water that will not overflow due to melting ice cubes,</u> so melting sea ice does not increase oceanic volume.

   (A) like a glass of water that will not overflow due to melting ice cubes,

   (B) like melting ice cubes that do not cause a glass of water to overflow,

   (C) a glass of water will not overflow because of melting ice cubes,

   (D) as melting ice cubes that do not cause a glass of water to overflow,

   (E) as melting ice cubes do not cause a glass of water to overflow,

Diction; Parallelism

The preposition *like* introduces nouns and noun phrases; the conjunction *as* introduces verbs or clauses, so *as* is required here. The comparative construction used here is *just as x so y*; *x* and *y* must be parallel. The *y* clause is written in effective subject-verb-object order: *melting sea ice does not increase oceanic volume.* The original wordy, awkward *x* clause is not parallel. To make it parallel, *melting ice cubes* should be the subject of the clause, *do not cause...to overflow* the verb phrase, and a *glass of water* the object.

A   *Like* is used in place of *as*; the two elements of comparison are not parallel.

B   *Like* is used in place of *as*; *that* violates parallelism.

C   *As* or *just as* is needed to introduce the clause; the two clauses are not parallel.

D   *That* violates the parallelism of the two clauses and creates an ungrammatical construction.

E   **Correct.** This sentence has *just as* properly introducing the first clause, and the two clauses are parallel.

The correct answer is E.

4.0 Math Review

4.0 Math Review

Although this chapter provides a review of some of the mathematical concepts of arithmetic, algebra, and geometry, it is not intended to be a textbook. You should use this chapter to familiarize yourself with the kinds of topics that are tested in the GMAT® test. You may wish to consult an arithmetic, algebra, or geometry book for a more detailed discussion of some of the topics.

Section 4.1, "Arithmetic," includes the following topics:

1. Properties of Integers
2. Fractions
3. Decimals
4. Real Numbers
5. Ratio and Proportion
6. Percents
7. Powers and Roots of Numbers
8. Descriptive Statistics
9. Sets
10. Counting Methods
11. Discrete Probability

Section 4.2, "Algebra," does not extend beyond what is usually covered in a first-year high school algebra course. The topics included are as follows:

1. Simplifying Algebraic Expressions
2. Equations
3. Solving Linear Equations with One Unknown
4. Solving Two Linear Equations with Two Unknowns
5. Solving Equations by Factoring
6. Solving Quadratic Equations
7. Exponents
8. Inequalities
9. Absolute Value
10. Functions

Section 4.3, "Geometry," is limited primarily to measurement and intuitive geometry or spatial visualization. Extensive knowledge of theorems and the ability to construct proofs, skills that are usually developed in a formal geometry course, are not tested. The topics included in this section are the following:

1. Lines
2. Intersecting Lines and Angles
3. Perpendicular Lines
4. Parallel Lines
5. Polygons (Convex)
6. Triangles
7. Quadrilaterals
8. Circles
9. Rectangular Solids and Cylinders
10. Coordinate Geometry

Section 4.4, "Word Problems," presents examples of and solutions to the following types of word problems:

1. Rate Problems
2. Work Problems
3. Mixture Problems
4. Interest Problems
5. Discount
6. Profit
7. Sets
8. Geometry Problems
9. Measurement Problems
10. Data Interpretation

4.1 Arithmetic

1. Properties of Integers

An *integer* is any number in the set {. . . –3, –2, –1, 0, 1, 2, 3, . . .}. If x and y are integers and $x \neq 0$, then x is a *divisor* (*factor*) of y provided that $y = xn$ for some integer n. In this case, y is also said to be *divisible* by x or to be a *multiple* of x. For example, 7 is a divisor or factor of 28 since $28 = (7)(4)$, but 8 is not a divisor of 28 since there is no integer n such that $28 = 8n$.

If x and y are positive integers, there exist unique integers q and r, called the *quotient* and *remainder*, respectively, such that $y = xq + r$ and $0 \leq r < x$. For example, when 28 is divided by 8, the quotient is 3 and the remainder is 4 since $28 = (8)(3) + 4$. Note that y is divisible by x if and only if the remainder r is 0; for example, 32 has a remainder of 0 when divided by 8 because 32 is divisible by 8. Also, note that when a smaller integer is divided by a larger integer, the quotient is 0 and the remainder is the smaller integer. For example, 5 divided by 7 has the quotient 0 and the remainder 5 since $5 = (7)(0) + 5$.

Any integer that is divisible by 2 is an *even integer*; the set of even integers is {. . . –4, –2, 0, 2, 4, 6, 8, . . .}. Integers that are not divisible by 2 are *odd integers*; {. . . –3, –1, 1, 3, 5, . . .} is the set of odd integers.

If at least one factor of a product of integers is even, then the product is even; otherwise the product is odd. If two integers are both even or both odd, then their sum and their difference are even. Otherwise, their sum and their difference are odd.

A *prime* number is a positive integer that has exactly two different positive divisors, 1 and itself. For example, 2, 3, 5, 7, 11, and 13 are prime numbers, but 15 is not, since 15 has four different positive divisors, 1, 3, 5, and 15. The number 1 is not a prime number since it has only one positive divisor. Every integer greater than 1 either is prime or can be uniquely expressed as a product of prime factors. For example, $14 = (2)(7)$, $81 = (3)(3)(3)(3)$, and $484 = (2)(2)(11)(11)$.

The numbers –2, –1, 0, 1, 2, 3, 4, 5 are *consecutive integers*. Consecutive integers can be represented by n, $n + 1$, $n + 2$, $n + 3$, . . . , where n is an integer. The numbers 0, 2, 4, 6, 8 are *consecutive even integers*, and 1, 3, 5, 7, 9 are *consecutive odd integers*. Consecutive even integers can be represented by $2n$, $2n + 2$, $2n + 4$, . . . , and consecutive odd integers can be represented by $2n + 1$, $2n + 3$, $2n + 5$, . . . , where n is an integer.

Properties of the integer 1. If n is any number, then $1 \cdot n = n$, and for any number $n \neq 0$, $n \cdot \dfrac{1}{n} = 1$.

The number 1 can be expressed in many ways; for example, $\dfrac{n}{n} = 1$ for any number $n \neq 0$.

Multiplying or dividing an expression by 1, in any form, does not change the value of that expression.

Properties of the integer 0. The integer 0 is neither positive nor negative. If n is any number, then $n + 0 = n$ and $n \cdot 0 = 0$. Division by 0 is not defined.

2. Fractions

In a fraction $\frac{n}{d}$, n is the *numerator* and d is the *denominator*. The denominator of a fraction can never be 0, because division by 0 is not defined.

Two fractions are said to be *equivalent* if they represent the same number. For example, $\frac{8}{36}$ and $\frac{14}{63}$ are equivalent since they both represent the number $\frac{2}{9}$. In each case, the fraction is reduced to lowest terms by dividing both numerator and denominator by their *greatest common divisor* (gcd). The gcd of 8 and 36 is 4 and the gcd of 14 and 63 is 7.

Addition and subtraction of fractions.

Two fractions with the same denominator can be added or subtracted by performing the required operation with the numerators, leaving the denominators the same. For example, $\frac{3}{5} + \frac{4}{5} = \frac{3+4}{5} = \frac{7}{5}$ and $\frac{5}{7} - \frac{2}{7} = \frac{5-2}{7} = \frac{3}{7}$. If two fractions do not have the same denominator, express them as equivalent fractions with the same denominator. For example, to add $\frac{3}{5}$ and $\frac{4}{7}$, multiply the numerator and denominator of the first fraction by 7 and the numerator and denominator of the second fraction by 5, obtaining $\frac{21}{35}$ and $\frac{20}{35}$, respectively; $\frac{21}{35} + \frac{20}{35} = \frac{41}{35}$.

For the new denominator, choosing the *least common multiple* (lcm) of the denominators usually lessens the work. For $\frac{2}{3} + \frac{1}{6}$, the lcm of 3 and 6 is 6 (not $3 \times 6 = 18$), so

$$\frac{2}{3} + \frac{1}{6} = \frac{2}{3} \times \frac{2}{2} + \frac{1}{6} = \frac{4}{6} + \frac{1}{6} = \frac{5}{6}.$$

Multiplication and division of fractions.

To multiply two fractions, simply multiply the two numerators and multiply the two denominators.

For example, $\frac{2}{3} \times \frac{4}{7} = \frac{2 \times 4}{3 \times 7} = \frac{8}{21}$.

To divide by a fraction, invert the divisor (that is, find its *reciprocal*) and multiply. For example,

$$\frac{2}{3} \div \frac{4}{7} = \frac{2}{3} \times \frac{7}{4} = \frac{14}{12} = \frac{7}{6}.$$

In the problem above, the reciprocal of $\frac{4}{7}$ is $\frac{7}{4}$. In general, the reciprocal of a fraction $\frac{n}{d}$ is $\frac{d}{n}$, where n and d are not zero.

Mixed numbers.

A number that consists of a whole number and a fraction, for example, $7\frac{2}{3}$, is a mixed number: $7\frac{2}{3}$ means $7 + \frac{2}{3}$.

To change a mixed number into a fraction, multiply the whole number by the denominator of the fraction and add this number to the numerator of the fraction; then put the result over the

denominator of the fraction. For example, $7\frac{2}{3} = \frac{(3 \times 7) + 2}{3} = \frac{23}{3}$.

3. Decimals

In the decimal system, the position of the period or *decimal point* determines the place value of the digits. For example, the digits in the number 7,654.321 have the following place values:

Thousands		Hundreds	Tens	Ones or units		Tenths	Hundredths	Thousandths
7	,	6	5	4	.	3	2	1

Some examples of decimals follow.

$$0.321 = \frac{3}{10} + \frac{2}{100} + \frac{1}{1,000} = \frac{321}{1,000}$$

$$0.0321 = \frac{0}{10} + \frac{3}{100} + \frac{2}{1,000} + \frac{1}{10,000} = \frac{321}{10,000}$$

$$1.56 = 1 + \frac{5}{10} + \frac{6}{100} = \frac{156}{100}$$

Sometimes decimals are expressed as the product of a number with only one digit to the left of the decimal point and a power of 10. This is called *scientific notation*. For example, 231 can be written as 2.31×10^2 and 0.0231 can be written as 2.31×10^{-2}. When a number is expressed in scientific notation, the exponent of the 10 indicates the number of places that the decimal point is to be moved in the number that is to be multiplied by a power of 10 in order to obtain the product. The decimal point is moved to the right if the exponent is positive and to the left if the exponent is negative. For example, 2.013×10^4 is equal to 20,130 and 1.91×10^{-4} is equal to 0.000191.

Addition and subtraction of decimals.

To add or subtract two decimals, the decimal points of both numbers should be lined up. If one of the numbers has fewer digits to the right of the decimal point than the other, zeros may be inserted to the right of the last digit. For example, to add 17.6512 and 653.27, set up the numbers in a column and add:

$$
\begin{array}{r}
17.6512 \\
+\ 653.2700 \\
\hline
670.9212
\end{array}
$$

Likewise for 653.27 minus 17.6512:

$$
\begin{array}{r}
653.2700 \\
-\ 17.6512 \\
\hline
635.6188
\end{array}
$$

Multiplication of decimals.

To multiply decimals, multiply the numbers as if they were whole numbers and then insert the decimal point in the product so that the number of digits to the right of the decimal point is equal to the sum of the numbers of digits to the right of the decimal points in the numbers being multiplied. For example:

$$
\begin{array}{r}
2.09 \quad (2 \text{ digits to the right}) \\
\times\ 1.3 \quad (1 \text{ digit to the right}) \\
\hline
627 \quad\quad\quad \\
2090 \quad\quad\quad \\
\hline
2.717 \quad (2 + 1 = 3 \text{ digits to the right})
\end{array}
$$

Division of decimals.

To divide a number (the dividend) by a decimal (the divisor), move the decimal point of the divisor to the right until the divisor is a whole number. Then move the decimal point of the dividend the same number of places to the right, and divide as you would by a whole number. The decimal point in the quotient will be directly above the decimal point in the new dividend. For example, to divide 698.12 by 12.4:

$$
12.4\overline{)698.12}
$$

will be replaced by:

$$
124\overline{)6981.2}
$$

and the division would proceed as follows:

$$
\begin{array}{r}
56.3 \\
124\overline{)6981.2} \\
\underline{620} \\
781 \\
\underline{744} \\
372 \\
\underline{372} \\
0
\end{array}
$$

4. Real Numbers

All *real* numbers correspond to points on the number line and all points on the number line correspond to real numbers. All real numbers except zero are either positive or negative.

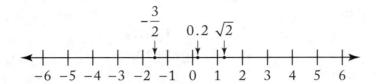

On a number line, numbers corresponding to points to the left of zero are negative and numbers corresponding to points to the right of zero are positive. For any two numbers on the number line, the number to the left is less than the number to the right; for example,

$$-4 < -3 < -\frac{3}{2} < -1, \text{ and } 1 < \sqrt{2} < 2.$$

To say that the number n is between 1 and 4 on the number line means that $n > 1$ and $n < 4$, that is, $1 < n < 4$. If n is "between 1 and 4, inclusive," then $1 \le n \le 4$.

The distance between a number and zero on the number line is called the *absolute value* of the number. Thus 3 and –3 have the same absolute value, 3, since they are both three units from zero. The absolute value of 3 is denoted $|3|$. Examples of absolute values of numbers are

$$|-5| = |5| = 5, \quad \left|-\frac{7}{2}\right| = \frac{7}{2}, \text{ and } |0| = 0.$$

Note that the absolute value of any nonzero number is positive.

Here are some properties of real numbers that are used frequently. If x, y, and z are real numbers, then

(1) $x + y = y + x$ and $xy = yx$.
For example, $8 + 3 = 3 + 8 = 11$, and $(17)(5) = (5)(17) = 85$.

(2) $(x + y) + z = x + (y + z)$ and $(xy)z = x(yz)$.
For example, $(7 + 5) + 2 = 7 + (5 + 2) = 7 + (7) = 14$, and $(5\sqrt{3})(\sqrt{3}) = (5)(\sqrt{3}\sqrt{3}) = (5)(3) = 15$.

(3) $xy + xz = x(y + z)$.
For example, $718(36) + 718(64) = 718(36 + 64) = 718(100) = 71{,}800$.

(4) If x and y are both positive, then $x + y$ and xy are positive.

(5) If x and y are both negative, then $x + y$ is negative and xy is positive.

(6) If x is positive and y is negative, then xy is negative.

(7) If $xy = 0$, then $x = 0$ or $y = 0$. For example, $3y = 0$ implies $y = 0$.

(8) $|x + y| \le |x| + |y|$. For example, if $x = 10$ and $y = 2$, then $|x + y| = |12| = 12 = |x| + |y|$; and if $x = 10$ and $y = -2$, then $|x + y| = |8| = 8 < 12 = |x| + |y|$.

5. Ratio and Proportion

The *ratio* of the number a to the number b $\left(b \neq 0\right)$ is $\frac{a}{b}$.

A ratio may be expressed or represented in several ways. For example, the ratio of 2 to 3 can be written as 2 to 3, 2:3, or $\frac{2}{3}$. The order of the terms of a ratio is important. For example, the ratio of the number of months with exactly 30 days to the number with exactly 31 days is $\frac{4}{7}$, not $\frac{7}{4}$.

A *proportion* is a statement that two ratios are equal; for example, $\frac{2}{3} = \frac{8}{12}$ is a proportion. One way to solve a proportion involving an unknown is to cross multiply, obtaining a new equality. For example, to solve for n in the proportion $\frac{2}{3} = \frac{n}{12}$, cross multiply, obtaining $24 = 3n$; then divide both sides by 3, to get $n = 8$.

6. Percents

Percent means *per hundred* or *number out of 100*. A percent can be represented as a fraction with a denominator of 100, or as a decimal. For example:

$$37\% = \frac{37}{100} = 0.37.$$

To find a certain percent of a number, multiply the number by the percent expressed as a decimal or fraction. For example:

$$20\% \text{ of } 90 = 0.2 \times 90 = 18$$

$$\text{or}$$

$$20\% \text{ of } 90 = \frac{20}{100} \times 90 = \frac{1}{5} \times 90 = 18.$$

Percents greater than 100%.

Percents greater than 100% are represented by numbers greater than 1. For example:

$$300\% = \frac{300}{100} = 3$$

$$250\% \text{ of } 80 = 2.5 \times 80 = 200.$$

Percents less than 1%.

The percent 0.5% means $\frac{1}{2}$ of 1 percent. For example, 0.5% of 12 is equal to $0.005 \times 12 = 0.06$.

Percent change.

Often a problem will ask for the percent increase or decrease from one quantity to another quantity. For example, "If the price of an item increases from \$24 to \$30, what is the percent increase in price?" To find the percent increase, first find the amount of the increase; then divide this increase by the original amount, and express this quotient as a percent. In the example above, the percent increase would be found in the following way: the amount of the increase is $\left(30 - 24\right) = 6$. Therefore, the percent increase is $\frac{6}{24} = 0.25 = 25\%$.

Likewise, to find the percent decrease (for example, the price of an item is reduced from $30 to $24), first find the amount of the decrease; then divide this decrease by the original amount, and express this quotient as a percent. In the example above, the amount of decrease is $(30 - 24) = 6$.

Therefore, the percent decrease is $\frac{6}{30} = 0.20 = 20\%$.

Note that the percent increase from 24 to 30 is not the same as the percent decrease from 30 to 24.

In the following example, the increase is greater than 100 percent: If the cost of a certain house in 1983 was 300 percent of its cost in 1970, by what percent did the cost increase?

If n is the cost in 1970, then the percent increase is equal to $\frac{3n - n}{n} = \frac{2n}{n} = 2$, or 200%.

7. Powers and Roots of Numbers

When a number k is to be used n times as a factor in a product, it can be expressed as k^n, which means the nth power of k. For example, $2^2 = 2 \times 2 = 4$ and $2^3 = 2 \times 2 \times 2 = 8$ are powers of 2.

Squaring a number that is greater than 1, or raising it to a higher power, results in a larger number; squaring a number between 0 and 1 results in a smaller number. For example:

$$3^2 = 9 \qquad \left(9 > 3\right)$$
$$\left(\frac{1}{3}\right)^2 = \frac{1}{9} \qquad \left(\frac{1}{9} < \frac{1}{3}\right)$$
$$\left(0.1\right)^2 = 0.01 \quad \left(0.01 < 0.1\right)$$

A *square root* of a number n is a number that, when squared, is equal to n. The square root of a negative number is not a real number. Every positive number n has two square roots, one positive and the other negative, but $\sqrt{n}$ denotes the positive number whose square is n. For example, $\sqrt{9}$ denotes 3. The two square roots of 9 are $\sqrt{9} = 3$ and $-\sqrt{9} = -3$.

Every real number r has exactly one real *cube root*, which is the number s such that $s^3 = r$. The real cube root of r is denoted by $\sqrt[3]{r}$. Since $2^3 = 8$, $\sqrt[3]{8} = 2$. Similarly, $\sqrt[3]{-8} = -2$, because $\left(-2\right)^3 = -8$.

8. Descriptive Statistics

A list of numbers, or numerical data, can be described by various statistical measures. One of the most common of these measures is the *average*, or *(arithmetic) mean*, which locates a type of "center" for the data. The average of n numbers is defined as the sum of the n numbers divided by n. For example, the average of 6, 4, 7, 10, and 4 is $\frac{6 + 4 + 7 + 10 + 4}{5} = \frac{31}{5} = 6.2$.

The *median* is another type of center for a list of numbers. To calculate the median of n numbers, first order the numbers from least to greatest; if n is odd, the median is defined as the middle number, whereas if n is even, the median is defined as the average of the two middle numbers. In the example above, the numbers, in order, are 4, 4, 6, 7, 10, and the median is 6, the middle number.

For the numbers 4, 6, 6, 8, 9, 12, the median is $\frac{6+8}{2} = 7$. Note that the mean of these numbers is 7.5.

The median of a set of data can be less than, equal to, or greater than the mean. Note that for a large set of data (for example, the salaries of 800 company employees), it is often true that about half of the data is less than the median and about half of the data is greater than the median; but this is not always the case, as the following data show.

3, 5, 7, 7, 7, 7, 7, 7, 8, 9, 9, 9, 9, 10, 10

Here the median is 7, but only $\frac{2}{15}$ of the data is less than the median.

The *mode* of a list of numbers is the number that occurs most frequently in the list. For example, the mode of 1, 3, 6, 4, 3, 5 is 3. A list of numbers may have more than one mode. For example, the list 1, 2, 3, 3, 3, 5, 7, 10, 10, 10, 20 has two modes, 3 and 10.

The degree to which numerical data are spread out or dispersed can be measured in many ways. The simplest measure of dispersion is the *range*, which is defined as the greatest value in the numerical data minus the least value. For example, the range of 11, 10, 5, 13, 21 is $21 - 5 = 16$. Note how the range depends on only two values in the data.

One of the most common measures of dispersion is the *standard deviation*. Generally speaking, the more the data are spread away from the mean, the greater the standard deviation. The standard deviation of n numbers can be calculated as follows: (1) find the arithmetic mean, (2) find the differences between the mean and each of the n numbers, (3) square each of the differences, (4) find the average of the squared differences, and (5) take the nonnegative square root of this average. Shown below is this calculation for the data 0, 7, 8, 10, 10, which have arithmetic mean 7.

x	$x - 7$	$(x-7)^2$
0	−7	49
7	0	0
8	1	1
10	3	9
10	3	9
	Total	68

Standard deviation $\sqrt{\dfrac{68}{5}} \approx 3.7$

Notice that the standard deviation depends on every data value, although it depends most on values that are farthest from the mean. This is why a distribution with data grouped closely around the mean will have a smaller standard deviation than will data spread far from the mean. To illustrate this, compare the data 6, 6, 6.5, 7.5, 9, which also have mean 7. Note that the numbers in the second set of data seem to be grouped more closely around the mean of 7 than the numbers in the first set. This is reflected in the standard deviation, which is less for the second set (approximately 1.1) than for the first set (approximately 3.7).

There are many ways to display numerical data that show how the data are distributed. One simple way is with a *frequency distribution*, which is useful for data that have values occurring with varying frequencies. For example, the 20 numbers

$$\begin{array}{cccccccccc} -4 & 0 & 0 & -3 & -2 & -1 & -1 & 0 & -1 & -4 \\ -1 & -5 & 0 & -2 & 0 & -5 & -2 & 0 & 0 & -1 \end{array}$$

are displayed on the next page in a frequency distribution by listing each different value x and the frequency f with which x occurs.

Data Value x	Frequency f
−5	2
−4	2
−3	1
−2	3
−1	5
0	7
Total	20

From the frequency distribution, one can readily compute descriptive statistics:

Mean: $= \dfrac{(-5)(2)+(-4)(2)+(-3)(1)+(-2)(3)+(-1)(5)+(0)(7)}{20} = -1.6$

Median: −1 (the average of the 10th and 11th numbers)

Mode: 0 (the number that occurs most frequently)

Range: $0 - (-5) = 5$

Standard deviation: $\sqrt{\dfrac{(-5+1.6)^2(2)+(-4+1.6)^2(2)+\ldots+(0+1.6)^2(7)}{20}} \approx 1.7$

9. Sets

In mathematics a *set* is a collection of numbers or other objects. The objects are called the *elements* of the set. If S is a set having a finite number of elements, then the number of elements is denoted by $|S|$. Such a set is often defined by listing its elements; for example, $S = \{-5, 0, 1\}$ is a set with $|S| = 3$. The order in which the elements are listed in a set does not matter; thus $\{-5, 0, 1\} = \{0, 1, -5\}$.

If all the elements of a set S are also elements of a set T, then S is a *subset* of T; for example, $S = \{-5, 0, 1\}$ is a subset of $T = \{-5, 0, 1, 4, 10\}$.

For any two sets A and B, the *union* of A and B is the set of all elements that are in A or in B or in both. The *intersection* of A and B is the set of all elements that are both in A *and* in B. The union is denoted by $A \cup B$ and the intersection is denoted by $A \cap B$. As an example, if $A = \{3, 4\}$ and $B = \{4, 5, 6\}$, then $A \cup B = \{3, 4, 5, 6\}$ and $A \cap B = \{4\}$. Two sets that have no elements in common are said to be *disjoint* or *mutually exclusive*.

The relationship between sets is often illustrated with a *Venn diagram* in which sets are represented by regions in a plane. For two sets S and T that are not disjoint and neither is a subset of the other, the intersection $S \cap T$ is represented by the shaded region of the diagram below.

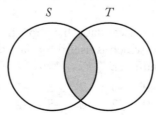

This diagram illustrates a fact about any two finite sets S and T: the number of elements in their union equals the sum of their individual numbers of elements minus the number of elements in their intersection (because the latter are counted twice in the sum); more concisely,

$$\left|S \cup T\right| = \left|S\right| + \left|T\right| - \left|S \cap T\right|.$$

This counting method is called the general addition rule for two sets. As a special case, if S and T are disjoint, then

$$\left|S \cup T\right| = \left|S\right| + \left|T\right|$$

since $\left|S \cap T\right| = 0$.

10. Counting Methods

There are some useful methods for counting objects and sets of objects without actually listing the elements to be counted. The following principle of multiplication is fundamental to these methods.

If an object is to be chosen from a set of m objects and a second object is to be chosen from a different set of n objects, then there are mn ways of choosing both objects simultaneously.

As an example, suppose the objects are items on a menu. If a meal consists of one entree and one dessert and there are 5 entrees and 3 desserts on the menu, then there are $5 \times 3 = 15$ different meals that can be ordered from the menu. As another example, each time a coin is flipped, there are two possible outcomes, heads and tails. If an experiment consists of 8 consecutive coin flips, then the experiment has 2^8 possible outcomes, where each of these outcomes is a list of heads and tails in some order.

A symbol that is often used with the multiplication principle is the *factorial*. If n is an integer greater than 1, then n factorial, denoted by the symbol $n!$, is defined as the product of all the integers from 1 to n. Therefore,

$$2! = (1)(2) = 2,$$
$$3! = (1)(2)(3) = 6,$$
$$4! = (1)(2)(3)(4) = 24, \text{ etc.}$$

Also, by definition, $0! = 1! = 1$.

The factorial is useful for counting the number of ways that a set of objects can be ordered. If a set of n objects is to be ordered from 1st to nth, then there are n choices for the 1st object, $n - 1$ choices for the 2nd object, $n - 2$ choices for the 3rd object, and so on, until there is only 1 choice for the nth object. Thus, by the multiplication principle, the number of ways of ordering the n objects is

$$n(n - 1)(n - 2) \cdots (3)(2)(1) = n!.$$

For example, the number of ways of ordering the letters A, B, and C is 3!, or 6:

ABC, ACB, BAC, BCA, CAB, and CBA.

These orderings are called the *permutations* of the letters A, B, and C.

A permutation can be thought of as a selection process in which objects are selected one by one in a certain order. If the order of selection is not relevant and only k objects are to be selected from a larger set of n objects, a different counting method is employed.

Specifically, consider a set of n objects from which a complete selection of k objects is to be made without regard to order, where $0 \le k \le n$. Then the number of possible complete selections of k objects is called the number of *combinations* of n objects taken k at a time and is denoted by $\binom{n}{k}$.

The value of $\binom{n}{k}$ is given by $\binom{n}{k} = \dfrac{n!}{k!(n-k)!}$.

Note that $\binom{n}{k}$ is the number of k-element subsets of a set with n elements. For example, if $S = \{A, B, C, D, E\}$, then the number of 2-element subsets of S, or the number of combinations of 5 letters taken 2 at a time, is $\binom{5}{2} = \dfrac{5!}{2!3!} = \dfrac{120}{(2)(6)} = 10$.

The subsets are $\{A, B\}$, $\{A, C\}$, $\{A, D\}$, $\{A, E\}$, $\{B, C\}$, $\{B, D\}$, $\{B, E\}$, $\{C, D\}$, $\{C, E\}$, and $\{D, E\}$.

Note that $\binom{5}{2} = 10 = \binom{5}{3}$ because every 2-element subset chosen from a set of 5 elements corresponds to a unique 3-element subset consisting of the elements *not* chosen.

In general, $\binom{n}{k} = \binom{n}{n-k}$.

11. Discrete Probability

Many of the ideas discussed in the preceding three topics are important to the study of discrete probability. Discrete probability is concerned with *experiments* that have a finite number of *outcomes*. Given such an experiment, an *event* is a particular set of outcomes. For example, rolling a number cube with faces numbered 1 to 6 (similar to a 6-sided die) is an experiment with 6 possible outcomes: 1, 2, 3, 4, 5, or 6. One event in this experiment is that the outcome is 4, denoted $\{4\}$; another event is that the outcome is an odd number: $\{1, 3, 5\}$.

The probability that an event E occurs, denoted by $P(E)$, is a number between 0 and 1, inclusive. If E has no outcomes, then E is *impossible* and $P(E) = 0$; if E is the set of all possible outcomes of the experiment, then E is *certain* to occur and $P(E) = 1$. Otherwise, E is possible but uncertain, and $0 < P(E) < 1$. If F is a subset of E, then $P(F) \le P(E)$. In the example above, if the probability of each of the 6 outcomes is the same, then the probability of each outcome is $\dfrac{1}{6}$, and the outcomes are said to be *equally likely*. For experiments in which all the individual outcomes are equally likely, the probability of an event E is

$$P(E) = \frac{\text{The number of outcomes in } E}{\text{The total number of possible outcomes}}.$$

In the example, the probability that the outcome is an odd number is

$$P(\{1, 3, 5\}) = \frac{|\{1, 3, 5\}|}{6} = \frac{3}{6} = \frac{1}{2}.$$

Given an experiment with events E and F, the following events are defined:
"*not E*" is the set of outcomes that are not outcomes in E;
"*E or F*" is the set of outcomes in E or F or both, that is, $E \cup F$;
"*E and F*" is the set of outcomes in both E and F, that is, $E \cap F$.

The probability that E does not occur is $P(\text{not } E) = 1 - P(E)$. The probability that "$E$ or F" occurs is $P(E \text{ or } F) = P(E) + P(F) - P(E \text{ and } F)$, using the general addition rule at the end of section 4.1.9 ("Sets"). For the number cube, if E is the event that the outcome is an odd number, {1, 3, 5}, and F is the event that the outcome is a prime number, {2, 3, 5}, then $P(E \text{ and } F) = P(\{3, 5\}) = \frac{2}{6} = \frac{1}{3}$ and so $P(E \text{ or } F) = P(E) + P(F) - P(E \text{ and } F) = \frac{3}{6} + \frac{3}{6} - \frac{2}{6} = \frac{4}{6} = \frac{2}{3}$.

Note that the event "E or F" is $E \cup F = \{1, 2, 3, 5\}$, and hence $P(E \text{ or } F) = \frac{|\{1, 2, 3, 5\}|}{6} = \frac{4}{6} = \frac{2}{3}$.

If the event "E and F" is impossible (that is, $E \cap F$ has no outcomes), then E and F are said to be *mutually exclusive* events, and $P(E \text{ and } F) = 0$. Then the general addition rule is reduced to $P(E \text{ or } F) = P(E) + P(F)$.

This is the special addition rule for the probability of two mutually exclusive events.

Two events A and B are said to be *independent* if the occurrence of either event does not alter the probability that the other event occurs. For one roll of the number cube, let $A = \{2, 4, 6\}$ and let $B = \{5, 6\}$. Then the probability that A occurs is $P(A) = \frac{|A|}{6} = \frac{3}{6} = \frac{1}{2}$, while, *presuming B occurs*, the probability that A occurs is

$$\frac{|A \cap B|}{|B|} = \frac{|\{6\}|}{|\{5, 6\}|} = \frac{1}{2}.$$

Similarly, the probability that B occurs is $P(B) = \frac{|B|}{6} = \frac{2}{6} = \frac{1}{3}$, while, *presuming A occurs*, the probability that B occurs is

$$\frac{|B \cap A|}{|A|} = \frac{|\{6\}|}{|\{2, 4, 6\}|} = \frac{1}{3}.$$

Thus, the occurrence of either event does not affect the probability that the other event occurs. Therefore, A and B are independent.

The following multiplication rule holds for any independent events E and F: $P(E \text{ and } F) = P(E)P(F)$.

For the independent events A and B above, $P(A \text{ and } B) = P(A)P(B) = \left(\frac{1}{2}\right)\left(\frac{1}{3}\right) = \left(\frac{1}{6}\right)$.

Note that the event "A and B" is $A \cap B = \{6\}$, and hence $P(A \text{ and } B) = P(\{6\}) = \frac{1}{6}$. It follows from the general addition rule and the multiplication rule above that if E and F are independent, then

$$P(E \text{ or } F) = P(E) + P(F) - P(E)P(F).$$

For a final example of some of these rules, consider an experiment with events A, B, and C for which $P(A) = 0.23$, $P(B) = 0.40$, and $P(C) = 0.85$. Also, suppose that events A and B are mutually exclusive and events B and C are independent. Then

$$P(A \text{ or } B) = P(A) + P(B) \quad (\text{since } A \text{ or } B \text{ are mutually exclusive})$$
$$= 0.23 + 0.40$$
$$= 0.63$$
$$P(B \text{ or } C) = P(B) + P(C) - P(B)P(C) \quad (\text{by independence})$$
$$= 0.40 + 0.85 - (0.40)(0.85)$$
$$= 0.91$$

Note that $P(A$ or $C)$ and $P(A$ and $C)$ cannot be determined using the information given. But it can be determined that A and C are *not* mutually exclusive since $P(A) + P(C) = 1.08$, which is greater than 1, and therefore cannot equal $P(A$ or $C)$; from this it follows that $P(A \text{ and } C) \geq 0.08$. One can also deduce that $P(A \text{ and } C) \leq P(A) = 0.23$, since $A \cap C$ is a subset of A, and that $P(A \text{ or } C) \geq P(C) = 0.85$ since C is a subset of $A \cup C$. Thus, one can conclude that $0.85 \leq P(A \text{ or } C) \leq 1$ and $0.08 \leq P(A \text{ and } C) \leq 0.23$.

4.2 Algebra

Algebra is based on the operations of arithmetic and on the concept of an *unknown quantity*, or *variable*. Letters such as x or n are used to represent unknown quantities. For example, suppose Pam has 5 more pencils than Fred. If F represents the number of pencils that Fred has, then the number of pencils that Pam has is $F + 5$. As another example, if Jim's present salary S is increased by 7%, then his new salary is $1.07S$. A combination of letters and arithmetic operations, such as

$F + 5$, $\dfrac{3x^2}{2x - 5}$, and $19x^2 - 6x + 3$, is called an *algebraic expression*.

The expression $19x^2 - 6x + 3$ consists of the *terms* $19x^2$, $-6x$, and 3, where 19 is the *coefficient* of x^2, -6 is the coefficient of x^1, and 3 is a *constant term* (or coefficient of $x^0 = 1$). Such an expression is called a *second degree* (or *quadratic*) *polynomial in x* since the highest power of x is 2. The expression $F + 5$ is a *first degree* (or *linear*) *polynomial in F* since the highest power of F is 1. The expression $\dfrac{3x^2}{2x - 5}$ is not a polynomial because it is not a sum of terms that are each powers of x multiplied by coefficients.

1. Simplifying Algebraic Expressions

Often when working with algebraic expressions, it is necessary to simplify them by factoring or combining *like* terms. For example, the expression $6x + 5x$ is equivalent to $(6 + 5)x$, or $11x$. In the expression $9x - 3y$, 3 is a factor common to both terms: $9x - 3y = 3(3x - y)$. In the expression $5x^2 + 6y$, there are no like terms and no common factors.

If there are common factors in the numerator and denominator of an expression, they can be divided out, provided that they are not equal to zero.

For example, if $x \neq 3$, then $\dfrac{x - 3}{x - 3}$ is equal to 1; therefore,

$$\frac{3xy - 9y}{x - 3} = \frac{3y(x - 3)}{x - 3}$$
$$= (3y)(1)$$
$$= 3y$$

To multiply two algebraic expressions, each term of one expression is multiplied by each term of the other expression. For example:

$$(3x - 4)(9y + x) = 3x(9y + x) - 4(9y + x)$$
$$= (3x)(9y) + (3x)(x) + (-4)(9y) + (-4)(x)$$
$$= 27xy + 3x^2 - 36y - 4x$$

An algebraic expression can be evaluated by substituting values of the unknowns in the expression. For example, if $x = 3$ and $y = -2$, then $3xy - x^2 + y$ can be evaluated as

$$3(3)(-2) - (3)^2 + (-2) = -18 - 9 - 2 = -29$$

2. Equations

A major focus of algebra is to solve equations involving algebraic expressions. Some examples of such equations are

$$5x - 2 = 9 - x \quad \left(\text{a linear equation with one unknown}\right)$$
$$3x + 1 = y - 2 \quad \left(\text{a linear equation with two unknowns}\right)$$
$$5x^2 + 3x - 2 = 7x \quad \left(\text{a quadratic equation with one unknown}\right)$$
$$\frac{x(x - 3)(x^2 + 5)}{x - 4} = 0 \quad \left(\text{an equation that is factored on one side with 0 on the other}\right)$$

The *solutions* of an equation with one or more unknowns are those values that make the equation true, or "satisfy the equation," when they are substituted for the unknowns of the equation. An equation may have no solution or one or more solutions. If two or more equations are to be solved together, the solutions must satisfy all the equations simultaneously.

Two equations having the same solution(s) are *equivalent equations*. For example, the equations

$$2 + x = 3$$
$$4 + 2x = 6$$

each have the unique solution $x = 1$. Note that the second equation is the first equation multiplied by 2. Similarly, the equations

$$3x - y = 6$$
$$6x - 2y = 12$$

have the same solutions, although in this case each equation has infinitely many solutions. If any value is assigned to x, then $3x - 6$ is a corresponding value for y that will satisfy both equations; for example, $x = 2$ and $y = 0$ is a solution to both equations, as is $x = 5$ and $y = 9$.

3. Solving Linear Equations with One Unknown

To solve a linear equation with one unknown (that is, to find the value of the unknown that satisfies the equation), the unknown should be isolated on one side of the equation. This can be done by performing the same mathematical operations on both sides of the equation. Remember that if the same number is added to or subtracted from both sides of the equation, this does not change the equality; likewise, multiplying or dividing both sides by the same nonzero number does not change the equality. For example, to solve the equation $\frac{5x-6}{3} = 4$ for x, the variable x can be isolated using the following steps:

$$5x - 6 = 12 \quad \left(\text{multiplying by 3}\right)$$
$$5x = 18 \quad \left(\text{adding 6}\right)$$
$$x = \frac{18}{5} \quad \left(\text{dividing by 5}\right)$$

The solution, $\frac{18}{5}$, can be checked by substituting it for x in the original equation to determine whether it satisfies that equation:

$$\frac{5\left(\frac{18}{5}\right) - 6}{3} = \frac{18 - 6}{3} = \frac{12}{3} = 4$$

Therefore, $x = \frac{18}{5}$ is the solution.

4. Solving Two Linear Equations with Two Unknowns

For two linear equations with two unknowns, if the equations are equivalent, then there are infinitely many solutions to the equations, as illustrated at the end of section 4.2.2 ("Equations"). If the equations are not equivalent, then they have either one unique solution or no solution. The latter case is illustrated by the two equations:

$$3x + 4y = 17$$
$$6x + 8y = 35$$

Note that $3x + 4y = 17$ implies $6x + 8y = 34$, which contradicts the second equation. Thus, no values of x and y can simultaneously satisfy both equations.

There are several methods of solving two linear equations with two unknowns. With any method, if a contradiction is reached, then the equations have no solution; if a trivial equation such as $0 = 0$ is reached, then the equations are equivalent and have infinitely many solutions. Otherwise, a unique solution can be found.

One way to solve for the two unknowns is to express one of the unknowns in terms of the other using one of the equations, and then substitute the expression into the remaining equation to obtain an equation with one unknown. This equation can be solved and the value of the unknown substituted into either of the original equations to find the value of the other unknown. For example, the following two equations can be solved for x and y.

$$\begin{pmatrix} 1 \end{pmatrix} \ 3x + 2y = 11$$
$$\begin{pmatrix} 2 \end{pmatrix} \quad x - y = 2$$

In equation (2), $x = 2 + y$. Substitute $2 + y$ in equation (1) for x:

$$3(2 + y) + 2y = 11$$
$$6 + 3y + 2y = 11$$
$$6 + 5y = 11$$
$$5y = 5$$
$$y = 1$$

If $y = 1$, then $x - 1 = 2$ and $x = 2 + 1 = 3$.

There is another way to solve for x and y by eliminating one of the unknowns. This can be done by making the coefficients of one of the unknowns the same (disregarding the sign) in both equations and either adding the equations or subtracting one equation from the other. For example, to solve the equations

$$\begin{pmatrix} 1 \end{pmatrix} \ 6x + 5y = 29$$
$$\begin{pmatrix} 2 \end{pmatrix} \ 4x - 3y = -6$$

by this method, multiply equation (1) by 3 and equation (2) by 5 to get

$$18x + 15y = 87$$
$$20x - 15y = -30$$

Adding the two equations eliminates y, yielding $38x = 57$, or $x = \dfrac{3}{2}$. Finally, substituting $\dfrac{3}{2}$ for x in one of the equations gives $y = 4$. These answers can be checked by substituting both values into both of the original equations.

5. Solving Equations by Factoring

Some equations can be solved by factoring. To do this, first add or subtract expressions to bring all the expressions to one side of the equation, with 0 on the other side. Then try to factor the nonzero side into a product of expressions. If this is possible, then using property (7) in section 4.1.4 ("Real Numbers") each of the factors can be set equal to 0, yielding several simpler equations that possibly can be solved. The solutions of the simpler equations will be solutions of the factored equation. As an example, consider the equation $x^3 - 2x^2 + x = -5(x-1)^2$:

$$x^3 - 2x^2 + x + 5(x-1)^2 = 0$$
$$x(x^2 + 2x + 1) + 5(x-1)^2 = 0$$
$$x(x-1)^2 + 5(x-1)^2 = 0$$
$$(x+5)(x-1)^2 = 0$$
$$x + 5 = 0 \text{ or } (x-1)^2 = 0$$
$$x = -5 \text{ or } x = 1.$$

For another example, consider $\dfrac{x(x-3)(x^2+5)}{x-4} = 0$. A fraction equals 0 if and only if its numerator equals 0. Thus, $x(x-3)(x^2+5) = 0$:

$$x = 0 \text{ or } x - 3 = 0 \text{ or } x^2 + 5 = 0$$
$$x = 0 \text{ or } x = 3 \text{ or } x^2 + 5 = 0.$$

But $x^2 + 5 = 0$ has no real solution because $x^2 + 5 > 0$ for every real number. Thus, the solutions are 0 and 3.

The solutions of an equation are also called the *roots* of the equation. These roots can be checked by substituting them into the original equation to determine whether they satisfy the equation.

6. Solving Quadratic Equations

The standard form for a *quadratic equation* is

$$ax^2 + bx + c = 0,$$

where a, b, and c are real numbers and $a \neq 0$; for example:

$$x^2 + 6x + 5 = 0$$
$$3x^2 - 2x = 0, \text{ and}$$
$$x^2 + 4 = 0$$

Some quadratic equations can easily be solved by factoring. For example:

$$(1) \qquad x^2 + 6x + 5 = 0$$
$$(x + 5)(x + 1) = 0$$
$$x + 5 = 0 \text{ or } x + 1 = 0$$
$$x = -5 \text{ or } x = -1$$

$$(2) \qquad 3x^2 - 3 = 8x$$
$$3x^2 - 8x - 3 = 0$$
$$(3x + 1)(x - 3) = 0$$
$$3x + 1 = 0 \text{ or } x - 3 = 0$$
$$x = -\frac{1}{3} \text{ or } x = 3$$

A quadratic equation has at most two real roots and may have just one or even no real root. For example, the equation $x^2 - 6x + 9 = 0$ can be expressed as $(x - 3)^2 = 0$, or $(x - 3)(x - 3) = 0$; thus the only root is 3. The equation $x^2 + 4 = 0$ has no real root; since the square of any real number is greater than or equal to zero, $x^2 + 4$ must be greater than zero.

An expression of the form $a^2 - b^2$ can be factored as $(a - b)(a + b)$.

For example, the quadratic equation $9x^2 - 25 = 0$ can be solved as follows.

$$(3x - 5)(3x + 5) = 0$$
$$3x - 5 = 0 \text{ or } 3x + 5 = 0$$
$$x = \frac{5}{3} \text{ or } x = -\frac{5}{3}$$

If a quadratic expression is not easily factored, then its roots can always be found using the *quadratic formula*: If $ax^2 + bx + c = 0\,(a \neq 0)$, then the roots are

$$x = \frac{-b + \sqrt{b^2 - 4ac}}{2a} \text{ and } x = \frac{-b - \sqrt{b^2 - 4ac}}{2a}$$

These are two distinct real numbers unless $b^2 - 4ac \leq 0$. If $b^2 - 4ac = 0$, then these two expressions for x are equal to $-\dfrac{b}{2a}$, and the equation has only one root. If $b^2 - 4ac < 0$, then $\sqrt{b^2 - 4ac}$ is not a real number and the equation has no real roots.

7. Exponents

A positive integer exponent of a number or a variable indicates a product, and the positive integer is the number of times that the number or variable is a factor in the product. For example, x^5 means $(x)(x)(x)(x)(x)$; that is, x is a factor in the product 5 times.

Some rules about exponents follow.

Let x and y be any positive numbers, and let r and s be any positive integers.

(1) $\left(x^r\right)\left(x^s\right) = x^{(r+s)}$; for example, $\left(2^2\right)\left(2^3\right) = 2^{(2+3)} = 2^5 = 32$.

(2) $\dfrac{x^r}{x^s} = x^{(r-s)}$; for example, $\dfrac{4^5}{4^2} = 4^{5-2} = 4^3 = 64$.

(3) $\left(x^r\right)\left(y^r\right) = (xy)^r$; for example, $\left(3^3\right)\left(4^3\right) = 12^3 = 1{,}728$.

(4) $\left(\dfrac{x}{y}\right)^r = \dfrac{x^r}{y^r}$; for example, $\left(\dfrac{2}{3}\right)^3 = \dfrac{2^3}{3^3} = \dfrac{8}{27}$.

(5) $\left(x^r\right)^s = x^{rs} = \left(x^s\right)^r$; for example, $\left(x^3\right)^4 = x^{12} = \left(x^4\right)^3$.

(6) $x^{-r} = \dfrac{1}{x^r}$; for example, $3^{-2} = \dfrac{1}{3^2} = \dfrac{1}{9}$.

(7) $x^0 = 1$; for example, $6^0 = 1$.

(8) $x^{\frac{r}{s}} = \left(x^{\frac{1}{s}}\right)^r = \left(x^r\right)^{\frac{1}{s}} = \sqrt[s]{x^r}$; for example, $8^{\frac{2}{3}} = \left(8^{\frac{1}{3}}\right)^2 = \left(8^2\right)^{\frac{1}{3}} = \sqrt[3]{8^2} = \sqrt[3]{64} = 4$ and $9^{\frac{1}{2}} = \sqrt{9} = 3$.

It can be shown that rules 1–6 also apply when r and s are not integers and are not positive, that is, when r and s are any real numbers.

8. Inequalities

An *inequality* is a statement that uses one of the following symbols:

$\neq$ not equal to

$>$ greater than

$\geq$ greater than or equal to

$<$ less than

$\leq$ less than or equal to

Some examples of inequalities are $5x - 3 < 9$, $6x \geq y$, and $\frac{1}{2} < \frac{3}{4}$. Solving a linear inequality with one unknown is similar to solving an equation; the unknown is isolated on one side of the inequality. As in solving an equation, the same number can be added to or subtracted from both sides of the inequality, or both sides of an inequality can be multiplied or divided by a positive number without changing the truth of the inequality. However, multiplying or dividing an inequality by a negative number reverses the order of the inequality. For example, $6 > 2$, but $(-1)(6) < (-1)(2)$.

To solve the inequality $3x - 2 > 5$ for x, isolate x by using the following steps:

$$3x - 2 > 5$$
$$3x > 7 \quad \left(\text{adding 2 to both sides}\right)$$
$$x > \frac{7}{3} \quad \left(\text{dividing both sides by 3}\right)$$

To solve the inequality $\frac{5x - 1}{-2} < 3$ for x, isolate x by using the following steps:

$$\frac{5x - 1}{-2} < 3$$
$$5x - 1 > -6 \quad \left(\text{multiplying both sides by } -2\right)$$
$$5x > -5 \quad \left(\text{adding 1 to both sides}\right)$$
$$x > -1 \quad \left(\text{dividing both sides by 5}\right)$$

9. Absolute Value

The absolute value of x, denoted $|x|$, is defined to be x if $x \geq 0$ and $-x$ if $x < 0$. Note that $\sqrt{x^2}$ denotes the nonnegative square root of x^2, and so $\sqrt{x^2} = |x|$.

10. Functions

An algebraic expression in one variable can be used to define a *function* of that variable. A function is denoted by a letter such as f or g along with the variable in the expression. For example, the expression $x^3 - 5x^2 + 2$ defines a function f that can be denoted by

$$f(x) = x^3 - 5x^2 + 2.$$

The expression $\frac{2z + 7}{\sqrt{z + 1}}$ defines a function g that can be denoted by

$$g(z) = \frac{2z + 7}{\sqrt{z + 1}}.$$

The symbols "$f(x)$" or "$g(z)$" do not represent products; each is merely the symbol for an expression, and is read "f of x" or "g of z."

Function notation provides a short way of writing the result of substituting a value for a variable. If $x = 1$ is substituted in the first expression, the result can be written $f(1) = -2$, and $f(1)$ is called the "value of f at $x = 1$." Similarly, if $z = 0$ is substituted in the second expression, then the value of g at $z = 0$ is $g(0) = 7$.

Once a function $f(x)$ is defined, it is useful to think of the variable x as an input and $f(x)$ as the corresponding output. In any function there can be no more than one output for any given input. However, more than one input can give the same output; for example, if $h(x) = |x + 3|$, then $h(-4) = 1 = h(-2)$.

The set of all allowable inputs for a function is called the *domain* of the function. For f and g defined above, the domain of f is the set of all real numbers and the domain of g is the set of all numbers greater than –1. The domain of any function can be arbitrarily specified, as in the function defined by "$h(x) = 9x - 5$ for $0 \leq x \leq 10$." Without such a restriction, the domain is assumed to be all values of x that result in a real number when substituted into the function.

The domain of a function can consist of only the positive integers and possibly 0. For example,

$$a(n) = n^2 + \frac{n}{5} \text{ for } n = 0, 1, 2, 3, \ldots.$$

Such a function is called a *sequence* and $a(n)$ is denoted by a_n. The value of the sequence a_n at $n = 3$ is $a_3 = 3^2 + \frac{3}{5} = 9.60$. As another example, consider the sequence defined by $b_n = (-1)^n (n!)$ for $n = 1, 2, 3, \ldots$. A sequence like this is often indicated by listing its values in the order $b_1, b_2, b_3, \ldots, b_n, \ldots$ as follows:

$-1, 2, -6, \ldots, (-1)^n(n!), \ldots$, and $(-1)^n(n!)$ is called the nth term of the sequence.

4.3 Geometry

1. Lines

In geometry, the word "line" refers to a straight line that extends without end in both directions.

$$\overline{\underset{\bullet}{\underset{P}{}} \qquad \underset{\bullet}{\underset{Q}{}}} \ell$$

The line above can be referred to as line PQ or line ℓ. The part of the line from P to Q is called a *line segment*. P and Q are the *endpoints* of the segment. The notation $\overline{PQ}$ is used to denote line segment PQ and PQ is used to denote the length of the segment.

2. Intersecting Lines and Angles

If two lines intersect, the opposite angles are called *vertical angles* and have the same measure. In the figure

$\angle PRQ$ and $\angle SRT$ are vertical angles and $\angle QRS$ and $\angle PRT$ are vertical angles. Also, $x + y = 180°$ since PRS is a straight line.

3. Perpendicular Lines

An angle that has a measure of $90°$ is a *right angle*. If two lines intersect at right angles, the lines are *perpendicular*. For example:

ℓ_1 and ℓ_2 above are perpendicular, denoted by $\ell_1 \perp \ell_2$. A right angle symbol in an angle of intersection indicates that the lines are perpendicular.

4. Parallel Lines

If two lines that are in the same plane do not intersect, the two lines are *parallel*. In the figure

lines ℓ_1 and ℓ_2 are parallel, denoted by $\ell_1 \parallel \ell_2$. If two parallel lines are intersected by a third line, as shown below, then the angle measures are related as indicated, where $x + y = 180°$.

5. Polygons (Convex)

A *polygon* is a closed plane figure formed by three or more line segments, called the *sides* of the polygon. Each side intersects exactly two other sides at their endpoints. The points of intersection of the sides are *vertices*. The term "polygon" will be used to mean a convex polygon, that is, a polygon in which each interior angle has a measure of less than $180°$.

The following figures are polygons:

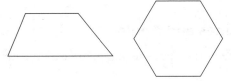

The following figures are not polygons:

A polygon with three sides is a *triangle*; with four sides, a *quadrilateral*; with five sides, a *pentagon*; and with six sides, a *hexagon*.

The sum of the interior angle measures of a triangle is 180°. In general, the sum of the interior angle measures of a polygon with n sides is equal to $(n - 2)180°$. For example, this sum for a pentagon is $(5 - 2)180° = (3)180° = 540°$.

Note that a pentagon can be partitioned into three triangles and therefore the sum of the angle measures can be found by adding the sum of the angle measures of three triangles.

The *perimeter* of a polygon is the sum of the lengths of its sides.

The commonly used phrase "area of a triangle" (or any other plane figure) is used to mean the area of the region enclosed by that figure.

6. Triangles

There are several special types of triangles with important properties. But one property that all triangles share is that the sum of the lengths of any two of the sides is greater than the length of the third side, as illustrated below.

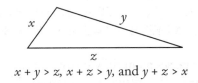

$x + y > z$, $x + z > y$, and $y + z > x$

An *equilateral* triangle has all sides of equal length. All angles of an equilateral triangle have equal measure. An *isosceles* triangle has at least two sides of the same length. If two sides of a triangle have the same length, then the two angles opposite those sides have the same measure. Conversely, if two angles of a triangle have the same measure, then the sides opposite those angles have the same length. In isosceles triangle *PQR* below, $x = y$ since $PQ = QR$.

A triangle that has a right angle is a *right* triangle. In a right triangle, the side opposite the right angle is the *hypotenuse*, and the other two sides are the *legs*. An important theorem concerning right triangles is the *Pythagorean theorem*, which states: In a right triangle, the square of the length of the hypotenuse is equal to the sum of the squares of the lengths of the legs.

In the figure above, $\triangle RST$ is a right triangle, so $\left(RS\right)^2 + \left(RT\right)^2 = \left(ST\right)^2$. Here, $RS = 6$ and $RT = 8$, so $ST = 10$, since $6^2 + 8^2 = 36 + 64 = 100 = \left(ST\right)^2$ and $ST = \sqrt{100}$. Any triangle in which the lengths of the sides are in the ratio 3:4:5 is a right triangle. In general, if a, b, and c are the lengths of the sides of a triangle and $a^2 + b^2 = c^2$, then the triangle is a right triangle.

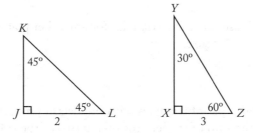

In $45°- 45°- 90°$ triangles, the lengths of the sides are in the ratio $1:1:\sqrt{2}$. For example, in $\triangle JKL$, if $JL = 2$, then $JK = 2$ and $KL = 2\sqrt{2}$. In $30°- 60°- 90°$ triangles, the lengths of the sides are in the ratio $1:\sqrt{3}:2$. For example, in $\triangle XYZ$, if $XZ = 3$, then $XY = 3\sqrt{3}$ and $YZ = 6$.

The *altitude* of a triangle is the segment drawn from a vertex perpendicular to the side opposite that vertex. Relative to that vertex and altitude, the opposite side is called the *base*.

The area of a triangle is equal to:

$$\frac{\left(\text{the length of the altitude}\right) \times \left(\text{the length of the base}\right)}{2}$$

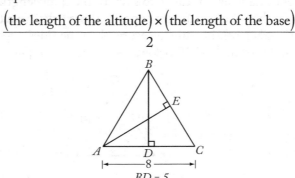

In $\triangle ABC$, $\overline{BD}$ is the altitude to base $\overline{AC}$ and $\overline{AE}$ is the altitude to base $\overline{BC}$. The area of $\triangle ABC$ is equal to

$$\frac{BD \times AC}{2} = \frac{5 \times 8}{2} = 20.$$

The area is also equal to $\frac{AE \times BC}{2}$. If $\triangle ABC$ above is isosceles and $AB = BC$, then altitude $\overline{BD}$ bisects the base; that is, $AD = DC = 4$. Similarly, any altitude of an equilateral triangle bisects the side to which it is drawn.

In equilateral triangle DEF, if $DE = 6$, then $DG = 3$ and $EG = 3\sqrt{3}$. The area of $\triangle DEF$ is equal to $\frac{3\sqrt{3} \times 6}{2} = 9\sqrt{3}$.

7. Quadrilaterals

A polygon with four sides is a *quadrilateral*. A quadrilateral in which both pairs of opposite sides are parallel is a *parallelogram*. The opposite sides of a parallelogram also have equal length.

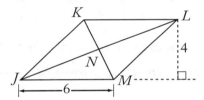

In parallelogram $JKLM$, $\overline{JK} \parallel \overline{LM}$ and $JK = LM$; $\overline{KL} \parallel \overline{JM}$ and $KL = JM$.

The diagonals of a parallelogram bisect each other (that is, $KN = NM$ and $JN = NL$).

The area of a parallelogram is equal to

$$(\text{the length of the altitude}) \times (\text{the length of the base}).$$

The area of $JKLM$ is equal to $4 \times 6 = 24$.

A parallelogram with right angles is a *rectangle*, and a rectangle with all sides of equal length is a *square*.

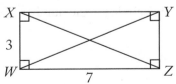

The perimeter of $WXYZ = 2(3) + 2(7) = 20$ and the area of $WXYZ$ is equal to $3 \times 7 = 21$.

The diagonals of a rectangle are equal; therefore $WY = XZ = \sqrt{9 + 49} = \sqrt{58}$.

A quadrilateral with two sides that are parallel, as shown above, is a *trapezoid*. The area of trapezoid *PQRS* may be calculated as follows:

$$\frac{1}{2}(\text{the sum of the lengths of the bases})(\text{the height}) = \frac{1}{2}(QR + PS)(8) = \frac{1}{2}(28 \times 8) = 112.$$

8. Circles

A *circle* is a set of points in a plane that are all located the same distance from a fixed point (the *center* of the circle).

A *chord* of a circle is a line segment that has its endpoints on the circle. A chord that passes through the center of the circle is a *diameter* of the circle. A *radius* of a circle is a segment from the center of the circle to a point on the circle. The words "diameter" and "radius" are also used to refer to the lengths of these segments.

The *circumference* of a circle is the distance around the circle. If r is the radius of the circle, then the circumference is equal to $2\pi r$, where π is approximately $\frac{22}{7}$ or 3.14. The *area* of a circle of radius r is equal to πr^2.

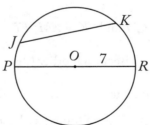

In the circle above, O is the center of the circle and $\overline{JK}$ and $\overline{PR}$ are chords. $\overline{PR}$ is a diameter and $\overline{OR}$ is a radius. If $OR = 7$, then the circumference of the circle is $2\pi(7) = 14\pi$ and the area of the circle is $\pi(7)^2 = 49\pi$.

The number of degrees of arc in a circle (or the number of degrees in a complete revolution) is 360.

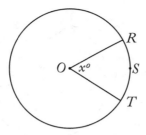

In the circle with center O above, the length of arc RST is $\dfrac{x}{360}$ of the circumference of the circle;

for example, if $x = 60$, then arc RST has length $\dfrac{1}{6}$ of the circumference of the circle.

A line that has exactly one point in common with a circle is said to be *tangent* to the circle, and that common point is called the *point of tangency*. A radius or diameter with an endpoint at the point of tangency is perpendicular to the tangent line, and, conversely, a line that is perpendicular to a radius or diameter at one of its endpoints is tangent to the circle at that endpoint.

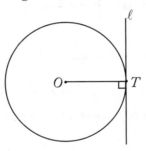

The line ℓ above is tangent to the circle and radius $\overline{OT}$ is perpendicular to ℓ.

If each vertex of a polygon lies on a circle, then the polygon is *inscribed* in the circle and the circle is *circumscribed* about the polygon. If each side of a polygon is tangent to a circle, then the polygon is *circumscribed* about the circle and the circle is *inscribed* in the polygon.

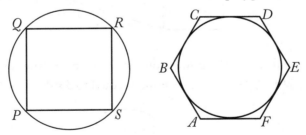

In the figure above, quadrilateral $PQRS$ is inscribed in a circle and hexagon $ABCDEF$ is circumscribed about a circle.

If a triangle is inscribed in a circle so that one of its sides is a diameter of the circle, then the triangle is a right triangle.

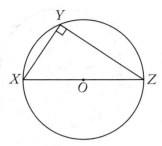

In the circle above, $\overline{XZ}$ is a diameter and the measure of $\angle XYZ$ is $90°$.

9. Rectangular Solids and Cylinders

A *rectangular solid* is a three-dimensional figure formed by 6 rectangular surfaces, as shown below. Each rectangular surface is a *face*. Each solid or dotted line segment is an *edge*, and each point at which the edges meet is a *vertex*. A rectangular solid has 6 faces, 12 edges, and 8 vertices. Opposite faces are parallel rectangles that have the same dimensions. A rectangular solid in which all edges are of equal length is a *cube*.

The *surface area* of a rectangular solid is equal to the sum of the areas of all the faces. The *volume* is equal to

$$(\text{length}) \times (\text{width}) \times (\text{height});$$

in other words, $(\text{area of base}) \times (\text{height})$.

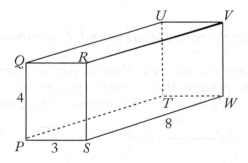

In the rectangular solid above, the dimensions are 3, 4, and 8. The surface area is equal to $2(3 \times 4) + 2(3 \times 8) + 2(4 \times 8) = 136$. The volume is equal to $3 \times 4 \times 8 = 96$.

The figure above is a right circular *cylinder*. The two bases are circles of the same size with centers O and P, respectively, and altitude (height) $\overline{OP}$ is perpendicular to the bases. The surface area of a right circular cylinder with a base of radius r and height h is equal to $2(\pi r^2) + 2\pi rh$ (the sum of the areas of the two bases plus the area of the curved surface).

The volume of a cylinder is equal to $\pi r^2 h$, that is,

$$(\text{area of base}) \times (\text{height}).$$

In the cylinder above, the surface area is equal to

$$2(25\pi) + 2\pi(5)(8) = 130\pi,$$

and the volume is equal to

$$25\pi(8) = 200\pi.$$

10. Coordinate Geometry

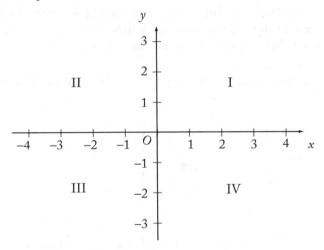

The figure above shows the (rectangular) *coordinate plane*. The horizontal line is called the *x-axis* and the perpendicular vertical line is called the *y-axis*. The point at which these two axes intersect, designated *O*, is called the *origin*. The axes divide the plane into four quadrants, I, II, III, and IV, as shown.

Each point in the plane has an *x-coordinate* and a *y-coordinate*. A point is identified by an ordered pair (x,y) of numbers in which the x-coordinate is the first number and the y-coordinate is the second number.

In the graph above, the (x,y) coordinates of point P are $(2,3)$ since P is 2 units to the right of the y-axis (that is, $x = 2$) and 3 units above the x-axis (that is, $y = 3$). Similarly, the (x,y) coordinates of point Q are $(-4,-3)$. The origin O has coordinates $(0,0)$.

One way to find the distance between two points in the coordinate plane is to use the Pythagorean theorem.

To find the distance between points R and S using the Pythagorean theorem, draw the triangle as shown. Note that Z has (x,y) coordinates $(-2,-3)$, $RZ = 7$, and $ZS = 5$. Therefore, the distance between R and S is equal to

$$\sqrt{7^2 + 5^2} = \sqrt{74}.$$

For a line in the coordinate plane, the coordinates of each point on the line satisfy a linear equation of the form $y = mx + b$ (or the form $x = a$ if the line is vertical). For example, each point on the line on the next page satisfies the equation $y = -\frac{1}{2}x + 1$. One can verify this for the points $(-2,2)$, $(2,0)$, and $(0,1)$ by substituting the respective coordinates for x and y in the equation.

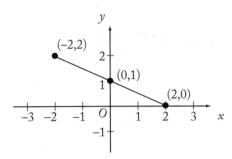

In the equation $y = mx + b$ of a line, the coefficient m is the *slope* of the line and the constant term b is the *y-intercept* of the line. For any two points on the line, the slope is defined to be the ratio of the difference in the y-coordinates to the difference in the x-coordinates. Using $(-2, 2)$ and $(2, 0)$ above, the slope is

$$\frac{\text{The difference in the } y\text{-coordinates}}{\text{The difference in the } x\text{-coordinates}} = \frac{0 - 2}{2 - (-2)} = \frac{-2}{4} = -\frac{1}{2}.$$

The y-intercept is the y-coordinate of the point at which the line intersects the y-axis. For the line above, the y-intercept is 1, and this is the resulting value of y when x is set equal to 0 in the equation $y = -\frac{1}{2}x + 1$. The *x-intercept* is the x-coordinate of the point at which the line intersects the x-axis. The x-intercept can be found by setting $y = 0$ and solving for x. For the line $y = -\frac{1}{2}x + 1$, this gives

$$-\frac{1}{2}x + 1 = 0$$

$$-\frac{1}{2}x = -1$$

$$x = 2.$$

Thus, the x-intercept is 2.

Given any two points (x_1, y_1) and (x_2, y_2) with $x_1 \neq x_2$, the equation of the line passing through these points can be found by applying the definition of slope. Since the slope is $m = \frac{y_2 - y_1}{x_2 - x_1}$, then using a point known to be on the line, say (x_1, y_1), any point (x, y) on the line must satisfy $\frac{y - y_1}{x - x_1} = m$, or $y - y_1 = m(x - x_1)$. (Using (x_2, y_2) as the known point would yield an equivalent equation.) For example, consider the points $(-2, 4)$ and $(3, -3)$ on the line below.

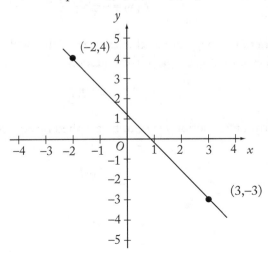

The slope of this line is

The Official Guide for GMAT® Review 12th Edition

The slope of this line is $\dfrac{-3-4}{3-(-2)} = \dfrac{-7}{5}$, so an equation of this line can be found using the point $(3,-3)$ as follows:

$$y - (-3) = -\frac{7}{5}(x - 3)$$

$$y + 3 = -\frac{7}{5}x + \frac{21}{5}$$

$$y = -\frac{7}{5}x + \frac{6}{5}$$

The y-intercept is $\dfrac{6}{5}$. The *x-intercept* can be found as follows:

$$0 = -\frac{7}{5}x + \frac{6}{5}$$

$$\frac{7}{5}x = \frac{6}{5}$$

$$x = \frac{6}{7}$$

Both of these intercepts can be seen on the graph.

If the slope of a line is negative, the line slants downward from left to right; if the slope is positive, the line slants upward. If the slope is 0, the line is horizontal; the equation of such a line is of the form $y = b$ since $m = 0$. For a vertical line, slope is not defined, and the equation is of the form $x = a$, where a is the x-intercept.

There is a connection between graphs of lines in the coordinate plane and solutions of two linear equations with two unknowns. If two linear equations with unknowns x and y have a unique solution, then the graphs of the equations are two lines that intersect in one point, which is the solution. If the equations are equivalent, then they represent the same line with infinitely many points or solutions. If the equations have no solution, then they represent parallel lines, which do not intersect.

There is also a connection between functions (see section 4.2.10) and the coordinate plane. If a function is graphed in the coordinate plane, the function can be understood in different and useful ways. Consider the function defined by

$$f(x) = -\frac{7}{5}x + \frac{6}{5}.$$

If the value of the function, $f(x)$, is equated with the variable y, then the graph of the function in the xy-coordinate plane is simply the graph of the equation

$$y = -\frac{7}{5}x + \frac{6}{5}$$

shown above. Similarly, any function $f(x)$ can be graphed by equating y with the value of the function:

$$y = f(x).$$

So for any x in the domain of the function f, the point with coordinates $(x, f(x))$ is on the graph of f, and the graph consists entirely of these points.

As another example, consider a quadratic polynomial function defined by $f(x) = x^2 - 1$. One can plot several points $(x, f(x))$ on the graph to understand the connection between a function and its graph:

x	$f(x)$
-2	3
-1	0
0	-1
1	0
2	3

If all the points were graphed for $-2 \leq x \leq 2$, then the graph would appear as follows.

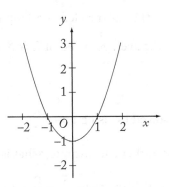

The graph of a quadratic function is called a *parabola* and always has the shape of the curve above, although it may be upside down or have a greater or lesser width. Note that the roots of the equation $f(x) = x^2 - 1 = 0$ are $x = 1$ and $x = -1$; these coincide with the x-intercepts since x-intercepts are found by setting $y = 0$ and solving for x. Also, the y-intercept is $f(0) = -1$ because this is the value of y corresponding to $x = 0$. For any function f, the x-intercepts are the solutions of the equation $f(x) = 0$ and the y-intercept is the value $f(0)$.

4.4 Word Problems

Many of the principles discussed in this chapter are used to solve word problems. The following discussion of word problems illustrates some of the techniques and concepts used in solving such problems.

1. Rate Problems

The distance that an object travels is equal to the product of the average speed at which it travels and the amount of time it takes to travel that distance, that is,

$$\text{Rate} \times \text{Time} = \text{Distance}.$$

Example 1: If a car travels at an average speed of 70 kilometers per hour for 4 hours, how many kilometers does it travel?

Solution: Since rate × time = distance, simply multiply 70 km/hour × 4 hours. Thus, the car travels 280 kilometers in 4 hours.

To determine the average rate at which an object travels, divide the total distance traveled by the total amount of traveling time.

Example 2: On a 400-mile trip, Car X traveled half the distance at 40 miles per hour (mph) and the other half at 50 mph. What was the average speed of Car X ?

Solution: First it is necessary to determine the amount of traveling time. During the first 200 miles, the car traveled at 40 mph; therefore, it took $\frac{200}{40} = 5$ hours to travel the first 200 miles.

During the second 200 miles, the car traveled at 50 mph; therefore, it took $\frac{200}{50} = 4$ hours to travel the second 200 miles. Thus, the average speed of Car X was $\frac{400}{9} = 44\frac{4}{9}$ mph. Note that the average speed is *not* $\frac{40 + 50}{2} = 45$.

Some rate problems can be solved by using ratios.

Example 3: If 5 shirts cost $44, then, at this rate, what is the cost of 8 shirts?

Solution: If c is the cost of the 8 shirts, then $\frac{5}{44} = \frac{8}{c}$. Cross multiplication results in the equation

$$5c = 8 \times 44 = 352$$

$$c = \frac{352}{5} = 70.40$$

The 8 shirts cost $70.40.

2. Work Problems

In a work problem, the rates at which certain persons or machines work alone are usually given, and it is necessary to compute the rate at which they work together (or vice versa).

The basic formula for solving work problems is $\frac{1}{r} + \frac{1}{s} = \frac{1}{h}$, where r and s are, for example, the number of hours it takes Rae and Sam, respectively, to complete a job when working alone, and h is the number of hours it takes Rae and Sam to do the job when working together. The reasoning is that in 1 hour Rae does $\frac{1}{r}$ of the job, Sam does $\frac{1}{s}$ of the job, and Rae and Sam together do $\frac{1}{h}$ of the job.

Example 1: If Machine X can produce 1,000 bolts in 4 hours and Machine Y can produce 1,000 bolts in 5 hours, in how many hours can Machines X and Y, working together at these constant rates, produce 1,000 bolts?

Solution:

$$\frac{1}{4} + \frac{1}{5} = \frac{1}{h}$$

$$\frac{5}{20} + \frac{4}{20} = \frac{1}{h}$$

$$\frac{9}{20} = \frac{1}{h}$$

$$9h = 20$$

$$h = \frac{20}{9} = 2\frac{2}{9}$$

Working together, Machines X and Y can produce 1,000 bolts in $2\frac{2}{9}$ hours.

Example 2: If Art and Rita can do a job in 4 hours when working together at their respective constant rates and Art can do the job alone in 6 hours, in how many hours can Rita do the job alone?

Solution:

$$\frac{1}{6} + \frac{1}{R} = \frac{1}{4}$$

$$\frac{R+6}{6R} = \frac{1}{4}$$

$$4R + 24 = 6R$$

$$24 = 2R$$

$$12 = R$$

Working alone, Rita can do the job in 12 hours.

3. Mixture Problems

In mixture problems, substances with different characteristics are combined, and it is necessary to determine the characteristics of the resulting mixture.

Example 1: If 6 pounds of nuts that cost $1.20 per pound are mixed with 2 pounds of nuts that cost $1.60 per pound, what is the cost per pound of the mixture?

Solution: The total cost of the 8 pounds of nuts is

$$6(\$1.20) + 2(\$1.60) = \$10.40.$$

The cost per pound is $\dfrac{\$10.40}{8} = \$1.30.$

Example 2: How many liters of a solution that is 15 percent salt must be added to 5 liters of a solution that is 8 percent salt so that the resulting solution is 10 percent salt?

Solution: Let n represent the number of liters of the 15% solution. The amount of salt in the 15% solution [$0.15n$] plus the amount of salt in the 8% solution [$(0.08)(5)$] must be equal to the amount of salt in the 10% mixture $\left[0.10(n + 5)\right]$. Therefore,

$$0.15n + 0.08(5) = 0.10(n + 5)$$
$$15n + 40 = 10n + 50$$
$$5n = 10$$
$$n = 2 \text{ liters}$$

Two liters of the 15% salt solution must be added to the 8% solution to obtain the 10% solution.

4. Interest Problems

Interest can be computed in two basic ways. With simple annual interest, the interest is computed on the principal only and is equal to $(\text{principal}) \times (\text{interest rate}) \times (\text{time})$. If interest is compounded, then interest is computed on the principal as well as on any interest already earned.

Example 1: If $8,000 is invested at 6 percent simple annual interest, how much interest is earned after 3 months?

Solution: Since the annual interest rate is 6%, the interest for 1 year is

$$(0.06)(\$8,000) = \$480.$$

The interest earned in 3 months is $\dfrac{3}{12}(\$480) = \$120.$

Example 2: If $10,000 is invested at 10 percent annual interest, compounded semiannually, what is the balance after 1 year?

Solution: The balance after the first 6 months would be

$$10,000 + (10,000)(0.05) = \$10,500.$$

The balance after one year would be $\quad 10,500 + (10,500)(0.05) = \$11,025.$

Note that the interest rate for each 6-month period is 5%, which is half of the 10% annual rate. The balance after one year can also be expressed as

$$10,000\left(1+\frac{0.10}{2}\right)^2 \text{ dollars.}$$

5. Discount

If a price is discounted by n percent, then the price becomes $(100 - n)$ percent of the original price.

Example 1: A certain customer paid $24 for a dress. If that price represented a 25 percent discount on the original price of the dress, what was the original price of the dress?

Solution: If p is the original price of the dress, then $0.75p$ is the discounted price and $0.75p = \$24$, or $p = \$32$. The original price of the dress was $32.

Example 2: The price of an item is discounted by 20 percent and then this reduced price is discounted by an additional 30 percent. These two discounts are equal to an overall discount of what percent?

Solution: If p is the original price of the item, then $0.8p$ is the price after the first discount. The price after the second discount is $(0.7)(0.8)p = 0.56p$. This represents an overall discount of 44 percent $(100\% - 56\%)$.

6. Profit

Gross profit is equal to revenues minus expenses, or selling price minus cost.

Example: A certain appliance costs a merchant $30. At what price should the merchant sell the appliance in order to make a gross profit of 50 percent of the cost of the appliance?

Solution: If s is the selling price of the appliance, then $s - 30 = (0.5)(30)$, or $s = \$45$. The merchant should sell the appliance for $45.

7. Sets

If S is the set of numbers 1, 2, 3, and 4, you can write $S = \{1,\ 2,\ 3,\ 4\}$. Sets can also be represented by Venn diagrams. That is, the relationship among the members of sets can be represented by circles.

Example 1: Each of 25 people is enrolled in history, mathematics, or both. If 20 are enrolled in history and 18 are enrolled in mathematics, how many are enrolled in both history and mathematics?

Solution: The 25 people can be divided into three sets: those who study history only, those who study mathematics only, and those who study history and mathematics. Thus a Venn diagram may be drawn as follows, where n is the number of people enrolled in both courses, $20 - n$ is the number enrolled in history only, and $18 - n$ is the number enrolled in mathematics only.

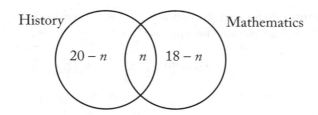

Since there is a total of 25 people, $(20 - n) + n + (18 - n) = 25$, or $n = 13$. Thirteen people are enrolled in both history and mathematics. Note that $20 + 18 - 13 = 25$, which is the general addition rule for two sets (see section 4.1.9).

Example 2: In a certain production lot, 40 percent of the toys are red and the remaining toys are green. Half of the toys are small and half are large. If 10 percent of the toys are red and small, and 40 toys are green and large, how many of the toys are red and large.

Solution: For this kind of problem, it is helpful to organize the information in a table:

	Red	Green	Total
Small	10%		50%
Large			50%
Total	40%	60%	100%

The numbers in the table are the percentages given. The following percentages can be computed on the basis of what is given:

	Red	Green	Total
Small	10%	40%	50%
Large	30%	20%	50%
Total	40%	60%	100%

Since 20% of the number of toys (n) are green and large, $0.20n = 40$ (40 toys are green and large), or $n = 200$. Therefore, 30% of the 200 toys, or $(0.3)(200) = 60$, are red and large.

8. Geometry Problems

The following is an example of a word problem involving geometry.
Example:

200 meters

The figure above shows an aerial view of a piece of land. If all angles shown are right angles, what is the perimeter of the piece of land?

Solution: For reference, label the figure as

If all the angles are right angles, then $QR + ST + UV = PW$, and $RS + TU + VW = PQ$. Hence, the perimeter of the land is $2PW + 2PQ = 2 \times 200 + 2 \times 200 = 800$ meters.

9. Measurement Problems

Some questions on the GMAT involve metric units of measure, whereas others involve English units of measure. However, except for units of time, if a question requires conversion from one unit of measure to another, the relationship between those units will be given.

Example: A train travels at a constant rate of 25 meters per second. How many kilometers does it travel in 5 minutes? $\left(1 \text{ kilometer} = 1,000 \text{ meters}\right)$

Solution: In 1 minute the train travels $\left(25\right)\left(60\right) = 1,500$ meters, so in 5 minutes it travels 7,500 meters. Since 1 kilometer = 1,000 meters, it follows that 7,500 meters equals $\frac{7,500}{1,000}$, or 7.5 kilometers.

10. Data Interpretation

Occasionally a question or set of questions will be based on data provided in a table or graph. Some examples of tables and graphs are given below.

Example 1:

Population by Age Group
(in thousands)

Age	Population
17 years and under	63,376
18–44 years	86,738
45–64 years	43,845
65 years and over	24,054

How many people are 44 years old or younger?

Solution: The figures in the table are given in thousands. The answer in thousands can be obtained by adding 63,376 thousand and 86,738 thousand. The result is 150,114 thousand, which is 150,114,000.

Example 2:

AVERAGE TEMPERATURE AND
PRECIPITATION IN CITY X

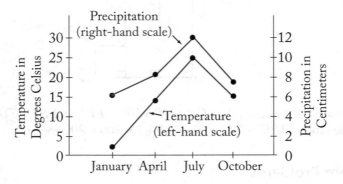

What are the average temperature and precipitation in City X during April?

Solution: Note that the scale on the left applies to the temperature line graph and the one on the right applies to the precipitation line graph. According to the graph, during April the average temperature is approximately 14° Celsius and the average precipitation is approximately 8 centimeters.

Example 3:

DISTRIBUTION OF AL'S WEEKLY NET SALARY

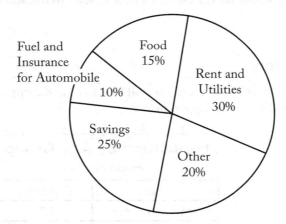

Al's weekly net salary is $350. To how many of the categories listed was at least $80 of Al's weekly net salary allocated?

Solution: In the circle graph, the relative sizes of the sectors are proportional to their corresponding values and the sum of the percents given is 100%. Note that $\frac{80}{350}$ is approximately 23%, so at least $80 was allocated to each of 2 categories—Rent and Utilities, and Savings—since their allocations are each greater than 23%.

5.0 Problem Solving

5.0 Problem Solving

The Quantitative section of the GMAT® test uses problem solving and data sufficiency questions to gauge your skill level. This chapter focuses on problem solving questions. Remember that quantitative questions require knowledge of the following:

- Arithmetic
- Elementary algebra
- Commonly known concepts of geometry

Problem solving questions are designed to test your basic mathematical skills and understanding of elementary mathematical concepts, as well as your ability to reason quantitatively, solve quantitative problems, and interpret graphic data. The mathematics knowledge required to answer the questions is no more advanced than what is generally taught in secondary school (or high school) mathematics classes.

In these questions, you are asked to solve each problem and select the best of the five answer choices given. Begin by reading the question thoroughly to determine exactly what information is given and to make sure you understand what is being asked. Scan the answer choices to understand your options. If the problem seems simple, take a few moments to see whether you can determine the answer. Then check your answer against the choices provided.

If you do not see your answer among the choices, or if the problem is complicated, take a closer look at the answer choices and think again about what the problem is asking. See whether you can eliminate some of the answer choices and narrow down your options. If you are still unable to narrow the answer down to a single choice, reread the question. Keep in mind that the answer will be based solely on the information provided in the question—don't allow your own experience and assumptions to interfere with your ability to find the correct answer to the question.

If you find yourself stuck on a question or unable to select the single correct answer, keep in mind that you have about two minutes to answer each quantitative question. You may run out of time if you take too long to answer any one question, so you may simply need to pick the answer that seems to make the most sense. Although guessing is generally not the best way to achieve a high GMAT score, making an educated guess is a good strategy for answering questions you are unsure of. Even if your answer to a particular question is incorrect, your answers to other questions will allow the test to accurately gauge your ability level.

The following pages include test-taking strategies, directions that will apply to questions of this type, sample questions, an answer key, and explanations for all the problems. These explanations present problem solving strategies that could be helpful in answering the questions.

5.1 Test-Taking Strategies

1. **Pace yourself.**

   Consult the on-screen timer periodically. Work as carefully as possible, but do not spend valuable time checking answers or pondering problems that you find difficult.

2. **Use the erasable notepad provided.**

   Working a problem out may help you avoid errors in solving the problem. If diagrams or figures are not presented, it may help if you draw your own.

3. **Read each question carefully to determine what is being asked.**

   For word problems, take one step at a time, reading each sentence carefully and translating the information into equations or other useful mathematical representations.

4. **Scan the answer choices before attempting to answer a question.**

   Scanning the answers can prevent you from putting answers in a form that is not given (e.g., finding the answer in decimal form, such as 0.25, when the choices are given in fractional form, such as $\frac{1}{4}$). Also, if the question requires approximations, a shortcut could serve well (e.g., you may be able to approximate 48 percent of a number by using half).

5. **Don't waste time trying to solve a problem that is too difficult for you.**

   Make your best guess and move on to the next question.

5.2 The Directions

These directions are very similar to those you will see for problem solving questions when you take the GMAT test. If you read them carefully and understand them clearly before sitting for the GMAT test, you will not need to spend too much time reviewing them once the test begins.

Solve the problem and indicate the best of the answer choices given.

Numbers: All numbers used are real numbers.

Figures: A figure accompanying a problem solving question is intended to provide information useful in solving the problem. Figures are drawn as accurately as possible. Exceptions will be clearly noted. Lines shown as straight are straight, and lines that appear jagged are also straight. The positions of points, angles, regions, etc., exist in the order shown, and angle measures are greater than zero. All figures lie in a plane unless otherwise indicated.

5.3 Sample Questions

Solve the problem and indicate the best of the answer choices given.

<u>Numbers:</u> All numbers used are real numbers.

<u>Figures:</u> A figure accompanying a problem solving question is intended to provide information useful in solving the problem. Figures are drawn as accurately as possible. Exceptions will be clearly noted. Lines shown as straight are straight, and lines that appear jagged are also straight. The positions of points, angles, regions, etc., exist in the order shown, and angle measures are greater than zero. All figures lie in a plane unless otherwise indicated.

1. A project scheduled to be carried out over a single fiscal year has a budget of $12,600, divided into 12 equal monthly allocations. At the end of the fourth month of that fiscal year, the total amount actually spent on the project was $4,580. By how much was the project over its budget?

   (A) $ 380
   (B) $ 540
   (C) $1,050
   (D) $1,380
   (E) $1,430

2. If the sum of 5, 8, 12, and 15 is equal to the sum of 3, 4, x, and x + 3, what is the value of x ?

   (A) 14
   (B) 15
   (C) 16
   (D) 17
   (E) 18

3. For which of the following values of n is $\dfrac{100 + n}{n}$ NOT an integer?

   (A) 1
   (B) 2
   (C) 3
   (D) 4
   (E) 5

4. Rectangular Floors X and Y have equal area. If Floor X is 12 feet by 18 feet and Floor Y is 9 feet wide, what is the length of Floor Y, in feet?

   (A) $13\dfrac{1}{2}$
   (B) 18
   (C) $18\dfrac{3}{4}$
   (D) 21
   (E) 24

PAYROLL AT COMPANY X	
Number of Employees	Salary
5	$20,000
4	$22,000
8	$25,000
3	$30,000

5. The table above shows the number of employees at each of four salary levels at Company X. What is the average (arithmetic mean) salary for the 20 employees?

   (A) $23,500
   (B) $23,750
   (C) $23,900
   (D) $24,125
   (E) $24,250

6.   A case contains c cartons. Each carton contains b boxes, and each box contains 100 paper clips. How many paper clips are contained in 2 cases?

(A) $100bc$

(B) $\dfrac{100b}{c}$

(C) $200bc$

(D) $\dfrac{200b}{c}$

(E) $\dfrac{200}{bc}$

7.   The sum of prime numbers that are greater than 60 but less than 70 is

(A)   67
(B)   128
(C)   191
(D)   197
(E)   260

8.   A rainstorm increased the amount of water stored in State J reservoirs from 124 billion gallons to 138 billion gallons. If the storm increased the amount of water in the reservoirs to 82 percent of total capacity, approximately how many billion gallons of water were the reservoirs short of total capacity prior to the storm?

(A)   9
(B)   14
(C)   25
(D)   30
(E)   44

9.   On the graph above, when $x = \dfrac{1}{2}$, $y = 2$; and when $x = 1$, $y = 1$. The graph is symmetric with respect to the vertical line at $x = 2$. According to the graph, when $x = 3$, $y =$

(A) -1

(B) $-\dfrac{1}{2}$

(C) 0

(D) $\dfrac{1}{2}$

(E) 1

10.   When $\dfrac{1}{10}$ percent of 5,000 is subtracted from $\dfrac{1}{10}$ of 5,000, the difference is

(A)   0
(B)   50
(C)   450
(D)   495
(E)   500

11.   Which of the following is the value of $\sqrt{\sqrt[3]{0.000064}}$?

(A)   0.004
(B)   0.008
(C)   0.02
(D)   0.04
(E)   0.2

12. Raffle tickets numbered consecutively from 101 through 350 are placed in a box. What is the probability that a ticket selected at random will have a number with a hundreds digit of 2 ?

(A) $\dfrac{2}{5}$

(B) $\dfrac{2}{7}$

(C) $\dfrac{33}{83}$

(D) $\dfrac{99}{250}$

(E) $\dfrac{100}{249}$

13. When Leo imported a certain item, he paid a 7 percent import tax on the portion of the total value of the item in excess of $1,000. If the amount of the import tax that Leo paid was $87.50, what was the total value of the item?

(A) $1,600
(B) $1,850
(C) $2,250
(D) $2,400
(E) $2,750

14. On Monday, a person mailed 8 packages weighing an average (arithmetic mean) of $12\dfrac{3}{8}$ pounds, and on Tuesday, 4 packages weighing an average of $15\dfrac{1}{4}$ pounds. What was the average weight, in pounds, of all the packages the person mailed on both days?

(A) $13\dfrac{1}{3}$

(B) $13\dfrac{13}{16}$

(C) $15\dfrac{1}{2}$

(D) $15\dfrac{15}{16}$

(E) $16\dfrac{1}{2}$

15. $0.1 + (0.1)^2 + (0.1)^3 =$

(A) 0.1
(B) 0.111
(C) 0.1211
(D) 0.2341
(E) 0.3

16. A carpenter constructed a rectangular sandbox with a capacity of 10 cubic feet. If the carpenter were to make a similar sandbox twice as long, twice as wide, and twice as high as the first sandbox, what would be the capacity, in cubic feet, of the second sandbox?

(A) 20
(B) 40
(C) 60
(D) 80
(E) 100

17. A bakery opened yesterday with its daily supply of 40 dozen rolls. Half of the rolls were sold by noon, and 80 percent of the remaining rolls were sold between noon and closing time. How many dozen rolls had not been sold when the bakery closed yesterday?

(A) 1
(B) 2
(C) 3
(D) 4
(E) 5

18. If the area of a square region having sides of length 6 centimeters is equal to the area of a rectangular region having width 2.5 centimeters, then the length of the rectangle, in centimeters, is

(A) 8.5
(B) 9.5
(C) 9.6
(D) 10.5
(E) 14.4

19. 150 is what percent of 30?

   (A) 5%
   (B) 20%
   (C) 50%
   (D) 200%
   (E) 500%

20. The ratio 2 to $\frac{1}{3}$ is equal to the ratio

   (A) 6 to 1
   (B) 5 to 1
   (C) 3 to 2
   (D) 2 to 3
   (E) 1 to 6

21. Running at the same constant rate, 6 identical machines can produce a total of 270 bottles per minute. At this rate, how many bottles could 10 such machines produce in 4 minutes?

   (A) 648
   (B) 1,800
   (C) 2,700
   (D) 10,800
   (E) 64,800

22. Of the five coordinates associated with points A, B, C, D, and E on the number line above, which has the greatest absolute value?

   (A) A
   (B) B
   (C) C
   (D) D
   (E) E

23. If n is a prime number greater than 3, what is the remainder when n^2 is divided by 12 ?

   (A) 0
   (B) 1
   (C) 2
   (D) 3
   (E) 5

24. $\dfrac{1}{1+\frac{1}{3}} - \dfrac{1}{1+\frac{1}{2}} =$

   (A) $-\dfrac{1}{3}$
   (B) $-\dfrac{1}{6}$
   (C) $-\dfrac{1}{12}$
   (D) $\dfrac{1}{12}$
   (E) $\dfrac{1}{3}$

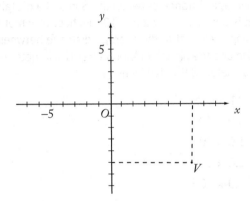

25. In the figure above, the coordinates of point V are

   (A) $(-7,5)$
   (B) $(-5,7)$
   (C) $(5,7)$
   (D) $(7,5)$
   (E) $(7,-5)$

26. A rope 40 feet long is cut into two pieces. If one piece is 18 feet longer than the other, what is the length, in feet, of the shorter piece?

   (A)   9
   (B)   11
   (C)   18
   (D)   22
   (E)   29

27. A student's average (arithmetic mean) test score on 4 tests is 78. What must be the student's score on a 5th test for the student's average score on the 5 tests to be 80 ?

   (A)   80
   (B)   82
   (C)   84
   (D)   86
   (E)   88

28. The average distance between the Sun and a certain planet is approximately 2.3×10^{14} inches. Which of the following is closest to the average distance between the Sun and the planet, in kilometers? (1 kilometer is approximately 3.9×10^4 inches.)

   (A) 7.1×10^8
   (B) 5.9×10^9
   (C) 1.6×10^{10}
   (D) 1.6×10^{11}
   (E) 5.9×10^{11}

29. If the quotient $\dfrac{a}{b}$ is positive, which of the following must be true?

   (A) $a > 0$
   (B) $b > 0$
   (C) $ab > 0$
   (D) $a - b > 0$
   (E) $a + b > 0$

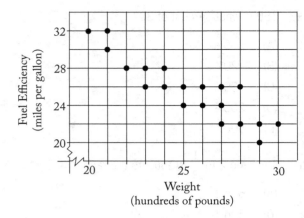

30. The dots on the graph above indicate the weights and fuel efficiency ratings for 20 cars. How many of the cars weigh more than 2,500 pounds and also get more than 22 miles per gallon?

   (A)   3
   (B)   5
   (C)   8
   (D)   10
   (E)   11

31. How many minutes does it take John to type y words if he types at the rate of x words per minute?

   (A) $\dfrac{x}{y}$

   (B) $\dfrac{y}{x}$

   (C) xy

   (D) $\dfrac{60x}{y}$

   (E) $\dfrac{y}{60x}$

32. $\sqrt{(16)(20) + (8)(32)} =$

   (A) $4\sqrt{20}$
   (B)   24
   (C)   25
   (D) $4\sqrt{20} + 8\sqrt{2}$
   (E)   32

33. If O is the center of the circle above, what fraction of the circular region is shaded?

(A) $\dfrac{1}{12}$

(B) $\dfrac{1}{9}$

(C) $\dfrac{1}{6}$

(D) $\dfrac{1}{4}$

(E) $\dfrac{1}{3}$

34. If Juan takes 11 seconds to run y yards, how many seconds will it take him to run x yards at the same rate?

(A) $\dfrac{11x}{y}$

(B) $\dfrac{11y}{x}$

(C) $\dfrac{x}{11y}$

(D) $\dfrac{11}{xy}$

(E) $\dfrac{xy}{11}$

35. John has 10 pairs of matched socks. If he loses 7 individual socks, what is the greatest number of pairs of matched socks he can have left?

(A) 7

(B) 6

(C) 5

(D) 4

(E) 3

36. What is the lowest positive integer that is divisible by each of the integers 1 through 7, inclusive?

(A) 420

(B) 840

(C) 1,260

(D) 2,520

(E) 5,040

37. $\dfrac{1}{0.75-1} =$

(A) -4

(B) -0.25

(C) 0.25

(D) 0.75

(E) 4

38. If $\dfrac{1.5}{0.2+x} = 5$, then $x =$

(A) -3.7

(B) 0.1

(C) 0.3

(D) 0.5

(E) 2.8

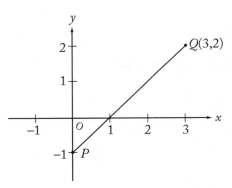

39. In the figure above, the point on segment PQ that is twice as far from P as from Q is

(A) (3,1)

(B) (2,1)

(C) (2,−1)

(D) (1.5,0.5)

(E) (1,0)

40. If n is an integer, which of the following must be even?

    (A) $n + 1$
    (B) $n + 2$
    (C) $2n$
    (D) $2n + 1$
    (E) n^2

41. If 4 is one solution of the equation $x^2 + 3x + k = 10$, where k is a constant, what is the other solution?

    (A) -7
    (B) -4
    (C) -3
    (D) 1
    (E) 6

42. If $\begin{vmatrix} a & b \\ c & d \end{vmatrix} = ad - bc$ for all numbers a, b, c, and d, then

    $\begin{vmatrix} 3 & 5 \\ -2 & 4 \end{vmatrix} =$

    (A) -22
    (B) -2
    (C) 2
    (D) 7
    (E) 22

43. The sum $\frac{7}{8} + \frac{1}{9}$ is between

    (A) $\frac{1}{2}$ and $\frac{3}{4}$
    (B) $\frac{3}{4}$ and 1
    (C) 1 and $1\frac{1}{4}$
    (D) $1\frac{1}{4}$ and $1\frac{1}{2}$
    (E) $1\frac{1}{2}$ and 2

44. If $x = 1 - 3t$ and $y = 2t - 1$, then for what value of t does $x = y$?

    (A) $\frac{5}{2}$
    (B) $\frac{3}{2}$
    (C) $\frac{2}{3}$
    (D) $\frac{2}{5}$
    (E) 0

45. $1 - \left(\frac{1}{2} - \frac{2}{3} \right) =$

    (A) $\frac{6}{5}$
    (B) $\frac{7}{6}$
    (C) $\frac{6}{7}$
    (D) $\frac{5}{6}$
    (E) 0

46. $\frac{(0.3)^5}{(0.3)^3} =$

    (A) 0.001
    (B) 0.01
    (C) 0.09
    (D) 0.9
    (E) 1.0

47. In a horticultural experiment, 200 seeds were planted in plot I and 300 were planted in plot II. If 57 percent of the seeds in plot I germinated and 42 percent of the seeds in plot II germinated, what percent of the total number of planted seeds germinated?

    (A) 45.5%
    (B) 46.5%
    (C) 48.0%
    (D) 49.5%
    (E) 51.0%

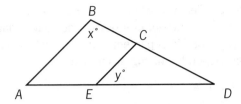

Note: Figure not drawn to scale.

48. In the figure above, if $\overline{AB} \parallel \overline{CE}$, $CE = DE$, and $y = 45$, then $x =$

(A)   45
(B)   60
(C)   67.5
(D)   112.5
(E)   135

49. How many integers n are there such that $1 < 5n + 5 < 25$?

(A)   Five
(B)   Four
(C)   Three
(D)   Two
(E)   One

50. If y is an integer, then the least possible value of $|23 - 5y|$ is

(A)   1
(B)   2
(C)   3
(D)   4
(E)   5

51. $\left(\sqrt{7} + \sqrt{7}\right)^2 =$

(A)   98
(B)   49
(C)   28
(D)   21
(E)   14

52. In a certain population, there are 3 times as many people aged 21 or under as there are people over 21. The ratio of those 21 or under to the total population is

(A)   1 to 2
(B)   1 to 3
(C)   1 to 4
(D)   2 to 3
(E)   3 to 4

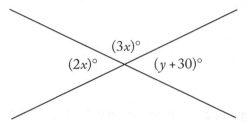

53. In the figure above, the value of y is

(A)   6
(B)   12
(C)   24
(D)   36
(E)   42

54. $\sqrt{80} + \sqrt{125} =$

(A) $9\sqrt{5}$
(B) $20\sqrt{5}$
(C) $41\sqrt{5}$
(D) $\sqrt{205}$
(E)   100

55. Kelly and Chris packed several boxes with books. If Chris packed 60 percent of the total number of boxes, what was the ratio of the number of boxes Kelly packed to the number of boxes Chris packed?

(A)   1 to 6
(B)   1 to 4
(C)   2 to 5
(D)   3 to 5
(E)   2 to 3

56. Of the following, which is the closest approximation of $\dfrac{50.2 \times 0.49}{199.8}$?

    (A) $\dfrac{1}{10}$

    (B) $\dfrac{1}{8}$

    (C) $\dfrac{1}{4}$

    (D) $\dfrac{5}{4}$

    (E) $\dfrac{25}{2}$

57. The average (arithmetic mean) of 10, 30, and 50 is 5 more than the average of 20, 40, and

    (A) 15
    (B) 25
    (C) 35
    (D) 45
    (E) 55

$$y = kx + 3$$

58. In the equation above, k is a constant. If $y = 17$ when $x = 2$, what is the value of y when $x = 4$?

    (A) 34
    (B) 31
    (C) 14
    (D) 11
    (E) 7

59. Each week, Harry is paid x dollars per hour for the first 30 hours and $1.5x$ dollars for each additional hour worked that week. Each week, James is paid x dollars per hour for the first 40 hours and $2x$ dollars for each additional hour worked that week. Last week James worked a total of 41 hours. If Harry and James were paid the same amount last week, how many hours did Harry work last week?

    (A) 35
    (B) 36
    (C) 37
    (D) 38
    (E) 39

60. A glass was filled with 10 ounces of water, and 0.01 ounce of the water evaporated each day during a 20-day period. What percent of the original amount of water evaporated during this period?

    (A) 0.002%
    (B) 0.02%
    (C) 0.2%
    (D) 2%
    (E) 20%

61. A glucose solution contains 15 grams of glucose per 100 cubic centimeters of solution. If 45 cubic centimeters of the solution were poured into an empty container, how many grams of glucose would be in the container?

    (A) 3.00
    (B) 5.00
    (C) 5.50
    (D) 6.50
    (E) 6.75

62. In the figure above, if $PQRS$ is a parallelogram, then $y - x =$

    (A) 30
    (B) 35
    (C) 40
    (D) 70
    (E) 100

63. If 1 kilometer is approximately 0.6 mile, which of the following best approximates the number of kilometers in 2 miles?

(A) $\dfrac{10}{3}$

(B) 3

(C) $\dfrac{6}{5}$

(D) $\dfrac{1}{3}$

(E) $\dfrac{3}{10}$

64. Lucy invested $10,000 in a new mutual fund account exactly three years ago. The value of the account increased by 10 percent during the first year, increased by 5 percent during the second year, and decreased by 10 percent during the third year. What is the value of the account today?

(A) $10,350
(B) $10,395
(C) $10,500
(D) $11,500
(E) $12,705

65. A certain fruit stand sold apples for $0.70 each and bananas for $0.50 each. If a customer purchased both apples and bananas from the stand for a total of $6.30, what total number of apples and bananas did the customer purchase?

(A) 10
(B) 11
(C) 12
(D) 13
(E) 14

66. At a certain school, the ratio of the number of second graders to the number of fourth graders is 8 to 5, and the ratio of the number of first graders to the number of second graders is 3 to 4. If the ratio of the number of third graders to the number of fourth graders is 3 to 2, what is the ratio of the number of first graders to the number of third graders?

(A) 16 to 15
(B) 9 to 5
(C) 5 to 16
(D) 5 to 4
(E) 4 to 5

$$A = \{2, 3, 4, 5\}$$
$$B = \{4, 5, 6, 7, 8\}$$

67. Two integers will be randomly selected from the sets above, one integer from set A and one integer from set B. What is the probability that the sum of the two integers will equal 9 ?

(A) 0.15
(B) 0.20
(C) 0.25
(D) 0.30
(E) 0.33

68. At a certain instant in time, the number of cars, N, traveling on a portion of a certain highway can be estimated by the formula

$$N = \frac{20Ld}{600 + s^2}$$

where L is the number of lanes in the same direction, d is the length of the portion of the highway, in feet, and s is the average speed of the cars, in miles per hour. Based on the formula, what is the estimated number of cars traveling on a $\dfrac{1}{2}$-mile portion of the highway if the highway has 2 lanes in the same direction and the average speed of the cars is 40 miles per hour? (5,280 feet = 1 mile)

(A) 155
(B) 96
(C) 80
(D) 48
(E) 24

NUMBER OF SHIPMENTS OF MANUFACTURED HOMES
IN THE UNITED STATES, 1990–2000

69. According to the chart shown, which of the following is closest to the median annual number of shipments of manufactured homes in the United States for the years from 1990 to 2000, inclusive?

(A) 250,000
(B) 280,000
(C) 310,000
(D) 325,000
(E) 340,000

70. If $y\left(\dfrac{3x-5}{2}\right) = y$ and $y \neq 0$, then $x =$

(A) $\dfrac{2}{3}$

(B) $\dfrac{5}{3}$

(C) $\dfrac{7}{3}$

(D) 1

(E) 4

71. If $x + 5 > 2$ and $x - 3 < 7$, the value of x must be between which of the following pairs of numbers?

(A) −3 and 10
(B) −3 and 4
(C) 2 and 7
(D) 3 and 4
(E) 3 and 10

72. A gym class can be divided into 8 teams with an equal number of players on each team or into 12 teams with an equal number of players on each team. What is the lowest possible number of students in the class?

(A) 20
(B) 24
(C) 36
(D) 48
(E) 96

73. If $r = 0.345$, $s = (0.345)^2$, and $t = \sqrt{0.345}$, which of the following is the correct ordering of r, s, and t?

(A) $r < s < t$
(B) $r < t < s$
(C) $s < t < r$
(D) $s < r < t$
(E) $t < r < s$

74. A total of n trucks and cars are parked in a lot. If the number of cars is $\dfrac{1}{4}$ the number of trucks, and $\dfrac{2}{3}$ of the trucks are pickups, how many pickups, in terms of n, are parked in the lot?

(A) $\dfrac{1}{6}n$

(B) $\dfrac{5}{12}n$

(C) $\dfrac{1}{2}n$

(D) $\dfrac{8}{15}n$

(E) $\dfrac{11}{12}n$

75. At least $\dfrac{2}{3}$ of the 40 members of a committee must vote in favor of a resolution for it to pass. What is the greatest number of members who could vote against the resolution and still have it pass?

(A) 19
(B) 17
(C) 16
(D) 14
(E) 13

76. In the Johnsons' monthly budget, the dollar amounts allocated to household expenses, food, and miscellaneous items are in the ratio 5:2:1, respectively. If the total amount allocated to these three categories is $1,800, what is the amount allocated to food?

    (A) $900
    (B) $720
    (C) $675
    (D) $450
    (E) $225

77. There are 4 more women than men on Centerville's board of education. If there are 10 members on the board, how many are women?

    (A) 3
    (B) 4
    (C) 6
    (D) 7
    (E) 8

78. Leona bought a 1-year, $10,000 certificate of deposit that paid interest at an annual rate of 8 percent compounded semiannually. What was the total amount of interest paid on this certificate at maturity?

    (A) $10,464
    (B) $ 864
    (C) $ 816
    (D) $ 800
    (E) $ 480

79. $\dfrac{(0.0036)(2.8)}{(0.04)(0.1)(0.003)} =$

    (A) 840.0
    (B) 84.0
    (C) 8.4
    (D) 0.84
    (E) 0.084

80. Machine A produces bolts at a uniform rate of 120 every 40 seconds, and Machine B produces bolts at a uniform rate of 100 every 20 seconds. If the two machines run simultaneously, how many seconds will it take for them to produce a total of 200 bolts?

    (A) 22
    (B) 25
    (C) 28
    (D) 32
    (E) 56

Amount of Bacteria Present	
Time	Amount
1:00 P.M.	10.0 grams
4:00 P.M.	x grams
7:00 P.M.	14.4 grams

81. Data for a certain biology experiment are given in the table above. If the amount of bacteria present increased by the same factor during each of the two 3-hour periods shown, how many grams of bacteria were present at 4:00 P.M. ?

    (A) 12.0
    (B) 12.1
    (C) 12.2
    (D) 12.3
    (E) 12.4

82. If n is an integer greater than 6, which of the following must be divisible by 3 ?

    (A) $n(n + 1)(n - 4)$
    (B) $n(n + 2)(n - 1)$
    (C) $n(n + 3)(n - 5)$
    (D) $n(n + 4)(n - 2)$
    (E) $n(n + 5)(n - 6)$

83. The total cost for Company X to produce a batch of tools is $10,000 plus $3 per tool. Each tool sells for $8. The gross profit earned from producing and selling these tools is the total income from sales minus the total production cost. If a batch of 20,000 tools is produced and sold, then Company X's gross profit per tool is

    (A) $3.00
    (B) $3.75
    (C) $4.50
    (D) $5.00
    (E) $5.50

84. A dealer originally bought 100 identical batteries at a total cost of q dollars. If each battery was sold at 50 percent above the original cost per battery, then, in terms of q, for how many dollars was each battery sold?

    (A) $\dfrac{3q}{200}$

    (B) $\dfrac{3q}{2}$

    (C) $150q$

    (D) $\dfrac{q}{100} + 50$

    (E) $\dfrac{150}{q}$

85. In an increasing sequence of 10 consecutive integers, the sum of the first 5 integers is 560. What is the sum of the last 5 integers in the sequence?

    (A) 585
    (B) 580
    (C) 575
    (D) 570
    (E) 565

86. Machine A produces 100 parts twice as fast as Machine B does. Machine B produces 100 parts in 40 minutes. If each machine produces parts at a constant rate, how many parts does Machine A produce in 6 minutes?

    (A) 30
    (B) 25
    (C) 20
    (D) 15
    (E) 7.5

87. A necklace is made by stringing N individual beads together in the repeating pattern red bead, green bead, white bead, blue bead, and yellow bead. If the necklace design begins with a red bead and ends with a white bead, then N could equal

    (A) 16
    (B) 32
    (C) 41
    (D) 54
    (E) 68

88. In the xy-coordinate system, if (a,b) and (a + 3,b + k) are two points on the line defined by the equation x = 3y − 7, then k =

    (A) 9
    (B) 3
    (C) $\dfrac{7}{3}$
    (D) 1
    (E) $\dfrac{1}{3}$

89. If s is the product of the integers from 100 to 200, inclusive, and t is the product of the integers from 100 to 201, inclusive, what is $\dfrac{1}{s} + \dfrac{1}{t}$ in terms of t?

    (A) $\dfrac{(201)^2}{t}$

    (B) $\dfrac{(202)(201)}{t}$

    (C) $\dfrac{201}{t}$

    (D) $\dfrac{202}{t}$

    (E) $\dfrac{(202)(201)}{t^2}$

90. If Jake loses 8 pounds, he will weigh twice as much as his sister. Together they now weigh 278 pounds. What is Jake's present weight, in pounds?

    (A) 131
    (B) 135
    (C) 139
    (D) 147
    (E) 188

91. A certain store sells all maps at one price and all books at another price. On Monday the store sold 12 maps and 10 books for a total of $38.00, and on Tuesday the store sold 20 maps and 15 books for a total of $60.00. At this store, how much less does a map sell for than a book?

(A) $0.25
(B) $0.50
(C) $0.75
(D) $1.00
(E) $1.25

92. A store reported total sales of $385 million for February of this year. If the total sales for the same month last year was $320 million, approximately what was the percent increase in sales?

(A) 2%
(B) 17%
(C) 20%
(D) 65%
(E) 83%

List I: 3, 6, 8, 19

List II: x, 3, 6, 8, 19

93. If the median of the numbers in list I above is equal to the median of the numbers in list II above, what is the value of x ?

(A) 6
(B) 7
(C) 8
(D) 9
(E) 10

94. In a certain city, 60 percent of the registered voters are Democrats and the rest are Republicans. In a mayoral race, if 75 percent of the registered voters who are Democrats and 20 percent of the registered voters who are Republicans are expected to vote for Candidate A, what percent of the registered voters are expected to vote for Candidate A ?

(A) 50%
(B) 53%
(C) 54%
(D) 55%
(E) 57%

95. $\frac{1}{2} + \left[\left(\frac{2}{3} \times \frac{3}{8} \right) \div 4 \right] - \frac{9}{16} =$

(A) $\frac{29}{16}$
(B) $\frac{19}{16}$
(C) $\frac{15}{16}$
(D) $\frac{9}{13}$
(E) 0

96. Water consists of hydrogen and oxygen, and the approximate ratio, by mass, of hydrogen to oxygen is 2:16. Approximately how many grams of oxygen are there in 144 grams of water?

(A) 16
(B) 72
(C) 112
(D) 128
(E) 142

97. If $x(2x + 1) = 0$ and $\left(x + \frac{1}{2} \right)(2x - 3) = 0$, then x =

(A) −3
(B) $-\frac{1}{2}$
(C) 0
(D) $\frac{1}{2}$
(E) $\frac{3}{2}$

98. On a scale that measures the intensity of a certain phenomenon, a reading of $n + 1$ corresponds to an intensity that is 10 times the intensity corresponding to a reading of n. On that scale, the intensity corresponding to a reading of 8 is how many times as great as the intensity corresponding to a reading of 3 ?

    (A)   5
    (B)   50
    (C) 10^5
    (D) 5^{10}
    (E) $8^{10} - 3^{10}$

99. For the positive numbers, $n, n + 1, n + 2, n + 4$, and $n + 8$, the mean is how much greater than the median?

    (A)   0
    (B)   1
    (C) $n + 1$
    (D) $n + 2$
    (E) $n + 3$

100. If $T = \dfrac{5}{9}(K - 32)$, and if $T = 290$, then $K =$

    (A) $\dfrac{1,738}{9}$
    (B)   322
    (C)   490
    (D)   554
    (E) $\dfrac{2,898}{5}$

101. The water from one outlet, flowing at a constant rate, can fill a swimming pool in 9 hours. The water from a second outlet, flowing at a constant rate, can fill the same pool in 5 hours. If both outlets are used at the same time, approximately what is the number of hours required to fill the pool?

    (A)   0.22
    (B)   0.31
    (C)   2.50
    (D)   3.21
    (E)   4.56

102. If a square mirror has a 20-inch diagonal, what is the approximate perimeter of the mirror, in inches?

    (A)   40
    (B)   60
    (C)   80
    (D)   100
    (E)   120

103. The present ratio of students to teachers at a certain school is 30 to 1. If the student enrollment were to increase by 50 students and the number of teachers were to increase by 5, the ratio of students to teachers would then be 25 to 1. What is the present number of teachers?

    (A)   5
    (B)   8
    (C)   10
    (D)   12
    (E)   15

104. What is the smallest integer n for which $25^n > 5^{12}$?

    (A)   6
    (B)   7
    (C)   8
    (D)   9
    (E)   10

105. Sixty percent of the members of a study group are women, and 45 percent of those women are lawyers. If one member of the study group is to be selected at random, what is the probability that the member selected is a woman lawyer?

    (A)   0.10
    (B)   0.15
    (C)   0.27
    (D)   0.33
    (E)   0.45

106. When positive integer x is divided by positive integer y, the remainder is 9. If $\dfrac{x}{y} = 96.12$, what is the value of y?

(A) 96
(B) 75
(C) 48
(D) 25
(E) 12

107. If x is the product of the positive integers from 1 to 8, inclusive, and if i, k, m, and p are positive integers such that $x = 2^i 3^k 5^m 7^p$, then $i + k + m + p =$

(A) 4
(B) 7
(C) 8
(D) 11
(E) 12

108. If $t = \dfrac{1}{2^9 \times 5^3}$ is expressed as a terminating decimal, how many zeros will t have between the decimal point and the first nonzero digit to the right of the decimal point?

(A) Three
(B) Four
(C) Five
(D) Six
(E) Nine

109. A pharmaceutical company received $3 million in royalties on the first $20 million in sales of the generic equivalent of one of its products and then $9 million in royalties on the next $108 million in sales. By approximately what percent did the ratio of royalties to sales decrease from the first $20 million in sales to the next $108 million in sales?

(A) 8%
(B) 15%
(C) 45%
(D) 52%
(E) 56%

110. If p is the product of the integers from 1 to 30, inclusive, what is the greatest integer k for which 3^k is a factor of p?

(A) 10
(B) 12
(C) 14
(D) 16
(E) 18

111. If candy bars that regularly sell for $0.40 each are on sale at two for $0.75, what is the percent reduction in the price of two such candy bars purchased at the sale price?

(A) $2\dfrac{1}{2}\%$
(B) $6\dfrac{1}{4}\%$
(C) $6\dfrac{2}{3}\%$
(D) 8%
(E) $12\dfrac{1}{2}\%$

112. If $s > 0$ and $\sqrt{\dfrac{r}{s}} = s$, what is r in terms of s?

(A) $\dfrac{1}{s}$
(B) $\sqrt{s}$
(C) $s\sqrt{s}$
(D) s^3
(E) $s^2 - s$

113. The front of a 6-foot-by-8-foot rectangular door has brass rectangular trim, as indicated by the shading in the figure above. If the trim is uniformly 1 foot wide, what fraction of the door's front surface is covered by the trim?

   (A) $\dfrac{13}{48}$

   (B) $\dfrac{5}{12}$

   (C) $\dfrac{1}{2}$

   (D) $\dfrac{7}{12}$

   (E) $\dfrac{5}{8}$

114. If $a = -0.3$, which of the following is true?

   (A) $a < a^2 < a^3$
   (B) $a < a^3 < a^2$
   (C) $a^2 < a < a^3$
   (D) $a^2 < a^3 < a$
   (E) $a^3 < a < a^2$

115. Mary's income is 60 percent more than Tim's income, and Tim's income is 40 percent less than Juan's income. What percent of Juan's income is Mary's income?

   (A) 124%
   (B) 120%
   (C) 96%
   (D) 80%
   (E) 64%

	City A	City B	City C	City D	City E
City A		•	•	•	•
City B			•	•	•
City C				•	•
City D					•
City E					

116. Each • in the mileage table above represents an entry indicating the distance between a pair of the five cities. If the table were extended to represent the distances between all pairs of 30 cities and each distance were to be represented by only one entry, how many entries would the table then have?

   (A) 60
   (B) 435
   (C) 450
   (D) 465
   (E) 900

117. If n is positive, which of the following is equal to $\dfrac{1}{\sqrt{n+1} - \sqrt{n}}$?

   (A) 1

   (B) $\sqrt{2n+1}$

   (C) $\dfrac{\sqrt{n+1}}{\sqrt{n}}$

   (D) $\sqrt{n+1} - \sqrt{n}$

   (E) $\sqrt{n+1} + \sqrt{n}$

118. The ratio of the length to the width of a rectangular advertising display is approximately 3.3 to 2. If the width of the display is 8 meters, what is the approximate length of the display, in meters?

   (A) 7
   (B) 11
   (C) 13
   (D) 16
   (E) 26

119. Which of the following is equivalent to the pair of inequalities $x + 6 > 10$ and $x - 3 \leq 5$?

    (A) $2 \leq x < 16$
    (B) $2 \leq x < 4$
    (C) $2 < x \leq 8$
    (D) $4 < x \leq 8$
    (E) $4 \leq x < 16$

120. David has d books, which is 3 times as many as Jeff and $\frac{1}{2}$ as many as Paula. How many books do the three of them have altogether, in terms of d ?

    (A) $\frac{5}{6}d$
    (B) $\frac{7}{3}d$
    (C) $\frac{10}{3}d$
    (D) $\frac{7}{2}d$
    (E) $\frac{9}{2}d$

121. There are 8 teams in a certain league and each team plays each of the other teams exactly once. If each game is played by 2 teams, what is the total number of games played?

    (A) 15
    (B) 16
    (C) 28
    (D) 56
    (E) 64

122. An operation θ is defined by the equation $a \theta b = \frac{a - b}{a + b}$, for all numbers a and b such that $a \neq -b$. If $a \neq -c$ and $a \theta c = 0$, then $c =$

    (A) $-a$
    (B) $-\frac{1}{a}$
    (C) 0
    (D) $\frac{1}{a}$
    (E) a

123. The price of lunch for 15 people was $207.00, including a 15 percent gratuity for service. What was the average price per person, EXCLUDING the gratuity?

    (A) $11.73
    (B) $12.00
    (C) $13.80
    (D) $14.00
    (E) $15.87

124. In Town X, 64 percent of the population are employed, and 48 percent of the population are employed males. What percent of the employed people in Town X are females?

    (A) 16%
    (B) 25%
    (C) 32%
    (D) 40%
    (E) 52%

125. If $\frac{p}{q} < 1$, and p and q are positive integers, which of the following must be greater than 1 ?

    (A) $\sqrt{\frac{p}{q}}$
    (B) $\frac{p}{q^2}$
    (C) $\frac{p}{2q}$
    (D) $\frac{q}{p^2}$
    (E) $\frac{q}{p}$

126. It would take one machine 4 hours to complete a large production order and another machine 3 hours to complete the same order. How many hours would it take both machines, working simultaneously at their respective constant rates, to complete the order?

(A) $\dfrac{7}{12}$

(B) $1\dfrac{1}{2}$

(C) $1\dfrac{5}{7}$

(D) $3\dfrac{1}{2}$

(E) 7

127. To mail a package, the rate is x cents for the first pound and y cents for each additional pound, where x > y. Two packages weighing 3 pounds and 5 pounds, respectively, can be mailed separately or combined as one package. Which method is cheaper, and how much money is saved?

(A) Combined, with a savings of x – y cents

(B) Combined, with a savings of y – x cents

(C) Combined, with a savings of x cents

(D) Separately, with a savings of x – y cents

(E) Separately, with a savings of y cents

128. If money is invested at r percent interest, compounded annually, the amount of the investment will double in approximately $\dfrac{70}{r}$ years. If Pat's parents invested $5,000 in a long-term bond that pays 8 percent interest, compounded annually, what will be the approximate total amount of the investment 18 years later, when Pat is ready for college?

(A) $20,000

(B) $15,000

(C) $12,000

(D) $10,000

(E) $ 9,000

129. On a recent trip, Cindy drove her car 290 miles, rounded to the nearest 10 miles, and used 12 gallons of gasoline, rounded to the nearest gallon. The actual number of miles per gallon that Cindy's car got on this trip must have been between

(A) $\dfrac{290}{12.5}$ and $\dfrac{290}{11.5}$

(B) $\dfrac{295}{12}$ and $\dfrac{285}{11.5}$

(C) $\dfrac{285}{12}$ and $\dfrac{295}{12}$

(D) $\dfrac{285}{12.5}$ and $\dfrac{295}{11.5}$

(E) $\dfrac{295}{12.5}$ and $\dfrac{285}{11.5}$

130. Which of the following inequalities is an algebraic expression for the shaded part of the number line above?

(A) $|x| \le 3$

(B) $|x| \le 5$

(C) $|x - 2| \le 3$

(D) $|x - 1| \le 4$

(E) $|x + 1| \le 4$

131. A factory has 500 workers, 15 percent of whom are women. If 50 additional workers are to be hired and all of the present workers remain, how many of the additional workers must be women in order to raise the percent of women employees to 20 percent?

(A) 3

(B) 10

(C) 25

(D) 30

(E) 35

132. In a small snack shop, the average (arithmetic mean) revenue was $400 per day over a 10-day period. During this period, if the average daily revenue was $360 for the first 6 days, what was the average daily revenue for the last 4 days?

    (A) $420
    (B) $440
    (C) $450
    (D) $460
    (E) $480

133. A certain country had a total annual expenditure of 1.2×10^{12} last year. If the population of the country was 240 million last year, what was the per capita expenditure?

    (A) $ 500
    (B) $1,000
    (C) $2,000
    (D) $3,000
    (E) $5,000

134. A certain rectangular window is twice as long as it is wide. If its perimeter is 10 feet, then its dimensions in feet are

    (A) $\dfrac{3}{2}$ by $\dfrac{7}{2}$

    (B) $\dfrac{5}{3}$ by $\dfrac{10}{3}$

    (C) 2 by 4

    (D) 3 by 6

    (E) $\dfrac{10}{3}$ by $\dfrac{20}{3}$

135. The diagram above shows the various paths along which a mouse can travel from point X, where it is released, to point Y, where it is rewarded with a food pellet. How many different paths from X to Y can the mouse take if it goes directly from X to Y without retracing any point along a path?

    (A) 6
    (B) 7
    (C) 12
    (D) 14
    (E) 17

136. If the operation $\odot$ is defined by $x \odot y = \sqrt{xy}$ for all positive numbers x and y, then $(5 \odot 45) \odot 60 =$

    (A) 30
    (B) 60
    (C) 90
    (D) $30\sqrt{15}$
    (E) $60\sqrt{15}$

137. A bar over a sequence of digits in a decimal indicates that the sequence repeats indefinitely.

    What is the value of $(10^4 - 10^2)(0.00\overline{12})$?

    (A) 0
    (B) $0.\overline{12}$
    (C) 1.2
    (D) 10
    (E) 12

138. At a loading dock, each worker on the night crew loaded $\dfrac{3}{4}$ as many boxes as each worker on the day crew. If the night crew has $\dfrac{4}{5}$ as many workers as the day crew, what fraction of all the boxes loaded by the two crews did the day crew load?

    (A) $\dfrac{1}{2}$

    (B) $\dfrac{2}{5}$

    (C) $\dfrac{3}{5}$

    (D) $\dfrac{4}{5}$

    (E) $\dfrac{5}{8}$

139. A restaurant meal cost $35.50 and there was no tax. If the tip was more than 10 percent but less than 15 percent of the cost of the meal, then the total amount paid must have been between

   (A) $40 and $42
   (B) $39 and $41
   (C) $38 and $40
   (D) $37 and $39
   (E) $36 and $37

140. In a weight-lifting competition, the total weight of Joe's two lifts was 750 pounds. If twice the weight of his first lift was 300 pounds more than the weight of his second lift, what was the weight, in pounds, of his first lift?

   (A)   225
   (B)   275
   (C)   325
   (D)   350
   (E)   400

141. A club collected exactly $599 from its members. If each member contributed at least $12, what is the greatest number of members the club could have?

   (A)   43
   (B)   44
   (C)   49
   (D)   50
   (E)   51

142. If y is the smallest positive integer such that 3,150 multiplied by y is the square of an integer, then y must be

   (A)   2
   (B)   5
   (C)   6
   (D)   7
   (E)   14

143. If [x] is the greatest integer less than or equal to x, what is the value of $[-1.6] + [3.4] + [2.7]$?

   (A)   3
   (B)   4
   (C)   5
   (D)   6
   (E)   7

144. If $\dfrac{4 - x}{2 + x} = x$, what is the value of $x^2 + 3x - 4$?

   (A) -4
   (B) -1
   (C)   0
   (D)   1
   (E)   2

145. The trapezoid shown in the figure above represents a cross section of the rudder of a ship. If the distance from A to B is 13 feet, what is the area of the cross section of the rudder in square feet?

   (A)   39
   (B)   40
   (C)   42
   (D)   45
   (E)   46.5

146. In a certain sequence, the term x_n is given by the formula $x_n = 2x_{n-1} - \dfrac{1}{2}(x_{n-2})$ for all $n \geq 2$. If $x_0 = 3$ and $x_1 = 2$, what is the value of x_3 ?

   (A)   2.5
   (B)   3.125
   (C)   4
   (D)   5
   (E)   6.75

147. In the figure above, *V* represents an observation point at one end of a pool. From *V*, an object that is actually located on the bottom of the pool at point *R* appears to be at point *S*. If *VR* = 10 feet, what is the distance *RS*, in feet, between the actual position and the perceived position of the object?

(A) $10 - 5\sqrt{3}$

(B) $10 - 5\sqrt{2}$

(C)   2

(D) $2\frac{1}{2}$

(E)   4

148. If *x*, *y*, and *k* are positive numbers such that

$$\left(\frac{x}{x+y}\right)(10) + \left(\frac{y}{x+y}\right)(20) = k \text{ and if } x < y,$$

which of the following could be the value of *k* ?

(A)   10

(B)   12

(C)   15

(D)   18

(E)   30

149. During a trip, Francine traveled *x* percent of the total distance at an average speed of 40 miles per hour and the rest of the distance at an average speed of 60 miles per hour. In terms of *x*, what was Francine's average speed for the entire trip?

(A) $\dfrac{180 - x}{2}$

(B) $\dfrac{x + 60}{4}$

(C) $\dfrac{300 - x}{5}$

(D) $\dfrac{600}{115 - x}$

(E) $\dfrac{12{,}000}{x + 200}$

150. If *x* = –1, then $\dfrac{x^4 - x^3 + x^2}{x - 1} =$

(A) $-\dfrac{3}{2}$

(B) $-\dfrac{1}{2}$

(C)   0

(D) $\dfrac{1}{2}$

(E) $\dfrac{3}{2}$

151. A toy store regularly sells all stock at a discount of 20 percent to 40 percent. If an additional 25 percent were deducted from the discount price during a special sale, what would be the lowest possible price of a toy costing $16 before any discount?

(A) $ 5.60

(B) $ 7.20

(C) $ 8.80

(D) $ 9.60

(E) $15.20

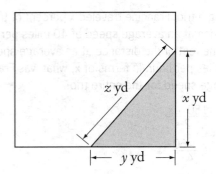

152. The shaded portion of the rectangular lot shown above represents a flower bed. If the area of the bed is 24 square yards and x = y + 2, then z equals

    (A) $\sqrt{13}$
    (B) $2\sqrt{13}$
    (C)   6
    (D)   8
    (E)   10

153. Jack is now 14 years older than Bill. If in 10 years Jack will be twice as old as Bill, how old will Jack be in 5 years?

    (A)   9
    (B)   19
    (C)   21
    (D)   23
    (E)   33

154. An empty pool being filled with water at a constant rate takes 8 hours to fill to $\frac{3}{5}$ of its capacity. How much more time will it take to finish filling the pool?

    (A)   5 hr 30 min
    (B)   5 hr 20 min
    (C)   4 hr 48 min
    (D)   3 hr 12 min
    (E)   2 hr 40 min

155. A positive number x is multiplied by 2, and this product is then divided by 3. If the positive square root of the result of these two operations equals x, what is the value of x ?

    (A) $\frac{9}{4}$

    (B) $\frac{3}{2}$

    (C) $\frac{4}{3}$

    (D) $\frac{2}{3}$

    (E) $\frac{1}{2}$

156. A tank contains 10,000 gallons of a solution that is 5 percent sodium chloride by volume. If 2,500 gallons of water evaporate from the tank, the remaining solution will be approximately what percent sodium chloride?

    (A)   1.25%
    (B)   3.75%
    (C)   6.25%
    (D)   6.67%
    (E)   11.7%

157. For any positive integer n, the sum of the first n positive integers equals $\frac{n(n+1)}{2}$. What is the sum of all the even integers between 99 and 301 ?

    (A)   10,100
    (B)   20,200
    (C)   22,650
    (D)   40,200
    (E)   45,150

158. A committee is composed of w women and m men. If 3 women and 2 men are added to the committee, and if one person is selected at random from the enlarged committee, then the probability that a woman is selected can be represented by

(A) $\dfrac{w}{m}$

(B) $\dfrac{w}{w+m}$

(C) $\dfrac{w+3}{m+2}$

(D) $\dfrac{w+3}{w+m+3}$

(E) $\dfrac{w+3}{w+m+5}$

159. How many prime numbers between 1 and 100 are factors of 7,150 ?

(A) One
(B) Two
(C) Three
(D) Four
(E) Five

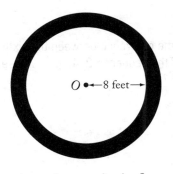

160. The figure above shows a circular flower bed, with its center at O, surrounded by a circular path that is 3 feet wide. What is the area of the path, in square feet?

(A) 25π
(B) 38π
(C) 55π
(D) 57π
(E) 64π

161. The positive integer n is divisible by 25. If $\sqrt{n}$ is greater than 25, which of the following could be the value of $\dfrac{n}{25}$?

(A) 22
(B) 23
(C) 24
(D) 25
(E) 26

162. A fruit-salad mixture consists of apples, peaches, and grapes in the ratio 6:5:2, respectively, by weight. If 39 pounds of the mixture is prepared, the mixture includes how many more pounds of apples than grapes?

(A) 15
(B) 12
(C) 9
(D) 6
(E) 4

163. This year Henry will save a certain amount of his income, and he will spend the rest. Next year Henry will have no income, but for each dollar that he saves this year, he will have $1 + r$ dollars available to spend. In terms of r, what fraction of his income should Henry save this year so that next year the amount he has available to spend will be equal to half the amount that he spends this year?

(A) $\dfrac{1}{r+2}$
(B) $\dfrac{1}{2r+2}$
(C) $\dfrac{1}{3r+2}$
(D) $\dfrac{1}{r+3}$
(E) $\dfrac{1}{2r+3}$

164. If $m^{-1} = -\dfrac{1}{3}$, then m^{-2} is equal to

(A) -9
(B) -3
(C) $-\dfrac{1}{9}$
(D) $\dfrac{1}{9}$
(E) 9

165. Lois has x dollars more than Jim has, and together they have a total of y dollars. Which of the following represents the number of dollars that Jim has?

(A) $\dfrac{y - x}{2}$

(B) $y - \dfrac{x}{2}$

(C) $\dfrac{y}{2} - x$

(D) $2y - x$

(E) $y - 2x$

166. During a certain season, a team won 80 percent of its first 100 games and 50 percent of its remaining games. If the team won 70 percent of its games for the entire season, what was the total number of games that the team played?

(A) 180
(B) 170
(C) 156
(D) 150
(E) 105

167. Of 30 applicants for a job, 14 had at least 4 years' experience, 18 had degrees, and 3 had less than 4 years' experience and did not have a degree. How many of the applicants had at least 4 years' experience and a degree?

(A) 14
(B) 13
(C) 9
(D) 7
(E) 5

168. If $1 + \dfrac{1}{x} = 2 - \dfrac{2}{x}$, then x =

(A) −1

(B) $\dfrac{1}{3}$

(C) $\dfrac{2}{3}$

(D) 2

(E) 3

169. Last year, for every 100 million vehicles that traveled on a certain highway, 96 vehicles were involved in accidents. If 3 billion vehicles traveled on the highway last year, how many of those vehicles were involved in accidents? (1 billion = 1,000,000,000)

(A) 288
(B) 320
(C) 2,880
(D) 3,200
(E) 28,800

170. Thirty percent of the members of a swim club have passed the lifesaving test. Among the members who have *not* passed the test, 12 have taken the preparatory course and 30 have not taken the course. How many members are there in the swim club?

(A) 60
(B) 80
(C) 100
(D) 120
(E) 140

171. What is the difference between the sixth and the fifth terms of the sequence 2, 4, 7, … whose nth term is $n + 2^{n-1}$?

(A) 2
(B) 3
(C) 6
(D) 16
(E) 17

172. If $(x - 1)^2 = 400$, which of the following could be the value of x − 5 ?

(A) 15
(B) 14
(C) −24
(D) −25
(E) −26

173. Which of the following describes all values of x for which $1 - x^2 \geq 0$?

(A) $x \geq 1$
(B) $x \leq -1$
(C) $0 \leq x \leq 1$
(D) $x \leq -1$ or $x \geq 1$
(E) $-1 \leq x \leq 1$

174. The probability is $\frac{1}{2}$ that a certain coin will turn up heads on any given toss. If the coin is to be tossed three times, what is the probability that on at least one of the tosses the coin will turn up tails?

(A) $\frac{1}{8}$

(B) $\frac{1}{2}$

(C) $\frac{3}{4}$

(D) $\frac{7}{8}$

(E) $\frac{15}{16}$

175. Of the final grades received by the students in a certain math course, $\frac{1}{5}$ are A's, $\frac{1}{4}$ are B's, $\frac{1}{2}$ are C's, and the remaining 10 grades are D's. What is the number of students in the course?

(A) 80
(B) 110
(C) 160
(D) 200
(E) 400

176. As x increases from 165 to 166, which of the following must increase?

I. $2x - 5$

II. $1 - \frac{1}{x}$

III. $\frac{1}{x^2 - x}$

(A) I only
(B) III only
(C) I and II
(D) I and III
(E) II and III

177. A rectangular box is 10 inches wide, 10 inches long, and 5 inches high. What is the greatest possible (straight-line) distance, in inches, between any two points on the box?

(A) 15
(B) 20
(C) 25
(D) $10\sqrt{2}$
(E) $10\sqrt{3}$

Club	Number of Students
Chess	40
Drama	30
Math	25

178. The table above shows the number of students in three clubs at McAuliffe School. Although no student is in all three clubs, 10 students are in both Chess and Drama, 5 students are in both Chess and Math, and 6 students are in both Drama and Math. How many different students are in the three clubs?

(A) 68
(B) 69
(C) 74
(D) 79
(E) 84

179. The ratio of two quantities is 3 to 4. If each of the quantities is increased by 5, what is the ratio of these two new quantities?

(A) $\frac{3}{4}$

(B) $\frac{8}{9}$

(C) $\frac{18}{19}$

(D) $\frac{23}{24}$

(E) It cannot be determined from the information given.

180. If the average (arithmetic mean) of x and y is 60 and the average (arithmetic mean) of y and z is 80, what is the value of z − x ?

   (A) 70
   (B) 40
   (C) 20
   (D) 10
   (E) It cannot be determined from the information given.

181. If $\frac{1}{2}$ of the air in a tank is removed with each stroke of a vacuum pump, what fraction of the original amount of air has been removed after 4 strokes?

   (A) $\frac{15}{16}$
   (B) $\frac{7}{8}$
   (C) $\frac{1}{4}$
   (D) $\frac{1}{8}$
   (E) $\frac{1}{16}$

182. If the two-digit integers M and N are positive and have the same digits, but in reverse order, which of the following CANNOT be the sum of M and N ?

   (A) 181
   (B) 165
   (C) 121
   (D) 99
   (E) 44

183. Car X and Car Y traveled the same 80-mile route. If Car X took 2 hours and Car Y traveled at an average speed that was 50 percent faster than the average speed of Car X, how many hours did it take Car Y to travel the route?

   (A) $\frac{2}{3}$
   (B) 1
   (C) $1\frac{1}{3}$
   (D) $1\frac{3}{5}$
   (E) 3

184. If the average (arithmetic mean) of the four numbers K, 2K + 3, 3K − 5, and 5K + 1 is 63, what is the value of K ?

   (A) 11
   (B) $15\frac{3}{4}$
   (C) 22
   (D) 23
   (E) $25\frac{3}{10}$

185. If p is an even integer and q is an odd integer, which of the following must be an odd integer?

   (A) $\frac{p}{q}$
   (B) pq
   (C) 2p + q
   (D) 2(p + q)
   (E) $\frac{3p}{q}$

186. Drum X is $\frac{1}{2}$ full of oil and Drum Y, which has twice the capacity of Drum X, is $\frac{2}{3}$ full of oil. If all of the oil in Drum X is poured into Drum Y, then Drum Y will be filled to what fraction of its capacity?

   (A) $\frac{3}{4}$
   (B) $\frac{5}{6}$
   (C) $\frac{11}{12}$
   (D) $\frac{7}{6}$
   (E) $\frac{11}{6}$

187. If $x > 0$, $\dfrac{x}{50} + \dfrac{x}{25}$ is what percent of x ?

    (A)   6%
    (B)   25%
    (C)   37%
    (D)   60%
    (E)   75%

188. If the operation ⊛ is defined for all a and b by the equation $a \circledast b = \dfrac{a^2b}{3}$, then $2 \circledast (3 \circledast -1) =$

    (A)   4
    (B)   2
    (C) $-\dfrac{4}{3}$
    (D) -2
    (E) -4

189. The inside dimensions of a rectangular wooden box are 6 inches by 8 inches by 10 inches. A cylindrical canister is to be placed inside the box so that it stands upright when the closed box rests on one of its six faces. Of all such canisters that could be used, what is the radius, in inches, of the one that has maximum volume?

    (A)   3
    (B)   4
    (C)   5
    (D)   6
    (E)   8

190. What is the units digit of $(13)^4(17)^2(29)^3$?

    (A)   9
    (B)   7
    (C)   5
    (D)   3
    (E)   1

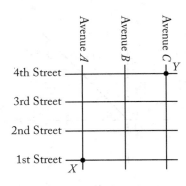

191. Pat will walk from Intersection X to Intersection Y along a route that is confined to the square grid of four streets and three avenues shown in the map above. How many routes from X to Y can Pat take that have the minimum possible length?

    (A)   6
    (B)   8
    (C)   10
    (D)   14
    (E)   16

192. The ratio, by volume, of soap to alcohol to water in a certain solution is 2:50:100. The solution will be altered so that the ratio of soap to alcohol is doubled while the ratio of soap to water is halved. If the altered solution will contain 100 cubic centimeters of alcohol, how many cubic centimeters of water will it contain?

    (A)   50
    (B)   200
    (C)   400
    (D)   625
    (E)   800

193. If 75 percent of a class answered the first question on a certain test correctly, 55 percent answered the second question on the test correctly, and 20 percent answered neither of the questions correctly, what percent answered both correctly?

    (A)   10%
    (B)   20%
    (C)   30%
    (D)   50%
    (E)   65%

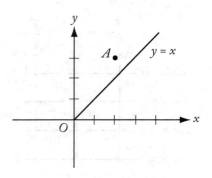

194. In the rectangular coordinate system above, the line $y = x$ is the perpendicular bisector of segment *AB* (not shown), and the *x*-axis is the perpendicular bisector of segment *BC* (not shown). If the coordinates of point *A* are (2,3), what are the coordinates of point *C* ?

   (A)   (–3,–2)
   (B)   (–3,2)
   (C)   (2,–3)
   (D)   (3,–2)
   (E)   (2,3)

195. A store currently charges the same price for each towel that it sells. If the current price of each towel were to be increased by $1, 10 fewer of the towels could be bought for $120, excluding sales tax. What is the current price of each towel?

   (A) $ 1
   (B) $ 2
   (C) $ 3
   (D) $ 4
   (E) $12

Number of Solid-Colored Marbles in Three Jars			
Jar	Number of red marbles	Number of green marbles	Total number of red and green marbles
P	x	y	80
Q	y	z	120
R	x	z	160

196. In the table above, what is the number of green marbles in Jar R ?

   (A)   70
   (B)   80
   (C)   90
   (D)   100
   (E)   110

197. A point on the edge of a fan blade that is rotating in a plane is 10 centimeters from the center of the fan. What is the distance traveled, in centimeters, by this point in 15 seconds when the fan runs at the rate of 300 revolutions per minute?

   (A) 750π
   (B) $1,500\pi$
   (C) $1,875\pi$
   (D) $3,000\pi$
   (E) $7,500\pi$

198. If $n = 4p$, where *p* is a prime number greater than 2, how many different positive <u>even</u> divisors does *n* have, including *n* ?

   (A)   Two
   (B)   Three
   (C)   Four
   (D)   Six
   (E)   Eight

   I.   72, 73, 74, 75, 76
   II.   74, 74, 74, 74, 74
   III. 62, 74, 74, 74, 89

199. The data sets I, II, and III above are ordered from greatest standard deviation to least standard deviation in which of the following?

   (A)   I, II, III
   (B)   I, III, II
   (C)   II, III, I
   (D)   III, I, II
   (E)   III, II, I

200. Of the 50 researchers in a workgroup, 40 percent will be assigned to Team A and the remaining 60 percent to Team B. However, 70 percent of the researchers prefer Team A and 30 percent prefer Team B. What is the lowest possible number of researchers who will NOT be assigned to the team they prefer?

(A)   15
(B)   17
(C)   20
(D)   25
(E)   30

201. If m is the average (arithmetic mean) of the first 10 positive multiples of 5 and if M is the median of the first 10 positive multiples of 5, what is the value of $M - m$?

(A)   −5
(B)   0
(C)   5
(D)   25
(E)   27.5

202. If $m > 0$ and x is m percent of y, then, in terms of m, y is what percent of x?

(A) $100m$

(B) $\dfrac{1}{100m}$

(C) $\dfrac{1}{m}$

(D) $\dfrac{10}{m}$

(E) $\dfrac{10,000}{m}$

203. What is the 25th digit to the right of the decimal point in the decimal form of $\dfrac{6}{11}$?

(A)   3
(B)   4
(C)   5
(D)   6
(E)   7

204. John and Mary were each paid x dollars in advance to do a certain job together. John worked on the job for 10 hours and Mary worked 2 hours less than John. If Mary gave John y dollars of her payment so that they would have received the same hourly wage, what was the dollar amount, in terms of y, that John was paid in advance?

(A) $4y$
(B) $5y$
(C) $6y$
(D) $8y$
(E) $9y$

205. In the rectangular coordinate system above, if point R (not shown) lies on the positive y-axis and the area of triangle ORP is 12, what is the y-coordinate of point R?

(A)   3
(B)   6
(C)   9
(D)   12
(E)   24

206. Car A is 20 miles behind Car B, which is traveling in the same direction along the same route as Car A. Car A is traveling at a constant speed of 58 miles per hour and Car B is traveling at a constant speed of 50 miles per hour. How many hours will it take for Car A to overtake and drive 8 miles ahead of Car B?

(A)   1.5
(B)   2.0
(C)   2.5
(D)   3.0
(E)   3.5

207. For the past n days, the average (arithmetic mean) daily production at a company was 50 units. If today's production of 90 units raises the average to 55 units per day, what is the value of n?

(A) 30
(B) 18
(C) 10
(D) 9
(E) 7

$$\left(\frac{x+1}{x-1}\right)^2$$

208. If $x \neq 0$ and $x \neq 1$, and if x is replaced by $\frac{1}{x}$ everywhere in the expression above, then the resulting expression is equivalent to

(A) $\left(\dfrac{x+1}{x-1}\right)^2$

(B) $\left(\dfrac{x-1}{x+1}\right)^2$

(C) $\dfrac{x^2+1}{1-x^2}$

(D) $\dfrac{x^2-1}{x^2+1}$

(E) $-\left(\dfrac{x-1}{x+1}\right)^2$

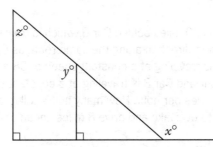

209. In the figure above, if z = 50, then x + y =

(A) 230
(B) 250
(C) 260
(D) 270
(E) 290

210. In the coordinate system above, which of the following is the equation of line ℓ?

(A) 2x − 3y = 6
(B) 2x + 3y = 6
(C) 3x + 2y = 6
(D) 2x − 3y = −6
(E) 3x − 2y = −6

211. If a two-digit positive integer has its digits reversed, the resulting integer differs from the original by 27. By how much do the two digits differ?

(A) 3
(B) 4
(C) 5
(D) 6
(E) 7

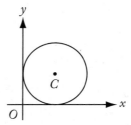

212. The circle with center C shown above is tangent to both axes. If the distance from O to C is equal to k, what is the radius of the circle, in terms of k?

(A) k

(B) $\dfrac{k}{\sqrt{2}}$

(C) $\dfrac{k}{\sqrt{3}}$

(D) $\dfrac{k}{2}$

(E) $\dfrac{k}{3}$

213. In an electric circuit, two resistors with resistances x and y are connected in parallel. In this case, if r is the combined resistance of these two resistors, then the reciprocal of r is equal to the sum of the reciprocals of x and y. What is r in terms of x and y?

(A) xy

(B) $x + y$

(C) $\dfrac{1}{x + y}$

(D) $\dfrac{xy}{x + y}$

(E) $\dfrac{x + y}{xy}$

214. Xavier, Yvonne, and Zelda each try independently to solve a problem. If their individual probabilities for success are $\dfrac{1}{4}$, $\dfrac{1}{2}$, and $\dfrac{5}{8}$, respectively, what is the probability that Xavier and Yvonne, but not Zelda, will solve the problem?

(A) $\dfrac{11}{8}$

(B) $\dfrac{7}{8}$

(C) $\dfrac{9}{64}$

(D) $\dfrac{5}{64}$

(E) $\dfrac{3}{64}$

215. If $\dfrac{1}{x} - \dfrac{1}{x + 1} = \dfrac{1}{x + 4}$, then x could be

(A) 0
(B) −1
(C) −2
(D) −3
(E) −4

216. $\left(\dfrac{1}{2}\right)^{-3} \left(\dfrac{1}{4}\right)^{-2} \left(\dfrac{1}{16}\right)^{-1} =$

(A) $\left(\dfrac{1}{2}\right)^{-48}$

(B) $\left(\dfrac{1}{2}\right)^{-11}$

(C) $\left(\dfrac{1}{2}\right)^{-6}$

(D) $\left(\dfrac{1}{8}\right)^{-11}$

(E) $\left(\dfrac{1}{8}\right)^{-6}$

217. In a certain game, a large container is filled with red, yellow, green, and blue beads worth, respectively, 7, 5, 3, and 2 points each. A number of beads are then removed from the container. If the product of the point values of the removed beads is 147,000, how many red beads were removed?

(A) 5
(B) 4
(C) 3
(D) 2
(E) 0

218. If $\dfrac{2}{1 + \dfrac{2}{y}} = 1$, then $y =$

(A) −2

(B) $-\dfrac{1}{2}$

(C) $\dfrac{1}{2}$

(D) 2

(E) 3

219. If *a*, *b*, and *c* are consecutive positive integers and
a < *b* < *c*, which of the following must be true?

  I.   *c* – *a* = 2

  II. *abc* is an even integer.

  III. $\frac{a + b + c}{3}$ is an integer.

  (A) I only
  (B) II only
  (C) I and II only
  (D) II and III only
  (E) I, II, and III

220. A part-time employee whose hourly wage was
increased by 25 percent decided to reduce the
number of hours worked per week so that the
employee's total weekly income would remain
unchanged. By what percent should the number of
hours worked be reduced?

  (A) 12.5%
  (B) 20%
  (C) 25%
  (D) 50%
  (E) 75%

221. Of the 200 students at College T majoring in one or
more of the sciences, 130 are majoring in chemistry
and 150 are majoring in biology. If at least 30 of the
students are not majoring in either chemistry or
biology, then the number of students majoring in *both*
chemistry and biology could be any number from

  (A) 20 to 50
  (B) 40 to 70
  (C) 50 to 130
  (D) 110 to 130
  (E) 110 to 150

222. If $5 - \frac{6}{x} = x$, then *x* has how many possible values?

  (A) None
  (B) One
  (C) Two
  (D) A finite number greater than two
  (E) An infinite number

223. Seed mixture X is 40 percent ryegrass and 60 percent
bluegrass by weight; seed mixture Y is 25 percent
ryegrass and 75 percent fescue. If a mixture of X and
Y contains 30 percent ryegrass, what percent of the
weight of the mixture is X ?

  (A) 10%
  (B) $33\frac{1}{3}$%
  (C) 40%
  (D) 50%
  (E) $66\frac{2}{3}$%

224. If *n* is a positive integer, then *n*(*n* + 1)(*n* + 2) is

  (A) even only when *n* is even
  (B) even only when *n* is odd
  (C) odd whenever *n* is odd
  (D) divisible by 3 only when *n* is odd
  (E) divisible by 4 whenever *n* is even

225. A straight pipe 1 yard in length was marked off in
fourths and also in thirds. If the pipe was then cut into
separate pieces at each of these markings, which of
the following gives all the different lengths of the
pieces, in fractions of a yard?

  (A) $\frac{1}{6}$ and $\frac{1}{4}$ only
  (B) $\frac{1}{4}$ and $\frac{1}{3}$ only
  (C) $\frac{1}{6}, \frac{1}{4},$ and $\frac{1}{3}$
  (D) $\frac{1}{12}, \frac{1}{6},$ and $\frac{1}{4}$
  (E) $\frac{1}{12}, \frac{1}{6},$ and $\frac{1}{3}$

226. If $\frac{0.0015 \times 10^m}{0.03 \times 10^k} = 5 \times 10^7$, then *m* – *k* =

  (A) 9
  (B) 8
  (C) 7
  (D) 6
  (E) 5

227. If $x + y = a$ and $x - y = b$, then $2xy =$

(A) $\dfrac{a^2 - b^2}{2}$

(B) $\dfrac{b^2 - a^2}{2}$

(C) $\dfrac{a - b}{2}$

(D) $\dfrac{ab}{2}$

(E) $\dfrac{a^2 + b^2}{2}$

$$p, r, s, t, u$$

228. An arithmetic sequence is a sequence in which each term after the first is equal to the sum of the preceding term and a constant. If the list of letters shown above is an arithmetic sequence, which of the following must also be an arithmetic sequence?

   I. $2p, 2r, 2s, 2t, 2u$

   II. $p - 3, r - 3, s - 3, t - 3, u - 3$

   III. p^2, r^2, s^2, t^2, u^2

(A) I only

(B) II only

(C) III only

(D) I and II

(E) II and III

229. Right triangle PQR is to be constructed in the xy-plane so that the right angle is at P and $\overline{PR}$ is parallel to the x-axis. The x- and y-coordinates of P, Q, and R are to be integers that satisfy the inequalities $-4 \le x \le 5$ and $6 \le y \le 16$. How many different triangles with these properties could be constructed?

(A)   110

(B)   1,100

(C)   9,900

(D) 10,000

(E) 12,100

230. The value of $\dfrac{2^{-14} + 2^{-15} + 2^{-16} + 2^{-17}}{5}$ is how many times the value of 2^{-17} ?

(A) $\dfrac{3}{2}$

(B) $\dfrac{5}{2}$

(C) 3

(D) 4

(E) 5

5.4 Answer Key

1.	A	31.	B	61.	E	91.	B
2.	B	32.	B	62.	A	92.	C
3.	C	33.	C	63.	A	93.	B
4.	E	34.	A	64.	B	94.	B
5.	C	35.	B	65.	B	95.	E
6.	C	36.	A	66.	E	96.	D
7.	B	37.	A	67.	B	97.	B
8.	E	38.	B	68.	D	98.	C
9.	E	39.	B	69.	C	99.	B
10.	D	40.	C	70.	C	100.	D
11.	E	41.	A	71.	A	101.	D
12.	A	42.	E	72.	B	102.	B
13.	C	43.	B	73.	D	103.	E
14.	A	44.	D	74.	D	104.	B
15.	B	45.	B	75.	E	105.	C
16.	D	46.	C	76.	D	106.	B
17.	D	47.	C	77.	D	107.	D
18.	E	48.	C	78.	C	108.	B
19.	E	49.	B	79.	A	109.	C
20.	A	50.	B	80.	B	110.	C
21.	B	51.	C	81.	A	111.	B
22.	A	52.	E	82.	A	112.	D
23.	B	53.	E	83.	C	113.	D
24.	D	54.	A	84.	A	114.	B
25.	E	55.	E	85.	A	115.	C
26.	B	56.	B	86.	A	116.	B
27.	E	57.	A	87.	E	117.	E
28.	B	58.	B	88.	D	118.	C
29.	C	59.	D	89.	D	119.	D
30.	B	60.	D	90.	E	120.	C

121. C	151. B	181. A	211. A
122. E	152. E	182. A	212. B
123. B	153. D	183. C	213. D
124. B	154. B	184. D	214. E
125. E	155. D	185. C	215. C
126. C	156. D	186. C	216. B
127. A	157. B	187. A	217. D
128. A	158. E	188. E	218. D
129. D	159. D	189. B	219. E
130. E	160. D	190. E	220. B
131. E	161. E	191. C	221. D
132. D	162. B	192. E	222. C
133. E	163. E	193. D	223. B
134. B	164. D	194. D	224. E
135. C	165. A	195. C	225. D
136. A	166. D	196. D	226. A
137. E	167. E	197. B	227. A
138. E	168. E	198. C	228. D
139. B	169. C	199. D	229. C
140. D	170. A	200. A	230. C
141. C	171. E	201. B	
142. E	172. C	202. E	
143. A	173. E	203. C	
144. C	174. D	204. E	
145. C	175. D	205. B	
146. C	176. C	206. E	
147. A	177. A	207. E	
148. D	178. C	208. A	
149. E	179. E	209. D	
150. A	180. B	210. B	

5.5 Answer Explanations

The following discussion is intended to familiarize you with the most efficient and effective approaches to the kinds of problems common to problem solving questions. The particular questions in this chapter are generally representative of the kinds of problem solving questions you will encounter on the GMAT. Remember that it is the problem solving strategy that is important, not the specific details of a particular question.

1. A project scheduled to be carried out over a single fiscal year has a budget of $12,600, divided into 12 equal monthly allocations. At the end of the fourth month of that fiscal year, the total amount actually spent on the project was $4,580. By how much was the project over its budget?

    (A) $ 380
    (B) $ 540
    (C) $1,050
    (D) $1,380
    (E) $1,430

    Arithmetic Operations with rational numbers

    The budget for four months is
    $\frac{\$12,600}{12} \times 4 = \$4,200$. Thus, the project was
    $4,580 - $4,200 = $380 over budget for the first four months.

    The correct answer is A.

2. If the sum of 5, 8, 12, and 15 is equal to the sum of 3, 4, x, and $x + 3$, what is the value of x ?

    (A)   14
    (B)   15
    (C)   16
    (D)   17
    (E)   18

    Algebra First-degree equations

    Convert the words into symbols and solve the equation:

$$5 + 8 + 12 + 15 = 3 + 4 + x + (x + 3)$$
$$40 = 2x + 10$$
$$30 = 2x$$
$$15 = x$$

The correct answer is B.

3. For which of the following values of n is $\frac{100 + n}{n}$ NOT an integer?

    (A)   1
    (B)   2
    (C)   3
    (D)   4
    (E)   5

    Arithmetic Properties of numbers

    Substitute the value for n given in each answer choice into the expression, and then simplify to determine whether or not that value results in an integer.

A	$\frac{100+1}{1} = \frac{101}{1} = 101$	Integer
B	$\frac{100+2}{2} = \frac{102}{2} = 51$	Integer
C	$\frac{100+3}{3} = \frac{103}{3} = 34.333...$	NOT an integer
D	$\frac{100+4}{4} = \frac{104}{4} = 26$	Integer
E	$\frac{100+5}{5} = \frac{105}{5} = 21$	Integer

Another method is to rewrite the given expression, $\dfrac{100+n}{n}$, as $\dfrac{100}{n}+\dfrac{n}{n}=\dfrac{100}{n}+1$. This shows that the given expression is an integer exactly when $\dfrac{100}{n}$ is an integer. Since 100 is not divisible by 3, but 100 is divisible by 1, 2, 4, and 5, it follows that $n = 3$.

The correct answer is C.

4. Rectangular Floors X and Y have equal area. If Floor X is 12 feet by 18 feet and Floor Y is 9 feet wide, what is the length of Floor Y, in feet?

(A) $13\dfrac{1}{2}$

(B) 18

(C) $18\dfrac{3}{4}$

(D) 21

(E) 24

Geometry Area

Since Floor X is a rectangle, its area is (width)(length) = (12)(18). It is given that this is also the area of Floor Y, so if L is the length of Floor Y, it follows that $9L$ = (12)(18), or

$$L = \dfrac{(12)(18)}{9} = \dfrac{(12)(\cancel{9})(2)}{\cancel{9}} = (12)(2) = 24.$$

The correct answer is E.

PAYROLL AT COMPANY X	
Number of Employees	Salary
5	$20,000
4	$22,000
8	$25,000
3	$30,000

5. The table above shows the number of employees at each of four salary levels at Company X. What is the average (arithmetic mean) salary for the 20 employees?

(A) $23,500
(B) $23,750
(C) $23,900
(D) $24,125
(E) $24,250

Arithmetic Statistics

From the table, there are 5 employees each with a salary of $20,000, 4 employees each with a salary of $22,000, and so on. The average (arithmetic mean) for all 20 employees is then

$$\dfrac{5(20,000)+4(22,000)+8(25,000)+3(30,000)}{20}$$

$$=\dfrac{100,000+88,000+200,000+90,000}{20}$$

$$=\dfrac{478,000}{20}$$

$$= 23,900$$

The correct answer is C.

6. A case contains c cartons. Each carton contains b boxes, and each box contains 100 paper clips. How many paper clips are contained in 2 cases?

(A) $100bc$

(B) $\dfrac{100b}{c}$

(C) $200bc$

(D) $\dfrac{200b}{c}$

(E) $\dfrac{200}{bc}$

Algebra Simplifying algebraic expressions

Each case has bc boxes, each of which has 100 paper clips. The total number of paper clips in 2 cases is thus $2(bc)(100) = 200bc$.

The correct answer is C.

7. The sum of prime numbers that are greater than 60 but less than 70 is

 (A) 67
 (B) 128
 (C) 191
 (D) 197
 (E) 260

Arithmetic Properties of numbers

A prime number is a positive integer divisible by exactly two different positive divisors, 1 and itself. Note that 62, 64, 66, and 68 are also divisible by 2; 63, 66, and 69 are also divisible by 3; and 65 is also divisible by 5. The only prime numbers between 60 and 70 are 61 and 67, and 61 + 67 = 128.

The correct answer is B.

8. A rainstorm increased the amount of water stored in State J reservoirs from 124 billion gallons to 138 billion gallons. If the storm increased the amount of water in the reservoirs to 82 percent of total capacity, approximately how many billion gallons of water were the reservoirs short of total capacity prior to the storm?

 (A) 9
 (B) 14
 (C) 25
 (D) 30
 (E) 44

Algebra Applied problems

Let t be the total capacity of the reservoirs in billions of gallons. The information that the post-storm water amount of 138 billion gallons represented 82 percent of total capacity can be expressed as $0.82t = 138$. Solve for t and then estimate the value of t: $t = \frac{138}{0.82} \approx \frac{140}{0.8} = \frac{1,400}{8} =$ 175 billion gallons. Thus, the amount the reservoirs were short of total capacity prior to the storm, in billions of gallons, was approximately $175 - 124 = 51$, so E is the best choice. A more accurate calculation gives $168.3 - 124 = 44.3$.

The correct answer is E.

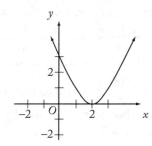

9. On the graph above, when $x = \frac{1}{2}$, $y = 2$; and when $x = 1$, $y = 1$. The graph is symmetric with respect to the vertical line at $x = 2$. According to the graph, when $x = 3$, $y =$

 (A) -1
 (B) $-\frac{1}{2}$
 (C) 0
 (D) $\frac{1}{2}$
 (E) 1

Arithmetic; Algebra Interpretation of graphs; Second-degree equations

Since the graph is symmetric with respect to $x = 2$, the y value when $x = 3$ will be the same as the y value when $x = 1$, which is 1.

The correct answer is E.

10. When $\frac{1}{10}$ percent of 5,000 is subtracted from $\frac{1}{10}$ of 5,000 the difference is

 (A) 0
 (B) 50
 (C) 450
 (D) 495
 (E) 500

Arithmetic Percents

Since $\frac{1}{10}$ percent is $\frac{1}{1,000}$, the difference asked for is $\left(\frac{1}{10}\right)(5,000) - \left(\frac{1}{1,000}\right)(5,000) =$ $500 - 5 = 495$.

The correct answer is D.

11. Which of the following is the value of $\sqrt{\sqrt[3]{0.000064}}$?

    (A) 0.004
    (B) 0.008
    (C) 0.02
    (D) 0.04
    (E) 0.2

Arithmetic Operations on radical expressions

The square root and cube root evaluations are more easily carried out when 0.000064 is rewritten as 64×10^{-6}. Using this rewritten form, the value asked for is

$$\sqrt{\sqrt[3]{0.000064}} = \sqrt{\sqrt[3]{64 \times 10^{-6}}}$$
$$= \sqrt{\sqrt[3]{64} \times \sqrt[3]{10^{-6}}}$$
$$= \sqrt{4 \times 10^{-2}}$$
$$= \sqrt{4} \times \sqrt{10^{-2}}$$
$$= 2 \times 10^{-1}$$
$$= 0.2$$

The correct answer is E.

12. Raffle tickets numbered consecutively from 101 through 350 are placed in a box. What is the probability that a ticket selected at random will have a number with a hundreds digit of 2 ?

    (A) $\dfrac{2}{5}$
    (B) $\dfrac{2}{7}$
    (C) $\dfrac{33}{83}$
    (D) $\dfrac{99}{250}$
    (E) $\dfrac{100}{249}$

Arithmetic Probability

There are 250 integers from 101 to 350 inclusive, 100 of which (that is, 200 through 299) have a hundreds digit of 2. Therefore, the probability that a ticket selected from the box at random

will have a hundreds digit of 2 can be expressed as $\dfrac{100}{250} = \dfrac{2}{5}$.

The correct answer is A.

13. When Leo imported a certain item, he paid a 7 percent import tax on the portion of the total value of the item in excess of $1,000. If the amount of the import tax that Leo paid was $87.50, what was the total value of the item?

    (A) $1,600
    (B) $1,850
    (C) $2,250
    (D) $2,400
    (E) $2,750

Algebra First-degree equations

Letting x represent the total value of the item, convert the words to symbols and solve the equation.

7% of value in excess of $1,000 = 87.50

$$0.07(x - 1,000) = 87.50$$
$$x - 1,000 = 1,250$$
$$x = 2,250$$

The correct answer is C.

14. On Monday, a person mailed 8 packages weighing an average (arithmetic mean) of $12\frac{3}{8}$ pounds, and on Tuesday, 4 packages weighing an average of $15\frac{1}{4}$ pounds. What was the average weight, in pounds, of all the packages the person mailed on both days?

    (A) $13\frac{1}{3}$
    (B) $13\frac{13}{16}$
    (C) $15\frac{1}{2}$
    (D) $15\frac{15}{16}$
    (E) $16\frac{1}{2}$

Arithmetic Statistics

Since average = $\dfrac{\text{sum of values}}{\text{number of values}}$,

the information about the two shipments of packages can be expressed as

$$\text{average} = \frac{8\left(12\dfrac{3}{8}\right) + 4\left(15\dfrac{1}{4}\right)}{12} = \frac{8\left(\dfrac{99}{8}\right) + 4\left(\dfrac{61}{4}\right)}{12}$$

$$= \frac{99 + 61}{12} = \frac{160}{12} = 13\frac{1}{3}.$$

The correct answer is A.

15. $0.1 + (0.1)^2 + (0.1)^3 =$

   (A)   0.1
   (B)   0.111
   (C)   0.1211
   (D)   0.2341
   (E)   0.3

Arithmetic Operations on rational numbers

Calculate the squared and the cubed term, and then add the three terms.

$0.1 + (0.1)^2 + (0.1)^3 = 0.1 + 0.01 + 0.001 = 0.111$

The correct answer is B.

16. A carpenter constructed a rectangular sandbox with a capacity of 10 cubic feet. If the carpenter were to make a similar sandbox twice as long, twice as wide, and twice as high as the first sandbox, what would be the capacity, in cubic feet, of the second sandbox?

   (A)   20
   (B)   40
   (C)   60
   (D)   80
   (E)   100

Geometry Volume

When all the dimensions of a three-dimensional object are changed by a factor of 2, the capacity, or volume, changes by a factor of $(2)(2)(2) = 2^3 = 8$. Thus the capacity of the second sandbox is $10(8) = 80$ cubic feet.

The correct answer is D.

17. A bakery opened yesterday with its daily supply of 40 dozen rolls. Half of the rolls were sold by noon, and 80 percent of the remaining rolls were sold between noon and closing time. How many dozen rolls had not been sold when the bakery closed yesterday?

   (A)   1
   (B)   2
   (C)   3
   (D)   4
   (E)   5

Arithmetic Operations on rational numbers; Percents

Since half of the 40 dozen rolls were sold by noon, then $\dfrac{1}{2}(40) = 20$ dozen rolls were left to be sold after noon. Because 80 percent of those 20 were sold, $100 - 80 = 20$ percent of them or $20(0.20) = 4$ dozen rolls had not been sold when the bakery closed.

The correct answer is D.

18. If the area of a square region having sides of length 6 centimeters is equal to the area of a rectangular region having width 2.5 centimeters, then the length of the rectangle, in centimeters, is

   (A)   8.5
   (B)   9.5
   (C)   9.6
   (D)   10.5
   (E)   14.4

Geometry Quadrilaterals

The area of a square region with side length 6 is 36 and the area of a rectangular region with width 2.5 and length x is $2.5x$. The two areas are equal, so

$$36 = 2.5x$$
$$36 = \frac{5}{2}x$$
$$36 \cdot \frac{2}{5} = x$$
$$\frac{72}{5} = x$$
$$14.4 = x$$

The correct answer is E.

19. 150 is what percent of 30 ?

    (A)   5%
    (B)   20%
    (C)   50%
    (D)   200%
    (E)   500%

Arithmetic Percents

Let x be the desired percent in the problem. The given information can be expressed by the following equation, which can then be solved for x.

$$150 = 30x$$
$$\frac{(15)(10)}{(3)(10)} = x$$
$$5 = x$$

Then, 5 expressed as a percent is 500%.

The correct answer is E.

20. The ratio 2 to $\frac{1}{3}$ is equal to the ratio

    (A)   6 to 1
    (B)   5 to 1
    (C)   3 to 2
    (D)   2 to 3
    (E)   1 to 6

Arithmetic Operations on rational numbers

The ratio 2 to $\frac{1}{3}$ is the same as $\frac{2}{\frac{1}{3}} = 2\left(\frac{3}{1}\right) = 6$, which is the same as a ratio of 6 to 1.

The correct answer is A.

21. Running at the same constant rate, 6 identical machines can produce a total of 270 bottles per minute. At this rate, how many bottles could 10 such machines produce in 4 minutes?

    (A)   648
    (B)   1,800
    (C)   2,700
    (D)   10,800
    (E)   64,800

Arithmetic Operations on rational numbers

Since there are 6 machines, each machine does $\frac{1}{6}$ of the work. Each machine can produce $270\left(\frac{1}{6}\right) = 45$ bottles per minute, so 10 machines can produce 45(10) = 450 bottles per minute. Therefore, the 10 machines can produce 450(4) = 1,800 bottles in 4 minutes.

The correct answer is B.

22. Of the five coordinates associated with points A, B, C, D, and E on the number line above, which has the greatest absolute value?

    (A) A
    (B) B
    (C) C
    (D) D
    (E) E

Arithmetic Properties of numbers

The absolute value of a number x is the distance between x and 0 on the number line. Point A is farthest from 0 and thus its coordinate has the greatest absolute value.

The correct answer is A.

23. If n is a prime number greater than 3, what is the remainder when n^2 is divided by 12 ?

    (A)   0
    (B)   1
    (C)   2
    (D)   3
    (E)   5

Arithmetic Properties of numbers

The simplest way to solve this problem is to choose a prime number greater than 3 and divide its square by 12 to see what the remainder is. For example, if $n = 5$, then $n^2 = 25$, and the remainder is 1 when 25 is divided by 12. A second prime number can be used to check the result. For example, if $n = 7$, then $n^2 = 49$, and the remainder is 1 when 49 is divided by 12. Because only one of the answer choices can be correct, the remainder must be 1.

For the more mathematically inclined, consider the remainder when each prime number n greater than 3 is divided by 6. The remainder cannot be 0 because that would imply that n is divisible by 6, which is impossible since n is a prime number. The remainder cannot be 2 or 4 because that would imply that n is even, which is impossible since n is a prime number greater than 3. The remainder cannot be 3 because that would imply that n is divisible by 3, which is impossible since n is a prime number greater than 3. Therefore, the only possible remainders when a prime number n greater than 3 is divided by 6 are 1 and 5. Thus, n has the form $6q + 1$ or $6q + 5$, where q is an integer, and, therefore, n^2 has the form $36q^2 + 12q + 1 = 12(3q^2 + q) + 1$ or $36q^2 + 60q + 25 = 12(3q^2 + 5q + 2) + 1$. In either case, n^2 has a remainder of 1 when divided by 12.

The correct answer is B.

24. $\dfrac{1}{1+\dfrac{1}{3}} - \dfrac{1}{1+\dfrac{1}{2}} =$

(A) $-\dfrac{1}{3}$

(B) $-\dfrac{1}{6}$

(C) $-\dfrac{1}{12}$

(D) $\dfrac{1}{12}$

(E) $\dfrac{1}{3}$

Arithmetic Operations with rational numbers

Perform the arithmetic calculations as follows:

$$\frac{1}{1+\frac{1}{3}} - \frac{1}{1+\frac{1}{2}} = \frac{1}{\frac{4}{3}} - \frac{1}{\frac{3}{2}}$$

$$= \frac{3}{4} - \frac{2}{3}$$

$$= \frac{9}{12} - \frac{8}{12}$$

$$= \frac{9-8}{12}$$

$$= \frac{1}{12}$$

The correct answer is D.

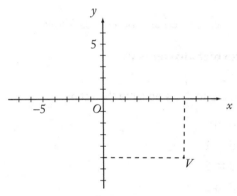

25. In the figure above, the coordinates of point V are

(A) $(-7,5)$
(B) $(-5,7)$
(C) $(5,7)$
(D) $(7,5)$
(E) $(7,-5)$

Geometry Coordinate geometry

The x-coordinate of V is 7, and the y-coordinate of V is -5. Thus, the coordinates, (x,y), of V are $(7,-5)$.

The correct answer is E.

26. A rope 40 feet long is cut into two pieces. If one piece is 18 feet longer than the other, what is the length, in feet, of the shorter piece?

    (A)   9
    (B)   11
    (C)   18
    (D)   22
    (E)   29

Algebra First-degree equations

Build an equation to express the given information and solve for the answer.

Let x = length of the shorter piece of rope in feet.

Then $x + 18$ = length of the longer piece of rope in feet.

Thus $x + (x + 18) = 40$ is the entire length of the rope in feet.

$2x + 18 = 40$ combine like terms

$2x = 22$ subtract 18 from both sides

$x = 11$ divide both sides by 2

The correct answer is B.

27. A student's average (arithmetic mean) test score on 4 tests is 78. What must be the student's score on a 5th test for the student's average score on the 5 tests to be 80 ?

    (A)   80
    (B)   82
    (C)   84
    (D)   86
    (E)   88

Arithmetic Statistics

The average of the student's first 4 test scores is 78, so the sum of the first 4 test scores is 4(78) = 312. If x represents the fifth test score, then the sum of all 5 test scores is 312 + x and the average of all 5 test scores is $\frac{312+x}{5}$. But the average of all 5 test scores is 80 so

$$\frac{312+x}{5} = 80$$

$$312 + x = 400$$

$$x = 88$$

The correct answer is E.

28. The average distance between the Sun and a certain planet is approximately 2.3×10^{14} inches. Which of the following is closest to the average distance between the Sun and the planet, in kilometers? (1 kilometer is approximately 3.9×10^4 inches.)

    (A) 7.1×10^8
    (B) 5.9×10^9
    (C) 1.6×10^{10}
    (D) 1.6×10^{11}
    (E) 5.9×10^{11}

Arithmetic Measurement conversion

Convert to kilometers and then estimate.

$$(2.3 \times 10^{14} \text{ in}) \left(\frac{1 \text{ km}}{3.9 \times 10^4 \text{ in}} \right) = \frac{2.3 \times 10^{14}}{3.9 \times 10^4} \text{ km}$$

$$= \frac{2.3}{3.9} \times 10^{14-4} \text{ km}$$

$$\approx \frac{2}{4} \times 10^{10}$$

$$= 0.5 \times 10^{10}$$

$$= 5 \times 10^9$$

The correct answer is B.

29. If the quotient $\frac{a}{b}$ is positive, which of the following must be true?

    (A) $a > 0$
    (B) $b > 0$
    (C) $ab > 0$
    (D) $a - b > 0$
    (E) $a + b > 0$

Arithmetic Properties of numbers

If the quotient $\frac{a}{b}$ is positive, then either a and b are both positive, or a and b are both negative.

A $a = -1$ and $b = -1$ show it NEED NOT BE TRUE that $a > 0$.

B $a = -1$ and $b = -1$ show it NEED NOT BE TRUE that $b > 0$.

C The condition that ab is positive is exactly the same condition that $\dfrac{a}{b}$ is positive. Thus, it MUST BE TRUE that $ab > 0$.

D $a = 1$ and $b = 2$ show it NEED NOT BE TRUE that $a - b > 0$.

E $a = -1$ and $b = -1$ show it NEED NOT BE TRUE that $a + b > 0$.

The correct answer is C.

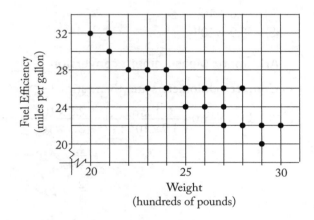

30. The dots on the graph above indicate the weights and fuel efficiency ratings for 20 cars. How many of the cars weigh more than 2,500 pounds and also get more than 22 miles per gallon?

(A)   3
(B)   5
(C)   8
(D)   10
(E)   11

Arithmetic Interpretation of graphs and tables

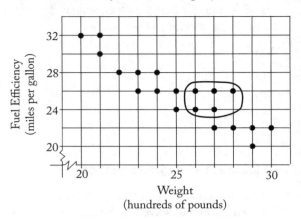

The only dots on the graph that meet the conditions of the problem are those to the right of 25 (that is, the car has a weight in excess of 2,500 pounds) and above 22 (that is, the car has a fuel efficiency over 22 miles per gallon) as shown.

The correct answer is B.

31. How many minutes does it take John to type y words if he types at the rate of x words per minute?

(A) $\dfrac{x}{y}$

(B) $\dfrac{y}{x}$

(C) xy

(D) $\dfrac{60x}{y}$

(E) $\dfrac{y}{60x}$

Algebra First-degree equations

Let m represent the number of minutes it takes John to type y words. In this rate problem, the number of words typed = (typing rate)(time). Thus, $y = xm$, or $m = \dfrac{y}{x}$.

The correct answer is B.

32. $\sqrt{(16)(20)+(8)(32)} =$

    (A) $4\sqrt{20}$
    (B) 24
    (C) 25
    (D) $4\sqrt{20}+8\sqrt{2}$
    (E) 32

Arithmetic Operations on radical expressions

Perform the indicated calculation. The following is one way to lessen the amount of arithmetic computation.

$$\sqrt{(16)(20)+(8)(32)} = \sqrt{(16)(20)+(16)(16)}$$

$$= \sqrt{(16)(20+16)}$$

$$= \sqrt{16}\sqrt{20+16}$$

$$= 4\sqrt{36}$$

$$= (4)(6)$$

$$= 24$$

The correct answer is B.

33. If O is the center of the circle above, what fraction of the circular region is shaded?

    (A) $\dfrac{1}{12}$

    (B) $\dfrac{1}{9}$

    (C) $\dfrac{1}{6}$

    (D) $\dfrac{1}{4}$

    (E) $\dfrac{1}{3}$

Geometry Circles and area

Vertical angles are congruent, so 150° + 150° = 300° of the circle is not shaded. Since there are 360° in a circle, this makes 360° − 300° = 60° of the circle shaded. The fraction of the circular region that is shaded is thus = $\dfrac{60}{360} = \dfrac{1}{6}$.

The correct answer is C.

34. If Juan takes 11 seconds to run y yards, how many seconds will it take him to run x yards at the same rate?

    (A) $\dfrac{11x}{y}$

    (B) $\dfrac{11y}{x}$

    (C) $\dfrac{x}{11y}$

    (D) $\dfrac{11}{xy}$

    (E) $\dfrac{xy}{11}$

Algebra Applied problems

Juan's running rate can be expressed as $\dfrac{y}{11}$ yards per second. Use this value in the formula distance = (rate)(time), letting t equal the time in seconds that it will take Juan to run the distance of x yards:

$$x = \frac{y}{11}t \quad \text{distance = (rate)(time)}$$

$$\frac{11x}{y} = t \quad \text{solve for } t \text{ by multiplying both sides by } \frac{11}{y}$$

The correct answer is A.

35. John has 10 pairs of matched socks. If he loses 7 individual socks, what is the greatest number of pairs of matched socks he can have left?

    (A) 7
    (B) 6
    (C) 5
    (D) 4
    (E) 3

Arithmetic Operations on rational numbers

Determine first the lowest number of pairs of matched socks that can be made from the 7 individual socks. The lowest number of pairs that 7 individual socks can come from is 3 full pairs plus one sock from a fourth pair. The greatest number of pairs of matched socks John can have left is therefore 10 − 4 = 6 fully matched pairs.

The correct answer is B.

36. What is the lowest positive integer that is divisible by each of the integers 1 through 7, inclusive?

   (A) 420
   (B) 840
   (C) 1,260
   (D) 2,520
   (E) 5,040

Arithmetic Operations on rational numbers

A number that is divisible by the integers from 1 through 7 inclusive must have 2, 3, 4, 5, 6, and 7 as factors. The lowest positive integer will have no duplication of factors. The lowest common multiple of 2, 3, 4, and 6 is 12, and 5 and 7 are prime, so the lowest positive integer that is divisible by each of the integers 1 through 7 inclusive is 12(5)(7) = 420.

The correct answer is A.

37. $\dfrac{1}{0.75-1} =$

   (A) −4
   (B) −0.25
   (C) 0.25
   (D) 0.75
   (E) 4

Arithmetic Operations with rational numbers

Perform the arithmetic calculations as follows:

$$\frac{1}{0.75-1} = \frac{1}{\frac{3}{4}-1}$$

$$= \frac{1}{-\frac{1}{4}}$$

$$= -4$$

The correct answer is A.

38. If $\dfrac{1.5}{0.2+x} = 5$, then $x =$

   (A) −3.7
   (B) 0.1
   (C) 0.3
   (D) 0.5
   (E) 2.8

Algebra First-degree equations

Work the problem to solve for x.

$$\frac{1.5}{0.2+x} = 5$$

$1.5 = 1 + 5x$ multiply both sides by 0.2 + x

$0.5 = 5x$ subtract 1 from both sides

$0.1 = x$ divide both sides by 5

The correct answer is B.

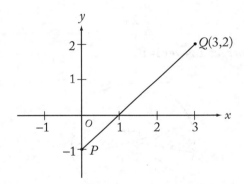

39. In the figure above, the point on segment PQ that is twice as far from P as from Q is

   (A) (3,1)
   (B) (2,1)
   (C) (2,−1)
   (D) (1.5,0.5)
   (E) (1,0)

Geometry Coordinate geometry

On a segment, a point that is twice as far from one end as the other is $\dfrac{1}{3}$ the distance from one end. The points (0,–1), (1,0), (2,1), and (3,2) are on segment PQ, and they divide the segment into three intervals of equal length as shown in the figure below.

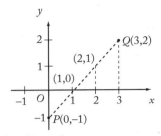

Note that the point (2,1) is twice as far from $P(0,-1)$ as from $Q(3,2)$ and also that it is $\frac{1}{3}$ the distance from Q.

The correct answer is B.

40. If n is an integer, which of the following must be even?

(A) $n + 1$
(B) $n + 2$
(C) $2n$
(D) $2n + 1$
(E) n^2

Arithmetic Properties of integers

A quick look at the answer choices reveals the expression $2n$ in answer choice C. $2n$ is a multiple of 2 and hence must be even.

Since only one answer choice can be correct, the other answer choices need not be checked. However, for completeness:

A $n + 1$ is odd if n is even and even if n is odd. Therefore, it is not true that $n + 1$ must be even.

B $n + 2$ is even if n is even and odd if n is odd. Therefore, it is not true that $n + 2$ must be even.

D $2n + 1$ is odd whether n is even or odd. Therefore, it is not true that $2n + 1$ must be even.

E n^2 is even if n is even and odd if n is odd. Therefore, it is not true that n^2 must be even.

The correct answer is C.

41. If 4 is one solution of the equation $x^2 + 3x + k = 10$, where k is a constant, what is the other solution?

(A) –7
(B) –4
(C) –3
(D) 1
(E) 6

Algebra Second-degree equations

If 4 is one solution of the equation, then substitute 4 for x and solve for k.

$$x^2 + 3x + k = 10$$
$$(4)^2 + 3(4) + k = 10$$
$$16 + 12 + k = 10$$
$$28 + k = 10$$
$$k = -18$$

Then, substitute –18 for k and solve for x.

$$x^2 + 3x - 18 = 10$$
$$x^2 + 3x - 28 = 0$$
$$(x + 7)(x - 4) = 0$$
$$x = -7, x = 4$$

The correct answer is A.

42. If $\begin{vmatrix} a & b \\ c & d \end{vmatrix} = ad - bc$ for all numbers a, b, c, and d, then $\begin{vmatrix} 3 & 5 \\ -2 & 4 \end{vmatrix} =$

(A) –22
(B) –2
(C) 2
(D) 7
(E) 22

Algebra Simplifying algebraic expressions

Using the given pattern, with $a = 3$, $b = 5$, $c = -2$, and $d = 4$, gives $\begin{vmatrix} 3 & 5 \\ -2 & 4 \end{vmatrix} = (3)(4) - (5)(-2) = 12 + 10 = 22$.

The correct answer is E.

(A)   45.5%
(B)   46.5%
(C)   48.0%
(D)   49.5%
(E)   51.0%

Arithmetic Percents

The total number of seeds that germinated was $200(0.57) + 300(0.42) = 114 + 126 = 240$. Because this was out of 500 seeds planted, the percent of the total planted that germinated was $\frac{240}{500} = 0.48$, or 48.0%.

The correct answer is C.

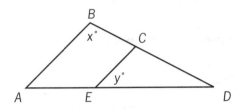

Note: Figure not drawn to scale.

48.   In the figure above, if $\overline{AB} \parallel \overline{CE}$, $CE = DE$, and $y = 45$, then $x =$

(A)   45
(B)   60
(C)   67.5
(D)   112.5
(E)   135

Geometry Angle measure in degrees; Triangles

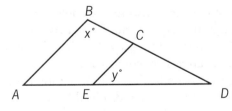

Note: Figure not drawn to scale.

Since $\overline{AB} \parallel \overline{CE}$, $\angle B$ and $\angle ECD$ are corresponding angles and, therefore, have the same measure. Since $CE = DE$, $\triangle CED$ is isosceles so $\angle D$ and $\angle ECD$ have the same measure. The

angles of $\triangle CED$ have degree measures x, x, and y, so $2x + y = 180$. Since $y = 45$,

$$2x + y = 180$$
$$2x + 45 = 180$$
$$2x = 135$$
$$x = 67.5$$

The correct answer is C.

49.   How many integers n are there such that $1 < 5n + 5 < 25$?

(A)   Five
(B)   Four
(C)   Three
(D)   Two
(E)   One

Algebra Inequalities

Isolate the variable in the inequalities to determine the range within which n lies.

$1 < 5n + 5 < 25$

$-4 < 5n < 20$ subtract 5 from all three values

$-\dfrac{4}{5} < n < 4$ divide all three values by 5

There are four integers between $-\dfrac{4}{5}$ and 4, namely 0, 1, 2, and 3.

The correct answer is B.

50.   If y is an integer, then the least possible value of $|23 - 5y|$ is

(A)   1
(B)   2
(C)   3
(D)   4
(E)   5

Arithmetic Absolute value; Operations with integers

Since y is an integer, $23 - 5y$ is also an integer. The task is to find the integer y for which $|23 - 5y|$ is the least. If $y \geq 0$, $-5y \leq 0$, and

$23 - 5y \le 23$. On the other hand, if $y \le 0$, $-5y \ge 0$, and $23 - 5y \ge 23$. Therefore, the least possible value of $|23 - 5y|$ occurs at a nonnegative value of y. From the chart below, it is clear that the least possible integer value of $|23 - 5y|$ is 2, which occurs when $y = 5$.

y	$|23 - 5y|$
0	23
1	18
2	13
3	8
4	3
5	2
6	7
7	12

Alternatively, since $|23 - 5y| \ge 0$, the minimum possible real value of $|23 - 5y|$ is 0. The integer value of y for which $|23 - 5y|$ is least is the integer closest to the solution of the equation $23 - 5y = 0$. The solution is $y = \dfrac{23}{5} = 4.6$ and the integer closest to 4.6 is 5.

The correct answer is B.

51. $\left(\sqrt{7} + \sqrt{7}\right)^{2} =$

(A) 98
(B) 49
(C) 28
(D) 21
(E) 14

Arithmetic Operations with radical expressions

Simplify the expression.

$$\left(\sqrt{7} + \sqrt{7}\right)^{2} = \left(2\sqrt{7}\right)^{2} = \left(2\right)^{2} \times \left(\sqrt{7}\right)^{2} =$$

$4 \times 7 = 28$

The correct answer is C.

52. In a certain population, there are 3 times as many people aged 21 or under as there are people over 21. The ratio of those 21 or under to the total population is

(A) 1 to 2
(B) 1 to 3
(C) 1 to 4
(D) 2 to 3
(E) 3 to 4

Algebra Applied problems

Let x represent the people over 21. Then $3x$ represents the number of people 21 or under, and $x + 3x = 4x$ represents the total population. Thus, the ratio of those 21 or under to the total population is $\dfrac{3x}{4x} = \dfrac{3}{4}$, or 3 to 4.

The correct answer is E.

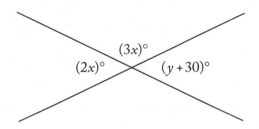

53. In the figure above, the value of y is

(A) 6
(B) 12
(C) 24
(D) 36
(E) 42

Geometry Angle measure in degrees

The sum of the measures of angles that form a straight line equals 180. From this, $2x + 3x = 180$ so $5x = 180$ and thus $x = 36$. Then, because vertical angles are congruent, their measures in degrees are equal. This can be expressed in the following equation and solved for y:

$2x = y + 30$	
$2(36) = y + 30$	substitute 36 for x
$72 = y + 30$	simplify
$42 = y$	subtract 30 from both sides

The correct answer is E.

54. $\sqrt{80} + \sqrt{125} =$

    (A) $9\sqrt{5}$

    (B) $20\sqrt{5}$

    (C) $41\sqrt{5}$

    (D) $\sqrt{205}$

    (E) 100

Arithmetic Operations with radical expressions

Rewrite each radical in the form $a\sqrt{b}$, where a and b are positive integers and b is as small as possible, and then add.

$$\begin{aligned}
\sqrt{80} + \sqrt{125} &= \sqrt{16(5)} + \sqrt{25(5)} \\
&= \left(\sqrt{16}\right)\left(\sqrt{5}\right) + \left(\sqrt{25}\right)\left(\sqrt{5}\right) \\
&= 4\sqrt{5} + 5\sqrt{5} \\
&= 9\sqrt{5}
\end{aligned}$$

The correct answer is A.

55. Kelly and Chris packed several boxes with books. If Chris packed 60 percent of the total number of boxes, what was the ratio of the number of boxes Kelly packed to the number of boxes Chris packed?

    (A) 1 to 6

    (B) 1 to 4

    (C) 2 to 5

    (D) 3 to 5

    (E) 2 to 3

Arithmetic Percents

If Chris packed 60 percent of the boxes, then Kelly packed $100 - 60 = 40$ percent of the boxes. The ratio of the number of boxes Kelly packed to the number Chris packed is $\dfrac{40\%}{60\%} = \dfrac{2}{3}$.

The correct answer is E.

56. Of the following, which is the closest approximation of $\dfrac{50.2 \times 0.49}{199.8}$?

    (A) $\dfrac{1}{10}$

    (B) $\dfrac{1}{8}$

    (C) $\dfrac{1}{4}$

    (D) $\dfrac{5}{4}$

    (E) $\dfrac{25}{2}$

Arithmetic Estimation

Simplify the expression using approximations.

$$\frac{50.2 \times 0.49}{199.8} \approx \frac{50 \times 0.5}{200} = \frac{25}{200} = \frac{1}{8}$$

The correct answer is B.

57. The average (arithmetic mean) of 10, 30, and 50 is 5 more than the average of 20, 40, and

    (A) 15

    (B) 25

    (C) 35

    (D) 45

    (E) 55

Arithmetic Statistics

Using the formula $\dfrac{\text{sum of } n \text{ values}}{n} = \text{average}$, the given information about the first set of numbers can be expressed in the equation $\dfrac{10 + 30 + 50}{3} = 30$. From the given information then, the average of the second set of numbers is $30 - 5 = 25$. Letting x represent the missing number, set up the equation for calculating the average for the second set of numbers, and solve for x.

$$\frac{20 + 40 + x}{3} = 25$$

$$\frac{60 + x}{3} = 25 \qquad \text{simplify}$$

$$60 + x = 75 \qquad \text{multiply both sides by 3}$$

$$x = 15 \qquad \text{subtract 60 from both sides}$$

The correct answer is A.

$$y = kx + 3$$

58. In the equation above, k is a constant. If $y = 17$ when $x = 2$, what is the value of y when $x = 4$?

(A)   34
(B)   31
(C)   14
(D)   11
(E)   7

Algebra First-degree equations

If $y = kx + 3$ and $y = 17$ when $x = 2$, then

$$17 = 2k + 3$$

$$14 = 2k$$

$$7 = k$$

Therefore, $y = 7x + 3$. When $x = 4$, $y = 7(4) + 3 = 31$.

The correct answer is B.

59. Each week, Harry is paid x dollars per hour for the first 30 hours and 1.5x dollars for each additional hour worked that week. Each week, James is paid x dollars per hour for the first 40 hours and 2x dollars for each additional hour worked that week. Last week James worked a total of 41 hours. If Harry and James were paid the same amount last week, how many hours did Harry work last week?

(A)   35
(B)   36
(C)   37
(D)   38
(E)   39

Algebra Systems of equations

Harry's pay, H, is given by

$$H = \begin{cases} xh \text{ for } h \le 30 \\ 30x + 1.5x\left(h - 30\right) \text{ for } h > 30 \end{cases}$$

and James's pay, J, is given by

$$J = \begin{cases} xh \text{ for } h \le 40 \\ 40x + 2x\left(h - 40\right) \text{ for } h > 40 \end{cases}$$

James worked 41 hours, for which his pay was $40x + 2x(41 - 40) = 42x$. Harry was paid the same amount as James, so Harry's pay was also $42x$. Thus,

$$42x = 30x + 1.5x(h - 30)$$

$$12x = 1.5x(h - 30)$$

$$8 = h - 30$$

$$38 = h$$

The correct answer is D.

60. A glass was filled with 10 ounces of water, and 0.01 ounce of the water evaporated each day during a 20-day period. What percent of the original amount of water evaporated during this period?

(A)   0.002%
(B)   0.02%
(C)   0.2%
(D)   2%
(E)   20%

Arithmetic Percents

Since 0.01 ounce of water evaporated each day for 20 days, a total of 20(0.01) = 0.2 ounce evaporated. Then, to find the percent of the original amount of water that evaporated, divide the amount that evaporated by the original amount and multiply by 100 to convert the decimal to a percent. Thus, $\frac{0.2}{10} \times 100 =$ 0.02 × 100 or 2%.

The correct answer is D.

61. A glucose solution contains 15 grams of glucose per 100 cubic centimeters of solution. If 45 cubic centimeters of the solution were poured into an empty container, how many grams of glucose would be in the container?

    (A) 3.00
    (B) 5.00
    (C) 5.50
    (D) 6.50
    (E) 6.75

Algebra Applied problems

Let x be the number of grams of glucose in the 45 cubic centimeters of solution. The proportion comparing the glucose in the 45 cubic centimeters to the given information about the 15 grams of glucose in the entire 100 cubic centimeters of solution can be expressed as $\dfrac{x}{45} = \dfrac{15}{100}$, and thus $100x = 675$ or $x = 6.75$.

The correct answer is E.

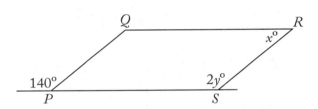

62. In the figure above, if $PQRS$ is a parallelogram, then $y - x =$

    (A)   30
    (B)   35
    (C)   40
    (D)   70
    (E)   100

Geometry Polygons

Since $PQRS$ is a parallelogram, the following must be true:

$140 = 2y$ corresponding angles are congruent

$2y + x = 180$ consecutive angles are supplementary (sum = 180°)

Solving the first equation for y gives $y = 70$. Substituting this into the second equation gives

$$2(70) + x = 180$$
$$140 + x = 180$$
$$x = 40$$

Thus, $y - x = 70 - 40 = 30$.

The correct answer is A.

63. If 1 kilometer is approximately 0.6 mile, which of the following best approximates the number of kilometers in 2 miles?

    (A) $\dfrac{10}{3}$

    (B) 3

    (C) $\dfrac{6}{5}$

    (D) $\dfrac{1}{3}$

    (E) $\dfrac{3}{10}$

Arithmetic Applied problems

Since 1 km ≈ 0.6 mi = $\dfrac{3}{5}$ mi, divide to find that $\left(1 \div \dfrac{3}{5}\right)$ km ≈ 1 mi, or $\dfrac{5}{3}$ km ≈ 1 mi. Therefore, $2\left(\dfrac{5}{3}\right)$ km ≈ 2 mi, or $\dfrac{10}{3}$ km ≈ 2 mi.

The correct answer is A.

64. Lucy invested $10,000 in a new mutual fund account exactly three years ago. The value of the account increased by 10 percent during the first year, increased by 5 percent during the second year, and decreased by 10 percent during the third year. What is the value of the account today?

    (A) $10,350
    (B) $10,395
    (C) $10,500
    (D) $11,500
    (E) $12,705

Arithmetic Percents

The first year's increase of 10 percent can be expressed as 1.10; the second year's increase of 5 percent can be expressed as 1.05; and the third year's decrease of 10 percent can be expressed as 0.90. Multiply the original value of the account by each of these yearly changes.

$$10,000(1.10)(1.05)(0.90) = 10,395$$

The correct answer is B.

65. A certain fruit stand sold apples for $0.70 each and bananas for $0.50 each. If a customer purchased both apples and bananas from the stand for a total of $6.30, what total number of apples and bananas did the customer purchase?

(A) 10
(B) 11
(C) 12
(D) 13
(E) 14

Algebra First-degree equations; Operations with integers

If each apple sold for $0.70, each banana sold for $0.50, and the total purchase price was $6.30, then $0.70x + 0.50y = 6.30$, where x and y are positive integers representing the number of apples and bananas, respectively, the customer purchased.

$$0.70x + 0.50y = 6.30$$

$$0.50y = 6.30 - 0.70x$$

$$0.50y = 0.70(9 - x)$$

$$y = \frac{7}{5}(9 - x)$$

Since y must be an integer, $9 - x$ must be divisible by 5. Furthermore, both x and y must be positive integers. For $x = 1, 2, 3, 4, 5, 6, 7, 8$, the corresponding values of $9 - x$ are 8, 7, 6, 5, 4, 3, 2, and 1. Only one of these, 5, is divisible by 5. Therefore, $x = 4$ and $y = \frac{7}{5}(9 - 4) = 7$ and the total number of apples and bananas the customer purchased is $4 + 7 = 11$.

The correct answer is B.

66. At a certain school, the ratio of the number of second graders to the number of fourth graders is 8 to 5, and the ratio of the number of first graders to the number of second graders is 3 to 4. If the ratio of the number of third graders to the number of fourth graders is 3 to 2, what is the ratio of the number of first graders to the number of third graders?

(A) 16 to 15
(B) 9 to 5
(C) 5 to 16
(D) 5 to 4
(E) 4 to 5

Arithmetic Ratio and proportion

If F, S, T, and R represent the number of first, second, third, and fourth graders, respectively, then the given ratios are: (i) $\frac{S}{R} = \frac{8}{5}$, (ii) $\frac{F}{S} = \frac{3}{4}$, and (iii) $\frac{T}{R} = \frac{3}{2}$. The desired ratio is $\frac{F}{T}$. From (i), $S = \frac{8}{5}R$, and from (ii), $F = \frac{3}{4}S$. Combining these results, $F = \frac{3}{4}S = \frac{3}{4}\left(\frac{8}{5}R\right) = \frac{6}{5}R$. From (iii), $T = \frac{3}{2}R$. Then $\frac{F}{T} = \frac{\frac{6}{5}R}{\frac{3}{2}R} = \frac{6}{5} \cdot \frac{2}{3} = \frac{4}{5}$. So, the ratio of the number of first graders to the number of third graders is 4 to 5.

The correct answer is E.

$$A = \{2, 3, 4, 5\}$$
$$B = \{4, 5, 6, 7, 8\}$$

67. Two integers will be randomly selected from the sets above, one integer from set A and one integer from set B. What is the probability that the sum of the two integers will equal 9 ?

(A) 0.15
(B) 0.20
(C) 0.25
(D) 0.30
(E) 0.33

Arithmetic; Algebra Probability;
Concepts of sets

The total number of different pairs of numbers, one from set A and one from set B is $(4)(5) = 20$. Of these 20 pairs of numbers, there are 4 possible pairs that sum to 9: 2 and 7, 3 and 6, 4 and 5, and 5 and 4. Thus, the probability that the sum of the two integers will be 9 is equal to $\frac{4}{20} = 0.20$.

The correct answer is B.

68. At a certain instant in time, the number of cars, N, traveling on a portion of a certain highway can be estimated by the formula

$$N = \frac{20Ld}{600 + s^2}$$

where L is the number of lanes in the same direction, d is the length of the portion of the highway, in feet, and s is the average speed of the cars, in miles per hour. Based on the formula, what is the estimated number of cars traveling on a $\frac{1}{2}$-mile portion of the highway if the highway has 2 lanes in the same direction and the average speed of the cars is 40 miles per hour? (5,280 feet = 1 mile)

(A)   155
(B)   96
(C)   80
(D)   48
(E)   24

Algebra Simplifying algebraic expressions

Substitute $L = 2$, $d = \frac{1}{2}(5,280)$, and $s = 40$ into the given formula and calculate the value for N.

$$N = \frac{20(2)\left(\frac{1}{2}\right)(5,280)}{600 + 40^2}$$

$$= \frac{20(5,280)}{600 + 1,600}$$

$$= \frac{20(5,280)}{2,200}$$

$$= \frac{2(528)}{22}$$

$$= \frac{528}{11}$$

$$= 48$$

The correct answer is D.

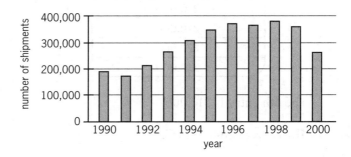

NUMBER OF SHIPMENTS OF MANUFACTURED HOMES
IN THE UNITED STATES, 1990–2000

69. According to the chart shown, which of the following is closest to the median annual number of shipments of manufactured homes in the United States for the years from 1990 to 2000, inclusive?

(A)   250,000
(B)   280,000
(C)   310,000
(D)   325,000
(E)   340,000

Arithmetic Interpretation of graphs and tables; Statistics

From the chart, the approximate numbers of shipments are as follows:

Year	Number of shipments
1990	190,000
1991	180,000
1992	210,000
1993	270,000
1994	310,000
1995	350,000
1996	380,000
1997	370,000
1998	390,000
1999	360,000
2000	270,000

Since there are 11 entries in the table and 11 is an odd number, the median of the numbers of shipments is the 6th entry when the numbers of shipments are arranged in order from least to greatest. In order, from least to greatest, the first 6 entries are:

Number of shipments
180,000
190,000
210,000
270,000
270,000
310,000

The 6th entry is 310,000.

The correct answer is C.

70. If $y\left(\dfrac{3x-5}{2}\right) = y$ and $y \neq 0$, then $x =$

(A) $\dfrac{2}{3}$

(B) $\dfrac{5}{3}$

(C) $\dfrac{7}{3}$

(D) 1

(E) 4

Algebra First-degree equations

Since $y \neq 0$, it is possible to simplify this equation and solve for x as follows:

$$y\left(\frac{3x-5}{2}\right) = y$$

$\dfrac{3x-5}{2} = 1$ divide both sides by y

$3x - 5 = 2$ multiply both sides by 2

$3x = 7$ solve for x

$x = \dfrac{7}{3}$

The correct answer is C.

71. If $x + 5 > 2$ and $x - 3 < 7$, the value of x must be between which of the following pairs of numbers?

(A) −3 and 10
(B) −3 and 4
(C) 2 and 7
(D) 3 and 4
(E) 3 and 10

Algebra Inequalities

Isolate x in each given inequality. Since $x + 5 > 2$, then $x > -3$. Since $x - 3 < 7$, then $x < 10$. Thus, $-3 < x < 10$, which means the value of x must be between −3 and 10.

The correct answer is A.

72. A gym class can be divided into 8 teams with an equal number of players on each team or into 12 teams with an equal number of players on each team. What is the lowest possible number of students in the class?

(A) 20
(B) 24
(C) 36
(D) 48
(E) 96

Arithmetic Properties of numbers

The lowest value that can be divided evenly by 8 and 12 is their least common multiple (LCM). Since $8 = 2^3$ and $12 = 2^2(3)$, the LCM is $2^3(3) = 24$.

The correct answer is B.

73. If $r = 0.345$, $s = (0.345)^2$, and $t = \sqrt{0.345}$, which of the following is the correct ordering of r, s, and t?

(A) $r < s < t$
(B) $r < t < s$
(C) $s < t < r$
(D) $s < r < t$
(E) $t < r < s$

Arithmetic Order

Given that $r = 0.345$, $s = (0.345)^2$, and $t = \sqrt{0.345}$, s and t can be expressed in terms of r as r^2 and $r^{\frac{1}{2}}$, respectively. Because $0 < r < 1$, the value of

r^x decreases as x increases. For example, $1 < 2$, but $\frac{1}{4} > \left(\frac{1}{4}\right)^2$. Therefore, since $\frac{1}{2} < 1 < 2$, $r^{\frac{1}{2}} > r > r^2$, and so $t > r > s$ or $s < r < t$.

The correct answer is D.

74. A total of n trucks and cars are parked in a lot. If the number of cars is $\frac{1}{4}$ the number of trucks, and $\frac{2}{3}$ of the trucks are pickups, how many pickups, in terms of n, are parked in the lot?

(A) $\frac{1}{6}n$

(B) $\frac{5}{12}n$

(C) $\frac{1}{2}n$

(D) $\frac{8}{15}n$

(E) $\frac{11}{12}n$

Algebra Simplifying algebraic expressions

It is given that n is the number of trucks and cars parked in the lot and the number of cars is $\frac{1}{4}$ the number of trucks, so if t represents the number of trucks and c represents the number of cars, $n = c + t$ and $c = \frac{1}{4}t$. Combining these two equations gives $n = \frac{1}{4}t + t = \frac{5}{4}t$. If p represents the number of pickups parked in the lot, then $p = \frac{2}{3}t$. Since $n = \frac{5}{4}t$, or equivalently $t = \frac{4}{5}n$, then $p = \frac{2}{3}t = \frac{2}{3}\left(\frac{4}{5}n\right) = \frac{8}{15}n$.

The correct answer is D.

75. At least $\frac{2}{3}$ of the 40 members of a committee must vote in favor of a resolution for it to pass. What is the greatest number of members who could vote against the resolution and still have it pass?

(A) 19
(B) 17
(C) 16
(D) 14
(E) 13

Arithmetic Operations on rational numbers

If at least $\frac{2}{3}$ of the members must vote in favor of a resolution, then no more than $\frac{1}{3}$ of the members can be voting against it. On this 40-member committee, $\frac{1}{3}(40) = 13\frac{1}{3}$, which means that no more than 13 members can vote against the resolution and still have it pass.

The correct answer is E.

76. In the Johnsons' monthly budget, the dollar amounts allocated to household expenses, food, and miscellaneous items are in the ratio 5:2:1, respectively. If the total amount allocated to these three categories is $1,800, what is the amount allocated to food?

(A) $900
(B) $720
(C) $675
(D) $450
(E) $225

Algebra Applied problems

Since the ratio is 5:2:1, let $5x$ be the money allocated to household expenses, $2x$ be the money allocated to food, and $1x$ be the money allocated to miscellaneous items. The given information can then be expressed in the following equation and solved for x.

$5x + 2x + 1x = \$1,800$

$8x = \$1,800$ combine like terms

$x = \$225$ divide both sides by 8

The money allocated to food is $2x = 2(\$225) = \$450$.

The correct answer is D.

77. There are 4 more women than men on Centerville's board of education. If there are 10 members on the board, how many are women?

(A)   3
(B)   4
(C)   6
(D)   7
(E)   8

Algebra Simultaneous equations; Applied problems

Let m be the number of men on the board and w be the number of women on the board. According to the problem,

$w = m + 4$ because there are 4 more women than men and

$w + m = 10$ because the board has a total of 10 members.

Substituting $m + 4$ for w in the second equation gives:

$m + m + 4 = 10$

$2m + 4 = 10$ combine like terms

$2m = 6$ subtract 4 from both sides

$m = 3$ divide both sides by 2

Using the first equation, $w = m + 4 = 3 + 4 = 7$ women on the board.

This problem can also be solved without algebra by listing the (m,w) possibilities for $w = m + 4$. These possibilities are $(0,4), (1,5), (2,6), (3,7)$, etc., and hence the pair in which $m + w = 10$ is $(3,7)$.

The correct answer is D.

78. Leona bought a 1-year, $10,000 certificate of deposit that paid interest at an annual rate of 8 percent compounded semiannually. What was the total amount of interest paid on this certificate at maturity?

(A) $10,464
(B) $ 864
(C) $ 816
(D) $ 800
(E) $ 480

Arithmetic Operations with rational numbers

Using the formula $A = P(1 + \frac{r}{n})^{nt}$, where A is the amount of money after t (1 year), P is the principal amount invested ($10,000), r is the annual interest rate (0.08), and n is the number of times compounding occurs annually (2), the given information can be expressed as follows and solved for A:

$A = (10,000)\left(1 + \frac{0.08}{2}\right)^{(2)(1)}$

$A = (10,000)(1.04)^2$

$A = (10,000)(1.0816)$

$A = 10,816$

Thus, since A is the final value of the certificate, the amount of interest paid at maturity is $10,816 - $10,000 = $816.

The correct answer is C.

79. $\dfrac{(0.0036)(2.8)}{(0.04)(0.1)(0.003)} =$

(A)   840.0
(B)   84.0
(C)   8.4
(D)   0.84
(E)   0.084

Arithmetic Operations with rational numbers

To make the calculations less tedious, convert the decimals to whole numbers times powers of 10 as follows:

$\dfrac{(0.0036)(2.8)}{(0.04)(0.1)(0.003)}$

$= \dfrac{(36 \times 10^{-4})(28 \times 10^{-1})}{(4 \times 10^{-2})(1 \times 10^{-1})(3 \times 10^{-3})}$

$= \dfrac{(36)(28)}{(4)(1)(3)} \times 10^{(-4-1)-(-2-1-3)}$

$= \dfrac{(36)(28)}{(4)(1)(3)} \times 10^{-5-(-6)}$

$$= \frac{(36)(28)}{(4)(1)(3)} \times 10^{-5+6}$$

$$= \left(\frac{36}{3}\right)\left(\frac{28}{4}\right) \times 10^{-5+6}$$

$$= (12)(7) \times 10^1$$

$$= 84 \times 10$$

$$= 840$$

The correct answer is A.

80. Machine A produces bolts at a uniform rate of 120 every 40 seconds, and Machine B produces bolts at a uniform rate of 100 every 20 seconds. If the two machines run simultaneously, how many seconds will it take for them to produce a total of 200 bolts?

(A) 22
(B) 25
(C) 28
(D) 32
(E) 56

Algebra Applied problems

Determine the production rates for each machine separately, and then calculate their production rate together.

$$\text{Rate of Machine A} = \frac{120}{40} = 3 \text{ bolts per second}$$

$$\text{Rate of Machine B} = \frac{100}{20} = 5 \text{ bolts per second}$$

Combined rate = 3 + 5 = 8 bolts per second

Build an equation with s = the number of seconds it takes to produce 200 bolts.

$8s = 200$ (rate)(time) = amount produced

$s = 25$ solve for s

The correct answer is B.

Amount of Bacteria Present	
Time	Amount
1:00 P.M.	10.0 grams
4:00 P.M.	x grams
7:00 P.M.	14.4 grams

81. Data for a certain biology experiment are given in the table above. If the amount of bacteria present increased by the same factor during each of the two 3-hour periods shown, how many grams of bacteria were present at 4:00 P.M. ?

(A) 12.0
(B) 12.1
(C) 12.2
(D) 12.3
(E) 12.4

Arithmetic Operations with rational numbers; Second-degree equations

Let f be the factor by which the amount of bacteria present increased every 3 hours. Then, from the table, $10.0f = x$ and $xf = 14.4$. Substituting $10.0f$ for x in the second equation gives

$$(10.0f)f = 14.4$$

$$10.0f^2 = 14.4$$

$$f^2 = 1.44$$

$$f = 1.2$$

and then $x = 10.0(1.2) = 12.0$.

The correct answer is A.

82. If n is an integer greater than 6, which of the following must be divisible by 3 ?

(A) $n(n + 1)(n - 4)$
(B) $n(n + 2)(n - 1)$
(C) $n(n + 3)(n - 5)$
(D) $n(n + 4)(n - 2)$
(E) $n(n + 5)(n - 6)$

Arithmetic Properties of numbers

The easiest and quickest way to do this problem is to choose an integer greater than 6, such as 7, and eliminate answer choices in which the value of the expression is not divisible by 3:

A $7(7 + 1)(7 - 4) = (7)(8)(3)$, which is divisible by 3, so A cannot be eliminated.

B $7(7 + 2)(7 - 1) = (7)(9)(6)$, which is divisible by 3, so B cannot be eliminated.

C $7(7 + 3)(7 - 5) = (7)(10)(2)$, which is not divisible by 3, so C can be eliminated.

D $7(7 + 4)(7 - 2) = (7)(11)(5)$, which is not divisible by 3, so D can be eliminated.

E $7(7 + 5)(7 - 6) = (7)(12)(1)$, which is divisible by 3, so E cannot be eliminated.

Choose another integer greater than 6, such as 8, and test the remaining answer choices:

A $8(8 + 1)(8 - 4) = (8)(9)(4)$, which is divisible by 3, so A cannot be eliminated.

B $8(8 + 2)(8 - 1) = (8)(10)(7)$, which is not divisible by 3, so B can be eliminated.

E $8(8 + 5)(8 - 6) = (8)(13)(2)$, which is not divisible by 3, so E can be eliminated.

Thus, A is the only answer choice that has not been eliminated.

For the more mathematically inclined, if n is divisible by 3, then the expression in each answer choice is divisible by 3. Assume, then, that n is not divisible by 3. If the remainder when n is divided by 3 is 1, then $n = 3q + 1$ for some integer q. All of the expressions $n - 4$, $n - 1$, $n + 2$, and $n + 5$ are divisible by 3 [i.e., $n - 4 = 3q - 3 = 3(q - 1)$, $n - 1 = 3q$, $n + 2 = 3q + 3 = 3(q + 1)$, $n + 5 = 3q + 6 = 3(q + 2)$], and none of the expressions $n - 6$, $n - 5$, $n - 2$, $n + 1$, $n + 3$, and $n + 4$ is divisible by 3. Therefore, if the remainder when n is divided by 3 is 1, only the expressions in answer choices A, B, and E are divisible by 3. On the other hand, if the remainder when n is divided by 3 is 2, then $n = 3q + 2$ for some integer q. All of the expressions $n - 5$, $n - 2$, $n + 1$, and $n + 4$ are divisible by 3 [i.e., $n - 5 = 3q - 3 = 3(q - 1)$, $n - 2 = 3q$, $n + 1 = 3q + 3 = 3(q + 1)$, $n + 4 = 3q + 6 = 3(q + 2)$], and none of the expressions $n - 6$, $n - 4$, $n - 1$, $n + 2$, $n + 3$, and $n + 5$ is divisible by 3. Therefore, if the remainder when n is divided by 3 is 2, only the expressions in answer choices A, C, and D are divisible by 3.

Only the expression in answer choice A is divisible by 3 regardless of whether n is divisible by 3, has a remainder of 1 when divided by 3, or has a remainder of 2 when divided by 3.

The correct answer is A.

83. The total cost for Company X to produce a batch of tools is $10,000 plus $3 per tool. Each tool sells for $8. The gross profit earned from producing and selling these tools is the total income from sales minus the total production cost. If a batch of 20,000 tools is produced and sold, then Company X's gross profit per tool is

(A) $3.00
(B) $3.75
(C) $4.50
(D) $5.00
(E) $5.50

Arithmetic Applied problems

The total cost to produce 20,000 tools is $10,000 + \$3(20,000) = \$70,000$. The revenue resulting from the sale of 20,000 tools is $\$8(20,000) = \$160,000$. The gross profit is $\$160,000 - \$70,000 = \$90,000$, and the gross profit per tool is $\dfrac{\$90,000}{20,000} = \$4.50$.

The correct answer is C.

84. A dealer originally bought 100 identical batteries at a total cost of q dollars. If each battery was sold at 50 percent above the original cost per battery, then, in terms of q, for how many dollars was each battery sold?

(A) $\dfrac{3q}{200}$

(B) $\dfrac{3q}{2}$

(C) $150q$

(D) $\dfrac{q}{100} + 50$

(E) $\dfrac{150}{q}$

Algebra Factoring and Simplifying algebraic expressions

Since 100 batteries cost q dollars, division by 100 shows that 1 battery costs $\frac{q}{100}$ dollars. Then, since the selling price is 50 percent above the original cost per battery, the selling price of each battery can be expressed as $\frac{q}{100}(1.50) = \frac{q}{100}\left(\frac{3}{2}\right) = \frac{3q}{200}$.

The correct answer is A.

85. In an increasing sequence of 10 consecutive integers, the sum of the first 5 integers is 560. What is the sum of the last 5 integers in the sequence?

   (A) 585
   (B) 580
   (C) 575
   (D) 570
   (E) 565

Algebra First-degree equations

Let the first 5 consecutive integers be represented by x, $x + 1$, $x + 2$, $x + 3$, and $x + 4$. Then, since the sum of the integers is 560, $x + (x + 1) + (x + 2) + (x + 3) + (x + 4) = 560$. Thus,

$5x + 10 = 560$

$5x = 550$ solve for x

$x = 110$

The first integer in the sequence is 110, so the next integers are 111, 112, 113, and 114. From this, the last 5 integers in the sequence, and thus their sum, can be determined. The sum of the 6th, 7th, 8th, 9th, and 10th integers is $115 + 116 + 117 + 118 + 119 = 585$.

This problem can also be solved without algebra: The sum of the last 5 integers exceeds the sum of the first 5 integers by $1 + 3 + 5 + 7 + 9 = 25$ because the 6th integer exceeds the 5th integer by 1, the 7th integer exceeds the 4th integer by 3, etc.

The correct answer is A.

86. Machine A produces 100 parts twice as fast as Machine B does. Machine B produces 100 parts in 40 minutes. If each machine produces parts at a constant rate, how many parts does Machine A produce in 6 minutes?

   (A) 30
   (B) 25
   (C) 20
   (D) 15
   (E) 7.5

Arithmetic Operations on rational numbers

If Machine A produces the parts twice as fast as Machine B does, then Machine A requires half as much time as Machine B does to produce 100 parts. So, if Machine B takes 40 minutes for the job, Machine A takes 20 minutes for the job. This is a rate of $\frac{100 \text{ parts}}{20 \text{ minutes}}$ = 5 parts per minute. At this rate, in 6 minutes Machine A will produce $5(6) = 30$ parts.

The correct answer is A.

87. A necklace is made by stringing N individual beads together in the repeating pattern red bead, green bead, white bead, blue bead, and yellow bead. If the necklace design begins with a red bead and ends with a white bead, then N could equal

   (A) 16
   (B) 32
   (C) 41
   (D) 54
   (E) 68

Algebra Applied problems

The bead pattern repeats after every fifth bead. Since the first bead in this design (or the first in the pattern) is red and the last bead in this design (or third in the pattern) is white, the number of beads in this design is 3 more than some multiple of 5. This can be expressed as $5n + 3$, where n is an integer. Test each of the answer choices to determine which is a multiple of 5 plus a value of 3. Of the options, only $68 = 5(13) + 3$ can be written in the form $5n + 3$.

The correct answer is E.

88. In the xy-coordinate system, if (a,b) and (a + 3,b + k) are two points on the line defined by the equation x = 3y – 7, then k =

    (A) 9

    (B) 3

    (C) $\dfrac{7}{3}$

    (D) 1

    (E) $\dfrac{1}{3}$

Geometry Simple coordinate geometry

Substituting the given coordinates for x and y in the equation $x = 3y - 7$ yields

$$a = 3b - 7$$

$$a + 3 = 3(b + k) - 7$$

Then substitute $3b - 7$ for a in second equation, and solve for k

$$3b - 7 + 3 = 3b + 3k - 7$$

$3b - 4 = 3b + 3k - 7$ combine like terms

$3 = 3k$ subtract $3b$ from and add 7 to both sides

$1 = k$ divide both sides by 3

The correct answer is D.

89. If s is the product of the integers from 100 to 200, inclusive, and t is the product of the integers from 100 to 201, inclusive, what is $\dfrac{1}{s} + \dfrac{1}{t}$ in terms of t?

    (A) $\dfrac{(201)^2}{t}$

    (B) $\dfrac{(202)(201)}{t}$

    (C) $\dfrac{201}{t}$

    (D) $\dfrac{202}{t}$

    (E) $\dfrac{(202)(201)}{t^2}$

Arithmetic Operations with rational numbers

Since $s = (100)(101)(102) \ldots (200)$ and $t = (100)(101)(102) \ldots (200)(201)$, $t = 201s$ or $s = \dfrac{t}{201}$. Then,

$$\frac{1}{s} + \frac{1}{t} = \frac{1}{\left(\dfrac{t}{201}\right)} + \frac{1}{t}$$

$$= \frac{201}{t} + \frac{1}{t}$$

$$= \frac{201 + 1}{t}$$

$$= \frac{202}{t}$$

The correct answer is D.

90. If Jake loses 8 pounds, he will weigh twice as much as his sister. Together they now weigh 278 pounds. What is Jake's present weight, in pounds?

    (A) 131
    (B) 135
    (C) 139
    (D) 147
    (E) 188

Algebra Systems of equations

Let J represent Jake's weight and S represent his sister's weight. Then $J - 8 = 2S$ and $J + S = 278$. Solve the second equation for S and get $S = 278 - J$. Substituting the expression for S into the first equation gives

$$J - 8 = 2(278 - J)$$

$$J - 8 = 556 - 2J$$

$$J + 2J = 556 + 8$$

$$3J = 564$$

$$J = 188$$

The correct answer is E.

91. A certain store sells all maps at one price and all books at another price. On Monday the store sold 12 maps and 10 books for a total of $38.00, and on Tuesday the store sold 20 maps and 15 books for a total of $60.00. At this store, how much less does a map sell for than a book?

   (A) $0.25
   (B) $0.50
   (C) $0.75
   (D) $1.00
   (E) $1.25

Algebra Systems of equations

Let m represent the price of each map and b represent the price of each book. Then the given information can be represented by the system $\begin{cases} 12m+10b=38 \\ 20m+15b=60 \end{cases}$. Multiplying the top equation by $-\dfrac{3}{2}$ gives $\begin{cases} -18m-15b=-57 \\ 20m+15b=60 \end{cases}$, and adding the two equations gives $2m = 3$ or $m = 1.5$.

Thus, each map sells for $1.50. Then,

$$12(1.50) + 10b = 38$$
$$18 + 10b = 38$$
$$10b = 20$$
$$b = 2$$

So, each book sells for $2.00 and each map sells for $1.50, which is $2.00 − $1.50 = $0.50 less than each book.

The correct answer is B.

92. A store reported total sales of $385 million for February of this year. If the total sales for the same month last year was $320 million, approximately what was the percent increase in sales?

   (A)   2%
   (B)   17%
   (C)   20%
   (D)   65%
   (E)   83%

Arithmetic Percents

The percent increase in sales from last year to this year is 100 times the quotient of the difference in sales for the two years divided by the sales last year. Thus, the percent increase is

$$\frac{385-320}{320} \times 100 = \frac{65}{320} \times 100$$

$$= \frac{13}{64} \times 100$$

$$\approx \frac{13}{65} \times 100$$

$$= \frac{1}{5} \times 100$$

$$= 20\%$$

The correct answer is C.

> List I: 3, 6, 8, 19
>
> List II: x, 3, 6, 8, 19

93. If the median of the numbers in list I above is equal to the median of the numbers in list II above, what is the value of x ?

   (A)   6
   (B)   7
   (C)   8
   (D)   9
   (E)   10

Arithmetic Statistics

Since list I has an even number of numbers, the median of list I is the average of the middle two numbers, so $\dfrac{6+8}{2}$ = 7 is the median of list I.
Since list II has an odd number of numbers, the median of list II will be the middle number when the five numbers are put in ascending order. Since the median of list II must be 7 (the median of list I) and since 7 is not in list II, then x = 7.

The correct answer is B.

94. In a certain city, 60 percent of the registered voters are Democrats and the rest are Republicans. In a mayoral race, if 75 percent of the registered voters who are Democrats and 20 percent of the registered voters who are Republicans are expected to vote for Candidate A, what percent of the registered voters are expected to vote for Candidate A ?

(A) 50%
(B) 53%
(C) 54%
(D) 55%
(E) 57%

Arithmetic; Algebra Percents;
Applied problems

Letting v be the number of registered voters in the city, then the information that 60% of the registered voters are Democrats can be expressed as $0.60v$. From this, it can be stated that $1.00v - 0.60v = 0.40v$ are Republicans. The percentage of Democrats and the percentage of Republicans who are expected to vote for Candidate A can then be expressed as $(0.75)(0.60v) + (0.20)(0.40v)$. Simplify the expression to determine the total percentage of voters expected to vote for Candidate A.

$(0.75)(0.60v) + (0.20)(0.40v)$

$= 0.45v + 0.08v$

$= 0.53v$

The correct answer is B.

95. $\dfrac{1}{2} + \left[\left(\dfrac{2}{3} \times \dfrac{3}{8} \right) \div 4 \right] - \dfrac{9}{16} =$

(A) $\dfrac{29}{16}$

(B) $\dfrac{19}{16}$

(C) $\dfrac{15}{16}$

(D) $\dfrac{9}{13}$

(E) 0

Arithmetic Operations on rational numbers

Perform the operations in the correct order, using least common denominators when adding or subtracting fractions:

$$\frac{1}{2} + \left[\left(\frac{2}{3} \times \frac{3}{8} \right) \div 4 \right] - \frac{9}{16} = \frac{1}{2} + \left[\left(\frac{\cancel{2}1}{\cancel{3}1} \times \frac{\cancel{3}1}{\cancel{8}4} \right) \div 4 \right] - \frac{9}{16}$$

$$= \frac{1}{2} + \left[\left(\frac{1}{4} \right) \div 4 \right] - \frac{9}{16}$$

$$= \frac{1}{2} + \frac{1}{16} - \frac{9}{16}$$

$$= \frac{8}{16} + \frac{1}{16} - \frac{9}{16}$$

$$= \frac{8 + 1 - 9}{16}$$

$$= \frac{0}{16}$$

$$= 0$$

The correct answer is E.

96. Water consists of hydrogen and oxygen, and the approximate ratio, by mass, of hydrogen to oxygen is 2:16. Approximately how many grams of oxygen are there in 144 grams of water?

(A) 16
(B) 72
(C) 112
(D) 128
(E) 142

Algebra Applied problems

The mass ratio of oxygen to water is $\dfrac{\text{oxygen}}{\text{oxygen + hydrogen}} = \dfrac{16}{16 + 2} = \dfrac{8}{9}$. Therefore, if x is the number of grams of oxygen in 144 grams of water, it follows that $\dfrac{x}{144} = \dfrac{8}{9}$. Now solve for x:

$$x = \frac{8}{9} \cdot \frac{144}{1} = \frac{(8)(\cancel{3})(4)(\cancel{3})(4)}{\cancel{9}} = (8)(4)(4) = 128.$$

The correct answer is D.

97. If $x(2x + 1) = 0$ and $\left(x + \dfrac{1}{2}\right)(2x - 3) = 0$, then $x =$

    (A) -3

    (B) $-\dfrac{1}{2}$

    (C) 0

    (D) $\dfrac{1}{2}$

    (E) $\dfrac{3}{2}$

Algebra Second-degree equations; Simultaneous equations

Setting each factor equal to 0, it can be seen that the solution set to the first equation is $\left\{0, -\dfrac{1}{2}\right\}$ and the solution set to the second equation is $\left\{-\dfrac{1}{2}, \dfrac{3}{2}\right\}$. Therefore, $-\dfrac{1}{2}$ is the solution to both equations.

The correct answer is B.

98. On a scale that measures the intensity of a certain phenomenon, a reading of $n + 1$ corresponds to an intensity that is 10 times the intensity corresponding to a reading of n. On that scale, the intensity corresponding to a reading of 8 is how many times as great as the intensity corresponding to a reading of 3 ?

    (A) 5
    (B) 50
    (C) 10^5
    (D) 5^{10}
    (E) $8^{10} - 3^{10}$

Arithmetic Operations on rational numbers

Since 8 can be obtained from 3 by "adding 1" five times, the intensity reading is greater by a factor of $(10)(10)(10)(10)(10) = 10^5$.

The correct answer is C.

99. For the positive numbers, n, $n + 1$, $n + 2$, $n + 4$, and $n + 8$, the mean is how much greater than the median?

    (A) 0
    (B) 1
    (C) $n + 1$
    (D) $n + 2$
    (E) $n + 3$

Algebra Statistics

Since the five positive numbers n, $n + 1$, $n + 2$, $n + 4$, and $n + 8$ are in ascending order, the median is the third number, which is $n + 2$. The mean of the five numbers is

$$\frac{n + (n+1) + (n+2) + (n+4) + (n+8)}{5}$$

$$= \frac{5n + 15}{5}$$

$$= n + 3$$

Since $(n + 3) - (n + 2) = 1$, the mean is 1 greater than the median.

The correct answer is B.

100. If $T = \dfrac{5}{9}(K - 32)$, and if $T = 290$, then $K =$

    (A) $\dfrac{1{,}738}{9}$

    (B) 322

    (C) 490

    (D) 554

    (E) $\dfrac{2{,}898}{5}$

Algebra First-degree equations

Substitute 290 for T in the equation, and solve for K.

$$T = \frac{5}{9}(K - 32)$$

$$290 = \frac{5}{9}(K - 32)$$

$$\frac{290}{1} \cdot \frac{9}{5} = K - 32$$

$$\frac{(29)(5)(2)}{1} \cdot \frac{9}{5} = K - 32$$

$$\frac{(29)(\cancel{5})(2)}{1} \cdot \frac{9}{\cancel{5}} = K - 32$$

$$522 = K - 32$$

$$554 = K$$

The correct answer is D.

101. The water from one outlet, flowing at a constant rate, can fill a swimming pool in 9 hours. The water from a second outlet, flowing at a constant rate, can fill the same pool in 5 hours. If both outlets are used at the same time, approximately what is the number of hours required to fill the pool?

(A)   0.22
(B)   0.31
(C)   2.50
(D)   3.21
(E)   4.56

Arithmetic Operations on rational numbers

The first outlet can fill the pool at a rate of $\frac{1}{9}$ of the pool per hour, and the second can fill the pool at a rate of $\frac{1}{5}$ of the pool per hour.

Together, they can fill the pool at a rate of $\frac{1}{9} + \frac{1}{5} = \frac{5}{45} + \frac{9}{45} = \frac{14}{45}$ of the pool per hour. Thus, when both outlets are used at the same time, they fill the pool in $\frac{45}{14} = 3.21$ hours.

The correct answer is D.

102. If a square mirror has a 20-inch diagonal, what is the approximate perimeter of the mirror, in inches?

(A)   40
(B)   60
(C)   80
(D)   100
(E)   120

Geometry Perimeter; Pythagorean theorem

Let x be the length of one of the sides of the square mirror.

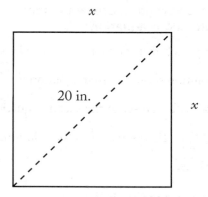

The triangles created by the diagonal are isosceles right triangles for which the Pythagorean theorem yields the following equation that can be solved for x.

$$x^2 + x^2 = 20^2$$
$$2x^2 = 400$$
$$x^2 = 200$$
$$x = \sqrt{200}$$

Therefore, the perimeter is $4x = 4\sqrt{200}$. To avoid estimating a value for $4\sqrt{200}$, note that $\left(4\sqrt{200}\right)^2 = (16)(200) = 3{,}200$, $(40)^2 = 1{,}600$, $(60)^2 = 3{,}600$, and $(80)^2 = 6{,}400$. The perimeter is closest to 60 because 3,200 is closer to 3,600 than it is to 1,600 or 6,400.

The correct answer is B.

103. The present ratio of students to teachers at a certain school is 30 to 1. If the student enrollment were to increase by 50 students and the number of teachers were to increase by 5, the ratio of students to

teachers would then be 25 to 1. What is the present number of teachers?

(A)   5
(B)   8
(C)   10
(D)   12
(E)   15

Algebra Applied problems

Let s be the present number of students, and let t be the present number of teachers. According to the problem, the following two equations apply:

$$\frac{30}{1} = \frac{s}{t} \qquad \text{Current student to teacher ratio}$$

$$\frac{s+50}{t+5} = \frac{25}{1} \qquad \text{Future student to teacher ratio}$$

Solving the first equation for s gives $s = 30t$. Substitute this value of s into the second equation, and solve for t.

$$\frac{30t+50}{t+5} = \frac{25}{1}$$

$30t + 50 = 25t + 125$ multiply both sides by $t + 5$

$\qquad 5t = 75$ simplify by subtraction

$\qquad\qquad t = 15$

The correct answer is E.

104. What is the smallest integer n for which $25^n > 5^{12}$?

(A)   6
(B)   7
(C)   8
(D)   9
(E)   10

Arithmetic Operations with rational numbers

Because $5^2 = 25$, a common base is 5. Rewrite the left side with 5 as a base: $25^n = (5^2)^n = 5^{2n}$. It follows that the desired integer is the least integer n for which $5^{2n} > 5^{12}$. This will be the least integer n for which $2n > 12$, or the least integer n for which $n > 6$, which is 7.

The correct answer is B.

105. Sixty percent of the members of a study group are women, and 45 percent of those women are lawyers. If one member of the study group is to be selected at random, what is the probability that the member selected is a woman lawyer?

(A)   0.10
(B)   0.15
(C)   0.27
(D)   0.33
(E)   0.45

Arithmetic Probability

For simplicity, suppose there are 100 members in the study group. Since 60 percent of the members are women, there are 60 women in the group. Also, 45 percent of the women are lawyers so there are $0.45(60) = 27$ women lawyers in the study group. Therefore the probability of selecting a woman lawyer is $\frac{27}{100} = 0.27$.

The correct answer is C.

106. When positive integer x is divided by positive integer y, the remainder is 9. If $\frac{x}{y} = 96.12$, what is the value of y ?

(A)   96
(B)   75
(C)   48
(D)   25
(E)   12

Arithmetic Properties of numbers

The remainder is 9 when x is divided by y, so $x = yq + 9$ for some positive integer q. Dividing both sides by y gives $\frac{x}{y} = q + \frac{9}{y}$. But, $\frac{x}{y} = 96.12 = 96 + 0.12$. Equating the two expressions for $\frac{x}{y}$ gives $q + \frac{9}{y} = 96 + 0.12$.

Thus, $q = 96$ and $\frac{9}{y} = 0.12$

$\qquad 9 = 0.12y$

$\qquad y = \dfrac{9}{0.12}$

$\qquad y = 75$

The correct answer is B.

107. If x is the product of the positive integers from 1 to 8, inclusive, and if i, k, m, and p are positive integers such that $x = 2^i 3^k 5^m 7^p$, then $i + k + m + p =$

(A)   4
(B)   7
(C)   8
(D)   11
(E)   12

Arithmetic Properties of numbers

The product of the positive integers from 1 to 8, inclusive, is

$$(1)(2)(3)(4)(5)(6)(7)(8) = (2^1)(3^1)(2^2)(5^1)(2^1)(3^1)(7^1)(2^3)$$

$$= (2^{1+2+1+3})(3^{1+1})(5^1)(7^1)$$

$$= (2^7)(3^2)(5^1)(7^1)$$

So, $i = 7$, $k = 2$, $m = 1$, $p = 1$, and
$i + k + m + p = 7 + 2 + 1 + 1 = 11$.

The correct answer is D.

108. If $t = \dfrac{1}{2^9 \times 5^3}$ is expressed as a terminating decimal, how many zeros will t have between the decimal point and the first nonzero digit to the right of the decimal point?

(A)   Three
(B)   Four
(C)   Five
(D)   Six
(E)   Nine

Arithmetic Exponents; Operations with rational numbers

Use properties of positive integer exponents to get

$$\frac{1}{2^9 \times 5^3} = \frac{1}{2^{6+3} \times 5^3}$$

$$= \frac{1}{\left(2^6 \times 2^3\right) \times 5^3}$$

$$= \frac{1}{2^6 \times \left(2^3 \times 5^3\right)}$$

$$= \frac{1}{2^6 \times 10^3}$$

$$= \frac{1}{2^6} \times \frac{1}{10^3}$$

$$= \frac{1}{2^6} \times 10^{-3}$$

$$= \frac{1}{64} \times 10^{-3}$$

So, $t = \dfrac{1}{64} \times 10^{-3}$.

Since $\dfrac{1}{100} \times 10^{-3} < \dfrac{1}{64} \times 10^{-3} < \dfrac{1}{10} \times 10^{-3}$, then

$$0.00001 < \frac{1}{64} \times 10^{-3} < 0.0001,$$

so $0.00001 < t < 0.0001$ and t has 4 zeros between the decimal point and the first nonzero digit to the right of the decimal point.

The correct answer is B.

109. A pharmaceutical company received $3 million in royalties on the first $20 million in sales of the generic equivalent of one of its products and then $9 million in royalties on the next $108 million in sales. By approximately what percent did the ratio of royalties to sales decrease from the first $20 million in sales to the next $108 million in sales?

(A)   8%
(B)   15%
(C)   45%
(D)   52%
(E)   56%

Arithmetic Percents

The ratio of royalties to sales for the first $20 million in sales is $\dfrac{3}{20}$, and the ratio of royalties to sales for the next $108 million in sales is $\dfrac{9}{108} = \dfrac{1}{12}$. The percent decrease in the royalties to sales ratios is 100 times the quotient of the difference in the ratios divided by the ratio of royalties to sales for the first $20 million in sales or

$$\frac{\dfrac{1}{12} - \dfrac{3}{20}}{\dfrac{3}{20}} \times 100 = \left(\frac{1}{12} - \frac{3}{20}\right) \times \frac{20}{3} \times 100$$

$$= \left(\frac{1}{12} \times \frac{20}{3} - 1\right) \times 100$$

$$= \left(\frac{5}{9} - 1\right) \times 100$$

$$= -\frac{4}{9} \times 100$$

$$\approx -0.44 \times 100$$

$$\approx 45\% \text{ decrease}$$

The correct answer is C.

110. If p is the product of the integers from 1 to 30, inclusive, what is the greatest integer k for which 3^k is a factor of p ?

   (A)   10
   (B)   12
   (C)   14
   (D)   16
   (E)   18

Arithmetic Properties of numbers

The table below shows the numbers from 1 to 30, inclusive, that have at least one factor of 3 and how many factors of 3 each has.

Multiples of 3 between 1 and 30	Number of factors of 3
3	1
6 = 2 × 3	1
9 = 3 × 3	2
12 = 2 × 2 × 3	1
15 = 3 × 5	1
18 = 2 × 3 × 3	2
21 = 3 × 7	1
24 = 2 × 2 × 2 × 3	1
27 = 3 × 3 × 3	3
30 = 2 × 3 × 5	1

The sum of the numbers in the right column is 14. Therefore, 3^{14} is the greatest power of 3 that is a factor of the product of the first 30 positive integers.

The correct answer is C.

111. If candy bars that regularly sell for $0.40 each are on sale at two for $0.75, what is the percent reduction in the price of two such candy bars purchased at the sale price?

   (A) $2\frac{1}{2}\%$
   (B) $6\frac{1}{4}\%$
   (C) $6\frac{2}{3}\%$
   (D)   8%
   (E) $12\frac{1}{2}\%$

Arithmetic Percents

Two candy bars at the regular price cost $2 \times \$0.40 = \$0.80$. The two candy bars at the sale price cost $\$0.80 - \$0.75 = \$0.05$ less. The percent of the reduction from the regular price can therefore be established as

$$\frac{\$0.05}{\$0.80} = 0.0625 = 6.25\% = 6\frac{1}{4}\%.$$

The correct answer is B.

112. If $s > 0$ and $\sqrt{\frac{r}{s}} = s$, what is r in terms of s ?

   (A) $\frac{1}{s}$
   (B) $\sqrt{s}$
   (C) $s\sqrt{s}$
   (D) s^3
   (E) $s^2 - s$

Algebra Equations

Solve the equation for r as follows:

$$\sqrt{\frac{r}{s}} = s$$

$\frac{r}{s} = s^2$ square both sides of the equation

$r = s^3$ multiply both sides by s

The correct answer is D.

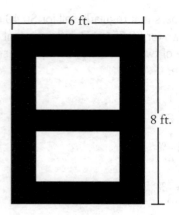

6 ft.

8 ft.

113. The front of a 6-foot-by-8-foot rectangular door has brass rectangular trim, as indicated by the shading in the figure above. If the trim is uniformly 1 foot wide, what fraction of the door's front surface is covered by the trim?

(A) $\dfrac{13}{48}$

(B) $\dfrac{5}{12}$

(C) $\dfrac{1}{2}$

(D) $\dfrac{7}{12}$

(E) $\dfrac{5}{8}$

Geometry Area

To determine the area of the trim, find the area of the unshaded portions of the door and subtract this from the door's total area. The width of each unshaded rectangle is the width of the door minus two trim strips, or 6 − 2 = 4 feet. The amount of height available for both unshaded rectangles is the height of the door minus three trim strips, or 8 − 3 = 5 feet. Thus, the area of the unshaded portions is 4 × 5 = 20 square feet. The area of the entire door is 6 × 8 = 48 square feet, so the area of the trim is 48 − 20 = 28 square feet. Therefore, the fraction of the door's front surface that is covered by the trim is $\dfrac{28}{48} = \dfrac{7}{12}$.

The correct answer is D.

114. If $a = -0.3$, which of the following is true?

(A) $a < a^2 < a^3$

(B) $a < a^3 < a^2$

(C) $a^2 < a < a^3$

(D) $a^2 < a^3 < a$

(E) $a^3 < a < a^2$

Arithmetic Operations on rational numbers

First, determine the relative values of a, a^2, and a^3, remembering that (negative)(negative) = positive. If $a = -0.3$ then $a^2 = (-0.3)^2 = (-0.3)(-0.3) = 0.09$, and $a^3 = (-0.3)^3 = (-0.3)(-0.3)(-0.3) = -0.027$.

Since $-0.3 < -0.027 < 0.09$, then $a < a^3 < a^2$.

The correct answer is B.

115. Mary's income is 60 percent more than Tim's income, and Tim's income is 40 percent less than Juan's income. What percent of Juan's income is Mary's income?

(A) 124%

(B) 120%

(C) 96%

(D) 80%

(E) 64%

Algebra; Arithmetic Applied problems; Percents

Let M be Mary's income, T be Tim's income, and J be Juan's income. Mary's income is 60 percent more than Tim's, so $M = T + 0.60T = 1.60T$. Since Tim's income is 40 percent less than Juan's income, Tim's income equals 100 − 40 = 60 percent of Juan's income, or $T = 0.6J$. Substituting $0.6J$ for T in the first equation gives $M = 1.6(0.6J)$ or $M = 0.96J$. Thus Mary's income is 96 percent of Juan's income.

The correct answer is C.

	City A	City B	City C	City D	City E
City A		•	•	•	•
City B			•	•	•
City C				•	•
City D					•
City E					

116. Each • in the mileage table above represents an entry indicating the distance between a pair of the five cities. If the table were extended to represent the distances between all pairs of 30 cities and each distance were to be represented by only one entry, how many entries would the table then have?

 (A) 60
 (B) 435
 (C) 450
 (D) 465
 (E) 900

Arithmetic Interpretation of tables

In a table with 30 cities, there are 30(30) = 900 boxes for entries. However, since a city does not need to have any entry for a distance to and from itself, 30 entries are not needed on the diagonal through the table. Thus, the necessary number of entries is reduced to 900 − 30 = 870 entries. Then, it is given that each pair of cities only needs one table entry, not two as the table allows; therefore, the table only needs to have $\dfrac{870}{2}$ = 435 entries.

The correct answer is B.

117. If n is positive, which of the following is equal to $\dfrac{1}{\sqrt{n+1}-\sqrt{n}}$?

 (A) 1
 (B) $\sqrt{2n+1}$
 (C) $\dfrac{\sqrt{n+1}}{\sqrt{n}}$
 (D) $\sqrt{n+1}-\sqrt{n}$
 (E) $\sqrt{n+1}+\sqrt{n}$

Algebra Computation with radical expressions

To rationalize the denominator, multiply the given expression by 1 using $\dfrac{\sqrt{n+1}+\sqrt{n}}{\sqrt{n+1}+\sqrt{n}}$, which is equivalent to 1.

$$\frac{1}{\sqrt{n+1}-\sqrt{n}} = \left(\frac{1}{\sqrt{n+1}-\sqrt{n}}\right)\left(\frac{\sqrt{n+1}+\sqrt{n}}{\sqrt{n+1}+\sqrt{n}}\right)$$

$$= \frac{\sqrt{n+1}+\sqrt{n}}{\left(\sqrt{n+1}\right)^2 - \sqrt{n}\sqrt{n+1} + \sqrt{n}\sqrt{n+1} - \left(\sqrt{n}\right)^2}$$

$$= \frac{\sqrt{n+1}+\sqrt{n}}{\left(\sqrt{n+1}\right)^2 - \left(\sqrt{n}\right)^2}$$

$$= \frac{\sqrt{n+1}+\sqrt{n}}{(n+1)-n}$$

$$= \sqrt{n+1}+\sqrt{n}$$

The correct answer is E.

118. The ratio of the length to the width of a rectangular advertising display is approximately 3.3 to 2. If the width of the display is 8 meters, what is the approximate length of the display, in meters?

 (A) 7
 (B) 11
 (C) 13
 (D) 16
 (E) 26

Algebra Applied problems

Letting l be the length of the advertising display, the proportion for the ratio of the length to the width can be expressed in the following equation, which can be solved for l:

$$\frac{3.3}{2} = \frac{l}{8}$$

13.2 = l multiply both sides by 8

The correct answer is C.

119. Which of the following is equivalent to the pair of inequalities $x + 6 > 10$ and $x - 3 \leq 5$?

    (A) $2 \leq x < 16$
    (B) $2 \leq x < 4$
    (C) $2 < x \leq 8$
    (D) $4 < x \leq 8$
    (E) $4 \leq x < 16$

    Algebra Inequalities

    Solve the inequalities separately and combine the results.

    $x + 6 > 10$

    $\qquad x > 4$

    $x - 3 \leq 5$

    $\qquad x \leq 8$

    Since $x > 4$, then $4 < x$. Combining $4 < x$ and $x \leq 8$ gives $4 < x \leq 8$.

    The correct answer is D.

120. David has d books, which is 3 times as many as Jeff and $\frac{1}{2}$ as many as Paula. How many books do the three of them have altogether, in terms of d ?

    (A) $\dfrac{5}{6}d$

    (B) $\dfrac{7}{3}d$

    (C) $\dfrac{10}{3}d$

    (D) $\dfrac{7}{2}d$

    (E) $\dfrac{9}{2}d$

    Algebra Applied problems; Simultaneous equations

    Let J be the number of books that Jeff has, and let P be the number of books Paula has. Then, the given information about David's books can be

expressed as $d = 3J$ and $d = \frac{1}{2}P$. Solving these two equations for J and P gives $\frac{d}{3} = J$ and $2d = P$.

Thus, $d + J + P = d + \frac{d}{3} + 2d = 3\frac{1}{3}d = \frac{10}{3}d$.

The correct answer is C.

121. There are 8 teams in a certain league and each team plays each of the other teams exactly once. If each game is played by 2 teams, what is the total number of games played?

    (A)   15
    (B)   16
    (C)   28
    (D)   56
    (E)   64

    Arithmetic Operations on rational numbers

    Since no team needs to play itself, each team needs to play 7 other teams. In addition, each game needs to be counted only once, rather than once for each team that plays that game. Since two teams play each game, $\frac{8 \times 7}{2} = 28$ games are needed.

    The correct answer is C.

122. An operation θ is defined by the equation $a \, \theta \, b = \dfrac{a - b}{a + b}$, for all numbers a and b such that $a \neq -b$. If $a \neq -c$ and $a \, \theta \, c = 0$, then $c =$

    (A) $-a$

    (B) $-\dfrac{1}{a}$

    (C) 0

    (D) $\dfrac{1}{a}$

    (E) a

    Algebra Simplifying algebraic expressions

    Substitute c for b and 0 for $a \, \theta \, c$ in the given equation, and solve for c.

$$0 = \frac{a-c}{a+c}$$

$0 = a - c$ multiply both sides by $a + c$

$c = a$ add c to both sides

The correct answer is E.

123. The price of lunch for 15 people was $207.00, including a 15 percent gratuity for service. What was the average price per person, EXCLUDING the gratuity?

    (A) $11.73
    (B) $12.00
    (C) $13.80
    (D) $14.00
    (E) $15.87

Arithmetic; Algebra Statistics; Applied problems

Let c be the total price of lunch for everyone excluding the gratuity. Since $207.00 is given as the total price including the 15% gratuity, the total price for the group lunch excluding the gratuity can be expressed as $207 = 1.15c$, or $\frac{\$207}{1.15} = \$180 = c$. The average price per person, or $\frac{\text{sum of } v \text{ values}}{v} = \text{average}$, was thus $\frac{\$180}{15} = \$12.00$ for each of the 15 individuals.

The correct answer is B.

124. In Town X, 64 percent of the population are employed, and 48 percent of the population are employed males. What percent of the employed people in Town X are females?

    (A)   16%
    (B)   25%
    (C)   32%
    (D)   40%
    (E)   52%

Arithmetic Percents

For simplicity, suppose that the population of Town X is 100. If 64% of the population are employed, then 64 people are employed. If 48% of the population are employed males, then 48 of the town's people are employed males. Then, there are $64 - 48 = 16$ employed females in Town X. The percent of the employed people who are females is then $\frac{16}{64} \times 100 = 25\%$.

The correct answer is B.

125. If $\frac{p}{q} < 1$, and p and q are positive integers, which of the following must be greater than 1?

    (A) $\sqrt{\dfrac{p}{q}}$

    (B) $\dfrac{p}{q^2}$

    (C) $\dfrac{p}{2q}$

    (D) $\dfrac{q}{p^2}$

    (E) $\dfrac{q}{p}$

Arithmetic Properties of numbers

Since p and q are positive integers, $0 < \dfrac{p}{q} < 1$.

A   Since $\dfrac{p}{q} < 1$, then $q > p$. Taking the square root of both sides of the inequality gives $\sqrt{q} > \sqrt{p}$. Then, $\sqrt{\dfrac{p}{q}} = \dfrac{\sqrt{p}}{\sqrt{q}}$, so here the denominator will still be larger than the numerator. CANNOT be greater than 1

B   Squaring the denominator increases the denominator, which decreases the value of the fraction. CANNOT be greater than 1

C   Multiplying the denominator by 2 increases the denominator, which decreases the value of the fraction. CANNOT be greater than 1

D   Since $\dfrac{p}{q} < 1$, then $q > p$. When $p^2 < q$, this expression will be greater than 1, but p^2 need not be less than q. For example, if $p = 2$ and $q = 100$, $\dfrac{p}{q} = \dfrac{2}{100}$ and

$$\dfrac{q}{p^2} = \dfrac{100}{2^2} = \dfrac{100}{4} = 25 > 1.$$

However, if $p = 3$ and $q = 4$, then $\dfrac{p}{q} = \dfrac{3}{4}$ and $\dfrac{q}{p^2} = \dfrac{4}{3^2} = \dfrac{4}{9} < 1$. NEED NOT be greater than 1

E   Again, since $\dfrac{p}{q} < 1$, then $q > p$. Thus, the reciprocal, $\dfrac{q}{p}$, always has a value greater than 1 because the numerator will always be a larger positive integer than the denominator. MUST be greater than 1

The correct answer is E.

126. It would take one machine 4 hours to complete a large production order and another machine 3 hours to complete the same order. How many hours would it take both machines, working simultaneously at their respective constant rates, to complete the order?

(A) $\dfrac{7}{12}$

(B) $1\dfrac{1}{2}$

(C) $1\dfrac{5}{7}$

(D) $3\dfrac{1}{2}$

(E)   7

Arithmetic Operations on rational numbers

The first machine can complete $\dfrac{1}{4}$ of the production order in one hour, and the second machine can complete $\dfrac{1}{3}$ of the same order in one hour. Thus, working together they can complete $\dfrac{1}{4} + \dfrac{1}{3} = \dfrac{3}{12} + \dfrac{4}{12} = \dfrac{7}{12}$ of the order in one hour. Therefore, it will take $\dfrac{12}{7} = 1\dfrac{5}{7}$ hours for the two machines working simultaneously to complete the production order.

The correct answer is C.

127. To mail a package, the rate is x cents for the first pound and y cents for each additional pound, where x > y. Two packages weighing 3 pounds and 5 pounds, respectively, can be mailed separately or combined as one package. Which method is cheaper, and how much money is saved?

(A)   Combined, with a savings of x – y cents

(B)   Combined, with a savings of y – x cents

(C)   Combined, with a savings of x cents

(D)   Separately, with a savings of x – y cents

(E)   Separately, with a savings of y cents

Algebra Applied problems

Shipping the two packages separately would cost $1x + 2y$ for the 3-pound package and $1x + 4y$ for the 5-pound package. Shipping them together (as a single 8-pound package) would cost $1x + 7y$. By calculating the sum of the costs for shipping the two packages separately minus the cost for shipping the one combined package, it is possible to determine the difference in cost, as shown.

$((1x + 2y) + (1x + 4y)) - (1x + 7y)$	(cost for 3 lb. + cost for 5 lb.) – cost for 8 lb.
$= (2x + 6y) - (1x + 7y)$	combine like terms
$= 2x + 6y - 1x - 7y$	distribute the negative
$= x - y$	combine like terms

Since x > y, this value is positive, which means it costs more to ship two packages separately. Thus it is cheaper to mail one combined package at a cost savings of x – y cents.

The correct answer is A.

128. If money is invested at r percent interest, compounded annually, the amount of the investment will double in approximately $\frac{70}{r}$ years. If Pat's parents invested $5,000 in a long-term bond that pays 8 percent interest, compounded annually, what will be the approximate total amount of the investment 18 years later, when Pat is ready for college?

(A) $20,000
(B) $15,000
(C) $12,000
(D) $10,000
(E) $ 9,000

Algebra Applied problems

Since the investment will double in $\frac{70}{r} = \frac{70}{8} = 8.75 \approx 9$ years, the value of the investment over 18 years can be approximated by doubling its initial value twice. Therefore, the approximate value will be ($5,000)(2)(2) = $20,000.

The correct answer is A.

129. On a recent trip, Cindy drove her car 290 miles, rounded to the nearest 10 miles, and used 12 gallons of gasoline, rounded to the nearest gallon. The actual number of miles per gallon that Cindy's car got on this trip must have been between

(A) $\frac{290}{12.5}$ and $\frac{290}{11.5}$

(B) $\frac{295}{12}$ and $\frac{285}{11.5}$

(C) $\frac{285}{12}$ and $\frac{295}{12}$

(D) $\frac{285}{12.5}$ and $\frac{295}{11.5}$

(E) $\frac{295}{12.5}$ and $\frac{285}{11.5}$

Arithmetic Estimation

The lowest number of miles per gallon can be calculated using the lowest possible miles and the highest amount of gasoline. Also, the highest number of miles per gallon can be calculated using the highest possible miles and the lowest amount of gasoline.

Since the miles are rounded to the nearest 10 miles, the number of miles is between 285 and 295. Since the gallons are rounded to the nearest gallon, the number of gallons is between 11.5 and 12.5. Therefore, the lowest number of miles per gallon is $\frac{\text{lowest miles}}{\text{highest gallons}} = \frac{285}{12.5}$ and the highest number of miles per gallon is $\frac{\text{highest miles}}{\text{lowest gallons}} = \frac{295}{11.5}$.

The correct answer is D.

130. Which of the following inequalities is an algebraic expression for the shaded part of the number line above?

(A) $|x| \leq 3$
(B) $|x| \leq 5$
(C) $|x - 2| \leq 3$
(D) $|x - 1| \leq 4$
(E) $|x + 1| \leq 4$

Algebra Inequalities

The number line above shows $-5 \leq x \leq 3$. To turn this into absolute value notation, as all the choices are written, the numbers need to be opposite signs of the same value.

Since the distance between -5 and 3 is 8 $(3 - (-5) = 8)$, that distance needs to be split in half with -4 to one side and 4 to the other. Each of these two values is 1 more than the values in the inequality above, so adding 1 to all terms in the inequality gives $-4 \leq x + 1 \leq 4$, which is the same as $|x + 1| \leq 4$.

The correct answer is E.

131. A factory has 500 workers, 15 percent of whom are women. If 50 additional workers are to be hired and all of the present workers remain, how many of the additional workers must be women in order to raise the percent of women employees to 20 percent?

(A)   3
(B)   10
(C)   25
(D)   30
(E)   35

**Arithmetic; Algebra Percents;
Applied problems**

Let w be the number of additional workers who must be women to satisfy the problem. It can be stated that, initially, $500(0.15) = 75$ of the workers were women. Since 50 more workers are to be hired, the total workforce will increase to $500 + 50 = 550$ employees. The information that the percentage of women employees will be 20 percent after this increase can be expressed in the following equation and solved for w.

$$\frac{75 + w}{550} = 0.20$$

$75 + w = 110$ multiply both sides by 550

$w = 35$ subtract 75 from both sides

The correct answer is E.

132. In a small snack shop, the average (arithmetic mean) revenue was $400 per day over a 10-day period. During this period, if the average daily revenue was $360 for the first 6 days, what was the average daily revenue for the last 4 days?

(A) $420
(B) $440
(C) $450
(D) $460
(E) $480

**Arithmetic; Algebra Statistics;
Applied problems**

Let x be the average daily revenue for the last 4 days. Using the formula

$$\text{average} = \frac{\text{sum of values}}{\text{number of values}},$$ the information

regarding the average revenues for the 10-day and 6-day periods can be expressed as follows and solved for x:

$$\$400 = \frac{6(\$360) + 4x}{10}$$

$\$4,000 = \$2,160 + 4x$ multiply both sides by 10

$\$1,840 = 4x$ subtract $2,160 from both sides

$\$460 = x$ divide both sides by 4

The correct answer is D.

133. A certain country had a total annual expenditure of 1.2×10^{12} last year. If the population of the country was 240 million last year, what was the per capita expenditure?

(A) $ 500
(B) $1,000
(C) $2,000
(D) $3,000
(E) $5,000

Arithmetic Operations on rational numbers

The per capita expenditure can be calculated as follows:

$$\frac{\$1.2 \times 10^{12}}{240 \text{ million}} = \frac{\$12 \times 10^{11}}{24 \times 10^{7}}$$

$$= \$\frac{12}{24} \times \frac{10^{11}}{10^{7}}$$

$$= \$\frac{1}{2} \times 10^{11-7}$$

$$= \$0.5 \times 10^{4}$$

$$= \$5,000$$

The correct answer is E.

134. A certain rectangular window is twice as long as it is wide. If its perimeter is 10 feet, then its dimensions in feet are

(A) $\frac{3}{2}$ by $\frac{7}{2}$

(B) $\frac{5}{3}$ by $\frac{10}{3}$

(C)   2 by 4

(D)   3 by 6

(E) $\frac{10}{3}$ by $\frac{20}{3}$

Geometry Perimeter

Let l and w be the length and width in feet, respectively, of the window. Then the information in the problem can be expressed in the following two equations: $l = 2w$ since the length is twice the width and $2l + 2w = 10$ since the perimeter is 10. Substitute l for $2w$ in the second equation to get $2l + l = 10$. Therefore, $3l = 10$, or $l = \dfrac{10}{3}$. Then $\dfrac{10}{3} = 2w$ so $w = \dfrac{5}{3}$.

The correct answer is B.

135. The diagram above shows the various paths along which a mouse can travel from point X, where it is released, to point Y, where it is rewarded with a food pellet. How many different paths from X to Y can the mouse take if it goes directly from X to Y without retracing any point along a path?

(A) 6
(B) 7
(C) 12
(D) 14
(E) 17

Arithmetic Elementary combinatorics

The total number of different paths can be found by multiplying the number of possible routes that can be taken from each intersection point of the paths to their next point of intersection. Refer to the figure below.

The total number of ways to get from X to A is 2, since there are only 2 paths to choose from. There are also only 2 ways to get from A to B. To get from B to Y, there are 3 possible choices. Thus, the total number of different paths is $(2)(2)(3) = 12$.

The correct answer is C.

136. If the operation $\odot$ is defined by $x \odot y = \sqrt{xy}$ for all positive numbers x and y, then $(5 \odot 45) \odot 60 =$

(A) 30
(B) 60
(C) 90
(D) $30\sqrt{15}$
(E) $60\sqrt{15}$

Arithmetic Operations on rational numbers

Substitute the values into the formula and simplify:

$$
\begin{aligned}
(5 \odot 45) \odot 60 &= \sqrt{(5)(45)} \odot 60 \\
&= \sqrt{(5)(5)(9)} \odot 60 \\
&= (5)(3) \odot 60 \\
&= 15 \odot 60 \\
&= \sqrt{(15)(60)} \\
&= \sqrt{(15)(15)(4)} \\
&= (15)(2) \\
&= 30
\end{aligned}
$$

The correct answer is A.

137. A bar over a sequence of digits in a decimal indicates that the sequence repeats indefinitely.

What is the value of $(10^4 - 10^2)(0.00\overline{12})$?

(A) 0
(B) $0.\overline{12}$
(C) 1.2
(D) 10
(E) 12

Arithmetic Operations on rational numbers

Distribute and simplify.

$(10^4 - 10^2)(0.00\overline{12})$

$= 10^4(0.00\overline{12}) - 10^2(0.00\overline{12})$ distribute the $(0.00\overline{12})$

$= 10,000(0.00\overline{12}) - 100(0.00\overline{12})$ $10^4 = 10,000$, and $10^2 = 100$

$= 12.\overline{12} - 0.\overline{12}$ multiply by multiples of 10 to move the decimals

$= 12$

The correct answer is E.

138. At a loading dock, each worker on the night crew loaded $\frac{3}{4}$ as many boxes as each worker on the day crew. If the night crew has $\frac{4}{5}$ as many workers as the day crew, what fraction of all the boxes loaded by the two crews did the day crew load?

(A) $\frac{1}{2}$

(B) $\frac{2}{5}$

(C) $\frac{3}{5}$

(D) $\frac{4}{5}$

(E) $\frac{5}{8}$

Arithmetic Operations on rational numbers

From this, the workers on the night crew will load $\frac{3}{4}\left(\frac{4}{5}\right) = \frac{3}{5}$ as many boxes as the day crew. The total loaded by both the day and night crews is thus $1 + \frac{3}{5} = \frac{5}{5} + \frac{3}{5} = \frac{8}{5}$ of the day crew's work. Therefore, the fraction of all the boxes loaded by the two crews that was done by the day crew was $\frac{1}{\frac{8}{5}} = 1\left(\frac{5}{8}\right) = \frac{5}{8}$.

The correct answer is E.

139. A restaurant meal cost $35.50 and there was no tax. If the tip was more than 10 percent but less than 15 percent of the cost of the meal, then the total amount paid must have been between

(A) $40 and $42
(B) $39 and $41
(C) $38 and $40
(D) $37 and $39
(E) $36 and $37

Arithmetic Estimation and percent

First calculate the actual total amount for the meal with a 10 percent tip and a 15 percent tip. To calculate each, multiply the cost of the meal by (1 + the percent as a decimal).

10 percent tip: 15 percent tip:

$35.50(1.10) $35.50(1.15)

$39.05 $40.825

The only answer choice that includes all values between $39.05 and $40.83 is B.

The correct answer is B.

140. In a weight-lifting competition, the total weight of Joe's two lifts was 750 pounds. If twice the weight of his first lift was 300 pounds more than the weight of his second lift, what was the weight, in pounds, of his first lift?

(A) 225
(B) 275
(C) 325
(D) 350
(E) 400

Algebra Applied problems

Let F and S be the weights, in pounds, of Joe's first and second lifts, respectively. Use these variables to set up two equations and then solve them.

$F + S = 750$ weight of two lifts was 750 pounds

$2F = S + 300$ twice the weight of first lift was 300 pounds more than the weight of second

$F = 750 - S$ solve the first equation for F

$2(750 - S) = S + 300$ substitute $750 - S$ for F in the second equation

$1{,}500 - 2S = S + 300$

$1{,}200 = 3S$ solve for S

$400 = S$

Substituting this value of S back into the first equation gives $F + 400 = 750$, or $F = 350$.

The correct answer is D.

141. A club collected exactly $599 from its members. If each member contributed at least $12, what is the greatest number of members the club could have?

(A)   43
(B)   44
(C)   49
(D)   50
(E)   51

Algebra Applied problems

To determine the greatest possible number of members, first recognize that each member had to contribute the lowest amount given. Write an inequality for the individual contributions and the total amount collected, with n representing the number of members in the club. Then solve for n.

$12n \leq 599$ (least contribution)(number of members) $\leq$ total collected

$n \leq 49\dfrac{11}{12}$ solve for n

Since n represents individual people, it must be a whole number; the greatest possible value of n is thus 49.

This problem can also be solved as follows: The inequality $12n \leq 599$, where n is restricted to the set of positive integers, is equivalent to $12n < 600$.

Therefore, $n < \dfrac{600}{12} = \dfrac{(12)(5)(10)}{12} = (5)(10) = 50$, and the greatest such value that is an integer is 49.

The correct answer is C.

142. If y is the smallest positive integer such that 3,150 multiplied by y is the square of an integer, then y must be

(A)   2
(B)   5
(C)   6
(D)   7
(E)   14

Arithmetic Properties of numbers

To find the smallest positive integer y such that $3{,}150y$ is the square of an integer, first find the prime factorization of 3,150 by a method similar to the following:

$3{,}150 = 10 \times 315$

$= (2 \times 5) \times (3 \times 105)$

$= 2 \times 5 \times 3 \times (5 \times 21)$

$= 2 \times 5 \times 3 \times 5 \times (3 \times 7)$

$= 2 \times 3^2 \times 5^2 \times 7$

To be a perfect square, $3{,}150y$ must have an even number of each of its prime factors. At a minimum, y must have one factor of 2 and one factor of 7 so that $3{,}150y$ has two factors of each of the primes 2, 3, 5, and 7. The smallest positive integer value of y is then $(2)(7) = 14$.

The correct answer is E.

143. If [x] is the greatest integer less than or equal to x, what is the value of [–1.6] + [3.4] + [2.7] ?

(A)   3
(B)   4
(C)   5
(D)   6
(E)   7

Arithmetic Computation with integers

The greatest integer that is less than or equal to –1.6 is –2. It cannot be –1 because –1 is greater than –1.6. The greatest integer that is less than or equal to 3.4 is 3. It cannot be 4 because 4 is greater than 3.4. The greatest integer that is less than or equal to 2.7 is 2. It cannot be 3 because 3 is greater than 2.7. Therefore, [–1.6] + [3.4] + [2.7] = –2 + 3 + 2 = 3.

The correct answer is A.

144. If $\dfrac{4-x}{2+x} = x$, what is the value of $x^2 + 3x - 4$?

   (A)   –4
   (B)   –1
   (C)   0
   (D)   1
   (E)   2

Algebra Second-degree equations

Work the problem.

$$\frac{4-x}{2+x} = x$$

$4 - x = x(2 + x)$ multiply both sides by $(2 + x)$

$4 - x = 2x + x^2$ distribute the x

$0 = x^2 + 3x - 4$ move all terms to right side

The correct answer is C.

145. The trapezoid shown in the figure above represents a cross section of the rudder of a ship. If the distance from A to B is 13 feet, what is the area of the cross section of the rudder in square feet?

   (A)   39
   (B)   40
   (C)   42
   (D)   45
   (E)   46.5

Geometry Triangles and the Pythagorean theorem

The formula for calculating the area of a trapezoid is

$$\text{Area} = \frac{1}{2}(\text{base 1} + \text{base 2})(\text{height}).$$

The bases of the trapezoid are given as 2 feet and 5 feet, so only the height (AQ) needs to be found. Since the dashed line $AB = 13$ feet, and triangle BQA is a right triangle, use the Pythagorean theorem to calculate AQ. Thus,

$$AQ = \sqrt{13^2 - 5^2} = \sqrt{144}, \text{ or } AQ = 12 \text{ feet.}$$

Substituting the values into the formula for calculating the area of a trapezoid:

$$\text{Area} = \frac{1}{2}(2 + 5)(12)$$

Area = 42 square feet.

The correct answer is C.

146. In a certain sequence, the term x_n is given by the formula $x_n = 2x_{n-1} - \dfrac{1}{2}(x_{n-2})$ for all $n \ge 2$. If $x_0 = 3$ and $x_1 = 2$, what is the value of x_3 ?

   (A)   2.5
   (B)   3.125
   (C)   4
   (D)   5
   (E)   6.75

Algebra Simplifying algebraic expressions

Given the formula $x_n = 2x_{n-1} - \dfrac{1}{2}x_{n-2}$ with $x_0 = 3$ and $x_1 = 2$, then

$$x_2 = 2x_1 - \frac{1}{2}x_0$$

$$= 2(2) - \frac{1}{2}(3)$$

$$= \frac{5}{2}$$

$$x_3 = 2x_2 - \frac{1}{2}x_1$$

$$= 2\left(\frac{5}{2}\right) - \frac{1}{2}(2)$$

$$= 5 - 1$$

$$= 4$$

The correct answer is C.

147. In the figure above, V represents an observation point at one end of a pool. From V, an object that is actually located on the bottom of the pool at point R appears to be at point S. If $VR = 10$ feet, what is the distance RS, in feet, between the actual position and the perceived position of the object?

(A) $10 - 5\sqrt{3}$

(B) $10 - 5\sqrt{2}$

(C)   2

(D) $2\frac{1}{2}$

(E)   4

Geometry Pythagorean theorem

Let P be the point 5 feet directly below V. ΔVPR is thus a right triangle.

$VP^2 + PR^2 = VR^2$	Pythagorean theorem applied to ΔVPR.
$5^2 + PR^2 = 10^2$	substitute known quantities
$25 + PR^2 = 100$	solve for PR
$PR^2 = 75$	
$PR = 5\sqrt{3}$	

Note that $\sqrt{75} = \sqrt{25 \cdot 3} = \sqrt{25}\sqrt{3} = 5\sqrt{3}$; thus, $RS = PS - PR = 10 - 5\sqrt{3}$.

The correct answer is A.

148. If x, y, and k are positive numbers such that $\left(\dfrac{x}{x+y}\right)(10) + \left(\dfrac{y}{x+y}\right)(20) = k$ and if $x < y$, which of the following could be the value of k?

(A)   10

(B)   12

(C)   15

(D)   18

(E)   30

Algebra Simplifying algebraic expressions

Simplify the expression for k as follows:

$$k = \left(\frac{x}{x+y}\right)(10) + \left(\frac{y}{x+y}\right)(20)$$

$$= \frac{10x + 20y}{x+y}$$

$$= \frac{10(x+y) + 10y}{x+y}$$

$$= \frac{10(x+y)}{x+y} + \frac{10y}{x+y}$$

$$= 10 + \frac{10y}{x+y}$$

Then since $0 < x < y$,

$$0 + y < x + y < y + y$$

$$y < x + y < 2y$$

$$\frac{1}{2y} < \frac{1}{x+y} < \frac{1}{y}$$

$$\frac{10y}{2y} < \frac{10y}{x+y} < \frac{10y}{y}$$

$$5 < \frac{10y}{x+y} < 10$$

$$15 < 10 + \frac{10y}{x+y} < 20$$

$$15 < k < 20$$

The only answer choice between 15 and 20 is 18, so 18 is the only answer choice that could be the value of k.

The correct answer is D.

149. During a trip, Francine traveled x percent of the total distance at an average speed of 40 miles per hour and the rest of the distance at an average speed of 60 miles per hour. In terms of x, what was Francine's average speed for the entire trip?

(A) $\dfrac{180 - x}{2}$

(B) $\dfrac{x + 60}{4}$

(C) $\dfrac{300 - x}{5}$

(D) $\dfrac{600}{115 - x}$

(E) $\dfrac{12,000}{x + 200}$

Algebra Applied problems

Assume for simplicity that the total distance of Francine's trip is 100 miles. Then the table below gives all of the pertinent information.

Distance	Rate	Time $= \dfrac{\text{Distance}}{\text{Rate}}$
x	40	$\dfrac{x}{40}$
$100 - x$	60	$\dfrac{100 - x}{60}$

The total time for Francine's trip is

$$\frac{x}{40} + \frac{100 - x}{60} = \frac{3x}{120} + \frac{2(100 - x)}{120}$$

$$= \frac{3x + 2(100 - x)}{120}$$

$$= \frac{3x + 200 - 2x}{120}$$

$$= \frac{x + 200}{120}$$

Francine's average speed over the entire trip is

$$\frac{\text{total distance}}{\text{total time}} = \frac{100}{\dfrac{x + 200}{120}} = \frac{12,000}{x + 200}.$$

The correct answer is E.

150. If $x = -1$, then $\dfrac{x^4 - x^3 + x^2}{x - 1} =$

(A) $-\dfrac{3}{2}$

(B) $-\dfrac{1}{2}$

(C) 0

(D) $\dfrac{1}{2}$

(E) $\dfrac{3}{2}$

Arithmetic Operations on rational numbers

Substituting the value of -1 for x in the expression results in

$$\frac{(-1)^4 - (-1)^3 + (-1)^2}{(-1) - 1} = \frac{1 - (-1) + 1}{-2} = -\frac{3}{2}$$

The correct answer is A.

151. A toy store regularly sells all stock at a discount of 20 percent to 40 percent. If an additional 25 percent were deducted from the discount price during a special sale, what would be the lowest possible price of a toy costing $16 before any discount?

(A) $ 5.60
(B) $ 7.20
(C) $ 8.80
(D) $ 9.60
(E) $15.20

Arithmetic Percents

The lowest possible price is paid when the maximum initial discount of 40% is received.

$16(0.6) = 9.60 calculate the first
                    40% discount

$9.60(0.75) = 7.20 calculate the second
                        25% discount

The correct answer is B.

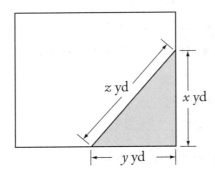

152. The shaded portion of the rectangular lot shown above represents a flower bed. If the area of the bed is 24 square yards and x = y + 2, then z equals

(A) $\sqrt{13}$
(B) $2\sqrt{13}$
(C) 6
(D) 8
(E) 10

Geometry Area and the Pythagorean theorem

Using the known area of the triangular flower bed and the known length of side x of the triangle, determine the length of side z of the triangle by applying the formula for calculating the area of a triangle:

Area of a triangle = $\frac{1}{2}$(base)(height)

$A = \frac{1}{2}xy$

$24 = \frac{1}{2}(y+2)(y)$ substitute 24 for area and y + 2 for x

$48 = y^2 + 2y$ solve for y

$0 = y^2 + 2y - 48$

$0 = (y+8)(y-6)$

$y + 8 = 0 \quad y - 6 = 0$

$y = -8 \quad\quad y = 6$ eliminate y = − 8 since it has to be a positive length

$x = 6 + 2 = 8$

Since the legs y and x of the right triangle are 6 and 8 yards long, respectively, the hypotenuse, z, must be 10 yards because 6-8-10 is a Pythagorean triple. Alternatively, the Pythagorean theorem can also be used to solve for z, where $x^2 + y^2 = z^2$. Thus, $8^2 + 6^2 = 64 + 36 = 100 = z^2$, and $\sqrt{100} = 10$.

The correct answer is E.

153. Jack is now 14 years older than Bill. If in 10 years Jack will be twice as old as Bill, how old will Jack be in 5 years?

(A) 9
(B) 19
(C) 21
(D) 23
(E) 33

Algebra Applied problems

Let J and B be Jack's and Bill's current ages. Then the information from the problem can be expressed in the following two equations:

$J = B + 14$, or equivalently $B = J - 14$ and $J + 10 = 2(B + 10)$.

Since Jack's age is to be determined, replace B in the second equation with $J - 14$ to get an equation that can be solved for J:

$J + 10 = 2(J - 14 + 10)$

$J + 10 = 2J - 8$

$18 = J$

Therefore, Jack's current age is 18, and hence Jack's age in 5 years will be 18 + 5 = 23.

The correct answer is D.

154. An empty pool being filled with water at a constant rate takes 8 hours to fill to $\frac{3}{5}$ of its capacity. How much more time will it take to finish filling the pool?

(A) 5 hr 30 min
(B) 5 hr 20 min
(C) 4 hr 48 min
(D) 3 hr 12 min
(E) 2 hr 40 min

Algebra Applied problems

Build an equation to express the given information and solve for the answer.

Let t = the total time needed to fill the pool.

Since it is given that it takes 8 hours to fill $\frac{3}{5}$ of the pool:

$$\frac{3}{5}t = 8$$

$$t = \frac{40}{3} \qquad \text{solve for } t$$

$$t = 13\frac{1}{3}$$

Thus, to calculate the time it will take to finish filling the pool:

$13\frac{1}{3} - 8 = 5\frac{1}{3}$ hours, or 5 hours 20 minutes.

The correct answer is B.

155. A positive number x is multiplied by 2, and this product is then divided by 3. If the positive square root of the result of these two operations equals x, what is the value of x ?

   (A) $\dfrac{9}{4}$

   (B) $\dfrac{3}{2}$

   (C) $\dfrac{4}{3}$

   (D) $\dfrac{2}{3}$

   (E) $\dfrac{1}{2}$

Algebra Second-degree equations

Set up an equation according to the given information, and then solve for x.

First, multiply x by 2, divide that by 3, and set the square root of that equal to x:

$$\sqrt{\frac{2x}{3}} = x$$

To solve this equation:

$$\frac{2x}{3} = x^2 \qquad \text{square both sides}$$

$$2x = 3x^2$$

$$0 = 3x^2 - 2x \qquad \text{solve for possible values of } x$$

$$0 = x(3x - 2)$$

$$x = 0, \ 3x - 2 = 0$$

since $x > 0$, use $3x - 2 = 0$ to solve for x:

$$3x - 2 = 0$$

$$3x = 2$$

$$x = \frac{2}{3}$$

The correct answer is D.

156. A tank contains 10,000 gallons of a solution that is 5 percent sodium chloride by volume. If 2,500 gallons of water evaporate from the tank, the remaining solution will be approximately what percent sodium chloride?

   (A)   1.25%
   (B)   3.75%
   (C)   6.25%
   (D)   6.67%
   (E)   11.7%

Arithmetic Operations on rational numbers; Percents

Before the evaporation occurs, the tank contains 10,000 (0.05) = 500 gallons of sodium chloride. After the evaporation occurs, the tank contains 10,000 – 2,500 = 7,500 gallons of solution, of which 500 gallons are known to be sodium chloride. Calculate the percentage based on these postevaporation amounts:

$$\frac{500}{7,500} = 0.0667 = 6.67\%$$

The correct answer is D.

157. For any positive integer n, the sum of the first n positive integers equals $\dfrac{n(n+1)}{2}$. What is the sum of all the even integers between 99 and 301 ?

(A)   10,100
(B)   20,200
(C)   22,650
(D)   40,200
(E)   45,150

Algebra Simplifying expressions; **Arithmetic** Computation with integers

The given formula translates into $1 + 2 + \ldots + n = \sum_{k=1}^{n} k = \frac{n(n+1)}{2}$. The sum of the even integers between 99 and 301 is the sum of the even integers from 100 through 300, or the sum of the 50th even integer through the 150th even integer. To get this sum, find the sum of the first 150 even integers and subtract the sum of the first 49 even integers. In symbols,

$$\sum_{k=1}^{150} 2k - \sum_{k=1}^{49} 2k = 2\sum_{k=1}^{150} k - 2\sum_{k=1}^{49} k$$

$$= 2\left(\frac{150(150+1)}{2}\right) - 2\left(\frac{49(49+1)}{2}\right)$$

$$= 150(151) - 49(50)$$

$$= 50[3(151) - 49]$$

$$= 50(453 - 49)$$

$$= 50(404)$$

$$= 20,200$$

The correct answer is B.

158. A committee is composed of w women and m men. If 3 women and 2 men are added to the committee, and if one person is selected at random from the enlarged committee, then the probability that a woman is selected can be represented by

(A) $\dfrac{w}{m}$

(B) $\dfrac{w}{w+m}$

(C) $\dfrac{w+3}{m+2}$

(D) $\dfrac{w+3}{w+m+3}$

(E) $\dfrac{w+3}{w+m+5}$

Arithmetic Probability

Set up an equation according to the given information regarding the values of w and m. The total number of women on the enlarged committee can be expressed as $w + 3$. The total number of members on the enlarged committee can be expressed as $w + m + 3 + 2$ or thus $w + m + 5$. Then, the probability that the one person selected at random from the enlarged committee is a woman is equal to

$$\frac{\text{the number of women}}{\text{the total number of members}} = \frac{w+3}{w+m+5}.$$

The correct answer is E.

159. How many prime numbers between 1 and 100 are factors of 7,150 ?

(A)   One
(B)   Two
(C)   Three
(D)   Four
(E)   Five

Arithmetic Properties of numbers

To find the number of prime numbers between 1 and 100 that are factors of 7,150, find the prime factorization of 7,150 using a method similar to the following:

$7,150 = 10 \times 715$

$\qquad = (2 \times 5) \times (5 \times 143)$

$\qquad = 2 \times 5 \times 5 \times (11 \times 13)$

Thus, 7,150 has four prime factors: 2, 5, 11, and 13.

The correct answer is D.

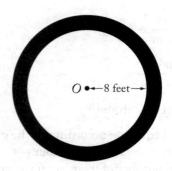

160. The figure above shows a circular flower bed, with its center at O, surrounded by a circular path that is 3 feet wide. What is the area of the path, in square feet?

    (A) 25π
    (B) 38π
    (C) 55π
    (D) 57π
    (E) 64π

Geometry Area (Circles)

The flower bed and the path form two concentric circles. Since the path is 3 feet wide, the radius of the outer circle is 8 feet + 3 feet = 11 feet. The area of a circle can be determined using the formula: area = $\pi(\text{radius})^2$.

The area of the path can thus be found by subtracting the area of the inner circle, A_1, from the area of the outer circle, A_2.

$A_2 - A_1 = \pi(11)^2 - \pi(8)^2 = 121\pi - 64\pi = 57\pi$

The correct answer is D.

161. The positive integer n is divisible by 25. If $\sqrt{n}$ is greater than 25, which of the following could be the value of $\dfrac{n}{25}$?

    (A) 22
    (B) 23
    (C) 24
    (D) 25
    (E) 26

Arithmetic Operations on radical expressions

If $\sqrt{n} > 25$, then $n > 25^2$. Therefore, $\dfrac{n}{25} > \dfrac{25^2}{25} = 25$ and the only answer choice that is greater than 25 is 26.

The correct answer is E.

162. A fruit-salad mixture consists of apples, peaches, and grapes in the ratio 6:5:2, respectively, by weight. If 39 pounds of the mixture is prepared, the mixture includes how many more pounds of apples than grapes?

    (A) 15
    (B) 12
    (C) 9
    (D) 6
    (E) 4

Algebra Applied problems

Using the given ratios, the information about the fruits in the mixture can be expressed as $6x + 5x + 2x = 39$, or $13x = 39$ and thus $x = 3$. There are $6x$ or $6(3) = 18$ pounds of apples and $2x$ or $2(3) = 6$ pounds of grapes. Therefore, there are $18 - 6 = 12$ more pounds of apples than pounds of grapes in 39 pounds of the mixture.

The correct answer is B.

163. This year Henry will save a certain amount of his income, and he will spend the rest. Next year Henry will have no income, but for each dollar that he saves this year, he will have $1 + r$ dollars available to spend. In terms of r, what fraction of his income should Henry save this year so that next year the amount he has available to spend will be equal to half the amount that he spends this year?

    (A) $\dfrac{1}{r+2}$
    (B) $\dfrac{1}{2r+2}$
    (C) $\dfrac{1}{3r+2}$
    (D) $\dfrac{1}{r+3}$
    (E) $\dfrac{1}{2r+3}$

Algebra Simplifying algebraic expressions

Let s be the amount Henry will save this year and let I be Henry's income this year. Then, $I - s$ is the amount he will spend this year. For each of the s dollars he saves this year, he will have $(1 + r)$ dollars to spend next year. Thus, he will have

$s(1 + r)$ dollars to spend next year. This amount is to be $\frac{1}{2}$ the amount he spends this year. The task is to find $\frac{s}{I}$, where I and s satisfy the condition $s(1 + r) = \frac{1}{2}(I - s)$. Solve for I as follows:

$$s(1 + r) = \frac{1}{2}(I - s)$$
$$2s(1 + r) = I - s$$
$$2s + 2rs = I - s$$
$$3s + 2rs = I$$
$$s(3 + 2r) = I$$

Then, $\frac{s}{I} = \frac{s}{s(3 + 2r)} = \frac{1}{2r + 3}$.

The correct answer is E.

164. If $m^{-1} = -\frac{1}{3}$, then m^{-2} is equal to

(A) -9
(B) -3
(C) $-\frac{1}{9}$
(D) $\frac{1}{9}$
(E) 9

Arithmetic Negative exponents

Using rules of exponents, $m^{-2} = m^{-1 \cdot 2} = (m^{-1})^2$, and since $m^{-1} = -\frac{1}{3}$, $m^{-2} = \left(-\frac{1}{3}\right)^2 = \frac{1}{9}$.

The correct answer is D.

165. Lois has x dollars more than Jim has, and together they have a total of y dollars. Which of the following represents the number of dollars that Jim has?

(A) $\frac{y - x}{2}$
(B) $y - \frac{x}{2}$
(C) $\frac{y}{2} - x$
(D) $2y - x$
(E) $y - 2x$

Algebra Simplifying algebraic expressions

Let J be the number of dollars that Jim has. Then, the amount that Lois has can be expressed as $J + x$ dollars. If Lois and Jim together have a total of y dollars, then:

$y = J + (J + x)$ total dollars = Jim's dollars + Lois's dollars

Solve this for J to determine the number of dollars that Jim has:

$$y = 2J + x$$
$$y - x = 2J$$
$$\frac{y - x}{2} = J$$

The correct answer is A.

166. During a certain season, a team won 80 percent of its first 100 games and 50 percent of its remaining games. If the team won 70 percent of its games for the entire season, what was the total number of games that the team played?

(A)   180
(B)   170
(C)   156
(D)   150
(E)   105

Arithmetic; Algebra Percents; Applied problems

Let G equal the number of games played by the team this season. The given information can be expressed as $(0.80)(100) + 0.50(G - 100) = 0.70G$, that is, 80 percent of the first 100 games plus 50 percent of the remaining games equals 70 percent of the total number of games played. This equation can be solved for G to determine the answer to the problem:

$$(0.80)(100) + 0.50(G - 100) = 0.70G$$

$80 + 0.50G - 50 = 0.70G$ simplify and distribute

$30 = 0.20G$ simplify and subtract $0.05G$ from both sides

$150 = G$ multiply by 5

The correct answer is D.

167. Of 30 applicants for a job, 14 had at least 4 years' experience, 18 had degrees, and 3 had less than 4 years' experience and did not have a degree. How many of the applicants had at least 4 years' experience and a degree?

    (A) 14
    (B) 13
    (C)   9
    (D)   7
    (E)   5

Arithmetic Operations on rational numbers

The problem classified the job applicants into two categories: whether they had more or less than 4 years' experience, and whether they had a degree. The given information can be summarized in the following table:

	At least 4 years' experience	Less than 4 years' experience	Total
Degree			18
No degree		3	
Total	14		30

Thus, according to the given information, $30 - 14 = 16$ applicants had less than 4 years' experience. Then, of those applicants with less than 4 years' experience, it is given that 3 applicants did not have a degree, so $16 - 3 = 13$ applicants had less than 4 years' experience and had a degree. Therefore, out of the given 18 applicants that had degrees, 13 applicants had less than 4 years' experience, so $18 - 13 = 5$ applicants had at least 4 years' experience with a degree. These results are shown in the following table.

	At least 4 years' experience	Less than 4 years' experience	Total
Degree	5	13	18
No degree		3	
Total	14	16	30

The correct answer is E.

168. If $1 + \dfrac{1}{x} = 2 - \dfrac{2}{x}$, then $x =$

    (A) -1
    (B) $\dfrac{1}{3}$
    (C) $\dfrac{2}{3}$
    (D) 2
    (E) 3

Algebra First-degree equations

Work the problem to solve the equation for x.

$$1 + \frac{1}{x} = 2 - \frac{2}{x}$$

$x + 1 = 2x - 2$ multiply through by x

$3 = x$ solve for x by adding 2 to and subtracting x from both sides

The correct answer is E.

169. Last year, for every 100 million vehicles that traveled on a certain highway, 96 vehicles were involved in accidents. If 3 billion vehicles traveled on the highway last year, how many of those vehicles were involved in accidents? (1 billion = 1,000,000,000)

    (A)   288
    (B)   320
    (C)   2,880
    (D)   3,200
    (E) 28,800

Arithmetic Operations on rational numbers

According to the given information, 96 out of every 100 million vehicles were in an accident last year. Thus, of the 3 billion vehicles on the highway last year, the number of vehicles involved in accidents was:

$$\frac{96}{100,000,000} \times 3,000,000,000 =$$

$$\frac{96}{100} \times 3,000 = 96 \times 30 = 2,880 \text{ vehicles}$$

The correct answer is C.

170. Thirty percent of the members of a swim club have passed the lifesaving test. Among the members who have *not* passed the test, 12 have taken the preparatory course and 30 have not taken the course. How many members are there in the swim club?

    (A) 60
    (B) 80
    (C) 100
    (D) 120
    (E) 140

Algebra Applied problems

If 30 percent of the club members have passed the test, then 70 percent have not. Among the members who have not passed the test, 12 have taken the course and 30 have not, for a total of 12 + 30 = 42 members who have not passed the test. Letting x represent the total number of members in the swim club, this information can be expressed as $0.70x = 42$, and so $x = 60$.

The correct answer is A.

171. What is the difference between the sixth and the fifth terms of the sequence 2, 4, 7, … whose nth term is $n + 2^{n-1}$?

    (A) 2
    (B) 3
    (C) 6
    (D) 16
    (E) 17

Algebra Simplifying algebraic expressions

According to the given formula, the sixth term of the sequence is $6 + 2^{6-1} = 6 + 2^5$ and the fifth term is $5 + 2^{5-1} = 5 + 2^4$. Then,

$(6 + 2^5) - (5 + 2^4) = (6 - 5) + (2^5 - 2^4)$

$= 1 + 2^4(2 - 1)$

$= 1 + 2^4$

$= 1 + 16$

$= 17$

The correct answer is E.

172. If $(x - 1)^2 = 400$, which of the following could be the value of $x - 5$?

    (A) 15
    (B) 14
    (C) -24
    (D) -25
    (E) -26

Algebra Second-degree equations

Work the problem by taking the square root of both sides and solving for x.

$(x - 1)^2 = 400$

$x - 1 = \pm 20$

$x - 1 = -20$, or $x - 1 = 20$

$x = -19$, or $x = 21$

Thus, $x - 5 = -24$ or 16.

The correct answer is C.

173. Which of the following describes all values of x for which $1 - x^2 \geq 0$?

    (A) $x \geq 1$
    (B) $x \leq -1$
    (C) $0 \leq x \leq 1$
    (D) $x \leq -1$ or $x \geq 1$
    (E) $-1 \leq x \leq 1$

Algebra Inequalities

The expression $1 - x^2$ can be factored as $(1 - x)(1 + x)$. The product is positive when both factors are positive (this happens if $1 \geq x$ and $x \geq -1$, or equivalently if $-1 \leq x \leq 1$) or both factors are negative (this happens if $1 \leq x$ and $x \leq 1$, which cannot happen), and therefore the solution is $-1 \leq x \leq 1$.

The correct answer is E.

174. The probability is $\frac{1}{2}$ that a certain coin will turn up heads on any given toss. If the coin is to be tossed three times, what is the probability that on at least one of the tosses the coin will turn up tails?

(A) $\dfrac{1}{8}$

(B) $\dfrac{1}{2}$

(C) $\dfrac{3}{4}$

(D) $\dfrac{7}{8}$

(E) $\dfrac{15}{16}$

Arithmetic Probability

Another way of stating that a coin toss will turn up tails at least once is to say that it will not turn up heads every time. The probability that on at least one of the tosses the coin will not turn up heads is 1 minus the probability that the coin will turn up heads on all three tosses. Each toss is an independent event, and so the probability of getting heads all three times is $\left(\dfrac{1}{2}\right)^3 = \dfrac{1}{8}$.

Thus, the probability of not getting heads all three times (that is, getting tails at least once) is $1 - \dfrac{1}{8} = \dfrac{7}{8}$.

The correct answer is D.

175. Of the final grades received by the students in a certain math course, $\dfrac{1}{5}$ are A's, $\dfrac{1}{4}$ are B's, $\dfrac{1}{2}$ are C's, and the remaining 10 grades are D's. What is the number of students in the course?

(A) 80
(B) 110
(C) 160
(D) 200
(E) 400

Algebra Applied problems

Let x be the number of students in the course. Then $\left(\dfrac{1}{5} + \dfrac{1}{4} + \dfrac{1}{2}\right)x$ or $\left(\dfrac{4}{20} + \dfrac{5}{20} + \dfrac{10}{20}\right)x$ or $\left(\dfrac{19}{20}\right)x$ of the students received grades of A, B, or C.

This means the 10 remaining grades represent $\dfrac{1}{20}$ of the students in the course. Thus, $\dfrac{1}{20}x = 10$, and $x = 200$.

The correct answer is D.

176. As x increases from 165 to 166, which of the following must increase?

I. $2x - 5$

II. $1 - \dfrac{1}{x}$

III. $\dfrac{1}{x^2 - x}$

(A) I only
(B) III only
(C) I and II
(D) I and III
(E) II and III

Algebra Simplifying algebraic expressions

Investigate each of the functions to determine if they increase from $x = 165$ to $x = 166$.

I.   Graphically, this represents a line with positive slope. Therefore, the function increases between any two values of x. A direct computation can also be used: $[2(166) - 5] - [2(165) - 5] = 2(166 - 165) = 2$, which is positive, and thus the function increases from $x = 165$ to $x = 166$.

II. Between any two positive values of x, $\dfrac{1}{x}$ decreases, and hence both $-\dfrac{1}{x}$ and $1 - \dfrac{1}{x}$ increase. A direct computation can also be used:

$$\left[1 - \dfrac{1}{166}\right] - \left[1 - \dfrac{1}{165}\right] =$$

$$\dfrac{1}{165} - \dfrac{1}{166} = \dfrac{166 - 165}{(165)(166)} = \dfrac{1}{(165)(166)},$$

which is positive, and thus the function increases from $x = 165$ to $x = 166$.

III. For $x = 165$, the denominator is $165^2 - 165 = (165)(165 - 1) = (165)(164)$, and for $x = 166$, the denominator is $166^2 - 166 = (166)(166 - 1) = (166)(165)$. Therefore,

$166^2 - 166 > 165^2 - 165$, and hence

$$\frac{1}{166^2 - 166} < \frac{1}{165^2 - 165},$$

which shows that $\dfrac{1}{x^2 - x}$ decreases from

$x = 165$ to $x = 166$.

The correct answer is C.

177. A rectangular box is 10 inches wide, 10 inches long, and 5 inches high. What is the greatest possible (straight-line) distance, in inches, between any two points on the box?

(A) 15
(B) 20
(C) 25
(D) $10\sqrt{2}$
(E) $10\sqrt{3}$

Geometry Pythagorean theorem

The greatest possible distance between any two points in a rectangular solid is the space diagonal

$(\overline{AD})$ of the rectangular solid as shown below.

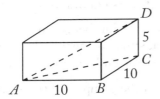

To compute the length of $\overline{AD}$, the Pythagorean theorem must be used twice as follows:

For $\triangle ABC$:

$AC^2 = AB^2 + BC^2$

$AC^2 = 10^2 + 10^2$

$AC^2 = 200$

$AC = \sqrt{200}$

For $\triangle ACD$:

$AD^2 = AC^2 + CD^2$

$AD^2 = \left(\sqrt{200}\right)^2 + 5^2$

$AD^2 = 200 + 25$

$AD^2 = 225$

$AD = 15$

The correct answer is A.

Club	Number of Students
Chess	40
Drama	30
Math	25

178. The table above shows the number of students in three clubs at McAuliffe School. Although no student is in all three clubs, 10 students are in both Chess and Drama, 5 students are in both Chess and Math, and 6 students are in both Drama and Math. How many different students are in the three clubs?

(A) 68
(B) 69
(C) 74
(D) 79
(E) 84

Arithmetic Interpretation of graphs and tables

A good way to solve this problem is to create a Venn diagram. To determine how many students to put in each section, begin by putting the given shared-student data in the overlapping sections. Put 0 in the intersection of all three clubs, 10 in the Chess and Drama intersection, 5 in the Chess and Math intersection, and 6 in the Drama and Math intersection, as shown in the Venn diagram below.

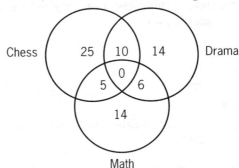

Subtracting the shared students from the totals in each club that are listed in the table establishes the members who belong only to that club. Through this process, it can be determined that the Chess club has 25 such members (40 − 10 − 5 = 25), the Drama club has 14 such members (30 − 10 − 6 = 14), and the Math club has 14 such members (25 − 5 − 6 = 14). Putting the number of unshared club members into the Venn diagram and then adding up all the sections of the diagram gives 25 + 14 + 14 + 10 + 5 + 6 = 74 students.

The correct answer is C.

179. The ratio of two quantities is 3 to 4. If each of the quantities is increased by 5, what is the ratio of these two new quantities?

(A) $\frac{3}{4}$

(B) $\frac{8}{9}$

(C) $\frac{18}{19}$

(D) $\frac{23}{24}$

(E) It cannot be determined from the information given.

Algebra Applied problems

Both 3 to 4 and 6 to 8 are examples of two quantities in the ratio 3 to 4. Increasing both numbers in each of these examples by 5 gives 8 to 9 and 11 to 13. Since $\frac{8}{9} \neq \frac{11}{13}$, the ratio of the two new quantities cannot be determined from the information given.

The correct answer is E.

180. If the average (arithmetic mean) of x and y is 60 and the average (arithmetic mean) of y and z is 80, what is the value of z – x?

(A) 70
(B) 40
(C) 20
(D) 10
(E) It cannot be determined from the information given.

Arithmetic; Algebra Statistics; Applied problems

The given information gives the following two equations:

$\frac{x+y}{2} = 60$ since the average of x and y is 60 and

$\frac{y+z}{2} = 80$ since the average of y and z is 80.

The two equations can be rewritten as $x + y = 120$ and $y + z = 160$. Subtracting the first equation from the second equation gives $(y + z) - (x + y) = 160 - 120$, or $z - x = 40$.

The correct answer is B.

181. If $\frac{1}{2}$ of the air in a tank is removed with each stroke of a vacuum pump, what fraction of the original amount of air has been removed after 4 strokes?

(A) $\frac{15}{16}$

(B) $\frac{7}{8}$

(C) $\frac{1}{4}$

(D) $\frac{1}{8}$

(E) $\frac{1}{16}$

Arithmetic Operations on rational numbers

With each stroke's removal of $\frac{1}{2}$ of the tank's air, the amount of air being removed from the tank on that stroke is equal to the amount of air remaining in the tank after that stroke. With the first stroke of the pump, $\frac{1}{2}$ of the air is removed; with the second stroke, $\frac{1}{2} \times \frac{1}{2} = \frac{1}{4}$ of the air is removed, leaving $\frac{1}{4}$ of the air. With the third stroke, $\frac{1}{2} \times \frac{1}{4} = \frac{1}{8}$ of the air is removed, leaving $\frac{1}{8}$ of the air, and with the fourth stroke, $\frac{1}{2} \times \frac{1}{8} = \frac{1}{16}$ of the air is removed. Therefore, with four strokes,

$\frac{1}{2} + \frac{1}{4} + \frac{1}{8} + \frac{1}{16} = \frac{8}{16} + \frac{4}{16} + \frac{2}{16} + \frac{1}{16} = \frac{15}{16}$ of the air has been removed.

The correct answer is A.

182. If the two-digit integers M and N are positive and have the same digits, but in reverse order, which of the following CANNOT be the sum of M and N?

   (A)   181
   (B)   165
   (C)   121
   (D)   99
   (E)   44

Algebra Applied problems

It is given that M and N have the same digits in reverse order. Let $M = 10t + u$ and $N = 10u + t$, where t and u are two digits. Then, $M + N = (10t + u) + (10u + t) = 11t + 11u = 11(t + u)$. This means that any sum of the two integers M and N must also be a multiple of 11. Of the answer choices, only 181 is not a multiple of 11 and thus cannot be the sum of M and N.

The correct answer is A.

183. Car X and Car Y traveled the same 80-mile route. If Car X took 2 hours and Car Y traveled at an average speed that was 50 percent faster than the average speed of Car X, how many hours did it take Car Y to travel the route?

   (A) $\dfrac{2}{3}$

   (B)   1

   (C) $1\dfrac{1}{3}$

   (D) $1\dfrac{3}{5}$

   (E)   3

Arithmetic Operations on rational numbers

Substituting the given information in the formula rate = $\dfrac{\text{distance}}{\text{time}}$, it can be determined that Car X traveled at a rate of $\dfrac{80 \text{ miles}}{2 \text{ hours}}$, or 40 miles per hour. Thus, Car Y traveled at 1.50(40) = 60 miles per hour. At this speed, Car Y would travel the 80-mile route in $\dfrac{80}{60} = \dfrac{4}{3} = 1\dfrac{1}{3}$ hours.

The correct answer is C.

184. If the average (arithmetic mean) of the four numbers K, $2K + 3$, $3K - 5$, and $5K + 1$ is 63, what is the value of K?

   (A)   11

   (B) $15\dfrac{3}{4}$

   (C)   22

   (D)   23

   (E) $25\dfrac{3}{10}$

Arithmetic Statistics

Using the formula $\dfrac{\text{sum of } n \text{ values}}{n}$ = average, the given information can be expressed in the following equation and solved for K.

$$\frac{K + (2K + 3) + (3K - 5) + (5K + 1)}{4} = 63$$

$$\frac{K + 2K + 3K + 5K + 3 - 5 + 1}{4} = 63$$

$$\frac{11K - 1}{4} = 63$$

$$11K - 1 = 252$$

$$11K = 253$$

$$K = 23$$

The correct answer is D.

185. If p is an even integer and q is an odd integer, which of the following must be an odd integer?

   (A) $\dfrac{p}{q}$

   (B) pq

   (C) $2p + q$

   (D) $2(p + q)$

   (E) $\dfrac{3p}{q}$

Arithmetic Properties of numbers

Since it is given that p is even and q is odd, use these properties to test the outcome of each answer choice to determine which one must be odd.

A $\dfrac{\text{even}}{\text{odd}}$ = even   must be even

B   (even)(odd) = even   must be even

C   2(even) + odd
    = even + odd = odd   must be odd

D   2(even + odd)
    = 2(odd) = even   must be even

E $\dfrac{3(\text{even})}{\text{odd}} = \dfrac{\text{even}}{\text{odd}}$ = even   must be even

The correct answer is C.

186. Drum X is $\dfrac{1}{2}$ full of oil and Drum Y, which has twice the capacity of Drum X, is $\dfrac{2}{3}$ full of oil. If all of the oil in Drum X is poured into Drum Y, then Drum Y will be filled to what fraction of its capacity?

(A) $\dfrac{3}{4}$

(B) $\dfrac{5}{6}$

(C) $\dfrac{11}{12}$

(D) $\dfrac{7}{6}$

(E) $\dfrac{11}{6}$

Algebra Applied problems

Let y represent the capacity of Drum Y. Since Y has twice the capacity of Drum X, Drum X has half the capacity of Drum Y, and thus the capacity of Drum X can be expressed as $\dfrac{1}{2}y$. Since Drum X is half full, the amount of oil in Drum X is equal to $\dfrac{1}{2}\left(\dfrac{1}{2}y\right)=\dfrac{1}{4}y$. According to the given information, the initial amount of oil in Drum Y is $\dfrac{2}{3}y$. When the oil in Drum X is poured into Drum Y, Drum Y thus contains $\dfrac{1}{4}y+\dfrac{2}{3}y=\dfrac{3}{12}y+\dfrac{8}{12}y=\dfrac{11}{12}y$, which is $\dfrac{11}{12}$ of its capacity.

The correct answer is C.

187. If x > 0, $\dfrac{x}{50}+\dfrac{x}{25}$ is what percent of x ?

(A)   6%
(B)   25%
(C)   37%
(D)   60%
(E)   75%

Algebra; Arithmetic Simplifying algebraic expressions; Percents

Because the question asks for a percent, use a common denominator of 100 to combine the two terms.

$\dfrac{x}{50}+\dfrac{x}{25}=\dfrac{2x}{100}+\dfrac{4x}{100}=\dfrac{6x}{100}=\left(\dfrac{6}{100}\right)x$, which is 6 percent of x.

The correct answer is A.

188. If the operation ⊛ is defined for all a and b by the equation $a \circledast b = \dfrac{a^2b}{3}$, then 2 ⊛ (3 ⊛ −1) =

(A)   4

(B)   2

(C) $-\dfrac{4}{3}$

(D)   −2

(E)   −4

Arithmetic Operations on rational numbers

Because 3 ⊛ −1 is within the parentheses, its value is computed first:

$$3 \circledast -1 = \dfrac{3^2(-1)}{3}$$
$$= \dfrac{9(-1)}{3}$$
$$= \dfrac{-9}{3}$$
$$= -3$$

Then, $2 \circledast (3 \circledast -1) = 2 \circledast -3$, which has the following value:

$$2 \circledast (3 \circledast -1) = 2 \circledast -3$$

$$= \frac{2^2(-3)}{3}$$

$$= \frac{4(-3)}{3}$$

$$= 4(-1)$$

$$= -4$$

The correct answer is E.

189. The inside dimensions of a rectangular wooden box are 6 inches by 8 inches by 10 inches. A cylindrical canister is to be placed inside the box so that it stands upright when the closed box rests on one of its six faces. Of all such canisters that could be used, what is the radius, in inches, of the one that has maximum volume?

    (A) 3
    (B) 4
    (C) 5
    (D) 6
    (E) 8

Geometry Volume

The largest cylinder that can fit in a rectangular box will have the same height as the box and a diameter equal to the smaller dimension of the top of the box. By definition, the diameter of the canister is twice its radius. One *possible* canister placement in the box is illustrated below.

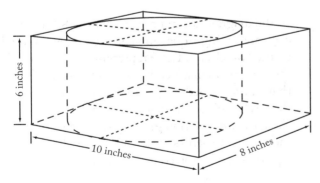

However, since the box can rest on any of three differently sized faces, it is necessary to consider

the volume of each possibility. The formula for calculating volume is volume = π(radius)^2(height), or $v = \pi r^2 h$; the possible volumes for the canister are those shown in the following table:

Dimensions of the box top	r	h	v
6 by 8	3	10	90π
6 by 10	3	8	72π
8 by 10	4	6	96π

Thus, the radius, in inches, of the canister having the maximum volume is 4.

The correct answer is B.

190. What is the units digit of $(13)^4(17)^2(29)^3$?

    (A) 9
    (B) 7
    (C) 5
    (D) 3
    (E) 1

Arithmetic Operations on rational numbers

The units digit of 13^4 is 1, since $3 \times 3 \times 3 \times 3 = 81$; the units digit of 17^2 is 9, since $7 \times 7 = 49$; and the units digit of 29^3 is 9, since $9 \times 9 \times 9 = 729$. Therefore, the units digit of $(13)^4(17)^2(29)^3$ is 1, since $1 \times 9 \times 9 = 81$.

The correct answer is E.

191. Pat will walk from Intersection X to Intersection Y along a route that is confined to the square grid of four streets and three avenues shown in the map above. How many routes from X to Y can Pat take that have the minimum possible length?

(A)   6
(B)   8
(C)   10
(D)   14
(E)   16

Arithmetic Elementary combinatorics

In order to walk from Intersection X to Intersection Y by one of the routes of minimum possible length, Pat must travel only upward or rightward between the intersections on the map. Let U represent upward movements and R represent rightward movements. It takes 3 upward and 2 rightward movements to complete the route.

The following 10 routes are possible:

$U\,U\,U\,R\,R$ $U\,R\,R\,U\,U$
$U\,U\,R\,U\,R$ $R\,R\,U\,U\,U$
$U\,U\,R\,R\,U$ $R\,U\,U\,U\,R$
$U\,R\,U\,U\,R$ $R\,U\,U\,R\,U$
$U\,R\,U\,R\,U$ $R\,U\,R\,U\,U$

The correct answer is C.

192. The ratio, by volume, of soap to alcohol to water in a certain solution is 2:50:100. The solution will be altered so that the ratio of soap to alcohol is doubled while the ratio of soap to water is halved. If the altered solution will contain 100 cubic centimeters of alcohol, how many cubic centimeters of water will it contain?

(A)   50
(B)   200
(C)   400
(D)   625
(E)   800

Arithmetic Operations on rational numbers

From $\dfrac{\text{soap}_{\text{original}}}{\text{alcohol}_{\text{original}}} = \dfrac{2}{50}$ we get

$$\frac{\text{soap}_{\text{altered}}}{\text{alcohol}_{\text{altered}}} = 2\left(\frac{\text{soap}_{\text{original}}}{\text{alcohol}_{\text{original}}}\right) = 2\left(\frac{2}{50}\right) = \frac{2}{25},$$

and from $\dfrac{\text{soap}_{\text{original}}}{\text{water}_{\text{original}}} = \dfrac{2}{100}$ we get

$$\frac{\text{soap}_{\text{altered}}}{\text{water}_{\text{altered}}} = \frac{1}{2}\left(\frac{\text{soap}_{\text{original}}}{\text{water}_{\text{original}}}\right) = \frac{1}{2}\left(\frac{2}{100}\right) = \frac{1}{100}.$$

Therefore, the amount of soap in the altered solution can be found by solving $\dfrac{\text{soap}_{\text{altered}}}{100} = \dfrac{2}{25}$, which gives $\text{soap}_{\text{altered}} = \dfrac{2}{25} \cdot \dfrac{100}{1} = 8$, and now the amount of water in the altered solution can be found by solving $\dfrac{8}{\text{water}_{\text{altered}}} = \dfrac{1}{100}$, which gives $\text{water}_{\text{altered}} = 800$.

The correct answer is E.

193. If 75 percent of a class answered the first question on a certain test correctly, 55 percent answered the second question on the test correctly, and 20 percent answered neither of the questions correctly, what percent answered both correctly?

(A)   10%
(B)   20%
(C)   30%
(D)   50%
(E)   65%

Arithmetic Percents

For questions of this type, it is convenient to draw a Venn diagram to represent the conditions in the problem. For example, the given information can be depicted:

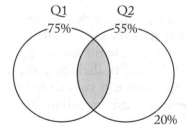

In the diagram it can be seen that the 80% of the class answering a question correctly is represented by the two circles. Let x represent the percent of the class that answered both questions correctly, that is, the shaded region above. Since the sum of the circles minus their overlap equals 80% of the class, the information given in the problem can then be expressed as 75% + 55% − x = 80%. This equation can be solved for x as follows:

$$75\% + 55\% - x = 80\%$$
$$130\% - x = 80\%$$
$$-x = -50\%$$
$$x = 50\%$$

The correct answer is D.

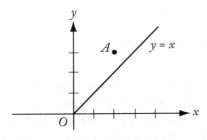

194. In the rectangular coordinate system above, the line $y = x$ is the perpendicular bisector of segment AB (not shown), and the x-axis is the perpendicular bisector of segment BC (not shown). If the coordinates of point A are (2,3), what are the coordinates of point C ?

(A) (–3,–2)
(B) (–3,2)
(C) (2,–3)
(D) (3,–2)
(E) (2,3)

Geometry Simple coordinate geometry

Since the line $y = x$ is the perpendicular bisector of $\overline{AB}$, B is the reflection of A through this line. In any reflection through the line $y = x$, the x-coordinate and the y-coordinate of a point become interchanged. Thus, if the coordinates of A are (2,3), the coordinates of B are (3,2).

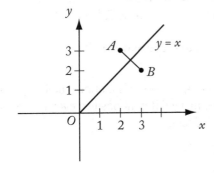

Since the x-axis is the perpendicular bisector of $\overline{BC}$, C is the reflection of B through the x-axis. In any reflection through the x-axis, the x-coordinate remains the same, and the sign of the y-coordinate changes.

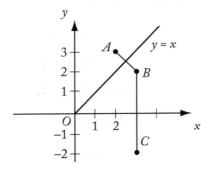

Since the coordinates of B are (3,2), the coordinates of C are therefore (3,–2).

The correct answer is D.

195. A store currently charges the same price for each towel that it sells. If the current price of each towel were to be increased by $1, 10 fewer of the towels could be bought for $120, excluding sales tax. What is the current price of each towel?

(A) $ 1
(B) $ 2
(C) $ 3
(D) $ 4
(E) $12

Algebra Applied problems

Let p be the current price per towel, and let n be the number of towels that can be bought for $120. Then the information in the problem can be expressed in the following equations:

(i) $pn = 120$

(ii) $(p + 1)(n - 10) = 120$ or equivalently

(iii) $pn + n - 10p - 10 = 120$.

Then replace pn in (iii) with 120 to get:

$$120 + n - 10p - 10 = 120$$

$$n - 10p - 10 = 0$$

$$n - 10(p + 1) = 0$$

$$n = 10(p + 1)$$

$$np = 10p(p + 1)$$

$$120 = 10p(p + 1)$$

$$12 = p(p + 1)$$

$$0 = p^2 + p - 12$$

$$0 = (p + 4)(p - 3)$$

$$p = 3$$

The correct answer is C.

Number of Solid-Colored Marbles in Three Jars			
Jar	Number of red marbles	Number of green marbles	Total number of red and green marbles
P	x	y	80
Q	y	z	120
R	x	z	160

196. In the table above, what is the number of green marbles in Jar R ?

(A) 70
(B) 80
(C) 90
(D) 100
(E) 110

Arithmetic; Algebra Interpretation of tables; Applied problems

First, set up an equation to find the total number of marbles in the three jars as follows:

$$x + y + y + z + x + z = 80 + 120 + 160$$

$$2x + 2y + 2z = 360 \quad \text{combine the like terms}$$

$$x + y + z = 180 \quad \text{divide both sides by 2}$$

Then, since it can be seen from the table that the number of green marbles in Jar R is z, solve for z to answer the problem. To do this most efficiently, use the information from the table for Jar P, which is that $x + y = 80$.

$$x + y + z = 180$$

$$80 + z = 180 \quad \text{substitute 80 for } x + y$$

$$z = 100$$

The correct answer is D.

197. A point on the edge of a fan blade that is rotating in a plane is 10 centimeters from the center of the fan. What is the distance traveled, in centimeters, by this point in 15 seconds when the fan runs at the rate of 300 revolutions per minute?

(A) 750π
(B) $1,500\pi$
(C) $1,875\pi$
(D) $3,000\pi$
(E) $7,500\pi$

Geometry Circles; Circumference; Applied problems

Since 15 seconds is $\dfrac{15}{60} = \dfrac{1}{4}$ minute, if the fan blade is rotating at the rate of 300 revolutions per minute, then in $\dfrac{1}{4}$ minute it rotates $\dfrac{300}{4} = 75$ revolutions. The distance the point on the edge of the fan blade rotates in 75 revolutions is 75 times the circumference of a circle with radius 10 centimeters. The circumference C of a circle with radius r is $C = 2\pi r$. Thus the distance the point travels is $75[2\pi(10)] = 1,500\pi$.

The correct answer is B.

198. If $n = 4p$, where p is a prime number greater than 2, how many different positive <u>even</u> divisors does n have, including n ?

(A) Two
(B) Three
(C) Four
(D) Six
(E) Eight

Arithmetic Properties of numbers

Since p is a prime greater than 2, p must be odd. Therefore, the possible even divisors of $n = 4p$ are 2, 4, $2p$, and $4p$. Alternatively, choose such a prime, for example $p = 3$, and determine the number of positive even divisors that $n = 4p = 12$ has.

The correct answer is C.

I.   72, 73, 74, 75, 76
II. 74, 74, 74, 74, 74
III. 62, 74, 74, 74, 89

199. The data sets I, II, and III above are ordered from greatest standard deviation to least standard deviation in which of the following?

(A)   I, II, III
(B)   I, III, II
(C)   II, III, I
(D)   III, I, II
(E)   III, II, I

Arithmetic Statistics

The data set with the least standard deviation will be the data set with elements most closely clustered around the mean of the data set, and the data set with the greatest standard deviation will be the data set with elements that are spread out farthest from the mean of the data set.

Because set I is symmetric about 74 (73 is 1 less than 74 and 75 is 1 more than 74; 72 is 2 less than 74 and 76 is 2 more than 74), the mean of set I is 74. Because every number in set II is 74, the mean of set II is 74. The mean of set III is $\frac{62 + 3(74) + 89}{5} = \frac{373}{5} = 74.6$.

The elements of set II do not deviate at all from 74, so set II has the least standard deviation. The most that any element of set I differs from 74 is 2, but there are elements of set III that differ from 74.6 by 12.6 and 14.4. Therefore, set III has a greater standard deviation than set I, which has a greater standard deviation than set II.

The correct answer is D.

200. Of the 50 researchers in a workgroup, 40 percent will be assigned to Team A and the remaining 60 percent to Team B. However, 70 percent of the researchers prefer Team A and 30 percent prefer Team B. What is the lowest possible number of researchers who will NOT be assigned to the team they prefer?

(A)   15
(B)   17
(C)   20
(D)   25
(E)   30

Arithmetic Percents

The number of researchers assigned to Team A will be $(0.40)(50) = 20$, and so 30 will be assigned to Team B. The number of researchers who prefer Team A is $(0.70)(50) = 35$, and the rest, 15, prefer Team B.

If all 15 who prefer Team B are assigned to Team B, which is to have 30 researchers, then 15 who prefer Team A will need to be assigned to Team B. Alternatively, since there are only 20 spots on Team A, $35 - 20 = 15$ who prefer Team A but will have to go to Team B instead.

The correct answer is A.

201. If m is the average (arithmetic mean) of the first 10 positive multiples of 5 and if M is the median of the first 10 positive multiples of 5, what is the value of $M - m$?

(A)   −5
(B)   0
(C)   5
(D)   25
(E)   27.5

Arithmetic Statistics

The first 10 positive multiples of 5 are 5, 10, 15, 20, 25, 30, 35, 40, 45, and 50. From this, the average (arithmetic mean) of the 10 multiples, that is, $\frac{\text{sum of values}}{\text{number of values}}$, can be calculated:

$$m = \frac{5 + 10 + 15 + 20 + 25 + 30 + 35 + 40 + 45 + 50}{10}$$

$$= \frac{275}{10} = 27.5.$$

Since there is an even number of multiples, the median, M, is the average of the middle two numbers, 25 and 30:

$$M = \frac{25 + 30}{2} = 27.5.$$

Therefore, the median minus the average is:

$$M - m = 27.5 - 27.5 = 0.$$

This problem can also be solved as follows. Since the values can be grouped in pairs (i.e., 5 and 50, 10 and 45, 15 and 40, etc.), each of which is symmetric with respect to the median, it follows that the average and median are equal.

The correct answer is B.

202. If $m > 0$ and x is m percent of y, then, in terms of m, y is what percent of x ?

   (A) $100m$

   (B) $\dfrac{1}{100m}$

   (C) $\dfrac{1}{m}$

   (D) $\dfrac{10}{m}$

   (E) $\dfrac{10{,}000}{m}$

Arithmetic Percents

The information that x is m percent of y can be expressed as $x = \dfrac{m}{100}\, y$ and solved for y as follows:

$$x = \frac{m}{100}\, y$$

$$\frac{100}{m}\, x = y$$

Then, to convert the fraction $\dfrac{100}{m}$ to an equivalent percent, multiply by 100, thus obtaining the value $\dfrac{10{,}000}{m}$.

The correct answer is E.

203. What is the 25th digit to the right of the decimal point in the decimal form of $\dfrac{6}{11}$?

   (A)   3
   (B)   4
   (C)   5
   (D)   6
   (E)   7

Arithmetic Properties of numbers

The fraction in its decimal form is $\dfrac{6}{11} = 0.545454\ldots$. Every odd-numbered digit to the right of the decimal point is 5, so the 25th digit must be 5.

The correct answer is C.

204. John and Mary were each paid x dollars in advance to do a certain job together. John worked on the job for 10 hours and Mary worked 2 hours less than John. If Mary gave John y dollars of her payment so that they would have received the same hourly wage, what was the dollar amount, in terms of y, that John was paid in advance?

   (A) $4y$
   (B) $5y$
   (C) $6y$
   (D) $8y$
   (E) $9y$

Algebra Applied problems

Let w be the amount of Mary and John's same hourly wage. To set their hourly pay equal, John, who worked 10 hours, needs to be paid $10w$, and Mary, who worked 8 hours, needs to be paid $8w$. Since Mary gave John y dollars, Mary now has $x - y$ dollars and John now has $x + y$ dollars. Their pay can thus be expressed as follows:

$x - y = 8w$	Mary's pay
$x + y = 10w$	John's pay

Subtract the first equation from the second and solve for w.

$$2y = 2w$$

$$y = w$$

Substitute y for w in the second equation, and solve for x, the amount each was paid in advance.

$$x + y = 10\,y$$
$$x = 9\,y$$

The correct answer is E.

205. In the rectangular coordinate system above, if point R (not shown) lies on the positive y-axis and the area of triangle ORP is 12, what is the y-coordinate of point R?

(A)   3
(B)   6
(C)   9
(D)   12
(E)   24

Geometry Simple coordinate geometry; Area

Since O and P of triangle ORP are already drawn and R has to be on the positive y-axis, the triangle is a right triangle with its base length the distance from the origin O (0,0) to P (4,0), which is 4.

Since the area of a triangle $= \dfrac{\text{(base)(height)}}{2}$, the information about the area and base can be expressed as follows and solved for the height of triangle OPR:

$$12 = \frac{(4)(\text{height})}{2}$$

$12 = 2(\text{height})$ simplify the right side

$6 = \text{height}$ solve for the height

On the y-axis, the x-coordinate is 0 and the y-coordinate is the distance above the axis that the point is located. In this case, the y-coordinate is the height of the triangle.

The correct answer is B.

206. Car A is 20 miles behind Car B, which is traveling in the same direction along the same route as Car A. Car A is traveling at a constant speed of 58 miles per hour and Car B is traveling at a constant speed of 50 miles per hour. How many hours will it take for Car A to overtake and drive 8 miles ahead of Car B?

(A)   1.5
(B)   2.0
(C)   2.5
(D)   3.0
(E)   3.5

Arithmetic Operations on rational numbers

Understand that Car A first has to travel 20 miles to catch up to Car B and then has to travel an additional 8 miles ahead of Car B, for a total of 28 extra miles to travel relative to Car B. It can be stated that Car A is traveling $58 - 50 = 8$ miles per hour faster than Car B. Solving the

distance = (rate)(time) formula for time yields

$$\frac{\text{distance}}{\text{rate}} = \text{time}.$$

By substitution into this formula, it will take

Car A $\dfrac{28 \text{ miles}}{8 \text{ miles per hour}} = 3.5$ hours to overtake

and drive 8 miles ahead of Car B.

The correct answer is E.

207. For the past n days, the average (arithmetic mean) daily production at a company was 50 units. If today's production of 90 units raises the average to 55 units per day, what is the value of n?

(A)   30
(B)   18
(C)   10
(D)   9
(E)   7

Arithmetic; Algebra Statistics; Applied problems; Simultaneous equations

Let x be the total production of the past n days.

Using the formula average $= \dfrac{\text{sum of values}}{\text{number of values}}$, the information in the problem can be expressed in the following two equations:

$$50 = \frac{x}{n}$$ daily average of 50 units over the past n days

$$55 = \frac{x+90}{n+1}$$ increased daily average when including today's 90 units

Solving the first equation for x gives $x = 50n$. Then substituting $50n$ for x in the second equation gives the following that can be solved for n:

$$55 = \frac{50n + 90}{n+1}$$

$55(n + 1) = 50n + 90$ multiply both sides by $(n + 1)$

$55n + 55 = 50n + 90$ distribute the 55

$5n = 35$ subtract $50n$ and 55 from both sides

$n = 7$ divide both sides by 5

The correct answer is E.

$$\left(\frac{x+1}{x-1}\right)^2$$

208. If $x \neq 0$ and $x \neq 1$, and if x is replaced by $\dfrac{1}{x}$ everywhere in the expression above, then the resulting expression is equivalent to

(A) $\left(\dfrac{x+1}{x-1}\right)^2$

(B) $\left(\dfrac{x-1}{x+1}\right)^2$

(C) $\dfrac{x^2+1}{1-x^2}$

(D) $\dfrac{x^2-1}{x^2+1}$

(E) $-\left(\dfrac{x-1}{x+1}\right)^2$

Algebra Simplifying algebraic expressions

Substitute $\dfrac{1}{x}$ for x in the expression and simplify.

$$\left(\frac{\frac{1}{x}+1}{\frac{1}{x}-1}\right)^2$$

Multiply the numerator and denominator inside the parentheses by x to eliminate the compound fractions.

$$\left(\frac{x\left(\frac{1}{x}+1\right)}{x\left(\frac{1}{x}-1\right)}\right)^2$$

Distribute the x's.

$$\left(\frac{1+x}{1-x}\right)^2$$

Since this is not one of the answer choices, it is necessary to simplify further. With the knowledge that $1 + x = x + 1$ and $1 - x = -(x - 1)$, it can be stated that

$$\left(\frac{1+x}{1-x}\right)^2 = \left(\frac{x+1}{-(x-1)}\right)^2 = \left(-\frac{x+1}{(x-1)}\right)^2 = \left(\frac{x+1}{x-1}\right)^2$$

because the negative, when squared, is positive.

The correct answer is A.

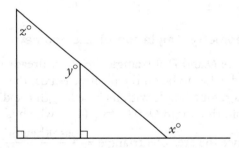

209. In the figure above, if $z = 50$, then $x + y =$

(A)   230
(B)   250
(C)   260
(D)   270
(E)   290

Geometry Angles; Measures of angles

Refer to the figure below.

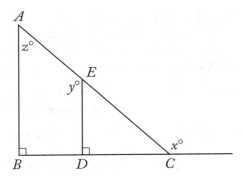

Triangle ABC is a right triangle, and segment AB is parallel to segment ED since they are both perpendicular to the same segment ($\overline{BC}$). Therefore, $m\angle DEC = m\angle BAC = z° = 50°$. So, since $\angle DEC$ and $\angle AED$ form a straight line at E, $y + 50 = 180$, or $y = 130$.

The measure of an exterior angle of a triangle is the sum of the measures of the nonadjacent interior angles. Thus,

$m\angle x = m\angle z + 90°$, or

$m\angle x = 50° + 90° = 140°$

Thus, $x + y = 140 + 130 = 270$.

The correct answer is D.

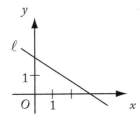

210. In the coordinate system above, which of the following is the equation of line ℓ?

(A) $2x - 3y = 6$
(B) $2x + 3y = 6$
(C) $3x + 2y = 6$
(D) $2x - 3y = -6$
(E) $3x - 2y = -6$

Geometry Simple coordinate geometry

The line is shown going through the points $(0,2)$ and $(3,0)$. The slope of the line can be found with the formula slope $= \dfrac{\text{change in } y}{\text{change in } x} = \dfrac{y_2 - y_1}{x_2 - x_1}$, for two points (x_1, y_1) and (x_2, y_2). Thus, the slope of this line equals $\dfrac{0-2}{3-0} = -\dfrac{2}{3}$. Using the formula for a line of $y = mx + b$, where m is the slope and b is the y-intercept (in this case, 2), an equation for this line is $y = -\dfrac{2}{3}x + 2$. Since this equation must be compared to the available answer choices, the following further steps should be taken:

$y = -\dfrac{2}{3}x + 2$

$3y = -2x + 6$ \qquad multiply both sides by 3

$2x + 3y = 6$ \qquad add $2x$ to both sides

This problem can also be solved as follows. From the graph, when $x = 0$, y is positive; when $y = 0$, x is positive. This eliminates all but B and C. Of these, B is the only line containing $(0,2)$. Still another way is to use $(0,2)$ to eliminate A, C, and E, and then use $(3,0)$ to eliminate D.

The correct answer is B.

211. If a two-digit positive integer has its digits reversed, the resulting integer differs from the original by 27. By how much do the two digits differ?

(A) 3
(B) 4
(C) 5
(D) 6
(E) 7

Algebra Applied problems

Let the one two-digit integer be represented by $10t + s$, where s and t are digits, and let the other integer with the reversed digits be represented by $10s + t$. The information that the difference between the integers is 27 can be expressed in the following equation, which can be solved for the answer.

$(10s + t) - (10t + s) = 27$

$10s + t - 10t - s = 27$ distribute the negative

$9s - 9t = 27$ combine like terms

$s - t = 3$ divide both sides by 9

Thus, it is seen that the two digits s and t differ by 3.

The correct answer is A.

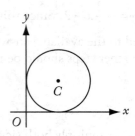

212. The circle with center C shown above is tangent to both axes. If the distance from O to C is equal to k, what is the radius of the circle, in terms of k ?

(A) k

(B) $\dfrac{k}{\sqrt{2}}$

(C) $\dfrac{k}{\sqrt{3}}$

(D) $\dfrac{k}{2}$

(E) $\dfrac{k}{3}$

Geometry Circles; Simple coordinate geometry

In a circle, all distances from the circle to the center are the same and called the radius, r.

Since the horizontal distance from C to the y-axis is also a radius, the base of the triangle drawn will be r as well. This creates a right triangle, and so the Pythagorean theorem (or $a^2 + b^2 = c^2$) applies.

$r^2 + r^2 = k^2$ substitute values into Pythagorean theorem;

$2r^2 = k^2$ combine like terms

$r^2 = \dfrac{k^2}{2}$ divide both sides by 2

$r = \sqrt{\dfrac{k^2}{2}}$ take the square root of both sides

$r = \dfrac{k}{\sqrt{2}}$ simplify the square root

The correct answer is B.

213. In an electric circuit, two resistors with resistances x and y are connected in parallel. In this case, if r is the combined resistance of these two resistors, then the reciprocal of r is equal to the sum of the reciprocals of x and y. What is r in terms of x and y ?

(A) xy

(B) $x + y$

(C) $\dfrac{1}{x + y}$

(D) $\dfrac{xy}{x + y}$

(E) $\dfrac{x + y}{xy}$

Algebra Applied problems

Note that two numbers are reciprocals of each other if and only if their product is 1. Thus the reciprocals of r, x, and y are $\dfrac{1}{r}$, $\dfrac{1}{x}$, and $\dfrac{1}{y}$, respectively. So, according to the problem, $\dfrac{1}{r} = \dfrac{1}{x} + \dfrac{1}{y}$. To solve this equation for r, begin by creating a common denominator on the right side by multiplying the first fraction by $\dfrac{y}{y}$ and the second fraction by $\dfrac{x}{x}$:

$$\frac{1}{r} = \frac{1}{x} + \frac{1}{y}$$

$$\frac{1}{r} = \frac{y}{xy} + \frac{x}{xy}$$

$$\frac{1}{r} = \frac{x+y}{xy} \qquad \text{combine the fractions on the right side}$$

$$r = \frac{xy}{x+y} \qquad \text{invert the fractions on both sides}$$

The correct answer is D.

214. Xavier, Yvonne, and Zelda each try independently to solve a problem. If their individual probabilities for success are $\frac{1}{4}$, $\frac{1}{2}$, and $\frac{5}{8}$, respectively, what is the probability that Xavier and Yvonne, but not Zelda, will solve the problem?

(A) $\frac{11}{8}$

(B) $\frac{7}{8}$

(C) $\frac{9}{64}$

(D) $\frac{5}{64}$

(E) $\frac{3}{64}$

Arithmetic Probability

Since the individuals' probabilities are independent, they can be multiplied to figure out the combined probability. The probability of Xavier's success is given as $\frac{1}{4}$, and the probability of Yvonne's success is given as $\frac{1}{2}$. Since the probability of Zelda's success is given as $\frac{5}{8}$, then the probability of her NOT solving the problem is $1 - \frac{5}{8} = \frac{3}{8}$. Thus, the combined probability is $\left(\frac{1}{4}\right)\left(\frac{1}{2}\right)\left(\frac{3}{8}\right) = \frac{3}{64}$.

The correct answer is E.

215. If $\frac{1}{x} - \frac{1}{x+1} = \frac{1}{x+4}$, then x could be

(A) 0
(B) −1
(C) −2
(D) −3
(E) −4

Algebra Second-degree equations

Solve the equation for x. Begin by multiplying all the terms by $x(x+1)(x+4)$ to eliminate the denominators.

$$\frac{1}{x} - \frac{1}{x+1} = \frac{1}{x+4}$$

$(x+1)(x+4) - x(x+4) = x(x+1)$

$(x+4)(x+1-x) = x(x+1)$ factor the $(x+4)$ out front on the left side

$(x+4)(1) = x(x+1)$ simplify

$x+4 = x^2 + x$ distribute the x on the right side

$4 = x^2$ subtract x from both sides

$\pm 2 = x$ take the square root of both sides

Both −2 and 2 are square roots of 4 since $(-2)^2 = 4$ and $(2)^2 = 4$. Thus, x could be −2.

This problem can also be solved as follows. Rewrite the left side as $\frac{(x+1)-x}{x(x+1)} = \frac{1}{x(x+1)}$, then set equal to the right side to get $\frac{1}{x(x+1)} = \frac{1}{x+4}$. Next, cross multiply: $(1)(x+4) = x(x+1)(1)$. Therefore, $x+4 = x^2 + x$, or $x^2 = 4$, so $x = \pm 2$.

The correct answer is C.

216. $\left(\dfrac{1}{2}\right)^{-3}\left(\dfrac{1}{4}\right)^{-2}\left(\dfrac{1}{16}\right)^{-1} =$

   (A) $\left(\dfrac{1}{2}\right)^{-48}$

   (B) $\left(\dfrac{1}{2}\right)^{-11}$

   (C) $\left(\dfrac{1}{2}\right)^{-6}$

   (D) $\left(\dfrac{1}{8}\right)^{-11}$

   (E) $\left(\dfrac{1}{8}\right)^{-6}$

Arithmetic Operations on rational numbers

It is clear from the answer choices that all three factors need to be written with a common denominator, and they thus become

$$\left(\dfrac{1}{2}\right)^{-3} = \left(\dfrac{1}{2}\right)^{-3}$$

$$\left(\dfrac{1}{4}\right)^{-2} = \left(\left(\dfrac{1}{2}\right)^{2}\right)^{-2} = \left(\dfrac{1}{2}\right)^{-4}$$

$$\left(\dfrac{1}{16}\right)^{-1} = \left(\left(\dfrac{1}{2}\right)^{4}\right)^{-1} = \left(\dfrac{1}{2}\right)^{-4}$$

So, $\left(\dfrac{1}{2}\right)^{-3}\left(\dfrac{1}{4}\right)^{-2}\left(\dfrac{1}{16}\right)^{-1} =$

$$\left(\dfrac{1}{2}\right)^{-3}\left(\dfrac{1}{2}\right)^{-4}\left(\dfrac{1}{2}\right)^{-4} = \left(\dfrac{1}{2}\right)^{-3-4-4} = \left(\dfrac{1}{2}\right)^{-11}.$$

The correct answer is B.

217. In a certain game, a large container is filled with red, yellow, green, and blue beads worth, respectively, 7, 5, 3, and 2 points each. A number of beads are then removed from the container. If the product of the point values of the removed beads is 147,000, how many red beads were removed?

   (A) 5
   (B) 4
   (C) 3
   (D) 2
   (E) 0

Arithmetic Properties of numbers

From this, the red beads represent factors of 7 in the total point value of 147,000. Since 147,000 = 147(1,000), and 1,000 = 10^3, then 147 is all that needs to be factored to determine the factors of 7. Factoring 147 yields 147 = (3)(49) = (3)(7^2). This means there are 2 factors of 7, or 2 red beads.

The correct answer is D.

218. If $\dfrac{2}{1+\dfrac{2}{y}} = 1$, then $y =$

   (A) -2

   (B) $-\dfrac{1}{2}$

   (C) $\dfrac{1}{2}$

   (D) 2

   (E) 3

Algebra First-degree equations

Solve for y.

$$\dfrac{2}{1+\dfrac{2}{y}} = 1$$

$1 + \dfrac{2}{y} = 2$ multiply both sides by $1+\dfrac{2}{y}$

$\dfrac{2}{y} = 1$ subtract 1 from each side

$y = 2$ solve for y

The correct answer is D.

219. If a, b, and c are consecutive positive integers and $a < b < c$, which of the following must be true?

   I. $c - a = 2$

   II. abc is an even integer.

   III. $\dfrac{a + b + c}{3}$ is an integer.

(A)   I only
(B)   II only
(C)   I and II only
(D)   II and III only
(E)   I, II, and III

Arithmetic Properties of numbers

Since a, b, and c are consecutive positive integers and $a < b < c$, then $b = a + 1$ and $c = a + 2$.

I. $c - a = (a + 2) - a = 2$ MUST be true

II.   (odd)(even)(odd) = even   MUST be true

   (even)(odd)(even) = even   MUST be true

III. $\dfrac{a + b + c}{3} = \dfrac{a + (a + 1) + (a + 2)}{3}$

   $= \dfrac{3a + 3}{3} = a + 1 = b$

   b is an integer   MUST be true

The correct answer is E.

---

220. A part-time employee whose hourly wage was increased by 25 percent decided to reduce the number of hours worked per week so that the employee's total weekly income would remain unchanged. By what percent should the number of hours worked be reduced?

(A)   12.5%
(B)   20%
(C)   25%
(D)   50%
(E)   75%

Algebra Applied problems

Let w represent the original hourly wage. Letting h be the original number of hours the employee worked per week, the original weekly income can be expressed as wh. Given a 25% increase in hourly wage, the employee's new wage is thus $1.25w$. Letting H be the reduced number of hours, the problem can then be expressed as:

$1.25wH = wh$ (new wage)(new hours) = (original wage)(original hours)

By dividing both sides by w, this equation can be solved for H:

$1.25H = h$

   $H = 0.8h$

Since the new hours should be $0.8 = 80\%$ of the original hours, the number of hours worked should be reduced by 20 percent.

The correct answer is B.

---

221. Of the 200 students at College T majoring in one or more of the sciences, 130 are majoring in chemistry and 150 are majoring in biology. If at least 30 of the students are not majoring in either chemistry or biology, then the number of students majoring in *both* chemistry and biology could be any number from

(A)   20 to 50
(B)   40 to 70
(C)   50 to 130
(D)   110 to 130
(E)   110 to 150

Arithmetic Operations on rational numbers

A Venn diagram will help with this problem. There are two extremes that need to be considered: (1) having the least number of students majoring in both chemistry and biology and (2) having the greatest number of students majoring in both chemistry and biology.

(1) If at least 30 science majors are not majoring in either chemistry or biology, then at most $200 - 30 = 170$ students can be majoring in either or both. Since there are $130 + 150 = 280$ biology and chemistry majors (some of whom are individual students majoring in both areas), then there are at least $280 - 170 = 110$ majoring in both. The diagram following shows this relationship.

170 TOTAL STUDENTS
FOR CHEMISTRY AND BIOLOGY MAJORS

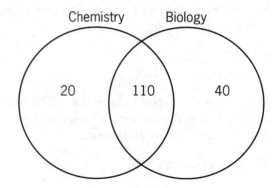

(2) The maximum number of students who can be majoring in both chemistry and biology is 130, since 130 is the number given as majoring in chemistry, the smaller of the two subject areas. Logically, there cannot be more double majors than there are majors in the smaller field. The diagram below shows this relationship in terms of the given numbers of majors in each subject area.

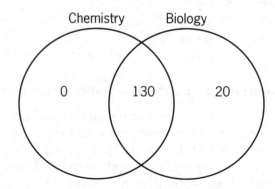

Additionally, from this diagram it can be seen that the total number of students who are majoring in chemistry, or in biology, or in both is 130 + 20 = 150. Thus, there are 200 − 150 = 50 students who are neither chemistry nor biology majors. This number is not in conflict with the condition that 30 is the minimum number of nonchemistry and nonbiology majors.

Thus, the number of students majoring in both chemistry and biology could be any number from a minimum of 110 to a maximum of 130.

The correct answer is D.

222. If $5 - \dfrac{6}{x} = x$, then x has how many possible values?

(A)   None
(B)   One
(C)   Two
(D)   A finite number greater than two
(E)   An infinite number

Algebra Second-degree equations

Solve the equation to determine how many values are possible for x.

$$5 - \frac{6}{x} = x$$
$$5x - 6 = x^2$$
$$0 = x^2 - 5x + 6$$
$$0 = (x - 3)(x - 2)$$
$$x = 3 \text{ or } 2$$

The correct answer is C.

223. Seed mixture X is 40 percent ryegrass and 60 percent bluegrass by weight; seed mixture Y is 25 percent ryegrass and 75 percent fescue. If a mixture of X and Y contains 30 percent ryegrass, what percent of the weight of the mixture is X ?

(A)   10%

(B) $33\dfrac{1}{3}$%

(C)   40%

(D)   50%

(E) $66\dfrac{2}{3}$%

Algebra Applied problems

Let X be the amount of seed mixture X in the final mixture, and let Y be the amount of seed mixture Y in the final mixture. The final mixture of X and Y needs to contain 30 percent ryegrass seed, so any other kinds of grass seed are irrelevant to the solution to this problem. The information about the ryegrass percentages for X, Y, and the final mixture can be expressed in the following equation and solved for X.

$0.40X + 0.25Y = 0.30(X + Y)$

$0.40X + 0.25Y = 0.30X + 0.30Y$	distribute the 0.30 on the right side
$0.10X = 0.05Y$	subtract $0.30X$ and $0.25Y$ from both sides
$X = 0.5Y$	divide both sides by 0.10

Using this, the percent of the weight of the combined mixture $(X + Y)$ that is X is

$$\frac{X}{X+Y} = \frac{0.5Y}{0.5Y + Y} = \frac{0.5Y}{1.5Y} = \frac{0.5}{1.5} = 0.33\overline{3} = 33\frac{1}{3}\%$$

The correct answer is B.

---

224. If n is a positive integer, then $n(n + 1)(n + 2)$ is

(A) even only when n is even
(B) even only when n is odd
(C) odd whenever n is odd
(D) divisible by 3 only when n is odd
(E) divisible by 4 whenever n is even

Arithmetic Properties of numbers

The numbers n, $n + 1$, and $n + 2$ are consecutive integers. Therefore, either their product is (odd)(even)(odd) = even, or their product is (even)(odd)(even) = even. In either case, the product of $n(n + 1)(n + 2)$ is even. Thus, each of answer choices A, B, and C is false.

A statement is false if a counterexample can be shown. Test the statement using an even multiple of 3 as the value of n in the equation. When $n = 6$, $n(n + 1)(n + 2) = 6(7)(8) = 336$. Since in this counterexample n is even but 336 is still divisible by 3, answer choice D is shown to be false.

When n is even (meaning divisible by 2), $n + 2$ is also even (and also divisible by 2). So $n(n + 1)(n + 2)$ is always divisible by 4.

The correct answer is E.

---

225. A straight pipe 1 yard in length was marked off in fourths and also in thirds. If the pipe was then cut into separate pieces at each of these markings, which of the following gives all the different lengths of the pieces, in fractions of a yard?

(A) $\frac{1}{6}$ and $\frac{1}{4}$ only

(B) $\frac{1}{4}$ and $\frac{1}{3}$ only

(C) $\frac{1}{6}, \frac{1}{4},$ and $\frac{1}{3}$

(D) $\frac{1}{12}, \frac{1}{6},$ and $\frac{1}{4}$

(E) $\frac{1}{12}, \frac{1}{6},$ and $\frac{1}{3}$

Arithmetic Operations on rational numbers

$$\begin{array}{ccccccc} A & B & C & D & E & F \\ \vdash & \mid & \mid & \mid & \mid\mid & & \dashv \\ 0 & \frac{1}{4} & \frac{1}{3} & \frac{1}{2} & \frac{2}{3} & \frac{3}{4} & 1 \end{array}$$

The number line above illustrates the markings on the pipe. Since the pipe is cut at the five markings, six pieces of pipe are produced. The length of each piece, as a fraction of a yard, is given in the following table.

Pipe piece	Length
A	$\frac{1}{4} - 0 = \frac{1}{4}$
B	$\frac{1}{3} - \frac{1}{4} = \frac{1}{12}$
C	$\frac{1}{2} - \frac{1}{3} = \frac{1}{6}$
D	$\frac{2}{3} - \frac{1}{2} = \frac{1}{6}$
E	$\frac{3}{4} - \frac{2}{3} = \frac{1}{12}$
F	$1 - \frac{3}{4} = \frac{1}{4}$

The correct answer is D.

226. If $\dfrac{0.0015 \times 10^m}{0.03 \times 10^k} = 5 \times 10^7$, then $m - k =$

(A) 9
(B) 8
(C) 7
(D) 6
(E) 5

Arithmetic Operations on rational numbers

The left side is easier to work with when the expressions are rewritten so that integers are involved:

$$\frac{0.0015 \times 10^m}{0.03 \times 10^k} = 5 \times 10^7$$

$$\frac{15 \times 10^{m-4}}{3 \times 10^{k-2}} = 5 \times 10^7$$

$$\frac{15}{3} \times \frac{10^{m-4}}{10^{k-2}} = 5 \times 10^7$$

$$5 \times \frac{10^{m-4}}{10^{k-2}} = 5 \times 10^7$$

$$\frac{10^{m-4}}{10^{k-2}} = 10^7$$

$$10^{m-4-(k-2)} = 10^7$$

$$m - 4 - (k - 2) = 7$$

$$m - k - 2 = 7$$

$$m - k = 9$$

The correct answer is A.

227. If $x + y = a$ and $x - y = b$, then $2xy =$

(A) $\dfrac{a^2 - b^2}{2}$

(B) $\dfrac{b^2 - a^2}{2}$

(C) $\dfrac{a - b}{2}$

(D) $\dfrac{ab}{2}$

(E) $\dfrac{a^2 + b^2}{2}$

Algebra Simplifying algebraic expressions

Begin by adding the two given equations to establish a value for x. Adding $x + y = a$ and $x - y = b$ gives $2x = a + b$ and thus $x = \dfrac{a+b}{2}$. Then, substitute this value of x into the first equation and solve for y:

$$\frac{a+b}{2} + y = a$$

$$y = a - \frac{a+b}{2}$$

$$y = \frac{2a}{2} - \frac{a+b}{2}$$

$$y = \frac{2a - a - b}{2}$$

$$y = \frac{a-b}{2}$$

Finally, solve the equation, substituting the values now established for x and y:

$$2xy = 2\left(\frac{a+b}{2}\right)\left(\frac{a-b}{2}\right)$$

$$2xy = \frac{2(a+b)(a-b)}{4}$$

$$2xy = \frac{a^2 - b^2}{2}$$

This problem can also be solved as follows: Since the squares of $x + y$ and $x - y$, when expanded, each include the expression $x^2 + y^2$ along with a multiple of xy, we can obtain a multiple of xy by subtracting these squares:

$$a^2 - b^2 = (x+y)^2 - (x-y)^2$$
$$= x^2 + 2xy + y^2 - (x^2 - 2xy + y^2)$$
$$= 4xy$$
$$= 2(2xy)$$
$$\frac{a^2 - b^2}{2} = 2xy$$

The correct answer is A.

$$p, r, s, t, u$$

228. An arithmetic sequence is a sequence in which each term after the first is equal to the sum of the preceding term and a constant. If the list of letters shown above is an arithmetic sequence, which of the following must also be an arithmetic sequence?

   I. $2p, 2r, 2s, 2t, 2u$

   II. $p - 3, r - 3, s - 3, t - 3, u - 3$

   III. p^2, r^2, s^2, t^2, u^2

   (A)   I only
   (B)   II only
   (C)   III only
   (D)   I and II
   (E)   II and III

Algebra Concepts of sets; Functions

It follows from the definition of arithmetic sequence given in the first sentence that there is a constant c such that $r - p = s - r = t - s = u - t = c$.

To test a sequence to determine whether it is arithmetic, calculate the difference of each pair of consecutive terms in that sequence to see if a constant difference is found.

I. $2r - 2p = 2(r - p) = 2c$
    $2s - 2r = 2(s - r) = 2c$
    $2t - 2s = 2(t - s) = 2c$
    $2u - 2t = 2(u - t) = 2c$ MUST be arithmetic

II. $(r - 3) - (p - 3) = r - p = c$ MUST be arithmetic

Since all values are just three less than the original, the same common difference applies.

III. $r^2 - p^2 = (r - p)(r + p) = c(r + p)$
     $s^2 - r^2 = (s - r)(s + r) = c(s + r)$ NEED NOT be arithmetic

Since $p, r, s, t,$ and u are an arithmetic sequence, $r + p \neq s + r$, because $p \neq s$ unless $c = 0$.

The correct answer is D.

229. Right triangle PQR is to be constructed in the xy-plane so that the right angle is at P and $\overline{PR}$ is parallel to the x-axis. The x- and y-coordinates of P, Q, and R are to be integers that satisfy the inequalities $-4 \leq x \leq 5$ and $6 \leq y \leq 16$. How many different triangles with these properties could be constructed?

   (A)   110
   (B)   1,100
   (C)   9,900
   (D)   10,000
   (E)   12,100

Geometry; Arithmetic Simple coordinate geometry; Elementary combinatorics

In the xy-plane, right triangle PQR is located in the rectangular region determined by $-4 \leq x \leq 5$ and $6 \leq y \leq 16$ (see following illustration).

Since the coordinates of points P, Q, and R are integers, there are 10 possible x values and 11 possible y values, so point P can be any one of $10(11) = 110$ points in the rectangular area.

Since $\overline{PR}$ has to be horizontal, R has the same y value as P and can have 9 other x values. $\overline{PQ}$ has to be vertical, so Q has the same x value as P and can have 10 other y values. This gives $110(9)(10) = 9,900$ possible triangles.

The correct answer is C.

230. The value of $\dfrac{2^{-14} + 2^{-15} + 2^{-16} + 2^{-17}}{5}$ is how many times the value of 2^{-17} ?

(A) $\dfrac{3}{2}$

(B) $\dfrac{5}{2}$

(C) 3

(D) 4

(E) 5

Arithmetic Negative exponents

If the value of $\dfrac{2^{-14} + 2^{-15} + 2^{-16} + 2^{-17}}{5}$ is x times the value of 2^{-17}, then

$$x(2^{-17}) = \dfrac{2^{-14} + 2^{-15} + 2^{-16} + 2^{-17}}{5}$$

$$x = \dfrac{\dfrac{2^{-14} + 2^{-15} + 2^{-16} + 2^{-17}}{5}}{2^{-17}}$$

$$= \dfrac{2^{-14} + 2^{-15} + 2^{-16} + 2^{-17}}{5} \times 2^{17}$$

$$= \dfrac{\left(2^{-14} + 2^{-15} + 2^{-16} + 2^{-17}\right) \times 2^{17}}{5}$$

$$= \dfrac{2^{-14+17} + 2^{-15+17} + 2^{-16+17} + 2^{-17+17}}{5}$$

$$= \dfrac{2^3 + 2^2 + 2^1 + 2^0}{5}$$

$$= \dfrac{8 + 4 + 2 + 1}{5}$$

$$= 3$$

The correct answer is C.

6.0 Data Sufficiency

6.0 Data Sufficiency

Data sufficiency questions appear in the Quantitative section of the GMAT® test. Multiple-choice data sufficiency questions are intermingled with problem solving questions throughout the section. You will have 75 minutes to complete the Quantitative section of the GMAT test, or about 2 minutes to answer each question. These questions require knowledge of the following topics:

- Arithmetic
- Elementary algebra
- Commonly known concepts of geometry

Data sufficiency questions are designed to measure your ability to analyze a quantitative problem, recognize which given information is relevant, and determine at what point there is sufficient information to solve a problem. In these questions, you are to classify each problem according to the five fixed answer choices, rather than find a solution to the problem.

Each data sufficiency question consists of a question, often accompanied by some initial information, and two statements, labeled (1) and (2), which contain additional information. You must decide whether the information in each statement is sufficient to answer the question or— if neither statement provides enough information—whether the information in the two statements together is sufficient. It is also possible that the statements in combination do not give enough information to answer the question.

Begin by reading the initial information and the question carefully. Next, consider the first statement. Does the information provided by the first statement enable you to answer the question? Go on to the second statement. Try to ignore the information given in the first statement when you consider whether the second statement provides information that, by itself, allows you to answer the question. Now you should be able to say, for each statement, whether it is sufficient to determine the answer.

Next, consider the two statements in tandem. Do they, together, enable you to answer the question?

Look again at your answer choices. Select the one that most accurately reflects whether the statements provide the information required to answer the question.

6.1 Test-Taking Strategies

1. Do not waste valuable time solving a problem.

You only need to determine whether sufficient information is given to solve it.

2. Consider each statement separately.

First, decide whether each statement alone gives sufficient information to solve the problem. Be sure to disregard the information given in statement (1) when you evaluate the information given in statement (2). If either, or both, of the statements give(s) sufficient information to solve the problem, select the answer corresponding to the description of which statement(s) give(s) sufficient information to solve the problem.

3. Judge the statements in tandem if neither statement is sufficient by itself.

It is possible that the two statements together do not provide sufficient information. Once you decide, select the answer corresponding to the description of whether the statements together give sufficient information to solve the problem.

4. Answer the question asked.

For example, if the question asks, "What is the value of y?" for an answer statement to be sufficient, you must be able to find one and only one value for y. Being able to determine minimum or maximum values for an answer (e.g., $y = x + 2$) is not sufficient, because such answers constitute a range of values rather than the specific value of y.

5. Be very careful not to make unwarranted assumptions based on the images represented.

Figures are not necessarily drawn to scale; they are generalized figures showing little more than intersecting line segments and the relationships of points, angles, and regions. So, for example, if a figure described as a rectangle looks like a square, do *not* conclude that it is, in fact, a square just by looking at the figure.

If statement 1 is sufficient, then the answer must be **A or D.**

If statement 2 is not sufficient, then the answer must be **A.**

If statement 2 is sufficient, then the answer must be **D.**

If statement 1 is not sufficient, then the answer must be **B, C, or E.**

If statement 2 is sufficient, then the answer must be **B.**

If statement 2 is not sufficient, then the answer must be **C or E.**

If both statements together are sufficient, then the answer must be **C.**

If both statements together are still not sufficient, then the answer must be **E.**

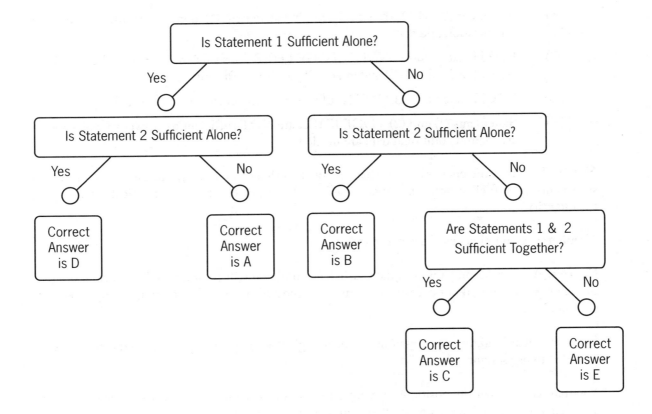

6.2 The Directions

These directions are similar to those you will see for data sufficiency questions when you take the GMAT test. If you read the directions carefully and understand them clearly before going to sit for the test, you will not need to spend much time reviewing them when you take the GMAT test.

Each data sufficiency problem consists of a question and two statements, labeled (1) and (2), that give data. You have to decide whether the data given in the statements are *sufficient* for answering the question. Using the data given in the statements *plus* your knowledge of mathematics and everyday facts (such as the number of days in July or the meaning of *counterclockwise*), you must indicate whether the data given in the statements are sufficient for answering the questions and then indicate one of the following answer choices:

(A)   Statement (1) ALONE is sufficient, but statement (2) alone is not sufficient to answer the question asked;

(B)   Statement (2) ALONE is sufficient, but statement (1) alone is not sufficient to answer the question asked;

(C)   BOTH statements (1) and (2) TOGETHER are sufficient to answer the question asked, but NEITHER statement ALONE is sufficient;

(D)   EACH statement ALONE is sufficient to answer the question asked;

(E)   Statements (1) and (2) TOGETHER are NOT sufficient to answer the question asked, and additional data are needed.

NOTE: In data sufficiency problems that ask for the value of a quantity, the data given in the statements are sufficient only when it is possible to determine exactly one numerical value for the quantity.

Numbers: All numbers used are real numbers.

Figures: A figure accompanying a data sufficiency problem will conform to the information given in the question but will not necessarily conform to the additional information given in statements (1) and (2).

Lines shown as straight can be assumed to be straight and lines that appear jagged can also be assumed to be straight.

You may assume that the positions of points, angles, regions, and so forth exist in the order shown and that angle measures are greater than zero degrees.

All figures lie in a plane unless otherwise indicated.

6.3 Sample Questions

Each <u>data sufficiency</u> problem consists of a question and two statements, labeled (1) and (2), which contain certain data. Using these data and your knowledge of mathematics and everyday facts (such as the number of days in July or the meaning of the word *counterclockwise*), decide whether the data given are sufficient for answering the question and then indicate one of the following answer choices:

A   Statement (1) ALONE is sufficient, but statement (2) alone is not sufficient.
B   Statement (2) ALONE is sufficient, but statement (1) alone is not sufficient.
C   BOTH statements TOGETHER are sufficient, but NEITHER statement ALONE is sufficient.
D   EACH statement ALONE is sufficient.
E   Statements (1) and (2) TOGETHER are not sufficient.

<u>Note:</u> In data sufficiency problems that ask for the value of a quantity, the data given in the statements are sufficient only when it is possible to determine exactly one numerical value for quantity.

<u>Example:</u>

In $\triangle PQR$, what is the value of x ?

(1) $PQ = PR$
(2) $y = 40$

<u>Explanation:</u> According to statement (1) $PQ = PR$; therefore, $\triangle PQR$ is isosceles and $y = z$. Since $x + y + z = 180$, it follows that $x + 2y = 180$. Since statement (1) does not give a value for y, you cannot answer the question using statement (1) alone. According to statement (2), $y = 40$; therefore, $x + z = 140$. Since statement (2) does not give a value for z, you cannot answer the question using statement (2) alone. Using both statements together, since $x + 2y = 180$ and the value of y is given, you can find the value of x. Therefore, BOTH statements (1) and (2) TOGETHER are sufficient to answer the questions, but NEITHER statement ALONE is sufficient.

<u>Numbers:</u> All numbers used are real numbers.

<u>Figures:</u>
- Figures conform to the information given in the question, but will not necessarily conform to the additional information given in statements (1) and (2).
- Lines shown as straight are straight, and lines that appear jagged are also straight.
- The positions of points, angles, regions, etc., exist in the order shown, and angle measures are greater than zero.
- All figures lie in a plane unless otherwise indicated.

1. What is the value of $|x|$?

    (1) $x = -|x|$
    (2) $x^2 = 4$

2. What percent of a group of people are women with red hair?

    (1) Of the women in the group, 5 percent have red hair.
    (2) Of the men in the group, 10 percent have red hair.

3. In a certain class, one student is to be selected at random to read. What is the probability that a boy will read?

    (1) Two-thirds of the students in the class are boys.
    (2) Ten of the students in the class are girls.

4. In College X the number of students enrolled in both a chemistry course and a biology course is how much less than the number of students enrolled in neither?

    (1) In College X there are 60 students enrolled in a chemistry course.
    (2) In College X there are 85 students enrolled in a biology course.

5. A certain expressway has Exits J, K, L, and M, in that order. What is the road distance from Exit K to Exit L ?

    (1) The road distance from Exit J to Exit L is 21 kilometers.
    (2) The road distance from Exit K to Exit M is 26 kilometers.

6. If n is an integer, is $n + 1$ odd?

    (1) $n + 2$ is an even integer.
    (2) $n - 1$ is an odd integer.

7. For which type of investment, J or K, is the annual rate of return greater?

    (1) Type J returns $115 per $1,000 invested for any one-year period and type K returns $300 per $2,500 invested for any one-year period.
    (2) The annual rate of return for an investment of type K is 12 percent.

8. A citrus fruit grower receives $15 for each crate of oranges shipped and $18 for each crate of grapefruit shipped. How many crates of oranges did the grower ship last week?

    (1) Last week the number of crates of oranges that the grower shipped was 20 more than twice the number of crates of grapefruit shipped.
    (2) Last week the grower received a total of $38,700 from the crates of oranges and grapefruit shipped.

9. If Pat saved $600 of his earnings last month, how much did Pat earn last month?

    (1) Pat spent $\frac{1}{2}$ of his earnings last month for living expenses and saved $\frac{1}{3}$ of the remainder.
    (2) Of his earnings last month, Pat paid twice as much in taxes as he saved.

10. Water is pumped into a partially filled tank at a constant rate through an inlet pipe. At the same time, water is pumped out of the tank at a constant rate through an outlet pipe. At what rate, in gallons per minute, is the amount of water in the tank increasing?

    (1) The amount of water initially in the tank is 200 gallons.
    (2) Water is pumped into the tank at a rate of 10 gallons per minute and out of the tank at a rate of 10 gallons every $2\frac{1}{2}$ minutes.

11. Is x a negative number?

    (1) $9x > 10x$
    (2) $x + 3$ is positive.

12. If i and j are integers, is $i + j$ an even integer?

    (1) $i < 10$
    (2) $i = j$

13. The charge for a telephone call between City R and City S is $0.42 for each of the first 3 minutes and $0.18 for each additional minute. A certain call between these two cities lasted for x minutes, where x is an integer. How many minutes long was the call?

    (1) The charge for the first 3 minutes of the call was $0.36 less than the charge for the remainder of the call.
    (2) The total charge for the call was $2.88.

14. If Car X followed Car Y across a certain bridge that is $\frac{1}{2}$ mile long, how many seconds did it take Car X to travel across the bridge?

    (1) Car X drove onto the bridge exactly 3 seconds after Car Y drove onto the bridge and drove off the bridge exactly 2 seconds after Car Y drove off the bridge.
    (2) Car Y traveled across the bridge at a constant speed of 30 miles per hour.

15. If $n + k = m$, what is the value of k?

    (1) $n = 10$
    (2) $m + 10 = n$

16. Is x an integer?

    (1) $\frac{x}{2}$ is an integer.
    (2) $2x$ is an integer.

17. Is the integer P odd?

    (1) The sum of P, $P + 4$, and $P + 11$ is even.
    (2) The sum of $P - 3$, P, and $P + 11$ is odd.

18. What is the maximum number of rectangular blocks, each with dimensions 12 centimeters by 6 centimeters by 4 centimeters, that will fit inside rectangular Box X?

    (1) When Box X is filled with the blocks and rests on a certain side, there are 25 blocks in the bottom layer.
    (2) The inside dimensions of Box X are 60 centimeters by 30 centimeters by 20 centimeters.

19. If sequence S has 200 terms, what is the 192nd term of S?

    (1) The first term of S is -40.
    (2) Each term of S after the first term is 3 less than the preceding term.

20. In $\triangle PQR$, if $PQ = x$, $QR = x + 2$, and $PR = y$, which of the three angles of $\triangle PQR$ has the greatest degree measure?

    (1) $y = x + 3$
    (2) $x = 2$

21. What percent of the drama club members enrolled at a certain school are female students?

    (1) Of the female students enrolled at the school, 40 percent are members of the drama club.
    (2) Of the male students enrolled at the school, 25 percent are members of the drama club.

22. A family-size box of cereal contains more cereal and costs more than the regular-size box of cereal. What is the cost per ounce of the family-size box of cereal?

    (1) The family-size box of cereal contains 10 ounces more than the regular-size box of cereal.
    (2) The family-size box of cereal costs $5.40.

23. The profit from the sale of a certain appliance increases, though not proportionally, with the number of units sold. Did the profit exceed $4 million on sales of 380,000 units?

    (1) The profit exceeded $2 million on sales of 200,000 units.
    (2) The profit exceeded $5 million on sales of 350,000 units.

24. If n is an integer, is n even?

    (1) $n^2 - 1$ is an odd integer.
    (2) $3n + 4$ is an even integer.

25. Carmen currently works 30 hours per week at her part-time job. If her gross hourly wage were to increase by $1.50, how many fewer hours could she work per week and still earn the same gross weekly pay as before the increase?

    (1) Her gross weekly pay is currently $225.00.
    (2) An increase of $1.50 would represent an increase of 20 percent of her current gross hourly wage.

26. The number n of units of its product that Company X is scheduled to produce in month t of its next fiscal year is given by the formula $n = \frac{900}{1 + c2^{-t}}$, where c is a constant and t is a positive integer between 1 and 6, inclusive. What is the number of units of its product that Company X is scheduled to produce in month 6 of its next fiscal year?

    (1) Company X is scheduled to produce 180 units of its product in month 1 of its next fiscal year.
    (2) Company X is scheduled to produce 300 units of its product in month 2 of its next fiscal year.

27. When 200 gallons of oil were removed from a tank, the volume of oil left in the tank was $\frac{3}{7}$ of the tank's capacity. What was the tank's capacity?

    (1) Before the 200 gallons were removed, the volume of oil in the tank was $\frac{1}{2}$ of the tank's capacity.
    (2) After the 200 gallons were removed, the volume of the oil left in the tank was 1,600 gallons less than the tank's capacity.

28. Division R of Company Q has 1,000 employees. What is the average (arithmetic mean) annual salary of the employees at Company Q?

    (1) The average annual salary of the employees in Division R is $30,000.
    (2) The average annual salary of the employees at Company Q who are <u>not</u> in Division R is $35,000.

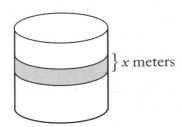

29. A circular tub has a band painted around its circumference, as shown above. What is the surface area of this painted band?

    (1) $x = 0.5$
    (2) The height of the tub is 1 meter.

30. What is the value of integer n?

    (1) $n(n + 1) = 6$
    (2) $2^{2n} = 16$

$$d = 0.43t7$$

31. If t denotes the thousandths digit in the decimal representation of d above, what digit is t?

    (1) If d were rounded to the nearest hundredth, the result would be 0.44.
    (2) If d were rounded to the nearest thousandth, the result would be 0.436.

32. Jerry bought 7 clothing items, including a coat, and the sum of the prices of these items was $365. If there was no sales tax on any clothing item with a price of less than $100 and a 7 percent sales tax on all other clothing items, what was the total sales tax on the 7 items that Jerry bought?

    (1) The price of the coat was $125.
    (2) The average (arithmetic mean) price for the 6 items other than the coat was $40.

33. What was the price at which a merchant sold a certain appliance?

    (1) The merchant's gross profit on the appliance was 20 percent of the price at which the merchant sold the appliance.
    (2) The price at which the merchant sold the appliance was $50 more than the merchant's cost of the appliance.

34. The inside of a rectangular carton is 48 centimeters long, 32 centimeters wide, and 15 centimeters high. The carton is filled to capacity with k identical cylindrical cans of fruit that stand upright in rows and columns, as indicated in the figure above. If the cans are 15 centimeters high, what is the value of k?

    (1) Each of the cans has a radius of 4 centimeters.
    (2) Six of the cans fit exactly along the length of the carton.

$$\begin{cases} x - 4 = z \\ y - x = 8 \\ 8 - z = t \end{cases}$$

35. For the system of equations given, what is the value of z?

    (1) $x = 7$
    (2) $t = 5$

36. For all integers n, the function f is defined by $f(n) = a^n$, where a is a constant. What is the value of $f(1)$?

    (1) $f(2) = 100$
    (2) $f(3) = -1,000$

37. The selling price of an article is equal to the cost of the article plus the markup. The markup on a certain television set is what percent of the selling price?

    (1) The markup on the television set is 25 percent of the cost.
    (2) The selling price of the television set is $250.

38. If p_1 and p_2 are the populations and r_1 and r_2 are the numbers of representatives of District 1 and District 2, respectively, the ratio of the population to the number of representatives is greater for which of the two districts?

    (1) $p_1 > p_2$
    (2) $r_2 > r_1$

39. In a random sample of 80 adults, how many are college graduates?

    (1) In the sample, the number of adults who are <u>not</u> college graduates is 3 times the number who are college graduates.
    (2) In the sample, the number of adults who are <u>not</u> college graduates is 40 more than the number who are college graduates.

	R	S	T	U
R	0	y	x	62
S	y	0	56	75
T	x	56	0	69
U	62	75	69	0

40. The table above shows the distance, in kilometers, by the most direct route, between any two of the four cities, R, S, T, and U. For example, the distance between City R and City U is 62 kilometers. What is the value of x ?

    (1) By the most direct route, the distance between S and T is twice the distance between S and R.
    (2) By the most direct route, the distance between T and U is 1.5 times the distance between R and T.

41. What is the value of the two-digit integer x ?

    (1) The sum of the two digits is 3.
    (2) x is divisible by 3.

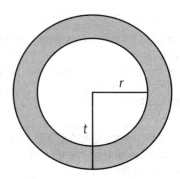

42. The figure above shows the circular cross section of a concrete water pipe. If the inside radius of the pipe is r feet and the outside radius of the pipe is t feet, what is the value of r ?

    (1) The ratio of $t - r$ to r is 0.15 and $t - r$ is equal to 0.3 foot.
    (2) The area of the concrete in the cross section is 1.29π square feet.

43. What is the tenths digit in the decimal representation of a certain number?

    (1) The number is less than $\frac{1}{3}$.
    (2) The number is greater than $\frac{1}{4}$.

44. Robots X, Y, and Z each assemble components at their respective constant rates. If r_x is the ratio of Robot X's constant rate to Robot Z's constant rate and r_y is the ratio of Robot Y's constant rate to Robot Z's constant rate, is Robot Z's constant rate the greatest of the three?

    (1) $r_x < r_y$
    (2) $r_y < 1$

45. If r is a constant and $a_n = rn$ for all positive integers n, for how many values of n is $a_n < 100$?

    (1) $a_{50} = 500$
    (2) $a_{100} + a_{105} = 2,050$

46. If r is represented by the decimal 0.t5, what is the digit t?

    (1) $r < \dfrac{1}{3}$

    (2) $r < \dfrac{1}{10}$

47. If the two floors in a certain building are 9 feet apart, how many steps are there in a set of stairs that extends from the first floor to the second floor of the building?

    (1) Each step is $\dfrac{3}{4}$ foot high.

    (2) Each step is 1 foot wide.

48. In June 1989, what was the ratio of the number of sales transactions made by Salesperson X to the number of sales transactions made by Salesperson Y?

    (1) In June 1989, Salesperson X made 50 percent more sales transactions than Salesperson Y did in May 1989.

    (2) In June 1989, Salesperson Y made 25 percent more sales transactions than in May 1989.

49. If $a < x < b$ and $c < y < d$, is $x < y$?

    (1) $a < c$

    (2) $b < c$

50. How many people are directors of both Company K and Company R?

    (1) There were 17 directors present at a joint meeting of the directors of Company K and Company R, and no directors were absent.

    (2) Company K has 12 directors and Company R has 8 directors.

51. If x and y are positive, is $\dfrac{x}{y}$ greater than 1?

    (1) $xy > 1$

    (2) $x - y > 0$

52. A clothing store acquired an item at a cost of x dollars and sold the item for y dollars. The store's gross profit from the item was what percent of its cost for the item?

    (1) $y - x = 20$

    (2) $\dfrac{y}{x} = \dfrac{5}{4}$

$$(n - x) + (n - y) + (n - z) + (n - k)$$

53. What is the value of the expression above?

    (1) The average (arithmetic mean) of x, y, z, and k is n.

    (2) x, y, z, and k are consecutive integers.

54. A taxi company charges f cents for the first mile of the taxi ride and m cents for each additional mile. How much does the company charge for a 10-mile taxi ride?

    (1) The company charges $0.90 for a 2-mile ride.

    (2) The company charges $1.20 for a 4-mile ride.

55. Guy's net income equals his gross income minus his deductions. By what percent did Guy's net income change on January 1, 1989, when both his gross income and his deductions increased?

    (1) Guy's gross income increased by 4 percent on January 1, 1989.

    (2) Guy's deductions increased by 15 percent on January 1, 1989.

56. What is the value of z in the triangle above?

    (1) $x + y = 139$

    (2) $y + z = 108$

57. Max has $125 consisting of bills each worth either $5 or $20. How many bills worth $5 does Max have?

    (1) Max has fewer than 5 bills worth $5 each.

    (2) Max has more than 5 bills worth $20 each.

58. If the ratio of the number of teachers to the number of students is the same in School District M and School District P, what is the ratio of the number of students in School District M to the number of students in School District P?

    (1) There are 10,000 more students in School District M than there are in School District P.

    (2) The ratio of the number of teachers to the number of students in School District M is 1 to 20.

59. If a total of 84 students are enrolled in two sections of a calculus course, how many of the 84 students are female?

   (1) $\frac{2}{3}$ of the students in Section 1 are female.

   (2) $\frac{1}{2}$ of the students in Section 2 are male.

60. What is the value of n in the equation $-25 + 19 + n = s$?

   (1) $s = 2$

   (2) $\frac{n}{s} = 4$

61. At a certain picnic, each of the guests was served either a single scoop or a double scoop of ice cream. How many of the guests were served a double scoop of ice cream?

   (1)   At the picnic, 60 percent of the guests were served a double scoop of ice cream.

   (2)   A total of 120 scoops of ice cream were served to all the guests at the picnic.

62. For a convention, a hotel charges a daily room rate of $120 for 1 person and x dollars for each additional person. What is the charge for each additional person?

   (1)   The daily cost per person for 4 people sharing the cost of a room equally is $45.

   (2)   The daily cost per person for 2 people sharing the cost of a room equally is $25 more than the corresponding cost for 4 people.

63. Stores L and M each sell a certain product at a different regular price. If both stores discount their regular price of the product, is the discount price at Store M less than the discount price at Store L ?

   (1)   At Store L the discount price is 10 percent less than the regular price; at Store M the discount price is 15 percent less than the regular price.

   (2)   At Store L the discount price is $5 less than the regular store price; at Store M the discount price is $6 less than the regular price.

64. If d denotes a decimal, is $d \geq 0.5$?

   (1)   When d is rounded to the nearest tenth, the result is 0.5.

   (2)   When d is rounded to the nearest integer, the result is 1.

65. How many integers are there between, but not including, integers r and s ?

   (1) $s - r = 10$

   (2)   There are 9 integers between, but not including, $r + 1$ and $s + 1$.

66. If n and t are positive integers, is n a factor of t ?

   (1) $n = 3^{n-2}$

   (2) $t = 3^n$

67. In a survey of 200 college graduates, 30 percent said they had received student loans during their college careers, and 40 percent said they had received scholarships. What percent of those surveyed said that they had received neither student loans nor scholarships during their college careers?

   (1)   25 percent of those surveyed said that they had received scholarships but no loans.

   (2)   50 percent of those surveyed who said that they had received loans also said that they had received scholarships.

68. Three machines, K, M, and P, working simultaneously and independently at their respective constant rates, can complete a certain task in 24 minutes. How long does it take Machine K, working alone at its constant rate, to complete the task?

   (1)   Machines M and P, working simultaneously and independently at their respective constant rates, can complete the task in 36 minutes.

   (2)   Machines K and P, working simultaneously and independently at their respective constant rates, can complete the task in 48 minutes.

69. Of the four numbers represented on the number line above, is r closest to zero?

   (1) $q = -s$

   (2) $-t < q$

70. Mary persuaded n friends to donate \$500 each to her election campaign, and then each of these n friends persuaded n more people to donate \$500 each to Mary's campaign. If no one donated more than once and if there were no other donations, what was the value of n?

    (1) The first n people donated $\frac{1}{16}$ of the total amount donated.
    (2) The total amount donated was \$120,000.

71. Carlotta can drive from her home to her office by one of two possible routes. If she must also return by one of these routes, what is the distance of the shorter route?

    (1) When she drives from her home to her office by the shorter route and returns by the longer route, she drives a total of 42 kilometers.
    (2) When she drives both ways, from her home to her office and back, by the longer route, she drives a total of 46 kilometers.

72. Is $x > y$?

    (1) $x = y + 2$
    (2) $\frac{x}{2} = y - 1$

73. If m is an integer, is m odd?

    (1) $\frac{m}{2}$ is <u>not</u> an even integer.
    (2) $m - 3$ is an even integer.

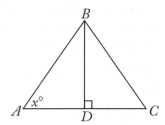

74. What is the area of triangular region ABC above?

    (1) The product of BD and AC is 20.
    (2) $x = 45$

75. In the xy-plane, the line with equation $ax + by + c = 0$, where $abc \neq 0$, has slope $\frac{2}{3}$. What is the value of b?

    (1) $a = 4$
    (2) $c = -6$

76. If m, p, and t are positive integers and $m < p < t$, is the product mpt an even integer?

    (1) $t - p = p - m$
    (2) $t - m = 16$

77. Each week a certain salesman is paid a fixed amount equal to \$300, plus a commission equal to 5 percent of the amount of his sales that week over \$1,000. What is the total amount the salesman was paid last week?

    (1) The total amount the salesman was paid last week is equal to 10 percent of the amount of his sales last week.
    (2) The salesman's sales last week totaled \$5,000.

78. A total of \$60,000 was invested for one year. Part of this amount earned simple annual interest at the rate of x percent per year, and the rest earned simple annual interest at the rate of y percent per year. If the total interest earned by the \$60,000 for that year was \$4,080, what is the value of x?

    (1) $x = \frac{3y}{4}$
    (2) The ratio of the amount that earned interest at the rate of x percent per year to the amount that earned interest at the rate of y percent per year was 3 to 2.

79. Leo can buy a certain computer for p_1 dollars in State A, where the sales tax is t_1 percent, or he can buy the same computer for p_2 dollars in State B, where the sales tax is t_2 percent. Is the total cost of the computer greater in State A than in State B?

    (1) $t_1 > t_2$
    (2) $p_1 t_1 > p_2 t_2$

80. If $r > 0$ and $s > 0$, is $\frac{r}{s} < \frac{s}{r}$?

    (1) $\frac{r}{3s} = \frac{1}{4}$
    (2) $s = r + 4$

$$k, n, 12, 6, 17$$

81. What is the value of n in the list above?

    (1) $k < n$
    (2) The median of the numbers in the list is 10.

82. If positive integer x is a multiple of 6 and positive integer y is a multiple of 14, is xy a multiple of 105 ?

   (1) x is a multiple of 9.

   (2) y is a multiple of 25.

83. What is the value of $b + c$?

   (1) $ab + cd + ac + bd = 6$

   (2) $a + d = 4$

84. What is the average (arithmetic mean) of j and k ?

   (1)   The average (arithmetic mean) of $j + 2$ and $k + 4$ is 11.

   (2)   The average (arithmetic mean) of j, k, and 14 is 10.

85. Paula and Sandy were among those people who sold raffle tickets to raise money for Club X. If Paula and Sandy sold a total of 100 of the tickets, how many of the tickets did Paula sell?

   (1)   Sandy sold $\frac{2}{3}$ as many of the raffle tickets as Paula did.

   (2)   Sandy sold 8 percent of all the raffle tickets sold for Club X.

86. A number of people each wrote down one of the first 30 positive integers. Were any of the integers written down by more than one of the people?

   (1)   The number of people who wrote down an integer was greater than 40.

   (2)   The number of people who wrote down an integer was less than 70.

87. Is the number of seconds required to travel d_1 feet at r_1 feet per second greater than the number of seconds required to travel d_2 feet at r_2 feet per second?

   (1) d_1 is 30 greater than d_2.

   (2) r_1 is 30 greater than r_2.

88. Last year, if Arturo spent a total of $12,000 on his mortgage payments, real estate taxes, and home insurance, how much did he spend on his real estate taxes?

   (1)   Last year, the total amount that Arturo spent on his real estate taxes and home insurance was $33\frac{1}{3}$ percent of the amount that he spent on his mortgage payments.

   (2)   Last year, the amount that Arturo spent on his real estate taxes was 20 percent of the total amount he spent on his mortgage payments and home insurance.

89. Is the number of members of Club X greater than the number of members of Club Y ?

   (1)   Of the members of Club X, 20 percent are also members of Club Y.

   (2)   Of the members of Club Y, 30 percent are also members of Club X.

90. If k, m, and t are positive integers and $\frac{k}{6} + \frac{m}{4} = \frac{t}{12}$, do t and 12 have a common factor greater than 1 ?

   (1) k is a multiple of 3.

   (2) m is a multiple of 3.

91. In the figure above, is $CD > BC$?

   (1) $AD = 20$

   (2) $AB = CD$

92. In a certain office, 50 percent of the employees are college graduates and 60 percent of the employees are over 40 years old. If 30 percent of those over 40 have master's degrees, how many of the employees over 40 have master's degrees?

   (1)   Exactly 100 of the employees are college graduates.

   (2)   Of the employees 40 years old or less, 25 percent have master's degrees.

93. On the number line above, p, q, r, s, and t are five consecutive even integers in increasing order. What is the average (arithmetic mean) of these five integers?

   (1) $q + s = 24$

   (2)   The average (arithmetic mean) of q and r is 11.

94. If line k in the xy-plane has equation $y = mx + b$, where m and b are constants, what is the slope of k?

    (1) k is parallel to the line with equation $y = (1 - m)x + b + 1$.
    (2) k intersects the line with equation $y = 2x + 3$ at the point (2,7).

95. Is $rst = 1$?

    (1) $rs = 1$
    (2) $st = 1$

TOTAL EXPENSES FOR THE FIVE DIVISIONS OF COMPANY H

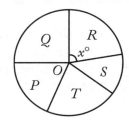

96. The figure above represents a circle graph of Company H's total expenses broken down by the expenses for each of its five divisions. If O is the center of the circle and if Company H's total expenses are $5,400,000, what are the expenses for Division R?

    (1) $x = 94$
    (2) The total expenses for Divisions S and T are twice as much as the expenses for Division R.

97. If x is negative, is $x < -3$?

    (1) $x^2 > 9$
    (2) $x^3 < -9$

98. Seven different numbers are selected from the integers 1 to 100, and each number is divided by 7. What is the sum of the remainders?

    (1) The range of the seven remainders is 6.
    (2) The seven numbers selected are consecutive integers.

r	s	t
u	v	w
x	y	z

99. Each of the letters in the table above represents one of the numbers 1, 2, or 3, and each of these numbers occurs exactly once in each row and exactly once in each column. What is the value of r?

    (1) $v + z = 6$
    (2) $s + t + u + x = 6$

100. If $[x]$ denotes the greatest integer less than or equal to x, is $[x] = 0$?

    (1) $5x + 1 = 3 + 2x$
    (2) $0 < x < 1$

101. Material A costs $3 per kilogram, and Material B costs $5 per kilogram. If 10 kilograms of Material K consists of x kilograms of Material A and y kilograms of Material B, is $x > y$?

    (1) $y > 4$
    (2) The cost of the 10 kilograms of Material K is less than $40.

102. While on a straight road, Car X and Car Y are traveling at different constant rates. If Car X is now 1 mile ahead of Car Y, how many minutes from now will Car X be 2 miles ahead of Car Y?

    (1) Car X is traveling at 50 miles per hour and Car Y is traveling at 40 miles per hour.
    (2) Three minutes ago Car X was $\frac{1}{2}$ mile ahead of Car Y.

103. If a certain animated cartoon consists of a total of 17,280 frames on film, how many minutes will it take to run the cartoon?

    (1) The cartoon runs without interruption at the rate of 24 frames per second.
    (2) It takes 6 times as long to run the cartoon as it takes to rewind the film, and it takes a total of 14 minutes to do both.

104. At what speed was a train traveling on a trip when it had completed half of the total distance of the trip?

    (1)   The trip was 460 miles long and took 4 hours to complete.
    (2)   The train traveled at an average rate of 115 miles per hour on the trip.

105. Tom, Jane, and Sue each purchased a new house. The average (arithmetic mean) price of the three houses was $120,000. What was the median price of the three houses?

    (1)   The price of Tom's house was $110,000.
    (2)   The price of Jane's house was $120,000.

106. If x and y are integers, is xy even?

    (1) $x = y + 1$
    (2) $\dfrac{x}{y}$ is an even integer.

107. A box contains only red chips, white chips, and blue chips. If a chip is randomly selected from the box, what is the probability that the chip will be either white or blue?

    (1)   The probability that the chip will be blue is $\dfrac{1}{5}$.

    (2)   The probability that the chip will be red is $\dfrac{1}{3}$.

108. If the successive tick marks shown on the number line above are equally spaced and if x and y are the numbers designating the end points of intervals as shown, what is the value of y?

    (1) $x = \dfrac{1}{2}$

    (2) $y - x = \dfrac{2}{3}$

109. In triangle ABC, point X is the midpoint of side AC and point Y is the midpoint of side BC. If point R is the midpoint of line segment XC and if point S is the midpoint of line segment YC, what is the area of triangular region RCS?

    (1)   The area of triangular region ABX is 32.
    (2)   The length of one of the altitudes of triangle ABC is 8.

110. The product of the units digit, the tens digit, and the hundreds digit of the positive integer m is 96. What is the units digit of m?

    (1)   m is odd.
    (2)   The hundreds digit of m is 8.

111. A department manager distributed a number of pens, pencils, and pads among the staff in the department, with each staff member receiving x pens, y pencils, and z pads. How many staff members were in the department?

    (1)   The numbers of pens, pencils, and pads that each staff member received were in the ratio 2:3:4, respectively.
    (2)   The manager distributed a total of 18 pens, 27 pencils, and 36 pads.

112. Machines X and Y produced identical bottles at different constant rates. Machine X, operating alone for 4 hours, filled part of a production lot; then Machine Y, operating alone for 3 hours, filled the rest of this lot. How many hours would it have taken Machine X operating alone to fill the entire production lot?

    (1)   Machine X produced 30 bottles per minute.
    (2)   Machine X produced twice as many bottles in 4 hours as Machine Y produced in 3 hours.

113. On a company-sponsored cruise, $\dfrac{2}{3}$ of the passengers were company employees and the remaining passengers were their guests. If $\dfrac{3}{4}$ of the company-employee passengers were managers, what was the number of company-employee passengers who were NOT managers?

    (1)   There were 690 passengers on the cruise.
    (2)   There were 230 passengers who were guests of the company employees.

114. The length of the edging that surrounds circular garden K is $\frac{1}{2}$ the length of the edging that surrounds circular garden G. What is the area of garden K? (Assume that the edging has negligible width.)

    (1) The area of G is 25π square meters.
    (2) The edging around G is 10π meters long.

115. For any integers x and y, min(x, y) and max(x, y) denote the minimum and the maximum of x and y, respectively. For example, min(5, 2) = 2 and max(5, 2) = 5. For the integer w, what is the value of min(10, w)?

    (1) w = max(20, z) for some integer z.
    (2) w = max(10, w)

116. During a 6-day local trade show, the least number of people registered in a single day was 80. Was the average (arithmetic mean) number of people registered per day for the 6 days greater than 90?

    (1) For the 4 days with the greatest number of people registered, the average (arithmetic mean) number registered per day was 100.
    (2) For the 3 days with the smallest number of people registered, the average (arithmetic mean) number registered per day was 85.

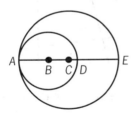

117. In the figure above, points A, B, C, D, and E lie on a line. A is on both circles, B is the center of the smaller circle, C is the center of the larger circle, D is on the smaller circle, and E is on the larger circle. What is the area of the region inside the larger circle and outside the smaller circle?

    (1) AB = 3 and BC = 2
    (2) CD = 1 and DE = 4

118. An employee is paid 1.5 times the regular hourly rate for each hour worked in excess of 40 hours per week, excluding Sunday, and 2 times the regular hourly rate for each hour worked on Sunday. How much was the employee paid last week?

    (1) The employee's regular hourly rate is $10.
    (2) Last week the employee worked a total of 54 hours but did not work more than 8 hours on any day.

119. What was the revenue that a theater received from the sale of 400 tickets, some of which were sold at the full price and the remainder of which were sold at a reduced price?

    (1) The number of tickets sold at the full price was $\frac{1}{4}$ of the total number of tickets sold.
    (2) The full price of a ticket was $25.

120. The annual rent collected by a corporation from a certain building was x percent more in 1998 than in 1997 and y percent less in 1999 than in 1998. Was the annual rent collected by the corporation from the building more in 1999 than in 1997?

    (1) $x > y$
    (2) $\frac{xy}{100} < x - y$

121. In the xy-plane, region R consists of all the points (x, y) such that $2x + 3y \leq 6$. Is the point (r, s) in region R?

    (1) $3r + 2s = 6$
    (2) $r \leq 3$ and $s \leq 2$

122. What is the volume of a certain rectangular solid?

    (1) Two adjacent faces of the solid have areas 15 and 24, respectively.
    (2) Each of two opposite faces of the solid has area 40.

123. Joanna bought only $0.15 stamps and $0.29 stamps. How many $0.15 stamps did she buy?

    (1) She bought $4.40 worth of stamps.
    (2) She bought an equal number of $0.15 stamps and $0.29 stamps.

	Favorable	Unfavorable	Not Sure
Candidate M	40	20	40
Candidate N	30	35	35

124. The table above shows the results of a survey of 100 voters who each responded "Favorable" or "Unfavorable" or "Not Sure" when asked about their impressions of Candidate M and of Candidate N. What was the number of voters who responded "Favorable" for both candidates?

    (1) The number of voters who did not respond "Favorable" for either candidate was 40.
    (2) The number of voters who responded "Unfavorable" for both candidates was 10.

125. If ° represents one of the operations +, −, and ×, is $k \circ (\ell + m) = (k \circ \ell) + (k \circ m)$ for all numbers k, ℓ, and m?

    (1) $k \circ 1$ is not equal to $1 \circ k$ for some numbers k.
    (2) ° represents subtraction.

126. How many of the 60 cars sold last month by a certain dealer had neither power windows nor a stereo?

    (1) Of the 60 cars sold, 20 had a stereo but not power windows.
    (2) Of the 60 cars sold, 30 had both power windows and a stereo.

127. In Jefferson School, 300 students study French or Spanish or both. If 100 of these students do not study French, how many of these students study both French and Spanish?

    (1) Of the 300 students, 60 do not study Spanish.
    (2) A total of 240 of the students study Spanish.

128. A school administrator will assign each student in a group of n students to one of m classrooms. If $3 < m < 13 < n$, is it possible to assign each of the n students to one of the m classrooms so that each classroom has the same number of students assigned to it?

    (1) It is possible to assign each of $3n$ students to one of m classrooms so that each classroom has the same number of students assigned to it.
    (2) It is possible to assign each of $13n$ students to one of m classrooms so that each classroom has the same number of students assigned to it.

129. What is the median number of employees assigned per project for the projects at Company Z ?

    (1) 25 percent of the projects at Company Z have 4 or more employees assigned to each project.
    (2) 35 percent of the projects at Company Z have 2 or fewer employees assigned to each project.

130. If Juan had a doctor's appointment on a certain day, was the appointment on a Wednesday?

    (1) Exactly 60 hours before the appointment, it was Monday.
    (2) The appointment was between 1:00 p.m. and 9:00 p.m.

131. When a player in a certain game tossed a coin a number of times, 4 more heads than tails resulted. Heads or tails resulted each time the player tossed the coin. How many times did heads result?

    (1) The player tossed the coin 24 times.
    (2) The player received 3 points each time heads resulted and 1 point each time tails resulted, for a total of 52 points.

132. What is the value of $x + y$ in the figure above?

    (1) $w = 95$
    (2) $z = 125$

133. Are all of the numbers in a certain list of 15 numbers equal?

    (1) The sum of all the numbers in the list is 60.
    (2) The sum of any 3 numbers in the list is 12.

134. A scientist recorded the number of eggs in each of 10 birds' nests. What was the standard deviation of the numbers of eggs in the 10 nests?

    (1) The average (arithmetic mean) number of eggs for the 10 nests was 4.
    (2) Each of the 10 nests contained the same number of eggs.

135. Quadrilateral *RSTU* shown above is a site plan for a parking lot in which side *RU* is parallel to side *ST* and *RU* is longer than *ST*. What is the area of the parking lot?

    (1)   *RU* = 80 meters

    (2)   *TU* = $20\sqrt{10}$ meters

136. If the average (arithmetic mean) of six numbers is 75, how many of the numbers are equal to 75 ?

    (1)   None of the six numbers is less than 75.

    (2)   None of the six numbers is greater than 75.

137. At a bakery, all donuts are priced equally and all bagels are priced equally. What is the total price of 5 donuts and 3 bagels at the bakery?

    (1)   At the bakery, the total price of 10 donuts and 6 bagels is $12.90.

    (2)   At the bakery, the price of a donut is $0.15 less than the price of a bagel.

138. What was the total amount of revenue that a theater received from the sale of 400 tickets, some of which were sold at *x* percent of full price and the rest of which were sold at full price?

    (1)   *x* = 50

    (2)   Full-price tickets sold for $20 each.

139. Any decimal that has only a finite number of nonzero digits is a terminating decimal. For example, 24, 0.82, and 5.096 are three terminating decimals. If *r* and *s* are positive integers and the ratio $\dfrac{r}{s}$ is expressed as a decimal, is $\dfrac{r}{s}$ a terminating decimal?

    (1) $90 < r < 100$

    (2) $s = 4$

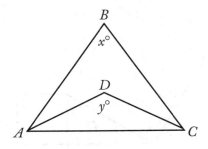

140. In the figure above, what is the value of *x* + *y* ?

    (1)   *x* = 70

    (2)   △*ABC* and △*ADC* are both isosceles triangles.

141. Committee X and Committee Y, which have no common members, will combine to form Committee Z. Does Committee X have more members than Committee Y ?

    (1)   The average (arithmetic mean) age of the members of Committee X is 25.7 years and the average age of the members of Committee Y is 29.3 years.

    (2)   The average (arithmetic mean) age of the members of Committee Z will be 26.6 years.

142. What amount did Jean earn from the commission on her sales in the first half of 1988 ?

    (1)   In 1988 Jean's commission was 5 percent of the total amount of her sales.

    (2)   The amount of Jean's sales in the second half of 1988 averaged $10,000 per month more than in the first half.

143. The price per share of Stock X increased by 10 percent over the same time period that the price per share of Stock Y decreased by 10 percent. The reduced price per share of Stock Y was what percent of the original price per share of Stock X ?

    (1)   The increased price per share of Stock X was equal to the original price per share of Stock Y.

    (2)   The increase in the price per share of Stock X was $\dfrac{10}{11}$ the decrease in the price per share of Stock Y.

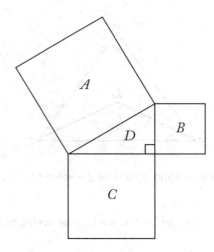

144. In the figure above, if the area of triangular region D is 4, what is the length of a side of square region A?

    (1) The area of square region B is 9.

    (2) The area of square region C is $\dfrac{64}{9}$.

145. If Sara's age is exactly twice Bill's age, what is Sara's age?

    (1) Four years ago, Sara's age was exactly 3 times Bill's age.

    (2) Eight years from now, Sara's age will be exactly 1.5 times Bill's age.

146. A report consisting of 2,600 words is divided into 23 paragraphs. A 2-paragraph preface is then added to the report. Is the average (arithmetic mean) number of words per paragraph for all 25 paragraphs less than 120?

    (1) Each paragraph of the preface has more than 100 words.

    (2) Each paragraph of the preface has fewer than 150 words.

147. A certain bookcase has 2 shelves of books. On the upper shelf, the book with the greatest number of pages has 400 pages. On the lower shelf, the book with the least number of pages has 475 pages. What is the median number of pages for all of the books on the 2 shelves?

    (1) There are 25 books on the upper shelf.

    (2) There are 24 books on the lower shelf.

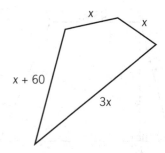

148. The figure above shows the number of meters in the lengths of the four sides of a jogging path. What is the total distance around the path?

    (1) One of the sides of the path is 120 meters long.

    (2) One of the sides of the path is twice as long as each of the two shortest sides.

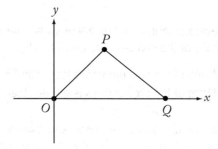

149. In the rectangular coordinate system above, if $OP < PQ$, is the area of region OPQ greater than 48?

    (1) The coordinates of point P are (6,8).

    (2) The coordinates of point Q are (13,0).

$$S = \dfrac{\dfrac{2}{n}}{\dfrac{1}{x} + \dfrac{2}{3x}}$$

150. In the expression above, if $xn \ne 0$, what is the value of S?

    (1) $x = 2n$

    (2) $n = \dfrac{1}{2}$

151. If n is a positive integer and $k = 5.1 \times 10^n$, what is the value of k?

    (1) $6{,}000 < k < 500{,}000$

    (2) $k^2 = 2.601 \times 10^9$

152. If Carmen had 12 more tapes, she would have twice as many tapes as Rafael. Does Carmen have fewer tapes than Rafael?

    (1) Rafael has more than 5 tapes.
    (2) Carmen has fewer than 12 tapes.

153. If x is an integer, is $x\,|x| < 2^x$?

    (1) $x < 0$
    (2) $x = -10$

154. If n is a positive integer, is the value of $b - a$ at least twice the value of $3^n - 2^n$?

    (1) $a = 2^{n+1}$ and $b = 3^{n+1}$
    (2) $n = 3$

155. The inflation index for the year 1989 relative to the year 1970 was 3.56, indicating that, on the average, for each dollar spent in 1970 for goods, $3.56 had to be spent for the same goods in 1989. If the price of a Model K mixer increased precisely according to the inflation index, what was the price of the mixer in 1970 ?

    (1) The price of the Model K mixer was $102.40 more in 1989 than in 1970.
    (2) The price of the Model K mixer was $142.40 in 1989.

156. Is 5^k less than 1,000 ?

    (1) $5^{k+1} > 3,000$
    (2) $5^{k-1} = 5^k - 500$

157. The hypotenuse of a right triangle is 10 cm. What is the perimeter, in centimeters, of the triangle?

    (1) The area of the triangle is 25 square centimeters.
    (2) The 2 legs of the triangle are of equal length.

158. Every member of a certain club volunteers to contribute equally to the purchase of a $60 gift certificate. How many members does the club have?

    (1) Each member's contribution is to be $4.
    (2) If 5 club members fail to contribute, the share of each contributing member will increase by $2.

159. If $x < 0$, is $y > 0$?

    (1) $\dfrac{x}{y} < 0$
    (2) $y - x > 0$

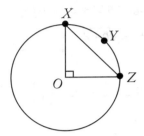

160. What is the circumference of the circle above with center O ?

    (1) The perimeter of $\triangle OXZ$ is $20 + 10\sqrt{2}$.
    (2) The length of arc XYZ is 5π.

161. Beginning in January of last year, Carl made deposits of $120 into his account on the 15th of each month for several consecutive months and then made withdrawals of $50 from the account on the 15th of each of the remaining months of last year. There were no other transactions in the account last year. If the closing balance of Carl's account for May of last year was $2,600, what was the range of the monthly closing balances of Carl's account last year?

    (1) Last year the closing balance of Carl's account for April was less than $2,625.
    (2) Last year the closing balance of Carl's account for June was less than $2,675.

162. If n and k are positive integers, is $\sqrt{n+k} > 2\sqrt{n}$?

    (1) $k > 3n$
    (2) $n + k > 3n$

163. In a certain business, production index p is directly proportional to efficiency index e, which is in turn directly proportional to investment index i. What is p if $i = 70$?

    (1) $e = 0.5$ whenever $i = 60$.
    (2) $p = 2.0$ whenever $i = 50$.

164. In the rectangular coordinate system, are the points (r,s) and (u,v) equidistant from the origin?

    (1) $r + s = 1$
    (2) $u = 1 - r$ and $v = 1 - s$

165. If x is an integer, is $9^x + 9^{-x} = b$?

    (1) $3^x + 3^{-x} = \sqrt{b + 2}$
    (2) $x > 0$

166. If n is a positive integer, is $\left(\frac{1}{10}\right)^n < 0.01$?

    (1) $n > 2$
    (2) $\left(\frac{1}{10}\right)^{n-1} < 0.1$

167. If n is a positive integer, what is the tens digit of n ?

    (1) The hundreds digit of $10n$ is 6.
    (2) The tens digit of $n + 1$ is 7.

168. What is the value of $\frac{2t + t - x}{t - x}$?

    (1) $\frac{2t}{t - x} = 3$
    (2) $t - x = 5$

169. Is n an integer?

    (1) n^2 is an integer.
    (2) $\sqrt{n}$ is an integer.

170. If n is a positive integer, is $n^3 - n$ divisible by 4 ?

    (1) $n = 2k + 1$, where k is an integer.
    (2) $n^2 + n$ is divisible by 6.

171. What is the tens digit of positive integer x ?

    (1) x divided by 100 has a remainder of 30.
    (2) x divided by 110 has a remainder of 30.

172. If x, y, and z are positive integers, is $x - y$ odd?

    (1) $x = z^2$
    (2) $y = (z - 1)^2$

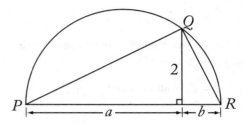

173. If arc PQR above is a semicircle, what is the length of diameter $\overline{PR}$?

    (1) $a = 4$
    (2) $b = 1$

174. Marcia's bucket can hold a maximum of how many liters of water?

    (1) The bucket currently contains 9 liters of water.
    (2) If 3 liters of water are added to the bucket when it is half full of water, the amount of water in the bucket will increase by $\frac{1}{3}$.

6.4 Answer Key

1.	B	36.	B	71.	C	106.	D	141.	C
2.	E	37.	A	72.	A	107.	B	142.	E
3.	A	38.	C	73.	B	108.	D	143.	D
4.	E	39.	D	74.	A	109.	A	144.	D
5.	E	40.	B	75.	A	110.	A	145.	D
6.	D	41.	E	76.	E	111.	E	146.	B
7.	A	42.	A	77.	D	112.	B	147.	C
8.	C	43.	E	78.	C	113.	D	148.	B
9.	A	44.	C	79.	E	114.	D	149.	A
10.	B	45.	D	80.	D	115.	D	150.	A
11.	A	46.	B	81.	C	116.	A	151.	D
12.	B	47.	A	82.	B	117.	D	152.	B
13.	D	48.	C	83.	C	118.	E	153.	D
14.	C	49.	B	84.	D	119.	E	154.	A
15.	B	50.	C	85.	A	120.	B	155.	D
16.	A	51.	B	86.	A	121.	E	156.	B
17.	D	52.	B	87.	E	122.	C	157.	D
18.	B	53.	A	88.	B	123.	A	158.	D
19.	C	54.	C	89.	C	124.	A	159.	A
20.	A	55.	E	90.	A	125.	D	160.	D
21.	E	56.	A	91.	E	126.	E	161.	C
22.	E	57.	D	92.	A	127.	D	162.	A
23.	B	58.	E	93.	D	128.	B	163.	B
24.	D	59.	E	94.	A	129.	C	164.	C
25.	D	60.	D	95.	E	130.	C	165.	A
26.	D	61.	C	96.	A	131.	D	166.	D
27.	D	62.	D	97.	A	132.	C	167.	A
28.	E	63.	C	98.	B	133.	B	168.	A
29.	E	64.	B	99.	D	134.	B	169.	B
30.	B	65.	D	100.	D	135.	D	170.	A
31.	B	66.	C	101.	B	136.	D	171.	A
32.	E	67.	D	102.	D	137.	A	172.	C
33.	C	68.	A	103.	D	138.	E	173.	D
34.	D	69.	A	104.	E	139.	B	174.	B
35.	D	70.	D	105.	B	140.	E		

6.5 Answer Explanations

The following discussion of data sufficiency is intended to familiarize you with the most efficient and effective approaches to the kinds of problems common to data sufficiency. The particular questions in this chapter are generally representative of the kinds of data sufficiency questions you will encounter on the GMAT. Remember that it is the problem solving strategy that is important, not the specific details of a particular question.

1. What is the value of $|x|$?

    (1) $x = -|x|$
    (2) $x^2 = 4$

    Arithmetic Absolute value

    (1) The absolute value of x, $|x|$, is always positive or 0, so this only determines that x is negative or 0; NOT sufficient.

    (2) Exactly two values of x ($x = \pm2$) are possible, each of which gives the value 2 for $|x|$; SUFFICIENT.

    **The correct answer is B;
    statement 2 alone is sufficient.**

2. What percent of a group of people are women with red hair?

    (1) Of the women in the group, 5 percent have red hair.
    (2) Of the men in the group, 10 percent have red hair.

    Arithmetic Percents

    In order to solve this problem, it is necessary to know the total number of people in the group and the number of women with red hair.

    (1) This indicates that 5 percent of the women have red hair, but neither the total number of women nor the total number of people in the group is known. Therefore, further information is needed; NOT sufficient.

    (2) This indicates the percent of men who have red hair, a fact that is irrelevant. It does not give information as to the total number in the group or the number of women with red hair; NOT sufficient.

With (1) and (2) taken together, the percent of men with red hair is known and the percent of the women with red hair is known, but not the percent of the group who are women with red hair. For example: if there are 100 women, including 5 red-haired women, and 100 men, including 10 red-haired men, then $\frac{5}{200}$ = 2.5 percent of the group are women with red hair. On the other hand, if there are 300 women, including 15 red-haired women and 100 men, including 10 red-haired men, then $\frac{15}{400}$ = 3.75 percent of the group are women with red hair.

**The correct answer is E;
both statements together are still not sufficient.**

3. In a certain class, one student is to be selected at random to read. What is the probability that a boy will read?

    (1) Two-thirds of the students in the class are boys.
    (2) Ten of the students in the class are girls.

    Arithmetic Probability

    (1) Since $\frac{2}{3}$ of the students in the class are boys, the probability that one student selected at random will be a boy is $\frac{2}{3}$; SUFFICIENT.

    (2) The desired probability is different for a class with 10 girls and 20 boys than it is for a class with 10 girls and 10 boys; NOT sufficient.

    **The correct answer is A;
    statement 1 alone is sufficient.**

4. In College X the number of students enrolled in both a chemistry course and a biology course is how much less than the number of students enrolled in neither?

    (1) In College X there are 60 students enrolled in a chemistry course.
    (2) In College X there are 85 students enrolled in a biology course.

Arithmetic Sets (Venn diagrams)

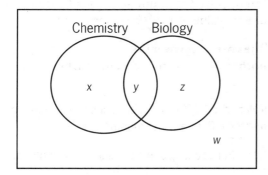

Consider the Venn diagram above, in which x represents the number of students in chemistry only, y represents the number of students in both chemistry and biology, z represents the number of students in biology only, and w represents the number of students in neither chemistry nor biology. Find the value for $w - y$.

    (1) Since there are 60 students enrolled in chemistry, $x + y = 60$, but there is no way to determine the value of y. Also, no information is given for determining w. For example, if $x = y = 30$ and $w = 30$, then $w - y = 0$. However, if $x = y = 30$ and $w = 40$, then $w - y = 10$; NOT sufficient.

    (2) Since there are 85 students enrolled in biology, $y + z = 85$, but there is no way to determine the value of y. Also, no information is given for determining w. For example, if $x = y = 30$, $z = 55$, and $w = 30$, then $w - y = 0$. However, if $x = y = 30$, $z = 55$, and $w = 40$, then $w - y = 10$; NOT sufficient.

Taking (1) and (2) together and subtracting the equation in (1) from the equation in (2) gives $z - x = 25$. Then, adding the equations gives $x + 2y + z = 145$, but neither gives information for

finding the value of w. For example, if $x = y = 30$, $z = 55$, and $w = 30$, then $w - y = 0$. However, if $x = y = 30$, $z = 55$, and $w = 40$, then $w - y = 10$.

**The correct answer is E;
both statements together are still not sufficient.**

5. A certain expressway has Exits J, K, L, and M, in that order. What is the road distance from Exit K to Exit L ?

    (1) The road distance from Exit J to Exit L is 21 kilometers.
    (2) The road distance from Exit K to Exit M is 26 kilometers.

Geometry Lines

Let JK, KL, and LM be the distances between adjacent exits.

    (1) It can only be determined that $KL = 21 - JK$; NOT sufficient.

    (2) It can only be determined that $KL = 26 - LM$; NOT sufficient.

Statements (1) and (2) taken together do not provide any of the distances JK, LM, or JM, which would give the needed information to find KL. For example, $KL = 1$ if $JK = 20$ and $LM = 25$, while $KL = 2$ if $JK = 19$ and $LM = 24$.

**The correct answer is E;
both statements together are still not sufficient.**

6. If n is an integer, is $n + 1$ odd?

    (1) $n + 2$ is an even integer.
    (2) $n - 1$ is an odd integer.

Arithmetic Properties of numbers

    (1) Since $n + 2$ is even, n is an even integer, and therefore $n + 1$ would be an odd integer; SUFFICIENT.

    (2) Since $n - 1$ is an odd integer, n is an even integer. Therefore $n + 1$ would be an odd integer; SUFFICIENT.

**The correct answer is D;
each statement alone is sufficient.**

7. For which type of investment, J or K, is the annual rate of return greater?

   (1) Type J returns $115 per $1,000 invested for any one-year period and type K returns $300 per $2,500 invested for any one-year period.
   (2) The annual rate of return for an investment of type K is 12 percent.

Arithmetic Percents

Compare the annual rates of return for Investments J and K.

   (1) For Investment J, the annual rate of return is $115 per $1,000 for any one-year period, which can be converted to a percent. For Investment K, the annual rate of return is $300 per $2,500 for any one-year period, which can also be converted to a percent. These two percents can be compared to determine which is larger; SUFFICIENT.
   (2) Investment K has an annual rate of return of 12 percent, but no information is given about the annual rate of return for Investment J; NOT sufficient.

The correct answer is A; statement 1 alone is sufficient.

8. A citrus fruit grower receives $15 for each crate of oranges shipped and $18 for each crate of grapefruit shipped. How many crates of oranges did the grower ship last week?

   (1) Last week the number of crates of oranges that the grower shipped was 20 more than twice the number of crates of grapefruit shipped.
   (2) Last week the grower received a total of $38,700 from the crates of oranges and grapefruit shipped.

Algebra Simultaneous equations

If x represents the number of crates of oranges and y represents the number of crates of grapefruit, find a unique value for x.

   (1) Translating from words into symbols gives $x = 2y + 20$, but there is no information about y and no way to find a unique value for x from this equation. For example, if $y = 10$, then $x = 40$, but if $y = 100$, then $x = 220$; NOT sufficient.

   (2) Translating from words to symbols gives $15x + 18y = 38,700$, but there is no way to find a unique value for x from this equation. For example, if $y = 2,150$, then $x = 0$ and if $y = 0$, then $x = 2,580$; NOT sufficient.

Taking (1) and (2) together gives a system of two equations in two unknowns. Substituting the equation from (1) into the equation from (2) gives a single equation in the variable y. This equation can be solved for a unique value of y from which a unique value of x can be determined.

The correct answer is C; both statements together are sufficient.

9. If Pat saved $600 of his earnings last month, how much did Pat earn last month?

   (1) Pat spent $\frac{1}{2}$ of his earnings last month for living expenses and saved $\frac{1}{3}$ of the remainder.
   (2) Of his earnings last month, Pat paid twice as much in taxes as he saved.

Arithmetic Operations with rational numbers

Let E be Pat's earnings last month. Find a unique value for E.

   (1) Pat spent $\frac{1}{2}E$ for living expenses and so $E - \frac{1}{2}E = \frac{1}{2}E$ remained. Pat saved $\frac{1}{3}$ of what remained, so Pat saved $\frac{1}{3}\left(\frac{1}{2}E\right) = \frac{1}{6}E$. But Pat saved $600, so $600 = \frac{1}{6}E$ and this gives a unique value for E; SUFFICIENT.
   (2) Pat saved $600 last month and paid 2($600) in taxes, but there is no way to determine Pat's earnings last month; NOT sufficient.

The correct answer is A; statement 1 alone is sufficient.

10. Water is pumped into a partially filled tank at a constant rate through an inlet pipe. At the same time, water is pumped out of the tank at a constant rate through an outlet pipe. At what rate, in gallons per minute, is the amount of water in the tank increasing?

(1) The amount of water initially in the tank is 200 gallons.

(2) Water is pumped into the tank at a rate of 10 gallons per minute and out of the tank at a rate of 10 gallons every $2\frac{1}{2}$ minutes.

Arithmetic Work Problem

If both the rate of the water being pumped into the tank and the rate of the water being pumped out of the tank are known, then the rate at which the total amount of water in the tank is changing can be determined, but not if only one of these quantities is known.

(1) This only gives the amount of water in the tank initially; NOT sufficient.

(2) This information provides both the needed rates. Since the water is being pumped out of the tank at the rate of 10 gallons every $2\frac{1}{2}$ minutes, that is, 4 gallons every minute, and since 10 gallons are pumped into the tank every minute, the rate at which the water is increasing in the tank is $10 - 4 = 6$ gallons per minute; SUFFICIENT.

The correct answer is B; statement 2 alone is sufficient.

11. Is x a negative number?

(1) $9x > 10x$

(2) $x + 3$ is positive.

Arithmetic Properties of numbers

(1) Subtracting $9x$ from both sides of $9x > 10x$ gives $0 > x$, which expresses the condition that x is negative; SUFFICIENT.

(2) Subtracting 3 from both sides of $x + 3 > 0$ gives $x > -3$, and $x > -3$ is true for some negative numbers (such as -2 and -1) and for some numbers that aren't negative (such as 0 and 1); NOT sufficient.

The correct answer is A; statement 1 alone is sufficient.

12. If i and j are integers, is $i + j$ an even integer?

(1) $i < 10$

(2) $i = j$

Arithmetic Properties of numbers

(1) Although $i < 10$, i could be an even number or an odd number less than 10. There is no information about j, so j could be an even number or an odd number. If i and j are both even integers, then $i + j$ is an even integer, and if i and j are both odd integers, then $i + j$ is an even integer. If, however, either i or j is an even integer and the other is an odd integer, then $i + j$ is an odd integer; NOT sufficient.

(2) If $i = j$, then $i + j$ can also be represented as $i + i$ when i is substituted for j in the expression. This can be simplified as $2i$, and since 2 times any integer produces an even integer, then $i + j$ must be an even integer; SUFFICIENT.

The correct answer is B; statement 2 alone is sufficient.

13. The charge for a telephone call between City R and City S is $0.42 for each of the first 3 minutes and $0.18 for each additional minute. A certain call between these two cities lasted for x minutes, where x is an integer. How many minutes long was the call?

(1) The charge for the first 3 minutes of the call was $0.36 less than the charge for the remainder of the call.

(2) The total charge for the call was $2.88.

Algebra First-degree equations

Let C be the charge for a phone call that lasts x minutes. Then $C = 0.42(3) + 0.18(x - 3)$, where $x \geq 3$. Find a unique value for x.

(1) The charge, in dollars, for the first 3 minutes of the call is $3(0.42) = 1.26$ and the charge for the remainder of the call is $0.18(x - 3)$. Then, $1.26 = 0.18(x - 3) - 0.36$, which can be solved for a unique value of x; SUFFICIENT.

(2) The charge, in dollars, for the call was 2.88, so $2.88 = 0.42(3) + 0.18(x - 3)$, which can be solved for a unique value of x; SUFFICIENT.

The correct answer is D; each statement alone is sufficient.

14. If Car X followed Car Y across a certain bridge that is $\frac{1}{2}$ mile long, how many seconds did it take Car X to travel across the bridge?

 (1) Car X drove onto the bridge exactly 3 seconds after Car Y drove onto the bridge and drove off the bridge exactly 2 seconds after Car Y drove off the bridge.
 (2) Car Y traveled across the bridge at a constant speed of 30 miles per hour.

Arithmetic Rate problem

Find the number of seconds that it took Car X to cross the $\frac{1}{2}$-mile bridge.

 (1) If Car X drove onto the bridge 3 seconds after Car Y and drove off the bridge 2 seconds after Car Y, then Car X took 1 second less to cross the bridge than Car Y. Since there is no information on how long Car Y took to cross the bridge, there is no way to determine how long Car X took to cross the bridge; NOT sufficient.
 (2) If the speed of Car Y was 30 miles per hour, it took Car Y $\frac{1}{60}$ hour = 1 minute = 60 seconds to cross the bridge. However, there is no information on how long Car X took to cross the bridge; NOT sufficient.

Taking (1) and (2) together, Car X took 1 second less than Car Y to cross the bridge and Car Y took 60 seconds to cross the bridge, so Car X took 60 − 1 = 59 seconds to cross the bridge.

**The correct answer is C;
both statements together are sufficient.**

15. If $n + k = m$, what is the value of k?

 (1) $n = 10$
 (2) $m + 10 = n$

Algebra First- and second-degree equations

It is given that $n + k = m$, so $k = m − n$. Thus, the question can be rephrased as: What is the value of $m − n$?

 (1) If $n = 10$, then $m − n = m − 10$, and the value of $m − 10$ can vary. For example, $m − 10 = 0$ if $m = 10$ and $m − 10 = 1$ if $m = 11$; NOT sufficient.
 (2) Subtracting both n and 10 from each side of $m + 10 = n$ gives $m − n = −10$, and hence the value of $m − n$ can be determined; SUFFICIENT.

**The correct answer is B;
statement 2 alone is sufficient.**

16. Is x an integer?

 (1) $\frac{x}{2}$ is an integer.
 (2) $2x$ is an integer.

Arithmetic Properties of numbers

 (1) If $\frac{x}{2}$ is an integer, it means that x can be divided by 2 without a remainder. This implies that x is an even integer; SUFFICIENT.
 (2) If $2x$ is an integer, then x could also be an integer. However, x could also be an odd number divided by 2, such as $\frac{1}{2}$ or $-\frac{1}{2}$ or $\frac{3}{2}$, none of which is an integer; NOT sufficient.

**The correct answer is A;
statement 1 alone is sufficient.**

17. Is the integer P odd?

 (1) The sum of P, $P + 4$, and $P + 11$ is even.
 (2) The sum of $P − 3$, P, and $P + 11$ is odd.

Arithmetic Properties of numbers

Determine if the integer P is odd.

 (1) If the sum of P, $P + 4$, and $P + 11$ is even, then $P + P + 4 + P + 11 = 3P + 15$ is even. Since 15 is odd, $3P$ must be odd in order for $3P + 15$ to be even. Then, if $3P$ is odd, P is odd because, if P were even, then $3P$ would be even; SUFFICIENT.

(2) If the sum of $P - 3$, P, and $P + 11$ is odd, then $P - 3 + P + P + 11 = 3P + 8$ is odd. Since 8 is even, $3P$ must be odd in order for $3P + 8$ to be odd. Then, as in (1), P is odd; SUFFICIENT.

**The correct answer is D;
each statement alone is sufficient.**

18. What is the maximum number of rectangular blocks, each with dimensions 12 centimeters by 6 centimeters by 4 centimeters, that will fit inside rectangular Box X ?

(1) When Box X is filled with the blocks and rests on a certain side, there are 25 blocks in the bottom layer.

(2) The inside dimensions of Box X are 60 centimeters by 30 centimeters by 20 centimeters.

Geometry Volume

Determine how many rectangular blocks will fit in a rectangular box.

(1) The side on which the box is resting could be 30 cm by 20 cm. If the blocks are resting on the side that is 6 cm by 4 cm, there would be $\frac{30}{6} \times \frac{20}{4} = 5 \times 5 = 25$ blocks on the bottom layer. If the box is 12 cm tall, a maximum of 25 blocks would fit inside the box. However, if the box is 48 cm tall, a maximum of 100 blocks would fit inside the box; NOT sufficient.

(2) If the box is resting on a side that is 30 cm by 20 cm, then $\frac{30}{6} \times \frac{20}{4} = 5 \times 5 = 25$ blocks will fit on the bottom layer. In this case, the height of the box is 60 cm and $\frac{60}{12} = 5$ layers will fit inside the box. If the box is resting on a side that is 60 cm by 30 cm, then $\frac{60}{12} \times \frac{30}{6} = 5 \times 5 = 25$ blocks will fit on the bottom layer. In this case, the height of the box is 20 cm and $\frac{20}{4} = 5$ layers will fit inside the box. If the box is resting on a side that is 60 cm by 20 cm, then $\frac{60}{12} \times \frac{20}{4} = 5 \times 5 = 25$ blocks will fit on the bottom layer. In this case, the height of the box is

30 cm and $\frac{30}{6} = 5$ layers will fit inside the box. In all cases, the maximum number of blocks that will fit inside the box is $5 \times 25 = 125$; SUFFICIENT.

**The correct answer is B;
statement 2 alone is sufficient.**

19. If sequence S has 200 terms, what is the 192nd term of S ?

(1) The first term of S is −40.

(2) Each term of S after the first term is 3 less than the preceding term.

Arithmetic Series and sequences

Determine the 192nd term of the 200-term sequence S.

(1) The first term of S is −40, but there is no way to determine any of the subsequent terms of S; NOT sufficient.

(2) Each term after the first term is 3 less than the preceding term, but there is no information on what the first term is and, therefore, no way to determine the 192nd term. For example, if the first term is 60, the 192nd term is $60 - 191(3) = -513$, but if the first term is 600, the 192nd term is $600 - 191(3) = 27$; NOT sufficient.

Taking (1) and (2) together, the first term is −40 and each term after the first is 3 less than the preceding term. Then, the second term is $-40 - 3 = -43$, the third term is $-43 - 3 = -40 - 2(3) = -46$, and the 192nd term is $-40 - 191(3) = -613$.

**The correct answer is C;
both statements together are sufficient.**

20. In $\triangle PQR$, if $PQ = x$, $QR = x + 2$, and $PR = y$, which of the three angles of $\triangle PQR$ has the greatest degree measure?

(1) $y = x + 3$

(2) $x = 2$

Geometry Triangles

In any triangle, the largest angle is opposite the longest side.

(1) Since $x + 2 > x$, the longest side is either $x + 2$ or y; therefore, it is sufficient to determine whether $y > x + 2$. If $y = x + 3$ and since $x + 3 > x + 2$, it follows by substitution that $y > x + 2$; SUFFICIENT.

(2) Substituting 2 for x yields that $PQ = 2$ and $QR = 4$, but no information is given as to the relationship of these sides with the value of y given for side PR; NOT sufficient.

The correct answer is A; statement 1 alone is sufficient.

21. What percent of the drama club members enrolled at a certain school are female students?

(1) Of the female students enrolled at the school, 40 percent are members of the drama club.

(2) Of the male students enrolled at the school, 25 percent are members of the drama club.

Arithmetic Percents

Determine what percent of drama club members are female.

(1) Knowing that 40 percent of the females enrolled at the school are in the drama club provides no information about the male/female breakdown of the drama club; NOT sufficient.

(2) Knowing that 25 percent of the males enrolled at the school are in the drama club provides no information about the male/female breakdown of the drama club; NOT sufficient.

Taking (1) and (2) together does not give enough information to determine what percent of drama club members are female. For example, if the school has 100 female students and 100 male students, then the drama club would have $0.40(100) + 0.25(100) = 40 + 25 = 65$ members, $\frac{40}{65} \approx 62$ percent of whom are female. On the other hand, if the school had 40 female students and 160 male students, the drama club would

have $0.40(40) + 0.25(160) = 16 + 40 = 56$ members, $\frac{16}{56} \approx 29$ percent of whom are female.

The correct answer is E; both statements together are still not sufficient.

22. A family-size box of cereal contains more cereal and costs more than the regular-size box of cereal. What is the cost per ounce of the family-size box of cereal?

(1) The family-size box of cereal contains 10 ounces more than the regular-size box of cereal.

(2) The family-size box of cereal costs $5.40.

Arithmetic Rate problem

Determine the cost per ounce of cereal in the family-size box.

(1) A family-size box contains 10 ounces more cereal than a regular-size box, but there is no information about how many ounces are contained in a regular-size box and no information about the cost of either size box, so there is no way to determine the cost per ounce of cereal in the family-size box; NOT sufficient.

(2) A family-size box costs $5.40, but there is no information about how many ounces of cereal a family-size box contains, so there is no way to determine the cost per ounce of cereal in the family-size box; NOT sufficient.

Taking (1) and (2) together, a family-size box costs $5.40 and contains 10 ounces more cereal than a regular-size box. However, there is no information about how much cereal a regular-size box contains and, therefore, no way to determine the cost per ounce of the cereal in a family-size box.

The correct answer is E; both statements together are still not sufficient.

23. The profit from the sale of a certain appliance increases, though not proportionally, with the number of units sold. Did the profit exceed $4 million on sales of 380,000 units?

(1) The profit exceeded $2 million on sales of 200,000 units.

(2) The profit exceeded $5 million on sales of 350,000 units.

Arithmetic Arithmetic operations; Proportions

(1) If the profits did increase proportionally, it might be reasonable to expect a profit of $4 million on sales of 400,000 units. However, it is given that the profits do not increase proportionally. Without knowing how the profits increase, it is impossible to tell the profits on sales of 380,000 units; NOT sufficient.

(2) It is given that the profits do increase with the number of units sold. Therefore, since the profit on sales of just 350,000 units well exceeded $4 million, then sales of 350,000 + 30,000 = 380,000 units would also have a profit exceeding $4 million; SUFFICIENT.

The correct answer is B; statement 2 alone is sufficient.

24. If n is an integer, is n even?

(1) $n^2 - 1$ is an odd integer.
(2) $3n + 4$ is an even integer.

Arithmetic Properties of numbers

Determine if the integer n is even.

(1) Since $n^2 - 1$ is odd, n^2 is even and so n is even; SUFFICIENT.

(2) Since $3n + 4$ is even, $3n$ is even and so n is even; SUFFICIENT.

The correct answer is D; each statement alone is sufficient.

25. Carmen currently works 30 hours per week at her part-time job. If her gross hourly wage were to increase by $1.50, how many fewer hours could she work per week and still earn the same gross weekly pay as before the increase?

(1) Her gross weekly pay is currently $225.00.
(2) An increase of $1.50 would represent an increase of 20 percent of her current gross hourly wage.

Arithmetic Operations with rational numbers

Let w be Carmen's gross hourly wage and let n be the number of hours fewer Carmen will need to work. Find a unique value for n such that $30w = (30 - n)(w + 1.50)$.

(1) Since Carmen's gross weekly pay is currently $225.00, then $30w = 225$ and $w = 7.50$. Substituting 7.50 for w gives $30(7.50) = (30 - n)(7.50 + 1.50)$, which can be solved for a unique value of n; SUFFICIENT.

(2) Since 1.50 is 20 percent of Carmen's current gross hourly pay, $1.50 = 0.20w$ and $w = 7.50$. This is the same information that was gained from statement (1) and will lead to the same result; SUFFICIENT.

The correct answer is D; each statement alone is sufficient.

26. The number n of units of its product that Company X is scheduled to produce in month t of its next fiscal year is given by the formula $n = \dfrac{900}{1 + c2^{-t}}$, where c is a constant and t is a positive integer between 1 and 6, inclusive. What is the number of units of its product that Company X is scheduled to produce in month 6 of its next fiscal year?

(1) Company X is scheduled to produce 180 units of its product in month 1 of its next fiscal year.
(2) Company X is scheduled to produce 300 units of its product in month 2 of its next fiscal year.

Algebra Formulas

Given the formula $n = \dfrac{900}{1 + c2^{-t}}$, determine the value of n when $t = 6$.

(1) Given that $n = 180$ when $t = 1$, then $180 = \dfrac{900}{1 + c\left(2^{-1}\right)}$. This equation can be solved for a unique value of c. Then, by substituting this value for c and 6 for t into $n = \dfrac{900}{1 + c2^{-t}}$, the value of n can be determined; SUFFICIENT.

(2) Given that $n = 300$ when $t = 2$, then $300 = \dfrac{900}{1 + c2^{-2}}$. This equation can be solved for a unique value of c. Then, by substituting this value for c and 6 for t into $n = \dfrac{900}{1 + c2^{-t}}$, the value of n can be determined; SUFFICIENT.

The correct answer is D; each statement alone is sufficient.

27. When 200 gallons of oil were removed from a tank, the volume of oil left in the tank was $\frac{3}{7}$ of the tank's capacity. What was the tank's capacity?

    (1) Before the 200 gallons were removed, the volume of oil in the tank was $\frac{1}{2}$ of the tank's capacity.

    (2) After the 200 gallons were removed, the volume of the oil left in the tank was 1,600 gallons less than the tank's capacity.

Arithmetic Operations with rational numbers

Let C be the capacity, in gallons, of the tank and let V be the volume of oil in the tank initially. Then $V - 200 = \frac{3}{7} C$. Find a unique value for C.

(1) Since the volume of oil in the tank initially was $\frac{1}{2}$ the tank's capacity, $V = \frac{1}{2}C$. Then, substituting $\frac{1}{2}C$ for V gives $\frac{1}{2}C - 200 = \frac{3}{7} C$, which can be solved for a unique value of C; SUFFICIENT.

(2) After the 200 gallons were removed, the volume of oil left in the tank was 1,600 gallons less than the tank's capacity. Therefore, since $V - 200 = \frac{3}{7} C$, $\frac{3}{7} C = C - 1,600$. This equation can be solved for a unique value of C; SUFFICIENT.

The correct answer is D; each statement alone is sufficient.

28. Division R of Company Q has 1,000 employees. What is the average (arithmetic mean) annual salary of the employees at Company Q ?

    (1) The average annual salary of the employees in Division R is $30,000.

    (2) The average annual salary of the employees at Company Q who are <u>not</u> in Division R is $35,000.

Arithmetic Statistics

Determine the average (arithmetic mean) annual salary of the employees at Company Q, given that Division R within Company Q has 1,000 employees.

(1) Although the average annual salary of the 1,000 employees in Division R is given, there is no information about the number of Company Q employees who are not in Division R or about their annual salaries. Therefore, it is impossible to determine the average annual salary of the employees at Company Q ; NOT sufficient.

(2) Although the average annual salary of the employees NOT in Division R is given, there is no information about the number of employees who are not in Division R. Therefore, it is impossible to determine the average annual salary of the employees at Company Q ; NOT sufficient.

Taking (1) and (2) together does not give the number of employees who are NOT in Division R, which is necessary to determine the average annual salary of the employees of Company Q.

The correct answer is E; both statements together are still not sufficient.

29. A circular tub has a band painted around its circumference, as shown above. What is the surface area of this painted band?

    (1) $x = 0.5$
    (2) The height of the tub is 1 meter.

Geometry Surface area

The surface area of the band is the product of the circumference of the band and the width of the band. If both factors are known, then the area can be determined, but not if only one of these factors is known.

(1) Only one factor, the width of the band, is known; NOT sufficient.

(2) The circumference or the means to find the circumference is not known; NOT sufficient.

With (1) and (2) taken together, there still is no information about the circumference of the tub.

The correct answer is E; both statements together are still not sufficient.

30. What is the value of integer n ?

    (1) $n(n + 1) = 6$
    (2) $2^{2n} = 16$

    Arithmetic; Algebra Arithmetic operations; First- and second-degree equations

    (1) If $(n + 1)$ is multiplied by n, the result is $n^2 + n = 6$. If 6 is subtracted from both sides, the equation becomes $n^2 + n - 6 = 0$. This in turn can be factored as $(n + 3)(n - 2) = 0$. Therefore, n could be either -3 or 2, but there is no further information for deciding between these two values; NOT sufficient.

    (2) From $2^{2n} = 16$, 2^{2n} must equal 2^4 (since $2 \times 2 \times 2 \times 2 = 16$). Therefore, $2n = 4$ and $n = 2$; SUFFICIENT.

    The correct answer is B; statement 2 alone is sufficient.

$$d = 0.43t\,7$$

31. If t denotes the thousandths digit in the decimal representation of d above, what digit is t ?

    (1) If d were rounded to the nearest hundredth, the result would be 0.44.
    (2) If d were rounded to the nearest thousandth, the result would be 0.436.

    Arithmetic Place value; Rounding

    Determine t, the thousandths digit of $d = 0.43t\,7$.

    (1) Since d rounded to the nearest hundredth is 0.44, t can be 5, 6, 7, 8, or 9 because each of 0.4357, 0.4367, 0.4377, 0.4387, and 0.4397 rounded to the nearest hundredth is 0.44; NOT sufficient.

    (2) Since d rounded to the nearest thousandth is 0.436 and the digit in ten-thousandths place of d is 7, the digit in thousandths place gets increased by 1 in the rounding process. Thus, $t + 1 = 6$ and $t = 5$; SUFFICIENT.

    The correct answer is B; statement 2 alone is sufficient.

32. Jerry bought 7 clothing items, including a coat, and the sum of the prices of these items was $365. If there was no sales tax on any clothing item with a price of less than $100 and a 7 percent sales tax on all other clothing items, what was the total sales tax on the 7 items that Jerry bought?

    (1) The price of the coat was $125.
    (2) The average (arithmetic mean) price for the 6 items other than the coat was $40.

    Arithmetic Applied problems

    Determine the amount of sales tax Jerry paid on the purchase of 7 items of clothing that included a coat and totaled $365, where there was no tax on any item with a price less than $100 and 7 percent tax on all other items.

    (1) Although Jerry paid sales tax on the price of the coat, which was $125, and the total price of the other 6 items was $365 − $125 = $240, no information is given on the individual prices of the other 6 items, which may or may not have been less than $100 and subject to sales tax; NOT sufficient.

    (2) Although the average price of the other 6 items was $40, no information is given on the individual prices of the other 6 items, which may or may not have been over $100, and therefore may or may not have been subject to sales tax; NOT sufficient.

    Taking (1) and (2) together, Jerry paid at least $0.07(125) = $8.75 in sales tax, but no information is given about whether any of the other 6 prices were subject to sales tax. If the price of each of the other 6 items was $40, then Jerry would have paid only $8.75 in sales tax. However, if the price of each of 2 items was $100 and the other 4 items were $10 each, Jerry would have paid a total of $0.07(125 + 100 + 100) = $22.75 in sales tax.

    The correct answer is E; both statements together are still not sufficient.

33. What was the price at which a merchant sold a certain appliance?

    (1) The merchant's gross profit on the appliance was 20 percent of the price at which the merchant sold the appliance.
    (2) The price at which the merchant sold the appliance was $50 more than the merchant's cost of the appliance.

Algebra Applied problems

Let R, C, and P be the appliance's selling price, the merchant's cost, and the gross profit, respectively. Determine the value of R.

    (1) Since $R - C = P$ and $P = 0.20R$, then $R - C = 0.2R$ and $0.8R = C$. No information is given about the value of C, so the value of R cannot be determined; NOT sufficient.
    (2) Although $R = C + 50$, no information is given about the value of C, so the value of R cannot be determined; NOT sufficient.

Taking (1) and (2) together and combining the two equations gives $R = 0.8R + 50$, which can be solved for a unique value of R.

**The correct answer is C;
both statements together are sufficient.**

34. The inside of a rectangular carton is 48 centimeters long, 32 centimeters wide, and 15 centimeters high. The carton is filled to capacity with k identical cylindrical cans of fruit that stand upright in rows and columns, as indicated in the figure above. If the cans are 15 centimeters high, what is the value of k?

    (1) Each of the cans has a radius of 4 centimeters.
    (2) Six of the cans fit exactly along the length of the carton.

Geometry Circles

    (1) If the radius of each can is 4 centimeters, the diameter of each can is 8 centimeters. Along the 48-centimeter length of the carton, 6 cans ($48 \div 8$) can be placed; along the 32-centimeter width of the carton, 4 cans ($32 \div 8$) can be placed. Hence, $k = 6 \times 4 = 24$; SUFFICIENT.
    (2) If 6 cans fit along the 48-centimeter length of the carton, this implies that the diameter of each can is 8 centimeters ($48 \div 6$). Along the 32 centimeter width, 4 cans can be placed, and again $k = 6 \times 4 = 24$; SUFFICIENT.

**The correct answer is D;
each statement alone is sufficient.**

$$\begin{cases} x - 4 = z \\ y - x = 8 \\ 8 - z = t \end{cases}$$

35. For the system of equations given, what is the value of z?

    (1) $x = 7$
    (2) $t = 5$

Algebra First- and second-degree equations

    (1) Since $x = 7$, then 7 can be substituted for x in the equation $x - 4 = z$, yielding $z = 3$; SUFFICIENT.
    (2) If $t = 5$, then the equation $8 - z = t$ can be used to solve this question:

$8 - z = 5$	substitute for t
$3 - z = 0$	subtract 5 from both sides
$3 = z$	add z to both sides; SUFFICIENT.

**The correct answer is D;
each statement alone is sufficient.**

36. For all integers n, the function f is defined by $f(n) = a^n$, where a is a constant. What is the value of $f(1)$?

    (1) $f(2) = 100$
    (2) $f(3) = -1{,}000$

Algebra Functions

Given $f(n) = a^n$, find the value of $f(1)$.

(1) Given that $f(2) = 100$, $a^2 = 100$, from which $a = 10$ or $a = -10$. Then, $f(1) = 10^1 = 10$ or $f(1) = (-10)^1 = -10$; NOT sufficient.

(2) Given that $f(3) = -1,000$, $a^3 = -1,000$, from which $a = -10$. Then, $f(1) = (-10)^1 = -10$; SUFFICIENT.

The correct answer is B; statement 2 alone is sufficient.

37. The selling price of an article is equal to the cost of the article plus the markup. The markup on a certain television set is what percent of the selling price?

(1) The markup on the television set is 25 percent of the cost.

(2) The selling price of the television set is $250.

Algebra Percents

Let S be the selling price of the television; C, the cost; and M, the markup, all in dollars. Then, $S = C + M$. Find the value of $\frac{M}{S}$ as a percent.

(1) Since the markup on the television is 25 percent of the cost, $M = 0.25C$. Then, $S = C + 0.25C = 1.25C$ and $\frac{M}{S} = \frac{0.25C}{1.25C} = 0.20$, which, as a percent is 20 percent; SUFFICIENT.

(2) The selling price of the television is $250, so $250 = S = C + M$. However, there is no information as to the values of either C or M. Therefore, it is impossible to determine the value of $\frac{M}{S}$. For example, if $C = 200$ and $M = 50$, then $\frac{M}{S} = 0.20$ or 20 percent, but if $C = 150$ and $M = 100$, then $\frac{M}{S} = 0.40$ or 40 percent; NOT sufficient.

The correct answer is A; statement 1 alone is sufficient.

38. If p_1 and p_2 are the populations and r_1 and r_2 are the numbers of representatives of District 1 and District 2, respectively, the ratio of the population to the number of representatives is greater for which of the two districts?

(1) $p_1 > p_2$

(2) $r_2 > r_1$

Algebra Ratios

Determine which ratio, $\frac{p_1}{r_1}$ or $\frac{p_2}{r_2}$, is greater.

(1) Even if $p_1 > p_2$, which ratio, $\frac{p_1}{r_1}$ or $\frac{p_2}{r_2}$, is greater depends of the values of r_1 and r_2. For example, if $p_1 = 1,000$, $p_2 = 500$, then $p_1 > p_2$. If $r_1 = 5$ and $r_2 = 2$, $\frac{p_1}{r_1} = \frac{1,000}{5} = 200$ and $\frac{p_2}{r_2} = \frac{500}{2} = 250$, so $\frac{p_2}{r_2} > \frac{p_1}{r_1}$. If however, $r_1 = 2$ and $r_2 = 5$, $\frac{p_1}{r_1} = \frac{1,000}{2} = 500$ and $\frac{p_2}{r_2} = \frac{500}{5} = 100$, so $\frac{p_1}{r_1} > \frac{p_2}{r_2}$; NOT sufficient.

(2) Even if $r_2 > r_1$, which ratio, $\frac{p_1}{r_1}$ or $\frac{p_2}{r_2}$, is greater depends of the values of p_1 and p_2. For example, if $r_1 = 2$, $r_2 = 5$, then $r_2 > r_1$. If $p_1 = 1,000$ and $p_2 = 500$, $\frac{p_1}{r_1} = \frac{1,000}{2} = 500$ and $\frac{p_2}{r_2} = \frac{500}{5} = 100$, so $\frac{p_1}{r_1} > \frac{p_2}{r_2}$. If however, $p_1 = 100$ and $p_2 = 1,000$, $\frac{p_1}{r_1} = \frac{100}{2} = 50$ and $\frac{p_2}{r_2} = \frac{1,000}{5} = 200$, so $\frac{p_2}{r_2} > \frac{p_1}{r_1}$; NOT sufficient.

Taking (1) and (2) together, $\frac{1}{r_2} < \frac{1}{r_1}$ because $r_2 > r_1$, and because populations can be assumed to be positive, $\frac{p_2}{r_2} < \frac{p_2}{r_1}$. Then, it follows that $\frac{p_2}{r_1} < \frac{p_1}{r_1}$ because $p_2 < p_1$. Combining $\frac{p_2}{r_2} < \frac{p_2}{r_1}$ and $\frac{p_2}{r_1} < \frac{p_1}{r_1}$ gives $\frac{p_2}{r_2} < \frac{p_1}{r_1}$.

The correct answer is C; both statements together are sufficient.

39. In a random sample of 80 adults, how many are college graduates?

    (1) In the sample, the number of adults who are <u>not</u> college graduates is 3 times the number who are college graduates.

    (2) In the sample, the number of adults who are <u>not</u> college graduates is 40 more than the number who are college graduates.

Algebra First-degree equations

Let C be the number of college graduates and let N be the number who are not college graduates. Then, $C + N = 80$. Find the value of C.

(1) Since the number who are not college graduates is 3 times the number who are, $N = 3C$. Then $C + 3C = 80$, $4C = 80$, and $C = 20$; SUFFICIENT.

(2) Since the number who are not college graduates is 40 more than the number who are college graduates, $N = C + 40$. Then $C + (C + 40) = 80$, $2C + 40 = 80$, $2C = 40$, and $C = 20$; SUFFICIENT.

The correct answer is D;
each statement alone is sufficient.

	R	S	T	U
R	0	y	x	62
S	y	0	56	75
T	x	56	0	69
U	62	75	69	0

40. The table above shows the distance, in kilometers, by the most direct route, between any two of the four cities, R, S, T, and U. For example, the distance between City R and City U is 62 kilometers. What is the value of x ?

    (1) By the most direct route, the distance between S and T is twice the distance between S and R.

    (2) By the most direct route, the distance between T and U is 1.5 times the distance between R and T.

Arithmetic; Algebra Tables; First-degree equations

The value of x is the distance between City R and City T; the value of y is the distance between City R and City S.

(1) From this, it can be determined only that $56 = 2y$. No information is given about x; NOT sufficient.

(2) This statement yields the equation $1.5x = 69$, which can be solved for x; SUFFICIENT.

The correct answer is B;
statement 2 alone is sufficient.

41. What is the value of the two-digit integer x ?

    (1) The sum of the two digits is 3.

    (2) x is divisible by 3.

Arithmetic Properties of numbers

In a problem of this kind, digits are the integers from 0 through 9, inclusive.

(1) From this, the two-digit integer must be 12, 21, or 30. However, a single numerical value of x cannot be determined; NOT sufficient.

(2) Since there are many two-digit integers divisible by 3, for example, 15, 24, and 27, once again a single numerical value of x cannot be determined; NOT sufficient.

Since all three numbers from (1) are also divisible by 3, (1) and (2) taken together do not provide sufficient information to identify the value of x.

The correct answer is E;
both statements together are still not sufficient.

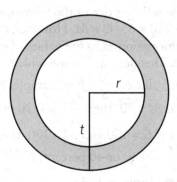

42. The figure above shows the circular cross section of a concrete water pipe. If the inside radius of the pipe is r feet and the outside radius of the pipe is t feet, what is the value of r ?

(1) The ratio of $t - r$ to r is 0.15 and $t - r$ is equal to 0.3 foot.

(2) The area of the concrete in the cross section is 1.29π square feet.

Geometry Circles; Area

Determine the value of r.

(1) Since $\frac{t-r}{r} = 0.15$ and $t - r = 0.3$, then $\frac{0.3}{r} = 0.15$ and $r = \frac{0.3}{0.15} = 2$; SUFFICIENT.

(2) The area of the concrete in the cross section is the area of the circular region with radius t minus the area of the circular region with radius r. The area of a circular region with radius R is πR^2, so the area of the concrete in the cross section is $\pi t^2 - \pi r^2$. This area is 1.29π, so $\pi t^2 - \pi r^2 = 1.29\pi$, and $t^2 - r^2 = 1.29$, from which it is impossible to determine a unique value for r. For example, if $t = \sqrt{2.29}$, then $r = 1$, but if $t = \sqrt{5.29}$, then $r = 2$; NOT sufficient.

The correct answer is A; statement 1 alone is sufficient.

43. What is the tenths digit in the decimal representation of a certain number?

(1) The number is less than $\frac{1}{3}$.

(2) The number is greater than $\frac{1}{4}$.

Arithmetic Properties of numbers

(1) Since the number is less than $\frac{1}{3}$, the tenths digit can be 0, 1, 2, or 3; NOT sufficient.

(2) Since the number is greater than $\frac{1}{4}$, the tenths digit can be 2, 3, 4, ..., 9; NOT sufficient.

From (1) and (2) taken together, the number, n, is greater than $\frac{1}{4}$ but less than $\frac{1}{3}$. The tenths digit can be 2 or 3.

The correct answer is E; both statements together are still not sufficient.

44. Robots X, Y, and Z each assemble components at their respective constant rates. If r_x is the ratio of Robot X's constant rate to Robot Z's constant rate and r_y is the ratio of Robot Y's constant rate to Robot Z's constant rate, is Robot Z's constant rate the greatest of the three?

(1) $r_x < r_y$

(2) $r_y < 1$

Algebra Ratios

Let X, Y, and Z represent the constant rates of Robots X, Y, and Z, respectively. Then $r_x = \frac{X}{Z}$ and $r_y = \frac{Y}{Z}$. Determine if Z is the greatest of X, Y, and Z.

(1) Since $r_x < r_y$, then $\frac{X}{Z} < \frac{Y}{Z}$ and $X < Y$. However, no information is given about the value of Z in relation to the values of X and Y; NOT sufficient.

(2) Since $r_y < 1$, then $\frac{Y}{Z} < 1$ and $Y < Z$. However, no information is given about the value of X in relation to the values of Y and Z; NOT sufficient.

Taking (1) and (2) together, $X < Y$ from (1) and $Y < Z$ from (2), so $X < Z$. Thus, Z is greater than both X and Y and is the greatest of the three.

The correct answer is C; both statements together are sufficient.

45. If r is a constant and $a_n = rn$ for all positive integers n, for how many values of n is $a_n < 100$?

(1) $a_{50} = 500$

(2) $a_{100} + a_{105} = 2{,}050$

Algebra Sequences and series

Determine how many values of n there are such that $a_n < 100$, where $a_n = rn$ and r is a constant.

(1) $a_{50} = 500$, so $50r = 500$ and $r = 10$. Thus, $a_n < 100$ for $n = 1, 2, 3, ..., 9$ and for no other values of n; SUFFICIENT.

(2) $a_{100} + a_{105} = 2,050$, so $100r + 105r = 2,050$. Then $205r = 2,050$ and $r = 10$. This is the same information obtained from (1), and because (1) is sufficient, so is (2); SUFFICIENT.

**The correct answer is D;
each statement alone is sufficient.**

46. If r is represented by the decimal $0.t5$, what is the digit t?

(1) $r < \dfrac{1}{3}$

(2) $r < \dfrac{1}{10}$

Arithmetic Place value

If $r = 0.t5$, find the digit t.

(1) If $r < \dfrac{1}{3}$, then t can be 0, 1, or 2 since $0.05 < \dfrac{1}{3}$, $0.15 < \dfrac{1}{3}$, and $0.25 < \dfrac{1}{3}$; NOT sufficient.

(2) If $r < \dfrac{1}{10}$, then t must be 0, because $0.15 > \dfrac{1}{10}$, $0.25 > \dfrac{1}{10}$, ..., $0.95 > \dfrac{1}{10}$; SUFFICIENT.

**The correct answer is B;
statement 2 alone is sufficient.**

47. If the two floors in a certain building are 9 feet apart, how many steps are there in a set of stairs that extends from the first floor to the second floor of the building?

(1) Each step is $\dfrac{3}{4}$ foot high.

(2) Each step is 1 foot wide.

Arithmetic Arithmetic operations

(1) If each step in the set of stairs is $\dfrac{3}{4}$ foot high and the set of stairs rises 9 feet from the first floor to the second, the number of steps must be $9 \div \dfrac{3}{4}$, or $\dfrac{9}{1} \times \dfrac{4}{3} = \dfrac{36}{3} = 12$; SUFFICIENT.

(2) This provides no information regarding the height of the steps, and so the question cannot be answered; NOT sufficient.

**The correct answer is A;
statement 1 alone is sufficient.**

48. In June 1989, what was the ratio of the number of sales transactions made by Salesperson X to the number of sales transactions made by Salesperson Y?

(1) In June 1989, Salesperson X made 50 percent more sales transactions than Salesperson Y did in May 1989.

(2) In June 1989, Salesperson Y made 25 percent more sales transactions than in May 1989.

Arithmetic Ratios; Percents

Let X_J be the number of sales transactions made by Salesperson X in June 1989 and let Y_J be the number of sales transactions made by Salesperson Y in June 1989. Find $\dfrac{X_J}{Y_J}$.

(1) Salesperson X made 50 percent more sales transactions in June 1989 than Salesperson Y made in May 1989, but no information is given about how many sales transactions Salesperson Y made in June 1989. Therefore, it is impossible to determine the value of $\dfrac{X_J}{Y_J}$; NOT sufficient.

(2) Salesperson Y made 25 percent more sales transactions in June 1989 than in May 1989, but no information is given about how many sales transactions Salesperson Y made in May 1989. Therefore, it is impossible to determine the value of Y_J and also impossible to determine the value of $\dfrac{X_J}{Y_J}$; NOT sufficient.

Taking (1) and (2) together, if X_M is the number of sales transactions made by Salesperson X in May 1989 and Y_M is the number of sales transactions made by Salesperson Y in May 1989, (1) gives $X_J = 1.5Y_M$ and (2) gives $Y_J = 1.25Y_M$.

Combining these two equations gives

$$\frac{X_J}{Y_J} = \frac{1.5Y_M}{1.25Y_M} = \frac{1.5}{1.25} = \frac{6}{5}.$$

The correct answer is C;
both statements together are sufficient.

49. If $a < x < b$ and $c < y < d$, is $x < y$?

    (1) $a < c$
    (2) $b < c$

Algebra Inequalities

Given $a < x < b$ and $c < y < d$, determine if $x < y$.

(1) Even though $a < c$, there is no information on the relative size of x and c. For example, if $a = 3$, $x = 10$, $b = 12$, $c = 4$, $y = 6$, and $d = 7$, $a < c$ because $3 < 4$ and $x > y$, since $10 > 6$. If, on the other hand, $a = 3$, $x = 4$, $b = 12$, $c = 4$, $y = 6$, and $d = 7$, $a < c$ because $3 < 4$ and $x < y$, since $4 < 6$. NOT sufficient.

(2) If $b < c$, then $a < x < b < c < y < d$ and so $x < y$; SUFFICIENT.

The correct answer is B;
statement 2 alone is sufficient.

50. How many people are directors of both Company K and Company R?

    (1) There were 17 directors present at a joint meeting of the directors of Company K and Company R, and no directors were absent.
    (2) Company K has 12 directors and Company R has 8 directors.

Algebra Sets

(1) This clarifies that Company K and Company R together have 17 individuals serving as directors. However, there is no information as to the distribution of the Company K directors, the Company R directors, and the joint directors; NOT sufficient.

(2) This gives the number of directors in each company but no information as to the number of joint directors; NOT sufficient.

Taking (1) and (2) together, it is known from (2) that there are 20 directorships in all. If at a joint meeting, there are only 17 people present, then $20 - 17 = 3$ people must be joint directors.

The correct answer is C;
both statements together are sufficient.

51. If x and y are positive, is $\dfrac{x}{y}$ greater than 1?

    (1) $xy > 1$
    (2) $x - y > 0$

Algebra Inequalities

Since, being positive, $y > 0$, it follows that $\dfrac{x}{y} > 1$ if and only if $x > y$.

(1) There are innumerable pairs of different numbers x and y whose product xy is greater than 1. The larger number in each pair can be either x or y; NOT sufficient.

(2) $x - y > 0$ is equivalent to $x > y$; SUFFICIENT.

The correct answer is B;
statement 2 alone is sufficient.

52. A clothing store acquired an item at a cost of x dollars and sold the item for y dollars. The store's gross profit from the item was what percent of its cost for the item?

    (1) $y - x = 20$
    (2) $\dfrac{y}{x} = \dfrac{5}{4}$

Algebra Applied problems

If the cost of an item of clothing is x and the selling price of the item is y, determine the value of $\dfrac{y - x}{x}$ as a percent.

(1) Although $y - x = 20$, there is no information to determine the value of x and therefore no way to determine the value of $\dfrac{y - x}{x}$; NOT sufficient.

(2) Since $\dfrac{y}{x} = \dfrac{5}{4}$, $y = \dfrac{5}{4}x$, and so $\dfrac{y - x}{x} =$

$\dfrac{\frac{5}{4}x - x}{x} = \dfrac{\frac{1}{4}x}{x} = \dfrac{1}{4}$, which is 25 percent; SUFFICIENT.

The correct answer is B;
statement 2 alone is sufficient.

$$(n - x) + (n - y) + (n - z) + (n - k)$$

53. What is the value of the expression above?

    (1) The average (arithmetic mean) of x, y, z, and k is n.

    (2) x, y, z, and k are consecutive integers.

Arithmetic Statistics

Determine the value of $(n - x) + (n - y) + (n - z) + (n - k)$, which can be rewritten as $4n - (x + y + z + k)$.

(1) Since the average of x, y, z, and k is n, then $\dfrac{x + y + z + k}{4} = n$ and $x + y + z + k = 4n$. Thus, $4n - (x + y + z + k) = 4n - 4n = 0$; SUFFICIENT.

(2) Even though x, y, z, and k are consecutive integers, no other information is given about the values of x, y, z, k, or n; NOT sufficient.

**The correct answer is A;
statement 1 alone is sufficient.**

54. A taxi company charges f cents for the first mile of the taxi ride and m cents for each additional mile. How much does the company charge for a 10-mile taxi ride?

    (1) The company charges $0.90 for a 2-mile ride.
    (2) The company charges $1.20 for a 4-mile ride.

Arithmetic Applied problems

If a taxi company charges f cents for the first mile and m cents for each additional mile, determine the charge for a 10-mile taxi ride, which can be expressed as $f + 9m$.

(1) Since the charge for a 2-mile ride is $0.90, $f + m = 0.90$, and so $f + 9m = 0.90 + 8m$, but the value of m is unknown; NOT sufficient.

(2) Since the charge for a 4-mile ride is $1.20, $f + 3m = 1.20$, and so $f + 9m = 1.20 + 6m$, but the value of m is unknown; NOT sufficient.

Taking (1) and (2) together and subtracting the equation in (1) from the equation in (2) gives $2m = 0.30$ from which $m = 0.15$. Then from (1), $f + 0.15 = 0.90$ and $f = 0.75$. Therefore, the charge for a 10-mile taxi ride is $0.75 + 9(\$0.15) = \$2.10$.

Alternatively, the graphs of $f + m = 0.90$ and $f + 3m = 1.20$ in the (f, m) coordinate plane are lines that intersect at exactly one point, and therefore values of f and m can be determined, from which $f + 9m$ can then be determined.

**The correct answer is C;
both statements together are sufficient.**

55. Guy's net income equals his gross income minus his deductions. By what percent did Guy's net income change on January 1, 1989, when both his gross income and his deductions increased?

    (1) Guy's gross income increased by 4 percent on January 1, 1989.

    (2) Guy's deductions increased by 15 percent on January 1, 1989.

Arithmetic Percents

Let g_b represent Guy's gross income and d_b Guy's deductions before January 1, 1989. Let g_a represent Guy's gross income and d_a Guy's deductions after January 1, 1989. Determine by what percent Guy's net income (gross income minus deductions) changed on January 1, 1989, when both his gross income and his deductions increased, or find $\dfrac{(g_a - d_a) - (g_b - d_b)}{g_b - d_b}$ as a percent.

(1) Guy's gross income increased by 4 percent on January 1, 1989, so $g_a = 1.04g_b$. Then, $\dfrac{(g_a - d_a) - (g_b - d_b)}{g_b - d_b} = \dfrac{(1.04g_b - d_a) - (g_b - d_b)}{g_b - d_b}$. However, no information is given about the values of g_b, d_a, or d_b, and so $\dfrac{(g_a - d_a) - (g_b - d_b)}{g_b - d_b}$ cannot be determined; NOT sufficient.

(2) Guy's deductions increased by 15 percent on January 1, 1989, so $d_a = 1.15d_b$. Then, $\dfrac{(g_a - d_a) - (g_b - d_b)}{g_b - d_b} = \dfrac{(g_a - 1.15d_b) - (g_b - d_b)}{g_b - d_b}$. However, no

information is given about the values of g_a, g_b, or d_b, and so $\dfrac{\left(g_a - d_a\right) - \left(g_b - d_b\right)}{g_b - d_b}$ cannot be determined; NOT sufficient.

Taking (1) and (2) together gives
$$\frac{\left(1.04g_b - 1.15d_b\right) - \left(g_b - d_b\right)}{g_b - d_b} = \frac{0.04g_b - 0.15d_b}{g_b - d_b},$$
which cannot be determined since the values of g_b and d_b are unknown.

**The correct answer is E;
both statements together are still not sufficient.**

56. What is the value of z in the triangle above?

(1) $x + y = 139$
(2) $y + z = 108$

Geometry Triangles

In any triangle the sum of the interior angles is $180°$; here, $x + y + z = 180$.

(1)   Since the sum of $x + y$ is known, the value of z can be determined by substituting 139 for $x + y$ in $x + y + z = 180$; SUFFICIENT.

(2)   Since the sum of $y + z$ is known, the value of x can be determined by substitution, but there is no way to determine the value of z in the sum $y + z$; NOT sufficient.

**The correct answer is A;
statement 1 alone is sufficient.**

57. Max has \$125 consisting of bills each worth either \$5 or \$20. How many bills worth \$5 does Max have?

(1)   Max has fewer than 5 bills worth \$5 each.
(2)   Max has more than 5 bills worth \$20 each.

Arithmetic Operations with integers

Let the integer x be the number of bills worth \$5 each and let the integer y be the number of bills

worth \$20 each. Then $5x + 20y = 125$. Determine the value of x.

(1)   Given that $x < 5$, then $x = 0$, 1, 2, 3, or 4. If x is even, then $5x + 20y$ is even and therefore cannot equal 125. If $x = 3$, then $15 + 20y = 125$, from which it follows that $20y = 110$. But, $\dfrac{110}{20}$ is not an integer and so $x \neq 3$. Thus, $x = 1$; SUFFICIENT.

(2)   Given that $y > 5$, then $y \geq 6$. If $y \geq 7$, then $20y \geq 140$ and so $5x + 20y \neq 125$. Therefore, $y = 6$ and $5x + 20(6) = 125$, so $x = 1$; SUFFICIENT.

**The correct answer is D;
each statement alone is sufficient.**

58. If the ratio of the number of teachers to the number of students is the same in School District M and School District P, what is the ratio of the number of students in School District M to the number of students in School District P?

(1)   There are 10,000 more students in School District M than there are in School District P.

(2)   The ratio of the number of teachers to the number of students in School District M is 1 to 20.

Algebra Ratios

Given that $\dfrac{T_M}{S_M} = \dfrac{T_P}{S_P}$, where T_M and S_M are the numbers of teachers and students, respectively, in District M, and T_P and S_P are the numbers of teachers and students, respectively, in District P, find the value of $\dfrac{S_M}{S_P}$.

(1)   Given that $S_M = S_P + 10,000$, then $\dfrac{S_M}{S_P} = \dfrac{S_P + 10,000}{S_P}$, but the value of S_P is unknown; NOT sufficient.

(2)   Given that $\dfrac{T_M}{S_M} = \dfrac{1}{20}$ and $\dfrac{T_M}{S_M} = \dfrac{T_P}{S_P}$, then $\dfrac{T_P}{S_P} = \dfrac{1}{20}$. Therefore, $S_P = 20T_P$ and $S_M = 20T_M$. It follows that $\dfrac{S_M}{S_P} = \dfrac{20T_M}{20T_P}$, but the values of T_M and T_P are unknown; NOT sufficient.

Taking (1) and (2) together, if $S_P = 1{,}000$,

$S_M = 1{,}000 + 10{,}000 = 11{,}000$, $T_P = \dfrac{1{,}000}{20} = 50$,

and $T_M = \dfrac{11{,}000}{20} = 550$, then $\dfrac{S_M}{S_P} = \dfrac{11}{1}$. However,

if $S_P = 5{,}000$, $S_M = 5{,}000 + 10{,}000, = 15{,}000$,

$T_P = \dfrac{5{,}000}{20} = 250$, and $T_M = \dfrac{15{,}000}{20} = 750$,

then $\dfrac{S_M}{S_P} = \dfrac{3}{1}$. Therefore, the value of $\dfrac{S_M}{S_P}$

cannot be determined.

The correct answer is E;
both statements together are still not sufficient.

59. If a total of 84 students are enrolled in two sections of a calculus course, how many of the 84 students are female?

   (1) $\dfrac{2}{3}$ of the students in Section 1 are female.

   (2) $\dfrac{1}{2}$ of the students in Section 2 are male.

Arithmetic Operations with rational numbers

Determine how many of the 84 students in two sections of a calculus course are female.

   (1) Even though it is known that $\dfrac{2}{3}$ of the students in Section 1 are female, no information is given about the number of students, male or female, in each of the two sections; NOT sufficient.

   (2) Even though it is known that $\dfrac{1}{2}$ of the students in Section 2 are male, no information is given about the number of students, male or female, in each of the two sections; NOT sufficient.

Taking (1) and (2) together, $\dfrac{2}{3}$ of the students in Section 1 are female and $\dfrac{1}{2}$ of the students in Section 2 are female. However, there is no information about how many of the 84 students in the two sections combined are in Section 1 and how many are in Section 2. Therefore, it is impossible to determine how many females there are among the 84 students. For example, if there are 42 students in each section, the number of

females is then $\left(\dfrac{2}{3} + \dfrac{1}{2} \right)(42) = \dfrac{7}{6}(42) = 49$. But if there are 24 students in Section 1 and 60 students in Section 2, then the number of females is $\dfrac{2}{3}(24) + \dfrac{1}{2}(60) = 16 + 30 = 46$.

The correct answer is E;
both statements together are still not sufficient.

60. What is the value of n in the equation $-25 + 19 + n = s$?

   (1) $s = 2$

   (2) $\dfrac{n}{s} = 4$

Algebra First- and second-degree equations

   (1) If $s = 2$, then the equation becomes $-25 + 19 + n = 2$ or $-6 + n = 2$ or $n = 8$; SUFFICIENT.

   (2) If $\dfrac{n}{s} = 4$, then $n = 4s$. By substituting this value of n in the given equation and simplifying, the equation becomes: $-25 + 19 + 4s = s$ or $-6 + 3s = 0$ or $s = 2$. Once s is found to be 2, the original equation can be solved as above; SUFFICIENT.

The correct answer is D;
each statement alone is sufficient.

61. At a certain picnic, each of the guests was served either a single scoop or a double scoop of ice cream. How many of the guests were served a double scoop of ice cream?

   (1) At the picnic, 60 percent of the guests were served a double scoop of ice cream.

   (2) A total of 120 scoops of ice cream were served to all the guests at the picnic.

Arithmetic Percents

   (1) The total number of guests is unknown, and thus 60% of the total is also unknown; NOT sufficient.

   (2) The total number of scoops served is known, but the ratio between single scoops and double scoops is unknown; NOT sufficient.

Using both statements, the ratio of the number of single scoops served to the number of double scoops served can be determined (1) and used with the total number of scoops served (2) to determine the total number of guests who were served a double scoop.

The correct answer is C;
both statements together are sufficient.

62. For a convention, a hotel charges a daily room rate of $120 for 1 person and x dollars for each additional person. What is the charge for each additional person?

    (1) The daily cost per person for 4 people sharing the cost of a room equally is $45.
    (2) The daily cost per person for 2 people sharing the cost of a room equally is $25 more than the corresponding cost for 4 people.

Algebra First-degree equations

If the daily room rate for a hotel is $120 for 1 person plus x dollars for each additional person, then the daily cost can be expressed as $120 + nx$, where n is the number of additional people staying in the room. Determine the value for x.

(1) For 4 people sharing the cost of a room equally, each person's share is $45. Therefore, the cost of the room, in dollars, is $120 + 3x = 45(4) = 180$. This equation can be solved for a unique value of x; SUFFICIENT.

(2) Since the cost per person for 2 people is $25 more than the cost per person for 4 people, then $\dfrac{120 + x}{2} = \dfrac{120 + 3x}{4} + 25$. This equation can be solved for a unique value of x; SUFFICIENT.

The correct answer is D;
each statement alone is sufficient.

63. Stores L and M each sell a certain product at a different regular price. If both stores discount their regular price of the product, is the discount price at Store M less than the discount price at Store L ?

    (1) At Store L the discount price is 10 percent less than the regular price; at Store M the discount price is 15 percent less than the regular price.

    (2) At Store L the discount price is $5 less than the regular store price; at Store M the discount price is $6 less than the regular price.

Arithmetic Percents

Let L_r and L_d be the regular and discounted prices, respectively, at Store L, and let M_r and M_d be the regular and discounted prices, respectively, at Store M. Determine if $M_d < L_d$.

(1) Knowing that $L_d = (1 - 0.10)L_r = 0.90L_r$ and that $M_d = (1 - 0.15)M_r = 0.85M_r$ gives no information for comparing M_d and L_d; NOT sufficient.

(2) Knowing that $L_d = L_r - 5$ and that $M_d = M_r - 6$ gives no information for comparing M_d and L_d; NOT sufficient.

Taking (1) and (2) together gives $0.90L_r = L_r - 5$ and $0.85M_r = M_r - 6$, from which it follows that $0.10L_r = 5$ or $L_r = 50$ and $0.15M_r = 6$ or $M_r = 40$. Then $L_d = 50 - 5 = 45$ and $M_d = 40 - 6 = 34$. Therefore, $M_d < L_d$.

The correct answer is C;
both statements together are sufficient.

64. If d denotes a decimal, is $d \geq 0.5$?

    (1) When d is rounded to the nearest tenth, the result is 0.5.

    (2) When d is rounded to the nearest integer, the result is 1.

Arithmetic Rounding; Estimating

(1) In this case, for example, the value of d could range from the decimal 0.45 to 0.54. Some of these, such as 0.51 or 0.52, are greater than or equal to 0.5, and others, such as 0.47 or 0.48, are less than 0.5; NOT sufficient.

(2) When the result of rounding d to the nearest integer is 1, d could range in value from the decimal 0.50 to 1.49, which are greater than or equal to 0.5; SUFFICIENT.

The correct answer is B;
statement 2 alone is sufficient.

65. How many integers are there between, but not including, integers r and s?

    (1) $s - r = 10$
    (2) There are 9 integers between, but not including, $r + 1$ and $s + 1$.

    Arithmetic Properties of numbers

    (1) Although the difference between s and r is 10, there are not 10 integers between them. For example, if s is 24 and r is 14, their difference is 10, but there are only 9 integers between them: 15, 16, 17, 18, 19, 20, 21, 22, and 23. This holds true for any two integers whose difference is 10; SUFFICIENT.

    (2) Since r and s are the same distance apart as $r + 1$ and $s + 1$, there would still be 9 integers between r and s in this case, although the integers themselves would change; SUFFICIENT.

    The correct answer is D; each statement alone is sufficient.

66. If n and t are positive integers, is n a factor of t?

    (1) $n = 3^{n-2}$
    (2) $t = 3^n$

    Algebra Exponents

    For positive integers n and t, determine if n is a factor of t.

    (1) If $n = 1$, then n is a factor of t, regardless of the value of t, because 1 is a factor of every positive integer. However, $n = 3^{n-2}$ implies that $n \neq 1$, because $3^{1-2} = 3^{-1} = \dfrac{1}{3}$ and $1 \neq \dfrac{1}{3}$. But, $n = 3^{n-2}$ provides no information about t to determine if n is a factor of t; NOT sufficient.

    (2) Knowing that $t = 3^n$ provides no information about n to determine if n is a factor of t. For example, if $n = 3$, then $t = 27$ and n is a factor of t. However, if $n = 2$, then $t = 9$ and 2 is not a factor of 9; NOT sufficient.

    Taking (1) and (2) together, $\dfrac{t}{n} = \dfrac{3^n}{3^{n-2}} = 3^{n-(n-2)} = 3^2 = 9$, which is an integer, so n is a factor of t; SUFFICIENT.

The correct answer is C; both statements together are sufficient.

67. In a survey of 200 college graduates, 30 percent said they had received student loans during their college careers, and 40 percent said they had received scholarships. What percent of those surveyed said that they had received neither student loans nor scholarships during their college careers?

    (1) 25 percent of those surveyed said that they had received scholarships but no loans.
    (2) 50 percent of those surveyed who said that they had received loans also said that they had received scholarships.

    Arithmetic Sets

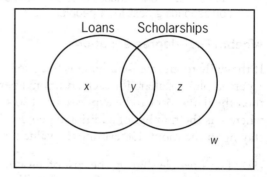

    Using the variables shown on the Venn diagram above, determine the value of w. According to the information given, 30 percent had received student loans, so $x + y = 0.3(200) = 60$ and $x = 60 - y$. Also, 40 percent had received scholarships, so $y + z = 0.4(200) = 80$ and $z = 80 - y$. Then, since $x + y + z + w = 200$, $w = 200 - x - y - z = 200 - (60 - y) - y - (80 - y) = 60 + y$. Thus, if the value of y can be determined, then the value of w can be determined.

    (1) Since 25 percent received scholarships but no loans, $z = 80 - y = 0.25(200) = 50$ and $y = 30$; SUFFICIENT.

    (2) Since 50 percent of those who had received loans had also received scholarships, $0.5(x + y) = y$ and so $0.5(60) = 30 = y$; SUFFICIENT.

The correct answer is D; each statement alone is sufficient.

68. Three machines, K, M, and P, working simultaneously and independently at their respective constant rates, can complete a certain task in 24 minutes. How long does it take Machine K, working alone at its constant rate, to complete the task?

    (1) Machines M and P, working simultaneously and independently at their respective constant rates, can complete the task in 36 minutes.
    (2) Machines K and P, working simultaneously and independently at their respective constant rates, can complete the task in 48 minutes.

Algebra Applied problems

Let k, m, and p be the numbers of minutes machines K, M, and P take, respectively, to complete the task. Then, Machine K can do $\frac{1}{k}$ of the task in 1 minute, Machine M can do $\frac{1}{m}$ of the task in 1 minute, and Machine P can do $\frac{1}{p}$ of the task in 1 minute. If all three machines working together can do the task in 24 minutes, then they can do $\frac{1}{24}$ of the task in 1 minute. So, $\frac{1}{k}+\frac{1}{m}+\frac{1}{p}=\frac{1}{24}$ and $\frac{1}{k}=\frac{1}{24}-\left(\frac{1}{m}+\frac{1}{p}\right)$. Determine k.

(1) Since M and P together can do the task in 36 minutes, they can do $\frac{1}{36}$ in 1 minute, and so $\frac{1}{m}+\frac{1}{p}=\frac{1}{36}$. Then $\frac{1}{k}=\frac{1}{24}-\frac{1}{36}$, which can be solved for a unique value of k; SUFFICIENT.

(2) Since K and P together can do the task in 48 minutes, they can do $\frac{1}{48}$ in 1 minute, and so $\frac{1}{k}+\frac{1}{p}=\frac{1}{48}$. From this information, there is no way to uniquely determine $\frac{1}{k}$ and therefore no way to uniquely determine k. For example, if $p=96$, then $\frac{1}{k}+\frac{1}{p}=\frac{1}{k}+\frac{1}{96}=\frac{1}{48}$ and $k=96$. On the other hand, if $p=60$, then $\frac{1}{k}+\frac{1}{p}=\frac{1}{k}+\frac{1}{60}=\frac{1}{48}$ and $k=240$. So, 96 and 240 are both possible values for k; NOT sufficient.

The correct answer is A; statement 1 alone is sufficient.

69. Of the four numbers represented on the number line above, is r closest to zero?

    (1) $q=-s$
    (2) $-t<q$

Algebra Order

Referring to the figure above, in which it may be assumed that q, r, s, and t are different numbers, determine if r is closest to 0.

(1) Since $q=-s$, one of q and s is positive and the other is negative. Since s is to the right of q, then s is positive and q is negative. Also, 0 is halfway between q and s, so q and s are the same distance from 0. If $r=0$, then, of q, r, s, and t, r is closest to 0 because it IS 0. If $r\neq0$, then either (i) $q<0<r<s<t$ or (ii) $q<r<0<s<t$.

(i) If $q<0<r<s<t$, as shown above, r is closer to 0 than s is because r is between 0 and s, and r is clearly closer to 0 than t is because t is farther away from 0 than s is. Also, since q and s are the same distance from 0 and r is closer to 0 than s is, then r is closer to 0 than q is. Therefore, r is closest to 0.

(ii) If $q<r<0<s<t$, as shown above, r is closer to 0 than q is because r is between 0 and q. Also, r is closer to 0 than s is because r is closer to 0 than q is and q and s are the same distance from 0. Moreover, r is closer to 0 than t is because t is farther away from 0 than s is. Therefore, r is closest to 0.

In each case, r is closest to 0; SUFFICIENT.

(2) If $-t<q$, then $-t$ is to the left of q. If $t=5$, $s=4$, $r=3$, and $q=-2$, then $-5<-2$, so (2) is satisfied. In this case, q is closest to 0. On

the other hand, if $t = 5$, $s = 4$, $r = -1$, and $q = -2$, then $-5 < -2$, so (2) is satisfied, but r is closest to 0; NOT sufficient.

The correct answer is A; statement 1 alone is sufficient.

70. Mary persuaded n friends to donate $500 each to her election campaign, and then each of these n friends persuaded n more people to donate $500 each to Mary's campaign. If no one donated more than once and if there were no other donations, what was the value of n?

    (1) The first n people donated $\frac{1}{16}$ of the total amount donated.
    (2) The total amount donated was $120,000.

Algebra Simultaneous equations

If n is the number of friends who each contributed $500 to Mary's campaign and each persuaded n more people to contribute $500 each to the campaign, then the amount contributed to the campaign was $\$500(n^2 + n)$. Assuming $n > 0$, determine the value of n.

(1) If the first n people contributed $\frac{1}{16}$ of the total amount, then
$$500n = \frac{1}{16}(500)(n^2 + n)$$
$$500n = \frac{1}{16}(500)(n)(n + 1)$$
$$16 = n + 1$$
$$15 = n; \text{ SUFFICIENT.}$$

(2) If the total amount contributed was $120,000, then
$$500(n^2 + n) = 120,000$$
$$n^2 + n = 240$$
$$n^2 + n - 240 = 0$$
$$(n + 16)(n - 15) = 0$$
$$n = 15; \text{ SUFFICIENT.}$$

Note that $n^2 + n = 240$ can be solved by inspection since $n^2 + n = n(n + 1)$ and the only consecutive positive integers whose product is 240 are 15 and 16, so $n = 15$.

Although it is not necessary to actually solve the quadratic equations in (1) and (2), it is necessary to analyze the nature of the solutions to make sure that there aren't two possible values for n.

The correct answer is D; each statement alone is sufficient.

71. Carlotta can drive from her home to her office by one of two possible routes. If she must also return by one of these routes, what is the distance of the shorter route?

    (1) When she drives from her home to her office by the shorter route and returns by the longer route, she drives a total of 42 kilometers.
    (2) When she drives both ways, from her home to her office and back, by the longer route, she drives a total of 46 kilometers.

Arithmetic Arithmetic operations

(1) Only the sum of the distances of the two routes (42 kilometers) is given and there are infinitely many pairs of numbers with a given sum; NOT sufficient.

(2) The distance of the longer route can be expressed as $\frac{46}{2}$ kilometers, but there is no information about the relationship between the two routes; NOT sufficient.

Using both statements together, the distance of the shorter route can be determined by subtracting the known distance of the longer route (2) from the known sum of the distances of the two routes (1). The distance of the shorter route is thus $42 - \frac{46}{2}$.

The correct answer is C; both statements together are sufficient.

72. Is $x > y$?

    (1) $x = y + 2$
    (2) $\frac{x}{2} = y - 1$

Algebra Inequalities

(1) $x = y + 2$ so $x - y = 2$ and since $2 > 0$, $x - y > 0$ and $x > y$; SUFFICIENT.

(2)   The equation given is equivalent to
$x = 2y - 2$, which is satisfied both by $x = 0$
and $y = 1$ ($x > y$ is false) and by $x = 4$ and
$y = 3$ ($x > y$ is true); NOT sufficient.

**The correct answer is A;
statement 1 alone is sufficient.**

73.   If m is an integer, is m odd?

(1) $\dfrac{m}{2}$ is <u>not</u> an even integer.

(2) $m - 3$ is an even integer.

Algebra Properties of numbers

(1)   Since m could be either the odd integer 3
or the even integer 10 and still satisfy this
condition, there is no information to show
definitively whether m is odd or even; NOT
sufficient.

(2)   If $m - 3$ is an even integer, then $m - 3 = 2k$
for some integer k and $m = 2k + 3 =$
$2(k + 1) + 1$, which is odd; SUFFICIENT.

**The correct answer is B;
statement 2 alone is sufficient.**

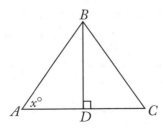

74.   What is the area of triangular region ABC above?

(1)   The product of BD and AC is 20.

(2) $x = 45$

Geometry Triangles; Area

The area of $\triangle ABC = \dfrac{BD \times AC}{2}$.

(1)   The product of BD and AC is given as 20,
so the area of $\triangle ABC$ is $\dfrac{20}{2}$ or 10;
SUFFICIENT.

(2)   With the measurement of x being 45, it is
concluded that $\triangle ABD$ is a 45-45-90 right
triangle, where the length of side BD is

equal to the length of side AD. However,
with no lengths of any side known, there is
not enough information to calculate the
area; NOT sufficient.

**The correct answer is A;
statement 1 alone is sufficient.**

75.   In the xy-plane, the line with equation $ax + by + c = 0$,
where $abc \neq 0$, has slope $\dfrac{2}{3}$. What is the value of b?

(1) $a = 4$

(2) $c = -6$

Arithmetic Coordinate geometry

If $ax + by + c = 0$, then $by = -ax - c$ and
$y = \dfrac{-a}{b}x - \dfrac{c}{b}$. The slope of the line with equation
$ax + by + c = 0$ is $\dfrac{-a}{b}$. Since the slope of this line
is $\dfrac{2}{3}$, then $\dfrac{-a}{b} = \dfrac{2}{3}$ or $b = \dfrac{-3a}{2}$. Determine the
value of b.

(1)   If $a = 4$, then $b = \dfrac{-3(4)}{2} = -6$;
SUFFICIENT.

(2)   If $c = -6$ and $a = 2$, then $b = -3$. However,
if $c = -6$ and $a = -2$, then $b = 3$; NOT
sufficient.

**The correct answer is A;
statement 1 alone is sufficient.**

76.   If m, p, and t are positive integers and $m < p < t$, is
the product mpt an even integer?

(1) $t - p = p - m$

(2) $t - m = 16$

Arithmetic Properties of numbers

Given integers m, p, and t, for which $m < p < t$,
determine if mpt is even.

(1)   Given that $t - p = p - m$, then $t + m = 2p$.
This means that $t + m$ is even, so both m
and t are odd or both are even and therefore
mt is either odd or even. If mt is even, then
mpt is even, regardless of the value of p.
However, if mt is odd, the evenness or
oddness of mpt depends on whether p is
even or odd; NOT sufficient.

(2) Given that $t - m = 16$, then m and t are either both odd or both even. This is the same situation as in (1); NOT sufficient.

Taking (1) and (2) together, m and t are both even or both odd, but no information is given about the evenness or oddness of p. Therefore, mpt could be even or odd.

The correct answer is E;
both statements together are still not sufficient.

77. Each week a certain salesman is paid a fixed amount equal to $300, plus a commission equal to 5 percent of the amount of his sales that week over $1,000. What is the total amount the salesman was paid last week?

(1) The total amount the salesman was paid last week is equal to 10 percent of the amount of his sales last week.

(2) The salesman's sales last week totaled $5,000.

Algebra Applied problems

Let P be the salesman's pay for last week and let S be the amount of his sales last week. Then $P = 300 + 0.05(S - 1,000)$. Determine the value of P.

(1) Given $P = 0.10S$, then $0.10S = 300 + 0.05(S - 1,000)$. This equation can be solved for a unique value of S, from which the value of P can be determined; SUFFICIENT.

(2) Given $S = 5,000$, then $P = 300 + 0.05(5,000 - 1,000)$; SUFFICIENT.

The correct answer is D;
each statement alone is sufficient.

78. A total of $60,000 was invested for one year. Part of this amount earned simple annual interest at the rate of x percent per year, and the rest earned simple annual interest at the rate of y percent per year. If the total interest earned by the $60,000 for that year was $4,080, what is the value of x?

(1) $x = \dfrac{3y}{4}$

(2) The ratio of the amount that earned interest at the rate of x percent per year to the amount that earned interest at the rate of y percent per year was 3 to 2.

Algebra Applied problems

Let X be the amount invested at x percent and let Y be the amount invested at y percent, where $X + Y = 60,000$. If $\dfrac{x}{100}X + \dfrac{y}{100}Y = 4,080$, determine the value of x.

(1) Given that $x = \dfrac{3}{4}y$, then $y = \dfrac{4}{3}x$. Since $X + Y = 60,000$, then $Y = 60,000 - X$. By substitution, $\dfrac{x}{100}X + \dfrac{y}{100}Y = 4,080$ becomes $\dfrac{x}{100}X + \dfrac{\frac{4}{3}x}{100}(60,000 - X) = 4,080$. However, because the value of X is unknown, it is impossible to determine a unique value for x; NOT sufficient.

(2) Given that $\dfrac{X}{Y} = \dfrac{3}{2}$, then $Y = \dfrac{2}{3}X$ and $Y = \dfrac{2}{3}(60,000 - Y)$, from which the values of Y and, in turn, X can be determined. However, since the value of y in the equation $\dfrac{x}{100}X + \dfrac{y}{100}Y = 4,080$ is still unknown, it is impossible to determine a unique value for x; NOT sufficient.

Taking (1) and (2) together,

$\dfrac{x}{100}X + \dfrac{y}{100}Y = 4,080$ from the stem becomes

$\dfrac{x}{100}X + \dfrac{\frac{4}{3}x}{100}Y = 4,080$, using the information from (1). Then, using the values of X and Y obtained from the information in (2) leaves an equation with x as the only unknown. This equation can be solved for a unique value of x; SUFFICIENT.

The correct answer is C;
both statements together are sufficient.

79. Leo can buy a certain computer for p_1 dollars in State A, where the sales tax is t_1 percent, or he can buy the same computer for p_2 dollars in State B, where the sales tax is t_2 percent. Is the total cost of the computer greater in State A than in State B?

    (1) $t_1 > t_2$
    (2) $p_1 t_1 > p_2 t_2$

Algebra Applied problems

Determine if $p_1 \left(1 + \dfrac{t_1}{0} \right)$ is greater than $p_2 \left(1 + \dfrac{t_2}{100} \right)$.

(1) Even if $t_1 > t_2$, no information is given about the size of p_1 or p_2, and it is impossible to tell if $p_1 \left(1 + \dfrac{t_1}{0} \right)$ is greater than $p_2 \left(1 + \dfrac{t_2}{100} \right)$.

For example, if $p_1 = 1,000$ and $p_2 = 1,200$ with $t_1 = 5$ and $t_2 = 4$, then $p_1 \left(1 + \dfrac{t_1}{0} \right) = 1,000(1 + 0.05) = 1,050$ and $p_2 \left(1 + \dfrac{t_2}{100} \right) = 1,200(1 + 0.04) = 1,248$, so $p_1 \left(1 + \dfrac{t_1}{0} \right)$ is not greater than $p_2 \left(1 + \dfrac{t_2}{100} \right)$. On the other hand, if $p_1 = 1,000$ and $p_2 = 900$ with $t_1 = 5$ and $t_2 = 4$, then $p_1 \left(1 + \dfrac{t_1}{0} \right) = 1,000(1 + 0.05) = 1,050$ and $p_2 \left(1 + \dfrac{t_2}{100} \right) = 900(1 + 0.04) = 936$, so $p_1 \left(1 + \dfrac{t_1}{0} \right)$ is greater than p_2; NOT sufficient.

(2) Even if $p_1 t_1 > p_2 t_2$, no information is given about the size of p_1 or p_2 and it is impossible to tell if $p_1 \left(1 + \dfrac{t_1}{0} \right)$ is greater than $p_2 \left(1 + \dfrac{t_2}{100} \right)$. For example, if $p_1 = 1,000$ and $p_2 = 1,200$ with $t_1 = 5$ and $t_2 = 4$, then $(1,000)(5) > (1,200)(4)$, but as shown above, $p_1 \left(1 + \dfrac{t_1}{0} \right)$ is not greater than $p_2 \left(1 + \dfrac{t_2}{100} \right)$. On the other hand, if $p_1 = 1,000$ and $p_2 = 900$ with $t_1 = 5$ and $t_2 = 4$, then $(1,000)(5) > (900)(4)$, but as shown above, $p_1 \left(1 + \dfrac{t_1}{0} \right)$ is greater than p_2; NOT sufficient.

Taking (1) and (2) together is of no more help than either (1) or (2) taken separately because the same examples used to show that (1) is not sufficient also show that (2) is not sufficient.

The correct answer is E; both statements together are still not sufficient.

80. If $r > 0$ and $s > 0$, is $\dfrac{r}{s} < \dfrac{s}{r}$?

    (1) $\dfrac{r}{3s} = \dfrac{1}{4}$
    (2) $s = r + 4$

Algebra Ratios

Given nonnegative numbers r and s, determine if $\dfrac{r}{s} < \dfrac{s}{r}$.

(1) If $\dfrac{r}{3s} = \dfrac{1}{4}$, then $\dfrac{r}{s} = \dfrac{3}{4}$, $\dfrac{s}{r} = \dfrac{4}{3}$, and so $\dfrac{r}{s} < \dfrac{s}{r}$, since $\dfrac{3}{4} < \dfrac{4}{3}$; SUFFICIENT.

(2) If $s = r + 4$, then $\dfrac{r}{s} = \dfrac{r}{r+4}$ and $\dfrac{s}{r} = \dfrac{r+4}{r}$. Since $r + 4 > r$, $\dfrac{r}{r+4} < 1$ and $\dfrac{r+4}{r} > 1$, so $\dfrac{r}{s} < \dfrac{s}{r}$; SUFFICIENT.

The correct answer is D; each statement alone is sufficient.

$$k, n, 12, 6, 17$$

81. What is the value of n in the list above?

    (1) $k < n$
    (2) The median of the numbers in the list is 10.

Arithmetic Statistics

Given the list k, n, 12, 6, 17, determine the value of n.

(1) Although $k < n$, no information is given about the value of k or n; NOT sufficient.

(2) Since the median of the numbers in the list is 10 and there are 5 numbers in the list, 10 is one of those 5 numbers. Therefore, $n = 10$ or $k = 10$. If $n = 10$, then the value of n has been determined. However, if $k = 10$, then n can be any number that is 10 or less, so the value of n cannot be determined; NOT sufficient.

Taking (1) and (2) together, if $k < n$ and the median of the list is 10, then 12 and 17 are to the right of the median and the list in ascending order is either 6, k, n, 12, 17 or k, 6, n, 12, 17. In either case, n is the middle number, and since the median is 10, $n = 10$; SUFFICIENT.

The correct answer is C; both statements together are sufficient.

82. If positive integer x is a multiple of 6 and positive integer y is a multiple of 14, is xy a multiple of 105 ?

(1) x is a multiple of 9.
(2) y is a multiple of 25.

Arithmetic Properties of numbers

Given that x is a multiple of 6, x has at least 1 factor of 2 and at least 1 factor of 3. Given that y is a multiple of 14, y has at least 1 factor of 2 and at least 1 factor of 7. So, xy has at least 1 factor of 2, at least 1 factor of 3, and at least 1 factor of 7 and can be expressed as $xy = (2)(3)(7)r = 42r$, where r is a positive integer. Determine if xy is a multiple of $105 = (3)(5)(7)$.

(1) If $x = (2)(3)(3)$, then x is a multiple of both 6 and 9. If $y = (2)(7)$ then y is a multiple of 14. In this case, $xy = (2)(3)(3)(2)(7) = (2^2)(3^2)(7)$ and is not a multiple of 105. However, if $x = (2)(3)(3)(5)$, then x is a multiple of both 6 and 9. If $y = (2)(7)$, then y is a multiple of 14. In this case, $xy = (2)(3)(3)(5)(14) = (2^2)(3^2)(5)(7)$ and is a multiple of 105; NOT sufficient.

(2) If $y = (2)(5)(5)(7)$, then y is a multiple of 14 and 25. If x is a multiple of 6, $x = (2)(3)q$ for some positive integer q. Then $xy = (2)(2)(3)(5)(5)(7)q$ and xy is a multiple of 105; SUFFICIENT.

The correct answer is B; statement 2 alone is sufficient.

83. What is the value of $b + c$?

(1) $ab + cd + ac + bd = 6$
(2) $a + d = 4$

Algebra First- and second-degree equations

(1) The equation $ab + cd + ac + bd = 6$ can be simplified to isolate $b + c$ by regrouping and then factoring as follows:

$$(ab + bd) + (ac + cd) = 6$$
$$b(a + d) + c(a + d) = 6$$
$$(a + d)(b + c) = 6$$

The value of $b + c$, however, cannot be determined unless the value of $a + d$ is known; NOT sufficient.

(2) This provides no information about b and c; NOT sufficient.

Since (2) provides the missing information about the needed value of $a + d$ in (1), the value of $b + c$ can be found when both (1) and (2) are used to complete the equation.

The correct answer is C; both statements together are sufficient.

84. What is the average (arithmetic mean) of j and k ?

(1) The average (arithmetic mean) of $j + 2$ and $k + 4$ is 11.
(2) The average (arithmetic mean) of j, k, and 14 is 10.

Arithmetic Statistics

The average of j and k is $\dfrac{j + k}{2}$, and this value can be determined if the value of $j + k$ can be determined.

(1) It is given that $\dfrac{(j+2)+(k+4)}{2} = 11$.

Therefore, $\dfrac{j+k+6}{2} = 11$, $j+k+6 = 22$;

$j+k = 16$; SUFFICIENT.

(2) It is given that $\dfrac{j+k+14}{3} = 10$. Therefore,

$j+k+14 = 30$, $j+k = 16$; SUFFICIENT.

The correct answer is D;
each statement alone is sufficient.

85. Paula and Sandy were among those people who sold raffle tickets to raise money for Club X. If Paula and Sandy sold a total of 100 of the tickets, how many of the tickets did Paula sell?

(1) Sandy sold $\dfrac{2}{3}$ as many of the raffle tickets as Paula did.

(2) Sandy sold 8 percent of all the raffle tickets sold for Club X.

Algebra Simultaneous equations

If Paula sold p tickets and Sandy sold s tickets, then $p + s = 100$.

(1) Since Sandy sold $\dfrac{2}{3}$ as many tickets as Paula, $s = \dfrac{2}{3}p$. The value of p can be determined by solving the two equations simultaneously; SUFFICIENT.

(2) Since the total number of the raffle tickets sold is unknown, the number of tickets that Sandy or Paula sold cannot be determined; NOT sufficient.

The correct answer is A;
statement 1 alone is sufficient.

86. A number of people each wrote down one of the first 30 positive integers. Were any of the integers written down by more than one of the people?

(1) The number of people who wrote down an integer was greater than 40.

(2) The number of people who wrote down an integer was less than 70.

Algebra Sets and functions

If the number of integers to be chosen from is smaller than the number of people making the choice, then at least one of the integers has to be chosen and written down by more than one person. If the number of integers to be chosen from is the same as or greater than the number of people making the choice, it is possible that no integer will be chosen and written down more than once.

(1) Because the number of people was greater than 30, at least one integer had to be written down by more than one person; SUFFICIENT.

(2) It is not helpful just to know that the number of people was less than 70. If, for instance, the number of people was 35, then at least one of the 30 integers had to be written down by more than one person. If the number of people was 25 instead, it is possible that no two people wrote down the same integer; NOT sufficient.

The correct answer is A;
statement 1 alone is sufficient.

87. Is the number of seconds required to travel d_1 feet at r_1 feet per second greater than the number of seconds required to travel d_2 feet at r_2 feet per second?

(1) d_1 is 30 greater than d_2.
(2) r_1 is 30 greater than r_2.

Algebra Applied problems

Determine if $\dfrac{d_1}{r_1}$ is greater than $\dfrac{d_2}{r_2}$.

(1) Although it is given that $d_1 = d_2 + 30$, without information about r_1 and r_2 it is impossible to determine if $\dfrac{d_1}{r_1}$ is greater than $\dfrac{d_2}{r_2}$. For example, if $d_1 = 60$, $d_2 = 30$, $r_1 = 90$, and $r_2 = 60$, then $d_1 = d_2 + 30$, but $\dfrac{d_1}{r_1} = \dfrac{2}{3}$ and $\dfrac{d_2}{r_2} = \dfrac{1}{2}$, so $\dfrac{d_1}{r_1}$ is greater than $\dfrac{d_2}{r_2}$. On the other hand, if $d_1 = 90$, $d_2 = 60$, $r_1 = 60$, and $r_2 = 30$, then $d_1 = d_2 + 30$, but $\dfrac{d_1}{r_1} = \dfrac{3}{2}$ and $\dfrac{d_2}{r_2} = 2$, so $\dfrac{d_1}{r_1}$ is not greater than $\dfrac{d_2}{r_2}$; NOT sufficient.

(2) Although it is given that $r_1 = r_2 + 30$, without information about d_1 and d_2 it is impossible to determine if $\dfrac{d_1}{r_1}$ is greater than $\dfrac{d_2}{r_2}$. For example, if $d_1 = 60$, $d_2 = 30$, $r_1 = 90$, and $r_2 = 60$, then $r_1 = r_2 + 30$, but $\dfrac{d_1}{r_1} = \dfrac{2}{3}$ and $\dfrac{d_2}{r_2} = \dfrac{1}{2}$, so $\dfrac{d_1}{r_1}$ is greater than $\dfrac{d_2}{r_2}$. On the other hand, if $d_1 = 90$, $d_2 = 60$, $r_1 = 60$, and $r_2 = 30$, then $r_1 = r_2 + 30$, but $\dfrac{d_1}{r_1} = \dfrac{3}{2}$ and $\dfrac{d_2}{r_2} = 2$, so $\dfrac{d_1}{r_1}$ is not greater than $\dfrac{d_2}{r_2}$; NOT sufficient.

Taking (1) and (2) together is of no more help than either of (1) or (2) taken separately because the same examples used to show that (1) is not sufficient also show that (2) is not sufficient.

The correct answer is E;
both statements together are still not sufficient.

88. Last year, if Arturo spent a total of $12,000 on his mortgage payments, real estate taxes, and home insurance, how much did he spend on his real estate taxes?

(1) Last year, the total amount that Arturo spent on his real estate taxes and home insurance was $33\dfrac{1}{3}$ percent of the amount that he spent on his mortgage payments.

(2) Last year, the amount that Arturo spent on his real estate taxes was 20 percent of the total amount he spent on his mortgage payments and home insurance.

Arithmetic Applied problems

Let M, R, and H be the amounts that Arturo spent last year on mortgage payments, real estate taxes, and home insurance, respectively. Given that $M + R + H = 12,000$, determine the value of R.

(1) Given that $R + H = \dfrac{1}{3}M$ and $M + R + H = 12,000$, then $M + \dfrac{1}{3}M = 12,000$, or $M = 9,000$. However, the value of R cannot

be determined, since it is possible that $R = 2,000$ (use $M = 9,000$ and $H = 1,000$) and it is possible that $R = 1,000$ (use $M = 9,000$ and $H = 2,000$); NOT sufficient.

(2) Given that $R = \dfrac{1}{5}(M + H)$, or $5R = M + H$ and $M + R + H = 12,000$, which can be rewritten as $(M + H) + R = 12,000$, then $5R + R = 12,000$, or $R = 2,000$; SUFFICIENT.

The correct answer is B;
statement 2 alone is sufficient.

89. Is the number of members of Club X greater than the number of members of Club Y?

(1) Of the members of Club X, 20 percent are also members of Club Y.

(2) Of the members of Club Y, 30 percent are also members of Club X.

Arithmetic Sets

Let a be the number of members in Club X that do not belong to Club Y, let b be the number of members in Club Y that do not belong to Club X, and let c be the number of members that belong to both Club X and to Club Y. Determine whether $a + c > b + c$, or equivalently, whether $a > b$.

(1) If $a = 80$, $b = 79$, and $c = 20$, then 20 percent of the members of Club X are also members of Club Y (because $c = 20$ is 20 percent of $a + c = 100$) and $a > b$ is true. However, if $a = 80$, $b = 80$, and $c = 20$, then 20 percent of the members of Club X are also members of Club Y (because $c = 20$ is 20 percent of $a + c = 100$) and $a > b$ is false. Therefore, it cannot be determined whether $a > b$; NOT sufficient.

(2) If $a = 71$, $b = 70$, and $c = 30$, then 30 percent of the members of Club Y are also members of Club X (because $c = 30$ is 30 percent of $b + c = 100$) and $a > b$ is true. However, if $a = 70$, $b = 70$, and $c = 30$, then 30 percent of the members of Club Y are also members of Club X (because $c = 30$ is 30 percent of $b + c = 100$) and $a > b$ is false. Therefore, it cannot be determined whether $a > b$; NOT sufficient.

Now assume both (1) and (2). From (1) it follows that $\dfrac{c}{a+c} = 0.20 = \dfrac{1}{5}$, or $5c = a + c$, and so $a = 4c$. From (2) it follows that $\dfrac{c}{b+c} = 0.30 = \dfrac{3}{10}$, or $10c = 3b + 3c$, and so $7c = 3b$ and $b = \dfrac{7}{3}c$. Since $4c > \dfrac{7}{3}c$ (from the statements it can be deduced that $c > 0$), it follows that $a > b$. Therefore, (1) and (2) together are sufficient.

The correct answer is C;
both statements together are sufficient.

90. If k, m, and t are positive integers and $\dfrac{k}{6} + \dfrac{m}{4} = \dfrac{t}{12}$, do t and 12 have a common factor greater than 1 ?

(1) k is a multiple of 3.
(2) m is a multiple of 3.

Arithmetic Properties of numbers

Using a common denominator and expressing the sum as a single fraction gives $\dfrac{2k}{12} + \dfrac{3m}{12} = \dfrac{t}{12}$. Therefore, it follows that $2k + 3m = t$. Determine if t and 12 have a common factor greater than 1.

(1) Given that k is a multiple of 3, then $2k$ is a multiple of 3. Since $3m$ is also a multiple of 3, and a sum of two multiples of 3 is a multiple of 3, it follows that t is a multiple of 3. Therefore, t and 12 have 3 as a common factor; SUFFICIENT.

(2) If $k = 3$ and $m = 3$, then m is a multiple of 3 and $t = 15$ (since $\dfrac{(2)(3)}{12} + \dfrac{(3)(3)}{12} = \dfrac{6+9}{12} = \dfrac{15}{12}$), so t and 12 have 3 as a common factor. However, if $k = 2$ and $m = 3$, then m is a multiple of 3 and $t = 13$ (since $\dfrac{(2)(2)}{12} + \dfrac{(3)(3)}{12} = \dfrac{4+9}{12} = \dfrac{13}{12}$), so t and 12 do not have a common factor greater than 1; NOT sufficient.

The correct answer is A;
statement 1 alone is sufficient.

91. In the figure above, is $CD > BC$?

(1) $AD = 20$
(2) $AB = CD$

Geometry Lines

(1) Information is given about the total length of the segment shown, which has no bearing on the relative sizes of CD and BC; NOT sufficient.

(2) Here, AB and CD are equal, which also has no bearing on the relative sizes of BC and CD; NOT sufficient.

It cannot be assumed that the figure is drawn to scale. Considering (1) and (2) together, if lengths AB and CD were each a little larger than pictured, for example,

then $BC < CD$. But if the reverse were true, and lengths AB and CD were instead a little smaller than pictured, then BC could be greater than CD.

The correct answer is E;
both statements together are still not sufficient.

92. In a certain office, 50 percent of the employees are college graduates and 60 percent of the employees are over 40 years old. If 30 percent of those over 40 have master's degrees, how many of the employees over 40 have master's degrees?

(1) Exactly 100 of the employees are college graduates.
(2) Of the employees 40 years old or less, 25 percent have master's degrees.

Arithmetic Percents

(1) It is given that 50 percent of the employees are college graduates. Here, it is now known that exactly 100 of the employees are college graduates. Thus, the total number of employees in the company is 200. It is also given that 60 percent of the

employees are over 40 years old, which would be (0.60)(200), or 120 employees. Since it is given that 30 percent of those over 40 have master's degrees, then (0.30)(120), or 36 employees are over 40 and have master's degrees; SUFFICIENT.

(2) There is no information regarding *how many* employees fall into any of the categories, and it thus cannot be determined how many employees there are in any category; NOT sufficient.

The correct answer is A;
statement 1 alone is sufficient.

93. On the number line above, *p*, *q*, *r*, *s*, and *t* are five consecutive even integers in increasing order. What is the average (arithmetic mean) of these five integers?

    (1) *q* + *s* = 24
    (2) The average (arithmetic mean) of *q* and *r* is 11.

Arithmetic Properties of numbers

Since *p*, *q*, *r*, *s*, and *t* are consecutive even integers listed in numerical order, the 5 integers can also be given as *p*, *p* + 2, *p* + 4, *p* + 6, and *p* + 8. Determine the average of these 5 integers, which is the value of $\dfrac{p+(p+2)+(p+4)+(p+6)+(p+8)}{5}$ = $\dfrac{5p+20}{5}$ = *p* + 4.

(1) Given that *q* + *s* = 24, then (*p* + 2) + (*p* + 6) = 24. Therefore, 2*p* + 8 = 24, or *p* = 8, and hence *p* + 4 = 12; SUFFICIENT.

(2) Given that $\dfrac{q+r}{2}$ = 11, then *q* + *r* = (2)(11) = 22, or (*p* + 2) + (*p* + 4) = 22. Therefore, 2*p* + 6 = 22, or *p* = 8, and hence *p* + 4 = 12; SUFFICIENT.

The correct answer is D;
each statement alone is sufficient.

94. If line *k* in the *xy*-plane has equation *y* = *mx* + *b*, where *m* and *b* are constants, what is the slope of *k* ?

    (1) *k* is parallel to the line with equation *y* = (1 − *m*)*x* + *b* + 1.
    (2) *k* intersects the line with equation *y* = 2*x* + 3 at the point (2,7).

Algebra Coordinate geometry

The slope of the line given by *y* = *mx* + *b* is *m*. Determine the value of *m*.

(1) Given that the slope of line *k* is equal to the slope of line given by *y* = (1 − *m*)*x* + *b* + 1, then *m* = 1 − *m*, 2*m* = 1, or *m* = $\dfrac{1}{2}$; SUFFICIENT.

(2) Since a line passing through the point (2,7) can have any value for its slope, it is impossible to determine the slope of line *k*. For example, *y* = *x* + 5 intersects *y* = 2*x* + 3 at (2,7) and has slope 1, while *y* = 3*x* + 1 intersects *y* = 2*x* + 3 at (2,7) and has slope 3; NOT sufficient.

The correct answer is A;
statement 1 alone is sufficient.

95. Is *rst* = 1 ?

    (1) *rs* = 1
    (2) *st* = 1

Arithmetic Properties of numbers

(1) This establishes that *rs* = 1, but since the value of *t* is unavailable, it is unknown if *rst* = 1; NOT sufficient.

(2) Similarly, this establishes the value of *st* but the value of *r* is unknown; NOT sufficient.

Both (1) and (2) taken together are still not sufficient to determine whether or not *rst* = 1. For example, it is true that if *r* = *s* = *t* = 1, then *rs* = 1, *st* = 1, and *rst* = 1. However, if *r* = *t* = 5, and *s* = $\dfrac{1}{5}$, then *rs* = 1, *st* = 1, but *rst* = 5.

The correct answer is E;
both statements together are still not sufficient.

TOTAL EXPENSES FOR THE FIVE DIVISIONS OF COMPANY H

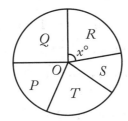

96. The figure above represents a circle graph of Company H's total expenses broken down by the expenses for each of its five divisions. If O is the center of the circle and if Company H's total expenses are $5,400,000, what are the expenses for Division R ?

    (1) $x = 94$
    (2)   The total expenses for Divisions S and T are twice as much as the expenses for Division R.

Geometry Circles

In this circle graph, the expenses of Division R are equal to the value of $\dfrac{x}{360}$ multiplied by $5,400,000, or $15,000x$. Therefore, it is necessary to know the value of x in order to determine the expenses for Division R.

    (1)   The value of x is given as 94, so the expenses of Division R can be determined; SUFFICIENT.

    (2)   This gives a comparison among the expenses of some of the divisions of Company H, but no information is given about the value of x; NOT sufficient.

**The correct answer is A;
statement 1 alone is sufficient.**

97. If x is negative, is $x < -3$?

    (1) $x^2 > 9$
    (2) $x^3 < -9$

Arithmetic Properties of numbers

    (1)   Given that $x^2 > 9$, it follows that $x < -3$ or $x > 3$, a result that can be obtained in a variety of ways. For example, consider the equivalent equation $(|x|)^2 > 9$ that reduces to $|x| > 3$, or consider when the two factors of

$x^2 - 9$ are both positive and when the two factors of $x^2 - 9$ are both negative, or consider where the graph of the parabola $y = x^2 - 9$ is above the x-axis, etc. Since it is also given that x is negative, it follows that $x < -3$; SUFFICIENT.

    (2)   Given that $x^3 < -9$, if $x = -4$, then $x^3 = -64$, and so $x^3 < -9$ and it is true that $x < -3$. However, if $x = -3$, then $x^3 = -27$, and so $x^3 < -9$, but it is not true that $x < -3$; NOT sufficient.

**The correct answer is A;
statement 1 alone is sufficient.**

98. Seven different numbers are selected from the integers 1 to 100, and each number is divided by 7. What is the sum of the remainders?

    (1)   The range of the seven remainders is 6.
    (2)   The seven numbers selected are consecutive integers.

Arithmetic Properties of numbers

    (1)   If the numbers are 6, 7, 14, 21, 28, 35, and 42, then the remainders when divided by 7 are 6, 0, 0, 0, 0, 0, and 0. Thus, the range of the remainders is 6 and the sum of the remainders is 6. However, if the numbers are 5, 6, 7, 14, 21, 28, and 35, then the remainders when divided by 7 are 5, 6, 0, 0, 0, 0, and 0. Thus, the range of the remainders is 6 and the sum of the remainders is 11. Therefore, it is not possible to determine the sum of the remainders given that the range of the remainders is 6; NOT sufficient.

    (2)   When a positive integer is divided by 7, the only possible remainders are 0, 1, 2, 3, 4, 5, and 6. Also, each of these remainders will occur exactly once when the terms in a sequence of 7 consecutive integers are divided by 7. For example, if n has remainder 4 upon division by 7 (for example, $n = 46$), then the remainders when n, $n + 1$, $n + 2$, $n + 3$, $n + 4$, $n + 5$, and $n + 6$ are divided by 7 will be 4, 5, 6, 0, 1, 2, and 3. Therefore, the sum of the remainders will always be $0 + 1 + 2 + 3 + 4 + 5 + 6$; SUFFICIENT.

**The correct answer is B;
statement 2 alone is sufficient.**

r	s	t
u	v	w
x	y	z

99. Each of the letters in the table above represents one of the numbers 1, 2, or 3, and each of these numbers occurs exactly once in each row and exactly once in each column. What is the value of r ?

   (1) $v + z = 6$
   (2) $s + t + u + x = 6$

Arithmetic Properties of numbers

In the following discussion, "row/column convention" means that each of the numbers 1, 2, and 3 appears exactly once in any given row and exactly once in any given column.

   (1) Given that $v + z = 6$, then both v and z are equal to 3, since no other sum of the possible values is equal to 6. Applying the row/column convention to row 2, and then to row 3, it follows that neither u nor x can be 3. Since neither u nor x can be 3, the row/column convention applied to column 1 forces r to be 3; SUFFICIENT.

   (2) If $u = 3$, then $s + t + x = 3$. Hence, $s = t = x = 1$, since the values these variables can have does not permit another possibility. However, this assignment of values would violate the row/column convention for row 1, and thus u cannot be 3. If $x = 3$, then $s + t + u = 3$. Hence, $s = t = u = 1$, since the values these variables can have does not permit another possibility. However, this assignment of values would violate the row/column convention for row 1, and thus x cannot be 3. Since neither u nor x can be 3, the row/column convention applied to column 1 forces r to be 3; SUFFICIENT.

**The correct answer is D;
each statement alone is sufficient.**

100. If [x] denotes the greatest integer less than or equal to x, is [x] = 0 ?

   (1) $5x + 1 = 3 + 2x$
   (2) $0 < x < 1$

Algebra Inequalities

It will be useful to observe that the condition $[x] = 0$ is equivalent to $0 \le x < 1$.

   (1) The solution to $5x + 1 = 3 + 2x$ is $x = \dfrac{2}{3}$, which satisfies $0 \le x < 1$; SUFFICIENT.

   (2) If $0 < x < 1$, then it follows that $0 \le x < 1$; SUFFICIENT.

**The correct answer is D;
each statement alone is sufficient.**

101. Material A costs $3 per kilogram, and Material B costs $5 per kilogram. If 10 kilograms of Material K consists of x kilograms of Material A and y kilograms of Material B, is $x > y$?

   (1) $y > 4$
   (2) The cost of the 10 kilograms of Material K is less than $40.

Algebra Inequalities

Since $x + y = 10$, the relation $x > y$ is equivalent to $x > 10 - x$, or $x > 5$.

   (1) The given information is consistent with $x = 5.5$ and $y = 4.5$, and the given information is also consistent with $x = y = 5$. Therefore, it is possible for $x > y$ to be true and it is possible for $x > y$ to be false; NOT sufficient.

   (2) Given that $3x + 5y < 40$, or $3x + 5(10 - x) < 40$, then $3x - 5x < 40 - 50$. It follows that $-2x < -10$, or $x > 5$; SUFFICIENT.

**The correct answer is B;
statement 2 alone is sufficient.**

102. While on a straight road, Car X and Car Y are traveling at different constant rates. If Car X is now 1 mile ahead of Car Y, how many minutes from now will Car X be 2 miles ahead of Car Y ?

   (1) Car X is traveling at 50 miles per hour and Car Y is traveling at 40 miles per hour.
   (2) Three minutes ago Car X was $\dfrac{1}{2}$ mile ahead of Car Y.

Arithmetic Rate problem

Simply stated, the question is how long will it take Car X to get one mile further ahead of Car Y than it is now.

(1)   At their constant rates, Car X would increase its distance from Car Y by 10 miles every hour or, equivalently, 1 mile every 6 minutes; SUFFICIENT.

(2)   This states that Car X increases its distance from Car Y by 0.5 mile every 3 minutes, or alternately 1 mile every 6 minutes; SUFFICIENT.

The correct answer is D; each statement alone is sufficient.

103.   If a certain animated cartoon consists of a total of 17,280 frames on film, how many minutes will it take to run the cartoon?

(1)   The cartoon runs without interruption at the rate of 24 frames per second.

(2)   It takes 6 times as long to run the cartoon as it takes to rewind the film, and it takes a total of 14 minutes to do both.

Arithmetic Arithmetic operations

(1)   Given the frames-per-second speed, it can be determined that it takes $\dfrac{17,280}{24 \times 60}$ minutes to run the cartoon; SUFFICIENT.

(2)   It is given both that it takes 14 minutes to run the cartoon and rewind the film and that, with the ratio 6:1 expressed as a fraction, the cartoon runs $\dfrac{6}{7}$ of the total time. Thus, it can be determined that running the cartoon takes $\dfrac{6}{7}$ of the 14 minutes; SUFFICIENT.

The correct answer is D; each statement alone is sufficient.

104.   At what speed was a train traveling on a trip when it had completed half of the total distance of the trip?

(1)   The trip was 460 miles long and took 4 hours to complete.

(2)   The train traveled at an average rate of 115 miles per hour on the trip.

Arithmetic Applied problems

Determine the speed of the train when it had completed half the total distance of the trip.

(1)   Given that the train traveled 460 miles in 4 hours, the train could have traveled at the constant rate of 115 miles per hour for 4 hours, and thus it could have been traveling 115 miles per hour when it had completed half the total distance of the trip. However, the train could have traveled 150 miles per hour for the first 2 hours (a distance of 300 miles) and 80 miles per hour for the last 2 hours (a distance of 160 miles), and thus it could have been traveling 150 miles per hour when it had completed half the total distance of the trip; NOT sufficient.

(2)   Given that the train traveled at an average rate of 115 miles per hour, each of the possibilities given in the explanation for (1) could occur, since 460 miles in 4 hours gives an average speed of $\dfrac{460}{4}$ = 115 miles per hour; NOT sufficient.

Assuming (1) and (2), each of the possibilities given in the explanation for (1) could occur. Therefore, (1) and (2) together are NOT sufficient.

The correct answer is E; both statements together are still not sufficient.

105.   Tom, Jane, and Sue each purchased a new house. The average (arithmetic mean) price of the three houses was $120,000. What was the median price of the three houses?

(1)   The price of Tom's house was $110,000.

(2)   The price of Jane's house was $120,000.

Arithmetic Statistics

Let T, J, and S be the purchase prices for Tom's, Jane's, and Sue's new houses. Given that the average purchase price is 120,000, or $T + J + S = (3)(120,000)$, determine the median purchase price.

(1) Given $T = 110,000$, the median could be 120,000 (if $J = 120,000$ and $S = 130,000$) or 125,000 (if $J = 125,000$ and $S = 125,000$); NOT sufficient.

(2) Given $J = 120,000$, the following two cases include every possibility consistent with $T + J + S = (3)(120,000)$, or $T + S = (2)(120,000)$.

(i) $T = S = 120,000$

(ii) One of T or S is less than 120,000 and the other is greater than 120,000.

In each case, the median is clearly 120,000; SUFFICIENT.

The correct answer is B; statement 2 alone is sufficient.

106. If x and y are integers, is xy even?

(1) $x = y + 1$

(2) $\dfrac{x}{y}$ is an even integer.

Arithmetic Properties of numbers

Determine if xy is even.

(1) Since x and y are consecutive integers, one of these two numbers is even, and hence their product is even. For example, if x is even, then $x = 2m$ for some integer m, and thus $xy = (2m)y = (my)(2)$, which is an integer multiple of 2, so xy is even; SUFFICIENT.

(2) If $\dfrac{x}{y}$ is even, then $\dfrac{x}{y} = 2n$ for some integer n, and thus $x = 2ny$. From this it follows that $xy = (2ny)(y) = (ny^2)(2)$, which is an integer multiple of 2, so xy is even; SUFFICIENT.

The correct answer is D; each statement alone is sufficient.

107. A box contains only red chips, white chips, and blue chips. If a chip is randomly selected from the box, what is the probability that the chip will be either white or blue?

(1) The probability that the chip will be blue is $\dfrac{1}{5}$.

(2) The probability that the chip will be red is $\dfrac{1}{3}$.

Arithmetic Probability

(1) Since the probability of drawing a blue chip is known, the probability of drawing a chip that is not blue (in other words, a red or white chip) can also be found. However, the probability of drawing a white or blue chip cannot be determined from this information; NOT sufficient.

(2) The probability that the chip will be either white or blue is the same as the probability that it will NOT be red. Thus, the probability is $1 - \dfrac{1}{3} = \dfrac{2}{3}$; SUFFICIENT.

The correct answer is B; statement 2 alone is sufficient.

108. If the successive tick marks shown on the number line above are equally spaced and if x and y are the numbers designating the end points of intervals as shown, what is the value of y?

(1) $x = \dfrac{1}{2}$

(2) $y - x = \dfrac{2}{3}$

Arithmetic Properties of numbers

(1) If 3 tick marks represent a value of $\dfrac{1}{2}$, then 6 tick marks would represent a value of 1. From this it can be established that each subdivision of the line represents $\dfrac{1}{6}$, so the value of y is $\dfrac{7}{6}$; SUFFICIENT.

(2) From this, the four equal subdivisions between y and x represent a total distance of $\frac{2}{3}$. This implies that each subdivision of the number line has the length $\frac{1}{4}\left(\frac{2}{3}\right) = \frac{1}{6}$, enabling the value of y to be found; SUFFICIENT.

The correct answer is D;
each statement alone is sufficient.

109. In triangle *ABC*, point *X* is the midpoint of side *AC* and point *Y* is the midpoint of side *BC*. If point *R* is the midpoint of line segment *XC* and if point *S* is the midpoint of line segment *YC*, what is the area of triangular region *RCS* ?

(1) The area of triangular region *ABX* is 32.
(2) The length of one of the altitudes of triangle *ABC* is 8.

Geometry Triangles; Area

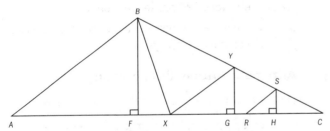

As shown in the figure above, *X* and *Y* are the midpoints of $\overline{AC}$ and $\overline{BC}$, respectively, of $\triangle ABC$, and *R* and *S* are the midpoints of $\overline{XC}$ and $\overline{YC}$, respectively. Thus, letting $AC = b$, it follows that $AX = XC = \frac{1}{2}b$ and $RC = \frac{1}{4}b$. Also, if $\overline{BF}$, $\overline{YG}$, and $\overline{SH}$ are perpendicular to $\overline{AC}$ as shown, then $\triangle BFC$, $\triangle YGC$, and $\triangle SHC$ are similar triangles, since their corresponding interior angles have the same measure. Thus, letting $BF = h$, it follows that $YG = \frac{1}{2}h$ and $SH = \frac{1}{4}h$. The area of $\triangle RCS$, which is $\frac{1}{2}\left(\frac{1}{4}b\right)\left(\frac{1}{4}h\right) = \frac{1}{32}bh$, can be determined exactly when the value of bh can be determined.

(1) Given that the area of $\triangle ABX$, which is $\frac{1}{2}(AX)(BF)$, or $\frac{1}{2}\left(\frac{1}{2}b\right)(h)$, is 32, then $bh = (4)(32)$; SUFFICIENT.

(2) Without knowing the length of the side to which the altitude is drawn, the area of $\triangle ABC$, and hence the value of bh, cannot be determined; NOT sufficient.

The correct answer is A;
statement 1 alone is sufficient.

110. The product of the units digit, the tens digit, and the hundreds digit of the positive integer *m* is 96. What is the units digit of *m* ?

(1) *m* is odd.
(2) The hundreds digit of *m* is 8.

Arithmetic Decimals

Let the hundreds, tens, and units digits of *m* be *a*, *b*, and *c*, respectively. Given that $abc = 96$, determine the value of *c*.

(1) Since *m* is odd, then $c = 1, 3, 5, 7,$ or 9. Also, because *c* is a factor of 96 and $96 = (2^5)(3)$, then $c = 1$ or $c = 3$. If $c = 1$, then $ab = 96$, but 96 cannot be expressed as a product of two 1-digit integers. Hence, $c \neq 1$, and thus, $c = 3$; SUFFICIENT.

(2) Given that $a = 8$, it is possible for *c* to be 3 (for example, $m = 843$) and it is possible for *c* to be 6 (for example, $m = 826$); NOT sufficient.

The correct answer is A;
statement 1 alone is sufficient.

111. A department manager distributed a number of pens, pencils, and pads among the staff in the department, with each staff member receiving *x* pens, *y* pencils, and *z* pads. How many staff members were in the department?

(1) The numbers of pens, pencils, and pads that each staff member received were in the ratio 2:3:4, respectively.
(2) The manager distributed a total of 18 pens, 27 pencils, and 36 pads.

Arithmetic Ratio and proportion

(1) Each of 10 staff members could have received 2 pens, 3 pencils, and 4 pads, or each of 20 staff members could have received 2 pens, 3 pencils, and 4 pads; NOT sufficient.

(2) There could have been 1 staff member who received 18 pens, 27 pencils, and 36 pads, or 3 staff members each of whom received 6 pens, 9 pencils, and 12 pads; NOT sufficient.

Assuming both (1) and (2), use the fact that 18:27:36 is equivalent to both 6:9:12 and 2:3:4 to obtain different possibilities for the number of staff. Each of 3 staff members could have received 6 pens, 9 pencils, and 12 pads, or each of 9 staff members could have received 2 pens, 3 pencils, and 4 pads. Therefore, (1) and (2) together are NOT sufficient.

**The correct answer is E;
both statements together are still not sufficient.**

112. Machines X and Y produced identical bottles at different constant rates. Machine X, operating alone for 4 hours, filled part of a production lot; then Machine Y, operating alone for 3 hours, filled the rest of this lot. How many hours would it have taken Machine X operating alone to fill the entire production lot?

(1) Machine X produced 30 bottles per minute.

(2) Machine X produced twice as many bottles in 4 hours as Machine Y produced in 3 hours.

Algebra Rate problem

Let r_X and r_Y be the rates, in numbers of bottles produced per hour, of Machine X and Machine Y. In 4 hours Machine X produces $4r_X$ bottles working alone and in 3 hours Machine Y produces $3r_Y$ bottles working alone. Thus, $4r_X + 3r_Y$ bottles are produced when Machine X operates alone for 4 hours followed by Machine Y operating alone for 3 hours. If t is the number of hours for Machine X to produce the same number of bottles, then $4r_X + 3r_Y = (r_X)t$.

(1) Given that Machine X produces 30 bottles per minute, then $r_X = (30)(60) = 1,800$. This

does not determine a unique value for t, since more than one positive value of t satisfies $(4)(1,800) + 3r_Y = (1,800)t$ when r_Y is allowed to vary over positive real numbers. For example, if $r_Y = 600$, then $t = 5$, and if $r_Y = 1,200$, then $t = 6$; NOT sufficient.

(2) Given that $4r_X = 2(3r_Y)$, so $r_X = \frac{3}{2} r_Y$. Therefore, from $4r_X + 3r_Y = (r_X)t$, it follows that $6r_Y + 3r_Y = \frac{3}{2} r_Y t$, or $6 + 3 = \frac{3}{2} t$, or $t = 6$; SUFFICIENT.

**The correct answer is B;
statement 2 alone is sufficient.**

113. On a company-sponsored cruise, $\frac{2}{3}$ of the passengers were company employees and the remaining passengers were their guests. If $\frac{3}{4}$ of the company-employee passengers were managers, what was the number of company-employee passengers who were NOT managers?

(1) There were 690 passengers on the cruise.

(2) There were 230 passengers who were guests of the company employees.

Arithmetic Arithmetic operations

(1) From this, since $\frac{2}{3}$ of the passengers were company employees, then $\frac{2}{3} \times 690 = 460$ passengers were company employees. Then, since $\frac{3}{4}$ of the company employees were managers, so $1 - \frac{3}{4} = \frac{1}{4}$ of the company-employee passengers were not managers. Therefore $\frac{1}{4} \times 460 = 115$ company employees who were not managers; SUFFICIENT.

(2) If 230 of the passengers were guests, then this represents $1 - \frac{2}{3} = \frac{1}{3}$ of the cruise passengers. Therefore, there were $230 \times 3 = 690$ passengers altogether, $690 - 230 = 460$ of whom were company employees. Since $1 - \frac{3}{4} = \frac{1}{4}$ of the company employees were

not managers, $\frac{1}{4} \times 460 = 115$ of the passengers who were company employees were not managers; SUFFICIENT.

**The correct answer is D;
each statement alone is sufficient.**

114. The length of the edging that surrounds circular garden K is $\frac{1}{2}$ the length of the edging that surrounds circular garden G. What is the area of garden K? (Assume that the edging has negligible width.)

    (1)   The area of G is 25π square meters.
    (2)   The edging around G is 10π meters long.

Geometry Circles; Area

Note that the length of the edging around a circular garden is equal to the circumference of the circle. The formula for the circumference of a circle, where C is the circumference and d is the diameter, is $C = \pi d$. The formula for the area of a circle, where A is the area and r is the radius, is $A = \pi r^2$. In any circle, r is equal to $\frac{1}{2}d$. If the length of the edging around K is equal to $\frac{1}{2}$ the length of the edging around G, then the circumference of K is equal to $\frac{1}{2}$ the circumference of G.

    (1)   Since the area of G is 25π square meters, $25\pi = \pi r^2$ or $25 = r^2$ and $5 = r$. So, if the radius of G is 5, the diameter is 10, and the circumference of G is equal to 10π. Since the circumference of K is $\frac{1}{2}$ that of G, then the circumference of K is 5π, making the diameter of K equal to 5. If the diameter of K is 5, the radius of K is 2.5, and the area of K is $\pi(2.5)^2$ or 6.25π; SUFFICIENT.

    (2)   If the edging around G is 10π meters long, then the circumference of G is 10π. The area of K can then by found by proceeding as in (1); SUFFICIENT.

**The correct answer is D;
each statement alone is sufficient.**

115. For any integers x and y, min(x, y) and max(x, y) denote the minimum and the maximum of x and y, respectively. For example, min(5, 2) = 2 and max(5, 2) = 5. For the integer w, what is the value of min(10, w)?

    (1) $w = $ max(20, z) for some integer z.
    (2) $w = $ max(10, w)

Arithmetic Properties of numbers

If $w \geq 10$, then min(10, w) = 10, and if $w < 10$, then min(10, w) = w. Therefore, the value of min(10, w) can be determined if the value of w can be determined.

    (1)   Given that $w = $ max(20, z), then $w \geq 20$. Hence, $w \geq 10$, and so min(10, w) = 10; SUFFICIENT.

    (2)   Given that $w = $ max(10, w), then $w \geq 10$, and so min(10, w) = 10; SUFFICIENT.

**The correct answer is D;
each statement alone is sufficient.**

116. During a 6-day local trade show, the least number of people registered in a single day was 80. Was the average (arithmetic mean) number of people registered per day for the 6 days greater than 90?

    (1)   For the 4 days with the greatest number of people registered, the average (arithmetic mean) number registered per day was 100.
    (2)   For the 3 days with the smallest number of people registered, the average (arithmetic mean) number registered per day was 85.

Arithmetic Statistics

Let a, b, c, d, and e be the numbers of people registered for the other 5 days, listed in increasing order. Determining if $\frac{80 + a + b + c + d + e}{6} > 90$ is equivalent to determining if $(80 + a + b + c + d + e) > (6)(90) = 540$, or if $a + b + c + d + e > 460$.

    (1)   Given that $\frac{b + c + d + e}{4} = 100$, then $b + c + d + e = 400$. Therefore, since $a \geq 80$ (because 80 is the least of the 6 daily registration numbers), it follows that $a + b + c + d + e \geq 80 + 400 = 480$, and hence $a + b + c + d + e > 460$; SUFFICIENT.

(2) Given that $\frac{80+a+b}{3}$ = 85, then $80 + a + b$ = (3)(85), or $a + b$ = 175. Note that this is possible with each of a and b being an integer that is at least 80, such as a = 87 and b = 88. From $a + b$ = 175, the condition $a + b + c + d + e > 460$ is equivalent to $175 + c + d + e > 460$, or $c + d + e > 285$. However, using 3 integers that are each at least 88 (recall that the values of c, d, and e must be at least the value of b), it is possible for $c + d + e > 285$ to hold (for example, $c = d = e = 100$) and it is possible for $c + d + e > 285$ not to hold (for example, $c = d = e = 90$); NOT sufficient.

**The correct answer is A;
statement 1 alone is sufficient.**

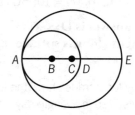

117. In the figure above, points A, B, C, D, and E lie on a line. A is on both circles, B is the center of the smaller circle, C is the center of the larger circle, D is on the smaller circle, and E is on the larger circle. What is the area of the region inside the larger circle and outside the smaller circle?

(1) AB = 3 and BC = 2
(2) CD = 1 and DE = 4

Geometry Circles

If R is the radius of the larger circle and r is the radius of the smaller circle, then the desired area is $\pi R^2 - \pi r^2$. Thus, if both the values of R and r can be determined, then the desired area can be determined.

(1) Given that $AB = r$ = 3 and BC = 2, then $AB + BC = R$ = 3 + 2 = 5; SUFFICIENT.

(2) Given that CD = 1 and DE = 4, then $CD + DE = R$ = 1 + 4 = 5. Since $\overline{AE}$ is a diameter of the larger circle, then $AD + DE = 2R$. Also, since $\overline{AD}$ is a

diameter of the smaller circle, then $AD = 2r$. Thus, $2r + DE = 2R$, or $2r + 4 = 10$, and so r = 3; SUFFICIENT.

**The correct answer is D;
each statement alone is sufficient.**

118. An employee is paid 1.5 times the regular hourly rate for each hour worked in excess of 40 hours per week, excluding Sunday, and 2 times the regular hourly rate for each hour worked on Sunday. How much was the employee paid last week?

(1) The employee's regular hourly rate is $10.
(2) Last week the employee worked a total of 54 hours but did not work more than 8 hours on any day.

Arithmetic Arithmetic operations

The employee's pay consists of at most 40 hours at the regular hourly rate, plus any overtime pay at either 1.5 or 2 times the regular hourly rate.

(1) From this, the employee's regular pay for a 40-hour week is $400. However, there is no information about overtime, and so the employee's total pay cannot be calculated; NOT sufficient.

(2) From this, the employee worked a total of 54 − 40 = 14 hours. However, there is no indication of how many hours were worked on Sunday (at 2 times the regular hourly rate) or another day (at 1.5 times the regular hourly rate); NOT sufficient.

With (1) and (2) taken together, there is still no way to calculate the amount of overtime pay.

**The correct answer is E;
both statements together are still not sufficient.**

119. What was the revenue that a theater received from the sale of 400 tickets, some of which were sold at the full price and the remainder of which were sold at a reduced price?

(1) The number of tickets sold at the full price was $\frac{1}{4}$ of the total number of tickets sold.
(2) The full price of a ticket was $25.

Arithmetic Arithmetic operations

(1) Since $\frac{1}{4}$ of the tickets were sold at full price, $\frac{3}{4} \times 400 = 300$ tickets were sold at a reduced price. However, the revenue cannot be determined from this information; NOT sufficient.

(2) Although a full-priced ticket cost \$25, the revenue cannot be determined without additional information; NOT sufficient.

When both (1) and (2) are taken together, the revenue from full-priced tickets was $100 \times \$25 = \$2,500$, but the cost of a reduced-priced ticket is still unknown, and the theater's revenues cannot be calculated.

**The correct answer is E;
both statements together are still not sufficient.**

120. The annual rent collected by a corporation from a certain building was x percent more in 1998 than in 1997 and y percent less in 1999 than in 1998. Was the annual rent collected by the corporation from the building more in 1999 than in 1997 ?

   (1) $x > y$

   (2) $\frac{xy}{100} < x - y$

Algebra Percents

Let A be the annual rent collected in 1997. Then the annual rent collected in 1998 is $\left(1 + \frac{x}{100}\right)A$ and the annual rent collected in 1999 is $\left(1 + \frac{x}{100}\right)\left(1 - \frac{y}{100}\right)A$. Determine if $A\left(1 + \frac{x}{100}\right)\left(1 - \frac{y}{100}\right) > A$, or equivalently, if $\left(1 + \frac{x}{100}\right)\left(1 - \frac{y}{100}\right) > 1$.

(1) Given that $x > y$, $\left(1 + \frac{x}{100}\right)\left(1 - \frac{y}{100}\right) > 1$ is possible by choosing $x = 100$ and $y = 10$, since $\left(1 + \frac{100}{100}\right)\left(1 - \frac{10}{100}\right) = (2)(0.9) = 1.8$,

and $\left(1 + \frac{x}{100}\right)\left(1 - \frac{y}{100}\right) \leq 1$ is possible by choosing $x = 100$ and $y = 90$, since $\left(1 + \frac{100}{100}\right)\left(1 - \frac{90}{100}\right) = (2)(0.1) = 0.2$; NOT sufficient.

(2) As shown below, the given inequality $\frac{xy}{100} < x - y$ is equivalent to the desired inequality, $\left(1 + \frac{x}{100}\right)\left(1 - \frac{y}{100}\right) > 1$, which can be justified by the following steps, where each step's inequality is equivalent to the previous step's inequality.

$\frac{xy}{10,000} < \frac{x}{100} - \frac{y}{100}$ divide both sides by 100

$0 < \frac{x}{100} - \frac{y}{100} - \frac{xy}{10,000}$ subtract $\frac{xy}{10,000}$ from both sides

$1 < 1 + \frac{x}{100} - \frac{y}{100} - \frac{xy}{10,000}$ add 1 to both sides

$1 < \left(1 + \frac{x}{100}\right)\left(1 - \frac{y}{100}\right)$ factor the right side; SUFFICIENT

**The correct answer is B;
statement 2 alone is sufficient.**

121. In the xy-plane, region R consists of all the points (x,y) such that $2x + 3y \leq 6$. Is the point (r,s) in region R ?

   (1) $3r + 2s = 6$

   (2) $r \leq 3$ and $s \leq 2$

Algebra Coordinate geometry

(1) Both $(r,s) = (2,0)$ and $(r,s) = (0,3)$ satisfy the equation $3r + 2s = 6$, since $3(2) + 2(0) = 6$ and $3(0) + 2(3) = 6$. However, $2(2) + 3(0) = 4$, so $(2,0)$ is in region R, while $2(0) + 3(3) = 9$, so $(0,3)$ is not in region R; NOT sufficient.

(2) Both $(r,s) = (0,0)$ and $(r,s) = (3,2)$ satisfy the inequalities $r \leq 3$ and $s \leq 2$. However, $2(0) + 3(0) = 0$, so $(0,0)$ is in region R, while $2(3) + 3(2) = 12$, so $(3,2)$ is not in region R; NOT sufficient.

Taking (1) and (2) together, it can be seen that both $(r,s) = (2,0)$ and $(r,s) = (1,1.5)$ satisfy $3r + 2s = 6$, $r \leq 3$ and $s \leq 2$. However, $2(2) + 3(0) = 4$, so $(2,0)$ is in region R, while $2(1) + 3(1.5) = 6.5$, so $(1,1.5)$ is not in region R. Therefore (1) and (2) together are NOT sufficient.

**The correct answer is E;
both statements together are still not sufficient.**

122. What is the volume of a certain rectangular solid?

    (1) Two adjacent faces of the solid have areas 15 and 24, respectively.
    (2) Each of two opposite faces of the solid has area 40.

Geometry Rectangular solids and cylinders

    (1) If the edge lengths of the rectangular solid are 3, 5, and 8, then two adjacent faces will have areas $(3)(5) = 15$ and $(3)(8) = 24$ and the volume of the rectangular solid will be $(3)(5)(8) = 120$. If the edge lengths of the rectangular solid are 1, 15, 24, then two adjacent faces will have areas $(1)(15) = 15$ and $(1)(24) = 24$ and the volume of the rectangular solid will be $(1)(15)(24) = 360$; NOT sufficient.

    (2) If the edge lengths of the rectangular solid are 5, 8, and x, where x is a positive real number, then the rectangular solid will have a pair of opposite faces of area 40, namely the two faces that are 5 by 8. However, the volume is $(5)(8)(x)$, which will vary as x varies; NOT sufficient.

Taking (1) and (2) together, if the edge lengths are denoted by x, y, and z, then $xy = 15$, $xz = 24$, and $yz = 40$, and so $(xy)(xz)(yz) = (15)(24)(40)$, or $(xyz)^2 = (15)(24)(40)$. Thus, the volume of the rectangular solid is $xyz = \sqrt{(15)(24)(40)}$. Therefore, (1) and (2) together are sufficient.

**The correct answer is C;
both statements together are sufficient.**

123. Joanna bought only $0.15 stamps and $0.29 stamps. How many $0.15 stamps did she buy?

    (1) She bought $4.40 worth of stamps.
    (2) She bought an equal number of $0.15 stamps and $0.29 stamps.

Algebra Simultaneous equations

Determine the value of x if x is the number of $0.15 stamps and y is the number of $0.29 stamps.

    (1) Given that $15x + 29y = 440$, then $29y = 440 - 15x$. Because x is an integer, $440 - 15x = 5(88 - 3x)$ is a multiple of 5. Therefore, $29y$ must be a multiple of 5, from which it follows that y must be a multiple of 5. Hence, the value of y must be among the numbers 0, 5, 10, 15, etc. To more efficiently test these values of y, note that $15x = 440 - 29y$, and hence $440 - 29y$ must be a multiple of 15, or equivalently, $440 - 29y$ must be a multiple of both 3 and 5. By computation, the values of $440 - 29y$ for y equal to 0, 5, 10, and 15 are 440, 295, 150, and 5. Of these, only 150, which corresponds to $y = 10$, is divisible by 3. From $15x = 440 - 29y$ it follows that $x = 10$ when $y = 10$. Therefore, $x = 10$ and $y = 10$; SUFFICIENT.

    (2) Although $x = y$, it is impossible to determine the value of x because there is no information on the total worth of the stamps Joanna bought. For example, if the total worth, in dollars, was $0.15 + 0.29$, then $x = 1$, but if the total worth was $2(0.15) + 2(0.29)$, then $x = 2$; NOT sufficient.

**The correct answer is A;
statement 1 alone is sufficient.**

	Favorable	Unfavorable	Not Sure
Candidate M	40	20	40
Candidate N	30	35	35

124. The table above shows the results of a survey of 100 voters who each responded "Favorable" or "Unfavorable" or "Not Sure" when asked about their impressions of Candidate M and of Candidate N. What was the number of voters who responded "Favorable" for both candidates?

(1)   The number of voters who did not respond "Favorable" for either candidate was 40.

(2)   The number of voters who responded "Unfavorable" for both candidates was 10.

Arithmetic Sets

If x is the number of voters who responded "Favorable" for both candidates, then it follows from the table that the number of voters who responded "Favorable" to at least one candidate is $40 + 30 - x = 70 - x$. This is because $40 + 30$ represents the number of voters who responded "Favorable" for Candidate M added to the number of voters who responded "Favorable" for Candidate N, a calculation that counts twice each of the x voters who responded "Favorable" for both candidates.

(1)   Given that there were 40 voters who did not respond "Favorable" for either candidate and there were 100 voters surveyed, the number of voters who responded "Favorable" to at least one candidate is $100 - 40 = 60$. Therefore, from the comments above, it follows that $70 - x = 60$, and hence $x = 10$; SUFFICIENT.

(2)   The information given affects only the numbers of voters in the categories "Unfavorable" for Candidate M only, "Unfavorable" for Candidate N only, and "Unfavorable" for both candidates. Thus, the numbers of voters in the categories "Favorable" for Candidate M only, "Favorable" for Candidate N only, and "Favorable" for both candidates are not affected. Since these latter categories are only constrained to have certain integer values that have a total sum of $70 - x$, more than one possibility exists for the value of x. For example, the numbers of voters in the categories "Favorable" for Candidate M only, "Favorable" for Candidate N only, and "Favorable" for both candidates could be 25, 15, and 15, respectively, which gives $70 - x = 25 + 15 + 15$, or $x = 15$. However, the numbers of voters in the categories "Favorable" for Candidate M only, "Favorable" for Candidate N only, and

"Favorable" for both candidates could be 30, 20, and 10, respectively, which gives $70 - x = 30 + 20 + 10$, or $x = 10$; NOT sufficient.

The correct answer is A; statement 1 alone is sufficient.

125. If $\circ$ represents one of the operations $+$, $-$, and $\times$, is $k \circ (\ell + m) = (k \circ \ell) + (k \circ m)$ for all numbers k, ℓ, and m?

(1) $k \circ 1$ is not equal to $1 \circ k$ for some numbers k.

(2) $\circ$ represents subtraction.

Arithmetic Properties of numbers

(1)   For operations $+$ and $\times$, $k \circ 1$ is equal to $1 \circ k$ since both $k + 1 = 1 + k$, and also $k \times 1 = 1 \times k$. Therefore, the operation represented must be subtraction. From this, it is possible to determine whether $k - (\ell + m) = (k - \ell) + (k - m)$ holds for all numbers k, ℓ, and m; SUFFICIENT.

(2)   The information is given directly that the operation represented is subtraction. Once again, it can be determined whether $k - (\ell + m) = (k - \ell) + (k - m)$ holds for all numbers k, ℓ, and m; SUFFICIENT.

The correct answer is D; each statement alone is sufficient.

126. How many of the 60 cars sold last month by a certain dealer had neither power windows nor a stereo?

(1)   Of the 60 cars sold, 20 had a stereo but not power windows.

(2)   Of the 60 cars sold, 30 had both power windows and a stereo.

Algebra Sets

(1)   With this information, there are three other categories of cars that are unknown: those equipped with both a stereo and power windows, with power windows but with no stereo, and with neither power windows nor a stereo; NOT sufficient.

(2)   Again there are three other categories that are unknown: those with a stereo but no power windows, with power windows with no stereo, and with neither power windows nor a stereo; NOT sufficient.

From (1) and (2) together, it can be deduced that there were 60 – 50 = 10 cars sold that did not have a stereo. However, it is unknown and cannot be concluded from this information how many of these cars did not have a stereo but did have power windows or did not have either a stereo or power windows.

**The correct answer is E;
both statements together are still not sufficient.**

127. In Jefferson School, 300 students study French or Spanish or both. If 100 of these students do not study French, how many of these students study both French and Spanish?

    (1)   Of the 300 students, 60 do not study Spanish.
    (2)   A total of 240 of the students study Spanish.

Algebra Sets (Venn diagrams)

One way to solve a problem of this kind is to represent the data regarding the 300 students by a Venn diagram. Let x be the number of students who study both French and Spanish, and let y be the number who do not study Spanish (i.e., those who study only French). It is given that there are 100 students who do not study French (i.e., those who study only Spanish). This information can be represented by the Venn diagram below, where $300 = x + y + 100$:

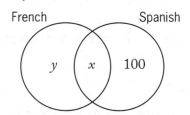

    (1)   This provides the value of y in the equation $300 = x + y + 100$, and the value of x (the number who study both languages) can thus be determined; SUFFICIENT.

(2)   Referring to the Venn diagram above, this provides the information that 240 is the sum of $x + 100$, the number of students who study Spanish. That is, 240 is equal to the number who study both French and Spanish (x) plus the number who study only Spanish (100). Since $240 = x + 100$, the value of x and thus the number who study both languages can be determined; SUFFICIENT.

**The correct answer is D;
each statement alone is sufficient.**

128. A school administrator will assign each student in a group of n students to one of m classrooms. If $3 < m < 13 < n$, is it possible to assign each of the n students to one of the m classrooms so that each classroom has the same number of students assigned to it?

    (1)   It is possible to assign each of $3n$ students to one of m classrooms so that each classroom has the same number of students assigned to it.
    (2)   It is possible to assign each of $13n$ students to one of m classrooms so that each classroom has the same number of students assigned to it.

Arithmetic Properties of numbers

Determine if n is divisible by m.

    (1)   Given that $3n$ is divisible by m, then n is divisible by m if $m = n = 9$ (note that $3n = 27$ and $m = 9$, so $3n$ is divisible by m) and n is not divisible by m if $m = 9$ and $n = 12$ (note that $3n = 36$ and $m = 9$, so $3n$ is divisible by m); NOT sufficient.

    (2)   Given that $13n$ is divisible by m, then $13n = qm$, or $\frac{n}{m} = \frac{q}{13}$, for some integer q. Since 13 is a prime number that divides qm (because $13n = qm$) and 13 does not divide m (because $m < 13$), it follows that 13 divides q. Therefore, $\frac{q}{13}$ is an integer, and since $\frac{n}{m} = \frac{q}{13}$, then $\frac{n}{m}$ is an integer. Thus, n is divisible by m; SUFFICIENT.

**The correct answer is B;
statement 2 alone is sufficient.**

129. What is the median number of employees assigned per project for the projects at Company Z ?

    (1) 25 percent of the projects at Company Z have 4 or more employees assigned to each project.
    (2) 35 percent of the projects at Company Z have 2 or fewer employees assigned to each project.

Arithmetic Statistics

(1) Although 25 percent of the projects have 4 or more employees, there is essentially no information about the middle values of the numbers of employees per project. For example, if there were a total of 100 projects, then the median could be 2 (75 projects that have exactly 2 employees each and 25 projects that have exactly 4 employees each) or the median could be 3 (75 projects that have exactly 3 employees each and 25 projects that have exactly 4 employees each); NOT sufficient.

(2) Although 35 percent of the projects have 2 or fewer employees, there is essentially no information about the middle values of the numbers of employees per project. For example, if there were a total of 100 projects, then the median could be 3 (35 projects that have exactly 2 employees each and 65 projects that have exactly 3 employees each) or the median could be 4 (35 projects that have exactly 2 employees each and 65 projects that have exactly 4 employees each); NOT sufficient.

Given both (1) and (2), $100 - (25 + 35)$ percent = 40 percent of the projects have exactly 3 employees. Therefore, when the numbers of employees per project are listed from least to greatest, 35 percent of the numbers are 2 or less and $(35 + 40)$ percent = 75 percent are 3 or less, and hence the median is 3.

The correct answer is C;
both statements together are sufficient.

130. If Juan had a doctor's appointment on a certain day, was the appointment on a Wednesday?

    (1) Exactly 60 hours before the appointment, it was Monday.
    (2) The appointment was between 1:00 p.m. and 9:00 p.m.

Arithmetic Arithmetic operations

(1) From this, it is not known at what point on Monday it was 60 hours before the appointment, and the day of the appointment cannot be known. If, for example, the specific point on Monday was 9:00 a.m., 60 hours later it would be 9:00 p.m. Wednesday, and the appointment would thus be on a Wednesday. If the specific point on Monday was instead 9:00 p.m., 60 hours later it would be 9:00 a.m. Thursday, and the appointment would instead fall on a Thursday rather than Wednesday; NOT sufficient.

(2) No information is given about the day of the appointment; NOT sufficient.

Using (1) and (2) together, it can be determined that the point 60 hours before any time from 1:00 p.m. to 9:00 p.m. on any particular day, as given in (2), is a time between 1:00 a.m. and 9:00 a.m. two days earlier. If 60 hours before an appointment in this 1:00 p.m.–9:00 p.m. time frame it was Monday as given in (1), then the appointment had to be on a Wednesday.

The correct answer is C;
both statements together are sufficient.

131. When a player in a certain game tossed a coin a number of times, 4 more heads than tails resulted. Heads or tails resulted each time the player tossed the coin. How many times did heads result?

    (1) The player tossed the coin 24 times.
    (2) The player received 3 points each time heads resulted and 1 point each time tails resulted, for a total of 52 points.

Arithmetic; Algebra Probability; Applied problems; Simultaneous equations

Let h represent the number of heads that resulted and t represent the number of tails obtained by the player. Then the information given can be expressed as $h = t + 4$.

(1) The additional information can be expressed as $h + t = 24$. When this equation is paired with the given information, $h = t + 4$, there are two linear equations in two unknowns. One way to conclude that we can determine the number of heads is to solve the equations simultaneously, thereby obtaining the number of heads and the number of tails: Solving $h = t + 4$ for t, which gives $t = h - 4$, and substituting the result in $h + t = 24$ gives $h + (h - 4) = 24$, which clearly can be solved for h. Another way to conclude that we can determine the number of heads is to note that the pair of equations represents two non-parallel lines in the coordinate plane; SUFFICIENT.

(2) The additional information provided can be expressed as $3h + t = 52$. The same comments in (1) apply here as well. For example, solving $h = t + 4$ for t, which gives $t = h - 4$, and substituting the result in $3h + t = 52$ gives $3h + (h - 4) = 52$, which clearly can be solved for h; SUFFICIENT.

**The correct answer is D;
each statement alone is sufficient.**

132. What is the value of $x + y$ in the figure above?

(1) $w = 95$
(2) $z = 125$

Geometry Angles

In the figure above, a, b, c, and d are the degree measures of the interior angles of the quadrilateral formed by the four lines and $a + b + c + d = 360$. Then

$$w + x + y + z$$

$$= (180 - a) + (180 - d) + (180 - c) + (180 - b)$$

$$= 720 - (a + b + c + d)$$

$$= 720 - 360$$

$$= 360.$$

Determine the value of $x + y$.

(1) Given that $w = 95$, then $95 + x + y + z = 360$ and $x + y + z = 265$. If $z = 65$, for example, then $x + y = 200$. On the other hand, if $z = 100$, then $x + y = 165$; NOT sufficient.

(2) Given that $z = 125$, then $w + x + y + 125 = 360$ and $w + x + y = 235$. If $w = 35$, for example, then $x + y = 200$. On the other hand, if $w = 100$, then $x + y = 135$; NOT sufficient.

Taking (1) and (2) together, $95 + x + y + 125 = 360$, and so $x + y = 140$. Therefore, (1) and (2) together are sufficient.

**The correct answer is C;
both statements together are sufficient.**

133. Are all of the numbers in a certain list of 15 numbers equal?

(1) The sum of all the numbers in the list is 60.
(2) The sum of any 3 numbers in the list is 12.

Arithmetic Properties of numbers

(1) If there are 15 occurrences of the number 4 in the list, then the sum of the numbers in the list is 60 and all the numbers in the list

are equal. If there are 13 occurrences of the number 4 in the list, 1 occurrence of the number 3 in the list, and 1 occurrence of the number 5 in the list, then the sum of the numbers in the list is 60 and not all the numbers in the list are equal; NOT sufficient.

(2) Given that the sum of any 3 numbers in the list is 12, arrange the numbers in the list in numerical order, from least to greatest: $a_1 \le a_2 \le a_3 \le \ldots \le a_{15}$.

If $a_1 < 4$, then $a_1 + a_2 + a_3 < 4 + a_2 + a_3$. Therefore, from (2), $12 < 4 + a_2 + a_3$, or $8 < a_2 + a_3$, and so at least one of the values a_2 and a_3 must be greater than 4. Because $a_2 \le a_3$, it follows that $a_3 > 4$. Since the numbers are arranged from least to greatest, it follows that $a_4 > 4$ and $a_5 > 4$. But then $a_3 + a_4 + a_5 > 4 + 4 + 4 = 12$, contrary to (2), and so $a_1 < 4$ is not true. Therefore, $a_1 \ge 4$. Since a_1 is the least of the 15 numbers, $a_n \ge 4$ for $n = 1, 2, 3, \ldots, 15$.

If $a_{15} > 4$, then $a_{13} + a_{14} + a_{15} > a_{13} + a_{14} + 4$. Therefore, from (2), $12 > a_{13} + a_{14} + 4$, or $8 > a_{13} + a_{14}$, and so at least one of the values a_{13} and a_{14} must be less than 4. Because $a_{13} \le a_{14}$, it follows that $a_{13} < 4$. Since the numbers are arranged from least to greatest, it follows that $a_{11} < 4$ and $a_{12} < 4$. But then $a_{11} + a_{12} + a_{13} < 4 + 4 + 4 = 12$, contrary to (2). Therefore, $a_{15} \le 4$. Since a_{15} is the greatest of the 15 numbers, $a_n \le 4$ for $n = 1, 2, 3, \ldots, 15$.

It has been shown that, for $n = 1, 2, 3, \ldots, 15$, each of $a_n \ge 4$ and $a_n \le 4$ is true. Therefore, $a_n = 4$ for $n = 1, 2, 3, \ldots, 15$; SUFFICIENT.

The correct answer is B; statement 2 alone is sufficient.

134. A scientist recorded the number of eggs in each of 10 birds' nests. What was the standard deviation of the numbers of eggs in the 10 nests?

(1) The average (arithmetic mean) number of eggs for the 10 nests was 4.

(2) Each of the 10 nests contained the same number of eggs.

Arithmetic Statistics

Note that if all the values in a data set are equal to the same number, say x, then the average of the data set is x, the difference between each data value and the average is $x - x = 0$, the sum of the squares of these differences is 0, and so the standard deviation is 0. On the other hand, if the values in a data set are not all equal to the same number, then the standard deviation will be positive.

(1) If each of the 10 nests had 4 eggs, then the average would be 4 and the standard deviation would be 0. If 8 nests had 4 eggs, 1 nest had 3 eggs, and 1 nest had 5 eggs, then the average would be 4 and the standard deviation would be positive; NOT sufficient.

(2) Since all of the data values are equal to the same number, the standard deviation is 0; SUFFICIENT.

The correct answer is B; statement 2 alone is sufficient.

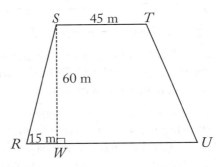

135. Quadrilateral $RSTU$ shown above is a site plan for a parking lot in which side RU is parallel to side ST and RU is longer than ST. What is the area of the parking lot?

(1) $RU = 80$ meters

(2) $TU = 20\sqrt{10}$ meters

Geometry Area

The area of a quadrilateral region that has parallel sides of lengths a and b and altitude h is $\frac{1}{2}(a + b)h$. Therefore, it is sufficient to know the lengths of the two parallel sides and the altitude in order to find the area. The altitude is shown to be 60 m and the length of one of the parallel sides is 45 m.

(1) The length of the base of the quadrilateral, that is, the length of the second parallel side, is given. Thus, the area of the quadrilateral region, in square meters, is $\frac{(45 + 80)}{2}(60)$; SUFFICIENT.

Alternatively, if the formula is unfamiliar, drawing the altitude from T, as shown in the figure below, can be helpful.

Since $ST = WX$ or 45 m, it can be seen that, in meters, $RU = 15 + 45 + XU$. Since $RU = 80$, then $80 = 15 + 45 + XU$, or $XU = 20$. The area of $RSTU$ is the sum of the areas $(\frac{1}{2}bh)$ of the two triangles ($\Delta SRW = 450$ m^2 and $\Delta TUX = 600$ m^2) and the area ($l \times w$) of the rectangle $STWX$ (2,700 m^2). Thus, the same conclusion can be drawn.

(2) Continue to refer to the supplemental figure showing the altitude drawn from T. Although the length of the base of the quadrilateral is not fully known, parts of the base (RW as well as $WX = ST$) are known. The only missing information is the length of $\overline{XU}$. This can be found using the Pythagorean theorem with ΔTUX. Since $\overline{ST}$ and $\overline{RU}$ are parallel, $TX = SW = 60$ m. It is given that $TU = 20\sqrt{10}$ m. Using the Pythagorean theorem, where $a^2 + b^2 = c^2$, yields $60^2 + XU^2 = TU^2 = (20\sqrt{10})^2$ and by simplification, $3{,}600 + XU^2 = 4{,}000$, and thus $XU^2 = 400$ and $XU = 20$. Then, the length of $\overline{RU}$, in meters, is $15 + 45 + 20 = 80$. Since this is the information given in (1), it can similarly be used to find the area of $RSTU$; SUFFICIENT.

**The correct answer is D;
each statement alone is sufficient.**

136. If the average (arithmetic mean) of six numbers is 75, how many of the numbers are equal to 75 ?

(1) None of the six numbers is less than 75.
(2) None of the six numbers is greater than 75.

Arithmetic Statistics

If the average of six numbers is 75, then $\frac{1}{6}$ of the sum of the numbers is 75. Therefore, the sum of the numbers is (6)(75).

(1) If one of the numbers is greater than 75, then we can write that number as $75 + x$ for some positive number x. Consequently, the sum of the 6 numbers must be at least $(5)(75) + (75 + x) = (6)(75) + x$, which is greater than (6)(75), contrary to the fact that the sum is equal to (6)(75). Hence, none of the numbers can be greater than 75. Since none of the numbers can be less than 75 (given information) and none of the numbers can be greater than 75, it follows that each of the numbers is equal to 75; SUFFICIENT.

(2) If one of the numbers is less than 75, then we can write that number as $75 - x$ for some positive number x. Consequently, the sum of the 6 numbers must be at most $(5)(75) + (75 - x) = (6)(75) - x$, which is less than (6)(75), contrary to the fact that the sum is equal to (6)(75). Hence, none of the numbers can be less than 75. Since none of the numbers can be less than 75 and none of the numbers can be greater than 75 (given information), it follows that each of the numbers is equal to 75; SUFFICIENT.

**The correct answer is D;
each statement alone is sufficient.**

137. At a bakery, all donuts are priced equally and all bagels are priced equally. What is the total price of 5 donuts and 3 bagels at the bakery?

(1) At the bakery, the total price of 10 donuts and 6 bagels is $12.90.
(2) At the bakery, the price of a donut is $0.15 less than the price of a bagel.

Algebra Simultaneous equations

Let x be the price, in dollars, of each donut and let y be the price, in dollars, of each bagel. Find the value of $5x + 3y$.

(1) Given that $10x + 6y = 12.90$, then $5x + 3y = \frac{1}{2}(10x + 6y)$, it follows that $5x + 3y = \frac{1}{2}(12.90)$; SUFFICIENT.

(2) Given that $x = y - 0.15$, then $5x + 3y = 5(y - 0.15) + 3y = 8y - 0.75$, which varies as y varies; NOT sufficient.

The correct answer is A; statement 1 alone is sufficient.

138. What was the total amount of revenue that a theater received from the sale of 400 tickets, some of which were sold at x percent of full price and the rest of which were sold at full price?

(1) $x = 50$
(2) Full-price tickets sold for $20 each.

Arithmetic Percents

(1) While this reveals that *some* of the 400 tickets were sold at 50 percent of full price and *some* were sold at full price, there is no information as to the amounts in either category, nor is there any information as to the cost of a full-price ticket; NOT sufficient.

(2) Although this specifies the price of the full-price tickets, it is still unknown how many tickets were sold at full price or at a discount. Moreover, the percent of the discount is not disclosed; NOT sufficient.

While (1) and (2) together show that full-price tickets were $20 and discount tickets were 50 percent of that or $10, the number or percentage of tickets sold at either price, and thus the theater's revenue, cannot be determined.

The correct answer is E; both statements together are still not sufficient.

139. Any decimal that has only a finite number of nonzero digits is a terminating decimal. For example, 24, 0.82, and 5.096 are three terminating decimals. If r and s are positive integers and the ratio $\frac{r}{s}$ is expressed as a decimal, is $\frac{r}{s}$ a terminating decimal?

(1) $90 < r < 100$
(2) $s = 4$

Arithmetic Properties of numbers

(1) This provides no information about the value of s. For example, $\frac{92}{5} = 18.4$, which terminates, but $\frac{92}{3} = 30.666\ldots$, which does not terminate; NOT sufficient.

(2) Division by the number 4 must terminate: the remainder when dividing by 4 must be 0, 1, 2, or 3, so the quotient must end with .0, .25, .5, or .75, respectively; SUFFICIENT.

The correct answer is B; statement 2 alone is sufficient.

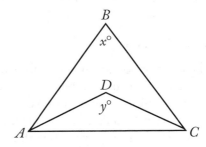

140. In the figure above, what is the value of x + y ?

(1) $x = 70$
(2) $\triangle ABC$ and $\triangle ADC$ are both isosceles triangles.

Geometry Triangles

(1) Even if $x = 70$, the location of point D can vary. As the location of D varies, the value of y will vary, and hence the value of $x + y$ will vary. Therefore, the value of $x + y$ cannot be determined; NOT sufficient.

(2)   If $\triangle ABC$ and $\triangle ADC$ are isosceles triangles, then $\angle BAC$ and $\angle BCA$ have the same measure, and $\angle DAC$ and $\angle DCA$ have the same measure. However, since no values are given for any of the angles, there is no way to evaluate $x + y$; NOT sufficient.

Taking (1) and (2) together, $x = 70$ and $\angle BAC$ and $\angle BCA$ have the same measure. Since the sum of the measures of the angles of a triangle is 180°, both $\angle BAC$ and $\angle BCA$ have measure 55° ($70 + 55 + 55 = 180$), but there is still no information about the value of y. Therefore, the value of $x + y$ cannot be determined.

**The correct answer is E;
both statements together are still not sufficient.**

141. Committee X and Committee Y, which have no common members, will combine to form Committee Z. Does Committee X have more members than Committee Y ?

(1)   The average (arithmetic mean) age of the members of Committee X is 25.7 years and the average age of the members of Committee Y is 29.3 years.

(2)   The average (arithmetic mean) age of the members of Committee Z will be 26.6 years.

Arithmetic Statistics

(1)   The information given allows for variations in the numbers of members in Committee X and Committee Y. For example, Committee X could have 10 members (8 age 25, 1 age 27, 1 age 30 with average age

$$\frac{(8)(25)+(1)(27)+(1)(30)}{10} = 25.7) \text{ and}$$

Committee Y could have 10 members (8 age 25, 1 age 40, 1 age 53 with average age

$$\frac{(8)(25)+(1)(40)+(1)(53)}{10} = 29.3), \text{ and}$$

so Committee X can fail to have more members than Committee Y. On the other hand, Committee X could have 100 members (80 age 25, 10 age 27, 10 age 30 with average age

$$\frac{(80)(25)+(10)(27)+(10)(30)}{100} = 25.7)$$

and Committee Y could have 10 members (8 age 25, 1 age 40, 1 age 53 with average

age $\dfrac{(8)(25)+(1)(40)+(1)(53)}{10} = 29.3$),

and so Committee X can have more members than Committee Y; NOT sufficient.

(2)   As above, the information given allows for variations in the numbers of members in Committee X and Committee Y. For example, Committee Z could have 10 members (8 age 25 and 2 age 33 with

average age $\dfrac{(8)(25)+(2)(33)}{10} = 26.6$). If

Committee X consists of the 2 members whose age is 33, then Committee X does not have more members than Committee Y. On the other hand, if Committee X consists of the 8 members whose age is 25, then Committee X has more members than Committee Y; NOT sufficient.

Given both (1) and (2), since 26.6 is closer to 25.7 than 29.3, it follows that Committee X has more members than Committee Y. This intuitively evident fact about averages can be proved algebraically. Let m and n be the numbers of members in Committees X and Y, respectively. Then it follows from (1) that the sum of the ages of the members in Committee X is $(25.7)m$ and the sum of the ages of the members in Committee Y is $(29.3)n$. Therefore, the average age of the members in Committee Z is

$\dfrac{(25.7)m+(29.3)n}{m+n}$, which is equal to 26.6 by (2):

$$\frac{(25.7)m+(29.3)n}{m+n} = 26.6$$

$$(25.7)m + (29.3)n = (26.6)(m + n)$$

$$(0.9)m = (2.7)n$$

$$m = 3n$$

Since both m and n are positive by (1), it follows that $m > n$; SUFFICIENT.

**The correct answer is C;
both statements together are sufficient.**

142. What amount did Jean earn from the commission on her sales in the first half of 1988 ?

    (1) In 1988 Jean's commission was 5 percent of the total amount of her sales.
    (2) The amount of Jean's sales in the second half of 1988 averaged $10,000 per month more than in the first half.

Arithmetic Applied problems

Let A be the amount of Jean's sales in the first half of 1988. Determine the value of A.

    (1) If the amount of Jean's sales in the first half of 1988 was $10,000, then her commission in the first half of 1988 would have been (5%)($10,000) = $500. On the other hand, if the amount of Jean's sales in the first half of 1988 was $100,000, then her commission in the first half of 1988 would have been (5%)($10,0000) = $5,000; NOT sufficient.

    (2) No information is given that relates the amount of Jean's sales to the amount of Jean's commission; NOT sufficient.

Given (1) and (2), from (1) the amount of Jean's commission in the first half of 1988 is (5%)A. From (2) the amount of Jean's sales in the second half of 1988 is A + $60,000. Both statements together do not give information to determine the value of A. Therefore, (1) and (2) together are NOT sufficient.

The correct answer is E; both statements together are still not sufficient.

143. The price per share of Stock X increased by 10 percent over the same time period that the price per share of Stock Y decreased by 10 percent. The reduced price per share of Stock Y was what percent of the original price per share of Stock X ?

    (1) The increased price per share of Stock X was equal to the original price per share of Stock Y.
    (2) The increase in the price per share of Stock X was $\frac{10}{11}$ the decrease in the price per share of Stock Y.

Arithmetic; Algebra Percents; Applied problems; Equations

Let x represent the original price per share of Stock X. The amount that Stock X increased per share can then be represented by $0.1x$ and the increased price per share of Stock X by $1.1x$. Let y represent the original price per share of Stock Y. The amount that Stock Y decreased per share can then be represented by $0.1y$ and the decreased price per share of Stock Y by $0.9y$. The reduced price per share of Stock Y as a percent of the original price per share of Stock X is

$$\left(\frac{0.9y}{x} \times 100\right)\% = \left(0.9 \times 100\right)\% \times \left(\frac{y}{x}\right).$$

Therefore, the question can be answered exactly when the value of $\frac{y}{x}$ can be determined.

    (1) The increased price per share of Stock X is $1.1x$, and this is given as equal to y. Thus, $1.1x = y$, from which the value of $\frac{y}{x}$ can be determined; SUFFICIENT.

    (2) The statement can be written as $0.1x = \frac{10}{11} \times 0.1y$, from which the value of $\frac{y}{x}$ can be determined; SUFFICIENT.

The correct answer is D; each statement alone is sufficient.

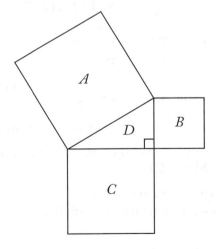

144. In the figure above, if the area of triangular region D is 4, what is the length of a side of square region A ?

    (1) The area of square region B is 9.
    (2) The area of square region C is $\frac{64}{9}$.

Geometry Area

The area of the triangular region D can be represented by $\frac{1}{2}bh$, where b is the base of the triangle (and is equal to the length of a side of the square region C) and h is the height of the triangle (and is equal to the length of a side of the square region B). The area of any square is equal to the length of a side squared. The Pythagorean theorem is used to find the length of a side of a right triangle, when the length of the other 2 sides of the triangle are known and is represented by $a^2 + b^2 = c^2$, where a and b are the lengths of the 2 perpendicular sides of the triangle and c is the length of the hypotenuse.

Although completed calculations are provided in what follows, keep in mind that completed calculations are not needed to solve this problem.

(1) If the area of B is 9, then the length of each side is 3. Therefore, $h = 3$. Then, b can be determined, since the area of the triangle is, by substitution, $4 = \frac{1}{2}(3b)$ or $8 = 3b$ or $\frac{8}{3} = b$. Once b is known, the Pythagorean theorem can be used: $\left(\frac{8}{3}\right)^2 + 3^2 = c^2$ or $\frac{64}{9} + 9 = c^2$ or $\frac{145}{9} = c^2$. The length of a side of A is thus $\sqrt{\frac{145}{9}}$; SUFFICIENT.

(2) If the area of C is $\frac{64}{9}$, then the length of each side is $\frac{8}{3}$. Therefore, $b = \frac{8}{3}$. The area of the triangle is $A = \frac{1}{2}bh$ so $4 = \frac{1}{2}\left(\frac{8}{3}h\right)$, $8 = \frac{8}{3}h$, and $3 = h$. Once h is known, the Pythagorean theorem can be used as above; SUFFICIENT.

**The correct answer is D;
each statement alone is sufficient.**

145. If Sara's age is exactly twice Bill's age, what is Sara's age?

(1) Four years ago, Sara's age was exactly 3 times Bill's age.

(2) Eight years from now, Sara's age will be exactly 1.5 times Bill's age.

Algebra Applied problems

If s and b represent Sara's and Bill's ages in years, then $s = 2b$.

(1) The additional information can be expressed as $s - 4 = 3(b - 4)$, or $s = 3b - 8$. When this equation is paired with the given information, $s = 2b$, there are two linear equations in two unknowns. One way to conclude that we can determine the value of s is to solve the equations simultaneously. Setting the two expressions for s equal to each other gives $3b - 8 = 2b$, or $b = 8$. Hence, $s = 2b = (2)(8) = 16$. Another way to conclude that we can determine the value of s is to note that the pair of equations represents two non-parallel lines in the coordinate plane; SUFFICIENT.

(2) The additional information provided can be expressed as $s + 8 = 1.5(b + 8)$. The same comments in (1) apply here as well. For example, multiplying both sides of $s + 8 = 1.5(b + 8)$ by 2 gives $2s + 16 = 3b + 24$ or, using $s = 2b$, $2(2b) + 16 = 3b + 24$. Therefore, $4b - 3b = 24 - 16$, or $b = 8$. Hence, $s = 2b = (2)(8) = 16$; SUFFICIENT.

**The correct answer is D;
each statement alone is sufficient.**

146. A report consisting of 2,600 words is divided into 23 paragraphs. A 2-paragraph preface is then added to the report. Is the average (arithmetic mean) number of words per paragraph for all 25 paragraphs less than 120 ?

(1) Each paragraph of the preface has more than 100 words.

(2) Each paragraph of the preface has fewer than 150 words.

Arithmetic Statistics

Determining if the average number of words for 25 paragraphs is less than 120 is equivalent to determining if the total number of words for the 25 paragraphs is less than $(25)(120) = (25)(4)(30) = (100)(30) = 3,000$. Since there are 2,600 words in the original 23 paragraphs, this is equivalent to determining if the total number of words in the 2 added paragraphs is less than $3,000 - 2,600 = 400$.

(1) The information provided implies only that the total number of words in the 2 added paragraphs is more than (2)(100) = 200. Therefore, the number of words could be 201, in which case the total number of added words is less than 400, or the number of words could be 400, in which case the number of added words is not less than 400; NOT sufficient.

(2) The information provided implies that the total number of words in the 2 added paragraphs is less than (2)(150) = 300, which in turn is less than 400; SUFFICIENT.

The correct answer is B;
statement 2 alone is sufficient.

147. A certain bookcase has 2 shelves of books. On the upper shelf, the book with the greatest number of pages has 400 pages. On the lower shelf, the book with the least number of pages has 475 pages. What is the median number of pages for all of the books on the 2 shelves?

(1) There are 25 books on the upper shelf.
(2) There are 24 books on the lower shelf.

Arithmetic Statistics

(1) The information given says nothing about the number of books on the lower shelf. If there are fewer than 25 books on the lower shelf, then the median number of pages will be the number of pages in one of the books on the upper shelf or the average number of pages in two books on the upper shelf. Hence, the median will be at most 400. If there are more than 25 books on the lower shelf, then the median number of pages will be the number of pages in one of the books on the lower shelf or the average number of pages in two books on the lower shelf. Hence, the median will be at least 475; NOT sufficient.

(2) An analysis very similar to that used in (1) shows the information given is not sufficient to determine the median; NOT sufficient.

Given both (1) and (2), it follows that there is a total of 49 books. Therefore, the median will be the 25th book when the books are ordered by number of pages. Since the 25th book in this ordering is the book on the upper shelf with the greatest number of pages, the median is 400. Therefore, (1) and (2) together are sufficient.

The correct answer is C;
both statements together are sufficient.

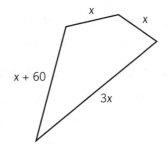

148. The figure above shows the number of meters in the lengths of the four sides of a jogging path. What is the total distance around the path?

(1) One of the sides of the path is 120 meters long.
(2) One of the sides of the path is twice as long as each of the two shortest sides.

Geometry Quadrilaterals

Determine the value of $6x + 60$, which can be determined exactly when the value of x can be determined.

(1) Given that one of the sides has length 120, it is possible that $x = 120$, that $3x = 120$, or $x + 60 = 120$. These possibilities generate more than one value for x; NOT sufficient.

(2) Since $x < x + 60$ and $x < 3x$ (the latter because x is positive), the two shortest side lengths are x. One of the two other side lengths is twice this, so it follows that $x + 60 = 2x$, or $x = 60$; SUFFICIENT.

The correct answer is B;
statement 2 alone is sufficient.

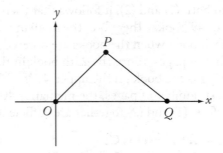

149. In the rectangular coordinate system above, if $OP < PQ$, is the area of region OPQ greater than 48 ?

(1) The coordinates of point P are (6,8).

(2) The coordinates of point Q are (13,0).

Geometry Coordinate Geometry; Triangles

The area of a triangle with base b and altitude h can be determined through the formula $\frac{1}{2}bh$. The altitude of a triangle is the line segment drawn from a vertex perpendicular to the side opposite that vertex. In a right triangle (formed here since it is given that the altitude is perpendicular to the side), the Pythagorean theorem states that the square of the length of the hypotenuse is equal to the sum of the squares of the lengths of the legs of the triangle.

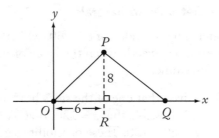

(1) The given information fixes the side lengths of $\triangle ORP$ as 6, 8, 10 (twice a 3-4-5 triangle), and the farther Q is from R (i.e., the greater the value of PQ), the greater the area of $\triangle PRQ$, and hence the greater the area of $\triangle OPQ$. If $PQ = 10$, then the area of $\triangle OPQ$ would be 48. Since it is known that $PQ > 10$ (because $10 = OP < PQ$), it follows that the area of $\triangle OPQ$ is greater than 48; SUFFICIENT.

(2) The given information implies that $OQ = 13$. However, no information is given about the height of P above the x-axis. Since the area of $\triangle ORP$ is $\frac{1}{2}$ the product of OQ and the

height of P above the x-axis, it cannot be determined whether the area of $\triangle ORP$ is greater than 48. For example, if this height were 2, then the area would be $\frac{1}{2}(2)(13) = 13$, and if this height were 8, then the area would be $\frac{1}{2}(8)(13) = 52$; NOT sufficient.

The correct answer is A; statement 1 alone is sufficient.

$$S = \dfrac{\dfrac{2}{n}}{\dfrac{1}{x} + \dfrac{2}{3x}}$$

150. In the expression above, if $xn \neq 0$, what is the value of S ?

(1) $x = 2n$

(2) $n = \dfrac{1}{2}$

Algebra First- and second-degree equations

It may be helpful to rewrite the given expression for S by multiplying its numerator and denominator by a common denominator of the secondary fractions (i.e., the common denominator of n, x, and $3x$):

$$\dfrac{\dfrac{2}{n}}{\dfrac{1}{x} + \dfrac{2}{3x}} \times \dfrac{3nx}{3nx} = \dfrac{6x}{3n + 2n} = \dfrac{6x}{5n} = \left(\dfrac{6}{5}\right)\left(\dfrac{x}{n}\right).$$

Therefore, the value of the expression can be determined exactly when the value of $\dfrac{x}{n}$ can be determined.

(1) From $x = 2n$ it follows that $\dfrac{x}{n} = 2$; SUFFICIENT.

(2) From $n = \dfrac{1}{2}$ it follows that $\dfrac{x}{n} = \dfrac{x}{\frac{1}{2}} = 2x$, which can vary; NOT sufficient.

The correct answer is A; statement 1 alone is sufficient.

151. If n is a positive integer and $k = 5.1 \times 10^n$, what is the value of k ?

(1) $6,000 < k < 500,000$

(2) $k^2 = 2.601 \times 10^9$

Arithmetic Properties of numbers

Given that $k = 5.1 \times 10^n$, where n is a positive integer, then the value of k must follow the pattern shown in the following table:

n	k
1	51
2	510
3	5,100
4	51,000
5	510,000
6	5,100,000
.	.
.	.
.	.

(1) Given that $6{,}000 < k < 500{,}000$, then k must have the value 51,000, and so $n = 4$; SUFFICIENT.

(2) Given that $k^2 = 2.601 \times 10^9$, then

$$k = \sqrt{2.601 \times 10^9} = \sqrt{2{,}601 \times 10^6} = \sqrt{2{,}601} \times \sqrt{10^6}$$
$$= 51 \times 10^3 = 51{,}000, \text{ and so } n = 4;$$
SUFFICIENT.

**The correct answer is D;
each statement alone is sufficient.**

152. If Carmen had 12 more tapes, she would have twice as many tapes as Rafael. Does Carmen have fewer tapes than Rafael?

  (1) Rafael has more than 5 tapes.
  (2) Carmen has fewer than 12 tapes.

Algebra Inequalities

If C and R are the numbers of tapes that Carmen and Rafael have, respectively, then $C + 12 = 2R$, or $C = 2R - 12$. To determine if $C < R$, it is equivalent to determining if $2R - 12 < R$, or equivalently, if $R < 12$.

(1) Given that $R > 5$, it is possible that $R < 12$ (for example, if $R = 8$ and $C = 4$) and it is possible that $R \not< 12$ (for example, if $R = 12$ and $C = 12$); NOT sufficient.

(2) Given that $C < 12$, it follows that $2R - 12 < 12$, or $R < 12$; SUFFICIENT.

**The correct answer is B;
statement 2 alone is sufficient.**

153. If x is an integer, is $x\,|x| < 2^x$?

  (1) $x < 0$
  (2) $x = -10$

Arithmetic Properties of numbers

Note that x^{-r} is equivalent to $\dfrac{1}{x^r}$; for example, $2^{-2} = \dfrac{1}{2^2} = \dfrac{1}{4}$.

(1) Since $|x| > 0$ when $x \neq 0$, it follows from $x < 0$ that $x|x|$ is the product of a negative number and a positive number, and hence $x|x|$ is negative. On the other hand, 2^x is positive for any number x. Since each negative number is less than each positive number, it follows that $x|x| < 2^x$; SUFFICIENT.

(2) The fact that $x = -10$ is a specific case of the argument in (1); SUFFICIENT.

**The correct answer is D;
each statement alone is sufficient.**

154. If n is a positive integer, is the value of $b - a$ at least twice the value of $3^n - 2^n$?

  (1) $a = 2^{n+1}$ and $b = 3^{n+1}$
  (2) $n = 3$

Algebra Exponents

If r, s, and x are real numbers with $x > 0$, then $x^{r+s} = (x^r)(x^s)$. Therefore, $2^{n+1} = (2^n)(2^1) = (2^n)(2)$ and $3^{n+1} = (3^n)(3^1) = (3^n)(3)$.

(1) From this, applying the properties of exponents:

$$b - a = 3^{n+1} - 2^{n+1} = 3(3^n) - 2(2^n)$$

Twice the value of the given expression $3^n - 2^n$ is equal to $2(3^n - 2^n)$ or $2(3^n) - 2(2^n)$. It is known that $b - a = 3(3^n) - 2(2^n)$, which is greater than $2(3^n) - 2(2^n)$. Thus, $b - a$ is at least twice the value of $3^n - 2^n$; SUFFICIENT.

(2) This statement gives no information about $b - a$; NOT sufficient.

**The correct answer is A;
statement 1 alone is sufficient.**

155. The inflation index for the year 1989 relative to the year 1970 was 3.56, indicating that, on the average, for each dollar spent in 1970 for goods, $3.56 had to be spent for the same goods in 1989. If the price of a Model K mixer increased precisely according to the inflation index, what was the price of the mixer in 1970 ?

(1) The price of the Model K mixer was $102.40 more in 1989 than in 1970.

(2) The price of the Model K mixer was $142.40 in 1989.

Arithmetic Proportions

The ratio of 1970 goods to 1989 goods is 1:3.56 or $\frac{1}{3.56}$. This ratio can be used to set up a proportion between 1970 goods and 1989 goods. Let x represent the 1970 price of the mixer. Although the 1970 price of the mixer is calculated in what follows, keep in mind that the object of this data sufficiency question is to determine whether the price can be calculated from the information given, not necessarily to actually calculate the price.

(1) From this, the 1989 price of the mixer can be expressed as $x + \$102.40$. Therefore a proportion can be set up and solved for x:

$$\frac{1}{3.56} = \frac{x}{x + \$102.40}$$

$x + \$102.40 = 3.56x$	cross multiply
$\$102.40 = 2.56x$	subtract x from both sides
$\$40 = x$	divide both sides by 2.56

The price of the mixer in 1970 was $40; SUFFICIENT.

(2) The following proportion can be set up using the information that the 1989 price of the mixer was $142.40:

$$\frac{1}{3.56} = \frac{x}{\$142.40}$$

$3.56x = \$142.40$	cross multiply
$x = \$40$	divide both sides by 3.56

The price of the mixer in 1970 was $40; SUFFICIENT.

The correct answer is D; each statement alone is sufficient.

156. Is 5^k less than 1,000 ?

(1) $5^{k+1} > 3,000$

(2) $5^{k-1} = 5^k - 500$

Arithmetic Arithmetic operations

If x is any positive number and r and s are any positive integers, then $x^{-r} = \frac{1}{x^r}$ and $x^{r+s} = (x^r)(x^s)$. Therefore, $5^{k+1} = 5^k(5^1)$. When both sides of this equation are divided by 5^1 (which equals 5), the resultant equation is $\frac{5^{k+1}}{5} = 5^k$.

(1) If both sides of this given inequality are divided by 5, it yields $\frac{5^{k+1}}{5} > \frac{3,000}{5}$ or $5^k > 600$. Although it is known that $5^k > 600$, it is unknown if 5^k is less than 1,000; NOT sufficient.

(2) It is given that $5^{k-1} = 5^k - 500$, thus:

$5^k - 5^{k-1} = 500$	subtract 5^k from both sides; divide all terms by -1
$5^k - 5^k(5^{-1}) = 500$	property of exponents
$5^k - 5^k\left(\frac{1}{5}\right) = 500$	substitute for 5^{-1}
$5^k\left(1 - \frac{1}{5}\right) = 500$	factor out 5^k
$5^k\left(\frac{4}{5}\right) = 500$	simplify
$5^k = 500\left(\frac{5}{4}\right)$	multiply both sides by $\left(\frac{5}{4}\right)$

$5^k = 625$, which is less than 1,000; SUFFICIENT.

The correct answer is B; statement 2 alone is sufficient.

157. The hypotenuse of a right triangle is 10 cm. What is the perimeter, in centimeters, of the triangle?

    (1) The area of the triangle is 25 square centimeters.
    (2) The 2 legs of the triangle are of equal length.

Geometry Triangles

If x and y are the lengths of the legs of the triangle, then it is given that $x^2 + y^2 = 100$. To determine the value of $x + y + 10$, the perimeter of the triangle, is equivalent to determining the value of $x + y$.

(1) Given that the area is 25, then $\frac{1}{2}xy = 25$, or $xy = 50$. Since $(x + y)^2 = x^2 + y^2 + 2xy$, it follows that $(x + y)^2 = 100 + 2(50)$, or $x + y = \sqrt{200}$; SUFFICIENT.

(2) Given that $x = y$, since $x^2 + y^2 = 100$, it follows that $2x^2 = 100$, or $x = \sqrt{50}$. Hence, $x + y = x + x = 2x = 2\sqrt{50}$; SUFFICIENT.

The correct answer is D; each statement alone is sufficient.

158. Every member of a certain club volunteers to contribute equally to the purchase of a $60 gift certificate. How many members does the club have?

    (1) Each member's contribution is to be $4.
    (2) If 5 club members fail to contribute, the share of each contributing member will increase by $2.

Arithmetic; Algebra Arithmetic operations; Simultaneous equations

(1) If each member's contribution is to be $4 and the total amount to be collected is $60, then $60 \div 4 = 15$ members in the club; SUFFICIENT.

(2) Let c represent each person's contribution, and let x represent the number of members in the club. From the given information, it is known that $\frac{60}{x} = c$. From this, it is also known that $\frac{60}{x - 5} = c + 2$.

These two equations can be solved simultaneously for x:

$$\frac{60}{x - 5} = \frac{60}{x} + 2 \qquad \text{substitute for } c$$

$$\frac{60}{x - 5} = \frac{60 + 2x}{x} \qquad \text{add fraction and whole number}$$

$$60x = (x - 5)(60 + 2x) \qquad \text{cross multiply}$$

$$60x = 2x^2 - 10x + 60x - 300 \qquad \text{multiply}$$

$$0 = 2x^2 - 10x - 300 \qquad \text{subtract } 60x \text{ from both sides}$$

$$0 = 2(x - 15)(x + 10) \qquad \text{factor}$$

Therefore, x could be 15 or −10. Since there cannot be −10 members, x must be 15; so there are 15 members in the club; SUFFICIENT.

The correct answer is D; each statement alone is sufficient.

159. If $x < 0$, is $y > 0$?

    (1) $\frac{x}{y} < 0$
    (2) $y - x > 0$

Algebra Inequalities

(1) In order for $x < 0$ and $\frac{x}{y} < 0$ to be true, y must be greater than 0. If $y = 0$, then $\frac{x}{y}$ would be undefined. If $y < 0$, then $\frac{x}{y}$ would be a positive number; SUFFICIENT.

(2) Here, if $x < 0$, then y could be 0. For example, if y was 0 and x was −3, then $y - x > 0$ would be $0 - (-3) > 0$ or $3 > 0$. The statement would also be true if y were less than 0 but greater than x. For example, if $y = -2$ and $x = -7$, then $-2 - (-7) > 0$ or $5 > 0$. Finally, this statement would also be true if $y > 0$. Without any further information, it is impossible to tell whether $y > 0$; NOT sufficient.

The correct answer is A; statement 1 alone is sufficient.

160. What is the circumference of the circle above with center O?

    (1) The perimeter of $\triangle OXZ$ is $20 + 10\sqrt{2}$.
    (2) The length of arc XYZ is 5π.

Geometry Circles

The circumference of the circle can be found if the radius r is known. $\triangle OXZ$ is a right triangle with $OX = OZ = r$ (since O is the center). The perimeter of $\triangle OXZ$ is the sum of OX (or r) + OZ (or r) + XZ, or the perimeter = $2r + XZ$. From the Pythagorean theorem,

$$XZ^2 = OX^2 + OZ^2$$
$$XZ^2 = r^2 + r^2$$
$$XZ = \sqrt{r^2 + r^2}$$
$$XZ = \sqrt{2r^2}$$
$$XZ = r\sqrt{2}$$

The perimeter of $\triangle OXZ$ is then $2r + r\sqrt{2}$.

    (1) The perimeter of $\triangle OXZ$ is $20 + 10\sqrt{2}$. Thus, $2r + r\sqrt{2} = 20 + 10\sqrt{2} = 2(10) + 10\sqrt{2}$, and $r = 10$. Since r is known, the circumference can be found; SUFFICIENT.

    (2) The length of arc XYZ is the measurement of angle XOZ divided by 360 and multiplied by the circumference. Since angle XOZ equals 90, the length of arc XYZ is thus $\frac{90}{360} = \frac{1}{4}$ of the circumference. Since $\frac{1}{4}$ of the circumference is given as equal to 5π, the circumference can be determined; SUFFICIENT.

**The correct answer is D;
each statement alone is sufficient.**

161. Beginning in January of last year, Carl made deposits of $120 into his account on the 15th of each month for several consecutive months and then made withdrawals of $50 from the account on the 15th of each of the remaining months of last year. There were no other transactions in the account last year. If the closing balance of Carl's account for May of last year was $2,600, what was the range of the monthly closing balances of Carl's account last year?

    (1) Last year the closing balance of Carl's account for April was less than $2,625.
    (2) Last year the closing balance of Carl's account for June was less than $2,675.

Arithmetic Statistics

    (1) If Carl began making $50 withdrawals on or before May 15, his account balance on April 16 would be at least $50 greater than it was on the last day of May. Thus, his account balance on April 16 would be at least $2,600 + $50 = $2,650, which is contrary to the information given in (1). Therefore, Carl did not begin making $50 withdrawals until June 15 or later. These observations can be used to give at least two possible ranges. Carl could have had an account balance of $2,000 on January 1, made $120 deposits in each of the first 11 months of the year, and then made a $50 withdrawal on December 15, which gives a range of monthly closing balances of (120)(10). Also, Carl could have had an account balance of $2,000 on January 1, made $120 deposits in each of the first 10 months of the year, and then made $50 withdrawals on November 15 and on December 15, which gives a range of monthly closing balances of (120)(9); NOT sufficient.

    (2) On June 1, Carl's account balance was the same as its closing balance was for May, namely $2,600. Depending on whether Carl made a $120 deposit or a $50 withdrawal on June 15, Carl's account balance on June 16 was either $2,720 or $2,550. It follows from the information given in (2) that Carl's balance on June 16 was $2,550. Therefore, Carl began making $50 withdrawals on or before June 15. These observations can be used to give at least two possible ranges. Carl could have had an account balance of

$2,680 on January 1, made one $120 deposit on January 15, and then made a $50 withdrawal in each of the remaining 11 months of the year (this gives a closing balance of $2,600 for May), which gives a range of monthly closing balances of (50)(11). Also, Carl could have had an account balance of $2,510 on January 1, made $120 deposits on January 15 and on February 15, and then made a $50 withdrawal in each of the remaining 10 months of the year (this gives a closing balance of $2,600 for May), which gives a range of monthly closing balances of (50)(10); NOT sufficient.

Given both (1) and (2), it follows from the remarks above that Carl began making $50 withdrawals on June 15. Therefore, the changes to Carl's account balance for each month of last year are known. Since the closing balance for May is given, it follows that the closing balances for each month of last year are known, and hence the range of these 12 known values can be determined. Therefore, (1) and (2) together are sufficient.

The correct answer is C; both statements together are sufficient.

162. If n and k are positive integers, is $\sqrt{n+k} > 2\sqrt{n}$?

(1) $k > 3n$
(2) $n + k > 3n$

Algebra Inequalities

Determine if $\sqrt{n+k} > 2\sqrt{n}$. Since each side is positive, squaring each side preserves the inequality, so $\sqrt{n+k} > 2\sqrt{n}$ is equivalent to $\left(\sqrt{n+k}\right)\left(\sqrt{n+k}\right) > \left(2\sqrt{n}\right)\left(2\sqrt{n}\right)$, which in turn is equivalent to $n + k > 4n$, or to $k > 3n$.

(1) Given that $k > 3n$, then $\sqrt{n+k} > 2\sqrt{n}$; SUFFICIENT.

(2) Given that $n + k > 3n$, then $k > 2n$. However, it is possible for $k > 2n$ to be true and $k > 3n$ to be false (for example, $k = 3$ and $n = 1$) and it is possible for $k > 2n$ to be true and $k > 3n$ to be true (for example, $k = 4$ and $n = 1$); NOT sufficient.

The correct answer is A; statement 1 alone is sufficient.

163. In a certain business, production index p is directly proportional to efficiency index e, which is in turn directly proportional to investment index i. What is p if $i = 70$?

(1) $e = 0.5$ whenever $i = 60$.
(2) $p = 2.0$ whenever $i = 50$.

Arithmetic Proportions

(1) This gives only values for e and i, and, while p is directly proportional to e, the nature of this proportion is unknown. Therefore, p cannot be determined; NOT sufficient.

(2) Since p is directly proportional to e, which is directly proportional to i, then p is directly proportional to i. Therefore, the following proportion can be set up: $\frac{p}{i} = \frac{2.0}{50}$. If $i = 70$, then $\frac{p}{70} = \frac{2.0}{50}$. Through cross multiplying, this equation yields $50p = 140$, or $p = 2.8$; SUFFICIENT.

The preceding approach is one method that can be used. Another approach is as follows: It is given that $p = Ke = K(Li) = (KL)i$, where K and L are the proportionality constants, and the value of $70KL$ is to be determined. Statement (1) allows us to determine the value of L, but gives nothing about K, and thus (1) is not sufficient. Statement (2) allows us to determine the value of KL, and thus (2) is sufficient.

The correct answer is B; statement 2 alone is sufficient.

164. In the rectangular coordinate system, are the points (r,s) and (u,v) equidistant from the origin?

(1) $r + s = 1$
(2) $u = 1 - r$ and $v = 1 - s$

Geometry Coordinate geometry

The distance from (r,s) to $(0,0)$ is $\sqrt{(r-0)^2 + (s-0)^2}$ or $\sqrt{r^2 + s^2}$. Similarly, the distance from (u,v) to $(0,0)$ is $\sqrt{u^2 + v^2}$. Therefore, if $r^2 + s^2 = u^2 + v^2$, the two points would be equidistant from the origin.

(1) This says nothing about coordinates u and v; NOT sufficient.

(2) Using this information, $u^2 = (1-r)^2$ or $1 - 2r + r^2$, and $v^2 = (1-s)^2$ or $1 - 2s + s^2$. Thus, $u^2 + v^2 = 1 - 2r + r^2 + 1 - 2s + s^2$, or $u^2 + v^2 = 2 - 2(r+s) + r^2 + s^2$, but there is no information about the value of $r + s$; NOT sufficient.

From (1) and (2) together, since $r + s = 1$, it follows by substitution that $u^2 + v^2 = 2 - 2(1) + r^2 + s^2$, or $u^2 + v^2 = r^2 + s^2$.

The correct answer is C; both statements together are sufficient.

165. If x is an integer, is $9^x + 9^{-x} = b$?

(1) $3^x + 3^{-x} = \sqrt{b+2}$
(2) $x > 0$

Algebra Exponents

When solving this problem it is helpful to note that $(x^r)(x^{-s}) = x^{r-s}$ and that $(x^r)^2 = x^{2r}$. Note also that $x^0 = 1$.

(1) From this, $3^x + 3^{-x} = \sqrt{b+2}$. Squaring both sides gives:

$$(3^x + 3^{-x})^2 = b + 2$$
$$3^{2x} + 2(3^x \times 3^{-x}) + 3^{-2x} = b + 2$$

$9^x + 2(3^0) + 9^{-x} = b + 2$ property of exponents

$9^x + 2 + 9^{-x} = b + 2$ property of exponents

$9^x + 9^{-x} = b$ subtract 2 from both sides; SUFFICIENT.

(2) This gives no information about the relationship between x and b; NOT sufficient.

The correct answer is A; statement 1 alone is sufficient.

166. If n is a positive integer, is $\left(\frac{1}{10}\right)^n < 0.01$?

(1) $n > 2$
(2) $\left(\frac{1}{10}\right)^{n-1} < 0.1$

Arithmetic; Algebra Properties of numbers; Inequalities

(1) $n > 2$

$-n < -2$

$10^{-n} < 10^{-2}$

$(10^{-1})^n < 10^{-2}$

$\left(\frac{1}{10}\right)^n < 10^{-2}$

$\left(\frac{1}{10}\right)^n < 0.01$

SUFFICIENT.

(2) $\left(\frac{1}{10}\right)^{n-1} < 0.1$

$\left(\frac{1}{10}\right)^{n-1} < 10^{-1}$

$(10^{-1})^{n-1} < 10^{-1}$

$(10)^{(-1)(n-1)} < 10^{-1}$

$(10)^{-n+1} < 10^{-1}$

$-n + 1 < -1$

$-n < -2$

$n > 2$

But, this is the inequality given in (1), which was sufficient; SUFFICIENT.

The correct answer is D; each statement alone is sufficient.

167. If n is a positive integer, what is the tens digit of n?

(1) The hundreds digit of $10n$ is 6.
(2) The tens digit of $n + 1$ is 7.

Arithmetic Properties of numbers

(1) Given that the hundreds digit of $10n$ is 6, the tens digit of n is 6, since the hundreds digit of $10n$ is always equal to the tens digit of n; SUFFICIENT.

(2) Given that the tens digit of $n + 1$ is 7, it is possible that the tens digit of n is 7 (for example, $n = 70$) and it is possible that the tens digit of n is 6 (for example, $n = 69$); NOT sufficient.

The correct answer is A; statement 1 alone is sufficient.

168. What is the value of $\dfrac{2t+t-x}{t-x}$?

(1) $\dfrac{2t}{t-x} = 3$

(2) $t - x = 5$

Algebra Simplifying algebraic expressions

Determine the value of $\dfrac{2t+t-x}{t-x}$.

(1) Since $\dfrac{2t}{t-x} = 3$ and

$\dfrac{2t+t-x}{t-x} = \dfrac{2t}{t-x} + \dfrac{t-x}{t-x} = \dfrac{2t}{t-x} + 1$,

it follows that $\dfrac{2t+t-x}{t-x} = 3 + 1$; SUFFICIENT.

(2) Given that $t - x = 5$, it follows that $\dfrac{2t+t-x}{t-x} = \dfrac{2t+5}{5} = \dfrac{2}{5}t + 1$, which can vary when the value of t varies. For example, $\dfrac{2}{5}t + 1 = 3$ if $t = 5$ (choose $x = 0$ to have $t - x = 5$) and $\dfrac{2}{5}t + 1 = 5$ if $t = 10$ (choose $x = 5$ to have $t - x = 5$); NOT sufficient.

The correct answer is A; statement 1 alone is sufficient.

169. Is n an integer?

(1) n^2 is an integer.

(2) $\sqrt{n}$ is an integer.

Arithmetic Properties of numbers

(1) Since 1^2 is an integer and $\left(\sqrt{2}\right)^2$ is an integer, the square of an integer can be an integer and the square of a non-integer can be an integer; NOT sufficient.

(2) If $\sqrt{n} = k$, where k is an integer, then $\left(\sqrt{n}\right)^2 = k^2$, or $n = k^2$. Therefore, n is the square of an integer, which in turn is an integer; SUFFICIENT.

The correct answer is B; statement 2 alone is sufficient.

170. If n is a positive integer, is $n^3 - n$ divisible by 4 ?

(1) $n = 2k + 1$, where k is an integer.

(2) $n^2 + n$ is divisible by 6.

Arithmetic Arithmetic operations; Properties of numbers

Since n is a positive integer and $n^3 - n = n(n^2 - 1) = n(n-1)(n+1)$, it follows that $n^3 - n$ is the product of the three consecutive integers $n - 1$, n, and $n + 1$.

(1) Since $2k$ is an even integer, then $n = 2k + 1$ must be an odd integer. Therefore, the consecutive integers, $n - 1$, n, and $n + 1$ are even, odd, and even, respectively. Two of the three numbers are therefore divisible by 2. When the product is broken down into factors, there are at least two factors of 2 in the product ($2 \times 2 = 4$) so the product of the three numbers must be divisible by 4; SUFFICIENT.

(2) The expression $n^2 + n$ can be factored as $n(n + 1)$, which represents the product of two consecutive integers. The fact that $n(n + 1)$ is divisible by 6 does not appear to ensure that $n(n-1)(n+1)$ is divisible by 4. For example, $(6)(7) = 42$ is divisible by 6, but $(5)(6)(7)$ is not divisible by 4. However, $(5)(6)$ is divisible by 6, and $(4)(5)(6)$ is divisible by 4. Since the exact value of n cannot be determined, it cannot be known whether $n^3 - n$ is divisible by 4; NOT sufficient.

The correct answer is A; statement 1 alone is sufficient.

171. What is the tens digit of positive integer x ?

    (1) x divided by 100 has a remainder of 30.
    (2) x divided by 110 has a remainder of 30.

    Arithmetic Properties of numbers

    (1)   Having a remainder of 30 when x is divided by 100 can only happen if x has a tens digit of 3 and a ones digit of 0, as in 130, 230, 630, and so forth; SUFFICIENT.

    (2)   When 140 is divided by 110, the quotient is 1 R30. However, 250 divided by 110 yields a quotient of 2 R30, and 360 divided by 110 gives a quotient of 3 R30. Since there is no consistency in the tens digit, more information is needed; NOT sufficient.

    The correct answer is A; statement 1 alone is sufficient.

172. If x, y, and z are positive integers, is $x - y$ odd?

    (1) $x = z^2$
    (2) $y = (z - 1)^2$

    Arithmetic Arithmetic operations; Properties of numbers

    (1)   This reveals the relationship between two of the variables but does not mention the relationship either has with y. Therefore the question cannot be answered; NOT sufficient.

    (2)   If $(z - 1)^2$ is expanded, the result is $z^2 - 2z + 1$. Since $y = z^2 - 2z + 1$, a substitution for y can be made in the expression $x - y$. It becomes $x - (z^2 - 2z + 1)$. However, without further information, it cannot be determined if $x - y$ is odd; NOT sufficient.

    When (1) and (2) are taken together, z^2, from (1), can be substituted for x in the expression $x - (z^2 - 2z + 1)$ from (2). It then yields $z^2 - z^2 + 2z - 1$, or simply $2z - 1$, which is always an odd number regardless of the value of z. So $x - y$ is odd.

    The correct answer is C; both statements together are sufficient.

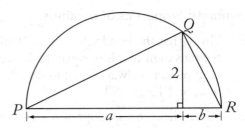

173. If arc PQR above is a semicircle, what is the length of diameter $\overline{PR}$?

    (1) $a = 4$
    (2) $b = 1$

    Geometry Circles

    Since angle PQR is inscribed in a semicircle, it is a right angle, and $\triangle PQR$ is a right triangle. $\triangle PQR$ is divided into two right triangles by the vertical line from Q to side $\overline{PR}$. Let $x = PQ$ and $y = QR$. The larger right triangle has hypotenuse x, so $x^2 = 4 + a^2$; the smaller right triangle has hypotenuse y, so $y^2 = 4 + b^2$. From $\triangle PQR$, $(a + b)^2 = x^2 + y^2$, so by substitution, $(a + b)^2 = (4 + a^2) + (4 + b^2)$, and by simplification, $a^2 + 2ab + b^2 = 8 + a^2 + b^2$ or $2ab = 8$ or $ab = 4$.

    (1)   If $a = 4$ is substituted in $ab = 4$, then b must be 1 and diameter PR is 5; SUFFICIENT.

    (2)   If $b = 1$ is substituted in $ab = 4$, then a must be 4 and diameter PR is 5; SUFFICIENT.

    The correct answer is D; each statement alone is sufficient.

174. Marcia's bucket can hold a maximum of how many liters of water?

    (1)   The bucket currently contains 9 liters of water.
    (2)   If 3 liters of water are added to the bucket when it is half full of water, the amount of water in the bucket will increase by $\frac{1}{3}$.

    Geometry Volume

    (1)   This statement only implies that the bucket will hold *at least* 9 liters, but the *maximum capacity* is still unknown; NOT sufficient.

    (2)   Letting c represent the maximum capacity of Marcia's bucket, the volume of water in the bucket when at half capacity can be expressed as $\frac{1}{2}c$, and if 3 liters are then

added, the present volume of water in the bucket can be expressed as $\frac{1}{2}c + 3$. It is given that, when the 3 liters are added, the volume of water will increase by $\frac{1}{3}$, which is equivalent to multiplying the present volume by $\frac{4}{3}$. This becomes the expression $\frac{4}{3}\left(\frac{1}{2}c\right)$.

Therefore, it is known that $\frac{1}{2}c + 3 = \frac{4}{3}\left(\frac{1}{2}c\right)$. This equation can be solved for c, through simplifying to $\frac{1}{2}c + 3 = \frac{2}{3}c$, then subtracting $\frac{1}{2}c$ from each side for $3 = \frac{2}{3}c - \frac{1}{2}c$, and then simplifying to $3 = \frac{1}{6}c$ or $18 = c$.

Thus the equation can be solved to determine the maximum capacity of the bucket; SUFFICIENT.

The correct answer is B; statement 2 alone is sufficient.

7.0   Reading Comprehension

7.0 Reading Comprehension

Reading comprehension questions appear in the Verbal section of the GMAT® test. The Verbal section uses multiple-choice questions to measure your ability to read and comprehend written material, to reason and evaluate arguments, and to correct written material to conform to standard written English. Because the Verbal section includes content from a variety of topics, you may be generally familiar with some of the material; however, neither the passages nor the questions assume knowledge of the topics discussed. Reading comprehension questions are intermingled with critical reasoning and sentence correction questions throughout the Verbal section of the test.

You will have 75 minutes to complete the Verbal section, or an average of about 1¾ minutes to answer each question. Keep in mind, however, that you will need time to read the written passages—and that time is not factored into the 1¾ minute average. You should therefore plan to proceed more quickly through the reading comprehension questions in order to give yourself enough time to read the passages thoroughly.

Reading comprehension questions begin with written passages up to 350 words long. The passages discuss topics from the social sciences, humanities, the physical or biological sciences, and such business-related fields as marketing, economics, and human resource management. The passages are accompanied by questions that will ask you to interpret the passage, apply the information you gather from the reading, and make inferences (or informed assumptions) based on the reading. For these questions, you will see a split computer screen. The written passage will remain visible on the left side as each question associated with that passage appears in turn on the right side. You will see only one question at a time, however. The number of questions associated with each passage may vary.

As you move through the reading comprehension sample questions, try to determine a process that works best for you. You might begin by reading a passage carefully and thoroughly, though some test takers prefer to skim the passages the first time through, or even to read the first question before reading the passage. You may want to reread any sentences that present complicated ideas or introduce terms that are new to you. Read each question and series of answers carefully. Make sure you understand exactly what the question is asking and what the answer choices are.

If you need to, you may go back to the passage and read any parts that are relevant to answering the question. Specific portions of the passages may be highlighted in the related questions.

The following pages describe what reading comprehension questions are designed to measure; present the directions that will precede questions of this type; and describe the various question types. This chapter also provides test-taking strategies, sample questions, and detailed explanations of all the questions. The explanations further illustrate the ways in which reading comprehension questions evaluate basic reading skills.

7.1 What Is Measured

Reading comprehension questions measure your ability to understand, analyze, and apply information and concepts presented in written form. All questions are to be answered on the basis of what is stated or implied in the reading material, and no specific prior knowledge of the material is required.

The GMAT reading comprehension questions evaluate your ability to do the following:

- **Understand words and statements.**
  Although the questions do not test your vocabulary (they will not ask you to define terms), they do test your ability to interpret special meanings of terms as they are used in the reading passages. The questions will also test your understanding of the English language. These questions may ask about the overall meaning of a passage.

- **Understand logical relationships between points and concepts.** This type of question may ask you to determine the strong and weak points of an argument or evaluate the relative importance of arguments and ideas in a passage.

- **Draw inferences from facts and statements.**
  The inference questions will ask you to consider factual statements or information presented in a reading passage and, on the basis of that information, reach conclusions.

- **Understand and follow the development of quantitative concepts as they are presented in written material.**
  This may involve the interpretation of numerical data or the use of simple arithmetic to reach conclusions about material in a passage.

There are six kinds of reading comprehension questions, each of which tests a different skill. The reading comprehension questions ask about the following areas:

Main idea

Each passage is a unified whole—that is, the individual sentences and paragraphs support and develop one main idea or central point. Sometimes you will be told the central point in the passage itself, and sometimes it will be necessary for you to determine the central point from the overall organization or development of the passage. You may be asked in this kind of question to

- recognize a correct restatement, or paraphrasing, of the main idea of a passage

- identify the author's primary purpose or objective in writing the passage

- assign a title that summarizes, briefly and pointedly, the main idea developed in the passage

Supporting ideas

These questions measure your ability to comprehend the supporting ideas in a passage and differentiate them from the main idea. The questions also measure your ability to differentiate ideas that are *explicitly stated* in a passage from ideas that are *implied* by the author but that are not explicitly stated. You may be asked about

- facts cited in a passage

- the specific content of arguments presented by the author in support of his or her views

- descriptive details used to support or elaborate on the main idea

Whereas questions about the main idea ask you to determine the meaning of a passage *as a whole*, questions about supporting ideas ask you to determine the meanings of individual sentences and paragraphs that *contribute* to the meaning of the passage as a whole. In other words, these questions ask for the main point of *one small part* of the passage.

Inferences

These questions ask about ideas that are not explicitly stated in a passage but are *implied* by the author. Unlike questions about supporting details, which ask about information that is directly stated in a passage, inference questions ask about ideas or meanings that must be inferred from information that is directly stated. Authors can make their points in indirect ways, suggesting ideas without actually stating them. Inference questions measure your ability to understand an author's intended meaning in parts of a passage where the meaning is only suggested. These questions do not ask about meanings or implications that are remote from the passage; rather, they ask about meanings that are developed indirectly or implications that are specifically suggested by the author.

To answer these questions, you may have to

- logically take statements made by the author one step beyond their literal meanings

- recognize an alternative interpretation of a statement made by the author

- identify the intended meaning of a word used figuratively in a passage

If a passage explicitly states an effect, for example, you may be asked to infer its cause. If the author compares two phenomena, you may be asked to infer the basis for the comparison. You may be asked to infer the characteristics of an old policy from an explicit description of a new one. When you read a passage, therefore, you should concentrate not only on the explicit meaning of the author's words, but also on the more subtle meaning implied by those words.

Applying information to a context outside the passage itself

These questions measure your ability to discern the relationships between situations or ideas presented by the author and other situations or ideas that might parallel those in the passage. In this kind of question, you may be asked to

- identify a hypothetical situation that is comparable to a situation presented in the passage

- select an example that is similar to an example provided in the passage

- apply ideas given in the passage to a situation not mentioned by the author

- recognize ideas that the author would probably agree or disagree with on the basis of statements made in the passage

Unlike inference questions, application questions use ideas or situations *not* taken from the passage. Ideas and situations given in a question are *like* those given in the passage, and they parallel ideas and situations in the passage; therefore, to answer the question, you must do more than recall what you read. You must recognize the essential attributes of ideas and situations presented in the passage when they appear in different words and in an entirely new context.

Logical structure

These questions require you to analyze and evaluate the organization and logic of a passage. They may ask you

- how a passage is constructed—for instance, does it define, compare or contrast, present a new idea, or refute an idea?
- how the author persuades readers to accept his or her assertions
- the reason behind the author's use of any particular supporting detail
- to identify assumptions that the author is making
- to assess the strengths and weaknesses of the author's arguments
- to recognize appropriate counterarguments

These questions measure your ability not only to comprehend a passage but also to evaluate it critically. However, it is important for you to realize that logical structure questions do not rely on any kind of formal logic, nor do they require you to be familiar with specific terms of logic or argumentation. You can answer these questions using only the information in the passage and careful reasoning.

About the style and tone

Style and tone questions ask about the expression of a passage and about the ideas in a passage that may be expressed through its diction—the author's choice of words. You may be asked to deduce the author's attitude to an idea, a fact, or a situation from the words that he or she uses to describe it. You may also be asked to select a word that accurately describes the tone of a passage—for instance, "critical," "questioning," "objective," or "enthusiastic."

To answer this type of question, you will have to consider the language of the passage as a whole. It takes more than one pointed, critical word to make the tone of an entire passage "critical." Sometimes, style and tone questions ask what audience the passage was probably intended for or what type of publication it probably appeared in. Style and tone questions may apply to one small part of the passage or to the passage as a whole. To answer them, you must ask yourself what meanings are contained in the words of a passage beyond the literal meanings. Did the author use certain words because of their emotional content, or because a particular audience would expect to hear them? Remember, these questions measure your ability to discern meaning expressed by the author through his or her choice of words.

7.2 Test-Taking Strategies

1. **Do not expect to be completely familiar with any of the material presented in reading comprehension passages.**

   You may find some passages easier to understand than others, but all passages are designed to present a challenge. If you have some familiarity with the material presented in a passage, do not let this knowledge influence your choice of answers to the questions. Answer all questions on the basis of what is *stated or implied* in the passage itself.

2. **Analyze each passage carefully, because the questions require you to have a specific and detailed understanding of the material.**
   You may find it easier to do the analysis first, before moving to the questions. Or, you may find that you prefer to skim the passage the first time and read more carefully once you understand what a question asks. You may even want to read the question before reading the passage. You should choose the method most suitable for you.

3. **Focus on key words and phrases, and make every effort to avoid losing the sense of what is discussed in the passage.**
   Keep the following in mind:

   • Note how each fact relates to an idea or an argument.

   • Note where the passage moves from one idea to the next.

   • Separate main ideas from supporting ideas.

   • Determine what conclusions are reached and why.

4. **Read the questions carefully, making certain that you understand what is asked.**
   An answer choice that accurately restates information in the passage may be incorrect if it does not answer the question. If you need to, refer back to the passage for clarification.

5. **Read all the choices carefully.**
   Never assume that you have selected the best answer without first reading all the choices.

6. **Select the choice that answers the question best in terms of the information given in the passage.**
   Do not rely on outside knowledge of the material to help you answer the questions.

7. **Remember that comprehension—not speed—is the critical success factor when it comes to reading comprehension questions.**

7.3 The Directions

These are the directions that you will see for reading comprehension questions when you take the GMAT test. If you read them carefully and understand them clearly before going to sit for the test, you will not need to spend too much time reviewing them once you are at the test center and the test is under way.

The questions in this group are based on the content of a passage. After reading the passage, choose the best answer to each question. Answer all questions following the passage on the basis of what is *stated or implied in the passage*.

7.4 Sample Questions

Each of the <u>reading comprehension</u> questions is based on the content of a passage. After reading the passage answer all questions pertaining to it on the basis of what is <u>stated</u> or <u>implied</u> in the passage. For each question, select the best answer of the choices given.

Line Ecoefficiency (measures to minimize environmental impact through the reduction or elimination of waste from production processes) has become a goal for companies worldwide, with many realizing significant
(5) cost savings from such innovations. Peter Senge and Goran Carstedt see this development as laudable but suggest that simply adopting ecoefficiency innovations could actually worsen environmental stresses in the future. Such innovations reduce
(10) production waste but do not alter the number of products manufactured nor the waste generated from their use and discard; indeed, most companies invest in ecoefficiency improvements in order to increase profits and growth. Moreover, there is no
(15) guarantee that increased economic growth from ecoefficiency will come in similarly ecoefficient ways, since in today's global markets, greater profits may be turned into investment capital that could easily be reinvested in old-style eco-inefficient industries. Even
(20) a vastly more ecoefficient industrial system could, were it to grow much larger, generate more total waste and destroy more habitat and species than would a smaller, less ecoefficient economy. Senge and Carstedt argue that to preserve the global
(25) environment and sustain economic growth, businesses must develop a new systemic approach that reduces total material use and total accumulated waste. Focusing exclusively on ecoefficiency, which offers a compelling business case according to
(30) established thinking, may distract companies from pursuing radically different products and business models.

Questions 1–3 refer to the passage above.

1. The primary purpose of the passage is to

   (A) explain why a particular business strategy has been less successful than was once anticipated

   (B) propose an alternative to a particular business strategy that has inadvertently caused ecological damage

   (C) present a concern about the possible consequences of pursuing a particular business strategy

   (D) make a case for applying a particular business strategy on a larger scale than is currently practiced

   (E) suggest several possible outcomes of companies' failure to understand the economic impact of a particular business strategy

2. The passage mentions which of the following as a possible consequence of companies' realization of greater profits through ecoefficiency?

   (A) The companies may be able to sell a greater number of products by lowering prices.

   (B) The companies may be better able to attract investment capital in the global market.

   (C) The profits may be reinvested to increase economic growth through ecoefficiency.

   (D) The profits may be used as investment capital for industries that are not ecoefficient.

   (E) The profits may encourage companies to make further innovations in reducing production waste.

3. The passage implies that which of the following is a possible consequence of a company's adoption of innovations that increase its ecoefficiency?

    (A) Company profits resulting from such innovations may be reinvested in that company with no guarantee that the company will continue to make further improvements in ecoefficiency.

    (B) Company growth fostered by cost savings from such innovations may allow that company to manufacture a greater number of products that will be used and discarded, thus worsening environmental stress.

    (C) A company that fails to realize significant cost savings from such innovations may have little incentive to continue to minimize the environmental impact of its production processes.

    (D) A company that comes to depend on such innovations to increase its profits and growth may be vulnerable in the global market to competition from old-style eco-inefficient industries.

    (E) A company that meets its ecoefficiency goals is unlikely to invest its increased profits in the development of new and innovative ecoefficiency measures.

Line   A recent study has provided clues to
predator-prey dynamics in the late Pleistocene
era. Researchers compared the number of tooth
fractures in present-day carnivores with tooth
(5)   fractures in carnivores that lived 36,000 to 10,000
years ago and that were preserved in the Rancho
La Brea tar pits in Los Angeles. The breakage
frequencies in the extinct species were strikingly
higher than those in the present-day species.

(10)   In considering possible explanations for this
finding, the researchers dismissed demographic bias
because older individuals were not overrepresented
in the fossil samples. They rejected preservational
bias because a total absence of breakage in two
(15)   extinct species demonstrated that the fractures
were not the result of abrasion within the pits.
They ruled out local bias because breakage data
obtained from other Pleistocene sites were similar
to the La Brea data. The explanation they consider
(20)   most plausible is behavioral differences between
extinct and present-day carnivores—in particular,
more contact between the teeth of predators and
the bones of prey due to more thorough
consumption of carcasses by the extinct species.
(25)   Such thorough carcass consumption implies to
the researchers either that prey availability was
low, at least seasonally, or that there was intense
competition over kills and a high rate of carcass
theft due to relatively high predator densities.

Questions 4–8 refer to the passage above.

4.   The primary purpose of the passage is to

    (A)   present several explanations for a well-known fact

    (B)   suggest alternative methods for resolving a debate

    (C)   argue in favor of a controversial theory

    (D)   question the methodology used in a study

    (E)   discuss the implications of a research finding

5.   According to the passage, compared with Pleistocene carnivores in other areas, Pleistocene carnivores in the La Brea area

    (A)   included the same species, in approximately the same proportions

    (B)   had a similar frequency of tooth fractures

    (C)   populated the La Brea area more densely

    (D)   consumed their prey more thoroughly

    (E)   found it harder to obtain sufficient prey

6.   According to the passage, the researchers believe that the high frequency of tooth breakage in carnivores found at La Brea was caused primarily by

    (A)   the aging process in individual carnivores

    (B)   contact between the fossils in the pits

    (C)   poor preservation of the fossils after they were removed from the pits

    (D)   the impact of carnivores' teeth against the bones of their prey

    (E)   the impact of carnivores' teeth against the bones of other carnivores during fights over kills

7. The researchers' conclusion concerning the absence of demographic bias would be most seriously undermined if it were found that

    (A)   the older an individual carnivore is, the more likely it is to have a large number of tooth fractures

    (B)   the average age at death of a present-day carnivore is greater than was the average age at death of a Pleistocene carnivore

    (C)   in Pleistocene carnivore species, older individuals consumed carcasses as thoroughly as did younger individuals

    (D)   the methods used to determine animals' ages in fossil samples tend to misidentify many older individuals as younger individuals

    (E)   data concerning the ages of fossil samples cannot provide reliable information about behavioral differences between extinct carnivores and present-day carnivores

8. According to the passage, if the researchers had NOT found that two extinct carnivore species were free of tooth breakage, the researchers would have concluded that

    (A)   the difference in breakage frequencies could have been the result of damage to the fossil remains in the La Brea pits

    (B)   the fossils in other Pleistocene sites could have higher breakage frequencies than do the fossils in the La Brea pits

    (C)   Pleistocene carnivore species probably behaved very similarly to one another with respect to consumption of carcasses

    (D)   all Pleistocene carnivore species differed behaviorally from present-day carnivore species

    (E)   predator densities during the Pleistocene era were extremely high

Line   Archaeology as a profession faces two major
       problems. First, it is the poorest of the poor.
       Only paltry sums are available for excavating and
       even less is available for publishing the results
(5)   and preserving the sites once excavated. Yet
       archaeologists deal with priceless objects every day.
       Second, there is the problem of illegal excavation,
       resulting in museum-quality pieces being sold to the
       highest bidder.
(10)   I would like to make an outrageous
       suggestion that would at one stroke provide
       funds for archaeology and reduce the amount
       of illegal digging. I would propose that scientific
       archaeological expeditions and governmental
(15)   authorities sell excavated artifacts on the open
       market. Such sales would provide substantial
       funds for the excavation and preservation of
       archaeological sites and the publication of results.
       At the same time, they would break the illegal
(20)   excavator's grip on the market, thereby decreasing
       the inducement to engage in illegal activities.
           You might object that professionals excavate to
       acquire knowledge, not money. Moreover, ancient
       artifacts are part of our global cultural heritage,
(25)   which should be available for all to appreciate, not
       sold to the highest bidder. I agree. Sell nothing that
       has unique artistic merit or scientific value. But,
       you might reply, everything that comes out of the
       ground has scientific value. Here we part company.
(30)   Theoretically, you may be correct in claiming
       that every artifact has potential scientific value.
       Practically, you are wrong.
           I refer to the thousands of pottery vessels and
       ancient lamps that are essentially duplicates of
(35)   one another. In one small excavation in Cyprus,
       archaeologists recently uncovered 2,000 virtually
       indistinguishable small jugs in a single courtyard.
       Even precious royal seal impressions known as
       l'melekh handles have been found in abundance
(40)   —more than 4,000 examples so far.
           The basements of museums are simply not
       large enough to store the artifacts that are likely
       to be discovered in the future. There is not enough
       money even to catalog the finds; as a result, they

(45)   cannot be found again and become as inaccessible
       as if they had never been discovered. Indeed, with
       the help of a computer, sold artifacts could be more
       accessible than are the pieces stored in bulging
       museum basements. Prior to sale, each could be
(50)   photographed and the list of the purchasers could
       be maintained on the computer. A purchaser could
       even be required to agree to return the piece if it
       should become needed for scientific purposes.
           It would be unrealistic to suggest that illegal
(55)   digging would stop if artifacts were sold on the
       open market. But the demand for the clandestine
       product would be substantially reduced. Who would
       want an unmarked pot when another was available
       whose provenance was known, and that was dated
(60)   stratigraphically by the professional archaeologist
       who excavated it?

Questions 9–11 refer to the passage above.

9. The primary purpose of the passage is to propose

   (A) an alternative to museum display of artifacts

   (B) a way to curb illegal digging while benefiting the archaeological profession

   (C) a way to distinguish artifacts with scientific value from those that have no such value

   (D) the governmental regulation of archaeological sites

   (E) a new system for cataloging duplicate artifacts

10. The author implies that all of the following statements about duplicate artifacts are true EXCEPT

    (A) a market for such artifacts already exists

    (B) such artifacts seldom have scientific value

    (C) there is likely to be a continuing supply of such artifacts

    (D) museums are well supplied with examples of such artifacts

    (E) such artifacts frequently exceed in quality those already cataloged in museum collections

11. Which of the following is mentioned in the passage as a disadvantage of storing artifacts in museum basements?

    (A) Museum officials rarely allow scholars access to such artifacts.

    (B) Space that could be better used for display is taken up for storage.

    (C) Artifacts discovered in one excavation often become separated from each other.

    (D) Such artifacts are often damaged by variations in temperature and humidity.

    (E) Such artifacts often remain uncataloged and thus cannot be located once they are put in storage.

Line   Traditionally, the first firm to commercialize a
new technology has benefited from the unique
opportunity to shape product definitions, forcing
followers to adapt to a standard or invest in
(5)   an unproven alternative. Today, however, the
largest payoffs may go to companies that lead in
developing integrated approaches for successful
mass production and distribution.
        Producers of the Beta format for videocassette
(10)   recorders (VCRs), for example, were first to develop
the VCR commercially in 1975, but producers of the
rival VHS (Video Home System) format proved to be
more successful at forming strategic alliances with
other producers and distributors to manufacture
(15)   and market their VCR format. Seeking to maintain
exclusive control over VCR distribution, Beta
producers were reluctant to form such alliances and
eventually lost ground to VHS in the competition for
the global VCR market.
(20)   Despite Beta's substantial technological head
start and the fact that VHS was neither technically
better nor cheaper than Beta, developers of VHS
quickly turned a slight early lead in sales into a
dominant position. Strategic alignments with
(25)   producers of prerecorded tapes reinforced the VHS
advantage. The perception among consumers that
prerecorded tapes were more available in VHS
format further expanded VHS's share of the market.
By the end of the 1980s, Beta was no longer in
(30)   production.

Questions 12–17 refer to the passage above.

12. The passage is primarily concerned with which of
the following?

(A)   Evaluating two competing technologies
(B)   Tracing the impact of a new technology by
      narrating a sequence of events
(C)   Reinterpreting an event from contemporary
      business history
(D)   Illustrating a business strategy by means of a
      case history
(E)   Proposing an innovative approach to business
      planning

13. According to the passage, today's successful firms,
unlike successful firms in the past, may earn the
greatest profits by

(A)   investing in research to produce cheaper
      versions of existing technology
(B)   being the first to market a competing technology
(C)   adapting rapidly to a technological standard
      previously set by a competing firm
(D)   establishing technological leadership in order to
      shape product definitions in advance of
      competing firms
(E)   emphasizing the development of methods for
      the mass production and distribution of a new
      technology

14. According to the passage, consumers began to
develop a preference for VCRs in the VHS format
because they believed which of the following?

(A)   VCRs in the VHS format were technically better
      than competing format VCRs.
(B)   VCRs in the VHS format were less expensive
      than competing format VCRs.
(C)   VHS was the first standard format for VCRs.
(D)   VHS prerecorded videotapes were more
      available than those in Beta format.
(E)   VCRs in the Beta format would soon cease to
      be produced.

15. The author implies that one way that VHS producers won control over the VCR market was by

    (A) carefully restricting access to VCR technology
    (B) giving up a slight early lead in VCR sales in order to improve long-term prospects
    (C) retaining a strict monopoly on the production of prerecorded videotapes
    (D) sharing control of the marketing of VHS format VCRs
    (E) sacrificing technological superiority over Beta format VCRs in order to remain competitive in price

16. The alignment of producers of VHS format VCRs with producers of prerecorded videotapes is most similar to which of the following?

    (A) The alignment of an automobile manufacturer with another automobile manufacturer to adopt a standard design for automobile engines
    (B) The alignment of an automobile manufacturer with an automotive glass company whereby the manufacturer agrees to purchase automobile windshields only from that one glass company
    (C) The alignment of an automobile manufacturer with a petroleum company to ensure the widespread availability of the fuel required by a new type of engine developed by the manufacturer
    (D) The alignment of an automobile manufacturer with its dealers to adopt a plan to improve automobile design
    (E) The alignment of an automobile dealer with an automobile rental chain to adopt a strategy for an advertising campaign to promote a new type of automobile

17. Which of the following best describes the relation of the first paragraph to the passage as a whole?

    (A) It makes a general observation to be exemplified.
    (B) It outlines a process to be analyzed.
    (C) It poses a question to be answered.
    (D) It advances an argument to be disputed.
    (E) It introduces conflicting arguments to be reconciled.

Line   In terrestrial environments, gravity places
special demands on the cardiovascular systems of
animals. Gravitational pressure can cause blood to
pool in the lower regions of the body, making it
(5)   difficult to circulate blood to critical organs such as
the brain. Terrestrial snakes, in particular, exhibit
adaptations that aid in circulating blood against the
force of gravity.
       The problem confronting terrestrial snakes is best
(10)   illustrated by what happens to sea snakes when
removed from their supportive medium. Because the
vertical pressure gradients within the blood vessels
are counteracted by similar pressure gradients in the
surrounding water, the distribution of blood
(15)   throughout the body of sea snakes remains about
the same regardless of their orientation in space,
provided they remain in the ocean. When removed
from the water and tilted at various angles with the
head up, however, blood pressure at their midpoint
(20)   drops significantly, and at brain level falls to zero.
That many terrestrial snakes in similar spatial
orientations do not experience this kind of circulatory
failure suggests that certain adaptations enable them
to regulate blood pressure more effectively in those
(25)   orientations.
       One such adaptation is the closer proximity of the
terrestrial snake's heart to its head, which helps to
ensure circulation to the brain, regardless of the
snake's orientation in space. The heart of sea snakes
(30)   can be located near the middle of the body, a
position that minimizes the work entailed in
circulating blood to both extremities. In arboreal
snakes, however, which dwell in trees and often
assume a vertical posture, the average distance

(35)   from the heart to the head can be as little as 15
percent of overall body length. Such a location
requires that blood circulated to the tail of the
snake travel a greater distance back to the heart,
a problem solved by another adaptation. When
(40)   climbing, arboreal snakes often pause
momentarily to wiggle their bodies, causing waves
of muscle contraction that advance from the lower
torso to the head. By compressing the veins and
forcing blood forward, these contractions
(45)   apparently improve the flow of venous blood
returning to the heart.

Questions 18–25 refer to the passage above.

18. The passage provides information in support of which of the following assertions?

  (A) The disadvantages of an adaptation to a particular feature of an environment often outweigh the advantages of such an adaptation.

  (B) An organism's reaction to being placed in an environment to which it is not well adapted can sometimes illustrate the problems that have been solved by the adaptations of organisms indigenous to that environment.

  (C) The effectiveness of an organism's adaptation to a particular feature of its environment can only be evaluated by examining the effectiveness with which organisms of other species have adapted to a similar feature of a different environment.

  (D) Organisms of the same species that inhabit strikingly different environments will often adapt in remarkably similar ways to the few features of those environments that are common.

  (E) Different species of organisms living in the same environment will seldom adapt to features of that environment in the same way.

19. According to the passage, one reason that the distribution of blood in the sea snake changes little while the creature remains in the ocean is that

  (A) the heart of the sea snake tends to be located near the center of its body

  (B) pressure gradients in the water surrounding the sea snake counter the effects of vertical pressure gradients within its blood vessels

  (C) the sea snake assumes a vertical posture less frequently than do the terrestrial and the arboreal snake

  (D) the sea snake often relies on waves of muscle contractions to help move blood from the torso to the head

  (E) the force of pressure gradients in the water surrounding the sea snake exceeds that of vertical pressure gradients within its circulatory system

20. It can be inferred from the passage that which of the following is true of species of terrestrial snakes that often need to assume a vertical posture?

  (A) They are more likely to be susceptible to circulatory failure in vertical postures than are sea snakes.

  (B) Their hearts are less likely to be located at the midpoint of their bodies than is the case with sea snakes.

  (C) They cannot counteract the pooling of blood in lower regions of their bodies as effectively as sea snakes can.

  (D) The blood pressure at their midpoint decreases significantly when they are tilted with their heads up.

  (E) They are unable to rely on muscle contractions to move venous blood from the lower torso to the head.

21. The author describes the behavior of the circulatory system of sea snakes when they are removed from the ocean (see lines 17–20) primarily in order to

    (A) illustrate what would occur in the circulatory system of terrestrial snakes without adaptations that enable them to regulate their blood pressure in vertical orientations

    (B) explain why arboreal snakes in vertical orientations must rely on muscle contractions to restore blood pressure to the brain

    (C) illustrate the effects of circulatory failure on the behavior of arboreal snakes

    (D) illustrate the superiority of the circulatory system of the terrestrial snake to that of the sea snake

    (E) explain how changes in spatial orientation can adversely affect the circulatory system of snakes with hearts located in relatively close proximity to their heads

22. It can be inferred from the passage that which of the following is a true statement about sea snakes?

    (A) They frequently rely on waves of muscle contractions from the lower torso to the head to supplement the work of the heart.

    (B) They cannot effectively regulate their blood pressure when placed in seawater and tilted at an angle with the head pointed downward.

    (C) They are more likely to have a heart located in close proximity to their heads than are arboreal snakes.

    (D) They become acutely vulnerable to the effects of gravitational pressure on their circulatory system when they are placed in a terrestrial environment.

    (E) Their cardiovascular system is not as complicated as that of arboreal snakes.

23. The author suggests that which of the following is a disadvantage that results from the location of a snake's heart in close proximity to its head?

    (A) A decrease in the efficiency with which the snake regulates the flow of blood to the brain

    (B) A decrease in the number of orientations in space that a snake can assume without loss of blood flow to the brain

    (C) A decrease in blood pressure at the snake's midpoint when it is tilted at various angles with its head up

    (D) An increase in the tendency of blood to pool at the snake's head when the snake is tilted at various angles with its head down

    (E) An increase in the amount of effort required to distribute blood to and from the snake's tail

24. The primary purpose of the third paragraph is to

    (A) introduce a topic that is not discussed earlier in the passage

    (B) describe a more efficient method of achieving an effect discussed in the previous paragraph

    (C) draw a conclusion based on information elaborated in the previous paragraph

    (D) discuss two specific examples of phenomena mentioned at the end of the previous paragraph

    (E) introduce evidence that undermines a view reported earlier in the passage

25. In the passage, the author is primarily concerned with doing which of the following?

(A) Explaining adaptations that enable the terrestrial snake to cope with the effects of gravitational pressure on its circulatory system

(B) Comparing the circulatory system of the sea snake with that of the terrestrial snake

(C) Explaining why the circulatory system of the terrestrial snake is different from that of the sea snake

(D) Pointing out features of the terrestrial snake's cardiovascular system that make it superior to that of the sea snake

(E) Explaining how the sea snake is able to neutralize the effects of gravitational pressure on its circulatory system

Line   During the 1960s and 1970s, the primary
economic development strategy of local
governments in the United States was to attract
manufacturing industries. Unfortunately, this
(5)   strategy was usually implemented at another
community's expense: many manufacturing facilities
were lured away from their moorings elsewhere
through tax incentives and slick promotional efforts.
Through the transfer of jobs and related revenues
(10) that resulted from this practice, one town's triumph
could become another town's tragedy.
    In the 1980s the strategy shifted from this
zero-sum game to one called "high-technology
development," in which local governments
(15) competed to attract newly formed high-technology
manufacturing firms. Although this approach was
preferable to victimizing other geographical areas
by taking their jobs, it also had its shortcomings:
high-tech manufacturing firms employ only a
(20) specially trained fraction of the manufacturing
workforce, and there simply are not enough
high-tech firms to satisfy all geographic areas.
    Recently, local governments have increasingly
come to recognize the advantages of yet a third
(25) strategy: the promotion of homegrown small
businesses. Small indigenous businesses are
created by a nearly ubiquitous resource, local
entrepreneurs. With roots in their communities,
these individuals are less likely to be enticed away
(30) by incentives offered by another community.
Indigenous industry and talent are kept at home,
creating an environment that both provides jobs
and fosters further entrepreneurship.

Questions 26–30 refer to the passage above.

26. The primary purpose of the passage is to

(A) advocate more effective strategies for encouraging the development of high-technology enterprises in the United States

(B) contrast the incentives for economic development offered by local governments with those offered by the private sector

(C) acknowledge and counter adverse criticism of programs being used to stimulate local economic development

(D) define and explore promotional efforts used by local governments to attract new industry

(E) review and evaluate strategies and programs that have been used to stimulate economic development

27. The passage suggests which of the following about the majority of United States manufacturing industries before the high-technology development era of the 1980s?

(A) They lost many of their most innovative personnel to small entrepreneurial enterprises.

(B) They experienced a major decline in profits during the 1960s and 1970s.

(C) They could provide real economic benefits to the areas in which they were located.

(D) They employed workers who had no specialized skills.

(E) They actively interfered with local entrepreneurial ventures.

28. The tone of the passage suggests that the author is most optimistic about the economic development potential of which of the following groups?

(A) Local governments
(B) High-technology promoters
(C) Local entrepreneurs
(D) Manufacturing industry managers
(E) Economic development strategists

29. The passage does NOT state which of the following about local entrepreneurs?

    (A) They are found nearly everywhere.

    (B) They encourage further entrepreneurship.

    (C) They attract out-of-town investors.

    (D) They employ local workers.

    (E) They are established in their communities.

30. The author of the passage mentions which of the following as an advantage of high-technology development?

    (A) It encourages the modernization of existing manufacturing facilities.

    (B) It promotes healthy competition between rival industries.

    (C) It encourages the growth of related industries.

    (D) It takes full advantage of the existing workforce.

    (E) It does not advantage one local workforce at the expense of another.

Line   In 1988 services moved ahead of manufacturing as the main product of the United States economy. But what is meant by "services"? Some economists define a service as something
(5)   that is produced and consumed simultaneously, for example, a haircut. The broader, classical definition is that a service is an intangible something that cannot be touched or stored. Yet electric utilities can store energy, and computer programmers
(10)   save information electronically. Thus, the classical definition is hard to sustain.

    The United States government's definition is more practical: services are the residual category that includes everything that is not agriculture or
(15)   industry. Under this definition, services includes activities as diverse as engineering and driving a bus. However, besides lacking a strong conceptual framework, this definition fails to recognize the distinction between service industries and service
(20)   occupations. It categorizes workers based on their company's final product rather than on the actual work the employees perform. Thus, the many service workers employed by manufacturers— bookkeepers or janitors, for example—would
(25)   fall under the industrial rather than the services category. Such ambiguities reveal the arbitrariness of this definition and suggest that, although practical for government purposes, it does not accurately reflect the composition of the current
(30)   United States economy.

Questions 31–35 refer to the passage above.

31. The author of the passage is primarily concerned with

    (A)   discussing research data underlying several definitions
    (B)   arguing for the adoption of a particular definition
    (C)   exploring definitions of a concept
    (D)   comparing the advantages of several definitions
    (E)   clarifying some ambiguous definitions

32. In comparing the United States government's definition of services with the classical definition, the author suggests that the classical definition is

    (A)   more pragmatic
    (B)   more difficult to apply
    (C)   less ambiguous
    (D)   more widely used
    (E)   more arbitrary

33. The passage suggests which of the following about service workers in the United States?

    (A)   The number of service workers may be underestimated by the definition of services used by the government.
    (B)   There were fewer service workers than agricultural workers before 1988.
    (C)   The number of service workers was almost equal to the number of workers employed in manufacturing until 1988.
    (D)   Most service workers are employed in service occupations rather than in service industries.
    (E)   Most service workers are employed in occupations where they provide services that do not fall under the classical definition of services.

34. The author of the passage mentions which of the following as one disadvantage of the United States government's definition of services?

    (A) It is less useful than the other definitions mentioned in the passage.

    (B) It is narrower in scope than the other definitions mentioned in the passage.

    (C) It is based on the final product produced rather than on the type of work performed.

    (D) It does not recognize the diversity of occupations within the service industries.

    (E) It misclassifies many workers who are employed in service industries.

35. The author refers to "service workers employed by manufacturers" (line 23) primarily in order to point out

    (A) a type of worker not covered by the United States government's system of classifying occupations

    (B) a flaw in the United States government's definition of services

    (C) a factor that has influenced the growth of the service economy in the United States

    (D) a type of worker who is classified on the basis of work performed rather than on the basis of the company's final product

    (E) the diversity of the workers who are referred to as service workers

Line   Current feminist theory, in validating women's own
stories of their experience, has encouraged scholars
of women's history to view the use of women's oral
narratives as the methodology, next to the use of
(5)   women's written autobiography, that brings historians
closest to the "reality" of women's lives. Such
narratives, unlike most standard histories, represent
experience from the perspective of women, affirm
the importance of women's contributions, and furnish
(10)   present-day women with historical continuity that is
essential to their identity, individually and collectively.
      Scholars of women's history should, however, be
as cautious about accepting oral narratives at face
value as they already are about written memories.
(15)   Oral narratives are no more likely than are written
narratives to provide a disinterested commentary on
events or people. Moreover, the stories people tell to
explain themselves are shaped by narrative devices
and storytelling conventions, as well as by other
(20)   cultural and historical factors, in ways that the
storytellers may be unaware of. The political rhetoric
of a particular era, for example, may influence
women's interpretations of the significance of their
experience. Thus a woman who views the Second
(25)   World War as pivotal in increasing the social
acceptance of women's paid work outside the home
may reach that conclusion partly and unwittingly
because of wartime rhetoric encouraging a positive
view of women's participation in such work.

Questions 36–41 refer to the passage above.

36.   The passage is primarily concerned with

(A)   contrasting the benefits of one methodology
with the benefits of another

(B)   describing the historical origins and inherent
drawbacks of a particular methodology

(C)   discussing the appeal of a particular
methodology and some concerns about its use

(D)   showing that some historians' adoption of a
particular methodology has led to criticism of
recent historical scholarship

(E)   analyzing the influence of current feminist views
on women's interpretations of their experience

37.   According to the passage, which of the following
shapes the oral narratives of women storytellers?

(A)   The conventions for standard histories in the
culture in which a woman storyteller lives

(B)   The conventions of storytelling in the culture in
which a woman storyteller lives

(C)   A woman storyteller's experience with distinctive
traditions of storytelling developed by the
women in her family of origin

(D)   The cultural expectations and experiences of
those who listen to oral narratives

(E)   A woman storyteller's familiarity with the stories
that members of other groups in her culture tell
to explain themselves

375 Reading Comprehension Sample Questions

38. The author of the passage would be most likely to make which of the following recommendations to scholars of women's history?

    (A) They should take into account their own life experiences when interpreting the oral accounts of women's historical experiences.

    (B) They should assume that the observations made in women's oral narratives are believed by the intended audience of the story.

    (C) They should treat skeptically observations reported in oral narratives unless the observations can be confirmed in standard histories.

    (D) They should consider the cultural and historical context in which an oral narrative was created before arriving at an interpretation of such a narrative.

    (E) They should rely on information gathered from oral narratives only when equivalent information is not available in standard histories.

39. Which of the following best describes the function of the last sentence of the passage?

    (A) It describes an event that historians view as crucial in recent women's history.

    (B) It provides an example of how political rhetoric may influence the interpretations of experience reported in women's oral narratives.

    (C) It provides an example of an oral narrative that inaccurately describes women's experience during a particular historical period.

    (D) It illustrates the point that some women are more aware than others of the social forces that shape their oral narratives.

    (E) It identifies the historical conditions that led to the social acceptance of women's paid work outside the home.

40. According to the passage, scholars of women's history should refrain from doing which of the following?

    (A) Relying on traditional historical sources when women's oral narratives are unavailable

    (B) Focusing on the influence of political rhetoric on women's perceptions to the exclusion of other equally important factors

    (C) Attempting to discover the cultural and historical factors that influence the stories women tell

    (D) Assuming that the conventions of women's written autobiographies are similar to the conventions of women's oral narratives

    (E) Accepting women's oral narratives less critically than they accept women's written histories

41. According to the passage, each of the following is a difference between women's oral narratives and most standard histories EXCEPT:

    (A) Women's oral histories validate the significance of women's achievements.

    (B) Women's oral histories depict experience from the point of view of women.

    (C) Women's oral histories acknowledge the influence of well-known women.

    (D) Women's oral histories present today's women with a sense of their historical relationship to women of the past.

    (E) Women's oral histories are crucial to the collective identity of today's women.

Line   In recent years, teachers of introductory
courses in Asian American studies have been facing
a dilemma nonexistent a few decades ago, when
hardly any texts in that field were available. Today,
(5)   excellent anthologies and other introductory texts
exist, and books on individual Asian American
nationality groups and on general issues important
for Asian Americans are published almost weekly.
Even professors who are experts in the field find
(10)   it difficult to decide which of these to assign to
students; nonexperts who teach in related areas
and are looking for writings for and by Asian
Americans to include in survey courses are in an
even worse position.
(15)   A complicating factor has been the continuing
lack of specialized one-volume reference works on
Asian Americans, such as biographical dictionaries
or desktop encyclopedias. Such works would
enable students taking Asian American studies
(20)   courses (and professors in related fields) to look
up basic information on Asian American individuals,
institutions, history, and culture without having
to wade through mountains of primary source
material. In addition, given such works, Asian
(25)   American studies professors might feel more free to
include more challenging Asian American material in
their introductory reading lists, since good reference
works allow students to acquire on their own the
background information necessary to interpret
(30)   difficult or unfamiliar material.

Questions 42–46 refer to the passage above.

42. The author of the passage is primarily concerned with
doing which of the following?

    (A)   Recommending a methodology
    (B)   Describing a course of study
    (C)   Discussing a problem
    (D)   Evaluating a past course of action
    (E)   Responding to a criticism

43. The "dilemma" mentioned in line 3 can best be
characterized as being caused by the necessity to
make a choice when faced with a

    (A)   lack of acceptable alternatives
    (B)   lack of strict standards for evaluating
    alternatives
    (C)   preponderance of bad alternatives as
    compared to good
    (D)   multitude of different alternatives
    (E)   large number of alternatives that are nearly
    identical in content

44. The passage suggests that the factor mentioned in lines 15–18 complicates professors' attempts to construct introductory reading lists for courses in Asian American studies in which of the following ways?

   (A) By making it difficult for professors to identify primary source material and to obtain standard information on Asian American history and culture

   (B) By preventing professors from identifying excellent anthologies and introductory texts in the field that are both recent and understandable to students

   (C) By preventing professors from adequately evaluating the quality of the numerous texts currently being published in the field

   (D) By making it more necessary for professors to select readings for their courses that are not too challenging for students unfamiliar with Asian American history and culture

   (E) By making it more likely that the readings professors assign to students in their courses will be drawn solely from primary sources

45. The passage implies that which of the following was true of introductory courses in Asian American studies a few decades ago?

   (A) The range of different textbooks that could be assigned for such courses was extremely limited.

   (B) The texts assigned as readings in such courses were often not very challenging for students.

   (C) Students often complained about the texts assigned to them in such courses.

   (D) Such courses were offered only at schools whose libraries were rich in primary sources.

   (E) Such courses were the only means then available by which people in the United States could acquire knowledge of the field.

46. According to the passage, the existence of good one-volume reference works about Asian Americans could result in

   (A) increased agreement among professors of Asian American studies regarding the quality of the sources available in their field

   (B) an increase in the number of students signing up for introductory courses in Asian American studies

   (C) increased accuracy in writings that concern Asian American history and culture

   (D) the use of introductory texts about Asian American history and culture in courses outside the field of Asian American studies

   (E) the inclusion of a wider range of Asian American material in introductory reading lists in Asian American studies

Line   In the seventeenth-century Florentine textile
industry, women were employed primarily in low-
paying, low-skill jobs. To explain this segregation
of labor by gender, economists have relied on
(5)   the useful theory of human capital. According
to this theory, investment in human capital—the
acquisition of difficult job-related skills—generally
benefits individuals by making them eligible to
engage in well-paid occupations. Women's role as
(10)   child bearers, however, results in interruptions in
their participation in the job market (as compared
with men's) and thus reduces their opportunities
to acquire training for highly skilled work. In
addition, the human capital theory explains why
(15)   there was a high concentration of women workers
in certain low-skill jobs, such as weaving, but not
in others, such as combing or carding, by positing
that because of their primary responsibility in child
rearing women took occupations that could be
(20)   carried out in the home.
    There were, however, differences in pay scales
that cannot be explained by the human capital
theory. For example, male construction workers
were paid significantly higher wages than female
(25)   taffeta weavers. The wage difference between
these two low-skill occupations stems from the
segregation of labor by gender: because a limited
number of occupations were open to women, there
was a large supply of workers in their fields, and
(30)   this "overcrowding" resulted in women receiving
lower wages and men receiving higher wages.

Questions 47–49 refer to the passage above.

47. The passage suggests that combing and carding differ
from weaving in that combing and carding were

(A) low-skill jobs performed primarily by women
employees
(B) low-skill jobs that were not performed in the
home
(C) low-skill jobs performed by both male and
female employees
(D) high-skill jobs performed outside the home
(E) high-skill jobs performed by both male and
female employees

48. Which of the following, if true, would most weaken the
explanation provided by the human capital theory for
women's concentration in certain occupations in
seventeenth-century Florence?

(A) Women were unlikely to work outside the home
even in occupations whose hours were flexible
enough to allow women to accommodate
domestic tasks as well as paid labor.
(B) Parents were less likely to teach occupational
skills to their daughters than they were to their
sons.
(C) Women's participation in the Florentine paid
labor force grew steadily throughout the
sixteenth and seventeenth centuries.
(D) The vast majority of female weavers in the
Florentine wool industry had children.
(E) Few women worked as weavers in the Florentine
silk industry, which was devoted to making
cloths that required a high degree of skill to
produce.

49. The author of the passage would be most likely to describe the explanation provided by the human capital theory for the high concentration of women in certain occupations in the seventeenth-century Florentine textile industry as

    (A)　well founded though incomplete

    (B)　difficult to articulate

    (C)　plausible but poorly substantiated

    (D)　seriously flawed

    (E)　contrary to recent research

(This passage was adapted from an article written in 1992.)

Line   Some observers have attributed the dramatic
        growth in temporary employment that occurred in
        the United States during the 1980s to increased
        participation in the workforce by certain groups,
(5)   such as first-time or reentering workers, who
        supposedly prefer such arrangements. However,
        statistical analyses reveal that demographic
        changes in the workforce did not correlate with
        variations in the total number of temporary
(10)   workers. Instead, these analyses suggest that
        factors affecting employers account for the rise
        in temporary employment. One factor is product
        demand: temporary employment is favored by
        employers who are adapting to fluctuating demand
(15)   for products while at the same time seeking
        to reduce overall labor costs. Another factor
        is labor's reduced bargaining strength, which
        allows employers more control over the terms of
        employment. Given the analyses, which reveal that
(20)   growth in temporary employment now far exceeds
        the level explainable by recent workforce entry
        rates of groups said to prefer temporary jobs, firms
        should be discouraged from creating excessive
        numbers of temporary positions. Government
(25)   policymakers should consider mandating benefit
        coverage for temporary employees, promoting pay
        equity between temporary and permanent workers,
        assisting labor unions in organizing temporary
        workers, and encouraging firms to assign temporary
(30)   jobs primarily to employees who explicitly indicate
        that preference.

Questions 50–56 refer to the passage above.

50. The primary purpose of the passage is to

(A) present the results of statistical analyses and propose further studies

(B) explain a recent development and predict its eventual consequences

(C) identify the reasons for a trend and recommend measures to address it

(D) outline several theories about a phenomenon and advocate one of them

(E) describe the potential consequences of implementing a new policy and argue in favor of that policy

51. According to the passage, which of the following is true of the "factors affecting employers" that are mentioned in lines 10–19?

(A) Most experts cite them as having initiated the growth in temporary employment that occurred during the 1980s.

(B) They may account for the increase in the total number of temporary workers during the 1980s.

(C) They were less important than demographic change in accounting for the increase of temporary employment during the 1980s.

(D) They included a sharp increase in the cost of labor during the 1980s.

(E) They are more difficult to account for than are other factors involved in the growth of temporary employment during the 1980s.

52. The passage suggests which of the following about the use of temporary employment by firms during the 1980s?

    (A) It enabled firms to deal with fluctuating product demand far more efficiently than they did before the 1980s.

    (B) It increased as a result of increased participation in the workforce by certain demographic groups.

    (C) It was discouraged by government-mandated policies.

    (D) It was a response to preferences indicated by certain employees for more flexible working arrangements.

    (E) It increased partly as a result of workers' reduced ability to control the terms of their employment.

53. The passage suggests which of the following about the workers who took temporary jobs during the 1980s?

    (A) Their jobs frequently led to permanent positions within firms.

    (B) They constituted a less demographically diverse group than has been suggested.

    (C) They were occasionally involved in actions organized by labor unions.

    (D) Their pay declined during the decade in comparison with the pay of permanent employees.

    (E) They did not necessarily prefer temporary employment to permanent employment.

54. The first sentence in the passage suggests that the "observers" mentioned in line 1 would be most likely to predict which of the following?

    (A) That the number of new temporary positions would decline as fewer workers who preferred temporary employment entered the workforce

    (B) That the total number of temporary positions would increase as fewer workers were able to find permanent positions

    (C) That employers would have less control over the terms of workers' employment as workers increased their bargaining strength

    (D) That more workers would be hired for temporary positions as product demand increased

    (E) That the number of workers taking temporary positions would increase as more workers in any given demographic group entered the workforce

55. In the context of the passage, the word "excessive" (line 23) most closely corresponds to which of the following phrases?

    (A) Far more than can be justified by worker preferences

    (B) Far more than can be explained by fluctuations in product demand

    (C) Far more than can be beneficial to the success of the firms themselves

    (D) Far more than can be accounted for by an expanding national economy

    (E) Far more than can be attributed to increases in the total number of people in the workforce

56. The passage mentions each of the following as an appropriate kind of governmental action EXCEPT

    (A) getting firms to offer temporary employment primarily to a certain group of people

    (B) encouraging equitable pay for temporary and permanent employees

    (C) facilitating the organization of temporary workers by labor unions

    (D) establishing guidelines on the proportion of temporary workers that firms should employ

    (E) ensuring that temporary workers obtain benefits from their employers

Line   In *Winters v. United States* (1908), the Supreme
Court held that the right to use waters flowing through
or adjacent to the Fort Belknap Indian Reservation
was reserved to American Indians by the treaty
(5)   establishing the reservation. Although this treaty did
not mention water rights, the Court ruled that the
federal government, when it created the reservation,
intended to deal fairly with American Indians by
reserving for them the waters without which their
(10)   lands would have been useless. Later decisions, citing
Winters, established that courts can find federal rights
to reserve water for particular purposes if (1) the land
in question lies within an enclave under exclusive
federal jurisdiction, (2) the land has been formally
(15)   withdrawn from federal public lands—i.e., withdrawn
from the stock of federal lands available for private
use under federal land use laws—and set aside or
reserved, and (3) the circumstances reveal the
government intended to reserve water as well as land
(20)   when establishing the reservation.
    Some American Indian tribes have also established
water rights through the courts based on their
traditional diversion and use of certain waters prior to
the United States' acquisition of sovereignty. For
(25)   example, the Rio Grande pueblos already existed when
the United States acquired sovereignty over New
Mexico in 1848. Although they at that time became
part of the United States, the pueblo lands never
formally constituted a part of federal public lands; in
(30)   any event, no treaty, statute, or executive order has
ever designated or withdrawn the pueblos from public
lands as American Indian reservations. This fact,
however, has not barred application of the *Winters*
doctrine. What constitutes an American Indian
(35)   reservation is a question of practice, not of legal
definition, and the pueblos have always been treated
as reservations by the United States. This pragmatic
approach is buttressed by *Arizona v. California* (1963),
wherein the Supreme Court indicated that the manner
(40)   in which any type of federal reservation is created
does not affect the application to it of the *Winters*
doctrine. Therefore, the reserved water rights of
Pueblo Indians have priority over other citizens' water
rights as of 1848, the year in which pueblos must be
(45)   considered to have become reservations.

Questions 57–63 refer to the passage above.

57. According to the passage, which of the following was true of the treaty establishing the Fort Belknap Indian Reservation?

(A) It was challenged in the Supreme Court a number of times.

(B) It was rescinded by the federal government, an action that gave rise to the *Winters* case.

(C) It cited American Indians' traditional use of the land's resources.

(D) It failed to mention water rights to be enjoyed by the reservation's inhabitants.

(E) It was modified by the Supreme Court in *Arizona v. California*.

58. The passage suggests that, if the criteria discussed in lines 10–20 were the only criteria for establishing a reservation's water rights, which of the following would be true?

(A) The water rights of the inhabitants of the Fort Belknap Indian Reservation would not take precedence over those of other citizens.

(B) Reservations established before 1848 would be judged to have no water rights.

(C) There would be no legal basis for the water rights of the Rio Grande pueblos.

(D) Reservations other than American Indian reservations could not be created with reserved water rights.

(E) Treaties establishing reservations would have to mention water rights explicitly in order to reserve water for a particular purpose.

59. Which of the following most accurately summarizes the relationship between *Arizona v. California* in lines 38–42, and the criteria citing the *Winters* doctrine in lines 10–20?

    (A) *Arizona v. California* abolishes these criteria and establishes a competing set of criteria for applying the *Winters* doctrine.

    (B) *Arizona v. California* establishes that the *Winters* doctrine applies to a broader range of situations than those defined by these criteria.

    (C) *Arizona v. California* represents the sole example of an exception to the criteria as they were set forth in the *Winters* doctrine.

    (D) *Arizona v. California* does not refer to the *Winters* doctrine to justify water rights, whereas these criteria do rely on the *Winters* doctrine.

    (E) *Arizona v. California* applies the criteria derived from the *Winters* doctrine only to federal lands other than American Indian reservations.

60. The "pragmatic approach" mentioned in lines 37–38 of the passage is best defined as one that

    (A) grants recognition to reservations that were never formally established but that have traditionally been treated as such

    (B) determines the water rights of all citizens in a particular region by examining the actual history of water usage in that region

    (C) gives federal courts the right to reserve water along with land even when it is clear that the government originally intended to reserve only the land

    (D) bases the decision to recognize the legal rights of a group on the practical effect such a recognition is likely to have on other citizens

    (E) dictates that courts ignore precedents set by such cases as *Winters v. United States* in deciding what water rights belong to reserved land

61. The author cites the fact that the Rio Grande pueblos were never formally withdrawn from public lands primarily in order to do which of the following?

    (A) Suggest why it might have been argued that the *Winters* doctrine ought not to apply to pueblo lands

    (B) Imply that the United States never really acquired sovereignty over pueblo lands

    (C) Argue that the pueblo lands ought still to be considered part of federal public lands

    (D) Support the argument that the water rights of citizens other than American Indians are limited by the *Winters* doctrine

    (E) Suggest that federal courts cannot claim jurisdiction over cases disputing the traditional diversion and use of water by Pueblo Indians

62. The primary purpose of the passage is to

    (A) trace the development of laws establishing American Indian reservations

    (B) explain the legal bases for the water rights of American Indian tribes

    (C) question the legal criteria often used to determine the water rights of American Indian tribes

    (D) discuss evidence establishing the earliest date at which the federal government recognized the water rights of American Indians

    (E) point out a legal distinction between different types of American Indian reservations

63. The passage suggests that the legal rights of citizens other than American Indians to the use of water flowing into the Rio Grande pueblos are

    (A) guaranteed by the precedent set in *Arizona v. California*

    (B) abolished by the *Winters* doctrine

    (C) deferred to the Pueblo Indians whenever treaties explicitly require this

    (D) guaranteed by federal land-use laws

    (E) limited by the prior claims of the Pueblo Indians

Line   Many United States companies have,
unfortunately, made the search for legal protection
from import competition into a major line of
work. Since 1980 the United States International
(5) Trade Commission (ITC) has received about 280
complaints alleging damage from imports that
benefit from subsidies by foreign governments.
Another 340 charge that foreign companies
"dumped" their products in the United States at
(10) "less than fair value." Even when no unfair practices
are alleged, the simple claim that an industry has
been injured by imports is sufficient grounds to
seek relief.
    Contrary to the general impression, this quest
(15) for import relief has hurt more companies than
it has helped. As corporations begin to function
globally, they develop an intricate web of marketing,
production, and research relationships. The complexity
of these relationships makes it unlikely that a system
(20) of import relief laws will meet the strategic needs of
all the units under the same parent company.
    Internationalization increases the danger that
foreign companies will use import relief laws against
the very companies the laws were designed to
(25) protect. Suppose a United States–owned company
establishes an overseas plant to manufacture
a product while its competitor makes the same
product in the United States. If the competitor can
prove injury from the imports—and that the United
(30) States company received a subsidy from a foreign
government to build its plant abroad—the United
States company's products will be uncompetitive in
the United States, since they would be subject to
duties.
(35)   Perhaps the most brazen case occurred when
the ITC investigated allegations that Canadian
companies were injuring the United States salt
industry by dumping rock salt, used to de-ice roads.
The bizarre aspect of the complaint was that a
(40) foreign conglomerate with United States operations
was crying for help against a United States
company with foreign operations. The "United
States" company claiming injury was a subsidiary
of a Dutch conglomerate, while the "Canadian"
(45) companies included a subsidiary of a Chicago firm
that was the second-largest domestic producer of
rock salt.

Questions 64–69 refer to the passage above.

64. The passage is chiefly concerned with

(A) arguing against the increased internationalization of United States corporations

(B) warning that the application of laws affecting trade frequently has unintended consequences

(C) demonstrating that foreign-based firms receive more subsidies from their governments than United States firms receive from the United States government

(D) advocating the use of trade restrictions for "dumped" products but not for other imports

(E) recommending a uniform method for handling claims of unfair trade practices

65. It can be inferred from the passage that the minimal basis for a complaint to the International Trade Commission is which of the following?

(A) A foreign competitor has received a subsidy from a foreign government.

(B) A foreign competitor has substantially increased the volume of products shipped to the United States.

(C) A foreign competitor is selling products in the United States at less than fair market value.

(D) The company requesting import relief has been injured by the sale of imports in the United States.

(E) The company requesting import relief has been barred from exporting products to the country of its foreign competitor.

66. The last paragraph performs which of the following functions in the passage?

    (A) It summarizes the discussion thus far and suggests additional areas for research.

    (B) It presents a recommendation based on the evidence presented earlier.

    (C) It discusses an exceptional case in which the results expected by the author of the passage were not obtained.

    (D) It introduces an additional area of concern not mentioned earlier.

    (E) It cites a specific case that illustrates a problem presented more generally in the previous paragraph.

67. The passage warns of which of the following dangers?

    (A) Companies in the United States may receive no protection from imports unless they actively seek protection from import competition.

    (B) Companies that seek legal protection from import competition may incur legal costs that far exceed any possible gain.

    (C) Companies that are United States owned but operate internationally may not be eligible for protection from import competition under the laws of the countries in which their plants operate.

    (D) Companies that are not United States owned may seek legal protection from import competition under United States import relief laws.

    (E) Companies in the United States that import raw materials may have to pay duties on those materials.

68. The passage suggests that which of the following is most likely to be true of United States trade laws?

    (A) They will eliminate the practice of "dumping" products in the United States.

    (B) They will enable manufacturers in the United States to compete more profitably outside the United States.

    (C) They will affect United States trade with Canada more negatively than trade with other nations.

    (D) Those that help one unit within a parent company will not necessarily help other units in the company.

    (E) Those that are applied to international companies will accomplish their intended result.

69. It can be inferred from the passage that the author believes which of the following about the complaint mentioned in the last paragraph?

    (A) The ITC acted unfairly toward the complainant in its investigation.

    (B) The complaint violated the intent of import relief laws.

    (C) The response of the ITC to the complaint provided suitable relief from unfair trade practices to the complainant.

    (D) The ITC did not have access to appropriate information concerning the case.

    (E) Each of the companies involved in the complaint acted in its own best interest.

Line   Milankovitch proposed in the early twentieth
century that the ice ages were caused by variations
in the Earth's orbit around the Sun. For some
time this theory was considered untestable,
(5)   largely because there was no sufficiently precise
chronology of the ice ages with which the orbital
variations could be matched.

To establish such a chronology it is necessary
to determine the relative amounts of land ice that
(10)   existed at various times in the Earth's past. A recent
discovery makes such a determination possible:
relative land-ice volume for a given period can be
deduced from the ratio of two oxygen isotopes,
16 and 18, found in ocean sediments. Almost
(15)   all the oxygen in water is oxygen 16, but a few
molecules out of every thousand incorporate the
heavier isotope 18. When an ice age begins, the
continental ice sheets grow, steadily reducing the
amount of water evaporated from the ocean that
(20)   will eventually return to it. Because heavier isotopes
tend to be left behind when water evaporates
from the ocean surfaces, the remaining ocean
water becomes progressively enriched in oxygen
18. The degree of enrichment can be determined
(25)   by analyzing ocean sediments of the period,
because these sediments are composed of calcium
carbonate shells of marine organisms, shells that
were constructed with oxygen atoms drawn from
the surrounding ocean. The higher the ratio of
(30)   oxygen 18 to oxygen 16 in a sedimentary specimen,
the more land ice there was when the sediment
was laid down.

As an indicator of shifts in the Earth's climate,
the isotope record has two advantages. First, it is
(35)   a global record: there is remarkably little variation
in isotope ratios in sedimentary specimens taken
from different continental locations. Second, it is
a more continuous record than that taken from
rocks on land. Because of these advantages,
(40)   sedimentary evidence can be dated with sufficient
accuracy by radiometric methods to establish a
precise chronology of the ice ages. The dated
isotope record shows that the fluctuations in
global ice volume over the past several hundred

(45)   thousand years have a pattern: an ice age occurs
roughly once every 100,000 years. These data have
established a strong connection between variations
in the Earth's orbit and the periodicity of the ice
ages.
(50)   However, it is important to note that other
factors, such as volcanic particulates or variations
in the amount of sunlight received by the Earth,
could potentially have affected the climate. The
advantage of the Milankovitch theory is that it
(55)   is testable; changes in the Earth's orbit can be
calculated and dated by applying Newton's laws
of gravity to progressively earlier configurations
of the bodies in the solar system. Yet the lack of
information about other possible factors affecting
(60)   global climate does not make them unimportant.

Questions 70–75 refer to the passage above.

70.   In the passage, the author is primarily interested in

(A)   suggesting an alternative to an outdated
research method
(B)   introducing a new research method that calls an
accepted theory into question
(C)   emphasizing the instability of data gathered
from the application of a new scientific method
(D)   presenting a theory and describing a new
method to test that theory
(E)   initiating a debate about a widely accepted
theory

71.   The author of the passage would be most likely to
agree with which of the following statements about the
Milankovitch theory?

(A)   It is the only possible explanation for the ice
ages.
(B)   It is too limited to provide a plausible explanation
for the ice ages, despite recent research
findings.
(C)   It cannot be tested and confirmed until further
research on volcanic activity is done.
(D)   It is one plausible explanation, though not the
only one, for the ice ages.
(E)   It is not a plausible explanation for the ice ages,
although it has opened up promising possibilities
for future research.

72. It can be inferred from the passage that the isotope record taken from ocean sediments would be less useful to researchers if which of the following were true?

    (A) It indicated that lighter isotopes of oxygen predominated at certain times.

    (B) It had far more gaps in its sequence than the record taken from rocks on land.

    (C) It indicated that climate shifts did not occur every 100,000 years.

    (D) It indicated that the ratios of oxygen 16 and oxygen 18 in ocean water were not consistent with those found in fresh water.

    (E) It stretched back for only a million years.

73. According to the passage, which of the following is true of the ratios of oxygen isotopes in ocean sediments?

    (A) They indicate that sediments found during an ice age contain more calcium carbonate than sediments formed at other times.

    (B) They are less reliable than the evidence from rocks on land in determining the volume of land ice.

    (C) They can be used to deduce the relative volume of land ice that was present when the sediment was laid down.

    (D) They are more unpredictable during an ice age than in other climatic conditions.

    (E) They can be used to determine atmospheric conditions at various times in the past.

74. It can be inferred from the passage that precipitation formed from evaporated ocean water has

    (A) the same isotopic ratio as ocean water

    (B) less oxygen 18 than does ocean water

    (C) less oxygen 18 than has the ice contained in continental ice sheets

    (D) a different isotopic composition than has precipitation formed from water on land

    (E) more oxygen 16 than has precipitation formed from fresh water

75. It can be inferred from the passage that calcium carbonate shells

    (A) are not as susceptible to deterioration as rocks

    (B) are less common in sediments formed during an ice age

    (C) are found only in areas that were once covered by land ice

    (D) contain radioactive material that can be used to determine a sediment's isotopic composition

    (E) reflect the isotopic composition of the water at the time the shells were formed

Line   Two works published in 1984 demonstrate
contrasting approaches to writing the history of
United States women. Buel and Buel's biography of
Mary Fish (1736–1818) makes little effort to place
(5)   her story in the context of recent historiography on
women. Lebsock, meanwhile, attempts not only to
write the history of women in one southern
community, but also to redirect two decades of
historiographical debate as to whether women
(10)   gained or lost status in the nineteenth century as
compared with the eighteenth century. Although
both books offer the reader the opportunity to
assess this controversy regarding women's status,
only Lebsock's deals with it directly. She examines
(15)   several different aspects of women's status, helping
to refine and resolve the issues. She concludes that
while women gained autonomy in some areas,
especially in the private sphere, they lost it in many
aspects of the economic sphere. More importantly,
(20)   she shows that the debate itself depends on frame
of reference: in many respects, women lost power
in relation to men, for example, as certain jobs
(delivering babies, supervising schools) were taken
over by men. Yet women also gained power in
(25)   comparison with their previous status, owning a
higher proportion of real estate, for example. In
contrast, Buel and Buel's biography provides ample
raw material for questioning the myth, fostered by
some historians, of a colonial golden age in the
(30)   eighteenth century but does not give the reader
much guidance in analyzing the controversy over
women's status.

Questions 76–81 refer to the passage above.

76.   The primary purpose of the passage is to

(A)   examine two sides of a historiographical debate

(B)   call into question an author's approach to a historiographical debate

(C)   examine one author's approach to a historiographical debate

(D)   discuss two authors' works in relationship to a historiographical debate

(E)   explain the prevalent perspective on a historiographical debate

77.   The author of the passage mentions the supervision of schools primarily in order to

(A)   remind readers of the role education played in the cultural changes of the nineteenth century in the United States

(B)   suggest an area in which nineteenth-century American women were relatively free to exercise power

(C)   provide an example of an occupation for which accurate data about women's participation are difficult to obtain

(D)   speculate about which occupations were considered suitable for United States women of the nineteenth century

(E)   illustrate how the answers to questions about women's status depend on particular contexts

78. With which of the following characterizations of Lebsock's contribution to the controversy concerning women's status in the nineteenth-century United States would the author of the passage be most likely to agree?

    (A) Lebsock has studied women from a formerly neglected region and time period.

    (B) Lebsock has demonstrated the importance of frame of reference in answering questions about women's status.

    (C) Lebsock has addressed the controversy by using women's current status as a frame of reference.

    (D) Lebsock has analyzed statistics about occupations and property that were previously ignored.

    (E) Lebsock has applied recent historiographical methods to the biography of a nineteenth-century woman.

79. According to the passage, Lebsock's work differs from Buel and Buel's work in that Lebsock's work

    (A) uses a large number of primary sources

    (B) ignores issues of women's legal status

    (C) refuses to take a position on women's status in the eighteenth century

    (D) addresses larger historiographical issues

    (E) fails to provide sufficient material to support its claims

80. The passage suggests that Lebsock believes that compared to nineteenth-century American women, eighteenth-century American women were

    (A) in many respects less powerful in relation to men

    (B) more likely to own real estate

    (C) generally more economically independent

    (D) more independent in conducting their private lives

    (E) less likely to work as school superintendents

81. The passage suggests that Buel and Buel's biography of Mary Fish provides evidence for which of the following views of women's history?

    (A) Women have lost power in relation to men since the colonial era.

    (B) Women of the colonial era were not as likely to be concerned with their status as were women in the nineteenth century.

    (C) The colonial era was not as favorable for women as some historians have believed.

    (D) Women had more economic autonomy in the colonial era than in the nineteenth century.

    (E) Women's occupations were generally more respected in the colonial era than in the nineteenth century.

Line   It was once believed that the brain was independent of metabolic processes occurring elsewhere in the body. In recent studies, however, we have discovered that the production and release

(5)   in brain neurons of the neurotransmitter serotonin (neurotransmitters are compounds that neurons use to transmit signals to other cells) depend directly on the food that the body processes.

Our first studies sought to determine whether

(10)   the increase in serotonin observed in rats given a large injection of the amino acid tryptophan might also occur after rats ate meals that change tryptophan levels in the blood. We found that, immediately after the rats began to eat, parallel

(15)   elevations occurred in blood tryptophan, brain tryptophan, and brain serotonin levels. These findings suggested that the production and release of serotonin in brain neurons were normally coupled with blood-tryptophan increases. In later studies we

(20)   found that injecting insulin into a rat's bloodstream also caused parallel elevations in blood and brain tryptophan levels and in serotonin levels. We then decided to see whether the secretion of the animal's own insulin similarly affected serotonin production.

(25)   We gave the rats a carbohydrate-containing meal that we knew would elicit insulin secretion. As we had hypothesized, the blood tryptophan level and the concentrations of tryptophan and of serotonin in the brain increased after the meal.

(30)   Surprisingly, however, when we added a large amount of protein to the meal, brain tryptophan and serotonin levels fell. Since protein contains tryptophan, why should it depress brain tryptophan levels? The answer lies in the mechanism that

(35)   provides blood tryptophan to the brain cells. This same mechanism also provides the brain cells with other amino acids found in protein, such as tyrosine and leucine. The consumption of protein increases blood concentration of the other amino acids much

(40)   more, proportionately, than it does that of tryptophan. The more protein is in a meal, the lower is the ratio of the resulting blood-tryptophan concentration to the concentration of competing amino acids, and the more slowly is tryptophan provided to the brain.

(45)   Thus the more protein in a meal, the less serotonin subsequently produced and released.

Questions 82–90 refer to the passage above.

82.   Which of the following titles best summarizes the contents of the passage?

(A)   Neurotransmitters: Their Crucial Function in Cellular Communication

(B)   Diet and Survival: An Old Relationship Reexamined

(C)   The Blood Supply and the Brain: A Reciprocal Dependence

(D)   Amino Acids and Neurotransmitters: The Connection between Serotonin Levels and Tyrosine

(E)   The Effects of Food Intake on the Production and Release of Serotonin: Some Recent Findings

83.   According to the passage, the speed with which tryptophan is provided to the brain cells of a rat varies with the

(A)   amount of protein present in a meal

(B)   concentration of serotonin in the brain before a meal

(C)   concentration of leucine in the blood rather than with the concentration of tyrosine in the blood after a meal

(D)   concentration of tryptophan in the brain before a meal

(E)   number of serotonin-containing neurons

84.   According to the passage, when the authors began their first studies, they were aware that

(A)   they would eventually need to design experiments that involved feeding rats high concentrations of protein

(B)   tryptophan levels in the blood were difficult to monitor with accuracy

(C)   serotonin levels increased after rats were fed meals rich in tryptophan

(D)   there were many neurotransmitters whose production was dependent on metabolic processes elsewhere in the body

(E)   serotonin levels increased after rats were injected with a large amount of tryptophan

85. According to the passage, one reason that the authors gave rats carbohydrates was to

    (A) depress the rats' tryptophan levels
    (B) prevent the rats from contracting diseases
    (C) cause the rats to produce insulin
    (D) demonstrate that insulin is the most important substance secreted by the body
    (E) compare the effect of carbohydrates with the effect of proteins

86. According to the passage, the more protein a rat consumes, the lower will be the

    (A) ratio of the rat's blood-tryptophan concentration to the amount of serotonin produced and released in the rat's brain
    (B) ratio of the rat's blood-tryptophan concentration to the concentration in its blood of the other amino acids contained in the protein
    (C) ratio of the rat's blood-tyrosine concentration to its blood-leucine concentration
    (D) number of neurotransmitters of any kind that the rat will produce and release
    (E) number of amino acids the rat's blood will contain

87. The authors' discussion of the "mechanism that provides blood tryptophan to the brain cells" (lines 34–35) is meant to

    (A) stimulate further research studies
    (B) summarize an area of scientific investigation
    (C) help explain why a particular research finding was obtained
    (D) provide supporting evidence for a controversial scientific theory
    (E) refute the conclusions of a previously mentioned research study

88. According to the passage, an injection of insulin was most similar in its effect on rats to an injection of

    (A) tyrosine
    (B) leucine
    (C) blood
    (D) tryptophan
    (E) protein

89. It can be inferred from the passage that which of the following would be LEAST likely to be a potential source of aid to a patient who was not adequately producing and releasing serotonin?

    (A) Meals consisting almost exclusively of protein
    (B) Meals consisting almost exclusively of carbohydrates
    (C) Meals that would elicit insulin secretion
    (D) Meals that had very low concentrations of tyrosine
    (E) Meals that had very low concentrations of leucine

90. It can be inferred from the passage that the authors initially held which of the following hypotheses about what would happen when they fed large amounts of protein to rats?

    (A) The rats' brain serotonin levels would not decrease.
    (B) The rats' brain tryptophan levels would decrease.
    (C) The rats' tyrosine levels would increase less quickly than would their leucine levels.
    (D) The rats would produce more insulin.
    (E) The rats would produce neurotransmitters other than serotonin.

Line   In 1955 Maurice Duverger published *The*
Political Role of Women, the first behavioralist,
multinational comparison of women's electoral
participation ever to use election data and survey
(5)   data together. His study analyzed women's patterns
of voting, political candidacy, and political activism
in four European countries during the first half of
the twentieth century. Duverger's research findings
were that women voted somewhat less frequently
(10)   than men (the difference narrowing the longer
women had the vote) and were slightly more
conservative.
     Duverger's work set an early standard for the
sensitive analysis of women's electoral activities.
(15)   Moreover, to Duverger's credit, he placed his
findings in the context of many of the historical
processes that had shaped these activities.
However, since these contexts have changed
over time, Duverger's approach has proved more
(20)   durable than his actual findings. In addition,
Duverger's discussion of his findings was hampered
by his failure to consider certain specific factors
important to women's electoral participation
at the time he collected his data: the influence
(25)   of political regimes, the effects of economic
factors, and the ramifications of political and
social relations between women and men. Given
this failure, Duverger's study foreshadowed the
enduring limitations of the behavioralist approach
(30)   to the multinational study of women's political
participation.

Questions 91–96 refer to the passage above.

91.   The primary purpose of the passage is to

(A)   evaluate a research study

(B)   summarize the history of a research area

(C)   report new research findings

(D)   reinterpret old research findings

(E)   reconcile conflicting research findings

92.   According to the passage, Duverger's study was
unique in 1955 in that it

(A)   included both election data and survey data

(B)   gathered data from sources never before used
in political studies

(C)   included an analysis of historical processes

(D)   examined the influence on voting behavior of the
relationships between women and men

(E)   analyzed not only voting and political candidacy
but also other political activities

93.   Which of the following characteristics of a country is
most clearly an example of a factor that Duverger, as
described in the passage, failed to consider in his
study?

(A)   A large population

(B)   A predominantly Protestant population

(C)   A predominantly urban population

(D)   A one-party government

(E)   Location in the heart of Europe

94. The author implies that Duverger's actual findings are

    (A) limited because they focus on only four
         countries
    (B) inaccurate in their description of the four
         countries in the early 1950s
    (C) out-of-date in that they are inapplicable in the
         four countries today
    (D) flawed because they are based on unsound data
    (E) biased by Duverger's political beliefs

95. The passage implies that, in comparing four European
    countries, Duverger found that the voting rates of
    women and men were most different in the country in
    which women

    (A) were most politically active
    (B) ran for office most often
    (C) held the most conservative political views
    (D) had the most egalitarian relations with men
    (E) had possessed the right to vote for the
         shortest time

96. The author implies that some behavioralist research
    involving the multinational study of women's political
    participation that followed Duverger's study did which
    of the following?

    (A) Ignored Duverger's approach
    (B) Suffered from faults similar to those in
         Duverger's study
    (C) Focused on political activism
    (D) Focused on the influences of political regimes
    (E) Focused on the political and social relations
         between women and men

Line   The majority of successful senior managers do
          not closely follow the classical rational model of first
          clarifying goals, assessing the problem, formulating
          options, estimating likelihoods of success, making a
(5)   decision, and only then taking action to implement
          the decision. Rather, in their day-by-day tactical
          maneuvers, these senior executives rely on what is
          vaguely termed "intuition" to manage a network of
          interrelated problems that require them to deal with
(10)   ambiguity, inconsistency, novelty, and surprise; and
          to integrate action into the process of thinking.
              Generations of writers on management have
          recognized that some practicing managers rely
          heavily on intuition. In general, however, such
(15)   writers display a poor grasp of what intuition is.
          Some see it as the opposite of rationality; others
          view it as an excuse for capriciousness.
              Isenberg's recent research on the cognitive
          processes of senior managers reveals that
(20)   managers' intuition is neither of these. Rather,
          senior managers use intuition in at least five distinct
          ways. First, they intuitively sense when a problem
          exists. Second, managers rely on intuition to
          perform well-learned behavior patterns rapidly. This
(25)   intuition is not arbitrary or irrational, but is based
          on years of painstaking practice and hands-on
          experience that build skills. A third function of
          intuition is to synthesize isolated bits of data and
          practice into an integrated picture, often in
(30)   an "Aha!" experience. Fourth, some managers use
          intuition as a check on the results of more rational
          analysis. Most senior executives are familiar with
          the formal decision analysis models and tools,
          and those who use such systematic methods
(35)   for reaching decisions are occasionally leery of
          solutions suggested by these methods which run
          counter to their sense of the correct course of
          action. Finally, managers can use intuition to bypass
          in-depth analysis and move rapidly to engender a
(40)   plausible solution. Used in this way, intuition is an
          almost instantaneous cognitive process in which a
          manager recognizes familiar patterns.
              One of the implications of the intuitive style
          of executive management is that "thinking" is
(45)   inseparable from acting. Since managers often "know"
          what is right before they can analyze and explain it,
          they frequently act first and explain later. Analysis is
          inextricably tied to action in thinking/acting cycles,
          in which managers develop thoughts about their

(50)   companies and organizations not by analyzing a
          problematic situation and then acting, but by acting
          and analyzing in close concert. Given the great
          uncertainty of many of the management issues that
          they face, senior managers often instigate a course
(55)   of action simply to learn more about an issue.
          They then use the results of the action to develop
          a more complete understanding of the issue. One
          implication of thinking/acting cycles is that action
          is often part of defining the problem, not just of
(60)   implementing the solution.

Questions 97–102 refer to the passage above.

97.   According to the passage, senior managers use
      intuition in all of the following ways EXCEPT to

      (A)   speed up the creation of a solution to a problem
      (B)   identify a problem
      (C)   bring together disparate facts
      (D)   stipulate clear goals
      (E)   evaluate possible solutions to a problem

98.   The passage suggests which of the following about
      the "writers on management" mentioned in line 12?

      (A)   They have criticized managers for not following
            the classical rational model of decision analysis.
      (B)   They have not based their analyses on a
            sufficiently large sample of actual managers.
      (C)   They have relied in drawing their conclusions on
            what managers say rather than on what
            managers do.
      (D)   They have misunderstood how managers use
            intuition in making business decisions.
      (E)   They have not acknowledged the role of intuition
            in managerial practice.

99. Which of the following best exemplifies "an 'Aha!' experience" (line 30) as it is presented in the passage?

    (A) A manager risks taking an action whose outcome is unpredictable to discover whether the action changes the problem at hand.

    (B) A manager performs well-learned and familiar behavior patterns in creative and uncharacteristic ways to solve a problem.

    (C) A manager suddenly connects seemingly unrelated facts and experiences to create a pattern relevant to the problem at hand.

    (D) A manager rapidly identifies the methodology used to compile data yielded by systematic analysis.

    (E) A manager swiftly decides which of several sets of tactics to implement in order to deal with the contingencies suggested by a problem.

100. According to the passage, the classical model of decision analysis includes all of the following EXCEPT

    (A) evaluation of a problem

    (B) creation of possible solutions to a problem

    (C) establishment of clear goals to be reached by the decision

    (D) action undertaken in order to discover more information about a problem

    (E) comparison of the probable effects of different solutions to a problem

101. It can be inferred from the passage that which of the following would most probably be one major difference in behavior between Manager X, who uses intuition to reach decisions, and Manager Y, who uses only formal decision analysis?

    (A) Manager X analyzes first and then acts; Manager Y does not.

    (B) Manager X checks possible solutions to a problem by systematic analysis; Manager Y does not.

    (C) Manager X takes action in order to arrive at the solution to a problem; Manager Y does not.

    (D) Manager Y draws on years of hands-on experience in creating a solution to a problem; Manager X does not.

    (E) Manager Y depends on day-to-day tactical maneuvering; Manager X does not.

102. The passage provides support for which of the following statements?

    (A) Managers who rely on intuition are more successful than those who rely on formal decision analysis.

    (B) Managers cannot justify their intuitive decisions.

    (C) Managers' intuition works contrary to their rational and analytical skills.

    (D) Logical analysis of a problem increases the number of possible solutions.

    (E) Intuition enables managers to employ their practical experience more efficiently.

Line   Frazier and Mosteller assert that medical
        research could be improved by a move toward
        larger, simpler clinical trials of medical treatments.
        Currently, researchers collect far more background
(5)   information on patients than is strictly required for
        their trials—substantially more than hospitals
        collect—thereby escalating costs of data
        collection, storage, and analysis. Although limiting
        information collection could increase the risk that
(10)   researchers will overlook facts relevant to a study,
        Frazier and Mosteller contend that such risk, never
        entirely eliminable from research, would still be
        small in most studies. Only in research on entirely
        new treatments are new and unexpected variables
(15)   likely to arise.
        Frazier and Mosteller propose not only that
        researchers limit data collection on individual
        patients but also that researchers enroll more
        patients in clinical trials, thereby obtaining a more
(20)   representative sample of the total population with
        the disease under study. Often researchers restrict
        study participation to patients who have no
        ailments besides those being studied. A treatment
        judged successful under these ideal conditions can
(25)   then be evaluated under normal conditions.
        Broadening the range of trial participants, Frazier
        and Mosteller suggest, would enable researchers to
        evaluate a treatment's efficacy for diverse patients
        under various conditions and to evaluate its
(30)   effectiveness for different patient subgroups. For
        example, the value of a treatment for a progressive
        disease may vary according to a patient's stage of
        disease. Patients' ages may also affect a
        treatment's efficacy.

Questions 103–107 refer to the passage above.

103.   The passage is primarily concerned with

       (A)   identifying two practices in medical research
             that may affect the accuracy of clinical trials

       (B)   describing aspects of medical research that
             tend to drive up costs

       (C)   evaluating an analysis of certain shortcomings
             of current medical research practices

       (D)   describing proposed changes to the ways in
             which clinical trials are conducted

       (E)   explaining how medical researchers have
             traditionally conducted clinical trials and how
             such trials are likely to change

104.   Which of the following can be inferred from the
       passage about a study of the category of patients
       referred to in lines 21–23?

       (A)   Its findings might have limited applicability.

       (B)   It would be prohibitively expensive in its attempt
             to create ideal conditions.

       (C)   It would be the best way to sample the total
             population of potential patients.

       (D)   It would allow researchers to limit information
             collection without increasing the risk that
             important variables could be overlooked.

       (E)   Its findings would be more accurate if it
             concerned treatments for a progressive disease
             than if it concerned treatments for a
             nonprogressive disease.

105. It can be inferred from the passage that a study limited to patients like those mentioned in lines 21–23 would have which of the following advantages over the kind of study proposed by Frazier and Mosteller?

    (A) It would yield more data and its findings would be more accurate.

    (B) It would cost less in the long term, though it would be more expensive in its initial stages.

    (C) It would limit the number of variables researchers would need to consider when evaluating the treatment under study.

    (D) It would help researchers to identify subgroups of patients with secondary conditions that might also be treatable.

    (E) It would enable researchers to assess the value of an experimental treatment for the average patient.

106. The author mentions patients' ages (line 33) primarily in order to

    (A) identify the most critical variable differentiating subgroups of patients

    (B) cast doubt on the advisability of implementing Frazier and Mosteller's proposals about medical research

    (C) indicate why progressive diseases may require different treatments at different stages

    (D) illustrate a point about the value of enrolling a wide range of patients in clinical trials

    (E) substantiate an argument about the problems inherent in enrolling large numbers of patients in clinical trials

107. According to the passage, which of the following describes a result of the way in which researchers generally conduct clinical trials?

    (A) They expend resources on the storage of information likely to be irrelevant to the study they are conducting.

    (B) They sometimes compromise the accuracy of their findings by collecting and analyzing more information than is strictly required for their trials.

    (C) They avoid the risk of overlooking variables that might affect their findings, even though doing so raises their research costs.

    (D) Because they attempt to analyze too much information, they overlook facts that could emerge as relevant to their studies.

    (E) In order to approximate the conditions typical of medical treatment, they base their methods of information collection on those used by hospitals.

Line   According to a recent theory, Archean-age
gold-quartz vein systems were formed more than
two billion years ago from magmatic fluids that
originated from molten granite-like bodies deep
(5)   beneath the surface of the Earth. This theory is
contrary to the widely held view that the systems
were deposited from metamorphic fluids, that is,
from fluids that formed during the dehydration of
wet sedimentary rocks.
(10)   The recently developed theory has considerable
practical importance. Most of the gold deposits
discovered during the original gold rushes were
exposed at the Earth's surface and were found
because they had shed trails of alluvial gold
(15)   that were easily traced by simple prospecting
methods. Although these same methods still lead
to an occasional discovery, most deposits not yet
discovered have gone undetected because they are
buried and have no surface expression.
(20)   The challenge in exploration is therefore to
unravel the subsurface geology of an area and
pinpoint the position of buried minerals. Methods
widely used today include analysis of aerial images
that yield a broad geological overview; geophysical
(25)   techniques that provide data on the magnetic,
electrical, and mineralogical properties of the
rocks being investigated; and sensitive chemical
tests that are able to detect the subtle chemical
halos that often envelop mineralization. However,
(30)   none of these high-technology methods are of any
value if the sites to which they are applied have
never mineralized, and to maximize the chances of
discovery the explorer must therefore pay particular
attention to selecting the ground formations most
(35)   likely to be mineralized. Such ground selection relies
to varying degrees on conceptual models, which
take into account theoretical studies of relevant
factors.
     These models are constructed primarily from
(40)   empirical observations of known mineral deposits
and from theories of ore-forming processes.
The explorer uses the models to identify those
geological features that are critical to the formation
of the mineralization being modeled, and then tries
(45)   to select areas for exploration that exhibit as many
of the critical features as possible.

Questions 108–114 refer to the passage above.

108. The author is primarily concerned with

    (A)   advocating a return to an older methodology
    (B)   explaining the importance of a recent theory
    (C)   enumerating differences between two widely
          used methods
    (D)   describing events leading to a discovery
    (E)   challenging the assumptions on which a theory
          is based

109. According to the passage, the widely held view of
     Archean-age gold-quartz vein systems is that such
     systems

    (A)   were formed from metamorphic fluids
    (B)   originated in molten granite-like bodies
    (C)   were formed from alluvial deposits
    (D)   generally have surface expression
    (E)   are not discoverable through chemical tests

110. The passage implies that which of the following steps
     would be the first performed by explorers who wish to
     maximize their chances of discovering gold?

    (A)   Surveying several sites known to have been
          formed more than two billion years ago
    (B)   Limiting exploration to sites known to have been
          formed from metamorphic fluid
    (C)   Using an appropriate conceptual model to select
          a site for further exploration
    (D)   Using geophysical methods to analyze rocks
          over a broad area
    (E)   Limiting exploration to sites where alluvial gold
          has previously been found

111. Which of the following statements about discoveries of gold deposits is supported by information in the passage?

    (A) The number of gold discoveries made annually has increased between the time of the original gold rushes and the present.

    (B) New discoveries of gold deposits are likely to be the result of exploration techniques designed to locate buried mineralization.

    (C) It is unlikely that newly discovered gold deposits will ever yield as much as did those deposits discovered during the original gold rushes.

    (D) Modern explorers are divided on the question of the utility of simple prospecting methods as a source of new discoveries of gold deposits.

    (E) Models based on the theory that gold originated from magmatic fluids have already led to new discoveries of gold deposits.

112. It can be inferred from the passage that which of the following is easiest to detect?

    (A) A gold-quartz vein system originating in magmatic fluids

    (B) A gold-quartz vein system originating in metamorphic fluids

    (C) A gold deposit that is mixed with granite

    (D) A gold deposit that has shed alluvial gold

    (E) A gold deposit that exhibits chemical halos

113. The theory mentioned in lines 1–5 relates to the conceptual models discussed in the passage in which of the following ways?

    (A) It may furnish a valid account of ore-forming processes, and, hence, can support conceptual models that have great practical significance.

    (B) It suggests that certain geological formations, long believed to be mineralized, are in fact mineralized, thus confirming current conceptual models.

    (C) It suggests that there may not be enough similarity across Archean-age gold-quartz vein systems to warrant the formulation of conceptual models.

    (D) It corrects existing theories about the chemical halos of gold deposits, and thus provides a basis for correcting current conceptual models.

    (E) It suggests that simple prospecting methods still have a higher success rate in the discovery of gold deposits than do more modern methods.

114. According to the passage, methods of exploring for gold that are widely used today are based on which of the following facts?

    (A) Most of the Earth's remaining gold deposits are still molten.

    (B) Most of the Earth's remaining gold deposits are exposed at the surface.

    (C) Most of the Earth's remaining gold deposits are buried and have no surface expression.

    (D) Only one type of gold deposit warrants exploration, since the other types of gold deposits are found in regions difficult to reach.

    (E) Only one type of gold deposit warrants exploration, since the other types of gold deposits are unlikely to yield concentrated quantities of gold.

Line   After evidence was obtained in the 1920s that
the universe is expanding, it became reasonable
to ask: Will the universe continue to expand
indefinitely, or is there enough mass in it for the
(5)   mutual attraction of its constituents to bring this
expansion to a halt? It can be calculated that
the critical density of matter needed to brake the
expansion and "close" the universe is equivalent
to three hydrogen atoms per cubic meter. But the
(10)   density of the observable universe—luminous matter
in the form of galaxies—comes to only a fraction
of this. If the expansion of the universe is to stop,
there must be enough invisible matter in the
universe to exceed the luminous matter in density
(15)   by a factor of roughly 70.
        Our contribution to the search for this "missing
matter" has been to study the rotational velocity
of galaxies at various distances from their center
of rotation. It has been known for some time that
(20)   outside the bright nucleus of a typical spiral galaxy
luminosity falls off rapidly with distance from the
center. If luminosity were a true indicator of mass,
most of the mass would be concentrated toward
the center. Outside the nucleus the rotational
(25)   velocity would decrease geometrically with distance
from the center, in conformity with Kepler's law.
Instead we have found that the rotational velocity
in spiral galaxies either remains constant with
increasing distance from the center or increases
(30)   slightly. This unexpected result indicates that the
falloff in luminous mass with distance from the
center is balanced by an increase in nonluminous
mass.
        Our findings suggest that as much as 90
(35)   percent of the mass of the universe is not radiating
at any wavelength with enough intensity to be
detected on the Earth. Such dark matter could be
in the form of extremely dim stars of low mass,
of large planets like Jupiter, or of black holes,
(40)   either small or massive. While it has not yet been
determined whether this mass is sufficient to
close the universe, some physicists consider it
significant that estimates are converging on the
critical value.

Questions 115–119 refer to the passage above.

115. The passage is primarily concerned with

    (A)   defending a controversial approach
    (B)   criticizing an accepted view
    (C)   summarizing research findings
    (D)   contrasting competing theories
    (E)   describing an innovative technique

116. The authors' study indicates that, in comparison with
the outermost regions of a typical spiral galaxy, the
region just outside the nucleus can be characterized
as having

    (A)   higher rotational velocity and higher luminosity
    (B)   lower rotational velocity and higher luminosity
    (C)   lower rotational velocity and lower luminosity
    (D)   similar rotational velocity and higher luminosity
    (E)   similar rotational velocity and similar luminosity

117. The authors' suggestion that "as much as 90 percent
of the mass of the universe is not radiating at any
wavelength with enough intensity to be detected on
the Earth" (lines 34–37) would be most weakened if
which of the following were discovered to be true?

    (A)   Spiral galaxies are less common than types of
          galaxies that contain little nonluminous matter.
    (B)   Luminous and nonluminous matter are
          composed of the same basic elements.
    (C)   The bright nucleus of a typical spiral galaxy also
          contains some nonluminous matter.
    (D)   The density of the observable universe is
          greater than most previous estimates have
          suggested.
    (E)   Some galaxies do not rotate or rotate too slowly
          for their rotational velocity to be measured.

118. It can be inferred from information presented in the passage that if the density of the universe were equivalent to significantly less than three hydrogen atoms per cubic meter, which of the following would be true as a consequence?

    (A) Luminosity would be a true indicator of mass.
    (B) Different regions in spiral galaxies would rotate at the same velocity.
    (C) The universe would continue to expand indefinitely.
    (D) The density of the invisible matter in the universe would have to be more than 70 times the density of the luminous matter.
    (E) More of the invisible matter in spiral galaxies would have to be located in their nuclei than in their outer regions.

119. The authors propose all of the following as possibly contributing to the "missing matter" in spiral galaxies EXCEPT

    (A) massive black holes
    (B) small black holes
    (C) small, dim stars
    (D) massive stars
    (E) large planets

Line   Jon Clark's study of the effect of the
modernization of a telephone exchange on exchange
maintenance work and workers is a solid
contribution to a debate that encompasses two
(5)   lively issues in the history and sociology of
technology: technological determinism and social
constructivism.
      Clark makes the point that the characteristics of a
technology have a decisive influence on job skills
(10)   and work organization. Put more strongly,
technology can be a primary determinant of social
and managerial organization. Clark believes this
possibility has been obscured by the recent
sociological fashion, exemplified by Braverman's
(15)   analysis, that emphasizes the way machinery
reflects social choices. For Braverman, the shape of
a technological system is subordinate to the
manager's desire to wrest control of the labor
process from the workers. Technological change is
(20)   construed as the outcome of negotiations among
interested parties who seek to incorporate their own
interests into the design and configuration of the
machinery. This position represents the new
mainstream called social constructivism.
(25)   The constructivists gain acceptance by
misrepresenting technological determinism:
technological determinists are supposed to believe,
for example, that machinery imposes appropriate
forms of order on society. The alternative to
(30)   constructivism, in other words, is to view technology
as existing outside society, capable of directly
influencing skills and work organization.
      Clark refutes the extremes of the constructivists
by both theoretical and empirical arguments.
(35)   Theoretically he defines "technology" in terms of
relationships between social and technical variables.
Attempts to reduce the meaning of technology to
cold, hard metal are bound to fail, for machinery is
just scrap unless it is organized functionally and
(40)   supported by appropriate systems of operation and
maintenance. At the empirical level Clark shows how
a change at the telephone exchange from
maintenance-intensive electromechanical switches
to semielectronic switching systems altered work
(45)   tasks, skills, training opportunities, administration,
and organization of workers. Some changes Clark
attributes to the particular way management and
labor unions negotiated the introduction of the
technology, whereas others are seen as arising from

(50)   the capabilities and nature of the technology itself.
Thus Clark helps answer the question: "When is
social choice decisive and when are the concrete
characteristics of technology more important?"

Questions 120–127 refer to the passage above.

120. The primary purpose of the passage is to

(A)   advocate a more positive attitude toward
technological change

(B)   discuss the implications for employees of the
modernization of a telephone exchange

(C)   consider a successful challenge to the
constructivist view of technological change

(D)   challenge the position of advocates of
technological determinism

(E)   suggest that the social causes of technological
change should be studied in real situations

121. Which of the following statements about the
modernization of the telephone exchange is supported
by information in the passage?

(A)   The new technology reduced the role of
managers in labor negotiations.

(B)   The modernization was implemented without the
consent of the employees directly affected by it.

(C)   The modernization had an impact that went
significantly beyond maintenance routines.

(D)   Some of the maintenance workers felt victimized
by the new technology.

(E)   The modernization gave credence to the view of
advocates of social constructivism.

122. Which of the following most accurately describes
Clark's opinion of Braverman's position?

(A)   He respects its wide-ranging popularity.

(B)   He disapproves of its misplaced emphasis on
the influence of managers.

(C)   He admires the consideration it gives to the
attitudes of the workers affected.

(D)   He is concerned about its potential to impede
the implementation of new technologies.

(E)   He is sympathetic to its concern about the
impact of modern technology on workers.

123. The information in the passage suggests that which of the following statements from hypothetical sociological studies of change in industry most clearly exemplifies the social constructivists' version of technological determinism?

    (A) It is the available technology that determines workers' skills, rather than workers' skills influencing the application of technology.

    (B) All progress in industrial technology grows out of a continuing negotiation between technological possibility and human need.

    (C) Some organizational change is caused by people; some is caused by computer chips.

    (D) Most major technological advances in industry have been generated through research and development.

    (E) Some industrial technology eliminates jobs, but educated workers can create whole new skills areas by the adaptation of the technology.

124. The information in the passage suggests that Clark believes that which of the following would be true if social constructivism had not gained widespread acceptance?

    (A) Businesses would be more likely to modernize without considering the social consequences of their actions.

    (B) There would be greater understanding of the role played by technology in producing social change.

    (C) Businesses would be less likely to understand the attitudes of employees affected by modernization.

    (D) Modernization would have occurred at a slower rate.

    (E) Technology would have played a greater part in determining the role of business in society.

125. According to the passage, constructivists employed which of the following to promote their argument?

    (A) Empirical studies of business situations involving technological change

    (B) Citation of managers supportive of their position

    (C) Construction of hypothetical situations that support their view

    (D) Contrasts of their view with a misstatement of an opposing view

    (E) Descriptions of the breadth of impact of technological change

126. The author of the passage uses the expression "are supposed to" in line 27 primarily in order to

    (A) suggest that a contention made by constructivists regarding determinists is inaccurate

    (B) define the generally accepted position of determinists regarding the implementation of technology

    (C) engage in speculation about the motivation of determinists

    (D) lend support to a comment critical of the position of determinists

    (E) contrast the historical position of determinists with their position regarding the exchange modernization

127. Which of the following statements about Clark's study of the telephone exchange can be inferred from information in the passage?

    (A) Clark's reason for undertaking the study was to undermine Braverman's analysis of the function of technology.

    (B) Clark's study suggests that the implementation of technology should be discussed in the context of conflict between labor and management.

    (C) Clark examined the impact of changes in the technology of switching at the exchange in terms of overall operations and organization.

    (D) Clark concluded that the implementation of new switching technology was equally beneficial to management and labor.

    (E) Clark's analysis of the change in switching systems applies only narrowly to the situation at the particular exchange that he studied.

Line All the cells in a particular plant start out with
the same complement of genes. How then can
these cells differentiate and form structures as
different as roots, stems, leaves, and fruits? The
(5) answer is that only a small subset of the genes in a
particular kind of cell are expressed, or turned on,
at a given time. This is accomplished by a complex
system of chemical messengers that in plants
include hormones and other regulatory molecules.
(10) Five major hormones have been identified: auxin,
abscisic acid, cytokinin, ethylene, and gibberellin.
Studies of plants have now identified a new class of
regulatory molecules called oligosaccharins.
Unlike the oligosaccharins, the five well-known
(15) plant hormones are pleiotropic rather than specific;
that is, each has more than one effect on the
growth and development of plants. The five have
so many simultaneous effects that they are not
very useful in artificially controlling the growth of
(20) crops. Auxin, for instance, stimulates the rate of
cell elongation, causes shoots to grow up and roots
to grow down, and inhibits the growth of lateral
shoots. Auxin also causes the plant to develop a
vascular system, to form lateral roots, and to
(25) produce ethylene.
The pleiotropy of the five well-studied plant
hormones is somewhat analogous to that of certain
hormones in animals. For example, hormones from
the hypothalamus in the brain stimulate the anterior
(30) lobe of the pituitary gland to synthesize and release
many different hormones, one of which stimulates
the release of hormones from the adrenal cortex.
These hormones have specific effects on target
organs all over the body. One hormone stimulates
(35) the thyroid gland, for example, another the ovarian
follicle cells, and so forth. In other words, there is a
hierarchy of hormones.
Such a hierarchy may also exist in plants. Oligosaccharins are fragments of the cell wall released
(40) by enzymes: different enzymes release different
oligosaccharins. There are indications that pleiotropic
plant hormones may actually function by activating
the enzymes that release these other, more specific
chemical messengers from the cell wall.

Questions 128–133 refer to the passage above.

128. According to the passage, the five well-known plant hormones are not useful in controlling the growth of crops because

   (A) it is not known exactly what functions the hormones perform
   (B) each hormone has various effects on plants
   (C) none of the hormones can function without the others
   (D) each hormone has different effects on different kinds of plants
   (E) each hormone works on only a small subset of a cell's genes at any particular time

129. The passage suggests that the place of hypothalamic hormones in the hormonal hierarchies of animals is similar to the place of which of the following in plants?

   (A) Plant cell walls
   (B) The complement of genes in each plant cell
   (C) A subset of a plant cell's gene complement
   (D) The five major hormones
   (E) The oligosaccharins

130. The passage suggests that which of the following is a function likely to be performed by an oligosaccharin?

   (A) To stimulate a particular plant cell to become part of a plant's root system
   (B) To stimulate the walls of a particular cell to produce other oligosaccharins
   (C) To activate enzymes that release specific chemical messengers from plant cell walls
   (D) To duplicate the gene complement in a particular plant cell
   (E) To produce multiple effects on a particular subsystem of plant cells

131. The author mentions specific effects that auxin has on plant development in order to illustrate the

    (A) point that some of the effects of plant hormones can be harmful

    (B) way in which hormones are produced by plants

    (C) hierarchical nature of the functioning of plant hormones

    (D) differences among the best-known plant hormones

    (E) concept of pleiotropy as it is exhibited by plant hormones

132. According to the passage, which of the following best describes a function performed by oligosaccharins?

    (A) Regulating the daily functioning of a plant's cells

    (B) Interacting with one another to produce different chemicals

    (C) Releasing specific chemical messengers from a plant's cell walls

    (D) Producing the hormones that cause plant cells to differentiate to perform different functions

    (E) Influencing the development of a plant's cells by controlling the expression of the cells' genes

133. The passage suggests that, unlike the pleiotropic hormones, oligosaccharins could be used effectively to

    (A) trace the passage of chemicals through the walls of cells

    (B) pinpoint functions of other plant hormones

    (C) artificially control specific aspects of the development of crops

    (D) alter the complement of genes in the cells of plants

    (E) alter the effects of the five major hormones on plant development

Line   In the two decades between 1910 and 1930, more than ten percent of the black population of the United States left the South, where the preponderance of the black population had been
(5)   located, and migrated to northern states, with the largest number moving, it is claimed, between 1916 and 1918. It has been frequently assumed, but not proved, that the majority of the migrants in what has come to be called the Great Migration
(10)   came from rural areas and were motivated by two concurrent factors: the collapse of the cotton industry following the boll weevil infestation, which began in 1898, and increased demand in the North for labor following the cessation of European
(15)   immigration caused by the outbreak of the First World War in 1914. This assumption has led to the conclusion that the migrants' subsequent lack of economic mobility in the North is tied to rural background, a background that implies unfamiliarity
(20)   with urban living and a lack of industrial skills.

   But the question of who actually left the South has never been rigorously investigated. Although numerous investigations document an exodus from rural southern areas to southern cities prior to the
(25)   Great Migration, no one has considered whether the same migrants then moved on to northern cities. In 1910 more than 600,000 black workers, or ten percent of the black workforce, reported themselves to be engaged in "manufacturing and mechanical
(30)   pursuits," the federal census category roughly encompassing the entire industrial sector. The Great Migration could easily have been made up entirely of this group and their families. It is perhaps surprising to argue that an employed population
(35)   could be enticed to move, but an explanation lies in the labor conditions then prevalent in the South.

   About thirty-five percent of the urban black population in the South was engaged in skilled trades. Some were from the old artisan class of
(40)   slavery—blacksmiths, masons, carpenters—which had had a monopoly of certain trades, but they were gradually being pushed out by competition, mechanization, and obsolescence. The remaining sixty-five percent, more recently urbanized, worked in
(45)   newly developed industries—tobacco, lumber, coal and iron manufacture, and railroads. Wages in the South, however, were low, and black workers were aware, through labor recruiters and the black press, that they could earn more even as unskilled

(50)   workers in the North than they could as artisans in the South. After the boll weevil infestation, urban black workers faced competition from the continuing influx of both black and white rural workers, who were driven to undercut the wages
(55)   formerly paid for industrial jobs. Thus, a move north would be seen as advantageous to a group that was already urbanized and steadily employed, and the easy conclusion tying their subsequent economic problems in the North to their rural background
(60)   comes into question.

Questions 134–139 refer to the passage above.

134. The author indicates explicitly that which of the following records has been a source of information in her investigation?

   (A)   United States Immigration Service reports from 1914 to 1930
   (B)   Payrolls of southern manufacturing firms between 1910 and 1930
   (C)   The volume of cotton exports between 1898 and 1910
   (D)   The federal census of 1910
   (E)   Advertisements of labor recruiters appearing in southern newspapers after 1910

135. In the passage, the author anticipates which of the following as a possible objection to her argument?

   (A)   It is uncertain how many people actually migrated during the Great Migration.
   (B)   The eventual economic status of the Great Migration migrants has not been adequately traced.
   (C)   It is not likely that people with steady jobs would have reason to move to another area of the country.
   (D)   It is not true that the term "manufacturing and mechanical pursuits" actually encompasses the entire industrial sector.
   (E)   Of the African American workers living in southern cities, only those in a small number of trades were threatened by obsolescence.

136. According to the passage, which of the following is true of wages in southern cities in 1910?

    (A) They were being pushed lower as a result of increased competition.

    (B) They had begun to rise so that southern industry could attract rural workers.

    (C) They had increased for skilled workers but decreased for unskilled workers.

    (D) They had increased in large southern cities but decreased in small southern cities.

    (E) They had increased in newly developed industries but decreased in the older trades.

137. The author cites each of the following as possible influences in an African American worker's decision to migrate north in the Great Migration EXCEPT

    (A) wage levels in northern cities

    (B) labor recruiters

    (C) competition from rural workers

    (D) voting rights in northern states

    (E) the African American press

138. It can be inferred from the passage that the "easy conclusion" mentioned in line 58 is based on which of the following assumptions?

    (A) People who migrate from rural areas to large cities usually do so for economic reasons.

    (B) Most people who leave rural areas to take jobs in cities return to rural areas as soon as it is financially possible for them to do so.

    (C) People with rural backgrounds are less likely to succeed economically in cities than are those with urban backgrounds.

    (D) Most people who were once skilled workers are not willing to work as unskilled workers.

    (E) People who migrate from their birthplaces to other regions of a country seldom undertake a second migration.

139. The primary purpose of the passage is to

    (A) support an alternative to an accepted methodology

    (B) present evidence that resolves a contradiction

    (C) introduce a recently discovered source of information

    (D) challenge a widely accepted explanation

    (E) argue that a discarded theory deserves new attention

7.5 Answer Key

1.	C	29.	C	57.	D	85.	C	113.	A
2.	D	30.	E	58.	C	86.	B	114.	C
3.	B	31.	C	59.	B	87.	C	115.	C
4.	E	32.	B	60.	A	88.	D	116.	D
5.	B	33.	A	61.	A	89.	A	117.	A
6.	D	34.	C	62.	B	90.	A	118.	C
7.	D	35.	B	63.	E	91.	A	119.	D
8.	A	36.	C	64.	B	92.	A	120.	C
9.	B	37.	B	65.	D	93.	D	121.	C
10.	E	38.	D	66.	E	94.	C	122.	B
11.	E	39.	B	67.	D	95.	E	123.	A
12.	D	40.	E	68.	D	96.	B	124.	B
13.	E	41.	C	69.	B	97.	D	125.	D
14.	D	42.	C	70.	D	98.	D	126.	A
15.	D	43.	D	71.	D	99.	C	127.	C
16.	C	44.	D	72.	B	100.	D	128.	B
17.	A	45.	A	73.	C	101.	C	129.	D
18.	B	46.	E	74.	B	102.	E	130.	A
19.	B	47.	B	75.	E	103.	D	131.	E
20.	B	48.	A	76.	D	104.	A	132.	E
21.	A	49.	A	77.	E	105.	C	133.	C
22.	D	50.	C	78.	B	106.	D	134.	D
23.	E	51.	B	79.	D	107.	A	135.	C
24.	D	52.	E	80.	C	108.	B	136.	A
25.	A	53.	E	81.	C	109.	A	137.	D
26.	E	54.	A	82.	E	110.	C	138.	C
27.	C	55.	A	83.	A	111.	B	139.	D
28.	C	56.	D	84.	E	112.	D		

7.6 Answer Explanations

The following discussion of reading comprehension is intended to familiarize you with the most efficient and effective approaches to the kinds of problems common to reading comprehension. The particular questions in this chapter are generally representative of the kinds of reading comprehension questions you will encounter on the GMAT. Remember that it is the problem solving strategy that is important, not the specific details of a particular question.

Questions 1–3 refer to the passage on page 358.

1. The primary purpose of the passage is to

    (A) explain why a particular business strategy has been less successful than was once anticipated

    (B) propose an alternative to a particular business strategy that has inadvertently caused ecological damage

    (C) present a concern about the possible consequences of pursuing a particular business strategy

    (D) make a case for applying a particular business strategy on a larger scale than is currently practiced

    (E) suggest several possible outcomes of companies' failure to understand the economic impact of a particular business strategy

Main idea

This question requires understanding the passage as a whole. The passage starts out defining a goal—ecoefficiency—that has become popular among companies throughout the world and that would be expected to bring overall ecological benefits. It then immediately introduces Senge and Carstedt, who have concerns about this idea. The rest of the passage is devoted to explaining their concerns, though the passage does not present a particular alternative strategy.

A   The passage never discusses whether ecoefficiency is or is not successful but only the possible consequences of it.

B   Lines 26–28 state that Senge and Carstedt believe that a *new systematic approach* must be found, but a particular alternative strategy is never offered.

C   **Correct.** After defining ecoefficiency, the rest of the passage is devoted to describing the concerns Senge and Carstedt have about it as a goal for companies.

D   The passage reports on particular concerns about the strategy and does not advocate expanding its adoption.

E   The passage is concerned with environmental impact, not economic impact.

The correct answer is C.

2. The passage mentions which of the following as a possible consequence of companies' realization of greater profits through ecoefficiency?

    (A) The companies may be able to sell a greater number of products by lowering prices.

    (B) The companies may be better able to attract investment capital in the global market.

    (C) The profits may be reinvested to increase economic growth through ecoefficiency.

    (D) The profits may be used as investment capital for industries that are not ecoefficient.

    (E) The profits may encourage companies to make further innovations in reducing production waste.

Supporting ideas

This question asks for identification of an example given in the passage of what could result from the greater profits that may come with ecoefficiency. Such profits are specifically mentioned only in lines 14 and 17. The increased growth and profits referred to in line 14 are associated with increased waste generated indirectly by ecoefficient companies. The growth and profits referred to in line 17 are associated with investment of this capital in industries that may not be ecoefficient.

A   The prices of companies' products are not mentioned in the passage.

B   Greater investment in ecoefficient companies by outside sources is not mentioned in the passage.

C   The passage mentions increased profits from ecoefficiency but not the use of these profits to then increase growth through further ecoefficiency.

D   Correct. Lines 14–19 state explicitly that company profits from ecoefficiency may be invested in eco-inefficient industries.

E   The passage does not discuss whether companies will use increased profits from ecoefficiency to become more ecoefficient.

The correct answer is D.

3.   The passage implies that which of the following is a possible consequence of a company's adoption of innovations that increase its ecoefficiency?

(A)   Company profits resulting from such innovations may be reinvested in that company with no guarantee that the company will continue to make further improvements in ecoefficiency.

(B)   Company growth fostered by cost savings from such innovations may allow that company to manufacture a greater number of products that will be used and discarded, thus worsening environmental stress.

(C)   A company that fails to realize significant cost savings from such innovations may have little incentive to continue to minimize the environmental impact of its production processes.

(D)   A company that comes to depend on such innovations to increase its profits and growth may be vulnerable in the global market to competition from old-style eco-inefficient industries.

(E)   A company that meets its ecoefficiency goals is unlikely to invest its increased profits in the development of new and innovative ecoefficiency measures.

Inference

The answer to this question will be an inference about what may result from a company's increased ecoefficiency. The passage suggests several outcomes from such an increase: a general worsening of the environment; a tendency for companies to manufacture more of particular products, which will then be thrown away by consumers; the possibility that increased profits will result in greater investment in industries that are not ecoefficient; and even the possibility that ecoefficiency might allow so much growth that more total waste will be produced and more overall wildlife habitat destroyed.

A   The passage suggests generally that ecoefficiency will increase companies' profits, but there is no suggestion that these companies will therefore then abandon ecoefficiency as a goal.

B   Correct. Lines 6–12 strongly suggest that it is possible that the increased growth that may come from ecoefficiency may result in more products being manufactured, which may result in more waste as those products are discarded by consumers.

C   The passage does not suggest that ecoefficiency may fail to increase a company's profits.

D   The passage suggests that ecoefficiency has allowed many companies to increase profits, but it does not suggest that eco-inefficient companies are more profitable or competitive in the global marketplace.

E   As with option (A), there is no suggestion that companies are likely to abandon ecoefficient strategies once they have realized increased profits from such strategies.

The correct answer is B.

Questions 4–8 refer to the passage on page 360.

4. The primary purpose of the passage is to

   (A) present several explanations for a well-known fact
   (B) suggest alternative methods for resolving a debate
   (C) argue in favor of a controversial theory
   (D) question the methodology used in a study
   (E) discuss the implications of a research finding

Main idea

This question depends on understanding the passage as a whole. The first paragraph reports the findings of a recent study. The second paragraph examines possible explanations for the findings, ruling out all but one of them. It then suggests some inferences that researchers have drawn based on the findings and the explanation.

A Several explanations are entertained, but only to be dismissed; the number of tooth fractures is not presented as a well-known fact.
B The passage does not mention alternative methods or a debate.
C The likely explanation for the tooth fractures is not shown to be controversial.
D The passage does not question the methodology of the study.
E **Correct.** The passage explores possible explanations for a recent research finding and some tentative inferences that it might support.

The correct answer is E.

5. According to the passage, compared with Pleistocene carnivores in other areas, Pleistocene carnivores in the La Brea area

   (A) included the same species, in approximately the same proportions
   (B) had a similar frequency of tooth fractures
   (C) populated the La Brea area more densely
   (D) consumed their prey more thoroughly
   (E) found it harder to obtain sufficient prey

Supporting ideas

Skim the passage to find a comparison of La Brea area carnivores with those from other areas. In lines 17–19, the numbers of tooth fractures, or *breakage data*, of Pleistocene carnivores at the La Brea site are compared with those at other sites. The carnivores at the La Brea site had about the same frequency of tooth fractures as the carnivores at other sites.

A Particular species are not compared in the passage.
B **Correct.** Tooth-fracture evidence at the La Brea site and other sites is similar.
C Population density at different sites is not compared.
D Thorough consumption is the most likely explanation of tooth fractures, but there is no evidence of any difference between La Brea and other Pleistocene sites.
E Difficulty of finding prey is implicated in the final sentence, but the La Brea site is not distinguished from other Pleistocene sites.

The correct answer is B.

6. According to the passage, the researchers believe that the high frequency of tooth breakage in carnivores found at La Brea was caused primarily by

   (A) the aging process in individual carnivores
   (B) contact between the fossils in the pits
   (C) poor preservation of the fossils after they were removed from the pits
   (D) the impact of carnivores' teeth against the bones of their prey
   (E) the impact of carnivores' teeth against the bones of other carnivores during fights over kills

Supporting ideas

As indicated by the phrase *according to the passage*, this question asks about ideas mentioned or expressed in the passage. After dismissing three possible causes of the tooth fractures, the author turns to the explanation researchers find *most plausible*: *more contact between the teeth of predators and the bones of prey due to more thorough consumption of carcasses* (lines 20–24).

A   Lines 11–12 dismiss aging as the cause.
B   Lines 13–16 rule out poor preservation within the pits.
C   Preservation after removal from the pits is not discussed.
D   Correct. Carnivores' tooth fractures were most likely caused by contact with the bones of their prey.
E   Line 28 mentions *competition over kills*, but does not link it to tooth fractures.

The correct answer is D.

7.   The researchers' conclusion concerning the absence of demographic bias would be most seriously undermined if it were found that

(A)   the older an individual carnivore is, the more likely it is to have a large number of tooth fractures

(B)   the average age at death of a present-day carnivore is greater than was the average age at death of a Pleistocene carnivore

(C)   in Pleistocene carnivore species, older individuals consumed carcasses as thoroughly as did younger individuals

(D)   the methods used to determine animals' ages in fossil samples tend to misidentify many older individuals as younger individuals

(E)   data concerning the ages of fossil samples cannot provide reliable information about behavioral differences between extinct carnivores and present-day carnivores

Logical structure

Begin by looking at the section on demographic bias. Lines 11–13 state that demographic bias has been ruled out as an explanation because *older individuals were not overrepresented in the fossil samples*. This implies that older carnivores would be expected to have more tooth fractures than younger ones. To answer this question, read each answer choice to find the one statement that undermines the researchers' conclusion. If the method to determine age in the fossil samples is faulty and older carnivores are misidentified as younger ones, then demographic bias cannot be dismissed.

A   This statement supports rather than undermines the researchers' conclusion.
B   This comparison between present-day and Pleistocene carnivores has no bearing on whether older Pleistocene individuals were overrepresented or not.
C   The comparison between older and younger individuals is irrelevant to the researchers' conclusion.
D   Correct. If older individuals have been misidentified as younger ones, then a higher proportion of older individuals undermines the researchers' conclusion.
E   Neither the differences nor the data are relevant to the researchers' conclusion about the proportion of older Pleistocene carnivores.

The correct answer is D.

8.   According to the passage, if the researchers had NOT found that two extinct carnivore species were free of tooth breakage, the researchers would have concluded that

(A)   the difference in breakage frequencies could have been the result of damage to the fossil remains in the La Brea pits

(B)   the fossils in other Pleistocene sites could have higher breakage frequencies than do the fossils in the La Brea pits

(C)   Pleistocene carnivore species probably behaved very similarly to one another with respect to consumption of carcasses

(D)   all Pleistocene carnivore species differed behaviorally from present-day carnivore species

(E)   predator densities during the Pleistocene era were extremely high

Logical structure

This question refers to the preservational bias explanation that the researchers reject (lines 13–16). Two extinct species had no tooth fractures. Thus, the breakage was almost certainly NOT caused by abrasion in the pits because the teeth of those two species would have showed fractures as well. If the researchers had not discovered the exception of the two species, then they could not have ruled out the possibility that the tooth breakage was caused by damage within the pits.

A **Correct.** If all species showed tooth fractures, then the breakage might have been caused by abrasion in the pits.
B The extinct species evidence was relevant to the issue of preservational bias, not local bias.
C Without the extinct species evidence, preservational bias is a strong explanation, and there is little need for the behavioral explanation.
D The passage does not say that all Pleistocene carnivore species were found in the La Brea pits; consequently no universal conclusion about all species can be made.
E The researchers cannot make a conclusion about the whole era based on one site.

The correct answer is A.

Questions 9–11 refer to the passage on page 362.

9. The primary purpose of the passage is to propose

(A) an alternative to museum display of artifacts
(B) a way to curb illegal digging while benefiting the archaeological profession
(C) a way to distinguish artifacts with scientific value from those that have no such value
(D) the governmental regulation of archaeological sites
(E) a new system for cataloging duplicate artifacts

Main idea

After identifying in the first paragraph two problems that the field of archaeology faces, the author begins the second paragraph by explicitly stating the purpose of the essay: *I would propose that scientific archaeological expeditions and governmental authorities sell excavated artifacts on the open market.* According to the author, this proposal would both benefit the field of archaeology (line 12) and reduce illegal digging for antiquities (lines 12–13).

A While explaining in paragraph 5 that museums often store countless artifacts unseen in their basements, the author proposes no alternative for museum display of these artifacts.
B **Correct.** The author argues that selling some antiquities would help archaeology and reduce illegal digging.
C No proposal for the grading of the artifacts is made in the passage.
D The author does not discuss governmental regulation of the sites.
E While the author supports one part of the proposal for selling antiquities by noting that sold artifacts could be cataloged on a computer, this is a detail rather than the main purpose of the passage.

The correct answer is B.

10. The author implies that all of the following statements about duplicate artifacts are true EXCEPT

(A) a market for such artifacts already exists
(B) such artifacts seldom have scientific value
(C) there is likely to be a continuing supply of such artifacts
(D) museums are well supplied with examples of such artifacts
(E) such artifacts frequently exceed in quality those already cataloged in museum collections

413

Inference

Duplicate artifacts are discussed throughout the passage. Because this question asks the reader to find the one statement that is NOT stated or implied in the passage, the best approach is to eliminate the four statements that are supported by the passage.

A In the closing sentence of the passage, the author implies that the market already exists.

B In lines 27–32, the author suggests selling artifacts that do not have *unique artistic merit or scientific value* and then states that while theoretically every artifact may have potential scientific value, in practice this is not the case. Paragraph 4 illustrates this by mentioning the many thousands of artifacts that are *essentially duplicates of one another*. Lines 51–53 imply that there are rare instances when duplicates do *become needed for scientific purposes*, so duplicates *seldom have scientific value*.

C This statement is implied in lines 41–43, where the author notes that museum basements are *simply not large enough to store the artifacts that are likely to be discovered in the future*.

D It can be inferred that if the duplicates cited in paragraph 4 are typical of the kinds of artifacts *stored in bulging museum basements* (lines 48–49), then museums are well supplied with such artifacts.

E **Correct.** The passage does not support the assertion that the quality of duplicate objects is higher than that of museum pieces.

The correct answer is E.

11. Which of the following is mentioned in the passage as a disadvantage of storing artifacts in museum basements?

(A) Museum officials rarely allow scholars access to such artifacts.

(B) Space that could be better used for display is taken up for storage.

(C) Artifacts discovered in one excavation often become separated from each other.

(D) Such artifacts are often damaged by variations in temperature and humidity.

(E) Such artifacts often remain uncataloged and thus cannot be located once they are put in storage.

Supporting ideas

This question asks for specific information stated in the passage, so begin by finding the discussion of museum storage in the fifth paragraph. There, the author exposes the problems museums face: too little room and too little money. Not enough funding exists to catalog artifacts, so the artifacts *become as inaccessible as if they had never been discovered* (lines 45–46).

A Restrictions on scholars' access to the museums' artifacts are not mentioned in the passage.

B The author does not argue that museums should use space differently.

C No mention is made of the separation of objects from the same excavation.

D The author does not discuss the conditions of storage.

E **Correct.** The author contends that many artifacts are left uncataloged and so, once shelved in the basements, they cannot be found

The correct answer is E.

Questions 12–17 refer to the passage on page 364.

12. The passage is primarily concerned with which of the following?

(A) Evaluating two competing technologies

(B) Tracing the impact of a new technology by narrating a sequence of events

(C) Reinterpreting an event from contemporary business history

(D) Illustrating a business strategy by means of a case history

(E) Proposing an innovative approach to business planning

Main idea

To figure out the primary concern of the passage, consider the passage as a whole. The first paragraph draws a contrast between past and present conditions and puts forward a beneficial strategy for businesses, *developing integrated approaches for successful mass production and distribution*. The second and third paragraphs then use a specific case to illustrate the benefits of this strategy.

A   The evaluation of VHS and Beta is used only as an example to illustrate the thesis stated in the first paragraph.

B   The passage does not discuss the impact of video recording technology in general.

C   *To reinterpret* an event implies that the author disagrees with an original interpretation, but no evidence indicates such a disagreement.

D   Correct. The first paragraph announces the business strategy, and the two subsequent paragraphs illustrate it with a particular case.

E   The author is observing, not proposing; no specific plan of action is proposed.

The correct answer is D.

13. According to the passage, today's successful firms, unlike successful firms in the past, may earn the greatest profits by

(A) investing in research to produce cheaper versions of existing technology

(B) being the first to market a competing technology

(C) adapting rapidly to a technological standard previously set by a competing firm

(D) establishing technological leadership in order to shape product definitions in advance of competing firms

(E) emphasizing the development of methods for the mass production and distribution of a new technology

Supporting ideas

The phrase *according to the passage* indicates that the answer is a claim made, explicitly or implicitly, in the passage. The question requires finishing a statement about firms in general; this is a clue to look at the first paragraph, the only place where firms in general are discussed. A contrast is drawn between past (lines 1–5) and present (lines 5–8) conditions. The companies that earn the greatest profits may be those *that lead in developing integrated approaches for successful mass production and distribution*.

A   Looking for ways to make cheaper versions is not discussed in the passage.

B   Being first was successful in the past, but might not be so now, the author argues.

C   The passage does not examine the advantage of rapid adaptation.

D   The author believes this method was successful in the past but might not be so in the present.

E   Correct. Developing the ways to get a new technology to the greatest number of consumers, through mass production and distribution, may lead to the greatest profits.

The correct answer is E.

14. According to the passage, consumers began to develop a preference for VCRs in the VHS format because they believed which of the following?

(A) VCRs in the VHS format were technically better than competing format VCRs.

(B) VCRs in the VHS format were less expensive than competing format VCRs.

(C) VHS was the first standard format for VCRs.

(D) VHS prerecorded videotapes were more available than those in Beta format.

(E) VCRs in the Beta format would soon cease to be produced.

Supporting ideas

The question's use of the phrase *according to the passage* means that the answer is a claim made, explicitly or implicitly, in the passage. Consumers' perceptions about the two formats are discussed in lines 26–28; consumers believed *that prerecorded tapes were more available in VHS format*.

A   The passage does not claim that consumers believed in the technical superiority of the VHS format.

B   The passage does not claim that consumers believed the VHS format was less expensive.

C   The passage does not claim that consumers thought that VHS was the first format.

D   **Correct.** The passage says that consumers believed prerecorded tapes were more available in the VHS format than in Beta.

E   The passage does not claim that consumers believed the Beta format would stop being produced.

The correct answer is D.

15.   The author implies that one way that VHS producers won control over the VCR market was by

(A)   carefully restricting access to VCR technology

(B)   giving up a slight early lead in VCR sales in order to improve long-term prospects

(C)   retaining a strict monopoly on the production of prerecorded videotapes

(D)   sharing control of the marketing of VHS format VCRs

(E)   sacrificing technological superiority over Beta format VCRs in order to remain competitive in price

Inference

By using the verb *implies*, this question indicates that the answer is not explicitly stated in the passage. The second paragraph contrasts the two approaches to marketing: Producers of the VHS format formed *strategic alliances with other producers and distributors to manufacture and market their VCR format*. The producers of Beta, on the other hand, did not form such alliances because they wanted *to maintain exclusive control over VCR distribution*. Taken together, these statements imply that the VHS producers shared control of marketing.

A   Restricting access to VCR technology was the unsuccessful strategy of Beta producers.

B   Lines 22–24 show that the VHS producers did not yield their *slight early lead in sales* but instead quickly turned it *into a dominant position*.

C   Lines 24–26 show just the reverse situation: VHS producers developed *strategic alignments with producers of prerecorded tapes*.

D   **Correct.** VHS producers shared control of marketing with other producers and distributors.

E   The passage does not suggest that VHS producers sacrificed technological superiority to remain competitive in price.

The correct answer is D.

16.   The alignment of producers of VHS format VCRs with producers of prerecorded videotapes is most similar to which of the following?

(A)   The alignment of an automobile manufacturer with another automobile manufacturer to adopt a standard design for automobile engines

(B)   The alignment of an automobile manufacturer with an automotive glass company whereby the manufacturer agrees to purchase automobile windshields only from that one glass company

(C)   The alignment of an automobile manufacturer with a petroleum company to ensure the widespread availability of the fuel required by a new type of engine developed by the manufacturer

(D)   The alignment of an automobile manufacturer with its dealers to adopt a plan to improve automobile design

(E)   The alignment of an automobile dealer with an automobile rental chain to adopt a strategy for an advertising campaign to promote a new type of automobile

Application

This question tests the reader's understanding of the relationship between the producers of VHS-format VCRs and the producers of prerecorded tapes by asking about an analogous relationship. The VHS machines and the tapes are mutually dependent products; a continual and widespread supply of tapes is necessary for a consumer's continuing use and enjoyment of the VHS equipment. In a similar way, a continual and widespread supply of fuel is necessary to a consumer's ongoing use and enjoyment of a car. The best parallel is an alignment of manufacturers to ensure the availability of mutually dependent products.

A   The alignment between producers of competing, rather than mutually dependent, products is not analogous.

B   This exclusive alignment would instead be analogous to one between a manufacturer of VHS-format VCRs and a manufacturer of one of the parts of the machine.

C   **Correct.** Prerecorded tapes are clearly analogous to fuel: both are products necessary to the consumer's successful utilization of the machines that depend on them. The alignment of the auto manufacturer with a petroleum company to ensure the availability of a specific fuel is analogous to the alignment of the producers of VHS-format VCRs and the producers of prerecorded tapes to ensure the availability of that entertainment medium.

D   This alignment would be analogous to one between manufacturers of VHS-format VCRs and distributors, not prerecorded tape producers.

E   This alignment between an equipment dealer and an equipment-rental business regarding adoption of an advertising strategy is not analogous.

The correct answer is C.

17. Which of the following best describes the relation of the first paragraph to the passage as a whole?

(A)   It makes a general observation to be exemplified.

(B)   It outlines a process to be analyzed.

(C)   It poses a question to be answered.

(D)   It advances an argument to be disputed.

(E)   It introduces conflicting arguments to be reconciled.

Logical structure

To answer this question, look at the structure of the author's argument. The first paragraph takes a position about firms in general. The second and third paragraphs illustrate that position with a specific example.

A   **Correct.** The first paragraph offers a general statement about all firms, and the subsequent paragraphs use an extended example to illustrate that statement.

B   The passage does not describe a process or invite further analysis.

C   The author is making a declaration (lines 5–8) rather than posing a question.

D   The position advanced in the first paragraph is supported, not disputed, by the rest of the passage.

E   The first paragraph contrasts past and present conditions, but does not show conflicting arguments.

The correct answer is A.

Questions 18–25 refer to the passage on page 366.

18. The passage provides information in support of which of the following assertions?

(A) The disadvantages of an adaptation to a particular feature of an environment often outweigh the advantages of such an adaptation.

(B) An organism's reaction to being placed in an environment to which it is not well adapted can sometimes illustrate the problems that have been solved by the adaptations of organisms indigenous to that environment.

(C) The effectiveness of an organism's adaptation to a particular feature of its environment can only be evaluated by examining the effectiveness with which organisms of other species have adapted to a similar feature of a different environment.

(D) Organisms of the same species that inhabit strikingly different environments will often adapt in remarkably similar ways to the few features of those environments that are common.

(E) Different species of organisms living in the same environment will seldom adapt to features of that environment in the same way.

Application

This question requires recognizing a principle underlying the passage's overall discussion. The passage makes a general claim about terrestrial animals' need to overcome the effect of gravity on their blood circulation systems, and it then uses the specific example of terrestrial snakes to illustrate this claim. To help identify the adaptations used by terrestrial snakes, the passage describes what happens to sea snakes, which are aquatic and less affected by gravity's influence, when they are subjected to a terrestrial environment. The specific problems faced by these snakes strongly suggest that terrestrial snakes have developed ways to overcome these problems. The passage then identifies specific physiological differences between sea snakes and terrestrial snakes that demonstrate how terrestrial snakes overcome gravity's influence.

A The passage discusses how species have successfully adapted to their specific environments and does not mention that these adaptations create disadvantages in that environment.

B Correct. The passage discusses the problems faced by sea snakes when they are subjected to a terrestrial environment and then examines terrestrial snakes to illustrate how certain adaptations solved these problems.

C The passage is not concerned with evaluating the effectiveness of species' adaptations to their environments; it takes for granted that these adaptations are effective.

D The passage is concerned with how species adapt differently to different environments and not with how adaptations to different environments are similar.

E The passage discusses how different environments affect how species have adapted, not how different species adapt to a similar environment.

The correct answer is B.

19. According to the passage, one reason that the distribution of blood in the sea snake changes little while the creature remains in the ocean is that

(A) the heart of the sea snake tends to be located near the center of its body

(B) pressure gradients in the water surrounding the sea snake counter the effects of vertical pressure gradients within its blood vessels

(C) the sea snake assumes a vertical posture less frequently than do the terrestrial and the arboreal snake

(D) the sea snake often relies on waves of muscle contractions to help move blood from the torso to the head

(E) the force of pressure gradients in the water surrounding the sea snake exceeds that of vertical pressure gradients within its circulatory system

Supporting ideas

This question asks for an identification of factual information in the passage. Given that the contrast between sea snakes and terrestrial snakes is being used to identify adaptations used by terrestrial animals to overcome the effect of gravity on their circulation systems, the passage needs initially to illustrate why it is that sea snakes are not confronted with the same problems that gravity causes for terrestrial snakes. This information therefore needs to come fairly early in the passage.

A   The passage identifies the location of a sea snake's heart as a factor that minimizes the effort required to pump blood to both extremities but not as a cause of the even distribution of blood in sea snakes.

B   **Correct.** The passage states explicitly in lines 11–17 that while sea snakes are in the ocean, the vertical pressure gradients in their blood vessels are counteracted by the pressure gradients in the water.

C   The passage does not discuss the frequency with which any snakes assume certain postures.

D   The passage discusses muscle contractions only in relation to arboreal snakes.

E   The passage states that the vertical pressures within sea snakes' blood vessels are *counteracted* (line 13) by the water's pressure, which suggests that the pressures are equalized, not that one force exceeds the other.

The correct answer is B.

20.   It can be inferred from the passage that which of the following is true of species of terrestrial snakes that often need to assume a vertical posture?

(A)   They are more likely to be susceptible to circulatory failure in vertical postures than are sea snakes.

(B)   Their hearts are less likely to be located at the midpoint of their bodies than is the case with sea snakes.

(C)   They cannot counteract the pooling of blood in lower regions of their bodies as effectively as sea snakes can.

(D)   The blood pressure at their midpoint decreases significantly when they are tilted with their heads up.

(E)   They are unable to rely on muscle contractions to move venous blood from the lower torso to the head.

Inference

This question requires using information given about how arboreal snakes, which are frequently in vertical postures, have adapted to gravity's influence to make an assumption that other terrestrial snakes that are frequently in these postures are likely to have similar adaptations. The passage implies that sea snakes have hearts at the midpoint of their bodies because the water's pressure gradients help distribute blood evenly. It then illustrates that arboreal snakes have hearts closer to their heads to help keep blood flowing to their brain when they are in vertical postures.

A   The passage does not suggest that any of the snakes mentioned are ill-adapted to their particular environments.

B   **Correct.** The passage states that arboreal snakes have hearts close to their heads and not at the midpoints of their bodies, so it is reasonable to conclude that any terrestrial snake that frequently assumes vertical postures would be unlikely to have hearts at their bodies' midpoint.

C   As with option (A), the passage does not suggest that any species of snake is ill-adapted to its environment.

D   The passage states that sea snakes lose pressure at their midpoints when they are tilted on land with heads up but that terrestrial snakes do not have this problem.

E   Because arboreal snakes use muscle contractions to circulate blood when they are vertical, it is likely that most terrestrial snakes that frequently assume vertical postures also have this capability.

The correct answer is B.

21. The author describes the behavior of the circulatory system of sea snakes when they are removed from the ocean (see lines 17–20) primarily in order to

    (A) illustrate what would occur in the circulatory system of terrestrial snakes without adaptations that enable them to regulate their blood pressure in vertical orientations

    (B) explain why arboreal snakes in vertical orientations must rely on muscle contractions to restore blood pressure to the brain

    (C) illustrate the effects of circulatory failure on the behavior of arboreal snakes

    (D) illustrate the superiority of the circulatory system of the terrestrial snake to that of the sea snake

    (E) explain how changes in spatial orientation can adversely affect the circulatory system of snakes with hearts located in relatively close proximity to their heads

Evaluation

Answering this question requires understanding why sea snakes have been brought into the passage's overall discussion about how terrestrial animals have overcome the influence of gravity on their blood circulation. The passage uses the effects that gravity has on sea snakes when they are taken out of water to identify problems that terrestrial snakes must have adapted to in order to survive.

A **Correct.** The passage uses the problems sea snakes have when taken out of water to illustrate that without certain adaptations, terrestrial snakes would likely have similar problems.

B The passage discusses sea snakes to illustrate problems faced by terrestrial snakes, not to explain how terrestrial snakes have adapted to gravity's influence.

C The passage does not discuss the effects of circulatory failure on arboreal snakes.

D The passage does not compare or contrast the effectiveness of the various adaptations used by different snakes.

E The passage does not imply that snakes with hearts close to their heads are adversely affected by spatial positions.

The correct answer is A.

22. It can be inferred from the passage that which of the following is a true statement about sea snakes?

    (A) They frequently rely on waves of muscle contractions from the lower torso to the head to supplement the work of the heart.

    (B) They cannot effectively regulate their blood pressure when placed in seawater and tilted at an angle with the head pointed downward.

    (C) They are more likely to have a heart located in close proximity to their heads than are arboreal snakes.

    (D) They become acutely vulnerable to the effects of gravitational pressure on their circulatory system when they are placed in a terrestrial environment.

    (E) Their cardiovascular system is not as complicated as that of arboreal snakes.

Inference

Answering this question requires understanding why sea snakes are discussed in the passage and what happens to them when they are taken out of water and subjected to the force of gravity. The second paragraph implies strongly that sea snakes will not survive certain terrestrial situations for which they are not adapted.

A The passage associates muscle contractions to circulate blood with arboreal snakes only.

B According to the passage, sea snakes' inability to regulate blood pressure occurs only when they are taken out of water.

C The passage states clearly that arboreal snakes have hearts closer to their heads than do sea snakes.

D **Correct.** The passage states that in certain postures, sea snakes placed in a terrestrial environment will lose all blood pressure at their brains, which is an acute vulnerability.

E The passage does not provide the information needed to compare the complexity of the various snakes discussed.

The correct answer is D.

23. The author suggests that which of the following is a disadvantage that results from the location of a snake's heart in close proximity to its head?

    (A) A decrease in the efficiency with which the snake regulates the flow of blood to the brain

    (B) A decrease in the number of orientations in space that a snake can assume without loss of blood flow to the brain

    (C) A decrease in blood pressure at the snake's midpoint when it is tilted at various angles with its head up

    (D) An increase in the tendency of blood to pool at the snake's head when the snake is tilted at various angles with its head down

    (E) An increase in the amount of effort required to distribute blood to and from the snake's tail

Inference

This question asks for an inference about the location of a snake's heart being closer to the brain than to the midpoint of its body. In the third paragraph, the passage states that in terrestrial snakes, which must fight the influence of gravity, the closer proximity of the heart to the head ensures blood circulation to the brain. The passage notes, however, that this makes it more difficult for such snakes to maintain blood circulation to the tail.

A The passage states that snakes have brains closer to their heads to more efficiently circulate blood to the brain.

B The passage suggests that having the heart close to the head increases the spatial orientations a snake can assume without losing blood flow to the brain, rather than decreases the number of orientations.

C The passage indicates that this is true only of sea snakes with hearts near their body's midpoint.

D The passage mentions blood pooling in the lower portions of a terrestrial organism's body but does not imply that blood can pool at a snake's head.

E **Correct.** Because, as the passage states, it is more difficult for a snake with its heart close to its head to circulate blood to the tail, and therefore its body is likely to put more effort into circulating blood to the tail.

The correct answer is E.

24. The primary purpose of the third paragraph is to

    (A) introduce a topic that is not discussed earlier in the passage

    (B) describe a more efficient method of achieving an effect discussed in the previous paragraph

    (C) draw a conclusion based on information elaborated in the previous paragraph

    (D) discuss two specific examples of phenomena mentioned at the end of the previous paragraph

    (E) introduce evidence that undermines a view reported earlier in the passage

Evaluation

Answering this question requires recognizing how the passage develops its main point. The first paragraph sets up a general claim about gravity's influence on terrestrial organisms. The second paragraph then describes the ill effects that gravity has on sea snakes to identify problems that terrestrial snakes have had to adapt to. The third paragraph then uses examples to illustrate how terrestrial snakes have adapted to gravity's influence.

A The topic of the third paragraph is the adaptations developed by terrestrial snakes to survive gravity's influence, which is part of the discussion in both the first and second paragraphs.

B There is no comparison in the passage of the efficiency of the different methods used by snakes to adapt to gravity's influence.

C The third paragraph is concerned with illustrating certain adaptations used by snakes and offers no conclusions about the problems terrestrial snakes have had to adapt to, which is the topic of the second paragraph.

D **Correct.** The end of the second paragraph refers to *certain adaptations* (line 23) that the third paragraph then goes on to identify and discuss.

E The third paragraph supports the main idea of the passage and is not used to counter any claim made earlier.

The correct answer is D.

25. In the passage, the author is primarily concerned with doing which of the following?

   (A) Explaining adaptations that enable the terrestrial snake to cope with the effects of gravitational pressure on its circulatory system

   (B) Comparing the circulatory system of the sea snake with that of the terrestrial snake

   (C) Explaining why the circulatory system of the terrestrial snake is different from that of the sea snake

   (D) Pointing out features of the terrestrial snake's cardiovascular system that make it superior to that of the sea snake

   (E) Explaining how the sea snake is able to neutralize the effects of gravitational pressure on its circulatory system

Main idea

Answering this question involves assessing what the passage as a whole is attempting to do. While the passage begins by making a general claim about gravity's influence on the cardiovascular systems of terrestrial animals, it immediately points to terrestrial snakes as a good example supporting this claim. The rest of the passage is then devoted to illustrating, using the observations involving sea snakes, how gravity's influence has shaped the cardiovascular systems of terrestrial snakes.

A   **Correct.** The entire passage is devoted to an explanation of how terrestrial snakes have adapted to gravity's influence.

B   While the passage does compare the systems of the two snakes, it does so for the larger purpose of demonstrating gravity's influence on terrestrial snakes.

C   The passage is more concerned with *how* the systems of the two snakes are different, rather than *why*, in order to identify how terrestrial snakes have adapted to gravity's influence.

D   There is no judgment in the passage as to the superiority of one snake's system over the other.

E   While the passage does explain how sea snakes do this, it does so only for the larger purpose of identifying how terrestrial snakes have adapted to gravity's influence.

The correct answer is A.

Questions 26–30 refer to the passage on page 370.

26. The primary purpose of the passage is to

   (A) advocate more effective strategies for encouraging the development of high-technology enterprises in the United States

   (B) contrast the incentives for economic development offered by local governments with those offered by the private sector

   (C) acknowledge and counter adverse criticism of programs being used to stimulate local economic development

   (D) define and explore promotional efforts used by local governments to attract new industry

   (E) review and evaluate strategies and programs that have been used to stimulate economic development

Main idea

To find the primary purpose, analyze the passage in its entirety. The passage discusses three different strategies or programs that local governments use to stimulate economic development, so the statement of the primary purpose must embrace all three strategies rather than focus on just one. The first paragraph describes how local governments attracted manufacturing industries in the 1960s and 1970s, with the result that one town prospered at another's expense. The second paragraph turns to the growth of high-technology manufacturing firms in the 1980s, which required a specialized workforce. The final paragraph shows the advantages of promoting local entrepreneurship.

A   High-technology development is only one of three kinds of economic development the passage discusses.

B   The private sector is not mentioned in the passage.

C   The passage acknowledges problems but does not counter criticism.

D   The passage examines the efforts to attract new industry in the first two paragraphs, but not in the third.

E   **Correct.** The passage describes and evaluates strategies and programs used by local governments to stimulate economic growth in their areas.

The correct answer is E.

27. The passage suggests which of the following about the majority of United States manufacturing industries before the high-technology development era of the 1980s?

    (A) They lost many of their most innovative personnel to small entrepreneurial enterprises.
    (B) They experienced a major decline in profits during the 1960s and 1970s.
    (C) They could provide real economic benefits to the areas in which they were located.
    (D) They employed workers who had no specialized skills.
    (E) They actively interfered with local entrepreneurial ventures.

Inference

This question directs attention to the manufacturing industries discussed in the first paragraph and asks for an inference about these industries. Because of *the transfer of jobs and related revenues*, attracting a manufacturer to a town was a *triumph*; losing such an industry was a *tragedy* (lines 9–11). In order for this conclusion to be true, it is logical to infer that these industries must have had a significant economic impact on the towns in which they were located.

A No information in the passage supports such a loss of personnel.
B The passage does not describe the industries' loss of profits.
C **Correct.** Transfer of jobs and related revenues to a community clearly provide real economic benefits to that community.
D The second paragraph mentions the *specially trained fraction of the manufacturing workforce* (lines 20–21) suitable for high-tech jobs, but that does not imply that workers in manufacturing industries were unskilled.
E The passage makes no suggestion that there was such interference.

The correct answer is C.

28. The tone of the passage suggests that the author is most optimistic about the economic development potential of which of the following groups?

    (A) Local governments
    (B) High-technology promoters
    (C) Local entrepreneurs
    (D) Manufacturing industry managers
    (E) Economic development strategists

Tone

To answer this question about the author's attitude, look at what the author says when evaluating the ways local governments try to stimulate economic growth. In the first two paragraphs, the author points out serious disadvantages in attracting manufacturing (lines 4–11) and high-technology industries (lines 19–22). The final paragraph, however, offers only advantages to promoting local entrepreneurship. The author does not mention any disadvantages here, which implies that the author is most optimistic about this third strategy, which *both provides jobs and fosters further entrepreneurship.*

A The local governments are part of the discussion of all three strategies, not just the one about which the author is most optimistic.
B In lines 18–22, the author points out the *shortcomings* of high-technology development.
C **Correct.** The author has only good things to say about local entrepreneurs.
D The author does not discuss managers of manufacturing industries.
E Other than local governments, the author does not mention economic development strategists.

The correct answer is C.

29. The passage does NOT state which of the following about local entrepreneurs?

    (A) They are found nearly everywhere.
    (B) They encourage further entrepreneurship.
    (C) They attract out-of-town investors.
    (D) They employ local workers.
    (E) They are established in their communities.

Supporting ideas

Use the process of elimination to discover the only characteristic of local entrepreneurs that is NOT explicitly stated in the passage. To do this, check each answer choice against the description of local entrepreneurs found in lines 28–33 of the passage.

A Line 27 does identify them as *a nearly ubiquitous resource*, meaning that they are found in most places.
B Line 33 says they create an environment that *fosters further entrepreneurship*.
C **Correct.** Out-of-town investors are not mentioned in the passage.
D Lines 31–32 say that *industry and talent are kept at home* and that they create an environment that *provides jobs*.
E Line 28 describes them as having *roots in their communities*.

The correct answer is C.

30. The author of the passage mentions which of the following as an advantage of high-technology development?

(A) It encourages the modernization of existing manufacturing facilities.
(B) It promotes healthy competition between rival industries.
(C) It encourages the growth of related industries.
(D) It takes full advantage of the existing workforce.
(E) It does not advantage one local workforce at the expense of another.

Supporting ideas

To answer this question, look for an advantage of high-technology development that is explicitly mentioned in the passage. In the second paragraph, the efforts of local governments to attract new high-technology firms are judged *preferable* to previous efforts to entice established manufacturing industries from another town to their own. Thus, the introduction of high technology made it possible for local governments to stop *victimizing other geographical areas by taking their jobs* (lines 17–18).

A The passage does not describe modernization of facilities.
B Competition between rival industries is not mentioned in the passage.
C The growth of related industries is not cited as an advantage.
D Lines 19–21 explain that high-tech manufacturing firms employ only a fraction of the workforce.
E **Correct.** The introduction of a new high-technology firm creates jobs for the local community without causing jobs to be lost elsewhere.

The correct answer is E.

Questions 31–35 refer to the passage on page 372.

31. The author of the passage is primarily concerned with

(A) discussing research data underlying several definitions
(B) arguing for the adoption of a particular definition
(C) exploring definitions of a concept
(D) comparing the advantages of several definitions
(E) clarifying some ambiguous definitions

Main idea

The author's primary concern is found by considering the passage as a whole. In the first paragraph, the author raises the central question regarding the meaning of *services* and then examines two definitions. The second paragraph analyzes the United States government's definition of *services* in more detail. The author is primarily interested in exploring different definitions of *services*.

A No research data are presented.
B The author points out the weakness of several definitions rather than giving reasons to adopt a particular one.
C **Correct.** The author considers several definitions of *services*.
D The author largely analyzes the disadvantages of the definitions.
E The author points out problems in the definitions rather than providing clarifications of the definitions themselves.

The correct answer is C.

32. In comparing the United States government's definition of services with the classical definition, the author suggests that the classical definition is

    (A) more pragmatic
    (B) more difficult to apply
    (C) less ambiguous
    (D) more widely used
    (E) more arbitrary

Inference

This question asks the reader to find information that is suggested but not directly stated in the passage. The author discusses the classical definition at the end of the first paragraph, pointing out two examples in which it does not apply and concluding that this definition is *hard to sustain*. By comparison, the government's definition is *more practical* because it is easy to apply; everything that is not agriculture or industry is defined as a service. An examination of the analysis of both definitions reveals that, according to the author, the classical definition is harder to apply.

A   The author describes the United States government's definition as *more practical* or pragmatic.
B   **Correct.** Citing two cases in which the classical definition does not apply, the author implies that this definition is harder to apply than the government's.
C   Although the United States government's definition is said to lead to *ambiguities*, the examples given to suggest difficulties with the classical definition indicate that it may be at least as ambiguous.
D   The author does not say that the classical definition is more widely used.
E   The author calls the government's definition arbitrary.

The correct answer is B.

33. The passage suggests which of the following about service workers in the United States?

    (A) The number of service workers may be underestimated by the definition of services used by the government.
    (B) There were fewer service workers than agricultural workers before 1988.
    (C) The number of service workers was almost equal to the number of workers employed in manufacturing until 1988.
    (D) Most service workers are employed in service occupations rather than in service industries.
    (E) Most service workers are employed in occupations where they provide services that do not fall under the classical definition of services.

Inference

The question's use of the word *suggests* means that the answer depends on making an inference. According to the author, one of the failures of the government's definition of services is that *the many service workers employed by manufacturers—bookkeepers or janitors, for example—would fall under the industrial rather than the services category* (lines 22–26). This example shows that the number of service workers is likely to be underestimated.

A   **Correct.** Because some service workers are included in the industrial category, it is possible that the total number of service workers may be underestimated.
B   The passage does not provide the information to support this statement.
C   The author says that services moved ahead of manufacturing as the *main product* in 1988 but does not discuss the number of workers in either area.
D   The passage does not provide the information to support this statement.
E   The passage does not provide the information to support this statement.

The correct answer is A.

34. The author of the passage mentions which of the following as one disadvantage of the United States government's definition of services?

    (A) It is less useful than the other definitions mentioned in the passage.

    (B) It is narrower in scope than the other definitions mentioned in the passage.

    (C) It is based on the final product produced rather than on the type of work performed.

    (D) It does not recognize the diversity of occupations within the service industries.

    (E) It misclassifies many workers who are employed in service industries.

Supporting ideas

This question is based on specific information explicitly stated in the passage. According to the author, the government's definition fails because *it categorizes workers based on their company's final product rather than on the actual work the employees perform* (lines 20–22).

A   The author calls this definition *practical for government purposes*, so for the government it is more useful than other definitions.

B   The definition *includes everything that is not agriculture or industry,* while the classical definition does not include occupations that are clearly services; the government's definition is thus not narrower.

C   **Correct.** Workers are categorized by the final product of their company rather than by the type of work they perform at that company.

D   Diversity of occupations within the service industries is not discussed.

E   The definition misclassifies service workers employed in manufacturing, not service industries.

The correct answer is C.

35. The author refers to "service workers employed by manufacturers" (line 23) primarily in order to point out

    (A) a type of worker not covered by the United States government's system of classifying occupations

    (B) a flaw in the United States government's definition of services

    (C) a factor that has influenced the growth of the service economy in the United States

    (D) a type of worker who is classified on the basis of work performed rather than on the basis of the company's final product

    (E) the diversity of the workers who are referred to as service workers

Logical structure

The author discusses *the many service workers employed by manufacturers* to illustrate the failure of the government's definition to distinguish between service industries and service occupations. The resulting ambiguities, in the author's view, reveal the *arbitrariness* of the definition and its inaccuracy in reflecting the composition of the economy.

A   The worker is covered but misclassified.

B   **Correct.** The author uses this example to point out a serious shortcoming in the government's definition.

C   The author mentions the growth of services at the beginning of the passage but does not explore the reasons for it.

D   The situation of service workers employed by manufacturers is just the reverse; they are categorized by the company's final product, not by the work they do.

E   The author had earlier cited and illustrated the diversity of service activities that are included in the government's residual category of services; the focus here is instead the arbitrariness and inaccuracy, in the author's view, of the government's definition.

The correct answer is B.

Questions 36–41 refer to the passage on page 374.

36. The passage is primarily concerned with

   (A) contrasting the benefits of one methodology with the benefits of another
   (B) describing the historical origins and inherent drawbacks of a particular methodology
   (C) discussing the appeal of a particular methodology and some concerns about its use
   (D) showing that some historians' adoption of a particular methodology has led to criticism of recent historical scholarship
   (E) analyzing the influence of current feminist views on women's interpretations of their experience

Main idea

This question asks for an abstract view of what the passage as a whole is primarily doing. The passage introduces a particular methodology that scholars of women's history have been encouraged to employ, explaining why the use of the methodology is supported. The passage then goes on to raise some concerns about the use of the methodology and cites one example in which caution is needed.

A   The passage is primarily concerned with only one methodology.
B   The passage mentions why the methodology had been encouraged but does not give the history of its origins; while it cautions historians to employ the methodology carefully, it is not concerned with drawbacks of its proper use.
C   **Correct.** The passage discusses why the use of a methodology is being encouraged and then offers some concerns about its use.
D   The passage does not discuss any criticism of recent scholarship in women's history.
E   There is no mention in the passage that feminist theory is influencing how women in general think about their experiences.

The correct answer is C.

37. According to the passage, which of the following shapes the oral narratives of women storytellers?

   (A) The conventions for standard histories in the culture in which a woman storyteller lives
   (B) The conventions of storytelling in the culture in which a woman storyteller lives
   (C) A woman storyteller's experience with distinctive traditions of storytelling developed by the women in her family of origin
   (D) The cultural expectations and experiences of those who listen to oral narratives
   (E) A woman storyteller's familiarity with the stories that members of other groups in her culture tell to explain themselves

Supporting ideas

This question asks for an identification of specific information provided by the passage. In the second paragraph, the passage describes certain concerns about using oral narratives. One of these concerns is that *the stories people tell to explain themselves are shaped by ... storytelling conventions* (lines 17–19) and other influences tied to the teller's cultural and historical context.

A   The passage uses *standard histories* (line 7) to refer to the usual work of scholars and not to something that influences oral narratives.
B   **Correct.** The passage raises as a concern that oral narratives may be influenced by storytelling conventions present in the culture of the speaker.
C   The passage does not mention the family of origin of women storytellers.
D   The passage does not mention the expectations of the listeners of oral narratives.
E   The passage does not discuss women storytellers' familiarity with the oral narratives belonging to other groups of women.

The correct answer is B.

38. The author of the passage would be most likely to make which of the following recommendations to scholars of women's history?

   (A) They should take into account their own life experiences when interpreting the oral accounts of women's historical experiences.
   (B) They should assume that the observations made in women's oral narratives are believed by the intended audience of the story.
   (C) They should treat skeptically observations reported in oral narratives unless the observations can be confirmed in standard histories.
   (D) They should consider the cultural and historical context in which an oral narrative was created before arriving at an interpretation of such a narrative.
   (E) They should rely on information gathered from oral narratives only when equivalent information is not available in standard histories.

Application

Answering this question involves recognizing what the author believes about oral narratives and then applying this belief to a hypothetical situation in which the author makes recommendations to scholars of women's history. While acknowledging the appeal of oral narratives to these scholars, in the second paragraph the author urges caution when using these narratives as sources of *disinterested commentary* (line 16). The passage then states that people's oral narratives are shaped by *cultural and historical factors* (line 20), which presumably relate to the cultural and historical context within which the narratives are spoken.

A   The passage does not mention the personal life experiences of scholars.
B   The passage does not mention the intended audiences of oral narratives.
C   The passage mentions *standard histories* (line 7) only as a reference to scholarly works that often have shortcomings.

D   **Correct.** The passage cautions that oral narratives may be biased due to cultural and historical factors, and it is therefore reasonable to suppose that the author would recommend that scholars consider this when using such information.
E   The passage does not refer to oral narratives as being valuable only for filling a gap in the available historical record.

The correct answer is D.

39. Which of the following best describes the function of the last sentence of the passage?

   (A) It describes an event that historians view as crucial in recent women's history.
   (B) It provides an example of how political rhetoric may influence the interpretations of experience reported in women's oral narratives.
   (C) It provides an example of an oral narrative that inaccurately describes women's experience during a particular historical period.
   (D) It illustrates the point that some women are more aware than others of the social forces that shape their oral narratives.
   (E) It identifies the historical conditions that led to the social acceptance of women's paid work outside the home.

Evaluation

This question requires recognizing how a particular part of the passage is related to the overall reasoning in the passage. The first paragraph introduces a methodology and describes the methodology's appeal. The second paragraph then raises concerns about the use of the methodology, drawing attention to the cultural and historical bias that may be present in oral narratives. In line 21, the passage refers specifically to the influence *political rhetoric* may have on a woman's understanding of her experience. In the final sentence, the passage provides a specific hypothetical example of a woman at the time of the Second World War to illustrate this concern.

A   The last sentence employs a hypothetical example and does not describe a particular event as being important to historians.

B   Correct. After contending that political rhetoric may influence oral narratives, the passage uses the example of the Second World War in the final sentence to support this claim.

C   The last sentence does not provide a particular example of an oral narrative.

D   The passage does not claim that some women are more aware than others of the social forces that may bear on them.

E   The passage does not claim that social conditions during the Second World War led to acceptance of women in the workplace.

The correct answer is B.

40. According to the passage, scholars of women's history should refrain from doing which of the following?

(A) Relying on traditional historical sources when women's oral narratives are unavailable

(B) Focusing on the influence of political rhetoric on women's perceptions to the exclusion of other equally important factors

(C) Attempting to discover the cultural and historical factors that influence the stories women tell

(D) Assuming that the conventions of women's written autobiographies are similar to the conventions of women's oral narratives

(E) Accepting women's oral narratives less critically than they accept women's written histories

Inference

Answering this question requires recognizing which option is directly inferable from information in the passage. After describing in the first paragraph why oral narratives are appealing to historians, the passage begins the second paragraph by imploring scholars of women's history to *be as cautious about accepting oral narratives ... as ... written memories* (lines 12–14). The passage then goes on to describe potential bias in oral narratives, suggesting that scholars should be as critical of them as they are of written sources.

A   The passage does not claim that traditional historical sources should be avoided by scholars.

B   The passage mentions the influence of political rhetoric merely as one example of potential bias.

C   The passage suggests that scholars *should* attempt to be aware of cultural and historical factors.

D   The passage does not discuss the conventions of women's written autobiographies.

E   Correct. The passage implies that written histories and oral narratives should receive the same level of critical scrutiny by scholars.

The correct answer is E.

41. According to the passage, each of the following is a difference between women's oral narratives and most standard histories EXCEPT:

(A) Women's oral histories validate the significance of women's achievements.

(B) Women's oral histories depict experience from the point of view of women.

(C) Women's oral histories acknowledge the influence of well-known women.

(D) Women's oral histories present today's women with a sense of their historical relationship to women of the past.

(E) Women's oral histories are crucial to the collective identity of today's women.

Supporting ideas

This question asks for information that is stated in the passage, and it requires a process of elimination. In line 7, oral narratives are presented as being *unlike most standard histories*, and the passage then goes on in lines 7–11 to list characteristics of oral histories that most standard histories do not have. The answer to this question will therefore contain a characteristic of women's oral histories that is not described in lines 7–11.

A   The passage states that, unlike most standard histories, women's oral histories *affirm the importance of women's contributions* (lines 8–9).

B   The passage states that, unlike most standard histories, women's oral histories *represent experience from the perspective of women* (lines 7–8).

C   **Correct.** The passage does not mention the influence of well-known women on women's oral histories.

D   The passage states that, unlike most standard histories, women's oral histories *furnish present-day women with historical continuity* (lines 9–10).

E   The passage states that, unlike most standard histories, women's oral histories furnish a historical sense that is *essential to their identity, individually and collectively* (line 11).

The correct answer is C.

Questions 42–46 refer to the passage on page 376.

42. The author of the passage is primarily concerned with doing which of the following?

    (A)   Recommending a methodology
    (B)   Describing a course of study
    (C)   Discussing a problem
    (D)   Evaluating a past course of action
    (E)   Responding to a criticism

Main idea

This question about the author's intent requires looking at the whole passage. The first paragraph introduces a problem unknown just a short time ago: an overabundance of materials. The second paragraph explains a complicating factor of this problem: the lack of reference works. A consideration of the passage as a whole shows that the author is most interested in discussing a problem.

A   A methodology is a system of principles and practices, or methods; no such system is recommended in this passage.

B   The author does not describe a particular course in Asian American studies, but rather points out a problem shared by all courses in the field.

C   **Correct.** The author discusses the problem created by the existence of too many materials and the nonexistence of easily usable reference works.

D   The author discusses a current situation, as the opening, *in recent years*, indicates.

E   If the author were responding to a criticism, the passage would likely cite the source of the criticism and discuss the basis of it; no such source is cited here.

The correct answer is C.

43. The "dilemma" mentioned in line 3 can best be characterized as being caused by the necessity to make a choice when faced with a

    (A)   lack of acceptable alternatives
    (B)   lack of strict standards for evaluating alternatives
    (C)   preponderance of bad alternatives as compared to good
    (D)   multitude of different alternatives
    (E)   large number of alternatives that are nearly identical in content

Logical structure

This question asks the reader to consider the context in which the author uses the word *dilemma*. The first sentence establishes that this dilemma did not exist previously, *when hardly any texts … were available*. The next sentence introduces the contrast to *today*, when so many excellent choices exist that it is difficult to select from among them.

A   As the second sentence makes clear, it is not a lack, but an abundance, of acceptable alternatives that creates the problem.
B   The context in which *dilemma* is used, the first two sentences, discusses a relative wealth of materials, not a lack of standards.
C   The author calls the anthologies *excellent* and does not describe any of the other materials in a negative light.
D   Correct. Teachers face the dilemma of choosing from the wealth of materials listed in the second sentence.
E   The second sentence identifies four different kinds of materials, all with varying content: anthologies, introductory texts, books on individual nationality groups, and books on general issues.

The correct answer is D.

44.   The passage suggests that the factor mentioned in lines 15–18 complicates professors' attempts to construct introductory reading lists for courses in Asian American studies in which of the following ways?

(A)   By making it difficult for professors to identify primary source material and to obtain standard information on Asian American history and culture

(B)   By preventing professors from identifying excellent anthologies and introductory texts in the field that are both recent and understandable to students

(C)   By preventing professors from adequately evaluating the quality of the numerous texts currently being published in the field

(D)   By making it more necessary for professors to select readings for their courses that are not too challenging for students unfamiliar with Asian American history and culture

(E)   By making it more likely that the readings professors assign to students in their courses will be drawn solely from primary sources

Inference

When a question asks what a passage *suggests* or *implies*, it is often necessary to look at more than one sentence or at sentences in different parts of the passage. The *complicating factor* cited at the beginning of the second paragraph is the lack of reference works. How this factor affects the way professors construct introductory reading lists is discussed in the final sentence of that paragraph. If students had good reference works to consult for *background information necessary to interpret difficult or unfamiliar material*, then their professors *might feel more free to include more challenging Asian American material in their introductory reading lists*. This sentence suggests that professors currently do not include challenging material on their reading lists because it is too difficult or unfamiliar for their students.

A   Identifying primary source material is not a problem; the author notes that there are *mountains* of it.
B   The lack of reference works does not prevent professors from identifying the recently published sources available in abundance to them; these sources are listed in the second sentence of the passage.
C   The author does not link the lack of reference materials to an inadequate evaluation of texts.
D   Correct. Because students cannot easily find basic information that would be available to them in reference works, professors might be inclined to select readings that are not too challenging for students unfamiliar with Asian American history and culture.
E   If reference works were available, students would not have to consult so many primary sources to find basic information; the passage does not indicate that the professors use solely primary materials.

The correct answer is D.

45. The passage implies that which of the following was true of introductory courses in Asian American studies a few decades ago?

    (A) The range of different textbooks that could be assigned for such courses was extremely limited.
    (B) The texts assigned as readings in such courses were often not very challenging for students.
    (C) Students often complained about the texts assigned to them in such courses.
    (D) Such courses were offered only at schools whose libraries were rich in primary sources.
    (E) Such courses were the only means then available by which people in the United States could acquire knowledge of the field.

Inference

This question requires information that is implied rather than explicitly stated in the passage. The comparison of introductory courses in Asian American studies taught now with those taught a few decades ago is made in the first sentence, where the author notes that *in recent years,* teachers have faced a *dilemma nonexistent a few decades ago, when hardly any texts … were available.* From this sentence, it is reasonable to infer that a few decades ago, teachers of introductory courses in this field had few texts to choose from.

A **Correct.** Because *hardly any texts were available*, teachers of introductory courses had few choices when they assigned textbooks to students.
B Currently, professors are prevented from assigning challenging works because students do not have reference works to consult for background information, but there is no indication about the difficulty of readings a few decades ago.
C The passage provides no information about student response to the readings.
D The passage does not discuss the primary-source materials available in school libraries.
E The author does not claim that these introductory courses were the sole means of acquiring knowledge in this field.

The correct answer is A.

46. According to the passage, the existence of good one-volume reference works about Asian Americans could result in

    (A) increased agreement among professors of Asian American studies regarding the quality of the sources available in their field
    (B) an increase in the number of students signing up for introductory courses in Asian American studies
    (C) increased accuracy in writings that concern Asian American history and culture
    (D) the use of introductory texts about Asian American history and culture in courses outside the field of Asian American studies
    (E) the inclusion of a wider range of Asian American material in introductory reading lists in Asian American studies

Supporting ideas

The phrase *according to the passage* indicates that this question concerns information that is explicitly stated in the passage. In the second paragraph, the author identifies two related advantages that would result if good one-volume reference works existed in this field: (1) students would be able to look up basic information easily, and (2) professors would be able to assign more challenging texts because of the students' resulting access to information required to understand those texts. Thus, introductory reading lists could include a wider range of materials than they do presently.

A The author neither indicates that reference works would promote a consensus of opinion on the quality of sources nor calls the quality of sources into question.
B The author does not link the availability of reference works to the popularity of courses.
C The author does not claim that the availability of reference works would increase accuracy in writing about the field.
D The passage mentions that nonexperts, professors who teach in related fields, might also benefit from using reference works, but there is no indication that the existence of a good one-volume work would result in the use of introductory texts in Asian American studies outside the field.

E   **Correct.** The existence of a good, easy-to-use reference work would allow professors to include a greater range of materials, including those that are more challenging, in their introductory reading lists.

The correct answer is E.

Questions 47–49 refer to the passage on page 378.

47.   The passage suggests that combing and carding differ from weaving in that combing and carding were

(A)   low-skill jobs performed primarily by women employees

(B)   low-skill jobs that were not performed in the home

(C)   low-skill jobs performed by both male and female employees

(D)   high-skill jobs performed outside the home

(E)   high-skill jobs performed by both male and female employees

Inference

Since the question uses the word *suggests*, the answer is probably not directly stated in the passage and therefore has to be inferred. How was weaving different from carding and combing? Lines 16–17 discuss weaving, combing, and carding; all three activities are characterized as low-skill jobs. As the human capital theory notes, there was a concentration of women in certain low-skill occupations because they *could be carried out in the home* (lines 19–20); weaving was one such occupation. Since the passage implies that relatively few women worked in carding and combing, these jobs presumably could *not* be carried out in the home. Thus the passage suggests that carding and combing were low-skill jobs, mostly done by men working outside the home.

A   Lines 15–17 imply that women predominated in weaving but that carding and combing were done mainly by men.

B   **Correct.** Carding and combing, unlike weaving, could not be done at home.

C   The passage suggests that weaving, carding, and combing were all low-skill jobs done by both men and women, although the concentrations of the genders in these jobs were different; this statement does not explain how the passage suggests that *combing and carding differ from weaving.*

D   Lines 16–17 characterize all three jobs as low-skill.

E   Lines 16–17 characterize all three jobs as low-skill.

The correct answer is B.

48.   Which of the following, if true, would most weaken the explanation provided by the human capital theory for women's concentration in certain occupations in seventeenth-century Florence?

(A)   Women were unlikely to work outside the home even in occupations whose hours were flexible enough to allow women to accommodate domestic tasks as well as paid labor.

(B)   Parents were less likely to teach occupational skills to their daughters than they were to their sons.

(C)   Women's participation in the Florentine paid labor force grew steadily throughout the sixteenth and seventeenth centuries.

(D)   The vast majority of female weavers in the Florentine wool industry had children.

(E)   Few women worked as weavers in the Florentine silk industry, which was devoted to making cloths that required a high degree of skill to produce.

Logical structure

To answer this question, examine the logic of the explanation. How does the human capital theory explain women's concentration in certain occupations? The theory says that women's roles in childbearing made it difficult for them to acquire the skills needed in high-skill jobs. Moreover, their role in child rearing made them choose occupations that could be carried out at home. Evidence against either of these points will weaken the explanation.

A **Correct.** If women of that time were generally unlikely to take any jobs outside the home, even those that allowed them to handle their domestic tasks, then these tasks are not the reason women predominated in jobs that they could do within the home, as the human capital theory posits.

B Different levels of teaching by parents may help perpetuate job segregation, but this is quite consistent with the socially defined role that women then had as childbearers and child rearers and the explanation provided by the human capital theory.

C The growth of women's participation in the paid labor force does not affect the explanation of occupational concentrations provided by the human capital theory.

D The explanation suggests the women chose weaving because they had children to raise at home. The fact that the majority of weavers had children actually supports, rather than weakens, the explanation.

E Silk weaving was a high-skill job, exactly the kind of job that women would not have in the human capital explanation. This point supports, rather than weakens, the explanation.

The correct answer is A.

49. The author of the passage would be most likely to describe the explanation provided by the human capital theory for the high concentration of women in certain occupations in the seventeenth-century Florentine textile industry as

(A) well founded though incomplete
(B) difficult to articulate
(C) plausible but poorly substantiated
(D) seriously flawed
(E) contrary to recent research

Logical structure

This question requires an evaluation of the author's point of view. What does the author think of the human capital explanation of women's occupational concentration in the Florentine textile industry? In line 5, the author characterizes the theory as *useful*, a positive word reflecting a positive evaluation. However, the entire second paragraph is devoted to examining *differences in pay scales that cannot be explained by the human capital theory.* The author's positive view of the theory is qualified by the theory's inability to explain an important point.

A **Correct.** This statement reflects the author's generally positive evaluation, as well as concerns about insufficiencies.

B The author articulates the theory without difficulty and does not criticize it as difficult to articulate.

C To substantiate the theory means to provide evidence that verifies the theory. The author regards the theory's explanations of high concentration of women in certain occupations as sound, and so is unlikely to regard the theory as *poorly substantiated*.

D If the author regarded the theory as *seriously flawed*, the passage would not describe it as *useful* (see line 5).

E The author does not mention recent research.

The correct answer is A.

Questions 50–56 refer to the passage on page 380.

50. The primary purpose of the passage is to

(A) present the results of statistical analyses and propose further studies
(B) explain a recent development and predict its eventual consequences
(C) identify the reasons for a trend and recommend measures to address it
(D) outline several theories about a phenomenon and advocate one of them
(E) describe the potential consequences of implementing a new policy and argue in favor of that policy

Main idea

Understanding the author's purpose comes from a careful consideration of the whole passage. The author begins by noting one explanation for the rise in temporary employment, but dismisses it, finding another explanation more likely. The author closes the passage by making specific recommendations to counter the problems caused by temporary employment.

A   The author uses statistical analyses as the basis of an explanation, but the analyses act only as support for the larger purpose of explaining a trend; no further studies are proposed.
B   The author explores possible reasons for a recent development but recommends ways to curb or change that development; the author does not predict the consequences if the situation is left unchanged or the recommendations unmet.
C   **Correct.** The author examines possible reasons for the rise in temporary employment and makes specific recommendations to change the current situation.
D   The use of the phrase *several theories* is enough to make this inaccurate. Two types of explanation are suggested: employee preference or employer self-interest.
E   The author makes recommendations but provides no arguments in support of those recommendations—merely suggesting that they are aimed at discouraging employers from creating too many temporary positions.

The correct answer is C.

51.   According to the passage, which of the following is true of the "factors affecting employers" that are mentioned in lines 10–19?

(A)   Most experts cite them as having initiated the growth in temporary employment that occurred during the 1980s.
(B)   They may account for the increase in the total number of temporary workers during the 1980s.

(C)   They were less important than demographic change in accounting for the increase of temporary employment during the 1980s.
(D)   They included a sharp increase in the cost of labor during the 1980s.
(E)   They are more difficult to account for than are other factors involved in the growth of temporary employment during the 1980s.

Supporting idea

This question is based on information explicitly stated in lines 10–12. The statistical analyses *suggest that factors affecting employers account for the rise in temporary employment.*

A   *Some observers* attribute the rise to the composition of the workforce; the passage does not identify what most experts believe.
B   **Correct.** The factors affecting employers may explain the rise in temporary employment.
C   The passage suggests that these factors were more important than demographic changes in explaining the rise.
D   Although there is some suggestion in lines 15–16 that employers at some point experienced difficulty from the cost of labor, the passage does not suggest that a sharp increase in that cost occurred in the 1980s—and even suggests that labor costs may have decreased because of labor's reduced bargaining strength.
E   The issue of how to *account for* those factors (i.e., explain why they occurred) is not raised in the passage—so the issue of whether those factors are more difficult to account for than other factors is not raised.

The correct answer is B.

52. The passage suggests which of the following about the use of temporary employment by firms during the 1980s?

    (A) It enabled firms to deal with fluctuating product demand far more efficiently than they did before the 1980s.

    (B) It increased as a result of increased participation in the workforce by certain demographic groups.

    (C) It was discouraged by government-mandated policies.

    (D) It was a response to preferences indicated by certain employees for more flexible working arrangements.

    (E) It increased partly as a result of workers' reduced ability to control the terms of their employment.

Inference

Since the word *suggests* is used in the question, the answer is probably not directly stated in the passage and therefore has to be inferred. The author believes that the rise in temporary employment during the 1980s can be explained by two factors affecting employers: *product demand* and *labor's reduced bargaining strength*. Temporary employment allows employers to adapt their workforce to the fluctuating demand for their product. At this time, *labor's reduced bargaining strength* left employers, not workers, in greater control of the terms of employment.

A   This goes too far beyond the information provided in the passage. The passage neither says nor implies anything about efficiency levels before the 1980s.

B   The author says that *demographic changes in the workforce did not correlate with variations in the total number of temporary workers*, ruling out this explanation.

C   In 1992, the author recommended government-mandated policies because they did not exist.

D   The author says that *growth in temporary employment now far exceeds the level explainable by ... groups said to prefer temporary jobs.*

E   **Correct.** *Labor's reduced bargaining power* resulted in employers' increased control over the terms of employment.

The correct answer is E.

53. The passage suggests which of the following about the workers who took temporary jobs during the 1980s?

    (A) Their jobs frequently led to permanent positions within firms.

    (B) They constituted a less demographically diverse group than has been suggested.

    (C) They were occasionally involved in actions organized by labor unions.

    (D) Their pay declined during the decade in comparison with the pay of permanent employees.

    (E) They did not necessarily prefer temporary employment to permanent employment.

Inference

The question's use of the word *suggests* indicates that the answer is probably not directly stated in the passage. The author says that the rise in temporary employment *now far exceeds the level explainable by recent workforce entry rates of groups said to prefer temporary jobs*. Thus, the number of workers employed on a temporary basis is far greater than the number of workers who actually do prefer temporary employment.

A   No evidence is presented that temporary jobs led to permanent positions.

B   The passage grants that there was *increased participation in the workforce by certain groups, such as first-time or reentering workers*. This suggests more rather than less demographic diversity.

C   The role of temporary workers in labor unions is not discussed.

D   The passage does suggest that the pay of temporary workers is less than that of permanent workers, but not that the pay of temporary workers *declined*.

E   **Correct.** The passage indicates that the number of workers in temporary jobs was higher than the number of workers who stated a preference for temporary work.

The correct answer is E.

54. The first sentence in the passage suggests that the "observers" mentioned in line 1 would be most likely to predict which of the following?

    (A) That the number of new temporary positions would decline as fewer workers who preferred temporary employment entered the workforce

    (B) That the total number of temporary positions would increase as fewer workers were able to find permanent positions

    (C) That employers would have less control over the terms of workers' employment as workers increased their bargaining strength

    (D) That more workers would be hired for temporary positions as product demand increased

    (E) That the number of workers taking temporary positions would increase as more workers in any given demographic group entered the workforce

Application

These observers specifically attribute the growth of temporary employment to *increased participation in the workforce by certain groups … who supposedly prefer such arrangements.* On the basis of the passage's first sentence, any prediction these observers might make must be about the relation between the number of workers in temporary employment and the preference of these workers for temporary employment. No other issue is discussed. A rise in temporary employment could be explained only by a rise in the number of new workers who prefer temporary jobs, and a decline in temporary employment only by a decline in the number of new workers who prefer temporary work.

A   **Correct.** By this rationale, the only reason for a decline in temporary employment would be a corresponding decline in the number of new workers who preferred temporary jobs.

B   According to the observers, temporary employment would increase only if a greater number of employers who preferred temporary jobs entered the workforce.

C   These observers are not said to consider control over the terms of employment.

D   These observers are not said to consider the relationship between product demand and temporary employment.

E   The number of workers taking temporary positions would rise only if they were composed of *certain groups, such as first-time or reentering workers,* who, the observers believe, prefer temporary work.

The correct answer is A.

55. In the context of the passage, the word "excessive" (line 23) most closely corresponds to which of the following phrases?

    (A) Far more than can be justified by worker preferences

    (B) Far more than can be explained by fluctuations in product demand

    (C) Far more than can be beneficial to the success of the firms themselves

    (D) Far more than can be accounted for by an expanding national economy

    (E) Far more than can be attributed to increases in the total number of people in the workforce

Logical structure

In its context in this passage, the word *excessive* indicates a value-judgment by the author. The author recommends that firms be *discouraged from creating excessive numbers of temporary positions* on the basis of the statistical analyses, which show that the rise in temporary employment *now far exceeds the level explainable by recent workforce entry rates of groups said to prefer temporary jobs.* In the context of lines 24–31, it is clear that the author believes that the large expansion in temporary employment exclusively serves employer interests at the expense of employee interests (including their preferences), and is, for that reason, excessive.

A **Correct.** An expansion of temporary employment that serves employer interests more than it serves employee interests (such as preferences) is considered by the author to be *excessive*.

B It is not because the expansion in temporary employment allows employers to respond to fluctuations in product demand that the author regards the expansion as *excessive*.

C The relation of temporary employment to the success of firms is not discussed.

D The relation of temporary employment to an expanding economy is not discussed.

E The author does not consider the issue of overall increases in the workforce as a whole, only the issue of increases in temporary employment.

The correct answer is A.

56. The passage mentions each of the following as an appropriate kind of governmental action EXCEPT

(A) getting firms to offer temporary employment primarily to a certain group of people

(B) encouraging equitable pay for temporary and permanent employees

(C) facilitating the organization of temporary workers by labor unions

(D) establishing guidelines on the proportion of temporary workers that firms should employ

(E) ensuring that temporary workers obtain benefits from their employers

Supporting ideas

The author closes the passage with a list of specific recommendations. Check that list against the possible answers. By the process of elimination, choose the one recommendation the author does not make. The author recommends that government policymakers consider: 1) *mandating benefit coverage for temporary employees*, 2) *promoting pay equity between temporary and permanent workers*, 3) *assisting labor unions in organizing temporary workers*, and 4) *encouraging firms to assign temporary jobs primarily to employees who explicitly indicate that preference*.

A The author does recommend that firms assign temporary jobs to workers who prefer temporary work.

B The author does recommend that pay equity between temporary and permanent workers be encouraged.

C The author does recommend that labor unions be assisted in organizing temporary workers.

D **Correct.** The author does not recommend that such guidelines be established.

E The author does recommend that benefit coverage for temporary workers be mandated.

The correct answer is D.

Questions 57–63 refer to the passage on page 382.

57. According to the passage, which of the following was true of the treaty establishing the Fort Belknap Indian Reservation?

(A) It was challenged in the Supreme Court a number of times.

(B) It was rescinded by the federal government, an action that gave rise to the *Winters* case.

(C) It cited American Indians' traditional use of the land's resources.

(D) It failed to mention water rights to be enjoyed by the reservation's inhabitants.

(E) It was modified by the Supreme Court in *Arizona v. California*.

Supporting ideas

This question requires recognizing information that is explicitly stated in the passage. In the first sentence, the passage states that the Fort Belknap Indian Reservation was established by treaty. The following sentence begins by stating that this treaty *did not mention water rights* (lines 5–6); in other words, the right to use the water flowing through the reservation was not established by treaty.

A   Although the Supreme Court ruled on water rights for the reservation established by the treaty, there is no evidence in the passage that the treaty itself was ever challenged in the Supreme Court.

B   Although the *Winters* case resulted in water rights for the reservation established by the treaty, there is no evidence in the passage that the treaty was ever rescinded.

C   The passage does not mention American Indians' traditional resource use as being tied to the treaty establishing the Fort Belknap Indian Reservation.

D   Correct. The passage states explicitly that the treaty establishing the Fort Belknap Indian Reservation did not mention the right to use water flowing through the reservation.

E   The passage does not mention the Fort Belknap Indian Reservation or the treaty that established it in relation to *Arizona v. California*.

The correct answer is D.

58. The passage suggests that, if the criteria discussed in lines 10–20 were the only criteria for establishing a reservation's water rights, which of the following would be true?

(A) The water rights of the inhabitants of the Fort Belknap Indian Reservation would not take precedence over those of other citizens.

(B) Reservations established before 1848 would be judged to have no water rights.

(C) There would be no legal basis for the water rights of the Rio Grande pueblos.

(D) Reservations other than American Indian reservations could not be created with reserved water rights.

(E) Treaties establishing reservations would have to mention water rights explicitly in order to reserve water for a particular purpose.

Inference

Answering this question requires making an inference based on information given in the passage. The question focuses on lines 10–20, where the passage provides a summary of the criteria used by the U.S. courts to establish water rights. The passage then explains that the Rio Grande pueblos used other means to establish water rights, noting that what *constitutes an American Indian reservation is a question of practice, not of legal definition* (lines 34–36). This strongly implies that establishing water rights for the Rio Grande pueblos required reference to legal language not contained in the criteria described in lines 10–20.

A   Since the passage says that decisions setting the criteria in lines 10–20 cited the *Winters* case—which gave water rights to the Fort Belknap Indian Reservation—one can infer that the Fort Belknap reservation met all of those criteria.

B   The criteria in lines 10–20 do not touch on specific dates of the transfer of sovereignty over particular lands.

C   Correct. The passage demonstrates that for the Rio Grande pueblos, it was necessary to establish water rights based on criteria not contained in lines 10–20.

D   The criteria described in lines 10–20 are not specific only to lands reserved for American Indians.

E   The passage illustrates that *Winters* established water rights in the absence of any explicit mention of water rights in the treaty.

The correct answer is C.

59. Which of the following most accurately summarizes the relationship between *Arizona v. California* in lines 38–42, and the criteria citing the *Winters* doctrine in lines 10–20?

   (A) *Arizona v. California* abolishes these criteria and establishes a competing set of criteria for applying the *Winters* doctrine.

   (B) *Arizona v. California* establishes that the *Winters* doctrine applies to a broader range of situations than those defined by these criteria.

   (C) *Arizona v. California* represents the sole example of an exception to the criteria as they were set forth in the *Winters* doctrine.

   (D) *Arizona v. California* does not refer to the *Winters* doctrine to justify water rights, whereas these criteria do rely on the *Winters* doctrine.

   (E) *Arizona v. California* applies the criteria derived from the *Winters* doctrine only to federal lands other than American Indian reservations.

Inference

This question requires inferring how one part of the passage bears on another part of the passage. The two parts referred to are the criteria described in lines 10–20 and *Arizona v. California*, which is referred to in lines 38–45. *Arizona v. California* shows that the establishment of water rights need not be tied to any previous legal definition of reservation lands but may be tied to the U.S. government's practice merely of treating the land as reserved for American Indians. The criteria described in lines 10–20 apply to situations in which the land in question has been legally identified as reservation land. So *Arizona v. California* broadened the scope of *Winters* in establishing water rights.

   A   The passage illustrates that *Arizona v. California* does not supersede or deny any of the criteria in lines 10–20.

   B   Correct. The passage suggests that *practice* and not *legal definition* (lines 34–36) allows *Winters* to be applied to situations not covered by the criteria in lines 10–20.

   C   In stating that *some American Indian tribes have also established water rights* by means other than the criteria in lines 10–20, the first sentence of the second paragraph makes clear that *Arizona v. California* is not the sole exception to the criteria.

   D   The passage states that *Arizona v. California* does refer to *Winters*.

   E   The passage illustrates that *Arizona v. California* was directly relevant to the Pueblo Indians' water rights.

The correct answer is B.

60. The "pragmatic approach" mentioned in lines 37–38 of the passage is best defined as one that

   (A) grants recognition to reservations that were never formally established but that have traditionally been treated as such

   (B) determines the water rights of all citizens in a particular region by examining the actual history of water usage in that region

   (C) gives federal courts the right to reserve water along with land even when it is clear that the government originally intended to reserve only the land

   (D) bases the decision to recognize the legal rights of a group on the practical effect such a recognition is likely to have on other citizens

   (E) dictates that courts ignore precedents set by such cases as *Winters v. United States* in deciding what water rights belong to reserved land

Supporting ideas

This question requires recognizing what a particular phrase in the passage is referring to. The pragmatic approach the question refers to is introduced by the passage as *this* pragmatic approach. It is therefore necessary to identify which approach the passage has already referred to in this context, which in this case is contained in the sentence just prior to the reference. This sentence states that establishing what is an American Indian reservation is a matter of the U.S. government's practice and not of any formal, legal definition.

   A   Correct. The approach referred to as *pragmatic* involves establishing American Indian reservations based not on formal law but on the government's established practice of treating the lands as such.

   B   The approach referred to as *pragmatic* is not specific to establishing water rights.

C   The approach referred to as *pragmatic* is not specific to establishing water rights.

D   The approach referred to as *pragmatic* does not refer to balancing the rights of some people with rights of others.

E   The approach referred to as *pragmatic* is shown to be consistent with and supportive of the rights established by *Winters*.

The correct answer is A.

61. The author cites the fact that the Rio Grande pueblos were never formally withdrawn from public lands primarily in order to do which of the following?

(A) Suggest why it might have been argued that the *Winters* doctrine ought not to apply to pueblo lands

(B) Imply that the United States never really acquired sovereignty over pueblo lands

(C) Argue that the pueblo lands ought still to be considered part of federal public lands

(D) Support the argument that the water rights of citizens other than American Indians are limited by the *Winters* doctrine

(E) Suggest that federal courts cannot claim jurisdiction over cases disputing the traditional diversion and use of water by Pueblo Indians

Evaluation

Answering this question involves recognizing how a particular part of the passage functions within the passage as a whole. The passage illustrates in the first paragraph that *Winters* was cited in the establishment of water rights based on a set of criteria that included the formal withdrawal of lands by the government. In the second paragraph, the case of the Rio Grande pueblos is introduced as an example of lands that had never been formally withdrawn by the government, raising the question of whether *Winters* would still be applicable in such situations. The passage then asserts that the situation of the pueblos *has not barred* (line 33) the application of *Winters*.

A   **Correct.** While the passage affirms the application of *Winters* to the situation with the pueblos, it recognizes that it may initially appear that *Winters* does not apply.

B   The passage states explicitly that the United States did gain official sovereignty over pueblo lands in 1848, when they *became part of the United States* (lines 27–28).

C   The passage states explicitly that *the pueblo lands never formally constituted a part of federal public lands* (lines 28–29) and takes no stand on the issue of whether particular lands ought to be considered public lands.

D   While one can infer that the rights of other citizens to use water could be limited by reserving water rights for residents of American Indian lands according to the *Winters* doctrine, the passage takes no stand on this issue.

E   The passage does not mention the rights of federal courts to claim jurisdiction over particular water rights cases.

The correct answer is A.

62. The primary purpose of the passage is to

(A) trace the development of laws establishing American Indian reservations

(B) explain the legal bases for the water rights of American Indian tribes

(C) question the legal criteria often used to determine the water rights of American Indian tribes

(D) discuss evidence establishing the earliest date at which the federal government recognized the water rights of American Indians

(E) point out a legal distinction between different types of American Indian reservations

Main idea

This question requires recognizing the main topic of the passage, which is about the establishment of water rights on American Indian lands. Its intent is to explain or describe, and it does not take sides on any issue.

A   The passage is primarily about establishing water rights, not establishing reservations.

B   Correct. The passage is an explanation of water rights on American Indian lands.

C   The passage describes legal criteria used to establish water rights on American Indian lands but does not take issue with them.

D   The passage does not discuss the earliest date for water rights on American Indian lands.

E   The passage is primarily about establishing water rights, not about types of reservations.

The correct answer is B.

63.   The passage suggests that the legal rights of citizens other than American Indians to the use of water flowing into the Rio Grande pueblos are

(A)   guaranteed by the precedent set in *Arizona v. California*

(B)   abolished by the *Winters* doctrine

(C)   deferred to the Pueblo Indians whenever treaties explicitly require this

(D)   guaranteed by federal land-use laws

(E)   limited by the prior claims of the Pueblo Indians

Inference

Answering this question requires recognizing what the passage implies. The passage illustrates at the beginning of the second paragraph that water rights were granted to Pueblo Indians based on their use of the water in the Rio Grande pueblos prior to U.S. sovereignty. The passage also later states that since the *Winters* doctrine applies, the water rights of Pueblo Indians *have priority over other citizens' water rights as of 1848* (lines 42–44), which implies that the water rights of citizens other than Pueblo Indians are limited.

A   The passage illustrates that *Arizona v. California* reinforced the water rights of citizens residing on American Indian

reservations; it does not imply a precedent ensuring water rights for other citizens.

B   The passage states that the water rights of citizens other than Pueblo Indians are lower in priority, not abolished altogether.

C   The passage does not mention that different water rights have been defined by different treaties.

D   The passage does not mention that the water rights of citizens other than Pueblo Indians are guaranteed on pueblo lands.

E   Correct. The passage states that the water rights of Pueblo Indians have priority over other citizens' water rights, which thereby limits the rights of those citizens.

The correct answer is E.

Questions 64–69 refer to the passage on page 384.

64.   The passage is chiefly concerned with

(A)   arguing against the increased internationalization of United States corporations

(B)   warning that the application of laws affecting trade frequently has unintended consequences

(C)   demonstrating that foreign-based firms receive more subsidies from their governments than United States firms receive from the United States government

(D)   advocating the use of trade restrictions for "dumped" products but not for other imports

(E)   recommending a uniform method for handling claims of unfair trade practices

Main idea

To answer this question, consider the passage as a whole. In the first sentence, the author sets off *unfortunately* in commas, drawing attention to the author's attitude about companies that seek legal protection from imports. In the next paragraph, the author says, *this quest for import relief has hurt more companies than it has helped*. The third paragraph creates a hypothetical situation to show how import relief might hurt American companies, and the last paragraph shows the actual, unintended, and unfortunate consequences of import relief laws.

A   Internationalization is accepted as a given (lines 16–18); no argument is made against it.

B   Correct. The author warns that American companies seeking relief from imports may suffer unexpected adverse consequences when the laws are applied to them.

C   The author does not make this comparison.

D   The author does not make this recommendation.

E   The author makes no recommendation but simply describes actual and possible consequences.

The correct answer is B.

65.   It can be inferred from the passage that the minimal basis for a complaint to the International Trade Commission is which of the following?

(A)   A foreign competitor has received a subsidy from a foreign government.

(B)   A foreign competitor has substantially increased the volume of products shipped to the United States.

(C)   A foreign competitor is selling products in the United States at less than fair market value.

(D)   The company requesting import relief has been injured by the sale of imports in the United States.

(E)   The company requesting import relief has been barred from exporting products to the country of its foreign competitor.

Inference

To make an inference about the minimal basis for a complaint, read what the passage says about complaints. The first paragraph describes two specific kinds of complaints the International Trade Commission (ITC) has received: *damage from imports that benefit from subsidies by foreign governments* and damage from imports *dumped at less than fair value.* The author contends that companies would complain even without any specific basis. In the current climate promoting import relief, *the simple claim that an industry has been injured by imports is sufficient grounds to seek relief.* Complaints are reviewed even when the complaining firm does not allege that dumping occurred—simply that the imports damaged its competitiveness.

A   This specific complaint is explicitly referred to in lines 4–7, but there is no suggestion that it is the minimal basis.

B   The scenario of a large increase in exports is not discussed in the passage.

C   This specific complaint is explicitly referred to in lines 8–10, but there is no suggestion that it is the minimal basis.

D   Correct. Lines 10–13 show that merely claiming to be injured by imports is enough for a company *to seek relief,* that is, to complain to the ITC.

E   This possibility is not discussed in the passage.

The correct answer is D.

66.   The last paragraph performs which of the following functions in the passage?

(A)   It summarizes the discussion thus far and suggests additional areas for research.

(B)   It presents a recommendation based on the evidence presented earlier.

(C)   It discusses an exceptional case in which the results expected by the author of the passage were not obtained.

(D)   It introduces an additional area of concern not mentioned earlier.

(E)   It cites a specific case that illustrates a problem presented more generally in the previous paragraph.

Logical structure

The first sentence of the last paragraph identifies its function when it introduces *the most brazen case*; this is a paragraph that will give an example. To discover what this *most brazen case* exemplifies, go back to the previous paragraph, where lines 22–25 provide a general statement about the danger of import laws being used against the companies the laws are supposed to protect. The last paragraph offers a specific example of the problem that is treated generally and hypothetically in the third paragraph.

A   It gives an example; it does not summarize.

B   It presents a specific case, not a recommendation.

C   It does discuss an exceptional case, but the author is using the case to illustrate consequences that the passage has already predicted could occur.

D   The last paragraph is discussing the same *area of concern* as the one discussed in the rest of the passage.

E   **Correct.** A potential danger of import laws, discussed hypothetically in the third paragraph, is illustrated by an actual case in the final paragraph.

The correct answer is E.

67.   The passage warns of which of the following dangers?

(A)   Companies in the United States may receive no protection from imports unless they actively seek protection from import competition.

(B)   Companies that seek legal protection from import competition may incur legal costs that far exceed any possible gain.

(C)   Companies that are United States owned but operate internationally may not be eligible for protection from import competition under the laws of the countries in which their plants operate.

(D)   Companies that are not United States owned may seek legal protection from import competition under United States import relief laws.

(E)   Companies in the United States that import raw materials may have to pay duties on those materials.

Supporting ideas

The passage as a whole warns against the potential dangers of import laws. Specifically, it points in lines 22–25 to *the danger that foreign companies will use import relief laws against the very companies the laws were designed to protect.* This specific danger is discussed at length in the third and fourth paragraphs.

A   The passage does not discuss this situation.

B   The passage does not discuss this situation.

C   The passage does not discuss this situation.

D   **Correct.** Foreign companies with operations in the United States may use the import relief laws to the detriment of American companies that have operations outside the United States.

E   The passage does not discuss this situation.

The correct answer is D.

68.   The passage suggests that which of the following is most likely to be true of United States trade laws?

(A)   They will eliminate the practice of "dumping" products in the United States.

(B)   They will enable manufacturers in the United States to compete more profitably outside the United States.

(C)   They will affect United States trade with Canada more negatively than trade with other nations.

(D)   Those that help one unit within a parent company will not necessarily help other units in the company.

(E)   Those that are applied to international companies will accomplish their intended result.

Inference

The use of *suggests* indicates that the answer is probably not directly stated in the passage. The second paragraph explains that global operations increase the complexity of a corporation's relationships, and this *intricate web* of relationships *makes it unlikely that a system of import relief laws will meet the strategic needs of all the units under the same parent company.* This statement leads the reader to infer that the trade laws may help one unit within a parent company, but not necessarily others.

A   The passage does not suggest that *dumping* will be eliminated.

B   The passage does not discuss this alternative.

C   The passage offers no evidence—even in its final paragraph—to support this inference.

D   **Correct.** The passage conveys this information in other words.

E   Lines 22–25 contend the reverse: Internationalization increases the likelihood that invoking import laws will have unintended consequences.

The correct answer is D.

69. It can be inferred from the passage that the author believes which of the following about the complaint mentioned in the last paragraph?

    (A) The ITC acted unfairly toward the complainant in its investigation.

    (B) The complaint violated the intent of import relief laws.

    (C) The response of the ITC to the complaint provided suitable relief from unfair trade practices to the complainant.

    (D) The ITC did not have access to appropriate information concerning the case.

    (E) Each of the companies involved in the complaint acted in its own best interest.

Inference

An inference requires going beyond the material explicitly stated in the passage. Reread the last paragraph to see what the author says about that specific complaint. In that case, a foreign competitor with American operations was seeking relief in these laws: *The bizarre aspect of the complaint was that a foreign conglomerate … was crying for help against a United States company.* The first sentence of the passage suggests that the author believes firms in the United States are making excessive use of trade-protection law. It does not suggest that the author opposes all trade-protection law—only that the laws should be used prudently, and in a manner consistent with their intended purpose. Lines 22–25 suggest that the author believes import relief laws are supposed to be protecting American companies from foreign competitors. The reader can infer that the author believes that the intent of these laws—the protection of American companies—is violated in the example described in the final paragraph.

A   The passage gives no information about how the ITC acted.

B   **Correct.** The author believes that the laws are supposed to protect American companies; the author's point in the final paragraph is that a foreign company may in fact invoke those laws against an American company.

C   The passage does not reveal the ITC's response to the complaint.

D   The passage does not discuss the ITC's access to information.

E   The inference concerns what the author thinks about the complaint itself rather than about the motivation of the companies.

The correct answer is B.

Questions 70–75 refer to the passage on page 386.

70. In the passage, the author is primarily interested in

    (A) suggesting an alternative to an outdated research method

    (B) introducing a new research method that calls an accepted theory into question

    (C) emphasizing the instability of data gathered from the application of a new scientific method

    (D) presenting a theory and describing a new method to test that theory

    (E) initiating a debate about a widely accepted theory

Main idea

This question concerns the main point of the passage. A careful examination of the overall structure of the passage will reveal the main point. In the first paragraph, the author briefly presents Milankovitch's theory and explains why it could not be tested early on. In the second and third paragraphs, the author describes how a new method allows testing of the theory and shows how evidence from the testing supports the theory. While the final paragraph acknowledges that other factors should be considered, the author's primary interest in this passage is in presenting Milankovitch's theory and the recently discovered method for testing it.

A   A new research method is described, but no previous method is discussed.

B   As described in the passage, the new method tests and confirms the theory; there is no mention that the theory is accepted or that the method casts doubt on it.

C   Nothing in the passage suggests that "instability of data" is an issue.

D   **Correct.** The author presents Milankovitch's theory and describes the oxygen isotope method of testing it.

E   The theory is nowhere said to be "widely accepted" and the author does not debate the theory.

The correct answer is D.

71. The author of the passage would be most likely to agree with which of the following statements about the Milankovitch theory?

   (A)   It is the only possible explanation for the ice ages.

   (B)   It is too limited to provide a plausible explanation for the ice ages, despite recent research findings.

   (C)   It cannot be tested and confirmed until further research on volcanic activity is done.

   (D)   It is one plausible explanation, though not the only one, for the ice ages.

   (E)   It is not a plausible explanation for the ice ages, although it has opened up promising possibilities for future research.

Application

The author's reaction to the statements about the Milankovitch theory must be based on how the author treats the theory in the passage. The first, second, and third paragraphs describe the theory and the use of a new research method to test the theory. The passage states that data from these tests *have established a strong connection between variations in the Earth's orbit and the periodicity of the ice ages,* suggesting that the author of the passage believes the theory is plausible. In the final paragraph, the author points to other factors that might be involved, suggesting that the theory might not provide a complete explanation.

A   In the last paragraph, the author suggests that because there are still other untested factors that may have effects on climate, other explanations are possible.

B   Though in the last paragraph the author points to other factors that may be involved, these are not presented by the author as indicating limitations that diminish the plausibility of the theory—they are acknowledged merely as possibilities that are not now understood—and nothing else in the passage suggests that the theory is "too limited."

C   The author shows how the theory has been tested; volcanic activity is not part of this theory.

D   **Correct.** The author's presentation of the theory and the tests of the theory show that the author finds the theory plausible; the mention of other factors shows the author does not think that all other explanations have been ruled out, even if they are as yet untested.

E   The theory was a plausible explanation from its beginning, but it was not testable until recently; scientists would be unlikely to try to devise means to test a theory that did not strike them as antecedently plausible.

The correct answer is D.

72. It can be inferred from the passage that the isotope record taken from ocean sediments would be less useful to researchers if which of the following were true?

   (A)   It indicated that lighter isotopes of oxygen predominated at certain times.

   (B)   It had far more gaps in its sequence than the record taken from rocks on land.

   (C)   It indicated that climate shifts did not occur every 100,000 years.

   (D)   It indicated that the ratios of oxygen 16 and oxygen 18 in ocean water were not consistent with those found in fresh water.

   (E)   It stretched back for only a million years.

Inference

To make an inference about the isotope record from ocean sediments, examine what the passage says about that record. The third paragraph discusses that record and lists its two advantages. First, it is a global record with *remarkably little variation* in samples from varied locations. Second, it is *more continuous* than the record from rocks. If either of these advantages were not true, then it is logical to infer that the record would be less useful.

A   According to lines 14–16, the lighter isotope does predominate; this is part of the record and does not affect its usefulness.

B   **Correct.** In lines 37–42, the author states that an advantage of the ocean record is that it is *a more continuous record than that taken from rocks on land*. If this were not true, the ocean record would be less useful.

C   If the record were to show that the shifts did not occur every 100,000 years, Milankovitch's theory would be weakened. This impact on the theory does not make the isotope record less useful to researchers. The record is useful precisely because it can offer evidence to confirm or refute such theories.

D   This inconsistency would not affect the usefulness of the ocean-water record. Researchers would simply need to accommodate the fresh-water inconsistency.

E   The record would still be useful. Lines 42–46 attest to the establishment of a pattern based on data from *the past several hundred thousand years*.

The correct answer is B.

73.   According to the passage, which of the following is true of the ratios of oxygen isotopes in ocean sediments?

(A)   They indicate that sediments found during an ice age contain more calcium carbonate than sediments formed at other times.

(B)   They are less reliable than the evidence from rocks on land in determining the volume of land ice.

(C)   They can be used to deduce the relative volume of land ice that was present when the sediment was laid down.

(D)   They are more unpredictable during an ice age than in other climatic conditions.

(E)   They can be used to determine atmospheric conditions at various times in the past.

Supporting ideas

The phrase *according to the passage* suggests that the answer to the question is most likely stated in the passage. Lines 12–14 state that the relative volume of land ice can be deduced from the ratio of oxygen 18 to oxygen 16 in ocean sediments.

A   There is no evidence in the passage about this point.

B   The ocean record is described in lines 38–39 as *more continuous*, so it is unlikely to be less reliable. In any case, reliability is not discussed.

C   **Correct.** Lines 12–14 explain that *the land-ice volume for a given period can be deduced from the ratio of two oxygen isotopes.*

D   There is no evidence in the passage to support this statement.

E   The passage does not discuss the use of this record in determining past atmospheric conditions.

The correct answer is C.

74.   It can be inferred from the passage that precipitation formed from evaporated ocean water has

(A)   the same isotopic ratio as ocean water

(B)   less oxygen 18 than does ocean water

(C)   less oxygen 18 than has the ice contained in continental ice sheets

(D)   a different isotopic composition than has precipitation formed from water on land

(E)   more oxygen 16 than has precipitation formed from fresh water

Inference

Any inference about precipitation from evaporated ocean water needs to be based on what the passage says. Lines 20–22 show that *heavier isotopes tend to be left behind when water evaporates from the ocean surfaces*. Therefore, the evaporated water would contain less oxygen 18 and the remaining ocean water would contain more. It is logical to infer that precipitation formed from this evaporated water would also contain less oxygen 18.

A   Lines 20–24 explain that the water remaining in the ocean after evaporation has more oxygen 18.

B   **Correct.** Since *the heavier isotopes tend to be left behind*, there will be less oxygen 18 in the evaporated water and in the precipitation that forms from it.

C   The passage suggests that the ocean water evaporates and through subsequent precipitation helps form the ice sheets, so the amount of oxygen 18 in the ice sheets should be similar to the amount in the precipitation formed from the evaporated water.

D   The passage does not discuss precipitation formed from water on land.

E   The passage does not discuss precipitation formed from fresh water.

The correct answer is B.

75.   It can be inferred from the passage that calcium carbonate shells

(A)   are not as susceptible to deterioration as rocks

(B)   are less common in sediments formed during an ice age

(C)   are found only in areas that were once covered by land ice

(D)   contain radioactive material that can be used to determine a sediment's isotopic composition

(E)   reflect the isotopic composition of the water at the time the shells were formed

Inference

Any inference about calcium carbonate shells needs to be based on what the passage says about these shells. Lines 24–32 explain the role of these shells in forming sediments and establishing a chronology for ice ages. The shells *were constructed with oxygen atoms drawn from the surrounding ocean*. Lines 29–32 make it clear that if the sediments reveal a higher ratio of oxygen 18, it is because more oxygen 18 had been left behind when the ocean water evaporated and contributed to the growth of continental ice sheets. It can thus be inferred that the shells that make up those sediments must reflect the proportion of oxygen 18 found in the ocean water at the time they were formed.

A   The only mention of rocks in the passage is a comparison of "gappiness" of the rock and sedimentary specimen records in lines 38–39; this information does not allow any firm inference to be made with respect to relative susceptibility to deterioration, though a more continuous record might be the result of less susceptibility to deterioration.

B   The passage does not make any reference to the relative abundance of these shells during ice ages; no such inference can be drawn.

C   The only information in the passage that might support this statement is found in lines 29–32, but that information, about the correlation between oxygen ratios in sediment specimens and land ice, describes a relation that implies nothing about distributions of such specimens.

D   Though the passage does indirectly indicate that the shells contained radioactive material, nothing in the passage suggests that radioactive material is used to determine isotopic composition.

E   **Correct.** The passage explains that oxygen atoms in the surrounding water are one of the building blocks of calcium carbonate shells. The isotopic composition of the surrounding water changes during the ice age cycles, so it is logical that the isotopic composition of the shells will change depending on when they were formed.

The correct answer is E.

Questions 76–81 refer to the passage on page 388.

76. The primary purpose of the passage is to

    (A) examine two sides of a historiographical debate
    (B) call into question an author's approach to a historiographical debate
    (C) examine one author's approach to a historiographical debate
    (D) discuss two authors' works in relationship to a historiographical debate
    (E) explain the prevalent perspective on a historiographical debate

Main idea

This question requires understanding what the passage as a whole is attempting to do. The passage opens by introducing two books published in 1984 that both concern the history of women in the United States. The passage then makes it clear that one book deals *directly* (line 14) with the issue of women's status, while the other does not. The passage then goes on to discuss the perspective that each book takes and what each book has to offer for an assessment of women's status in the eighteenth and nineteenth centuries.

A   The two books discussed in the passage do not take different sides on a particular debate but rather are described as being more or less useful to the debate itself.

B   The passage focuses on how two different books contain information useful to a particular historiographical debate but does not call into question the approach of either book.

C   The passage focuses on two authors' works, not one.

D   **Correct.** The passage discusses what two different books have to offer in relation to a particular historiographical debate.

E   The passage does not describe any perspective on a particular historiographical debate as being more prevalent than any other.

The correct answer is D.

77. The author of the passage mentions the supervision of schools primarily in order to

    (A) remind readers of the role education played in the cultural changes of the nineteenth century in the United States
    (B) suggest an area in which nineteenth-century American women were relatively free to exercise power
    (C) provide an example of an occupation for which accurate data about women's participation are difficult to obtain
    (D) speculate about which occupations were considered suitable for United States women of the nineteenth century
    (E) illustrate how the answers to questions about women's status depend on particular contexts

Evaluation

Answering this question depends on understanding what role a particular piece of information plays in the passage as a whole. The author implicitly supports Lebsock's contention (beginning at line 19) that different frames of reference can produce different perspectives on the debate about women's status in the eighteenth and nineteenth centuries. The author then summarizes different contexts cited by Lebsock to support the contention about frames of reference. As part of this summary, the author refers to *supervising schools* (line 23) as an example of a job that apparently showed women losing power.

A   The passage does not discuss the role of education in the nineteenth century.

B   The passage does mention some ways in which, according to Lebsock, *women … gained power* (line 24) in the nineteenth century, but *supervising schools* is not among them.

C   The passage does not discuss the difficulty of obtaining data about particular occupations.

D   The passage makes no judgments about the suitability for women of any jobs in the nineteenth century.

E   **Correct.** The passage mentions supervising schools as part of an illustration of Lebsock's claim that the debate about women's status depends on the context being examined.

The correct answer is E.

78. With which of the following characterizations of Lebsock's contribution to the controversy concerning women's status in the nineteenth-century United States would the author of the passage be most likely to agree?

    (A) Lebsock has studied women from a formerly neglected region and time period.

    (B) Lebsock has demonstrated the importance of frame of reference in answering questions about women's status.

    (C) Lebsock has addressed the controversy by using women's current status as a frame of reference.

    (D) Lebsock has analyzed statistics about occupations and property that were previously ignored.

    (E) Lebsock has applied recent historiographical methods to the biography of a nineteenth-century woman.

Supporting ideas

Answering this question requires recognizing information explicitly given in the passage. The passage introduces the work of Lebsock in line 6 and then goes on to describe several characteristics of Lebsock's book. In lines 19–21, the author introduces Lebsock's claim that the historiographical debate about women's status is dependent on frame of reference and calls that claim important; the passage then gives an example showing how frame of reference affects views of women's status. In so doing, the author displays an implicit agreement with Lebsock's discussion on this point.

A   The author of the passage portrays neither the place nor time period that Lebsock focuses on as having been neglected by historians.

B   Correct. The author describes as important Lebsock's idea that frame of reference informs the debate about women's status.

C   According to the passage, Lebsock's book deals with women's status in the eighteenth and nineteenth centuries, not the present status of women.

D   The passage does not mention or imply that Lebsock analyzed statistics in writing her book.

E   Although the passage does describe Lebsock's book as pertaining to an ongoing historiographical debate, it identifies the book's topic as *women in one southern community* (lines 7–8), not the life of a single woman.

The correct answer is B.

79. According to the passage, Lebsock's work differs from Buel and Buel's work in that Lebsock's work

    (A) uses a large number of primary sources

    (B) ignores issues of women's legal status

    (C) refuses to take a position on women's status in the eighteenth century

    (D) addresses larger historiographical issues

    (E) fails to provide sufficient material to support its claims

Supporting ideas

This question asks for recognition of information contained in the passage. In the first sentence, the passage states that Buel and Buel's work and Lebsock's work have *contrasting approaches*. The passage then proceeds, using descriptions of each work's approach, to illustrate how the works differ. The passage notes that Buel and Buel's work *makes little effort* to place its biographical subject *in the context of recent historiography on women* (lines 4–6), whereas Lebsock's work attempts *to redirect two decades of historiographical debate* about women's status.

A   Primary sources are not mentioned in the passage in relation to either work discussed.

B   The legal status of women is not mentioned in the passage.

C   Lebsock's work is described in the passage as attempting to redirect the debate about women's status in the eighteenth and nineteenth centuries.

D   **Correct.** The passage suggests that by not placing its subject's story in the context of historiography, Buel and Buel's work does not therefore address larger historiographical issues, as Lebsock's does.

E   The passage tends to support Lebsock's views and does not refer to any lack of support for the claims made in Lebsock's work.

The correct answer is D.

80. The passage suggests that Lebsock believes that compared to nineteenth-century American women, eighteenth-century American women were

(A)   in many respects less powerful in relation to men

(B)   more likely to own real estate

(C)   generally more economically independent

(D)   more independent in conducting their private lives

(E)   less likely to work as school superintendents

Inference

This question requires making an inference based on information given in the passage. As part of the passage's description of Lebsock's contribution to the historiographical debate about women's status in the eighteenth and nineteenth centuries, Lebsock's conclusions about women's autonomy are described. As part of this description, the passage cites Lebsock's conclusion that nineteenth-century women lost economic autonomy when compared to eighteenth-century women (lines 16–19).

A   The passage states that in many ways women in the nineteenth century *lost power in relation to men* (lines 21–22), which would imply that in those respects eighteenth-century women had more power in relation to men, not less. The only increase mentioned in nineteenth-century women's power is associated with owning more real estate.

B   The passage states that more nineteenth-century women owned real estate.

C   **Correct.** As the passage states, Lebsock concluded that nineteenth-century women lost economic autonomy compared to eighteenth-century women.

D   The passage states that nineteenth-century women gained more independence in their private lives.

E   The passage cites school superintendents as an example of an occupation more likely to be held by eighteenth-century women.

The correct answer is C.

81. The passage suggests that Buel and Buel's biography of Mary Fish provides evidence for which of the following views of women's history?

(A)   Women have lost power in relation to men since the colonial era.

(B)   Women of the colonial era were not as likely to be concerned with their status as were women in the nineteenth century.

(C)   The colonial era was not as favorable for women as some historians have believed.

(D)   Women had more economic autonomy in the colonial era than in the nineteenth century.

(E)   Women's occupations were generally more respected in the colonial era than in the nineteenth century.

Inference

This question requires understanding what the passage implies. The approach that Buel and Buel's work takes is specifically described in lines 3–6 and again in lines 27–32. In lines 27–30, the passage states that Buel and Buel's work *provides ample raw material for questioning the myth ... of a colonial golden age in the eighteenth century,* referring to a myth about women's status. In describing this golden age as a myth fostered by some historians, the passage suggests that this era was not as favorable to women as these historians suggest.

A The passage describes Lebsock's work as providing such evidence, not Buel and Buel's work.

B The passage does not pertain to the level of concern women had for their status.

C **Correct.** The final paragraph of the passage describes Buel and Buel's work as providing material that calls into question claims that the eighteenth century was especially favorable to women.

D The passage refers to the economic autonomy of women in relation to Lebsock's work, not Buel and Buel's work.

E The passage does not refer to whether any particular occupations held by women were more respected at one time or another.

The correct answer is C.

Questions 82–90 refer to the passage on page 390.

82. Which of the following titles best summarizes the contents of the passage?

(A) Neurotransmitters: Their Crucial Function in Cellular Communication

(B) Diet and Survival: An Old Relationship Reexamined

(C) The Blood Supply and the Brain: A Reciprocal Dependence

(D) Amino Acids and Neurotransmitters: The Connection between Serotonin Levels and Tyrosine

(E) The Effects of Food Intake on the Production and Release of Serotonin: Some Recent Findings

Main idea

Finding a title that best summarizes a passage requires examining the passage as a whole. This task is made easier by the fact that the second sentence of the first paragraph provides a topic sentence stating the main idea: *In recent studies, however, we have discovered that the production and release in brain neurons of the neurotransmitter serotonin … depend directly on the food that the body processes.* In the second paragraph, the authors cite the results of several studies relating neurotransmitter levels to eating meals and to injections of insulin. In the final paragraph, the authors discuss a study of the effect of a protein-rich meal on serotonin level. Thus, the correct title must show the relationship between food eaten and serotonin produced.

A The function of neurotransmitters is only briefly mentioned.

B The passage does not discuss the relation between diet and survival.

C There is no discussion of blood supply and the brain.

D While tyrosine is briefly mentioned, this was not a main focus of the studies.

E **Correct.** This title offers a summary of the article's contents.

The correct answer is E.

83. According to the passage, the speed with which tryptophan is provided to the brain cells of a rat varies with the

(A) amount of protein present in a meal

(B) concentration of serotonin in the brain before a meal

(C) concentration of leucine in the blood rather than with the concentration of tyrosine in the blood after a meal

(D) concentration of tryptophan in the brain before a meal

(E) number of serotonin-containing neurons

Supporting ideas

The phrase *according to the passage* suggests that the answer is likely stated in the passage. Look at the third paragraph, which discusses variations in the speed with which tryptophan is provided to the brain. Lines 41–44 state *the more protein is in a meal … the more slowly is tryptophan provided to the brain.*

A **Correct.** The greater the amount of protein, the more slowly tryptophan is provided.

B The relationship is not discussed in the passage, although the concentration of serotonin *after* a meal is measured.

C While leucine and tyrosine are mentioned, their concentrations in the blood are not compared.

D This relationship is not discussed in the passage, although the concentration of tryptophan *after* a meal is measured.

E The researchers do not consider the number of neurons.

The correct answer is A.

84. According to the passage, when the authors began their first studies, they were aware that

(A) they would eventually need to design experiments that involved feeding rats high concentrations of protein

(B) tryptophan levels in the blood were difficult to monitor with accuracy

(C) serotonin levels increased after rats were fed meals rich in tryptophan

(D) there were many neurotransmitters whose production was dependent on metabolic processes elsewhere in the body

(E) serotonin levels increased after rats were injected with a large amount of tryptophan

Supporting ideas

The phrase *according to the passage* suggests that the answer is likely stated in the passage. Look at the first sentence of the second paragraph where the focus of the authors' *first studies* is explained. The investigators wanted to see if an increase in serotonin levels would be observed after rats ate meals that changed tryptophan levels in the blood. Earlier research had already established that injecting tryptophan increased serotonin levels.

A The authors' decision to add protein came later in their studies, after they had seen the effects of eating in general.

B The passage does not identify any problems with monitoring tryptophan levels in the blood.

C This was the hypothesis of the first experiment, so the authors could not have known it beforehand.

D This point is irrelevant to the authors' work; only one neurotransmitter, serotonin, is discussed.

E **Correct.** Lines 9–12 show that this increase had already been observed.

The correct answer is E.

85. According to the passage, one reason that the authors gave rats carbohydrates was to

(A) depress the rats' tryptophan levels

(B) prevent the rats from contracting diseases

(C) cause the rats to produce insulin

(D) demonstrate that insulin is the most important substance secreted by the body

(E) compare the effect of carbohydrates with the effect of proteins

Supporting ideas

The phrase *according to the passage* suggests that the answer is likely stated in the passage. Look at lines 22–26, which say *We then decided to see whether the secretion of the animal's own insulin similarly affected serotonin production. We gave the rats a carbohydrate-containing meal that we knew would elicit insulin secretion.* These sentences together show that the authors gave carbohydrates to the rats to cause the rats to secrete insulin.

A   Lines 26–29 show that the carbohydrate increased the blood tryptophan level.
B   Preventing disease was not part of the study.
C   **Correct.** The authors had already tried injecting insulin; they then gave the rats carbohydrates to stimulate insulin production.
D   The authors make no such claim about insulin.
E   The study involving protein came later, so this could not have been the reason for giving the rats carbohydrates.

The correct answer is C.

86. According to the passage, the more protein a rat consumes, the lower will be the

(A) ratio of the rat's blood-tryptophan concentration to the amount of serotonin produced and released in the rat's brain
(B) ratio of the rat's blood-tryptophan concentration to the concentration in its blood of the other amino acids contained in the protein
(C) ratio of the rat's blood-tyrosine concentration to its blood-leucine concentration
(D) number of neurotransmitters of any kind that the rat will produce and release
(E) number of amino acids the rat's blood will contain

Supporting ideas

The phrase *according to the passage* suggests that the answer is likely stated in the passage. In lines 41–43, the authors state: *The more protein is in a meal, the lower is the ratio of the resulting blood-tryptophan concentration to the concentration of competing amino acids ….*

A   While lower levels of blood-tryptophan lead to lower serotonin levels, the relationship is not discussed in terms of a ratio.
B   **Correct.** Lines 41–43 show this to be the correct answer choice.
C   This relationship is not demonstrated in the passage.

D   This point is not made in the passage.
E   Lines 38–40 explain that *consumption of protein increases blood concentration of the other amino acids much more ….* Since proteins are made up of amino acids, eating protein would logically increase the number of amino acids.

The correct answer is B.

87. The authors' discussion of the "mechanism that provides blood tryptophan to the brain cells" (lines 34–35) is meant to

(A) stimulate further research studies
(B) summarize an area of scientific investigation
(C) help explain why a particular research finding was obtained
(D) provide supporting evidence for a controversial scientific theory
(E) refute the conclusions of a previously mentioned research study

Logical structure

To find the purpose of this discussion, look at the context in which this reference occurs. At the beginning of the third paragraph, the authors note that, *surprisingly*, adding protein led to lower brain tryptophan and serotonin levels. The question is why were the levels lowered? *The answer lies* in the mechanism cited in lines 34–35. Therefore, the discussion of the mechanism is meant to explain a surprising research finding.

A   No further studies are mentioned.
B   There are summaries of several studies, but there is no summary of an entire area of scientific investigation.
C   **Correct.** The mechanism helps explain the surprising finding about lower brain tryptophan and serotonin levels.
D   No theory is advanced, nor is any evidence about it provided.
E   There is no attempt to refute any other study.

The correct answer is C.

88. According to the passage, an injection of insulin was most similar in its effect on rats to an injection of

    (A) tyrosine
    (B) leucine
    (C) blood
    (D) tryptophan
    (E) protein

Supporting ideas

Since the question refers to information given in the passage, the answer can be found by careful reading. In order to find an injection with a similar effect, look first at the effect of injecting insulin. In lines 20–22, the authors state that *injecting insulin … caused parallel elevations in blood and brain tryptophan levels and in serotonin levels.* The only other reference to injection occurs earlier in lines 10–13 where rats injected with tryptophan had increased serotonin levels; injecting tryptophan would obviously cause tryptophan levels to increase. Thus, the effects of injecting insulin were similar to the effects on injecting tryptophan.

A   No evidence suggests that tyrosine injection would have similar effects.
B   The studies did not involve injecting leucine.
C   The studies did not involve injecting blood.
D   Correct. According to the passage, injecting tryptophan raises serotonin and tryptophan levels just as injecting insulin does.
E   The studies involved eating protein, not injecting it; eating protein did not raise serotonin levels.

The correct answer is D.

89. It can be inferred from the passage that which of the following would be LEAST likely to be a potential source of aid to a patient who was not adequately producing and releasing serotonin?

    (A) Meals consisting almost exclusively of protein
    (B) Meals consisting almost exclusively of carbohydrates
    (C) Meals that would elicit insulin secretion
    (D) Meals that had very low concentrations of tyrosine
    (E) Meals that had very low concentrations of leucine

Inference

Since this question asks for an inference, the answer is not directly stated in the passage; it must instead be derived from the information given. What kind of meals would NOT help a patient with low serotonin levels? Meals that increased serotonin would help the patient; meals that lowered serotonin would not. According to the last sentence in the passage, *the more protein in a meal, the less serotonin subsequently produced and released.* Therefore, high-protein meals would be LEAST likely to help the patient.

A   **Correct.** Meals with very high levels of protein would tend to lower serotonin and thus to be less beneficial for the patient with inadequate serotonin levels.
B   When rats ate a carbohydrate-containing meal, serotonin increased (lines 25–29). Therefore, these meals would tend to raise serotonin levels and so help the patient.
C   In the study, meals that elicited insulin secretion raised serotonin levels.
D   Since tyrosine is an amino acid found in protein, meals low in tyrosine would be low in protein and so would tend to raise serotonin levels and help the patient.
E   Since leucine is an amino acid found in protein, meals low in leucine would be low in protein and so would tend to raise serotonin levels and help the patient.

The correct answer is A.

90. It can be inferred from the passage that the authors initially held which of the following hypotheses about what would happen when they fed large amounts of protein to rats?

    (A) The rats' brain serotonin levels would not decrease.
    (B) The rats' brain tryptophan levels would decrease.
    (C) The rats' tyrosine levels would increase less quickly than would their leucine levels.
    (D) The rats would produce more insulin.
    (E) The rats would produce neurotransmitters other than serotonin.

Inference

When the authors discuss the results of adding protein to meals, they begin with the word *surprisingly* (line 30). The use of this word indicates that the results differed from the authors' initial hypotheses. The results showed lowered serotonin. It is reasonable to conclude that the researchers initially hypothesized that serotonin levels would not decrease.

A   **Correct.** The use of the word *surprisingly* in line 30 suggests that researchers thought serotonin levels would not decrease.

B   The researchers had expected that tryptophan levels would not decrease, *since protein contains tryptophan* (lines 32–34).

C   Since there is no discussion of the comparative levels of tyrosine and leucine, there was probably no hypothesis about these levels.

D   In the passage insulin is explicitly discussed in relation to carbohydrates, and plays no role at all in the discussion of protein; this very strongly suggests that insulin production played no role in the authors' decision to feed the rats large amounts of protein.

E   Serotonin is the only neurotransmitter discussed in the research, so it is unlikely that the researchers had an initial hypothesis involving other neurotransmitters.

The correct answer is A.

Questions 91–96 refer to the passage on page 392.

91.   The primary purpose of the passage is to

   (A)   evaluate a research study

   (B)   summarize the history of a research area

   (C)   report new research findings

   (D)   reinterpret old research findings

   (E)   reconcile conflicting research findings

Main idea

Determining the primary purpose comes from examining what the author does in the entire passage. In the first paragraph, the author explains Duverger's work on women's electoral participation. In the second paragraph the author points out both the successes and failures of that work. The purpose of this passage, then, is to evaluate Duverger's study.

A   **Correct.** The author evaluates Duverger's study of women's electoral activities.

B   This passage examines only one research study, not an entire research area.

C   Duverger's work was published in 1955; its findings are not new.

D   The author explains and evaluates Duverger's findings but does not reinterpret them.

E   The author's discussion of Duverger's work does not reveal or attempt to reconcile conflicting findings.

The correct answer is A.

92.   According to the passage, Duverger's study was unique in 1955 in that it

   (A)   included both election data and survey data

   (B)   gathered data from sources never before used in political studies

   (C)   included an analysis of historical processes

   (D)   examined the influence on voting behavior of the relationships between women and men

   (E)   analyzed not only voting and political candidacy but also other political activities

Supporting ideas

This question is based on information specifically stated in the first sentence of the passage. The author introduces Duverger's work by calling it the first study of *women's electoral participation ever to use election data and survey data together* (lines 3–5).

A   **Correct.** Duverger's work was unique because it used election data and survey data together.

B   The two data types had never before been used together in such a study; they may well have been used separately in many earlier political studies.

C   The second paragraph states that Duverger placed his findings in the context of historical processes, but not that he was unique in doing so (lines 15–17).

D   Duverger compared the frequency and direction of voting between men and women, not the effect that their relationships had on voting (line 27).

E   Duverger's work analyzed political activism, but the author does not claim that it was unique in doing so (lines 5–6).

The correct answer is A.

93.   Which of the following characteristics of a country is most clearly an example of a factor that Duverger, as described in the passage, failed to consider in his study?

(A)   A large population

(B)   A predominantly Protestant population

(C)   A predominantly urban population

(D)   A one-party government

(E)   Location in the heart of Europe

Inference

In the second paragraph, the author notes Duverger's *failure to consider … the influence of political regimes, the effects of economic factors, and the ramifications of political and social relations between women and men* (lines 22–27). This question requires checking this list from the passage against the possible answers; the only point of convergence is the system of government. A system of government in which there is only one political party is a type of political regime.

A   The author does not say that Duverger failed to consider the size of the population.

B   No evidence shows that Duverger failed to consider the predominance of a religion.

C   The author does not say that Duverger failed to consider the location of the population.

D   **Correct.** According to the author of the passage, Duverger failed to consider *the influence of political regimes*.

E   Duverger is not faulted for failing to consider the location of the countries that he studied.

The correct answer is D.

94.   The author implies that Duverger's actual findings are

(A)   limited because they focus on only four countries

(B)   inaccurate in their description of the four countries in the early 1950s

(C)   out-of-date in that they are inapplicable in the four countries today

(D)   flawed because they are based on unsound data

(E)   biased by Duverger's political beliefs

Inference

Since the question uses the word *implies*, the answer involves making an inference based on the information in the text. The second paragraph evaluates Duverger's work. The author notes that Duverger *placed his findings in the context of many of the historical processes*. Because these contexts have changed since 1955, the author holds that *Duverger's approach has proved more durable than his actual findings*. The actual findings, then, are out-of-date and irrelevant to the countries today.

A   The limitations the author brings up in the second paragraph have no connection to the number of countries studied.

B   The limitations the author brings up in the second paragraph do not suggest that the findings were inaccurate; rather, they were, in the author's view, significantly incomplete.

C   **Correct.** The actual findings, unlike the research method, are out-of-date and inapplicable today.

D   The limitations the author brings up in the second paragraph do not suggest that Duverger's data were unsound; rather, in the author's view, they were incomplete and have become dated.

E   The limitations the author brings up in the second paragraph do not suggest that Duverger's findings were politically biased; rather, in the author's view, they did not take full enough account of politics.

The correct answer is C.

95. The passage implies that, in comparing four European countries, Duverger found that the voting rates of women and men were most different in the country in which women

   (A) were most politically active
   (B) ran for office most often
   (C) held the most conservative political views
   (D) had the most egalitarian relations with men
   (E) had possessed the right to vote for the shortest time

Inference

The comparison of voting rates is discussed at the end of the first paragraph and forms the basis for the required inference. Duverger found that *women voted somewhat less frequently than men* but that this difference narrowed *the longer the women had the vote* (lines 9–11). That is, there was an ongoing process of convergence in voting rates for women and men, as the time period for which women had the vote lengthened. This suggests that at one end, when women had been voting for the shortest time, voting rates were most dissimilar, and at the other end, when women had been voting for the longest time, the rates were most similar.

A   Women's political activism is not suggested as a reason for the difference.
B   Women's political candidacy is not suggested as a reason for the difference.
C   Women's political views are not suggested as a reason for the difference.
D   Women's egalitarian relations with men are not suggested as a reason for the difference.
E   **Correct.** Duverger's finding is of (apparently steady, ongoing) convergence in voting-frequency rates between women and men over time. This supports the inference that the shorter the time period, the less convergence—i.e., the more divergence—there is in voting-frequency rates.

The correct answer is E.

96. The author implies that some behavioralist research involving the multinational study of women's political participation that followed Duverger's study did which of the following?

   (A) Ignored Duverger's approach
   (B) Suffered from faults similar to those in Duverger's study
   (C) Focused on political activism
   (D) Focused on the influences of political regimes
   (E) Focused on the political and social relations between women and men

Inference

The final sentence of the passage links Duverger's study to behavioralist work in general. After noting Duverger's failure to consider several important elements, the author observes, *Duverger's study foreshadowed the enduring limitations of the behavioralist approach to the multinational study of women's political participation* (lines 28–31). Thus, it is reasonable to infer that the author is of the opinion that the behavioralist research that followed Duverger's study suffered from the same limitations.

A   The author does not imply that other behavioralists ignored Duverger's approach.
B   **Correct.** The author says that Duverger's work revealed the *enduring limitations* also found in later behavioralist research.
C   This is not obviously a limitation at all, let alone one that Duverger's study suffered from.
D   This is not obviously a limitation at all, let alone one that Duverger's study suffered from.
E   This is not obviously a limitation at all, let alone one that Duverger's study suffered from.

The correct answer is B.

Questions 97–102 refer to the passage on page 394.

97. According to the passage, senior managers use intuition in all of the following ways EXCEPT to

   (A) speed up the creation of a solution to a problem
   (B) identify a problem
   (C) bring together disparate facts
   (D) stipulate clear goals
   (E) evaluate possible solutions to a problem

Supporting ideas

To answer this question, look for information explicitly stated in the passage. The third paragraph of the passage describes the five ways that senior managers use intuition. To find the one way that is NOT described, go back to the paragraph and check the possible answers against the list of the ways provided in the paragraph. The list includes all the answer choices except stipulating clear goals.

A   Lines 39–40 state that intuition allows managers to *move rapidly to engender a plausible solution.*

B   Lines 22–23 explain that managers use intuition to *sense when a problem exists.*

C   Lines 28–29 say the third function of intuition is *to synthesize isolated bits of data and practice into an integrated picture.*

D   **Correct.** Stipulating clear goals is not linked with managers' use of intuition.

E   Lines 30–38 show that managers use intuition *as a check on the results of more rational analysis,* when they are *leery of solutions suggested by these methods.*

The correct answer is D.

98.   The passage suggests which of the following about the "writers on management" mentioned in line 12?

(A)   They have criticized managers for not following the classical rational model of decision analysis.

(B)   They have not based their analyses on a sufficiently large sample of actual managers.

(C)   They have relied in drawing their conclusions on what managers say rather than on what managers do.

(D)   They have misunderstood how managers use intuition in making business decisions.

(E)   They have not acknowledged the role of intuition in managerial practice.

Inference

Answering this question depends on making an inference from the passage. The second paragraph dismisses most *writers on management* for displaying *a poor grasp of what intuition is* (line 15). The third paragraph, in contrast, describes Isenberg's research, which shows that *senior managers use intuition in at least five distinct ways* (lines 21–22), and those ways are then discussed in more detail. It can be inferred that Isenberg understands what most *writers on management* do not: how managers use intuition in making business decisions.

A   The passage does not link these writers with such a critique of managers.

B   No mention is made in the passage of the writers' methods.

C   The passage does not indicate that the writers have examined words at the expense of actions.

D   **Correct.** According to the passage, the writers do not understand what intuition is or how managers apply it.

E   According to lines 12–15, the writers have acknowledged that *some practicing managers rely heavily on intuition,* but the writers fail to understand how or why.

The correct answer is D.

99.   Which of the following best exemplifies "an 'Aha!' experience" (line 30) as it is presented in the passage?

(A)   A manager risks taking an action whose outcome is unpredictable to discover whether the action changes the problem at hand.

(B)   A manager performs well-learned and familiar behavior patterns in creative and uncharacteristic ways to solve a problem.

(C)   A manager suddenly connects seemingly unrelated facts and experiences to create a pattern relevant to the problem at hand.

(D)   A manager rapidly identifies the methodology used to compile data yielded by systematic analysis.

(E)   A manager swiftly decides which of several sets of tactics to implement in order to deal with the contingencies suggested by a problem.

Application

Finding an example involves applying the information in the passage to new situations. How do managers reach *an "Aha!" experience*? Lines 28–29 clearly explain that this experience is the result of the managers' ability *to synthesize isolated bits of data and practice into an integrated picture*. Managers connect apparently unrelated pieces of information and elements of their previous experience, and, through these unexpected connections, produce a unified picture or pattern.

A   This managerial style is mentioned in the last paragraph, but not as defining the *"Aha!" experience*.

B   Lines 23–27 indicate that managers use intuition *to perform well-learned behavior patterns rapidly*, but the result is not an *"Aha!" experience*.

C   Correct. Through an intuitive appreciation of the subtle interrelationships of disparate facts and experiences, the manager all at once perceives the coherent overarching pattern or picture formed by the interconnections, which lines 28–29 define as an *"Aha!" experience*.

D   Lines 34–38 show that managers do possess this ability, but it does not culminate in an *"Aha!" experience*.

E   This managerial style is also related to the second function of intuition, *to perform well-learned behavior patterns rapidly* (lines 23–27), but does not define an *"Aha!" experience*.

The correct answer is C.

100. According to the passage, the classical model of decision analysis includes all of the following EXCEPT

(A)   evaluation of a problem

(B)   creation of possible solutions to a problem

(C)   establishment of clear goals to be reached by the decision

(D)   action undertaken in order to discover more information about a problem

(E)   comparison of the probable effects of different solutions to a problem

Supporting ideas

What does the passage say about the classical model of decision analysis? The first sentence defines the classical model as *clarifying goals, assessing the problem, formulating options, estimating likelihoods of success, making a decision, and only then taking action to implement the decision.* To solve this process-of-elimination question, check the given list against the possible answers in order to find the one that does not match. Note that the exact wording in the answers may differ from that in the passage; the match is based on underlying meaning.

A   Evaluating a problem is identified as *assessing the problem*.

B   Creating solutions is identified as *formulating options*.

C   Establishing goals is identified as *clarifying goals*.

D   Correct. Acting in order to learn more about the problem is not identified in the passage as part of the rational classical model. It does appear as part of the acting/thinking cycle in the last paragraph.

E   Comparing probable effects is identified as *estimating likelihoods of success*.

The correct answer is D.

101. It can be inferred from the passage that which of the following would most probably be one major difference in behavior between Manager X, who uses intuition to reach decisions, and Manager Y, who uses only formal decision analysis?

(A)   Manager X analyzes first and then acts; Manager Y does not.

(B)   Manager X checks possible solutions to a problem by systematic analysis; Manager Y does not.

(C)   Manager X takes action in order to arrive at the solution to a problem; Manager Y does not.

(D)   Manager Y draws on years of hands-on experience in creating a solution to a problem; Manager X does not.

(E)   Manager Y depends on day-to-day tactical maneuvering; Manager X does not.

Application

To answer this question, apply the information in the passage to the specific examples of Manager X, an intuitive decision maker, and Manager Y, who relies exclusively on formal decision analysis. The first paragraph distinguishes between the process of formal decision analysis, in which a decision is made and then action is taken (lines 4–5), and the process of intuition, in which action is integrated into the process of thinking (lines 10–11). The last paragraph reinforces the definition of the intuitive manager as one for whom *"thinking" is inseparable from acting* and *action is often part of defining the problem.* Manager X is likely to act as part of the process of solving a problem, but Manager Y is not.

A   Acting only after analysis characterizes the rational model, not intuition.
B   Systematic analysis is typical of the rational model, not intuition.
C   **Correct.** An intuitive manager acts as a step within the problem-solving process, but a manager who depends on formal decision analysis acts only after making a decision.
D   Drawing on experience is linked in the passage with intuition rather than with rational analysis; the passage does not suggest that managers who use formal decision analysis would ignore their experience in so doing.
E   Day-to-day tactical maneuvers are required of all managers.

The correct answer is C.

102.   The passage provides support for which of the following statements?

(A)   Managers who rely on intuition are more successful than those who rely on formal decision analysis.

(B)   Managers cannot justify their intuitive decisions.

(C)   Managers' intuition works contrary to their rational and analytical skills.

(D)   Logical analysis of a problem increases the number of possible solutions.

(E)   Intuition enables managers to employ their practical experience more efficiently.

Logical structure

This question asks the reader to select the statement for which there is the most justification in the passage. The entire passage places value on the use of intuition, so the answer to this question is bound to show a benefit of intuition. Lines 25–27 reveal that intuition is based on *years of painstaking practice and hands-on experience* and lines 38–40 explain that, in contrast to formal decision analysis, intuition allows managers to *move rapidly to engender a plausible solution.* Thus, intuition enables managers to apply their experience quickly and productively, that is, efficiently.

A   The first paragraph acknowledges that most successful managers are intuitive, but it does not go so far as to make this comparison.
B   There is no support for or against this statement in the passage; Isenberg's research shows why intuition is beneficial, but does not address how managers justify their decisions.
C   Intuition does not compete with rational analysis, but complements it; line 25 provides an assurance that intuition is *not arbitrary or irrational.*
D   The passage does not support this claim for logical analysis.
E   **Correct.** Managers can reach decisions more efficiently through an intuitive approach based on experience than through time-consuming formal analyses.

The correct answer is E.

Questions 103–107 refer to the passage on page 396.

103.   The passage is primarily concerned with

(A)   identifying two practices in medical research that may affect the accuracy of clinical trials

(B)   describing aspects of medical research that tend to drive up costs

(C)   evaluating an analysis of certain shortcomings of current medical research practices

(D)   describing proposed changes to the ways in which clinical trials are conducted

(E)   explaining how medical researchers have traditionally conducted clinical trials and how such trials are likely to change

Main idea

This question requires an understanding of what the passage as a whole is doing. The passage introduces Frazier and Mosteller as proposing changes to the ways clinical trials in medical research are currently conducted. The rest of the passage then describes these proposed changes together with the support Frazier and Mosteller provide for adopting these changes.

A   The passage identifies practices in medical research to help illustrate the basis for Frazier and Mosteller's proposed changes.

B   The passage mentions medical research costs as one example within the larger description of Frazier and Mosteller's proposed changes.

C   The passage is not concerned with evaluating Frazier and Mosteller's proposed changes.

D   Correct. The passage describes the changes proposed by Frazier and Mosteller to the way clinical trials are conducted.

E   The passage is not concerned with establishing the likelihood of any changes to the way medical research is conducted.

The correct answer is D.

104. Which of the following can be inferred from the passage about a study of the category of patients referred to in lines 21–23?

(A)   Its findings might have limited applicability.

(B)   It would be prohibitively expensive in its attempt to create ideal conditions.

(C)   It would be the best way to sample the total population of potential patients.

(D)   It would allow researchers to limit information collection without increasing the risk that important variables could be overlooked.

(E)   Its findings would be more accurate if it concerned treatments for a progressive disease than if it concerned treatments for a nonprogressive disease.

Inference

This question requires drawing an inference from information given in the passage. In describing the proposals put forth by Frazier and Mosteller, the passage states in lines 16–21 that they propose using more patients in clinical trials than are currently being used, and that the trials would thereby obtain *a more representative sample of the total population with the disease under study.* The passage then states that researchers often *restrict* (lines 21–23) their trials to certain types of patients, therefore limiting the applicability of their findings.

A   Correct. The passage states that the researchers preferred to restrict the types of patients used in their studies, thereby using a less representative sample than if they used a more inclusive group of patients.

B   The passage mentions the added expense of clinical trials only in relation to data storage, collection, and analysis.

C   The passage describes the category of patients referred to as restricted and therefore unrepresentative of the total population.

D   While the passage does mention the amount of data collected about an individual patient, that topic is not connected to the category of patients referred to in lines 21–23.

E   The passage does not suggest that a study using the category of patients referred to would be more effective in investigating progressive diseases.

The correct answer is A.

105. It can be inferred from the passage that a study limited to patients like those mentioned in lines 21–23 would have which of the following advantages over the kind of study proposed by Frazier and Mosteller?

(A)   It would yield more data and its findings would be more accurate.

(B)   It would cost less in the long term, though it would be more expensive in its initial stages.

(C)   It would limit the number of variables researchers would need to consider when evaluating the treatment under study.

(D) It would help researchers to identify subgroups of patients with secondary conditions that might also be treatable.

(E) It would enable researchers to assess the value of an experimental treatment for the average patient.

Inference

This question requires understanding what the information in the passage implies. The passage explains that Frazier and Mosteller's proposal involves enrolling more patients in clinical trials (lines 18–19) than is the case with the category of patients referred to. The passage then explains that broadening the range of trial participants would allow an evaluation of particular treatments *under various conditions* and *for different patient subgroups* (lines 29–30). This strongly suggests that limiting the patients used to those described in the referred text would limit the number of variables researchers would need to consider.

A   The passage suggests that not limiting the patients used in clinical trials will yield more data than restricting them will.

B   The passage refers to the costs of clinical trials only as it concerns the collection, storage, and analysis of data collected from participants.

C   Correct. By limiting the patients used to those having the ailment under study, the passage suggests that researchers need to consider fewer variables in their assessment of a treatment.

D   The passage suggests that *not* limiting the types of patients used in clinical trials will better allow researchers to evaluate subgroups.

E   The passage suggests that limiting the types of patients available for clinical trials results in data for specific, rather than average, populations.

The correct answer is C.

106. The author mentions patients' ages (line 33) primarily in order to

(A) identify the most critical variable differentiating subgroups of patients

(B) cast doubt on the advisability of implementing Frazier and Mosteller's proposals about medical research

(C) indicate why progressive diseases may require different treatments at different stages

(D) illustrate a point about the value of enrolling a wide range of patients in clinical trials

(E) substantiate an argument about the problems inherent in enrolling large numbers of patients in clinical trials

Evaluation

Answering this question requires understanding how a particular piece of information functions in the passage as a whole. The passage is concerned with describing the proposals of Frazier and Mosteller. One of these proposals, described in the second paragraph, involves broadening the range of participants used in clinical trials. The passage states that in following this proposal, Frazier and Mosteller suggest that the effectiveness of treatments can be assessed for different patient subgroups. To affirm the value of broadening the range of participants, the passage then cites two examples of criteria by which relevant subgroups might be identified: disease stages and patients' ages.

A   The passage makes no judgment as to the value of the subgroups it refers to in relation to broadened participation in clinical trials.

B   The passage does not call into question the potential effectiveness of Frazier and Mosteller's proposals.

C   The passage's example of patients' ages is not intended to be causally connected to its previous example regarding progressive diseases.

D   Correct. Patients' ages are referred to in the passage to identify subgroups that could be evaluated if the range of participants in clinical trials were broadened.

E   The passage refers to patients' ages in support of Frazier and Mosteller's proposal that more patients be used in clinical trials.

The correct answer is D.

107. According to the passage, which of the following describes a result of the way in which researchers generally conduct clinical trials?

  (A) They expend resources on the storage of information likely to be irrelevant to the study they are conducting.

  (B) They sometimes compromise the accuracy of their findings by collecting and analyzing more information than is strictly required for their trials.

  (C) They avoid the risk of overlooking variables that might affect their findings, even though doing so raises their research costs.

  (D) Because they attempt to analyze too much information, they overlook facts that could emerge as relevant to their studies.

  (E) In order to approximate the conditions typical of medical treatment, they base their methods of information collection on those used by hospitals.

Supporting ideas

This question asks for an identification of specific information given in the passage. The passage describes the proposals of Frazier and Mosteller as attempting to improve the way clinical trials have generally been conducted. In describing how current trials are generally conducted, the passage states that researchers collect *far more background information on patients than is strictly required for their trials* (lines 4–6) and that they therefore escalate the costs of the trials.

A **Correct.** The passage states that researchers generally collect more information than they need to perform their clinical trials, which drives up the costs of the trials.

B The passage makes no judgment about the accuracy of the information collected by researchers who currently hold clinical trials.

C The passage states that the risk of overlooking relevant information in clinical trials is *never entirely eliminable* (lines 11–12).

D The passage states that researchers generally collect more information than is relevant, not that they overlook relevant information.

E The passage states that, in general, researchers currently collect more information than hospitals do (line 6).

The correct answer is A.

Questions 108–114 refer to the passage on page 398.

108. The author is primarily concerned with

  (A) advocating a return to an older methodology

  (B) explaining the importance of a recent theory

  (C) enumerating differences between two widely used methods

  (D) describing events leading to a discovery

  (E) challenging the assumptions on which a theory is based

Main idea

Examine the entire passage to find the author's primary concern. An analysis of this passage shows that the author introduces a recent theory in the first paragraph, explains the practical importance of the theory in the second, and discusses the methods of exploration the theory makes possible in the third and fourth paragraphs. The author is primarily concerned with presenting a new theory and showing why it is important.

A The only older methodology cited in the passage, *simple prospecting methods*, leads to only an *occasional discovery* (lines 15–17); there is no indication that the author favors this.

B **Correct.** The author describes a recent theory of ore formation and discusses its importance.

C Three methods of exploration are described in the third paragraph, but differences among them are not discussed.

D The passage describes a theory and the practice derived from it; it does not describe a series of events leading to a discovery.

E The author describes two theories of ore formation in the first paragraph but does not challenge the assumptions on which either one is based.

The correct answer is B.

109. According to the passage, the widely held view of Archean-age gold-quartz vein systems is that such systems

    (A) were formed from metamorphic fluids
    (B) originated in molten granite-like bodies
    (C) were formed from alluvial deposits
    (D) generally have surface expression
    (E) are not discoverable through chemical tests

Supporting ideas

This question asks for information explicitly stated in the first paragraph where Archean-age gold-quartz vein systems are discussed. The recent theory is *contrary* to the *widely held* theory that Archean-age gold-quartz vein systems *were deposited from metamorphic fluids* (lines 6–7).

A **Correct.** The widely held theory explains that the systems were *deposited from metamorphic fluids* (line 7).

B It is the recent theory that holds that the systems were formed *from magmatic fluids that originated from molten granite-like bodies* (lines 3–4); the recent theory is not *the widely held view.*

C Alluvial deposits are mentioned only in the context of *simple prospecting methods* (lines 14–16); there is nothing in the passage explicitly linking alluvial deposits to metamorphic fluids.

D Lines 17–19 explain that most deposits *not yet discovered … have no surface expression*, but there is no mention in the passage of widely held beliefs concerning surface expressions of the metamorphic fluids.

E *Sensitive chemical tests* are able to detect deposits where mineralization has occurred (lines 27–29).

The correct answer is A.

110. The passage implies that which of the following steps would be the first performed by explorers who wish to maximize their chances of discovering gold?

    (A) Surveying several sites known to have been formed more than two billion years ago
    (B) Limiting exploration to sites known to have been formed from metamorphic fluid

    (C) Using an appropriate conceptual model to select a site for further exploration
    (D) Using geophysical methods to analyze rocks over a broad area
    (E) Limiting exploration to sites where alluvial gold has previously been found

Inference

Since the question uses the word *implies*, the answer will be an inference based on what the passage says about exploration. The third and fourth paragraphs describe the process of exploration. The high-technology methods are of no use to the explorer if the sites have not mineralized, *and to maximize the chances of discovery the explorer must therefore pay particular attention to selecting the ground formations most likely to be mineralized* (lines 30–35). Conceptual models based on observation and ore-formation theories allow the explorer to identify the areas most likely to be mineralized (lines 39–46).

A Nothing in the passage indicates that a large portion of two-billion-year-old sites will have gold in them; it only indicates that if they are gold-quartz vein systems, they will be over two billion years old.

B The widely held view, rather than the recent theory that is the focus of the passage, argued that gold-quartz vein systems were formed from metamorphic fluids. The passage says the recent theory has *considerable practical importance*, suggesting the benefits of applying the recent theory rather than this widely held view.

C **Correct.** Conceptual models lead the explorer to the sites most likely to have mineralized.

D Geophysical techniques are of no use unless ground formations in an area have been mineralized (lines 24–32).

E The *simple prospecting methods* that find alluvial gold lead to only an *occasional discovery*; *most deposits not yet discovered … are buried* (lines 15–19).

The correct answer is C.

111. Which of the following statements about discoveries of gold deposits is supported by information in the passage?

    (A) The number of gold discoveries made annually has increased between the time of the original gold rushes and the present.

    (B) New discoveries of gold deposits are likely to be the result of exploration techniques designed to locate buried mineralization.

    (C) It is unlikely that newly discovered gold deposits will ever yield as much as did those deposits discovered during the original gold rushes.

    (D) Modern explorers are divided on the question of the utility of simple prospecting methods as a source of new discoveries of gold deposits.

    (E) Models based on the theory that gold originated from magmatic fluids have already led to new discoveries of gold deposits.

Supporting ideas

This question requires consideration of explicit information throughout the passage. The second paragraph explains that *most deposits not yet discovered … are buried* (lines 17–19), so the explorer's best means of discovering them is the use of *conceptual models* to identify the sites most likely to have buried minerals (lines 35–38). At that point, the explorer may use the high-technology methods possible when buried mineralization is present (lines 22–29).

A   The passage does not discuss the number of gold discoveries.

B   Correct. Since most gold deposits are buried, explorers must find the sites most likely to contain buried minerals.

C   The passage does not discuss the yield of gold discoveries.

D   While *simple prospecting methods* lead only to an *occasional discovery*, modern explorers are not said to dispute their utility (lines 15–17).

E   The passage does not say that gold deposits have already been found by using the models based on this recent theory.

The correct answer is B.

112. It can be inferred from the passage that which of the following is easiest to detect?

    (A) A gold-quartz vein system originating in magmatic fluids

    (B) A gold-quartz vein system originating in metamorphic fluids

    (C) A gold deposit that is mixed with granite

    (D) A gold deposit that has shed alluvial gold

    (E) A gold deposit that exhibits chemical halos

Application

To answer this question, apply what the passage says about gold deposits to the examples in the answer choices. The second paragraph states that the gold deposits discovered during the gold rushes were *exposed at the Earth's surface*; they were found because *they had shed trails of alluvial gold that were easily traced by simple prospecting methods* (lines 11–16). Most deposits have not been detected because they are buried and have *no surface expression*. Thus the simplest gold to find would be that in a deposit that had shed alluvial gold.

A   The recent theory holds that gold-quartz vein systems are formed from magmatic fluids, but does not say that these systems have easily detectable surface expressions; the passage states that they form deep beneath the surface of Earth, which makes it unlikely that they will be easy to find.

B   The widely held view contends that gold-quartz vein systems are formed from metamorphic fluids, but does not say if these have easily detectable surface expressions.

C   The passage does not comment on gold deposits mixed with granite, although the recent theory does mention *molten granite-like bodies deep beneath the surface of the Earth* (lines 4–5).

D   Correct. Finding gold deposits that have shed alluvial gold at the Earth's surface is far easier than finding buried gold deposits.

E   One complex, difficult subsurface exploration method involves chemical tests detecting the subtle chemical halos that surround mineralized areas; clearly this is not the *easiest* means of detecting gold deposits.

The correct answer is D.

113. The theory mentioned in lines 1–5 relates to the conceptual models discussed in the passage in which of the following ways?

    (A) It may furnish a valid account of ore-forming processes, and, hence, can support conceptual models that have great practical significance.

    (B) It suggests that certain geological formations, long believed to be mineralized, are in fact mineralized, thus confirming current conceptual models.

    (C) It suggests that there may not be enough similarity across Archean-age gold-quartz vein systems to warrant the formulation of conceptual models.

    (D) It corrects existing theories about the chemical halos of gold deposits, and thus provides a basis for correcting current conceptual models.

    (E) It suggests that simple prospecting methods still have a higher success rate in the discovery of gold deposits than do more modern methods.

Logical structure

This question requires considering the conceptual models described in lines 35–41 in light of the recent theory (lines 1–5), which the author assures the reader has *considerable practical importance* (lines 10–11). The conceptual models are derived from observation and from *theories of ore-forming processes*. Therefore, the recent theory may explain ore formation in a way that leads to the development of an updated model, and that model may then aid in the discovery of gold deposits.

A **Correct.** The theory provides an explanation of ore formation, which aids in creating a conceptual model that may help explorers find gold deposits.

B The theory does not confirm models, but contributes to forming them.

C The practical value of the theory is that it can help to formulate models.

D The theory does not challenge theories about chemical halos but rather contributes to the development of conceptual models that might allow for the broader application of chemical halos.

E The theory does not compare methods of discovering gold deposits.

The correct answer is A.

114. According to the passage, methods of exploring for gold that are widely used today are based on which of the following facts?

    (A) Most of the Earth's remaining gold deposits are still molten.

    (B) Most of the Earth's remaining gold deposits are exposed at the surface.

    (C) Most of the Earth's remaining gold deposits are buried and have no surface expression.

    (D) Only one type of gold deposit warrants exploration, since the other types of gold deposits are found in regions difficult to reach.

    (E) Only one type of gold deposit warrants exploration, since the other types of gold deposits are unlikely to yield concentrated quantities of gold.

Supporting ideas

This question concerns factual information stated in the passage. In contrast to the gold deposits discovered at the Earth's surface, *most deposits not yet discovered have gone undetected because they are buried and have no surface expression* (lines 17–19). The *methods widely used today* must search for buried minerals rather than minerals on the surface (lines 22–29).

A The passage mentions neither molten gold nor the method to detect it.

B The passage explicitly says that most deposits are buried.

C **Correct.** The passage explicitly states that most gold deposits are buried, leaving no traces at the Earth's surface.

D The passage neither distinguishes between types of gold nor describes inaccessible regions.

E The passage does not relate types of gold to yields of gold deposits.

The correct answer is C.

Questions 115–119 refer to the passage on page 400.

115. The passage is primarily concerned with

(A)   defending a controversial approach
(B)   criticizing an accepted view
(C)   summarizing research findings
(D)   contrasting competing theories
(E)   describing an innovative technique

Main idea

Figuring out the authors' primary concern depends on a careful review of the passage as a whole. The first paragraph identifies the larger question that is the context for the authors' investigation. The second paragraph presents the part of the question the authors researched, concluding with their unexpected results. The third paragraph explains the importance of these findings in relation to the larger question of the universe's possible *"close."* The authors' primary purpose in this passage is to summarize the findings of their research.

A   The authors do not discuss approaches to the question they research.
B   The authors mention that their findings do not conform to Kepler's law, but the passage's primary focus is on summarizing research findings and not on criticizing any particular view.
C   **Correct.** This passage presents a summation of the findings of the authors' research.
D   The authors do not contrast different theories in this passage.
E   The authors do not discuss new techniques in this passage.

The correct answer is C.

116. The authors' study indicates that, in comparison with the outermost regions of a typical spiral galaxy, the region just outside the nucleus can be characterized as having

(A)   higher rotational velocity and higher luminosity
(B)   lower rotational velocity and higher luminosity
(C)   lower rotational velocity and lower luminosity
(D)   similar rotational velocity and higher luminosity
(E)   similar rotational velocity and similar luminosity

Inference

In the second paragraph, the authors observe that *outside the bright nucleus of a typical spiral galaxy luminosity falls off rapidly* (lines 20–21); the region just outside the nucleus may thus be characterized as having higher luminosity than the outermost regions of a spiral galaxy. Their research finds that *the rotational velocity in spiral galaxies either remains constant with increasing distance from the center or increases slightly* (lines 27–30). The region just outside the nucleus may thus be characterized as sharing with the outermost regions of a spiral galaxy a similar rotational velocity.

A   This region was expected to have higher rotational velocity, but the research findings did not corroborate this hypothesis; it is correct that the region has higher luminosity.
B   The region does have higher luminosity, but not lower rotational velocity.
C   The region has neither lower luminosity nor lower rotational velocity.
D   **Correct.** The region has similar rotational velocity and higher luminosity.
E   The region has similar rotational velocity but higher luminosity.

The correct answer is D.

117. The authors' suggestion that "as much as 90 percent of the mass of the universe is not radiating at any wavelength with enough intensity to be detected on the Earth" (lines 34–37) would be most weakened if which of the following were discovered to be true?

   (A) Spiral galaxies are less common than types of galaxies that contain little nonluminous matter.

   (B) Luminous and nonluminous matter are composed of the same basic elements.

   (C) The bright nucleus of a typical spiral galaxy also contains some nonluminous matter.

   (D) The density of the observable universe is greater than most previous estimates have suggested.

   (E) Some galaxies do not rotate or rotate too slowly for their rotational velocity to be measured.

Application

The authors' conclusion about nonluminous matter is based on their study of the rotational velocity of spiral galaxies. If spiral galaxies were found to be atypical of galaxies, then it would be possible that, in those other galaxies, nonluminous matter does not increase as luminous matter decreases. If this were the case, the authors' conclusion would be based on a sample of galaxies not representative of the whole, and their argument would be seriously weakened.

A **Correct.** The authors' conclusion assumes that spiral galaxies are typical of all galaxies; information calling that assumption into question weakens the argument.

B The relation rather than the composition of luminous and nonluminous mass is relevant to the conclusion.

C Nonluminous mass increases as luminous mass decreases: This finding does not rule out that the nucleus contains some nonluminous mass; the argument is not affected.

D The density of the observable universe is only *a fraction* of the density needed to "*close*" the universe, so even if this density were greater, it is not likely to exceed the density of nonluminous matter.

E The authors are concerned only with measurable rotational velocity.

The correct answer is A.

118. It can be inferred from information presented in the passage that if the density of the universe were equivalent to significantly less than three hydrogen atoms per cubic meter, which of the following would be true as a consequence?

   (A) Luminosity would be a true indicator of mass.

   (B) Different regions in spiral galaxies would rotate at the same velocity.

   (C) The universe would continue to expand indefinitely.

   (D) The density of the invisible matter in the universe would have to be more than 70 times the density of the luminous matter.

   (E) More of the invisible matter in spiral galaxies would have to be located in their nuclei than in their outer regions.

Inference

An inference is drawn from stated information. This question refers to the first paragraph, where the authors explain that *the critical density of matter needed to brake the expansion and "close" the universe is equivalent to three hydrogen atoms per cubic meter* (lines 7–9). If the density is significantly less, then the universe will not "*close*" but continue to expand indefinitely.

A The authors' finding that luminosity is not a true indicator of mass is not derived from the conclusion that the density is less than three hydrogen atoms per cubic meter.

B The authors' finding that different regions rotate at similar velocities does not come from the hypothesis about the density of the universe.

C **Correct.** If the critical density needed to "*close*" the universe is equivalent to three hydrogen atoms per cubic meter, then a density of significantly less than this amount means that the universe will continue its expansion.

D This statement would be true of the hypothetical "*close*" of the universe, but if the density is less than three hydrogen atoms per cubic meter, the universe will continue its expansion.

E This statement cannot be inferred from the hypothesis about the density of the universe.

The correct answer is C.

119. The authors propose all of the following as possibly contributing to the "missing matter" in spiral galaxies EXCEPT

    (A) massive black holes
    (B) small black holes
    (C) small, dim stars
    (D) massive stars
    (E) large planets

Supporting ideas

This question asks the reader to find the list of possible explanations for the *"missing"* or *dark matter* that the authors give in the passage and to check that list against the possible answers. Using the process of elimination will show which answer is not included on the authors' list. In the final paragraph, the authors write, *Such dark matter could be in the form of extremely dim stars of low mass, of large planets like Jupiter, or of black holes, either small or massive* (lines 37–40).

A   The authors include massive black holes.
B   The authors include small black holes.
C   The authors include small, dim stars.
D   Correct. The authors do not include massive stars in their list of possible explanations for *"missing matter."*
E   The authors include large planets.

The correct answer is D.

Questions 120–127 refer to the passage on page 402.

120. The primary purpose of the passage is to

    (A) advocate a more positive attitude toward technological change
    (B) discuss the implications for employees of the modernization of a telephone exchange
    (C) consider a successful challenge to the constructivist view of technological change
    (D) challenge the position of advocates of technological determinism
    (E) suggest that the social causes of technological change should be studied in real situations

Main idea

This question asks for an assessment of what the passage as a whole is doing. The passage introduces Clark's study as a *solid contribution* (lines 3–4) to the debate between technological determinists and social constructivists. In the second paragraph, Braverman is introduced as holding a position of social constructivism, a position that Clark takes issue with. In the final paragraph, the passage holds that Clark *refutes the extremes of the constructivists* (line 33), and Clark's arguments challenging social constructivism are then described.

A   The passage takes no position on the merits of technological change but is concerned only with the role of such change in society.
B   The passage mentions telephone exchange workers as an example that helps illustrate the more central debate between determinists and constructivists.
C   Correct. The passage is mainly concerned with portraying Clark's view as a successful challenge to constructivism.
D   The passage describes Clark's view as a successful challenge to social constructivism, not technological determinism.
E   The passage is concerned with describing a challenge to social constructivism and not with suggesting the context in which technological change ought to be studied.

The correct answer is C.

121. Which of the following statements about the modernization of the telephone exchange is supported by information in the passage?

    (A) The new technology reduced the role of managers in labor negotiations.
    (B) The modernization was implemented without the consent of the employees directly affected by it.
    (C) The modernization had an impact that went significantly beyond maintenance routines.
    (D) Some of the maintenance workers felt victimized by the new technology.
    (E) The modernization gave credence to the view of advocates of social constructivism.

Supporting ideas

This question requires recognizing information contained in the passage. The passage states in the first paragraph that Clark's study focused on the modernization of a telephone exchange and the effect this had on maintenance work and workers. After describing Braverman's analysis in the second paragraph as being at odds with Clark's views, the passage discusses Clark's views in more detail in the final paragraph. As part of this discussion, the passage notes that Clark shows how a change from *maintenance-intensive electromechanical switches to semielectronic switching systems* at the telephone exchange *altered work tasks, skills, training opportunities, administration, and organization of workers* (lines 41–46). Thus, the passage shows that the modernization of the telephone exchange affected much more than maintenance routines.

A   The passage does not discuss whether new technology reduces the role of managers in labor negotiations.

B   The passage does not discuss the role of employee consent in the modernization of the telephone exchange.

C   **Correct.** The passage states that the modernization of the telephone exchange affected tasks, skills, training, administration, and the organization of workers.

D   The passage does not suggest that maintenance workers felt victimized by the modernization of the telephone exchange.

E   The passage describes modernization as a fact viewable from a perspective of social constructivism or technological determinism, but that does not in itself support either view.

The correct answer is C.

122. Which of the following most accurately describes Clark's opinion of Braverman's position?

(A)   He respects its wide-ranging popularity.

(B)   He disapproves of its misplaced emphasis on the influence of managers.

(C)   He admires the consideration it gives to the attitudes of the workers affected.

(D)   He is concerned about its potential to impede the implementation of new technologies.

(E)   He is sympathetic to its concern about the impact of modern technology on workers.

Inference

Answering this question requires inferring what the passage's author likely believes. The passage describes Braverman's position as one of mainstream social constructivism (lines 23–24), a position that Clark takes issue with. Although it describes Braverman's position, the rest of the passage is devoted to showing how Clark's position takes issue with Braverman's. In the second paragraph, the passage describes Clark as holding that *technology can be a primary determinant of social and managerial organization* (lines 11–12), which suggests that managers are sometimes subordinate to technological change. In lines 16–19, however, Braverman is described as holding that *the shape of a technological system is subordinate to the manager's desire to wrest control of the labor process from the workers*, which shows that Clark and Braverman are at odds on this point.

A   Since the passage says that Clark believes an important insight *has been obscured by the recent sociological fashion* that Braverman's views exemplify (lines 12–15), one cannot infer that Clark respects the popularity of Braverman's views.

B   **Correct.** The passage shows that Clark believes managers to have less influence over how technology affects an organization than Braverman claims that they have.

C   The passage does not indicate that Clark admires any aspect of Braverman's position.

D   The passage does not indicate that Clark considers impediments to modernization.

E   The passage does not indicate that Clark is sympathetic to any concerns attributed to Braverman.

The correct answer is B.

123. The information in the passage suggests that which of the following statements from hypothetical sociological studies of change in industry most clearly exemplifies the social constructivists' version of technological determinism?

(A)   It is the available technology that determines workers' skills, rather than workers' skills influencing the application of technology.

(B)   All progress in industrial technology grows out of a continuing negotiation between technological possibility and human need.

(C)   Some organizational change is caused by people; some is caused by computer chips.

(D)   Most major technological advances in industry have been generated through research and development.

(E)   Some industrial technology eliminates jobs, but educated workers can create whole new skills areas by the adaptation of the technology.

Application

This question requires understanding different points of view discussed in the passage. In the first paragraph, the passage mentions the debate involving technological determinism and social constructivism. In the second and third paragraphs, the passage uses Braverman's analysis to illustrate the social constructivists' position and in the third paragraph suggests that the constructivists are *misrepresenting technological determinism* (lines 25–26). In lines 31–32, the constructivists are reported to hold that technological determinism views technology as *existing outside society, capable of directly influencing skills and work organization.*

   A   **Correct.** This statement is consistent with the constructivists' view that technological determinism sees technology as outside of society, influencing workers' skills.
   B   The passage states that the constructivists hold that *technological determinists are supposed to believe ... that machinery imposes appropriate forms of order on society* (lines 27–29), suggesting that no negotiation is present.

C   According to the description of them in the passage, constructivists portray technological determinists as believing that technology, not people, drives organizational change.
D   The passage does not portray either constructivists or determinists as being concerned with technological research and development.
E   The passage does not portray either constructivists or determinists as being concerned with technology-driven job elimination or creation.

The correct answer is A.

124. The information in the passage suggests that Clark believes that which of the following would be true if social constructivism had not gained widespread acceptance?

(A)   Businesses would be more likely to modernize without considering the social consequences of their actions.

(B)   There would be greater understanding of the role played by technology in producing social change.

(C)   Businesses would be less likely to understand the attitudes of employees affected by modernization.

(D)   Modernization would have occurred at a slower rate.

(E)   Technology would have played a greater part in determining the role of business in society.

Inference

Answering this question involves understanding a point of view as it is described in the passage. The passage aligns Clark's study closely with the technological determinists, summarizing his view in lines 11–12: *technology can be a primary determinant of social and managerial organization.* In the following sentence, the passage states that Clark believes that *this possibility is obscured by the recent sociological fashion, exemplified by Braverman's analysis* (lines 12–15). After illustrating Braverman's analysis, the passage then states that it represents *social constructivism.*

A   According to the passage, Clark holds that constructivists obscure how modernization might have social consequences.

B   **Correct.** According to the passage, Clark sees constructivism as obscuring the possibility that technology plays a primary role in social change.

C   The passage does not discuss how the attitudes of employees are perceived by their employers.

D   The passage describes a debate about the history and sociology of technology; it does not suggest that sociological analyses affect the pace of modernization.

E   The passage describes a debate about the history and sociology of technology; it does not suggest that sociological analyses affect the role that technology plays in business.

The correct answer is B.

125. According to the passage, constructivists employed which of the following to promote their argument?

    (A)   Empirical studies of business situations involving technological change

    (B)   Citation of managers supportive of their position

    (C)   Construction of hypothetical situations that support their view

    (D)   Contrasts of their view with a misstatement of an opposing view

    (E)   Descriptions of the breadth of impact of technological change

Supporting ideas

Answering this question involves recognizing information given in the passage. The passage indicates that a debate exists between technological determinists and social constructivists, suggesting that these views are in opposition. The passage goes on to state that *constructivists gain acceptance by misrepresenting technological determinism* (lines 25–26). This misrepresentation is presented as the *alternative to constructivism* (lines 29–30), suggesting that constructivists promoted their own view by contrasting it with a misrepresentation of determinists' views.

A   The passage mentions empirical studies in relation to Clark's study but not Braverman's analysis.

B   The passage does not mention that managers were supportive of any particular point of view within the sociology of technology.

C   The passage does not mention any hypothetical situations as being used by the constructivists in support of their view.

D   **Correct.** The passage indicates that the constructivists have come into fashion by contrasting their own views with a misrepresentation of the views of technological determinists.

E   The passage does not describe the constructivists as making determinations regarding the degree of impact that technological change has on social or managerial organization.

The correct answer is D.

126. The author of the passage uses the expression "are supposed to" in line 27 primarily in order to

    (A)   suggest that a contention made by constructivists regarding determinists is inaccurate

    (B)   define the generally accepted position of determinists regarding the implementation of technology

    (C)   engage in speculation about the motivation of determinists

    (D)   lend support to a comment critical of the position of determinists

    (E)   contrast the historical position of determinists with their position regarding the exchange modernization

Evaluation

This question requires understanding how a particular phrase functions in the passage as a whole. In the third paragraph the passage states that *constructivists gain acceptance by misrepresenting technological determinism* (lines 25–26) and follows this claim with an example of this misrepresentation, stating that *technological determinists are supposed to believe, for example* (lines 27–28). This line implies that the constructivist view of the determinists is inaccurate.

A   **Correct.** The passage uses the expression in part to provide an example of the constructivists' misrepresentation of the determinists.

B   The passage indicates that the view attributed to the determinists is a misrepresentation, not one that is generally accepted by determinists.

C   The expression in the passage is part of a discussion about the motivation of constructivists, not determinists.

D   The expression in the passage is part of a discussion that is critical of the constructivists, not the determinists.

E   The passage does not describe either the historical position of determinists or their position on the exchange modernization.

The correct answer is A.

127. Which of the following statements about Clark's study of the telephone exchange can be inferred from information in the passage?

(A) Clark's reason for undertaking the study was to undermine Braverman's analysis of the function of technology.

(B) Clark's study suggests that the implementation of technology should be discussed in the context of conflict between labor and management.

(C) Clark examined the impact of changes in the technology of switching at the exchange in terms of overall operations and organization.

(D) Clark concluded that the implementation of new switching technology was equally beneficial to management and labor.

(E) Clark's analysis of the change in switching systems applies only narrowly to the situation at the particular exchange that he studied.

Inference

This question requires understanding what the passage implies in its discussion of a point of view. The details of Clark's views are discussed primarily in the final paragraph. The passage states that on an empirical level, Clark demonstrates that technological change regarding switches at the telephone exchange *altered work tasks, skills, training opportunities, administration, and organization of workers* (lines 44–46). The passage goes on to state Clark's contention that these changes even influenced negotiations between management and labor unions.

A   The passage indicates that Clark's study addressed the extremes of both technological determinism and social constructivism. It cites Braverman as a proponent of social constructivism but provides no evidence that Clark's motivation in beginning his study was specifically to target an analysis offered by Braverman.

B   The passage indicates that Clark attributed some organizational change to the way labor and management negotiated the introduction of technology but does not mention conflict between them.

C   **Correct.** According to the passage, Clark concludes that changes to the technology of switches had an influence on several aspects of the overall operations and organization of the telephone exchange.

D   The passage does not indicate that Clark assesses the benefits of technological change to either labor or management.

E   The passage indicates that Clark believes the change in switching technology influenced many aspects of the overall operations of the telephone exchange.

The correct answer is C.

Questions 128–133 refer to the passage on page 404.

128. According to the passage, the five well-known plant hormones are not useful in controlling the growth of crops because

   (A) it is not known exactly what functions the hormones perform
   (B) each hormone has various effects on plants
   (C) none of the hormones can function without the others
   (D) each hormone has different effects on different kinds of plants
   (E) each hormone works on only a small subset of a cell's genes at any particular time

Supporting ideas

To answer this question, look for information that is provided in the passage. Lines 16–20 explain that each of the five plant hormones *has more than one effect on the growth and development of plants*; for this reason, they *are not very useful in artificially controlling the growth of crops*.

A   Lines 20–25 describe in detail the multiple functions of the hormone auxin.
B   **Correct.** The hormones *have so many simultaneous effects* on plants that they are not useful in controlling the growth of crops.
C   The passage provides no evidence to support this reason.
D   No information is given in the passage to support this reason.
E   The hormones' multiple effects on plant growth, not their specific effect at the cellular level, make them ineffective at artificially controlling crop growth.

The correct answer is B.

129. The passage suggests that the place of hypothalamic hormones in the hormonal hierarchies of animals is similar to the place of which of the following in plants?

   (A) Plant cell walls
   (B) The complement of genes in each plant cell
   (C) A subset of a plant cell's gene complement
   (D) The five major hormones
   (E) The oligosaccharins

Inference

This question asks for information that is not directly stated in the passage. It requires examining the analogy between the action of hormones in animals and in plants, which is the subject of the third and fourth paragraphs. In animals, hypothalamic hormones stimulate the pituitary gland to synthesize and release many different hormones; this process causes hormones from the adrenal cortex to be released. A similar *hierarchy of hormones* may exist in plants. The pleiotropic plant hormones may activate the enzymes that, in turn, release oligosaccharins from the cell wall. It is reasonable to infer that, in triggering the action, the plant hormones may act in a way similar to the hypothalamic hormones in animals.

A   Plant cell walls do not activate enzymes as the hypothalamic hormones activate the pituitary gland.
B   The passage states that all cells of a plant start out with the same complement of genes (lines 1–2), but this statement is not part of the analogy.
C   Line 5 refers to the subset of genes, but it is not a part of the analogy.
D   **Correct.** Like hypothalamic hormones in animals, the five major plant hormones may be responsible for releasing the catalysts for growth.
E   The oligosaccharins are part of the hierarchy, but they are not equivalent to the hypothalamic hormones in releasing other hormones.

The correct answer is D.

130. The passage suggests that which of the following is a function likely to be performed by an oligosaccharin?

    (A) To stimulate a particular plant cell to become part of a plant's root system
    (B) To stimulate the walls of a particular cell to produce other oligosaccharins
    (C) To activate enzymes that release specific chemical messengers from plant cell walls
    (D) To duplicate the gene complement in a particular plant cell
    (E) To produce multiple effects on a particular subsystem of plant cells

Inference

Answering this question requires making an inference based on the information in the passage. The analogy between animal and plant hormones describes a process that ends, in animals, with *specific effects on target organs all over the body* (lines 33–34). While the pleiotropic plant hormones have multiple effects, the oligosaccharins are described as *more specific chemical messengers* (lines 43–44). It is reasonable to infer that oligosaccharins affect a specific part of a plant's growth.

A   **Correct.** This is the only response that gives an example of an effect on a specific aspect of plant growth and development.
B   The last paragraph explains that enzymes release oligosaccharins. The passage provides no evidence that oligosaccharins stimulate the release of other oligosaccharins.
C   The pleiotropic plant hormones, not the oligosaccharins, may activate the enzymes (lines 41–43).
D   The passage does not discuss such duplication.
E   The oligosaccharins, as *more specific chemical messengers*, have a specific effect, not multiple effects, on plant growth.

The correct answer is A.

131. The author mentions specific effects that auxin has on plant development in order to illustrate the

    (A) point that some of the effects of plant hormones can be harmful
    (B) way in which hormones are produced by plants
    (C) hierarchical nature of the functioning of plant hormones
    (D) differences among the best-known plant hormones
    (E) concept of pleiotropy as it is exhibited by plant hormones

Logical structure

To answer this question, reread the section where auxin is discussed. The second paragraph explains that each of the five major pleiotropic hormones, including auxin, *has more than one effect on the growth and development of plants*. The author then lists auxin's multiple effects as an example of the principle of pleiotropy in plants.

A   The passage does not discuss harmful effects.
B   The passage discusses the effects of hormones, not their production.
C   Auxin is used to exemplify the many different effects of a pleiotropic hormone, not its role in a hierarchy of hormones.
D   The differences among the five major hormones are not discussed.
E   **Correct.** The author lists auxin's multiple effects to illustrate how pleiotropic hormones affect plant growth.

The correct answer is E.

132. According to the passage, which of the following best describes a function performed by oligosaccharins?

(A) Regulating the daily functioning of a plant's cells
(B) Interacting with one another to produce different chemicals
(C) Releasing specific chemical messengers from a plant's cell walls
(D) Producing the hormones that cause plant cells to differentiate to perform different functions
(E) Influencing the development of a plant's cells by controlling the expression of the cells' genes

Supporting ideas

To answer this question, look for information that is provided in the passage. Oligosaccharins are *regulatory molecules* (line 13). They form part of the complex system that turns on, or expresses, a small subset of genes in a particular kind of cell. As explained in the first paragraph, this process allows plant cells to differentiate and form different plant structures. Unlike the five major plant hormones, the oligosaccharins affect a specific aspect of the plant's growth (lines 14–17).

A   The passage does not discuss the daily functioning of a plant's cells.
B   The passage provides no evidence of this interaction.
C   The oligosaccharins *are fragments of the cell wall* (line 39) and the *specific chemical messengers from the cell wall* (lines 43–44).
D   The oligosaccharins are not said to produce hormones.
E   **Correct.** Oligosaccharins are part of the system that turns on, or expresses, the subset of a cell's genes that allows cells to grow into different plant structures.

The correct answer is E.

133. The passage suggests that, unlike the pleiotropic hormones, oligosaccharins could be used effectively to

(A) trace the passage of chemicals through the walls of cells
(B) pinpoint functions of other plant hormones
(C) artificially control specific aspects of the development of crops
(D) alter the complement of genes in the cells of plants
(E) alter the effects of the five major hormones on plant development

Inference

The passage does not explicitly state how oligosaccharins could be used, but a use can be inferred. The second paragraph establishes that the pleiotropic hormones are not useful in artificially controlling crop growth because of their multiple, diverse effects. Oligosaccharins are contrasted with the hormones because they have specific effects. Thus it is reasonable to infer that oligosaccharins might be used to control specific aspects of crop growth.

A   Passage of chemicals through cell walls is not discussed.
B   The passage does not indicate that oligosaccharins act in this way.
C   **Correct.** Because the oligosaccharins have specific rather than multiple effects, they might have the potential to be used to control specific aspects of a crop's growth.
D   The oligosaccharins are not said to alter the cells' complement of genes.
E   The passage does not show that oligosaccharins alter the hormones' effects.

The correct answer is C.

Questions 134–139 refer to the passage on page 406.

134. The author indicates explicitly that which of the following records has been a source of information in her investigation?

    (A) United States Immigration Service reports from 1914 to 1930
    (B) Payrolls of southern manufacturing firms between 1910 and 1930
    (C) The volume of cotton exports between 1898 and 1910
    (D) The federal census of 1910
    (E) Advertisements of labor recruiters appearing in southern newspapers after 1910

Supporting ideas

Since the question uses the word *explicitly*, it is clear that the answer can be found in the passage. In lines 27–30, the author refers to the number of African American workers in *manufacturing and mechanical pursuits*, a phrase cited as coming from the federal census and indicating that she was using census data. While she probably used other sources as well, no other source is explicitly mentioned.

    A   Immigration Service reports are not mentioned in the passage.
    B   Payroll records are not mentioned in the passage.
    C   While the decline of the cotton industry is mentioned, records of exports are not.
    D   Correct. The federal census is indicated as a source of information on the employment of African American workers.
    E   Labor recruiters and the African American press are mentioned, but there is no mention of data being collected from labor recruiting ads.

The correct answer is D.

135. In the passage, the author anticipates which of the following as a possible objection to her argument?

    (A) It is uncertain how many people actually migrated during the Great Migration.
    (B) The eventual economic status of the Great Migration migrants has not been adequately traced.
    (C) It is not likely that people with steady jobs would have reason to move to another area of the country.
    (D) It is not true that the term "manufacturing and mechanical pursuits" actually encompasses the entire industrial sector.
    (E) Of the African American workers living in southern cities, only those in a small number of trades were threatened by obsolescence.

Logical structure

Answering questions about the author's line of argument requires following the steps in the logical structure of that argument. The author argues that many of the African American migrants to the North may have lived and worked in southern urban areas, not rural areas. In lines 33–36, she recognizes that some people may find it *surprising to argue* that African Americans with steady jobs would leave and proceeds to offer *an explanation* based on southern labor conditions. She thus anticipates the objection that workers would not leave steady jobs.

    A   The actual number of people migrating is not part of the author's argument, which concerns whether the migrants came from urban or rural backgrounds.
    B   The eventual economic status is outside the scope of the argument.
    C   Correct. The author anticipates this objection and answers it by citing southern labor conditions.
    D   The author claims that *"manufacturing and mechanical pursuits"* encompassed roughly *the entire industrial sector* (lines 29–31) but does not address—either explicitly or implicitly— any possible objections relating to this claim.

E   The number of industrial workers leaving southern cities specifically because of job obsolescence is not at issue and is thus not the basis for a potential objection. In the final paragraph, the author is simply presenting her case that wage pressures affected southern African American urban workers in general, in both artisan trades and newly developed industries.

The correct answer is C.

136. According to the passage, which of the following is true of wages in southern cities in 1910?

(A) They were being pushed lower as a result of increased competition.
(B) They had begun to rise so that southern industry could attract rural workers.
(C) They had increased for skilled workers but decreased for unskilled workers.
(D) They had increased in large southern cities but decreased in small southern cities.
(E) They had increased in newly developed industries but decreased in the older trades.

Supporting ideas

The information that this question asks for is stated in the passage and can be found by careful rereading. The last paragraph is about working conditions in the South. Lines 52–55 show that an influx of rural workers had increased competition for the available industrial jobs and driven wages lower.

A   **Correct.** Lines 52–55 indicate that wages were going down as more workers arrived from rural areas and competed for jobs.
B   Rural workers arrived in the city because of the boll weevil infestation, not because of the promise of higher wages, and their arrival depressed wages.
C   The passage refers to wages for industrial jobs but does not distinguish between the wages of skilled workers and unskilled workers in this respect.

D   The passage does not discuss wage differences between large and small southern cities.
E   The passage provides no information on differences in wages between older trades and new industries.

The correct answer is A.

137. The author cites each of the following as possible influences in an African American worker's decision to migrate north in the Great Migration EXCEPT

(A) wage levels in northern cities
(B) labor recruiters
(C) competition from rural workers
(D) voting rights in northern states
(E) the African American press

Supporting ideas

Use the process of elimination to answer this question regarding what specifically does NOT appear in the passage. Four of the five answers are mentioned as influences on migration, and one is not. Match each answer with its mention in the passage; the choice that does not have a match is the correct answer. In this case, the only answer not mentioned is *voting rights*.

A   Northern wage levels are mentioned in lines 49–51.
B   Labor recruiters are mentioned in line 48.
C   Competition from rural workers is mentioned in lines 52–54.
D   **Correct.** Voting rights in northern states are not mentioned in the passage; the author has not cited them as a possible influence on a migrant's decision.
E   The African American press is mentioned in lines 48–49.

The correct answer is D.

138. It can be inferred from the passage that the "easy conclusion" mentioned in line 58 is based on which of the following assumptions?

(A) People who migrate from rural areas to large cities usually do so for economic reasons.

(B) Most people who leave rural areas to take jobs in cities return to rural areas as soon as it is financially possible for them to do so.

(C) People with rural backgrounds are less likely to succeed economically in cities than are those with urban backgrounds.

(D) Most people who were once skilled workers are not willing to work as unskilled workers.

(E) People who migrate from their birthplaces to other regions of a country seldom undertake a second migration.

Inference

The question directs one's attention to line 58 and the phrase *easy conclusion*. In this context, *easy* has the negative connotation of "facile" or "simplistic" and suggests the author's disagreement with the conclusion that the economic problems of the migrants to northern urban areas were linked to their rural backgrounds. The *conclusion* derived from this link is first discussed in lines 17–19, where lack of economic success in the North is tied to a rural background.

A The author does assume economic motives for migration, but this assumption is not linked to the conclusion about difficulties arising from a rural background.
B This point is not discussed in the passage and is not related to the conclusion that a rural background is linked to economic problems.
C **Correct.** The conclusion referred to in line 58 is based on the assumption that rural background will hinder economic success in urban settings.
D The conclusion refers to all people from rural backgrounds and does not distinguish between skilled and unskilled workers.
E The conclusion about the economic difficulties of migrants from rural backgrounds makes no assumptions about whether people migrate more than once.

The correct answer is C.

139. The primary purpose of the passage is to

(A) support an alternative to an accepted methodology

(B) present evidence that resolves a contradiction

(C) introduce a recently discovered source of information

(D) challenge a widely accepted explanation

(E) argue that a discarded theory deserves new attention

Main idea

Answering questions about primary purpose requires thinking about the underlying structure of the passage. In the first paragraph, the author describes the Great Migration and mentions the assumption that most migrants came from rural areas. Some people then concluded that the migrants' economic difficulties were due to their rural background. In the second paragraph, the author speculates that many migrants could have come from urban areas, and in the third paragraph, she offers information that supports her position. Essentially, if the migrants came from urban areas, their subsequent economic difficulties cannot be attributed to their nonexistent rural background. An analysis of the structure of the passage thus reveals that the author is presenting a generally accepted view and then challenging it.

A The author is showing the weakness in an explanation; there is no discussion of a methodology or of an alternative methodology.
B The reasoning presented in the passage contradicts what the author describes as prevailing ideas but does not resolve any previous contradiction.
C The author does not mention any source of information that was previously unavailable. While census records are briefly mentioned, they are hardly a recently discovered source of information.
D **Correct.** The author first discusses a widely accepted explanation of the economic difficulties of African American migrants and then challenges that explanation.
E The author argues against an explanation she thinks should be discarded. She does not discuss any previously discarded theory.

The correct answer is D.

8.0 Critical Reasoning

8.0 Critical Reasoning

Critical reasoning questions appear in the Verbal section of the GMAT® test. The Verbal section uses multiple-choice questions to measure your ability to read and comprehend written material, to reason and to evaluate arguments, and to correct written material to conform to standard written English. Because the Verbal section includes content from a variety of topics, you may be generally familiar with some of the material; however, neither the passages nor the questions assume knowledge of the topics discussed. Critical reasoning questions are intermingled with reading comprehension and sentence correction questions throughout the Verbal section of the test.

You will have 75 minutes to complete the Verbal section, or about 1¾ minutes to answer each question. Although critical reasoning questions are based on written passages, these passages are shorter than reading comprehension passages. They tend to be less than 100 words in length and generally are followed by one or two questions. For these questions, you will see a split computer screen. The written passage will remain visible as each question associated with that passage appears in turn on the screen. You will see only one question at a time.

Critical reasoning questions are designed to test the reasoning skills involved in (1) making arguments, (2) evaluating arguments, and (3) formulating or evaluating a plan of action. The materials on which questions are based are drawn from a variety of sources. The GMAT test does not suppose any familiarity with the subject matter of those materials.

In these questions, you are to analyze the situation on which each question is based, and then select the answer choice that most appropriately answers the question. Begin by reading the passages carefully, then reading the five answer choices. If the correct answer is not immediately obvious to you, see whether you can eliminate some of the wrong answers. Reading the passage a second time may be helpful in illuminating subtleties that were not immediately evident.

Answering critical reasoning questions requires no specialized knowledge of any particular field; you don't have to have knowledge of the terminology and conventions of formal logic. The sample critical reasoning questions in this chapter illustrate the variety of topics the test may cover, the kinds of questions it may ask, and the level of analysis it requires.

The following pages describe what critical reasoning questions are designed to measure and present the directions that will precede questions of this type. Sample questions and explanations of the correct answers follow.

8.1 What Is Measured

Critical reasoning questions are designed to provide one measure of your ability to reason effectively in the following areas:

- **Argument construction**
  Questions in this category may ask you to recognize such things as the basic structure of an argument, properly drawn conclusions, underlying assumptions, well-supported explanatory hypotheses, and parallels between structurally similar arguments.

- **Argument evaluation**
  These questions may ask you to analyze a given argument and to recognize such things as factors that would strengthen or weaken the given argument; reasoning errors committed in making that argument; and aspects of the method by which the argument proceeds.

- **Formulating and evaluating a plan of action**
  This type of question may ask you to recognize such things as the relative appropriateness, effectiveness, or efficiency of different plans of action; factors that would strengthen or weaken the prospects of success of a proposed plan of action; and assumptions underlying a proposed plan of action.

8.2 Test-Taking Strategies

1. **Read very carefully the set of statements on which a question is based.**
   Pay close attention to

   - what is put forward as factual information

   - what is not said but necessarily follows from what is said

   - what is claimed to follow from facts that have been put forward

   - how well substantiated are any claims that a particular conclusion follows from the facts that have been put forward

   In reading the arguments, it is important to pay attention to the logical reasoning used; the actual truth of statements portrayed as fact is not important.

2. **Identify the conclusion.**
   The conclusion does not necessarily come at the end of the text; it may come somewhere in the middle or even at the beginning. Be alert to clues in the text that an argument follows logically from another statement or statements in the text.

3. **Determine exactly what each question asks.**
   You might find it helpful to read the question first, before reading the material on which it is based; don't assume that you know what you will be asked about an argument. An argument may have obvious flaws, and one question may ask you to detect them. But another question may direct you to select the one answer choice that does NOT describe a flaw in the argument.

4. **Read all the answer choices carefully.**
   Do not assume that a given answer is the best without first reading all the choices.

8.3 The Directions

These are the directions you will see for critical reasoning questions when you take the GMAT test. If you read them carefully and understand them clearly before going to sit for the test, you will not need to spend too much time reviewing them when you are at the test center and the test is under way.

For these questions, select the best of the answer choices given.

8.4 Sample Questions

Each of the <u>critical reasoning</u> questions is based on a short argument, a set of statements, or a plan of action. For each question, select the best answer of the choices given.

1. "Life expectancy" is the average age at death of the entire live-born population. In the middle of the nineteenth century, life expectancy in North America was 40 years, whereas now it is nearly 80 years. Thus, in those days, people must have been considered old at an age that we now consider the prime of life.

   Which of the following, if true, undermines the argument above?

   (A) In the middle of the nineteenth century, the population of North America was significantly smaller than it is today.

   (B) Most of the gains in life expectancy in the last 150 years have come from reductions in the number of infants who die in their first year of life.

   (C) Many of the people who live to an advanced age today do so only because of medical technology that was unknown in the nineteenth century.

   (D) The proportion of people who die in their seventies is significantly smaller today than is the proportion of people who die in their eighties.

   (E) More people in the middle of the nineteenth century engaged regularly in vigorous physical activity than do so today.

2. Scientists propose placing seismic stations on the floor of the Pacific Ocean to warn threatened coastal communities on the northwestern coast of the United States of approaching tidal waves caused by earthquakes. Since forewarned communities could take steps to evacuate, many of the injuries and deaths that would otherwise occur could be avoided if the government would implement this proposal.

   The answer to which of the following questions would be most important in determining whether implementing the proposal would be likely to achieve the desired result?

   (A) When was the last time that the coastal communities were threatened by an approaching tidal wave?

   (B) How far below sea level would the stations be located?

   (C) Would there be enough time after receiving warning of an approaching tidal wave for communities to evacuate safely?

   (D) How soon after a tidal wave hits land is it safe for evacuees to return to their communities?

   (E) Can the stations be equipped to collect and relay information about phenomena other than tidal waves caused by earthquakes?

3. Homeowners aged 40 to 50 are more likely to purchase ice cream and are more likely to purchase it in larger amounts than are members of any other demographic group. The popular belief that teenagers eat more ice cream than adults must, therefore, be false.

   The argument is flawed primarily because the author

   (A) fails to distinguish between purchasing and consuming

   (B) does not supply information about homeowners in age groups other than 40 to 50

   (C) depends on popular belief rather than on documented research findings

   (D) does not specify the precise amount of ice cream purchased by any demographic group

   (E) discusses ice cream rather than more nutritious and healthful foods

4. According to a prediction of the not-so-distant future published in 1940, electricity would revolutionize agriculture. Electrodes would be inserted into the soil, and the current between them would kill bugs and weeds and make crop plants stronger.

   Which of the following, if true, most strongly indicates that the logic of the prediction above is flawed?

(A) In order for farmers to avoid electric shock while working in the fields, the current could be turned off at such times without diminishing the intended effects.

(B) If the proposed plan for using electricity were put into practice, farmers would save on chemicals now being added to the soil.

(C) It cannot be taken for granted that the use of electricity is always beneficial.

(D) Since weeds are plants, electricity would affect weeds in the same way as it would affect crop plants.

(E) Because a planting machine would need to avoid coming into contact with the electrodes, new parts for planting machines would need to be designed.

5. A company is considering changing its policy concerning daily working hours. Currently, this company requires all employees to arrive at work at 8 a.m. The proposed policy would permit each employee to decide when to arrive—from as early as 6 a.m. to as late as 11 a.m.

The adoption of this policy would be most likely to decrease employees' productivity if the employees' job functions required them to

(A) work without interruption from other employees

(B) consult at least once a day with employees from other companies

(C) submit their work for a supervisor's eventual approval

(D) interact frequently with each other throughout the entire workday

(E) undertake projects that take several days to complete

6. The amount of time it takes for most of a worker's occupational knowledge and skills to become obsolete has been declining because of the introduction of advanced manufacturing technology (AMT). Given the rate at which AMT is currently being introduced in manufacturing, the average worker's old skills become obsolete and new skills are required within as little as five years.

Which of the following plans, if feasible, would allow a company to prepare most effectively for the rapid obsolescence of skills described above?

(A) The company will develop a program to offer selected employees the opportunity to receive training six years after they were originally hired.

(B) The company will increase its investment in AMT every year for a period of at least five years.

(C) The company will periodically survey its employees to determine how the introduction of AMT has affected them.

(D) Before the introduction of AMT, the company will institute an educational program to inform its employees of the probable consequences of the introduction of AMT.

(E) The company will ensure that it can offer its employees any training necessary for meeting their job requirements.

7. Traverton's city council wants to minimize the city's average yearly expenditures on its traffic signal lights and so is considering replacing the incandescent bulbs currently in use with arrays of light-emitting diodes (LEDs) as the incandescent bulbs burn out. Compared to incandescent bulbs, LED arrays consume significantly less energy and cost no more to purchase. Moreover, the costs associated with the conversion of existing fixtures so as to accept LED arrays would be minimal.

Which of the following would it be most useful to know in determining whether switching to LED arrays would be likely to help minimize Traverton's yearly maintenance costs?

(A) Whether the expected service life of LED arrays is at least as long as that of the currently used incandescent bulbs

(B) Whether any cities have switched from incandescent lights in their traffic signals to lighting elements other than LED arrays

(C) Whether the company from which Traverton currently buys incandescent bulbs for traffic signals also sells LED arrays

(D) Whether Traverton's city council plans to increase the number of traffic signal lights in Traverton

(E) Whether the crews that currently replace incandescent bulbs in Traverton's traffic signals know how to convert the existing fixtures so as to accept LED arrays

8. A report that many apples contain a cancer-causing preservative called Alar apparently had little effect on consumers. Few consumers planned to change their apple-buying habits as a result of the report. Nonetheless, sales of apples in grocery stores fell sharply in March, a month after the report was issued.

   Which of the following, if true, best explains the reason for the apparent discrepancy described above?

   (A) In March, many grocers removed apples from their shelves in order to demonstrate concern about their customers' health.

   (B) Because of a growing number of food-safety warnings, consumers in March were indifferent to such warnings.

   (C) The report was delivered on television and also appeared in newspapers.

   (D) The report did not mention that any other fruit contains Alar, although the preservative is used on other fruit.

   (E) Public health officials did not believe that apples posed a health threat because only minute traces of Alar were present in affected apples.

9. In order to reduce the number of items damaged while in transit to customers, packaging consultants recommended that the TrueSave mail-order company increase the amount of packing material so as to fill any empty spaces in its cartons. Accordingly, TrueSave officials instructed the company's packers to use more packing material than before, and the packers zealously acted on these instructions and used as much as they could. Nevertheless, customer reports of damaged items rose somewhat.

   Which of the following, if true, most helps to explain why acting on the consultants' recommendation failed to achieve its goal?

   (A) The change in packing policy led to an increase in expenditure on packing material and labor.

   (B) When packing material is compressed too densely, it loses some of its capacity to absorb shock.

   (C) The amount of packing material used in a carton does not significantly influence the ease with which a customer can unpack the package.

   (D) Most of the goods that TrueSave ships are electronic products that are highly vulnerable to being damaged in transit.

   (E) TrueSave has lost some of its regular customers as a result of the high number of damaged items they received.

10. Cable-television spokesperson: Subscriptions to cable television are a bargain in comparison to "free" television. Remember that "free" television is not really free. It is consumers, in the end, who pay for the costly advertising that supports "free" television.

    Which of the following, if true, is most damaging to the position of the cable-television spokesperson?

    (A) Consumers who do not own television sets are less likely to be influenced in their purchasing decisions by television advertising than are consumers who own television sets.

    (B) Subscriptions to cable television include access to some public-television channels, which do not accept advertising.

    (C) For locations with poor television reception, cable television provides picture quality superior to that provided by free television.

    (D) There is as much advertising on many cable-television channels as there is on "free" television channels.

    (E) Cable-television subscribers can choose which channels they wish to receive.

11. Wood smoke contains dangerous toxins that cause changes in human cells. Because wood smoke presents such a high health risk, legislation is needed to regulate the use of open-air fires and wood-burning stoves.

    Which of the following, if true, provides the most support for the argument above?

    (A) The amount of dangerous toxins contained in wood smoke is much less than the amount contained in an equal volume of automobile exhaust.

    (B) Within the jurisdiction covered by the proposed legislation, most heating and cooking is done with oil or natural gas.

(C)   Smoke produced by coal-burning stoves is significantly more toxic than smoke from wood-burning stoves.

(D)   No significant beneficial effect on air quality would result if open-air fires were banned within the jurisdiction covered by the proposed legislation.

(E)   In valleys where wood is used as the primary heating fuel, the concentration of smoke results in poor air quality.

12.   A certain automaker aims to increase its market share by deeply discounting its vehicles' prices for the next several months. The discounts will cut into profits, but because they will be heavily advertised the manufacturer hopes that they will attract buyers away from rival manufacturers' cars. In the longer term, the automaker envisions that customers initially attracted by the discounts may become loyal customers.

In assessing the plan's chances of achieving its aim, it would be most useful to know which of the following?

(A)   Whether the automaker's competitors are likely to respond by offering deep discounts on their own products

(B)   Whether the advertisements will be created by the manufacturer's current advertising agency

(C)   Whether some of the automaker's models will be more deeply discounted than others

(D)   Whether the automaker will be able to cut costs sufficiently to maintain profit margins even when the discounts are in effect

(E)   Whether an alternative strategy might enable the automaker to enhance its profitability while holding a constant or diminishing share of the market

13.   In Swartkans territory, archaeologists discovered charred bone fragments dating back one million years. Analysis of the fragments, which came from a variety of animals, showed that they had been heated to temperatures no higher than those produced in experimental campfires made from branches of white stinkwood, the most common tree around Swartkans.

Which of the following, if true, would, together with the information above, provide the best basis for the claim that the charred bone fragments are evidence of the use of fire by early hominids?

(A)   The white stinkwood tree is used for building material by the present-day inhabitants of Swartkans.

(B)   Forest fires can heat wood to a range of temperatures that occur in campfires.

(C)   The bone fragments were fitted together by the archaeologists to form the complete skeletons of several animals.

(D)   Apart from the Swartkans discovery, there is reliable evidence that early hominids used fire as many as 500,000 years ago.

(E)   The bone fragments were found in several distinct layers of limestone that contained primitive cutting tools known to have been used by early hominids.

14.   In Washington County, attendance at the movies is just large enough for the cinema operators to make modest profits. The size of the county's population is stable and is not expected to increase much. Yet there are investors ready to double the number of movie screens in the county within five years, and they are predicting solid profits both for themselves and for the established cinema operators.

Which of the following, if true about Washington County, most helps to provide a justification for the investors' prediction?

(A)   Over the next ten years, people in their teenage years, the prime moviegoing age, will be a rapidly growing proportion of the county's population.

(B)   As distinct from the existing cinemas, most of the cinemas being planned would be located in downtown areas, in hopes of stimulating an economic revitalization of those areas.

(C)   Spending on video purchases, as well as spending on video rentals, has been increasing modestly each year for the past ten years.

(D)   The average number of screens per cinema is lower among existing cinemas than it is among cinemas still in the planning stages.

(E)   The sale of snacks and drinks in cinemas accounts for a steadily growing share of most cinema operators' profits.

15. A conservation group in the United States is trying to change the long-standing image of bats as frightening creatures. The group contends that bats are feared and persecuted solely because they are shy animals that are active only at night.

Which of the following, if true, would cast the most serious doubt on the accuracy of the group's contention?

(A) Bats are steadily losing natural roosting places such as caves and hollow trees and are thus turning to more developed areas for roosting.

(B) Bats are the chief consumers of nocturnal insects and thus can help make their hunting territory more pleasant for humans.

(C) Bats are regarded as frightening creatures not only in the United States but also in Europe, Africa, and South America.

(D) Raccoons and owls are shy and active only at night, yet they are not generally feared and persecuted.

(E) People know more about the behavior of other greatly feared animal species, such as lions, alligators, and snakes, than they do about the behavior of bats.

16. Which of the following best completes the passage below?

People buy prestige when they buy a premium product. They want to be associated with something special. Mass-marketing techniques and price-reduction strategies should not be used because _____.

(A) affluent purchasers currently represent a shrinking portion of the population of all purchasers

(B) continued sales depend directly on the maintenance of an aura of exclusivity

(C) purchasers of premium products are concerned with the quality as well as with the price of the products

(D) expansion of the market niche to include a broader spectrum of consumers will increase profits

(E) manufacturing a premium brand is not necessarily more costly than manufacturing a standard brand of the same product

17. Hunter: **Many people blame hunters alone for the decline in Greenrock National Forest's deer population over the past ten years.** Yet clearly, black bears have also played an important role in this decline. In the past ten years, the forest's protected black bear population has risen sharply, and examination of black bears found dead in the forest during the deer hunting season showed that a number of them had recently fed on deer.

In the hunter's argument, the portion in boldface plays which of the following roles?

(A) It is the main conclusion of the argument.

(B) It is a finding that the argument seeks to explain.

(C) It is an explanation that the argument concludes is correct.

(D) It provides evidence in support of the main conclusion of the argument.

(E) It introduces a judgment that the argument opposes.

18. In Asia, where palm trees are nonnative, the trees' flowers have traditionally been pollinated by hand, which has kept palm fruit productivity unnaturally low. When weevils known to be efficient pollinators of palm flowers were introduced into Asia in 1980, palm fruit productivity increased—by up to 50 percent in some areas—but then decreased sharply in 1984.

Which of the following statements, if true, would best explain the 1984 decrease in productivity?

(A) Prices for palm fruit fell between 1980 and 1984 following the rise in production and a concurrent fall in demand.

(B) Imported trees are often more productive than native trees because the imported ones have left behind their pests and diseases in their native lands.

(C) Rapid increases in productivity tend to deplete trees of nutrients needed for the development of the fruit-producing female flowers.

(D) The weevil population in Asia remained at approximately the same level between 1980 and 1984.

(E) Prior to 1980 another species of insect pollinated the Asian palm trees, but not as efficiently as the species of weevil that was introduced in 1980.

19. Physician: The hormone melatonin has shown promise as a medication for sleep disorders when taken in synthesized form. Because the long-term side effects of synthetic melatonin are unknown, however, I cannot recommend its use at this time.

    Patient: Your position is inconsistent with your usual practice. You prescribe many medications that you know have serious side effects, so concern about side effects cannot be the real reason you will not prescribe melatonin.

    The patient's argument is flawed because it fails to consider that

    (A) the side effects of synthetic melatonin might be different from those of naturally produced melatonin

    (B) it is possible that the physician does not believe that melatonin has been conclusively shown to be effective

    (C) sleep disorders, if left untreated, might lead to serious medical complications

    (D) the side effects of a medication can take some time to manifest themselves

    (E) known risks can be weighed against known benefits, but unknown risks cannot

20. In recent years, many cabinetmakers have been winning acclaim as artists. But since furniture must be useful, cabinetmakers must exercise their craft with an eye to the practical utility of their product. For this reason, cabinetmaking is not art.

    Which of the following is an assumption that supports drawing the conclusion above from the reason given for that conclusion?

    (A) Some furniture is made to be placed in museums, where it will not be used by anyone.

    (B) Some cabinetmakers are more concerned than others with the practical utility of the products they produce.

    (C) Cabinetmakers should be more concerned with the practical utility of their products than they currently are.

    (D) An object is not an art object if its maker pays attention to the object's practical utility.

    (E) Artists are not concerned with the monetary value of their products.

21. Male bowerbirds construct elaborately decorated nests, or bowers. Basing their judgment on the fact that different local populations of bowerbirds of the same species build bowers that exhibit different building and decorative styles, researchers have concluded that the bowerbirds' building styles are a culturally acquired, rather than a genetically transmitted, trait.

    Which of the following, if true, would most strengthen the conclusion drawn by the researchers?

    (A) There are more common characteristics than there are differences among the bower-building styles of the local bowerbird population that has been studied most extensively.

    (B) Young male bowerbirds are inept at bower-building and apparently spend years watching their elders before becoming accomplished in the local bower style.

    (C) The bowers of one species of bowerbird lack the towers and ornamentation characteristic of the bowers of most other species of bowerbird.

    (D) Bowerbirds are found only in New Guinea and Australia, where local populations of the birds apparently seldom have contact with one another.

    (E) It is well known that the song dialects of some songbirds are learned rather than transmitted genetically.

22. Plan: Concerned about the welfare of its senior citizens, the government of Runagia decided two years ago to increase by 20 percent the government-provided pension paid to all Runagians age sixty-five and older.

    Result: Many Runagian senior citizens are no better off financially now than they were before the increase.

    Further information: The annual rate of inflation since the pension increase has been below 5 percent, and the increased pension has been duly received by all eligible Runagians.

    In light of the further information, which of the following, if true, does most to explain the result that followed implementation of the plan?

    (A) The majority of senior citizens whose financial position has not improved rely entirely on the government pension for their income.
    (B) The Runagian banking system is so inefficient that cashing a pension check can take as much as three weeks.
    (C) The prices of goods and services that meet the special needs of many senior citizens have increased at a rate much higher than the rate of inflation.
    (D) The pension increase occurred at a time when the number of Runagians age sixty-five and older who were living below the poverty level was at an all-time high.
    (E) The most recent pension increase was only the second such increase in the last ten years.

23. A drug that is highly effective in treating many types of infection can, at present, be obtained only from the bark of the ibora, a tree that is quite rare in the wild. It takes the bark of 5,000 trees to make one kilogram of the drug. It follows, therefore, that continued production of the drug must inevitably lead to the ibora's extinction.

    Which of the following, if true, most seriously weakens the argument above?

    (A) The drug made from ibora bark is dispensed to doctors from a central authority.
    (B) The drug made from ibora bark is expensive to produce.
    (C) The leaves of the ibora are used in a number of medical products.

    (D) The ibora can be propagated from cuttings and grown under cultivation.
    (E) The ibora generally grows in largely inaccessible places.

24. The Plexis Corporation, a leading computer chip manufacturer, is currently developing a new chip, which is faster and more efficient than any computer chip currently in use. The new chip will be released for sale in twelve months. Plexis' market research has shown that initial sales of the new chip would be maximized by starting to advertise it now, but the company has decided to wait another six months before doing so.

    Which of the following, if true, provides the Plexis Corporation with the best reason for postponing advertising its new chip?

    (A) Some computer users are reluctant to purchase new computer products when they are first released.
    (B) The cost of an advertising campaign capable of maximizing initial sales of the new chip would be no greater than campaigns previously undertaken by Plexis.
    (C) Advertising the new chip now will significantly decrease sales of Plexis' current line of computer chips.
    (D) Plexis' major rivals in the computer chip manufacturing business are developing a chip with capabilities that are comparable to those of Plexis' new chip.
    (E) Taking full advantage of the capacities of the new chip will require substantial adjustments in other segments of the computer industry.

25. Many breakfast cereals are fortified with vitamin supplements. Some of these cereals provide 100 percent of the recommended daily requirement of vitamins. Nevertheless, a well-balanced breakfast, including a variety of foods, is a better source of those vitamins than are such fortified breakfast cereals alone.

    Which of the following, if true, would most strongly support the position above?

(A)   In many foods, the natural combination of vitamins with other nutrients makes those vitamins more usable by the body than are vitamins added in vitamin supplements.

(B)   People who regularly eat cereals fortified with vitamin supplements sometimes neglect to eat the foods in which the vitamins occur naturally.

(C)   Foods often must be fortified with vitamin supplements because naturally occurring vitamins are removed during processing.

(D)   Unprocessed cereals are naturally high in several of the vitamins that are usually added to fortified breakfast cereals.

(E)   Cereals containing vitamin supplements are no harder to digest than similar cereals without added vitamins.

26. When a polygraph test is judged inconclusive, this is no reflection on the examinee. Rather, such a judgment means that the test has failed to show whether the examinee was truthful or untruthful. Nevertheless, employers will sometimes refuse to hire a job applicant because of an inconclusive polygraph test result.

Which of the following conclusions can most properly be drawn from the information above?

(A)   Most examinees with inconclusive polygraph test results are in fact untruthful.

(B)   Polygraph tests should not be used by employers in the consideration of job applicants.

(C)   An inconclusive polygraph test result is sometimes unfairly held against the examinee.

(D)   A polygraph test indicating that an examinee is untruthful can sometimes be mistaken.

(E)   Some employers have refused to consider the results of polygraph tests when evaluating job applicants.

27. For similar cars and comparable drivers, automobile insurance for collision damage has always cost more in Greatport than in Fairmont. Police studies, however, show that cars owned by Greatport residents are, on average, slightly less likely to be involved in a collision than cars in Fairmont. Clearly, therefore, insurance companies are making a greater profit on collision-damage insurance in Greatport than in Fairmont.

In evaluating the argument, it would be most useful to compare

(A)   the level of traffic congestion in Greatport with the level of traffic congestion in Fairmont

(B)   the cost of repairing collision damage in Greatport with the cost of repairing collision damage in Fairmont

(C)   the rates Greatport residents pay for other forms of insurance with the rates paid for similar insurance by residents of Fairmont

(D)   the condition of Greatport's roads and streets with the condition of Fairmont's roads and streets

(E)   the cost of collision-damage insurance in Greatport and Fairmont with that in other cities

28. The technological conservatism of bicycle manufacturers is a reflection of the kinds of demand they are trying to meet. The only cyclists seriously interested in innovation and willing to pay for it are bicycle racers. Therefore, innovation in bicycle technology is limited by what authorities will accept as standard for purposes of competition in bicycle races.

Which of the following is an assumption made in drawing the conclusion above?

(A)   The market for cheap, traditional bicycles cannot expand unless the market for high-performance competition bicycles expands.

(B)   High-performance bicycles are likely to be improved more as a result of technological innovations developed in small workshops than as a result of technological innovations developed in major manufacturing concerns.

(C)   Bicycle racers do not generate a strong demand for innovations that fall outside what is officially recognized as standard for purposes of competition.

(D)   The technological conservatism of bicycle manufacturers results primarily from their desire to manufacture a product that can be sold without being altered to suit different national markets.

(E)   The authorities who set standards for high-performance bicycle racing do not keep informed about innovative bicycle design.

29. Last year a record number of new manufacturing jobs were created. Will this year bring another record? Well, a new manufacturing job is created either within an existing company or by the start-up of a new company. Within existing firms, new jobs have been created this year at well below last year's record pace. At the same time, there is considerable evidence that the number of new companies starting up will be no higher this year than it was last year, and surely **the new companies starting up this year will create no more jobs per company than did last year's start-ups.** Clearly, it can be concluded that **the number of new jobs created this year will fall short of last year's record**.

In the argument given, the two portions in boldface play which of the following roles?

(A) The first is a prediction that, if accurate, would provide support for the main conclusion of the argument; the second is that main conclusion.

(B) The first is a prediction that, if accurate, would provide support for the main conclusion of the argument; the second is a conclusion drawn in order to support that main conclusion.

(C) The first is an objection that the argument rejects; the second is the main conclusion of the argument.

(D) The first is an objection that the argument rejects; the second presents a conclusion that could be drawn if that objection were allowed to stand.

(E) The first is a claim that has been advanced in support of a position that the argument opposes; the second is a claim advanced in support of the main conclusion of the argument.

30. Robot satellites relay important communications and identify weather patterns. Because the satellites can be repaired only in orbit, astronauts are needed to repair them. Without repairs, the satellites would eventually malfunction. Therefore, space flights carrying astronauts must continue.

Which of the following, if true, would most seriously weaken the argument above?

(A) Satellites falling from orbit because of malfunctions burn up in the atmosphere.

(B) Although satellites are indispensable in the identification of weather patterns, weather forecasters also make some use of computer projections to identify weather patterns.

(C) The government, responding to public pressure, has decided to cut the budget for space flights and put more money into social welfare programs.

(D) Repair of satellites requires heavy equipment, which adds to the amount of fuel needed to lift a spaceship carrying astronauts into orbit.

(E) Technical obsolescence of robot satellites makes repairing them more costly and less practical than sending new, improved satellites into orbit.

31. A company's two divisions performed with remarkable consistency over the past three years: in each of those years, the pharmaceuticals division has accounted for roughly 20 percent of dollar sales and 40 percent of profits, and the chemicals division for the balance.

Which of the following can properly be inferred regarding the past three years from the statement above?

(A) Total dollar sales for each of the company's divisions have remained roughly constant.

(B) The pharmaceuticals division has faced stiffer competition in its markets than has the chemicals division.

(C) The chemicals division has realized lower profits per dollar of sales than has the pharmaceuticals division.

(D) The product mix offered by each of the company's divisions has remained unchanged.

(E) Highly profitable products accounted for a higher percentage of the chemicals division's sales than those of the pharmaceuticals division's.

32. The Eurasian ruffe, a fish species inadvertently introduced into North America's Great Lakes in recent years, feeds on the eggs of lake whitefish, a native species, thus threatening the lakes' natural ecosystem. To help track the ruffe's spread, government agencies have produced wallet-sized cards about the ruffe. The cards contain pictures of the ruffe and explain the danger they pose; the cards also request anglers to report any ruffe they catch.

Which of the following, if true, would provide most support for the prediction that the agencies' action will have its intended effect?

(A) The ruffe has spiny fins that make it unattractive as prey.

(B) Ruffe generally feed at night, but most recreational fishing on the Great Lakes is done during daytime hours.

(C) Most people who fish recreationally on the Great Lakes are interested in the preservation of the lake whitefish because it is a highly prized game fish.

(D) The ruffe is one of several nonnative species in the Great Lakes whose existence threatens the survival of lake whitefish populations there.

(E) The bait that most people use when fishing for whitefish on the Great Lakes is not attractive to ruffe.

33. Advertisement: Today's customers expect high quality. Every advance in the quality of manufactured products raises customer expectations. The company that is satisfied with the current quality of its products will soon find that its customers are not. At MegaCorp, meeting or exceeding customer expectations is our goal.

Which of the following must be true on the basis of the statements in the advertisement above?

(A) MegaCorp's competitors will succeed in attracting customers only if those competitors adopt MegaCorp's goal as their own.

(B) A company that does not correctly anticipate the expectations of its customers is certain to fail in advancing the quality of its products.

(C) MegaCorp's goal is possible to meet only if continuing advances in product quality are possible.

(D) If a company becomes satisfied with the quality of its products, then the quality of its products is sure to decline.

(E) MegaCorp's customers are currently satisfied with the quality of its products.

34. Which of the following most logically completes the argument?

Ferber's syndrome, a viral disease that frequently affects cattle, is transmitted to these animals through infected feed. Even though chickens commercially raised for meat are often fed the type of feed identified as the source of infection in cattle, Ferber's syndrome is only rarely observed in chickens. This fact, however, does not indicate that most chickens are immune to the virus that causes Ferber's syndrome, since _____.

(A) chickens and cattle are not the only kinds of farm animal that are typically fed the type of feed liable to be contaminated with the virus that causes Ferber's syndrome

(B) Ferber's syndrome has been found in animals that have not been fed the type of feed liable to be contaminated with the virus that can cause the disease

(C) resistance to some infectious organisms such as the virus that causes Ferber's syndrome can be acquired by exposure to a closely related infectious organism

(D) chickens and cattle take more than a year to show symptoms of Ferber's syndrome, and chickens commercially raised for meat, unlike cattle, are generally brought to market during the first year of life

(E) the type of feed liable to be infected with the virus that causes Ferber's syndrome generally constitutes a larger proportion of the diet of commercially raised chickens than of commercially raised cattle

35. Last year the rate of inflation was 1.2 percent, but for the current year it has been 4 percent. We can conclude that inflation is on an upward trend and the rate will be still higher next year.

 Which of the following, if true, most seriously weakens the conclusion above?

 (A) The inflation figures were computed on the basis of a representative sample of economic data rather than all of the available data.

 (B) Last year a dip in oil prices brought inflation temporarily below its recent stable annual level of 4 percent.

 (C) Increases in the pay of some workers are tied to the level of inflation, and at an inflation rate of 4 percent or above, these pay raises constitute a force causing further inflation.

 (D) The 1.2 percent rate of inflation last year represented a 10-year low.

 (E) Government intervention cannot affect the rate of inflation to any significant degree.

36. Offshore oil-drilling operations entail an unavoidable risk of an oil spill, but importing oil on tankers presently entails an even greater such risk per barrel of oil. Therefore, if we are to reduce the risk of an oil spill without curtailing our use of oil, we must invest more in offshore operations and import less oil on tankers.

 Which of the following, if true, most seriously weakens the argument above?

 (A) Tankers can easily be redesigned so that their use entails less risk of an oil spill.

 (B) Oil spills caused by tankers have generally been more serious than those caused by offshore operations.

 (C) The impact of offshore operations on the environment can be controlled by careful management.

 (D) Offshore operations usually damage the ocean floor, but tankers rarely cause such damage.

 (E) Importing oil on tankers is currently less expensive than drilling for it offshore.

37. Thyrian lawmaker: Thyria's Cheese Importation Board inspects all cheese shipments to Thyria and rejects shipments not meeting specified standards. Yet only 1 percent is ever rejected. Therefore, since the health consequences and associated economic costs of not rejecting that 1 percent are negligible, whereas the board's operating costs are considerable, for economic reasons alone the board should be disbanded.

 Consultant: I disagree. The threat of having their shipments rejected deters many cheese exporters from shipping substandard product.

 The consultant responds to the lawmaker's argument by

 (A) rejecting the lawmaker's argument while proposing that the standards according to which the board inspects imported cheese should be raised

 (B) providing evidence that the lawmaker's argument has significantly overestimated the cost of maintaining the board

 (C) objecting to the lawmaker's introducing into the discussion factors that are not strictly economic

 (D) pointing out a benefit of maintaining the board, which the lawmaker's argument has failed to consider

 (E) shifting the discussion from the argument at hand to an attack on the integrity of the cheese inspectors

38. Which of the following best completes the passage below?

 The computer industry's estimate that it loses millions of dollars when users illegally copy programs without paying for them is greatly exaggerated. Most of the illegal copying is done by people with no serious interest in the programs. Thus, the loss to the industry is quite small, because _____.

 (A) many users who illegally copy programs never find any use for them

 (B) most people who illegally copy programs would not purchase them even if purchasing them were the only way to obtain them

(C)   even if the computer industry received all the revenue it claims to be losing, it would still be experiencing financial difficulties

(D)   the total market value of all illegal copies is low in comparison to the total revenue of the computer industry

(E)   the number of programs that are frequently copied illegally is low in comparison to the number of programs available for sale

39.   The growing popularity of computer-based activities was widely expected to result in a decline in television viewing, since it had been assumed that people lack sufficient free time to maintain current television-viewing levels while spending increasing amounts of free time on the computer. That assumption, however, is evidently false: In a recent mail survey concerning media use, a very large majority of respondents who report increasing time spent per week using computers report no change in time spent watching television.

Which of the following would it be most useful to determine in order to evaluate the argument?

(A)   Whether a large majority of the survey respondents reported watching television regularly

(B)   Whether the amount of time spent watching television is declining among people who report that they rarely or never use computers

(C)   Whether the type of television programs a person watches tends to change as the amount of time spent per week using computers increases

(D)   Whether a large majority of the computer owners in the survey reported spending increasing amounts of time per week using computers

(E)   Whether the survey respondents' reports of time spent using computers included time spent using computers at work

40.   In the last decade there has been a significant decrease in coffee consumption. During this same time, there has been increasing publicity about the adverse long-term effects on health of the caffeine in coffee. Therefore, the decrease in coffee consumption must have been caused by consumers' awareness of the harmful effects of caffeine.

Which of the following, if true, most seriously calls into question the explanation above?

(A)   On average, people consume 30 percent less coffee today than they did 10 years ago.

(B)   Heavy coffee drinkers may have mild withdrawal symptoms, such as headaches, for a day or so after significantly decreasing their coffee consumption.

(C)   Sales of specialty types of coffee have held steady as sales of regular brands have declined.

(D)   The consumption of fruit juices and caffeine-free herbal teas has increased over the past decade.

(E)   Coffee prices increased steadily in the past decade because of unusually severe frosts in coffee-growing nations.

41.   Which of the following best completes the passage below?

When the products of several competing suppliers are perceived by consumers to be essentially the same, classical economics predicts that price competition will reduce prices to the same minimal levels and all suppliers' profits to the same minimal levels. Therefore, if classical economics is true, and given suppliers' desire to make as much profit as possible, it should be expected that _____.

(A)   in a crowded market widely differing prices will be charged for products that are essentially the same as each other

(B)   as a market becomes less crowded as suppliers leave, the profits of the remaining suppliers will tend to decrease

(C)   each supplier in a crowded market will try to convince consumers that its product differs significantly from its competitors' products.

(D)   when consumers are unable to distinguish the products in a crowded market, consumers will judge that the higher-priced products are of higher quality

(E)   suppliers in crowded markets will have more incentive to reduce prices and thus increase sales than to introduce innovations that would distinguish their product from their competitors' products

42. Crowding on Mooreville's subway frequently leads to delays, because it is difficult for passengers to exit from the trains. Subway ridership is projected to increase by 20 percent over the next 10 years. The Mooreville Transit Authority plans to increase the number of daily train trips by only 5 percent over the same period. Officials predict that this increase is sufficient to ensure that the incidence of delays due to crowding does not increase.

Which of the following, if true, provides the strongest grounds for the officials' prediction?

(A) By changing maintenance schedules, the Transit Authority can achieve the 5 percent increase in train trips without purchasing any new subway cars.

(B) The Transit Authority also plans a 5 percent increase in the number of bus trips on routes that connect to subways.

(C) For most commuters who use the subway system, there is no practical alternative public transportation available.

(D) Most of the projected increase in ridership is expected to occur in off-peak hours when trains are now sparsely used.

(E) The 5 percent increase in the number of train trips can be achieved without an equal increase in Transit Authority operational costs.

43. Installing scrubbers in smokestacks and switching to cleaner-burning fuel are the two methods available to Northern Power for reducing harmful emissions from its plants. Scrubbers will reduce harmful emissions more than cleaner-burning fuels will. Therefore, by installing scrubbers, Northern Power will be doing the most that can be done to reduce harmful emissions from its plants.

Which of the following is an assumption on which the argument depends?

(A) Switching to cleaner-burning fuel will not be more expensive than installing scrubbers.

(B) Northern Power can choose from among various kinds of scrubbers, some of which are more effective than others.

(C) Northern Power is not necessarily committed to reducing harmful emissions from its plants.

(D) Harmful emissions from Northern Power's plants cannot be reduced more by using both methods together than by the installation of scrubbers alone.

(E) Aside from harmful emissions from the smokestacks of its plants, the activities of Northern Power do not cause significant air pollution.

44. Trancorp currently transports all its goods to Burland Island by truck. The only bridge over the channel separating Burland from the mainland is congested, and trucks typically spend hours in traffic. Trains can reach the channel more quickly than trucks, and freight cars can be transported to Burland by barges that typically cross the channel in an hour. Therefore, to reduce shipping time, Trancorp plans to switch to trains and barges to transport goods to Burland.

Which of the following would be most important to know in determining whether Trancorp's plan, if implemented, is likely to achieve its goal?

(A) Whether transportation by train and barge would be substantially less expensive than transportation by truck

(B) Whether there are boats that can make the trip between the mainland and Burland faster than barges can

(C) Whether loading the freight cars onto barges is very time consuming

(D) Whether the average number of vehicles traveling over the bridge into Burland has been relatively constant in recent years

(E) Whether most trucks transporting goods into Burland return to the mainland empty

45. Some anthropologists study modern-day societies of foragers in an effort to learn about our ancient ancestors who were also foragers. A flaw in this strategy is that forager societies are extremely varied. Indeed, any forager society with which anthropologists are familiar has had considerable contact with modern, non-forager societies.

Which of the following, if true, would most weaken the criticism made above of the anthropologists' strategy?

(A) All forager societies throughout history have had a number of important features in common that are absent from other types of societies.

(B) Most ancient forager societies either dissolved or made a transition to another way of life.

(C) All anthropologists study one kind or another of modern-day society.

(D) Many anthropologists who study modern-day forager societies do not draw inferences about ancient societies on the basis of their studies.

(E) Even those modern-day forager societies that have not had significant contact with modern societies are importantly different from ancient forager societies.

46. Contrary to earlier predictions, demand for sugarcane has not increased in recent years. Yet, even though prices and production amounts have also been stable during the last three years, sugarcane growers last year increased their profits by more than 10 percent over the previous year's level.

Any of the following statements, if true about last year, helps to explain the rise in profits EXCEPT:

(A) Many countries that are large consumers of sugarcane increased their production of sugarcane-based ethanol, yet their overall consumption of sugarcane decreased.

(B) Sugarcane growers have saved money on wages by switching from paying laborers an hourly wage to paying them by the amount harvested.

(C) The price of oil, the major energy source used by sugarcane growers in harvesting their crops, dropped by over 20 percent.

(D) Many small sugarcane growers joined together to form an association of sugarcane producers and began to buy supplies at low group rates.

(E) Rainfall in sugarcane-growing regions was higher than it had been during the previous year, allowing the growers to save money on expensive artificial irrigation.

47. Which of the following most logically completes the argument below?

Davison River farmers are currently deciding between planting winter wheat this fall or spring wheat next spring. Winter wheat and spring wheat are usually about equally profitable. Because of new government restrictions on the use of Davison River water for irrigation, per acre yields for winter wheat, though not for spring wheat, would be much lower than average. Therefore, planting spring wheat will be more profitable than planting winter wheat, since _____.

(A) the smaller-than-average size of a winter wheat harvest this year would not be compensated for by higher winter wheat prices

(B) new crops of spring wheat must be planted earlier than the time at which standing crops of winter wheat are ready to be harvested

(C) the spring wheat that farmers in the Davison River region plant is well adapted to the soil of the region

(D) spring wheat has uses that are different from those of winter wheat

(E) planting spring wheat is more profitable than planting certain other crops, such as rye

48. If the county continues to collect residential trash at current levels, landfills will soon be overflowing and parkland will need to be used in order to create more space. Charging each household a fee for each pound of trash it puts out for collection will induce residents to reduce the amount of trash they create; this charge will therefore protect the remaining county parkland.

Which of the following is an assumption made in drawing the conclusion above?

(A) Residents will reduce the amount of trash they put out for collection by reducing the number of products they buy.

(B) The collection fee will not significantly affect the purchasing power of most residents, even if their households do not reduce the amount of trash they put out.

(C) The collection fee will not induce residents to dump their trash in the parklands illegally.

(D) The beauty of county parkland is an important issue for most of the county's residents.

(E) Landfills outside the county's borders could be used as dumping sites for the county's trash.

49. Certain genetically modified strains of maize produce a powerful natural insecticide. The insecticide occurs throughout the plant, including its pollen. Maize pollen is dispersed by the wind and frequently blows onto milkweed plants that grow near maize fields. Caterpillars of monarch butterflies feed exclusively on milkweed leaves. When these caterpillars are fed milkweed leaves dusted with pollen from modified maize plants, they die. Therefore, by using genetically modified maize, farmers put monarch butterflies at risk.

Which of the following would it be most useful to determine in order to evaluate the argument?

(A) Whether the natural insecticide is as effective against maize-eating insects as commercial insecticides typically used on maize are

(B) Whether the pollen of genetically modified maize contains as much insecticide as other parts of these plants

(C) Whether monarch butterfly caterpillars are actively feeding during the part of the growing season when maize is releasing pollen

(D) Whether insects that feed on genetically modified maize plants are likely to be killed by insecticide from the plant's pollen

(E) Whether any maize-eating insects compete with monarch caterpillars for the leaves of milkweed plants growing near maize fields

50. Although computers can enhance people's ability to communicate, computer games are a cause of underdeveloped communication skills in children. After-school hours spent playing computer games are hours not spent talking with people. Therefore, children who spend all their spare time playing these games have less experience in interpersonal communication than other children have.

The argument depends on which of the following assumptions?

(A) Passive activities such as watching television and listening to music do not hinder the development of communication skills in children.

(B) Most children have other opportunities, in addition to after-school hours, in which they can choose whether to play computer games or to interact with other people.

(C) Children who do not spend all of their after-school hours playing computer games spend at least some of that time talking with other people.

(D) Formal instruction contributes little or nothing to children's acquisition of communication skills.

(E) The mental skills developed through playing computer games do not contribute significantly to children's intellectual development.

51. One variety of partially biodegradable plastic beverage container is manufactured from small bits of plastic bound together by a degradable bonding agent such as cornstarch. Since only the bonding agent degrades, leaving the small bits of plastic, no less plastic refuse per container is produced when such containers are discarded than when comparable nonbiodegradable containers are discarded.

Which of the following, if true, most strengthens the argument above?

(A) Both partially biodegradable and non-biodegradable plastic beverage containers can be crushed completely flat by refuse compactors.

(B) The partially biodegradable plastic beverage containers are made with more plastic than comparable nonbiodegradable ones in order to compensate for the weakening effect of the bonding agents.

(C) Many consumers are ecology-minded and prefer to buy a product sold in the partially biodegradable plastic beverage containers rather than in nonbiodegradable containers, even if the price is higher.

(D) The manufacturing process for the partially biodegradable plastic beverage containers results in less plastic waste than the manufacturing process for nonbiodegradable plastic beverage containers.

(E) Technological problems with recycling currently prevent the reuse as food or beverage containers of the plastic from either type of plastic beverage container.

52. Rye sown in the fall and plowed into the soil in early spring leaves a residue that is highly effective at controlling broad-leaved weeds, but unfortunately for only about forty-five days. No major agricultural crop matures from seed in as little as forty-five days. Synthetic herbicides, on the other hand, although not any longer-lasting, can be reapplied as the crop grows. Clearly, therefore, for major agricultural crops, plowing rye into the soil can play no part in effective weed control.

The argument is most vulnerable to the objection that it fails to

(A) consider that there might be minor, quick-growing crops that do mature in forty-five days or less

(B) identify any alternative method of weed control that could be used instead of the method it rejects

(C) distinguish among the various kinds of synthetic herbicides

(D) allow for the possibility of combining the two weed-control methods it mentions

(E) allow for the possibility that plants other than rye, handled the same way, might have the same effect

53. Most employees in the computer industry move from company to company, changing jobs several times in their careers. However, Summit Computers is known throughout the industry for retaining its employees. Summit credits its success in retaining employees to its informal, nonhierarchical work environment.

Which of the following, if true, most strongly supports Summit's explanation of its success in retaining employees?

(A) Some people employed in the computer industry change jobs if they become bored with their current projects.

(B) A hierarchical work environment hinders the cooperative exchange of ideas that computer industry employees consider necessary for their work.

(C) Many of Summit's senior employees had previously worked at only one other computer company.

(D) In a nonhierarchical work environment, people avoid behavior that might threaten group harmony and thus avoid discussing with their colleagues any dissatisfaction they might have with their jobs.

(E) The cost of living near Summit is relatively low compared to areas in which some other computer companies are located.

54. Journalist: In late 1994, the present government of the Republic of Bellam came into power. Each year since then, about thirty journalists have been imprisoned for printing articles that criticize the government. In 1994, under the old government, only six journalists were imprisoned for criticizing the government. So the old government was more tolerant of criticism by the press than the new one is.

Politician: But in 1994 only six journalists criticized the government, and now journalists routinely do.

The politician challenges the journalist's argument by doing which of the following?

(A) Presenting data that extend further into the past than the journalist's data

(B) Introducing evidence that undermines an assumption of the journalist's argument

(C) Questioning the accuracy of the evidence presented in support of the journalist's conclusion

(D) Pointing out that the argument illegitimately draws a general conclusion on the basis of a sample of only a few cases

(E) Stating that the argument treats information about some members of a group as if it applied to all members of that group

55. Insurance Company X is considering issuing a new policy to cover services required by elderly people who suffer from diseases that afflict the elderly. Premiums for the policy must be low enough to attract customers. Therefore, Company X is concerned that the income from the policies would not be sufficient to pay for the claims that would be made.

Which of the following strategies would be most likely to minimize Company X's losses on the policies?

(A) Attracting middle-aged customers unlikely to submit claims for benefits for many years

(B) Insuring only those individuals who did not suffer any serious diseases as children

(C) Including a greater number of services in the policy than are included in other policies of lower cost

(D) Insuring only those individuals who were rejected by other companies for similar policies

(E) Insuring only those individuals who are wealthy enough to pay for the medical services

56. The fewer restrictions there are on the advertising of legal services, the more lawyers there are who advertise their services, and the lawyers who advertise a specific service usually charge less for that service than the lawyers who do not advertise. Therefore, if the state removes any of its current restrictions, such as the one against advertisements that do not specify fee arrangements, overall consumer legal costs will be lower than if the state retains its current restrictions.

If the statements above are true, which of the following must be true?

(A) Some lawyers who now advertise will charge more for specific services if they do not have to specify fee arrangements in the advertisements.

(B) More consumers will use legal services if there are fewer restrictions on the advertising of legal services.

(C) If the restriction against advertisements that do not specify fee arrangements is removed, more lawyers will advertise their services.

(D) If more lawyers advertise lower prices for specific services, some lawyers who do not advertise will also charge less than they currently charge for those services.

(E) If the only restrictions on the advertising of legal services were those that apply to every type of advertising, most lawyers would advertise their services.

57. Which of the following most logically completes the argument given below?

People in isolated rain-forest communities tend to live on a largely vegetarian diet, and they eat little salt. Few of them suffer from high blood pressure, and their blood pressure does not tend to increase with age, as is common in industrialized countries. Such people often do develop high blood pressure when they move to cities and adopt high-salt diets. Though suggestive, these facts do not establish salt as the culprit in high blood pressure, however, because _____.

(A) genetic factors could account for the lack of increase of blood pressure with age among such people

(B) people eating high-salt diets and living from birth in cities in industrialized societies generally have a tendency to have high blood pressure

(C) it is possible to have a low-salt diet while living in a city in an industrialized country

(D) there are changes in other aspects of diet when such people move to the city

(E) salt is a necessity for human life, and death can occur when the body loses too much salt

58. Even though most universities retain the royalties from faculty members' inventions, the faculty members retain the royalties from books and articles they write. Therefore, faculty members should retain the royalties from the educational computer software they develop.

The conclusion above would be more reasonably drawn if which of the following were inserted into the argument as an additional premise?

(A) Royalties from inventions are higher than royalties from educational software programs.

(B) Faculty members are more likely to produce educational software programs than inventions.

(C)   Inventions bring more prestige to universities than do books and articles.

(D)   In the experience of most universities, educational software programs are more marketable than are books and articles.

(E)   In terms of the criteria used to award royalties, educational software programs are more nearly comparable to books and articles than to inventions.

59.   In order to withstand tidal currents, juvenile horseshoe crabs frequently burrow in the sand. Such burrowing discourages barnacles from clinging to their shells. When fully grown, however, the crabs can readily withstand tidal currents without burrowing, and thus they acquire substantial populations of barnacles. Surprisingly, in areas where tidal currents are very weak, juvenile horseshoe crabs are found not to have significant barnacle populations, even though they seldom burrow.

Which of the following, if true, most helps to explain the surprising finding?

(A)   Tidal currents do not themselves dislodge barnacles from the shells of horseshoe crabs.

(B)   Barnacles most readily attach themselves to horseshoe crabs in areas where tidal currents are weakest.

(C)   The strength of the tidal currents in a given location varies widely over the course of a day.

(D)   A very large barnacle population can significantly decrease the ability of a horseshoe crab to find food.

(E)   Until they are fully grown, horseshoe crabs shed their shells and grow new ones several times a year.

60.   Red blood cells in which the malarial-fever parasite resides are eliminated from a person's body after 120 days. Because the parasite cannot travel to a new generation of red blood cells, any fever that develops in a person more than 120 days after that person has moved to a malaria-free region is not due to the malarial parasite.

Which of the following, if true, most seriously weakens the conclusion above?

(A)   The fever caused by the malarial parasite may resemble the fever caused by flu viruses.

(B)   The anopheles mosquito, which is the principal insect carrier of the malarial parasite, has been eradicated in many parts of the world.

(C)   Many malarial symptoms other than the fever, which can be suppressed with antimalarial medication, can reappear within 120 days after the medication is discontinued.

(D)   In some cases, the parasite that causes malarial fever travels to cells of the spleen, which are less frequently eliminated from a person's body than are red blood cells.

(E)   In any region infested with malaria-carrying mosquitoes, there are individuals who appear to be immune to malaria.

61.   Neither a rising standard of living nor balanced trade, by itself, establishes a country's ability to compete in the international marketplace. Both are required simultaneously since standards of living can rise because of growing trade deficits and trade can be balanced by means of a decline in a country's standard of living.

If the facts stated in the passage above are true, a proper test of a country's ability to be competitive is its ability to

(A)   balance its trade while its standard of living rises

(B)   balance its trade while its standard of living falls

(C)   increase trade deficits while its standard of living rises

(D)   decrease trade deficits while its standard of living falls

(E)   keep its standard of living constant while trade deficits rise

62. When there is less rainfall than normal, the water level of Australian rivers falls and the rivers flow more slowly. Because algae whose habitat is river water grow best in slow-moving water, the amount of algae per unit of water generally increases when there has been little rain. By contrast, however, following a period of extreme drought, algae levels are low even in very slow-moving river water.

Which of the following, if true, does most to explain the contrast described above?

(A) During periods of extreme drought, the populations of some of the species that feed on algae tend to fall.

(B) The more slowly water moves, the more conducive its temperature is to the growth of algae.

(C) When algae populations reach very high levels, conditions within the river can become toxic for some of the other species that normally live there.

(D) Australian rivers dry up completely for short intervals in periods of extreme drought.

(E) Except during periods of extreme drought, algae levels tend to be higher in rivers in which the flow has been controlled by damming than in rivers that flow freely.

63. When hypnotized subjects are told that they are deaf and are then asked whether they can hear the hypnotist, they reply, "No." Some theorists try to explain this result by arguing that the selves of hypnotized subjects are dissociated into separate parts, and that the part that is deaf is dissociated from the part that replies.

Which of the following challenges indicates the most serious weakness in the attempted explanation described above?

(A) Why does the part that replies not answer, "Yes"?

(B) Why are the observed facts in need of any special explanation?

(C) Why do the subjects appear to accept the hypnotist's suggestion that they are deaf?

(D) Why do hypnotized subjects all respond the same way in the situation described?

(E) Why are the separate parts of the self the same for all subjects?

64. A prominent investor who holds a large stake in the Burton Tool Company has recently claimed that **the company is mismanaged**, citing as evidence the company's failure to slow production in response to a recent rise in its inventory of finished products. It is doubtful whether an investor's sniping at management can ever be anything other than counterproductive, **but in this case it is clearly not justified**. It is true that an increased inventory of finished products often indicates that production is outstripping demand, but in Burton's case it indicates no such thing. Rather, the increase in inventory is entirely attributable to products that have already been assigned to orders received from customers.

In the argument given, the two boldfaced portions play which of the following roles?

(A) The first states the position that the argument as a whole opposes; the second provides evidence to undermine the support for the position being opposed.

(B) The first states the position that the argument as a whole opposes; the second is evidence that has been used to support the position being opposed.

(C) The first states the position that the argument as a whole opposes; the second states the conclusion of the argument as a whole.

(D) The first is evidence that has been used to support a position that the argument as a whole opposes; the second provides information to undermine the force of that evidence.

(E) The first is evidence that has been used to support a position that the argument as a whole opposes; the second states the conclusion of the argument as a whole.

65. Excavation of the ancient city of Kourion on the island of Cyprus revealed a pattern of debris and collapsed buildings typical of towns devastated by earthquakes. Archaeologists have hypothesized that the destruction was due to a major earthquake known to have occurred near the island in A.D. 365.

Which of the following, if true, most strongly supports the archaeologists' hypothesis?

(A) Bronze ceremonial drinking vessels that are often found in graves dating from years preceding and following A.D. 365 were also found in several graves near Kourion.

(B) No coins minted after A.D. 365 were found in Kourion, but coins minted before that year were found in abundance.

(C) Most modern histories of Cyprus mention that an earthquake occurred near the island in A.D. 365.

(D) Several small statues carved in styles current in Cyprus in the century between A.D. 300 and A.D. 400 were found in Kourion.

(E) Stone inscriptions in a form of the Greek alphabet that was definitely used in Cyprus after A.D. 365 were found in Kourion.

66. To protect certain fledgling industries, the government of Country Z banned imports of the types of products those industries were starting to make. As a direct result, the cost of those products to the buyers, several export-dependent industries in Z, went up, sharply limiting the ability of those industries to compete effectively in their export markets.

Which of the following conclusions about Country Z's adversely affected export-dependent industries is best supported by the passage?

(A) Profit margins in those industries were not high enough to absorb the rise in costs mentioned above.

(B) Those industries had to contend with the fact that other countries banned imports from Country Z.

(C) Those industries succeeded in expanding the domestic market for their products.

(D) Steps to offset rising materials costs by decreasing labor costs were taken in those industries.

(E) Those industries started to move into export markets that they had previously judged unprofitable.

67. Several industries have recently switched at least partly from older technologies powered by fossil fuels to new technologies powered by electricity. It is thus evident that less fossil fuel is being used as a result of the operations of these industries than would have been used if these industries had retained their older technologies.

Which of the following, if true, most strengthens the argument above?

(A) Many of the industries that have switched at least partly to the new technologies have increased their output.

(B) Less fossil fuel was used to manufacture the machinery employed in the new technologies than was originally used to manufacture the machinery employed in the older technologies.

(C) More electricity is used by those industries that have switched at least partly to the new technologies than by those industries that have not switched.

(D) Some of the industries that have switched at least partly to the new technologies still use primarily technologies that are powered by fossil fuels.

(E) The amount of fossil fuel used to generate the electricity needed to power the new technologies is less than the amount that would have been used to power the older technologies.

68. The local board of education found that, because the current physics curriculum has little direct relevance to today's world, physics classes attracted few high school students. So to attract students to physics classes, the board proposed a curriculum that emphasizes principles of physics involved in producing and analyzing visual images.

Which of the following, if true, provides the strongest reason to expect that the proposed curriculum will be successful in attracting students?

(A) Several of the fundamental principles of physics are involved in producing and analyzing visual images.

(B) Knowledge of physics is becoming increasingly important in understanding the technology used in today's world.

(C) Equipment that a large producer of photographic equipment has donated to the high school could be used in the proposed curriculum.

(D) The number of students interested in physics today is much lower than the number of students interested in physics 50 years ago.

(E) In today's world the production and analysis of visual images is of major importance in communications, business, and recreation.

69. Scientists have modified feed corn genetically, increasing its resistance to insect pests. Farmers who tried out the genetically modified corn last season applied less insecticide to their corn fields and still got yields comparable to those they would have gotten with ordinary corn. Ordinary corn seed, however, costs less, and what these farmers saved on insecticide rarely exceeded their extra costs for seed. Therefore, for most feed-corn farmers, switching to genetically modified seed would be unlikely to increase profits.

Which of the following would it be most useful to know in order to evaluate the argument?

(A) Whether there are insect pests that sometimes reduce feed-corn yields, but against which commonly used insecticides and the genetic modification are equally ineffective

(B) Whether the price that farmers receive for feed corn has remained steady over the past few years

(C) Whether the insecticides typically used on feed corn tend to be more expensive than insecticides typically used on other crops

(D) Whether most of the farmers who tried the genetically modified corn last season applied more insecticide than was actually necessary

(E) Whether, for most farmers who plant feed corn, it is their most profitable crop

70. Although aspirin has been proven to eliminate moderate fever associated with some illnesses, many doctors no longer routinely recommend its use for this purpose. A moderate fever stimulates the activity of the body's disease-fighting white blood cells and also inhibits the growth of many strains of disease-causing bacteria.

If the statements above are true, which of the following conclusions is most strongly supported by them?

(A) Aspirin, an effective painkiller, alleviates the pain and discomfort of many illnesses.

(B) Aspirin can prolong a patient's illness by eliminating moderate fever helpful in fighting some diseases.

(C) Aspirin inhibits the growth of white blood cells, which are necessary for fighting some illnesses.

(D) The more white blood cells a patient's body produces, the less severe the patient's illness will be.

(E) The focus of modern medicine is on inhibiting the growth of disease-causing bacteria within the body.

71. Roland: The alarming fact is that 90 percent of the people in this country now report that they know someone who is unemployed.

Sharon: But a normal, moderate level of unemployment is 5 percent, with one out of 20 workers unemployed. So at any given time if a person knows approximately 50 workers, one or more will very likely be unemployed.

Sharon's argument relies on the assumption that

(A)   normal levels of unemployment are rarely exceeded

(B)   unemployment is not normally concentrated in geographically isolated segments of the population

(C)   the number of people who each know someone who is unemployed is always higher than 90 percent of the population

(D)   Roland is not consciously distorting the statistics he presents

(E)   knowledge that a personal acquaintance is unemployed generates more fear of losing one's job than does knowledge of unemployment statistics

72.   Community activist: If Morganville wants to keep its central shopping district healthy, it should prevent the opening of a huge SaveAll discount department store on the outskirts of Morganville. Records from other small towns show that whenever SaveAll has opened a store outside the central shopping district of a small town, within five years the town has experienced the bankruptcies of more than a quarter of the stores in the shopping district.

The answer to which of the following would be most useful for evaluating the community activist's reasoning?

(A)   Have community activists in other towns successfully campaigned against the opening of a SaveAll store on the outskirts of their towns?

(B)   Do a large percentage of the residents of Morganville currently do almost all of their shopping at stores in Morganville?

(C)   In towns with healthy central shopping districts, what proportion of the stores in those districts suffer bankruptcy during a typical five-year period?

(D)   What proportion of the employees at the SaveAll store on the outskirts of Morganville will be drawn from Morganville?

(E)   Do newly opened SaveAll stores ever lose money during their first five years of operation?

73.   In comparison to the standard typewriter keyboard, the EFCO keyboard, which places the most-used keys nearest the typist's strongest fingers, allows faster typing and results in less fatigue. Therefore, replacement of standard keyboards with the EFCO keyboard will result in an immediate reduction of typing costs.

Which of the following, if true, would most weaken the conclusion drawn above?

(A)   People who use both standard and EFCO keyboards report greater difficulty in the transition from the EFCO keyboard to the standard keyboard than in the transition from the standard keyboard to the EFCO keyboard.

(B)   EFCO keyboards are no more expensive to manufacture than are standard keyboards and require less frequent repair than do standard keyboards.

(C)   The number of businesses and government agencies that use EFCO keyboards is increasing each year.

(D)   The more training and experience an employee has had with the standard keyboard, the more costly it is to train that employee to use the EFCO keyboard.

(E)   Novice typists can learn to use the EFCO keyboard in about the same amount of time that it takes them to learn to use the standard keyboard.

74. In the past the country of Malvernia has relied heavily on imported oil. Malvernia recently implemented a program to convert heating systems from oil to natural gas. Malvernia currently produces more natural gas each year than it uses, and oil production in Malvernian oil fields is increasing at a steady pace. If these trends in fuel production and usage continue, therefore, Malvernian reliance on foreign sources for fuel is likely to decline soon.

Which of the following would it be most useful to establish in evaluating the argument?

(A) When, if ever, will production of oil in Malvernia outstrip production of natural gas?

(B) Is Malvernia among the countries that rely most on imported oil?

(C) What proportion of Malvernia's total energy needs is met by hydroelectric, solar, and nuclear power?

(D) Is the amount of oil used each year in Malvernia for generating electricity and fuel for transportation increasing?

(E) Have any existing oil-burning heating systems in Malvernia already been converted to natural-gas-burning heating systems?

75. An overly centralized economy, not the changes in the climate, is responsible for the poor agricultural production in Country X since its new government came to power. Neighboring Country Y has experienced the same climatic conditions, but while agricultural production has been falling in Country X, it has been rising in Country Y.

Which of the following, if true, would most weaken the argument above?

(A) Industrial production also is declining in Country X.

(B) Whereas Country Y is landlocked, Country X has a major seaport.

(C) Both Country X and Country Y have been experiencing drought conditions.

(D) The crops that have always been grown in Country X are different from those that have always been grown in Country Y.

(E) Country X's new government instituted a centralized economy with the intention of ensuring an equitable distribution of goods.

76. Because no employee wants to be associated with bad news in the eyes of a superior, information about serious problems at lower levels is progressively softened and distorted as it goes up each step in the management hierarchy. The chief executive is, therefore, less well informed about problems at lower levels than are his or her subordinates at those levels.

The conclusion drawn above is based on the assumption that

(A) problems should be solved at the level in the management hierarchy at which they occur

(B) employees should be rewarded for accurately reporting problems to their superiors

(C) problem-solving ability is more important at higher levels than it is at lower levels of the management hierarchy

(D) chief executives obtain information about problems at lower levels from no source other than their subordinates

(E) some employees are more concerned about truth than about the way they are perceived by their superiors

77. Although the earliest surviving Greek inscriptions written in an alphabet date from the eighth century B.C., **the fact that the text of these Greek inscriptions sometimes runs from right to left and sometimes from left to right** indicates that the Greeks adopted alphabetic writing at least two centuries before these inscriptions were produced. After all, the Greeks learned alphabetic writing from the Phoenicians, and presumably, along with the alphabet, they also adopted the then-current Phoenician practice with respect to the direction of text. **And although Phoenician writing was originally inconsistent in direction, by the eighth century B.C. Phoenician was consistently written from right to left and had been for about two centuries**.

In the argument given, the two portions in boldface play which of the following roles?

(A) The first and the second each describe evidence that has been used to challenge the position that the argument seeks to establish.

(B) The first is evidence that forms the basis for an objection to the position that the argument seeks to establish; the second is that position.

(C) The first is evidence that forms the basis for an objection to the position that the argument seeks to establish; the second is a consideration that is introduced to counter the force of that evidence.

(D) The first and the second each provide evidence in support of the position that the argument seeks to establish.

(E) The first provides evidence in support of the position that the argument seeks to establish; the second is that position.

78. A recent report determined that although only 3 percent of drivers on Maryland highways equipped their vehicles with radar detectors, 33 percent of all vehicles ticketed for exceeding the speed limit were equipped with them. Clearly, drivers who equip their vehicles with radar detectors are more likely to exceed the speed limit regularly than are drivers who do not.

The conclusion drawn above depends on which of the following assumptions?

(A) Drivers who equip their vehicles with radar detectors are less likely to be ticketed for exceeding the speed limit than are drivers who do not.

(B) Drivers who are ticketed for exceeding the speed limit are more likely to exceed the speed limit regularly than are drivers who are not ticketed.

(C) The number of vehicles that were ticketed for exceeding the speed limit was greater than the number of vehicles that were equipped with radar detectors.

(D) Many of the vehicles that were ticketed for exceeding the speed limit were ticketed more than once in the time period covered by the report.

(E) Drivers on Maryland highways exceeded the speed limit more often than did drivers on other state highways not covered in the report.

79. **In countries where automobile insurance includes compensation for whiplash injuries sustained in automobile accidents, reports of having suffered such injuries are twice as frequent as they are in countries where whiplash is not covered.** Presently, no objective test for whiplash exists, so it is true that spurious reports of whiplash injuries cannot be readily identified. Nevertheless, these facts do not warrant the conclusion drawn by some commentators that in the countries with the higher rates of reported whiplash injuries, half of the reported cases are spurious. Clearly, **in countries where automobile insurance does not include compensation for whiplash, people often have little incentive to report whiplash injuries that they actually have suffered.**

In the argument given, the two boldfaced portions play which of the following roles?

(A) The first is a claim that the argument disputes; the second is a conclusion that has been based on that claim.

(B) The first is a claim that has been used to support a conclusion that the argument accepts; the second is that conclusion.

(C) The first is evidence that has been used to support a conclusion for which the argument provides further evidence; the second is the main conclusion of the argument.

(D) The first is a finding whose implications are at issue in the argument; the second is a claim presented in order to argue against deriving certain implications from that finding.

(E) The first is a finding whose accuracy is evaluated in the argument; the second is evidence presented to establish that the finding is accurate.

80. Products sold under a brand name used to command premium prices because, in general, they were superior to nonbrand rival products. Technical expertise in product development has become so widespread, however, that special quality advantages are very hard to obtain these days and even harder to maintain. As a consequence, brand-name products generally neither offer higher quality nor sell at higher prices. Paradoxically, brand names are a bigger marketing advantage than ever.

Which of the following, if true, most helps to resolve the paradox outlined above?

(A) Brand names are taken by consumers as a guarantee of getting a product as good as the best rival products.

(B) Consumers recognize that the quality of products sold under invariant brand names can drift over time.

(C) In many acquisitions of one corporation by another, the acquiring corporation is interested more in acquiring the right to use certain brand names than in acquiring existing production facilities.

(D) In the days when special quality advantages were easier to obtain than they are now, it was also easier to get new brand names established.

(E) The advertising of a company's brand-name products is at times transferred to a new advertising agency, especially when sales are declining.

81. When demand for a factory's products is high, more money is spent at the factory for safety precautions and machinery maintenance than when demand is low. Thus the average number of on-the-job accidents per employee each month should be lower during periods when demand is high than when demand is low and less money is available for safety precautions and machinery maintenance.

Which of the following, if true about a factory when demand for its products is high, casts the most serious doubt on the conclusion drawn above?

(A) Its employees ask for higher wages than they do at other times.

(B) Its management hires new workers but lacks the time to train them properly.

(C) Its employees are less likely to lose their jobs than they are at other times.

(D) Its management sponsors a monthly safety award for each division in the factory.

(E) Its old machinery is replaced with modern, automated models.

82. A sudden increase in the production of elephant ivory artifacts on the Mediterranean coast of North Africa occurred in the tenth century. Historians explain this increase as the result of an area opening up as a new source of ivory and argue on this basis that the important medieval trade between North Africa and East Africa began at this period.

Each of the following, if true, provides some support for the historians' account described above EXCEPT:

(A) In East Africa gold coins from Mediterranean North Africa have been found at a tenth-century site but at no earlier sites.

(B) The many surviving letters of pre-tenth-century North African merchants include no mention of business transactions involving East Africa.

(C) Excavations in East Africa reveal a tenth-century change in architectural style to reflect North African patterns.

(D) Documents from Mediterranean Europe and North Africa that date back earlier than the tenth century show knowledge of East African animals.

(E) East African carvings in a style characteristic of the tenth century depict seagoing vessels very different from those used by local sailors but of a type common in the Mediterranean.

83. Journalist: In physics journals, the number of articles reporting the results of experiments involving particle accelerators was lower last year than it had been in previous years. Several of the particle accelerators at major research institutions were out of service the year before last for repairs, so it is likely that the low number of articles was due to the decline in availability of particle accelerators.

    Which of the following, if true, most seriously undermines the journalist's argument?

    (A) Every article based on experiments with particle accelerators that was submitted for publication last year actually was published.

    (B) The average time scientists must wait for access to a particle accelerator has declined over the last several years.

    (C) The number of physics journals was the same last year as in previous years.

    (D) Particle accelerators can be used for more than one group of experiments in any given year.

    (E) Recent changes in the editorial policies of several physics journals have decreased the likelihood that articles concerning particle-accelerator research will be accepted for publication.

84. Many people suffer an allergic reaction to certain sulfites, including those that are commonly added to wine as preservatives. However, since there are several winemakers who add sulfites to none of the wines they produce, people who would like to drink wine but are allergic to sulfites can drink wines produced by these winemakers without risking an allergic reaction to sulfites.

    Which of the following is an assumption on which the argument depends?

    (A) These winemakers have been able to duplicate the preservative effect produced by adding sulfites by means that do not involve adding any potentially allergenic substances to their wine.

    (B) Not all forms of sulfite are equally likely to produce the allergic reaction.

    (C) Wine is the only beverage to which sulfites are commonly added.

    (D) Apart from sulfites, there are no substances commonly present in wine that give rise to an allergic reaction.

    (E) Sulfites are not naturally present in the wines produced by these winemakers in amounts large enough to produce an allergic reaction in someone who drinks these wines.

85. Networks of blood vessels in bats' wings serve only to disperse heat generated in flight. This heat is generated only because bats flap their wings. Thus paleontologists' recent discovery that the winged dinosaur Sandactylus had similar networks of blood vessels in the skin of its wings provides evidence for the hypothesis that Sandactylus flew by flapping its wings, not just by gliding.

    In the passage, the author develops the argument by

    (A) forming the hypothesis that best explains several apparently conflicting pieces of evidence

    (B) reinterpreting evidence that had been used to support an earlier theory

    (C) using an analogy with a known phenomenon to draw a conclusion about an unknown phenomenon

    (D) speculating about how structures observed in present-day creatures might have developed from similar structures in creatures now extinct

    (E) pointing out differences in the physiological demands that flight makes on large, as opposed to small, creatures

86. Keith: Compliance with new government regulations requiring the installation of smoke alarms and sprinkler systems in all theaters and arenas will cost the entertainment industry $25 billion annually. Consequently, jobs will be lost and profits diminished. Therefore, these regulations will harm the country's economy.

    Laura: The $25 billion spent by some businesses will be revenue for others. Jobs and profits will be gained as well as lost.

    Laura responds to Keith by

    (A) demonstrating that Keith's conclusion is based on evidence that is not relevant to the issue at hand
    (B) challenging the plausibility of the evidence that serves as the basis for Keith's argument
    (C) suggesting that Keith's argument overlooks a mitigating consequence
    (D) reinforcing Keith's conclusion by supplying a complementary interpretation of the evidence Keith cites
    (E) agreeing with the main conclusion of Keith's argument but construing that conclusion as grounds for optimism rather than for pessimism

87. In the United States, of the people who moved from one state to another when they retired, the percentage who retired to Florida has decreased by three percentage points over the past ten years. Since many local businesses in Florida cater to retirees, these declines are likely to have a noticeably negative economic effect on these businesses and therefore on the economy of Florida.

    Which of the following, if true, most seriously weakens the argument given?

    (A) People who moved from one state to another when they retired moved a greater distance, on average, last year than such people did ten years ago.
    (B) People were more likely to retire to North Carolina from another state last year than people were ten years ago.

    (C) The number of people who moved from one state to another when they retired has increased significantly over the past ten years.
    (D) The number of people who left Florida when they retired to live in another state was greater last year than it was ten years ago.
    (E) Florida attracts more people who move from one state to another when they retire than does any other state.

88. Businesses are suffering because of a lack of money available for development loans. To help businesses, the government plans to modify the income-tax structure in order to induce individual taxpayers to put a larger portion of their incomes into retirement savings accounts, because as more money is deposited in such accounts, more money becomes available to borrowers.

    Which of the following, if true, raises the most serious doubt regarding the effectiveness of the government's plan to increase the amount of money available for development loans for businesses?

    (A) When levels of personal retirement savings increase, consumer borrowing always increases correspondingly.
    (B) The increased tax revenue the government would receive as a result of business expansion would not offset the loss in revenue from personal income taxes during the first year of the plan.
    (C) Even with tax incentives, some people will choose not to increase their levels of retirement savings.
    (D) Bankers generally will not continue to lend money to businesses whose prospective earnings are insufficient to meet their loan repayment schedules.
    (E) The modified tax structure would give all taxpayers, regardless of their incomes, the same tax savings for a given increase in their retirement savings.

89. Since it has become known that **several of a bank's top executives have been buying shares in their own bank,** the bank's depositors, who had been worried by rumors that the bank faced impending financial collapse, have been greatly relieved. They reason that, since top executives evidently have faith in the bank's financial soundness, those worrisome rumors must be false. Such reasoning might well be overoptimistic, however, since **corporate executives have been known to buy shares in their own company in a calculated attempt to dispel negative rumors about the company's health.**

In the argument given, the two boldfaced portions play which of the following roles?

(A) The first describes evidence that has been taken as supporting a conclusion; the second gives a reason for questioning that support.

(B) The first describes evidence that has been taken as supporting a conclusion; the second states a contrary conclusion that is the main conclusion of the argument.

(C) The first provides evidence in support of the main conclusion of the argument; the second states that conclusion.

(D) The first describes the circumstance that the argument as a whole seeks to explain; the second gives the explanation that the argument seeks to establish.

(E) The first describes the circumstance that the argument as a whole seeks to explain; the second provides evidence in support of the explanation that the argument seeks to establish.

90. A new law gives ownership of patents—documents providing exclusive right to make and sell an invention—to universities, not the government, when those patents result from government-sponsored university research. Administrators at Logos University plan to sell any patents they acquire to corporations in order to fund programs to improve undergraduate teaching.

Which of the following, if true, would cast the most doubt on the viability of the college administrators' plan described above?

(A) Profit-making corporations interested in developing products based on patents held by universities are likely to try to serve as exclusive sponsors of ongoing university research projects.

(B) Corporate sponsors of research in university facilities are entitled to tax credits under new federal tax-code guidelines.

(C) Research scientists at Logos University have few or no teaching responsibilities and participate little if at all in the undergraduate programs in their field.

(D) Government-sponsored research conducted at Logos University for the most part duplicates research already completed by several profit-making corporations.

(E) Logos University is unlikely to attract corporate sponsorship of its scientific research.

91. Environmentalist: The commissioner of the Fish and Game Authority would have the public believe that increases in the number of marine fish caught demonstrate that this resource is no longer endangered. This is a specious argument, as unsound as it would be to assert that the ever-increasing rate at which rain forests are being cut down demonstrates a lack of danger to that resource. The real cause of the increased fish-catch is a greater efficiency in using technologies that deplete resources.

The environmentalist's statements, if true, best support which of the following as a conclusion?

(A) The use of technology is the reason for the increasing encroachment of people on nature.

(B) It is possible to determine how many fish are in the sea in some way other than by catching fish.

(C) The proportion of marine fish that are caught is as high as the proportion of rain forest trees that are cut down each year.

(D) Modern technologies waste resources by catching inedible fish.

(E) Marine fish continue to be an endangered resource.

92. In the country of Veltria, the past two years' broad economic recession has included a business downturn in the clothing trade, where sales are down by about 7 percent as compared to two years ago. Clothing wholesalers have found, however, that the proportion of credit extended to retailers that was paid off on time fell sharply in the first year of the recession but returned to its prerecession level in the second year.

    Which of the following, if true, most helps to explain the change between the first and the second year of the recession in the proportion of credit not paid off on time?

    (A) The total amount of credit extended to retailers by clothing wholesalers increased between the first year of the recession and the second year.

    (B) Between the first and second years of the recession, clothing retailers in Veltria saw many of their costs, rent and utilities in particular, increase.

    (C) Of the considerable number of clothing retailers in Veltria who were having financial difficulties before the start of the recession, virtually all were forced to go out of business during its first year.

    (D) Clothing retailers in Veltria attempted to stimulate sales in the second year of the recession by discounting merchandise.

    (E) Relatively recession-proof segments of the clothing trade, such as work clothes, did not suffer any decrease in sales during the first year of the recession.

93. Commentator: The theory of trade retaliation states that countries closed out of any of another country's markets should close some of their own markets to the other country in order to pressure the other country to reopen its markets. If every country acted according to this theory, no country would trade with any other.

    The commentator's argument relies on which of the following assumptions?

    (A) No country actually acts according to the theory of trade retaliation.

    (B) No country should block any of its markets to foreign trade.

    (C) Trade disputes should be settled by international tribunal.

    (D) For any two countries, at least one has some market closed to the other.

    (E) Countries close their markets to foreigners to protect domestic producers.

94. Studies in restaurants show that the tips left by customers who pay their bill in cash tend to be larger when the bill is presented on a tray that bears a credit-card logo. Consumer psychologists hypothesize that simply seeing a credit-card logo makes many credit-card holders willing to spend more because it reminds them that their spending power exceeds the cash they have immediately available.

    Which of the following, if true, most strongly supports the psychologists' interpretation of the studies?

    (A) The effect noted in the studies is not limited to patrons who have credit cards.

    (B) Patrons who are under financial pressure from their credit-card obligations tend to tip less when presented with a restaurant bill on a tray with a credit-card logo than when the tray has no logo.

    (C) In virtually all of the cases in the studies, the patrons who paid bills in cash did not possess credit cards.

    (D) In general, restaurant patrons who pay their bills in cash leave larger tips than do those who pay by credit card.

    (E) The percentage of restaurant bills paid with a given brand of credit card increases when that credit card's logo is displayed on the tray with which the bill is presented.

95. Although parapsychology is often considered a pseudoscience, it is in fact a genuine scientific enterprise, for it uses scientific methods such as controlled experiments and statistical tests of clearly stated hypotheses to examine the questions it raises.

    The conclusion above is properly drawn if which of the following is assumed?

(A) If a field of study can conclusively answer the questions it raises, then it is a genuine science.

(B) Since parapsychology uses scientific methods, it will produce credible results.

(C) Any enterprise that does not use controlled experiments and statistical tests is not genuine science.

(D) Any field of study that employs scientific methods is a genuine scientific enterprise.

(E) Since parapsychology raises clearly statable questions, they can be tested in controlled experiments.

96. Hotco oil burners, designed to be used in asphalt plants, are so efficient that Hotco will sell one to the Clifton Asphalt plant for no payment other than the cost savings between the total amount the asphalt plant actually paid for oil using its former burner during the last two years and the total amount it will pay for oil using the Hotco burner during the next two years. On installation, the plant will make an estimated payment, which will be adjusted after two years to equal the actual cost savings.

Which of the following, if it occurred, would constitute a disadvantage for Hotco of the plan described above?

(A) Another manufacturer's introduction to the market of a similarly efficient burner

(B) The Clifton Asphalt plant's need for more than one new burner

(C) Very poor efficiency in the Clifton Asphalt plant's old burner

(D) A decrease in the demand for asphalt

(E) A steady increase in the price of oil beginning soon after the new burner is installed

97. **Delta Products Inc. has recently switched at least partly from older technologies using fossil fuels to new technologies powered by electricity.** The question has been raised whether it can be concluded that **for a given level of output Delta's operation now causes less fossil fuel to be consumed than it did formerly.** The answer, clearly, is yes, since the amount of fossil fuel used to generate the electricity needed to power the new technologies is less than the amount needed to power the older technologies, provided level of output is held constant.

In the argument given, the two boldfaced portions play which of the following roles?

(A) The first identifies the content of the conclusion of the argument; the second provides support for that conclusion.

(B) The first provides support for the conclusion of the argument; the second identifies the content of that conclusion.

(C) The first states the conclusion of the argument; the second calls that conclusion into question.

(D) The first provides support for the conclusion of the argument; the second calls that conclusion into question.

(E) Each provides support for the conclusion of the argument.

98. An experiment was done in which human subjects recognize a pattern within a matrix of abstract designs and then select another design that completes that pattern. The results of the experiment were surprising. The lowest expenditure of energy in neurons in the brain was found in those subjects who performed most successfully in the experiments.

Which of the following hypotheses best accounts for the findings of the experiment?

(A) The neurons of the brain react less when a subject is trying to recognize patterns than when the subject is doing other kinds of reasoning.

(B) Those who performed best in the experiment experienced more satisfaction when working with abstract patterns than did those who performed less well.

(C) People who are better at abstract pattern recognition have more energy-efficient neural connections.

(D) The energy expenditure of the subjects' brains increases when a design that completes the initially recognized pattern is determined.

(E) The task of completing a given design is more capably performed by athletes, whose energy expenditure is lower when they are at rest.

99. Which of the following most logically completes the argument?

   The irradiation of food kills bacteria and thus retards spoilage. However, it also lowers the nutritional value of many foods. For example, irradiation destroys a significant percentage of whatever vitamin B1 a food may contain. Proponents of irradiation point out that irradiation is no worse in this respect than cooking. However, this fact is either beside the point, since much irradiated food is eaten raw, or else misleading, since _____.

   (A) many of the proponents of irradiation are food distributors who gain from foods' having a longer shelf life

   (B) it is clear that killing bacteria that may be present on food is not the only effect that irradiation has

   (C) cooking is usually the final step in preparing food for consumption, whereas irradiation serves to ensure a longer shelf life for perishable foods

   (D) certain kinds of cooking are, in fact, even more destructive of vitamin B1 than carefully controlled irradiation is

   (E) for food that is both irradiated and cooked, the reduction of vitamin B1 associated with either process individually is compounded

100. One way to judge the performance of a company is to compare it with other companies. This technique, commonly called "benchmarking," permits the manager of a company to discover better industrial practices and can provide a justification for the adoption of good practices.

   Any of the following, if true, is a valid reason for benchmarking the performance of a company against companies with which it is not in competition rather than against competitors EXCEPT:

   (A) Comparisons with competitors are most likely to focus on practices that the manager making the comparisons already employs.

   (B) Getting "inside" information about the unique practices of competitors is particularly difficult.

   (C) Since companies that compete with each other are likely to have comparable levels of efficiency, only benchmarking against noncompetitors is likely to reveal practices that would aid in beating competitors.

   (D) Managers are generally more receptive to new ideas that they find outside their own industry.

   (E) Much of the success of good companies is due to their adoption of practices that take advantage of the special circumstances of their products or markets.

101. For a trade embargo against a particular country to succeed, a high degree of both international accord and ability to prevent goods from entering or leaving that country must be sustained. A total blockade of Patria's ports is necessary to an embargo, but such an action would be likely to cause international discord over the embargo.

   The claims above, if true, most strongly support which of the following conclusions?

   (A) The balance of opinion is likely to favor Patria in the event of a blockade.

   (B) As long as international opinion is unanimously against Patria, a trade embargo is likely to succeed.

   (C) A naval blockade of Patria's ports would ensure that no goods enter or leave Patria.

   (D) Any trade embargo against Patria would be likely to fail at some time.

   (E) For a blockade of Patria's ports to be successful, international opinion must be unanimous.

102. Theater Critic: The play *La Finestrina*, now at Central Theater, was written in Italy in the eighteenth century. The director claims that this production is as similar to the original production as is possible in a modern theater. Although the actor who plays Harlequin the clown gives a performance very reminiscent of the twentieth-century American comedian Groucho Marx, Marx's comic style was very much within the comic acting tradition that had begun in sixteenth-century Italy.

The considerations given best serve as part of an argument that

(A)   modern audiences would find it hard to tolerate certain characteristics of a historically accurate performance of an eighteenth-century play

(B)   Groucho Marx once performed the part of the character Harlequin in *La Finestrina*

(C)   in the United States the training of actors in the twentieth century is based on principles that do not differ radically from those that underlay the training of actors in eighteenth-century Italy

(D)   the performance of the actor who plays Harlequin in *La Finestrina* does not serve as evidence against the director's claim

(E)   the director of *La Finestrina* must have advised the actor who plays Harlequin to model his performance on comic performances of Groucho Marx

103.   The cost of producing radios in Country Q is 10 percent less than the cost of producing radios in Country Y. Even after transportation fees and tariff charges are added, it is still cheaper for a company to import radios from Country Q to Country Y than to produce radios in Country Y.

The statements above, if true, best support which of the following assertions?

(A)   Labor costs in Country Q are 10 percent below those in Country Y.

(B)   Importing radios from Country Q to Country Y will eliminate 10 percent of the manufacturing jobs in Country Y.

(C)   The tariff on a radio imported from Country Q to Country Y is less than 10 percent of the cost of manufacturing the radio in Country Y.

(D)   The fee for transporting a radio from Country Q to Country Y is more than 10 percent of the cost of manufacturing the radio in Country Q.

(E)   It takes 10 percent less time to manufacture a radio in Country Q than it does in Country Y.

104.   Although the discount stores in Goreville's central shopping district are expected to close within five years as a result of competition from a SpendLess discount department store that just opened, those locations will not stay vacant for long. In the five years since the opening of Colson's, a nondiscount department store, a new store has opened at the location of every store in the shopping district that closed because it could not compete with Colson's.

Which of the following, if true, most seriously weakens the argument?

(A)   Many customers of Colson's are expected to do less shopping there than they did before the SpendLess store opened.

(B)   Increasingly, the stores that have opened in the central shopping district since Colson's opened have been discount stores.

(C)   At present, the central shopping district has as many stores operating in it as it ever had.

(D)   Over the course of the next five years, it is expected that Goreville's population will grow at a faster rate than it has for the past several decades.

(E)   Many stores in the central shopping district sell types of merchandise that are not available at either SpendLess or Colson's.

105.   The average normal infant born in the United States weighs between 12 and 14 pounds at the age of three months. Therefore, if a three-month-old child weighs only 10 pounds, its weight gain has been below the United States average.

Which of the following indicates a flaw in the reasoning above?

(A)   Weight is only one measure of normal infant development.

(B)   Some three-month-old children weigh as much as 17 pounds.

(C)   It is possible for a normal child to weigh 10 pounds at birth.

(D)   The phrase "below average" does not necessarily mean insufficient.

(E)   Average weight gain is not the same as average weight.

106. Kale has more nutritional value than spinach. But since collard greens have more nutritional value than lettuce, it follows that kale has more nutritional value than lettuce.

Any of the following, if introduced into the argument as an additional premise, makes the argument above logically correct EXCEPT:

(A) Collard greens have more nutritional value than kale.

(B) Spinach has more nutritional value than lettuce.

(C) Spinach has more nutritional value than collard greens.

(D) Spinach and collard greens have the same nutritional value.

(E) Kale and collard greens have the same nutritional value.

107. Last year all refuse collected by Shelbyville city services was incinerated. This incineration generated a large quantity of residual ash. In order to reduce the amount of residual ash Shelbyville generates this year to half of last year's total, the city has revamped its collection program. This year city services will separate for recycling enough refuse to reduce the number of truckloads of refuse to be incinerated to half of last year's number.

Which of the following is required for the revamped collection program to achieve its aim?

(A) This year, no materials that city services could separate for recycling will be incinerated.

(B) Separating recyclable materials from materials to be incinerated will cost Shelbyville less than half what it cost last year to dispose of the residual ash.

(C) Refuse collected by city services will contain a larger proportion of recyclable materials this year than it did last year.

(D) The refuse incinerated this year will generate no more residual ash per truckload incinerated than did the refuse incinerated last year.

(E) The total quantity of refuse collected by Shelbyville city services this year will be no greater than that collected last year.

108. Although custom prosthetic bone replacements produced through a new computer-aided design process will cost more than twice as much as ordinary replacements, custom replacements should still be cost-effective. Not only will surgery and recovery time be reduced, but custom replacements should last longer, thereby reducing the need for further hospital stays.

Which of the following must be studied in order to evaluate the argument presented above?

(A) The amount of time a patient spends in surgery versus the amount of time spent recovering from surgery

(B) The amount by which the cost of producing custom replacements has declined with the introduction of the new technique for producing them

(C) The degree to which the use of custom replacements is likely to reduce the need for repeat surgery when compared with the use of ordinary replacements

(D) The degree to which custom replacements produced with the new technique are more carefully manufactured than are ordinary replacements

(E) The amount by which custom replacements produced with the new technique will drop in cost as the production procedures become standardized and applicable on a larger scale

109. Springfield Fire Commissioner: The vast majority of false fire alarms are prank calls made anonymously from fire alarm boxes on street corners. Since virtually everyone has access to a private telephone, these alarm boxes have outlived their usefulness. Therefore, we propose to remove the boxes. Removing the boxes will reduce the number of prank calls without hampering people's ability to report a fire.

Which of the following, if true, most strongly supports the claim that the proposal, if carried out, will have the announced effect?

(A) The fire department traces all alarm calls made from private telephones and records where they came from.

(B) Maintaining the fire alarm boxes costs Springfield approximately $5 million annually.

(C) A telephone call can provide the fire department with more information about the nature and size of a fire than can an alarm placed from an alarm box.

(D) Responding to false alarms significantly reduces the fire department's capacity for responding to fires.

(E) On any given day, a significant percentage of the public telephones in Springfield are out of service.

110. Correctly measuring the productivity of service workers is complex. Consider, for example, postal workers: they are often said to be more productive if more letters are delivered per postal worker. But is this really true? What if more letters are lost or delayed per worker at the same time that more are delivered?

The objection implied above to the productivity measure described is based on doubts about the truth of which of the following statements?

(A) Postal workers are representative of service workers in general.

(B) The delivery of letters is the primary activity of the postal service.

(C) Productivity should be ascribed to categories of workers, not to individuals.

(D) The quality of services rendered can appropriately be ignored in computing productivity.

(E) The number of letters delivered is relevant to measuring the productivity of postal workers.

111. The difficulty with the proposed high-speed train line is that a used plane can be bought for one-third the price of the train line, and the plane, which is just as fast, can fly anywhere. The train would be a fixed linear system, and we live in a world that is spreading out in all directions and in which consumers choose the free-wheel systems (cars, buses, aircraft), which do not have fixed routes. Thus a sufficient market for the train will not exist.

Which of the following, if true, most severely weakens the argument presented above?

(A) Cars, buses, and planes require the efforts of drivers and pilots to guide them, whereas the train will be guided mechanically.

(B) Cars and buses are not nearly as fast as the high-speed train will be.

(C) Planes are not a free-wheel system because they can fly only between airports, which are less convenient for consumers than the high-speed train's stations would be.

(D) The high-speed train line cannot use currently underutilized train stations in large cities.

(E) For long trips, most people prefer to fly rather than to take ground-level transportation.

112. The average hourly wage of television assemblers in Vernland has long been significantly lower than that in neighboring Borodia. Since Borodia dropped all tariffs on Vernlandian televisions three years ago, the number of televisions sold annually in Borodia has not changed. However, recent statistics show a drop in the number of television assemblers in Borodia. Therefore, updated trade statistics will probably indicate that the number of televisions Borodia imports annually from Vernland has increased.

Which of the following is an assumption on which the argument depends?

(A) The number of television assemblers in Vernland has increased by at least as much as the number of television assemblers in Borodia has decreased.

(B) Televisions assembled in Vernland have features that televisions assembled in Borodia do not have.

(C) The average number of hours it takes a Borodian television assembler to assemble a television has not decreased significantly during the past three years.

(D) The number of televisions assembled annually in Vernland has increased significantly during the past three years.

(E) The difference between the hourly wage of television assemblers in Vernland and the hourly wage of television assemblers in Borodia is likely to decrease in the next few years.

113. The pharmaceutical industry argues that because new drugs will not be developed unless heavy development costs can be recouped in later sales, the current 20 years of protection provided by patents should be extended in the case of newly developed drugs. However, in other industries new-product development continues despite high development costs, a fact that indicates that the extension is unnecessary.

Which of the following, if true, most strongly supports the pharmaceutical industry's argument against the challenge made above?

(A) No industries other than the pharmaceutical industry have asked for an extension of the 20-year limit on patent protection.

(B) Clinical trials of new drugs, which occur after the patent is granted and before the new drug can be marketed, often now take as long as 10 years to complete.

(C) There are several industries in which the ratio of research and development costs to revenues is higher than it is in the pharmaceutical industry.

(D) An existing patent for a drug does not legally prevent pharmaceutical companies from bringing to market alternative drugs, provided they are sufficiently dissimilar to the patented drug.

(E) Much recent industrial innovation has occurred in products—for example, in the computer and electronics industries—for which patent protection is often very ineffective.

114. Guidebook writer: I have visited hotels throughout the country and have noticed that in those built before 1930 the quality of the original carpentry work is generally superior to that in hotels built afterward. Clearly carpenters working on hotels before 1930 typically worked with more skill, care, and effort than carpenters who have worked on hotels built subsequently.

Which of the following, if true, most seriously weakens the guidebook writer's argument?

(A) The quality of original carpentry in hotels is generally far superior to the quality of original carpentry in other structures, such as houses and stores.

(B) Hotels built since 1930 can generally accommodate more guests than those built before 1930.

(C) The materials available to carpenters working before 1930 were not significantly different in quality from the materials available to carpenters working after 1930.

(D) The better the quality of original carpentry in a building, the less likely that building is to fall into disuse and be demolished.

(E) The average length of apprenticeship for carpenters has declined significantly since 1930.

115. Caterpillars of all species produce an identical hormone called "juvenile hormone" that maintains feeding behavior. Only when a caterpillar has grown to the right size for pupation to take place does a special enzyme halt the production of juvenile hormone. This enzyme can be synthesized and will, on being ingested by immature caterpillars, kill them by stopping them from feeding.

Which of the following, if true, most strongly supports the view that it would NOT be advisable to try to eradicate agricultural pests that go through a caterpillar stage by spraying croplands with the enzyme mentioned above?

(A) Most species of caterpillar are subject to some natural predation.

(B) Many agricultural pests do not go through a caterpillar stage.

(C) Many agriculturally beneficial insects go through a caterpillar stage.

(D) Since caterpillars of different species emerge at different times, several sprayings would be necessary.

(E) Although the enzyme has been synthesized in the laboratory, no large-scale production facilities exist as yet.

116. Firms adopting "profit-related-pay" (PRP) contracts pay wages at levels that vary with the firm's profits. In the metalworking industry last year, firms with PRP contracts in place showed productivity per worker on average 13 percent higher than that of their competitors who used more traditional contracts.

If, on the basis of the evidence above, it is argued that PRP contracts increase worker productivity, which of the following, if true, would most seriously weaken that argument?

(A) Results similar to those cited for the metalworking industry have been found in other industries where PRP contracts are used.

(B) Under PRP contracts costs other than labor costs, such as plant, machinery, and energy, make up an increased proportion of the total cost of each unit of output.

(C) Because introducing PRP contracts greatly changes individual workers' relationships to the firm, negotiating the introduction of PRP contracts is complex and time-consuming.

(D) Many firms in the metalworking industry have modernized production equipment in the last five years, and most of these introduced PRP contracts at the same time.

(E) In firms in the metalworking industry where PRP contracts are in place, the average take-home pay is 15 percent higher than it is in those firms where workers have more traditional contracts.

117. Scientists typically do their most creative work before the age of forty. It is commonly thought that this happens because aging by itself brings about a loss of creative capacity. However, studies show that **of scientists who produce highly creative work beyond the age of forty, a disproportionately large number entered their field at an older age than is usual**. Since by the age of forty the large majority of scientists have been working in their field for at least fifteen years, the studies' finding strongly suggests that the real reason why scientists over forty rarely produce highly creative work is not that they have aged but rather that **scientists over forty have generally spent too long in their field**.

In the argument given, the two portions in boldface play which of the following roles?

(A) The first is a claim, the accuracy of which is at issue in the argument; the second is a conclusion drawn on the basis of that claim.

(B) The first is an objection that has been raised against a position defended in the argument; the second is that position.

(C) The first is evidence that has been used to support an explanation that the argument challenges; the second is that explanation.

(D) The first is evidence that has been used to support an explanation that the argument challenges; the second is a competing explanation that the argument favors.

(E) The first provides evidence to support an explanation that the argument favors; the second is that explanation.

118. Northern Air has dozens of flights daily into and out of Belleville Airport, which is highly congested. Northern Air depends for its success on economy and quick turnaround and consequently is planning to replace its large planes with Skybuses, whose novel aerodynamic design is extremely fuel efficient. The Skybus's fuel efficiency results in both lower fuel costs and reduced time spent refueling.

Which of the following, if true, could present the most serious disadvantage for Northern Air in replacing their large planes with Skybuses?

(A) The Skybus would enable Northern Air to schedule direct flights to destinations that currently require stops for refueling.

(B) Aviation fuel is projected to decline in price over the next several years.

(C) The fuel efficiency of the Skybus would enable Northern Air to eliminate refueling at some of its destinations, but several mechanics would lose their jobs.

(D) None of Northern Air's competitors that use Belleville Airport are considering buying Skybuses.

(E) The aerodynamic design of the Skybus causes turbulence behind it when taking off that forces other planes on the runway to delay their takeoffs.

119. It is true of both men and women that those who marry as young adults live longer than those who never marry. This does not show that marriage causes people to live longer, since, as compared with other people of the same age, young adults who are about to get married have fewer of the unhealthy habits that can cause a person to have a shorter life, most notably smoking and immoderate drinking of alcohol.

Which of the following, if true, most strengthens the argument above?

(A) Marriage tends to cause people to engage less regularly in sports that involve risk of bodily harm.

(B) A married person who has an unhealthy habit is more likely to give up that habit than a person with the same habit who is unmarried.

(C) A person who smokes is much more likely than a nonsmoker to marry a person who smokes at the time of marriage, and the same is true for people who drink alcohol immoderately.

(D) Among people who marry as young adults, most of those who give up an unhealthy habit after marriage do not resume the habit later in life.

(E) Among people who as young adults neither drink alcohol immoderately nor smoke, those who never marry live as long as those who marry.

120. The earliest Mayan pottery found at Colha, in Belize, is about 3,000 years old. Recently, however, 4,500-year-old stone agricultural implements were unearthed at Colha. These implements resemble Mayan stone implements of a much later period, also found at Colha. Moreover, the implements' designs are strikingly different from the designs of stone implements produced by other cultures known to have inhabited the area in prehistoric times. Therefore, there were surely Mayan settlements in Colha 4,500 years ago.

Which of the following, if true, most seriously weakens the argument?

(A) Ceramic ware is not known to have been used by the Mayan people to make agricultural implements.

(B) Carbon-dating of corn pollen in Colha indicates that agriculture began there around 4,500 years ago.

(C) Archaeological evidence indicates that some of the oldest stone implements found at Colha were used to cut away vegetation after controlled burning of trees to open areas of swampland for cultivation.

(D) Successor cultures at a given site often adopt the style of agricultural implements used by earlier inhabitants of the same site.

(E) Many religious and social institutions of the Mayan people who inhabited Colha 3,000 years ago relied on a highly developed system of agricultural symbols.

121. Codex Berinensis, a Florentine copy of an ancient Roman medical treatise, is undated but contains clues to when it was produced. Its first 80 pages are by a single copyist, but the remaining 20 pages are by three different copyists, which indicates some significant disruption. Since a letter in handwriting identified as that of the fourth copyist mentions a plague that killed many people in Florence in 1148, Codex Berinensis was probably produced in that year.

Which of the following, if true, most strongly supports the hypothesis that Codex Berinensis was produced in 1148?

(A) Other than Codex Berinensis, there are no known samples of the handwriting of the first three copyists.

(B) According to the account by the fourth copyist, the plague went on for 10 months.

(C) A scribe would be able to copy a page of text the size and style of Codex Berinensis in a day.

(D) There was only one outbreak of plague in Florence in the 1100s.

(E) The number of pages of Codex Berinensis produced by a single scribe becomes smaller with each successive change of copyist.

122. The spacing of the four holes on a fragment of a bone flute excavated at a Neanderthal campsite is just what is required to play the third through sixth notes of the diatonic scale—the seven-note musical scale used in much of Western music since the Renaissance. Musicologists therefore hypothesize that the diatonic musical scale was developed and used thousands of years before it was adopted by Western musicians.

Which of the following, if true, most strongly supports the hypothesis?

(A) Bone flutes were probably the only musical instrument made by Neanderthals.

(B) No musical instrument that is known to have used a diatonic scale is of an earlier date than the flute found at the Neanderthal campsite.

(C) The flute was made from a cave-bear bone and the campsite at which the flute fragment was excavated was in a cave that also contained skeletal remains of cave bears.

(D) Flutes are the simplest wind instrument that can be constructed to allow playing a diatonic scale.

(E) The cave-bear leg bone used to make the Neanderthal flute would have been long enough to make a flute capable of playing a complete diatonic scale.

123. Outsourcing is the practice of obtaining from an independent supplier a product or service that a company has previously provided for itself. Since a company's chief objective is to realize the highest possible year-end profits, any product or service that can be obtained from an independent supplier for less than it would cost the company to provide the product or service on its own should be outsourced.

Which of the following, if true, most seriously weakens the argument?

(A) If a company decides to use independent suppliers for a product, it can generally exploit the vigorous competition arising among several firms that are interested in supplying that product.

(B) Successful outsourcing requires a company to provide its suppliers with information about its products and plans that can fall into the hands of its competitors and give them a business advantage.

(C) Certain tasks, such as processing a company's payroll, are commonly outsourced, whereas others, such as handling the company's core business, are not.

(D) For a company to provide a product or service for itself as efficiently as an independent supplier can provide it, the managers involved need to be as expert in the area of that product or service as the people in charge of that product or service at an independent supplier are.

(E) When a company decides to use an independent supplier for a product or service, the independent supplier sometimes hires members of the company's staff who formerly made the product or provided the service that the independent supplier now supplies.

124. Museums that house Renaissance oil paintings typically store them in environments that are carefully kept within narrow margins of temperature and humidity to inhibit any deterioration. Laboratory tests have shown that the kind of oil paint used in these paintings actually adjusts to climatic changes quite well. If, as some museum directors believe, **paint is the most sensitive substance in these works**, then by relaxing the standards for temperature and humidity control, **museums can reduce energy costs without risking damage to these paintings**. Museums would be rash to relax those standards, however, since results of preliminary tests indicate that gesso, a compound routinely used by Renaissance artists to help paint adhere to the canvas, is unable to withstand significant variations in humidity.

In the argument above, the two portions in boldface play which of the following roles?

(A) The first is an objection that has been raised against the position taken by the argument; the second is the position taken by the argument.

(B) The first is the position taken by the argument; the second is the position that the argument calls into question.

(C) The first is a judgment that has been offered in support of the position that the argument calls into question; the second is a circumstance on which that judgment is, in part, based.

(D) The first is a judgment that has been offered in support of the position that the argument calls into question; the second is that position.

(E) The first is a claim that the argument calls into question; the second is the position taken by the argument.

8.5 Answer Key

1.	B	32.	C	63.	A	94.	B
2.	C	33.	C	64.	C	95.	D
3.	A	34.	D	65.	B	96.	E
4.	D	35.	B	66.	A	97.	B
5.	D	36.	A	67.	E	98.	C
6.	E	37.	D	68.	E	99.	E
7.	A	38.	B	69.	D	100.	E
8.	A	39.	E	70.	B	101.	D
9.	B	40.	E	71.	B	102.	D
10.	D	41.	C	72.	C	103.	C
11.	E	42.	D	73.	D	104.	B
12.	A	43.	D	74.	D	105.	E
13.	E	44.	C	75.	D	106.	A
14.	A	45.	A	76.	D	107.	D
15.	D	46.	A	77.	D	108.	C
16.	B	47.	A	78.	B	109.	A
17.	E	48.	C	79.	D	110.	D
18.	C	49.	C	80.	A	111.	C
19.	E	50.	C	81.	B	112.	C
20.	D	51.	B	82.	D	113.	B
21.	B	52.	D	83.	E	114.	D
22.	C	53.	B	84.	E	115.	C
23.	D	54.	B	85.	C	116.	D
24.	C	55.	A	86.	C	117.	E
25.	A	56.	C	87.	C	118.	E
26.	C	57.	D	88.	A	119.	E
27.	B	58.	E	89.	A	120.	D
28.	C	59.	E	90.	D	121.	D
29.	A	60.	D	91.	E	122.	E
30.	E	61.	A	92.	C	123.	B
31.	C	62.	D	93.	D	124.	D

8.6 Answer Explanations

The following discussion is intended to familiarize you with the most efficient and effective approaches to critical reasoning questions. The particular questions in this chapter are generally representative of the kinds of critical reasoning questions you will encounter on the GMAT. Remember that it is the problem solving strategy that is important, not the specific details of a particular question.

1. "Life expectancy" is the average age at death of the entire live-born population. In the middle of the nineteenth century, life expectancy in North America was 40 years, whereas now it is nearly 80 years. Thus, in those days, people must have been considered old at an age that we now consider the prime of life.

    Which of the following, if true, undermines the argument above?

    (A)   In the middle of the nineteenth century, the population of North America was significantly smaller than it is today.
    (B)   Most of the gains in life expectancy in the last 150 years have come from reductions in the number of infants who die in their first year of life.
    (C)   Many of the people who live to an advanced age today do so only because of medical technology that was unknown in the nineteenth century.
    (D)   The proportion of people who die in their seventies is significantly smaller today than is the proportion of people who die in their eighties.
    (E)   More people in the middle of the nineteenth century engaged regularly in vigorous physical activity than do so today.

    Argument Evaluation

    Situation   Life expectancy in mid-nineteenth century North America was 40 years; now it is almost 80. What we think of as the prime of life must have been considered old in that earlier era.

    Reasoning   *What point weakens this argument?* The argument is discussing life expectancy over the entire population of those born alive. The argument relies on the idea that if 40 years was the average life expectancy, then the usual length of life must have been around 40. But averages can be misleading. What if, in the nineteenth century, the number of infants born alive but not surviving their first year was far higher than it is today? If this were so, it would significantly reduce the *average age at time of death* of the population as a whole—but of course that population could have contained many who lived well into their seventies or eighties. Thus, if we add the information that first-year infant mortality was quite high 150 years ago, the conclusion that 40 years was considered old then would be much less well supported.

    A   The size of the population is irrelevant to the argument.
    B   **Correct.** Greatly reducing first-year infant mortality will have a large impact on the average life expectancy of the population as a whole. That, rather than grown adults living twice as long, is enough to account for a large portion of the doubling in average life expectancy.
    C   This point supports rather than weakens the argument.
    D   This point supports the argument.
    E   Exercise may have helped some nineteenth century people to live longer than they otherwise would. How many people—and what percentage of the population? Did this help them live past 40? If so, how long? If we had some of this information, it might affect the argument. But since this option does not provide these answers, it has little effect on the argument.

    The correct answer is B.

2. Scientists propose placing seismic stations on the floor of the Pacific Ocean to warn threatened coastal communities on the northwestern coast of the United States of approaching tidal waves caused by earthquakes. Since forewarned communities could take steps to evacuate, many of the injuries and deaths that would otherwise occur could be avoided if the government would implement this proposal.

    The answer to which of the following questions would be most important in determining whether implementing the proposal would be likely to achieve the desired result?

    (A)   When was the last time that the coastal communities were threatened by an approaching tidal wave?

    (B)   How far below sea level would the stations be located?

    (C)   Would there be enough time after receiving warning of an approaching tidal wave for communities to evacuate safely?

    (D)   How soon after a tidal wave hits land is it safe for evacuees to return to their communities?

    (E)   Can the stations be equipped to collect and relay information about phenomena other than tidal waves caused by earthquakes?

Evaluation of a Plan

Situation Scientists plan to place on the floor of the Pacific Ocean seismic stations that can sense earthquakes and warn threatened coastal communities when they will be threatened by tidal waves. Communities that receive warning that tidal waves are approaching could evacuate, and injuries and deaths that the tidal wave would most likely cause could be avoided, under this plan.

Reasoning *What would it be most important to know in determining whether implementing the plan will achieve its desired result, preventing injuries and deaths?* Communities must actually evacuate for the plan to achieve the desired result, and that evacuation must be accomplished without itself causing injuries or deaths. For this to happen, the proposed seismic stations' warnings must come early enough to enable the communities to perform a safe evacuation.

A   Knowing the last time that coastal communities were threatened by an approaching tidal wave might be useful in determining whether the seismic stations are a good use of resources (because it might indicate how often tidal waves pose a threat), but it does not help determine whether the stations' warnings would lead to evacuations preventing injuries and deaths when a tidal wave does hit.

B   The plan is to install the seismic stations on the floor of the Pacific Ocean. Knowing the floor's depth would not help determine whether the seismic stations would help prevent injuries and deaths when a tidal wave hits.

C   **Correct.** If the answer to this question is yes, it will indicate that the plan is more likely to achieve its desired result. If the answer is no, it will show that the plan will not do so.

D   Knowing when evacuees could safely return to their communities is irrelevant to the desired result of the plan as described in the passage.

E   While it might be useful to know whether the seismic stations could be used to gather data on phenomena other than tidal waves, this does not speak to the issue of whether the stations would help prevent injuries and deaths caused by tidal waves.

The correct answer is C.

3.   Homeowners aged 40 to 50 are more likely to purchase ice cream and are more likely to purchase it in larger amounts than are members of any other demographic group. The popular belief that teenagers eat more ice cream than adults must, therefore, be false.

The argument is flawed primarily because the author

(A)   fails to distinguish between purchasing and consuming

(B)   does not supply information about homeowners in age groups other than 40 to 50

(C)   depends on popular belief rather than on documented research findings

(D)   does not specify the precise amount of ice cream purchased by any demographic group

(E)   discusses ice cream rather than more nutritious and healthful foods

Argument Evaluation

Situation   Adults aged 40 to 50 buy more ice cream than does any other demographic group (for example, teenagers). Does this mean that adults consume more ice cream than teenagers do?

Reasoning   *A flawed assumption underlies the reasoning: the assumption that the buyers of the ice cream are also the eaters of the ice cream.* Although the demographic group homeowners aged 40 to 50 purchases more ice cream than does any other demographic group, it is quite likely that much of the ice cream purchased by those homeowners is for consumption by family members rather than for exclusive consumption by the purchaser. This leaves open the possibility that teenagers may indeed be the largest consumers of ice cream.

A   **Correct.** The failure to make this distinction led to the making of the flawed assumption.

B   This is false: The argument tells us (indirectly) that homeowners aged 40 to 50 buy more ice cream than does any other group—which allows us to infer that they buy more than do homeowners aged 30 to 40, for example. But even if the argument had stated such information explicitly, it would not have offered any better support for its conclusion.

C   There is nothing in the argument to suggest that the information given is based on popular belief.

D   Providing precise information about the quantity of ice cream purchased by homeowners aged 40 to 50 would not improve the argument at all.

E   The subject is ice cream, not nutrition, so this point is irrelevant.

The correct answer is A.

4. According to a prediction of the not-so-distant future published in 1940, electricity would revolutionize agriculture. Electrodes would be inserted into the soil, and the current between them would kill bugs and weeds and make crop plants stronger.

    Which of the following, if true, most strongly indicates that the logic of the prediction above is flawed?

    (A) In order for farmers to avoid electric shock while working in the fields, the current could be turned off at such times without diminishing the intended effects.

    (B) If the proposed plan for using electricity were put into practice, farmers would save on chemicals now being added to the soil.

    (C) It cannot be taken for granted that the use of electricity is always beneficial.

    (D) Since weeds are plants, electricity would affect weeds in the same way as it would affect crop plants.

    (E) Because a planting machine would need to avoid coming into contact with the electrodes, new parts for planting machines would need to be designed.

Evaluation of a Plan

Situation   In 1940, electricity was predicted to revolutionize agriculture. This prediction suggested that electric current running between electrodes inserted into the soil would kill bugs and weeds while encouraging the growth of crop plants.

Reasoning   *Which point most suggests that the logic used in formulating the prediction is flawed?* Electricity will revolutionize agriculture, it is said, because current can be run through electrodes placed in the soil. This current will kill bugs and weeds while strengthening plants. But how will the current accomplish this feat? More specifically, how will it kill one kind of plant (weeds) while strengthening another (crop plants)?

A   The logic of the prediction has nothing to do with whether the current can be turned on and off; rather, it is concerned with the current itself and its effects.

B   Rather than suggesting that the logic of the prediction is flawed, this serves to support the prediction: Farmers' saving on chemicals would be part of the predicted agricultural revolution.

C   The argument does not take for granted that the use of electricity is always beneficial; it merely suggests that it would be of great benefit to agriculture.

D   **Correct.** This statement properly identifies a problem with the prediction: It provides no reason to believe that the electricity would affect crop plants and weeds differently.

E   Rather than suggesting that the logic of the prediction is flawed, this serves to support the prediction: Changes in planting machines would be part of the predicted agricultural revolution.

The correct answer is D.

5. A company is considering changing its policy concerning daily working hours. Currently, this company requires all employees to arrive at work at 8 a.m. The proposed policy would permit each employee to decide when to arrive—from as early as 6 a.m. to as late as 11 a.m.

The adoption of this policy would be most likely to decrease employees' productivity if the employees' job functions required them to

(A) work without interruption from other employees

(B) consult at least once a day with employees from other companies

(C) submit their work for a supervisor's eventual approval

(D) interact frequently with each other throughout the entire workday

(E) undertake projects that take several days to complete

Evaluation of a Plan

Situation A company considers changing all employees' starting time from 8 a.m. to individually flexible arrival hours, anytime from 6 to 11 a.m.

Reasoning *Under what conditions could this plan cause employees' productivity to decline?* Consider the job functions defined in the answer choices and determine which entails requirements that would most likely be in conflict with the proposed plan. A plan that allows a five-hour range of start times would make it far more difficult for employees to coordinate their schedules. This would make it difficult, if not impossible, for employees to collaborate with each other throughout the workday and could well decrease productivity.

A Working without interruption would likely mean improved productivity.

B Assuming that all employees are in the same time zone (we are not told otherwise), the flexible hours would still leave plenty of time for at least one daily consultation during the regular business hours of the workday.

C *Eventual approval* indicates that the flexibility exists to permit employees' submissions at any time.

D Correct. The wide range of flexibility in regards to working hours would make frequent interaction difficult, if not impossible, and would be likely to decrease employees' productivity.

E We are not told that the projects involve significant interaction; so such projects would be accomplished just as easily on the proposed flexible schedule.

The correct answer is D.

6. The amount of time it takes for most of a worker's occupational knowledge and skills to become obsolete has been declining because of the introduction of advanced manufacturing technology (AMT). Given the rate at which AMT is currently being introduced in manufacturing, the average worker's old skills become obsolete and new skills are required within as little as five years.

Which of the following plans, if feasible, would allow a company to prepare most effectively for the rapid obsolescence of skills described above?

(A) The company will develop a program to offer selected employees the opportunity to receive training six years after they were originally hired.

(B) The company will increase its investment in AMT every year for a period of at least five years.

(C) The company will periodically survey its employees to determine how the introduction of AMT has affected them.

(D) Before the introduction of AMT, the company will institute an educational program to inform its employees of the probable consequences of the introduction of AMT.

(E) The company will ensure that it can offer its employees any training necessary for meeting their job requirements.

Evaluation of a Plan

Situation The introduction of AMT is making workers' occupational skills obsolete within as little as five years.

Reasoning *Which plan will be most effective in helping the company prepare for the expected rapid obsolescence in occupational knowledge and skills?* It should be clear that some type of training or retraining will be involved, since (at least in certain types of industry) it is unlikely that any company in that industry can afford to avoid introducing AMT if its market competitors are doing so.

A Providing training only to *selected* employees and only after their skills have already become obsolete is not likely to be an effective response.

B This plan only accelerates the problem and does not address the employees' skills.

C Periodic surveys may provide information to employers but will not be enough to prevent employees' skills from becoming obsolete.

D Having knowledge of the consequences does not prevent those consequences; employees' skills will still become obsolete.

E **Correct.** This would ensure that all employees have the most current occupational knowledge and skills needed for their jobs

The correct answer is E.

7. Traverton's city council wants to minimize the city's average yearly expenditures on its traffic signal lights and so is considering replacing the incandescent bulbs currently in use with arrays of light-emitting diodes (LEDs) as the incandescent bulbs burn out. Compared to incandescent bulbs, LED arrays consume significantly less energy and cost no more to purchase. Moreover, the costs associated with the conversion of existing fixtures so as to accept LED arrays would be minimal.

Which of the following would it be most useful to know in determining whether switching to LED arrays would be likely to help minimize Traverton's yearly maintenance costs?

(A) Whether the expected service life of LED arrays is at least as long as that of the currently used incandescent bulbs

(B) Whether any cities have switched from incandescent lights in their traffic signals to lighting elements other than LED arrays

(C) Whether the company from which Traverton currently buys incandescent bulbs for traffic signals also sells LED arrays

(D) Whether Traverton's city council plans to increase the number of traffic signal lights in Traverton

(E) Whether the crews that currently replace incandescent bulbs in Traverton's traffic signals know how to convert the existing fixtures so as to accept LED arrays

Evaluation of a Plan

Situation   The city council of Traverton is considering replacing burned-out incandescent traffic signal lights with LED arrays. The LED arrays consume less energy than incandescent bulbs do while costing no more than those bulbs. Further, the cost of converting existing fixtures to accept LED arrays would be minimal.

Reasoning   *What would it be most important to know in determining whether the switch to LEDs would minimize the city's yearly maintenance costs?* LEDs cost no more than incandescent bulbs, and they consume less energy. This suggests that the overall cost of LEDs is lower than that of incandescent bulbs. Is there any circumstance under which the costs associated with LEDs might be higher? They might be higher if more LEDs than incandescent bulbs had to be purchased every year—and that would be necessary if LEDs burn out more quickly than incandescent bulbs do.

A   **Correct.** Unless the answer to this question were yes rather than no, the switch to LED arrays would not help minimize Traverton's yearly maintenance costs. So it is essential to know the answer to this question in order to determine whether switching to LEDs would help.

B   The existence of another possible alternative to incandescent lights does not have any bearing on the question of whether switching from incandescent lights to LEDs would help.

C   The source from which Traverton acquires its lights, be they incandescent or LEDs, is unimportant.

D   Increasing the number of traffic signal lights in Traverton would probably increase the city's yearly maintenance costs, but it would do so regardless of whether those lights use LEDs or incandescent bulbs.

E   Since the goal of switching to LED arrays is to help minimize yearly expenditures on maintenance, a potential one-time cost—that of training workers to convert the existing fixtures—is not relevant. Further, it is not necessarily the case that the crews that currently replace the incandescent bulbs would be the ones converting the existing fixtures—and even if they were, the account of the plan states that conversion costs would be minimal.

The correct answer is A.

8.   A report that many apples contain a cancer-causing preservative called Alar apparently had little effect on consumers. Few consumers planned to change their apple-buying habits as a result of the report. Nonetheless, sales of apples in grocery stores fell sharply in March, a month after the report was issued.

Which of the following, if true, best explains the reason for the apparent discrepancy described above?

(A)   In March, many grocers removed apples from their shelves in order to demonstrate concern about their customers' health.

(B)   Because of a growing number of food-safety warnings, consumers in March were indifferent to such warnings.

(C)   The report was delivered on television and also appeared in newspapers.

(D)   The report did not mention that any other fruit contains Alar, although the preservative is used on other fruit.

(E)   Public health officials did not believe that apples posed a health threat because only minute traces of Alar were present in affected apples.

Argument Construction

Situation   Despite a report that Alar, used to preserve many apples, could cause cancer, few consumers planned to stop buying apples. However, sales of apples in grocery stores fell sharply a month after the report.

Reasoning   *How can this apparent discrepancy be explained?* If consumers did not intend to change their buying habits, then some other change must have been responsible for the decline in apple sales. If apples were not available to buy in grocery stores, then retail sales would obviously fall. The decision of many grocers to remove apples from their shelves in the month following the report would explain the decline in retail sales.

A   **Correct.** This would be sufficient to explain why sales fell even though consumers did not plan to stop buying apples.

B   This point explains why consumers did not intend to change their apple-buying habits—but not why sales fell.

C   How consumers may have heard about the report throws no light on the discrepancy between their response and the decline in sales.

D   Fruits other than apples are not a part of the discussion.

E   The health officials' opinion, if indeed known to consumers, would likely lead to stable apple sales—so this point does not explain the decline in apple sales.

The correct answer is A.

9. In order to reduce the number of items damaged while in transit to customers, packaging consultants recommended that the TrueSave mail-order company increase the amount of packing material so as to fill any empty spaces in its cartons. Accordingly, TrueSave officials instructed the company's packers to use more packing material than before, and the packers zealously acted on these instructions and used as much as they could. Nevertheless, customer reports of damaged items rose somewhat.

Which of the following, if true, most helps to explain why acting on the consultants' recommendation failed to achieve its goal?

(A) The change in packing policy led to an increase in expenditure on packing material and labor.

(B) When packing material is compressed too densely, it loses some of its capacity to absorb shock.

(C) The amount of packing material used in a carton does not significantly influence the ease with which a customer can unpack the package.

(D) Most of the goods that TrueSave ships are electronic products that are highly vulnerable to being damaged in transit.

(E) TrueSave has lost some of its regular customers as a result of the high number of damaged items they received.

Evaluation of a Plan

Situation   Mail-order company TrueSave wants to reduce the number of items damaged while in transit to customers. Packaging consultants recommended that to achieve this goal, the company should use more packing material to fill empty spaces in its cartons. The company's packers began using as much packing material as they could, yet reports of damaged items rose rather than fell.

Reasoning   *What would help explain why the company's acting on the recommendation did not achieve its goal?* The recommendation involved increasing the amount of packing material, so there must have been something about that increase that led to more damage. More damage would be likely to result if stuffing more packing material into shipping boxes made the packaging less effective.

A   An increase in expenditure on packing material and labor might affect the company's profitability, but it would have no effect on whether items were damaged in transit.

B   Correct. This statement adequately explains why more items, rather than fewer, were damaged in transit.

C   If customers were able to remove their items just as easily from boxes filled with more packing material as from boxes using less packing material, the items would be unaffected by an increase in the amount of packing material used.

D   The kind of goods TrueSave ships most frequently is not relevant to the question of why increasing the amount of packing material failed to reduce the number of items damaged in transit, since they most likely shipped this same kind of goods both before and after making the recommended change.

E   The loss of regular customers helps explain why TrueSave turned to the packaging consultants for help, but it does not help explain why those consultants' recommendation failed to reduce the number of items damaged in transit.

The correct answer is B.

10. Cable-television spokesperson: Subscriptions to cable television are a bargain in comparison to "free" television. Remember that "free" television is not really free. It is consumers, in the end, who pay for the costly advertising that supports "free" television.

    Which of the following, if true, is most damaging to the position of the cable-television spokesperson?

    (A) Consumers who do not own television sets are less likely to be influenced in their purchasing decisions by television advertising than are consumers who own television sets.
    (B) Subscriptions to cable television include access to some public-television channels, which do not accept advertising.
    (C) For locations with poor television reception, cable television provides picture quality superior to that provided by free television.
    (D) There is as much advertising on many cable-television channels as there is on "free" television channels.
    (E) Cable-television subscribers can choose which channels they wish to receive.

Argument Evaluation

Situation   A cable-television spokesperson argues that cable fees are a bargain since so-called "free" television is actually paid for by consumers who underwrite the cost of advertising.

Reasoning   *Which point weakens the spokesperson's argument?* The spokesperson's argument compares the bargain price of a subscription to cable television with the "price" of the costly advertising on "free" television. Consider what situation would undermine this comparison. What if cable television, in addition to its subscription fee, airs just as much advertising as does "free" television? Then the cable subscriber is paying twice, and the spokesperson's argument that cable television is a bargain in comparison to "free" television is weakened.

A   People who do not watch television are irrelevant to the argument.

B   The fact that cable television subscriptions include access to advertising-free public-television channels does not weaken the argument that "free" television is not free.

C   The picture quality of cable and free television are not at issue in this argument.

D   Correct. This statement properly identifies a factor that weakens the spokesperson's argument: If the cost of the advertising on "free" television is ultimately passed on to consumers in the prices they pay for the advertised product, and many cable channels have comparable amounts of advertising, then cable television will necessarily have the same kind of hidden cost as "free" television.

E   Television viewers who do not watch cable channels have a choice as to which channels and programs they view. For example, they could watch channels with no advertising. So this information does not differentiate cable-television viewers from "free"-television viewers.

The correct answer is D.

11. Wood smoke contains dangerous toxins that cause changes in human cells. Because wood smoke presents such a high health risk, legislation is needed to regulate the use of open-air fires and wood-burning stoves.

Which of the following, if true, provides the most support for the argument above?

(A) The amount of dangerous toxins contained in wood smoke is much less than the amount contained in an equal volume of automobile exhaust.

(B) Within the jurisdiction covered by the proposed legislation, most heating and cooking is done with oil or natural gas.

(C) Smoke produced by coal-burning stoves is significantly more toxic than smoke from wood-burning stoves.

(D) No significant beneficial effect on air quality would result if open-air fires were banned within the jurisdiction covered by the proposed legislation.

(E) In valleys where wood is used as the primary heating fuel, the concentration of smoke results in poor air quality.

Argument Construction

Situation   Wood smoke is hazardous, so restrictive legislation is needed.

Reasoning   *Which point supports the need for legislation?* The argument for legislation is based on the position that wood smoke is hazardous to people's health. Any evidence of physical harm resulting from wood smoke supports the argument that legislation is needed. Undoubtedly, poor air quality caused by a high concentration of wood smoke presents just such a health risk.

A   If wood smoke were as dangerous as car exhaust, this might support the idea of regulating it just as exhaust emissions are regulated; but this statement tells us it is less dangerous.

B   This point suggests less of a need for legislation.

C   This information provides no support for the idea that the use of wood-burning stoves should be regulated.

D   The lack of benefit from banning open-air fires is a point against the legislation.

E   **Correct.** This supports the argument in favor of legislation.

The correct answer is E.

12. A certain automaker aims to increase its market share by deeply discounting its vehicles' prices for the next several months. The discounts will cut into profits, but because they will be heavily advertised the manufacturer hopes that they will attract buyers away from rival manufacturers' cars. In the longer term, the automaker envisions that customers initially attracted by the discounts may become loyal customers.

In assessing the plan's chances of achieving its aim, it would be most useful to know which of the following?

(A) Whether the automaker's competitors are likely to respond by offering deep discounts on their own products

(B) Whether the advertisements will be created by the manufacturer's current advertising agency

(C) Whether some of the automaker's models will be more deeply discounted than others

(D) Whether the automaker will be able to cut costs sufficiently to maintain profit margins even when the discounts are in effect

(E) Whether an alternative strategy might enable the automaker to enhance its profitability while holding a constant or diminishing share of the market

Evaluation of a Plan

Situation An automaker is planning to offer deep discounts on its vehicles' prices in order to increase its market share. The automaker's profit margins will be reduced by this action. By advertising the discounts, the automaker hopes to attract customers who might otherwise be inclined to buy rival manufacturers' cars. These customers would ideally then develop loyalty to the automaker's cars.

Reasoning *What would it be most useful to know in assessing whether offering deep discounts will enable the automaker to increase its market share?* To achieve an increase in market share, the automaker would have to take customers away from other automakers. Under what circumstances would other automakers be able to retain their customers, if those customers are more likely to purchase cars from automakers that offer deep discounts (and then remain loyal to those automakers)? The other automakers might try to retain their customers by matching the discounts. Thus it would be useful to know whether the other automakers would indeed offer such discounts.

A **Correct.** If the answer to this question were yes, the plan would probably not achieve its aim of increasing market share. If the answer were no, the plan would have a good chance of succeeding.

B Since there is no information about the effectiveness of the automaker's current advertising, it would not be useful to know whether the same advertising agency will produce the ads publicizing the discount.

C Knowing whether some models will be more deeply discounted than others might help in assessing which of the automaker's models will sell best, but it would not help in assessing the overall chance of the automaker increasing its market share.

D The discounts the automaker plans to offer will cut into profits, according to the information given, so the question of whether the automaker can maintain profit margins while the discounts are in effect has already been answered.

E While it might be useful to the automaker to know about alternative strategies, such knowledge does not help in assessing the likelihood that the plan under discussion will achieve its aim.

The correct answer is A.

13. In Swartkans territory, archaeologists discovered charred bone fragments dating back one million years. Analysis of the fragments, which came from a variety of animals, showed that they had been heated to temperatures no higher than those produced in experimental campfires made from branches of white stinkwood, the most common tree around Swartkans.

    Which of the following, if true, would, together with the information above, provide the best basis for the claim that the charred bone fragments are evidence of the use of fire by early hominids?

    (A) The white stinkwood tree is used for building material by the present-day inhabitants of Swartkans.

    (B) Forest fires can heat wood to a range of temperatures that occur in campfires.

    (C) The bone fragments were fitted together by the archaeologists to form the complete skeletons of several animals.

    (D) Apart from the Swartkans discovery, there is reliable evidence that early hominids used fire as many as 500,000 years ago.

    (E) The bone fragments were found in several distinct layers of limestone that contained primitive cutting tools known to have been used by early hominids.

Argument Evaluation

Situation Archaeologists analyzed charred bone fragments dating back to one million years ago and found that the fire that burned the fragments had been no hotter than a campfire fueled by stinkwood would be. It is claimed that the fragments show that early hominids used fire.

Reasoning *Which additional piece of information would strengthen the argument?* Any physical evidence that links the early hominids to the charred bone fragments strengthens the argument. If these bone fragments were found in conjunction with some other evidence of the presence of early hominids, then the evidence from the Swartkans location could be used to support the claim that early hominids used fire.

A   Today's use of stinkwood for building is irrelevant to the argument.

B   This suggests that forest fires could have been responsible for the charring, so it weakens the argument.

C   This information offers no support to the argument that early hominids used fire.

D   The fragments date back one million years, so evidence from 500,000 years ago is irrelevant.

E   **Correct.** This information links early hominids to these bone fragments and so strengthens the argument.

The correct answer is E.

14. In Washington County, attendance at the movies is just large enough for the cinema operators to make modest profits. The size of the county's population is stable and is not expected to increase much. Yet there are investors ready to double the number of movie screens in the county within five years, and they are predicting solid profits both for themselves and for the established cinema operators.

   Which of the following, if true about Washington County, most helps to provide a justification for the investors' prediction?

   (A) Over the next ten years, people in their teenage years, the prime moviegoing age, will be a rapidly growing proportion of the county's population.
   (B) As distinct from the existing cinemas, most of the cinemas being planned would be located in downtown areas, in hopes of stimulating an economic revitalization of those areas.
   (C) Spending on video purchases, as well as spending on video rentals, has been increasing modestly each year for the past ten years.
   (D) The average number of screens per cinema is lower among existing cinemas than it is among cinemas still in the planning stages.
   (E) The sale of snacks and drinks in cinemas accounts for a steadily growing share of most cinema operators' profits.

Evaluation of a Plan

Situation   Movie attendance in Washington County is large enough (though barely so) to allow the cinemas to make a modest profit. The county's population is expected to remain approximately the same. Despite this, investors wish to double the number of movie screens in the county. They expect both that the new screens will be profitable and that the established cinema operators will continue to maintain their profits.

Reasoning   *What piece of information would most help justify the investors' expectation?* To make twice the number of movie screens profitable, movie attendance in Washington County would have to increase. But how could this happen, given that the county's population is not expected to change? Clearly, some people in Washington County will need to go to the movies more often than they do now. This might happen if some of the population of Washington County were to age into a demographic that is likely to go to the movies more frequently.

   A   **Correct.** This statement tells us that over the next ten years, a larger proportion of the population will probably be moviegoers and this could significantly increase movie attendance in Washington County.
   B   While stimulating downtown revitalization is a worthy goal, this does not help explain why more people would be likely to go to the movies in Washington County. Further, it raises the question of whether theaters in a revitalized downtown would draw business away from theaters in other locations, thus reducing the established cinema operators' profits.
   C   This provides a reason to doubt the investors' prediction, because if spending on videos is increasing, people are probably less likely to see movies in movie theaters.
   D   Regardless of how many screens each new cinema has relative to the established cinemas, none of them will be profitable if they cannot attract sufficient numbers of cinemagoers.
   E   Cinemas' profitability depending on their sales of snacks and drinks does not explain why more people would go to the cinema in the first place.

The correct answer is A.

15. A conservation group in the United States is trying to change the long-standing image of bats as frightening creatures. The group contends that bats are feared and persecuted solely because they are shy animals that are active only at night.

Which of the following, if true, would cast the most serious doubt on the accuracy of the group's contention?

(A) Bats are steadily losing natural roosting places such as caves and hollow trees and are thus turning to more developed areas for roosting.

(B) Bats are the chief consumers of nocturnal insects and thus can help make their hunting territory more pleasant for humans.

(C) Bats are regarded as frightening creatures not only in the United States but also in Europe, Africa, and South America.

(D) Raccoons and owls are shy and active only at night, yet they are not generally feared and persecuted.

(E) People know more about the behavior of other greatly feared animal species, such as lions, alligators, and snakes, than they do about the behavior of bats.

Argument Evaluation

Situation   A conservation group claims that bats are feared and persecuted only because they are shy, nocturnal animals.

Reasoning   *What casts doubt on the proposed explanation for people's fear and persecution of bats?* If people fear bats only because these animals are shy and active at night, then other species that share those same attributes should be equally feared. Yet raccoons and owls, similarly shy and nocturnal, do not elicit the same reaction from people.

A   This information seems to refer to recent changes in bats' habitats—but the passage tells us that the fear being discussed is "long-standing." A long-standing fear cannot be adequately explained by recent changes.

B   The fact that bats provide a benefit for humans does not explain humans' fear of them.

C   This tells us the fear is widespread but throws no light on what causes it.

D   Correct. This suggests that one or more factors other than bats' shyness and nocturnal habits are needed to explain humans' reactions to bats. For example, false beliefs about bats would be one such factor.

E   This suggests that more knowledge about the characteristics of some animal species may produce more, not less fear. But this is quite compatible with the idea that lack of knowledge about the behavior of bats could explain people's fearful reaction to them. One effect of lack of knowledge, for example, is allowing false beliefs to flourish.

The correct answer is D.

16. Which of the following best completes the passage below?

People buy prestige when they buy a premium product. They want to be associated with something special. Mass-marketing techniques and price-reduction strategies should not be used because _____.

(A) affluent purchasers currently represent a shrinking portion of the population of all purchasers

(B) continued sales depend directly on the maintenance of an aura of exclusivity

(C) purchasers of premium products are concerned with the quality as well as with the price of the products

(D) expansion of the market niche to include a broader spectrum of consumers will increase profits

(E) manufacturing a premium brand is not necessarily more costly than manufacturing a standard brand of the same product

Argument Construction

Situation Consumers seek prestige when they buy premium products, that is to say, expensive, top-quality products. Mass-marketing techniques and price-reduction strategies are not appropriate tools to sell these products to consumers seeking to be associated with something special.

Reasoning The correct answer will be the option that best answers the following question: *Why are these tools NOT appropriate for selling these products to this group of consumers?* Consider that these consumers want to feel that the premium product they are buying is out of the ordinary. Any strategy that makes the premium product seem more common or easier to own reduces that product's appeal to this group. By definition, mass-marketing techniques appeal to a huge number of people, rather than a small, select group. Further, reducing prices reduces any associated prestige as well because the product becomes more broadly obtainable.

A This information suggests that the percentage of the population who would buy high-prestige, expensive products may be shrinking. However, the point of the argument is not what the size of the market segment is but rather, what marketing strategies are most effective in selling to that market segment, given the motivations that drive its buying behavior.

B **Correct.** This information, if true, provides a good reason for the avoidance of mass marketing techniques and price-reduction strategies.

C Using mass-marketing techniques and price-reduction strategies could sometimes suggest low quality (and reduce the snob-appeal of the products)—but this issue is addressed more directly and explicitly in (B). The passage does not assume that all mass-marketed products must be of low quality.

D This statement provides a reason why broader marketing should be employed, rather than supporting an argument that it should be avoided.

E Manufacturing costs are not discussed and so are irrelevant.

The correct answer is B.

17. Hunter: **Many people blame hunters alone for the decline in Greenrock National Forest's deer population over the past ten years.** Yet clearly, black bears have also played an important role in this decline. In the past ten years, the forest's protected black bear population has risen sharply, and examination of black bears found dead in the forest during the deer hunting season showed that a number of them had recently fed on deer.

In the hunter's argument, the portion in boldface plays which of the following roles?

(A) It is the main conclusion of the argument.

(B) It is a finding that the argument seeks to explain.

(C) It is an explanation that the argument concludes is correct.

(D) It provides evidence in support of the main conclusion of the argument.

(E) It introduces a judgment that the argument opposes.

Argument Construction

Situation The hunter claims that hunters have been identified by many people as the sole cause of the decline in Greenrock National Forest's deer population. But the hunter argues that black bears have also contributed to the deer population decline. Black bears are protected and have increased in number, and they have been found to have fed recently on deer.

Reasoning *What role in the argument is played by the hunter's statement that many people blame hunters alone for the decline in the national forest's deer population?* In this statement, the hunter claims that many people have judged hunters responsible for the decline. The hunter then goes on to offer evidence supporting a different judgment: that hunters are *not* solely responsible, but that black bears are also to blame.

A The hunter's main conclusion is that black bears have also contributed to the decline in the deer population.

B The argument seeks to offer a reason for the finding that the deer population has declined, not the finding that people blame hunters for that decline.

C The hunter does not conclude that blaming hunters for the decline in the deer population is correct; rather, the hunter suggests that black bears should also be blamed.

D The hunter believes that hunters are *not* solely responsible for the decline in the deer population, so people's suggestion that they *are* responsible does not support the hunter's main conclusion.

E **Correct.** The boldfaced statement cites a judgment that the hunter attributes to many people, and that the hunter argues is incorrect. The hunter opposes the judgment that hunters alone are responsible for the decline in the deer population.

The correct answer is E.

18. In Asia, where palm trees are nonnative, the trees' flowers have traditionally been pollinated by hand, which has kept palm fruit productivity unnaturally low. When weevils known to be efficient pollinators of palm flowers were introduced into Asia in 1980, palm fruit productivity increased—by up to 50 percent in some areas—but then decreased sharply in 1984.

Which of the following statements, if true, would best explain the 1984 decrease in productivity?

(A) Prices for palm fruit fell between 1980 and 1984 following the rise in production and a concurrent fall in demand.

(B) Imported trees are often more productive than native trees because the imported ones have left behind their pests and diseases in their native lands.

(C) Rapid increases in productivity tend to deplete trees of nutrients needed for the development of the fruit-producing female flowers.

(D) The weevil population in Asia remained at approximately the same level between 1980 and 1984.

(E) Prior to 1980 another species of insect pollinated the Asian palm trees, but not as efficiently as the species of weevil that was introduced in 1980.

Argument Construction

Situation   In 1980, the introduction of weevils to pollinate palms trees in Asia resulted in increased palm fruit productivity. This productivity decreased sharply in 1984.

Reasoning   *What explains the sudden decrease in 1984?* The palm trees had experienced a sudden burst of productivity beginning in 1980. What if an aftereffect of that spurt was the cause? If that burst of productivity had used up the trees' nutrients, then the trees would be unable to produce the flowers that are pollinated in order to produce fruit. This sudden exhaustion of the tree's resources could adequately explain the sudden decrease in productivity.

A   Falling prices and falling demand do not explain the falling productivity of the trees.

B   The lack of pests and diseases among imported trees does not explain the sharply decreased productivity.

C   **Correct.** If there are fewer fruit-producing female flowers, there is likely to be less fruit.

D   If the weevil population pollinating the trees remained the same, one would expect that productivity would have remained the same, rather than declining. So this cannot provide an adequate explanation.

E   This information is unlikely to be relevant to the change that occurred in 1984.

The correct answer is C.

19.   Physician: The hormone melatonin has shown promise as a medication for sleep disorders when taken in synthesized form. Because the long-term side effects of synthetic melatonin are unknown, however, I cannot recommend its use at this time.

Patient: Your position is inconsistent with your usual practice. You prescribe many medications that you know have serious side effects, so concern about side effects cannot be the real reason you will not prescribe melatonin.

The patient's argument is flawed because it fails to consider that

(A)   the side effects of synthetic melatonin might be different from those of naturally produced melatonin
(B)   it is possible that the physician does not believe that melatonin has been conclusively shown to be effective
(C)   sleep disorders, if left untreated, might lead to serious medical complications
(D)   the side effects of a medication can take some time to manifest themselves
(E)   known risks can be weighed against known benefits, but unknown risks cannot

Argument Evaluation

Situation   The physician refuses to prescribe synthetic melatonin to treat sleep disorders despite this medication's promise. The reason the physician offers for this refusal is that the long-term side effects of synthetic melatonin are unknown. The patient responds that because the physician prescribes other medications that are known to have serious side effects, it cannot be a concern for synthetic melatonin's side effects that is prompting the physician's refusal to prescribe that medication.

Reasoning   *What does the patient's argument fail to consider?* The patient says that the inconsistency in the physician's position lies in the physician's unwillingness to prescribe synthetic melatonin coupled with a willingness to prescribe other medications that are known to have serious side effects. But notice that the physician does not say that synthetic melatonin has *serious* side effects; rather, the physician points out that the long-term side effects of synthetic melatonin are unknown. The physician most likely prescribes medications that have serious side effects because the medications' benefits outweigh the risks posed by their side effects. In the case of synthetic melatonin, however, this kind of decision cannot be made.

A   The patient's argument has to do with whether the physician's refusal to prescribe synthetic melatonin is consistent with the physician's usual prescription practices. The question of whether naturally produced melatonin has different side effects than synthetic melatonin has no bearing on that argument.

B   It is quite reasonable for the patient's argument not to mention this possibility, especially since the physician expresses a belief that synthetic melatonin may be effective—but expresses no belief about whether or not it has been conclusively shown to be effective.

C   Awareness that sleep disorders can lead to serious medical complications most likely prompts the patient's desire for treatment—but the patient's not mentioning this possible consequence of sleep disorders does not indicate a flaw in the argument.

D   The patient makes clear that the physician prescribes medications that have serious side effects; the time those side effects take to manifest themselves is not relevant to the argument.

E   **Correct.** The patient's argument is flawed in failing to consider this key difference between known risks and unknown risks. If the patient had considered this key difference, the patient would have realized that the physician's position is not at all inconsistent, and that the physician's refusal to prescribe is genuinely based on a concern about an unknown risk.

The correct answer is E.

20. In recent years, many cabinetmakers have been winning acclaim as artists. But since furniture must be useful, cabinetmakers must exercise their craft with an eye to the practical utility of their product. For this reason, cabinetmaking is not art.

Which of the following is an assumption that supports drawing the conclusion above from the reason given for that conclusion?

(A) Some furniture is made to be placed in museums, where it will not be used by anyone.

(B) Some cabinetmakers are more concerned than others with the practical utility of the products they produce.

(C) Cabinetmakers should be more concerned with the practical utility of their products than they currently are.

(D) An object is not an art object if its maker pays attention to the object's practical utility.

(E) Artists are not concerned with the monetary value of their products.

Argument Construction

Situation   Cabinetmaking is not art because furniture must be made with an eye to its usefulness.

Reasoning   *What assumption is made in the argument?* The argument claims that cabinetmakers, when making furniture, must take usefulness into account. It concludes that cabinetmaking is not art. However, the reasoning has a gap: Some information that is not explicitly stated is needed to make the argument succeed. This need for additional information can be met, at least in part, by adding an assumption such as this: Nothing created with a view to its usefulness is a work of art.

A   The destination of the object after its creation is not the issue.

B   The extent to which some cabinetmakers *actually consider* utility is irrelevant, since the reasoning claims that utility must be considered in the successful manufacture of furniture.

C   The argument primarily concerns truly successful cabinetmaking, whether it is art or not, and the role utility plays in (successful) cabinetmaking. It does not address the issue of whether or not current cabinetmakers give adequate consideration to utility or whether or not today's cabinetmakers produce truly successful and useful furniture.

D   Correct. This option, unlike the other four, provides information that helps fill the gap in the argument.

E   The issue of monetary value is not raised at all in the argument.

The correct answer is D.

21. Male bowerbirds construct elaborately decorated nests, or bowers. Basing their judgment on the fact that different local populations of bowerbirds of the same species build bowers that exhibit different building and decorative styles, researchers have concluded that the bowerbirds' building styles are a culturally acquired, rather than a genetically transmitted, trait.

Which of the following, if true, would most strengthen the conclusion drawn by the researchers?

(A) There are more common characteristics than there are differences among the bower-building styles of the local bowerbird population that has been studied most extensively.

(B) Young male bowerbirds are inept at bower-building and apparently spend years watching their elders before becoming accomplished in the local bower style.

(C) The bowers of one species of bowerbird lack the towers and ornamentation characteristic of the bowers of most other species of bowerbird.

(D) Bowerbirds are found only in New Guinea and Australia, where local populations of the birds apparently seldom have contact with one another.

(E) It is well known that the song dialects of some songbirds are learned rather than transmitted genetically.

Argument Evaluation

Situation   Male bowerbirds of the same species but living in different habitats build nests of widely varying styles. Researchers conclude that this nest-building behavior is culturally acquired rather than genetically transmitted.

Reasoning   *What evidence supports the researchers' conclusion?* The researchers base their conclusion upon the different styles of nests and probably the assumption that the nests would all be similar if the bower-building behavior was only transmitted through the genes of the species. What would lend support to this reasoning? If young male bowerbirds have no inherent aptitude for nest building and must learn it over a period of years by watching older male bowerbirds, then the argument that bowerbirds acquire their nest-building preferences culturally rather than genetically is strengthened.

A   The greater number of similarities than differences in style in one population could be attributed to either cultural acquisition or genetic transmission, so the conclusion is not strengthened.

B   **Correct.** Compared with the other options, this information provides the most additional support for the researchers' conclusion.

C   The cited differences are among populations of the same species; differences between species are outside the scope of the conclusion.

D   Since no information is given about the nest-building styles of these populations (whether or not they are of the same species), the fact that they have little contact neither strengthens nor weakens the conclusion.

E   This statement provides an example of learned bird behavior, and so provides a little additional support for the conclusion, but not as much additional support as does (B).

The correct answer is B.

22. **Plan:** Concerned about the welfare of its senior citizens, the government of Runagia decided two years ago to increase by 20 percent the government-provided pension paid to all Runagians age sixty-five and older.

Result: Many Runagian senior citizens are no better off financially now than they were before the increase.

Further information: The annual rate of inflation since the pension increase has been below 5 percent, and the increased pension has been duly received by all eligible Runagians.

In light of the further information, which of the following, if true, does most to explain the result that followed implementation of the plan?

(A) The majority of senior citizens whose financial position has not improved rely entirely on the government pension for their income.

(B) The Runagian banking system is so inefficient that cashing a pension check can take as much as three weeks.

(C) The prices of goods and services that meet the special needs of many senior citizens have increased at a rate much higher than the rate of inflation.

(D) The pension increase occurred at a time when the number of Runagians age sixty-five and older who were living below the poverty level was at an all-time high.

(E) The most recent pension increase was only the second such increase in the last ten years.

Evaluation of a Plan

Situation Two years ago, Runagia's government attempted to improve senior citizens' welfare by increasing senior citizens' pensions by 20 percent. Unfortunately, many of those senior citizens' welfare did not improve. This result occurred despite inflation being relatively low—below 5 percent—and all appropriate people receiving their increased pensions.

Reasoning *What would do most to explain why many of Runagia's senior citizens are no better off than they were before their pensions increased?* Many of Runagia's senior citizens were not helped by receiving more money. Clearly, these senior citizens used nearly 20 percent more money than they did before to maintain the same standard of living. Usually, this could be explained by high inflation—but the further information informs us that the annual rate of inflation was well below the percentage of the pension increase. The annual rate of inflation is, however, an average calculated over a large number of goods and services. The prices of some goods and services rise more than the prices of other goods and services. It could be the case that the goods and services senior citizens need are those that have risen most in price. If this were the case, their pension increase could have been insufficient to raise their standard of living.

A Regardless of what someone relies on for their income, a 20 percent increase in that income would be expected to raise that person's standard of living.

B The 20 percent increase in pensions occurred two years ago. Whatever problems a three-week delay in the cashing of pension checks caused would be unlikely to persist over two years.

C **Correct.** This statement properly identifies a reason why the plan's result was that many Runagian senior citizens were no better off than they were before the increase.

D Even if it were true that an all-time high number of Runagians over sixty-five were living below the poverty line at the time of the pension increase, it would still be expected that such an increase would leave them better off financially than they were before the increase.

E Regardless of how many pension increases there were in the past, the current 20 percent increase could reasonably be expected to leave its recipients better off financially than they were before the increase.

The correct answer is C.

23.　A drug that is highly effective in treating many types of infection can, at present, be obtained only from the bark of the ibora, a tree that is quite rare in the wild. It takes the bark of 5,000 trees to make one kilogram of the drug. It follows, therefore, that continued production of the drug must inevitably lead to the ibora's extinction.

Which of the following, if true, most seriously weakens the argument above?

(A)　The drug made from ibora bark is dispensed to doctors from a central authority.

(B)　The drug made from ibora bark is expensive to produce.

(C)　The leaves of the ibora are used in a number of medical products.

(D)　The ibora can be propagated from cuttings and grown under cultivation.

(E)　The ibora generally grows in largely inaccessible places.

Argument Evaluation

Situation　The extinction of the rare ibora tree is inevitable if production of an effective infection-fighting drug continues.

Reasoning　*Which point most weakens the argument?* The production of the drug requires such an enormous amount of bark that, the argument concludes, the continuing existence of the rare tree is in jeopardy. But the argument assumes that killing the trees in the wild is the only way to obtain the needed bark. Can the tree be cultivated? If so, the majority of the trees in the wild could be left to flourish.

A　The method of the drug's distribution is irrelevant, unless the central authority can limit the drug's production from the bark of wild ibora trees. But this information is not provided.

B　The cost of producing the drug does not affect the outcome for the tree unless it deters production.

C　The existence of uses for other parts of the tree opens the possibility that the ibora-bark drug would cause no increase in destruction of trees other than what exists already. If this information were provided, it would weaken support for the conclusion. Since it is not provided, this option does not significantly weaken the argument.

D　**Correct.** This information most weakens the argument.

E　Difficulty of access to the trees could provide a disincentive to their harvesting—but we are not told that it would prevent their harvesting.

The correct answer is D.

24. The Plexis Corporation, a leading computer chip manufacturer, is currently developing a new chip, which is faster and more efficient than any computer chip currently in use. The new chip will be released for sale in twelve months. Plexis' market research has shown that initial sales of the new chip would be maximized by starting to advertise it now, but the company has decided to wait another six months before doing so.

Which of the following, if true, provides the Plexis Corporation with the best reason for postponing advertising its new chip?

(A) Some computer users are reluctant to purchase new computer products when they are first released.

(B) The cost of an advertising campaign capable of maximizing initial sales of the new chip would be no greater than campaigns previously undertaken by Plexis.

(C) Advertising the new chip now will significantly decrease sales of Plexis' current line of computer chips.

(D) Plexis' major rivals in the computer chip manufacturing business are developing a chip with capabilities that are comparable to those of Plexis' new chip.

(E) Taking full advantage of the capacities of the new chip will require substantial adjustments in other segments of the computer industry.

Argument Construction

Situation   Plexis' new computer chip, which will go on sale in twelve months, bests all those currently on the market in terms of speed and efficiency. According to market research, advertising the chip now will maximize its initial sales. The company, however, has decided to wait six months before starting to advertise.

Reasoning   *What reason could there be for Plexis postponing its advertising?* Plexis would probably postpone the advertising if there were a downside to it that outweighed the boost in initial sales that advertising now would provide. Since the boost in initial sales would presumably increase Plexis' profits, the downside to the advertising would most likely be something that would reduce Plexis' profits.

A   Advertising would probably be likely to persuade computer users to purchase the new product; thus this provides a reason why Plexis should start its advertising now rather than delay it for six months.

B   The advertising campaign's cost, if it is particularly high, might be a reason for Plexis to delay it—but that the cost will not be significantly different from that of other ad campaigns provides no compelling reason for delay.

C   **Correct.** This statement properly identifies a reason for Plexis to postpone its ad campaign: Its profits might be adversely affected by an early start to the campaign.

D   This provides a reason for Plexis to begin advertising the new chip as soon as possible—to get out ahead of the competition.

E   If the new chip will require other segments of the computer industry to adjust, it would be to Plexis' benefit to publicize the new chip as soon as possible, so that those adjustments can be made before the new chip comes on the market.

The correct answer is C.

25.   Many breakfast cereals are fortified with vitamin supplements. Some of these cereals provide 100 percent of the recommended daily requirement of vitamins. Nevertheless, a well-balanced breakfast, including a variety of foods, is a better source of those vitamins than are such fortified breakfast cereals alone.

Which of the following, if true, would most strongly support the position above?

(A)   In many foods, the natural combination of vitamins with other nutrients makes those vitamins more usable by the body than are vitamins added in vitamin supplements.

(B)   People who regularly eat cereals fortified with vitamin supplements sometimes neglect to eat the foods in which the vitamins occur naturally.

(C)   Foods often must be fortified with vitamin supplements because naturally occurring vitamins are removed during processing.

(D)   Unprocessed cereals are naturally high in several of the vitamins that are usually added to fortified breakfast cereals.

(E)   Cereals containing vitamin supplements are no harder to digest than similar cereals without added vitamins.

Argument Evaluation

Situation   A well-balanced breakfast with a variety of foods is a better source of vitamins than a breakfast of cereal fortified with vitamin supplements.

Reasoning   *What strengthens the argument in favor of a balanced breakfast as a better source of vitamins?* The argument compares a breakfast consisting of cereal that has been fortified with vitamins to a well-balanced breakfast that includes foods with naturally occurring vitamins. What would make the foods with naturally occurring vitamins a better source of those vitamins than cereal fortified with those vitamins? If the combination of the naturally occurring vitamins with other nutrients in the foods allows the body to better use those vitamins, a balanced breakfast of those foods would be a better source of those vitamins than a breakfast of fortified cereal alone.

A   **Correct.** This information strengthens the argument more than the information in any of the other options.

B   This statement explains that some who eat fortified cereal sometimes omit other foods from their diet. But this bit of sociological information is irrelevant to the scientific issue of which type of breakfast is a better source of vitamins.

C   This statement provides an answer to the question, "Why are some foods fortified with vitamins?" It does not address the question at issue, "Which type of breakfast is a better source of vitamins?"

D   This information is not evidence that a well-balanced breakfast is a better source of certain vitamins than is fortified cereal alone.

E   This information tells us that fortified cereal is not especially hard to digest—but does not indicate that a breakfast of fortified cereal alone is an inferior source of vitamins.

The correct answer is A.

26. When a polygraph test is judged inconclusive, this is no reflection on the examinee. Rather, such a judgment means that the test has failed to show whether the examinee was truthful or untruthful. Nevertheless, employers will sometimes refuse to hire a job applicant because of an inconclusive polygraph test result.

    Which of the following conclusions can most properly be drawn from the information above?

    (A) Most examinees with inconclusive polygraph test results are in fact untruthful.
    (B) Polygraph tests should not be used by employers in the consideration of job applicants.
    (C) An inconclusive polygraph test result is sometimes unfairly held against the examinee.
    (D) A polygraph test indicating that an examinee is untruthful can sometimes be mistaken.
    (E) Some employers have refused to consider the results of polygraph tests when evaluating job applicants.

Argument Construction

Situation Employers sometimes refuse to hire job applicants because of inconclusive polygraph tests, even though inconclusive tests reveal only the failure of the test itself to determine the truthfulness or untruthfulness of the person tested.

Reasoning *What conclusion can be drawn from this information?* Inconclusive polygraph results do not reveal anything about the person tested; they reveal only the failure of the polygraph test. Nevertheless, employers may choose not to hire an applicant whose polygraph test has had an inconclusive result. It is reasonable to conclude that these employers unfairly treat the lack of firm polygraph results as counting against the candidate—not against the polygraph test.

A This statement makes a judgment that is explicitly contradicted in the passage, which states that an inconclusive polygraph result *is no reflection on the examinee.*

B This sweeping conclusion is not as well supported by the passage as is (C). The passage discusses only inconclusive polygraph results.

C **Correct.** Given the information in the passage, one can infer that inconclusive polygraph tests are sometimes used unfairly against job applicants—if one makes the reasonable assumption that judging a job applicant unsuitable is unfair if the judgment is based merely on the failure of a particular technique to provide reliable evidence.

D The passage is concerned only with inconclusive tests, not cases when the polygraph test is mistaken.

E Information about employers who do not consider polygraph tests is irrelevant to the discussion.

The correct answer is C.

27. For similar cars and comparable drivers, automobile insurance for collision damage has always cost more in Greatport than in Fairmont. Police studies, however, show that cars owned by Greatport residents are, on average, slightly less likely to be involved in a collision than cars in Fairmont. Clearly, therefore, insurance companies are making a greater profit on collision-damage insurance in Greatport than in Fairmont.

In evaluating the argument, it would be most useful to compare

(A) the level of traffic congestion in Greatport with the level of traffic congestion in Fairmont

(B) the cost of repairing collision damage in Greatport with the cost of repairing collision damage in Fairmont

(C) the rates Greatport residents pay for other forms of insurance with the rates paid for similar insurance by residents of Fairmont

(D) the condition of Greatport's roads and streets with the condition of Fairmont's roads and streets

(E) the cost of collision-damage insurance in Greatport and Fairmont with that in other cities

Argument Evaluation

Situation A particular kind of insurance, that for collision damage, costs more in Greatport than in Fairmont. The cars of Greatport residents are, however, less likely to be involved in collisions than are cars of Fairmont residents. So insurance companies must be making a greater profit on collision-damage insurance in Greatport than in Fairmont.

Reasoning *What would it help to consider in evaluating the argument?* Insurance companies would make greater profits on collision-damage insurance in Greatport than they make in Fairmont if they pay out less money in response to Greatport residents' claims than they do in response to Fairmont's residents' claims. That Greatport residents' cars are involved in fewer collisions than are Fairmont's residents' cars supports this—if there are fewer collisions overall, then the insurance companies might pay out less money overall. But the number of collisions is only one factor contributing to how much money an insurance company pays out in response to claims; another factor is the amount of damage inflicted on the cars involved in collisions and how much it costs to repair that damage. These costs would need to be considered before concluding that insurance companies' profits on collision-damage insurance are greater in Greatport than in Fairmont.

A The level of traffic congestion probably contributes to the frequency of collisions in each town. The information given, however, includes the statement that Greatport cars are less likely to be involved in collisions than are Fairmont cars. Why this occurs—whether, for example, traffic congestion is a contributory factor—is not relevant.

B **Correct.** This is clearly a factor that would affect the profitability of insurance in the two towns—and is therefore highly relevant to evaluating the argument, especially its conclusion.

C The argument's conclusion is about insurance companies' profits on collision-damage insurance alone, so other types of insurance, and the rates paid for them, are not relevant.

D The condition of the roads and streets in each town probably contributes to the frequency of collisions in each town. The information given, however, includes the statement that Greatport cars are less likely to be involved in collisions than are Fairmont cars. Why this is so—whether, for example, the condition of the roads is a contributory cause—is not relevant.

E Since the argument is concerned solely with collision-insurance costs and profits in Greatport and Fairmont, comparing the cost of insurance in those towns with the cost of insurance elsewhere would provide no useful insight.

The correct answer is B.

28. The technological conservatism of bicycle manufacturers is a reflection of the kinds of demand they are trying to meet. The only cyclists seriously interested in innovation and willing to pay for it are bicycle racers. Therefore, innovation in bicycle technology is limited by what authorities will accept as standard for purposes of competition in bicycle races.

    Which of the following is an assumption made in drawing the conclusion above?

    (A) The market for cheap, traditional bicycles cannot expand unless the market for high-performance competition bicycles expands.

    (B) High-performance bicycles are likely to be improved more as a result of technological innovations developed in small workshops than as a result of technological innovations developed in major manufacturing concerns.

    (C) Bicycle racers do not generate a strong demand for innovations that fall outside what is officially recognized as standard for purposes of competition.

    (D) The technological conservatism of bicycle manufacturers results primarily from their desire to manufacture a product that can be sold without being altered to suit different national markets.

    (E) The authorities who set standards for high-performance bicycle racing do not keep informed about innovative bicycle design.

Argument Construction

Situation   Bicycle racers are the only consumers willing to pay for innovations in bicycle technology. Manufacturers therefore limit innovation to the standards established for competitive bicycle racing.

Reasoning   *What is being assumed in this argument?* This argument implies a connection between what bicycle racers want and what bicycle manufacturers make. The passage states that only racers are interested in innovation and willing to pay for it. The conclusion is drawn that innovation is limited by the standards laid down by racing authorities. But there is a gap in the reasoning here—information needed to enable the conclusion to be properly drawn. The drawing of the conclusion is justified if the information that bicycle racers buy only innovations that are approved by racing authorities is added.

A   The argument concerns innovation in bicycle technology. It is not about the entire market for all bicycles, so this claim about traditional bicycles is not assumed.

B   The passage does not discuss where the best innovations are likely to be created, so no assumption about small workshops versus large manufacturers is made.

C   **Correct.** This statement identifies information that appropriately fills the gap in the reasoning as stated in the passage.

D   This claim provides an explanation of manufacturers' technological conservatism that is quite different from the explanation indicated in the passage.

E   The passage does not indicate what the racing authorities do or do not know about bicycle innovation—even though it suggests that they may be reluctant to approve every possible innovation for racing purposes.

The correct answer is C.

29. Last year a record number of new manufacturing jobs were created. Will this year bring another record? Well, a new manufacturing job is created either within an existing company or by the start-up of a new company. Within existing firms, new jobs have been created this year at well below last year's record pace. At the same time, there is considerable evidence that the number of new companies starting up will be no higher this year than it was last year; and surely **the new companies starting up this year will create no more jobs per company than did last year's start-ups**. Clearly, it can be concluded that **the number of new jobs created this year will fall short of last year's record**.

In the argument given, the two portions in boldface play which of the following roles?

(A) The first is a prediction that, if accurate, would provide support for the main conclusion of the argument; the second is that main conclusion.

(B) The first is a prediction that, if accurate, would provide support for the main conclusion of the argument; the second is a conclusion drawn in order to support that main conclusion.

(C) The first is an objection that the argument rejects; the second is the main conclusion of the argument.

(D) The first is an objection that the argument rejects; the second presents a conclusion that could be drawn if that objection were allowed to stand.

(E) The first is a claim that has been advanced in support of a position that the argument opposes; the second is a claim advanced in support of the main conclusion of the argument.

Argument Construction

Situation The question posed is whether this year will, like last year, see a record number of new manufacturing jobs. Among the evidence presented is the assertion that any new manufacturing job is created by an existing company or as part of the start-up of a new company. New jobs have been created by existing firms at a slower pace than last year. It is unlikely that more new companies will be started up this year than were started last year; further, the argument suggests that this year's new companies are unlikely to create more jobs per company than did last year's new companies. For all these reasons, the argument concludes, this year's job creation will not equal that of last year.

Reasoning *What roles do the two portions in boldface play in the argument?* The first boldfaced portion states that this year's new companies will create no more jobs per company than did last year's new companies. The speaker does not know this for a fact, since it has not yet happened; it is thus a prediction. If it turns out to be the case, it would support the idea that job creation this year will fall short of last year's—which is, in turn, the conclusion that the argument reaches.

A **Correct.** This statement properly identifies the roles played in the argument by the two portions in boldface.

B This properly identifies the role played in the argument by the first portion in boldface. The second is, of course, a conclusion, but it is not drawn in order to support the main conclusion; rather, it is the main conclusion.

C This properly identifies the role played by the second portion in boldface. The first portion in boldface, however, states that companies starting up this year will create no more jobs than last year's start-ups. The argument does not reject this idea; rather, it relies on it.

D The first portion in boldface states that companies starting up this year will create no more jobs than last year's start-ups. The argument does not reject this idea; rather, it relies on it. The second portion in boldface does present a conclusion, but since the first portion is not an objection, any description that relies on that mischaracterization is in error.

E The second portion in boldface is not merely a claim; it is, rather, the main conclusion of the argument. The first portion in boldface is a claim, but it is not advanced in support of a position that the argument opposes; rather, it supports the argument's main conclusion.

The correct answer is A.

30. Robot satellites relay important communications and identify weather patterns. Because the satellites can be repaired only in orbit, astronauts are needed to repair them. Without repairs, the satellites would eventually malfunction. Therefore, space flights carrying astronauts must continue.

Which of the following, if true, would most seriously weaken the argument above?

(A) Satellites falling from orbit because of malfunctions burn up in the atmosphere.

(B) Although satellites are indispensable in the identification of weather patterns, weather forecasters also make some use of computer projections to identify weather patterns.

(C) The government, responding to public pressure, has decided to cut the budget for space flights and put more money into social welfare programs.

(D) Repair of satellites requires heavy equipment, which adds to the amount of fuel needed to lift a spaceship carrying astronauts into orbit.

(E) Technical obsolescence of robot satellites makes repairing them more costly and less practical than sending new, improved satellites into orbit.

Argument Evaluation

Situation   Robot satellites used to predict weather patterns must be repaired in orbit by astronauts, so space flights carrying astronauts must continue.

Reasoning   *What information would most weaken the argument?* The passage provides the information that the satellites would probably malfunction unless they are repaired and that to perform those repairs, astronauts are needed. The conclusion is that space flights with astronauts must continue. The unstated assumption is that there is no good alternative to repairing the satellites. Any information that challenges this assumption will weaken the argument. A less expensive and more practical way of preventing the problems that would arise from failure to repair rapidly obsolescing satellites is to replace them with new, improved satellites. This suggestion of a better alternative weakens the argument more than do any of the other options.

A   This tells us that a malfunction can destroy the satellite—information that provides some additional support to the argument.

B   Since satellites are judged to be *indispensable*, this statement suggests that their repair continues to be necessary—this somewhat strengthens the argument.

C   The argument does not assume that space flights are funded by the government, but this statement tells us that they are at least partly government-funded, and that at least some of that funding is to be eliminated. This makes it less likely that needed space flights with astronauts would occur—but it does not undermine the claim that such flights are needed.

D   Increased fuel costs do not weaken the claim that space flights with astronauts are needed.

E   **Correct.** This information challenges the assumption in the argument that there is no good alternative to repairing the satellites.

The correct answer is E.

31. A company's two divisions performed with remarkable consistency over the past three years: in each of those years, the pharmaceuticals division has accounted for roughly 20 percent of dollar sales and 40 percent of profits, and the chemicals division for the balance.

    Which of the following can properly be inferred regarding the past three years from the statement above?

    (A) Total dollar sales for each of the company's divisions have remained roughly constant.
    (B) The pharmaceuticals division has faced stiffer competition in its markets than has the chemicals division.
    (C) The chemicals division has realized lower profits per dollar of sales than has the pharmaceuticals division.
    (D) The product mix offered by each of the company's divisions has remained unchanged.
    (E) Highly profitable products accounted for a higher percentage of the chemicals division's sales than those of the pharmaceuticals division's.

    Argument Construction

    Situation   For three years, the pharmaceutical division of a company has accounted for 20 percent of the dollar sales and 40 percent of the profits, and the chemicals division for 80 percent of the sales and 60 percent of the profits.

    Reasoning   *What can be inferred from these numbers?* The income from sales of the chemicals division was four times the sales income of the pharmaceutical division, but the chemicals division's profit (income minus costs) was only one-and-a-half times the pharmaceutical division's profit. Clearly the pharmaceuticals division made more profit per dollar of sales income than the chemicals division did.

    A   The information is about percentages, not total dollars; the percentages could have remained the same for each of three years even though sales income increased each year.
    B   There is no information about the competition faced by either division; the higher profit margin for the pharmaceutical division would suggest, if anything, less intense competition in its markets.
    C   **Correct.** If the information in the passage is true, then this must also be true.
    D   Since there is no information about the product mix, no inference about it is possible.
    E   The passage does not distinguish between highly profitable products and other products, so this inference cannot be drawn from the information.

    The correct answer is C.

32. The Eurasian ruffe, a fish species inadvertently introduced into North America's Great Lakes in recent years, feeds on the eggs of lake whitefish, a native species, thus threatening the lakes' natural ecosystem. To help track the ruffe's spread, government agencies have produced wallet-sized cards about the ruffe. The cards contain pictures of the ruffe and explain the danger they pose; the cards also request anglers to report any ruffe they catch.

    Which of the following, if true, would provide most support for the prediction that the agencies' action will have its intended effect?

    (A) The ruffe has spiny fins that make it unattractive as prey.

    (B) Ruffe generally feed at night, but most recreational fishing on the Great Lakes is done during daytime hours.

    (C) Most people who fish recreationally on the Great Lakes are interested in the preservation of the lake whitefish because it is a highly prized game fish.

    (D) The ruffe is one of several nonnative species in the Great Lakes whose existence threatens the survival of lake whitefish populations there.

    (E) The bait that most people use when fishing for whitefish on the Great Lakes is not attractive to ruffe.

Evaluation of a Plan

Situation   The Eurasian ruffe, a species not native to the Great Lakes, is threatening the native lake whitefish. Government agencies hope that wallet-sized cards identifying the ruffe, explaining the danger they pose, and asking anglers to report their ruffe catches will help them track the ruffe's spread.

Reasoning   *What point would support the idea that the agencies' action will have its intended effect?* The cards are intended to help government agencies track the ruffe's spread. They will be useful for this purpose only if anglers actually report the ruffe they catch. Thus anything that increases the odds of anglers' doing such reporting would make it more likely that the cards will have their intended effect.

A   If ruffe are unattractive as prey, they will probably spread more quickly in the Great Lakes. This will most likely have little effect on whether the wallet-sized cards will help government agencies track the ruffe.

B   If ruffe feed at night, while fishing is done in the daytime, it is unlikely that anglers would catch ruffe. Thus few catches would be reported to government agencies, making it more difficult for those agencies to track the spread of ruffe.

C   **Correct.** This statement properly identifies a point that supports the prediction that the agencies' action will have its intended effect—that is, those who are interested in preserving the lake whitefish will be likely to report catches of ruffe, which threaten whitefish, thus enabling the agencies' tracking of the spread of ruffe.

D   That the ruffe is one of several nonnative species threatening the Great Lakes lessens the odds that the whitefish will survive, but this has no effect on the question of whether the wallet-sized cards will help government agencies track the ruffe's spread.

E   This would make it likely that anglers would catch few ruffe. If anglers do not catch many ruffe, there will not be many to report to government agencies, which would in turn make it more difficult for those agencies to track the ruffe's spread.

The correct answer is C.

33. Advertisement: Today's customers expect high quality. Every advance in the quality of manufactured products raises customer expectations. The company that is satisfied with the current quality of its products will soon find that its customers are not. At MegaCorp, meeting or exceeding customer expectations is our goal.

Which of the following must be true on the basis of the statements in the advertisement above?

(A) MegaCorp's competitors will succeed in attracting customers only if those competitors adopt MegaCorp's goal as their own.

(B) A company that does not correctly anticipate the expectations of its customers is certain to fail in advancing the quality of its products.

(C) MegaCorp's goal is possible to meet only if continuing advances in product quality are possible.

(D) If a company becomes satisfied with the quality of its products, then the quality of its products is sure to decline.

(E) MegaCorp's customers are currently satisfied with the quality of its products.

Argument Construction

Situation   An advertisement for MegaCorp observes that every advance in quality raises customer expectations; it is not enough for a company to be satisfied with current quality.

Reasoning   *What can be inferred from the assertions in the advertisement?* The advertisement tells us that meeting or exceeding customer expectations is MegaCorp's goal. Since advances in quality are said to increase expectations, meeting expectations implies a need to make further advances. This in turn implies that MegaCorp can meet its goal only if a continually increasing level of product quality is possible.

A   This is not well supported. MegaCorp's competitors could attract customers by having a different or more ambitious goal than MegaCorp's—for example, always exceeding customer expectations.

B   This is not well supported. The passage leaves open the possibility that a company that advances the quality of its products would still fail to meet the expectations of its customers.

C   **Correct.** Given the information in the passage, MegaCorp's goal could not be achieved unless increasing customer expectations could be fulfilled through increasing advances in product quality.

D   While the ad implies that a company should not be satisfied with current quality, it does not go so far as to say that such an attitude causes quality to decline.

E   This is probably true if MegaCorp is meeting its stated goal—but the passage does not tell us that the goal is being met.

The correct answer is C.

34. Which of the following most logically completes the argument?

Ferber's syndrome, a viral disease that frequently affects cattle, is transmitted to these animals through infected feed. Even though chickens commercially raised for meat are often fed the type of feed identified as the source of infection in cattle, Ferber's syndrome is only rarely observed in chickens. This fact, however, does not indicate that most chickens are immune to the virus that causes Ferber's syndrome, since _____.

(A) chickens and cattle are not the only kinds of farm animal that are typically fed the type of feed liable to be contaminated with the virus that causes Ferber's syndrome

(B) Ferber's syndrome has been found in animals that have not been fed the type of feed liable to be contaminated with the virus that can cause the disease

(C) resistance to some infectious organisms such as the virus that causes Ferber's syndrome can be acquired by exposure to a closely related infectious organism

(D) chickens and cattle take more than a year to show symptoms of Ferber's syndrome, and chickens commercially raised for meat, unlike cattle, are generally brought to market during the first year of life

(E) the type of feed liable to be infected with the virus that causes Ferber's syndrome generally constitutes a larger proportion of the diet of commercially raised chickens than of commercially raised cattle

Argument Construction

Situation   Certain feed given to cows and to chickens commercially raised for meat is infected with the virus that causes Ferber's syndrome. Cows are frequently affected by this disease, while it is rarely observed in chickens. But (for a reason the argument omits) this does not suggest that chickens are immune to the virus.

Reasoning   *What point would most logically complete the argument?* How could it be the case that chickens are infected, yet Ferber's syndrome is only rarely observed in them? The important point here is that Ferber's syndrome is not *observed* in chickens. A disease is usually observed to be present on the basis of its symptoms. Those symptoms might not be present, or might not *yet* be present, in chickens that are infected with the virus. If the chickens were used for meat before they began showing symptoms, then they would not be observed to have Ferber's syndrome, but this would not indicate that they were immune to the virus.

A   That other animals are fed the potentially contaminated feed is not relevant to the question of whether chickens are immune to the virus.

B   The idea that there could be a source of the virus other than contaminated feed does not have any bearing on whether chickens are immune to the virus.

C   The idea that there is a way for animals to acquire a resistance to the virus that causes Ferber's syndrome suggests that some animals, possibly chickens, might be immune to the virus. This is the opposite of what the argument is trying to establish.

D   **Correct.** This statement properly identifies a point that logically completes the argument: It provides a reason why infected chickens would fail to show symptoms of Ferber's syndrome.

E   If chickens' diets contain proportionally more of the potentially infected feed than cattle's diets do, it is even more surprising that Ferber's syndrome is not observed in chickens—far from providing a reason not to conclude that chickens are immune to the virus; this makes it seem even more likely that they are immune.

The correct answer is D.

35. Last year the rate of inflation was 1.2 percent, but for the current year it has been 4 percent. We can conclude that inflation is on an upward trend and the rate will be still higher next year.

Which of the following, if true, most seriously weakens the conclusion above?

(A) The inflation figures were computed on the basis of a representative sample of economic data rather than all of the available data.

(B) Last year a dip in oil prices brought inflation temporarily below its recent stable annual level of 4 percent.

(C) Increases in the pay of some workers are tied to the level of inflation, and at an inflation rate of 4 percent or above, these pay raises constitute a force causing further inflation.

(D) The 1.2 percent rate of inflation last year represented a 10-year low.

(E) Government intervention cannot affect the rate of inflation to any significant degree.

Argument Evaluation

Situation   The rate of inflation was 1.2 percent last year but is 4 percent in the current year. It is therefore expected to rise above 4 percent next year.

Reasoning   *What point most weakens this conclusion?* The conclusion is based on an *upward trend* that is derived from data for two years. Data from only two years provide rather weak evidence of a *trend*. Additional evidence that provides a context for the annual inflation rates during the most recent two-year period will promote a more solid evaluation of this prediction of next year's inflation rate. If inflation has recently been *stable* at 4 percent, and the temporary drop the previous year is accounted for by lower oil prices, then the basis for the prediction seems quite weak.

A   As long as the sample was representative, the figures should be accurate. This point does not weaken the conclusion.

B   **Correct.** This statement suggests that the 1.2 percent inflation rate is an unusual occurrence in recent years. Especially because the dip below the stable 4 percent rate was *temporary*, this unusual occurrence cannot be used as the basis for predicting a trend.

C   This statement explains one process by which inflation increases and tends to support the conclusion that inflation will continue to rise.

D   This information implies, for example, that two years ago, the inflation rate was higher than 1.2 percent. This raises the possibility (without stating it) that last year and the year preceding mark a trend of declining inflation (and that the current year's 4 percent is an aberration). However, if the inflation rate two years ago was only slightly higher than 1.2 percent (for example, 1.25 percent), then it would be difficult to regard these two numbers as signaling a trend of declining inflation. We do not have enough information here to regard this as a significant weakener. The information is sufficient to justify a little doubt about the argument's conclusion—but not at all specific enough to undermine the argument's conclusion as much as does (B).

E   The failure of government intervention to affect the rate of inflation could be seen to support, not weaken, the conclusion.

The correct answer is B.

36. Offshore oil-drilling operations entail an unavoidable risk of an oil spill, but importing oil on tankers presently entails an even greater such risk per barrel of oil. Therefore, if we are to reduce the risk of an oil spill without curtailing our use of oil, we must invest more in offshore operations and import less oil on tankers.

Which of the following, if true, most seriously weakens the argument above?

(A) Tankers can easily be redesigned so that their use entails less risk of an oil spill.
(B) Oil spills caused by tankers have generally been more serious than those caused by offshore operations.
(C) The impact of offshore operations on the environment can be controlled by careful management.
(D) Offshore operations usually damage the ocean floor, but tankers rarely cause such damage.
(E) Importing oil on tankers is currently less expensive than drilling for it offshore.

Argument Evaluation

Situation   Currently, the risk of an oil spill is greater from oil tankers than it is from offshore oil drilling. In order to reduce the risk of an oil spill, we should expand offshore operations and import less oil on tankers.

Reasoning   *What point most weakens this argument?* The argument is based on the current situation, but present conditions need not continue in the future if they can be improved. What if oil tankers can be redesigned so that they pose less of a risk of an oil spill? If it were so, then adding that information would weaken the argument. The lowered risk of oil spills resulting from improved oil tanker design could make tankers less problematic than offshore operations.

A   **Correct.** The addition of this information to the argument would weaken the argument more than would the information in any of the other options.
B   The more serious nature of the oil spills caused by tankers strengthens the argument.
C   Careful management controlling the environmental impact of offshore operations supports the argument rather than weakens it.
D   While offshore operations may cause other environmental damage, this point is not relevant to the argument, which concerns just oil spills.
E   Importing oil on tankers may be an attractive economic alternative, but because this point is unrelated to oil spills, it does not weaken the argument.

The correct answer is A.

37. Thyrian lawmaker: Thyria's Cheese Importation Board inspects all cheese shipments to Thyria and rejects shipments not meeting specified standards. Yet only 1 percent is ever rejected. Therefore, since the health consequences and associated economic costs of not rejecting that 1 percent are negligible, whereas the board's operating costs are considerable, for economic reasons alone the board should be disbanded.

Consultant: I disagree. The threat of having their shipments rejected deters many cheese exporters from shipping substandard product.

The consultant responds to the lawmaker's argument by

(A) rejecting the lawmaker's argument while proposing that the standards according to which the board inspects imported cheese should be raised

(B) providing evidence that the lawmaker's argument has significantly overestimated the cost of maintaining the board

(C) objecting to the lawmaker's introducing into the discussion factors that are not strictly economic

(D) pointing out a benefit of maintaining the board, which the lawmaker's argument has failed to consider

(E) shifting the discussion from the argument at hand to an attack on the integrity of the cheese inspectors

Argument Construction

Situation   The Thyrian lawmaker argues that the Cheese Importation Board should be disbanded, because its operating costs are high and it rejects only a small percentage of the cheese it inspects. The consultant disagrees, pointing out that the board's inspections deter those who export cheese to Thyria from shipping substandard cheese.

Reasoning   *What strategy does the consultant use in the counterargument?* The consultant indicates to the lawmaker that there is a reason to retain the board that the lawmaker has not considered. The benefit the board provides is not that it identifies a great deal of substandard cheese and rejects it (thus keeping the public healthy), but that the possibility that their cheese could be found substandard is what keeps exporters from attempting to export low-quality cheese to Thyria.

A   The consultant does reject the lawmaker's argument, but the consultant does not propose higher standards. Indeed, in suggesting that the board should be retained, the consultant implies that the board's standards are appropriate.

B   The consultant does not provide any evidence related to the board's cost.

C   The only point the lawmaker raises that is not strictly economic is about the health consequences of disbanding the board, but the consultant does not address this point at all.

D   **Correct.** This statement properly identifies the strategy the consultant employs in his or her counterargument. The consultant points out that the board provides a significant benefit that the lawmaker did not consider.

E   The consultant does not attack the integrity of the cheese inspectors; to the contrary, the consultant says that their inspections deter the cheese exporters from shipping substandard cheese.

The correct answer is D.

38. Which of the following best completes the passage below?

The computer industry's estimate that it loses millions of dollars when users illegally copy programs without paying for them is greatly exaggerated. Most of the illegal copying is done by people with no serious interest in the programs. Thus, the loss to the industry is quite small, because _____.

(A) many users who illegally copy programs never find any use for them

(B) most people who illegally copy programs would not purchase them even if purchasing them were the only way to obtain them

(C) even if the computer industry received all the revenue it claims to be losing, it would still be experiencing financial difficulties

(D) the total market value of all illegal copies is low in comparison to the total revenue of the computer industry

(E) the number of programs that are frequently copied illegally is low in comparison to the number of programs available for sale

Argument Construction

Situation   The computer industry's estimate of its losses due to illegally copied programs is exaggerated—and actually quite small—because most of the illegal copying is done by people who are not greatly interested in the programs.

Reasoning   *Why would the loss to the industry be said to be small?* The industry's loss due to illegal copying of programs must be evaluated in terms of the sales lost; the actual loss to the industry is directly related to the legitimate sales opportunities that have been lost. Would the people illegally copying the programs buy them if they could not otherwise obtain them? If it were true that most of them have *no serious interest in the programs,* they would be unlikely to purchase them. In this case, few sales would be lost and the loss to the industry could be considered small.

A   What users do (or do not do) with programs once they have them does not help to show that the loss to the industry is small.

B   **Correct.** This information provides a reason supporting the claim that the industry has not lost potential sales.

C   The greater financial difficulties of the industry do not help to show that the loss incurred because of the illegally copied programs is small.

D   This comparison is faulty: The loss is not being considered in the context of total industry revenues but in the context of total sales of programs.

E   This information does not provide a good reason for the claim that the loss to the industry is small. Even if the number of programs frequently copied is low, the number of copies made from each program might be huge (for the most popular programs).

The correct answer is B.

39. The growing popularity of computer-based activities was widely expected to result in a decline in television viewing, since it had been assumed that people lack sufficient free time to maintain current television-viewing levels while spending increasing amounts of free time on the computer. That assumption, however, is evidently false: In a recent mail survey concerning media use, a very large majority of respondents who report increasing time spent per week using computers report no change in time spent watching television.

Which of the following would it be most useful to determine in order to evaluate the argument?

(A) Whether a large majority of the survey respondents reported watching television regularly

(B) Whether the amount of time spent watching television is declining among people who report that they rarely or never use computers

(C) Whether the type of television programs a person watches tends to change as the amount of time spent per week using computers increases

(D) Whether a large majority of the computer owners in the survey reported spending increasing amounts of time per week using computers

(E) Whether the survey respondents' reports of time spent using computers included time spent using computers at work

Argument Evaluation

Situation   The argument is intended to debunk the assumption that people lack sufficient free time to maintain television-viewing levels while spending increasing amounts of free time on the computer. To do so, it cites a survey of media use in which a large majority of respondents who spend increasing amounts of time using computers also claim to have not altered the amount of time they spend watching television.

Reasoning   *What would it be most useful to know in order to evaluate the argument?* The argument uses the survey results to claim that people have enough free time to both maintain their television viewing levels and spend increasing amounts of free time on the computer. But the survey, as reported here, did not address whether people are spending their *free time* on the computer; the respondents reported increasing *time* spent per week using computers. Since the argument is about free time, it is important to know whether this is actually what the respondents were reporting.

A   The argument is concerned with the *change* in the amount of television watched by those whose computer use increased, so whether the survey's respondents reported watching television regularly is irrelevant.

B   The argument is concerned with the change in the amount of television watched by those whose computer use has increased, so it does not matter whether the amount of time spent watching television among people who do not use computers is declining, remaining the same, or increasing.

C   The argument is concerned with the *amount* of television watched by those whose computer use has increased, not the type of television programs such a person does or does not watch.

D   The argument here is concerned with people who report spending increasing amounts of time on the computer; what computer owners do is a separate question.

E   **Correct.** This statement properly identifies something that would be useful to know in evaluating the argument: whether the survey data included time spent using computers at work—if it did, this would make the data misleading as evidence for the argument's conclusion.

The correct answer is E.

40. In the last decade there has been a significant decrease in coffee consumption. During this same time, there has been increasing publicity about the adverse long-term effects on health of the caffeine in coffee. Therefore, the decrease in coffee consumption must have been caused by consumers' awareness of the harmful effects of caffeine.

Which of the following, if true, most seriously calls into question the explanation above?

(A) On average, people consume 30 percent less coffee today than they did 10 years ago.
(B) Heavy coffee drinkers may have mild withdrawal symptoms, such as headaches, for a day or so after significantly decreasing their coffee consumption.
(C) Sales of specialty types of coffee have held steady as sales of regular brands have declined.
(D) The consumption of fruit juices and caffeine-free herbal teas has increased over the past decade.
(E) Coffee prices increased steadily in the past decade because of unusually severe frosts in coffee-growing nations.

Argument Evaluation

Situation The decrease in coffee consumption in the last decade can be explained by consumers' increased awareness of the detrimental effects of the caffeine in coffee.

Reasoning *What point weakens this explanation?* A conclusion offering an explanation for some occurrence may be weakened when another explanation at least as compelling as the original is offered. Coffee consumption may have decreased over the decade for some reason other than consumers' awareness of the adverse health effects of caffeine. If the price of coffee has increased in the same period that consumption has decreased, then the decrease may well be the result of consumers' attention to price rather than their attention to health. Higher prices would offer a good alternative explanation that would weaken the original explanation.

A This point merely tells us how much coffee consumption has decreased; it does not make the explanation offered in the conclusion any less likely to be correct.

B Withdrawal symptoms would occur only after decreased consumption has occurred and so cannot explain why the decrease occurred.

C Suppose that the specialty coffees that had their sales hold steady were all caffeine-free coffees; note that nothing rules this out. If this were the case, the explanation would remain plausible.

D An increase in the consumption of these drinks could plausibly be the result of some coffee drinkers switching to these drinks to avoid the negative effects of caffeine.

E **Correct.** This statement properly identifies a plausible alternative explanation and therefore undermines the given explanation.

The correct answer is E.

41. Which of the following best completes the passage below?

When the products of several competing suppliers are perceived by consumers to be essentially the same, classical economics predicts that price competition will reduce prices to the same minimal levels and all suppliers' profits to the same minimal levels. Therefore, if classical economics is true, and given suppliers' desire to make as much profit as possible, it should be expected that _____.

(A) in a crowded market widely differing prices will be charged for products that are essentially the same as each other

(B) as a market becomes less crowded as suppliers leave, the profits of the remaining suppliers will tend to decrease

(C) each supplier in a crowded market will try to convince consumers that its product differs significantly from its competitors' products.

(D) when consumers are unable to distinguish the products in a crowded market, consumers will judge that the higher-priced products are of higher quality

(E) suppliers in crowded markets will have more incentive to reduce prices and thus increase sales than to introduce innovations that would distinguish their product from their competitors' products

Argument Construction

Situation Classical economics holds that prices and profits are minimal when consumers perceive the products of competing suppliers to be the same.

Reasoning *According to classical economics, what strategy are suppliers most likely to use to maximize profits in such a situation?* The given information states that the force driving prices and profits down in this case is the consumers' perception that the competing products are *essentially the same.* It is reasonable to assume that, with prices already at *minimal levels*, it is not possible to lower them any more. What can be done? The suppliers' most likely strategy would then be to change the consumers' perception of their products. It can be expected that an individual supplier would try to convince consumers that its product greatly differs from (and is certainly preferable to) the products of its competitors.

A   According to classical economics, *prices* will be reduced by competition *to the same minimal levels* as long as the products *are perceived by consumers to be essentially the same*, and nothing indicates that they will not be; therefore there is no reason to believe that prices will differ widely.

B   The passage discusses the conditions of a crowded market, not a market that is becoming less crowded.

C   **Correct.** This statement properly suggests that the most likely strategy for any one supplier in a crowded market is convincing consumers that its product is very different from those of its competitors.

D   According to classical economics, *prices* will be reduced *to the same minimal levels* when consumers are unable to distinguish among the products; therefore none of the products will be priced higher than any others.

E   The passage gives no indication of what classical economics says about the attractiveness to suppliers of reducing prices versus introducing innovations.

The correct answer is C.

42. Crowding on Mooreville's subway frequently leads to delays, because it is difficult for passengers to exit from the trains. Subway ridership is projected to increase by 20 percent over the next 10 years. The Mooreville Transit Authority plans to increase the number of daily train trips by only 5 percent over the same period. Officials predict that this increase is sufficient to ensure that the incidence of delays due to crowding does not increase.

Which of the following, if true, provides the strongest grounds for the officials' prediction?

(A) By changing maintenance schedules, the Transit Authority can achieve the 5 percent increase in train trips without purchasing any new subway cars.

(B) The Transit Authority also plans a 5 percent increase in the number of bus trips on routes that connect to subways.

(C) For most commuters who use the subway system, there is no practical alternative public transportation available.

(D) Most of the projected increase in ridership is expected to occur in off-peak hours when trains are now sparsely used.

(E) The 5 percent increase in the number of train trips can be achieved without an equal increase in Transit Authority operational costs.

Argument Construction

Situation Ridership on the Mooreville subway, which often experiences delays due to crowding, is expected to increase 20 percent over the next 10 years. Despite plans to increase the number of daily trains only 5 percent during those 10 years, officials predict that delays due to crowding will not increase.

Reasoning *What would provide the strongest grounds for the officials' prediction that delays due to crowding will not increase?* Delays due to crowding probably would increase if the extra 20 percent total ridership occurred at typically busy times, even if the total 5 percent increase in the number of daily trains were to occur at those typically busy times. The increases in daily trains would clearly not be enough to absorb the extra ridership. If the increase in ridership were to occur at other times of day, however, perhaps when the subway trains were less crowded overall, the system would be able to absorb the extra passengers without an increase in delays due to crowding.

A While this supports the idea that the Transit Authority can economically increase the number of train trips, it provides no information about whether the trains will be crowded.

B Increasing the number of bus trips on routes that connect to subways would be likely to lead to more people to ride the subways. This makes it less likely that the officials' prediction—that delays due to overcrowding will not increase—will turn out to have been accurate.

C This suggests that subway ridership will remain high, and thus that delays caused by overcrowding will continue.

D **Correct.** This statement properly identifies a situation in which the officials' prediction is likely to turn out to have been accurate. The ridership will be increasing during times when more passengers will not create delays, since they will merely fill empty seats on existing trains.

E While this supports the idea that the Transit Authority can economically increase the number of train trips, it provides no information about whether the trains will be crowded.

The correct answer is D.

43. Installing scrubbers in smokestacks and switching to cleaner-burning fuel are the two methods available to Northern Power for reducing harmful emissions from its plants. Scrubbers will reduce harmful emissions more than cleaner-burning fuels will. Therefore, by installing scrubbers, Northern Power will be doing the most that can be done to reduce harmful emissions from its plants.

Which of the following is an assumption on which the argument depends?

(A)   Switching to cleaner-burning fuel will not be more expensive than installing scrubbers.

(B)   Northern Power can choose from among various kinds of scrubbers, some of which are more effective than others.

(C)   Northern Power is not necessarily committed to reducing harmful emissions from its plants.

(D)   Harmful emissions from Northern Power's plants cannot be reduced more by using both methods together than by the installation of scrubbers alone.

(E)   Aside from harmful emissions from the smokestacks of its plants, the activities of Northern Power do not cause significant air pollution.

Argument Construction

Situation   A power plant can reduce emissions by installing scrubbers and also by switching to cleaner-burning fuel; installing scrubbers reduces emissions more than switching fuels. By installing scrubbers, the company is doing the most that it can do.

Reasoning   *What assumption does the argument depend on?* The assumption will be a statement that has to be true in order for the argument's premises to provide a solid reason for believing its conclusion. Here, the conclusion that the company is doing the most that it can do is based on believing that choosing one or the other of the two options will be more effective than choosing both options together. This argument assumes, then, that installing the scrubbers alone is just as effective as both installing scrubbers *and* switching to cleaner-burning fuel.

A   The relative costs of the two options indicate nothing about whether by installing scrubbers the company will have done the most that it can to reduce harmful emissions.

B   Even if the company installs the most efficient scrubbers, it may be that there is more that Northern Power could do to reduce harmful emissions.

C   Even if the company is fully committed to reducing harmful emissions, it could be that installing scrubbers is the most it can do to reduce harmful emissions.

D   Correct. If harmful emissions could be reduced even more by using both methods, then installing scrubbers alone will not be the most that the company can do to reduce harmful emissions.

E   Even if this were not assumed and the company's other activities did cause significant air pollution, it could still be that installing scrubbers is the most that the company can do to reduce harmful emissions *from its plants*; perhaps any of its other activities that do cause significant air pollution have nothing to do with its plants—for example, pollution coming from trucks the company uses.

The correct answer is D.

44. Trancorp currently transports all its goods to Burland Island by truck. The only bridge over the channel separating Burland from the mainland is congested, and trucks typically spend hours in traffic. Trains can reach the channel more quickly than trucks, and freight cars can be transported to Burland by barges that typically cross the channel in an hour. Therefore, to reduce shipping time, Trancorp plans to switch to trains and barges to transport goods to Burland.

    Which of the following would be most important to know in determining whether Trancorp's plan, if implemented, is likely to achieve its goal?

    (A) Whether transportation by train and barge would be substantially less expensive than transportation by truck

    (B) Whether there are boats that can make the trip between the mainland and Burland faster than barges can

    (C) Whether loading the freight cars onto barges is very time consuming

    (D) Whether the average number of vehicles traveling over the bridge into Burland has been relatively constant in recent years

    (E) Whether most trucks transporting goods into Burland return to the mainland empty

Evaluation of a Plan

Situation Transporting goods to Burland Island by truck takes many hours, because the trucks must take the congested single bridge that reaches the island. Trains can get goods to the channel separating Burland from the mainland more quickly than trucks can, and the freight cars can then be loaded onto barges that can cross the channel in an hour. Trancorp plans to reduce shipping time by switching from trucks to trains and barges.

Reasoning *What would it be most important to know in determining whether Trancorp will achieve its goal of reducing shipping time?* Trancorp's plan could fail to reduce shipping time if there were some aspect of the new shipping process, involving the trains and the barges, that took more time than anticipated.

A The goal of Trancorp's plan is to reduce shipping time. This might lower costs—but whether or not it does so is not directly relevant to whether or not the plan's goal is achieved.

B Trancorp's plan involves the use of barges. If some boats can make the trip between the mainland and Burland faster than barges can, that might be something to consider for the future, but it has nothing to do with whether the current plan will reduce shipping time.

C **Correct.** This statement properly identifies something that would be important in determining whether Trancorp's plan for reducing shipping time will achieve its goal—that is, whether loading the freight cars onto the barges will use up all the time saved by not using trucks.

D Regardless of variation in traffic, the bridge, according to the information provided in the passage, is congested and typically causes trucking delays. Given this information, the degree of variation is not helpful in evaluating Transcorp's plan.

E The state of the trucks returning to the mainland has nothing to do with whether Trancorp's plan for reducing shipping time will achieve its goal.

The correct answer is C.

45. Some anthropologists study modern-day societies of foragers in an effort to learn about our ancient ancestors who were also foragers. A flaw in this strategy is that forager societies are extremely varied. Indeed, any forager society with which anthropologists are familiar has had considerable contact with modern, non-forager societies.

Which of the following, if true, would most weaken the criticism made above of the anthropologists' strategy?

(A) All forager societies throughout history have had a number of important features in common that are absent from other types of societies.

(B) Most ancient forager societies either dissolved or made a transition to another way of life.

(C) All anthropologists study one kind or another of modern-day society.

(D) Many anthropologists who study modern-day forager societies do not draw inferences about ancient societies on the basis of their studies.

(E) Even those modern-day forager societies that have not had significant contact with modern societies are importantly different from ancient forager societies.

Argument Evaluation

Situation Studying contemporary foraging societies in order to understand ancient foragers is flawed because forager societies are so widely varied and also because the contemporary foragers have had so much contact with modern societies.

Reasoning *Which point weakens this argument?* The argument rejects the comparison of modern-day foraging societies to ancient ones because of the variety of existing forager societies and because the modern-day foragers have been in contact with other modern cultures. What situation would support making this comparison? What if modern-day foragers remain similar to ancient foragers because of nonchanging features of foraging societies throughout history? If these are features that are not shared with other cultures, then the argument that anthropologists cannot learn about ancient foragers by studying their modern counterparts is weakened.

A **Correct.** This statement properly identifies the factor that weakens the argument: A comparison could well be a valuable source of understanding if all foraging societies are shown to share certain features not found in other societies.

B This point slightly strengthens, rather than weakens, the argument.

C This point does not address the issue of comparing a modern society to an ancient society.

D The reason for this could be that these anthropologists know that such a comparison is not useful; thus this point does not weaken the argument.

E This point strengthens, rather than weakens, the argument.

The correct answer is A.

46. Contrary to earlier predictions, demand for sugarcane has not increased in recent years. Yet, even though prices and production amounts have also been stable during the last three years, sugarcane growers last year increased their profits by more than 10 percent over the previous year's level.

    Any of the following statements, if true about last year, helps to explain the rise in profits EXCEPT:

    (A) Many countries that are large consumers of sugarcane increased their production of sugarcane-based ethanol, yet their overall consumption of sugarcane decreased.

    (B) Sugarcane growers have saved money on wages by switching from paying laborers an hourly wage to paying them by the amount harvested.

    (C) The price of oil, the major energy source used by sugarcane growers in harvesting their crops, dropped by over 20 percent.

    (D) Many small sugarcane growers joined together to form an association of sugarcane producers and began to buy supplies at low group rates.

    (E) Rainfall in sugarcane-growing regions was higher than it had been during the previous year, allowing the growers to save money on expensive artificial irrigation.

Argument Construction

Situation   Even though demand for sugar cane has not increased, and although prices and production amounts have been stable, sugarcane growers experienced a 10 percent rise in profits last year.

Reasoning   *Which piece of information does NOT help to explain the rise in profits?* All the answer choices will show a reason that profits rose except one. Consider each one to determine which situation would NOT be likely to contribute to increased profits. Any changes that lowered costs for the sugarcane growers WOULD be able to contribute to a rise in their profits. On the other hand, if it is true that many historically large consumers of sugarcane reduced their overall consumption last year, then the lower demand for sugarcane would be unlikely to drive increases in profits. Such a decrease in total consumption would be more likely to drive prices and profits down than up.

A   **Correct.** This statement properly identifies a factor that does not explain a rise in profits; it indicates a drop in consumption among certain countries without indicating a corresponding increase in consumption elsewhere or any decreases in costs for growers.

B   Saving money on wages would lower costs and thus contribute to a rise in profits.

C   Saving money on oil would lower costs and thus contribute to a rise in profits.

D   Saving money on supplies bought at a lower rate would lower costs and thus contribute to a rise in profits.

E   Saving money on irrigation would lower costs and thus contribute to a rise in profits.

The correct answer is A.

47. Which of the following most logically completes the argument below?

Davison River farmers are currently deciding between planting winter wheat this fall or spring wheat next spring. Winter wheat and spring wheat are usually about equally profitable. Because of new government restrictions on the use of Davison River water for irrigation, per acre yields for winter wheat, though not for spring wheat, would be much lower than average. Therefore, planting spring wheat will be more profitable than planting winter wheat, since _____.

(A) the smaller-than-average size of a winter wheat harvest this year would not be compensated for by higher winter wheat prices

(B) new crops of spring wheat must be planted earlier than the time at which standing crops of winter wheat are ready to be harvested

(C) the spring wheat that farmers in the Davison River region plant is well adapted to the soil of the region

(D) spring wheat has uses that are different from those of winter wheat

(E) planting spring wheat is more profitable than planting certain other crops, such as rye

Argument Construction

Situation   Farmers in the Davison River region must choose between planting winter wheat in the fall and planting spring wheat next spring. The crops tend to be equally profitable. This year's winter wheat crop yield is likely to be lower than average. The spring wheat yield should not be lower than average. Thus, for these reasons (plus one that the argument omits), spring wheat will be more profitable than winter wheat.

Reasoning   *Which point would logically complete the argument?* What would ensure spring wheat's profitability over winter wheat? Since the yield per acre of winter wheat is likely to be lower than usual, there will most likely be less winter wheat to sell. Winter wheat could match its usual profitability if the price farmers receive for it were to rise. If its price does not rise, however, it is unlikely to match its usual profitability. It would thus be unlikely to match spring wheat's profitability.

A   **Correct.** If this is true, it would mean that smaller-than-average winter wheat yields would translate into lower-than-usual profits on winter wheat (while spring wheat would be as profitable as winter wheat would normally be). This would justify the conclusion that spring wheat will be more profitable than winter wheat.

B   This provides support for the idea that farmers must choose between planting winter wheat and planting spring wheat, but it does not help determine which would be more profitable to plant.

C   This does not help explain why spring wheat is likely to be more profitable than winter wheat, because it gives no information about how well winter wheat is adapted to the soil of the region.

D   That spring wheat and winter wheat have different uses is not helpful in supporting a conclusion about which kind of wheat will be more profitable. It might help to know which of their uses are more profitable than others.

E   Since the question is whether it will be more profitable to plant winter wheat or to plant spring wheat, the fact that spring wheat is more profitable than nonwheat crops is not relevant.

The correct answer is A.

48. If the county continues to collect residential trash at current levels, landfills will soon be overflowing and parkland will need to be used in order to create more space. Charging each household a fee for each pound of trash it puts out for collection will induce residents to reduce the amount of trash they create; this charge will therefore protect the remaining county parkland.

Which of the following is an assumption made in drawing the conclusion above?

(A) Residents will reduce the amount of trash they put out for collection by reducing the number of products they buy.

(B) The collection fee will not significantly affect the purchasing power of most residents, even if their households do not reduce the amount of trash they put out.

(C) The collection fee will not induce residents to dump their trash in the parklands illegally.

(D) The beauty of county parkland is an important issue for most of the county's residents.

(E) Landfills outside the county's borders could be used as dumping sites for the county's trash.

Argument Construction

Situation Landfills will overflow and parkland will have to be used instead if current trash collection levels continue. Charging fees per pound of trash collected will inhibit trash growth and protect parkland.

Reasoning *What assumption underlies the conclusion?* The assumption will be a statement that has to be true in order for the argument's premises to provide a solid reason for believing its conclusion. To reach the conclusion that the plan will protect the parkland, the argument must assume that county residents will comply with the new fee, reducing both the trash they generate and the need to convert parkland to landfills. It is assumed that residents will not resort to some illegal means of avoiding the new fee, and it is certainly assumed that they will not contribute to the destruction of parklands by dumping trash in them illegally.

A Even though the fee may indirectly have this effect, the argument need not assume that it will; perhaps residents will continue to buy as much, but will make longer use of the product, or recycle it.

B The argument would be stronger if this were assumed NOT to be true.

C **Correct.** This statement properly identifies the fact that the argument rests on the assumption that the fee will not create illegal dumping.

D The argument need not assume this, and nothing in the argument indicates that it does. Financial incentives could be enough to make the desired outcome happen even if residents are indifferent to the parkland's beauty.

E The argument assumes that residents will reduce the amount of trash that they create, not that they will find other places to dispose of it.

The correct answer is C.

49. Certain genetically modified strains of maize produce a powerful natural insecticide. The insecticide occurs throughout the plant, including its pollen. Maize pollen is dispersed by the wind and frequently blows onto milkweed plants that grow near maize fields. Caterpillars of monarch butterflies feed exclusively on milkweed leaves. When these caterpillars are fed milkweed leaves dusted with pollen from modified maize plants, they die. Therefore, by using genetically modified maize, farmers put monarch butterflies at risk.

Which of the following would it be most useful to determine in order to evaluate the argument?

(A) Whether the natural insecticide is as effective against maize-eating insects as commercial insecticides typically used on maize are

(B) Whether the pollen of genetically modified maize contains as much insecticide as other parts of these plants

(C) Whether monarch butterfly caterpillars are actively feeding during the part of the growing season when maize is releasing pollen

(D) Whether insects that feed on genetically modified maize plants are likely to be killed by insecticide from the plant's pollen

(E) Whether any maize-eating insects compete with monarch caterpillars for the leaves of milkweed plants growing near maize fields

Argument Evaluation

Situation Monarch butterfly caterpillars die when fed milkweed leaves dusted with the pollen of certain genetically modified strains of maize. A natural insecticide occurs throughout the maize plant and in its pollen, which blows onto milkweed growing near maize fields. Caterpillars of monarch butterflies eat only milkweed leaves, so farmers who use this genetically modified maize are endangering monarch butterflies.

Reasoning *What would it be most useful to know in evaluating the argument?* We know that the caterpillars eat only milkweed leaves, but we do not know when, in the course of their development, they do so. Monarch butterflies would be at risk only if the caterpillars were to eat the milkweed leaves when those leaves had maize pollen on them. So it would be useful to know if the caterpillars eat milkweed leaves when maize pollen is likely to be present.

A The argument addresses whether farmers put monarch butterflies at risk by using genetically modified maize. The effectiveness of the natural insecticide that maize produces, relative to other insecticides, is not relevant to determining whether monarch butterflies are being endangered.

B The amount of insecticide in the rest of the plant, as opposed to in its pollen, has nothing to do with whether the use of the maize puts monarch butterflies at risk. All that matters is the amount of insecticide in the pollen, and we know that this is sufficient to kill the caterpillars.

C **Correct.** This question properly identifies something that it would be useful to know in evaluating whether monarch butterflies are actually at risk—that is, whether caterpillars will be eating milkweed leaves when those leaves are likely to have pollen on them.

D Since the issue at hand is whether farmers are endangering monarch butterflies, the question of the maize pollen's impact on other insects—that is, those that feed on maize—is irrelevant.

E Competition from maize-eating insects attracted to the area by the planting of maize might affect the monarch butterfly population, but simply knowing that such insects might compete with the caterpillars for milkweed leaves does not give any information on whether they would be able to compete *successfully* for those leaves.

The correct answer is C.

50. Although computers can enhance people's ability to communicate, computer games are a cause of underdeveloped communication skills in children. After-school hours spent playing computer games are hours not spent talking with people. Therefore, children who spend all their spare time playing these games have less experience in interpersonal communication than other children have.

    The argument depends on which of the following assumptions?

    (A) Passive activities such as watching television and listening to music do not hinder the development of communication skills in children.
    (B) Most children have other opportunities, in addition to after-school hours, in which they can choose whether to play computer games or to interact with other people.
    (C) Children who do not spend all of their after-school hours playing computer games spend at least some of that time talking with other people.
    (D) Formal instruction contributes little or nothing to children's acquisition of communication skills.
    (E) The mental skills developed through playing computer games do not contribute significantly to children's intellectual development.

Argument Construction

Situation   Spending after-school hours playing computer games does not enhance communication skills because children are not talking with other people during this time. Children who spend all their spare time playing computer games do not have as much interpersonal communication as other children do.

Reasoning   *What assumption does this argument depend on?* The unstated assumption in an argument will be a statement that has to be true in order for the argument's premises to provide a solid reason for believing its conclusion. Here, playing computer games is said to replace talking with people. Thus the argument assumes that children who do not spend all their spare time playing computer games instead spend at least some of that time talking with people.

A   This need not be assumed. The argument is not committed to any claim about the effects that watching television or listening to music may have on the development of communication skills in children.

B   The argument is limited to after-school hours or spare time.

C   **Correct.** This statement properly identifies the assumption on which the argument is based.

D   This could be false and the argument could still be sound; perhaps children who spend all their spare time playing computer games receive no formal instruction.

E   This could be false and the argument could still be sound as long as the intellectual development the games contribute to does not contribute to the development of communication skills.

The correct answer is C.

51. One variety of partially biodegradable plastic beverage container is manufactured from small bits of plastic bound together by a degradable bonding agent such as cornstarch. Since only the bonding agent degrades, leaving the small bits of plastic, no less plastic refuse per container is produced when such containers are discarded than when comparable nonbiodegradable containers are discarded.

Which of the following, if true, most strengthens the argument above?

(A) Both partially biodegradable and nonbiodegradable plastic beverage containers can be crushed completely flat by refuse compactors.

(B) The partially biodegradable plastic beverage containers are made with more plastic than comparable nonbiodegradable ones in order to compensate for the weakening effect of the bonding agents.

(C) Many consumers are ecology-minded and prefer to buy a product sold in the partially biodegradable plastic beverage containers rather than in nonbiodegradable containers, even if the price is higher.

(D) The manufacturing process for the partially biodegradable plastic beverage containers results in less plastic waste than the manufacturing process for nonbiodegradable plastic beverage containers.

(E) Technological problems with recycling currently prevent the reuse as food or beverage containers of the plastic from either type of plastic beverage container.

Argument Evaluation

Situation   One kind of partially biodegradable beverage container produces as much plastic refuse per container as a nonbiodegradable container does because only the bonding agent, not the plastic, degrades once the container is discarded.

Reasoning   *Which point strengthens the argument?* The information that strengthens the argument will help rule out a possible objection to the argument. In this case, one possible objection would be that the partially biodegradable containers might contain less plastic given that the container is made up in part of the degradable bonding agent. So, discovering that the partially biodegradable containers actually use more plastic than comparable nonbiodegradable ones in order to compensate for the weakness of the biodegradable bonding agent would strengthen the argument.

A   Nonbiodegradable plastic containers can be crushed completely flat. To say that biodegradable ones can be completely crushed also is perfectly compatible with saying that they contain less plastic.

B   **Correct.** This statement properly identifies a point that strengthens the argument by saying that the container actually produces more plastic refuse.

C   Consumers' preferences are not relevant to the argument about residual plastic.

D   The argument is not concerned with waste from manufacturing processes, but only with the product itself.

E   No reason is given to indicate that the inability to reuse the plastic from either type of container is related to the amount of plastic in either container.

The correct answer is B.

52. Rye sown in the fall and plowed into the soil in early spring leaves a residue that is highly effective at controlling broad-leaved weeds, but unfortunately for only about forty-five days. No major agricultural crop matures from seed in as little as forty-five days. Synthetic herbicides, on the other hand, although not any longer-lasting, can be reapplied as the crop grows. Clearly, therefore, for major agricultural crops, plowing rye into the soil can play no part in effective weed control.

The argument is most vulnerable to the objection that it fails to

(A) consider that there might be minor, quick-growing crops that do mature in forty-five days or less

(B) identify any alternative method of weed control that could be used instead of the method it rejects

(C) distinguish among the various kinds of synthetic herbicides

(D) allow for the possibility of combining the two weed-control methods it mentions

(E) allow for the possibility that plants other than rye, handled the same way, might have the same effect

Argument Evaluation

Situation   Broad-leaved weeds can be controlled in the spring for forty-five days by plowing fall-sown rye into the soil. But major agricultural crops take more than forty-five days to mature, and the rye-sowing process cannot be repeated. Synthetic herbicides last no longer than forty-five days, but they can be reapplied as necessary. Based on these facts, it is concluded that plowing rye into the soil cannot be part of effective weed control for major crops.

Reasoning   *To what objection is the argument vulnerable?* Note that the conclusion of the argument is emphatic: Plowing rye into the soil can play *no* part in effective weed control. Does the argument support this strong a conclusion? The argument fails to address whether it would be feasible to use plowed-in rye to control weeds for the first forty-five days of crop growth, and use applications of herbicide for the rest of the growing season. This might not be the case, but it should be addressed before it is concluded that plowing rye into the soil *cannot* be part of effective weed control.

A   The argument is concerned with whether plowing rye into the soil can be used in weed control for major crops, so the existence of minor crops for which rye could be used, because its weed-controlling qualities would last throughout their maturation, is irrelevant.

B   The argument *does* identify a method of weed control that can be used instead of rye: synthetic herbicides.

C   That there are many types of synthetic herbicides is not important to the argument; what is important is that at least some of them can be reapplied as crops grow.

D   Correct. This statement properly identifies a possibility that the argument fails to consider.

E   The argument is concerned with whether rye can be used to control weeds. That there might be other plants that could have the same effect is not relevant.

The correct answer is D.

53. Most employees in the computer industry move from company to company, changing jobs several times in their careers. However, Summit Computers is known throughout the industry for retaining its employees. Summit credits its success in retaining employees to its informal, nonhierarchical work environment.

Which of the following, if true, most strongly supports Summit's explanation of its success in retaining employees?

(A) Some people employed in the computer industry change jobs if they become bored with their current projects.

(B) A hierarchical work environment hinders the cooperative exchange of ideas that computer industry employees consider necessary for their work.

(C) Many of Summit's senior employees had previously worked at only one other computer company.

(D) In a nonhierarchical work environment, people avoid behavior that might threaten group harmony and thus avoid discussing with their colleagues any dissatisfaction they might have with their jobs.

(E) The cost of living near Summit is relatively low compared to areas in which some other computer companies are located.

Argument Evaluation

Situation   A computer company attributes its success in retaining employees to its informal, nonhierarchical work environment.

Reasoning   *Which point most supports the company's explanation?* The company says that employees stay at the company for one reason: its work environment. The explanation can therefore be supported only by a point that relates to the specific work environment. If employees feel that a more formal, hierarchical structure would interfere with their ability to do their jobs, the argument is strengthened.

A   Neither this point nor the passage indicates that an informal, nonhierarchical work environment would be less boring than others.

B   **Correct.** This statement properly identifies a point that strengthens the company's argument, relating the work environment to job satisfaction and therefore to employees' remaining at the company.

C   The previous work experience of senior employees is irrelevant.

D   While this point shows how the work environment might reduce discussion of job dissatisfaction, it does not indicate that there will be less dissatisfaction.

E   This point presents an alternate explanation—employees stay due to low cost of living—and so tends to weaken the company's argument.

The correct answer is B.

54.   Journalist: In late 1994, the present government of the Republic of Bellam came into power. Each year since then, about thirty journalists have been imprisoned for printing articles that criticize the government. In 1994, under the old government, only six journalists were imprisoned for criticizing the government. So the old government was more tolerant of criticism by the press than the new one is.

Politician: But in 1994 only six journalists criticized the government, and now journalists routinely do.

The politician challenges the journalist's argument by doing which of the following?

(A)   Presenting data that extend further into the past than the journalist's data

(B)   Introducing evidence that undermines an assumption of the journalist's argument

(C)   Questioning the accuracy of the evidence presented in support of the journalist's conclusion

(D)   Pointing out that the argument illegitimately draws a general conclusion on the basis of a sample of only a few cases

(E)   Stating that the argument treats information about some members of a group as if it applied to all members of that group

Argument Construction

Situation   The journalist argues that because more journalists who have printed articles critical of the government have been imprisoned under the new government than under the old government, the old government was more tolerant of criticism. The politician points out that journalists routinely criticize the government now, while under the old government far fewer did so, and all of those who did were imprisoned.

Reasoning   *How does the politician challenge the journalist's argument?* The politician brings up a fact that the journalist did not mention: that the six journalists who were imprisoned under the old government were the only journalists who criticized the government. The politician also points out that journalists now routinely criticize the government. The journalist assumes that the number of journalists imprisoned is an indicator of the government's tolerance of criticism, but the politician points to evidence that weakens that assumption.

A   The politician's data extend exactly as far back as the journalist's: to 1994.

B   **Correct.** This statement properly identifies the politician's challenge to the journalist's argument. The journalist assumes that the more journalists that are imprisoned annually, the less tolerant the government is. The politician's response suggests that the criterion should be, rather, how frequently journalists criticize the government.

C   The politician does not dispute the numbers of imprisoned journalists cited by the journalist.

D   The politician does not suggest that the journalist is looking at too few cases; rather, the politician suggests that the journalist has misunderstood the significance of the cases cited.

E   Rather than suggesting that the journalist is using specific information too generally, the politician suggests that the journalist is not using the proper specific information—that is, that the six journalists imprisoned under the older government were the only ones who criticized the government.

The correct answer is B.

55. Insurance Company X is considering issuing a new policy to cover services required by elderly people who suffer from diseases that afflict the elderly. Premiums for the policy must be low enough to attract customers. Therefore, Company X is concerned that the income from the policies would not be sufficient to pay for the claims that would be made.

Which of the following strategies would be most likely to minimize Company X's losses on the policies?

(A) Attracting middle-aged customers unlikely to submit claims for benefits for many years

(B) Insuring only those individuals who did not suffer any serious diseases as children

(C) Including a greater number of services in the policy than are included in other policies of lower cost

(D) Insuring only those individuals who were rejected by other companies for similar policies

(E) Insuring only those individuals who are wealthy enough to pay for the medical services

Evaluation of a Plan

Situation An insurance company considers an affordable policy for the elderly, but the company's income from the policies must exceed expenditures on claims.

Reasoning *What strategy will minimize the company's losses?* The insurance company's proposed plan would include a high-risk group, the elderly, who are likely to submit claims immediately. By expanding the customer base to include those who are less likely to submit claims for many years, the company will increase its income and thus minimize its losses.

A **Correct.** This statement properly identifies a strategy that minimizes policy losses.

B No connection is made between childhood diseases and geriatric diseases, so this point is irrelevant.

C Offering more services would tend to increase costs, and thus losses.

D Individuals rejected by other companies are more likely to make claims that would increase losses.

E People who are wealthy enough to pay for the services themselves would buy insurance only if the policies were reasonably priced and they planned to make claims on the policies; this point is irrelevant.

The correct answer is A.

56. The fewer restrictions there are on the advertising of legal services, the more lawyers there are who advertise their services, and the lawyers who advertise a specific service usually charge less for that service than the lawyers who do not advertise. Therefore, if the state removes any of its current restrictions, such as the one against advertisements that do not specify fee arrangements, overall consumer legal costs will be lower than if the state retains its current restrictions.

If the statements above are true, which of the following must be true?

(A) Some lawyers who now advertise will charge more for specific services if they do not have to specify fee arrangements in the advertisements.

(B) More consumers will use legal services if there are fewer restrictions on the advertising of legal services.

(C) If the restriction against advertisements that do not specify fee arrangements is removed, more lawyers will advertise their services.

(D) If more lawyers advertise lower prices for specific services, some lawyers who do not advertise will also charge less than they currently charge for those services.

(E) If the only restrictions on the advertising of legal services were those that apply to every type of advertising, most lawyers would advertise their services.

Argument Construction

Situation   Consumer legal costs will be reduced if the state removes even one restriction on lawyers' advertisements because the fewer the restrictions, the greater the number of lawyers who advertise, and lawyers who advertise charge less than lawyers who do not advertise.

Reasoning   *What conclusion can logically be drawn?* The argument sets up an inverse proportion: the fewer the number of restrictions on ads, the greater the number of lawyers who advertise. This is true of all restrictions and all lawyers. Therefore, removing any one restriction necessarily increases the number of lawyers who advertise.

A   The lawyers may charge more, but nothing in the passage rules out the possibility that no lawyer will charge more.

B   No evidence in the passage indicates that there will be an increased use of legal services.

C   **Correct.** This statement properly identifies a conclusion that logically follows, because reducing any restriction will increase the number of lawyers who advertise.

D   Nothing in the passage indicates that lawyers who continue not to advertise will be compelled to lower their fees.

E   The argument concerns numbers of advertisers rather than types; it remains possible that few lawyers would advertise.

The correct answer is C.

57. Which of the following most logically completes the argument given below?

People in isolated rain-forest communities tend to live on a largely vegetarian diet, and they eat little salt. Few of them suffer from high blood pressure, and their blood pressure does not tend to increase with age, as is common in industrialized countries. Such people often do develop high blood pressure when they move to cities and adopt high-salt diets. Though suggestive, these facts do not establish salt as the culprit in high blood pressure, however, because _____.

(A) genetic factors could account for the lack of increase of blood pressure with age among such people

(B) people eating high-salt diets and living from birth in cities in industrialized societies generally have a tendency to have high blood pressure

(C) it is possible to have a low-salt diet while living in a city in an industrialized country

(D) there are changes in other aspects of diet when such people move to the city

(E) salt is a necessity for human life, and death can occur when the body loses too much salt

Argument Construction

Situation People in isolated communities who eat low-salt diets tend not to have high blood pressure or to experience age-related increases in blood pressure. When these people move to industrialized areas and adopt high-salt diets, many do develop high blood pressure. Nevertheless, (for a reason the argument omits) one cannot conclude that salt causes high blood pressure.

Reasoning *What idea would logically complete the argument?* It may seem reasonable to say that salt causes high blood pressure when it is observed that when people who eat little salt begin eating salt, they develop high blood pressure. But look more closely at the circumstances under which these people began eating more salt: They moved from isolated rain-forest communities, where they ate vegetarian diets, to cities. It is most likely the case that such a move would entail dietary changes other than just an increase in salt consumption, and so it is possible that those changes contribute to their developing high blood pressure.

A If genetic factors accounted for such people's lack of increase of blood pressure with age, then their blood pressure would not increase when they moved to cities and adopted high-salt diets.

B If people who eat high-salt diets tend to have high blood pressure, it would support the idea that salt is indeed the culprit in high blood pressure.

C The argument is concerned with what happens when people from rain-forest communities move to cities *and adopt high-salt diets*, so the fact that it is possible to have a low-salt diet in a city is not relevant.

D **Correct.** This statement properly identifies a reason why salt might not be responsible for high blood pressure: There could be some other dietary factor that, when adopted, causes high blood pressure.

E The argument is concerned with the effects of high-salt diets. The fact that consuming too little salt can cause death says nothing about whether consuming too much salt is harmful.

The correct answer is D.

58. Even though most universities retain the royalties from faculty members' inventions, the faculty members retain the royalties from books and articles they write. Therefore, faculty members should retain the royalties from the educational computer software they develop.

    The conclusion above would be more reasonably drawn if which of the following were inserted into the argument as an additional premise?

    (A) Royalties from inventions are higher than royalties from educational software programs.
    (B) Faculty members are more likely to produce educational software programs than inventions.
    (C) Inventions bring more prestige to universities than do books and articles.
    (D) In the experience of most universities, educational software programs are more marketable than are books and articles.
    (E) In terms of the criteria used to award royalties, educational software programs are more nearly comparable to books and articles than to inventions.

Argument Construction

Situation Faculty members get the royalties from their books, but universities get the royalties from faculty inventions. Faculty members should get the royalties from their educational computer software.

Reasoning *What premise should be added to the argument?* This argument does not support its conclusion very well without an underlying assumption regarding the nature of computer programs. If, in terms of the criteria used to award royalties, educational computer programs are more like books and articles than like inventions, faculty members should retain the royalties. On the other hand, if they are more like inventions, then universities should retain the royalties. The conclusion states that faculty members should receive royalties for educational software without stating that software is more comparable to books and articles than to inventions. The missing premise must show the relationship between educational software and either inventions or books and articles.

A   The same may be true of books and articles.
B   This point does not indicate whether educational software is more comparable to inventions or to books and articles.
C   This point could be true even if, with regard to the relevant criteria, educational software is more comparable to inventions than to books and articles.
D   This point does not indicate whether educational software is more comparable to inventions or to books and articles.
E   **Correct.** This statement properly identifies a premise that establishes the relationship required to complete the argument.

The correct answer is E.

59. In order to withstand tidal currents, juvenile horseshoe crabs frequently burrow in the sand. Such burrowing discourages barnacles from clinging to their shells. When fully grown, however, the crabs can readily withstand tidal currents without burrowing, and thus they acquire substantial populations of barnacles. Surprisingly, in areas where tidal currents are very weak, juvenile horseshoe crabs are found not to have significant barnacle populations, even though they seldom burrow.

Which of the following, if true, most helps to explain the surprising finding?

(A) Tidal currents do not themselves dislodge barnacles from the shells of horseshoe crabs.

(B) Barnacles most readily attach themselves to horseshoe crabs in areas where tidal currents are weakest.

(C) The strength of the tidal currents in a given location varies widely over the course of a day.

(D) A very large barnacle population can significantly decrease the ability of a horseshoe crab to find food.

(E) Until they are fully grown, horseshoe crabs shed their shells and grow new ones several times a year.

Argument Construction

Situation   Juvenile horseshoe crabs withstand tidal currents by burrowing in the sand. This action makes barnacles less likely to cling to their shells. Adult horseshoe crabs can withstand currents, so they do not burrow, and barnacles become more likely to cling to their shells. Surprisingly, however, juvenile horseshoe crabs that do not burrow, because tidal currents do not threaten them, do not have significant numbers of barnacles clinging to their shells.

Reasoning   *What would most help explain the finding that nonburrowing juvenile horseshoe crabs do not have significant barnacle populations?* The finding suggests that there is some way in which nonburrowing juvenile horseshoe crabs either discourage barnacles from clinging to their shells, or get rid of the barnacles that do cling to their shells. Identifying how this is accomplished will explain the finding.

A   This gives a reason why juvenile horseshoe crabs that do not burrow *would* have significant barnacle populations.

B   If barnacles in areas of weak tidal currents readily attach themselves to horseshoe crabs, then it would be more likely for juvenile horseshoe crabs in such areas to have significant barnacle populations.

C   The areas under discussion are those where tidal currents are very weak. The strength of currents may vary widely there, but presumably they are still weak compared to other areas.

D   The surprising finding under discussion is why certain juvenile horseshoe crabs do not have significant barnacle populations, despite failing to engage in behavior that dislodges barnacles. That a very large barnacle population can hurt a horseshoe crab does not help explain such a finding.

E   **Correct.** This statement properly identifies something that helps explain the surprising finding: If juvenile horseshoe crabs regularly shed their shells, they also regularly shed the barnacles that cling to those shells. Thus juvenile horseshoe crabs would most likely be found not to have significant barnacle populations.

The correct answer is E.

60. Red blood cells in which the malarial-fever parasite resides are eliminated from a person's body after 120 days. Because the parasite cannot travel to a new generation of red blood cells, any fever that develops in a person more than 120 days after that person has moved to a malaria-free region is not due to the malarial parasite.

Which of the following, if true, most seriously weakens the conclusion above?

(A) The fever caused by the malarial parasite may resemble the fever caused by flu viruses.

(B) The anopheles mosquito, which is the principal insect carrier of the malarial parasite, has been eradicated in many parts of the world.

(C) Many malarial symptoms other than the fever, which can be suppressed with antimalarial medication, can reappear within 120 days after the medication is discontinued.

(D) In some cases, the parasite that causes malarial fever travels to cells of the spleen, which are less frequently eliminated from a person's body than are red blood cells.

(E) In any region infested with malaria-carrying mosquitoes, there are individuals who appear to be immune to malaria.

Argument Evaluation

Situation   The malarial-fever parasite lives in red blood cells, but these cells are eliminated after 120 days. If the infected person moves to a malaria-free region, any new fever that occurs after 120 days cannot be due to the malarial-fever parasite.

Reasoning   *What weakens the conclusion?* The passage says that the malarial parasites that reside in red blood cells are eliminated after 120 days. What if malarial parasites can also reside in other places in a person's body? If for instance the parasites can reside in the spleen, from which they are not eliminated as frequently, as well as in red blood cells, they may not be eliminated within 120 days. Therefore, they could cause malarial fever after the 120-day period. In that case, the conclusion ruling out a new generation of malarial parasites as the cause of new fever is unfounded.

A   The issue is not about a similarity of symptoms but about where the parasites reside.

B   The existence of malaria-free regions is not in question.

C   The argument gives no reason to postulate any significant connection between the discontinuation of medication and the issue of whether symptoms can persist after a patient has been in a malaria-free region for 120 days.

D   Correct. This statement properly identifies a point that weakens the conclusion.

E   This tells us only that some individuals are immune; it does not help us determine whether those who are not can have symptoms occur more than 120 days after moving into a malaria-free area.

The correct answer is D.

61. Neither a rising standard of living nor balanced trade, by itself, establishes a country's ability to compete in the international marketplace. Both are required simultaneously since standards of living can rise because of growing trade deficits and trade can be balanced by means of a decline in a country's standard of living.

    If the facts stated in the passage above are true, a proper test of a country's ability to be competitive is its ability to

    (A) balance its trade while its standard of living rises
    (B) balance its trade while its standard of living falls
    (C) increase trade deficits while its standard of living rises
    (D) decrease trade deficits while its standard of living falls
    (E) keep its standard of living constant while trade deficits rise

    Argument Evaluation

    Situation   A country's ability to compete in the international marketplace depends on both a rising standard of living and balanced trade.

    Reasoning   *What must a country do to be considered competitive?* The passage states that there are two conditions that must be met simultaneously: The standard of living must rise, and trade must be balanced. While it is possible for the standard of living to rise when trade is not balanced and for trade to be balanced while the standard of living is falling, neither of these situations allows the country to be considered competitive internationally. The country must both balance trade and have a rising standard of living.

    A   **Correct.** This statement properly identifies the two requirements the country must meet at the same time.
    B   One of the two conditions is not met; the standard of living must be rising, not falling.
    C   One of the two conditions is not met; trade must be balanced.
    D   Neither of the conditions is met; trade must be balanced, and the standard of living must be rising.
    E   Neither of the conditions is met; the standard of living must be rising, not constant, and trade must be balanced.

    The correct answer is A.

62. When there is less rainfall than normal, the water level of Australian rivers falls and the rivers flow more slowly. Because algae whose habitat is river water grow best in slow-moving water, the amount of algae per unit of water generally increases when there has been little rain. By contrast, however, following a period of extreme drought, algae levels are low even in very slow-moving river water.

Which of the following, if true, does most to explain the contrast described above?

(A) During periods of extreme drought, the populations of some of the species that feed on algae tend to fall.

(B) The more slowly water moves, the more conducive its temperature is to the growth of algae.

(C) When algae populations reach very high levels, conditions within the river can become toxic for some of the other species that normally live there.

(D) Australian rivers dry up completely for short intervals in periods of extreme drought.

(E) Except during periods of extreme drought, algae levels tend to be higher in rivers in which the flow has been controlled by damming than in rivers that flow freely.

Argument Construction

Situation When Australian rivers flow slowly due to little rain, algae populations in those rivers increase. But after periods of extreme drought, algae levels are low even in water moving at speeds that would normally show population increases.

Reasoning *What would explain the contrast between algae levels in slow-moving water resulting from little rain and slow-moving water after a drought?* There must be some difference between what happens during periods in which there is simply less rainfall than normal and periods in which there is extreme drought, a difference that affects the algae population.

A This indicates one of the consequences of drought, and slightly suggests that this might be due to a lower algae level. But it does nothing to explain why algae levels might be lower after a drought.

B This could explain why some rivers that are slow-moving and have little water might have a high algae level—but not why the algae level is low in such rivers after a period of drought.

C This explains why levels of other species might be low when algae populations are high, not why algae populations are high when there is little rain, but low following a period of extreme drought.

D Correct. This statement properly identifies something that helps explain the contrast. According to the information given, the habitat of the algae under discussion is river water. If the river dries up, the algae will probably not survive. Then after the drought, algae population levels would likely take a while to rise again.

E This emphasizes that there is a contrast between what happens to algae during periods of extreme drought and what happens to them at other times, but it does not help explain that contrast.

The correct answer is D.

63. When hypnotized subjects are told that they are deaf and are then asked whether they can hear the hypnotist, they reply, "No." Some theorists try to explain this result by arguing that the selves of hypnotized subjects are dissociated into separate parts, and that the part that is deaf is dissociated from the part that replies.

    Which of the following challenges indicates the most serious weakness in the attempted explanation described above?

    (A) Why does the part that replies not answer, "Yes"?
    (B) Why are the observed facts in need of any special explanation?
    (C) Why do the subjects appear to accept the hypnotist's suggestion that they are deaf?
    (D) Why do hypnotized subjects all respond the same way in the situation described?
    (E) Why are the separate parts of the self the same for all subjects?

Argument Evaluation

Situation   People under hypnosis are told they are deaf. When asked by the hypnotist if they can hear, they hear the question and respond, "No." A theory explains this puzzling result by stating that the hypnotized subjects dissociate the part of themselves that is deaf from the part that replies to the question.

Reasoning   *Which question points to a weakness in the theory?* According to the theory, hypnotized people dissociate themselves into separate parts: the hearing part and the deaf part. Then, they must be using the hearing part of themselves when they respond to the hypnotist's question; obviously, if they were using the deaf part of themselves at that point, they would not hear or thus respond at all. So, if they are using the hearing part of themselves, as the theorists maintain, why would they respond "No" to the question, "Can you hear me?" The hearing part would more logically answer "Yes."

A   **Correct.** This statement properly identifies a challenge that demonstrates the weakness in the theory.

B   This question does not address a weakness in the explanation; instead it asks why there needs to be an explanation at all.

C   The theorists' explanation, if true, can help answer this question, so this challenge does not indicate a weakness.

D   The theorists' explanation, if true, can help answer this question, so this challenge does not indicate a weakness.

E   The theorists' explanation does not address why the parts of the self are the same for all subjects, so this question does not get to a weakness of their argument.

The correct answer is A.

64. A prominent investor who holds a large stake in the Burton Tool Company has recently claimed that **the company is mismanaged**, citing as evidence the company's failure to slow production in response to a recent rise in its inventory of finished products. It is doubtful whether an investor's sniping at management can ever be anything other than counterproductive, **but in this case it is clearly not justified**. It is true that an increased inventory of finished products often indicates that production is outstripping demand, but in Burton's case it indicates no such thing. Rather, the increase in inventory is entirely attributable to products that have already been assigned to orders received from customers.

In the argument given, the two boldfaced portions play which of the following roles?

(A) The first states the position that the argument as a whole opposes; the second provides evidence to undermine the support for the position being opposed.

(B) The first states the position that the argument as a whole opposes; the second is evidence that has been used to support the position being opposed.

(C) The first states the position that the argument as a whole opposes; the second states the conclusion of the argument as a whole.

(D) The first is evidence that has been used to support a position that the argument as a whole opposes; the second provides information to undermine the force of that evidence.

(E) The first is evidence that has been used to support a position that the argument as a whole opposes; the second states the conclusion of the argument as a whole.

Argument Evaluation

Situation   An investor states that Burton Tool must be mismanaged because it has failed to slow production in response to increasing inventory of finished products. This criticism is unjustified because the finished inventory has already been assigned to orders received.

Reasoning   *Which option identifies the roles played by the boldfaced portions?* The first boldfaced portion expresses the investor's claim that the company is mismanaged. The argument asserts, in the second boldfaced portion, that this claim by the investor is unjustified. The passage then goes on to support this assertion.

A   The second boldfaced portion does not provide evidence to undermine the support for the position being opposed; instead, it states that this position is unjustified.

B   The second boldfaced portion is not said to have been used as evidence for the position being opposed; instead, it states that this position is unjustified.

C   **Correct.** This option correctly identifies the roles played in the argument by the boldfaced portions.

D   The first boldfaced portion is not *evidence for* the position being opposed; it *is* that position.

E   Again, first is not *evidence for* the position being opposed; it *is* that position.

The correct answer is C.

65. Excavation of the ancient city of Kourion on the island of Cyprus revealed a pattern of debris and collapsed buildings typical of towns devastated by earthquakes. Archaeologists have hypothesized that the destruction was due to a major earthquake known to have occurred near the island in A.D. 365.

Which of the following, if true, most strongly supports the archaeologists' hypothesis?

(A) Bronze ceremonial drinking vessels that are often found in graves dating from years preceding and following A.D. 365 were also found in several graves near Kourion.

(B) No coins minted after A.D. 365 were found in Kourion, but coins minted before that year were found in abundance.

(C) Most modern histories of Cyprus mention that an earthquake occurred near the island in A.D. 365.

(D) Several small statues carved in styles current in Cyprus in the century between A.D. 300 and A.D. 400 were found in Kourion.

(E) Stone inscriptions in a form of the Greek alphabet that was definitely used in Cyprus after A.D. 365 were found in Kourion.

Argument Evaluation

Situation   The excavation of Kourion reveals a pattern of destruction typical in towns destroyed by earthquakes. Archaeologists suggest Kourion was destroyed when an earthquake hit nearby in A.D. 365.

Reasoning   *Which statement best supports the archaeologists' hypothesis?* An earthquake struck near Cyprus in A.D. 365; this fact is not disputed. If this earthquake is the one responsible for the devastation of Kourion, then there should be evidence of active occupation before A.D. 365, but no evidence of activity after that date. The dates on the coins found on the site suggest that life in Kourion was flourishing before A.D. 365; the total lack of coins after the year of the earthquake supports the idea that the city had been destroyed.

A   The existence of vessels made both before and after A.D. 365 suggests that Kourion was not destroyed by the earthquake.

B   **Correct.** This statement properly identifies evidence that supports the archaeologists' hypothesis.

C   The occurrence of the earthquake is not in question; this statement simply confirms a fact already assumed in the argument.

D   The existence of statues carved in styles current after the date of the earthquake (A.D. 365–A.D. 400) argues against the town's destruction in A.D. 365.

E   The existence of inscriptions using an alphabet common only after the earthquake argues against the theory that the earthquake destroyed Kourion.

The correct answer is B.

66. To protect certain fledgling industries, the government of Country Z banned imports of the types of products those industries were starting to make. As a direct result, the cost of those products to the buyers, several export-dependent industries in Z, went up, sharply limiting the ability of those industries to compete effectively in their export markets.

Which of the following conclusions about Country Z's adversely affected export-dependent industries is best supported by the passage?

(A) Profit margins in those industries were not high enough to absorb the rise in costs mentioned above.

(B) Those industries had to contend with the fact that other countries banned imports from Country Z.

(C) Those industries succeeded in expanding the domestic market for their products.

(D) Steps to offset rising materials costs by decreasing labor costs were taken in those industries.

(E) Those industries started to move into export markets that they had previously judged unprofitable.

Argument Construction

Situation   Country Z bans the importation of products that would compete with those that some of its new industries are beginning to make. Consequently, the export-dependent local industries that buy these products must pay more for them, and these exporters are now less competitive in their markets.

Reasoning   *What conclusion can be drawn about the export-dependent industries?* Any conclusion must be supported by the facts in the passage. The export-dependent industries could no longer compete effectively when they had to purchase necessary products at greater expense from local industries. The export-dependent industries' inability to adjust successfully to the rise in costs suggests that staying competitive in their markets required tight cost control to maintain their profit margins. It is reasonable to conclude then that their profit margins were not high enough for them to be able to absorb the increased costs caused by their new need to purchase domestically made products.

A   **Correct.** This statement properly identifies the conclusion that the export-dependent industries were low-margin businesses that could not successfully accommodate the higher prices of the domestically made products.

B   No information about other countries' ban of imports from Country Z is given in the passage.

C   Not enough information is given in the passage to support this conclusion.

D   No information about cutting labor costs is given in the passage.

E   No information about the industries' moving into different markets is given in the passage.

The correct answer is A.

67.   Several industries have recently switched at least partly from older technologies powered by fossil fuels to new technologies powered by electricity. It is thus evident that less fossil fuel is being used as a result of the operations of these industries than would have been used if these industries had retained their older technologies.

Which of the following, if true, most strengthens the argument above?

(A)   Many of the industries that have switched at least partly to the new technologies have increased their output.

(B)   Less fossil fuel was used to manufacture the machinery employed in the new technologies than was originally used to manufacture the machinery employed in the older technologies.

(C)   More electricity is used by those industries that have switched at least partly to the new technologies than by those industries that have not switched.

(D)   Some of the industries that have switched at least partly to the new technologies still use primarily technologies that are powered by fossil fuels.

(E)   The amount of fossil fuel used to generate the electricity needed to power the new technologies is less than the amount that would have been used to power the older technologies.

Argument Evaluation

Situation   Several industries have now switched, at least partly, to technologies using electricity rather than fossil fuels. Thus, less fossil fuel will be consumed as a result of the operation of these industries than otherwise would have been.

Reasoning   *Which option most strengthens the argument?* One way to strengthen an argument is to eliminate or minimize one of its flaws or weaknesses. Because the conclusion is stated in terms of "fossil fuel consumed *as a result* of the operation of these industries," the claim would encompass even any fossil fuel that might be used to generate the electricity that the newer technologies use. Yet the premise of the argument does not address this issue. So the argument is strengthened if it turns out that less fossil fuel was used to produce the electricity than would have been used to power the older technologies.

A   In an indirect way, this option slightly weakens rather than strengthens the argument. For *if* fossil fuels are used to produce the electricity now used by the industries and *if* it is because of these newer technologies that output has increased, the argument's conclusion is *less* likely.

B   It does not matter how much fossil fuel was used to manufacture the older technologies *originally*. That has no bearing on whether more fossil fuel would have been expended as a result of the *continued operation* of the industries if the partial switch to newer technologies had not occurred.

C   This is what we would expect, but it in no way strengthens the argument.

D   This may seem to weaken the argument by indicating that the switch from older technologies will have less of an impact on fossil fuel consumption by these industries than we might have assumed. But since the conclusion makes no claim about how much consumption has been reduced, it is not clear that this option has any bearing on the strength of the argument one way or the other.

E   **Correct.** This is the option that most strengthens the argument.

The correct answer is E.

68. The local board of education found that, because the current physics curriculum has little direct relevance to today's world, physics classes attracted few high school students. So to attract students to physics classes, the board proposed a curriculum that emphasizes principles of physics involved in producing and analyzing visual images.

Which of the following, if true, provides the strongest reason to expect that the proposed curriculum will be successful in attracting students?

(A) Several of the fundamental principles of physics are involved in producing and analyzing visual images.
(B) Knowledge of physics is becoming increasingly important in understanding the technology used in today's world.
(C) Equipment that a large producer of photographic equipment has donated to the high school could be used in the proposed curriculum.
(D) The number of students interested in physics today is much lower than the number of students interested in physics 50 years ago.
(E) In today's world the production and analysis of visual images is of major importance in communications, business, and recreation.

Evaluation of a Plan

Situation Low enrollment in physics classes is blamed on the lack of relevance of the current curriculum to the current world. To attract more students, the board proposes a new curriculum emphasizing the principles of physics involved in producing and analyzing visual images.

Reasoning *What is the best reason for the success of this plan?* To attract more students, the class must be relevant to today's world. Evidence that the proposed content of the curriculum is indeed relevant would provide strong support for the plan. If producing and analyzing visual images is of major importance in communications, business, and recreation, the curriculum has clear relevance to today's world and should therefore attract more students.

A Given other claims made in the argument, this statement would not help explain why students would be attracted to the class unless producing and analyzing images is directly relevant to today's world. Nothing in the passage indicates that they are.

B This statement explains why students should take physics, but not why they would be attracted to the class.

C The availability of appropriate equipment is important once students are registered for the class, but it does not explain why they would be attracted to the class in the first place.

D The downward trend in enrollment does not suggest much success for the new class.

E **Correct.** This statement properly identifies a factor that would contribute to the success of the proposed plan to increase enrollment.

The correct answer is E.

69. Scientists have modified feed corn genetically, increasing its resistance to insect pests. Farmers who tried out the genetically modified corn last season applied less insecticide to their corn fields and still got yields comparable to those they would have gotten with ordinary corn. Ordinary corn seed, however, costs less, and what these farmers saved on insecticide rarely exceeded their extra costs for seed. Therefore, for most feed-corn farmers, switching to genetically modified seed would be unlikely to increase profits.

Which of the following would it be most useful to know in order to evaluate the argument?

(A) Whether there are insect pests that sometimes reduce feed-corn yields, but against which commonly used insecticides and the genetic modification are equally ineffective

(B) Whether the price that farmers receive for feed corn has remained steady over the past few years

(C) Whether the insecticides typically used on feed corn tend to be more expensive than insecticides typically used on other crops

(D) Whether most of the farmers who tried the genetically modified corn last season applied more insecticide than was actually necessary

(E) Whether, for most farmers who plant feed corn, it is their most profitable crop

Argument Evaluation

Situation   Farmers who grew feed corn genetically engineered to be pest resistant got yields comparable to those of farmers growing ordinary feed corn, but did so while using less pesticide. Since the amount saved on pesticide was rarely in excess of the extra costs for the genetically modified corn, most farmers will probably not increase profits by choosing the genetically engineered variety.

Reasoning   *Which would be most useful to know in evaluating the argument?* To answer a question such as this, one should look for information that would strengthen or weaken the argument. If one had information that the farmers growing the genetically modified corn could have increased their yields last year at lower cost, this would be helpful in evaluating the argument, because this would show that the argument is weak.

A   It does not matter to the argument whether there are pests against which pesticides and genetic resistance are equally ineffective, because that is compatible with there being pests against which they are not equally effective.

B   Whether prices of feed corn go up or down affects the comparison groups equally.

C   The relative cost of insecticides for other crops has no bearing on the argument because the argument is concerned with only feed corn.

D   **Correct.** This option provides the information that it would be most useful to know in evaluating the argument. It shows that farmers growing genetically modified corn last year could have attained higher profits than they in fact did.

E   The argument concerns only the relative profitability of growing one variety of feed corn versus another.

The correct answer is D.

70. Although aspirin has been proven to eliminate moderate fever associated with some illnesses, many doctors no longer routinely recommend its use for this purpose. A moderate fever stimulates the activity of the body's disease-fighting white blood cells and also inhibits the growth of many strains of disease-causing bacteria.

If the statements above are true, which of the following conclusions is most strongly supported by them?

(A) Aspirin, an effective painkiller, alleviates the pain and discomfort of many illnesses.
(B) Aspirin can prolong a patient's illness by eliminating moderate fever helpful in fighting some diseases.
(C) Aspirin inhibits the growth of white blood cells, which are necessary for fighting some illnesses.
(D) The more white blood cells a patient's body produces, the less severe the patient's illness will be.
(E) The focus of modern medicine is on inhibiting the growth of disease-causing bacteria within the body.

Argument Construction

Situation   Many doctors do not recommend taking aspirin for moderate fever associated with illness because moderate fever activates the immune systems and hinders the growth of disease-carrying bacteria.

Reasoning   *Which claim is best supported by this information?* This passage maintains that moderate fever can help fight some diseases by activating the immune system and inhibiting the growth of some bacteria that cause disease. Aspirin suppresses moderate fever. By doing so, aspirin can be viewed as hindering a beneficial process and prolonging an illness.

A   Though this may be true, the passage says nothing that supports the claim.
B   **Correct.** This statement properly identifies a conclusion that can be drawn from the information.
C   Since moderate fever promotes the *activity* of the white blood cells, it is fair to conclude that suppressing the fever with aspirin affects the *activity* of the white blood cells. The passage gives no evidence, however, regarding whether this suppression has anything to do with aspirin's effect, if any, on the *growth* of white blood cells.
D   The passage does not provide enough information to conclude that the greater the number of white blood cells, the less severe the illness.
E   The passage is compatible with saying that inhibiting the growth of disease-causing bacteria within the body is one of many concerns of modern medicine, in which case saying that this is *the focus of modern medicine* would be an overstatement.

The correct answer is B.

71. Roland: The alarming fact is that 90 percent of the people in this country now report that they know someone who is unemployed.

Sharon: But a normal, moderate level of unemployment is 5 percent, with one out of 20 workers unemployed. So at any given time if a person knows approximately 50 workers, one or more will very likely be unemployed.

Sharon's argument relies on the assumption that

(A) normal levels of unemployment are rarely exceeded

(B) unemployment is not normally concentrated in geographically isolated segments of the population

(C) the number of people who each know someone who is unemployed is always higher than 90 percent of the population

(D) Roland is not consciously distorting the statistics he presents

(E) knowledge that a personal acquaintance is unemployed generates more fear of losing one's job than does knowledge of unemployment statistics

Argument Construction

Situation Roland is alarmed that 90 percent of the population knows someone who is out of work. Sharon replies that a normal level of unemployment is 5 percent, illustrating her point by saying that if a person knows 50 workers, at least one of them is likely to be unemployed.

Reasoning *What assumption does Sharon make in putting together her argument?* Sharon makes a general statement claiming that if a person knows 50 workers, it is likely that at least one of them is unemployed. Sharon's generalization would not likely be true if unemployment were concentrated in certain geographically isolated areas.

A Sharon's argument is about a normal level of unemployment; how rarely or frequently that level is exceeded is outside the scope of her argument.

B **Correct.** This statement properly identifies an assumption that underlies Sharon's argument.

C Although Sharon's argument is compatible with saying that even more than 90 percent of the population knows someone who is unemployed, nothing suggests that she assumes that this is true.

D Sharon's argument is not based on the figure Roland cites and does not assume its accuracy or inaccuracy; her argument merely points out that his figure is not inconsistent with a normal rate of unemployment.

E The fear of losing a job is not part of Sharon's argument; this statement is irrelevant.

The correct answer is B.

72. Community activist: If Morganville wants to keep its central shopping district healthy, it should prevent the opening of a huge SaveAll discount department store on the outskirts of Morganville. Records from other small towns show that whenever SaveAll has opened a store outside the central shopping district of a small town, within five years the town has experienced the bankruptcies of more than a quarter of the stores in the shopping district.

The answer to which of the following would be most useful for evaluating the community activist's reasoning?

(A) Have community activists in other towns successfully campaigned against the opening of a SaveAll store on the outskirts of their towns?

(B) Do a large percentage of the residents of Morganville currently do almost all of their shopping at stores in Morganville?

(C) In towns with healthy central shopping districts, what proportion of the stores in those districts suffer bankruptcy during a typical five-year period?

(D) What proportion of the employees at the SaveAll store on the outskirts of Morganville will be drawn from Morganville?

(E) Do newly opened SaveAll stores ever lose money during their first five years of operation?

Argument Evaluation

Situation   Morganville should stop SaveAll from opening a store on its outskirts if it wants to keep its shopping district healthy. Other small towns have experienced bankruptcies in 25 percent of the stores in their central shopping district within five years after such openings.

Reasoning   *Which option provides the information that it would be most useful to know in evaluating the argument?* The argument contends that if SaveAll opens a store in Morganville, then that will somehow undermine the health of the shopping district. Two basic questions arise when evaluating the bankruptcy data from other small towns: (1) Did the opening of SaveAlls cause any of these bankruptcies? No information is given about bankruptcy rates in small towns without SaveAlls. (2) Is a 25 percent bankruptcy rate over five years *unhealthy?*

A   This has to do with the likelihood that the SaveAll will open; and not with what will happen if it does.

B   The conclusion would be supported just as well—or as poorly—if this question were answered with a yes as with a no.

C   **Correct.** This option provides the information that it would be most useful to know in evaluating the argument.

D   This may be important in determining the effect the SaveAll would have on Morganville residents, but the argument has only to do with SaveAll's effect on the economic health of the shopping district.

E   Whether SaveAlls tend to make or lose money in their first five years has no obvious bearing on whether they are apt to undermine the health of the town's shopping districts.

The correct answer is C.

73. In comparison to the standard typewriter keyboard, the EFCO keyboard, which places the most-used keys nearest the typist's strongest fingers, allows faster typing and results in less fatigue. Therefore, replacement of standard keyboards with the EFCO keyboard will result in an immediate reduction of typing costs.

Which of the following, if true, would most weaken the conclusion drawn above?

(A) People who use both standard and EFCO keyboards report greater difficulty in the transition from the EFCO keyboard to the standard keyboard than in the transition from the standard keyboard to the EFCO keyboard.

(B) EFCO keyboards are no more expensive to manufacture than are standard keyboards and require less frequent repair than do standard keyboards.

(C) The number of businesses and government agencies that use EFCO keyboards is increasing each year.

(D) The more training and experience an employee has had with the standard keyboard, the more costly it is to train that employee to use the EFCO keyboard.

(E) Novice typists can learn to use the EFCO keyboard in about the same amount of time that it takes them to learn to use the standard keyboard.

Argument Evaluation

Situation   Compared to the standard typewriter keyboard, the EFCO keyboard promotes faster typing while producing less fatigue. Replacing standard keyboards with EFCO keyboards promises immediate reduction of typing costs.

Reasoning   *What point would weaken the conclusion about reduced typing costs?* Whenever a word like *immediate* is part of an argument, it is wise to be alert. Given the comparison with the standard keyboard, it could well be that over the longer term the EFCO keyboard will save money. What problems might there be initially, however, that would counteract the possibility of *immediate* savings? Personnel must first be retrained on the new EFCO keyboard, and it is possible that the costs of the training could offset any short-term savings. If the more experience employees have had with the standard keyboard, the more costly the initial training, then adopting the new keyboard could have high short-term costs that preclude *immediate* savings.

A   The greater ease of changing from the standard keyboard to the EFCO keyboard for typists experienced in both would support, not weaken, the conclusion.

B   The fewer repairs required by EFCO keyboards should save money in the long run; immediate costs will not go up since the price of both keyboards is the same. The conclusion is not weakened.

C   The increasing use of EFCO keyboards supports the conclusion, because it suggests that other offices have found the switch advantageous.

D   **Correct.** This statement properly identifies information that weakens the conclusion that savings will be immediate.

E   For new typists, training time is the same for both keyboards; this statement does not weaken the conclusion.

The correct answer is D.

74. In the past the country of Malvernia has relied heavily on imported oil. Malvernia recently implemented a program to convert heating systems from oil to natural gas. Malvernia currently produces more natural gas each year than it uses, and oil production in Malvernian oil fields is increasing at a steady pace. If these trends in fuel production and usage continue, therefore, Malvernian reliance on foreign sources for fuel is likely to decline soon.

Which of the following would it be most useful to establish in evaluating the argument?

(A) When, if ever, will production of oil in Malvernia outstrip production of natural gas?

(B) Is Malvernia among the countries that rely most on imported oil?

(C) What proportion of Malvernia's total energy needs is met by hydroelectric, solar, and nuclear power?

(D) Is the amount of oil used each year in Malvernia for generating electricity and fuel for transportation increasing?

(E) Have any existing oil-burning heating systems in Malvernia already been converted to natural-gas-burning heating systems?

Argument Evaluation

Situation   Malvernia has relied heavily on imported oil, but recently began a program to convert heating systems from oil to natural gas. Malvernia produces more natural gas than it uses, so it will probably reduce its reliance on imported oils if these trends continue.

Reasoning   *Which option provides the information that it would be most useful to know in evaluating the argument?* In other words, we are looking for the option which—depending on whether it was answered yes or no—would either most weaken or most strengthen the argument. The argument indicates that Malvernia will be using less oil for heating and will be producing more oil domestically. But the conclusion that Malvernia's reliance on foreign oil will decline, assuming the current trends mentioned continue, would be seriously undermined if there was something in the works that was bound to offset these trends, for instance, if it turned out that the country's need for oil was going to rise drastically in the coming years.

A   Since both counteract the need for imported oil, it makes little difference to the argument whether domestic oil production exceeds domestic natural gas.

B   Whether there are many countries that rely more on foreign oil than Malvernia would have little impact on whether Malvernia's need for foreign oil can be expected to decline.

C   Since there is no information in the argument about whether Malvernia can expect an increase or decrease from these other energy sources, it does not matter how much they now provide.

D   Correct. This option provides the information that it would be most useful to know in evaluating the argument.

E   The argument tells us that a program has begun *recently* to convert heating systems from oil to gas. So, even if no such conversions have been completed, the argument still indicates that they can be expected to occur.

The correct answer is D.

75. An overly centralized economy, not the changes in the climate, is responsible for the poor agricultural production in Country X since its new government came to power. Neighboring Country Y has experienced the same climatic conditions, but while agricultural production has been falling in Country X, it has been rising in Country Y.

Which of the following, if true, would most weaken the argument above?

(A) Industrial production also is declining in Country X.

(B) Whereas Country Y is landlocked, Country X has a major seaport.

(C) Both Country X and Country Y have been experiencing drought conditions.

(D) The crops that have always been grown in Country X are different from those that have always been grown in Country Y.

(E) Country X's new government instituted a centralized economy with the intention of ensuring an equitable distribution of goods.

Argument Evaluation

Situation   Two countries sharing similar climate conditions differ widely in agricultural production, one experiencing a rise and the other a decline. The decline is blamed on an overly centralized economy.

Reasoning   *What point most weakens the argument that the economy is to blame?* If a factor other than the economy could account for the differences in agricultural production, then the argument is weakened. If the two countries grow different kinds of crops that may react differently to the same climate conditions, then the types of crops, rather than the economy could be responsible for the differences in production.

A   This weakly suggests that the overly centralized economy of Country X is to blame for its poor agricultural production; this strengthens the argument more than it weakens it.

B   The availability of a seaport does not explain the differences in agricultural production.

C   Similar climate conditions have already been established in the argument.

D   Correct. This statement properly identifies a factor that weakens the argument.

E   The government's intention when instituting the economy does not have any bearing on whether the economy is responsible for the decline or not.

The correct answer is D.

76. Because no employee wants to be associated with bad news in the eyes of a superior, information about serious problems at lower levels is progressively softened and distorted as it goes up each step in the management hierarchy. The chief executive is, therefore, less well informed about problems at lower levels than are his or her subordinates at those levels.

    The conclusion drawn above is based on the assumption that

    (A) problems should be solved at the level in the management hierarchy at which they occur
    (B) employees should be rewarded for accurately reporting problems to their superiors
    (C) problem-solving ability is more important at higher levels than it is at lower levels of the management hierarchy
    (D) chief executives obtain information about problems at lower levels from no source other than their subordinates
    (E) some employees are more concerned about truth than about the way they are perceived by their superiors

Argument Construction

Situation   No employee wants to report bad news to a superior, so information about problems is softened and distorted as it goes up the ranks of management. As a result, chief executives know less about problems at lower levels than their subordinates do.

Reasoning   *What assumption is being made in this argument?* This passage contends that information travels step by step upward through an organization, and that information becomes increasingly distorted along the route with each additional individual's reluctance to be candid with a superior about problems. What must be true about this information flow to support the conclusion? In order to conclude that chief executives are *less well informed* about problems than their subordinates, the argument must logically assume that they have no source of information except their subordinates.

A   This argument is not about how problems should be solved, only about how chief executives learn of them.

B   No recommendation for solving the problem is assumed; only the method of discovering the problem is assumed.

C   Problem-solving ability plays no role in the argument.

D   **Correct.** This statement properly identifies an assumption that underlies the argument.

E   This statement undermines the assertion made in the first sentence of the passage and so cannot be assumed.

The correct answer is D.

77. Although the earliest surviving Greek inscriptions written in an alphabet date from the eighth century B.C., **the fact that the text of these Greek inscriptions sometimes runs from right to left and sometimes from left to right** indicates that the Greeks adopted alphabetic writing at least two centuries before these inscriptions were produced. After all, the Greeks learned alphabetic writing from the Phoenicians, and presumably, along with the alphabet, they also adopted the then-current Phoenician practice with respect to the direction of text. **And although Phoenician writing was originally inconsistent in direction, by the eighth century B.C. Phoenician was consistently written from right to left and had been for about two centuries**.

In the argument given, the two portions in boldface play which of the following roles?

(A) The first and the second each describe evidence that has been used to challenge the position that the argument seeks to establish.

(B) The first is evidence that forms the basis for an objection to the position that the argument seeks to establish; the second is that position.

(C) The first is evidence that forms the basis for an objection to the position that the argument seeks to establish; the second is a consideration that is introduced to counter the force of that evidence.

(D) The first and the second each provide evidence in support of the position that the argument seeks to establish.

(E) The first provides evidence in support of the position that the argument seeks to establish; the second is that position.

Argument Evaluation

Situation   The oldest surviving Greek inscriptions written in an alphabet are from the eighth century B.C. and run from both left to right and right to left. Therefore, it is likely that the Greeks adopted alphabetic writing at least two centuries before these inscriptions were made. The Greeks adopted their alphabet from the Phoenicians, who wrote in both directions up until two centuries prior to the eighth century.

Reasoning   *What roles do the two boldfaced portions play in the argument?* The conclusion of the argument is that the Greeks adopted alphabetic writing at least two centuries before the oldest surviving Greek inscriptions were written in the eighth century B.C. The first and second boldfaced portions work together to support this conclusion.

A   The first and second portions are not used to challenge the position the argument seeks to establish, but to support it.

B   The first is evidence for the conclusion, not for an objection to it; the second is as well.

C   The first is evidence for the conclusion, not for an objection to it; the second is as well.

D   Correct. This option correctly identifies the roles played by the boldfaced portions.

E   The second boldfaced portion is not the conclusion, but evidence for that conclusion.

The correct answer is D.

78. A recent report determined that although only 3 percent of drivers on Maryland highways equipped their vehicles with radar detectors, 33 percent of all vehicles ticketed for exceeding the speed limit were equipped with them. Clearly, drivers who equip their vehicles with radar detectors are more likely to exceed the speed limit regularly than are drivers who do not.

The conclusion drawn above depends on which of the following assumptions?

(A) Drivers who equip their vehicles with radar detectors are less likely to be ticketed for exceeding the speed limit than are drivers who do not.

(B) Drivers who are ticketed for exceeding the speed limit are more likely to exceed the speed limit regularly than are drivers who are not ticketed.

(C) The number of vehicles that were ticketed for exceeding the speed limit was greater than the number of vehicles that were equipped with radar detectors.

(D) Many of the vehicles that were ticketed for exceeding the speed limit were ticketed more than once in the time period covered by the report.

(E) Drivers on Maryland highways exceeded the speed limit more often than did drivers on other state highways not covered in the report.

Argument Construction

Situation   Although only 3 percent of drivers on Maryland's highways have radar detectors in their vehicles, 33 percent of vehicles recently ticketed for driving over the speed limit on Maryland highways have had radar detectors. Drivers who have radar detectors are thus more likely to exceed the speed limit regularly than drivers who do not.

Reasoning   *What assumption must be true for the conclusion to be drawn?* The argument moves from a particular example, that is, the percentage of vehicles ticketed for exceeding the speed limit that were equipped with radar detectors, to a generalization about the regular driving behaviors of all drivers who have radar detectors in their vehicles. The reasoning links the example to the generalization with an assumption. What can the assumption be? Only if the drivers ticketed in this instance are assumed to make a regular habit of exceeding the speed limit can the conclusion be drawn that drivers with radar detectors are more likely to do so *regularly* than drivers who are not ticketed.

A   While this statement about being ticketed may be true, the conclusion pertains to the recurrent exceeding of the speed limit, so this statement is not relevant.

B   **Correct.** This statement properly identifies the conclusion's necessary assumption about ticketed drivers' being more likely to drive in excess of the speed limit than nonticketed drivers.

C   This statement is about the number of vehicles ticketed, not about the regular habits of drivers, so it is not assumed for the conclusion.

D   While this additional information could help support the conclusion, it is not a necessary assumption in the conclusion because it is about the particular example of the drivers in Maryland, not about drivers' habits in general.

E   Learning that Maryland drivers are not representative of other drivers undermines the conclusion about all drivers, so it is clearly not assumed.

The correct answer is B.

79. **In countries where automobile insurance includes compensation for whiplash injuries sustained in automobile accidents, reports of having suffered such injuries are twice as frequent as they are in countries where whiplash is not covered.** Presently, no objective test for whiplash exists, so it is true that spurious reports of whiplash injuries cannot be readily identified. Nevertheless, these facts do not warrant the conclusion drawn by some commentators that in the countries with the higher rates of reported whiplash injuries, half of the reported cases are spurious. Clearly, **in countries where automobile insurance does not include compensation for whiplash, people often have little incentive to report whiplash injuries that they actually have suffered.**

In the argument given, the two boldfaced portions play which of the following roles?

(A) The first is a claim that the argument disputes; the second is a conclusion that has been based on that claim.

(B) The first is a claim that has been used to support a conclusion that the argument accepts; the second is that conclusion.

(C) The first is evidence that has been used to support a conclusion for which the argument provides further evidence; the second is the main conclusion of the argument.

(D) The first is a finding whose implications are at issue in the argument; the second is a claim presented in order to argue against deriving certain implications from that finding.

(E) The first is a finding whose accuracy is evaluated in the argument; the second is evidence presented to establish that the finding is accurate.

Argument Evaluation

Situation   Reported whiplash injuries are twice as common in countries where car insurance companies pay compensation for such injuries as they are in countries where insurance companies do not. Although there is no objective test for whiplash, this does not mean, as some suggest, that half of the reports of such injuries are fake. It could simply be that where insurance will not pay for such injuries, people are less inclined to report them.

Reasoning   *What roles do the two boldfaced portions play in the argument?* The first portion tells us about the correlation between reported cases of whiplash in countries and the willingness of insurance companies in those countries to compensate for whiplash injuries. The argument next states that whiplash is difficult to objectively verify. The argument then asserts that *although* this last fact, taken together with the first boldfaced portion, has led some to infer that over half of the reported cases in countries with the highest whiplash rates are spurious, such an inference is unwarranted. The second boldfaced portion then helps to explain why such an inference is not necessarily warranted by offering an alternative explanation.

A   The claim made in the first boldfaced portion is never disputed in the argument; at dispute is how to account for the fact that this claim is true. The second is not the argument's conclusion.

B   In a manner of speaking, perhaps, the argument uses the first portion to support its conclusion; but there is no indication that it has been used elsewhere to do so. In any case, the second boldfaced portion is not the argument's conclusion.

C   The first has been used to support a conclusion that the argument *rejects*; the second boldfaced portion is not the argument's conclusion.

D   Correct. This option correctly identifies the roles played in the argument by the boldfaced portions.

E   The accuracy of the first boldfaced portion is never questioned in the argument; nor is the second intended to somehow help show that the first is accurate. Rather, the argument assumes that the first portion is accurate.

The correct answer is D.

80. Products sold under a brand name used to command premium prices because, in general, they were superior to nonbrand rival products. Technical expertise in product development has become so widespread, however, that special quality advantages are very hard to obtain these days and even harder to maintain. As a consequence, brand-name products generally neither offer higher quality nor sell at higher prices. Paradoxically, brand names are a bigger marketing advantage than ever.

Which of the following, if true, most helps to resolve the paradox outlined above?

(A) Brand names are taken by consumers as a guarantee of getting a product as good as the best rival products.

(B) Consumers recognize that the quality of products sold under invariant brand names can drift over time.

(C) In many acquisitions of one corporation by another, the acquiring corporation is interested more in acquiring the right to use certain brand names than in acquiring existing production facilities.

(D) In the days when special quality advantages were easier to obtain than they are now, it was also easier to get new brand names established.

(E) The advertising of a company's brand-name products is at times transferred to a new advertising agency, especially when sales are declining.

Argument Evaluation

Situation   In both quality and price, brand-name and nonbrand products have now become similar. Yet brand names offer a bigger marketing advantage than ever.

Reasoning   *How can this paradox be explained?* It is given that a brand-name product's only distinction from its rival products is likely to be a recognizable name. How, then, can brand names give products a bigger marketing advantage? Could consumers be relying on their outdated knowledge and believing that brand names continue to guarantee that a product's quality is at least as good as, and possibly higher than, that of the rival products at the same price? If so, they would choose to purchase the brand-name product trusting they would, at a minimum, get comparable quality for the same price.

A   **Correct.** This statement correctly identifies the consumer behavior that explains the marketing advantage of brand names.

B   Consumers would be less likely to buy brand-name products if they were unsure of their quality, so this statement does not resolve the paradox.

C   Corporations value brand names, but this statement does not say why, nor does it explain the marketing advantage of brand names.

D   Although it was easier in the past both to obtain special quality advantages and to establish new brand names, these facts are not linked other than coincidentally and do not explain why brand names are a marketing advantage now.

E   The shift from one advertising agency to another to counteract falling sales does not account for the general marketing advantage brand names enjoy.

The correct answer is A.

81. When demand for a factory's products is high, more money is spent at the factory for safety precautions and machinery maintenance than when demand is low. Thus the average number of on-the-job accidents per employee each month should be lower during periods when demand is high than when demand is low and less money is available for safety precautions and machinery maintenance.

Which of the following, if true about a factory when demand for its products is high, casts the most serious doubt on the conclusion drawn above?

(A) Its employees ask for higher wages than they do at other times.

(B) Its management hires new workers but lacks the time to train them properly.

(C) Its employees are less likely to lose their jobs than they are at other times.

(D) Its management sponsors a monthly safety award for each division in the factory.

(E) Its old machinery is replaced with modern, automated models.

Argument Evaluation

Situation Because more money is spent on safety precautions and machinery maintenance at a factory when demand for its product is high, the average number of job-related accidents per employee at the factory should be lower when demand is high.

Reasoning *What point casts doubt on the conclusion?* Consider what other conditions can result from high demand for a factory's products. What if, when demand is high, more employees are hired to meet the demand? If, in the effort to increase production, there is not enough time for proper training, then it is likely that the new, poorly trained employees will have more job-related accidents than experienced, well-trained workers.

A If employers consented to employees' request and diverted money from safety to wages, this statement might cast doubt on the conclusion. However, no such reallocation of resources is implied, and the passage conclusively states that more money *is* spent on safety precautions and machinery maintenance when demand for the product is high. Therefore this statement is irrelevant.

B Correct. This statement properly identifies a point that undermines the conclusion.

C Increased job security could result in an increased number of workers, which might increase the total number of accidents. However, the conclusion is about the number of accidents *per employee*, so this point is irrelevant.

D Actively promoting safety with an award would tend to support the argument, not weaken it.

E Replacing outdated machinery with more modern machinery could result in a safer workplace; this point could strengthen the conclusion.

The correct answer is B.

82. A sudden increase in the production of elephant ivory artifacts on the Mediterranean coast of North Africa occurred in the tenth century. Historians explain this increase as the result of an area opening up as a new source of ivory and argue on this basis that the important medieval trade between North Africa and East Africa began at this period.

    Each of the following, if true, provides some support for the historians' account described above EXCEPT:

    (A) In East Africa gold coins from Mediterranean North Africa have been found at a tenth-century site but at no earlier sites.

    (B) The many surviving letters of pre-tenth-century North African merchants include no mention of business transactions involving East Africa.

    (C) Excavations in East Africa reveal a tenth-century change in architectural style to reflect North African patterns.

    (D) Documents from Mediterranean Europe and North Africa that date back earlier than the tenth century show knowledge of East African animals.

    (E) East African carvings in a style characteristic of the tenth century depict seagoing vessels very different from those used by local sailors but of a type common in the Mediterranean.

Argument Evaluation

Situation   There was a sudden increase in the production of ivory artifacts in an area of North Africa in the tenth century. Historians say this was brought about by a new source of ivory opening up, and argue from this that important trade between North Africa and East Africa began at this time.

Reasoning   *Which option does NOT provide support for the historians' account?* The historians' account posits new trade between North and East Africa opening in the tenth century and infers this from the increase in ivory production in North Africa that occurred at about this time. Thus, an option that identifies some connection between North and East Africa which predates the tenth century would not support but rather undermine the historians' account.

A   That gold coins may have first been traded between East Africa and North Africa supports the idea that important trade between these areas opened up at this time.

B   This is support for the historians' conclusion, because if there had been important trade between East Africa and North Africa prior to the tenth century, there likely would have been some mention of it in at least some of the letters that survive from that period.

C   This change in architectural design suggests that North Africa began to influence East Africa around this time. Opening up of new trade would explain the emergence of this new influence.

D   Correct. This is the one option that does not support the historians' account.

E   The fact that East African carvings that are possibly from tenth century depict ships not from East Africa but possibly from North Africa would support the idea that trade was occurring at this time.

The correct answer is D.

83. Journalist: In physics journals, the number of articles reporting the results of experiments involving particle accelerators was lower last year than it had been in previous years. Several of the particle accelerators at major research institutions were out of service the year before last for repairs, so it is likely that the low number of articles was due to the decline in availability of particle accelerators.

Which of the following, if true, most seriously undermines the journalist's argument?

(A) Every article based on experiments with particle accelerators that was submitted for publication last year actually was published.

(B) The average time scientists must wait for access to a particle accelerator has declined over the last several years.

(C) The number of physics journals was the same last year as in previous years.

(D) Particle accelerators can be used for more than one group of experiments in any given year.

(E) Recent changes in the editorial policies of several physics journals have decreased the likelihood that articles concerning particle-accelerator research will be accepted for publication.

Argument Evaluation

Situation   A journalist attributes the low number of articles about particle accelerators in physics journals to the fact that several accelerators at major research institutions had been out of service the previous year.

Reasoning   *What point undermines the journalist's argument?* The journalist assumes that the researchers' lack of access to the accelerators is responsible for the decline in the number of articles. What else could explain fewer articles? What if the decline is due, not to the availability of the accelerators for experiments, but to policies regarding publishing articles related to such experiments? An alternate explanation is that changes in the editorial policies of physics journals, rather than the effect of the out-of-service accelerators, could well be responsible for the lower number of published articles about particle-accelerator research.

A   This statement rules out the possibility that submitted articles were not published, and eliminating this alternate explanation tends to support the argument.

B   A decline in waiting time would seem to promote more articles about accelerator research being written and published, not fewer.

C   While the decline in articles could be explained by a decline in the number of journals, this statement eliminates that alternate explanation.

D   If the accelerators can be used for multiple experiments, then it is reasonable to expect more articles related to them, not fewer.

E   **Correct.** This statement properly identifies a point that undermines the journalist's reasoning.

The correct answer is E.

84. Many people suffer an allergic reaction to certain sulfites, including those that are commonly added to wine as preservatives. However, since there are several winemakers who add sulfites to none of the wines they produce, people who would like to drink wine but are allergic to sulfites can drink wines produced by these winemakers without risking an allergic reaction to sulfites.

Which of the following is an assumption on which the argument depends?

(A) These winemakers have been able to duplicate the preservative effect produced by adding sulfites by means that do not involve adding any potentially allergenic substances to their wine.

(B) Not all forms of sulfite are equally likely to produce the allergic reaction.

(C) Wine is the only beverage to which sulfites are commonly added.

(D) Apart from sulfites, there are no substances commonly present in wine that give rise to an allergic reaction.

(E) Sulfites are not naturally present in the wines produced by these winemakers in amounts large enough to produce an allergic reaction in someone who drinks these wines.

Argument Construction

Situation   People who are allergic to certain sulfites can avoid risking an allergic reaction by drinking wine from one of the several producers that does not add sulfites.

Reasoning   *On what assumption does the argument depend?* Drinking wine to which no sulfites have been *added* will not prevent exposure to sulfites if, for instance, sulfites occur naturally in wines. In particular, if the wines that do not have sulfites added have sulfites present naturally in quantities sufficient to produce an allergic reaction, drinking these wines will not prevent an allergic reaction. The argument therefore depends on assuming that this is not the case.

A   The argument does not require this because the conclusion does not address allergic reactions to substances other than sulfites.

B   The argument specifically refers to "certain sulfites" producing allergic reactions. It is entirely compatible with certain other forms of sulfites not producing allergic reactions in anyone.

C   This is irrelevant. The argument does not claim that one can avoid having an allergic reaction to sulfites *from any source* just by restricting one's wine consumption to those varieties to which no sulfites have been added.

D   Once again, the argument's conclusion does not address allergic reactions to substances other than sulfites in wine.

E   **Correct.** The argument relies on this assumption.

The correct answer is E.

85. Networks of blood vessels in bats' wings serve only to disperse heat generated in flight. This heat is generated only because bats flap their wings. Thus paleontologists' recent discovery that the winged dinosaur Sandactylus had similar networks of blood vessels in the skin of its wings provides evidence for the hypothesis that Sandactylus flew by flapping its wings, not just by gliding.

In the passage, the author develops the argument by

(A) forming the hypothesis that best explains several apparently conflicting pieces of evidence
(B) reinterpreting evidence that had been used to support an earlier theory
(C) using an analogy with a known phenomenon to draw a conclusion about an unknown phenomenon
(D) speculating about how structures observed in present-day creatures might have developed from similar structures in creatures now extinct
(E) pointing out differences in the physiological demands that flight makes on large, as opposed to small, creatures

Argument Evaluation

Situation The network of blood vessels in bats' wings is compared with a similar structure in the wings of the dinosaur Sandactylus to explain how the dinosaur flew.

Reasoning *How is this argument developed?* The author first shows that a physical characteristic of bats' wings is directly related to their style of flight. The author then argues that the similar structure found in the wings of Sandactylus is evidence that the dinosaur had a style of flight similar to that of bats. The structure of this argument is a comparison, or analogy, between a known phenomenon (bats) and an unknown one (Sandactylus).

A The evidence of the blood vessels in the wings does not conflict with other evidence.
B The evidence of the blood vessels in the wings is used to support only one theory—that Sandactylus flew by flapping its wings as well as by gliding; no evidence is discussed in relation to any earlier theory.
C **Correct.** This statement properly identifies how the argument compares the wings of bats and of Sandactylus in order to draw a conclusion about how the dinosaur flew.
D The argument is not about how the structures in the bats developed from the structures in the dinosaurs, but rather about how Sandactylus flew.
E The comparison between bats and Sandactylus points out similarities, not differences.

The correct answer is C.

86. Keith: Compliance with new government regulations requiring the installation of smoke alarms and sprinkler systems in all theaters and arenas will cost the entertainment industry $25 billion annually. Consequently, jobs will be lost and profits diminished. Therefore, these regulations will harm the country's economy.

    Laura: The $25 billion spent by some businesses will be revenue for others. Jobs and profits will be gained as well as lost.

    Laura responds to Keith by

    (A) demonstrating that Keith's conclusion is based on evidence that is not relevant to the issue at hand
    (B) challenging the plausibility of the evidence that serves as the basis for Keith's argument
    (C) suggesting that Keith's argument overlooks a mitigating consequence
    (D) reinforcing Keith's conclusion by supplying a complementary interpretation of the evidence Keith cites
    (E) agreeing with the main conclusion of Keith's argument but construing that conclusion as grounds for optimism rather than for pessimism

Argument Construction

Situation   Keith argues that the cost of new regulations will result in a loss of jobs and profits, hurting the national economy. Laura points out that while one industry will suffer, others will gain by supplying the goods and services required by the regulations.

Reasoning   *What is the strategy Laura uses in the counterargument?* Laura uses the same evidence, the $25 billion spent on meeting new regulations, but comes to a different conclusion. While Keith focuses on the losses to one industry, Laura looks at the gains to other industries. By suggesting a consequence that Keith did not mention, she places the outcome in a more positive light.

A   Laura accepts the relevance of Keith's evidence and uses it herself when she replies that *the $25 billion spent by some businesses will be revenue for others.*

B   Laura does not challenge Keith's evidence; she uses the same evidence as the basis of her own argument.

C   **Correct.** This statement properly identifies the strategy Laura employs in her counterargument. Laura points out that Keith did not consider that, in this case, losses for one industry mean gains for others.

D   Laura rejects rather than reinforces Keith's conclusion; while he notes the losses in jobs and profits that will harm the economy, she points out that *jobs and profits will be gained as well as lost.*

E   Laura does not agree with Keith's main conclusion that the regulations will harm the national economy; she argues instead that gains in other industries will compensate for the losses in one industry.

The correct answer is C.

87. In the United States, of the people who moved from one state to another when they retired, the percentage who retired to Florida has decreased by three percentage points over the past ten years. Since many local businesses in Florida cater to retirees, these declines are likely to have a noticeably negative economic effect on these businesses and therefore on the economy of Florida.

Which of the following, if true, most seriously weakens the argument given?

(A) People who moved from one state to another when they retired moved a greater distance, on average, last year than such people did ten years ago.

(B) People were more likely to retire to North Carolina from another state last year than people were ten years ago.

(C) The number of people who moved from one state to another when they retired has increased significantly over the past ten years.

(D) The number of people who left Florida when they retired to live in another state was greater last year than it was ten years ago.

(E) Florida attracts more people who move from one state to another when they retire than does any other state.

Argument Evaluation

Situation   Of those people who move to another state when they retire, the percentage moving to Florida has declined. This trend is apt to harm Florida's economy because many businesses there cater to retirees.

Reasoning   *Which of the options most weakens the argument?* The argument draws its conclusion from data about the *proportion* of emigrating retirees moving to Florida. Yet what matters more directly to the conclusion (and to Florida's economy) is the *absolute number* of retirees immigrating to Florida. That number could have remained constant or even risen if the absolute number of emigrating retirees itself increased while the proportion going to Florida decreased.

A   This has no obvious bearing on the argument one way or another. It makes it more likely, perhaps, that a person in a distant state will retire to Florida, but less likely that one in a neighboring state will do so.

B   This has no bearing whether fewer people have been retiring to Florida over the last ten years.

C   **Correct.** This is the option that most seriously weakens the argument.

D   This makes it *more* likely that Florida's economy will be harmed because of decreasing numbers of retirees, but has no real bearing on the argument which concludes specifically that *declines in the proportion of emigrating retirees moving to Florida* will have a negative effect on the state's economy.

E   This is irrelevant. At issue is how the numbers of retirees in Florida from one year compare to the next, not how those numbers compare with numbers of retirees in other states.

The correct answer is C.

88. Businesses are suffering because of a lack of money available for development loans. To help businesses, the government plans to modify the income-tax structure in order to induce individual taxpayers to put a larger portion of their incomes into retirement savings accounts, because as more money is deposited in such accounts, more money becomes available to borrowers.

Which of the following, if true, raises the most serious doubt regarding the effectiveness of the government's plan to increase the amount of money available for development loans for businesses?

(A) When levels of personal retirement savings increase, consumer borrowing always increases correspondingly.

(B) The increased tax revenue the government would receive as a result of business expansion would not offset the loss in revenue from personal income taxes during the first year of the plan.

(C) Even with tax incentives, some people will choose not to increase their levels of retirement savings.

(D) Bankers generally will not continue to lend money to businesses whose prospective earnings are insufficient to meet their loan repayment schedules.

(E) The modified tax structure would give all taxpayers, regardless of their incomes, the same tax savings for a given increase in their retirement savings.

Evaluation of a Plan

Situation   Because the lack of available money for development loans is harming businesses, the government plans to modify the income-tax structure, encouraging taxpayers to put more money into retirement accounts. This plan is intended to ensure that with more money put into these accounts, more money will in turn be available to business borrowers.

Reasoning   *What potential flaw in this plan might prevent it from being effective?* What is the expectation behind the plan? The government's plan supposes that the money invested in retirement accounts will be available to business borrowers in the form of development loans. Consider what circumstances might hinder that availability. What if consumer borrowers compete with businesses? If it is known that, historically, increased savings in personal retirement accounts corresponds with increased consumer borrowing, then the government's effort to target businesses as the beneficiaries of this plan could well fail.

A   **Correct.** This statement properly identifies a reason that the government's plan could be less effective in meeting its goal.

B   A predicted revenue shortfall does not directly affect the plan's effectiveness in reaching its stated goal, and might be deemed an acceptable cost of achieving that goal.

C   As long as the total amount deposited in personal retirement accounts increases sufficiently, the decision of *some people* not to increase their contributions will not keep the plan from achieving its goal.

D   The plan would increase the money available specifically for development loans, not existing loans.

E   The universal tax savings does not affect the effectiveness of the plan.

The correct answer is A.

89. Since it has become known that **several of a bank's top executives have been buying shares in their own bank**, the bank's depositors, who had been worried by rumors that the bank faced impending financial collapse, have been greatly relieved. They reason that, since top executives evidently have faith in the bank's financial soundness, those worrisome rumors must be false. Such reasoning might well be overoptimistic, however, since **corporate executives have been known to buy shares in their own company in a calculated attempt to dispel negative rumors about the company's health**.

    In the argument given, the two boldfaced portions play which of the following roles?

    (A) The first describes evidence that has been taken as supporting a conclusion; the second gives a reason for questioning that support.

    (B) The first describes evidence that has been taken as supporting a conclusion; the second states a contrary conclusion that is the main conclusion of the argument.

    (C) The first provides evidence in support of the main conclusion of the argument; the second states that conclusion.

    (D) The first describes the circumstance that the argument as a whole seeks to explain; the second gives the explanation that the argument seeks to establish.

    (E) The first describes the circumstance that the argument as a whole seeks to explain; the second provides evidence in support of the explanation that the argument seeks to establish.

Argument Evaluation

Situation   Top executives at a bank that has been rumored to be in financial trouble have been buying shares in the bank. Bank depositors see this as a good sign, because they believe that it indicates that the executives have faith in the bank. However, corporate executives sometimes do this just to dispel rumors about a company's health.

Reasoning   *What is the role that the two boldfaced portions play in the argument?* The first boldfaced portion states that bank executives are buying bank shares, which the passage indicates is taken by bank depositors to be evidence of the executives' faith in the bank. The passage then tells us what some have inferred from this, and finally offers in the second boldfaced statement evidence that undermines this inference.

A   **Correct.** This option correctly identifies the roles played by the boldfaced portions.

B   This correctly describes the first statement's role, but the second statement is not offered as a conclusion—no evidence is given for it; rather it is evidence for something else.

C   Again, the second statement is not offered as a conclusion; no evidence is given for it.

D   The second statement is not itself offered as an explanation of why these bank executives are investing in the bank; if it were, that would mean that the bank executives are doing so *because* corporate executives are known to do such things in a calculated effort to dispel worries. Furthermore the argument does not conclude that this other explanation (which the boldfaced portion points to) is correct, only that the one inferred by depositors may not be.

E   Again, the argument is not so much seeking to establish an explanation of its own as it is trying to undermine that inferred by the depositors.

The correct answer is A.

90. A new law gives ownership of patents—documents providing exclusive right to make and sell an invention—to universities, not the government, when those patents result from government-sponsored university research. Administrators at Logos University plan to sell any patents they acquire to corporations in order to fund programs to improve undergraduate teaching.

Which of the following, if true, would cast the most doubt on the viability of the college administrators' plan described above?

(A) Profit-making corporations interested in developing products based on patents held by universities are likely to try to serve as exclusive sponsors of ongoing university research projects.

(B) Corporate sponsors of research in university facilities are entitled to tax credits under new federal tax-code guidelines.

(C) Research scientists at Logos University have few or no teaching responsibilities and participate little if at all in the undergraduate programs in their field.

(D) Government-sponsored research conducted at Logos University for the most part duplicates research already completed by several profit-making corporations.

(E) Logos University is unlikely to attract corporate sponsorship of its scientific research.

Evaluation of a Plan

Situation   Universities own the patents resulting from government-sponsored research at their institutions. One university plans to sell its patents to corporations to fund a program to improve teaching.

Reasoning   *Which point casts doubt on the university's plan?* The university's plan assumes there will be a market for its patents, and that the corporations will want to buy them. What might make this untrue? If some of the corporations have already done the same or similar research, they will not be prospective buyers of the university's patents.

A   This point is irrelevant to the plan to sell patents in order to fund a program.

B   The university plans to sell the patents to the corporations, not to invite the corporations to sponsor research.

C   This point is irrelevant to the university's plan to sell off patents since the plan does not specify that the research scientists will be involved in the programs to improve undergraduate teaching.

D   Correct. This statement properly identifies a factor that casts doubt on the university's plan to sell its patents to corporations.

E   The plan concerns selling patents resulting from government-sponsored research, not attracting corporate sponsorship for research.

The correct answer is D.

91. Environmentalist: The commissioner of the Fish and Game Authority would have the public believe that increases in the number of marine fish caught demonstrate that this resource is no longer endangered. This is a specious argument, as unsound as it would be to assert that the ever-increasing rate at which rain forests are being cut down demonstrates a lack of danger to that resource. The real cause of the increased fish-catch is a greater efficiency in using technologies that deplete resources.

The environmentalist's statements, if true, best support which of the following as a conclusion?

(A) The use of technology is the reason for the increasing encroachment of people on nature.

(B) It is possible to determine how many fish are in the sea in some way other than by catching fish.

(C) The proportion of marine fish that are caught is as high as the proportion of rain forest trees that are cut down each year.

(D) Modern technologies waste resources by catching inedible fish.

(E) Marine fish continue to be an endangered resource.

Argument Construction

Situation   A public official argues that increased catches show that marine fish are no longer endangered. An environmentalist attacks the position and cites technology as the cause of the increased catch.

Reasoning   *What conclusion do the environmentalist's statements support?* The environmentalist casts doubt by saying the commissioner *would have the public believe* that the increased catch shows that the fish are no longer endangered; the phrasing indicates that the environmentalist believes just the reverse. The environmentalist does believe the marine fish are endangered, and, after attacking the commissioner's argument as *specious,* or false, and offering an analogy to make that argument look ridiculous, the environmentalist gives an alternate explanation for the increased catch that is consistent with that belief.

A   Although the environmentalist claims that technology causes people's greater encroachment on nature in this single instance, there is nothing in the argument to suggest that such encroachment caused by technology is a general trend.

B   The environmentalist's claims imply that the number of fish caught is not a reliable indicator of how many are left in the ocean but do not give any indication that it is possible to find out by any other means, either.

C   The environmentalist creates an analogy between fish caught and rain forest trees cut down but does not compare their proportion.

D   Nothing about how the fish can be used, including whether they are edible or inedible, plays any role in the environmentalist's argument.

E   **Correct.** This statement properly identifies a conclusion supported by the environmentalist's statements: The marine fish are endangered.

The correct answer is E.

92. In the country of Veltria, the past two years' broad economic recession has included a business downturn in the clothing trade, where sales are down by about 7 percent as compared to two years ago. Clothing wholesalers have found, however, that the proportion of credit extended to retailers that was paid off on time fell sharply in the first year of the recession but returned to its prerecession level in the second year.

    Which of the following, if true, most helps to explain the change between the first and the second year of the recession in the proportion of credit not paid off on time?

    (A) The total amount of credit extended to retailers by clothing wholesalers increased between the first year of the recession and the second year.

    (B) Between the first and second years of the recession, clothing retailers in Veltria saw many of their costs, rent and utilities in particular, increase.

    (C) Of the considerable number of clothing retailers in Veltria who were having financial difficulties before the start of the recession, virtually all were forced to go out of business during its first year.

    (D) Clothing retailers in Veltria attempted to stimulate sales in the second year of the recession by discounting merchandise.

    (E) Relatively recession-proof segments of the clothing trade, such as work clothes, did not suffer any decrease in sales during the first year of the recession.

Argument Evaluation

Situation   Two years of recession in Veltria included a downturn in the clothing trade where sales are down 7 percent from two years ago. Yet, in the second year of the recession, the proportion of credit extended from clothing wholesalers to retailers that was paid off on time has returned to its prerecession level, after having fallen sharply during the first year.

Reasoning   *Which option would most help to explain the change between the first and second year in the proportion of credit paid off on time?* The apparent discrepancy in the passage that needs explaining is between the downturn in the clothing trade over the last two years and the return to prerecession rates in the proportion of credit extended to clothing retailers that was paid on time. How can the proportion this past year be similar to what it would be in a normal year? After all, one would expect retailers to have a harder time paying off credit in a recession. And what changed in the past year to bring this about? If the first year of the recession drove out of business many of the retailers who were most apt to get behind in their payments to wholesalers, then that would explain how the rate at which credit was being paid on time could be as high in the second year of the recession as it was before the recession.

A   The fact that the absolute amount of credit that was extended to retailers went up in the second year does not help to explain why the *proportion that was paid on time* also went up.

B   If anything, this would suggest that more retailers would have trouble paying their credit to wholesalers on time.

C   **Correct.** This is the option that most helps to explain the phenomenon.

D   Just because retailers *tried* to stimulate sales does not mean that they succeeded, and the passage tells us that the downturn in sales in the clothing trade continued into the second year.

E   This does not change the fact that there was a downturn in sales of clothing during the first year. Furthermore, the question is why the rate of unpaid credit dropped in the *second* year of the recession.

The correct answer is C.

93. Commentator: The theory of trade retaliation states that countries closed out of any of another country's markets should close some of their own markets to the other country in order to pressure the other country to reopen its markets. If every country acted according to this theory, no country would trade with any other.

The commentator's argument relies on which of the following assumptions?

(A) No country actually acts according to the theory of trade retaliation.

(B) No country should block any of its markets to foreign trade.

(C) Trade disputes should be settled by international tribunal.

(D) For any two countries, at least one has some market closed to the other.

(E) Countries close their markets to foreigners to protect domestic producers.

Argument Construction

Situation The theory of trade retaliation is explained as the action and reaction of closing markets between trading nations; no country would ever trade with another, the observation is offered, if every country acted according to the theory.

Reasoning *What assumption underlies this argument?* What makes the commentator conclude that no country would be trading if the theory were operative? The commentator must perceive of some condition as a given here. The argument assumes an initial action, a country's closing of a market to a trading partner, that is followed by a reaction, the retaliatory closing of a market by that partner. In this unending pattern of action-reaction, at least one of the two countries must have a market closed to the other.

A The argument does not assume that no country acts according to the theory, just that not all countries do so.

B The commentator's argument is about what the theory of trade retaliation predicts, not about what trade policies countries ought to follow, and a statement about the latter is not an assumption for the former.

C This alternative scenario—trade disputes settled by international tribunal rather than by trade retaliation—plays no role in the argument.

D Correct. This statement properly identifies the assumption required to create the never-ending action-reaction pattern.

E The argument does not pertain to countries' initial reasons for closing their markets to foreign trade, only to the consequences of doing so.

The correct answer is D.

94. Studies in restaurants show that the tips left by customers who pay their bill in cash tend to be larger when the bill is presented on a tray that bears a credit-card logo. Consumer psychologists hypothesize that simply seeing a credit-card logo makes many credit-card holders willing to spend more because it reminds them that their spending power exceeds the cash they have immediately available.

Which of the following, if true, most strongly supports the psychologists' interpretation of the studies?

(A) The effect noted in the studies is not limited to patrons who have credit cards.

(B) Patrons who are under financial pressure from their credit-card obligations tend to tip less when presented with a restaurant bill on a tray with a credit-card logo than when the tray has no logo.

(C) In virtually all of the cases in the studies, the patrons who paid bills in cash did not possess credit cards.

(D) In general, restaurant patrons who pay their bills in cash leave larger tips than do those who pay by credit card.

(E) The percentage of restaurant bills paid with a given brand of credit card increases when that credit card's logo is displayed on the tray with which the bill is presented.

Argument Evaluation

Situation   Studies have found that restaurant customers give more generous tips when their bills are brought on trays bearing a credit-card logo. Psychologists speculate that this is because the logo reminds customers of their ability to spend more money than they have.

Reasoning   *Which of the options most helps to support the psychologists' explanation of the studies?* The psychologists' hypothesis is that the credit-card logos on the trays bring to the minds of those who tip more the fact that they have more purchasing power than merely the cash that they have at hand. This explanation would not be valid even if those people who are *not* reminded of their own excess purchasing power—if in fact they have any such power—when they see such a logo nonetheless tip more in such trays. Thus, if restaurant patrons who are under financial pressure from their credit-card obligations do not tip more when their bills are presented on trays bearing credit-card logos, then the psychologists' interpretation of the studies is supported.

A   This undermines the psychologists' interpretation, for it shows that the same phenomenon occurs even when the alleged cause has been removed.

B   **Correct.** This option identifies the result that would most strengthen the psychologists' interpretation.

C   This undermines the psychologists' interpretation by showing that the same phenomenon occurs even when the alleged cause has been removed; patrons cannot be reminded of something that is not there.

D   To the extent that this bears on the interpretation of the study, it weakens it. Patrons *using* credit cards are surely aware that they have credit, and yet they spend *less* generously.

E   This does not support the idea that being reminded that one has a credit card induces one to be *more generous*, only that it induces one to *use* that credit card.

The correct answer is B.

95. Although parapsychology is often considered a pseudoscience, it is in fact a genuine scientific enterprise, for it uses scientific methods such as controlled experiments and statistical tests of clearly stated hypotheses to examine the questions it raises.

The conclusion above is properly drawn if which of the following is assumed?

(A) If a field of study can conclusively answer the questions it raises, then it is a genuine science.

(B) Since parapsychology uses scientific methods, it will produce credible results.

(C) Any enterprise that does not use controlled experiments and statistical tests is not genuine science.

(D) Any field of study that employs scientific methods is a genuine scientific enterprise.

(E) Since parapsychology raises clearly statable questions, they can be tested in controlled experiments.

Argument Construction

Situation   The argument states that parapsychology is a genuine science because it uses scientific methods.

Reasoning   *What assumption does the argument make?* The argument asserts that parapsychology is a science, *for it uses scientific methods.* The argument thus assumes that the use of scientific methods proves that a field of study is a genuine science.

A   The argument is based on an assumption about how the questions are investigated rather than on how well they are answered.

B   The argument is not about whether the results are credible, so this assumption is irrelevant.

C   The argument does not concern what is *not* genuine science, so there is no need for this assumption.

D   **Correct.** This statement properly identifies the argument's assumption that the use of scientific method is sufficient to make an enterprise genuine science.

E   This assumption does not make the connection required by the argument between the use of scientific methods and a field of study's status as genuine science.

The correct answer is D.

96. Hotco oil burners, designed to be used in asphalt plants, are so efficient that Hotco will sell one to the Clifton Asphalt plant for no payment other than the cost savings between the total amount the asphalt plant actually paid for oil using its former burner during the last two years and the total amount it will pay for oil using the Hotco burner during the next two years. On installation, the plant will make an estimated payment, which will be adjusted after two years to equal the actual cost savings.

Which of the following, if it occurred, would constitute a disadvantage for Hotco of the plan described above?

(A) Another manufacturer's introduction to the market of a similarly efficient burner

(B) The Clifton Asphalt plant's need for more than one new burner

(C) Very poor efficiency in the Clifton Asphalt plant's old burner

(D) A decrease in the demand for asphalt

(E) A steady increase in the price of oil beginning soon after the new burner is installed

Evaluation of a Plan

Situation   Hotco produces a very efficient oil burner. It sells a burner to an asphalt plant, stating that the price of the burner is how much money the plant saves on oil using the new burner.

Reasoning   *Hotco will be at a disadvantage if which of the following occurs?* Hotco is to be paid based on how much money the plant saves on oil over a two-year period. There is an assumption that a number of factors will remain relatively stable from the previous two years to the next two years. What is a factor that could cause a disadvantage for Hotco? If the price of oil goes up, then the plant will experience smaller savings than Hotco anticipated, despite the plant's using less oil than previously because of its new, more efficient burners. If the plant's savings go down, Hotco will not get the payment it is expecting.

A   The burner is already installed, so a competitor is not a problem.

B   The plant's need for multiple burners should be an opportunity for Hotco, not a disadvantage.

C   If the old burner was very inefficient, the new burner should save a great deal of money that would ultimately go to Hotco.

D   If demand decreases, less oil would need to be purchased, and Hotco would get more money.

E   **Correct.** This statement properly identifies a factor that would constitute a disadvantage for the plan: since the payment for the burner is based on savings in oil purchases, any increases in the price of oil will decrease savings and thus decrease payments to Hotco.

The correct answer is E.

97. **Delta Products Inc. has recently switched at least partly from older technologies using fossil fuels to new technologies powered by electricity.** The question has been raised whether it can be concluded that **for a given level of output Delta's operation now causes less fossil fuel to be consumed than it did formerly.** The answer, clearly, is yes, since the amount of fossil fuel used to generate the electricity needed to power the new technologies is less than the amount needed to power the older technologies, provided level of output is held constant.

In the argument given, the two boldfaced portions play which of the following roles?

(A) The first identifies the content of the conclusion of the argument; the second provides support for that conclusion.

(B) The first provides support for the conclusion of the argument; the second identifies the content of that conclusion.

(C) The first states the conclusion of the argument; the second calls that conclusion into question.

(D) The first provides support for the conclusion of the argument; the second calls that conclusion into question.

(E) Each provides support for the conclusion of the argument.

Argument Evaluation

Situation   Delta switched from technologies using fossil fuels to ones using electricity. It has been asked whether this results in less fossil fuel used per level of output. The answer is that it does.

Reasoning   *What roles do the two boldfaced portions play in the argument?* The first boldfaced statement is simply asserted by the passage. But the second boldfaced statement, when it is first introduced, is not asserted to be true, but rather is identified as something that might be inferred from the first statement. By the end of the passage the argument concludes that the second statement is true.

A   This option simply reverses the roles that the statements play in the argument.

B   **Correct.** This option identifies the roles the boldfaced portions play.

C   Nothing in the passage is intended to support the first statement; and the second statement is not supposed to call the first into question.

D   This correctly identifies the role of the first statement, but the second boldfaced portion does not call the argument's conclusion into question—it is part of a sentence that refers to the question whether that conclusion can be drawn from the first statement.

E   Again, this is only half right. The second boldfaced portion is not offered as support for the conclusion; if it were offered as such support, the argument would be guilty of circular reasoning, since the second boldfaced portion states exactly what the argument concludes.

The correct answer is B.

98. An experiment was done in which human subjects recognize a pattern within a matrix of abstract designs and then select another design that completes that pattern. The results of the experiment were surprising. The lowest expenditure of energy in neurons in the brain was found in those subjects who performed most successfully in the experiments.

    Which of the following hypotheses best accounts for the findings of the experiment?

    (A) The neurons of the brain react less when a subject is trying to recognize patterns than when the subject is doing other kinds of reasoning.
    (B) Those who performed best in the experiment experienced more satisfaction when working with abstract patterns than did those who performed less well.
    (C) People who are better at abstract pattern recognition have more energy-efficient neural connections.
    (D) The energy expenditure of the subjects' brains increases when a design that completes the initially recognized pattern is determined.
    (E) The task of completing a given design is more capably performed by athletes, whose energy expenditure is lower when they are at rest.

Argument Construction

Situation   Experimental subjects worked with pattern recognition and completion. The subjects who performed best showed the lowest expenditure of energy in neurons in the brain.

Reasoning   *Which hypothesis best accounts for the findings?* In order to account for the findings, the hypothesis must suggest a plausible link between successful performance and the energy expenditure of neurons in the brain. Consider each answer choice, and evaluate its plausibility and logic. Where is there a reasonably direct relationship between the given factors and the conclusion that is drawn? Understand that hypotheses based on factors not included in the experiment cannot be used to account for the findings.

A   The experiment did not compare types of reasoning so this hypothesis does not account for the results.

B   No information is provided about subjects' satisfaction, so this hypothesis is not warranted.

C   **Correct.** This statement properly identifies a hypothesis that connects subjects' performance with their energy expenditure and so could account for the experiment's results.

D   The most successful subjects would presumably not have completed fewer patterns than average, so the posited increase in energy would likely lead to higher energy expenditures for them, not lower.

E   No information is offered on the subjects, so no hypothesis about athletes is warranted.

The correct answer is C.

99. Which of the following most logically completes the argument?

The irradiation of food kills bacteria and thus retards spoilage. However, it also lowers the nutritional value of many foods. For example, irradiation destroys a significant percentage of whatever vitamin B1 a food may contain. Proponents of irradiation point out that irradiation is no worse in this respect than cooking. However, this fact is either beside the point, since much irradiated food is eaten raw, or else misleading, since _____.

(A) many of the proponents of irradiation are food distributors who gain from foods' having a longer shelf life

(B) it is clear that killing bacteria that may be present on food is not the only effect that irradiation has

(C) cooking is usually the final step in preparing food for consumption, whereas irradiation serves to ensure a longer shelf life for perishable foods

(D) certain kinds of cooking are, in fact, even more destructive of vitamin B1 than carefully controlled irradiation is

(E) for food that is both irradiated and cooked, the reduction of vitamin B1 associated with either process individually is compounded

Argument Construction

Situation Irradiation kills bacteria but it also lowers the amount of nutrients—including vitamin B1—in foods. Proponents try to dismiss this concern by arguing that cooking destroys B1 as well. That point is said to be misleading.

Reasoning *Which option most logically completes the argument?* For the proponents' claim to be misleading it needs to be suggesting something about irradiation that is false. By stating that irradiation destroys no more B1 than cooking does, the proponent seems to be suggesting that any food that is going to be cooked might as well be irradiated because it will end up with the same amount of B1 either way. But if the effects of radiation and cooking combine to destroy more B1 than cooking or irradiation alone would, then the proponents' claim suggests something that is false.

A This might make the assurances of the proponents less credible but it does not make their claim misleading.

B Nothing about the proponents' claim suggests that the only effect irradiation has is to kill bacteria.

C The fact that cooking and irradiation have different purposes does not indicate that the proponents' claim suggests something that is false.

D If anything, this strengthens the proponents' point by minimizing the relative damage caused by irradiation.

E **Correct.** This option most logically completes the argument.

The correct answer is E.

100. One way to judge the performance of a company is to compare it with other companies. This technique, commonly called "benchmarking," permits the manager of a company to discover better industrial practices and can provide a justification for the adoption of good practices.

Any of the following, if true, is a valid reason for benchmarking the performance of a company against companies with which it is not in competition rather than against competitors EXCEPT:

(A) Comparisons with competitors are most likely to focus on practices that the manager making the comparisons already employs.

(B) Getting "inside" information about the unique practices of competitors is particularly difficult.

(C) Since companies that compete with each other are likely to have comparable levels of efficiency, only benchmarking against noncompetitors is likely to reveal practices that would aid in beating competitors.

(D) Managers are generally more receptive to new ideas that they find outside their own industry.

(E) Much of the success of good companies is due to their adoption of practices that take advantage of the special circumstances of their products or markets.

Argument Construction

Situation   "Benchmarking" is a technique for judging the performance of a company by comparing it with other companies. The goal is to find and adopt better industrial practices.

Reasoning   *Which one condition does NOT recommend benchmarking against noncompetitors? Which one condition IS a well-founded reason to benchmark against competitors?* First, sort through the given information and the answer choices for the question to gain an understanding of the potential advantages or disadvantages of comparing a company to its competitors or to noncompetitors. What are the reasons in favor of benchmarking against noncompetitors? Information about noncompeting companies is easier to obtain; it can offer new insights; and it may be easier to put into practice. Why then might a manager choose to benchmark against competitors? Competing companies do share special circumstances involving products and markets. If companies are often successful because of practices related to these special circumstances within their industry, then benchmarking against competitors will reveal these practices and so be more fruitful than benchmarking against noncompetitors.

A   Since benchmarking against competitors would yield few new practices, it would be better to benchmark against noncompetitors.

B   If information about competitors is hard to obtain, benchmarking against noncompetitors is preferable.

C   Since benchmarking against noncompetitors would yield practices useful in beating competitors, benchmarking against noncompetitors is preferable.

D   If managers are more likely to adopt new practices learned from benchmarking against noncompetitors, then this technique is preferable.

E   **Correct.** This statement properly identifies the rationale that supports a company's benchmarking against its competitors.

The correct answer is E.

101. For a trade embargo against a particular country to succeed, a high degree of both international accord and ability to prevent goods from entering or leaving that country must be sustained. A total blockade of Patria's ports is necessary to an embargo, but such an action would be likely to cause international discord over the embargo.

The claims above, if true, most strongly support which of the following conclusions?

(A) The balance of opinion is likely to favor Patria in the event of a blockade.

(B) As long as international opinion is unanimously against Patria, a trade embargo is likely to succeed.

(C) A naval blockade of Patria's ports would ensure that no goods enter or leave Patria.

(D) Any trade embargo against Patria would be likely to fail at some time.

(E) For a blockade of Patria's ports to be successful, international opinion must be unanimous.

Argument Construction

Situation   The success of a trade embargo requires both international accord and the ability to enforce the embargo. In the case of Patria, an embargo would require a total blockade of the ports, but the blockade itself would likely lead to international discord.

Reasoning   *What conclusion can be drawn from this information?* A conclusion must be based only on the information provided. Since the given information discusses the general conditions for a successful trade embargo and the conditions specific to the possible embargo in Patria, the conclusion should be about the likelihood of success for a trade embargo against Patria. Since international accord is necessary for the success of an embargo but the blockade required in this case would create international discord, the contradictions of this paradoxical situation make any embargo unlikely to succeed.

A   Although international discord would likely result from a blockade, no information allows a conclusion to be drawn about the balance of opinion.

B   This conclusion is not justified because a successful embargo requires both international accord and the ability to enforce the embargo.

C   This statement simply defines the purpose of a blockade; it is not a conclusion from the information given.

D   **Correct.** This statement properly identifies a conclusion supported by the claims.

E   The necessary condition for success is *a high degree of international accord*, not unanimity, so this conclusion cannot be justified.

The correct answer is D.

102. Theater Critic: The play *La Finestrina*, now at Central Theater, was written in Italy in the eighteenth century. The director claims that this production is as similar to the original production as is possible in a modern theater. Although the actor who plays Harlequin the clown gives a performance very reminiscent of the twentieth-century American comedian Groucho Marx, Marx's comic style was very much within the comic acting tradition that had begun in sixteenth-century Italy.

The considerations given best serve as part of an argument that

(A) modern audiences would find it hard to tolerate certain characteristics of a historically accurate performance of an eighteenth-century play

(B) Groucho Marx once performed the part of the character Harlequin in *La Finestrina*

(C) in the United States the training of actors in the twentieth century is based on principles that do not differ radically from those that underlay the training of actors in eighteenth-century Italy

(D) the performance of the actor who plays Harlequin in *La Finestrina* does not serve as evidence against the director's claim

(E) the director of *La Finestrina* must have advised the actor who plays Harlequin to model his performance on comic performances of Groucho Marx

Argument Construction

Situation The director of the local production of *La Finestrina* says it is as similar to the original production as is possible in a modern theater. The actor playing Harlequin gives a performance reminiscent of Groucho Marx, whose comic style falls within an acting tradition which began in sixteenth-century Italy.

Reasoning *For which of the options would the consideration given best serve as an argument?* The actor's performance was reminiscent of someone who fell within a tradition going back to sixteenth-century Italy. The play was written, and therefore was likely first performed, in eighteenth-century Italy. All of this suggests that there could be a similarity between the performances of Harlequin in the local production and in the original production. While the two performances *might* have been quite dissimilar, there is nothing *here* that supports that.

A   Regardless of how plausible this option might be on its own merits, the passage provides no support for it because the passage provides no information about the characteristics of a historically accurate performance of an eighteenth-century play.

B   The passage neither says this nor implies it.

C   The passage says nothing about the training of actors, so this option would be supported by the passage only in a very roundabout, indirect way.

D   **Correct.** This is the option that the considerations most support.

E   That the performance reminded the theater critic of Groucho Marx hardly shows that the similarity was intentional, let alone that it was at the director's instruction.

The correct answer is D.

103. The cost of producing radios in Country Q is 10 percent less than the cost of producing radios in Country Y. Even after transportation fees and tariff charges are added, it is still cheaper for a company to import radios from Country Q to Country Y than to produce radios in Country Y.

The statements above, if true, best support which of the following assertions?

(A) Labor costs in Country Q are 10 percent below those in Country Y.

(B) Importing radios from Country Q to Country Y will eliminate 10 percent of the manufacturing jobs in Country Y.

(C) The tariff on a radio imported from Country Q to Country Y is less than 10 percent of the cost of manufacturing the radio in Country Y.

(D) The fee for transporting a radio from Country Q to Country Y is more than 10 percent of the cost of manufacturing the radio in Country Q.

(E) It takes 10 percent less time to manufacture a radio in Country Q than it does in Country Y.

Argument Construction

Situation   One country's manufacturing costs for a product are 10 percent higher than another country's. Even with tariffs and transportation costs, importing is a less expensive option than local production.

Reasoning   *What conclusion can be drawn from this information?* Because production costs are 10 percent higher in Country Y than in Country Q, importing radios is less expensive only if the combined costs of tariffs and transportation are less than 10 percent of the manufacturing costs.

A   Lower labor costs may explain the lower production costs in Country Q, but there may be a variety of other reasons as well.

B   It is possible that manufacturing jobs would be decreased, but no evidence in the passage leads to that conclusion.

C   **Correct.** This statement properly identifies the point that, for importing to be less expensive, tariffs and transportation costs together must be less than 10 percent of manufacturing costs. Therefore, tariffs alone must be less than 10 percent

D   If transportation costs were more than 10 percent, importing would be more expensive, not less.

E   Less production time may explain the lower costs in Country Q, but there may be a variety of other reasons as well.

The correct answer is C.

104. Although the discount stores in Goreville's central shopping district are expected to close within five years as a result of competition from a SpendLess discount department store that just opened, those locations will not stay vacant for long. In the five years since the opening of Colson's, a nondiscount department store, a new store has opened at the location of every store in the shopping district that closed because it could not compete with Colson's.

Which of the following, if true, most seriously weakens the argument?

(A) Many customers of Colson's are expected to do less shopping there than they did before the SpendLess store opened.

(B) Increasingly, the stores that have opened in the central shopping district since Colson's opened have been discount stores.

(C) At present, the central shopping district has as many stores operating in it as it ever had.

(D) Over the course of the next five years, it is expected that Goreville's population will grow at a faster rate than it has for the past several decades.

(E) Many stores in the central shopping district sell types of merchandise that are not available at either SpendLess or Colson's.

Argument Evaluation

Situation Due to competition from a recently opened SpendLess discount department store, discount stores in Goreville's central shopping district are expected to close within five years. But those locations will not be vacant long, for new stores have replaced all those that closed because of the opening five years ago of a Colson's nondiscount department store.

Reasoning *The question is which option would most weaken the argument?* The arguer infers that stores that leave because of the SpendLess will be replaced in their locations by other stores because that is what happened after the Colson's department came in. Since the reasoning relies on a presumed similarity between the two cases, any information that brings to light a relevant dissimilarity would weaken the argument. If the stores that were driven out by Colson's were replaced mostly by discount stores, that suggests that the stores were replaced because of a need that no longer exists after the opening of SpendLess.

A The fact that Colson's may be seeing fewer customers does not mean that the discount stores that close will not be replaced; they might be replaced by stores that in no way compete with Colson's or SpendLess.

B **Correct.** This option most seriously weakens the argument.

C If anything, this strengthens the argument by indicating that Goreville's central shopping district is thriving.

D This, too, strengthens the argument because one is more likely to open a new store in an area with a growing population.

E Because this statement does not indicate whether any of these stores that offer goods not sold at SpendLess or Colson's will be among those that are closing, it is not possible to determine what effect it has on the strength of the argument.

The correct answer is B.

105. The average normal infant born in the United States weighs between 12 and 14 pounds at the age of three months. Therefore, if a three-month-old child weighs only 10 pounds, its weight gain has been below the United States average.

Which of the following indicates a flaw in the reasoning above?

(A)   Weight is only one measure of normal infant development.
(B)   Some three-month-old children weigh as much as 17 pounds.
(C)   It is possible for a normal child to weigh 10 pounds at birth.
(D)   The phrase "below average" does not necessarily mean insufficient.
(E)   Average weight gain is not the same as average weight.

Argument Evaluation

Situation   An infant's low weight at three months, compared with the national average, shows that the child's weight gain has not been average.

Reasoning   *How is this reasoning flawed?* The conclusion relies on a direct connection between average weight and average weight gain. While the infant's weight is known to be below average for a three-month-old child, no conclusion can be drawn about this infant's weight gain. No information is given about average birth weights or average weight gains.

A   The passage does not say that weight is the sole measure of development; this statement fails to point out any error in the reasoning.

B   The greater weight of some infants would be calculated in reaching the average.

C   This birth weight may be consistent with the weight range at three months; not enough information is provided to make a judgment.

D   The passage does not claim that *below average* is the same as *insufficient*, so pointing out the distinction does not show an error in the reasoning.

E   **Correct.** This statement properly identifies the logical flaw in the reasoning, which takes evidence about average weight to draw a conclusion about average weight gain. The two measures are not the same.

The correct answer is E.

106. Kale has more nutritional value than spinach. But since collard greens have more nutritional value than lettuce, it follows that kale has more nutritional value than lettuce.

Any of the following, if introduced into the argument as an additional premise, makes the argument above logically correct EXCEPT:

(A) Collard greens have more nutritional value than kale.

(B) Spinach has more nutritional value than lettuce.

(C) Spinach has more nutritional value than collard greens.

(D) Spinach and collard greens have the same nutritional value.

(E) Kale and collard greens have the same nutritional value.

Argument Construction

Situation   Using the symbol > to mean "has (or have) more nutritional value than," this statement can be expressed as kale > spinach, and collard greens > lettuce. The conclusion that kale > lettuce remains valid if all but one of the premises is added.

Reasoning   *Which premise makes the conclusion incorrect?* The information given in the passage is that kale > spinach and that collard greens > lettuce. This is not enough to conclude that kale > lettuce; another premise is needed to establish the relative nutritional value of kale and lettuce. Look at each premise offered in the answers to see whether the conclusion kale > lettuce remains valid. The ranking of vegetables may change with the additional premises; the conclusion, kale > lettuce, must not change. Find the one answer that does NOT support the conclusion.

A   **Correct.** This statement properly identifies an additional premise that would invalidate the argument. If collard greens > kale, then it is possible that lettuce > kale, because the ranking could be collard greens > lettuce > kale > spinach.

B   If spinach > lettuce, then kale > lettuce because kale > spinach.

C   If spinach > collard greens, then kale > lettuce because the ranking would then be kale > spinach > collard greens > lettuce.

D   If spinach = collard greens, then kale > lettuce because the ranking would be kale > spinach = collard greens > lettuce.

E   If kale = collard greens, then kale > lettuce because kale = collard greens > lettuce.

The correct answer is A.

107. Last year all refuse collected by Shelbyville city services was incinerated. This incineration generated a large quantity of residual ash. In order to reduce the amount of residual ash Shelbyville generates this year to half of last year's total, the city has revamped its collection program. This year city services will separate for recycling enough refuse to reduce the number of truckloads of refuse to be incinerated to half of last year's number.

Which of the following is required for the revamped collection program to achieve its aim?

(A) This year, no materials that city services could separate for recycling will be incinerated.

(B) Separating recyclable materials from materials to be incinerated will cost Shelbyville less than half what it cost last year to dispose of the residual ash.

(C) Refuse collected by city services will contain a larger proportion of recyclable materials this year than it did last year.

(D) The refuse incinerated this year will generate no more residual ash per truckload incinerated than did the refuse incinerated last year.

(E) The total quantity of refuse collected by Shelbyville city services this year will be no greater than that collected last year.

Argument Construction

Situation   To cut in half the residual ash produced at its incinerator, the city will separate for recycling enough refuse to cut in half the number of truckloads of refuse going to the incinerator.

Reasoning   *Which option is required if the city's revamped collection program is to achieve its aim?* Cutting the number of truckloads of refuse in half must reduce the amount of residual ash to half last year's level. But if removal of the recycled refuse does not proportionately reduce the amount of ash, this will not happen. So if the amount of residual ash produced per truckload increases after recycling, then the amount of ash produced will not be cut in half by cutting in half the number of truckloads.

A   This merely indicates that no further reduction of ash through recycling could be achieved this year; it indicates nothing about how much the ash will be reduced.

B   This suggests a further benefit from recycling, but does not bear on the amount of ash that will be produced.

C   Since no information is provided about how much, if any, recyclable materials were removed from the refuse last year, this does not affect the reasoning.

D   Correct. This states a requirement for the collection program to achieve its aim.

E   This is not a requirement because even if the city collects more refuse this year, it could still cut in half the amount of residual ash by cutting in half the number of truckloads going to the incinerator.

The correct answer is D.

108. Although custom prosthetic bone replacements produced through a new computer-aided design process will cost more than twice as much as ordinary replacements, custom replacements should still be cost-effective. Not only will surgery and recovery time be reduced, but custom replacements should last longer, thereby reducing the need for further hospital stays.

Which of the following must be studied in order to evaluate the argument presented above?

(A) The amount of time a patient spends in surgery versus the amount of time spent recovering from surgery

(B) The amount by which the cost of producing custom replacements has declined with the introduction of the new technique for producing them

(C) The degree to which the use of custom replacements is likely to reduce the need for repeat surgery when compared with the use of ordinary replacements

(D) The degree to which custom replacements produced with the new technique are more carefully manufactured than are ordinary replacements

(E) The amount by which custom replacements produced with the new technique will drop in cost as the production procedures become standardized and applicable on a larger scale

Argument Evaluation

Situation   Custom prosthetic bone replacements, although twice as expensive as ordinary replacements, should be cost-effective because they reduce the time of surgery, recovery, and potential future hospitalizations.

Reasoning   *What research study would help in evaluating this argument?* The custom replacements must be compared with the ordinary replacements on the basis of the costs of surgery, recovery, and potential repeat hospitalizations. Repeat surgery involves all three kinds of costs; the extent to which such repeat surgery can be avoided is a sound measure of the cost-effectiveness of the two types of replacements.

A   Comparing time in surgery with time in recovery does not lead to a conclusion about the two kinds of replacements and their cost-effectiveness.

B   The cost-effectiveness of the custom replacements is being projected in the current moment; a previous decline in production costs would already have been taken into account.

C   **Correct.** This statement properly identifies evidence of cost-effectiveness that would assist in evaluating the argument.

D   The analysis is about cost-effectiveness; it is not about the level of care taken in manufacture.

E   Anticipating a future drop in production costs is outside the scope of the analysis, which should be based on current conditions.

The correct answer is C.

109. Springfield Fire Commissioner: The vast majority of false fire alarms are prank calls made anonymously from fire alarm boxes on street corners. Since virtually everyone has access to a private telephone, these alarm boxes have outlived their usefulness. Therefore, we propose to remove the boxes. Removing the boxes will reduce the number of prank calls without hampering people's ability to report a fire.

Which of the following, if true, most strongly supports the claim that the proposal, if carried out, will have the announced effect?

(A) The fire department traces all alarm calls made from private telephones and records where they came from.

(B) Maintaining the fire alarm boxes costs Springfield approximately $5 million annually.

(C) A telephone call can provide the fire department with more information about the nature and size of a fire than can an alarm placed from an alarm box.

(D) Responding to false alarms significantly reduces the fire department's capacity for responding to fires.

(E) On any given day, a significant percentage of the public telephones in Springfield are out of service.

Argument Evaluation

Situation   It is proposed that fire alarm boxes on street corners be removed. Doing so will reduce the number of prank calls without hampering people's ability to report fires. Most false alarms are prank calls made from these boxes. They have outlived their usefulness, as most people now have private telephones.

Reasoning   *Which option most strongly supports the claim that removing the alarm boxes will reduce the number of prank calls without hampering people's ability to report a fire?* The argument already provides some evidence that (1) removing the boxes will reduce prank calls—because that is where most such call are now made from—and that (2) doing so will not hamper people's ability to report fires—virtually everyone already has a private telephone from which they could report a fire. So for an option to be correct it must support either (1) or (2) or both, and provide more such support than the other options. If prank calls from private telephones are traced back to their origin, that should deter people from making such calls.

A   **Correct.** This option provides the most support for the claim.

B   This may provide a reason for supporting the proposal, but it provides no support for either (1) or (2).

C   This indicates that it is better to receive fire calls from telephones than from alarm boxes—other things being equal—but that supports neither (1) nor (2). There is still the possibility that the only person aware that a fire has started is near an alarm box but lacks access to a telephone.

D   This merely indicates that it would be good if the proposal had the intended effects.

E   This actually *weakens* support for (2), by enhancing the possibility that the only person aware that a fire has started is near an alarm box but lacks access to a working telephone.

The correct answer is A.

110. Correctly measuring the productivity of service workers is complex. Consider, for example, postal workers: they are often said to be more productive if more letters are delivered per postal worker. But is this really true? What if more letters are lost or delayed per worker at the same time that more are delivered?

The objection implied above to the productivity measure described is based on doubts about the truth of which of the following statements?

(A) Postal workers are representative of service workers in general.

(B) The delivery of letters is the primary activity of the postal service.

(C) Productivity should be ascribed to categories of workers, not to individuals.

(D) The quality of services rendered can appropriately be ignored in computing productivity.

(E) The number of letters delivered is relevant to measuring the productivity of postal workers.

Argument Evaluation

Situation   In considering how best to measure productivity, the assumption is made that the more letters postal workers deliver, the more productive they are. This assumption is then challenged: What if the number of delayed and lost letters increases proportionately with the number of letters delivered?

Reasoning   *Which statement would NOT be accepted by those objecting to the measure?* The point of the objection is that the number of letters delivered is, by itself, an inadequate measure of postal workers' productivity. The challenge introduces the issue of the quality of the work being performed by suggesting that the number of misdirected letters should also be taken into account. The challenge is based on rejecting the idea that quality can be ignored when measuring productivity.

A   The argument uses postal workers as an example; the challenge does not question the fairness of the example.

B   Letter delivery is assumed to be the primary activity of postal workers because their productivity is measured on that basis; the challenge does not reject this point.

C   The argument does discuss a category of workers, postal workers, rather than individuals; the challenge does not reject this point.

D   **Correct.** This statement properly identifies the point that is the basis of the challenge to the measure; the objection does NOT accept the position that quality can be ignored in evaluating productivity.

E   There is no doubt that counting letters delivered is part of measuring productivity; the challenge is to its being the only measure.

The correct answer is D.

111. The difficulty with the proposed high-speed train line is that a used plane can be bought for one-third the price of the train line, and the plane, which is just as fast, can fly anywhere. The train would be a fixed linear system, and we live in a world that is spreading out in all directions and in which consumers choose the free-wheel systems (cars, buses, aircraft), which do not have fixed routes. Thus a sufficient market for the train will not exist.

Which of the following, if true, most severely weakens the argument presented above?

(A) Cars, buses, and planes require the efforts of drivers and pilots to guide them, whereas the train will be guided mechanically.

(B) Cars and buses are not nearly as fast as the high-speed train will be.

(C) Planes are not a free-wheel system because they can fly only between airports, which are less convenient for consumers than the high-speed train's stations would be.

(D) The high-speed train line cannot use currently underutilized train stations in large cities.

(E) For long trips, most people prefer to fly rather than to take ground-level transportation.

Argument Evaluation

Situation   A free-wheel system of transportation, the airplane, is as fast as a fixed linear system, the high-speed train. Because people prefer free-wheel systems that do not have fixed routes, the high-speed train will never find a sufficient market.

Reasoning   *What is the potential weakness in this argument?* The passage argues that consumers will choose to fly rather than use the high-speed train. The argument is based upon a consumer preference for free-wheel systems over fixed linear systems. The definition of a free-wheel system is one that does *not have fixed routes.* The argument is weakened by any challenge to the definition of flying as a free-wheel transportation system. It is true that airplanes may be able to go almost anywhere, but commercial airlines do establish fixed routes and necessarily must travel to and from airports. Furthermore, if airports are less conveniently located for consumers than are train terminals, consumers might well prefer the more convenient of the two fixed-route alternatives.

A   The method of guidance is irrelevant to the argument about free-wheel versus fixed linear systems.

B   The passage compares the speed and system models of airplanes and high-speed trains. The argument does not incorporate buses and cars, which are included only to give examples of free-wheel systems, and so this statement is irrelevant.

C   Correct. This statement properly identifies the weakness in the argument: Airplanes are not truly a free-wheel system because they are restricted to traveling between airports. Additionally, airports tend to be less conveniently located than train terminals, which has further potential to weaken the argument in favor of airplanes.

D   The inability of high-speed trains to use some convenient train stations strengthens, rather than weakens, the argument in favor of airplanes.

E   Consumer preference for air travel over ground travel on long trips strengthens, rather than weakens, the argument in favor of airplanes.

The correct answer is C.

112. The average hourly wage of television assemblers in Vernland has long been significantly lower than that in neighboring Borodia. Since Borodia dropped all tariffs on Vernlandian televisions three years ago, the number of televisions sold annually in Borodia has not changed. However, recent statistics show a drop in the number of television assemblers in Borodia. Therefore, updated trade statistics will probably indicate that the number of televisions Borodia imports annually from Vernland has increased.

Which of the following is an assumption on which the argument depends?

(A) The number of television assemblers in Vernland has increased by at least as much as the number of television assemblers in Borodia has decreased.

(B) Televisions assembled in Vernland have features that televisions assembled in Borodia do not have.

(C) The average number of hours it takes a Borodian television assembler to assemble a television has not decreased significantly during the past three years.

(D) The number of televisions assembled annually in Vernland has increased significantly during the past three years.

(E) The difference between the hourly wage of television assemblers in Vernland and the hourly wage of television assemblers in Borodia is likely to decrease in the next few years.

Argument Construction

Situation Television assemblers in Vernland are paid less than those in neighboring Borodia. The number of televisions sold in Borodia has not dropped since its tariffs on Borodian TVs were lowered three years ago, but the number of TV assemblers in Borodia has. So TV imports from Vernland have likely increased.

Reasoning *What assumption does the argument depend on?* The fact that fewer individuals in Borodia are working as TV assemblers is offered as evidence that TV imports from Vernland into Borodia have likely increased. That piece of evidence is relevant *only* as an indication that the number of TVs being produced within Borodia has decreased. But a drop in the number of TV assemblers does not indicate a drop in the number of TVs being assembled *if* the number of TVs an average assembler puts together has increased. Thus, the argument must be assuming that the average time it takes an assembler to put together a TV has not significantly decreased.

A The argument does not rely on any information about the number of television assemblers in Vernland nor for that matter on the number of TVs assembled in Vernland.

B The argument need not assume there is any difference in the features of the TVs produced in the two countries. Increased sales of Vernlandian TVs in Borodia could be due to any number of other reasons, such as price or quality.

C **Correct.** This option states an assumption on which the argument depends.

D The argument does not depend upon this being so: Vernland's domestic TV sales (or perhaps its exports to countries other than Borodia) may have decreased by more than its imports into Borodia have increased.

E The argument's conclusion addresses what *has* happened; the argument in no way relies on any assumptions about what may or may not happen in the coming years.

The correct answer is C.

113. The pharmaceutical industry argues that because new drugs will not be developed unless heavy development costs can be recouped in later sales, the current 20 years of protection provided by patents should be extended in the case of newly developed drugs. However, in other industries new-product development continues despite high development costs, a fact that indicates that the extension is unnecessary.

Which of the following, if true, most strongly supports the pharmaceutical industry's argument against the challenge made above?

(A) No industries other than the pharmaceutical industry have asked for an extension of the 20-year limit on patent protection.

(B) Clinical trials of new drugs, which occur after the patent is granted and before the new drug can be marketed, often now take as long as 10 years to complete.

(C) There are several industries in which the ratio of research and development costs to revenues is higher than it is in the pharmaceutical industry.

(D) An existing patent for a drug does not legally prevent pharmaceutical companies from bringing to market alternative drugs, provided they are sufficiently dissimilar to the patented drug.

(E) Much recent industrial innovation has occurred in products—for example, in the computer and electronics industries—for which patent protection is often very ineffective.

Argument Evaluation

Situation   The pharmaceutical industry argues for longer patents for new drugs to offset high development costs, claiming that no new drugs can be developed profitably otherwise. Its critics argue that the patent extension is unnecessary because other industries with high development costs keep developing new products.

Reasoning   *How can the pharmaceutical industry best answer the challenge concerning other industries?* The pharmaceutical industry must explain how it differs from other industries. Unlike other industries, it must wait for clinical trials of new drugs before those drugs can be marketed. The clinical trials may take half the patent period, so the pharmaceutical industry may have only half the time allowed to other industries to market new products and recover development costs.

A   Other industries' failure to ask for the same extension does not justify the pharmaceutical industry request.

B   **Correct.** This statement properly identifies evidence that supports the pharmaceutical industry's argument.

C   Pointing out that other industries may have even higher ratios of costs to revenues weakens the pharmaceutical industry's argument.

D   If alternative drugs can rival a patented drug, then the extended patent protection the pharmaceutical industry seeks would appear to be useless.

E   Innovation's effects on patent protection in other industries do not explain why the pharmaceutical industry needs longer patent protection.

The correct answer is B.

114. Guidebook writer: I have visited hotels throughout the country and have noticed that in those built before 1930 the quality of the original carpentry work is generally superior to that in hotels built afterward. Clearly carpenters working on hotels before 1930 typically worked with more skill, care, and effort than carpenters who have worked on hotels built subsequently.

Which of the following, if true, most seriously weakens the guidebook writer's argument?

(A) The quality of original carpentry in hotels is generally far superior to the quality of original carpentry in other structures, such as houses and stores.

(B) Hotels built since 1930 can generally accommodate more guests than those built before 1930.

(C) The materials available to carpenters working before 1930 were not significantly different in quality from the materials available to carpenters working after 1930.

(D) The better the quality of original carpentry in a building, the less likely that building is to fall into disuse and be demolished.

(E) The average length of apprenticeship for carpenters has declined significantly since 1930.

Argument Evaluation

Situation The original carpentry in hotels built before 1930 shows superior care, skill, and effort to that in hotels built after 1930. This leads to the conclusion that carpenters working on hotels before 1930 were superior in skill, care, and effort to those that came after.

Reasoning *Which option most seriously weakens the argument?* The argument draws an inference from a comparison between carpentry in hotels of different eras to a judgment about the carpenters working on hotels in those eras. One way to weaken this inference is by finding some way in which the carpentry in the hotels may be unrepresentative of the skill, care, and effort of the carpenters working in the eras. The comparison is between the carpentry evident in hotels of the two eras *that still exist*. Thus, if there is some reason to think that hotels with good carpentry survive longer than those with bad carpentry, then still-existing hotels from the older era will have disproportionately more good carpentry, even assuming no difference between the skill, care, and effort of the carpenters from the two eras.

A   This option applies equally to both eras, so it has no bearing on the argument.

B   It is not clear whether carpenters working on larger hotels would exercise more, less, or the same skill and care as those working on smaller hotels; thus this option does not weaken the argument.

C   The argument does not rely, even implicitly, on there being any difference in the quality of materials used in the two eras, so it does not weaken the argument to point out that no such difference exists.

D   **Correct.** This weakens the reasoning in the argument by showing a respect in which the comparison between *existing* hotels is unrepresentative.

E   The longer a carpenter works as an apprentice, the more skill he or she is apt to have upon becoming a full-fledged carpenter. So this option would tend to slightly strengthen rather than weaken the argument.

The correct answer is D.

115. Caterpillars of all species produce an identical hormone called "juvenile hormone" that maintains feeding behavior. Only when a caterpillar has grown to the right size for pupation to take place does a special enzyme halt the production of juvenile hormone. This enzyme can be synthesized and will, on being ingested by immature caterpillars, kill them by stopping them from feeding.

Which of the following, if true, most strongly supports the view that it would NOT be advisable to try to eradicate agricultural pests that go through a caterpillar stage by spraying croplands with the enzyme mentioned above?

(A) Most species of caterpillar are subject to some natural predation.

(B) Many agricultural pests do not go through a caterpillar stage.

(C) Many agriculturally beneficial insects go through a caterpillar stage.

(D) Since caterpillars of different species emerge at different times, several sprayings would be necessary.

(E) Although the enzyme has been synthesized in the laboratory, no large-scale production facilities exist as yet.

Argument Evaluation

Situation The feeding behavior of immature caterpillars of all species is regulated by the *juvenile hormone*; an enzyme stops the production of this hormone when the caterpillars have reached an appropriate level of growth. At any earlier time in their development, ingesting this enzyme, which can be produced synthetically, kills the immature caterpillars because they stop feeding. What sort of evidence would count against the advisability of spraying croplands with this enzyme to eradicate agricultural pests that undergo a caterpillar stage?

Reasoning *What evidence strengthens the argument that the synthetic enzyme should <u>not</u> be sprayed on croplands?* Spraying the enzyme will kill all insects that go through a caterpillar stage. If the goal is to eradicate insect pests by killing them at the caterpillar stage, why is this spraying inadvisable? The relationship between crops and insects is complicated; while some insects harm crops, others benefit them. If the spraying kills all susceptible insects, regardless of whether they harm or help the crops, it can also destroy agriculturally beneficial insects. This is a good reason to doubt whether the spraying would be advisable.

A   Spraying would eradicate all pests that go through a caterpillar stage and so is more effective than natural predators are. This statement provides no reason not to spray.

B   Spraying affects only those agricultural pests that do go through a caterpillar stage, so this statement is irrelevant.

C   **Correct.** This statement properly identifies evidence that strengthens the argument against spraying.

D   The need to spray repeatedly does not provide any significant evidence that spraying is inadvisable, but simply suggests that the process will be more complicated.

E   The mere lack of *current* production facilities does not mean that it would be inadvisable to develop and use the spray in the future.

The correct answer is C.

116. Firms adopting "profit-related-pay" (PRP) contracts pay wages at levels that vary with the firm's profits. In the metalworking industry last year, firms with PRP contracts in place showed productivity per worker on average 13 percent higher than that of their competitors who used more traditional contracts.

If, on the basis of the evidence above, it is argued that PRP contracts increase worker productivity, which of the following, if true, would most seriously weaken that argument?

(A) Results similar to those cited for the metalworking industry have been found in other industries where PRP contracts are used.

(B) Under PRP contracts costs other than labor costs, such as plant, machinery, and energy, make up an increased proportion of the total cost of each unit of output.

(C) Because introducing PRP contracts greatly changes individual workers' relationships to the firm, negotiating the introduction of PRP contracts is complex and time-consuming.

(D) Many firms in the metalworking industry have modernized production equipment in the last five years, and most of these introduced PRP contracts at the same time.

(E) In firms in the metalworking industry where PRP contracts are in place, the average take-home pay is 15 percent higher than it is in those firms where workers have more traditional contracts.

Argument Evaluation

Situation Last year, firms using profit-related-pay (PRP) contracts found that productivity per worker increased significantly as compared to firms that used traditional wage contracts.

Reasoning *What point weakens the argument that PRP contracts increase productivity?* The argument directly attributes increased productivity to the existence of PRP contracts. Any information that other factors might have contributed to the increase in productivity would weaken the argument. If production equipment was modernized during the same period that the new contracts took effect, then it is possible that the modernized equipment was responsible for the higher level of productivity.

A   Similar findings in other industries strengthen rather than weaken the argument.

B   If workers are more productive, labor costs are a smaller proportion of total costs and nonlabor costs are a greater proportion. This point does not weaken the argument.

C   The difficulty of negotiating the contracts is irrelevant to a conclusion about what happens once the contracts are in place.

D   Correct. This statement properly identifies information that weakens the argument.

E   The higher pay of workers on PRP contracts is consistent with their higher productivity. This statement does not weaken the argument.

The correct answer is D.

117. Scientists typically do their most creative work before the age of forty. It is commonly thought that this happens because aging by itself brings about a loss of creative capacity. However, studies show that **of scientists who produce highly creative work beyond the age of forty, a disproportionately large number entered their field at an older age than is usual**. Since by the age of forty the large majority of scientists have been working in their field for at least fifteen years, the studies' finding strongly suggests that the real reason why scientists over forty rarely produce highly creative work is not that they have aged but rather that **scientists over forty have generally spent too long in their field**.

In the argument given, the two portions in boldface play which of the following roles?

(A) The first is a claim, the accuracy of which is at issue in the argument; the second is a conclusion drawn on the basis of that claim.

(B) The first is an objection that has been raised against a position defended in the argument; the second is that position.

(C) The first is evidence that has been used to support an explanation that the argument challenges; the second is that explanation.

(D) The first is evidence that has been used to support an explanation that the argument challenges; the second is a competing explanation that the argument favors.

(E) The first provides evidence to support an explanation that the argument favors; the second is that explanation.

Argument Evaluation

Situation   It is generally thought that the reason scientists tend to do their most creative work before age forty is that creative capacity declines with age. Yet those scientists who do creative work after forty tend, disproportionately, to have started their careers in science later in life. So a better explanation is that many scientists over forty have just been at it too long.

Reasoning   *What roles do the two portions of the argument that are in boldface play?* The argument describes a phenomenon and what is commonly thought to explain it. Then, the first boldfaced statement introduces evidence that suggests that there may be another explanation. After this evidence is further developed, the argument then concludes that there is indeed a better explanation for the phenomenon; that explanation is stated in the second boldfaced portion.

A   The accuracy of the first statement is never called into question by the argument; rather, it is relied upon as the basis for the argument's conclusion.

B   The first statement is not an objection against the position the argument defends; instead, it is a basis for that position.

C   The first statement is not used to support a position the argument challenges, and the second statement is the explanation the argument supports, not the one it challenges.

D   The second statement is indeed an explanation that the argument favors; but the first statement is not used to support a competing explanation that the argument challenges.

E   **Correct.** This option correctly identifies the roles played by the boldfaced portions of the argument.

The correct answer is E.

118. Northern Air has dozens of flights daily into and out of Belleville Airport, which is highly congested. Northern Air depends for its success on economy and quick turnaround and consequently is planning to replace its large planes with Skybuses, whose novel aerodynamic design is extremely fuel efficient. The Skybus's fuel efficiency results in both lower fuel costs and reduced time spent refueling.

Which of the following, if true, could present the most serious disadvantage for Northern Air in replacing their large planes with Skybuses?

(A) The Skybus would enable Northern Air to schedule direct flights to destinations that currently require stops for refueling.

(B) Aviation fuel is projected to decline in price over the next several years.

(C) The fuel efficiency of the Skybus would enable Northern Air to eliminate refueling at some of its destinations, but several mechanics would lose their jobs.

(D) None of Northern Air's competitors that use Belleville Airport are considering buying Skybuses.

(E) The aerodynamic design of the Skybus causes turbulence behind it when taking off that forces other planes on the runway to delay their takeoffs.

Evaluation of a Plan

Situation   An airline flies in and out of a highly congested airport many times a day. Because the airline's success depends on low costs and quick turnaround, it plans to replace its current planes with Skybuses, whose more fuel-efficient design will reduce both fuel costs and the time spent refueling.

Reasoning   *What could be a serious disadvantage of the plan?* Since it is given that the Skybuses provide fuel economy and quicker refueling, what could be a disadvantage of the proposed plan? What if the use of the particular aircraft somehow contributed to the congestion at the busy airport or caused slower turnaround? While the Skybus's design promotes fuel economy, if it also creates turbulence on takeoff, the turbulence would then delay the takeoffs of any other planes. Since the airport is congested and the airline flies through it many times a day, such takeoff delays would ultimately impede Northern Air's turnaround time, as well as its success.

A   The ability to schedule direct flights would be an advantage, not a disadvantage.

B   The decline in the price of aviation fuel might make the plan seem less pressing, and it could conceivably complicate the issue of whether the expected savings would justify the investment in new planes. However, lower fuel costs would not diminish the crucial time-saving advantage of Skybuses, and any hypotheses about their relevance to the overall decision are purely speculative.

C   The ability to eliminate refueling is an advantage to the airline. The loss of jobs could, in theory, have some negative effect on the airline due to lowered morale among remaining employees. However, *several* does not support a hypothesis that the effect would be very significant, and any hypotheses about whether it might override the benefits are purely speculative.

D   The decisions made by other airlines are irrelevant to the plan.

E   **Correct.** This statement properly identifies a potentially serious disadvantage to the plan.

The correct answer is E.

119. It is true of both men and women that those who marry as young adults live longer than those who never marry. This does not show that marriage causes people to live longer, since, as compared with other people of the same age, young adults who are about to get married have fewer of the unhealthy habits that can cause a person to have a shorter life, most notably smoking and immoderate drinking of alcohol.

Which of the following, if true, most strengthens the argument above?

(A) Marriage tends to cause people to engage less regularly in sports that involve risk of bodily harm.

(B) A married person who has an unhealthy habit is more likely to give up that habit than a person with the same habit who is unmarried.

(C) A person who smokes is much more likely than a nonsmoker to marry a person who smokes at the time of marriage, and the same is true for people who drink alcohol immoderately.

(D) Among people who marry as young adults, most of those who give up an unhealthy habit after marriage do not resume the habit later in life.

(E) Among people who as young adults neither drink alcohol immoderately nor smoke, those who never marry live as long as those who marry.

Argument Evaluation

Situation We should not conclude that getting married causes one to live longer based merely on the fact that those who marry young tend to live longer than those who never marry at all. Those who marry young tend to have fewer unhealthy habits to begin with, such as drinking and smoking, than do those who will never marry.

Reasoning *Which of the options most strengthens the argument?* The argument is trying to show that the difference in longevity between the two groups need not be *caused by* marital status. The argument relies on the fact that even before marriage those who will be married tend to live healthier lifestyles than those who will never marry. Yet, even if those who are apt to live longer are more apt to marry young, it could still be that marriage *further enhances* one's longevity. So, by showing that a person who gets married young tends to live about as long as one who had been living an equally healthy lifestyle as a young adult but who never got married, the argument is greatly strengthened.

A To the extent that risk of bodily harm decreases longevity, this weakens rather than strengthens the argument.

B This option, too, weakens the argument rather than strengthens it, since it suggests that marriage does indeed enhance one's longevity.

C Even if a person with unhealthy habits who marries is more likely to wind up with a spouse with unhealthy habits than is a person with healthy habits who marries, that tells us nothing about whether the average person who gets married gets a boost in longevity.

D This option does not tell us whether it is also true of those who never marry that most of them who give up an unhealthy habit as a young adult ever resume that habit later in life. Thus, by itself, this option has no bearing on the strength of the argument.

E **Correct.** This strengthens the argument against the causal connection between marriage and longevity by showing that the longevity difference disappears when the longevity of those who marry young is compared with young adults with similar health habits who will never marry.

The correct answer is E.

120. The earliest Mayan pottery found at Colha, in Belize, is about 3,000 years old. Recently, however, 4,500-year-old stone agricultural implements were unearthed at Colha. These implements resemble Mayan stone implements of a much later period, also found at Colha. Moreover, the implements' designs are strikingly different from the designs of stone implements produced by other cultures known to have inhabited the area in prehistoric times. Therefore, there were surely Mayan settlements in Colha 4,500 years ago.

Which of the following, if true, most seriously weakens the argument?

(A) Ceramic ware is not known to have been used by the Mayan people to make agricultural implements.

(B) Carbon-dating of corn pollen in Colha indicates that agriculture began there around 4,500 years ago.

(C) Archaeological evidence indicates that some of the oldest stone implements found at Colha were used to cut away vegetation after controlled burning of trees to open areas of swampland for cultivation.

(D) Successor cultures at a given site often adopt the style of agricultural implements used by earlier inhabitants of the same site.

(E) Many religious and social institutions of the Mayan people who inhabited Colha 3,000 years ago relied on a highly developed system of agricultural symbols.

Argument Evaluation

Situation   Recently, 4,500-year-old stone agricultural implements have been found in Colha, a location where 3,000-year-old Mayan pottery had previously been found. The implements resemble other Mayan implements of a much later time that were also found in Colha, and they are unlike the implements used by other local cultures in prehistoric times. These recently discovered implements thus prove that Mayan culture was established in Colha 4,500 years ago.

Reasoning   *Which point weakens the argument?* First, identify a crucial underlying assumption. The argument assumes the distinctive 4,500-year-old implements must be Mayan because they are similar to implements the Mayans are known to have used there much later. What if there is another reason for the similarity? What if a culture that comes to an already inhabited site tends to adapt its implements to the style of the resident culture's implements? In that case, the Mayans could have come to the already established community of Colha at some later point, and the later Mayan agricultural tools could be copies of the earlier culture's tools.

A   The argument does not suggest that the Mayans used ceramics for implements, so this point does not weaken the argument; it is irrelevant to it.

B   Since the point of the argument is who, specifically, established a settlement in Colha 4,500 years ago, the evidence that some unidentified people were practicing agriculture there at that time neither strengthens nor weakens the argument.

C   Discovering how the implements were used does not explain who was using them, so this information is not relevant to the conclusion.

D   **Correct.** This statement properly identifies the weakness in the argument that the similarity between the 4,500-year-old implements and the later Mayan implements may be attributed to the Mayans' adopting the style of implements used earlier by another culture.

E   That the Mayans relied on agricultural symbols at that time is nearly irrelevant to the issue of whether the earlier implements belonged to their culture. To the extent that this is relevant, it very slightly supports, rather than weakens, the argument; *highly developed* suggests that Mayans had been practicing agriculture for a long time.

The correct answer is D.

121. Codex Berinensis, a Florentine copy of an ancient Roman medical treatise, is undated but contains clues to when it was produced. Its first 80 pages are by a single copyist, but the remaining 20 pages are by three different copyists, which indicates some significant disruption. Since a letter in handwriting identified as that of the fourth copyist mentions a plague that killed many people in Florence in 1148, Codex Berinensis was probably produced in that year.

Which of the following, if true, most strongly supports the hypothesis that Codex Berinensis was produced in 1148?

(A)   Other than Codex Berinensis, there are no known samples of the handwriting of the first three copyists.

(B)   According to the account by the fourth copyist, the plague went on for 10 months.

(C)   A scribe would be able to copy a page of text the size and style of Codex Berinensis in a day.

(D)   There was only one outbreak of plague in Florence in the 1100s.

(E)   The number of pages of Codex Berinensis produced by a single scribe becomes smaller with each successive change of copyist.

Argument Evaluation

Situation   The Florentine copy of an ancient Roman work is undated but provides clues as to the time it was produced. The first 80 pages of Codex Berinenis are the work of one copyist. The fact that the last 20 pages are the work of a succession of three different copyists is an indication of serious turmoil at the time the copying was done. Since a letter in the fourth copyist's handwriting reveals that a plague killed many people there in 1148, Codex Berinenis was probably produced in that year.

Reasoning   *Which information supports the hypothesis dating the Codex to 1148?* Consider the basis of the hypothesis: the succession of copyists indicating the work was significantly disrupted, and the fourth copyist's letter indicating the plague of 1148 caused serious loss of life. From this it is argued that the plague of 1148 was the reason for the multiple copyists and that the work can thus be dated to that year. What if there were multiple plagues? In that case, Codex Berinensis could have been produced at another time. If instead only one plague occurred in the 1100s, the elimination of that possibility supports the hypothesis that the work was done in 1148.

A   Examples of the copyists' handwriting might help date Codex Berinensis; the absence of handwriting samples does not help support 1148 as the date.

B   The length of the plague, while it may account for the succession of copyists, does not help support the particular year the work was done.

C   The amount of work a copyist could achieve each day does not provide any information about the year the work appeared.

D   **Correct.** This statement properly identifies a circumstance that supports the hypothesis.

E   The productivity or tenure of the various copyists is irrelevant to establishing the date.

The correct answer is D.

122. The spacing of the four holes on a fragment of a bone flute excavated at a Neanderthal campsite is just what is required to play the third through sixth notes of the diatonic scale—the seven-note musical scale used in much of Western music since the Renaissance. Musicologists therefore hypothesize that the diatonic musical scale was developed and used thousands of years before it was adopted by Western musicians.

Which of the following, if true, most strongly supports the hypothesis?

(A) Bone flutes were probably the only musical instrument made by Neanderthals.

(B) No musical instrument that is known to have used a diatonic scale is of an earlier date than the flute found at the Neanderthal campsite.

(C) The flute was made from a cave-bear bone and the campsite at which the flute fragment was excavated was in a cave that also contained skeletal remains of cave bears.

(D) Flutes are the simplest wind instrument that can be constructed to allow playing a diatonic scale.

(E) The cave-bear leg bone used to make the Neanderthal flute would have been long enough to make a flute capable of playing a complete diatonic scale.

Argument Evaluation

Situation   The arrangement of the holes in a bone fragment from a Neanderthal campsite match part of the scale used in Western music since the Renaissance. Musicologists hypothesize from this that the scale was developed thousands of years before Western musicians adopted it.

Reasoning   *Which of the options, if true, would provide the most support for the musicologists' hypothesis?* One way to approach this question is to ask yourself, "If this option were false, would the hypothesis be *less* likely to be true?" If the Neanderthal bone fragment could *not* have been part of a flute that encompassed *the entire* seven-note diatonic scale, then the bone fragment's existence would not provide strong support for the hypothesis.

A   To the extent that this is even relevant, it tends to weaken the hypothesis; it makes less likely the possibility that Neanderthals used other types of musical instruments employing the diatonic scale.

B   This also weakens the hypothesis, because it states that there is no known evidence of a certain type that would support the hypothesis.

C   The fact that the cave-bear bone fragment that was apparently a flute came from a site where many other cave-bear skeletal remains were found has little bearing on the hypothesis, and in no way supports it.

D   This does not strengthen the hypothesis, for even if the option were false—even if a simpler instrument could be constructed that employed the diatonic scale—the existence of a flute employing the diatonic scale would provide no less support for the hypothesis.

E   **Correct.** This option most strongly supports the hypothesis.

The correct answer is E.

123. Outsourcing is the practice of obtaining from an independent supplier a product or service that a company has previously provided for itself. Since a company's chief objective is to realize the highest possible year-end profits, any product or service that can be obtained from an independent supplier for less than it would cost the company to provide the product or service on its own should be outsourced.

Which of the following, if true, most seriously weakens the argument?

(A) If a company decides to use independent suppliers for a product, it can generally exploit the vigorous competition arising among several firms that are interested in supplying that product.

(B) Successful outsourcing requires a company to provide its suppliers with information about its products and plans that can fall into the hands of its competitors and give them a business advantage.

(C) Certain tasks, such as processing a company's payroll, are commonly outsourced, whereas others, such as handling the company's core business, are not.

(D) For a company to provide a product or service for itself as efficiently as an independent supplier can provide it, the managers involved need to be as expert in the area of that product or service as the people in charge of that product or service at an independent supplier are.

(E) When a company decides to use an independent supplier for a product or service, the independent supplier sometimes hires members of the company's staff who formerly made the product or provided the service that the independent supplier now supplies.

Argument Evaluation

Situation   In order to realize the highest year-end profits, a company should outsource any service or product that can be obtained from an independent supplier for less than it would cost the company to provide that service or product itself.

Reasoning   *What weakens this argument?* When could outsourcing a service or product result in a business disadvantage or lower profits? It is clear that the company must give independent suppliers enough information to enable them to provide the contracted products and services, but this means that the company can lose control over who has possession of such critical information. If the information becomes known to the company's competitors and gives them a business advantage, the company's profitability may be harmed rather than helped by outsourcing. This possibility weakens the argument.

A   This would strengthen the argument since the pricing competition among independent suppliers is an advantage for the company.

B   **Correct.** This statement properly identifies one disadvantage of outsourcing: the company no longer controls access to its information and plans. With the increased possibility of competitors' gaining access to its proprietary information, the company's business is put at risk.

C   Providing examples of the tasks typically outsourced or handled internally does not affect the argument.

D   Expertise in a particular area is an advantage of outsourcing and thus a strength of the argument.

E   The supplier's hiring of members of the company's staff to handle work no longer performed within the company is not shown to be a disadvantage.

The correct answer is B.

124. Museums that house Renaissance oil paintings typically store them in environments that are carefully kept within narrow margins of temperature and humidity to inhibit any deterioration. Laboratory tests have shown that the kind of oil paint used in these paintings actually adjusts to climatic changes quite well. If, as some museum directors believe, **paint is the most sensitive substance in these works**, then by relaxing the standards for temperature and humidity control, **museums can reduce energy costs without risking damage to these paintings**. Museums would be rash to relax those standards, however, since results of preliminary tests indicate that gesso, a compound routinely used by Renaissance artists to help paint adhere to the canvas, is unable to withstand significant variations in humidity.

In the argument above, the two portions in boldface play which of the following roles?

(A) The first is an objection that has been raised against the position taken by the argument; the second is the position taken by the argument.

(B) The first is the position taken by the argument; the second is the position that the argument calls into question.

(C) The first is a judgment that has been offered in support of the position that the argument calls into question; the second is a circumstance on which that judgment is, in part, based.

(D) The first is a judgment that has been offered in support of the position that the argument calls into question; the second is that position.

(E) The first is a claim that the argument calls into question; the second is the position taken by the argument.

Argument Evaluation

Situation   Museums house Renaissance paintings under strictly controlled climatic conditions to prevent deterioration. This is costly. But the paint in these works actually adjusts well to climate changes. On the other hand, another compound routinely used in these paintings, gesso, does not react well to changes in humidity.

Reasoning   *What roles do the two boldfaced statements play in the argument?* The first statement is not asserted by the author of the argument, but rather attributed as a belief to some museum directors. What the argument itself asserts is that IF this belief is true THEN the second boldfaced statement is true. But the argument then goes on to offer evidence that the first statement is false and so concludes that museum directors would be ill-advised to assume that the second statement was true.

A   This option mistakenly claims that the argument adopts the second statement as its position, when in fact the argument calls this position into question.

B   Rather than adopting the first statement, the argument offers evidence that calls it into question.

C   This option contends that the first statement is a judgment that is based on the second; in fact the opposite is true.

D   **Correct.** This option properly identifies the roles the two portions in boldface play in the argument.

E   While the argument does call the first statement into question, it also calls the second statement into question.

The correct answer is D.

9.0 Sentence Correction

9.0 Sentence Correction

Sentence correction questions appear in the Verbal section of the GMAT® test. The Verbal section uses multiple-choice questions to measure your ability to read and comprehend written material, to reason and evaluate arguments, and to correct written material to conform to standard written English. Because the Verbal section includes passages from several different content areas, you may be generally familiar with some of the material; however, neither the passages nor the questions assume detailed knowledge of the topics discussed. Sentence correction questions are intermingled with critical reasoning and reading comprehension questions throughout the Verbal section of the test. You will have 75 minutes to complete the Verbal section, or about 1¾ minutes to answer each question.

Sentence correction questions present a statement in which words are underlined. The questions ask you to select from the answer options the best expression of the idea or relationship described in the underlined section. The first answer choice always repeats the original phrasing, whereas the other four provide alternatives. In some cases, the original phrasing is the best choice. In other cases, the underlined section has obvious or subtle errors that require correction. These questions require you to be familiar with the stylistic conventions and grammatical rules of standard written English and to demonstrate your ability to improve incorrect or ineffective expressions.

You should begin these questions by reading the sentence carefully. Note whether there are any obvious grammatical errors as you read the underlined section. Then read the five answer choices carefully. If there was a subtle error you did not recognize the first time you read the sentence, it may become apparent after you have read the answer choices. If the error is still unclear, see whether you can eliminate some of the answers as being incorrect. Remember that in some cases, the original selection may be the best answer.

9.1 Basic English Grammar Rules

Sentence correction questions ask you to recognize and potentially correct at least one of the following grammar rules. However, these rules are not exhaustive. If you are interested in learning more about English grammar as a way to prepare for the GMAT test, there are several resources available on the Web.

Agreement

Standard English requires elements within a sentence to be consistent. There are two types of agreement: noun-verb and pronoun.

Noun-verb agreement: Singular subjects take singular verbs, whereas plural subjects take plural verbs.
Examples:
Correct: "I walk to the store." Incorrect: "I walks to the store."
Correct: "We go to school." Incorrect: "We goes to school."
Correct: "The number of residents has grown." Incorrect: "The number of residents have grown."
Correct: "The masses have spoken." Incorrect: "The masses has spoken."

Pronoun agreement: A pronoun must agree with the noun or pronoun it refers to in person, number, and gender.

Examples:

Correct: "When you dream, you are usually asleep." Incorrect: "When one dreams, you are usually asleep."

Correct: "When the kids went to sleep, they slept like logs." Incorrect: "When the kids went to sleep, he slept like a log."

Diction

Words should be chosen to reflect correctly and effectively the appropriate part of speech. There are several words that are commonly used incorrectly. When answering sentence correction questions, pay attention to the following conventions.

Among/between: *Among* is used to refer to relationships involving more than two objects. *Between* is used to refer to relationships involving only two objects.

Examples:

Correct: "We divided our winnings among the three of us." Incorrect: "We divided our winnings between the three of us."

Correct: "She and I divided the cake between us." Incorrect: "She and I divided the cake among us."

As/like: As can be a preposition meaning "in the capacity of," but more often is a conjunction of manner and is followed by a verb. *Like* is generally used as a preposition, and therefore is followed by a noun, an object pronoun, or a verb ending in *ing.*

Examples:

Correct: "I work as a librarian." Incorrect: "I work like a librarian."

Correct: "Do as I say, not as I do." Incorrect: "Do like I say, not like I do."

Correct: "It felt like a dream." Incorrect: "It felt as a dream."

Correct: "People like you inspire me." Incorrect: "People as you inspire me."

Correct: "There's nothing like biking on a warm, autumn day." Incorrect: "There's nothing as biking on a warm autumn day."

Mass and count words: Mass words are nouns quantified by an amount rather than by a number. *Count* nouns can be quantified by a number.

Examples:

Correct: "We bought a loaf of bread." Incorrect: "We bought one bread."

Correct: "He wished me much happiness." Incorrect: "He wished me many happinesses."

Correct: "We passed many buildings." Incorrect: "We passed much buildings."

Pronouns: Myself should not be used as a substitute for *I* or *me.*

Examples:

Correct: "Mom and I had to go to the store." Incorrect: "Mom and myself had to go to the store."

Correct: "He gave the present to Dad and me." Incorrect: "He gave the present to Dad and myself."

Grammatical Construction

Good grammar requires complete sentences. Be on the lookout for improperly formed constructions.

Fragments: Parts of a sentence that are disconnected from the main clause are called fragments.
Example:
Correct: "We saw the doctor and his nurse at the party." Incorrect: "We saw the doctor at the party. And his nurse."

Run-on sentences: A run-on sentence is two independent clauses that run together without proper punctuation.
Examples:
Correct: "Jose Canseco is still a feared batter; most pitchers don't want to face him."
Incorrect: "Jose Canseco is still a feared batter most pitchers don't want to face him."

Constructions: Avoid wordy, redundant constructions.
Example:
Correct: "We could not come to the meeting because of a conflict." Incorrect: "The reason we could not come to the meeting is because of a conflict."

Idiom

It is important to avoid nonstandard expressions, although English idioms sometimes do not follow conventional grammatical rules. Be careful to use the correct idiom when using the constructions and parts of speech.

Prepositions: Specific prepositions have specific purposes.
Examples:
Correct: "She likes to jog in the morning." Incorrect: "She likes to jog on the morning."
Correct: "They ranged in age from 10 to 15." Incorrect: "They ranged in age from 10 up to 15."

Correlatives: Word combinations such as "not only … but also" should be followed by an element of the same grammatical type.
Examples:
Correct: "I have called not only to thank her but also to tell her about the next meeting."
Incorrect: "I have called not only to thank her but also I told her about the next meeting."

Forms of comparison: Many forms follow precise constructions. *Fewer* refers to a specific number, whereas *less than* refers to a continuous quantity. *Between … and* is the correct form to designate a choice. *Farther* refers to distance, whereas *further* refers to degree.
Examples:
Correct: "There were fewer children in my class this year." Incorrect: "There were less children in my class this year."
Correct: "There was less devastation than I was told." Incorrect: "There was fewer devastation than I was told."
Correct: "We had to choose between chocolate and vanilla." Incorrect: "We had to choose between chocolate or vanilla." (It is also correct to say, "We had to choose chocolate or vanilla.")
Correct: "I ran farther than John, but he took his weight training further than I did."
Incorrect: "I ran further than John, but he took his weight training farther than I did."

Logical Predication

Watch out for phrases that detract from the logical argument.

Modification problems: Modifiers should be positioned so it is clear what word or words they are meant to modify. If modifiers are not positioned clearly, they can cause illogical references or comparisons, or distort the meaning of the statement.
Examples:
Correct: "I put the cake that I baked by the door." Incorrect: "I put the cake by the door that I baked."
Correct: "Reading my mind, she gave me the delicious cookie." Incorrect: "Reading my mind, the cookie she gave me was delicious."
Correct: "In the Middle Ages, the world was believed to be flat." Incorrect: "In the Middle Ages, the world was flat."

Parallelism

Constructing a sentence that is parallel in structure depends on making sure that the different elements in the sentence balance each other; this is a little bit like making sure that the two sides of a mathematical equation are balanced. To make sure that a sentence is grammatically correct, check to see that phrases, clauses, verbs, and other sentence elements parallel each other.

Examples:
Correct: "I took a bath, went to sleep, and woke up refreshed." Incorrect: "I took a bath, sleeping, and waking up refreshed."
Correct: "The only way to know is to take the plunge." Incorrect: "The only way to know is taking the plunge."

Rhetorical Construction

Good sentence structure avoids constructions that are awkward, wordy, redundant, imprecise, or unclear, even when they are free of grammatical errors.
Example:
Correct: "Before we left on vacation, we watered the plants, checked to see that the stove was off, and set the burglar alarm." Incorrect: "Before we left to go on our vacation, we watered, checked to be sure that the stove had been turned off, and set it."

Verb Form

In addition to watching for problems of agreement or parallelism, make sure that verbs are used in the correct tense. Be alert to whether a verb should reflect past, present, or future tense.
Example:
Correct: "I went to school yesterday." "I go to school every weekday." "I will go to school tomorrow."

Each tense also has a perfect form (used with the past participle—e.g., walked, ran), a progressive form (used with the present participle—e.g., walking, running), and a perfect progressive form (also used with the present participle—e.g., walking, running).

Present perfect: Used with *has* or *have*, the present perfect tense describes an action that occurred at an indefinite time in the past or that began in the past and continues into the present.
Examples:
Correct: "I have traveled all over the world." (at an indefinite time)
Correct: "He has gone to school since he was five years old." (continues into the present)

Past perfect: This verb form is used with *had* to show the order of two events that took place in the past.
Example:
Correct: "By the time I left for school, the cake had been baked."

Future perfect: Used with *will have*, this verb form describes an event in the future that will precede another event.
Example:
Correct: "By the end of the day, I will have studied for all my tests."

Present progressive: Used with *am, is,* or *are,* this verb form describes an ongoing action that is happening now.
Example:
Correct: "I am studying for exams." "The student is studying for exams." "We are studying for exams."

Past progressive: Used with *was* or *were,* this verb form describes something that was happening when another action occurred.
Example:
Correct: "The student was studying when the fire alarm rang." "They were studying when the fire broke out."

Future progressive: Used with *will be* or *shall be,* this verb tense describes an ongoing action that will continue into the future.
Example:
Correct: "The students will be studying for exams throughout the month of December."

Present perfect progressive: Used with *have been* or *has been,* this verb tense describes something that began in the past, continues into the present, and may continue into the future.
Example:
Correct: "The student has been studying hard in the hope of acing the test."

Past perfect progressive: Used with *had been,* this verb form describes an action of some duration that was completed before another past action occurred.
Example:
Correct: "Before the fire alarm rang, the student had been studying."

Future perfect progressive: Used with *will have been,* this verb form describes a future, ongoing action that will occur before a specified time.
Example:
Correct: "By the end of next year, the students will have been studying math for five years."

9.2 Study Suggestions

There are two basic ways you can study for sentence correction questions:

- **Read material that reflects standard usage.**
  One way to gain familiarity with the basic conventions of standard written English is simply to read. Suitable material will usually be found in good magazines and nonfiction books, editorials in outstanding newspapers, and the collections of essays used by many college and university writing courses.

- **Review basic rules of grammar and practice with writing exercises.**
  Begin by reviewing the grammar rules laid out in this chapter. Then, if you have school assignments (such as essays and research papers) that have been carefully evaluated for grammatical errors, it may be helpful to review the comments and corrections.

9.3 What Is Measured

Sentence correction questions test three broad aspects of language proficiency:

- **Correct expression**
  A correct sentence is grammatically and structurally sound. It conforms to all the rules of standard written English, including noun-verb agreement, noun-pronoun agreement, pronoun consistency, pronoun case, and verb tense sequence. A correct sentence will not have dangling, misplaced, or improperly formed modifiers; unidiomatic or inconsistent expressions; or faults in parallel construction.

- **Effective expression**
  An effective sentence expresses an idea or relationship clearly and concisely as well as grammatically. This does not mean that the choice with the fewest and simplest words is necessarily the best answer. It means that there are no superfluous words or needlessly complicated expressions in the best choice.

- **Proper diction**
  An effective sentence also uses proper diction. (Diction refers to the standard dictionary meanings of words and the appropriateness of words in context.) In evaluating the diction of a sentence, you must be able to recognize whether the words are well chosen, accurate, and suitable for the context.

9.4 Test-Taking Strategies

1. **Read the entire sentence carefully.**
   Try to understand the specific idea or relationship that the sentence should express.

2. **Evaluate the underlined passage for errors and possible corrections before reading the answer choices.**
   This strategy will help you discriminate among the answer choices. Remember, in some cases the underlined passage is correct.

3. **Read each answer choice carefully.**
   The first answer choice always repeats the underlined portion of the original sentence. Choose this answer if you think that the sentence is best as originally written, but do so *only after* examining all the other choices.

4. **Try to determine how to correct what you consider to be wrong with the original sentence.**
   Some of the answer choices may change things that are not wrong, whereas others may not change everything that is wrong.

5. **Make sure that you evaluate the sentence and the choices thoroughly.**
   Pay attention to general clarity, grammatical and idiomatic usage, economy and precision of language, and appropriateness of diction.

6. **Read the whole sentence, substituting the choice that you prefer for the underlined passage.**
   A choice may be wrong because it does not fit grammatically or structurally with the rest of the sentence. Remember that some sentences will require no correction. When the given sentence requires no correction, choose the first answer.

9.5 The Directions

These are the directions that you will see for sentence correction questions when you take the GMAT test. If you read them carefully and understand them clearly before going to sit for the test, you will not need to spend too much time reviewing them once you are at the test center and the test is under way.

Sentence correction questions present a sentence, part or all of which is underlined. Beneath the sentence, you will find five ways of phrasing the underlined passage. The first answer choice repeats the original underlined passage; the other four are different. If you think the original phrasing is best, choose the first answer; otherwise choose one of the others.

This type of question tests your ability to recognize the correctness and effectiveness of expression in standard written English. In choosing your answer, follow the requirements of standard written English; that is, pay attention to grammar, choice of words, and sentence construction. Choose the answer that produces the most effective sentence; this answer should be clear and exact, without awkwardness, ambiguity, redundancy, or grammatical error.

9.6 Sample Questions

Each of the <u>sentence correction</u> questions presents a sentence, part or all of which is underlined. Beneath the sentence you will find five ways of phrasing the underlined part. The first of these repeats the original; the other four are different. Follow the requirements of standard written English to choose your answer, paying attention to grammar, word choice, and sentence construction. Select the answer that produces the most effective sentence; your answer should make the sentence clear, exact, and free of grammatical error. It should also minimize awkwardness, ambiguity, and redundancy.

1. The Glass House Mountains in Queensland, Australia, were sighted in 1770 by the English navigator Captain James Cook, <u>by whom they were named supposedly because its</u> sheer wet rocks glistened like glass.

    (A) by whom they were named supposedly because its
    (B) by whom they were named supposedly and their
    (C) naming them supposedly since their
    (D) who so named them supposedly because their
    (E) who so named it since supposedly their

2. Although a surge in retail sales <u>have raised hopes that there is a recovery finally</u> under way, many economists say that without a large amount of spending the recovery might not last.

    (A) have raised hopes that there is a recovery finally
    (B) raised hopes for there being a recovery finally
    (C) had raised hopes for a recovery finally being
    (D) has raised hopes that a recovery is finally
    (E) raised hopes for a recovery finally

3. Although various eighteenth- and nineteenth-century American poets had professed an interest in Native American poetry and had pretended to imitate Native American forms in their own works, <u>until almost 1900, scholars and critics did not begin seriously to study</u> traditional Native American poetry in native languages.

    (A) until almost 1900, scholars and critics did not begin seriously to study
    (B) until almost 1900 scholars and critics had not begun seriously studying
    (C) not until almost 1900 were scholars and critics to begin seriously to study

    (D) it was not almost until 1900 when scholars and critics began to seriously study
    (E) it was not until almost 1900 that scholars and critics seriously began studying

4. Of all the vast tides of migration that have swept through history, <u>maybe none is more concentrated as</u> the wave that brought 12 million immigrants onto American shores in little more than three decades.

    (A) maybe none is more concentrated as
    (B) it may be that none is more concentrated as
    (C) perhaps it is none that is more concentrated than
    (D) maybe it is none that was more concentrated than
    (E) perhaps none was more concentrated than

5. Diabetes, together with its serious complications, <u>ranks as the nation's third leading cause of death, surpassed only</u> by heart disease and cancer.

    (A) ranks as the nation's third leading cause of death, surpassed only
    (B) rank as the nation's third leading cause of death, only surpassed
    (C) has the rank of the nation's third leading cause of death, only surpassed
    (D) are the nation's third leading causes of death, surpassed only
    (E) have been ranked as the nation's third leading causes of death, only surpassed

6. In late 1997, the chambers inside the pyramid of the Pharaoh Menkaure at Giza were closed to visitors for cleaning and repair due to moisture exhaled by tourists, which raised its humidity to such levels so that salt from the stone was crystallizing and fungus was growing on the walls.

   (A) due to moisture exhaled by tourists, which raised its humidity to such levels so that salt from the stone was crystallizing

   (B) due to moisture that tourists had exhaled, thereby raising its humidity to such levels that salt from the stone would crystallize

   (C) because tourists were exhaling moisture, which had raised the humidity within them to levels such that salt from the stone would crystallize

   (D) because of moisture that was exhaled by tourists raising the humidity within them to levels so high as to make the salt from the stone crystallize

   (E) because moisture exhaled by tourists had raised the humidity within them to such levels that salt from the stone was crystallizing

7. As its sales of computer products have surpassed those of measuring instruments, the company has become increasingly willing to compete for the mass market sales they would in the past have conceded to rivals.

   (A) they would in the past have conceded to rivals

   (B) they would have conceded previously to their rivals

   (C) that in the past would have been conceded previously to rivals

   (D) it previously would have conceded to rivals in the past

   (E) it would in the past have conceded to rivals

8. The widely accepted big bang theory holds that the universe began in an explosive instant ten to twenty billion years ago and has been expanding ever since.

   (A) that the universe began in an explosive instant ten to twenty billion years ago and has been expanding

   (B) that the universe had begun in an explosive instant ten to twenty billion years ago and had been expanding

   (C) that the beginning of the universe was an explosive instant ten to twenty billion years ago that has expanded

   (D) the beginning of the universe to have been an explosive instant ten to twenty billion years ago that is expanding

   (E) the universe to have begun in an explosive instant ten to twenty billion years ago and has been expanding

9. Like the idolization accorded the Brontës and Brownings, James Joyce and Virginia Woolf are often subjected to the kind of veneration that blurs the distinction between the artist and the human being.

   (A) Like the idolization accorded the Brontës and Brownings,

   (B) As the Brontës' and Brownings' idolization,

   (C) Like that accorded to the Brontës and Brownings,

   (D) As it is of the Brontës and Brownings,

   (E) Like the Brontës and Brownings,

10. Carnivorous mammals can endure what would otherwise be lethal levels of body heat because they have a heat-exchange network which kept the brain from getting too hot.

    (A) which kept

    (B) that keeps

    (C) which has kept

    (D) that has been keeping

    (E) having kept

11. There are several ways to build solid walls using just mud or clay, but the most extensively used method has been the forming of bricks out of mud or clay, and, after some preliminary air drying or sun drying, they are laid in the wall in mud mortar.

    (A) the forming of bricks out of mud or clay, and, after some preliminary air drying or sun drying, they are laid

    (B) forming the mud or clay into bricks, and, after some preliminary air drying or sun drying, to lay them

    (C) having bricks formed from mud or clay, and, after some preliminary air drying or sun drying, they were laid

    (D) to form the mud or clay into bricks, and, after some preliminary air drying or sun drying, to lay them

    (E) that bricks were formed from mud or clay, which, after some preliminary air drying or sun drying, were laid

12. Rising inventories, <u>when unaccompanied correspondingly by increases in sales, can lead</u> to production cutbacks that would hamper economic growth.

    (A) when unaccompanied correspondingly by increases in sales, can lead
    (B) when not accompanied by corresponding increases in sales, possibly leads
    (C) when they were unaccompanied by corresponding sales increases, can lead
    (D) if not accompanied by correspondingly increased sales, possibly leads
    (E) if not accompanied by corresponding increases in sales, can lead

13. A surge in new home sales and a drop in weekly unemployment <u>claims suggest that the economy might not be as weak as some analysts previously thought</u>.

    (A) claims suggest that the economy might not be as weak as some analysts previously thought
    (B) claims suggests that the economy might not be so weak as some analysts have previously thought
    (C) claims suggest that the economy might not be as weak as have been previously thought by some analysts
    (D) claims, suggesting about the economy that it might not be so weak as previously thought by some analysts
    (E) claims, suggesting the economy might not be as weak as previously thought to be by some analysts

14. Sunspots, vortices of gas associated with strong electromagnetic activity, <u>are visible as dark spots on the surface of the Sun but have never been sighted on</u> the Sun's poles or equator.

    (A) are visible as dark spots on the surface of the Sun but have never been sighted on
    (B) are visible as dark spots that never have been sighted on the surface of the Sun
    (C) appear on the surface of the Sun as dark spots although never sighted at
    (D) appear as dark spots on the surface of the Sun, although never having been sighted at
    (E) appear as dark spots on the Sun's surface, which have never been sighted on

15. Warning that computers in the United States are not secure, the National Academy of Sciences has urged the nation to revamp computer security procedures, institute new emergency response teams, <u>creating a special nongovernment organization to take</u> charge of computer security planning.

    (A) creating a special nongovernment organization to take
    (B) creating a special nongovernment organization that takes
    (C) creating a special nongovernment organization for taking
    (D) and create a special nongovernment organization for taking
    (E) and create a special nongovernment organization to take

16. Retail sales rose 0.8 of 1 percent in August, intensifying expectations <u>that personal spending in the July–September quarter more than doubled that of</u> the 1.4 percent growth rate in personal spending for the previous quarter.

    (A) that personal spending in the July–September quarter more than doubled that of
    (B) that personal spending in the July–September quarter would more than double
    (C) of personal spending in the July–September quarter, that it more than doubled
    (D) of personal spending in the July–September quarter more than doubling that of
    (E) of personal spending in the July–September quarter, that it would more than double that of

17. The commission has directed advertisers to restrict the use of the word "natural" to foods that do not contain color or flavor additives, chemical preservatives, <u>or nothing that has been</u> synthesized.

    (A) or nothing that has been
    (B) or that has been
    (C) and nothing that is
    (D) or anything that has been
    (E) and anything

18. Plants are more efficient at acquiring carbon than are fungi, in the form of carbon dioxide, and converting it to energy-rich sugars.

    (A) Plants are more efficient at acquiring carbon than are fungi,

    (B) Plants are more efficient at acquiring carbon than fungi,

    (C) Plants are more efficient than fungi at acquiring carbon,

    (D) Plants, more efficient than fungi at acquiring carbon,

    (E) Plants acquire carbon more efficiently than fungi,

19. The Iroquois were primarily planters, but supplementing their cultivation of maize, squash, and beans with fishing and hunting.

    (A) but supplementing

    (B) and had supplemented

    (C) and even though they supplemented

    (D) although they supplemented

    (E) but with supplementing

20. As contrasted with the honeybee, the yellow jacket can sting repeatedly without dying and carries a potent venom that can cause intense pain.

    (A) As contrasted with the honeybee,

    (B) In contrast to the honeybee's,

    (C) Unlike the sting of the honeybee,

    (D) Unlike that of the honeybee,

    (E) Unlike the honeybee,

21. Neuroscientists, having amassed a wealth of knowledge over the past twenty years about the brain and its development from birth to adulthood, are now drawing solid conclusions about how the human brain grows and how babies acquire language.

    (A) Neuroscientists, having amassed a wealth of knowledge over the past twenty years about the brain and its development from birth to adulthood, are

    (B) Neuroscientists, having amassed a wealth of knowledge about the brain and its development from birth to adulthood over the past twenty years, and are

    (C) Neuroscientists amassing a wealth of knowledge about the brain and its development from birth to adulthood over the past twenty years, and are

    (D) Neuroscientists have amassed a wealth of knowledge over the past twenty years about the brain and its development from birth to adulthood,

    (E) Neuroscientists have amassed, over the past twenty years, a wealth of knowledge about the brain and its development from birth to adulthood,

22. None of the attempts to specify the causes of crime explains why most of the people exposed to the alleged causes do not commit crimes and, conversely, why so many of those not so exposed have.

    (A) have

    (B) has

    (C) shall

    (D) do

    (E) could

23. In a previous design, the weight of the discus used in track competition is concentrated in a metal center, but now it is lined with lead around the perimeter, thereby improving stability in flight and resulting in longer throws.

    (A) In a previous design, the weight of the discus used in track competition is concentrated in a metal center, but now it is

    (B) According to a previous design, the weight of the discus used in track competition was concentrated in a metal center, but now it is

    (C) Once designed with its weight concentrated in a metal center, the discus used in track competition is now

    (D) The discus used in track competition, once designed with its weight concentrated in a metal center, but now

    (E) The discus used in track competition was once designed having its weight concentrated in a metal center and now

24. In virtually all types of tissue in every animal species, dioxin induces the production of enzymes that are the organism's <u>trying to metabolize, or render harmless, the chemical that is irritating it</u>.

    (A) trying to metabolize, or render harmless, the chemical that is irritating it
    (B) trying that it metabolize, or render harmless, the chemical irritant
    (C) attempt to try to metabolize, or render harmless, such a chemical irritant
    (D) attempt to try and metabolize, or render harmless, the chemical irritating it
    (E) attempt to metabolize, or render harmless, the chemical irritant

25. <u>Based on accounts of various ancient writers,</u> scholars have painted a sketchy picture of the activities of an all-female cult that, perhaps as early as the sixth century B.C., worshipped a goddess known in Latin as Bona Dea, "the good goddess."

    (A) Based on accounts of various ancient writers,
    (B) Basing it on various ancient writers' accounts,
    (C) With accounts of various ancient writers used for a basis,
    (D) By the accounts of various ancient writers they used,
    (E) Using accounts of various ancient writers,

26. Emily Dickinson's letters to Susan Huntington <u>Dickinson were written over a period beginning a few years before Susan's marriage to Emily's brother and ending shortly before Emily's death in 1886, outnumbering</u> her letters to anyone else.

    (A) Dickinson were written over a period beginning a few years before Susan's marriage to Emily's brother and ending shortly before Emily's death in 1886, outnumbering
    (B) Dickinson were written over a period that begins a few years before Susan's marriage to Emily's brother and ended shortly before Emily's death in 1886, outnumber
    (C) Dickinson, written over a period beginning a few years before Susan's marriage to Emily's brother and that ends shortly before Emily's death in 1886 and outnumbering

    (D) Dickinson, which were written over a period beginning a few years before Susan's marriage to Emily's brother, ending shortly before Emily's death in 1886, and outnumbering
    (E) Dickinson, which were written over a period beginning a few years before Susan's marriage to Emily's brother and ending shortly before Emily's death in 1886, outnumber

27. Paleontologists believe that fragments of a primate jawbone unearthed in Burma and estimated <u>at 40 to 44 million years old provide evidence of</u> a crucial step along the evolutionary path that led to human beings.

    (A) at 40 to 44 million years old provide evidence of
    (B) as being 40 to 44 million years old provides evidence of
    (C) that it is 40 to 44 million years old provides evidence of what was
    (D) to be 40 to 44 million years old provide evidence of
    (E) as 40 to 44 million years old provides evidence of what was

28. Building on civilizations that preceded them in coastal Peru, the Mochica developed their own elaborate society, <u>based on cultivating such crops like corn and beans, the harvesting of fish and shellfish, and exploiting</u> other wild and domestic resources.

    (A) based on cultivating such crops like corn and beans, the harvesting of fish and shellfish, and exploiting
    (B) based on the cultivation of such crops as corn and beans, the harvesting of fish and seafood, and the exploitation of
    (C) and basing it on the cultivation of crops like corn and beans, harvesting fish and seafood, and the exploiting of
    (D) and they based it on their cultivation of crops such as corn and beans, the harvest of fish and seafood, and exploiting
    (E) and they based it on their cultivating such crops like corn and beans, their harvest of fish and shellfish, and they exploited

29. The end of the eighteenth century saw the emergence of prize-stock breeding, with individual bulls and cows receiving awards, fetching unprecedented prices, and <u>excited</u> enormous interest whenever they were put on show.

    (A) excited
    (B) it excited
    (C) exciting
    (D) would excite
    (E) it had excited

30. For members of the seventeenth-century Ashanti nation in Africa, animal-hide shields with wooden frames were essential items of military equipment, <u>a method to protect</u> warriors against enemy arrows and spears.

    (A) a method to protect
    (B) as a method protecting
    (C) protecting
    (D) as a protection of
    (E) to protect

31. <u>Unlike the conviction held by many of her colleagues that genes were</u> relatively simple and static, Barbara McClintock adhered to her own more complicated ideas about how genes might operate, and in 1983, at the age of 81, was awarded a Nobel Prize for her discovery that the genes in corn are capable of moving from one chromosomal site to another.

    (A) Unlike the conviction held by many of her colleagues that genes were
    (B) Although many of her colleagues were of the conviction of genes being
    (C) Contrary to many of her colleagues being convinced that genes were
    (D) Even though many of her colleagues were convinced that genes were
    (E) Even with many of her colleagues convinced of genes being

32. Galileo was convinced that natural phenomena, as manifestations of the laws of physics, would appear the same to someone on the deck of a ship moving smoothly and uniformly through the <u>water as a</u> person standing on land.

    (A) water as a
    (B) water as to a
    (C) water; just as it would to a
    (D) water, as it would to the
    (E) water; just as to the

33. <u>Because an oversupply of computer chips has sent prices plunging,</u> the manufacturer has announced that it will cut production by closing its factories for two days a month.

    (A) Because an oversupply of computer chips has sent prices plunging,
    (B) Because of plunging prices for computer chips, which is due to an oversupply,
    (C) Because computer chip prices have been sent plunging, which resulted from an oversupply,
    (D) Due to plunging computer chip prices from an oversupply,
    (E) Due to an oversupply, with the result that computer chip prices have been sent plunging,

34. Beyond the immediate cash flow crisis that the museum faces, its survival depends on <u>if it can broaden its membership and leave</u> its cramped quarters for a site where it can store and exhibit its more than 12,000 artifacts.

    (A) if it can broaden its membership and leave
    (B) whether it can broaden its membership and leave
    (C) whether or not it has the capability to broaden its membership and can leave
    (D) its ability for broadening its membership and leaving
    (E) the ability for it to broaden its membership and leave

35. Along with the drop in producer prices announced yesterday, the strong retail sales figures released today seem <u>like it is indicative that</u> the economy, although growing slowly, is not nearing a recession.

    (A) like it is indicative that
    (B) as if to indicate
    (C) to indicate that
    (D) indicative of
    (E) like an indication of

36. Dressed as a man and using the name Robert Shurtleff, Deborah Sampson, the first woman to draw a soldier's pension, joined the Continental Army in 1782 at the age of <u>22, was injured three times, and was discharged in 1783 because she had become</u> too ill to serve.

    (A) 22, was injured three times, and was discharged in 1783 because she had become
    (B) 22, was injured three times, while being discharged in 1783 because she had become
    (C) 22 and was injured three times, and discharged in 1783, being
    (D) 22, injured three times, and was discharged in 1783 because she was
    (E) 22, having been injured three times and discharged in 1783, being

37. Although schistosomiasis is not often fatal, <u>it is so debilitating that it has become an economic</u> drain on many developing countries.

    (A) it is so debilitating that it has become an economic
    (B) it is of such debilitation, it has become an economical
    (C) so debilitating is it as to become an economic
    (D) such is its debilitation, it becomes an economical
    (E) there is so much debilitation that it has become an economical

38. In 1850, Lucretia Mott published her *Discourse on Women*, <u>arguing in a treatise for women to have equal political and legal rights</u> and for changes in the married women's property laws.

    (A) arguing in a treatise for women to have equal political and legal rights
    (B) arguing in a treatise for equal political and legal rights for women
    (C) a treatise that advocates women's equal political and legal rights
    (D) a treatise advocating women's equal political and legal rights
    (E) a treatise that argued for equal political and legal rights for women

39. In 1527 King Henry VIII sought to have his marriage to Queen Catherine annulled <u>so as to marry</u> Anne Boleyn.

    (A) so as to marry
    (B) and so could be married to
    (C) to be married to
    (D) so that he could marry
    (E) in order that he would marry

40. Dr. Tonegawa won the Nobel Prize for discovering how the body can constantly change its genes to fashion a <u>seeming unlimited number of antibodies, each specifically targeted at</u> an invading microbe or foreign substance.

    (A) seeming unlimited number of antibodies, each specifically targeted at
    (B) seeming unlimited number of antibodies, each targeted specifically to
    (C) seeming unlimited number of antibodies, all specifically targeted at
    (D) seemingly unlimited number of antibodies, all of them targeted specifically to
    (E) seemingly unlimited number of antibodies, each targeted specifically at

41. To develop more accurate population forecasts, demographers <u>have to know a great deal more than now about the social and economic</u> determinants of fertility.

    (A) have to know a great deal more than now about the social and economic
    (B) have to know a great deal more than they do now about the social and economical
    (C) would have to know a great deal more than they do now about the social and economical
    (D) would have to know a great deal more than they do now about the social and economic
    (E) would have to know a great deal more than now about the social and economic

42. Scientists have recently discovered what could be the largest and oldest living organism on Earth, a giant fungus that is an interwoven filigree of mushrooms and rootlike tentacles spawned by a single fertilized spore some 10,000 years ago and <u>extending</u> for more than 30 acres in the soil of a Michigan forest.

    (A) extending
    (B) extends
    (C) extended
    (D) it extended
    (E) is extending

43. Laos has a land area <u>about the same as Great Britain but only four million in population, where many</u> are members of hill tribes ensconced in the virtually inaccessible mountain valleys of the north.

    (A) about the same as Great Britain but only four million in population, where many
    (B) of about the same size as Great Britain is, but in Laos there is a population of only four million, and many
    (C) that is about the same size as Great Britain's land area, but in Laos with a population of only four million people, many of them
    (D) comparable to the size of Great Britain, but only four million in population, and many
    (E) comparable to that of Great Britain but a population of only four million people, many of whom

44. The plot of *The Bostonians* centers on the <u>rivalry between Olive Chancellor, an active feminist, with her charming and cynical cousin, Basil Ransom,</u> when they find themselves drawn to the same radiant young woman whose talent for public speaking has won her an ardent following.

    (A) rivalry between Olive Chancellor, an active feminist, with her charming and cynical cousin, Basil Ransom,
    (B) rivals Olive Chancellor, an active feminist, against her charming and cynical cousin, Basil Ransom,
    (C) rivalry that develops between Olive Chancellor, an active feminist, and Basil Ransom, her charming and cynical cousin,
    (D) developing rivalry between Olive Chancellor, an active feminist, with Basil Ransom, her charming and cynical cousin,
    (E) active feminist, Olive Chancellor, and the rivalry with her charming and cynical cousin Basil Ransom,

45. Quasars, at billions of light-years from Earth the most distant observable objects in the universe, <u>believed to be</u> the cores of galaxies in an early stage of development.

    (A) believed to be
    (B) are believed to be
    (C) some believe them to be
    (D) some believe they are
    (E) it is believed that they are

46. In ancient Thailand, <u>much of the local artisans' creative energy was expended for the creation of Buddha images and when they constructed and decorated the temples that enshrined them</u>.

    (A) much of the local artisans' creative energy was expended for the creation of Buddha images and when they constructed and decorated the temples that enshrined them
    (B) much of the local artisans' creative energy was expended on the creation of Buddha images and on construction and decoration of the temples in which they were enshrined
    (C) much of the local artisans' creative energy was expended on the creation of Buddha images as well as constructing and decoration of the temples in which they were enshrined
    (D) creating images of Buddha accounted for much of the local artisans' creative energy, and also constructing and decorating the temples enshrining them
    (E) the creation of Buddha images accounted for much of the local artisans' creative energy as well as construction and decoration of the temples that enshrined them

47. Five fledgling sea eagles left their nests in western Scotland this summer, <u>bringing</u> to 34 the number of wild birds successfully raised since transplants from Norway began in 1975.

    (A) bringing
    (B) and brings
    (C) and it brings
    (D) and it brought
    (E) and brought

48. In 1713, Alexander Pope began <u>his translation of the *Iliad*, a work that, taking him seven years until completion, and that literary critic Samuel Johnson, Pope's contemporary, pronounced</u> the greatest translation in any language.

    (A) his translation of the *Iliad*, a work that, taking him seven years until completion, and that literary critic Samuel Johnson, Pope's contemporary, pronounced
    (B) his translation of the *Iliad*, a work that took him seven years to complete and that literary critic Samuel Johnson, Pope's contemporary, pronounced
    (C) his translation of the *Iliad*, a work that had taken seven years to complete and that literary critic Samuel Johnson, Pope's contemporary, pronounced it as
    (D) translating the *Iliad*, a work that took seven years until completion and that literary critic Samuel Johnson, Pope's contemporary, pronounced it as
    (E) translating the *Iliad*, a work that had taken seven years to complete and literary critic Samuel Johnson, Pope's contemporary, pronounced it

49. The automotive conveyor-belt system, which Henry Ford modeled after an assembly-line technique introduced by Ransom Olds, reduced <u>from a day and a half to 93 minutes the required time of assembling a Model T</u>.

    (A) from a day and a half to 93 minutes the required time of assembling a Model T
    (B) the time being required to assemble a Model T, from a day and a half down to 93 minutes
    (C) the time being required to assemble a Model T, a day and a half to 93 minutes

    (D) the time required to assemble a Model T from a day and a half to 93 minutes
    (E) from a day and a half to 93 minutes, the time required for the assembling of a Model T

50. According to some analysts, the gains in the stock market reflect growing confidence <u>that the economy will avoid the recession that many had feared earlier in the year and instead come</u> in for a "soft landing," followed by a gradual increase in business activity.

    (A) that the economy will avoid the recession that many had feared earlier in the year and instead come
    (B) in the economy to avoid the recession, what many feared earlier in the year, rather to come
    (C) in the economy's ability to avoid the recession, something earlier in the year many had feared, and instead to come
    (D) in the economy to avoid the recession many were fearing earlier in the year, and rather to come
    (E) that the economy will avoid the recession that was feared earlier this year by many, with it instead coming

51. A new study suggests that the conversational pace of everyday life may be so brisk <u>it hampers the ability of some children for distinguishing discrete sounds and words and, the result is, to make</u> sense of speech.

    (A) it hampers the ability of some children for distinguishing discrete sounds and words and, the result is, to make
    (B) that it hampers the ability of some children to distinguish discrete sounds and words and, as a result, to make
    (C) that it hampers the ability of some children to distinguish discrete sounds and words and, the result of this, they are unable to make
    (D) that it hampers the ability of some children to distinguish discrete sounds and words, and results in not making
    (E) as to hamper the ability of some children for distinguishing discrete sounds and words, resulting in being unable to make

52. To Josephine Baker, Paris was her home long before it was fashionable to be an expatriate, and she remained in France during the Second World War as a performer and an intelligence agent for the Resistance.

    (A) To Josephine Baker, Paris was her home long before it was fashionable to be an expatriate,

    (B) For Josephine Baker, long before it was fashionable to be an expatriate, Paris was her home,

    (C) Josephine Baker made Paris her home long before to be an expatriate was fashionable,

    (D) Long before it was fashionable to be an expatriate, Josephine Baker made Paris her home,

    (E) Long before it was fashionable being an expatriate, Paris was home to Josephine Baker,

53. The nineteenth-century chemist Humphry Davy presented the results of his early experiments in his "Essay on Heat and Light," a critique of all chemistry since Robert Boyle as well as a vision of a new chemistry that Davy hoped to found.

    (A) a critique of all chemistry since Robert Boyle as well as a vision of a

    (B) a critique of all chemistry following Robert Boyle and also his envisioning of a

    (C) a critique of all chemistry after Robert Boyle and envisioning as well

    (D) critiquing all chemistry from Robert Boyle forward and also a vision of

    (E) critiquing all the chemistry done since Robert Boyle as well as his own envisioning of

54. The report recommended that the hospital should eliminate unneeded beds, expensive services should be consolidated, and use space in other hospitals.

    (A) should eliminate unneeded beds, expensive services should be consolidated, and use space in other hospitals

    (B) should eliminate unneeded beds, expensive services should be consolidated, and other hospitals' space be used

    (C) should eliminate unneeded beds, expensive services should be consolidated, and to use space in other hospitals

    (D) eliminate unneeded beds, consolidate expensive services, and other hospitals' space used

    (E) eliminate unneeded beds, consolidate expensive services, and use space in other hospitals

55. Many house builders offer rent-to-buy programs that enable a family with insufficient savings for a conventional down payment to be able to move into new housing and to apply part of the rent to a purchase later.

    (A) programs that enable a family with insufficient savings for a conventional down payment to be able to move into new housing and to apply

    (B) programs that enable a family with insufficient savings for a conventional down payment to move into new housing and to apply

    (C) programs; that enables a family with insufficient savings for a conventional down payment to move into new housing, to apply

    (D) programs, which enables a family with insufficient savings for a conventional down payment to move into new housing, applying

    (E) programs, which enable a family with insufficient savings for a conventional down payment to be able to move into new housing, applying

56. Many of the earliest known images of Hindu deities in India date from the time of the Kushan Empire, fashioned either from the spotted sandstone of Mathura or Gandharan grey schist.

    (A) Empire, fashioned either from the spotted sandstone of Mathura or

    (B) Empire, fashioned from either the spotted sandstone of Mathura or from

    (C) Empire, either fashioned from the spotted sandstone of Mathura or

    (D) Empire and either fashioned from the spotted sandstone of Mathura or from

    (E) Empire and were fashioned either from the spotted sandstone of Mathura or from

57. That educators have not anticipated the impact of microcomputer technology can hardly be said that it is their fault: Alvin Toffler, one of the most prominent students of the future, did not even mention microcomputers in *Future Shock*, published in 1970.

    (A) That educators have not anticipated the impact of microcomputer technology can hardly be said that it is their fault

    (B) That educators have not anticipated the impact of microcomputer technology can hardly be said to be at fault

    (C) It can hardly be said that it is the fault of educators who have not anticipated the impact of microcomputer technology

    (D) It can hardly be said that educators are at fault for not anticipating the impact of microcomputer technology

    (E) The fact that educators are at fault for not anticipating the impact of microcomputer technology can hardly be said

58. A leading figure in the Scottish Enlightenment, Adam Smith's two major books are to democratic capitalism what Marx's *Das Kapital* is to socialism.

    (A) Adam Smith's two major books are to democratic capitalism what

    (B) Adam Smith's two major books are to democratic capitalism like

    (C) Adam Smith's two major books are to democratic capitalism just as

    (D) Adam Smith wrote two major books that are to democratic capitalism similar to

    (E) Adam Smith wrote two major books that are to democratic capitalism what

59. The Olympic Games helped to keep peace among the pugnacious states of the Greek world in that a sacred truce was proclaimed during the festival's month.

    (A) world in that a sacred truce was proclaimed during the festival's month

    (B) world, proclaiming a sacred truce during the festival's month

    (C) world when they proclaimed a sacred truce for the festival month

    (D) world, for a sacred truce was proclaimed during the month of the festival

    (E) world by proclamation of a sacred truce that was for the month of the festival

60. While all states face similar industrial waste problems, the predominating industries and the regulatory environment of the states obviously determines the types and amounts of waste produced, as well as the cost of disposal.

    (A) all states face similar industrial waste problems, the predominating industries and the regulatory environment of the states obviously determines

    (B) each state faces a similar industrial waste problem, their predominant industries and regulatory environment obviously determine

    (C) all states face a similar industrial waste problem; their predominating industries and regulatory environment obviously determines

    (D) each state faces similar industrial waste problems, the predominant industries and the regulatory environment of each state obviously determines

    (E) all states face similar industrial waste problems, the predominant industries and the regulatory environment of each state obviously determine

61. Rivaling the pyramids of Egypt or even the ancient cities of the Maya as an achievement, the army of terra-cotta warriors created to protect Qin Shi Huang, China's first emperor, in his afterlife is more than 2,000 years old and took 700,000 artisans more than 36 years to complete.

    (A) the army of terra-cotta warriors created to protect Qin Shi Huang, China's first emperor, in his afterlife is more than 2,000 years old and took 700,000 artisans more than 36 years to complete

    (B) Qin Shi Huang, China's first emperor, was protected in his afterlife by an army of terra-cotta warriors that was created more than 2,000 years ago by 700,000 artisans who took more than 36 years to complete it

    (C) it took 700,000 artisans more than 36 years to create an army of terra-cotta warriors more than 2,000 years ago that would protect Qin Shi Huang, China's first emperor, in his afterlife

    (D) more than 2,000 years ago, 700,000 artisans worked more than 36 years to create an army of terra-cotta warriors to protect Qin Shi Huang, China's first emperor, in his afterlife

    (E) more than 36 years were needed to complete the army of terra-cotta warriors that 700,000 artisans created 2,000 years ago to protect Qin Shi Huang, China's first emperor, in his afterlife

62. When Congress reconvenes, some newly elected members from rural states will try and establish tighter restrictions for the amount of grain farmers are to be allowed to grow and to encourage more aggressive sales of United States farm products overseas.

    (A) and establish tighter restrictions for the amount of grain farmers are to be allowed to grow and to encourage

    (B) and establish tighter restrictions on the amount of grain able to be grown by farmers and encouraging

    (C) establishing tighter restrictions for the amount of grain farmers are allowed to grow and to encourage

    (D) to establish tighter restrictions on the amount of grain capable of being grown by farmers and encouraging

    (E) to establish tighter restrictions on the amount of grain farmers will be allowed to grow and to encourage

63. The yield of natural gas from Norway's Troll gas field is expected to increase annually until the year 2005 and then to stabilize at six billion cubic feet a day, which will allow such an extraction rate at least for 50 years' production.

    (A) 2005 and then to stabilize at six billion cubic feet a day, which will allow such an extraction rate at least for

    (B) 2005 and then to stabilize at six billion cubic feet a day, an extraction rate that will allow at least

    (C) 2005 and then stabilizing at six billion cubic feet a day, with such an extraction rate at the least allowing

    (D) 2005, then stabilizing at six billion cubic feet a day, allowing such an extraction rate for at least

    (E) 2005, then stabilizing at six billion cubic feet a day, which will allow such an extraction rate for at least

64. Doctors generally agree that such factors as cigarette smoking, eating rich foods high in fats, and alcohol consumption not only do damage by themselves but also aggravate genetic predispositions toward certain diseases.

    (A) not only do damage by themselves but also aggravate

    (B) do damage by themselves but also are aggravating to

    (C) are damaging by themselves but also are aggravating

    (D) not only do damage by themselves, they are also aggravating to

    (E) are doing damage by themselves, and they are also aggravating

65. In a plan to stop the erosion of East Coast beaches, the Army Corps of Engineers proposed building parallel to shore a breakwater of rocks that would rise six feet above the waterline and act as a buffer, so that it absorbs the energy of crashing waves and protecting the beaches.

    (A) act as a buffer, so that it absorbs

    (B) act like a buffer so as to absorb

    (C) act as a buffer, absorbing

    (D) acting as a buffer, absorbing

    (E) acting like a buffer, absorb

66. The 32 species that make up the dolphin family are closely related to whales and in fact include the animal known as the killer whale, which can grow to be 30 feet long and is famous for its aggressive hunting pods.

    (A) include the animal known as the killer whale, which can grow to be 30 feet long and is

    (B) include the animal known as the killer whale, growing as big as 30 feet long and

    (C) include the animal known as the killer whale, growing up to 30 feet long and being

    (D) includes the animal known as the killer whale, which can grow as big as 30 feet long and is

    (E) includes the animal known as the killer whale, which can grow to be 30 feet long and it is

67. Affording strategic proximity to the Strait of Gibraltar, Morocco was also of interest to the French throughout the first half of the twentieth century because they assumed that if they did not hold it, their grip on Algeria was always insecure.

    (A) if they did not hold it, their grip on Algeria was always insecure
    (B) without it their grip on Algeria would never be secure
    (C) their grip on Algeria was not ever secure if they did not hold it
    (D) without that, they could never be secure about their grip on Algeria
    (E) never would their grip on Algeria be secure if they did not hold it

68. The first trenches that were cut into a 500-acre site at Tell Hamoukar, Syria, have yielded strong evidence for centrally administered complex societies in northern regions of the Middle East that were arising simultaneously with but independently of the more celebrated city-states of southern Mesopotamia, in what is now southern Iraq.

    (A) that were cut into a 500-acre site at Tell Hamoukar, Syria, have yielded strong evidence for centrally administered complex societies in northern regions of the Middle East that were arising simultaneously with but
    (B) that were cut into a 500-acre site at Tell Hamoukar, Syria, yields strong evidence that centrally administered complex societies in northern regions of the Middle East were arising simultaneously with but also
    (C) having been cut into a 500-acre site at Tell Hamoukar, Syria, have yielded strong evidence that centrally administered complex societies in northern regions of the Middle East were arising simultaneously but
    (D) cut into a 500-acre site at Tell Hamoukar, Syria, yields strong evidence of centrally administered complex societies in northern regions of the Middle East arising simultaneously but also
    (E) cut into a 500-acre site at Tell Hamoukar, Syria, have yielded strong evidence that centrally administered complex societies in northern regions of the Middle East arose simultaneously with but

69. Once they had seen the report from the medical examiner, the investigators did not doubt whether the body recovered from the river was the man who had attempted to escape from the state prison.

    (A) did not doubt whether the body recovered from the river was
    (B) have no doubt whether the body recovered from the river was
    (C) had not doubted that the body recovered from the river was
    (D) have no doubt whether the body recovered from the river was that of
    (E) had no doubt that the body recovered from the river was that of

70. His studies of ice-polished rocks in his Alpine homeland, far outside the range of present-day glaciers, led Louis Agassiz in 1837 to propose the concept of an age in which great ice sheets had existed in now currently temperate areas.

    (A) in which great ice sheets had existed in now currently temperate areas
    (B) in which great ice sheets existed in what are now temperate areas
    (C) when great ice sheets existed where there were areas now temperate
    (D) when great ice sheets had existed in current temperate areas
    (E) when great ice sheets existed in areas now that are temperate

71. Unlike the original National Museum of Science and Technology in Italy, where the models are encased in glass or operated only by staff members, the Virtual Leonardo Project, an online version of the museum, encourages visitors to "touch" each exhibit, which thereby activates the animated functions of the piece.

    (A) exhibit, which thereby activates
    (B) exhibit, in turn an activation of
    (C) exhibit, and it will activate
    (D) exhibit and thereby activate
    (E) exhibit which, as a result, activates

72. More and more in recent years, cities are stressing the arts as a means to greater economic development and investing millions of dollars in cultural activities, despite strained municipal budgets and fading federal support.

    (A) to greater economic development and investing
    (B) to greater development economically and investing
    (C) of greater economic development and invest
    (D) of greater development economically and invest
    (E) for greater economic development and the investment of

73. Combining enormous physical strength with higher intelligence, the Neanderthals appear as equipped for facing any obstacle the environment could put in their path, but their relatively sudden disappearance during the Paleolithic era indicates that an inability to adapt to some environmental change led to their extinction.

    (A) appear as equipped for facing any obstacle the environment could put in their path,
    (B) appear to have been equipped to face any obstacle the environment could put in their path,
    (C) appear as equipped to face any obstacle the environment could put in their paths,
    (D) appeared as equipped to face any obstacle the environment could put in their paths,
    (E) appeared to have been equipped for facing any obstacle the environment could put in their path,

74. A 1972 agreement between Canada and the United States reduced the amount of phosphates that municipalities had been allowed to dump into the Great Lakes.

    (A) reduced the amount of phosphates that municipalities had been allowed to dump
    (B) reduced the phosphate amount that municipalities had been dumping
    (C) reduces the phosphate amount municipalities have been allowed to dump
    (D) reduced the amount of phosphates that municipalities are allowed to dump
    (E) reduces the amount of phosphates allowed for dumping by municipalities

75. A proposal has been made to trim the horns from rhinoceroses to discourage poachers; the question is whether tourists will continue to visit game parks and see rhinoceroses after their horns are trimmed.

    (A) whether tourists will continue to visit game parks and see rhinoceroses after their horns are
    (B) whether tourists will continue to visit game parks to see one once their horns are
    (C) whether tourists will continue to visit game parks to see rhinoceroses once the animals' horns have been
    (D) if tourists will continue to visit game parks and see rhinoceroses once the animals' horns are
    (E) if tourists will continue to visit game parks to see one after the animals' horns have been

76. Retailers reported moderate gains in their November sales, as much because of their sales of a year earlier being so bad as that shoppers were getting a head start on buying their holiday gifts.

    (A) of their sales of a year earlier being so bad as that
    (B) of their sales a year earlier having been as bad as because
    (C) of their sales a year earlier being as bad as because
    (D) their sales a year earlier had been so bad as because
    (E) their sales of a year earlier were as bad as that

77. The only way for growers to salvage frozen citrus is to process them quickly into juice concentrate before they rot when warmer weather returns.

    (A) to process them quickly into juice concentrate before they rot when warmer weather returns
    (B) if they are quickly processed into juice concentrate before warmer weather returns to rot them
    (C) for them to be processed quickly into juice concentrate before the fruit rots when warmer weather returns
    (D) if the fruit is quickly processed into juice concentrate before they rot when warmer weather returns
    (E) to have it quickly processed into juice concentrate before warmer weather returns and rots the fruit

78. Fossils of the arm of a <u>sloth found in Puerto Rico in 1991, and dated at 34 million years old, made it the earliest known mammal of</u> the Greater Antilles Islands.

   (A) sloth found in Puerto Rico in 1991, and dated at 34 million years old, made it the earliest known mammal of

   (B) sloth, that they found in Puerto Rico in 1991, has been dated at 34 million years old, thus making it the earliest mammal known on

   (C) sloth that was found in Puerto Rico in 1991, was dated at 34 million years old, making this the earliest known mammal of

   (D) sloth, found in Puerto Rico in 1991, have been dated at 34 million years old, making the sloth the earliest known mammal on

   (E) sloth which, found in Puerto Rico in 1991, was dated at 34 million years old, made the sloth the earliest known mammal of

79. Defense attorneys have occasionally argued that their clients' misconduct stemmed from a reaction to something ingested, but <u>in attributing criminal or delinquent behavior to some food allergy,</u> the perpetrators are in effect told that they are not responsible for their actions.

   (A) in attributing criminal or delinquent behavior to some food allergy,

   (B) if criminal or delinquent behavior is attributed to an allergy to some food,

   (C) in attributing behavior that is criminal or delinquent to an allergy to some food,

   (D) if some food allergy is attributed as the cause of criminal or delinquent behavior,

   (E) in attributing a food allergy as the cause of criminal or delinquent behavior,

80. A report by the American Academy for the Advancement of Science has concluded that <u>much of the currently uncontrolled dioxins to which North Americans are exposed comes</u> from the incineration of wastes.

   (A) much of the currently uncontrolled dioxins to which North Americans are exposed comes

   (B) much of the currently uncontrolled dioxins that North Americans are exposed to come

   (C) much of the dioxins that are currently uncontrolled and that North Americans are exposed to comes

   (D) many of the dioxins that are currently uncontrolled and North Americans are exposed to come

   (E) many of the currently uncontrolled dioxins to which North Americans are exposed come

81. Recently physicians have determined that stomach ulcers are <u>not caused by stress, alcohol, or rich foods, but</u> a bacterium that dwells in the mucous lining of the stomach.

   (A) not caused by stress, alcohol, or rich foods, but

   (B) not caused by stress, alcohol, or rich foods, but are by

   (C) caused not by stress, alcohol, or rich foods, but by

   (D) caused not by stress, alcohol, and rich foods, but

   (E) caused not by stress, alcohol, and rich foods, but are by

82. According to a recent poll, owning and living in a freestanding house on its own land is still a goal of a majority of young adults, <u>like that of earlier generations</u>.

   (A) like that of earlier generations

   (B) as that for earlier generations

   (C) just as earlier generations did

   (D) as have earlier generations

   (E) as it was of earlier generations

83. In 2000, a mere two dozen products accounted for half the increase in spending on prescription drugs, <u>a phenomenon that is explained not just because of more expensive drugs but by the fact that doctors are writing</u> many more prescriptions for higher-cost drugs.

   (A) a phenomenon that is explained not just because of more expensive drugs but by the fact that doctors are writing

   (B) a phenomenon that is explained not just by the fact that drugs are becoming more expensive but also by the fact that doctors are writing

   (C) a phenomenon occurring not just because of drugs that are becoming more expensive but because of doctors having also written

   (D) which occurred not just because drugs are becoming more expensive but doctors are also writing

   (E) which occurred not just because of more expensive drugs but because doctors have also written

84. Often visible as smog, <u>ozone is formed in the atmosphere from</u> hydrocarbons and nitrogen oxides, two major pollutants emitted by automobiles, react with sunlight.

    (A) ozone is formed in the atmosphere from
    (B) ozone is formed in the atmosphere when
    (C) ozone is formed in the atmosphere, and when
    (D) ozone, formed in the atmosphere when
    (E) ozone, formed in the atmosphere from

85. Salt deposits and moisture threaten to destroy the Mohenjo-Daro excavation in Pakistan, the site of an ancient civilization <u>that flourished at the same time as the civilizations</u> in the Nile Delta and the river valleys of the Tigris and Euphrates.

    (A) that flourished at the same time as the civilizations
    (B) that had flourished at the same time as had the civilizations
    (C) that flourished at the same time those had
    (D) flourishing at the same time as those did
    (E) flourishing at the same time as those were

86. The results of the company's cost-cutting measures are evident in its profits, <u>which increased 5 percent during the first 3 months of this year after it fell</u> over the last two years.

    (A) which increased 5 percent during the first 3 months of this year after it fell
    (B) which had increased 5 percent during the first 3 months of this year after it had fallen
    (C) which have increased 5 percent during the first 3 months of this year after falling
    (D) with a 5 percent increase during the first 3 months of this year after falling
    (E) with a 5 percent increase during the first 3 months of this year after having fallen

87. In an effort to reduce their inventories, Italian vintners have cut prices; their wines <u>have been priced to sell, and they are</u>.

    (A) have been priced to sell, and they are
    (B) are priced to sell, and they have
    (C) are priced to sell, and they do
    (D) are being priced to sell, and have
    (E) had been priced to sell, and they have

88. <u>Thelonious Monk, who was a jazz pianist and composer, produced a body of work both rooted</u> in the stride-piano tradition of Willie (The Lion) Smith and Duke Ellington, yet in many ways he stood apart from the mainstream jazz repertory.

    (A) Thelonious Monk, who was a jazz pianist and composer, produced a body of work both rooted
    (B) Thelonious Monk, the jazz pianist and composer, produced a body of work that was rooted both
    (C) Jazz pianist and composer Thelonious Monk, who produced a body of work rooted
    (D) Jazz pianist and composer Thelonious Monk produced a body of work that was rooted
    (E) Jazz pianist and composer Thelonious Monk produced a body of work rooted both

89. Dirt roads may evoke the bucolic simplicity of another century, but financially strained townships point out that <u>dirt roads cost twice as much as maintaining paved roads</u>.

    (A) dirt roads cost twice as much as maintaining paved roads
    (B) dirt roads cost twice as much to maintain as paved roads do
    (C) maintaining dirt roads costs twice as much as paved roads do
    (D) maintaining dirt roads costs twice as much as it does for paved roads
    (E) to maintain dirt roads costs twice as much as for paved roads

90. Although early soap operas <u>were first aired on evening radio in the 1920s, they had moved to the daytime hours of the 1930s</u> when the evening schedule became crowded with comedians and variety shows.

    (A) were first aired on evening radio in the 1920s, they had moved to the daytime hours of the 1930s
    (B) were first aired on evening radio in the 1920s, they were moved to the daytime hours in the 1930s
    (C) were aired first on evening radio in the 1920s, moving to the daytime hours in the 1930s
    (D) were aired first in the evening on 1920s radio, they moved to the daytime hours of the 1930s
    (E) aired on evening radio first in the 1920s, they were moved to the 1930s in the daytime hours

91. Nobody knows exactly how many languages there are in the world, partly because of the difficulty of distinguishing between a language <u>and the sublanguages or dialects within it, but those who have tried to count typically have found</u> about five thousand.

    (A) and the sublanguages or dialects within it, but those who have tried to count typically have found

    (B) and the sublanguages or dialects within them, with those who have tried counting typically finding

    (C) and the sublanguages or dialects within it, but those who have tried counting it typically find

    (D) or the sublanguages or dialects within them, but those who tried to count them typically found

    (E) or the sublanguages or dialects within them, with those who have tried to count typically finding

92. The energy source on *Voyager 2* is not a nuclear reactor, in which atoms are actively broken <u>apart; rather</u> a kind of nuclear battery that uses natural radioactive decay to produce power.

    (A) apart; rather
    (B) apart, but rather
    (C) apart, but rather that of
    (D) apart, but that of
    (E) apart; it is that of

93. <u>Heating-oil prices are expected to be higher this year than last because refiners are paying about $5 a barrel more for crude oil than they were</u> last year.

    (A) Heating-oil prices are expected to be higher this year than last because refiners are paying about $5 a barrel more for crude oil than they were

    (B) Heating-oil prices are expected to rise higher this year over last because refiners pay about $5 a barrel for crude oil more than they did

    (C) Expectations are for heating-oil prices to be higher this year than last year's because refiners are paying about $5 a barrel for crude oil more than they did

    (D) It is the expectation that heating-oil prices will be higher for this year over last because refiners are paying about $5 a barrel more for crude oil now than what they were

    (E) It is expected that heating-oil prices will rise higher this year than last year's because refiners pay about $5 a barrel for crude oil more than they did

94. The recent surge in the number of airplane flights has clogged the nation's air-traffic control system, <u>to lead to 55 percent more delays at airports, and prompts</u> fears among some officials that safety is being compromised.

    (A) to lead to 55 percent more delays at airports, and prompts

    (B) leading to 55 percent more delay at airports and prompting

    (C) to lead to a 55 percent increase in delay at airports and prompt

    (D) to lead to an increase of 55 percent in delays at airports, and prompted

    (E) leading to a 55 percent increase in delays at airports and prompting

95. The peaks of a mountain range, acting like rocks in a streambed, produce ripples in the air flowing over them; the resulting flow pattern, with <u>crests and troughs that remain stationary although the air that forms them is moving rapidly, are</u> known as "standing waves."

    (A) crests and troughs that remain stationary although the air that forms them is moving rapidly, are

    (B) crests and troughs that remain stationary although they are formed by rapidly moving air, are

    (C) crests and troughs that remain stationary although the air that forms them is moving rapidly, is

    (D) stationary crests and troughs although the air that forms them is moving rapidly, are

    (E) stationary crests and troughs although they are formed by rapidly moving air, is

96. One of the primary distinctions <u>between our intelligence with that of other primates may lay not so much in any specific skill but</u> in our ability to extend knowledge gained in one context to new and different ones.

    (A) between our intelligence with that of other primates may lay not so much in any specific skill but

    (B) between our intelligence with that of other primates may lie not so much in any specific skill but instead

    (C) between our intelligence and that of other primates may lie not so much in any specific skill as

    (D) our intelligence has from that of other primates may lie not in any specific skill as

    (E) of our intelligence to that of other primates may lay not in any specific skill but

97. Unlike <u>Schoenberg's 12-tone system that dominated</u> the music of the postwar period, Bartók founded no school and left behind only a handful of disciples.

    (A) Schoenberg's 12-tone system that dominated

    (B) Schoenberg and his 12-tone system which dominated

    (C) Schoenberg, whose 12-tone system dominated

    (D) the 12-tone system of Schoenberg that has dominated

    (E) Schoenberg and the 12-tone system, dominating

98. <u>Even though Clovis points, spear points with longitudinal grooves chipped onto their faces, have been found all over North America, they are named for the New Mexico site where they were first discovered in 1932.</u>

    (A) Even though Clovis points, spear points with longitudinal grooves chipped onto their faces, have been found all over North America, they are named for the New Mexico site where they were first discovered in 1932.

    (B) Although named for the New Mexico site where first discovered in 1932, Clovis points are spear points of longitudinal grooves chipped onto their faces and have been found all over North America.

    (C) Named for the New Mexico site where they have been first discovered in 1932, Clovis points, spear points of longitudinal grooves chipped onto the faces, have been found all over North America.

    (D) Spear points with longitudinal grooves that are chipped onto the faces, Clovis points, even though named for the New Mexico site where first discovered in 1932, but were found all over North America.

    (E) While Clovis points are spear points whose faces have longitudinal grooves chipped into them, they have been found all over North America, and named for the New Mexico site where they have been first discovered in 1932.

99. Ranked as one of the most important of Europe's young playwrights, Franz Xaver Kroetz has written 40 plays; his works—translated into more than 30 languages—are produced more often <u>than any</u> contemporary German dramatist.

    (A) than any

    (B) than any other

    (C) than are any

    (D) than those of any other

    (E) as are those of any

100. <u>The stars, some of them at tremendous speeds, are in motion just as the planets are, yet being</u> so far away from Earth that their apparent positions in the sky do not change enough for their movement to be observed during a single human lifetime.

    (A) The stars, some of them at tremendous speeds, are in motion just as the planets are, yet being

    (B) Like the planets, the stars are in motion, some of them at tremendous speeds, but they are

    (C) Although like the planets the stars are in motion, some of them at tremendous speeds, yet

    (D) As the planets, the stars are in motion, some of them at tremendous speeds, but they are

    (E) The stars are in motion like the planets, some of which at tremendous speeds are in motion but

101. Heavy commitment by an executive to a course of action, especially if it has worked well in the past, makes it likely to miss signs of incipient trouble or misinterpret them when they do appear.

   (A) Heavy commitment by an executive to a course of action, especially if it has worked well in the past, makes it likely to miss signs of incipient trouble or misinterpret them when they do appear.

   (B) An executive who is heavily committed to a course of action, especially one that worked well in the past, makes missing signs of incipient trouble or misinterpreting ones likely when they do appear.

   (C) An executive who is heavily committed to a course of action is likely to miss or misinterpret signs of incipient trouble when they do appear, especially if it has worked well in the past.

   (D) Executives' being heavily committed to a course of action, especially if it has worked well in the past, makes them likely to miss signs of incipient trouble or misinterpreting them when they do appear.

   (E) Being heavily committed to a course of action, especially one that has worked well in the past, is likely to make an executive miss signs of incipient trouble or misinterpret them when they do appear.

102. As rainfall began to decrease in the Southwest about the middle of the twelfth century, most of the Monument Valley Anasazi abandoned their homes to join other clans whose access to water was less limited.

   (A) whose access to water was less limited

   (B) where there was access to water that was less limited

   (C) where they had less limited water access

   (D) with less limitations on water access

   (E) having less limitations to water access

103. Yellow jackets number among the 900 or so species of the world's social wasps, wasps living in a highly cooperative and organized society where they consist almost entirely of females—the queen and her sterile female workers.

   (A) wasps living in a highly cooperative and organized society where they consist almost entirely of

   (B) wasps that live in a highly cooperative and organized society consisting almost entirely of

   (C) which means they live in a highly cooperative and organized society, almost all

   (D) which means that their society is highly cooperative, organized, and it is almost entirely

   (E) living in a society that is highly cooperative, organized, and it consists of almost all

104. El Niño, the periodic abnormal warming of the sea surface off Peru, a phenomenon in which changes in the ocean and atmosphere combine allowing the warm water that has accumulated in the western Pacific to flow back to the east.

   (A) a phenomenon in which changes in the ocean and atmosphere combine allowing the warm water that has accumulated

   (B) a phenomenon where changes in the ocean and atmosphere are combining to allow the warm water that is accumulating

   (C) a phenomenon in which ocean and atmosphere changes combine and which allows the warm water that is accumulated

   (D) is a phenomenon in which changes in the ocean and atmosphere combine to allow the warm water that has accumulated

   (E) is a phenomenon where ocean and atmosphere changes are combining and allow the warm water accumulating

105. Beatrix Potter, in her book illustrations, carefully coordinating them with her narratives, capitalized on her keen observation and love of the natural world.

   (A) Beatrix Potter, in her book illustrations, carefully coordinating them with her narratives,

   (B) In her book illustrations, carefully coordinating them with her narratives, Beatrix Potter

   (C) In her book illustrations, which she carefully coordinated with her narratives, Beatrix Potter

   (D) Carefully coordinated with her narratives, Beatrix Potter, in her book illustrations

   (E) Beatrix Potter, in her book illustrations, carefully coordinated them with her narratives and

106. Marconi's conception of the radio was as a substitute for the telephone, a tool for private conversation; instead, it is precisely the opposite, a tool for communicating with a large, public audience.

    (A) Marconi's conception of the radio was as a substitute for the telephone, a tool for private conversation; instead, it is

    (B) Marconi conceived of the radio as a substitute for the telephone, a tool for private conversation, but which is

    (C) Marconi conceived of the radio as a tool for private conversation that could substitute for the telephone; instead, it has become

    (D) Marconi conceived of the radio to be a tool for private conversation, a substitute for the telephone, which has become

    (E) Marconi conceived of the radio to be a substitute for the telephone, a tool for private conversation, other than what it is,

107. Originally developed for detecting air pollutants, a technique called proton-induced X-ray emission, which can quickly analyze the chemical elements in almost any substance without destroying it, is finding uses in medicine, archaeology, and criminology.

    (A) Originally developed for detecting air pollutants, a technique called proton-induced X-ray emission, which can quickly analyze the chemical elements in almost any substance without destroying it,

    (B) Originally developed for detecting air pollutants, having the ability to analyze the chemical elements in almost any substance without destroying it, a technique called proton-induced X-ray emission

    (C) A technique originally developed for detecting air pollutants, called proton-induced X-ray emission, which can quickly analyze the chemical elements in almost any substance without destroying it,

    (D) A technique originally developed for detecting air pollutants, called proton-induced X-ray emission, which has the ability to analyze the chemical elements in almost any substance quickly and without destroying it,

    (E) A technique that was originally developed for detecting air pollutants and has the ability to analyze the chemical elements in almost any substance quickly and without destroying the substance, called proton-induced X-ray emission,

108. Authoritative parents are more likely than permissive parents to have children who as adolescents are self-confident, high in self-esteem, and responsibly independent.

    (A) Authoritative parents are more likely than permissive parents to have children who as adolescents are self-confident, high in self-esteem, and responsibly independent.

    (B) Authoritative parents who are more likely than permissive parents to have adolescent children that are self-confident, high in self-esteem, and responsibly independent.

    (C) Children of authoritative parents, rather than permissive parents, are the more likely to be self-confident, have a high self-esteem, and to be responsibly independent as adolescents.

    (D) Children whose parents are authoritative rather than being permissive, are more likely to have self-confidence, a high self-esteem, and be responsibly independent when they are an adolescent.

    (E) Rather than permissive parents, the children of authoritative parents are the more likely to have self-confidence, a high self-esteem, and to be responsibly independent as an adolescent.

109. Among the objects found in the excavated temple were small terra-cotta effigies left by suppliants who were either asking the goddess Bona Dea's aid in healing physical and mental ills or thanking her for such help.

    (A) in healing physical and mental ills or thanking her for such help

    (B) in healing physical and mental ills and to thank her for helping

    (C) in healing physical and mental ills, and thanking her for helping

    (D) to heal physical and mental ills or to thank her for such help

    (E) to heal physical and mental ills or thanking her for such help

110. Published in Harlem, the owner and editor of *The Messenger* were two young journalists, Chandler Owen and A. Philip Randolph, who would later make his reputation as a labor leader.

   (A) Published in Harlem, the owner and editor of *The Messenger* were two young journalists, Chandler Owen and A. Philip Randolph, who would later make his reputation as a labor leader.
   (B) Published in Harlem, two young journalists, Chandler Owen and A. Philip Randolph, who would later make his reputation as a labor leader, were the owner and editor of *The Messenger*.
   (C) Published in Harlem, *The Messenger* was owned and edited by two young journalists, A. Philip Randolph, who would later make his reputation as a labor leader, and Chandler Owen.
   (D) *The Messenger* was owned and edited by two young journalists, Chandler Owen and A. Philip Randolph, who would later make his reputation as a labor leader, and published in Harlem.
   (E) The owner and editor being two young journalists, Chandler Owen and A. Philip Randolph, who would later make his reputation as a labor leader, *The Messenger* was published in Harlem.

111. Construction of the Roman Colosseum, which was officially known as the Flavian Amphitheater, began in A.D. 69, during the reign of Vespasian, was completed a decade later, during the reign of Titus, who opened the Colosseum with a one-hundred-day cycle of religious pageants, gladiatorial games, and spectacles.

   (A) which was officially known as the Flavian Amphitheater, began in A.D. 69, during the reign of Vespasian,
   (B) officially known as the Flavian Amphitheater, begun in A.D. 69, during the reign of Vespasian, and
   (C) which was officially known as the Flavian Amphitheater, began in A.D. 69, during the reign of Vespasian, and
   (D) officially known as the Flavian Amphitheater and begun in A.D. 69, during the reign of Vespasian it
   (E) officially known as the Flavian Amphitheater, which was begun in A.D. 69, during the reign of Vespasian, and

112. As a baby emerges from the darkness of the womb with a rudimentary sense of vision, it would be rated about 20/500, or legally blind if it were an adult with such vision.

   (A) As a baby emerges from the darkness of the womb with a rudimentary sense of vision, it would be rated about 20/500, or legally blind if it were an adult with such vision.
   (B) A baby emerges from the darkness of the womb with a rudimentary sense of vision that would be rated about 20/500, or legally blind as an adult.
   (C) As a baby emerges from the darkness of the womb, its rudimentary sense of vision would be rated about 20/500; qualifying it to be legally blind if an adult.
   (D) A baby emerges from the darkness of the womb with a rudimentary sense of vision that would be rated about 20/500; an adult with such vision would be deemed legally blind.
   (E) As a baby emerges from the darkness of the womb, its rudimentary sense of vision, which would deemed legally blind for an adult, would be rated about 20/500.

113. Because there are provisions of the new maritime code that provide that even tiny islets can be the basis for claims to the fisheries and oil fields of large sea areas, they have already stimulated international disputes over uninhabited islands.

   (A) Because there are provisions of the new maritime code that provide that even tiny islets can be the basis for claims to the fisheries and oil fields of large sea areas, they have already stimulated
   (B) Because the new maritime code provides that even tiny islets can be the basis for claims to the fisheries and oil fields of large sea areas, it has already stimulated
   (C) Even tiny islets can be the basis for claims to the fisheries and oil fields of large sea areas under provisions of the new maritime code, already stimulating
   (D) Because even tiny islets can be the basis for claims to the fisheries and oil fields of large sea areas under provisions of the new maritime code, this has already stimulated
   (E) Because even tiny islets can be the basis for claims to the fisheries and oil fields of large sea areas under provisions of the new maritime code, which is already stimulating

114. The original building and loan associations were organized as limited life funds, whose members made monthly payments on their share subscriptions, then taking turns drawing on the funds for home mortgages.

    (A)   subscriptions, then taking turns drawing
    (B)   subscriptions, and then taking turns drawing
    (C)   subscriptions and then took turns drawing
    (D)   subscriptions and then took turns, they drew
    (E)   subscriptions and then drew, taking turns

115. Gall's hypothesis of there being different mental functions localized in different parts of the brain is widely accepted today.

    (A)   of there being different mental functions localized in different parts of the brain is widely accepted today
    (B)   of different mental functions that are localized in different parts of the brain is widely accepted today
    (C)   that different mental functions are localized in different parts of the brain is widely accepted today
    (D)   which is that there are different mental functions localized in different parts of the brain is widely accepted today
    (E)   which is widely accepted today is that there are different mental functions localized in different parts of the brain

116. Mauritius was a British colony for almost 200 years, excepting for the domains of administration and teaching, the English language was never really spoken on the island.

    (A)   excepting for
    (B)   except in
    (C)   but except in
    (D)   but excepting for
    (E)   with the exception of

117. George Sand (Aurore Lucile Dupin) was one of the first European writers to consider the rural poor to be legitimate subjects for literature and portray these with sympathy and respect in her novels.

    (A)   to be legitimate subjects for literature and portray these
    (B)   should be legitimate subjects for literature and portray these
    (C)   as being legitimate subjects for literature and portraying them
    (D)   as if they were legitimate subjects for literature and portray them
    (E)   legitimate subjects for literature and to portray them

118. The World Wildlife Fund has declared that global warming, a phenomenon most scientists agree to be caused by human beings in burning fossil fuels, will create havoc among migratory birds by altering the environment in ways harmful to their habitats.

    (A)   a phenomenon most scientists agree to be caused by human beings in burning fossil fuels,
    (B)   a phenomenon most scientists agree that is caused by fossil fuels burned by human beings,
    (C)   a phenomenon that most scientists agree is caused by human beings' burning of fossil fuels,
    (D)   which most scientists agree on as a phenomenon caused by human beings who burn fossil fuels,
    (E)   which most scientists agree to be a phenomenon caused by fossil fuels burned by human beings,

119. New theories propose that catastrophic impacts of asteroids and comets may have caused reversals in the Earth's magnetic field, the onset of ice ages, splitting apart continents 80 million years ago, and great volcanic eruptions.

    (A)   splitting apart continents
    (B)   the splitting apart of continents
    (C)   split apart continents
    (D)   continents split apart
    (E)   continents that were split apart

120. A firm that specializes in the analysis of handwriting claims <u>from a one-page writing sample that it can assess</u> more than 300 personality traits, including enthusiasm, imagination, and ambition.

    (A) from a one-page writing sample that it can assess
    (B) from a one-page writing sample it has the ability of assessing
    (C) the ability, from a one-page writing sample, of assessing
    (D) to be able, from a one-page writing sample, to assess
    (E) being able to assess, from a one-page writing sample

121. Sales of wines declined in the late 1980s, but <u>they began to grow again after the 1991 report that linked moderate consumption of alcohol, and particularly of red wine, with a reduced risk of heart disease.</u>

    (A) they began to grow again after the 1991 report that linked moderate consumption of alcohol, and particularly of red wine, with a reduced risk of heart disease
    (B) after the 1991 report that linked a reduced risk of heart disease with a moderate alcohol consumption, particularly red wine, they began growing again
    (C) in a 1991 report, moderate alcohol consumption, and particularly of red wine, which was linked with a reduced risk of heart disease, caused them to begin to grow again
    (D) with a reduced risk of heart disease linked in a 1991 report with moderate alcohol consumption, in particular red wine, they began growing again
    (E) a reduced risk of heart disease linked to moderate alcohol consumption in a 1991 report, and in particular red wine, started them growing again

122. A wildlife expert predicts that the reintroduction of the caribou into northern Minnesota <u>would fail if the density of the timber wolf population in that region is more numerous</u> than one wolf for every 39 square miles.

    (A) would fail if the density of the timber wolf population in that region is more numerous
    (B) would fail provided the density of the timber wolf population in that region is more
    (C) should fail if the timber wolf density in that region was greater
    (D) will fail if the density of the timber wolf population in that region is greater
    (E) will fail if the timber wolf density in that region were more numerous

123. <u>She was less successful after she had emigrated to New York compared to</u> her native Germany, photographer Lotte Jacobi nevertheless earned a small group of discerning admirers, and her photographs were eventually exhibited in prestigious galleries across the United States.

    (A) She was less successful after she had emigrated to New York compared to
    (B) Being less successful after she had emigrated to New York as compared to
    (C) Less successful after she emigrated to New York than she had been in
    (D) Although she was less successful after emigrating to New York when compared to
    (E) She had been less successful after emigrating to New York than in

124. Found throughout Central and South America, <u>sloths hang from trees by long rubbery limbs and sleep 15 hours a day, moving infrequently enough</u> that two species of algae grow on its coat and between its toes.

    (A) sloths hang from trees by long rubbery limbs and sleep 15 hours a day, moving infrequently enough
    (B) sloths hang from trees by long rubbery limbs, they sleep 15 hours a day, and with such infrequent movements
    (C) sloths use their long rubbery limbs to hang from trees, sleep 15 hours a day, and move so infrequently
    (D) the sloth hangs from trees by its long rubbery limbs, sleeping 15 hours a day and moving so infrequently
    (E) the sloth hangs from trees by its long rubbery limbs, sleeps 15 hours a day, and it moves infrequently enough

125. Today, because of improvements in agricultural technology, the same amount of acreage produces <u>double the apples that it has</u> in 1910.

    (A) double the apples that it has
    (B) twice as many apples as it did
    (C) as much as twice the apples it has
    (D) two times as many apples as there were
    (E) a doubling of the apples that it did

126. The use of lie detectors is based on the assumption that lying produces emotional reactions in an individual <u>that, in turn, create unconscious physiological responses</u>.

    (A) that, in turn, create unconscious physiological responses
    (B) that creates unconscious physiological responses in turn
    (C) creating, in turn, unconscious physiological responses
    (D) to create, in turn, physiological responses that are unconscious
    (E) who creates unconscious physiological responses in turn

127. Joan of Arc, a young Frenchwoman who claimed to be divinely inspired, turned the tide of English victories in her country by liberating the city of Orléans and <u>she persuaded Charles VII of France to claim his throne</u>.

    (A) she persuaded Charles VII of France to claim his throne
    (B) persuaded Charles VII of France in claiming his throne
    (C) persuading that the throne be claimed by Charles VII of France
    (D) persuaded Charles VII of France to claim his throne
    (E) persuading that Charles VII of France should claim the throne

128. Australian embryologists have found evidence <u>that suggests that the elephant is descended from an aquatic animal, and its trunk originally evolving</u> as a kind of snorkel.

    (A) that suggests that the elephant is descended from an aquatic animal, and its trunk originally evolving
    (B) that has suggested the elephant descended from an aquatic animal, its trunk originally evolving
    (C) suggesting that the elephant had descended from an aquatic animal with its trunk originally evolved
    (D) to suggest that the elephant had descended from an aquatic animal and its trunk originally evolved
    (E) to suggest that the elephant is descended from an aquatic animal and that its trunk originally evolved

129. Cajuns speak a dialect brought to southern Louisiana by the 4,000 Acadians who migrated there in 1755; their language is basically seventeenth-century French <u>to which has been added English, Spanish, and Italian words</u>.

    (A) to which has been added English, Spanish, and Italian words
    (B) added to which is English, Spanish, and Italian words
    (C) to which English, Spanish, and Italian words have been added
    (D) with English, Spanish, and Italian words having been added to it
    (E) and, in addition, English, Spanish, and Italian words are added

130. One view of the economy contends that a large drop in oil prices should eventually lead to <u>lowering interest rates, as well as lowering fears about inflation,</u> a rally in stocks and bonds, and a weakening of the dollar.

    (A) lowering interest rates, as well as lowering fears about inflation,
    (B) a lowering of interest rates and of fears about inflation,
    (C) a lowering of interest rates, along with fears about inflation,
    (D) interest rates being lowered, along with fears about inflation,
    (E) interest rates and fears about inflation being lowered, with

131. Over 75 percent of the energy produced in France derives from nuclear power, <u>while in Germany it is just over 33 percent</u>.

    (A) while in Germany it is just over 33 percent
    (B) compared to Germany, which uses just over 33 percent
    (C) whereas nuclear power accounts for just over 33 percent of the energy produced in Germany
    (D) whereas just over 33 percent of the energy comes from nuclear power in Germany
    (E) compared with the energy from nuclear power in Germany, where it is just over 33 percent

132. Although the term "psychopath" is popularly applied to an especially brutal criminal, in psychology <u>it is someone who is</u> apparently incapable of feeling compassion or the pangs of conscience.

    (A) it is someone who is
    (B) it is a person
    (C) they are people who are
    (D) it refers to someone who is
    (E) it is in reference to people

133. Last week local shrimpers held a news conference to take some credit for the resurgence of the rare Kemp's ridley turtle, saying that their compliance with laws <u>requiring that turtle-excluder devices be on shrimp nets protect</u> adult sea turtles.

    (A) requiring that turtle-excluder devices be on shrimp nets protect
    (B) requiring turtle-excluder devices on shrimp nets is protecting
    (C) that require turtle-excluder devices on shrimp nets protect
    (D) to require turtle-excluder devices on shrimp nets are protecting
    (E) to require turtle-excluder devices on shrimp nets is protecting

134. Recently implemented "shift-work equations" based on studies of the human sleep cycle have reduced sickness, sleeping on the job, <u>fatigue among shift workers, and have raised</u> production efficiency in various industries.

    (A) fatigue among shift workers, and have raised
    (B) fatigue among shift workers, and raised
    (C) and fatigue among shift workers while raising
    (D) lowered fatigue among shift workers, and raised
    (E) and fatigue among shift workers was lowered while raising

135. Spanning more than 50 years, Friedrich <u>Müller began his career in an unpromising apprenticeship as</u> a Sanskrit scholar and culminated in virtually every honor that European governments and learned societies could bestow.

    (A) Müller began his career in an unpromising apprenticeship as
    (B) Müller's career began in an unpromising apprenticeship as
    (C) Müller's career began with the unpromising apprenticeship of being
    (D) Müller had begun his career with the unpromising apprenticeship of being
    (E) the career of Müller has begun with an unpromising apprenticeship of

136. <u>Whereas in mammals the tiny tubes that convey nutrients to bone cells are arrayed in parallel lines, in birds the tubes</u> form a random pattern.

    (A) Whereas in mammals the tiny tubes that convey nutrients to bone cells are arrayed in parallel lines, in birds the tubes
    (B) Whereas the tiny tubes for the conveying of nutrients to bone cells are arrayed in mammals in parallel lines, birds have tubes that
    (C) Unlike mammals, where the tiny tubes for conveying nutrients to bone cells are arrayed in parallel lines, birds' tubes
    (D) Unlike mammals, in whom the tiny tubes that convey nutrients to bone cells are arrayed in parallel lines, the tubes in birds
    (E) Unlike the tiny tubes that convey nutrients to bone cells, which in mammals are arrayed in parallel lines, in birds the tubes

137. Joachim Raff and Giacomo Meyerbeer are examples of the kind of composer who receives popular acclaim while living, often goes into decline after death, and never regains popularity again.

    (A) often goes into decline after death, and never regains popularity again
    (B) whose reputation declines after death and never regains its status again
    (C) but whose reputation declines after death and never regains its former status
    (D) who declines in reputation after death and who never regained popularity again
    (E) then has declined in reputation after death and never regained popularity

138. In no other historical sighting did Halley's Comet cause such a worldwide sensation as did its return in 1910–1911.

    (A) did its return in 1910–1911
    (B) had its 1910–1911 return
    (C) in its return of 1910–1911
    (D) its return of 1910–1911 did
    (E) its return in 1910–1911

139. The company announced that its profits declined much less in the second quarter than analysts had expected it to and its business will improve in the second half of the year.

    (A) had expected it to and its business will improve
    (B) had expected and that its business would improve
    (C) expected it would and that it will improve its business
    (D) expected them to and its business would improve
    (E) expected and that it will have improved its business

140. Rock samples taken from the remains of an asteroid about twice the size of the 6-mile-wide asteroid that eradicated the dinosaurs has been dated to be 3.47 billion years old and thus is evidence of the earliest known asteroid impact on Earth.

    (A) has been dated to be 3.47 billion years old and thus is
    (B) has been dated at 3.47 billion years old and thus
    (C) have been dated to be 3.47 billion years old and thus are
    (D) have been dated as being 3.47 billion years old and thus
    (E) have been dated at 3.47 billion years old and thus are

9.7 Answer Key

1.	D	36.	A	71.	D	106.	C
2.	D	37.	A	72.	A	107.	A
3.	E	38.	E	73.	B	108.	A
4.	E	39.	D	74.	D	109.	A
5.	A	40.	E	75.	C	110.	C
6.	E	41.	D	76.	D	111.	C
7.	E	42.	A	77.	E	112.	D
8.	A	43.	E	78.	D	113.	B
9.	E	44.	C	79.	B	114.	C
10.	B	45.	B	80.	E	115.	C
11.	D	46.	B	81.	C	116.	C
12.	E	47.	A	82.	E	117.	E
13.	A	48.	B	83.	B	118.	C
14.	A	49.	D	84.	B	119.	B
15.	E	50.	A	85.	A	120.	D
16.	B	51.	B	86.	C	121.	A
17.	D	52.	D	87.	C	122.	D
18.	C	53.	A	88.	D	123.	C
19.	D	54.	E	89.	B	124.	D
20.	E	55.	B	90.	B	125.	B
21.	A	56.	E	91.	A	126.	A
22.	D	57.	D	92.	B	127.	D
23.	C	58.	E	93.	A	128.	E
24.	E	59.	D	94.	E	129.	C
25.	E	60.	E	95.	C	130.	B
26.	E	61.	A	96.	C	131.	C
27.	D	62.	E	97.	C	132.	D
28.	B	63.	B	98.	A	133.	B
29.	C	64.	A	99.	D	134.	C
30.	C	65.	C	100.	B	135.	B
31.	D	66.	A	101.	E	136.	A
32.	B	67.	B	102.	A	137.	C
33.	A	68.	E	103.	B	138.	C
34.	B	69.	E	104.	D	139.	B
35.	C	70.	B	105.	C	140.	E

9.8 Answer Explanations

The following discussion of sentence correction is intended to familiarize you with the most efficient and effective approaches to these kinds of questions. The particular questions in this chapter are generally representative of the kinds of sentence correction questions you will encounter on the GMAT.

1. The Glass House Mountains in Queensland, Australia, were sighted in 1770 by the English navigator Captain James Cook, <u>by whom they were named supposedly because its</u> sheer wet rocks glistened like glass.

   (A) by whom they were named supposedly because its
   (B) by whom they were named supposedly and their
   (C) naming them supposedly since their
   (D) who so named them supposedly because their
   (E) who so named it since supposedly their

   Agreement; Rhetorical construction

   To avoid a wordy and confusing series of passive clauses, the relative clause explaining what James Cook did should be an active-voice construction (*who so named* rather than *by whom they were named*). The possessive pronoun referring to *the Glass House Mountains* should be plural (*their* rather than *its*), to agree with the plural antecedent.

   A   *By whom they were supposedly named* is a passive construction that is unnecessarily indirect and wordy, especially immediately following another passive construction; the singular *its* does not agree with the plural antecedent *the Glass House Mountains*.

   B   This version of the sentence loses the causal connection, failing to explain why James Cook gave the mountains their particular name.

   C   As the object of a preposition and not the subject of the clause, *James Cook* does not work as the noun that the verbal phrase beginning with *naming* can describe; the preposition *since* loses the important causal logic of the sentence.

   D   **Correct.** This concise sentence uses active-voice construction in the relative clause and maintains agreement between the pronoun *their* and its antecedent.

   E   The pronoun *it* does not agree with the plural *Mountains* and the following pronoun *their*.

   The correct answer is D.

2. Although a surge in retail sales <u>have raised hopes that there is a recovery finally</u> under way, many economists say that without a large amount of spending the recovery might not last.

   (A) have raised hopes that there is a recovery finally
   (B) raised hopes for there being a recovery finally
   (C) had raised hopes for a recovery finally being
   (D) has raised hopes that a recovery is finally
   (E) raised hopes for a recovery finally

   Agreement; Rhetorical construction

   The subject of the first clause, the singular noun *surge*, must take the singular verb *has raised* rather than the plural *have raised*. It is superfluous and pointless to say that people hope both that *there is* a recovery and that such a recovery *is underway*. In this context, *there is* adds nothing and can be omitted to create a more concise sentence.

   A   Subject and verb do not agree; *there is … finally underway* is awkward and wordy.

   B   *For there being* is awkward and wordy.

   C   *Had raised* is the wrong verb tense; *for … being* is awkward and wordy.

   D   **Correct.** In this sentence, the subject and verb agree, and the verb is in the appropriate tense; *a recovery is finally* is clear and concise.

   E   *For a recovery finally* is awkward and—to the extent that it can be seen as grammatical—does not make sense.

   The correct answer is D.

3. Although various eighteenth- and nineteenth-century American poets had professed an interest in Native American poetry and had pretended to imitate Native American forms in their own works, <u>until almost 1900, scholars and critics did not begin seriously to study</u> traditional Native American poetry in native languages.

    (A) until almost 1900, scholars and critics did not begin seriously to study

    (B) until almost 1900 scholars and critics had not begun seriously studying

    (C) not until almost 1900 were scholars and critics to begin seriously to study

    (D) it was not almost until 1900 when scholars and critics began to seriously study

    (E) it was not until almost 1900 that scholars and critics seriously began studying

Verb form; Rhetorical construction

The past-perfect verbs *had professed* and *had pretended* designate a time (eighteenth and nineteenth century) earlier than simple past tense, so the second clause, explaining what happened around 1900, must use the past tense. The placement of the phrase *until almost 1900* at the beginning of the second clause is confusing. Does it refer back to the first verb or forward to the next verb?

A   The tenses are fine in this version, but the placement of *until almost 1900* is problematic.

B   The tense of the second clause needs to be simple past, not past perfect.

C   The sequence of infinitives (*to begin seriously to study*) is awkward and wordy.

D   *Not almost until* is a nonsensical sequence of modifiers.

E   **Correct.** The phrase *not until almost 1900* is properly placed, and the verb in the main clause is in the simple past tense.

The correct answer is E.

4. Of all the vast tides of migration that have swept through history, <u>maybe none is more concentrated as</u> the wave that brought 12 million immigrants onto American shores in little more than three decades.

    (A) maybe none is more concentrated as

    (B) it may be that none is more concentrated as

    (C) perhaps it is none that is more concentrated than

    (D) maybe it is none that was more concentrated than

    (E) perhaps none was more concentrated than

Idiom; Verb form

This sentence depends on the comparative structure *x is more than y*. Here, an idiomatically incorrect construction *x (none) is more as y (the wave)* is used. In addition, the second part of the sentence uses the past tense verb *brought*, indicating that the event is over. The verb used in the comparative construction must also be past tense, *x (none) was more concentrated than y (the wave)*. *Maybe* and *perhaps* are interchangeable; *perhaps* is slightly more formal.

A   Incorrect idiom is used for comparison; *is concentrated* is the wrong tense.

B   Incorrect idiom is used for comparison; *it may be that* is wordy.

C   *It is none that is more ...* is wordy; also, in this context, *it* must refer to something (unlike in phrases such as "it is clear that ..."), yet it does not plausibly refer to anything.

D   As in C, *it is none that was more ...* is wordy; *it* must refer to something, yet it does not plausibly refer to anything.

E   **Correct.** The correct comparative construction is used in this sentence; the verb is past tense.

The correct answer is E.

5. Diabetes, together with its serious complications, <u>ranks as the nation's third leading cause of death, surpassed only</u> by heart disease and cancer.

    (A) ranks as the nation's third leading cause of death, surpassed only

    (B) rank as the nation's third leading cause of death, only surpassed

    (C) has the rank of the nation's third leading cause of death, only surpassed

    (D) are the nation's third leading causes of death, surpassed only

    (E) have been ranked as the nation's third leading causes of death, only surpassed

Agreement; Logical predication

This sentence correctly matches the singular verb, *ranks*, with the singular subject, *diabetes*, and uses the present tense to indicate a current situation. The phrase following *diabetes* is set off by a pair of commas, indicating that it is descriptive information that may be dropped from the sentence; it is not a part of the subject. *Only* is placed with precision next to the group of words it actually limits, *by heart disease and cancer*. Placed before *surpassed*, *only* would more ambiguously limit *surpassed*.

A   **Correct.** In the original sentence, the subject and verb agree, and the proper tense is used; *only* is correctly placed next to the phrase it limits.

B   *Rank* does not agree with *diabetes*; *only* limits *surpassed* rather than *by heart disease and cancer*.

C   *Has the rank of* is wordy and unidiomatic; *only* limits *surpassed* rather than *by heart disease and cancer*.

D   Construction *are … causes* does not agree with *diabetes*.

E   Construction *have been ranked … causes* does not agree with *diabetes* and uses the wrong verb tense; *only* limits *surpassed* rather than *by heart disease and cancer*.

The correct answer is A.

6.   In late 1997, the chambers inside the pyramid of the Pharaoh Menkaure at Giza were closed to visitors for cleaning and repair <u>due to moisture exhaled by tourists, which raised its humidity to such levels so that salt from the stone was crystallizing</u> and fungus was growing on the walls.

(A)   due to moisture exhaled by tourists, which raised its humidity to such levels so that salt from the stone was crystallizing

(B)   due to moisture that tourists had exhaled, thereby raising its humidity to such levels that salt from the stone would crystallize

(C)   because tourists were exhaling moisture, which had raised the humidity within them to levels such that salt from the stone would crystallize

(D)   because of moisture that was exhaled by tourists raising the humidity within them to levels so high as to make the salt from the stone crystallize

(E)   because moisture exhaled by tourists had raised the humidity within them to such levels that salt from the stone was crystallizing

Agreement; Parallelism

The plural subject *chambers* requires plural pronouns. The sentence explains a causal sequence: visitors' breath introduced moisture that caused salt to crystallize, which caused the chambers to be closed for cleaning and repair. The phrase *due to* makes this causal sequence somewhat ambiguous, seeming to suggest that the repairs were due to humidity from visitors' breath.

A   *Due to* is an imprecise expression of the causal connection between the tourists' breath and the closing of the museum for cleaning; the singular pronoun *its* does not agree with the plural antecedent *chambers*.

B   It is not at all clear what the reference is for the pronoun *its*; *fungus was growing* should be parallel to *salt … was crystallizing* (not *would crystallize*) because it is another effect of the humidity.

C   The pronoun *them* seems to refer to *tourists*, which is nonsensical; the entire construction is awkward and wordy; *would crystallize* is not parallel to *was growing*.

D   Once again, *them* seems to refer to tourists; the entire construction is awkward, wordy, and ambiguous; *crystallize* is not parallel to *was growing*.

E   **Correct.** The causal sequence is clear, and *them* clearly refers to *chambers*.

The correct answer is E.

7. As its sales of computer products have surpassed those of measuring instruments, the company has become increasingly willing to compete for the mass market sales <u>they would in the past have conceded to rivals</u>.

    (A) they would in the past have conceded to rivals
    (B) they would have conceded previously to their rivals
    (C) that in the past would have been conceded previously to rivals
    (D) it previously would have conceded to rivals in the past
    (E) it would in the past have conceded to rivals

    Agreement; Rhetorical construction

    When a number of words intervene between a pronoun and its referent, an error such as the one in this sentence is easy to make. The subject of the main clause is the singular noun *company*, so the pronoun referring to the company must also be singular. Even if *the company* might be thought of as referring to the members of a business, the singular verb *(has become increasingly willing)* establishes that the noun is singular in this sentence.

    A Plural pronoun *they* does not agree with singular *the company*.
    B Plural pronouns *they* and *their* do not agree with *the company*.
    C *Previously* repeats the idea of *in the past*; the passive-voice construction in this context is weak and ambiguous.
    D The placement of *in the past* makes it unclear whether it is supposed to modify *rivals* or *would have conceded*; if the latter, then it is redundant.
    E **Correct.** In this concise sentence, the singular pronoun *it* agrees with the singular referent *the company*.

    The correct answer is E.

8. The widely accepted big bang theory holds <u>that the universe began in an explosive instant ten to twenty billion years ago and has been expanding</u> ever since.

    (A) that the universe began in an explosive instant ten to twenty billion years ago and has been expanding
    (B) that the universe had begun in an explosive instant ten to twenty billion years ago and had been expanding
    (C) that the beginning of the universe was an explosive instant ten to twenty billion years ago that has expanded
    (D) the beginning of the universe to have been an explosive instant ten to twenty billion years ago that is expanding
    (E) the universe to have begun in an explosive instant ten to twenty billion years ago and has been expanding

    Logical predication; Verb form

    The sentence describes the central tenet of a theory about how the universe began. The focus of the second clause should be consistently on the subject *the universe*, and all verbs in the clause beginning with *that* must describe what the universe did at the initial explosive moment.

    A **Correct.** Both verbs in the second clause correctly take *universe* as their subject.
    B *Had begun* is the wrong tense because it describes action that occurred farther in the past than some other, specified past action.
    C The relative clause *that has expanded* describes *instant*, which makes no sense.
    D *The beginning of the universe to have been …* is unnecessarily indirect and wordy; illogically suggests that *beginning* is expanding, not the universe.
    E The verb phrases *to have begun* and *has been expanding* both reference the same subject of the clause, *universe*, and therefore need to be parallel.

    The correct answer is A.

9. Like the idolization accorded the Brontës and Brownings, James Joyce and Virginia Woolf are often subjected to the kind of veneration that blurs the distinction between the artist and the human being.

    (A) Like the idolization accorded the Brontës and Brownings,
    (B) As the Brontës' and Brownings' idolization,
    (C) Like that accorded to the Brontës and Brownings,
    (D) As it is of the Brontës and Brownings,
    (E) Like the Brontës and Brownings,

Logical predication

This sentence intends to compare nineteenth- and twentieth-century writers. Instead the comparison becomes ambiguous and illogical. *Like* must be used to compare similar elements: *Joyce* and *Woolf* are *like* the *Brontës* and the *Brownings*; they are not *like* the *idolization*.

A   *The idolization accorded* is not comparable to Joyce and Woolf.

B   The conjunction *as* may introduce a clause but not a phrase; Joyce and Woolf are compared to *idolization* rather than to the writers.

C   *That* is ambiguous, and Joyce and Woolf are compared to *that* rather than to the writers.

D   *It* is ambiguous; *as it is of* is awkward and wordy; the twentieth-century writers are compared to *it* rather than to the nineteenth-century writers.

E   **Correct.** In this sentence, *like* introduces a clear and concise comparison that correctly links the nineteenth-and twentieth-century writers.

The correct answer is E.

10. Carnivorous mammals can endure what would otherwise be lethal levels of body heat because they have a heat-exchange network which kept the brain from getting too hot.

    (A) which kept
    (B) that keeps
    (C) which has kept
    (D) that has been keeping
    (E) having kept

Verb form; Rhetorical construction

The use of the past tense (*kept*) is incorrect because a current situation is discussed; the present tense (*keeps*) is consistent with the other verbs in the sentence. In (A) and (C), *which* introduces a restrictive clause. Some writers follow the convention that *which* can only be used for nonrestrictive clauses, but insistence on this rule is controversial, and both (A) and (C) can be rejected on other grounds.

A   *Kept* is the wrong tense.

B   **Correct.** The verb *keeps* indicates a current situation and is consistent with the other verbs in the sentence. The sentence is clear and concise.

C   Mistaken shift in tense: In this sentence the present tense expresses a timeless general principle; in contrast, *has kept* indicates a more definite context and time period and suggests that the heat-exchange network may no longer have this effect.

D   *Has been keeping* is the wrong tense.

E   *Having* is awkward and imprecise; *kept* is the wrong tense.

The correct answer is B.

11. There are several ways to build solid walls using just mud or clay, but the most extensively used method has been <u>the forming of bricks out of mud or clay, and, after some preliminary air drying or sun drying, they are laid</u> in the wall in mud mortar.

    (A) the forming of bricks out of mud or clay, and, after some preliminary air drying or sun drying, they are laid

    (B) forming the mud or clay into bricks, and, after some preliminary air drying or sun drying, to lay them

    (C) having bricks formed from mud or clay, and, after some preliminary air drying or sun drying, they were laid

    (D) to form the mud or clay into bricks, and, after some preliminary air drying or sun drying, to lay them

    (E) that bricks were formed from mud or clay, which, after some preliminary air drying or sun drying, were laid

Parallelism; Verb form

The purpose of the sentence is to describe the historically most popular method of building walls. The first clause announces this topic and the second clause describes the particular method. The clearest, most efficient way to accomplish these two pieces of business is to use a parallel structure. The *ways to build* in the first clause is narrowed to the single way *to form* and *to lay* in the second clause. There is no need to alternate the verb phrases between active and passive voice or to shift tenses.

A   The active gerund phrase *the forming of bricks* does not fit with the passive verb phrase that follows (*they are laid*).

B   The verb phrases *forming the mud …* and *to lay them* are not parallel.

C   In addition to faulty parallelism between *having bricks formed* and *they were laid*, the tense in the second half of the sentence unaccountably shifts from present to past.

D   Correct. The phrases *to form* and *to lay* in the second clause are parallel to *to build* in the first clause.

E   The relative clause beginning with *which* apparently (but nonsensically) describes the closest nouns, *mud or clay*, rather than *bricks*.

The correct answer is D.

12. Rising inventories, <u>when unaccompanied correspondingly by increases in sales, can lead</u> to production cutbacks that would hamper economic growth.

    (A) when unaccompanied correspondingly by increases in sales, can lead

    (B) when not accompanied by corresponding increases in sales, possibly leads

    (C) when they were unaccompanied by corresponding sales increases, can lead

    (D) if not accompanied by correspondingly increased sales, possibly leads

    (E) if not accompanied by corresponding increases in sales, can lead

Diction; Agreement

The modifying phrase *when … sales* is needlessly difficult to understand. The adverb *correspondingly* is incorrectly and ambiguously used; using the adjective *corresponding* to modify *increases in sales* makes the intended meaning clearer. *Unaccompanied* is not wrong but *not accompanied* more effectively expresses the intended negation.

A   *Unaccompanied correspondingly* is awkward and ambiguous.

B   Plural subject *inventories* does not agree with the singular verb *leads*.

C   Wrong tense: past tense *were* indicates a completed event, but *can lead* indicates a possibility that continues.

D   *Correspondingly increased sales* is awkward and unclear; verb (*leads*) does not agree with the subject (*inventories*).

E   Correct. *Not accompanied* emphasizes the negative and is preferable to *unaccompanied* in this usage; *corresponding* modifies *increases in sales*; the modifier is clear and comprehensible, and there is no subject-verb agreement problem.

The correct answer is E.

13. A surge in new home sales and a drop in weekly unemployment <u>claims suggest that the economy might not be as weak as some analysts previously thought</u>.

   (A) claims suggest that the economy might not be as weak as some analysts previously thought

   (B) claims suggests that the economy might not be so weak as some analysts have previously thought

   (C) claims suggest that the economy might not be as weak as have been previously thought by some analysts

   (D) claims, suggesting about the economy that it might not be so weak as previously thought by some analysts

   (E) claims, suggesting the economy might not be as weak as previously thought to be by some analysts

Agreement; Grammatical construction

The plural subject of this sentence (*surge* and *drop*) requires a plural verb, *suggest*. The object of this verb, the clause beginning with *that*, should be presented in as clear and direct a manner as possible.

A **Correct.** The plural subject is matched with a plural verb.

B The singular verb *suggests* does not match the plural subject of the sentence.

C The sentence offers no plural subject to fit the passive verb *have been thought*.

D This construction is awkward, wordy, and imprecise; it also lacks a main verb; there is no reason to use passive voice, and *suggesting about the economy that it might* ... introduces extra words that contribute nothing to the meaning of this sentence fragment.

E The passive construction makes this unnecessarily wordy; the lack of a main verb makes this a sentence fragment.

The correct answer is A.

14. Sunspots, vortices of gas associated with strong electromagnetic activity, <u>are visible as dark spots on the surface of the Sun but have never been sighted on</u> the Sun's poles or equator.

   (A) are visible as dark spots on the surface of the Sun but have never been sighted on

   (B) are visible as dark spots that never have been sighted on the surface of the Sun

   (C) appear on the surface of the Sun as dark spots although never sighted at

   (D) appear as dark spots on the surface of the Sun, although never having been sighted at

   (E) appear as dark spots on the Sun's surface, which have never been sighted on

Logical predication; Parallelism

The correct parallel structure in the original sentence emphasizes the contrast between where sunspots are found (*are visible ... Sun*) and where they are not (*have never been sighted ... equator*). *Sunspots* is the subject of the sentence; *are* is the verb of the first part of the contrast, and *have been sighted* is the verb of the second. (The adjective *visible* is a complement and is parallel to the past participle *sighted*.) Both parts of the sentence conclude with phrases indicating location. The contrast itself is indicated by the conjunction *but*.

A **Correct.** This sentence clearly and correctly draws a contrast between where sunspots are found and where they are not.

B The modifying clause *that never ... Sun* distorts the meaning of the sentence; also, without punctuation, the phrase *on the surface of the Sun the Sun's poles or equator* is ungrammatical and makes no sense.

C *Although* typically introduces a subordinate clause, which has a subject and a verb, but here there is no subject and *sighted* is not a complete verb.

D *Although* usually introduces a subordinate clause, but there is no subject of the clause and *having been sighted* is not a complete verb phrase.

E This phrasing makes the sentence somewhat awkward and unclear.

The correct answer is A.

15. Warning that computers in the United States are not secure, the National Academy of Sciences has urged the nation to revamp computer security procedures, institute new emergency response teams, <u>creating a special nongovernment organization to take</u> charge of computer security planning.

    (A) creating a special nongovernment organization to take
    (B) creating a special nongovernment organization that takes
    (C) creating a special nongovernment organization for taking
    (D) and create a special nongovernment organization for taking
    (E) and create a special nongovernment organization to take

Parallelism; Grammatical construction

This sentence contains a list of three elements, all of which should be parallel. The last element should be preceded by the conjunction *and*. In this sentence, the last element must be made parallel to the previous two: *to* (1) *revamp computer security procedures*, (2) *institute new emergency response teams, and* (3) *create a special nongovernment organization to take charge of computer security planning*. Omitting *and* causes the reader to anticipate still another element in the series when there is none. Using the participle *creating* not only violates parallelism but also causes misreading since the participial phrase could modify the first part of the sentence. *To* does not need to be repeated with *institute* and *create* because it is understood.

A   *Creating* is not parallel to *to revamp* and *institute*; *and* is needed in this series.

B   *Creating* violates the parallelism of the previous two elements; *and* is needed in this series; since the organization does not yet exist, *that takes* is illogical.

C   *Creating* is not parallel to *to revamp* and *institute*; *and* is needed in this series; *to* has the sense of *in order to*, but *for taking* is neither precise nor idiomatic.

D   In the construction *create ... to take*, the sense of *to* is *in order to*; *for taking* is not idiomatically correct.

E   **Correct.** The three elements in the series are parallel in this sentence, and the last is preceded by *and*.

The correct answer is E.

16. Retail sales rose 0.8 of 1 percent in August, intensifying expectations <u>that personal spending in the July–September quarter more than doubled that of</u> the 1.4 percent growth rate in personal spending for the previous quarter.

    (A) that personal spending in the July–September quarter more than doubled that of
    (B) that personal spending in the July–September quarter would more than double
    (C) of personal spending in the July–September quarter, that it more than doubled
    (D) of personal spending in the July–September quarter more than doubling that of
    (E) of personal spending in the July–September quarter, that it would more than double that of

Verb form; Logical predication

The sentence explains the expectations that resulted from a past retail sales trend. Since expectations look to the future but are not yet realized, the relative clause explaining these expectations should be conditional, employing the auxiliary verb *would*.

A   The simple past-tense verb form does not express the forward-looking sense of *expectations*.

B   **Correct.** By using the verb *would double*, this concise sentence indicates that the expectation has not yet been realized.

C   This construction is awkward, announcing the topic (*personal spending*) and then elaborating in a relative clause that restates this topic as *it*.

D   Although this option is not technically wrong, it is less clear and graceful than B.

E   Like option C, this sentence is awkward and unnecessarily wordy, announcing the topic and then using an additional clause to elaborate on it.

The correct answer is B.

17. The commission has directed advertisers to restrict the use of the word "natural" to foods that do not contain color or flavor additives, chemical preservatives, or nothing that has been synthesized.

(A)   or nothing that has been
(B)   or that has been
(C)   and nothing that is
(D)   or anything that has been
(E)   and anything

Idiom; Logical predication

The use of *do not* and *nothing* in the same sentence creates a double negative and reverses the intended meaning. *Anything* should be used instead of *nothing*. Logically, a "natural" food cannot contain any prohibited ingredient, so the list of prohibited ingredients must be connected by *or*.

A   The use of *nothing* creates a double negative.

B   *That has been synthesized* distorts the meaning by referring to foods, rather than to something added to a food.

C   The use of *nothing* creates a double negative; *and* should be *or*.

D   **Correct.** This sentence correctly avoids a double negative and uses parallel elements.

E   *And* distorts the meaning of the sentence.

The correct answer is D.

18. Plants are more efficient at acquiring carbon than are fungi, in the form of carbon dioxide, and converting it to energy-rich sugars.

(A)   Plants are more efficient at acquiring carbon than are fungi,
(B)   Plants are more efficient at acquiring carbon than fungi,
(C)   Plants are more efficient than fungi at acquiring carbon,
(D)   Plants, more efficient than fungi at acquiring carbon,
(E)   Plants acquire carbon more efficiently than fungi,

Logical predication; Grammatical construction

This sentence compares how efficiently plants and fungi acquire carbon and convert it into sugars. The sentence construction needs to make clear that plants and fungi are the two topics being compared, and it must also clarify that *in the form of carbon dioxide* refers to *carbon* rather than to either *plants* or *fungi*.

A   According to the sentence grammar, *in the form of carbon dioxide* describes *fungi*, which is nonsensical.

B   This sentence claims that plants acquire carbon more efficiently than they acquire fungi, which is also nonsensical; *the form of carbon dioxide* still modifies *fungi*.

C   **Correct.** The sentence clearly compares plants to fungi, and *in the form of carbon dioxide* correctly modifies *carbon*.

D   This sentence is grammatically incomplete; there is no verb for the subject *plants*.

E   As in B, this sentence claims that plants acquire carbon more efficiently than they acquire fungi; it is also grammatically incomplete because *and converting* does not clearly refer to anything.

The correct answer is C.

19. The Iroquois were primarily planters, <u>but supplementing</u> their cultivation of maize, squash, and beans with fishing and hunting.

    (A) but supplementing
    (B) and had supplemented
    (C) and even though they supplemented
    (D) although they supplemented
    (E) but with supplementing

Grammatical construction; Verb form

The participle *supplementing* would normally be expected to modify the first clause, describing or extending its meaning, but the logic of this sentence demands a contrast, not an extension. Consequently, the second part of the sentence must be revised to emphasize the contrast properly. The logic of the sentence also argues against a construction that would set the two clauses and the importance of their content equal when they clearly should not be. The best solution is to have the main clause describe the primary activity, and a subordinate clause, *although they supplemented*, describe the supplementary activity.

A The construction using *supplementing* fails to support the intended meaning of the sentence.

B *And* does not convey contrast; *had supplemented* is the past perfect tense but the simple past is required to match *were*.

C *And* does not convey contrast and should be omitted; *and even though* creates a sentence fragment.

D Correct. Using *although* creates a subordinate clause in this sentence and logically links that clause with the main clause; the simple past *supplemented* parallels the simple past *were*.

E *But with* is awkward and unclear; *supplementing* is a modifier when a contrasting clause is needed.

The correct answer is D.

20. <u>As contrasted with the honeybee,</u> the yellow jacket can sting repeatedly without dying and carries a potent venom that can cause intense pain.

    (A) As contrasted with the honeybee,
    (B) In contrast to the honeybee's,
    (C) Unlike the sting of the honeybee,
    (D) Unlike that of the honeybee,
    (E) Unlike the honeybee,

Idiom; Logical predication

The intent of the sentence is to contrast the honeybee and the yellow jacket. Correct idioms for such a contrast include *in contrast with x, y; in contrast to x, y;* and *unlike x, y.* In all these idioms, *x* and *y* must be grammatically and logically parallel. *As contrasted with* is not a correct idiom.

A *As contrasted with* is not a correct idiom.

B Because of its apostrophe, *the honeybee's* is not parallel to *the yellow jacket.*

C *The sting of the honeybee* is not parallel to *the yellow jacket.*

D *That of the honeybee* is not parallel to *the yellow jacket.*

E Correct. This sentence uses a correct idiom, and *the honeybee* is properly parallel to *the yellow jacket.*

The correct answer is E.

21. <u>Neuroscientists, having amassed a wealth of knowledge over the past twenty years about the brain and its development from birth to adulthood, are</u> now drawing solid conclusions about how the human brain grows and how babies acquire language.

    (A) Neuroscientists, having amassed a wealth of knowledge over the past twenty years about the brain and its development from birth to adulthood, are
    (B) Neuroscientists, having amassed a wealth of knowledge about the brain and its development from birth to adulthood over the past twenty years, and are

(C)   Neuroscientists amassing a wealth of knowledge about the brain and its development from birth to adulthood over the past twenty years, and are

(D)   Neuroscientists have amassed a wealth of knowledge over the past twenty years about the brain and its development from birth to adulthood,

(E)   Neuroscientists have amassed, over the past twenty years, a wealth of knowledge about the brain and its development from birth to adulthood,

Grammatical construction; Logical predication

This sentence introduces the subject (*Neuroscientists*), pauses to explain what neuroscientists have accomplished in the past twenty years, and then concludes by explaining what neuroscientists are presently doing as a result of their past accomplishments. The second part of the sentence—the explanation—interrupts the flow of the sentence from the subject (*Neuroscientists*) to the predicate (*are now drawing solid conclusions …*); it should therefore be bracketed by commas. The sentence construction should provide a main verb for the subject *neuroscientists*.

A   **Correct.** The explanatory phrase between the subject and predicate is set off by commas, and the main clause contains both a subject (*Neuroscientists*) and a corresponding verb (*are now drawing*).

B   *And are* indicates that *are* follows a previous verb, but in fact the sentence has not yet provided a first main verb for the subject *Neuroscientists*; the sentence is therefore incomplete; *over the … years* appears to be modifying *adulthood*.

C   *Amassing*, like *having amassed*, functions as an adjective, not a verb; the sentence therefore lacks the first main verb implied by the compound verb construction *and are now drawing.…*

D   The final descriptor in present tense, *now drawing conclusions …* does not fit the opening clause, which is in present-perfect tense (*have amassed a wealth …*) and seems to modify *adulthood*.

E   Like D, this sentence attempts to attach a present-tense descriptor to a present-perfect clause.

The correct answer is A.

22.   None of the attempts to specify the causes of crime explains why most of the people exposed to the alleged causes do not commit crimes and, conversely, why so many of those not so exposed have.

(A)   have
(B)   has
(C)   shall
(D)   do
(E)   could

Grammatical construction; Parallelism

The sentence compares one group of people, *most of the people exposed to the alleged causes*, with another group of people, *so many of those not so exposed*. To maintain the comparison, the verb in the second part should match the verb in the first part. Since the first verb is *do not commit*, the second verb should be the parallel *do*. There is no need to repeat *commit crimes* since it is understood in this construction.

A   Verb should be *do*, not *have*.

B   Verb should be *do*, not *has*.

C   Verb should be *do*, not *shall*.

D   **Correct.** This sentence correctly uses the verb *do* to complete the comparison and maintain the parallelism with *do not commit*.

E   Verb should be *do*, not *could*.

The correct answer is D.

23. In a previous design, the weight of the discus used in track competition is concentrated in a metal center, but now it is lined with lead around the perimeter, thereby improving stability in flight and resulting in longer throws.

    (A) In a previous design, the weight of the discus used in track competition is concentrated in a metal center, but now it is
    (B) According to a previous design, the weight of the discus used in track competition was concentrated in a metal center, but now it is
    (C) Once designed with its weight concentrated in a metal center, the discus used in track competition is now
    (D) The discus used in track competition, once designed with its weight concentrated in a metal center, but now
    (E) The discus used in track competition was once designed having its weight concentrated in a metal center and now

Verb Form; Grammatical construction; Logical predication

The sentence requires two tenses—past tense to describe the previous design and present tense to describe the current design of the discus. In the sentence presented here, the grammatical subject is *weight*, not *discus*, so the pronoun *it* grammatically refers to *weight*, which makes no sense.

A   The verb tense describing the *previous design* should be past, not present; the pronoun *it* refers to the subject of the first clause, *weight*, and it does not make sense to say that the weight of the discus is lined with lead.

B   Although the tense of the verb in the first clause is appropriately past, the pronoun in the second clause is still referring to *weight* instead of *discus*.

C   **Correct.** The introductory phrase describes the past design of the discus with a past participle (*designed*) that modifies the subject of the main clause (*the discus*); the main verb *is lined* is in present tense.

D   This version of the sentence is a fragment because it has no main verb.

E   The sentence is missing a main verb in the final phrase; *was once designed* must be followed by *is now lined*.

The correct answer is C.

24. In virtually all types of tissue in every animal species, dioxin induces the production of enzymes that are the organism's trying to metabolize, or render harmless, the chemical that is irritating it.

    (A) trying to metabolize, or render harmless, the chemical that is irritating it
    (B) trying that it metabolize, or render harmless, the chemical irritant
    (C) attempt to try to metabolize, or render harmless, such a chemical irritant
    (D) attempt to try and metabolize, or render harmless, the chemical irritating it
    (E) attempt to metabolize, or render harmless, the chemical irritant

Diction; Rhetorical construction

The *-ing* form of a verb can be used as a noun (e.g., *running* is her favorite sport), but it is often awkward, particularly when used with a possessive, as in this case. Substituting the noun *attempt* for the gerund *trying* eliminates the problem. While *chemical that is irritating it* and *chemical irritating it* are both grammatically correct and could be appropriate in some usages, they are excessively wordy for this context.

A   *Trying* is awkward, especially in this construction with *organism's*.

B   *Trying that it metabolize* is ungrammatical.

C   *Attempt to try* is redundant.

D   *Attempt to try and* is redundant.

E   **Correct.** In this sentence, the noun *attempt* replaces the gerund *trying* in this construction with *organism's*.

The correct answer is E.

25. Based on accounts of various ancient writers, scholars have painted a sketchy picture of the activities of an all-female cult that, perhaps as early as the sixth century B.C., worshipped a goddess known in Latin as Bona Dea, "the good goddess."

    (A) Based on accounts of various ancient writers,
    (B) Basing it on various ancient writers' accounts,
    (C) With accounts of various ancient writers used for a basis,
    (D) By the accounts of various ancient writers they used,
    (E) Using accounts of various ancient writers,

    Logical predication; Rhetorical construction

    The underlined phrase is a modifier; it functions as an adjective to describe the noun that immediately follows it. In this case, the phrase incorrectly modifies *scholars*, which does not make any sense. What are the scholars doing? When the modifier begins with *using*, it correctly links the scholars with the modifier that describes their activity.

    A   *Based on …* incorrectly modifies *scholars*.
    B   The pronoun *it* does not have a clear reference.
    C   This choice is wordy and awkward.
    D   This choice is wordy and awkward.
    E   **Correct.** In this sentence, *using accounts of various ancient writers* correctly modifies *scholars* in a clear and concise expression of their activity.

    The correct answer is E.

26. Emily Dickinson's letters to Susan Huntington Dickinson were written over a period beginning a few years before Susan's marriage to Emily's brother and ending shortly before Emily's death in 1886, outnumbering her letters to anyone else.

    (A) Dickinson were written over a period beginning a few years before Susan's marriage to Emily's brother and ending shortly before Emily's death in 1886, outnumbering
    (B) Dickinson were written over a period that begins a few years before Susan's marriage to Emily's brother and ended shortly before Emily's death in 1886, outnumber
    (C) Dickinson, written over a period beginning a few years before Susan's marriage to Emily's brother and that ends shortly before Emily's death in 1886 and outnumbering
    (D) Dickinson, which were written over a period beginning a few years before Susan's marriage to Emily's brother, ending shortly before Emily's death in 1886, and outnumbering
    (E) Dickinson, which were written over a period beginning a few years before Susan's marriage to Emily's brother and ending shortly before Emily's death in 1886, outnumber

    Parallelism; Grammatical construction

    The main point of the sentence is that Dickinson's letters to her sister-in-law outnumber her letters to anyone else. To emphasize this point, *outnumber* should be the main verb, and the description introduced by the passive verb *were written* needs to be changed from a main clause to an adjectival phrase.

    A   The long, wordy opening clause gives too much emphasis to the period when Dickinson's letters were written; it is unclear what *outnumbering* refers to.
    B   The verbs describing the letter-writing period (*begins* and *ended*) are not parallel.
    C   The verbs describing the letter-writing period need to be in parallel form and agree in tense—e.g., *beginning* and *ending* or *that began* and *that ended*; this is a fragment because it lacks a main verb for *letters*.
    D   The lack of a main verb for the subject of the sentence, *letters*, makes this a fragment.
    E   **Correct.** The information about the period when Dickinson's letters were written is contained in an adjectival phrase set off by commas, and the main verb *outnumber* refers clearly to *letters*.

    The correct answer is E.

27. Paleontologists believe that fragments of a primate jawbone unearthed in Burma and estimated <u>at 40 to 44 million years old provide evidence of</u> a crucial step along the evolutionary path that led to human beings.

(A) at 40 to 44 million years old provide evidence of

(B) as being 40 to 44 million years old provides evidence of

(C) that it is 40 to 44 million years old provides evidence of what was

(D) to be 40 to 44 million years old provide evidence of

(E) as 40 to 44 million years old provides evidence of what was

Idiom; Agreement

The verb *estimated* should be followed by the infinitive *to be*, not the preposition *at*—unless the writer intends to indicate a location at which someone made the estimate. The jawbone fragments *were estimated to be* a certain age. The plural subject *fragments* requires the plural verb *provide*.

A   *Estimated* is incorrectly followed by *at*.

B   *Estimated* should be followed by *to be*, not *as being*; the singular verb *provides* incorrectly follows the plural subject *fragments*.

C   Introducing a clause, *that it is …* , creates an ungrammatical sentence; the singular verb *provides* does not agree with the plural subject *fragments*.

D   Correct. In this sentence, the verb *estimated* is correctly followed by the infinitive *to be*.

E   The singular verb *provides* does not match the plural subject *fragments*.

The correct answer is D.

28. Building on civilizations that preceded them in coastal Peru, the Mochica developed their own elaborate society, <u>based on cultivating such crops like corn and beans, the harvesting of fish and shellfish, and exploiting</u> other wild and domestic resources.

(A) based on cultivating such crops like corn and beans, the harvesting of fish and shellfish, and exploiting

(B) based on the cultivation of such crops as corn and beans, the harvesting of fish and seafood, and the exploitation of

(C) and basing it on the cultivation of crops like corn and beans, harvesting fish and seafood, and the exploiting of

(D) and they based it on their cultivation of crops such as corn and beans, the harvest of fish and seafood, and exploiting

(E) and they based it on their cultivating such crops like corn and beans, their harvest of fish and shellfish, and they exploited

Diction; Parallelism

The sentence describes the elaborate society of the Mochica with a series of three features, the first of which contains an example. The three features must be presented in parallel structures—e.g., *cultivating*, *harvesting*, and *exploiting*. The use of *such* to introduce the examples of crops requires that the comparison be completed with *as* instead of *like*.

A   The second item in the series violates the parallelism required for the series; *like* is the incorrect word to complete the introduction of examples.

B   Correct. The three items in the series are in parallel form, and *such crops* is correctly followed by *as*.

C   *And basing it on …* must come before the main verb in order to make this version a complete sentence.

D   The items in the description of the society are not in parallel form.

E   *Like* is the wrong word to introduce the examples; *based it on their cultivating such crops …* is awkward and wordy; *they based* is parallel to *they exploited*, but for this sentence to work, *and* would have to be inserted before *their harvest of fish*.

The correct answer is B.

9.8 Sentence Correction Answer Explanations

29. The end of the eighteenth century saw the emergence of prize-stock breeding, with individual bulls and cows receiving awards, fetching unprecedented prices, and <u>excited</u> enormous interest whenever they were put on show.

    (A) excited
    (B) it excited
    (C) exciting
    (D) would excite
    (E) it had excited

Parallelism

The bulls and cows are described in a series of participial phrases. Items in a series should be parallel: *receiving awards* is parallel to *fetching unprecedented prices*, but *excited* must be changed to *exciting* to make the third phrase, *exciting enormous interest*, parallel to the first two.

A   *Excited* is not parallel to *receiving* and *fetching*.

B   Unclear referent for *it*; sentence construction relying on the introduction of a new independent clause is awkward and creates new errors in the first sentence; *it excited* is not parallel to *receiving* and *fetching*.

C   **Correct.** In this sentence, *exciting* is parallel to *receiving* and *fetching*.

D   *Would excite* is not parallel to *receiving* and *fetching*.

E   Unclear referent for *it*; sentence construction relying on the introduction of a new independent clause is awkward and creates new errors in the first sentence; *it had excited* is not parallel to *receiving* and *fetching*.

The correct answer is C.

30. For members of the seventeenth-century Ashanti nation in Africa, animal-hide shields with wooden frames were essential items of military equipment, <u>a method to protect</u> warriors against enemy arrows and spears.

    (A) a method to protect
    (B) as a method protecting
    (C) protecting
    (D) as a protection of
    (E) to protect

Logical predication; Rhetorical construction

The underlined part of the sentence begins a phrase describing *items of military equipment*. It is awkward and inaccurate to describe *items* themselves as *a method*. Replacing the underlined phrase with the participle *protecting* creates a modifying phrase that clearly explains the purpose of the *items of military equipment*.

A   *A method to protect* is awkward and inaccurate in reference to *items*.

B   The singular *method* should not refer to the plural *items*; *as a method protecting* is awkward and not idiomatic.

C   **Correct.** In this sentence, *protecting* properly introduces a modifying phrase revealing the purpose of the *items*.

D   The prepositional phrase *as a protection of warriors* is awkward and imprecise; using the noun form *protection* creates wordiness and is awkward in reference to *items*.

E   Although the infinitive *to protect* would work if it were not preceded by a comma, it cannot act as a nonrestrictive adjectival phrase modifying *items*.

The correct answer is C.

31. <u>Unlike the conviction held by many of her colleagues that genes were</u> relatively simple and static, Barbara McClintock adhered to her own more complicated ideas about how genes might operate, and in 1983, at the age of 81, was awarded a Nobel Prize for her discovery that the genes in corn are capable of moving from one chromosomal site to another.

    (A) Unlike the conviction held by many of her colleagues that genes were
    (B) Although many of her colleagues were of the conviction of genes being
    (C) Contrary to many of her colleagues being convinced that genes were
    (D) Even though many of her colleagues were convinced that genes were
    (E) Even with many of her colleagues convinced of genes being

Rhetorical construction; Idiom; Logical predication

The sentence compares a widely held conviction about genes with McClintock's adherence to her own ideas, then goes on to describe McClintock's accomplishments. The sentence must not compare widespread convictions with McClintock herself. The clearest and most efficient way to make the comparison is to introduce McClintock's colleagues' convictions in a dependent clause, followed by a main clause that introduces McClintock's different way of doing things and goes on to explain how successful she was.

A   Incorrect comparison between *conviction* and *Barbara McClintock*.
B   *Were of the conviction of genes being relatively simple* is wordy and awkward.
C   *Contrary to many of her colleagues being convinced* is wordy and awkward.
D   Correct. A dependent clause describing the beliefs of McClintock's colleagues is followed by the main clause presenting the contrasting beliefs of McClintock.
E   *Even with many of her colleagues …* is wordy and indirect.

The correct answer is D.

32. Galileo was convinced that natural phenomena, as manifestations of the laws of physics, would appear the same to someone on the deck of a ship moving smoothly and uniformly through the <u>water as a</u> person standing on land.

    (A) water as a
    (B) water as to a
    (C) water; just as it would to a
    (D) water, as it would to the
    (E) water; just as to the

Idiom; Parallelism

The second part of this sentence is a comparison. The correct, parallel, and idiomatic structure makes the comparison clear. In this case, a phenomenon appears *the same to x (someone) as to y (a person)*. The two parts of the comparison must be parallel.

A   Without the preposition *to*, the sentence is neither idiomatic nor parallel.
B   Correct. The sentence uses the correct idiom, and the two parts of the comparison are parallel.
C   The use of a semicolon creates a sentence fragment.
D   The idiom is *the same to x as to y*, but this change would make it incorrect: *the same to x, as it would to y*, which also introduces a problem of agreement between the plural *phenomena* and the singular *it*.
E   The use of a semicolon introduces a sentence fragment.

The correct answer is B.

33. <u>Because an oversupply of computer chips has sent prices plunging,</u> the manufacturer has announced that it will cut production by closing its factories for two days a month.

    (A) Because an oversupply of computer chips has sent prices plunging,
    (B) Because of plunging prices for computer chips, which is due to an oversupply,
    (C) Because computer chip prices have been sent plunging, which resulted from an oversupply,

(D)   Due to plunging computer chip prices from an oversupply,

(E)   Due to an oversupply, with the result that computer chip prices have been sent plunging,

Agreement; Rhetorical construction

This sentence describes a causal sequence of events: The oversupply of chips caused prices to plunge, which in turn caused the manufacturer to announce factory closings to cut production. The clearest, most efficient way to express this sequence is to present the events in chronological order, as they occurred.

A   **Correct.** Events are presented concisely, in chronological order.

B   Because *which* refers to plural *prices*, it should be followed by *are*, not *is*.

C   The violation of chronological order is confusing; reference of *which* is ambiguous.

D   This backward description of the events behind the announcement of factory closings is confusing and awkward.

E   *Due to* followed by *with the result* is redundant and unnecessarily wordy.

The correct answer is A.

34.   Beyond the immediate cash flow crisis that the museum faces, its survival depends on <u>if it can broaden its membership and leave</u> its cramped quarters for a site where it can store and exhibit its more than 12,000 artifacts.

(A)   if it can broaden its membership and leave

(B)   whether it can broaden its membership and leave

(C)   whether or not it has the capability to broaden its membership and can leave

(D)   its ability for broadening its membership and leaving

(E)   the ability for it to broaden its membership and leave

Idiom; Verb form

This sentence requires the correct use of an idiom: *Depends on* should be followed by *whether*, not *if*, because this is an interrogative clause following a preposition.

A   *Depends on if* is not a correct idiomatic expression.

B   **Correct.** *Depends on whether* is the correct idiom to use in this sentence.

C   Adding *it has the capability to* creates an unnecessarily wordy construction.

D   *Its ability* should be followed by *to broaden*, not *for broadening*.

E   *The ability for it to broaden* is wordy, awkward, and ungrammatical.

The correct answer is B.

35.   Along with the drop in producer prices announced yesterday, the strong retail sales figures released today seem <u>like it is indicative that</u> the economy, although growing slowly, is not nearing a recession.

(A)   like it is indicative that

(B)   as if to indicate

(C)   to indicate that

(D)   indicative of

(E)   like an indication of

Grammatical construction; Agreement

In this sentence, the verb *seem* should be followed by an infinitive, *to indicate*; the relative pronoun *that* correctly introduces the clause, but *it* does not agree with *sales figures*.

A   Singular *it* does not agree with plural *sales figures*.

B   Verb *seem* may be followed by *as if* in some contexts, but here the result is an ungrammatical and illogical construction.

C   **Correct.** In this sentence, the verb *seem* is correctly followed by the infinitive *to indicate*, and the pronoun *that* correctly introduces a clause.

D   *Indicative of* cannot introduce a clause.

E   *An indication of* is wordy and cannot introduce a clause.

The correct answer is C.

36. Dressed as a man and using the name Robert Shurtleff, Deborah Sampson, the first woman to draw a soldier's pension, joined the Continental Army in 1782 at the age of <u>22, was injured three times, and was discharged in 1783 because she had become</u> too ill to serve.

    (A) 22, was injured three times, and was discharged in 1783 because she had become

    (B) 22, was injured three times, while being discharged in 1783 because she had become

    (C) 22 and was injured three times, and discharged in 1783, being

    (D) 22, injured three times, and was discharged in 1783 because she was

    (E) 22, having been injured three times and discharged in 1783, being

    Parallelism; Logical predication

    This sentence introduces Deborah Sampson with a description of Sampson when she first enlisted, and goes on to describe her career in the Continental Army. The information about her historical significance interrupts the chronological flow of the sentence and must therefore be set off with commas. The sequence of events that marks her career must be presented as a parallel series of items.

    A **Correct.** The phrase that describes Deborah Sampson as *the first woman to draw a soldier's pension* intervenes between the subject and predicate of the main verb and thus is appropriately set off with commas; the three verbs in the main clause are in parallel form.

    B *While being* … indicates that Sampson was injured at the same time she was discharged from the Army.

    C *Discharged* should be in passive voice—*was discharged*—because Sampson did not do this herself.

    D *Injured* needs to be in passive voice.

    E *having been injured* … indicates that all Sampson's injuries as well as her discharge occurred in 1783.

    The correct answer is A.

37. Although schistosomiasis is not often fatal, <u>it is so debilitating that it has become an economic</u> drain on many developing countries.

    (A) it is so debilitating that it has become an economic

    (B) it is of such debilitation, it has become an economical

    (C) so debilitating is it as to become an economic

    (D) such is its debilitation, it becomes an economical

    (E) there is so much debilitation that it has become an economical

    Idiom

    This sentence correctly uses the idiomatic construction *so x that y* where *y* is a subordinate clause that explains or describes *x*: *So debilitating that it has become.…* *It* clearly refers to *schistosomiasis*, which is correctly modified by the adjective *debilitating*.

    A **Correct.** In this sentence, the pronoun reference is clear, and the *so x that y* construction is concise.

    B The noun *debilitation* creates an awkward, wordy alternative and a slight change in meaning; the subordinate clause is not introduced by *that*; *economical* does not have the same meaning as *economic*.

    C The construction *so x as to y* is not a correct idiom.

    D The construction introduced by *such* is awkward and wordy; *debilitation* is also awkward and slightly different in meaning; *that* is omitted; *economical* does not have the same meaning as *economic*.

    E The noun *debilitation* creates an awkward, wordy alternative and a slight change in meaning; *economical* does not have the same meaning as *economic*.

    The correct answer is A.

38. In 1850, Lucretia Mott published her *Discourse on Women*, <u>arguing in a treatise for women to have equal political and legal rights</u> and for changes in the married women's property laws.

    (A) arguing in a treatise for women to have equal political and legal rights

    (B) arguing in a treatise for equal political and legal rights for women

    (C) a treatise that advocates women's equal political and legal rights

    (D) a treatise advocating women's equal political and legal rights

    (E) a treatise that argued for equal political and legal rights for women

Parallelism; Rhetorical construction

Mott's *Discourse* was a treatise, and it is redundant and confusing to present her as both publishing her *Discourse* and *arguing in a treatise,* as though they were two separate things. The verb *arguing* must be followed by a prepositional phrase beginning with *for,* but the verb *advocating* simply takes a direct object.

A   After *published her Discourse … arguing in a treatise* is wordy and imprecise.

B   *Arguing in a treatise* is redundant and awkward.

C   The verb *advocates* does not work idiomatically with the prepositional phrase *for changes….*

D   The verbal *advocating* does not work idiomatically with the prepositional phrase *for changes….*

E   **Correct.** The title of Mott's publication is followed by a phrase describing the treatise, and *argued* is followed by *for.*

The correct answer is E.

39. In 1527 King Henry VIII sought to have his marriage to Queen Catherine annulled <u>so as to marry</u> Anne Boleyn.

    (A) so as to marry

    (B) and so could be married to

    (C) to be married to

    (D) so that he could marry

    (E) in order that he would marry

Grammatical construction; Idiom

This sentence should use the construction *x happened so that y could happen*; *so* introduces a clause of purpose, explaining the reason for the action in the main clause. *Henry … sought to have his marriage … annulled so that he could marry Anne Boleyn.* The relationship between the two clauses is clear.

A   *So as to marry* is not idiomatically correct; it does not identify who will marry.

B   This alternative is ungrammatical and illogical: Henry could not marry simply on the basis of seeking an annulment.

C   The infinitive here should be preceded by a conjunction (*in order*); *to marry* is preferable to the wordier *to be married to.*

D   **Correct.** This sentence's construction clearly shows the reason that Henry sought an annulment; *could* is more appropriate than *would* because the annulment would not ensure his marriage—it would only enable him to marry.

E   The conditional *would marry* is incorrect.

The correct answer is D.

40. Dr. Tonegawa won the Nobel Prize for discovering how the body can constantly change its genes to fashion a seeming unlimited number of antibodies, each specifically targeted at an invading microbe or foreign substance.

   (A) seeming unlimited number of antibodies, each specifically targeted at
   (B) seeming unlimited number of antibodies, each targeted specifically to
   (C) seeming unlimited number of antibodies, all specifically targeted at
   (D) seemingly unlimited number of antibodies, all of them targeted specifically to
   (E) seemingly unlimited number of antibodies, each targeted specifically at

Diction; Idiom

Adjectives modify nouns and pronouns. Adverbs modify adjectives, verbs, and other adverbs. The adverb *seemingly*, not the adjective *seeming*, should be used to modify the adjective *unlimited*. The idiomatic form to be used here is *targeted ... at* rather than *targeted ... to*. Logic requires that *each* antibody is meant to deal individually with *an invading microbe or foreign substance*.

A   The adjective *seeming* should instead be the adverb *seemingly*.
B   The adjective *seeming* should instead be the adverb *seemingly*.
C   The adjective *seeming* should instead be the adverb *seemingly*; the use of *all* instead of *each* does not make sense.
D   The use of *all* instead of *each* does not make sense.
E   **Correct.** This sentence correctly uses *seemingly* instead of *seeming* and *each* instead of *all*.

The correct answer is E.

41. To develop more accurate population forecasts, demographers have to know a great deal more than now about the social and economic determinants of fertility.

   (A) have to know a great deal more than now about the social and economic
   (B) have to know a great deal more than they do now about the social and economical
   (C) would have to know a great deal more than they do now about the social and economical
   (D) would have to know a great deal more than they do now about the social and economic
   (E) would have to know a great deal more than now about the social and economic

Verb form; Logical predication

This sentence explains a hypothetical situation and therefore calls for a conditional—or contrary-to-fact—construction, because in order to more accurately predict population, demographers *would have to know* more than they presently know. A present-tense verb is required to describe the current state of demographers' knowledge, and the comparison made by the sentence must be between current and conditional knowledge, not between knowledge and time of knowing (*now*).

A   Wrong comparison—between knowledge and time (*now*); conditional verb is needed.
B   Conditional verb is needed; *economical* is the wrong adjective.
C   *Economical* is the wrong adjective.
D   **Correct.** Conditional knowledge, indicated by *would have to know*, is correctly compared to current knowledge.
E   Wrong comparison—between what demographers need to know and *now*.

The correct answer is D.

42. Scientists have recently discovered what could be the largest and oldest living organism on Earth, a giant fungus that is an interwoven filigree of mushrooms and rootlike tentacles spawned by a single fertilized spore some 10,000 years ago and <u>extending</u> for more than 30 acres in the soil of a Michigan forest.

    (A) extending
    (B) extends
    (C) extended
    (D) it extended
    (E) is extending

Parallelism; Verb form

The original sentence is correctly written. The giant fungus is described as an *interwoven filigree spawned … some 10,000 years ago and extending for more than 30 acres*. The present participle *extending* parallels the past participle *spawned*.

A   Correct. This sentence has the participles *spawned* and *extending* in a correct parallel construction. *Spawned* refers to something that happened in the past, while *extending* refers to something that continues into the present.

B   *Extends* is a present tense verb, not the participle needed for parallel structure; the ostensible parallel between *extends* and the distant verb *is* is superficial and would result in an awkward and unclear sentence.

C   *Extended* looks parallel to *spawned*, but this phrase would mean that the fungus extended only in the past when the fungus clearly lives on in the present.

D   *It extended* is not parallel to *spawned* and indicates an event completed in the past.

E   *Is extending* is the progressive form of the present tense verb, not the participle required for parallelism.

The correct answer is A.

43. Laos has a land area <u>about the same as Great Britain but only four million in population, where many</u> are members of hill tribes ensconced in the virtually inaccessible mountain valleys of the north.

    (A) about the same as Great Britain but only four million in population, where many
    (B) of about the same size as Great Britain is, but in Laos there is a population of only four million, and many
    (C) that is about the same size as Great Britain's land area, but in Laos with a population of only four million people, many of them
    (D) comparable to the size of Great Britain, but only four million in population, and many
    (E) comparable to that of Great Britain but a population of only four million people, many of whom

Logical predication; Grammatical construction

The comparison in this sentence is between the land area of Laos and the land area of Great Britain, not between the land area of Laos and Great Britain. The phrase about the population of Laos is most clearly and efficiently expressed in an appositive using a relative pronoun to refer back to *people* rather than the more abstract *population*. Using this construction keeps the appropriate emphasis on the two main claims being made about Laos, one describing its land area and the other its sparse population.

A   The comparison between land area and Great Britain is incorrect; *where* is an inappropriate referent to *population*, which does not designate a place.

B   Inappropriate comparison between land area and Great Britain; the *there is …* construction is wordy and imprecise.

C   The reference of *them* is unclear and the expression is generally awkward.

D   The coordinating conjunction *and* gives undue emphasis to the claim that many of the people in Laos live in inaccessible places.

E   **Correct.** The land area of Laos is correctly compared to *that of* Great Britain; *whom* refers appropriately to *people*.

The correct answer is E.

44. The plot of *The Bostonians* centers on the <u>rivalry between Olive Chancellor, an active feminist, with her charming and cynical cousin, Basil Ransom,</u> when they find themselves drawn to the same radiant young woman whose talent for public speaking has won her an ardent following.

   (A) rivalry between Olive Chancellor, an active feminist, with her charming and cynical cousin, Basil Ransom,

   (B) rivals Olive Chancellor, an active feminist, against her charming and cynical cousin, Basil Ransom,

   (C) rivalry that develops between Olive Chancellor, an active feminist, and Basil Ransom, her charming and cynical cousin,

   (D) developing rivalry between Olive Chancellor, an active feminist, with Basil Ransom, her charming and cynical cousin,

   (E) active feminist, Olive Chancellor, and the rivalry with her charming and cynical cousin Basil Ransom,

Idiom; Rhetorical construction

Olive Chancellor and Basil Ransom are rivals. The situation can be expressed with the construction *the rivalry between x and y* or the construction *the rivals x and y*. The construction *rivalry between … with* is incorrect.

A *With* is incorrect in the construction *the rivalry between x and y*.

B *Against* is incorrect in the construction *the rivals x and y*.

C **Correct.** This sentence uses the construction *the rivalry between x and y* correctly; it also clearly identifies both parties in the rivalry.

D *With* is incorrect in the construction *the rivalry between x and y*.

E This sentence does not make it clear that Olive is a party to the rivalry.

The correct answer is C.

45. Quasars, at billions of light-years from Earth the most distant observable objects in the universe, <u>believed to be</u> the cores of galaxies in an early stage of development.

   (A) believed to be
   (B) are believed to be
   (C) some believe them to be
   (D) some believe they are
   (E) it is believed that they are

Grammatical construction

The original sentence is not actually a sentence; it is a sentence fragment since it lacks a verb: *believed to be* on its own is a participial phrase. The verb *are* must be placed before *believed to be* to create a complete sentence.

A This sentence fragment lacks a verb.

B **Correct.** The verb *are believed to be* grammatically completes the sentence and connects *quasars* to *cores*.

C The clause *some believe them to be* does not supply a verb to accompany *quasars* as the subject of the sentence, and the clause supplies an object *them* so that *quasars* cannot be the object, making the sentence ungrammatical.

D The clause *some believe they are* does not complete the clause begun by *quasars*, making the sentence ungrammatical.

E The clause *it is believed that they are* does not complete the clause begun by *quasars*, making the sentence ungrammatical.

The correct answer is B.

46. In ancient Thailand, <u>much of the local artisans' creative energy was expended for the creation of Buddha images and when they constructed and decorated the temples that enshrined them.</u>

(A)   much of the local artisans' creative energy was expended for the creation of Buddha images and when they constructed and decorated the temples that enshrined them

(B)   much of the local artisans' creative energy was expended on the creation of Buddha images and on construction and decoration of the temples in which they were enshrined

(C)   much of the local artisans' creative energy was expended on the creation of Buddha images as well as constructing and decoration of the temples in which they were enshrined

(D)   creating images of Buddha accounted for much of the local artisans' creative energy, and also constructing and decorating the temples enshrining them

(E)   the creation of Buddha images accounted for much of the local artisans' creative energy as well as construction and decoration of the temples that enshrined them

Idiom; Parallelism; Rhetorical construction

The main point of the sentence is that artisans in ancient Thailand spent most of their creative energy on three tasks: creating Buddha images, and constructing and decorating temples to enshrine the Buddhas. These three tasks must be described in parallel forms. The verb *expended* should be followed by the preposition *on*, not *for*.

A   *For* is the wrong preposition; the *and when* … clause introduces faulty parallelism; it is unclear what *they* refers to.

B   **Correct.** The three activities are presented in parallel form: creation of Buddha images and construction and *decoration of the temples.*

C   *Constructing* violates the parallelism otherwise maintained by *creation* and *decoration.*

D   The *and also* phrase is awkwardly set apart from the main claim of the sentence—which is that all three tasks consumed much of the artisans' energy.

E   This construction is awkward and unnecessarily wordy and says something different—that the images accounted for the construction and decoration of temples.

The correct answer is B.

47.   Five fledgling sea eagles left their nests in western Scotland this summer, <u>bringing</u> to 34 the number of wild birds successfully raised since transplants from Norway began in 1975.

(A)   bringing

(B)   and brings

(C)   and it brings

(D)   and it brought

(E)   and brought

Verb form; Grammatical construction

Bringing is the present participle of the verb *to bring.* As used here, it correctly describes an action that happens at the same time as the action in the main clause; *bringing* indicates that the number of wild birds became 34 when the five eagles left their nests.

A   **Correct.** The participle *bringing* correctly links the two ideas in the sentence.

B   In this construction, the subject of the second verb must be the same as the subject of the first verb, but *five eagles* cannot grammatically or logically be the subject of *brings.*

C   *It brings* is the wrong tense.

D   There are too many possible referents for *it.*

E   *Five eagles* can be the grammatical subject of *brought*, but not the logical one; it was not the eagles themselves but rather the entire action of their leaving their nests that brought the number to 34.

The correct answer is A.

48. In 1713, Alexander Pope began his translation of the *Iliad*, a work that, taking him seven years until completion, and that literary critic Samuel Johnson, Pope's contemporary, pronounced the greatest translation in any language.

(A) his translation of the *Iliad*, a work that, taking him seven years until completion, and that literary critic Samuel Johnson, Pope's contemporary, pronounced

(B) his translation of the *Iliad*, a work that took him seven years to complete and that literary critic Samuel Johnson, Pope's contemporary, pronounced

(C) his translation of the *Iliad*, a work that had taken seven years to complete and that literary critic Samuel Johnson, Pope's contemporary, pronounced it as

(D) translating the *Iliad*, a work that took seven years until completion and that literary critic Samuel Johnson, Pope's contemporary, pronounced it as

(E) translating the *Iliad*, a work that had taken seven years to complete and literary critic Samuel Johnson, Pope's contemporary, pronounced it

Logical predication; Grammatical construction

Pope's translation of the *Iliad*, not the *Iliad* itself, took seven years to complete. The main point of the sentence is that Pope began this translation in 1713, and every other comment about it must be subordinated to that opening claim, in parallel relative clauses.

A   *A work that* ... requires a verb; without it, the sentence is a fragment.

B   **Correct.** Pope's *translation* is described as *a work*, which is then described concisely in two dependent clauses.

C   The pronoun *it* after *pronounced* is redundant, an ungrammatical reference to *a work*, which has already been referenced by the relative pronoun *that*.

D   The appositive phrase *a work* ... incorrectly refers to the *Iliad*, not Pope's translation.

E   The appositive phrase *a work* ... incorrectly refers to the *Iliad*; the coordinating conjunction introduces inappropriate emphasis on Johnson's description, and the expression is awkward and unclear.

The correct answer is B.

49. The automotive conveyor-belt system, which Henry Ford modeled after an assembly-line technique introduced by Ransom Olds, reduced from a day and a half to 93 minutes the required time of assembling a Model T.

(A) from a day and a half to 93 minutes the required time of assembling a Model T

(B) the time being required to assemble a Model T, from a day and a half down to 93 minutes

(C) the time being required to assemble a Model T, a day and a half to 93 minutes

(D) the time required to assemble a Model T from a day and a half to 93 minutes

(E) from a day and a half to 93 minutes, the time required for the assembling of a Model T

Rhetorical construction; Idiom

The underlined portion of the original sentence is awkward because the verb *reduced* is followed by a prepositional phrase rather than the direct object *time*. Changing this structure so that the object immediately follows the verb, *reduced the time*, also allows an idiomatic error to be corrected. *Required* should be followed by an infinitive, *to assemble*, rather than a prepositional phrase, *of assembling*. The phrase indicating time should be used to complete the sentence: *reduced the time required to assemble a Model T from a day and a half to 93 minutes*.

A   Placement of phrases creates an awkward construction; *required ... of assembling* is not idiomatic.

B   *Being required* and *down to* are wordy constructions; the comma is unnecessary.

C   *Being required* is wordy; the construction *from ... to* indicates time, not *to* alone.

D   Correct. This sentence has a clear, concise, and idiomatic construction.

E   Beginning with the prepositional phrase is awkward; the comma is unnecessary; *required for the assembling of* is wordy and awkward.

The correct answer is D.

50. According to some analysts, the gains in the stock market reflect growing confidence <u>that the economy will avoid the recession that many had feared earlier in the year and instead come</u> in for a "soft landing," followed by a gradual increase in business activity.

(A)   that the economy will avoid the recession that many had feared earlier in the year and instead come

(B)   in the economy to avoid the recession, what many feared earlier in the year, rather to come

(C)   in the economy's ability to avoid the recession, something earlier in the year many had feared, and instead to come

(D)   in the economy to avoid the recession many were fearing earlier in the year, and rather to come

(E)   that the economy will avoid the recession that was feared earlier this year by many, with it instead coming

Grammatical construction; Rhetorical construction

The original sentence successfully avoids the problems that may occur in a long sentence with multiple modifiers. Two subordinate clauses begin with *that*, and one of them is contained within another. *That many had feared earlier in the year* clearly defines *the recession*. *That the economy will avoid ... and instead (will* understood) *come...* is the subordinate clause that follows the main clause; its subject, *economy*, is followed by two parallel verbs, *will avoid* and (*will* understood) *come*. *Instead* before the second verb properly indicates contrast.

A   Correct. This sentence contains two correct subordinate clauses introduced by *that*.

B   *What* cannot replace *that*; *the economy to avoid the recession* is awkward and unclear; *rather to come* does not complete the second part of the sentence idiomatically.

C   *Earlier in the year* should follow *many had feared*, rather than preceding it; *instead to come* does not complete the second part of the sentence idiomatically.

D   *The recession* must be followed by *that*; *were fearing* is the wrong tense; *rather to come* does not complete the second part of the sentence idiomatically.

E   The passive voice construction *that was feared ...* is weak and wordy; *with it instead coming* is awkward, wordy, and ungrammatical.

The correct answer is A.

51. A new study suggests that the conversational pace of everyday life may be so brisk <u>it hampers the ability of some children for distinguishing discrete sounds and words and, the result is, to make</u> sense of speech.

    (A) it hampers the ability of some children for distinguishing discrete sounds and words and, the result is, to make
    (B) that it hampers the ability of some children to distinguish discrete sounds and words and, as a result, to make
    (C) that it hampers the ability of some children to distinguish discrete sounds and words and, the result of this, they are unable to make
    (D) that it hampers the ability of some children to distinguish discrete sounds and words, and results in not making
    (E) as to hamper the ability of some children for distinguishing discrete sounds and words, resulting in being unable to make

Rhetorical construction; Parallelism; Diction

The sentence describes a hypothesized causal series: The fast conversational pace impairs children's ability to distinguish individual sounds and words, and this, in turn, impairs their ability to make sense of speech. These two consequences, both impaired abilities, are most clearly and efficiently expressed in parallel infinitive phrases (*to distinguish* and *to make*). The explanatory phrase *as a result* before the second infinitive clarifies the sequence. The term *ability* should be followed by the preposition *to*, not *for*.

A   *For* is the wrong preposition to follow *ability*; the phrase *and, the result, is* introduces a new clause which indicates that children's inability to distinguish sounds enables them to make sense of speech.

B   **Correct.** The two abilities hampered by the fast pace of conversation are described with the parallel infinitive phrases *to distinguish* and *to make*.

C   *The result of this* is a new subject that grammatically requires a new verb; the phrase is wordy and unclear.

D   This version of the sentence nonsensically suggests that the pace of speech results in not making sense of speech, removing the children from the picture as the ones who are affected.

E   The phrase is awkward, wordy, and unclear; *for* is the incorrect preposition to follow ability.

The correct answer is B.

52. <u>To Josephine Baker, Paris was her home long before it was fashionable to be an expatriate,</u> and she remained in France during the Second World War as a performer and an intelligence agent for the Resistance.

    (A) To Josephine Baker, Paris was her home long before it was fashionable to be an expatriate,
    (B) For Josephine Baker, long before it was fashionable to be an expatriate, Paris was her home,
    (C) Josephine Baker made Paris her home long before to be an expatriate was fashionable,
    (D) Long before it was fashionable to be an expatriate, Josephine Baker made Paris her home,
    (E) Long before it was fashionable being an expatriate, Paris was home to Josephine Baker,

Rhetorical construction; Parallelism

This compound sentence (consisting of two independent clauses joined by the coordinating conjunction *and*) would be most clearly expressed if Josephine Baker were the subject of the first clause since *she* is the subject of the second clause: *Josephine Baker made Paris her home* would clearly parallel *she remained in France*. The adverb clause *long ... expatriate* is best placed before the main clause.

A   *To Josephine Baker ... her* is redundant and awkward; the subject of the first main clause is *Paris* rather than *Baker*.

B   *For Josephine Baker ... her* is redundant and awkward; putting two introductory elements together before the main clause is awkward.

C   Inversion of the expected word order in *to be an expatriate was unfashionable* is awkward.

D   **Correct.** The clearest, most economical order for this sentence is to put the adverb clause first, and make *Baker* the subject of the first main clause, parallel to *she* in the second.

E *Being* is awkward; *Baker* should be the subject of the first main clause, parallel to *she* in the second main clause.

The correct answer is D.

53. The nineteenth-century chemist Humphry Davy presented the results of his early experiments in his "Essay on Heat and Light," <u>a critique of all chemistry since Robert Boyle as well as a vision of a</u> new chemistry that Davy hoped to found.

(A) a critique of all chemistry since Robert Boyle as well as a vision of a

(B) a critique of all chemistry following Robert Boyle and also his envisioning of a

(C) a critique of all chemistry after Robert Boyle and envisioning as well

(D) critiquing all chemistry from Robert Boyle forward and also a vision of

(E) critiquing all the chemistry done since Robert Boyle as well as his own envisioning of

Parallelism; Rhetorical construction

The main objective of the sentence is to describe "Essay on Heat and Light" as Davy's presentation of his own experiments and to further explain that the essay served as both a critique of previous chemistry and a vision of a new kind of chemistry. The clearest, most effective form for providing this explanation of the essay's function is to make *critique* and *vision* both appositives of "Essay on Heat and Light," and to present them in a parallel structure.

A **Correct.** The phrases describing the essay's function are presented in parallel form.

B *Critique* and *his envisioning* are not parallel; the phrase *and also his envisioning* is unnecessarily wordy; it is also unclear to whom *his* refers.

C The two descriptors are not parallel.

D The two descriptors are not parallel.

E The meaning is confused in the assertion that Davy critiqued his own vision of chemistry.

The correct answer is A.

54. The report recommended that the hospital <u>should eliminate unneeded beds, expensive services should be consolidated, and use space in other hospitals.</u>

(A) should eliminate unneeded beds, expensive services should be consolidated, and use space in other hospitals

(B) should eliminate unneeded beds, expensive services should be consolidated, and other hospitals' space be used

(C) should eliminate unneeded beds, expensive services should be consolidated, and to use space in other hospitals

(D) eliminate unneeded beds, consolidate expensive services, and other hospitals' space used

(E) eliminate unneeded beds, consolidate expensive services, and use space in other hospitals

Grammatical construction; Parallelism

The underlined portion of the sentence is incoherent and runs together two sentences (*the ... beds*; *expensive ... consolidated*). Making the report's three recommendations into a series of three grammatically parallel elements corrects this problem. Since the report *recommended*, it is redundant to use *should*. Each of the three parallel elements may consist of a verb and an object: 1) *eliminate unneeded beds*, 2) *consolidate expensive services*, and 3) *use space in other hospitals*.

A Incoherent construction includes a run-on sentence; following *recommended*, *should* is redundant.

B Following *recommended*, *should* is redundant; three elements in the series are not parallel.

C Following *recommended*, *should* is redundant; the second and third elements are not parallel to the first.

D *Other hospitals' space* used is awkward and not parallel to the other two elements.

E **Correct.** In this concise sentence, each of the three parallel elements in the series consists of a verb and an object.

The correct answer is E.

55. Many house builders offer rent-to-buy <u>programs that enable a family with insufficient savings for a conventional down payment to be able to move into new housing and to apply</u> part of the rent to a purchase later.

    (A)   programs that enable a family with insufficient savings for a conventional down payment to be able to move into new housing and to apply
    (B)   programs that enable a family with insufficient savings for a conventional down payment to move into new housing and to apply
    (C)   programs; that enables a family with insufficient savings for a conventional down payment to move into new housing, to apply
    (D)   programs, which enables a family with insufficient savings for a conventional down payment to move into new housing, applying
    (E)   programs, which enable a family with insufficient savings for a conventional down payment to be able to move into new housing, applying

Rhetorical construction; Logical predication

In a lengthy sentence consisting of many phrases, it is essential to determine which phrases and words are necessary to the sentence and which words may be eliminated because they are unnecessary. The relative pronoun *that* correctly refers to *programs* and introduces the subordinate clause; *family* is followed by two phrases that are clear and correct. *To be able to move*, however, is needlessly wordy, repeating the meaning of *enable*, and can be reduced to *to move*. This creates a parallel construction in which *programs ... enable a family ... to move ... and to apply*.

A   *To be able to move* is wordy and *able* is redundant after *enable*; *to apply* is not logically parallel to the infinitive phrase *(able) to move*.

B   Correct. In this sentence, eliminating the wordy construction *to be able* allows *to move* to be parallel to *to apply*.

C   Insofar as this is grammatical, using a semicolon here causes *that* to refer too broadly to the entire previous clause rather than specifically to *programs*; the two infinitives should be joined by the conjunction *and*, not separated by a comma.

D   *Enables* does not agree with the plural subject; *applying* following a nonrestrictive clause suggests incorrectly that the builders, not the family, are applying the rent.

E   The comma after *programs* is incorrect because the clause is meant to be restrictive; as in D, *applying* will alter the meaning of the sentence.

The correct answer is B.

56. Many of the earliest known images of Hindu deities in India date from the time of the Kushan <u>Empire, fashioned either from the spotted sandstone of Mathura or</u> Gandharan grey schist.

    (A)   Empire, fashioned either from the spotted sandstone of Mathura or
    (B)   Empire, fashioned from either the spotted sandstone of Mathura or from
    (C)   Empire, either fashioned from the spotted sandstone of Mathura or
    (D)   Empire and either fashioned from the spotted sandstone of Mathura or from
    (E)   Empire and were fashioned either from the spotted sandstone of Mathura or from

Logical predication; Parallelism

The sentence makes two claims about the earliest known images of Hindu deities in India: They date from the Kushan Empire, and they are made from sandstone or schist. The clearest, most effective way to incorporate these two claims into a single sentence is to provide two parallel predicates for the single subject, *the earliest known images of Hindu deities in India*. The two options of media, presented as either/or choices, must also be given in parallel structure: *either from ... or from ...* or *from either ... or....*

A   Placement of the modifier *fashioned …* suggests that the *Empire* (the closest noun), not the images of the deities, was fashioned out of these materials; to parallel *either from*, the preposition *from* should also follow *or*.

B   Parallelism requires that *either* precede the first appearance of *from* or that the second appearance of *from* be eliminated.

C   As in A and B, the placement of the modifier after *Empire* is misleading; parallelism requires that the phrase *fashioned from*, or another comparable verb and preposition, follow *or*.

D   Parallelism requires that a verb follow *or*, since a verb follows *either*.

E   **Correct.** Two verbs, *date* and *were fashioned*, introduce parallel predicates for the subject, *earliest known images*; the choices of media are correctly presented with the structure *either from … or from*.

The correct answer is E.

57.   That educators have not anticipated the impact of microcomputer technology can hardly be said that it is their fault: Alvin Toffler, one of the most prominent students of the future, did not even mention microcomputers in *Future Shock*, published in 1970.

(A)   That educators have not anticipated the impact of microcomputer technology can hardly be said that it is their fault

(B)   That educators have not anticipated the impact of microcomputer technology can hardly be said to be at fault

(C)   It can hardly be said that it is the fault of educators who have not anticipated the impact of microcomputer technology

(D)   It can hardly be said that educators are at fault for not anticipating the impact of microcomputer technology

(E)   The fact that educators are at fault for not anticipating the impact of microcomputer technology can hardly be said

Grammatical construction; Rhetorical construction

Although it is possible to begin a sentence with a subordinate clause beginning with *that*, this inverted construction often results in errors such as those found here. In the original sentence, the subordinate clause *that … technology* is followed by the main verb, *can … be said*, but then the verb is followed by yet another subordinate clause, *that it is their fault*. The best way to solve this problem is by putting the sentence in the expected order, with the main clause (*It can hardly be said*) preceding the subordinate clause (*that …*). For greater clarity and concision, the two subordinate clauses should be condensed into one: *educators are at fault for not anticipating the impact of microcomputer technology*.

A   Inverting the usual order results in an ungrammatical construction in which the main verb is both preceded and followed by a subordinate clause.

B   *Can hardly be said to be at fault* does not grammatically complete the subordinate clause.

C   Construction *that it is … who have not* is wordy and awkward; it also distorts meaning and lacks completion.

D   **Correct.** This sentence has the main clause followed by one subordinate clause correctly introduced by *that*.

E   *The fact* is wordy; the inverted construction does not successfully convey the meaning of the sentence.

The correct answer is D.

58. A leading figure in the Scottish Enlightenment, <u>Adam Smith's two major books are to democratic capitalism what</u> Marx's *Das Kapital* is to socialism.

   (A) Adam Smith's two major books are to democratic capitalism what
   (B) Adam Smith's two major books are to democratic capitalism like
   (C) Adam Smith's two major books are to democratic capitalism just as
   (D) Adam Smith wrote two major books that are to democratic capitalism similar to
   (E) Adam Smith wrote two major books that are to democratic capitalism what

Idiom; Logical predication

A leading figure in the Scottish Enlightenment describes Adam Smith, not his two books, so the name of Adam Smith must immediately follow the opening phrase. The comparison between Smith's books and Marx's book is expressed as a ratio, so the correct idiomatic expression is *x is to y what a is to b.*

A   The opening phrase is a dangling modifier because it describes Smith, not his books.
B   The opening phrase is a dangling modifier; *like* is an incorrect word for making the comparison.
C   The opening phrase is a dangling modifier; *just as* is an incorrect term for the comparison.
D   *Similar to* is an incorrect conclusion to the comparison introduced by *are to.*
E   **Correct.** The opening phrase is followed by the subject that it modifies, Adam Smith, and the comparison of the two men's work is presented idiomatically.

The correct answer is E.

59. The Olympic Games helped to keep peace among the pugnacious states of the Greek <u>world in that a sacred truce was proclaimed during the festival's month.</u>

   (A) world in that a sacred truce was proclaimed during the festival's month
   (B) world, proclaiming a sacred truce during the festival's month
   (C) world when they proclaimed a sacred truce for the festival month
   (D) world, for a sacred truce was proclaimed during the month of the festival
   (E) world by proclamation of a sacred truce that was for the month of the festival

Idiom; Rhetorical construction

This sentence depends on using the correct conjunction to join two independent clauses. *In that* is a conjunction that means *inasmuch as*; because *in that* has largely gone out of use, it is considered stilted and overly formal. It also uses two words when one would do. In this sentence, the second clause explains the first one, so the conjunction *for*, meaning *because*, is the most appropriate choice for joining the two independent clauses of the compound sentence. *Festival's month* is an awkward and imprecise use of the possessive; *during the month of the festival* is clearer.

A   *In that* is stilted and overly formal.
B   It is not clear who would be doing the *proclaiming*; a clause is preferable to a phrase here.
C   *They* is ambiguous, possibly referring to either the *states* or the *Games.* The phrase *truce for the festival month* loses the sense that it's to take place for the duration of the month.
D   **Correct.** In this sentence, the conjunction *for* joins the two clauses correctly and economically.
E   Wordy and awkward construction.

The correct answer is D.

60. While <u>all states face similar industrial waste problems, the predominating industries and the regulatory environment of the states obviously determines</u> the types and amounts of waste produced, as well as the cost of disposal.

   (A) all states face similar industrial waste problems, the predominating industries and the regulatory environment of the states obviously determines
   (B) each state faces a similar industrial waste problem, their predominant industries and regulatory environment obviously determine
   (C) all states face a similar industrial waste problem; their predominating industries and regulatory environment obviously determines

(D) each state faces similar industrial waste problems, the predominant industries and the regulatory environment of each state obviously determines

(E) all states face similar industrial waste problems, the predominant industries and the regulatory environment of each state obviously determine

Agreement; Grammatical construction

This sentence requires careful attention to number and agreement. The main clause has a compound subject, *the predominating industries and the regulatory environment*, which must take a plural verb, *determine*, rather than the singular verb shown in the original sentence. The sentence begins with the conjunction *while*, here used to mean *although*, and contrasts the similar situation of *all states* with the varying conditions of *each state*. The point of the main clause is that all *states* do not share the same *predominating industries* and *regulatory environment*, so it is more logical and correct to have the *regulatory environment* of *each state*.

A   Compound subject does not agree with the singular verb *determines*; main clause should call attention to the conditions of *each state*, not *the states*.

B   *Each state* must be compared to all other states; *their* does not agree with *each*.

C   Using a semicolon results in a sentence fragment; subject and verb do not agree.

D   *Each state* must be compared to all other states; subject and verb do not agree.

E   **Correct.** This sentence makes the clear distinction between the problem *all states* share and the conditions *each state* faces; subject and verb agree.

The correct answer is E.

61. Rivaling the pyramids of Egypt or even the ancient cities of the Maya as an achievement, <u>the army of terra-cotta warriors created to protect Qin Shi Huang, China's first emperor, in his afterlife is more than 2,000 years old and took 700,000 artisans more than 36 years to complete.</u>

(A) the army of terra-cotta warriors created to protect Qin Shi Huang, China's first emperor, in his afterlife is more than 2,000 years old and took 700,000 artisans more than 36 years to complete

(B) Qin Shi Huang, China's first emperor, was protected in his afterlife by an army of terra-cotta warriors that was created more than 2,000 years ago by 700,000 artisans who took more than 36 years to complete it

(C) it took 700,000 artisans more than 36 years to create an army of terra-cotta warriors more than 2,000 years ago that would protect Qin Shi Huang, China's first emperor, in his afterlife

(D) more than 2,000 years ago, 700,000 artisans worked more than 36 years to create an army of terra-cotta warriors to protect Qin Shi Huang, China's first emperor, in his afterlife

(E) more than 36 years were needed to complete the army of terra-cotta warriors that 700,000 artisans created 2,000 years ago to protect Qin Shi Huang, China's first emperor, in his afterlife

Logical predication; Rhetorical construction

The opening modifier, *Rivaling the pyramids …* describes *the army of terra-cotta warriors*, which must immediately follow the modifier. The placement of the predicates that follow is important; they must clarify two things about the army of terra-cotta warriors: how old it is and how long it took to complete. The clearest and most effective way to express these two assertions is as parallel verb phrases, *is more than 2,000 years old* and *took … more than 36 years to complete.*

A   **Correct.** The opening phrase correctly modifies the subject, *the army of terra-cotta warriors*; the placement of modifiers and predicates in the main clause makes the meaning of the sentence clear.

B   Opening phrase is a dangling modifier because it does not describe the subject *Qin Shi Huang*; in addition, the sentence is awkward and unclear.

C   Opening phrase is a dangling modifier because it does not describe the subject *it*; the sequence of information presented is confusing and unclear.

D   Opening phrase is a dangling modifier because it does not describe the subject *700,000 artisans*.

E   Opening phrase is a dangling modifier because it does not describe the subject *more than 36 years*.

The correct answer is A.

62. When Congress reconvenes, some newly elected members from rural states will try <u>and establish tighter restrictions for the amount of grain farmers are to be allowed to grow and to encourage</u> more aggressive sales of United States farm products overseas.

    (A) and establish tighter restrictions for the amount of grain farmers are to be allowed to grow and to encourage

    (B) and establish tighter restrictions on the amount of grain able to be grown by farmers and encouraging

    (C) establishing tighter restrictions for the amount of grain farmers are allowed to grow and to encourage

    (D) to establish tighter restrictions on the amount of grain capable of being grown by farmers and encouraging

    (E) to establish tighter restrictions on the amount of grain farmers will be allowed to grow and to encourage

Idiom; Parallelism

Although *try and* is an idiom often used in colloquial language, in this sentence, *to* is needed after *will try* to maintain parallelism: *to establish* and *to encourage*. The correct preposition following *restrictions* is not *for* but *on*. *Are to be allowed to grow* is wordy; the infinitive *to be* should be omitted for a tighter and clearer expression.

A   *To* should replace *and* before *establish*; *restrictions* is incorrectly followed by *for* rather than *on*; *to be* is wordy and should be omitted.

B   Here, the passive-voice construction *able to be grown by* is weak and wordy; the constructions *and establish … and encouraging …* are not parallel.

C   *Will try establishing* does not show intent or purpose; *restrictions* must be followed by *on*, not *for*; parallelism is lost.

D   Passive-voice construction *capable of being grown by* is weak and wordy; *encouraging* and *to establish* are not parallel.

E   **Correct.** *To establish* indicates purpose and parallels *to encourage*; *restrictions* is correctly followed by *on*; the wordiness of the verb phrase has been eliminated.

The correct answer is E.

63. The yield of natural gas from Norway's Troll gas field is expected to increase annually until the year <u>2005 and then to stabilize at six billion cubic feet a day, which will allow such an extraction rate at least for</u> 50 years' production.

    (A) 2005 and then to stabilize at six billion cubic feet a day, which will allow such an extraction rate at least for

    (B) 2005 and then to stabilize at six billion cubic feet a day, an extraction rate that will allow at least

    (C) 2005 and then stabilizing at six billion cubic feet a day, with such an extraction rate at the least allowing

    (D) 2005, then stabilizing at six billion cubic feet a day, allowing such an extraction rate for at least

    (E) 2005, then stabilizing at six billion cubic feet a day, which will allow such an extraction rate for at least

Rhetorical construction; Verb form; Logical predication

The sentence is about predictions that Troll gas field's yield would increase until it stabilized at a particular extraction rate in 2005. The term *extraction rate* refers to *six billion cubic feet a day*, so it is redundant and confusingly circular to rename *six billion cubic feet* with the relative pronoun *which* in the subject position and then reintroduce *extraction rate* as the object.

A   The relative phrase beginning with *which* is nonsensical, since the pronoun reference is inaccurate, and the phrase essentially says that the extraction rate enables the extraction rate.

B   **Correct.** The infinitive *to stabilize* parallels *to increase*; information about the *six billion cubic feet a day* is expressed clearly and concisely in an appositive phrase containing a relative clause (*an extraction rate that will allow …*).

C   The phrasing is awkward and unclear; *stabilizing* is an incorrect verb form; it should be an infinitive to parallel *to increase*.

D   *Stabilizing* is an incorrect verb form; it should be an infinitive to parallel *to increase*; the subsequent phrase is awkward and confusing because it is not clear what noun *allowing* is supposed to modify.

E   *Stabilizing* violates the requirement of parallelism, and *which* introduces a nonsensical redundancy, effectively making the claim that the extraction rate (*six billion cubic feet*) enables the extraction rate.

The correct answer is B.

64. Doctors generally agree that such factors as cigarette smoking, eating rich foods high in fats, and alcohol consumption <u>not only do damage by themselves but also aggravate</u> genetic predispositions toward certain diseases.

(A) not only do damage by themselves but also aggravate

(B) do damage by themselves but also are aggravating to

(C) are damaging by themselves but also are aggravating

(D) not only do damage by themselves, they are also aggravating to

(E) are doing damage by themselves, and they are also aggravating

Verb form; Logical predication

This correctly written sentence uses the construction *not only x … but also y*; *x* is the simple present verb *do damage* and *y* is the parallel verb *aggravate*. The simple present tense should be used for a general statement such as this one. When used as a verb, *aggravate* clearly means to make worse; the adjective *aggravating* is instead widely interpreted to mean *annoying*.

A   **Correct.** This sentence correctly uses the *not only … but also* construction to explain the parallel effects of the factors.

B   *Are aggravating to* is not parallel to *do damage*; *aggravating* suggests a different meaning than does *aggravate*; using *but also* without using *not only* is incorrect.

C   The form *are aggravating* distorts the meaning of the sentence; using *but also* without using *not only* is incorrect.

D   Using *not only* without using *but also* is incorrect; *are aggravating to* is not parallel to *do damage*; *aggravating* suggests a different meaning.

E   Simple present tense, rather than the present progressive, should be used to present a general statement; *aggravating* distorts meaning.

The correct answer is A.

65. In a plan to stop the erosion of East Coast beaches, the Army Corps of Engineers proposed building parallel to shore a breakwater of rocks that would rise six feet above the waterline and <u>act as a buffer, so that it absorbs</u> the energy of crashing waves and protecting the beaches.

(A) act as a buffer, so that it absorbs

(B) act like a buffer so as to absorb

(C) act as a buffer, absorbing

(D) acting as a buffer, absorbing

(E) acting like a buffer, absorb

Parallelism; Idiom

The last part of the sentence describes the breakwater and should consist of two grammatically parallel phrases, *absorbing … and protecting*, in order to show two equal functions. *Act* followed by *like* means *to behave or comport oneself* and describes the action of a person: *He acted like a fool*. Here, *act as* describes the function of a thing; *the breakwater … acts as a buffer*. As an inanimate object, a breakwater cannot "behave" itself; it must be performing some function.

A   *So that it absorbs* should be *absorbing* to parallel *protecting*.

B   *Act as* is the proper idiom to describe things; *so as to absorb* is awkward and should be changed to *absorbing* to be parallel to *protecting*.

C   **Correct.** The idiom *act as* is used correctly in this sentence; *absorbing* is properly parallel to *protecting*.

D   Modifying clause is *that would rise … and* (*would* understood) *act*; *acting* cannot be used instead of *act*.

E   Modifying clause is *that would rise … and* (*would* understood) *act*; *acting* cannot be used instead of *act*; *absorb* is not parallel to *protecting*.

The correct answer is C.

66. The 32 species that make up the dolphin family are closely related to whales and in fact <u>include the animal known as the killer whale, which can grow to be 30 feet long and is</u> famous for its aggressive hunting pods.

(A) include the animal known as the killer whale, which can grow to be 30 feet long and is

(B) include the animal known as the killer whale, growing as big as 30 feet long and

(C) include the animal known as the killer whale, growing up to 30 feet long and being

(D) includes the animal known as the killer whale, which can grow as big as 30 feet long and is

(E) includes the animal known as the killer whale, which can grow to be 30 feet long and it is

Rhetorical construction; Agreement

The subject of the sentence is *the 32 species that make up the dolphin family*, and the sentence makes two claims about them: They are closely related, and they include the killer whale. The relative pronoun *which* restates the object of the second verb, reintroducing *the animal known as the killer whale* as the subject of a relative clause followed by two parallel verbs: *can grow* and *is famous*.

A **Correct.** In this concise sentence, verbs agree in number with their subjects and the relative pronoun *which* indicates clearly that *the animal known as the killer whale* is the subject of the verbs in the dependent clause.

B Changing the verb to the participial *growing* introduces ambiguity, because it could refer back to the subject of the sentence (*32 species*).

C The participial *growing* might refer to *the 32 species*; the introduction of *being* is unnecessarily wordy and adds nothing in terms of meaning.

D *as big as* is an idiomatically incorrect expression of the comparison; the plural verb form *include* is needed to match the plural subject *the 32 species*.

E *It* simply restates the subject of the previous phrase, introducing more words but no additional meaning; the singular verb form *includes* should be the plural form *include*.

The correct answer is A.

67. Affording strategic proximity to the Strait of Gibraltar, Morocco was also of interest to the French throughout the first half of the twentieth century because they assumed that <u>if they did not hold it, their grip on Algeria was always insecure</u>.

(A) if they did not hold it, their grip on Algeria was always insecure

(B) without it their grip on Algeria would never be secure

(C) their grip on Algeria was not ever secure if they did not hold it

(D) without that, they could never be secure about their grip on Algeria

(E) never would their grip on Algeria be secure if they did not hold it

Rhetorical construction; Verb form

Conditional constructions require specific verb tenses. For a past condition, the subordinate clause introduced by *if* uses the past indicative, and the main clause uses the conditional *if x happened, then y would happen*.

A Verb *was* should be the conditional *would be*; wordy and imprecise.

B **Correct.** This clear, concise sentence correctly uses the conditional *would never be*.

C Verb *was* should be the conditional *would be*; pronoun *it* is ambiguous and could refer to either *Morocco* or *Algeria*.

D *It*, not *that*, should be used to refer back to *Morocco*; *could never be secure about their grip* is awkward.

E Inverted word order is awkward and confusing; *it* could refer to either *Morocco* or *Algeria*.

The correct answer is B.

68. The first trenches <u>that were cut into a 500-acre site at Tell Hamoukar, Syria, have yielded strong evidence for centrally administered complex societies in northern regions of the Middle East that were arising simultaneously with but</u> independently of the more celebrated city-states of southern Mesopotamia, in what is now southern Iraq.

(A) that were cut into a 500-acre site at Tell Hamoukar, Syria, have yielded strong evidence for centrally administered complex societies in northern regions of the Middle East that were arising simultaneously with but

(B) that were cut into a 500-acre site at Tell Hamoukar, Syria, yields strong evidence that centrally administered complex societies in northern regions of the Middle East were arising simultaneously with but also

(C) having been cut into a 500-acre site at Tell Hamoukar, Syria, have yielded strong evidence that centrally administered complex societies in northern regions of the Middle East were arising simultaneously but

(D) cut into a 500-acre site at Tell Hamoukar, Syria, yields strong evidence of centrally administered complex societies in northern regions of the Middle East arising simultaneously but also

(E) cut into a 500-acre site at Tell Hamoukar, Syria, have yielded strong evidence that centrally administered complex societies in northern regions of the Middle East arose simultaneously with but

Rhetorical construction; Agreement; Grammatical construction

This sentence, explaining interconnections among a number of events, needs to be streamlined as much as possible in order to become understandable. To this end, unnecessary words and structures should be eliminated. Prominent among these are the relative clauses beginning with *that*. Additionally, the subject of this sentence is the plural *trenches*, which requires a plural verb.

A *That were cut …* and *that were arising …* are unnecessarily wordy and create an unnecessarily complicated and confusing sentence structure.

B In addition to the unnecessarily wordy relative clauses, the singular verb *yields* does not agree with the plural subject *trenches*.

C *Having been cut …* is unnecessarily wordy; *arising simultaneously* must be followed by the preposition *with* in order to make sense.

D The singular verb *yields* does not agree with the plural subject *trenches*; *also* adds no meaning to the sentence.

E **Correct.** Unnecessary clauses and phrases are avoided, and the subject and verb of the main clause agree in number.

The correct answer is E.

69. Once they had seen the report from the medical examiner, the investigators <u>did not doubt whether the body recovered from the river was</u> the man who had attempted to escape from the state prison.

(A) did not doubt whether the body recovered from the river was

(B) have no doubt whether the body recovered from the river was

(C) had not doubted that the body recovered from the river was

(D) have no doubt whether the body recovered from the river was that of

(E) had no doubt that the body recovered from the river was that of

Diction; Verb form

As it is used in the opening clause, the past perfect verb tense indicates that an action in the past was completed before another action in the past: *Once x had happened, then y happened.* To maintain proper verb sequence, the verb in the main clause must therefore be in the simple past tense. When *doubt* is used in a negative context such as *there is no doubt* or *he does not doubt*, it should be followed by *that*. A dead *body* cannot be a *man*; the body is *that of* a *man*.

A *Whether* should be *that*; the body is *that of* a man.

B Incorrect use of present verb *have* instead of *had*; *whether* should be *that*; the body is *that of* a man.

C Incorrect use of past-perfect verb *had not doubted* instead of *did not doubt*; the body is *that of* a man.

D Incorrect use of present verb *have* instead of *had*; *whether* should be *that*.

E **Correct.** In this sentence, *had no doubt* is the proper tense and is correctly followed by *that*; *that of* is used to refer to the body of a man.

The correct answer is E.

70. His studies of ice-polished rocks in his Alpine homeland, far outside the range of present-day glaciers, led Louis Agassiz in 1837 to propose the concept of an age <u>in which great ice sheets had existed in now currently temperate areas</u>.

(A) in which great ice sheets had existed in now currently temperate areas

(B) in which great ice sheets existed in what are now temperate areas

(C) when great ice sheets existed where there were areas now temperate

(D) when great ice sheets had existed in current temperate areas

(E) when great ice sheets existed in areas now that are temperate

Verb form; Rhetorical construction

In which or *when* can be used interchangeably in this sentence. The verb form here should be the simple past *existed* rather than the past perfect *had existed*. *Now currently* is redundant because both adverbs express the same idea.

A *Had existed* should be *existed; now currently* is redundant.

B Correct. The simple past verb tense is correctly used in this sentence; *now* is placed and used correctly.

C *Where there were areas now temperate* is wordy and confusing.

D *Had existed* should be *existed; current* should be *currently; in current temperate areas* is unclear.

E *Now* is an adverb and should be placed just after the verb *are*.

The correct answer is B.

71. Unlike the original National Museum of Science and Technology in Italy, where the models are encased in glass or operated only by staff members, the Virtual Leonardo Project, an online version of the museum, encourages visitors to "touch" each <u>exhibit, which thereby activates</u> the animated functions of the piece.

(A) exhibit, which thereby activates

(B) exhibit, in turn an activation of

(C) exhibit, and it will activate

(D) exhibit and thereby activate

(E) exhibit which, as a result, activates

Grammatical construction; Logical predication

The relative pronoun *which* requires an antecedent, and there is none provided in this sentence. It makes more sense to make the visitors the agents responsible for the action of both the verbs—*touch* and *activate*. Because to "touch" is an infinitive, the second verb form must be, as well, though the *to* may be implied.

A *Which* has no antecedent in the sentence, so it is unclear what activated the display.

B *In turn an activation* ... seems to be the subject of a new clause, but it has no verb, so the sentence is incomplete.

C There is no antecedent for *it* because *touch* is a verb.

D Correct. The agent of the action is clearly indicated by the grammatical structure of the sentence; visitors are encouraged *to "touch"* ... *and thereby (to) activate*.

E *Which* has no antecedent in this sentence.

The correct answer is D.

72. More and more in recent years, cities are stressing the arts as a means <u>to greater economic development and investing</u> millions of dollars in cultural activities, despite strained municipal budgets and fading federal support.

    (A) to greater economic development and investing
    (B) to greater development economically and investing
    (C) of greater economic development and invest
    (D) of greater development economically and invest
    (E) for greater economic development and the investment of

    Diction; Parallelism

    The idiom *as a means to* correctly communicates that *stressing the arts* is a method for achieving *greater economic development*. The idiom *as a means of* would incorrectly suggest that *stressing the arts* is a kind of *greater economic development*. The adjective *economic* is needed to modify the noun *development*, and *investing* must be parallel to *stressing*.

    A **Correct.** The idiom *as a means to* is correct in this sentence; *stressing* and *investing* are parallel.
    B Adverb *economically* is the wrong part of speech and conveys the incorrect meaning.
    C *Of* should be *to* to form the correct idiom; *invest* should be *investing* to parallel *stressing*.
    D *Of* should be *to* to form the correct idiom; adverb *economically* is the wrong part of speech and conveys the incorrect meaning; *invest* should be *investing* to parallel *stressing*.
    E *As a means for* is not idiomatic; *the investment of* is awkward and is not parallel to *stressing*.

    The correct answer is A.

73. Combining enormous physical strength with higher intelligence, the Neanderthals <u>appear as equipped for facing any obstacle the environment could put in their path,</u> but their relatively sudden disappearance during the Paleolithic era indicates that an inability to adapt to some environmental change led to their extinction.

    (A) appear as equipped for facing any obstacle the environment could put in their path,
    (B) appear to have been equipped to face any obstacle the environment could put in their path,
    (C) appear as equipped to face any obstacle the environment could put in their paths,
    (D) appeared as equipped to face any obstacle the environment could put in their paths,
    (E) appeared to have been equipped for facing any obstacle the environment could put in their path,

    Verb form; Diction

    Because Neanderthals "disappeared," the verb describing their apparent abilities cannot be present tense, so *as equipped* must be changed to *to have been equipped*. The expression *equipped to face* is clearer and more direct than *equipped for facing*.

    A *As equipped* indicates that Neanderthals still appear this way; *equipped* should be followed by an infinitive form instead of a prepositional phrase.
    B **Correct.** The verb tense clearly indicates that the current evidence is about Neanderthals in the past.
    C *As equipped* does not indicate that Neanderthals appeared this way in the past; while individual Neanderthals may well have followed different paths, this sentence is about the single evolutionary path taken by Neanderthals as a species.
    D Present-tense *appear* is needed to parallel present-tense *indicates* and to reinforce that this is current evidence about Neanderthals in the past; as in C, *paths* should be singular.
    E *For facing* is an incorrect substitution of a prepositional phrase for an infinitive.

    The correct answer is B.

74. A 1972 agreement between Canada and the United States <u>reduced the amount of phosphates that municipalities had been allowed to dump</u> into the Great Lakes.

   (A) reduced the amount of phosphates that municipalities had been allowed to dump
   (B) reduced the phosphate amount that municipalities had been dumping
   (C) reduces the phosphate amount municipalities have been allowed to dump
   (D) reduced the amount of phosphates that municipalities are allowed to dump
   (E) reduces the amount of phosphates allowed for dumping by municipalities

Verb form; Idiom

An agreement that occurred in 1972 is correctly described with the past tense verb *reduced*. Since the dumping continued after the date of the agreement, the past perfect verb *had been allowed* should instead be the present *are allowed* (if the agreement remained in effect when the sentence was written) or the past *were allowed* (if the agreement was no longer in effect when the sentence was written). Since *were allowed* does not appear in any of the options, we can assume that the correct verb tense is *are allowed*. The phrase *amount of phosphates* is clear and idiomatically correct, whereas *phosphate amount* is not idiomatic.

A *Had been allowed* should be *are allowed*.

B *The phosphate amount* should be *the amount of phosphates*; the omission of some form of *allow* is incorrect since the agreement changed not the amount dumped, but the amount permitted to be dumped.

C Present tense *reduces* should be the past tense *reduced*; *the phosphate amount* should be *the amount of phosphates*; *have been allowed* should be *are allowed*.

D **Correct.** The past tense *reduced* is correctly used in this sentence to describe a past action, and the present tense *are allowed* is used to describe the present situation.

E Present tense *reduces* should be the past tense *reduced*; *allowed for dumping* is an incorrect idiom; *allowed for dumping by municipalities* is awkward.

The correct answer is D.

75. A proposal has been made to trim the horns from rhinoceroses to discourage poachers; the question is <u>whether tourists will continue to visit game parks and see rhinoceroses after their horns are</u> trimmed.

   (A) whether tourists will continue to visit game parks and see rhinoceroses after their horns are
   (B) whether tourists will continue to visit game parks to see one once their horns are
   (C) whether tourists will continue to visit game parks to see rhinoceroses once the animals' horns have been
   (D) if tourists will continue to visit game parks and see rhinoceroses once the animals' horns are
   (E) if tourists will continue to visit game parks to see one after the animals' horns have been

Logical predication; Diction; Verb form

The tourists are visiting for the purpose of seeing the rhinoceroses; purpose is expressed by using *to*, not *and*. Since *their* could refer to either *tourists* or *rhinoceroses*, *animals' horns* is needed to avoid the ludicrous suggestion that the visitors' horns are being trimmed. The verb following *after* should be the present-perfect *have been trimmed* to reflect that the trimming must occur before the tourists arrive.

A *And see* should be *to see*; *their* is ambiguous; *are* should be *have been*.

B *One* is ambiguous; *their* clearly and absurdly refers to *tourists*; *are* should be *have been*.

C **Correct.** In this sentence, *to* correctly precedes *see*; it is clear that the horns belong to the animals; and *have been* is the correct tense following *once*.

D *And see* should be *to see*; *are* should be *have been*.

E *One* is ambiguous.

The correct answer is C.

76. Retailers reported moderate gains in their November sales, as much because <u>of their sales of a year earlier being so bad as that</u> shoppers were getting a head start on buying their holiday gifts.

    (A) of their sales of a year earlier being so bad as that

    (B) of their sales a year earlier having been as bad as because

    (C) of their sales a year earlier being as bad as because

    (D) their sales a year earlier had been so bad as because

    (E) their sales of a year earlier were as bad as that

Rhetorical construction; Parallelism

This sentence gives two equally plausible reasons for the moderate gains retailers reported in November sales. These two reasons are introduced with a formula that requires parallel structure: *As much because x as because y.* The clearest, most efficient way to fill this formula is to follow *because* with clauses with active verbs, thereby eliminating the wordiness that accompanies prepositional phrases (*because of ...*) followed by participial phrases (e.g., *being so bad* or *having been as bad*).

A   The participial phrase *being so bad ...* is wordy and awkward; the elements following *because* are not parallel.

B   Participial phrases make this version of the sentence wordy and awkward.

C   This version makes an incorrect comparison between previous sales and shoppers' strategies in November; the participial phrase is wordy and awkward.

D   Correct. The comparison is clearly expressed with concise, parallel clauses.

E   This makes an incorrect comparison between previous sales and shoppers' strategies in November.

The correct answer is D.

77. The only way for growers to salvage frozen citrus is <u>to process them quickly into juice concentrate before they rot when warmer weather returns.</u>

    (A) to process them quickly into juice concentrate before they rot when warmer weather returns

    (B) if they are quickly processed into juice concentrate before warmer weather returns to rot them

    (C) for them to be processed quickly into juice concentrate before the fruit rots when warmer weather returns

    (D) if the fruit is quickly processed into juice concentrate before they rot when warmer weather returns

    (E) to have it quickly processed into juice concentrate before warmer weather returns and rots the fruit

Parallelism; Agreement

Parallelism requires that the same word forms perform the same functions in the sentence. Here, the linking verb *is* requires two infinitives: *to salvage ... to process* (or *to have ... processed*). A pronoun must match the noun it refers to. *Citrus* is singular and requires the singular pronoun *it*, not the plural pronouns *them* and *they*.

A   *Citrus* does not agree with *them* and *they*.

B   *If they are quickly processed* is not parallel to the infinitive *to salvage*; *they* does not agree with *citrus*.

C   *For them to be processed quickly* is not parallel to the infinitive *to salvage*; *them* does not agree with *citrus*.

D   *If the fruit is quickly processed* is not parallel to the infinitive *to salvage*; *they* does not agree with *fruit*.

E   Correct. This sentence has correct parallel infinitives and uses the words *it* and *fruit* to refer unambiguously to *citrus*. The use of *before* rather than *when* also clearly establishes the cause-and-effect relationship between weather and rotting.

The correct answer is E.

78. Fossils of the arm of a <u>sloth found in Puerto Rico in 1991, and dated at 34 million years old, made it the earliest known mammal of</u> the Greater Antilles Islands.

    (A) sloth found in Puerto Rico in 1991, and dated at 34 million years old, made it the earliest known mammal of
    (B) sloth, that they found in Puerto Rico in 1991, has been dated at 34 million years old, thus making it the earliest mammal known on
    (C) sloth that was found in Puerto Rico in 1991, was dated at 34 million years old, making this the earliest known mammal of
    (D) sloth, found in Puerto Rico in 1991, have been dated at 34 million years old, making the sloth the earliest known mammal on
    (E) sloth which, found in Puerto Rico in 1991, was dated at 34 million years old, made the sloth the earliest known mammal of

Agreement; Logical predication

The subject of the sentence is the plural *fossils*, not *sloth*, and therefore requires a plural verb. *It* therefore does not have a singular antecedent. To clarify the identification of the oldest known mammal, the noun *the sloth* must be explicitly identified.

A   Because *sloth* is the object of a preposition and not the subject of the sentence, there is no reasonable antecedent for the pronoun *it*; in this construction, the subject of *made* is *fossils*, but it makes no sense to say that the *fossils* made it the earliest known mammal.

B   The introduction of the mysterious *they*, a pronoun without a reference, adds confusion to this sentence; the singular verb does not agree with the plural subject.

C   The relative clause *that was* … is wordy and awkward; the singular verb does not agree with the plural subject.

D   **Correct.** The plural verb agrees with its plural subject, and *the sloth* is explicitly identified as *the earliest known mammal*.

E   The singular verb does not agree with the plural subject.

The correct answer is D.

79. Defense attorneys have occasionally argued that their clients' misconduct stemmed from a reaction to something ingested, but <u>in attributing criminal or delinquent behavior to some food allergy,</u> the perpetrators are in effect told that they are not responsible for their actions.

    (A) in attributing criminal or delinquent behavior to some food allergy,
    (B) if criminal or delinquent behavior is attributed to an allergy to some food,
    (C) in attributing behavior that is criminal or delinquent to an allergy to some food,
    (D) if some food allergy is attributed as the cause of criminal or delinquent behavior,
    (E) in attributing a food allergy as the cause of criminal or delinquent behavior,

Logical predication; Idiom

The original sentence contains a misplaced modifier. The modifying phrase (*in attributing …*) incorrectly describes *perpetrators* when it should describe *defense attorneys*. The correct idiom in the active voice is one *attributes x* (an effect) *to y* (a cause). In the passive voice, *x* (the effect) *is attributed to y* (the cause). The best way to correct the sentence is to transform the modifying phrase into a subordinate clause that uses the idiom correctly: *criminal or delinquent behavior* (*x*) *is attributed to* (verb phrase) *an allergy to some food* (*y*).

A   Misplaced modifier.

B   **Correct.** In this sentence, the modification error has been eliminated with the use of the correct idiom, *is attributed to*.

C   Modifier describes *perpetrators*, not *attorneys*; wordy and imprecise.

D   *X is attributed as the cause of y* is not the correct idiom.

E   Modifier incorrectly describes *perpetrators*; idiom is misused.

The correct answer is B.

80. A report by the American Academy for the Advancement of Science has concluded that <u>much of the currently uncontrolled dioxins to which North Americans are exposed comes</u> from the incineration of wastes.

    (A) much of the currently uncontrolled dioxins to which North Americans are exposed comes
    (B) much of the currently uncontrolled dioxins that North Americans are exposed to come
    (C) much of the dioxins that are currently uncontrolled and that North Americans are exposed to comes
    (D) many of the dioxins that are currently uncontrolled and North Americans are exposed to come
    (E) many of the currently uncontrolled dioxins to which North Americans are exposed come

Diction; Agreement

Much is used for an uncountable quantity such as effort or rain; *many* must be used for a countable quantity such as people or *dioxins*. As the subject of the subordinate clause, *many* must then be followed by the plural verb *come* rather than the singular *comes*.

A   *Much* is used instead of *many*.
B   *Much* is used instead of *many*.
C   *Much* is used instead of *many*; *that are* is wordy.
D   *That are* is wordy; to maintain the parallel in this construction, *that* would have to be repeated in the clause *that North Americans are exposed to.*
E   **Correct.** In this concise sentence, *many* is correctly used with *dioxins*, and the subject and verb agree.

The correct answer is E.

81. Recently physicians have determined that stomach ulcers are <u>not caused by stress, alcohol, or rich foods, but</u> a bacterium that dwells in the mucous lining of the stomach.

    (A) not caused by stress, alcohol, or rich foods, but
    (B) not caused by stress, alcohol, or rich foods, but are by
    (C) caused not by stress, alcohol, or rich foods, but by
    (D) caused not by stress, alcohol, and rich foods, but
    (E) caused not by stress, alcohol, and rich foods, but are by

Parallelism; Diction

The formula used in this sentence *not this but that* requires parallel elements following *not* and *but*. This means that *not by stress, alcohol, or rich foods* must be balanced by *but by a bacterium* … There is no need to repeat the verb *are caused*, or even the auxiliary verb *are*, because the verb precedes the *not by … but by …* formula. The substitution of the conjunction *and* for the conjunction *or* changes the meaning of the sentence: *Stress, alcohol and rich foods* identifies the combination of these three factors as a suggested cause of stomach ulcers, whereas *stress, alcohol, or rich foods* offers three individual possibilities. There is no way to tell which one of these is the intended meaning of the sentence.

A   To preserve parallelism, *but* should be followed by *by.*
B   There is no reason to repeat the auxiliary verb *are.*
C   **Correct.** This sentence correctly uses the *not by … but by …* formula.
D   To preserve parallelism, *but* should be followed by *by.*
E   To preserve parallelism, *but* should be followed by *by.*

The correct answer is C.

82. According to a recent poll, owning and living in a freestanding house on its own land is still a goal of a majority of young adults, <u>like that of earlier generations</u>.

    (A) like that of earlier generations
    (B) as that for earlier generations
    (C) just as earlier generations did
    (D) as have earlier generations
    (E) as it was of earlier generations

Parallelism

This sentence compares a single goal shared by generations. The second part of the sentence must have the same structure as the first part: a clause with a subject and a verb. The phrase *owning … land* is the subject of the first clause; in the correct sentence, the pronoun *it* refers back to this phrase and is the subject of the second clause. The first verb *is* also parallels the second verb *was*. The prepositional phrases *of a majority of young adults* and *of earlier generations* are parallel and correct.

A   Phrase, without subject and verb, is not parallel to the main clause.

B   Phrase, without subject and verb, is not parallel to the main clause.

C   Subject and verb of the second clause—*earlier generations did*—are not parallel to those of the main clause.

D   The verb *have* is not parallel to *is* in the main clause and also does not make sense without a past participle.

E   **Correct.** In this sentence *as* shows comparison and introduces a subordinate clause in which all grammatical elements correspond to those in the main clause.

The correct answer is E.

83. In 2000, a mere two dozen products accounted for half the increase in spending on prescription drugs, <u>a phenomenon that is explained not just because of more expensive drugs but by the fact that doctors are writing</u> many more prescriptions for higher-cost drugs.

    (A) a phenomenon that is explained not just because of more expensive drugs but by the fact that doctors are writing
    (B) a phenomenon that is explained not just by the fact that drugs are becoming more expensive but also by the fact that doctors are writing
    (C) a phenomenon occurring not just because of drugs that are becoming more expensive but because of doctors having also written
    (D) which occurred not just because drugs are becoming more expensive but doctors are also writing
    (E) which occurred not just because of more expensive drugs but because doctors have also written

Rhetorical construction; Idiom

This sentence explains that a few high-cost products account for increased spending for two reasons—rising drug prices and more prescriptions for high-priced drugs. To present these two causes, the sentence employs a formula that requires parallel elements: *not just because of x, but because of y*, with *x* and *y* assuming the same grammatical form. One way to create this parallelism is to phrase both contributing causes as noun clauses beginning with *the fact that*. To streamline the sentence, unnecessary words and redundancies should be eliminated. One such redundancy is the repetition of meaning in *explained* and *because of*.

A   It is redundant and confusing to say that the phenomenon in question is *explained … because of*; the sentence structure is not parallel.

B   **Correct.** This sentence correctly uses parallel structure.

C   The phrasing *drugs that are becoming* and *doctors having also written* are awkward and confusing; the placement of *also* is incorrect.

D   The structure of this sentence is not parallel.

E   The placement of *also* is incorrect; the structure of the sentence is not parallel.

The correct answer is B.

84. Often visible as smog, <u>ozone is formed in the atmosphere from</u> hydrocarbons and nitrogen oxides, two major pollutants emitted by automobiles, react with sunlight.

(A)   ozone is formed in the atmosphere from

(B)   ozone is formed in the atmosphere when

(C)   ozone is formed in the atmosphere, and when

(D)   ozone, formed in the atmosphere when

(E)   ozone, formed in the atmosphere from

Grammatical construction; Idiom

The preposition *from* is incorrect because *ozone is formed from x and y react* is not a grammatical structure. Replacing *from* with the subordinating conjunction *when* makes the sentence complete: *Ozone is formed when x and y react.* A main clause is followed by a subordinate clause.

A   The preposition *from* introduces an incoherent and ungrammatical construction.

B   **Correct.** The conjunction *when* introduces a subordinate clause, which completes the sentence correctly and coherently.

C   *And when* distorts the meaning, suggesting that ozone is formed in two ways.

D   Omitting the main verb, *is*, results in a sentence fragment.

E   These changes result in a sentence fragment.

The correct answer is B.

85. Salt deposits and moisture threaten to destroy the Mohenjo-Daro excavation in Pakistan, the site of an ancient civilization <u>that flourished at the same time as the civilizations</u> in the Nile Delta and the river valleys of the Tigris and Euphrates.

(A)   that flurished at the same time as the civilizations

(B)   that had flourished at the same time as had the civilizations

(C)   that flourished at the same time those had

(D)   flourishing at the same time as those did

(E)   flourishing at the same time as those were

Verb form; Agreement

The underlined portion of the sentence is a relative clause that describes *an ancient civilization*; the clause correctly uses the simple past tense, *flourished*, to describe civilizations that existed simultaneously.

A   **Correct.** In this sentence, the relative clause correctly uses the simple past tense.

B   Use of the past perfect, *had flourished*, is incorrect because it indicates a time prior to another action; the second *had* is redundant and unnecessary.

C   Plural pronoun *those* cannot refer to the singular *civilization* and thus lacks a referent; *as* is missing but necessary; *had* is the wrong verb tense.

D   Plural pronoun *those* cannot refer to the singular *civilization* and thus lacks a referent; *did* is awkward and unnecessary.

E   Plural pronoun *those* cannot refer to the singular *civilization* and thus lacks a referent; *were* is awkward and unnecessary.

The correct answer is A.

86. The results of the company's cost-cutting measures are evident in its profits, <u>which increased 5 percent during the first 3 months of this year after it fell</u> over the last two years.

    (A) which increased 5 percent during the first 3 months of this year after it fell
    (B) which had increased 5 percent during the first 3 months of this year after it had fallen
    (C) which have increased 5 percent during the first 3 months of this year after falling
    (D) with a 5 percent increase during the first 3 months of this year after falling
    (E) with a 5 percent increase during the first 3 months of this year after having fallen

Verb form; Agreement; Idiom

This sentence describes two sequentially ordered indicators by which the results of a company's cost-cutting measures can be seen. The first indicator to be identified, a 5 percent increase in profits, occurred <u>after</u> the indicator mentioned next. The sentence therefore needs to clarify the sequence by presenting the first-identified indicator in a clause with a verb tense that indicates a later time period than the verb tense in the clause presenting the second-identified indicator. The subject of the relative clause, *which*, refers to the plural noun *profits*, so subsequent pronouns referring to these profits must also be plural.

A   The verb tenses do not distinguish between the times at which these indicators occurred; the singular *it* does not agree with the plural *profits*.

B   The verb tenses do not distinguish between the times when the indicators occurred; the singular *it* does not agree with the plural *profits*.

C   **Correct.** The verb tenses clearly indicate the sequence of events.

D   It is not clear what connection is being described by *with*; the prepositional phrase makes the sentence wordy and unclear.

E   It is not clear what connection is being described by *with*; the prepositional phrase makes the sentence wordy and unclear.

The correct answer is C.

87. In an effort to reduce their inventories, Italian vintners have cut prices; their wines <u>have been priced to sell, and they are.</u>

    (A) have been priced to sell, and they are
    (B) are priced to sell, and they have
    (C) are priced to sell, and they do
    (D) are being priced to sell, and have
    (E) had been priced to sell, and they have

Verb form

In the underlined segment, the second verb does not need to repeat the word *sell* because it is understood from the previous verb phrase *priced to sell*. However, the second verb must be correctly conjugated with the understood *sell*. *They are sell* is not a correct verb form; *they do sell* is correct.

A   *They are* would require *selling* to complete it, not *sell*.

B   *They have* would require *sold* to complete it, not *sell*.

C   **Correct.** This sentence properly uses *they do* in place of *they do sell*, a grammatically correct verb.

D   *Have* would require *sold* to complete it, not *sell*; omitting the subject *they* requires that the comma be omitted as well.

E   *They have* would require *sold* to complete it, not *sell*; the past-perfect *had been priced* suggests illogically that the wines were already *priced to sell* before the vintners cut prices; moreover, since the past-perfect tense indicates that one event in the past occurred prior to another event in the past, the past-tense *did* would be required rather than the present-tense *have*.

The correct answer is C.

88. <u>Thelonious Monk, who was a jazz pianist and composer, produced a body of work both rooted</u> in the stride-piano tradition of Willie (The Lion) Smith and Duke Ellington, yet in many ways he stood apart from the mainstream jazz repertory.

(A) Thelonious Monk, who was a jazz pianist and composer, produced a body of work both rooted

(B) Thelonious Monk, the jazz pianist and composer, produced a body of work that was rooted both

(C) Jazz pianist and composer Thelonious Monk, who produced a body of work rooted

(D) Jazz pianist and composer Thelonious Monk produced a body of work that was rooted

(E) Jazz pianist and composer Thelonious Monk produced a body of work rooted both

Grammatical construction; Rhetorical construction

The subject of the sentence is *Thelonious Monk*, and the sentence tells about two things that he did: *produced* and *stood apart*. The work he produced was rooted in the mainstream (*stride piano*) jazz tradition, yet at the same time, he deviated from this tradition. The use of a relative clause (*who was a jazz pianist …*) or an appositive (*the jazz pianist …*) introduces unnecessary wordiness and grammatical complexity. Since only one point is being made about Monk's body of work, the appearance of the word *both* in the clause presenting the claim about Monk's work is deceptive as well as grammatically incorrect.

A The relative clause introduces wordiness and confusion.

B The appositive introduces wordiness and unnecessary grammatical complexity.

C The sentence is a fragment because the main subject, *Thelonious Monk*, has no verb.

D Correct. The sentence concisely identifies Thelonious Monk and expresses the single point about his work without unnecessary or misleading words.

E The appearance of *both* is misleading, since only one point is being made about where Monk's musical roots are located.

The correct answer is D.

89. Dirt roads may evoke the bucolic simplicity of another century, but financially strained townships point out that dirt roads cost twice as much as maintaining paved roads.

(A) dirt roads cost twice as much as maintaining paved roads

(B) dirt roads cost twice as much to maintain as paved roads do

(C) maintaining dirt roads costs twice as much as paved roads do

(D) maintaining dirt roads costs twice as much as it does for paved roads

(E) to maintain dirt roads costs twice as much as for paved roads

Logical predication; Parallelism

This sentence intends to compare the costs necessary *to maintain* two kinds of roads, but it compares *dirt roads* generally with *maintaining paved roads*. For the correct focus, the comparison must be formulated *x costs twice as much to maintain as y* rather than *x costs twice as much as maintaining y*. X (*dirt roads*) and *y* (*paved roads*) must appear in grammatically parallel constructions.

A *Dirt roads* are compared to *maintaining paved roads*.

B Correct. The costs *to maintain* the roads are emphasized in this sentence construction; *dirt roads cost* and *paved roads do* (*cost* understood) are parallel.

C *Maintaining dirt roads* is compared to *paved roads* in general.

D *It* has no logical referent; the elements being compared are not parallel.

E *To maintain dirt roads* is not parallel to *for paved roads*.

The correct answer is B.

90. Although early soap operas <u>were first aired on evening radio in the 1920s, they had moved to the daytime hours of the 1930s</u> when the evening schedule became crowded with comedians and variety shows.

    (A) were first aired on evening radio in the 1920s, they had moved to the daytime hours of the 1930s
    (B) were first aired on evening radio in the 1920s, they were moved to the daytime hours in the 1930s
    (C) were aired first on evening radio in the 1920s, moving to the daytime hours in the 1930s
    (D) were aired first in the evening on 1920s radio, they moved to the daytime hours of the 1930s
    (E) aired on evening radio first in the 1920s, they were moved to the 1930s in the daytime hours

Verb form; Parallelism

The two clauses about soap operas should be parallel. The first verb *were … aired* should be balanced by another passive-voice verb in the simple past tense, *were moved*. The past perfect *had moved* indicates action completed before the action in the simple past *were aired*, suggesting illogically that the 1930s were finished sometime during the 1920s. The prepositional phrase *in the 1920s* should be balanced by the parallel phrase *in the 1930s*.

A   *Had moved* is neither parallel to *were aired* nor correct in tense; *in* is preferable to *of* for creating parallelism in the prepositional phrases.
B   **Correct.** In this sentence, the two verbs are parallel, as are the two prepositional phrases.
C   Use of the participle *moving*, rather than the verb *moved*, results in a sentence fragment.
D   *Moved* is not parallel to *were aired*; the prepositional phrases are not parallel.
E   *Aired* is not parallel to *were moved*; the prepositional phrases are not parallel.

The correct answer is B.

91. Nobody knows exactly how many languages there are in the world, partly because of the difficulty of distinguishing between a language <u>and the sublanguages or dialects within it, but those who have tried to count typically have found</u> about five thousand.

    (A) and the sublanguages or dialects within it, but those who have tried to count typically have found
    (B) and the sublanguages or dialects within them, with those who have tried counting typically finding
    (C) and the sublanguages or dialects within it, but those who have tried counting it typically find
    (D) or the sublanguages or dialects within them, but those who tried to count them typically found
    (E) or the sublanguages or dialects within them, with those who have tried to count typically finding

Agreement; Idiom

This sentence first introduces a condition that makes it difficult to count languages and then, with the conjunction *but*, introduces the topic of those who defy these difficulties and try to count the world's languages anyway. Connecting these two parts of the sentence with *but* indicates that the second clause of the sentence is counter to expectation. The challenges of the task are explained using the example of a single language and its many sublanguages or dialects. When this example is referred to with a pronoun, the pronoun should be singular; when the languages being counted are referred to with a pronoun, this pronoun must be plural.

A   **Correct.** The pronoun *it* agrees in number to its singular antecedent, and *but* indicates that the idea expressed in the final clause defies expectations.
B   The plural pronoun *them* incorrectly refers to the singular antecedent *language*; connecting the two clauses with the preposition *with* loses the sense that counting languages despite the difficulties defies expectations.
C   The second appearance of *it*, referring to world languages, is incorrect because it does not agree in number with *languages*.

D   The conjunction *or* is incorrect—the idiomatic expression is *distinguishing between x and y*; the plural pronoun *them* does not agree with the singular antecedent *language*.

E   The plural pronoun *them* incorrectly refers to the singular antecedent, *language; with* is an imprecise connector for the two clauses, losing the *counter-to-expectation* relationship between them.

The correct answer is A.

92. The energy source on *Voyager 2* is not a nuclear reactor, in which atoms are actively broken <u>apart; rather</u> a kind of nuclear battery that uses natural radioactive decay to produce power.

(A) apart; rather
(B) apart, but rather
(C) apart, but rather that of
(D) apart, but that of
(E) apart; it is that of

Grammatical construction

This sentence focuses on a contrast by using the construction *not x, but rather y; x* and *y* are parallel. In this sentence *not x* (*a nuclear reactor*), should be followed by *but rather y* (*a kind of nuclear battery*). A comma, not a semicolon, should separate the two parallel parts of the contrast; use of a semicolon would require a subject and verb in the construction.

A   Subject and verb are needed after the semicolon; *not x* should be balanced by *but rather y*.

B   **Correct.** In this sentence, the contrast is clearly drawn in the correct construction *not a nuclear reactor ... , but rather a kind of nuclear battery.*

C   *That of* has no referent and results in an illogical, ungrammatical construction.

D   *Rather* should be included to emphasize contrast; *that of* has no referent.

E   No word is used to indicate contrast; *that of* has no referent.

The correct answer is B.

93. <u>Heating-oil prices are expected to be higher this year than last because refiners are paying about $5 a barrel more for crude oil than they were</u> last year.

(A) Heating-oil prices are expected to be higher this year than last because refiners are paying about $5 a barrel more for crude oil than they were

(B) Heating-oil prices are expected to rise higher this year over last because refiners pay about $5 a barrel for crude oil more than they did

(C) Expectations are for heating-oil prices to be higher this year than last year's because refiners are paying about $5 a barrel for crude oil more than they did

(D) It is the expectation that heating-oil prices will be higher for this year over last because refiners are paying about $5 a barrel more for crude oil now than what they were

(E) It is expected that heating-oil prices will rise higher this year than last year's because refiners pay about $5 a barrel for crude oil more than they did

Rhetorical construction; Idiom

The sentence connects a comparison between this year's and last year's heating-oil prices with a comparison between this year's and last year's crude-oil prices. The most efficient, parallel expression of those comparisons is to use two comparative expressions, *higher than* and *more than*.

A   **Correct.** This sentence expresses the comparison in succinct, parallel phrases.

B   The comparative form, *higher*, anticipates the comparative term *than*, not *over*; in the second clause, the comparative terms *more than* should immediately follow *$5 a barrel*.

C   *Expectations are for ...* is an unnecessarily wordy and indirect expression; the possessive *year's* is not parallel with the adverbial phrase *this year*.

D   *It is the expectation that ...* is wordy and awkward; *for* and *what* are unnecessary.

E   *It is expected that ...* is wordy and awkward; the possessive *last year's* does not parallel the adverbial phrase *this year*.

The correct answer is A.

94. The recent surge in the number of airplane flights has clogged the nation's air-traffic control system, <u>to lead to 55 percent more delays at airports, and prompts</u> fears among some officials that safety is being compromised.

   (A) to lead to 55 percent more delays at airports, and prompts
   (B) leading to 55 percent more delay at airports and prompting
   (C) to lead to a 55 percent increase in delay at airports and prompt
   (D) to lead to an increase of 55 percent in delays at airports, and prompted
   (E) leading to a 55 percent increase in delays at airports and prompting

Parallelism; Diction

The intent of the sentence is to show two effects of the surge in flights. These effects should be stated in parallel ways, instead of the construction *to lead ...* and *prompts ...* used in the original sentence. Using participial phrases introduced by *leading* and *prompting* solves this problem. The phrase *55 percent more delays* is not as clear as the phrase *a 55 percent increase in delays*.

A *To lead* and *prompts* are not parallel; *55 percent more delays* is not clear.
B *55 percent more delay* is unclear.
C *To lead* and *prompt* are not parallel; the meaning of *55 percent increase in delay* is not clear.
D Participial phrase introduced by *leading* is preferable to the unclear infinitive phrase *to lead to*; *an increase of 55 percent in delays* is awkward and wordy.
E **Correct.** *Leading* and *prompting* are parallel in this sentence; the phrase *a 55 percent increase in delays* is clear and concise.

The correct answer is E.

95. The peaks of a mountain range, acting like rocks in a streambed, produce ripples in the air flowing over them; the resulting flow pattern, with <u>crests and troughs that remain stationary although the air that forms them is moving rapidly, are</u> known as "standing waves."

   (A) crests and troughs that remain stationary although the air that forms them is moving rapidly, are
   (B) crests and troughs that remain stationary although they are formed by rapidly moving air, are
   (C) crests and troughs that remain stationary although the air that forms them is moving rapidly, is
   (D) stationary crests and troughs although the air that forms them is moving rapidly, are
   (E) stationary crests and troughs although they are formed by rapidly moving air, is

Agreement

The subject of the second independent clause is *the resulting flow pattern*; this singular subject requires the singular verb *is known*, not the plural verb *are known*. While the long descriptive construction between the subject and verb may make it difficult to see this relationship, notice that the modifying phrase is set off with commas. The use of the active voice in the verbs of the subordinate clauses provides greater clarity of meaning.

A Plural verb does not agree with the singular subject.
B Plural verb does not agree with the singular subject; the subordinate clause in the passive voice following *although* is awkward and unclear.
C **Correct.** In this sentence, the singular verb *is known* agrees with the subject *the resulting flow pattern*.
D Plural verb does not agree with the singular subject.
E The subordinate clause in the passive voice following *although* is awkward and unclear.

The correct answer is C.

96. One of the primary distinctions <u>between our intelligence with that of other primates may lay not so much in any specific skill but</u> in our ability to extend knowledge gained in one context to new and different ones.

    (A) between our intelligence with that of other primates may lay not so much in any specific skill but

    (B) between our intelligence with that of other primates may lie not so much in any specific skill but instead

    (C) between our intelligence and that of other primates may lie not so much in any specific skill as

    (D) our intelligence has from that of other primates may lie not in any specific skill as

    (E) of our intelligence to that of other primates may lay not in any specific skill but

Diction; Idiom

When using the term *distinction* to indicate difference, the correct preposition to use is *between*. In this sentence, the distinction *may lie* in a certain ability that humans do not share with other primates. The verb *may lay* is transitive, requiring a direct object.

A *With* is the incorrect comparative term to follow *distinctions between*; *lay* is the incorrect verb.

B *With* is the incorrect comparative term to follow *distinctions between*.

C **Correct.** The preposition *between* and the intransitive verb *may lie* are correct in this sentence.

D *From* is the incorrect preposition to use with *distinction*; without *so much*, which is used in C, *as* seems to introduce a comparison for *specific skill* rather than a distinction.

E *Of* is the incorrect preposition to use with *distinction*, and *to* is an incorrect comparative term; *lay* is the incorrect verb.

The correct answer is C.

97. Unlike <u>Schoenberg's 12-tone system that dominated</u> the music of the postwar period, Bartók founded no school and left behind only a handful of disciples.

    (A) Schoenberg's 12-tone system that dominated

    (B) Schoenberg and his 12-tone system which dominated

    (C) Schoenberg, whose 12-tone system dominated

    (D) the 12-tone system of Schoenberg that has dominated

    (E) Schoenberg and the 12-tone system, dominating

Logical predication

The original sentence makes the logical error of comparing *Bartók* to the *twelve-tone system*. The lack of clarity results in the implication that the *system* might have founded a school or left behind disciples. The sentence must clearly indicate that it is the individuals, *Bartók* and *Schoenberg*, who are being compared. It must also make it plain that it was the *system* that dominated the music of the postwar period.

A Illogically compares *Bartók* to the *12-tone system*, rather than to *Schoenberg*.

B Incorrect use of *and* illogically compares *Bartók* to the *system* as well as *Schoenberg*.

C **Correct.** This sentence makes the logical comparison between the individuals, and the relative clause clarifies that it is the *system* that dominated the music of the postwar period.

D Illogically compares *Bartók* to the *system*, rather than to *Schoenberg*; perfect verb form *has dominated* distorts the meaning by indicating that the system continues to dominate music today.

E Incorrect use of *and* illogically compares *Bartók* to the *system* as well as *Schoenberg*; introduces confusion about what *dominating* modifies.

The correct answer is C.

98. <u>Even though Clovis points, spear points with longitudinal grooves chipped onto their faces, have been found all over North America, they are named for the New Mexico site where they were first discovered in 1932.</u>

   (A) Even though Clovis points, spear points with longitudinal grooves chipped onto their faces, have been found all over North America, they are named for the New Mexico site where they were first discovered in 1932.

   (B) Although named for the New Mexico site where first discovered in 1932, Clovis points are spear points of longitudinal grooves chipped onto their faces and have been found all over North America.

   (C) Named for the New Mexico site where they have been first discovered in 1932, Clovis points, spear points of longitudinal grooves chipped onto the faces, have been found all over North America.

   (D) Spear points with longitudinal grooves that are chipped onto the faces, Clovis points, even though named for the New Mexico site where first discovered in 1932, but were found all over North America.

   (E) While Clovis points are spear points whose faces have longitudinal grooves chipped into them, they have been found all over North America, and named for the New Mexico site where they have been first discovered in 1932.

Verb form; Rhetorical construction; Logical predication

Even though, *although*, and *while* introduce clauses that <u>appear</u> to be logically incompatible but in fact are not. In this sentence, the apparent incompatibility that must be clearly expressed is that although the spear points are named for a particular place in New Mexico, they are in fact found throughout North America. Because their discovery took place in 1932 and is not ongoing, the correct verb tense is simple past, not present perfect.

A **Correct.** The *even though* clause expresses clearly that the seeming incompatibility is between where the spear points have been found (*all over North America*) and the naming of the spear points for a single site in New Mexico.

B The sentence structure indicates that the expected incompatibility is between the geographically based name of the points and their physical properties, which makes no sense; *where discovered* is missing a subject—the correct form is *where they were first discovered*.

C *Have been first discovered* is the wrong tense, since the discovery is a discrete event completed in the past.

D The sequence of information in this sentence is confusing; *even though* and *but* both introduce information that is contrary to expectation, so to use them both to describe a single apparent contradiction is redundant and nonsensical.

E *While* introduces a description of Clovis points and suggests that this appears incompatible with their appearance all over North America, which makes no sense; *have been first discovered* is the wrong tense.

The correct answer is A.

99. Ranked as one of the most important of Europe's young playwrights, Franz Xaver Kroetz has written 40 plays; his works—translated into more than 30 languages—are produced more often <u>than any</u> contemporary German dramatist.

   (A) than any
   (B) than any other
   (C) than are any
   (D) than those of any other
   (E) as are those of any

Logical predication

The original sentence says Kroetz's *works ... are produced more often than any ... dramatist*. A *dramatist* cannot be *produced* and cannot be compared to *works*. Kroetz's *works* must be compared to *works* of other dramatists: *Kroetz's works ... are produced more often than those* (works) *of any other dramatist*.

A   Illogical comparison between *works* and *dramatist*.

B   Illogical comparison between *works* and *any other dramatist*.

C   Illogical comparison between *works* and *dramatist*.

D   Correct. In this sentence, Kroetz's *works* are compared to *those* (the pronoun referring to *works*), of other dramatists.

E   *More often* must be completed by *than*, not as; the phrase *those of any* illogically includes Kroetz's works.

The correct answer is D.

100. The stars, some of them at tremendous speeds, are in motion just as the planets are, yet being so far away from Earth that their apparent positions in the sky do not change enough for their movement to be observed during a single human lifetime.

(A)   The stars, some of them at tremendous speeds, are in motion just as the planets are, yet being

(B)   Like the planets, the stars are in motion, some of them at tremendous speeds, but they are

(C)   Although like the planets the stars are in motion, some of them at tremendous speeds, yet

(D)   As the planets, the stars are in motion, some of them at tremendous speeds, but they are

(E)   The stars are in motion like the planets, some of which at tremendous speeds are in motion but

Grammatical construction; Rhetorical construction

The first part of the original sentence intends to compare stars and planets; the comparison would be more effective at the beginning of the sentence: *Like the planets, the stars*. This alternative construction would lead the reader to expect the verb *are* immediately following the subject, and then the completion of the clause, *in motion*. The modifying phrase, *some of them at tremendous speeds*, is best placed after *motion*. This whole construction, *Like the planets, the stars are in motion, some of them at tremendous speeds*, is a main clause and must be followed by a comma before a coordinating conjunction (such as *yet* or *but*) introduces a second main clause. The second clause must have a subject and a verb; *being* is neither and must be replaced with *they are*.

A   Placements of the modifying phrase and the comparison are awkward and ineffective; *being* provides neither a subject nor a verb for the second main clause.

B   Correct. The comparison is clear and effective in this sentence; the second clause includes a subject and a verb.

C   Both *although* and *yet* indicate contrast, so only one of them may be used; wordy, awkward phrasing leads to an ungrammatical construction that lacks a subject and verb for the second clause.

D   The preposition *like* must be used for a comparison of two nouns; the subordinating conjunction *as* would need to introduce a subordinate clause.

E   Placement of *like the planets* is awkward; *some of which* is awkward and ambiguous; *are in motion* is said twice; subject and verb of the second clause are omitted.

The correct answer is B.

101. Heavy commitment by an executive to a course of action, especially if it has worked well in the past, makes it likely to miss signs of incipient trouble or misinterpret them when they do appear.

    (A) Heavy commitment by an executive to a course of action, especially if it has worked well in the past, makes it likely to miss signs of incipient trouble or misinterpret them when they do appear.

    (B) An executive who is heavily committed to a course of action, especially one that worked well in the past, makes missing signs of incipient trouble or misinterpreting ones likely when they do appear.

    (C) An executive who is heavily committed to a course of action is likely to miss or misinterpret signs of incipient trouble when they do appear, especially if it has worked well in the past.

    (D) Executives' being heavily committed to a course of action, especially if it has worked well in the past, makes them likely to miss signs of incipient trouble or misinterpreting them when they do appear.

    (E) Being heavily committed to a course of action, especially one that has worked well in the past, is likely to make an executive miss signs of incipient trouble or misinterpret them when they do appear.

Rhetorical construction; Logical predication

This sentence explains that an executive who is blindly committed to a proven course of action is likely to overlook or misinterpret indicators that the plan may no longer be working. The sentence needs to make clear *who* may misinterpret these indicators.

A   The passive construction causes the sentence to be wordy and confusing; the reference for *it* is ambiguous, leaving the reader with questions about who or what is likely to miss these signs.

B   The sentence structure indicates that the *executive*, not his or her strategy, causes signs to be overlooked; the modifier *when they do appear* is misplaced.

C   The reference for the pronoun *it* is unclear because many nouns have intervened between the appearance of the logical referent (*course of action*) and *it*.

D   *Misinterpreting* should be an infinitive verb form to parallel *miss*; the phrasing throughout the sentence is wordy and awkward.

E   **Correct.** The grammatical structure of this sentence and the appropriate placement of modifiers expresses the meaning clearly and concisely.

The correct answer is E.

102. As rainfall began to decrease in the Southwest about the middle of the twelfth century, most of the Monument Valley Anasazi abandoned their homes to join other clans whose access to water was less limited.

    (A) whose access to water was less limited
    (B) where there was access to water that was less limited
    (C) where they had less limited water access
    (D) with less limitations on water access
    (E) having less limitations to water access

Diction; Logical predication

In the original sentence, the underlined clause provides a clear, correct, and succinct comparison, explaining the reason for the migration. The possessive pronoun *whose* correctly refers to its immediate antecedent, *clans*, and modifies *access*. For those other clans, access to water was *less limited* than it was for the Anasazi.

A   **Correct.** This sentence uses a clear, concise clause that correctly connects *access to water* with *clans* by using the possessive pronoun *whose*.

B   *Where there was … that was* is awkward, wordy, and redundant.

C   *They* is ambiguous and might refer to either the *Anasazi* or *other clans*; *less limited water access* is awkward.

D   *Limitations* is a countable quantity, so it must be modified by *fewer*, not *less*.

E   *Limitations* is a countable quantity, so it must be modified by *fewer*, not *less*.

The correct answer is A.

103. Yellow jackets number among the 900 or so species of the world's social wasps, <u>wasps living in a highly cooperative and organized society where they consist almost entirely of</u> females—the queen and her sterile female workers.

 (A) wasps living in a highly cooperative and organized society where they consist almost entirely of
 (B) wasps that live in a highly cooperative and organized society consisting almost entirely of
 (C) which means they live in a highly cooperative and organized society, almost all
 (D) which means that their society is highly cooperative, organized, and it is almost entirely
 (E) living in a society that is highly cooperative, organized, and it consists of almost all

Idiom; Logical predication; Rhetorical construction

This sentence identifies yellow jackets as one of 900 types of social wasps and provides an explanation of the term *social wasps*. In this explanation, the society or population—not the individual wasps themselves—consists almost entirely of females. The three descriptors of social wasps (*cooperative*, *organized*, and *consisting almost entirely of females*) are most effectively expressed in parallel structures.

 A *They*, referring to wasps, is an incorrect subject for *consist*.
 B **Correct.** The three descriptors of the wasp society are in parallel form, and *consisting* properly modifies *society*.
 C The sentence structure makes it unclear what *almost all females* describes.
 D *And it is* … violates the parallelism of the three descriptors of social wasps.
 E *And it consists* … violates the parallelism of the three descriptors.

The correct answer is B.

104. El Niño, the periodic abnormal warming of the sea surface off Peru, <u>a phenomenon in which changes in the ocean and atmosphere combine allowing the warm water that has accumulated</u> in the western Pacific to flow back to the east.

 (A) a phenomenon in which changes in the ocean and atmosphere combine allowing the warm water that has accumulated
 (B) a phenomenon where changes in the ocean and atmosphere are combining to allow the warm water that is accumulating
 (C) a phenomenon in which ocean and atmosphere changes combine and which allows the warm water that is accumulated
 (D) is a phenomenon in which changes in the ocean and atmosphere combine to allow the warm water that has accumulated
 (E) is a phenomenon where ocean and atmosphere changes are combining and allow the warm water accumulating

Grammatical construction; Logical predication

This accumulation of phrases and clauses results in a sentence fragment; there is no main verb. This problem is easily solved by inserting the verb to be: *El Niño … is a phenomenon….* The clause defining *phenomenon* is clear (*in which changes in the ocean and atmosphere combine*), but the subsequent phrase, *allowing …* is not. If the participial phrase were to modify the previous clause, a comma would have to be inserted between *combine* and *allowing*. A better choice would be to follow *combine* with *to allow*, showing purpose. In this sense, the environmental changes *combine* (intransitive) in order to allow the water to flow back east.

 A Lacking a main verb, this construction is a sentence fragment; *allowing* should be replaced by *to allow*.
 B This construction is a sentence fragment; present progressive verb form (*are combining, is accumulating*) indicates action in progress, which does not accurately describe a periodically occurring phenomenon.
 C This construction is a sentence fragment; making a separate clause *and which allows …* prevents the relationships from being easily understood.
 D **Correct.** The addition of *is* completes the sentence; *combine to allow* shows the purpose of the changes.
 E *Where* cannot correctly refer to *phenomenon*; *are combining* is the wrong verb form; the relationships among the parts of the sentence are unclear.

The correct answer is D.

105. <u>Beatrix Potter, in her book illustrations, carefully coordinating them with her narratives,</u> capitalized on her keen observation and love of the natural world.

(A) Beatrix Potter, in her book illustrations, carefully coordinating them with her narratives,
(B) In her book illustrations, carefully coordinating them with her narratives, Beatrix Potter
(C) In her book illustrations, which she carefully coordinated with her narratives, Beatrix Potter
(D) Carefully coordinated with her narratives, Beatrix Potter, in her book illustrations
(E) Beatrix Potter, in her book illustrations, carefully coordinated them with her narratives and

Logical predication; Rhetorical construction

This sentence awkwardly presents two phrases intended to modify *Beatrix Potter* and loses the clarity and logic of the meaning. In the original sentence, these modifiers sound choppy and create too much separation between the subject, *Beatrix Potter*, and the verb *capitalized*. Beginning the sentence with *In her book illustrations* and following that phrase with the relative clause *which she carefully coordinated with her narratives* allows the subject, *Beatrix Potter*, to be united with the verb, *capitalized*, for a stronger main clause.

A   The participial phrase does not clearly modify the noun in the preceding phrase; use of the present progressive form of the verb confuses the sequence of time with respect to the past tense of the main verb *capitalized*.
B   Phrase *carefully coordinating* ... illogically modifies the noun that immediately precedes it: *book illustrations*; Potter, not the illustrations, did the coordinating.
C   **Correct.** The correct placement of the modifying elements makes this sentence easier to understand; the use of *which* clearly links the two elements.
D   *Carefully coordinated* ... absurdly modifies *Beatrix Potter* rather than *her illustrations*.
E   The participial phrase does not clearly modify *book illustrations*; the relationships among the parts of the sentence are unclear.

The correct answer is C.

106. <u>Marconi's conception of the radio was as a substitute for the telephone, a tool for private conversation; instead, it is</u> precisely the opposite, a tool for communicating with a large, public audience.

(A) Marconi's conception of the radio was as a substitute for the telephone, a tool for private conversation; instead, it is
(B) Marconi conceived of the radio as a substitute for the telephone, a tool for private conversation, but which is
(C) Marconi conceived of the radio as a tool for private conversation that could substitute for the telephone; instead, it has become
(D) Marconi conceived of the radio to be a tool for private conversation, a substitute for the telephone, which has become
(E) Marconi conceived of the radio to be a substitute for the telephone, a tool for private conversation, other than what it is,

Rhetorical construction; Logical predication

The main point of this sentence is to explain that while Marconi felt the radio would substitute for the phone as an instrument of private communication, in fact it has become an instrument of mass communication. It is less wordy to use *Marconi* as the subject of the active verb *conceived* than to use the subject *conception* with the static verb *was*. The pronoun *it* positioned as the subject of the final verb *has become* refers back to *radio*. Versions of the sentence that use the relative pronoun *which* indicate that the telephone has become a mass medium.

A   The nominalized subject, *conception*, leads to a wordy and awkward sentence.
B   The reference for the relative pronoun *which* is ambiguous; the sentence as a whole is awkward.
C   **Correct.** An active verb makes the first clause more concise; *it* in the second clause clearly refers to *the radio*.
D   *Conceived of* ... should be followed by *as* rather than *to be*.

E   *Conceived of* ... should be followed by *as* rather than *to be*; *other than what it is* is awkward, wordy, and redundant, overlapping the meaning of *precisely the opposite.* ...

The correct answer is C.

107. Originally developed for detecting air pollutants, a technique called proton-induced X-ray emission, which can quickly analyze the chemical elements in almost any substance without destroying it, is finding uses in medicine, archaeology, and criminology.

(A) Originally developed for detecting air pollutants, a technique called proton-induced X-ray emission, which can quickly analyze the chemical elements in almost any substance without destroying it,

(B) Originally developed for detecting air pollutants, having the ability to analyze the chemical elements in almost any substance without destroying it, a technique called proton-induced X-ray emission

(C) A technique originally developed for detecting air pollutants, called proton-induced X-ray emission, which can quickly analyze the chemical elements in almost any substance without destroying it,

(D) A technique originally developed for detecting air pollutants, called proton-induced X-ray emission, which has the ability to analyze the chemical elements in almost any substance quickly and without destroying it,

(E) A technique that was originally developed for detecting air pollutants and has the ability to analyze the chemical elements in almost any substance quickly and without destroying the substance, called proton-induced X-ray emission,

Rhetorical construction

The original sentence successfully avoids the problems that may occur in a long sentence with multiple modifiers. The sentence opens with the modifier *originally developed for detecting air pollutants*. This participial phrase is immediately followed by the word *technique* that it modifies; *technique* is in turn followed by the phrase *called proton-induced X-ray emission*. Finally, the nonrestrictive clause *which ... destroying it* is correctly placed next to *emission* and set off from the rest of the sentence by a pair of commas.

A   **Correct.** The modifiers are all correctly placed and punctuated; the meaning is clear.

B   Placement of two long modifiers at the beginning of the sentence is awkward and makes it difficult to locate the subject; second modifier (*having...*) actually modifies the first modifier.

C   *Called proton-induced X-ray emission* should be placed next to *a technique* and should not be set off by commas; relative clause introduced by *which* incorrectly and illogically modifies *emission*.

D   *Called proton-induced X-ray emission* should be placed next to *a technique* and should not be set off by commas; relative clause introduced by *which* incorrectly and illogically modifies *emission*; *has the ability to* is wordy.

E   *Called proton-induced X-ray emission* should be placed next to *a technique* and should not be set off by commas; *has the ability to* is wordy.

The correct answer is A.

108. <u>Authoritative parents are more likely than permissive parents to have children who as adolescents are self-confident, high in self-esteem, and responsibly independent.</u>

   (A) Authoritative parents are more likely than permissive parents to have children who as adolescents are self-confident, high in self-esteem, and responsibly independent.

   (B) Authoritative parents who are more likely than permissive parents to have adolescent children that are self-confident, high in self-esteem, and responsibly independent.

   (C) Children of authoritative parents, rather than permissive parents, are the more likely to be self-confident, have a high self-esteem, and to be responsibly independent as adolescents.

   (D) Children whose parents are authoritative rather than being permissive, are more likely to have self-confidence, a high self-esteem, and be responsibly independent when they are an adolescent.

   (E) Rather than permissive parents, the children of authoritative parents are the more likely to have self-confidence, a high self-esteem, and to be responsibly independent as an adolescent.

Grammatical construction; Logical predication

The sentence compares authoritative parents to permissive parents in terms of the kinds of adolescent children they are likely to have. Versions of the sentence that compare parents to children are nonsensical. The three characteristics most likely exemplified by children of authoritative parents should be presented in parallel structure.

   A **Correct.** The sentence effectively compares authoritative parents to permissive parents and expresses the characteristics of the children in parallel form.

   B The sentence is a fragment, since the main subject, *authoritative parents*, has no verb.

   C To preserve parallelism, the infinitive marker *to* should appear only before the first verb in the series OR it should appear before all three verbs; the sentence seems to be comparing children and parents.

   D The word *being* destroys the parallelism between *authoritative* and *permissive*; the single predicate noun *adolescent* does not agree with the plural subject *they*.

   E This sentence unintentionally compares children and parents.

The correct answer is A.

109. Among the objects found in the excavated temple were small terra-cotta effigies left by supplicants who were either asking the goddess Bona Dea's aid <u>in healing physical and mental ills or thanking her for such help.</u>

   (A) in healing physical and mental ills or thanking her for such help

   (B) in healing physical and mental ills and to thank her for helping

   (C) in healing physical and mental ills, and thanking her for helping

   (D) to heal physical and mental ills or to thank her for such help

   (E) to heal physical and mental ills or thanking her for such help

Parallelism; Idiom

This correct sentence uses parallel structure to explain that *supplicants were either asking ... or thanking*. The correlative pair *either/or* is correctly used since each element is followed by the same part of speech: *either asking ... or thanking*. The pair of correlative conjunctions *either ... or* always work together; *either* may only be followed by *or*. The noun *aid* is correctly followed by *in healing* rather than by the infinitive *to heal*.

A   **Correct.** The original sentence uses parallel structure to make its point; the idioms are correctly used.

B   *And* is incorrect following *either*, and its use changes the meaning of the sentence; *to thank* is not parallel to *asking*; *for helping* is awkward.

C   No comma should be used following *ills*; *and* is incorrect following *either*, and its use changes the meaning of the sentence; *for helping* is awkward.

D   *To heal* is incorrect following *aid*; *to thank* is not parallel to *asking*.

E   *To heal* is incorrect following *aid*.

The correct answer is A.

110. Published in Harlem, the owner and editor of *The Messenger* were two young journalists, Chandler Owen and A. Philip Randolph, who would later make his reputation as a labor leader.

(A) Published in Harlem, the owner and editor of *The Messenger* were two young journalists, Chandler Owen and A. Philip Randolph, who would later make his reputation as a labor leader.

(B) Published in Harlem, two young journalists, Chandler Owen and A. Philip Randolph, who would later make his reputation as a labor leader, were the owner and editor of *The Messenger*.

(C) Published in Harlem, *The Messenger* was owned and edited by two young journalists, A. Philip Randolph, who would later make his reputation as a labor leader, and Chandler Owen.

(D) *The Messenger* was owned and edited by two young journalists, Chandler Owen and A. Philip Randolph, who would later make his reputation as a labor leader, and published in Harlem.

(E) The owner and editor being two young journalists, Chandler Owen and A. Philip Randolph, who would later make his reputation as a labor leader, *The Messenger* was published in Harlem.

Logical predication; agreement

A modifying phrase must be placed near the word it modifies. Here, the incorrect placement of the modifying phrase *published in Harlem* makes the phrase describe *the owner and editor* when it should describe *The Messenger*. The use of the singular *owner and editor* is puzzling: did one journalist own and the other edit? Or did they jointly own and edit? It is also unclear which of the two journalists is described in the clause beginning *who*.

A   *Published in Harlem* incorrectly modifies *the owner and editor*; references are unclear.

B   *Published in Harlem* incorrectly modifies *two young journalists*; references are unclear.

C   **Correct.** In this sentence, the modifier correctly describes *The Messenger*; the verbs indicate that both journalists played both roles; and the relative clause clearly shows Randolph, not Owen, as the owner of the reputation.

D   The relative clause (*who ... leader*) lacks a clear antecedent; placement of *published in Harlem* is awkward and unclear.

E   *Being* introduces an awkward construction; the relative clause (*who ... leader*) does not have a clear antecedent.

The correct answer is C.

111. Construction of the Roman Colosseum, <u>which was officially known as the Flavian Amphitheater, began in A.D. 69, during the reign of Vespasian,</u> was completed a decade later, during the reign of Titus, who opened the Colosseum with a one-hundred-day cycle of religious pageants, gladiatorial games, and spectacles.

(A) which was officially known as the Flavian Amphitheater, began in A.D. 69, during the reign of Vespasian,

(B) officially known as the Flavian Amphitheater, begun in A.D. 69, during the reign of Vespasian, and

(C) which was officially known as the Flavian Amphitheater, began in A.D. 69, during the reign of Vespasian, and

(D) officially known as the Flavian Amphitheater and begun in A.D. 69, during the reign of Vespasian it

(E) officially known as the Flavian Amphitheater, which was begun in A.D. 69, during the reign of Vespasian, and

Grammatical construction; Verb form

The main subject of the sentence is *Construction*, and it has two main verbs: *began* and *was completed*. These two verbs should be connected by the conjunction *and* to preserve their equal grammatical status. Both verbs should be in simple past tense.

A   The conjunction is missing before the second main verb, *was completed*.

B   *Begun* is the wrong verb form.

C   Correct. The two verbs of the main clause are in simple past tense and are joined with *and*.

D   There is no need to use the pronoun *it* as the subject of *was completed*, because *Roman Colosseum* (modified by phrases describing its name and the time it was begun) already serves as the subject of the final verb.

E   The appearance of the relative pronoun as the subject of the main verbs deprives the term *construction* of a verb and makes this sentence a fragment.

The correct answer is C.

112. <u>As a baby emerges from the darkness of the womb with a rudimentary sense of vision, it would be rated about 20/500, or legally blind if it were an adult with such vision.</u>

(A) As a baby emerges from the darkness of the womb with a rudimentary sense of vision, it would be rated about 20/500, or legally blind if it were an adult with such vision.

(B) A baby emerges from the darkness of the womb with a rudimentary sense of vision that would be rated about 20/500, or legally blind as an adult.

(C) As a baby emerges from the darkness of the womb, its rudimentary sense of vision would be rated about 20/500; qualifying it to be legally blind if an adult.

(D) A baby emerges from the darkness of the womb with a rudimentary sense of vision that would be rated about 20/500; an adult with such vision would be deemed legally blind.

(E) As a baby emerges from the darkness of the womb, its rudimentary sense of vision, which would deemed legally blind for an adult, would be rated about 20/500.

Grammatical construction

This sentence fails to convey its meaning because its construction is faulty. It begins with a subordinate clause, whose subject is *a baby*; the subject of the main clause, *it* appears to refer back to *baby*. However, reading the main clause reveals that *it* is intended to refer to the *sense of vision* the first time it is used and to the *baby* the second time. The whole sentence must be revised, and the relationships between the two parts of the sentence must be clarified.

A   Repeated use of *it* creates confusion because the referent is not clear.

B   The final phrase is awkwardly and ambiguously attached to the sentence.

C   The use of a semicolon instead of a comma creates a sentence fragment.

D   Correct. One independent clause describes a baby's vision, the other an adult's; the two independent but linked main clauses are correctly separated with a semicolon in this version of the sentence.

E   Subordinate clause beginning with *which* is awkward and ambiguous.

The correct answer is D.

113. <u>Because there are provisions of the new maritime code that provide that even tiny islets can be the basis for claims to the fisheries and oil fields of large sea areas, they have already stimulated</u> international disputes over uninhabited islands.

    (A) Because there are provisions of the new maritime code that provide that even tiny islets can be the basis for claims to the fisheries and oil fields of large sea areas, they have already stimulated

    (B) Because the new maritime code provides that even tiny islets can be the basis for claims to the fisheries and oil fields of large sea areas, it has already stimulated

    (C) Even tiny islets can be the basis for claims to the fisheries and oil fields of large sea areas under provisions of the new maritime code, already stimulating

    (D) Because even tiny islets can be the basis for claims to the fisheries and oil fields of large sea areas under provisions of the new maritime code, this has already stimulated

    (E) Because even tiny islets can be the basis for claims to the fisheries and oil fields of large sea areas under provisions of the new maritime code, which is already stimulating

Logical predication; Grammatical construction

In this sentence, the *there are ... that ...* construction contributes nothing more than unnecessary words. The sentence needs to make clear whether *provisions* or *code* is the subject of the main verb *stimulated*.

A The *there are ... that ...* construction is unnecessarily wordy; in the predicate nominative instead of the subject position, *provisions* is not an obvious referent for the pronoun *they*.

B Correct. In this sentence, *the new maritime code* is clearly the antecedent of *it* in the main clause and thus the subject of *has already stimulated*.

C *Under provisions of the new maritime code* is a misplaced modifier, seeming to describe *sea areas*; the sentence does not make clear what is *stimulating ... disputes*.

D The referent of *this* is unclear.

E The sentence is a fragment, opening with a dependent clause (*Because ... code*) and concluding with a relative clause, but lacking a main, independent clause.

The correct answer is B.

114. The original building and loan associations were organized as limited life funds, whose members made monthly payments on their share <u>subscriptions, then taking turns drawing</u> on the funds for home mortgages.

    (A) subscriptions, then taking turns drawing

    (B) subscriptions, and then taking turns drawing

    (C) subscriptions and then took turns drawing

    (D) subscriptions and then took turns, they drew

    (E) subscriptions and then drew, taking turns

Verb form; Parallelism

The *members* performed a sequence of two actions: first they *made monthly payments ...* and then *took turns drawing*. The two actions must be expressed by the parallel past tense verbs *made* and *took*. The substitution of *taking* for *took* disrupts the parallelism and makes the sentence hard to understand.

A The participle *taking* is not parallel to the verb *made*.

B Adding *and* does not solve the lack of parallelism.

C Correct. In this sentence, the second verb, *took*, is parallel to the first verb, *made*; the two verbs are correctly joined by *and* as compound verbs with the same subject, *members*.

D Illogical construction creates a run-on sentence.

E Construction is illogical, failing to show what the members *drew*; the final phrase makes no sense.

The correct answer is C.

115. Gall's hypothesis <u>of there being different mental functions localized in different parts of the brain is widely accepted today</u>.

    (A)   of there being different mental functions localized in different parts of the brain is widely accepted today

    (B)   of different mental functions that are localized in different parts of the brain is widely accepted today

    (C)   that different mental functions are localized in different parts of the brain is widely accepted today

    (D)   which is that there are different mental functions localized in different parts of the brain is widely accepted today

    (E)   which is widely accepted today is that there are different mental functions localized in different parts of the brain

Grammatical construction

Gall's hypothesis is contained in the clause *that different mental functions are localized in different parts of the brain* (noun + marker *that* + content clause). A series of phrases provides neither the same clarity nor grammatical correctness.

A   *Of there being* is not a precise expression; a clause identifying Gall's hypothesis is needed: *that* introduces a clause that complements the noun *hypothesis*.

B   This construction distorts meaning by separating parts of the description.

C   **Correct.** This sentence uses a clause that identifies Gall's hypothesis clearly and correctly.

D   *Which is* and *there are* introduce a wordy and awkward construction.

E   *Which is widely accepted today* implies that Gall's other theories are not accepted today, distorting the meaning of the sentence.

The correct answer is C.

116. Mauritius was a British colony for almost 200 years, <u>excepting for</u> the domains of administration and teaching, the English language was never really spoken on the island.

    (A)   excepting for

    (B)   except in

    (C)   but except in

    (D)   but excepting for

    (E)   with the exception of

Idiom; Grammatical construction

This two-clause sentence describes an apparent incompatibility: as a British colony, Mauritius might be expected to be English-speaking, but in fact it was not. To describe this apparent contradiction and to avoid a comma splice, the clauses should be joined by the conjunction *but*. *Domains* describes places *in* which English is spoken; *for* is the incorrect preposition. *Excepting* is not idiomatic English in this case.

A   The lack of a conjunction causes a comma splice; *excepting for* is non-idiomatic.

B   The lack of a conjunction causes a comma splice.

C   **Correct.** The two independent clauses are separated by *but*, and *except in* is an appropriate idiom.

D   *Excepting for* is non-idiomatic.

E   The lack of a conjunction causes a comma splice.

The correct answer is C.

117. George Sand (Aurore Lucile Dupin) was one of the first European writers to consider the rural poor <u>to be legitimate subjects for literature and portray these</u> with sympathy and respect in her novels.

(A) to be legitimate subjects for literature and portray these

(B) should be legitimate subjects for literature and portray these

(C) as being legitimate subjects for literature and portraying them

(D) as if they were legitimate subjects for literature and portray them

(E) legitimate subjects for literature and to portray them

Idiom; Diction; Parallelism

When *consider* means *think of* or *believe after careful deliberation*, it does not require *as* or any other expression before the object. The most concise phrase is *to consider the rural poor legitimate subjects for literature*. This phrase should have a parallel in *to portray them with sympathy and respect*. While it is not essential to repeat *to*, the repetition elegantly reinforces the parallelism. The correct pronoun must follow *portray*: Sand portrayed *them*. The pronoun *them* refers to the rural poor and is the direct object. *These* (pl. of *this*) is a demonstrative pronoun, and here it is unclear what it is pointing to as its antecedent: *Subjects* is the nearest plural noun antecedent, but *these* could also point to something not in the sentence, an unknown noun. Only the objective form of the pronoun (*them*) clearly points back to its antecedent *the rural poor*.

A   *To be* is unnecessary; *these* must be replaced by *them*.

B   *Should be* is wordy and requires *that* following *consider*; *these* should be *them*.

C   *As being* is awkward and unnecessary; *portraying* and *to consider* are not parallel.

D   *As if they were* distorts the meaning.

E   **Correct.** In this sentence, the correct idiom is used with the verb *consider*; the correct pronoun, *them*, replaces the incorrect *these*; *to consider* and *to portray* are parallel.

The correct answer is E.

118. The World Wildlife Fund has declared that global warming, <u>a phenomenon most scientists agree to be caused by human beings in burning fossil fuels,</u> will create havoc among migratory birds by altering the environment in ways harmful to their habitats.

(A) a phenomenon most scientists agree to be caused by human beings in burning fossil fuels,

(B) a phenomenon most scientists agree that is caused by fossil fuels burned by human beings,

(C) a phenomenon that most scientists agree is caused by human beings' burning of fossil fuels,

(D) which most scientists agree on as a phenomenon caused by human beings who burn fossil fuels,

(E) which most scientists agree to be a phenomenon caused by fossil fuels burned by human beings,

Logical predication; Rhetorical construction

The underlined portion of the sentence is an appositive defining *global warming* as a phenomenon caused by the burning of fossil fuels by humans. Because this appositive intervenes between the subject (*global warming*) and verb (*will create*) of a clause, it should be expressed as clearly and economically as possible so as not to confuse the meaning of the sentence as a whole.

A   *To be caused* and *in burning* are wordy, awkward, and indirect.

B   *That is* should immediately follow *phenomenon*, not *agree*.

C   **Correct.** The phrase *human beings' burning* is more economical than constructions with prepositional phrases or relative clauses.

D   The phrasing is wordy and indirect.

E   The phrasing is wordy and the meaning is imprecise; it is not fossil fuels that cause global warming—it is the burning of fossil fuels by humans.

The correct answer is C.

119. New theories propose that catastrophic impacts of asteroids and comets may have caused reversals in the Earth's magnetic field, the onset of ice ages, splitting apart continents 80 million years ago, and great volcanic eruptions.

    (A) splitting apart continents
    (B) the splitting apart of continents
    (C) split apart continents
    (D) continents split apart
    (E) continents that were split apart

    Parallelism

    This sentence lists four effects of catastrophic impacts; each effect, except the one included in the underlined portion, is given in noun form: *reversals, the onset, eruptions. Splitting* is a verb and thus not parallel to the other nouns in the series; in the second option *splitting* is a noun. *Splitting* may be transformed into a noun by adding the article *the*.

    A *Splitting*, a verb, is not parallel to *reversals*, *the onset*, and *eruptions*, and its role as a member in the series is unclear.
    B Correct. *The splitting* is a gerund, or noun form, and is properly used in this sentence; it is parallel to the other nouns.
    C Verb *split* is not parallel to *reversals*, *the onset*, and *eruptions*.
    D If the impacts truly caused continents the verb *created* would be used, but it makes no sense to say impacts caused continents and this phrase is not parallel to the other noun phrases.
    E This option is similar to the previous option: *continents* cannot be said to be *caused*.

    The correct answer is B.

120. A firm that specializes in the analysis of handwriting claims from a one-page writing sample that it can assess more than 300 personality traits, including enthusiasm, imagination, and ambition.

    (A) from a one-page writing sample that it can assess
    (B) from a one-page writing sample it has the ability of assessing

    (C) the ability, from a one-page writing sample, of assessing
    (D) to be able, from a one-page writing sample, to assess
    (E) being able to assess, from a one-page writing sample

    Idiom; Rhetorical construction

    The meaning of this sentence becomes lost in an awkward and ungrammatical construction. The verb *claims* may be followed by one of two correct constructions: *claims that* + a subordinate clause, or *claims* + the infinitive. When the prepositional phrase *from a one-page writing sample* is placed between *claims* and *that*, the result confuses and distorts the meaning by suggesting that the claim is contained in the writing sample. Instead, the firm claims *to be able ... to assess*. The prepositional phrase should be placed between a pair of commas to show clearly that it is additional information not crucial to understanding the sentence.

    A Prepositional phrase following the verb distorts the meaning of the sentence.
    B Placing the prepositional phrase after *claims* distorts meaning; *that* is omitted; *the ability of assessing* is wordy and awkward.
    C *The ability ... of assessing* is wordy and awkward.
    D Correct. The correct idiomatic construction (*claims to be able to assess*) is used in this sentence, and the prepositional phrase is set off in a pair of commas to prevent misreading.
    E *Claims ... being able* is not a correct idiom.

    The correct answer is D.

121. Sales of wines declined in the late 1980s, but they began to grow again after the 1991 report that linked moderate consumption of alcohol, and particularly of red wine, with a reduced risk of heart disease.

    (A) they began to grow again after the 1991 report that linked moderate consumption of alcohol, and particularly of red wine, with a reduced risk of heart disease
    (B) after the 1991 report that linked a reduced risk of heart disease with a moderate alcohol consumption, particularly red wine, they began growing again

(C)   in a 1991 report, moderate alcohol consumption, and particularly of red wine, which was linked with a reduced risk of heart disease, caused them to begin to grow again

(D)   with a reduced risk of heart disease linked in a 1991 report with moderate alcohol consumption, in particular red wine, they began growing again

(E)   a reduced risk of heart disease linked to moderate alcohol consumption in a 1991 report, and in particular red wine, started them growing again

Logical predication; Rhetorical construction

This sentence explains why a trend of declining wine sales reversed after the publication of a 1991 report suggesting that moderate consumption of red wine correlated with reduced risk of heart disease. The phrase *particularly of red wine* modifies *consumption of alcohol*, and the sentence must make clear that it is *moderate consumption*, not *red wine* that the report links to *reduced risk*.

A   **Correct.** In the second clause, *they* refers correctly to *sales of wines*; the relative clause beginning with *that* clearly indicates that the report *linked moderate consumption … with a reduced risk.*

B   *Particularly red wine* cannot describe consumption—the preposition *of* is needed; the placement of *they* so far from the position of the antecedent *Sales* makes the sentence awkward and difficult to decode.

C   The clause beginning with *which* refers to *red wine* in this construction, erroneously suggesting that wine rather than *moderate consumption* of alcohol correlates with reduced risk of heart disease; *particularly of red wine* is not parallel to *moderate alcohol consumption*; it needs to follow *moderate consumption of alcohol* to make sense.

D   Without the preposition *of*, the sentence indicates that red wine is a kind of consumption—which makes no sense.

E   The incorrect placement of the modifier *in a 1991 report* suggests that wine is being consumed (albeit in moderation) in the report itself.

The correct answer is A.

122.   A wildlife expert predicts that the reintroduction of the caribou into northern Minnesota would fail if the density of the timber wolf population in that region is more numerous than one wolf for every 39 square miles.

(A)   would fail if the density of the timber wolf population in that region is more numerous

(B)   would fail provided the density of the timber wolf population in that region is more

(C)   should fail if the timber wolf density in that region was greater

(D)   will fail if the density of the timber wolf population in that region is greater

(E)   will fail if the timber wolf density in that region were more numerous

Verb form; Diction

A prediction is made about a future event, which can be restated using the construction *y will happen if x happens first* (an alternate form is *if x happens, y will happen*). The subjunctive verb form *would* expresses remoteness and thus casts some doubt on the likelihood of *x*. The verb form *will fail* expresses the likelihood *x* with greater certainty. *Density* is not a countable quantity, so it cannot be modified by *more numerous*, which is used solely for countable quantities; *greater* is correct.

A   *Would fail* expresses doubt about the future outcome; *density* should be modified by *greater*.

B   This construction requires *will fail*, not *would fail*; *if* is preferred to *provided*; *density* should be modified by *greater*.

C   *Will fail*, not *should fail*, is required; *timber wolf density* does not clearly refer to the population; the tense of the final verb is incorrect.

D   **Correct.** The verb form *will fail* better expresses the certainty of the prediction; *density* is appropriately modified by *greater*.

E   *Timber wolf density* does not clearly refer to the population; the tense and number of the final verb are incorrect; *density* cannot be modified by *numerous*.

The correct answer is D.

123. She <u>was less successful after she had emigrated to</u>
<u>New York compared to</u> her native Germany,
photographer Lotte Jacobi nevertheless earned a
small group of discerning admirers, and her
photographs were eventually exhibited in prestigious
galleries across the United States.

(A) She was less successful after she had
emigrated to New York compared to

(B) Being less successful after she had emigrated
to New York as compared to

(C) Less successful after she emigrated to New
York than she had been in

(D) Although she was less successful after
emigrating to New York when compared to

(E) She had been less successful after emigrating
to New York than in

Idiom; Grammatical construction; Logical predication

This sentence compares the success Jacobi
experienced after moving to New York to the
success she had previously experienced in
Germany. The phrase *less successful* anticipates the
conclusion of the comparison with the phrase
than.... The main subject of the sentence is
photographer Lotte Jacobi, and the main verb is
earned. The opening clause *She was less successful ...*
therefore creates a comma splice if the comma is
not followed by a conjunction. The most efficient
way to incorporate the information about Jacobi's
comparative successes in Germany and in New
York is to turn this clause into an adjectival phrase
describing Jacobi.

A *Less successful ...* anticipates *than* rather than
compared to ...; a comma is insufficient to
join two independent clauses into a single
sentence.

B *As compared to* is an incorrect way to
complete the comparison introduced by *less;*
Being ... is unnecessarily wordy and
awkward.

C **Correct.** The idiomatic construction *less*
successful ... than is incorporated into an
introductory adjectival phrase modifying
Lotte Jacobi.

D *When compared to* is an incorrect phrase to
complete the comparison introduced by *less.*

E A comma is insufficient to join two
independent clauses into a single sentence;
past-perfect tense is misleading, since it refers
to Jacobi's experience in New York, which in
fact followed her experience in Germany.

The correct answer is C.

124. Found throughout Central and South America,
<u>sloths hang from trees by long rubbery limbs and</u>
<u>sleep 15 hours a day, moving infrequently enough</u>
that two species of algae grow on its coat and
between its toes.

(A) sloths hang from trees by long rubbery limbs and
sleep 15 hours a day, moving infrequently enough

(B) sloths hang from trees by long rubbery limbs,
they sleep 15 hours a day, and with such
infrequent movements

(C) sloths use their long rubbery limbs to hang from
trees, sleep 15 hours a day, and move so
infrequently

(D) the sloth hangs from trees by its long rubbery
limbs, sleeping 15 hours a day and moving so
infrequently

(E) the sloth hangs from trees by its long rubbery
limbs, sleeps 15 hours a day, and it moves
infrequently enough

Agreement; Idiom

The plural *sloths* in the underlined section of
the sentence does not agree with the singular
its (*its coat, its toes*) in the given section of the
sentence, and so *sloths* must be replaced by *the*
sloth. When *its* is then inserted before *long rubbery*
limbs, it becomes clear that the limbs belong to
the sloth, not the trees. The phrase *moving*
infrequently enough that is not idiomatic. The
correct construction is *so x that y: moving so*
infrequently that two species....

A *Sloths* does not agree with *its*; *moving*
infrequently enough is not the correct idiom.

B *Sloths* does not agree with *its*; *hang ... they*
sleep ... with such infrequent movements
introduces a comma splice and is awkward,
wordy, and not parallel.

C *Sloths* does not agree with *its*; this structure
says that sloths use their *long rubbery limbs*
to ... sleep.

D **Correct.** *The sloth* agrees with *its*; the construction *moving so x that y* is properly used in this sentence.

E *Hangs … sleeps … it moves* is not a parallel construction; *infrequently enough that* is not a correct idiom.

The correct answer is D.

125. Today, because of improvements in agricultural technology, the same amount of acreage produces <u>double the apples that it has</u> in 1910.

    (A) double the apples that it has
    (B) twice as many apples as it did
    (C) as much as twice the apples it has
    (D) two times as many apples as there were
    (E) a doubling of the apples that it did

Logical predication; Diction; Verb form

The sentence compares the number of apples produced today with the number of apples produced in 1910. The phrase *double the apples* is not very exact but it could be understood to mean *twice as many* or *as many as*; the verb form *has* confounds the sequence of events and makes the comparison illogical. An action that occurred in 1910 requires a verb in the past tense. The two elements being compared must be grammatically parallel. *The same amount … produces* is paralleled by *as it did* (*produce* understood). The subjects *amount* and *it* are parallel, as are the verbs *produces* and *did* (*produce*).

A The comparative construction *as many as* is needed; the verb tense *has* is incorrect with *in 1910*.

B **Correct.** *As many as* is used for a countable quantity; the two elements being compared are parallel; the verb is in the past tense.

C *Much* is used where *many* is required; the verb tense *has* is incorrect with *in 1910*.

D *Two times* is wordy; *there were* is vague because it does not refer to *amount of acreage*.

E *A doubling of the apples* is awkward and, when joined with *that it did*, suggests doubling the apples themselves, not the amount of apples.

The correct answer is B.

126. The use of lie detectors is based on the assumption that lying produces emotional reactions in an individual <u>that, in turn, create unconscious physiological responses</u>.

    (A) that, in turn, create unconscious physiological responses
    (B) that creates unconscious physiological responses in turn
    (C) creating, in turn, unconscious physiological responses
    (D) to create, in turn, physiological responses that are unconscious
    (E) who creates unconscious physiological responses in turn

Agreement; Rhetorical construction; Logical predication

This sentence describes a cause-and-effect sequence; in the underlined portion of the sentence, the relative pronoun *that* refers to the plural noun *reactions*. The verb in the relative clause must therefore be a plural verb. The causal sequence is most clearly expressed by a relative clause that turns the object *emotional reactions* (from the clause *lying causes emotional reactions in an individual*) into the subject (*that*) of a new clause (*that in turn create unconscious physiological responses*). *In turn* is best placed before the verb of the second relative clause, *create*, to clarify that a chain of events is being described.

A **Correct.** This construction clearly indicates the causal sequence.

B The singular verb *creates* does not agree with the subject referenced by the relative pronoun *that (reactions)*.

C This construction is less successful at clarifying the chain of events because *creating* seems to refer back to *lying*; if used as a participial, *creating* would have to be preceded by a comma.

D This construction does not make clear the causal chain of events, because it is unclear which noun *to create* should attach to; the infinitive construction implies intent, which does not really make sense.

E Because *reactions* is not a person, *who* is the wrong relative pronoun to use.

The correct answer is A.

127. Joan of Arc, a young Frenchwoman who claimed to be divinely inspired, turned the tide of English victories in her country by liberating the city of Orléans and she persuaded Charles VII of France to claim his throne.

    (A) she persuaded Charles VII of France to claim his throne
    (B) persuaded Charles VII of France in claiming his throne
    (C) persuading that the throne be claimed by Charles VII of France
    (D) persuaded Charles VII of France to claim his throne
    (E) persuading that Charles VII of France should claim the throne

Parallelism

Because this sentence consists of many parts, including lengthy modifiers (*a young Frenchwoman* ... ; *by liberating* ...), it is crucial to make the basic structure of it—the subject and verbs of the main clause—as clear and as concisely expressed as possible. *Joan of Arc* is the subject, *turned* is the first verb of the main clause, and *persuaded* is the second verb; so the sentence should be *Joan ... turned ... and persuaded.* Inserting *she* before the second verb both violates the parallelism and adds an unnecessary word.

A   *Persuaded,* not *she persuaded,* is parallel to *turned.*

B   The idiomatic construction is *persuade x to do y,* not *persuade x in doing y.*

C   Here *persuading* is linked to *liberating,* but even if it were said that Joan did *turn the tide of English victories* by *persuading* Charles to claim the throne, a person cannot be said to *persuade* a clause (*that the thrown be claimed*), a person persuades another person or other entity; *be claimed by* is wordy.

D   **Correct.** In this sentence, *persuaded* is parallel to *turned,* and the idiomatic construction *persuade x to do y* is used.

E   Parallel form links *persuading* and *liberating* when *persuaded* should be parallel to *turned*; *persuading that x* is not a correct idiom: a person can only persuade another person or other entity.

The correct answer is D.

128. Australian embryologists have found evidence that suggests that the elephant is descended from an aquatic animal, and its trunk originally evolving as a kind of snorkel.

    (A) that suggests that the elephant is descended from an aquatic animal, and its trunk originally evolving
    (B) that has suggested the elephant descended from an aquatic animal, its trunk originally evolving
    (C) suggesting that the elephant had descended from an aquatic animal with its trunk originally evolved
    (D) to suggest that the elephant had descended from an aquatic animal and its trunk originally evolved
    (E) to suggest that the elephant is descended from an aquatic animal and that its trunk originally evolved

Parallelism; Verb form

The clearest, most economical way of expressing the two things suggested by Australian embryologists' evidence is to format them as relative clauses serving as parallel direct objects of the verb *suggest.* It is awkward and confusing to string together relative clauses: *evidence that suggests that the elephant....* A clearer way of making this connection is to turn the verb *suggests* into a participle modifying *evidence.* The word *descended* is a predicate adjective following the present-tense verb *is* and describing the present-day elephant. The verb *evolved* should be past tense because it describes how the trunk of the elephant *originally* evolved, not how it is evolving today.

A   The string of relative phrases is awkward and confusing; the phrase following the conjunction *and* is not parallel with the relative clause *that the elephant is descended....*

B   The evidence *still* suggests these things about the evolution of the elephant and its trunk, so the present-perfect verb tense is inaccurate.

C   *Had descended* is the wrong verb tense; *with* cannot be followed by an independent clause.

D   *Had descended* is the wrong tense; the phrase following the conjunction *and* does not parallel the relative clause that precedes the conjunction.

E **Correct.** The two dependent clauses beginning with *that* are in parallel form and contain verbs in the correct tenses.

The correct answer is E.

129. Cajuns speak a dialect brought to southern Louisiana by the 4,000 Acadians who migrated there in 1755; their language is basically seventeenth-century French to which has been added English, Spanish, and Italian words.

    (A) to which has been added English, Spanish, and Italian words
    (B) added to which is English, Spanish, and Italian words
    (C) to which English, Spanish, and Italian words have been added
    (D) with English, Spanish, and Italian words having been added to it
    (E) and, in addition, English, Spanish, and Italian words are added

Agreement; Logical predication

The sentence describes the Cajun language as *seventeenth-century French* and then modifies that description by noting the addition of words from other languages. Since *words* is a plural noun, a plural verb is required. The inverted word order in the original sentence is awkward.

A The singular *has* does not agree in number with *English, Spanish, and Italian words*; the verb should be the plural *have*; the inversion of the subject and the verb is awkward.

B Verb must be plural; since the action began in the past, the present perfect form *have been added* is required.

C **Correct.** The relative clause in this sentence has the correct verb form, and its placement makes it clear that it modifies the noun *French*. The clause also follows normal subject-verb word order.

D *With* does not concisely modify the noun *French*; *having been added to it* is a wordy expression.

E Verb tense is incorrect; it is not clear that the construction modifies the noun *French*.

The correct answer is C.

130. One view of the economy contends that a large drop in oil prices should eventually lead to lowering interest rates, as well as lowering fears about inflation, a rally in stocks and bonds, and a weakening of the dollar.

    (A) lowering interest rates, as well as lowering fears about inflation,
    (B) a lowering of interest rates and of fears about inflation,
    (C) a lowering of interest rates, along with fears about inflation,
    (D) interest rates being lowered, along with fears about inflation,
    (E) interest rates and fears about inflation being lowered, with

Parallelism; Diction

The sentence uses parallel structure to describe the anticipated effects of a drop in oil prices. Parallel noun phrases list two effects, *a rally ... and a weakening*, so the first effect in the series must be written as *a lowering*. *Lowering* is a participle, whereas *a lowering* is a gerund and functions as a noun. For the sake of both clarity and conciseness, the effects on interest rates and fears should be combined into a single noun phrase: *a lowering of interest rates and of fears about inflation*.

A Each noun in the parallel series should be introduced by the indefinite article *a*; *lowering*, a verb form, needs to be made into the noun *a lowering*; rates and fears should be combined.

B **Correct.** The series *a lowering ... a rally ... and a weakening* uses parallel structure correctly; *a lowering of interest rates and of fears* gracefully combines two effects in this sentence.

C Parallelism is maintained with *a lowering*, but the use of *along with* makes it unclear that *fears* is parallel to *rates*.

D Parallelism is not maintained due to use of *along with* as in the previous option; the phrase *interest rates being lowered* is awkward.

E Parallelism is not maintained; the phrase *interest rates and fears about inflation being lowered* is awkward.

The correct answer is B.

131. Over 75 percent of the energy produced in France derives from nuclear power, while in Germany it is just over 33 percent.

    (A) while in Germany it is just over 33 percent
    (B) compared to Germany, which uses just over 33 percent
    (C) whereas nuclear power accounts for just over 33 percent of the energy produced in Germany
    (D) whereas just over 33 percent of the energy comes from nuclear power in Germany
    (E) compared with the energy from nuclear power in Germany, where it is just over 33 percent

Rhetorical construction; Logical predication

This sentence compares percentages and uses the prepositional phrases *in France* and *in Germany* to distinguish the percentage of energy in each country coming from nuclear power. This information is most efficiently and clearly presented in two clauses joined by the conjunction *whereas*, which signifies a difference between the situations in the two countries. Each clause must identify what the percentage refers to—that is, the portion of the respective country's energy that comes from nuclear power.

A *While* is somewhat ambiguous, since it might indicate simultaneity rather than contrast; the referent of *it* is ambiguous, raising questions about just what two things are being compared.

B This sentence compares *75 percent* to *Germany;* it is not clear what *33 percent* refers to.

C **Correct.** The two clauses joined by *whereas* indicate clearly that the comparison is between the different percentages of energy coming from nuclear power.

D The use of the definite article *the* makes it seem as though the energy being referred to in this part of the sentence is that of France.

E This construction is wordy and unclear; the referent of *it* is ambiguous.

The correct answer is C.

132. Although the term "psychopath" is popularly applied to an especially brutal criminal, in psychology it is someone who is apparently incapable of feeling compassion or the pangs of conscience.

    (A) it is someone who is
    (B) it is a person
    (C) they are people who are
    (D) it refers to someone who is
    (E) it is in reference to people

Logical predication; Grammatical construction; Agreement

The intent of the sentence is to define the term "psychopath." In this sentence, the pronoun *it* refers back to *the term* and seems illogically to refer forward to *someone.* Logically, an inanimate *term* cannot be *a person* or *someone.* The sentence needs to be reworded so that it is clear that "psychopath" is a term used to define a specific kind of person.

A This construction illogically asserts that *the term* is a person.

B This construction illogically asserts that *the term* is a person.

C Plural pronoun *they* does not agree with the singular noun *the term* and cannot refer to *psychopath;* this construction also asserts that *the term* is a person.

D **Correct.** In this sentence, the verb *refers* clearly links the term to a particular kind of person; the alignment of pronouns and antecedents is both logical and grammatical.

E To be correct, this construction needs a main verb such as *used;* the construction *is used in reference to* is awkward and much wordier than the single word *refers;* the plural *people* should be singular.

The correct answer is D.

133. Last week local shrimpers held a news conference to take some credit for the resurgence of the rare Kemp's ridley turtle, saying that their compliance with laws requiring that turtle-excluder devices be on shrimp nets protect adult sea turtles.

   (A) requiring that turtle-excluder devices be on shrimp nets protect
   (B) requiring turtle-excluder devices on shrimp nets is protecting
   (C) that require turtle-excluder devices on shrimp nets protect
   (D) to require turtle-excluder devices on shrimp nets are protecting
   (E) to require turtle-excluder devices on shrimp nets is protecting

Rhetorical construction; Agreement

The subject of the clause introduced by *saying that* is the singular noun *compliance*. This subject requires the singular form of the verb *protect*. The clearest, most economical way to describe the laws in question is to follow the word *laws* with a present participle *requiring*. To use an infinitive, *to require*, seems to indicate that requiring these devices is the objective of the laws, when in fact the objective is to protect the sea turtles.

A   The plural verb *protect* does not agree with the singular subject *compliance*.

B   Correct. The singular verb *is protecting* agrees with the singular subject *compliance*, and the participial phrase beginning with *requiring* concisely and accurately describes the laws.

C   The relative clause *that require* introduces unnecessary wordiness; the plural verb *protect* does not agree with the singular subject *compliance*.

D   *To require* obscures the purpose of the laws; the plural verb phrase *are protecting* does not agree with the singular subject *compliance*.

E   *To require* obscures the purpose of the laws.

The correct answer is B.

134. Recently implemented "shift-work equations" based on studies of the human sleep cycle have reduced sickness, sleeping on the job, fatigue among shift workers, and have raised production efficiency in various industries.

   (A) fatigue among shift workers, and have raised
   (B) fatigue among shift workers, and raised
   (C) and fatigue among shift workers while raising
   (D) lowered fatigue among shift workers, and raised
   (E) and fatigue among shift workers was lowered while raising

Grammatical construction

Implementing the equations has reduced *sickness, sleeping on the job,* and *fatigue*; at the same time, it has increased *efficiency*. The three parallel elements (*have reduced x, y,* and *z*) require *and* before the final element.

A   The omission of *and* before *fatigue* creates an unclear sentence.

B   The omission of *and* before *fatigue* creates an unclear sentence.

C   Correct. The use of *and* in this sentence unites the three parallel elements; the phrase *while raising* provides a clear contrast with *have reduced*.

D   *And* is required to link the parallel elements; the verb *reduced* applies to all three parallel elements, so inserting *lowered* before *fatigue* illogically suggests that fatigue actually increased.

E   The insertion of *was lowered* destroys the parallel structure, and thus *while raising* has no logical referent here.

The correct answer is C.

135. Spanning more than 50 years, Friedrich <u>Müller</u>
<u>began his career in an unpromising apprenticeship</u>
<u>as</u> a Sanskrit scholar and culminated in virtually
every honor that European governments and
learned societies could bestow.

(A) Müller began his career in an unpromising
apprenticeship as

(B) Müller's career began in an unpromising
apprenticeship as

(C) Müller's career began with the unpromising
apprenticeship of being

(D) Müller had begun his career with the
unpromising apprenticeship of being

(E) the career of Müller has begun with an
unpromising apprenticeship of

Logical predication; Idiom

What spanned more than 50 years? It was
Müller's career that spanned 50 years and
culminated in virtually every honor. The correct
subject of the sentence must be *Müller's career.*

A   *Müller's career*, not *Müller*, should be the
subject of the sentence.

B   **Correct.** Using *Müller's career* as the subject
of the sentence solves the modification
problem with *spanning ...* and provides a
logical subject for *culminated.*

C   *Apprenticeship of being* is an incorrect idiom;
apprenticeship as is correct.

D   *Müller's career*, not *Müller*, should be the
subject of the sentence; past perfect tense is
inappropriate; *apprenticeship of being* is an
incorrect idiom.

E   *Müller's career* is preferable to *the career of*
Müller; present perfect tense is incorrect;
apprenticeship of should be *apprenticeship as.*

The correct answer is B.

136. <u>Whereas in mammals the tiny tubes that convey</u>
<u>nutrients to bone cells are arrayed in parallel lines, in</u>
<u>birds the tubes</u> form a random pattern.

(A) Whereas in mammals the tiny tubes that convey
nutrients to bone cells are arrayed in parallel
lines, in birds the tubes

(B) Whereas the tiny tubes for the conveying of
nutrients to bone cells are arrayed in mammals
in parallel lines, birds have tubes that

(C) Unlike mammals, where the tiny tubes for
conveying nutrients to bone cells are arrayed in
parallel lines, birds' tubes

(D) Unlike mammals, in whom the tiny tubes that
convey nutrients to bone cells are arrayed in
parallel lines, the tubes in birds

(E) Unlike the tiny tubes that convey nutrients to
bone cells, which in mammals are arrayed in
parallel lines, in birds the tubes

Idiom; Rhetorical construction; Parallelism

Whereas introduces two contrasting situations
or events and should be followed by parallel
structures. In this sentence, *whereas* is
immediately followed by a clause beginning
with the prepositional phrase *in mammals*; this
means that the second part of the sentence must
also be a clause that opens with a preposition that
functions in the same way—in this case, *in birds*.
This structure clarifies that the things being
contrasted are the *tubes* in mammals and the *tubes*
in birds. Incorrect versions of the sentence
grammatically contrast *tubes* and *birds*, *mammals*
and *tubes*, or *birds* and *mammals*.

A   **Correct.** Parallel structures make clear that
the tubes in mammals are being contrasted
with the tubes in birds.

B   The faulty parallelism results in a sentence
that is confusing and unnecessarily wordy.

C   The sentence compares *mammals* and *birds'*
tubes.

D   Because of faulty parallelism, this sentence
also compares *mammals* and *tubes in birds.*

E   This structure is wordy and confusing
because of faulty parallelism.

The correct answer is A.

137. Joachim Raff and Giacomo Meyerbeer are examples of the kind of composer who receives popular acclaim while living, <u>often goes into decline after death, and never regains popularity again</u>.

    (A) often goes into decline after death, and never regains popularity again
    (B) whose reputation declines after death and never regains its status again
    (C) but whose reputation declines after death and never regains its former status
    (D) who declines in reputation after death and who never regained popularity again
    (E) then has declined in reputation after death and never regained popularity

Verb tense; Parallelism

Faulty parallelism in the relative clause *who receives … goes … regains …* makes it unclear who or what is being described. The original clause begins by describing a certain kind of composer. As written, with *who* as the subject of *goes* and *regains*, the last two descriptions illogically continue to refer to the kind of composer. Logically it must be the reputation that declines after the composer's death.

A   Illogically suggests the composer goes into decline after death; redundant *again*.

B   The two clauses are not parallel, lack a coordinating conjunction, and do not describe the same thing; redundant *again*.

C   **Correct.** This sentence presents the proper logic while maintaining parallel structure and consistent verb tense.

D   The verb tenses are inconsistent with present tense used in the first phrase; redundant *again*.

E   The verb tenses are inconsistent with present tense used in the first phrase; to maintain parallelism, the verbs must be *receives … declines … regains*.

The correct answer is C.

138. In no other historical sighting did Halley's Comet cause such a worldwide sensation as <u>did its return in 1910–1911</u>.

    (A) did its return in 1910–1911
    (B) had its 1910–1911 return
    (C) in its return of 1910–1911
    (D) its return of 1910–1911 did
    (E) its return in 1910–1911

Parallelism; Verb form; Logical predication

The single subject of this sentence is *Halley's Comet*, and its single verb phrase is *did cause*. The comparison presented by the sentence is between adverbial phrases describing times when the comet was seen. Grammatically, the items being compared are parallel prepositional phrases beginning with the preposition *in: in no other sighting* and *in its return in 1910–1911*. This is the clearest, most economical way of presenting the information. The options that introduce a second verb (*did* or *had*) violate the parallelism and introduce a comparison between the comet itself (subject of the verb *did cause*) and the comet's return (subject of the verb *did* or *had*).

A   This sentence implies a comparison between the comet and its return.

B   This sentence implies a comparison between the comet and its return; *had* is the wrong auxiliary verb form because it must be followed by *caused* instead of *cause*.

C   **Correct.** The parallel prepositional phrases in this sentence correctly compare times when the comet was sighted.

D   This sentence implies a comparison between the comet and its return.

E   This sentence violates parallelism, implying a comparison between a prepositional phrase and a noun phrase.

The correct answer is C.

139. The company announced that its profits declined much less in the second quarter than analysts had expected it to and its business will improve in the second half of the year.

(A) had expected it to and its business will improve
(B) had expected and that its business would improve
(C) expected it would and that it will improve its business
(D) expected them to and its business would improve
(E) expected and that it will have improved its business

Parallelism, verb tense, antecedent

The original sentence has three problems. The sentence must clarify that the analysts held their expectations before the company's announcement. That is, it must use the past perfect *had expected* to show action prior to the past tense of *announced*. The sentence must also use *would* rather than *will* for the company's uncertain business improvement in the future. Secondly, the use of the singular pronoun *it* to refer to plural *profits* is incorrect. Finally, two parallel clauses are needed because the company made two announcements: one about the decline of profits and one about the future of its business.

A   Use of *it* to refer to *profits* is incorrect; use of *will* is incorrect; the second announcement is not clear.

B   **Correct.** Removal of *it to* avoids the error in grammar and eliminates unnecessary words in this sentence. The addition of *that* before *its business would* creates another parallel clause associated with *announced* and clarifies that there is a second announcement. Finally, this sentence properly uses *had expected* and *would*.

C   Incorrectly uses *expected*; use of *it* to refer to *profits* is incorrect, and *would* is unnecessary; the overuse of *it* and *its* is confusing; *will* is incorrectly used instead of *would*.

D   Incorrectly uses *expected*; *them to* is both unnecessary and awkward; also, a second announcement is not made clear.

E   Incorrectly uses *expected*; incorrectly uses the future perfect (*will have improved*) that implies the action will be completed rather than ongoing.

The correct answer is B.

140. Rock samples taken from the remains of an asteroid about twice the size of the 6-mile-wide asteroid that eradicated the dinosaurs has been dated to be 3.47 billion years old and thus is evidence of the earliest known asteroid impact on Earth.

(A) has been dated to be 3.47 billion years old and thus is
(B) has been dated at 3.47 billion years old and thus
(C) have been dated to be 3.47 billion years old and thus are
(D) have been dated as being 3.47 billion years old and thus
(E) have been dated at 3.47 billion years old and thus are

Agreement; Idiom

The plural subject of this sentence, *Rock samples*, requires plural verb phrases—*have been dated* and *are* rather than *has been dated* and *is*. The idiomatic way of expressing estimation of age is with the phrase *dated at*.

A   The subject and verbs do not agree; *dated to be ...* is not idiomatic.
B   The subject and verb do not agree; the conjunction *and thus* should be followed by a verb.
C   *Dated to be* is not idiomatic.
D   *As being* is not idiomatic; the conjunction *and thus* should be followed by a verb.
E   **Correct.** The plural verbs match the plural subject, and the wording of the sentence is idiomatic.

The correct answer is E.

10.0 Analytical Writing Assessment

10.0 Analytical Writing Assessment

The Analytical Writing Assessment (AWA) consists of two 30-minute writing tasks:

- **Analysis of an Argument**
  You must read a brief argument, analyze the reasoning behind it, and then write a critique of the argument. In this task, you are not asked to state your opinion but rather to analyze the one given. You may, for example, consider what questionable assumptions underlie the author's thinking, what alternative explanations or counterexamples might weaken the conclusion, or what sort of evidence could help strengthen or refute the argument.

- **Analysis of an Issue**
  You must analyze a given issue or opinion and then explain your point of view on the subject by citing relevant reasons and/or examples drawn from your experience, observations, or reading.

For both tasks, you will use the computer keyboard to type in your response. You will be able to use typical word-processing functions—that is, you can cut, copy, paste, undo, and redo. These functions can be accessed either by using the keyboard or by using the mouse to click on icons on the screen. You will be able to take notes when planning your response.

It is important that you plan carefully before you begin writing. Read the specific analytical writing task several times to make sure you understand exactly what is expected. Think about how you might present your analysis. You may want to sketch an outline to help you plan and organize. Keep in mind the 30-minute time limit as you plan your response—keep your analysis brief enough to give you plenty of time to write a first draft, read it over carefully, and make any necessary corrections or revisions before you run out of time. As you write, try to keep your language clear, your sentences concise, and the flow of your ideas logical. State your premise clearly at the beginning, and make sure you present a strong conclusion at the end.

10.1 What Is Measured

The Analytical Writing Assessment is designed as a direct measure of your ability to think critically and communicate your ideas. More specifically, the Analysis of an Issue task tests your ability to explore the complexities of an issue or opinion and, if appropriate, to take a position that is informed by your understanding of those complexities. The Analysis of an Argument task tests your ability to formulate an appropriate and constructive critique of a specific conclusion based upon a specific line of thinking.

The issue and argument that you will find on the test concern topics of general interest, some related to business and some pertaining to a variety of other subjects. It is important to note, however, that no AWA question presupposes any specific knowledge of business or other specific content areas. Only your capacity to write analytically is assessed.

College and university faculty members from various subject-matter areas, including but not limited to management education, will evaluate your AWA essays. For information on how readers are qualified, visit www.mba.com. Readers are trained to be sensitive and fair in evaluating the responses of nonnative speakers of English. A computer scoring program will also evaluate your essays. Your responses will be scored on the basis of:

- the overall quality of your ideas

- your ability to organize, develop, and express those ideas

- how well you provide relevant supporting reasons and examples

- your ability to control the elements of standard written English

10.2 Test-Taking Strategies

General

1. **Read the question carefully.**
   Make sure you have taken all parts of a question into account before you begin to respond to it.

2. **Do not start to write immediately.**
   Take a few minutes to think about the question and plan a response before you begin writing. You may find it helpful to write a brief outline or jot down some ideas on the erasable notepad provided. Take care to organize your ideas and develop them fully, but leave time to reread your response and make any revisions that you think would improve it.

Analysis of an Issue

1. **Be careful about taking a position.**
   Although many Analysis of an Issue questions require you to take a position, think carefully before you do so. Readers will assess your ability to think and write critically. Try to show that you recognize and understand the complexities of an issue or an opinion before you take a position on it. Consider the issue from different perspectives, and think about your own experiences and things you have read that relate to the issue. Rather than announce a position, your answer should develop a position logically.

2. **Avoid presenting a "catalog" of examples.**
   It is essential to illustrate and develop your ideas by means of examples drawn from your observations, experiences, and reading, but keep in mind that one or two well-chosen, well-developed examples are much more effective than a long list.

Analysis of an Argument

1. **Focus on the task of analyzing and critiquing a line of thinking or reasoning.**
   Get used to asking yourself questions such as the following: *What questionable assumptions might underlie the thinking? What alternative explanations might be given? What counterexamples might be raised? What additional evidence might prove useful in fully and fairly evaluating the reasoning?*

2. **Develop fully any examples you use.**
   Do not simply list your examples—explain how they illustrate your point.

3. **Discuss alternative explanations or counterexamples.**
   These techniques allow you to introduce illustrations and examples drawn from your observations, experiences, and reading.

4. **Make sure your response reads like a narrative.**
   Your response should not read like an outline. It should use full sentences, a coherent organizational scheme, logical transitions between points, and appropriately introduced and developed examples.

10.3 The Directions

These are the directions that you will see for the Analytical Writing Assessment. If you read them carefully and understand them clearly before going to sit for the test, you will not need to spend too much time reviewing them when you take the GMAT® test. They read as follows:

ANALYSIS OF AN ISSUE

In this section, you will need to analyze the issue presented and explain your views on it. There is no "correct" answer. Instead, you should consider various perspectives as you develop your own position on the issue.

Writing Your Response: Take a few minutes to think about the issue and plan a response before you begin writing. Be sure to organize your ideas and develop them fully, but leave time to reread your response and make any revisions that you think are necessary.

Evaluation of Your Response: Scores will take into account how well you:

- organize, develop, and express your ideas about the issue presented

- provide relevant supporting reasons and examples

- control the elements of standard written English

ANALYSIS OF AN ARGUMENT

In this section, you will be asked to write a critique of the argument presented. *You are* not *asked to present your own views on the subject.*

Writing Your Response: Take a few minutes to evaluate the argument and plan a response before you begin writing. Be sure to leave enough time to reread your response and make any revisions that you think are necessary.

Evaluation of Your Response: Scores will reflect how well you:

- organize, develop, and express your ideas about the argument presented

- provide relevant supporting reasons and examples

- control the elements of standard written English

10.4 GMAT® Scoring Guide: Analysis of an Issue

6 Outstanding

A 6 paper presents a cogent, well-articulated analysis of the complexities of the issue and demonstrates mastery of the elements of effective writing.

A typical paper in this category exhibits the following characteristics:

- explores ideas and develops a position on the issue with insightful reasons and/or persuasive examples
- is clearly well organized
- demonstrates superior control of language, including diction and syntactic variety
- demonstrates superior facility with the conventions (grammar, usage, and mechanics) of standard written English but may have minor flaws

5 Strong

A 5 paper presents a well-developed analysis of the complexities of the issue and demonstrates a strong control of the elements of effective writing.

A typical paper in this category exhibits the following characteristics:

- develops a position on the issue with well-chosen reasons and/or examples
- is generally well organized
- demonstrates clear control of language, including diction and syntactic variety
- demonstrates facility with the conventions of standard written English but may have minor flaws

4 Adequate

A 4 paper presents a competent analysis of the issue and demonstrates adequate control of the elements of writing.

A typical paper in this category exhibits the following characteristics:

- develops a position on the issue with relevant reasons and/or examples
- is adequately organized
- demonstrates adequate control of language, including diction and syntax, but may lack syntactic variety
- displays control of the conventions of standard written English but may have some flaws

3 Limited

A 3 paper demonstrates some competence in its analysis of the issue and in its control of the elements of writing but is clearly flawed.

A typical paper in this category exhibits one or more of the following characteristics:

- is vague or limited in developing a position on the issue
- is poorly organized
- is weak in the use of relevant reasons or examples
- uses language imprecisely and/or lacks sentence variety
- contains occasional major errors or frequent minor errors in grammar, usage, and mechanics

2 Seriously Flawed

A 2 paper demonstrates serious weaknesses in analytical writing skills.

A typical paper in this category exhibits one or more of the following characteristics:

- is unclear or seriously limited in presenting or developing a position on the issue
- is disorganized
- provides few, if any, relevant reasons or examples
- has serious and frequent problems in the use of language and sentence structure
- contains numerous errors in grammar, usage, or mechanics that interfere with meaning

1 Fundamentally Deficient

A 1 paper demonstrates fundamental deficiencies in analytical writing skills.

A typical paper in this category exhibits one or more of the following characteristics:

- provides little evidence of the ability to develop or organize a coherent response to the topic
- has severe and persistent errors in language and sentence structure
- contains a pervasive pattern of errors in grammar, usage, and mechanics that severely interferes with meaning

0 No Score

A paper in this category is off topic, not written in English, is merely attempting to copy the topic, or consists only of keystroke characters.

NR Blank

10.5 Sample: Analysis of an Issue

Read the statement and the instructions that follow it and then make any notes that will help you plan your response.

"People often complain that products are not made to last. They feel that making products that wear out fairly quickly wastes both natural and human resources. What they fail to see, however, is that such manufacturing practices keep costs down for the consumer and stimulate demand."

Which do you find more compelling: the complaint about products that do not last or the response to it? Explain your positions using relevant reasons and/or examples from your own experience, observations, or reading.

Sample Paper 6

Many people feel that products are not made to last, and correspondingly, many natural and human resources are wasted. On the other hand, it can be noted that such manufacturing practices keep costs down and hence stimulate demand. In this discussion, I shall present arguments favoring the former statement and refuting the latter statement.

Products that are not made to last waste a great deal of natural and human resources. The exact amount of wasted natural resources depends on the specific product. For example in the automobile industry, the Yugo is the classic example of an underpriced vehicle that was not made to last. Considering that the average Yugo had (not "has" since they are no longer produced!) a life expectancy of two years and 25,000 miles, it was a terrible waste.

Automobile industry standards today create vehicles that are warrantied for about five years and 50,000 miles. By producing cheap Yugos that last less than half as long as most cars are warrantied, the Yugo producer is wasting valuable natural resources. These same resources could be used by Ford or Toyota to produce an Escort or Tercel that will last twice as long, thereby reducing the usage of natural resources by a factor of two.

Human resources in this example are also wasteful. On the production side, manufacturers of a poor quality automobile, like the Yugo, get no personal or profession satisfaction from the fact that their product is the worst automobile in the United States. This knowledge adversely affects the productivity of the Yugo workers.

Conversely, the workers at the Saturn plants constantly receive positive feedback on their successful products. Saturn prides itself with its reputation for quality and innovation—as is seen in its recent massive recall to fix a defect. This recall was handled so well that Saturn's image was actually bolstered. Had a recall occurred at a Yugo plant, the bad situation would have become even worse.

Another factor in the human resources area is the reaction by the consumer. A great deal of human resources have been wasted by Yugo owners waiting for the dreaded tow truck to show up to haul away the Yugo carcass. Any vehicle owner who is uncertain of his/her vehicle's performance at 7 a.m. as he/she is about to drive to work, senses a great deal of despair. This is a great waste of human resources for the consumer.

While the consumer senses the waste of natural and human resources in a poor quality product, so does the manufacturer. People who argue that low quality manufacturing processes keep costs low for the consumer and hence stimulate demand should look at the Yugo example. In the mid 1980s the Yugo was by far the cheapest car in the United States at $3,995. By 1991, the Yugo was no longer sold here and was synonymous with the word "lemon."

Explanation of Score 6

The response above is ambitious and somewhat unusual in its focusing on just one example, the lesson of the now defunct Yugo. Responses, especially outstanding ones, typically discuss several different examples that build support for the writer's position on the issue. This sample response, then, should not be taken as necessarily endorsing a one-example writing strategy. What it does serve to underscore is how much is to be gained by developing, not just listing, examples. The strength of the response lies in the organized and thorough way in which it explores the related aspects of the example it cites. The clear organizational scheme (two major points, with the second point subdivided) is readily apparent: Yugo's substandard cars (1) waste natural resources and (2) waste human resources by (a) destroying worker morale and productivity and (b) inconveniencing and upsetting customers. The persuasiveness of the writer's thinking is especially evident in the discussion of the second major point, the waste of human resources. Here the writer not only considers customers as well as workers, but also introduces the matter of the Saturn recall in order to show, by contrast with the case of Yugo, how a superior product, satisfied workers, and a company image good for marketing are interrelated.

The response complements its outstanding organizational clarity and thorough development with some syntactic variety and an occasional rhetorical flair (e.g., the image of the despairing Yugo owner waiting for "the dreaded tow truck … to haul away the Yugo carcass" in paragraph 6). It is important to point out, however, that the writing is not perfect. For one thing, the opening paragraph is essentially a repeat of the question. In addition, the writing is not—and is not expected to be—entirely free from minor flaws (e.g., "profession satisfaction" [paragraph 4] should obviously be "professional satisfaction," and "Saturn prides itself with" [paragraph 5] should be "Saturn prides itself on"). Nevertheless, these occasional flaws are not serious enough to detract from the general impression that this is an excellent response to the question.

Sample Paper 4

I find the response to the complaint more compelling. Although the complaint is valid, it is most often the case the building a product to last forever will indeed cost more than the average consumer is willing to pay. Creating such a product would require more materials and/or more heavy-duty wear resistant materials which inherently are more expensive. Another factor that would drive costs up is the fact that demand for products would decrease. The demand would decrease since people do not have to replace old products with new product as often. With the increased variable costs for materials combined with a reduction in the production volume associated with lower demand, manufacturers must raise prices to break even or maintain the current level of profits.

Although a few producers may make products to last, it is understandable how these companies can be driven out of existence. If a new competitor enters the market with a similar product that has a shorter life but a substantially lower price, then they will probably steal major portions of the other company's market share. The effects depend heavily upon the consumers' perception of quality and what the customers requirements from the product actually are.

For example, consumers may decide between two types of automobiles. One car may be built to last a long time but may not have the performance or be as comfortable as another car that is cheaper. So most consumers would purchase the cheaper car even though it may not last as long as the heavy-duty car. Consumers may not realize that the more expensive car is of higher quality in the sense that it will last longer and will not be willing to pay the extra cost.

Consumer decisions also depend on what consumers are actually looking for in a product. Consumers typically get tired of driving the same car for many years and want to buy new cars fairly often. This tendency forces producers to keep costs low enough to allow low enough prices for people to buy cars often. People don't want cars to last forever.

In conclusion, producers are in the situation that they're in due to external forces from the consumers. Producers must compete and they have found the best way satisfy the majority of the consumers.

Explanation of Score 4

This response presents a competent analysis of the issue. It develops its position by explaining some of the ways in which the factors mentioned in the question—manufacturing costs and consumer demand—are affected by making products that do not last very long. By way of illustration, the response cites the example of consumers choosing automobiles. Although this example is relevant, it lacks specificity: no actual types of cars are described in terms of the key issue, durability, and no contrast between more and less durable types is developed to prove a point.

Although the response is competently organized and therefore generally easy to follow in its main lines, its clarity is marred by an awkward transition from the second paragraph to the third. The main idea of the second paragraph is that many consumers will abandon a made-to-last expensive product in favor of a substantially cheaper version with a shorter life. But the last sentence of this paragraph, a sentence that is signally unclear, marks an ill-prepared-for change in the direction of the entire response. The "effects" (the word, used loosely and unclearly, seems to refer to the consumer's final decisions about what to buy) are seen to depend not only upon the simple choice between cost and quality but also upon a complex of new forces—aspects of consumer psychology and "requirements" (consumer needs?)—that now suddenly and puzzlingly face the reader. Although the third and fourth paragraphs go on to develop the writer's views about these new forces, the reader never quite recovers from the sense that the response has abruptly changed course. What is more, the consideration of consumer psychology and "requirements" can cause the writer to stray into side issues. For example, pointing out that customers may choose a car on the basis of performance and comfort rather than durability has no direct bearing on the complaint that products are not made to last.

The wording of this response is generally appropriate, although the language is occasionally awkward, as in "keep costs low enough to allow low enough prices" (paragraph 4) and "producers are in the situation that they're in" (paragraph 5).

Sample Paper 2

I find the response better than the complaint of people. The response seems to originate without much thought involved. It is more of an emotional complaint than one anchored in logic or thought. Yes, it is a waste of human resources but that is without consideration to the benefits: lower costs and stimulated demand. Thus, the response fails to recognize the benefits.

The strength of the response is that it forces the reader to reconsider the complaint. It adds a new dimension to the argument. It, however, fails to address the issue of wasting human resources. Does this mean the responder agrees with the notion of wasting resources.

In all actuality both the response and complaint as ineffective. The complaint doesn't recognize or address the benefits, like the response doesn't address the issue of wasting resources. The response, however, does bring in a new dimension and thus weakens the argument of the complaint.

Explanation of Score 2

In this piece of writing, the writer's purpose seems to waver between defending "the response" against "the complaint" and weighing the relative strengths and limitations of both. In addition, the writer offers no new reasons or specific examples and so ends up merely repeating assertions made in "the complaint" and "the response."

The writing is marked throughout by vagueness. The writer's decision to adopt the topic's terms "response" and "complaint" as a convenient shorthand for the two positions articulated leads immediately to a confusing lack of specificity, compounded in the first paragraph by the fact that the two terms are mixed up (e.g., "response" in the second and the fifth sentences is meant to refer to "complaint"). The first paragraph is made even more confusing because the pronouns "it" and "that" lack antecedents in the sentence "Yes, it is a waste of human resources but that is without consideration to the benefits."

The general lack of clarity is aggravated by errors in conventional English grammar and usage, most of them concentrated in paragraph 3. The first sentence begins with an unidiomatic phrase ("In all actuality") and lacks a verb ("both the response and complaint as ineffective"). The second sentence incorrectly uses "like" instead of "just as": "The complaint doesn't recognize or address … like the response doesn't address." In short, the writing fits the description of seriously flawed prose in the scoring guide: it displays "serious and frequent problems in the use of language and sentence structure."

10.6 Analysis of an Issue Sample Topics

"In some countries, television and radio programs are carefully censored for offensive language and behavior. In other countries, there is little or no censorship."

In your view, to what extent should government or any other group be able to censor television or radio programs? Explain, giving relevant reasons and/or examples to support your position.

"It is unrealistic to expect individual nations to make, independently, the sacrifices necessary to conserve energy. International leadership and worldwide cooperation are essential if we expect to protect the world's energy resources for future generations."

Discuss the extent to which you agree or disagree with the opinion stated above. Support your views with reasons and/or examples from your own experience, observations, or reading.

"Corporations and other businesses should try to eliminate the many ranks and salary grades that classify employees according to their experience and expertise. A 'flat' organizational structure is more likely to encourage collegiality and cooperation among employees."

Discuss the extent to which you agree or disagree with the opinion stated above. Support your views with reasons and/or examples from your own experience, observations, or reading.

"Of all the manifestations* of power, restraint in the use of that power impresses people most."

*manifestations: apparent signs or indicators

Explain what you think this quotation means and discuss the extent to which you agree or disagree with it. Develop your position with reasons and/or specific examples drawn from history, current events, or your own experience, observations, or reading.

"All groups and organizations should function as teams in which everyone makes decisions and shares responsibilities and duties. Giving one person central authority and responsibility for a project or task is not an effective way to get work done."

To what extent do you agree or disagree with the opinion expressed above? Support your views with reasons and/or specific examples drawn from your own work or school experiences, your observations, or your reading.

"There is only one definition of success—to be able to spend your life in your own way."

To what extent do you agree or disagree with this definition of success? Support your position by using reasons and examples from your reading, your own experience, or your observation of others.

"The best way to give advice to other people is to find out what they want and then advise them how to attain it."

Discuss the extent to which you agree or disagree with the opinion expressed above. Support your point of view with reasons and/or examples from your own experience, observations, or reading.

"For hundreds of years, the monetary system of most countries has been based on the exchange of metal coins and printed pieces of paper. However, because of recent developments in technology, the international community should consider replacing the entire system of coins and paper with a system of electronic accounts of credits and debits."

Discuss the extent to which you agree or disagree with the opinion stated above. Support your views with reasons and/or examples from your own experience, observations, or reading.

"Employees should keep their private lives and personal activities as separate as possible from the workplace."

Discuss the extent to which you agree or disagree with the opinion stated above. Support your views with reasons and/or examples from your own experience, observations, or reading.

"In any enterprise, the process of making or doing something is ultimately more important than the final product."

Discuss the extent to which you agree or disagree with the opinion expressed above. Support your point of view with reasons and/or examples from your own experience, observations, or reading.

"When someone achieves greatness in any field—such as the arts, science, politics, or business—that person's achievements are more important than any of his or her personal faults."

Discuss the extent to which you agree or disagree with the opinion stated above. Support your views with reasons and/or examples from your own experience, observations, or reading.

"Education has become the main provider of individual opportunity in our society. Just as property and money once were the keys to success, education has now become the element that most ensures success in life."

In your opinion, how accurate is the view expressed above? Explain, using reasons and examples based on your own experience, observations, or reading.

"Responsibility for preserving the natural environment ultimately belongs to each individual person, not to government."

Discuss the extent to which you agree or disagree with the opinion stated above. Support your views with reasons and/or examples from your own experience, observations, or reading.

"Organizations should be structured in a clear hierarchy in which the people at each level, from top to bottom, are held accountable for completing a particular component of the work. Any other organizational structure goes against human nature and will ultimately prove fruitless."

Discuss the extent to which you agree or disagree with the opinion expressed above. Support your point of view with reasons and/or examples from your own experience, observations, or reading.

"Nations should cooperate to develop regulations that limit children's access to adult material on the Internet."

Discuss the extent to which you agree or disagree with the opinion stated above. Support your views with reasons and/or examples from your own experience, observations, or reading.

"Public buildings reveal much about the attitudes and values of the society that builds them. Today's new schools, courthouses, airports, and libraries, for example, reflect the attitudes and values of today's society."

Discuss the extent to which you agree or disagree with the opinion stated above. Support your views with reasons and/or examples from your own experience, observations, or reading.

"Some people believe that the best approach to effective time management is to make detailed daily and long-term plans and then to adhere to them. However, this highly structured approach to work is counterproductive. Time management needs to be flexible so that employees can respond to unexpected problems as they arise."

Discuss the extent to which you agree or disagree with the opinion expressed above. Support your point of view with reasons and/or examples from your own experience, observations, or reading.

"If the primary duty and concern of a corporation is to make money, then conflict is inevitable when the corporation must also acknowledge a duty to serve society."

From your perspective, how accurate is the above statement? Support your position with reasons and/or examples from your own experience, observations, or reading.

"Some employers who recruit recent college graduates for entry-level jobs evaluate applicants only on their performance in business courses such as accounting, marketing, and economics. However, other employers also expect applicants to have a broad background in such courses as history, literature, and philosophy."

Do you think that, in the application process, employers should emphasize one type of background—either specialization in business courses or a more varied academic preparation—over the other? Why or why not? Develop your position by using reasons and/or examples from your own experience, observations, or reading.

"In this age of automation, many people complain that humans are becoming subservient to machines. But, in fact, machines are continually improving our lives."

Discuss the extent to which you agree or disagree with the opinion expressed above. Support your point of view with reasons and/or examples from your own experience, observations, or reading.

"Job security and salary should be based on employee performance, not on years of service. Rewarding employees primarily for years of service discourages people from maintaining consistently high levels of productivity."

Discuss the extent to which you agree or disagree with the opinion stated above. Support your views with reasons and/or examples from your own experience, observations, or reading.

"Clearly, government has a responsibility to support the arts. However, if that support is going to produce anything of value, government must place no restrictions on the art that is produced."

To what extent do you agree or disagree with the opinion expressed above? Develop your position by giving specific reasons and/or examples from your own experience, observations, or reading.

"Schools should be responsible only for teaching academic skills and not for teaching ethical and social values."

Discuss the extent to which you agree or disagree with the opinion expressed above. Support your point of view with reasons and/or examples from your own experience, observations, or reading.

"A powerful business leader has far more opportunity to influence the course of a community or a nation than does any government official."

Discuss the extent to which you agree or disagree with the opinion stated above. Support your views with reasons and/or examples from your own experience, observations, or reading.

"The best strategy for managing a business, or any enterprise, is to find the most capable people and give them as much authority as possible."

Discuss the extent to which you agree or disagree with the opinion stated above. Support your views with reasons and/or examples from your own experience, observations, or reading.

"Location has traditionally been one of the most important determinants of a business's success. The importance of location is not likely to change, no matter how advanced the development of computer communications and others kinds of technology becomes."

Discuss the extent to which you agree or disagree with the opinion stated above. Support your views with reasons and/or examples from your own experience, observations, or reading.

"A company's long-term success is primarily dependent on the job satisfaction and the job security felt by the company's employees."

Discuss the extent to which you agree or disagree with the opinion stated above. Support your views with reasons and/or examples from your own experience, observations, or reading.

"Because businesses use high-quality advertising to sell low-quality products, schools should give students extensive training in how to make informed decisions before making purchases."

Discuss the extent to which you agree or disagree with the opinion expressed above. Support your point of view with reasons and/or examples from your own experience, observations, or reading.

"Too many people think only about getting results. The key to success, however, is to focus on the specific task at hand and not to worry about results."

What do you think this piece of advice means, and do you think that it is, on the whole, worth following? Support your views with reasons and/or examples drawn from your own experience, observations, or reading.

"Companies benefit when they discourage employees from working extra hours or taking work home. When employees spend their leisure time without 'producing' something for the job, they will be more focused and effective when they return to work."

Discuss the extent to which you agree or disagree with the opinion expressed above. Support your point of view with reasons and/or examples from your own experience, observations, or reading.

"Financial gain should be the most important factor in choosing a career."

Discuss the extent to which you agree or disagree with the opinion stated above. Support your views with reasons and/or examples from your own experience, observations, or reading.

"You can tell the ideas of a nation by its advertisements."

Explain what you think this quotation means and discuss the extent to which you agree or disagree with it. Develop your position with reasons and/or specific examples drawn from history, current events, or your own experience, observations, or reading.

"People are likely to accept as a leader only someone who has demonstrated an ability to perform the same tasks that he or she expects others to perform."

Discuss the extent to which you agree or disagree with the opinion stated above. Support your views with reasons and/or examples from your own experience, observations, or reading.

"All citizens should be required to perform a specified amount of public service. Such service would benefit not only the country as a whole but also the individual participants."

Discuss the extent to which you agree or disagree with the opinion stated above. Support your views with reasons and/or examples from your own experience, observations, or reading.

"Business relations are infected through and through with the disease of short-sighted motives. We are so concerned with immediate results and short-term goals that we fail to look beyond them."

Assuming that the term "business relations" can refer to the decisions and actions of any organization—for instance, a small family business, a community association, or a large international corporation—explain the extent to which you think that this criticism is valid. In your discussion of the issue, use reasons and/or examples from your own experience, your observation of others, or your reading.

"Businesses and other organizations have overemphasized the importance of working as a team. Clearly, in any human group, it is the strong individual, the person with the most commitment and energy, who gets things done."

Discuss the extent to which you agree or disagree with the opinion stated above. Support your views with reasons and/or examples from your own experience, observations, or reading.

"Since science and technology are becoming more and more essential to modern society, schools should devote more time to teaching science and technology and less to teaching the arts and humanities."

Discuss the extent to which you agree or disagree with the opinion stated above. Support your views with reasons and/or examples from your own experience, observations, or reading.

"Courtesy is rapidly disappearing from everyday interactions, and as a result, we are all the poorer for it."

From your perspective, is this an accurate observation? Why or why not? Explain, using reasons and/or examples from your own experience, observations, or reading.

"It is difficult for people to achieve professional success without sacrificing important aspects of a fulfilling personal life."

Discuss the extent to which you agree or disagree with the opinion stated above. Support your views with reasons and/or examples from your own experience, observations, or reading.

"With the increasing emphasis on a global economy and international cooperation, people need to understand that their role as citizens of the world is more important than their role as citizens of a particular country."

Discuss the extent to which you agree or disagree with the opinion stated above. Support your views with reasons and/or examples from your own experience, observations, or reading.

"The best way to preserve the natural environment is to impose penalties—whether fines, imprisonment, or other punishments—on those who are most responsible for polluting or otherwise damaging it."

Discuss the extent to which you agree or disagree with the opinion expressed above. Support your point of view with reasons and/or examples from your own experience, observations, or reading.

"Scientists are continually redefining the standards for what is beneficial or harmful to the environment. Since these standards keep shifting, companies should resist changing their products and processes in response to each new recommendation until those recommendations become government regulations."

Discuss the extent to which you agree or disagree with the opinion stated above. Support your views with reasons and/or examples from your own experience, observations, or reading.

"The most important reason for studying history is not that knowledge of history can make us better people or a better society but that it can provide clues to solving the societal problems that we face today."

Discuss the extent to which you agree or disagree with the opinion expressed above. Support your point of view with reasons and/or examples from your own experience, observations, or reading.

"All companies should invest heavily in advertising because high-quality advertising can sell almost any product or service."

Discuss the extent to which you agree or disagree with the opinion expressed above. Support your point of view with reasons and/or examples from your own experience, observations, or reading.

"The most effective way for a businessperson to maximize profits over a long period of time is to follow the highest standards of ethics."

Discuss the extent to which you agree or disagree with the opinion stated above. Support your views with reasons and/or examples from your own experience, observations, or reading.

"Businesses are as likely as are governments to establish large bureaucracies, but bureaucracy is far more damaging to a business than it is to a government."

Discuss the extent to which you agree or disagree with the opinion expressed above. Support your point of view with reasons and/or examples from your own experience, observations, or reading.

"The primary responsibility for preventing environmental damage belongs to government, not to individuals or private industry."

Discuss the extent to which you agree or disagree with the opinion expressed above. Support your point of view with reasons and/or examples from your own experience, observations, or reading.

"In matching job candidates with job openings, managers must consider not only such variables as previous work experience and educational background but also personality traits and work habits, which are more difficult to judge."

What do you consider essential in an employee or colleague? Explain, using reasons and/or examples from your work or work-like experiences, or from your observations of others.

"Ask most older people to identify the key to success, and they are likely to reply 'hard work.' Yet, I would tell people starting off in a career that work in itself is not the key. In fact, you have to approach work cautiously—too much or too little can be self-defeating."

To what extent do you agree or disagree with this view of work? Develop your position by using reasons and/or examples from your reading, experience, or observations.

"How far should a supervisor go in criticizing the performance of a subordinate? Some highly successful managers have been known to rely on verbal abuse and intimidation. Do you think that this is an effective means of communicating expectations? If not, what alternative should a manager use in dealing with someone whose work is less than satisfactory?"

Explain your views on this issue. Be sure to support your position with reasons and/or examples from your own experience, observations, or reading.

"The presence of a competitor is always beneficial to a company. Competition forces a company to change itself in ways that improve its practices."

Discuss the extent to which you agree or disagree with the opinion stated above. Support your views with reasons and/or examples from your own experience, observations, or reading.

"Successful individuals typically set their next goal somewhat—but not too much—above their last achievement. In this way, they steadily raise their level of aspiration."

In your opinion, how accurate is this statement? Explain, using specific reasons and examples from your reading, your own experience, or your observation of others.

"The term 'user-friendly' is usually applied to the trouble-free way that computer software moves people from screen to screen, function to function. However, the term can also refer to a government office, a library, public transportation, or anything designed to provide information or services in an easy, friendly way. Just as all societies have many striking examples of user-friendly services, so do they abound in examples of user-unfriendly systems."

Identify a system or service that you have found to be either "user-friendly" or "user-unfriendly." Discuss, from the user's perspective, in what way the system either is or is not easy to use and explain the consequences or effect of such a system.

"Popular entertainment is overly influenced by commercial interests. Superficiality, obscenity, and violence characterize films and television today because those qualities are commercially successful."

Discuss the extent to which you agree or disagree with this opinion. To support your position, use reasons and/or examples from your reading, your observations, or your experiences as a consumer of popular entertainment.

———————————————

"Never tell people how to do things. Tell them what to do, and they will surprise you with their ingenuity." To what extent do you agree or disagree with the opinion expressed above?

Explain your point of view by giving reasons and/or examples from your own experience, observations, or reading.

———————————————

"The secret of business is to know something that nobody else knows."

Explain what you think the above quotation means and discuss the extent to which you agree or disagree with it. Support your position with relevant reasons and/or examples from your own experience, observations, or reading.

———————————————

"Everywhere, it seems, there are clear and positive signs that people are becoming more respectful of one another's differences."

In your opinion, how accurate is the view expressed above? Use reasons and/or examples from your own experience, observations, or reading to develop your position.

———————————————

"What is the final objective of business? It is to make the obtaining of a living—the obtaining of food, clothing, shelter, and a minimum of luxuries—so mechanical and so little time-consuming that people shall have time for other things." — A business leader, circa 1930

Explain what you think the quotation above means and discuss the extent to which you agree or disagree with the view of business it expresses. Support your views with reasons and/or examples from your own experience, observations, or reading.

———————————————

"Juvenile crime is a serious social problem, and businesses must become more involved in helping to prevent it."

Discuss the extent to which you agree or disagree with the opinion expressed above. Support your point of view with reasons and/or examples from your own experience, observations, or reading.

———————————————

"Employers should have no right to obtain information about their employees' health or other aspects of their personal lives without the employees' permission."

Discuss the extent to which you agree or disagree with the opinion stated above. Support your views with reasons and/or examples from your own experience, observations, or reading.

"Even at its best, a government is a tremendous burden to business, though a necessary one."

Discuss the extent to which you agree or disagree with the opinion expressed above. Support your point of view with reasons and/or examples from your own experience, observations, or reading.

"What education fails to teach us is to see the human community as one. Rather than focus on the unique differences that separate one nation from another, education should focus on the similarities among all people and places on Earth."

What do you think of the view of education expressed above? Explain, using reasons and/or specific examples from your own experience, observations, or reading.

"As government bureaucracy increases, citizens become more and more separated from their government."

Discuss the extent to which you agree or disagree with the opinion expressed above. Support your point of view with reasons and/or examples from your own experience, observations, or reading.

"The goal of business should not be to make as big a profit as possible. Instead, business should also concern itself with the well-being of the public."

Discuss the extent to which you agree or disagree with the opinion expressed above. Support your point of view with reasons and/or examples from your own experience, observations, or reading.

"The rise of multinational corporations is leading to global homogeneity.* Because people everywhere are beginning to want the same products and services, regional differences are rapidly disappearing."

* homogeneity: sameness, similarity

Discuss the extent to which you agree or disagree with the opinion expressed above. Support your point of view with reasons and/or examples from your own experience, observations, or reading.

"Manufacturers are responsible for ensuring that their products are safe. If a product injures someone, for whatever reason, the manufacturer should be held legally and financially accountable for the injury."

Discuss the extent to which you agree or disagree with the opinion expressed above. Support your point of view with reasons and/or examples from your own experience, observations, or reading.

"Work greatly influences people's personal lives—their special interests, their leisure activities, even their appearance away from the workplace."

Discuss the extent to which you agree or disagree with the opinion expressed above. Support your point of view with reasons and/or examples from your own experience, observations, or reading.

"Since the physical work environment affects employee productivity and morale, the employees themselves should have the right to decide how their workplace is designed."

Discuss the extent to which you agree or disagree with the opinion stated above. Support your views with reasons and/or examples from your own experience, observations, or reading.

"The most important quality in an employee is not specific knowledge or technical competence. Instead, it is the ability to work well with other employees."

Discuss the extent to which you agree or disagree with the opinion expressed above. Support your point of view with reasons and/or examples from your own experience, observations, or reading.

"So long as no laws are broken, there is nothing unethical about doing whatever you need to do to promote existing products or to create new products."

Discuss the extent to which you agree or disagree with the opinion expressed above. Support your point of view with reasons and/or examples from your own experience, observations, or reading.

"Commercialism has become too widespread. It has even crept into schools and places of worship. Every nation should place limits on what kinds of products, if any, can be sold at certain events or places."

Discuss the extent to which you agree or disagree with the opinion expressed above. Support your point of view with reasons and/or examples from your own experience, observations, or reading.

"Companies should not try to improve employees' performance by giving incentives—for example, awards or gifts. These incentives encourage negative kinds of behavior instead of encouraging a genuine interest in doing the work well."

Discuss the extent to which you agree or disagree with the opinion stated above. Support your views with reasons and/or examples from your own experience, observations, or reading.

"People often give the following advice: "Be yourself. Follow your instincts and behave in a way that feels natural."

Do you think that, in general, this is good advice? Why or why not? Develop your point of view by giving reasons and/or examples from your own experience, observations, or reading.

"The people we remember best are the ones who broke the rules."

Discuss the extent to which you agree or disagree with the opinion expressed above. Support your point of view with reasons and/or examples from your own experience, observations, or reading.

"There are essentially two forces that motivate people: self-interest and fear."

Discuss the extent to which you agree or disagree with the opinion stated above. Support your position with reasons and/or examples from your own experience, observations, or reading.

"For a leader there is nothing more difficult, and therefore more important, than to be able to make decisions."

Discuss the extent to which you agree or disagree with the opinion expressed above. Support your point of view with reasons and/or examples from your own experience, observations, or reading.

"Although 'genius' is difficult to define, one of the qualities of genius is the ability to transcend traditional modes of thought and create new ones."

Explain what you think the above statement means and discuss the extent to which you agree or disagree with this definition of genius. In your discussion, be sure to include at least one example of someone who, in your opinion, exemplifies genius or a particular characteristic of genius.

"Most people would agree that buildings represent a valuable record of any society's past, but controversy arises when old buildings stand on ground that modern planners feel could be better used for modern purposes."

In your opinion, which is more important—preserving historic buildings or encouraging modern development? Explain your position, using reasons and examples based on your own experiences, observations, or reading.

"The ability to deal with people is as purchasable a commodity as sugar or coffee, and it is worth more than any other commodity under the sun."

Explain what you think the above quotation means and discuss the extent to which you agree or disagree with it. Support your position with relevant reasons and/or examples from your own experience, observations, or reading.

"As individuals, people save too little and borrow too much."

From your perspective, how accurate is the view expressed above? In your discussion, be sure to consider the conditions under which it is appropriate to save money and the conditions under which it is appropriate to borrow. Develop your position using reasons and/or examples from your own experience, observations, or reading.

"No one can possibly achieve any real and lasting success or 'get rich' in business by conforming to conventional practices or ways of thinking."

Discuss the extent to which you agree or disagree with the opinion stated above. Support your views with reasons and/or examples from your own experience, observations, or reading.

"Business and government must do more, much more, to meet the needs and goals of women in the workplace."

What do you think of the opinion expressed above? In your discussion, be sure to use reasons and/or examples from your own experience, observations, or reading.

"We shape our buildings and afterward our buildings shape us."

Explain what you think this statement means and discuss the extent to which you do or do not agree with it. Support your views with reasons and/or specific examples from your experience, observations, or reading.

"A business should not be held responsible for providing customers with complete information about its products or services; customers should have the responsibility of gathering information about the products or services they may want to buy."

Discuss the extent to which you agree or disagree with the opinion stated above. Support your views with reasons and/or examples from your own experience, observations, or reading.

"Advertising is the most influential and therefore the most important artistic achievement of the twentieth century."

Discuss the extent to which you agree or disagree with the opinion expressed above. Support your point of view with reasons and/or examples from your own experience, observations, or reading.

"Whether promoting a product, an event, or a person, an advertising campaign is most effective when it appeals to emotion rather than to reason."

Discuss the extent to which you agree or disagree with the opinion expressed above. Support your point of view with reasons and/or examples from your own experience, observations, or reading.

"As technologies and the demand for certain services change, many workers will lose their jobs. The responsibility for those people to adjust to such change should belong to the individual worker, not to government or to business."

Discuss the extent to which you agree or disagree with the opinion stated above. Support your position with specific reasons and/or examples drawn from your reading, your observations, or your own experience.

"Each generation must accept blame not only for the hateful words and actions of some of its members but also for the failure of other members to speak out against those words and actions."

Discuss the extent to which you agree or disagree with the opinion expressed above. Support your point of view with reasons and/or examples from your own experience, observations, or reading.

"The study of history is largely a waste of time because it prevents us from focusing on the challenges of the present."

Discuss the extent to which you agree or disagree with the opinion expressed above. Support your point of view with reasons and/or examples from your own experience, observations, or reading.

"People often complain that products are not made to last. They feel that making products that wear out fairly quickly wastes both natural and human resources. What they fail to see, however, is that such manufacturing practices keep costs down for the consumer and stimulate demand."

Which do you find more compelling: the complaint about products that do not last or the response to it? Explain your position using relevant reasons and/or examples drawn from your own experience, observations, or reading.

"Government should establish regulations to reduce or eliminate any suspected health hazards in the environment, even when the scientific studies of these health hazards are incomplete or contradictory."

Discuss the extent to which you agree or disagree with the opinion stated above. Support your views with reasons and/or examples from your own experience, observations, or reading.

"Employees should show loyalty to their company by fully supporting the company's managers and policies, even when the employees believe that the managers and policies are misguided."

Discuss the extent to which you agree or disagree with the opinion stated above. Support your views with reasons and/or examples from your own experience, observations, or reading.

"To be successful, companies should trust their workers and give them as much freedom as possible. Any company that tries to control employees' behavior through a strict system of rewards and punishments will soon find that such controls have a negative effect on employee morale and, consequently, on the company's success."

Discuss the extent to which you agree or disagree with the opinion stated above. Support your views with reasons and/or examples from your own experience, observations, or reading.

"If parents want to prepare their children to succeed in life, teaching the children self-discipline is more important than teaching them self-esteem."

Discuss the extent to which you agree or disagree with the opinion stated above. Support your views with reasons and/or examples from your own experience, observations, or reading.

"Companies are never justified in employing young children, even if the child's family would benefit from the income."

Discuss the extent to which you agree or disagree with the opinion stated above. Support your views with reasons and/or examples from your own experience, observations, or reading.

"In order to understand a society, we must examine the contents of its museums and the subjects of its memorials. What a society chooses to preserve, display, and commemorate is the truest indicator of what the society values."

Discuss the extent to which you agree or disagree with the opinion stated above. Support your views with reasons and/or examples from your own experience, observations, or reading.

"In business, more than in any other social arena, men and women have learned how to share power effectively."

Discuss the extent to which you agree or disagree with the opinion stated above. Support your views with reasons and/or examples from your own experience, observations, or reading.

"In order to accommodate the increasing number of undergraduate students, colleges and universities should offer most courses through distance learning, such as videotaped instruction that can be accessed through the Internet or cable television. Requiring students to appear at a designated time and place is no longer an effective or efficient way of teaching most undergraduate courses."

Discuss the extent to which you agree or disagree with the opinion stated above. Support your views with reasons and/or examples from your own experience, observations, or reading.

"If a nation is to ensure its own economic success, it must maintain a highly competitive educational system in which students compete among themselves and against students from other countries."

Discuss the extent to which you agree or disagree with the opinion stated above. Support your views with reasons and/or examples from your own experience, observations, or reading.

"In order to force companies to improve policies and practices considered unethical or harmful, society should rely primarily on consumer action—such as refusal to buy product—rather than legislative action."

Discuss the extent to which you agree or disagree with the opinion stated above. Support your views with reasons and/or examples from your own experience, observations, or reading.

"The automobile has caused more problems than it has solved. Most societies would probably be much better off if the automobile had never been invented."

Discuss the extent to which you agree or disagree with the opinion stated above. Support your views with reasons and/or examples from your own experience, observations, or reading.

"An advanced degree may help someone get a particular job. Once a person begins working, however, the advanced degree and the formal education it represents are rarely relevant to success on the job."

Discuss the extent to which you agree or disagree with the opinion stated above. Support your views with reasons and/or examples from your own experience, observations, or reading.

"Most people today place too much emphasis on satisfying their immediate desires. The overall quality of life would be greatly improved if we all focused instead on meeting our long-term needs."

Discuss the extent to which you agree or disagree with the opinion stated above. Support your views with reasons and/or examples from your own experience, observations, or reading.

"The value of any nation should be measured more by its scientific and artistic achievements than by its business successes."

Discuss the extent to which you agree or disagree with the opinion stated above. Support your views with reasons and/or examples from your own experience, observations, or reading.

"All archaeological treasures should remain in the country in which they were originally discovered. These works should not be exported, even if museums in other parts of the world are better able to preserve and display them."

Discuss the extent to which you agree or disagree with the opinion stated above. Support your views with reasons and/or examples from your own experience, observations, or reading.

"The most effective way for managers to assign work is to divide complex tasks into their simpler component parts. This way, each worker completes a small portion of the task but contributes to the whole."

Discuss the extent to which you agree or disagree with the opinion stated above. Support your views with reasons and/or examples from your own experience, observations, or reading.

"People are overwhelmed by the increasing amount of information available on the computer. Therefore, the immediate goal of the information technology industry should be to help people learn how to obtain the information they need efficiently and wisely."

Discuss the extent to which you agree or disagree with the opinion stated above. Support your views with reasons and/or examples from your own experience, observations, or reading.

"Employees should not have full access to their own personnel files. If, for example, employees were allowed to see certain confidential materials, the people supplying that information would not be likely to express their opinions candidly."

Discuss the extent to which you agree or disagree with the opinion stated above. Support your views with reasons and/or examples from your own experience, observations, or reading.

"All personnel evaluations at a company should be multidirectional—that is, people at every level of the organization should review not only those working 'under' them but also those working 'over' them."

Discuss the extent to which you agree or disagree with the opinion stated above. Support your views with reasons and/or examples from your own experience, observations, or reading.

———————————————

"The most effective business leaders are those who maintain the highest ethical standards."

Discuss the extent to which you agree or disagree with the opinion stated above. Support your views with reasons and/or examples from your own experience, observations, or reading.

———————————————

"Because of recent advancements in business and technology, the overall quality of life in most societies has never been better than at the present time."

Discuss the extent to which you agree or disagree with the opinion stated above. Support your views with reasons and/or examples from your own experience, observations, or reading.

———————————————

"In most fields—including education, politics, and business—the prevailing philosophy never stays in place very long. This pattern of constantly shifting from one theoretical position to another is an inevitable reflection of human nature: people soon tire of the status quo."

Discuss the extent to which you agree or disagree with the opinion stated above. Support your views with reasons and/or examples from your own experience, observations, or reading.

———————————————

"It is essential that the nations of the world increase spending on the building of space stations and on the exploration of other planets, even if that means spending less on other government programs."

Discuss the extent to which you agree or disagree with the opinion stated above. Support your views with reasons and/or examples from your own experience, observations, or reading.

———————————————

"Technology ultimately separates and alienates people more than it serves to bring them together."

Discuss the extent to which you agree or disagree with the opinion stated above. Support your views with reasons and/or examples from your own experience, observations, or reading.

———————————————

"All employees should help decide how the profits of their company or business should be used."

Discuss the extent to which you agree or disagree with the opinion stated above. Support your views with reasons and/or examples from your own experience, observations, or reading.

———————————————

"A government should provide funding for the arts, but only for those artistic works that reflect the values and attitudes of the majority of the population."

Discuss the extent to which you agree or disagree with the opinion stated above. Support your views with reasons and/or examples from your own experience, observations, or reading.

"The well-being of a society depends more on the success of small businesses than on the success of a few large, high-profile corporations."

Discuss the extent to which you agree or disagree with the opinion stated above. Support your views with reasons and/or examples from your own experience, observations, or reading.

"People's loyalty to political parties and political leaders significantly hinders their ability to form their own opinions about an issue."

Discuss the extent to which you agree or disagree with the opinion stated above. Support your views with reasons and/or examples from your own experience, observations, or reading.

"It makes no sense for people with strong technological skills to go to college if they know that they can earn a good salary without a college degree."

Discuss the extent to which you agree or disagree with the opinion stated above. Support your views with reasons and/or examples from your own experience, observations, or reading.

"Companies should not allow the trend toward informality in dress and conduct at the workplace to continue; formality in dress and behavior helps create a more disciplined and productive work environment."

Discuss the extent to which you agree or disagree with the opinion stated above. Support your views with reasons and/or examples from your own experience, observations, or reading.

"Whether people accept or reject an idea depends more on the way it is presented to them than on the merits of the idea itself."

Discuss the extent to which you agree or disagree with the opinion stated above. Support your views with reasons and/or examples from your own experience, observations, or reading.

"Schools should not teach specialized information and techniques, which might soon become outdated. Instead, schools should encourage a more general approach to learning."

Discuss the extent to which you agree or disagree with the opinion stated above. Support your views with reasons and/or examples from your own experience, observations, or reading.

"The current trend of moving frequently from company to company has negative consequences: it causes instability in the workplace and, as a result, instability in society. Therefore, companies should require employees to make a long-term commitment to the organization."

Discuss the extent to which you agree or disagree with the opinion stated above. Support your views with reasons and/or examples from your own experience, observations, or reading.

"The most effective leaders are those who can solve complex problems by finding simple, immediate solutions."

Discuss the extent to which you agree or disagree with the opinion stated above. Support your views with reasons and/or examples from your own experience, observations, or reading.

———————————————

"Formal education should not come to an end when people graduate from college. Instead, people should frequently enroll in courses throughout their lives."

Discuss the extent to which you agree or disagree with the opinion stated above. Support your views with reasons and/or examples from your own experience, observations, or reading.

———————————————

"Laws pertaining to relatively minor crimes must be vigorously enforced if a society hopes to stop more serious crimes."

Discuss the extent to which you agree or disagree with the opinion stated above. Support your views with reasons and/or examples from your own experience, observations, or reading.

———————————————

"In general, a company's most valuable employees are those who are concerned more with efficiency than with quality."

Discuss the extent to which you agree or disagree with the opinion stated above. Support your views with reasons and/or examples from your own experience, observations, or reading.

———————————————

"Instead of relying on the advice of outside experts, organizations should place greater value on the advice that can come only from their own highly experienced employees."

Discuss the extent to which you agree or disagree with the opinion stated above. Support your views with reasons and/or examples from your own experience, observations, or reading.

———————————————

"When judging the qualifications of potential employees, business employers should rely solely on objective information, such as a candidate's résumé and education. Personal interviews are much too subjective and are therefore not a valid basis on which to judge a person's qualifications for a job."

Discuss the extent to which you agree or disagree with the opinion stated above. Support your views with reasons and/or examples from your own experience, observations, or reading.

———————————————

"We can learn more about a society by observing how its people spend their leisure time than by observing them at work."

Discuss the extent to which you agree or disagree with the opinion stated above. Support your views with reasons and/or examples from your own experience, observations, or reading.

"Governments should not be responsible for regulating businesses and other organizations. Instead, society would benefit if the organizations themselves assumed most of the responsibility for establishing and enforcing their own standards and regulations."

Discuss the extent to which you agree or disagree with the opinion stated above. Support your views with reasons and/or examples from your own experience, observations, or reading.

"In any business or other organization, it is better to have managers with strong leadership skills than managers with expertise and work experience in a particular field."

Discuss the extent to which you agree or disagree with the opinion stated above. Support your views with reasons and/or examples from your own experience, observations, or reading.

"Employees should not be asked to provide formal evaluations of their supervisor because they have little basis for judging or even understanding their supervisor's performance."

Discuss the extent to which you agree or disagree with the opinion stated above. Support your views with reasons and/or examples from your own experience, observations, or reading.

"Although many people object to advertisements and solicitations that intrude into their lives through such means as the telephone, the Internet, and television, companies and organizations must have the right to contact potential customers and donors whenever and however they wish."

Discuss the extent to which you agree or disagree with the opinion stated above. Support your views with reasons and/or examples from your own experience, observations, or reading.

"In business courses, professors should teach only factual information and skills, not ethics."

Discuss the extent to which you agree or disagree with the opinion stated above. Support your views with reasons and/or examples from your own experience, observations, or reading.

"In some companies, employees are allowed to express their feelings and opinions about the company by sending electronic messages to everyone in the company. In other companies, this type of communication is strictly prohibited."

What restrictions, if any, do you think companies should place on employees' electronic communications? Support your views with reasons and/or examples from your own experience, observations, or reading.

"Some people claim that in order to protect national parks and historical sites, public access to them should be greatly restricted. Others argue that there should be few restrictions, if any, because such places were intended for everyone to use."

Explain your position on this issue. Support your views with reasons and/or examples from your own experience, observations, or reading.

———————————————————————

"Some people claim that the growth of mass media has stifled intellectual curiosity. Others, however, argue that the availability of so much information and entertainment has encouraged individuals to expand their intellect and creativity."

Explain your position on this issue. Support your views with reasons and/or examples from your own experience, observations, or reading.

———————————————————————

"Some experts maintain that students learn best in a highly structured environment, one that emphasizes discipline, punctuality, and routine. Others insist that educators, if they are to help students maximize their potential, ought to maintain an atmosphere of relative freedom and spontaneity."

Explain your position on the issue of structure versus freedom in an ideal learning environment. Support your views with reasons and/or examples from your own experience, observations, or reading.

———————————————————————

10.7 GMAT® Scoring Guide: Analysis of an Argument

6 Outstanding

A 6 paper presents a cogent, well-articulated critique of the argument and demonstrates mastery of the elements of effective writing.

A typical paper in this category exhibits the following characteristics:

- clearly identifies important features of the argument and analyzes them insightfully
- develops ideas cogently, organizes them logically, and connects them with clear transitions
- effectively supports the main points of the critique
- demonstrates control of language, including diction and syntactic variety
- demonstrates facility with the conventions of standard written English but may have minor flaws

5 Strong

A 5 paper presents a well-developed critique of the argument and demonstrates good control of the elements of effective writing.

A typical paper in this category exhibits the following characteristics:

- clearly identifies important features of the argument and analyzes them in a generally thoughtful way
- develops ideas clearly, organizes them logically, and connects them with appropriate transitions
- sensibly supports the main points of the critique
- demonstrates control of language, including diction and syntactic variety
- demonstrates facility with the conventions of standard written English but may have occasional flaws

4 Adequate

A 4 paper presents a competent critique of the argument and demonstrates adequate control of the elements of writing.

A typical paper in this category exhibits the following characteristics:

- identifies and analyzes important features of the argument
- develops and organizes ideas satisfactorily but may not connect them with transitions
- supports the main points of the critique
- demonstrates sufficient control of language to convey ideas with reasonable clarity
- generally follows the conventions of standard written English but may have some flaws

3 Limited

A 3 paper demonstrates some competence in analytical writing skills and in its control of the elements of writing but is plainly flawed.

A typical paper in this category exhibits one or more of the following characteristics:

- does not identify or analyze most of the important features of the argument, although some analysis of the argument is present
- mainly analyzes tangential or irrelevant matters, or reasons poorly
- is limited in the logical development and organization of ideas
- offers support of little relevance and value for points of the critique
- does not convey meaning clearly
- contains occasional major errors or frequent minor errors in grammar, usage, and mechanics

2 Seriously Flawed

A 2 paper demonstrates serious weaknesses in analytical writing skills.

A typical paper in this category exhibits one or more of the following characteristics:

- does not present a critique based on logical analysis, but may instead present the writer's own views on the subject
- does not develop ideas, or is disorganized and illogical
- provides little, if any, relevant or reasonable support
- has serious and frequent problems in the use of language and in sentence structure
- contains numerous errors in grammar, usage, and mechanics that interfere with meaning

1 Fundamentally Deficient

A 1 paper demonstrates fundamental deficiencies in analytical writing skills.

A typical paper in this category exhibits more than one of the following characteristics:

- provides little evidence of the ability to understand and analyze the argument
- provides little evidence of the ability to develop an organized response
- has severe and persistent errors in language and sentence structure
- contains a pervasive pattern of errors in grammar, usage, and mechanics that results in incoherence

0 No Score

A paper in this category is off topic, not written in English, is merely attempting to copy the topic, or consists only of keystroke characters.

NR Blank

10.8 Sample: Analysis of an Argument

Read the statement and the instructions that follow it, and then make any notes that will help you plan your response.

The following appeared as part of an article in a daily newspaper:

"The computerized on-board warning system that will be installed in commercial airliners will virtually solve the problem of midair plane collisions. One plane's warning system can receive signals from another's transponder—a radio set that signals a plane's course—in order to determine the likelihood of a collision and recommend evasive action."

Discuss how well reasoned you find this argument. In your discussion, be sure to analyze the line of reasoning and the use of evidence in the argument. For example, you may need to consider what questionable assumptions underlie the thinking and what alternative explanations or counterexamples might weaken the conclusion. You can also discuss what sort of evidence would strengthen or refute the argument, what changes in the argument would make it more logically sound, and what, if anything, would help you better evaluate its conclusion.

Sample Paper 6

The argument that this warning system will virtually solve the problem of midair plane collisions omits some important concerns that must be addressed to substantiate the argument. The statement that follows the description of what this warning system will do simply describes the system and how it operates. This alone does not constitute a logical argument in favor of the warning system, and it certainly does not provide support or proof of the main argument.

Most conspicuously, the argument does not address the cause of the problem of midair plane collisions, the use of the system by pilots and flight specialists, or who is involved in the midair plane collisions. First, the argument assumes that the cause of the problem is that the planes' courses, the likelihood of collisions, and actions to avoid collisions are unknown or inaccurate. In a weak attempt to support its claim, the argument describes a system that makes all of these things accurately known. But if the cause of the problem of midair plane collisions is that pilots are not paying attention to their computer systems or flight operations, the warning system will not solve the collision problem. Second, the argument never addresses the interface between individuals and the system and how this will affect the warning system's objective of obliterating the problem of collisions. If the pilot or flight specialist does not conform to what the warning system suggests, midair collisions will not be avoided. Finally, if planes other than commercial airliners are involved in the collisions, the problem of these collisions cannot be solved by a warning system that will not be installed on non-commercial airliners. The argument also does not address what would happen in the event that the warning system collapses, fails, or does not work properly.

Because the argument leaves out several key issues, it is not sound or persuasive. If it included the items discussed above instead of solely explaining what the system supposedly does, the argument would have been more thorough and convincing.

Explanation of Score 6

This response is, as the scoring guide requires of a 6, "cogent" and "well articulated": all the points made not only bear directly on the argument to be analyzed, but also contribute to a single, integrated development of the writer's critique. The writer begins by making the controlling point that a mere description of the warning system's mode of operation cannot serve as a true argument proving the system's effectiveness, since the description overlooks several major considerations. The writer then identifies these considerations—what causes midair collisions, how pilots will actually use the commercial airline warning system, what kinds of airplanes are typically involved in midair collisions—and, citing appropriate counterexamples (e.g., what if pilots do not pay attention to their instruments?), explains fully how each oversight undermines the conclusion that the warning system will virtually eliminate midair plane collisions.

Throughout, the writer complements the logically organized development of this critique with good, clear prose that demonstrates the ability not only to control language and vary sentence structure but also to express ideas forcibly (e.g., "the argument never addresses the interface between individuals and the system"). Of course, as in any response written under time constraints, occasional minor flaws can be found. For example, "the argument assumes that the cause of the problem is that the planes' courses, the likelihood of collisions, and actions to avoid collisions are unknown or inaccurate" is wordy and imprecise: how can a course, a likelihood, or actions be inaccurate? But flaws such as these, minor and infrequent, do not interfere with the overall clarity and forcefulness of this outstanding response.

Sample Paper 4

The argument is not logically convincing. It does not state whether all planes can receive signals from each other. It does not state whether planes constantly receive signals. If they only receive signals once every certain time interval, collisions will not definitely be prevented. Further if they receive a signal right before they are about to crash, they cannot avoid each other.

The main flaw in the argument is that it assumes that the two planes, upon receiving each other's signals, will know which evasive action to take. For example, the two planes could be going towards each other and then receive the signals. If one turns at an angle to the left and the other turns at an angle to the right, the two planes will still crash. Even if they receive an updated signal, they will not have time to avoid each other.

The following argument would be more sound and persuasive. The new warning system will solve the problem of midair plane collisions. Each plane will receive constant, continual signals from each other. If the two planes are headed in a direction where they will crash, the system will coordinate the signals, and tell one plane to go one way, and the other plane to go another way. The new system will ensure that the two planes will turn in different directions so they don't crash by trying to prevent the original crash. In addition, the two planes will be able to see themselves and the other on a computer screen, to aid in the evasive action.

Explanation of Score 4

This response competently cites a number of deficiencies in the argument presented: the information given about the nature of the signals sent and received and the evasive action recommended does not warrant the conclusion that the onboard warning system "will virtually solve the problem of midair plane collisions." However, in discussing these insufficiencies in the argument, the response reveals an unevenness in the quality of its reasoning. For example, while it is perfectly legitimate to point out that the argument assumes too much and says too little about the evasive action that will be recommended by the warning system, it is farfetched to suggest that the system might be so poorly designed as to route two approaching airplanes to the same spot. Likewise, while it is fair to question the effectiveness of a warning signal about which the argument says so little, it is not reasonable to assume that the system would be designed to space signals so far apart that they would prove useless. Rather than invent implausibly bad versions of the warning system to prove that it might be ineffective, a stronger response would analyze unexplored possibilities inherent in the information that is given—for example, the possibility that pilots might not be able to respond quickly and effectively to the radio signals the argument says they will receive when the new system is installed. The "more sound and persuasive argument" in the last paragraph, while an improvement on the original, continues to overlook this possibility and also assumes that other types of aircraft without transponders will pose no problems.

The organization of ideas, while generally sound, is sometimes weakened by needless repetition of the same points, as in sentences 4 and 5 of the last paragraph. The writing contains minor instances of awkwardness (e.g., "Each plane will receive constant, continual signals from each other" in paragraph 3), but is free of flaws that make understanding difficult. However, though the writing is generally clean and clear, the syntax does not show much variety. A few sentences begin with "if" clauses, but almost all the rest, even those that begin with a transitional phrase such as "for example" or "in addition," conform to a "subject, verb, complement" pattern. The first paragraph, in which the second and third sentences begin the same way ("It does not state"), is particularly repetitious.

Sample Paper 2

This argument has no information about air collisions. I think most cases happen in new airports because the air traffic I heavy. In this case sound airport control could solve the problem.

I think this argument is logically reasonable. Its assumption is that plane collisions are caused by planes that don't know each others positions. So pilots can do nothing, if they know each others position through the system it will solve the problem.

If it can provide evidence the problem is lack of knowledge of each others positions, it will be more sound and persuasive.

More information about air collisions is helpful, (the reason for air collisions).

Explanation of Score 2

This response is seriously flawed in several ways. First of all, it has very little substance. The writer appears to make only one point—that while it seems reasonable to assume that midair collisions would be less likely if pilots were sure of each other's positions, readers cannot adequately judge this assumption without more information about where, why, and how such collisions occur. This point, furthermore, is neither explained by a single reason beyond what is given in the topic nor supported by a single example. Legitimate though it is, it cannot, alone and undeveloped, serve as an adequate response to the argument.

Aside from being undeveloped, the response is confusing. At the outset, it seems to be critical of the argument. The writer begins by pointing to the inadequacy of the information given; then speculates, without evidence, that "most cases happen in new airports"; and then suggests that the problem should be addressed by improving "airport control," not (it is implied) by installing onboard warning systems. After criticizing the argument in the first paragraph, the writer confusingly seems to endorse it in the second. Then, in the remainder of the response, the writer returns to a critical stance.

The general lack of coherence is reflected in the serious and frequent writing problems that make meaning hard to determine—for example, the elliptical and ungrammatical "So pilots can do nothing, if they know each others position through the system it will solve the problem" (paragraph 2) or "If it can provide evidence the problem is lack of knowledge of each others positions, it will be more sound and persuasive" (paragraph 3). The prose suffers from a variety of basic errors in grammar, usage, and mechanics.

10.9 Analysis of an Argument Sample Topics

The following appeared as part of an annual report sent to stockholders by Olympic Foods, a processor of frozen foods:

"Over time, the costs of processing go down because as organizations learn how to do things better, they become more efficient. In color film processing, for example, the cost of a 3-by-5-inch print fell from 50 cents for five-day service in 1970 to 20 cents for one-day service in 1984. The same principle applies to the processing of food. And since Olympic Foods will soon celebrate its 25th birthday, we can expect that our long experience will enable us to minimize costs and thus maximize profits."

Discuss how well reasoned you find this argument. In your discussion be sure to analyze the line of reasoning and the use of evidence in the argument. For example, you may need to consider what questionable assumptions underlie the thinking and what alternative explanations or counterexamples might weaken the conclusion. You can also discuss what sort of evidence would strengthen or refute the argument, what changes in the argument would make it more logically sound, and what, if anything, would help you better evaluate its conclusion.

The following appeared in a memorandum from the business department of the Apogee Company:

"When the Apogee Company had all its operations in one location, it was more profitable than it is today. Therefore, the Apogee Company should close down its field offices and conduct all its operations from a single location. Such centralization would improve profitability by cutting costs and helping the company maintain better supervision of all employees."

Discuss how well reasoned … etc.

The following appeared in a memorandum issued by a large city's council on the arts:

"In a recent citywide poll, 15 percent more residents said that they watch television programs about the visual arts than was the case in a poll conducted five years ago. During these past five years, the number of people visiting our city's art museums has increased by a similar percentage. Since the corporate funding that supports public television, where most of the visual arts programs appear, is now being threatened with severe cuts, we can expect that attendance at our city's art museums will also start to decrease. Thus some of the city's funds for supporting the arts should be reallocated to public television."

Discuss how well reasoned … etc.

The following appeared in a report presented for discussion at a meeting of the directors of a company that manufactures parts for heavy machinery:

"The falling revenues that the company is experiencing coincide with delays in manufacturing. These delays, in turn, are due in large part to poor planning in purchasing metals. Consider further that the manager of the department that handles purchasing of raw materials has an excellent background in general business, psychology, and sociology, but knows little about the properties of metals. The company should, therefore, move the purchasing manager to the sales department and bring in a scientist from the research division to be manager of the purchasing department."

Discuss how well reasoned … etc.

The following appeared in an announcement issued by the publisher of *The Mercury*, a weekly newspaper:

"Since a competing lower-priced newspaper, *The Bugle*, was started five years ago, *The Mercury*'s circulation has declined by 10,000 readers. The best way to get more people to read *The Mercury* is to reduce its price below that of *The Bugle*, at least until circulation increases to former levels. The increased circulation of *The Mercury* will attract more businesses to buy advertising space in the paper."

Discuss how well reasoned ... etc.

The following appeared as part of an article in a magazine devoted to regional life:

"Corporations should look to the city of Helios when seeking new business opportunities or a new location. Even in the recent recession, Helios's unemployment rate was lower than the regional average. It is the industrial center of the region, and historically it has provided more than its share of the region's manufacturing jobs. In addition, Helios is attempting to expand its economic base by attracting companies that focus on research and development of innovative technologies."

Discuss how well reasoned ... etc.

The following appeared in the health section of a magazine on trends and lifestyles:

"People who use the artificial sweetener aspartame are better off consuming sugar, since aspartame can actually contribute to weight gain rather than weight loss. For example, high levels of aspartame have been shown to trigger a craving for food by depleting the brain of a chemical that registers satiety, or the sense of being full. Furthermore, studies suggest that sugars, if consumed after at least 45 minutes of continuous exercise, actually enhance the body's ability to burn fat. Consequently, those who drink aspartame-sweetened juices after exercise will also lose this calorie-burning benefit. Thus it appears that people consuming aspartame rather than sugar are unlikely to achieve their dietary goals."

Discuss how well reasoned ... etc.

The following appeared in the editorial section of a corporate newsletter:

"The common notion that workers are generally apathetic about management issues is false, or at least outdated: a recently published survey indicates that 79 percent of the nearly 1,200 workers who responded to survey questionnaires expressed a high level of interest in the topics of corporate restructuring and redesign of benefits programs."

Discuss how well reasoned ... etc.

The following appeared in the opinion column of a financial magazine:

"On average, middle-aged consumers devote 39 percent of their retail expenditure to department store products and services, while for younger consumers the average is only 25 percent. Since the number of middle-aged people will increase dramatically within the next decade, department stores can expect retail sales to increase significantly during that period. Furthermore, to take advantage of the trend, these stores should begin to replace some of those products intended to attract the younger consumer with products intended to attract the middle-aged consumer."

Discuss how well reasoned ... etc.

The following appeared in the editorial section of a local newspaper:

"This past winter, 200 students from Waymarsh State College traveled to the state capitol building to protest against proposed cuts in funding for various state college programs. The other 12,000 Waymarsh students evidently weren't so concerned about their education: they either stayed on campus or left for winter break. Since the group who did not protest is far more numerous, it is more representative of the state's college students than are the protesters. Therefore the state legislature need not heed the appeals of the protesting students."

Discuss how well reasoned ... etc.

The following appeared in the editorial section of a local newspaper:

"In the first four years that Montoya has served as mayor of the city of San Perdito, the population has decreased and the unemployment rate has increased. Two businesses have closed for each new business that has opened. Under Varro, who served as mayor for four years before Montoya, the unemployment rate decreased and the population increased. Clearly, the residents of San Perdito would be best served if they voted Montoya out of office and reelected Varro."

Discuss how well reasoned ... etc.

The following appeared as part of a promotional campaign to sell advertising space in the *Daily Gazette* to grocery stores in the Marston area:

"Advertising the reduced price of selected grocery items in the *Daily Gazette* will help you increase your sales. Consider the results of a study conducted last month. Thirty sale items from a store in downtown Marston were advertised in *The Gazette* for four days. Each time one or more of the 30 items was purchased, clerks asked whether the shopper had read the ad. Two-thirds of the 200 shoppers asked answered in the affirmative. Furthermore, more than half the customers who answered in the affirmative spent over $100 at the store."

Discuss how well reasoned ... etc.

The following appeared as part of a campaign to sell advertising time on a local radio station to local businesses:

"The Cumquat Café began advertising on our local radio station this year and was delighted to see its business increase by 10 percent over last year's totals. Their success shows you how you can use radio advertising to make your business more profitable."

Discuss how well reasoned … etc.

The following appeared as part of a newspaper editorial:

"Two years ago Nova High School began to use interactive computer instruction in three academic subjects. The school dropout rate declined immediately, and last year's graduates have reported some impressive achievements in college. In future budgets the school board should use a greater portion of the available funds to buy more computers, and all schools in the district should adopt interactive computer instruction throughout the curriculum."

Discuss how well reasoned … etc.

The following appeared as a part of an advertisement for Adams, who is seeking re-election as governor:

"Re-elect Adams, and you will be voting for proven leadership in improving the state's economy. Over the past year alone, 70 percent of the state's workers have had increases in their wages, 5,000 new jobs have been created, and six corporations have located their headquarters here. Most of the respondents in a recent poll said they believed that the economy is likely to continue to improve if Adams is re-elected. Adams's opponent, Zebulon, would lead our state in the wrong direction, because Zebulon disagrees with many of Adams's economic policies."

Discuss how well reasoned … etc.

The following appeared as part of an article in the education section of a Waymarsh city newspaper:

"Throughout the last two decades, those who earned graduate degrees found it very difficult to get jobs teaching their academic specialties at the college level. Those with graduate degrees from Waymarsh University had an especially hard time finding such jobs. But better times are coming in the next decade for all academic job seekers, including those from Waymarsh. Demographic trends indicate that an increasing number of people will be reaching college age over the next 10 years; consequently, we can expect that the job market will improve dramatically for people seeking college-level teaching positions in their fields."

Discuss how well reasoned … etc.

The following appeared in an article in a consumer-products magazine:

"Two of today's best-selling brands of full-strength prescription medication for the relief of excess stomach acid, Acid-Ease and Pepticaid, are now available in milder nonprescription forms. Doctors have written 76 million more prescriptions for full-strength Acid-Ease than for full-strength Pepticaid. So people who need an effective but milder nonprescription medication for the relief of excess stomach acid should choose Acid-Ease."

Discuss how well reasoned ... etc.

The following is an excerpt from a memo written by the head of a governmental department:

"Neither stronger ethics regulations nor stronger enforcement mechanisms are necessary to ensure ethical behavior by companies doing business with this department. We already have a code of ethics that companies doing business with this department are urged to abide by, and virtually all of these companies have agreed to follow it. We also know that the code is relevant to the current business environment because it was approved within the last year, and in direct response to specific violations committed by companies with which we were then working—not in abstract anticipation of potential violations, as so many such codes are."

Discuss how well reasoned ... etc.

The following appeared as part of an article in the travel section of a newspaper:

"Over the past decade, the restaurant industry in the country of Spiessa has experienced unprecedented growth. This surge can be expected to continue in the coming years, fueled by recent social changes: personal incomes are rising, more leisure time is available, single-person households are more common, and people have a greater interest in gourmet food, as evidenced by a proliferation of publications on the subject."

Discuss how well reasoned ... etc.

The following appeared in an article in a health and fitness magazine:

"Laboratory studies show that Saluda Natural Spring Water contains several of the minerals necessary for good health and that it is completely free of bacteria. Residents of Saluda, the small town where the water is bottled, are hospitalized less frequently than the national average. Even though Saluda Natural Spring Water may seem expensive, drinking it instead of tap water is a wise investment in good health."

Discuss how well reasoned ... etc.

The following appeared as part of an editorial in an industry newsletter:

"While trucking companies that deliver goods pay only a portion of highway maintenance costs and no property tax on the highways they use, railways spend billions per year maintaining and upgrading their facilities. The government should lower the railroad companies' property taxes, since sending goods by rail is clearly a more appropriate mode of ground transportation than highway shipping. For one thing, trains consume only a third of the fuel a truck would use to carry the same load, making them a more cost-effective and environmentally sound mode of transport. Furthermore, since rail lines already exist, increases in rail traffic would not require building new lines at the expense of taxpaying citizens."

Discuss how well reasoned ... etc.

The following appeared in the editorial section of a newspaper:

"As public concern over drug abuse has increased, authorities have become more vigilant in their efforts to prevent illegal drugs from entering the country. Many drug traffickers have consequently switched from marijuana, which is bulky, or heroin, which has a market too small to justify the risk of severe punishment, to cocaine. Thus enforcement efforts have ironically resulted in an observed increase in the illegal use of cocaine."

Discuss how well reasoned ... etc.

The following appeared in a speech delivered by a member of the city council:

"Twenty years ago, only half of the students who graduated from Einstein High School went on to attend a college or university. Today, two-thirds of the students who graduate from Einstein do so. Clearly, Einstein has improved its educational effectiveness over the past two decades. This improvement has occurred despite the fact that the school's funding, when adjusted for inflation, is about the same as it was 20 years ago. Therefore, we do not need to make any substantial increase in the school's funding at this time."

Discuss how well reasoned ... etc.

The following appeared in a memo from the customer service division to the manager of Mammon Savings and Loan:

"We believe that improved customer service is the best way for us to differentiate ourselves from competitors and attract new customers. We can offer our customers better service by reducing waiting time in teller lines from an average of six minutes to an average of three. By opening for business at 8:30 instead of 9:00, and by remaining open for an additional hour beyond our current closing time, we will be better able to accommodate the busy schedules of our customers. These changes will enhance our bank's image as the most customer-friendly bank in town and give us the edge over our competition."

Discuss how well reasoned ... etc.

The following appeared as part of an article in a magazine on lifestyles:

"Two years ago, City L was listed fourteenth in an annual survey that ranks cities according to the quality of life that can be enjoyed by those living in them. This information will enable people who are moving to the state in which City L is located to confidently identify one place, at least, where schools are good, housing is affordable, people are friendly, the environment is safe, and the arts flourish."

Discuss how well reasoned ... etc.

The following appeared in a memorandum from a member of a financial management and consulting firm:

"We have learned from an employee of Windfall, Ltd., that its accounting department, by checking about 10 percent of the last month's purchasing invoices for errors and inconsistencies, saved the company some $10,000 in overpayments. In order to help our clients increase their net gains, we should advise each of them to institute a policy of checking all purchasing invoices for errors. Such a recommendation could also help us get the Windfall account by demonstrating to Windfall the rigorousness of our methods."

Discuss how well reasoned ... etc.

The following appeared in a newspaper editorial:

"As violence in movies increases, so do crime rates in our cities. To combat this problem we must establish a board to censor certain movies, or we must limit admission to persons over 21 years of age. Apparently our legislators are not concerned about this issue since a bill calling for such actions recently failed to receive a majority vote."

Discuss how well reasoned ... etc.

The following appeared in the editorial section of a local newspaper:

"Commuter use of the new subway train is exceeding the transit company's projections. However, commuter use of the shuttle buses that transport people to the subway stations is below the projected volume. If the transit company expects commuters to ride the shuttle buses to the subway rather than drive there, it must either reduce the shuttle bus fares or increase the price of parking at the subway stations."

Discuss how well reasoned ... etc.

The following was excerpted from the speech of a spokesperson for Synthetic Farm Products, Inc.:

"Many farmers who invested in the equipment needed to make the switch from synthetic to organic fertilizers and pesticides feel that it would be too expensive to resume synthetic farming at this point. But studies of farmers who switched to organic farming last year indicate that their current crop yields are lower. Hence their purchase of organic farming equipment, a relatively minor investment compared to the losses that would result from continued lower crop yields, cannot justify persisting on an unwise course. And the choice to farm organically is financially unwise, given that it was motivated by environmental rather than economic concerns."

Discuss how well reasoned ... etc.

The following appeared in a newspaper story giving advice about investments:

"As overall life expectancy continues to rise, the population of our country is growing increasingly older. For example, more than 20 percent of the residents of one of our more populated regions are now at least 65 years old, and occupancy rates at resort hotels in that region declined significantly during the past six months. Because of these two related trends, a prudent investor would be well advised to sell interest in hotels and invest in hospitals and nursing homes instead."

Discuss how well reasoned … etc.

The following appeared as part of the business plan of an investment and financial consulting firm:

"Studies suggest that an average coffee drinker's consumption of coffee increases with age, from age 10 through age 60. Even after age 60, coffee consumption remains high. The average cola drinker's consumption of cola, however, declines with increasing age. Both of these trends have remained stable for the past 40 years. Given that the number of older adults will significantly increase as the population ages over the next 20 years, it follows that the demand for coffee will increase and the demand for cola will decrease during this period. We should, therefore, consider transferring our investments from Cola Loca to Early Bird Coffee."

Discuss how well reasoned … etc.

The following appeared in the editorial section of a West Cambria newspaper:

"A recent review of the West Cambria volunteer ambulance service revealed a longer average response time to accidents than was reported by a commercial ambulance squad located in East Cambria. In order to provide better patient care for accident victims and to raise revenue for our town by collecting service fees for ambulance use, we should disband our volunteer service and hire a commercial ambulance service."

Discuss how well reasoned … etc.

The following is part of a business plan being discussed at a board meeting of the Perks Company:

"It is no longer cost-effective for the Perks Company to continue offering its employees a generous package of benefits and incentives year after year. In periods when national unemployment rates are low, Perks may need to offer such a package in order to attract and keep good employees, but since national unemployment rates are now high, Perks does not need to offer the same benefits and incentives. The money thus saved could be better used to replace the existing plant machinery with more technologically sophisticated equipment, or even to build an additional plant."

Discuss how well reasoned … etc.

The following appeared as part of a plan proposed by an executive of the Easy Credit Company to the president:

"The Easy Credit Company would gain an advantage over competing credit card services if we were to donate a portion of the proceeds from the use of our cards to a well-known environmental organization in exchange for the use of its symbol or logo on our card. Since a recent poll shows that a large percentage of the public is concerned about environmental issues, this policy would attract new customers, increase use among existing customers, and enable us to charge interest rates that are higher than the lowest ones available."

Discuss how well reasoned ... etc.

The following appeared as part of a recommendation from the financial planning office to the administration of Fern Valley University:

"In the past few years, Fern Valley University has suffered from a decline in both enrollments and admissions applications. The reason can be discovered from our students, who most often cite poor teaching and inadequate library resources as their chief sources of dissatisfaction with Fern Valley. Therefore, in order to increase the number of students attending our university, and hence to regain our position as the most prestigious university in the greater Fern Valley metropolitan area, it is necessary to initiate a fund-raising campaign among the alumni that will enable us to expand the range of subjects we teach and to increase the size of our library facilities."

Discuss how well reasoned ... etc.

The following appeared in an article in a college departmental newsletter:

"Professor Taylor of Jones University is promoting a model of foreign language instruction in which students receive 10 weeks of intensive training, then go abroad to live with families for 10 weeks. The superiority of the model, Professor Taylor contends, is proved by the results of a study in which foreign language tests given to students at 25 other colleges show that first-year foreign language students at Jones speak more fluently after only 10 to 20 weeks in the program than do 9 out of 10 foreign language majors elsewhere at the time of their graduation."

Discuss how well reasoned ... etc.

The following appeared as part of an article in the business section of a local newspaper:

"Motorcycle X has been manufactured in the United States for more than 70 years. Although one foreign company has copied the motorcycle and is selling it for less, the company has failed to attract motorcycle X customers—some say because its product lacks the exceptionally loud noise made by motorcycle X. But there must be some other explanation. After all, foreign cars tend to be quieter than similar American-made cars, but they sell at least as well. Also, television advertisements for motorcycle X highlight its durability and sleek lines, not its noisiness, and the ads typically have voice-overs or rock music rather than engine-roar on the sound track."

Discuss how well reasoned ... etc.

The following appeared in the editorial section of a campus newspaper:

"Because occupancy rates for campus housing fell during the last academic year, so did housing revenues. To solve the problem, campus housing officials should reduce the number of available housing units, thereby increasing the occupancy rates. Also, to keep students from choosing to live off-campus, housing officials should lower the rents, thereby increasing demand."

Discuss how well reasoned ... etc.

The following appeared in an Avia Airlines departmental memorandum:

"On average, 9 out of every 1,000 passengers who traveled on Avia Airlines last year filed a complaint about our baggage-handling procedures. This means that although some 1 percent of our passengers were unhappy with those procedures, the overwhelming majority were quite satisfied with them; thus it would appear that a review of the procedures is not important to our goal of maintaining or increasing the number of Avia's passengers."

Discuss how well reasoned ... etc.

The following appeared as part of an article in a weekly newsmagazine:

"The country of Sacchar can best solve its current trade deficit problem by lowering the price of sugar, its primary export. Such an action would make Sacchar better able to compete for markets with other sugar-exporting countries. The sale of Sacchar's sugar abroad would increase, and this increase would substantially reduce Sacchar's trade deficit."

Discuss how well reasoned ... etc.

The following appeared as part of an article in a trade publication:

"Stronger laws are needed to protect new kinds of home-security systems from being copied and sold by imitators. With such protection, manufacturers will naturally invest in the development of new home-security products and production technologies. Without stronger laws, therefore, manufacturers will cut back on investment. From this will follow a corresponding decline not only in product quality and marketability, but also in production efficiency, and thus ultimately a loss of manufacturing jobs in the industry."

Discuss how well reasoned ... etc.

The following appeared in the opinion section of a national newsmagazine:

"To reverse the deterioration of the postal service, the government should raise the price of postage stamps. This solution will no doubt prove effective, since the price increase will generate larger revenues and will also reduce the volume of mail, thereby eliminating the strain on the existing system and contributing to improved morale."

Discuss how well reasoned ... etc.

The following appeared in an article in the health section of a newspaper:

"There is a common misconception that university hospitals are better than community or private hospitals. This notion is unfounded, however: the university hospitals in our region employ 15 percent fewer doctors, have a 20 percent lower success rate in treating patients, make far less overall profit, and pay their medical staff considerably less than do private hospitals. Furthermore, many doctors at university hospitals typically divide their time among teaching, conducting research, and treating patients. From this it seems clear that the quality of care at university hospitals is lower than that at other kinds of hospitals."

Discuss how well reasoned ... etc.

The following is part of a business plan created by the management of the Megamart grocery store:

"Our total sales have increased this year by 20 percent since we added a pharmacy section to our grocery store. Clearly, the customer's main concern is the convenience afforded by one-stop shopping. The surest way to increase our profits over the next couple of years, therefore, is to add a clothing department along with an automotive supplies and repair shop. We should also plan to continue adding new departments and services, such as a restaurant and a garden shop, in subsequent years. Being the only store in the area that offers such a range of services will give us a competitive advantage over other local stores."

Discuss how well reasoned ... etc.

The following appeared as part of a column in a popular entertainment magazine:

"The producers of the forthcoming movie *3003* will be most likely to maximize their profits if they are willing to pay Robin Good several million dollars to star in it—even though that amount is far more than any other person involved with the movie will make. After all, Robin has in the past been paid a similar amount to work in several films that were very financially successful."

Discuss how well reasoned ... etc.

The following appeared in a memorandum from the directors of a security and safety consulting service:

"Our research indicates that over the past six years no incidents of employee theft have been reported within ten of the companies that have been our clients. In analyzing the security practices of these ten companies, we have further learned that each of them requires its employees to wear photo identification badges while at work. In the future, therefore, we should recommend the use of such identification badges to all of our clients."

Discuss how well reasoned ... etc.

The following appeared as part of an article in the business section of a local newspaper:

"The owners of the Cumquat Café evidently made a good business decision in moving to a new location, as can be seen from the fact that the Café will soon celebrate its second anniversary there. Moreover, it appears that businesses are not likely to succeed at the old location: since the Café's move, three different businesses— a tanning salon, an antique emporium, and a pet-grooming shop—have occupied its former spot."

Discuss how well reasoned ... etc.

The following appeared in the editorial section of a local newspaper:

"The profitability of Croesus Company, recently restored to private ownership, is a clear indication that businesses fare better under private ownership than under public ownership."

Discuss how well reasoned ... etc.

The following appeared in the editorial section of a local newspaper:

"If the paper from every morning edition of the nation's largest newspaper were collected and rendered into paper pulp that the newspaper could reuse, about 5 million trees would be saved each year. This kind of recycling is unnecessary, however, since the newspaper maintains its own forests to ensure an uninterrupted supply of paper."

Discuss how well reasoned ... etc.

The following appeared as part of a business plan recommended by the new manager of a musical rock group called Zapped:

"To succeed financially, Zapped needs greater name recognition. It should therefore diversify its commercial enterprises. The rock group Zonked plays the same type of music that Zapped plays, but it is much better known than Zapped because, in addition to its concert tours and four albums, Zonked has a series of posters, a line of clothing and accessories, and a contract with a major advertising agency to endorse a number of different products."

Discuss how well reasoned ... etc.

The following appeared in a magazine article on trends and lifestyles:

"In general, people are not as concerned as they were a decade ago about regulating their intake of red meat and fatty cheeses. Walk into the Heart's Delight, a store that started selling organic fruits and vegetables and whole-grain flours in the 1960s, and you will also find a wide selection of cheeses made with high butterfat content. Next door, the owners of the Good Earth Café, an old vegetarian restaurant, are still making a modest living, but the owners of the new House of Beef across the street are millionaires."

Discuss how well reasoned ... etc.

The following editorial appeared in the Elm City paper:

"The construction last year of a shopping mall in downtown Oak City was a mistake. Since the mall has opened, a number of local businesses have closed, and the downtown area suffers from an acute parking shortage, and arrests for crime and vagrancy have increased in the nearby Oak City Park. Elm City should pay attention to the example of the Oak City mall and deny the application to build a shopping mall in Elm City."

Discuss how well reasoned ... etc.

The following appeared as part of an editorial in a weekly newsmagazine:

"Historically, most of this country's engineers have come from our universities; recently, however, our university-age population has begun to shrink, and decreasing enrollments in our high schools clearly show that this drop in numbers will continue throughout the remainder of the decade. Consequently, our nation will soon be facing a shortage of trained engineers. If we are to remain economically competitive in the world marketplace, then we must increase funding for education—and quickly."

Discuss how well reasoned … etc.

The following appeared in an Excelsior Company memorandum:

"The Excelsior Company plans to introduce its own brand of coffee. Since coffee is an expensive food item, and since there are already many established brands of coffee, the best way to gain customers for the Excelsior brand is to do what Superior, the leading coffee company, did when it introduced the newest brand in its line of coffees: conduct a temporary sales promotion that offers free samples, price reductions, and discount coupons for the new brand."

Discuss how well reasoned … etc.

The following appeared as part of an article in a health club trade publication:

"After experiencing a decline in usage by its members, Healthy Heart fitness center built an indoor pool. Since usage did not increase significantly, it appears that health club managers should adopt another approach—lowering membership fees rather than installing expensive new features."

Discuss how well reasoned … etc.

The following appeared as part of an article in a popular arts-and-leisure magazine:

"The safety codes governing the construction of public buildings are becoming far too strict. The surest way for architects and builders to prove that they have met the minimum requirements established by these codes is to construct buildings by using the same materials and methods that are currently allowed. But doing so means that there will be very little significant technological innovation within the industry, and hence little evolution of architectural styles and design—merely because of the strictness of these safety codes."

Discuss how well reasoned … etc.

The following is from a campaign by Big Boards Inc. to convince companies in River City that their sales will increase if they use Big Boards billboards for advertising their locally manufactured products:

"The potential of Big Boards to increase sales of your products can be seen from an experiment we conducted last year. We increased public awareness of the name of the current national women's marathon champion by publishing her picture and her name on billboards in River City for a period of three months. Before this time, although the champion had just won her title and was receiving extensive national publicity, only five percent of 15,000 randomly surveyed residents of River City could correctly name the champion when shown her picture; after the three-month advertising experiment, 35 percent of respondents from a second survey could supply her name."

Discuss how well reasoned ... etc.

The following appeared as part of an article on government funding of environmental regulatory agencies:

"When scientists finally learn how to create large amounts of copper from other chemical elements, the regulation of copper mining will become unnecessary. For one thing, since the amount of potentially available copper will no longer be limited by the quantity of actual copper deposits, the problem of over-mining will quickly be eliminated altogether. For another, manufacturers will not need to use synthetic copper substitutes, the production of which creates pollutants. Thus, since two problems will be settled—over-mining and pollution— it makes good sense to reduce funding for mining regulation and either save the money or reallocate it where it is needed more."

Discuss how well reasoned ... etc.

The following appeared as part of an article in a popular science magazine:

"Scientists must typically work 60 to 80 hours a week if they hope to further their careers; consequently, good and affordable all-day child care must be made available to both male and female scientists if they are to advance in their fields. Moreover, requirements for career advancement must be made more flexible so that preschool-age children can spend a significant portion of each day with a parent."

Discuss how well reasoned ... etc.

The following appeared as part of a recommendation by one of the directors of the Beta Company:

"The Alpha Company has just reduced its workforce by laying off 15 percent of its employees in all divisions and at all levels, and it is encouraging early retirement for other employees. As you know, the Beta Company manufactures some products similar to Alpha's, but our profits have fallen over the last few years. To improve Beta's competitive position, we should try to hire a significant number of Alpha's former workers, since these experienced workers can provide valuable information about Alpha's successful methods, will require little training, and will be particularly motivated to compete against Alpha."

Discuss how well reasoned ... etc.

The following appeared in the letters-to-the-editor section of a local newspaper:

"*Muscle Monthly,* a fitness magazine that regularly features pictures of bodybuilders using state-of-the-art exercise machines, frequently sells out, according to the owner of Skyview Newsstand. To help maximize fitness levels in our town's residents, we should, therefore, equip our new community fitness center with such machines."

Discuss how well reasoned ... etc.

The following appeared as part of an article in the business section of a local newspaper:

"The Cumquat Café made a mistake in moving to a new location. After one year at the new spot, it is doing about the same volume of business as before, but the owners of the RoboWrench plumbing supply wholesale outlet that took over its old location are apparently doing better: RoboWrench is planning to open a store in a neighboring city."

Discuss how well reasoned ... etc.

The following appeared in a memorandum from the director of human resources to the executive officers of Company X:

"Last year, we surveyed our employees on improvements needed at Company X by having them rank, in order of importance, the issues presented in a list of possible improvements. Improved communications between employees and management was consistently ranked as the issue of highest importance by the employees who responded to the survey. As you know, we have since instituted regular communications sessions conducted by high-level management, which the employees can attend on a voluntary basis. Therefore, it is likely that most employees at Company X now feel that the improvement most needed at the company has been made."

Discuss how well reasoned ... etc.

The following appeared in a memorandum from the vice president of Road Food, an international chain of fast-food restaurants:

"This past year, we spent almost as much on advertising as did our main competitor, Street Eats, which has fewer restaurants than we do. Although it appeared at first that our advertising agency had created a campaign along the lines we suggested, in fact our total profits were lower than those of Street Eats. In order to motivate our advertising agency to perform better, we should start basing the amount that we pay it on how much total profit we make each year."

Discuss how well reasoned ... etc.

The following appeared in the promotional literature for Cerberus dog food:

"Obesity is a great problem among pet dogs, just as it is among their human owners. Obesity in humans is typically caused by consuming more calories than the body needs. For humans, a proper diet for losing weight is a reduced-calorie diet that is high in fiber and carbohydrates but low in fat. Therefore, the best way for dog owners to help their dogs lose weight in a healthy way is to restrict the dog's diet to Cerberus reduced-calorie dog food, which is high in fiber and carbohydrates but low in fat."

Discuss how well reasoned ... etc.

The following appeared in an article in a travel magazine:

"After the airline industry began requiring airlines to report their on-time rates, Speedee Airlines achieved the number one on-time rate, with more than 89 percent of its flights arriving on time each month. And now Speedee is offering more flights to more destinations than ever before. Clearly, Speedee is the best choice for today's business traveler."

Discuss how well reasoned … etc.

The following appeared in a memorandum to the planning department of an investment firm:

"Costs have begun dropping for several types of equipment currently used to convert solar energy into electricity. Moreover, some exciting new technologies for converting solar energy are now being researched and developed. Hence we can expect that solar energy will soon become more cost efficient and attractive than coal or oil as a source of electrical power. We should, therefore, encourage investment in Solario, a new manufacturer of solar-powered products. After all, Solario's chief executive was once on the financial planning team for Ready-to-Ware, a software engineering firm that has shown remarkable growth since its recent incorporation."

Discuss how well reasoned … etc.

The following appeared in a memorandum from a company's marketing department:

"Since our company started manufacturing and marketing a deluxe air filter six months ago, sales of our economy filter—and company profits—have decreased significantly. The deluxe air filter sells for 50 percent more than the economy filter, but the economy filter lasts for only one month while the deluxe filter can be used for two months before it must be replaced. To increase repeat sales of our economy filter and maximize profits, we should discontinue the deluxe air filter and concentrate all our advertising efforts on the economy filter."

Discuss how well reasoned … etc.

The following appeared in a memorandum from the president of a company that makes shampoo:

"A widely publicized study claims that HR2, a chemical compound in our shampoo, can contribute to hair loss after prolonged use. This study, however, involved only 500 subjects. Furthermore, we have received no complaints from our customers during the past year, and some of our competitors actually use more HR2 per bottle of shampoo than we do. Therefore, we do not need to consider replacing the HR2 in our shampoo with a more expensive alternative."

Discuss how well reasoned … etc.

The following appeared in the editorial section of a local newspaper:

"The tragic crash of a medical helicopter last week points out a situation that needs to be addressed. The medical-helicopter industry supposedly has more stringent guidelines for training pilots and maintaining equipment than do most other airline industries, but these guidelines do not appear to be working: statistics reveal that the rate of medical-helicopter accidents is much higher than the rate of accidents for nonmedical helicopters or commercial airliners."

Discuss how well reasoned ... etc.

The following appeared as part of a recommendation from the business manager of a department store:

"Local clothing stores reported that their profits decreased, on average, for the three-month period between August 1 and October 31. Stores that sell products for the home reported that, on average, their profits increased during this same period. Clearly, consumers are choosing to buy products for their homes instead of clothing. To take advantage of this trend, we should reduce the size of our clothing departments and enlarge our home furnishings and household products departments."

Discuss how well reasoned ... etc.

The following appeared in a letter to the editor of a regional newspaper:

"In response to petitions from the many farmers and rural landowners throughout our region, the legislature has spent valuable time and effort enacting severe laws to deter motorists from picking fruit off the trees, trampling through the fields, and stealing samples of foliage. But how can our local lawmakers occupy themselves with such petty vandalism when crime and violence plague the nation's cities? The fate of apples and leaves is simply too trivial to merit their attention."

Discuss how well reasoned ... etc.

The following appeared as part of an editorial in a campus newspaper:

"With an increasing demand for highly skilled workers, this nation will soon face a serious labor shortage. New positions in technical and professional occupations are increasing rapidly, while at the same time the total labor force is growing slowly. Moreover, the government is proposing to cut funds for aid to education in the near future."

Discuss how well reasoned ... etc.

The following appeared as part of a memorandum from a government agency:

"Given the limited funding available for the building and repair of roads and bridges, the government should not spend any money this year on fixing the bridge that crosses the Styx River. This bridge is located near a city with a weakening economy, so it is not as important as other bridges; moreover, the city population is small and thus unlikely to contribute a significant enough tax revenue to justify the effort of fixing the bridge."

Discuss how well reasoned ... etc.

The following appeared as part of an article in an entertainment magazine:

"A series of books based on the characters from a popular movie are consistently best sellers in local bookstores. Seeking to capitalize on the books' success, Vista Studios is planning to produce a movie sequel based on the books. Due to the success of the books and the original movie, the sequel will undoubtedly be profitable."

Discuss how well reasoned … etc.

The following appeared in a letter to the editor of a popular science and technology magazine:

"It is a popular myth that consumers are really benefiting from advances in agricultural technology. Granted, consumers are, on the average, spending a decreasing proportion of their income on food. But consider that the demand for food does not rise in proportion with real income. As real income rises, therefore, consumers can be expected to spend a decreasing proportion of their income on food. Yet agricultural technology is credited with having made our lives better."

Discuss how well reasoned … etc.

The following appeared in the editorial section of a local newspaper:

"This city should be able to improve existing services and provide new ones without periodically raising the taxes of the residents. Instead, the city should require that the costs of services be paid for by developers who seek approval for their large new building projects. After all, these projects can be highly profitable to the developers, but they can also raise a city's expenses and increase the demand for its services."

Discuss how well reasoned … etc.

The following appeared in the editorial section of a local newspaper:

"In order to avoid the serious health threats associated with many landfills, our municipality should build a plant for burning trash. An incinerator could offer economic as well as ecological advantages over the typical old-fashioned type of landfill: incinerators can be adapted to generate moderate amounts of electricity, and ash residue from some types of trash can be used to condition garden soil."

Discuss how well reasoned … etc.

The following appeared in the editorial section of a monthly business newsmagazine:

"Most companies would agree that as the risk of physical injury occurring on the job increases, the wages paid to employees should also increase. Hence it makes financial sense for employers to make the workplace safer: they could thus reduce their payroll expenses and save money."

Discuss how well reasoned … etc.

The following appeared as part of a company memorandum:

"Adopting an official code of ethics regarding business practices may in the long run do our company more harm than good in the public eye. When one of our competitors received unfavorable publicity for violating its own code of ethics, it got more attention from the media than it would have if it had had no such code. Rather than adopt an official code of ethics, therefore, we should instead conduct a publicity campaign that stresses the importance of protecting the environment and assisting charitable organizations."

Discuss how well reasoned … etc.

_____

The following appeared in the editorial section of a daily newspaper:

"Although forecasts of presidential elections based on opinion polls measure current voter preference, many voters keep changing their minds about whom they prefer until the last few days before the balloting. Some do not even make a final decision until they enter the voting booth. Forecasts based on opinion polls are therefore little better at predicting election outcomes than a random guess would be."

Discuss how well reasoned … etc.

_____

The following appeared in the editorial section of a newspaper in the country of West Cambria:

"The practice of officially changing speed limits on the highways—whether by increasing or decreasing them—is a dangerous one. Consider what happened over the past decade whenever neighboring East Cambria changed its speed limits: an average of 3 percent more automobile accidents occurred during the week following the change than had occurred during the week preceding it—even when the speed limit was lowered. This statistic shows that the change in speed limit adversely affected the alertness of drivers."

Discuss how well reasoned … etc.

_____

The following appeared as part of a memorandum from the vice president of Nostrum, a large pharmaceutical corporation:

"The proposal to increase the health and retirement benefits that our employees receive should not be implemented at this time. An increase in these benefits is not only financially unjustified, since our last year's profits were lower than those of the preceding year, but also unnecessary, since our chief competitor, Panacea, offers its employees lower health and retirement benefits than we currently offer. We can assume that our employees are reasonably satisfied with the health and retirement benefits that they now have since a recent survey indicated that two-thirds of the respondents viewed them favorably."

Discuss how well reasoned … etc.

The following appeared as part of an article on trends in television:

"A recent study of viewers' attitudes toward prime-time television programs shows that many of the programs that were judged by their viewers to be of high quality appeared on (noncommercial) television networks, and that, on commercial television, the most popular shows are typically sponsored by the bestselling products. Thus, it follows that businesses who use commercial television to promote their products will achieve the greatest advertising success by sponsoring only highly rated programs—and, ideally, programs resembling the highly rated noncommercial programs on public channels as much as possible."

Discuss how well reasoned ... etc.

The following appeared as part of an article in the business section of a daily newspaper:

"Company A has a large share of the international market in video-game hardware and software. Company B, the pioneer in these products, was once a $12 billion-a-year giant but collapsed when children became bored with its line of products. Thus Company A can also be expected to fail, especially given the fact that its games are now in so many American homes that the demand for them is nearly exhausted."

Discuss how well reasoned ... etc.

The following appeared as part of an article in a photography magazine:

"When choosing whether to work in color or in black-and-white, the photographer who wishes to be successful should keep in mind that because color photographs are more true to life, magazines use more color photographs than black-and-white ones, and many newspapers are also starting to use color photographs. The realism of color also accounts for the fact that most portrait studios use more color film than black-and-white film. Furthermore, there are more types of color film than black-and-white film available today. Clearly, photographers who work in color have an advantage over those who work in black-and-white."

Discuss how well reasoned ... etc.

The following appeared as part of a letter to the editor of a local newspaper:

"It makes no sense that in most places 15-year-olds are not eligible for their driver's license while people who are far older can retain all of their driving privileges by simply renewing their license. If older drivers can get these renewals, often without having to pass another driving test, then 15-year-olds should be eligible to get a license. Fifteen-year-olds typically have much better eyesight, especially at night; much better hand-eye coordination; and much quicker reflexes. They are also less likely to feel confused by unexpected developments or disoriented in unfamiliar surroundings, and they recover from injuries more quickly."

Discuss how well reasoned ... etc.

The following appeared in an ad for a book titled *How to Write a Screenplay for a Movie*:

"Writers who want to succeed should try to write film screenplays rather than books, since the average film tends to make greater profits than does even a best-selling book. It is true that some books are also made into films. However, our nation's film producers are more likely to produce movies based on original screenplays than to produce films based on books, because in recent years the films that have sold the most tickets have usually been based on original screenplays."

Discuss how well reasoned ... etc.

The following appeared as part of an article in a daily newspaper:

"The computerized onboard warning system that will be installed in commercial airliners will virtually solve the problem of midair plane collisions. One plane's warning system can receive signals from another's transponder—a radio set that signals a plane's course—in order to determine the likelihood of a collision and recommend evasive action."

Discuss how well reasoned ... etc.

The following appeared in a memorandum from the ElectroWares company's marketing department:

"Since our company started manufacturing and marketing a deluxe light bulb six months ago, sales of our economy light bulb—and company profits—have decreased significantly. Although the deluxe light bulb sells for 50 percent more than the economy bulb, it lasts twice as long. Therefore, to increase repeat sales and maximize profits, we should discontinue the deluxe light bulb."

Discuss how well reasoned ... etc.

The following is taken from an editorial in a local newspaper:

"Over the past decade, the price per pound of citrus fruit has increased substantially. Eleven years ago, Megamart charged 15 cents a pound for lemons, but today it commonly charges over a dollar a pound. In only one of these last 11 years was the weather unfavorable for growing citrus crops. Evidently, then, citrus growers have been responsible for the excessive increase in the price of citrus fruit, and strict pricing regulations are needed to prevent them from continuing to inflate prices."

Discuss how well reasoned ... etc.

The following appeared as part of an article in a local newspaper:

"Over the past three years the tartfish industry has changed markedly: fishing technology has improved significantly, and the demand for tartfish has grown in both domestic and foreign markets. As this trend continues, the tartfish industry on Shrimp Island can expect to experience the same overfishing problems that are already occurring with mainland fishing industries: without restrictions on fishing, fishers see no reason to limit their individual catches. As the catches get bigger, the tartfish population will be dangerously depleted while the surplus of tartfish will devalue the catch for fishers. Government regulation is the only answer: tartfish-fishing should be allowed only during the three-month summer season, when tartfish reproduce and thus are most numerous, rather than throughout the year."

Discuss how well reasoned ... etc.

The following appeared in a proposal from the development office at Platonic University:

"Because Platonic University has had difficulty in meeting its expenses over the past three years, we need to find new ways to increase revenues. We should consider following the example of Greene University, which recently renamed itself after a donor who gave it $100 million. If Platonic University were to advertise to its alumni and other wealthy people that it will rename either individual buildings or the entire university itself after the donors who give the most money, the amount of donations would undoubtedly increase."

Discuss how well reasoned ... etc.

The following appeared as part of an article in the business section of a local newspaper:

"Hippocrene Plumbing Supply recently opened a wholesale outlet in the location once occupied by the Cumquat Café. Hippocrene has apparently been quite successful there because it is planning to open a large outlet in a nearby city. But the Cumquat Café, one year after moving to its new location, has seen its volume of business drop somewhat from the previous year's. Clearly, the former site was the better business location, and the Cumquat Café has made a mistake in moving to its new address."

Discuss how well reasoned ... etc.

The following appeared in the editorial section of a local paper:

"Applications for advertising spots on KMTV, our local cable television channel, decreased last year. Meanwhile a neighboring town's local channel, KOOP, changed its focus to farming issues and reported an increase in advertising applications for the year. To increase applications for its advertisement spots, KMTV should focus its programming on farming issues as well."

Discuss how well reasoned ... etc.

The following appeared as part of an article in a computer magazine:

"A year ago Apex Manufacturing bought its managers computers for their homes and paid for telephone connections so that they could access Apex computers and data files from home after normal business hours. Since last year, productivity at Apex has increased by 15 percent. Other companies can learn from the success at Apex: given home computers and access to company resources, employees will work additional hours at home and thereby increase company profits."

Discuss how well reasoned ... etc.

The following was excerpted from an article in a farming trade publication:

"Farmers who switched from synthetic to organic farming last year have seen their crop yields decline. Many of these farmers feel that it would be too expensive to resume synthetic farming at this point, given the money that they invested in organic farming supplies and equipment. But their investments will be relatively minor compared to the losses from continued lower crop yields. Organic farmers should switch to synthetic farming rather than persist in an unwise course. And the choice to farm organically is financially unwise, given that it was motivated by environmental rather than economic concerns."

Discuss how well reasoned ... etc.

The following appeared in a letter to prospective students from the admissions office at Plateau College:

"Every person who earned an advanced degree in science or engineering from Olympus University last year received numerous offers of excellent jobs. Typically, many graduates of Plateau College have gone on to pursue advanced degrees at Olympus. Therefore, enrolling as an undergraduate at Plateau College is a wise choice for students who wish to ensure success in their careers."

Discuss how well reasoned ... etc.

The following appeared in a memorandum sent by a vice-president of the Nadir Company to the company's human resources department:

"Nadir does not need to adopt the costly 'family-friendly' programs that have been proposed, such as part-time work, work at home, and jobsharing. When these programs were made available at the Summit Company, the leader in its industry, only a small percentage of employees participated in them. Rather than adversely affecting our profitability by offering these programs, we should concentrate on offering extensive training that will enable employees to increase their productivity."

Discuss how well reasoned ... etc.

The following appeared as part of an article in a trade magazine for breweries:

"Magic Hat Brewery recently released the results of a survey of visitors to its tasting room last year. Magic Hat reports that the majority of visitors asked to taste its low-calorie beers. To boost sales, other small breweries should brew low-calorie beers as well."

Discuss how well reasoned ... etc.

The following appeared in an editorial from a newspaper serving the town of Saluda:

"The Saluda Consolidated High School offers more than 200 different courses from which its students can choose. A much smaller private school down the street offers a basic curriculum of only 80 different courses, but it consistently sends a higher proportion of its graduating seniors on to college than Consolidated does. By eliminating at least half of the courses offered there and focusing on a basic curriculum, we could improve student performance at Consolidated and also save many tax dollars."

Discuss how well reasoned ... etc.

The following appeared as part of an article in the book section of a newspaper:

"Currently more and more books are becoming available in electronic form—either free-of-charge on the Internet or for a very low price-per-book on compact disc. Thus literary classics are likely to be read more widely than ever before. People who couldn't have purchased these works at bookstore prices will now be able to read them for little or no money; similarly, people who find it inconvenient to visit libraries and wait for books to be returned by other patrons will now have access to whatever classic they choose from their home or work computers. This increase in access to literary classics will radically affect the public taste in reading, creating a far more sophisticated and learned reading audience than has ever existed before."

Discuss how well reasoned ... etc.

The following appeared as an editorial in a magazine concerned with educational issues:

"In our country, the real earnings of men who have only a high-school degree have decreased significantly over the past 15 years, but those of male college graduates have remained about the same. Therefore, the key to improving the earnings of the next generation of workers is to send all students to college. Our country's most important educational goal, then, should be to establish enough colleges and universities to accommodate all high school graduates."

Discuss how well reasoned ... etc.

The following appeared as part of a business plan created by the management of the Take Heart Fitness Center:

"After opening the new swimming pool early last summer, Take Heart saw a 12 percent increase in the use of the center by its members. Therefore, in order to increase membership in Take Heart, we should continue to add new recreational facilities in subsequent years: for example, a multipurpose game room, a tennis court, and a miniature golf course. Being the only center in the area offering this range of activities would give us a competitive advantage in the health and recreation market."

Discuss how well reasoned ... etc.

The following appeared in a letter from a staff member in the office of admissions at Argent University:

"The most recent nationwide surveys show that undergraduates choose their major field primarily based on their perception of job prospects in that field. At our university, economics is now the most popular major, so students must perceive this field as having the best job prospects. Therefore, we can increase our enrollment if we focus our advertising and recruiting on publicizing the accomplishments of our best-known economics professors and the success of our economics graduates in finding employment."

Discuss how well reasoned ... etc.

The following appeared as part of a memorandum from the loan department of the Frostbite National Bank:

"We should not approve the business loan application of the local group that wants to open a franchise outlet for the Kool Kone chain of ice cream parlors. Frostbite is known for its cold winters, and cold weather can mean slow ice cream sales. For example, even though Frostbite is a town of 10,000 people, it has only one ice cream spot— the Frigid Cow. Despite the lack of competition, the Frigid Cow's net revenues fell by 10 percent last winter."

Discuss how well reasoned ... etc.

_____

The following appeared as part of a letter to the editor of a local newspaper:

"Bayview High School is considering whether to require all of its students to wear uniforms while at school. Students attending Acorn Valley Academy, a private school in town, earn higher grades on average and are more likely to go on to college. Moreover, Acorn Valley reports few instances of tardiness, absenteeism, or discipline problems. Since Acorn Valley requires its students to wear uniforms, Bayview High School would do well to follow suit and require its students to wear uniforms as well."

Discuss how well reasoned ... etc.

_____

The following appeared in a memo to the Saluda town council from the town's business manager:

"Research indicates that those who exercise regularly are hospitalized less than half as often as those who don't exercise. By providing a well-equipped gym for Saluda's municipal employees, we should be able to reduce the cost of our group health insurance coverage by approximately 50 percent and thereby achieve a balanced town budget."

Discuss how well reasoned ... etc.

_____

The following appeared in a memorandum written by the assistant manager of a store that sells gourmet food items from various countries:

"A local wine store made an interesting discovery last month: it sold more French than Italian wine on days when it played recordings of French accordion music, but it sold more Italian than French wine on days when Italian songs were played. Therefore, I recommend that we put food specialties from one particular country on sale for a week at a time and play only music from that country while the sale is going on. By this means we will increase our profits in the same way that the wine store did, and we will be able to predict more precisely what items we should stock at any given time."

Discuss how well reasoned ... etc.

The following appeared in a memorandum from the director of research and development at Ready-to-Ware, a software engineering firm:

"The package of benefits and incentives that Ready-to-Ware offers to professional staff is too costly. Our quarterly profits have declined since the package was introduced two years ago, at the time of our incorporation. Moreover, the package had little positive effect, as we have had only marginal success in recruiting and training high-quality professional staff. To become more profitable again, Ready-to-Ware should, therefore, offer the reduced benefits package that was in place two years ago and use the savings to fund our current research and development initiatives."

Discuss how well reasoned … etc.

The following appeared as a memorandum from the vice-president of the Dolci candy company:

"Given the success of our premium and most expensive line of chocolate candies in a recent taste test and the consequent increase in sales, we should shift our business focus to producing additional lines of premium candy rather than our lower-priced, ordinary candies. When the current economic boom ends and consumers can no longer buy major luxury items, such as cars, they will still want to indulge in small luxuries, such as expensive candies."

Discuss how well reasoned … etc.

The following appeared in a memorandum from the business office of the Lovin' Cupful, a national restaurant chain:

"The Lovin' Cupful franchises in our northeast region have begun serving customers Almost, a brand new powdered instant tea, in place of brewed tea. Waiters report that only about 2 percent of the customers have complained, and that customers who want refills typically ask for 'more tea.' It appears, then, that 98 percent of the customers are perfectly happy with the switch, or else they cannot tell powdered instant from brewed tea. Therefore, in order to take advantage of the lower price per pound of Almost, all of our restaurants should begin substituting it for brewed tea."

Discuss how well reasoned … etc.

The following appeared in a memorandum from the director of marketing for a pharmaceutical company:

"According to a survey of 5,000 urban residents, the prevalence of stress headaches increases with educational level, so that stress headaches occur most often among people with graduate-school degrees. It is well established that, nationally, higher educational levels usually correspond with higher levels of income. Therefore, in marketing our new pain remedy, Omnilixir, we should send free samples primarily to graduate students and to people with graduate degrees, and we should concentrate on advertising in professional journals rather than in general interest magazines."

Discuss how well reasoned … etc.

The following appeared as part of an editorial in the Waymarsh city newspaper:

"Last year the parents of first graders in our school district expressed satisfaction with the reading skills their children developed but complained strongly about their children's math skills. To remedy this serious problem and improve our district's elementary education, everyone in the teacher-training program at Waymarsh University should be required to take more courses in mathematics."

Discuss how well reasoned ... etc.

The following appeared in a letter to the editor of a River City newspaper:

"The Clio Development Group should not be permitted to build a multilevel parking garage on Dock Street since most of the buildings on the block would have to be demolished. Because these buildings were erected decades ago, they have historic significance and must therefore be preserved as economic assets in the effort to revitalize a restored riverfront area. Recall how Lakesburg has benefited from business increases in its historic downtown center. Moreover, there is plenty of vacant land for a parking lot elsewhere in River City."

Discuss how well reasoned ... etc.

The following appeared in a corporate planning memorandum for a company that develops amusement parks:

"Because travel from our country to foreign countries has increased dramatically in recent years, our next project should be a 'World Tour' theme park with replicas of famous foreign buildings, rides that have international themes, and refreshment stands serving only foods from the country represented by the nearest ride. The best location would be near our capital city, which has large percentages of international residents and of children under the age of 16. Given the advantages of this site and the growing interest in foreign countries, the 'World Tour' theme park should be as successful as our space-travel theme park, where attendance has increased tenfold over the past decade."

Discuss how well reasoned ... etc.

The following appeared in a memorandum from the publisher to the staff of The Clarion, a large metropolitan newspaper:

"During the recent campaign for mayor, a clear majority of city readers who responded to our survey indicated a desire for more news about city government. To increase circulation, and thus our profits, we should therefore consistently devote a greater proportion of space in all editions of The Clarion to coverage of local news."

Discuss how well reasoned ... etc.

The following appeared in a memorandum from the assistant manager of Pageturner Books:

"Over the past two years, Pageturner's profits have decreased by 5 percent, even though we have added a popular café as well as a music section selling CDs and tapes. At the same time, we have experienced an increase in the theft of merchandise. We should therefore follow the example of Thoreau Books, which increased its profits after putting copies of its most frequently stolen books on a high shelf behind the payment counter. By doing likewise with copies of the titles that our staff reported stolen last year, we too can increase profitability."

Discuss how well reasoned ... etc.

The following appeared in a letter to the editor of a River City newspaper:

"The Clio Development Group's plan for a multilevel parking garage on Dock Street should be approved in order to strengthen the economy of the surrounding area. Although most of the buildings on the block would have to be demolished, they are among the oldest in the city and thus of little current economic value. Those who oppose the project should realize that historic preservation cannot be the only consideration: even Athens or Jerusalem will knock down old buildings to put up new ones that improve the local economy."

Discuss how well reasoned ... etc.

The following appeared in a memorandum from the owner of Carlo's Clothing to the staff:

"Since Disc Depot, the music store on the next block, began a new radio advertising campaign last year, its business has grown dramatically, as evidenced by the large increase in foot traffic into the store. While the Disc Depot's owners have apparently become wealthy enough to retire, profits at Carlo's Clothing have remained stagnant for the past three years. In order to boost our sales and profits, we should therefore switch from newspaper advertising to frequent radio advertisements like those for Disc Depot."

Discuss how well reasoned ... etc.

The following appeared as part of the business plan of the Capital Idea investment firm:

"Across town in the Park Hill district, the Thespian Theater, Pizzazz Pizza, and the Niblick Golf Club have all had business increases over the past two years. Capital Idea should therefore invest in the Roxy Playhouse, the Slice-o'-Pizza, and the Divot Golf Club, three new businesses in the Irongate district. As a condition, we should require them to participate in a special program: Any customer who patronizes two of the businesses will receive a substantial discount at the third. By motivating customers to patronize all three, we will thus contribute to the profitability of each and maximize our return."

Discuss how well reasoned ... etc.

The following appeared as part of an article in a newsletter for farmers:

"Users of Solacium, a medicinal herb now grown mainly in Asia, report that it relieves tension and promotes deep sleep. A recent study indicates that a large number of college students who took pills containing one of the ingredients in Solacium suffered less anxiety. To satisfy the anticipated demands for this very promising therapeutic herb and to reap the financial benefits, farmers in this country should begin growing it."

Discuss how well reasoned ... etc.

The following appeared in a memorandum from the president of Aurora, a company that sells organic milk (milk produced without the use of chemical additives):

"Sales of organic food products in this country have tripled over the past five years. If Aurora is to profit from this continuing trend, we must diversify and start selling products such as organic orange juice and organic eggs in addition to our regular product line. With the recent increase of articles in health magazines questioning the safety of milk and other food products, customers are even more likely to buy our line of organic products. And to help ensure our successful expansion, we should hire the founder of a chain of health-food stores to serve as our vice president of marketing."

Discuss how well reasoned ... etc.

The following appeared in a memorandum from the human resources department of Diversified Manufacturing:

"Managers at our central office report that their employees tend to be most productive in the days immediately preceding a vacation. To help counteract our declining market share, we could increase the productivity of our professional staff members, who currently receive four weeks paid vacation a year, by limiting them to a maximum of one week's continuous vacation time. They will thus take more vacation breaks during a year and give us more days of maximum productivity."

Discuss how well reasoned ... etc.

The following appeared in a memorandum from a regional supervisor of post office operations:

"During a two-week study of postal operations, the Presto City post office handled about twice as many items as the Lento City post office, even though the cities are about the same size. Moreover, customer satisfaction appears to be higher in Presto City, since the study found fewer complaints regarding the Presto City post office. Therefore, the postmasters at these two offices should exchange assignments: the Presto City postmaster will solve the problems of inefficiency and customer dissatisfaction at the Lento City office while the Lento City postmaster learns firsthand the superior methods of Presto City."

Discuss how well reasoned ... etc.

The following appeared in a memorandum written by the managing director of the Exeunt Theater Company:

"Now that we have moved to a larger theater, we can expect to increase our revenues from ticket sales. To further increase profits, we should start producing the plays that have been most successful when they were performed in our nation's largest cities. In addition, we should hire the Adlib Theater Company's director of fund-raising, since corporate contributions to Adlib have increased significantly over the three years that she has worked for Adlib."

Discuss how well reasoned … etc.

_____

The following appeared in a memorandum from the human resources department of HomeStyle, a house remodeling business:

"This year, despite HomeStyle's move to new office space, we have seen a decline in both company morale and productivity, and a corresponding increase in administrative costs. To rectify these problems, we should begin using a newly developed software package for performance appraisal and feedback. Managers will save time by simply choosing comments from a preexisting list; then the software will automatically generate feedback for the employee. The human resources department at CounterBalance, the manufacturer of the countertops we install, reports satisfaction with the package."

Discuss how well reasoned … etc.

_____

The following appeared as part of an article in a weekly newsmagazine:

"The country of Oleum can best solve the problem of its balance-of-trade deficit by further increasing the tax on its major import, crude oil. After Oleum increased the tax on imported crude oil four months ago, consumption of gasoline declined by 20 percent. Therefore, by imposing a second and significantly higher tax increase next year, Oleum will dramatically decrease its balance of trade deficit."

Discuss how well reasoned … etc.

_____

The following appeared as part of a business plan by the Capital Idea investment firm:

"In recent years the worldwide demand for fish has grown, and improvements in fishing technology have made larger catches, and thus increased supply, possible: for example, last year's tuna catch was 9 percent greater than the previous year's. To capitalize on these trends, we should therefore invest in the new tartfish processing plant on Tartfish Island, where increasing revenues from tourism indicate a strong local economy."

Discuss how well reasoned … etc.

The following appeared in a speech by a stockholder of Consolidated Industries at the company's annual stockholders' meeting:

"In the computer hardware division last year, profits fell significantly below projections, the product line decreased from 20 to only 5 items, and expenditures for employee benefits increased by 15 percent. Nevertheless, Consolidated's board of directors has approved an annual salary of more than $1 million for our company's chief executive officer. The present board members should be replaced because they are unconcerned about the increasing costs of employee benefits and salaries, in spite of the company's problems generating income."

Discuss how well reasoned ... etc.

The following appeared in a memorandum from the business planning department of Avia Airlines:

"Of all the cities in their region, Beaumont and Fletcher are showing the fastest growth in the number of new businesses. Therefore, Avia should establish a commuter route between them as a means of countering recent losses on its main passenger routes. And to make the commuter route more profitable from the outset, Avia should offer a 1/3 discount on tickets purchased within two days of the flight. Unlike tickets bought earlier, discount tickets will be nonrefundable, and so gain from their sale will be greater."

Discuss how well reasoned ... etc.

The following appeared in a memorandum from the vice president of Gigantis, a development company that builds and leases retail store facilities:

"Nationwide over the past five years, sales have increased significantly at outlet stores that deal exclusively in reduced-price merchandise. Therefore, we should publicize the new mall that we are building at Pleasantville as a central location for outlet shopping and rent store space only to outlet companies. By taking advantage of the success of outlet stores, this plan should help ensure full occupancy of the mall and enable us to recover quickly the costs of building the mall."

Discuss how well reasoned ... etc.

The following appeared in a memorandum written by the chair of the music department to the president of Omega University:

"Mental health experts have observed that symptoms of mental illness are less pronounced in many patients after group music-therapy sessions, and job openings in the music-therapy field have increased during the past year. Consequently, graduates from our degree program for music therapists should have no trouble finding good positions. To help improve the financial status of Omega University, we should therefore expand our music-therapy degree program by increasing its enrollment targets."

Discuss how well reasoned ... etc.

The following appeared in a memorandum to the work-group supervisors of the GBS Company:

"The CoffeeCart beverage and food service located in the lobby of our main office building is not earning enough in sales to cover its costs, and so the cart may discontinue operating at GBS. Given the low staff morale, as evidenced by the increase in the number of employees leaving the company, the loss of this service could present a problem, especially since the staff morale questionnaire showed widespread dissatisfaction with the snack machines. Therefore, supervisors should remind the employees in their group to patronize the cart—after all, it was leased for their convenience so that they would not have to walk over to the cafeteria on breaks."

Discuss how well reasoned … etc.

The following appeared as part of an article in a trade magazine:

"During a recent trial period in which government inspections at selected meat-processing plants were more frequent, the amount of bacteria in samples of processed chicken decreased by 50 percent on average from the previous year's level. If the government were to institute more frequent inspections, the incidence of stomach and intestinal infections throughout the country could thus be cut in half. In the meantime, consumers of Excel Meats should be safe from infection because Excel's main processing plant has shown more improvement in eliminating bacterial contamination than any other plant cited in the government report."

Discuss how well reasoned … etc.

Appendix A   Percentile Ranking Tables

Table 1
Percentages of Examinees Tested from January 2005 through December 2007 (including Repeaters) Who Scored Below Specified Verbal Scores

Verbal Scaled Score	Percentage Below	Verbal Scaled Score	Percentage Below
46–60	99	26	40
45	98	25	36
43	96	24	33
42	95	23	29
41	92	22	27
40	89	21	23
39	87	20	19
38	83	19	16
37	81	18	15
36	78	17	12
35	74	16	10
34	69	15	8
33	66	14	7
32	64	13	5
31	58	12	4
30	56	11	3
29	53	10	2
28	48	7–9	1
27	43	0–6	0

Number of Candidates = 650,395
Mean = 27.8
Standard deviation = 9.1

Table 2

Percentages of Examinees Tested from January 2005 through December 2007 (including Repeaters) Who Scored Below Specified Quantitative Scores

Quantitative Scaled Score	Percentage Below	Quantitative Scaled Score	Percentage Below
51–60	99	30	29
50	94	29	25
49	88	28	24
48	84	27	20
47	79	26	19
46	77	25	16
45	75	24	15
44	70	23	13
43	68	22	11
42	63	21	10
41	61	20	9
40	59	19	8
39	55	18	7
38	53	17	5
37	51	16	4
36	46	15	4
35	42	14	4
34	40	13	3
33	38	11–12	2
32	34	7–10	1
31	30	0–6	0

Number of Candidates = 650,395
Mean = 35.6
Standard deviation = 10.7

Table 3

Percentages of Examinees Tested from January 2005 through December 2007 (including Repeaters) Who Scored Below Specified Total Scores

Total Scaled Score	Percentage Below	Total Scaled Score	Percentage Below
760–800	99	500	36
750	98	490	34
740	97	480	31
730	96	470	29
720	95	460	25
710	92	450	23
700	90	440	21
690	88	430	19
680	86	420	17
670	85	410	15
660	83	400	13
650	80	390	12
640	76	380	10
630	75	370	9
620	72	360	8
610	69	350	7
600	66	340	6
590	63	330	5
580	60	320	4
570	58	310	3
560	54	300	3
550	51	290	3
540	48	280	2
530	44	270	2
520	42	230–250	1
510	39	200–220	0

Number of Candidates = 650,395
Mean = 535.2
Standard deviation = 120.1

Table 4
Percentages of Examinees Tested from January 2005 through December 2007 (including Repeaters) Who Scored Below Specified AWA Scores

AWA Scaled Score	Percentage Below
6.0	87
5.5	80
5.0	55
4.5	42
4.0	21
3.5	13
3.0	6
2.5	4
2.0	3
1.5	3
1.0	3
0.5	3
0.0	0

Number of Candidates = 650,395
Mean = 4.4
Standard deviation = 1.2

Appendix B   Answer Sheets

Diagnostic Answer Sheet - Quantitative

1.	27.
2.	28.
3.	29.
4.	30.
5.	31.
6.	32.
7.	33.
8.	34.
9.	35.
10.	36.
11.	37.
12.	38.
13.	39.
14.	40.
15.	41.
16.	42.
17.	43.
18.	44.
19.	45.
20.	46.
21.	47.
22.	48.
23.	
24.	
25.	
26.	

Diagnostic Answer Sheet - Verbal

1.	27.
2.	28.
3.	29.
4.	30.
5.	31.
6.	32.
7.	33.
8.	34.
9.	35.
10.	36.
11.	37.
12.	38.
13.	39.
14.	40.
15.	41.
16.	42.
17.	43.
18.	44.
19.	45.
20.	46.
21.	47.
22.	48.
23.	49.
24.	50.
25.	51.
26.	52.

Problem Solving Answer Sheet

1.	32.	63.	94.	125.	156.	187.	218.
2.	33.	64.	95.	126.	157.	188.	219.
3.	34.	65.	96.	127.	158.	189.	220.
4.	35.	66.	97.	128.	159.	190.	221.
5.	36.	67.	98.	129.	160.	191.	222.
6.	37.	68.	99.	130.	161.	192.	223.
7.	38.	69.	100.	131.	162.	193.	224.
8.	39.	70.	101.	132.	163.	194.	225.
9.	40.	71.	102.	133.	164.	195.	226.
10.	41.	72.	103.	134.	165.	196.	227.
11.	42.	73.	104.	135.	166.	197.	228.
12.	43.	74.	105.	136.	167.	198.	229.
13.	44.	75.	106.	137.	168.	199.	230.
14.	45.	76.	107.	138.	169.	200.	
15.	46.	77.	108.	139.	170.	201.	
16.	47.	78.	109.	140.	171.	202.	
17.	48.	79.	110.	141.	172.	203.	
18.	49.	80.	111.	142.	173.	204.	
19.	50.	81.	112.	143.	174.	205.	
20.	51.	82.	113.	144.	175.	206.	
21.	52.	83.	114.	145.	176.	207.	
22.	53.	84.	115.	146.	177.	208.	
23.	54.	85.	116.	147.	178.	209.	
24.	55.	86.	117.	148.	179.	210.	
25.	56.	87.	118.	149.	180.	211.	
26.	57.	88.	119.	150.	181.	212.	
27.	58.	89.	120.	151.	182.	213.	
28.	59.	90.	121.	152.	183.	214.	
29.	60.	91.	122.	153.	184.	215.	
30.	61.	92.	123.	154.	185.	216.	
31.	62.	93.	124.	155.	186.	217.	

Data Sufficiency Answer Sheet

1.	36.	71.	106.	141.
2.	37.	72.	107.	142.
3.	38.	73.	108.	143.
4.	39.	74.	109.	144.
5.	40.	75.	110.	145.
6.	41.	76.	111.	146.
7.	42.	77.	112.	147.
8.	43.	78.	113.	148.
9.	44.	79.	114.	149.
10.	45.	80.	115.	150.
11.	46.	81.	116.	151.
12.	47.	82.	117.	152.
13.	48.	83.	118.	153.
14.	49.	84.	119.	154.
15.	50.	85.	120.	155.
16.	51.	86.	121.	156.
17.	52.	87.	122.	157.
18.	53.	88.	123.	158.
19.	54.	89.	124.	159.
20.	55.	90.	125.	160.
21.	56.	91.	126.	161.
22.	57.	92.	127.	162.
23.	58.	93.	128.	163.
24.	59.	94.	129.	164.
25.	60.	95.	130.	165.
26.	61.	96.	131.	166.
27.	62.	97.	132.	167.
28.	63.	98.	133.	168.
29.	64.	99.	134.	169.
30.	65.	100.	135.	170.
31.	66.	101.	136.	171.
32.	67.	102.	137.	172.
33.	68.	103.	138.	173.
34.	69.	104.	139.	174.
35.	70.	105.	140.	

Reading Comprehension Answer Sheet

1.	32.	63.	94.	125.
2.	33.	64.	95.	126.
3.	34.	65.	96.	127.
4.	35.	66.	97.	128.
5.	36.	67.	98.	129.
6.	37.	68.	99.	130.
7.	38.	69.	100.	131.
8.	39.	70.	101.	132.
9.	40.	71.	102.	133.
10.	41.	72.	103.	134.
11.	42.	73.	104.	135.
12.	43.	74.	105.	136.
13.	44.	75.	106.	137.
14.	45.	76.	107.	138.
15.	46.	77.	108.	139.
16.	47.	78.	109.	
17.	48.	79.	110.	
18.	49.	80.	111.	
19.	50.	81.	112.	
20.	51.	82.	113.	
21.	52.	83.	114.	
22.	53.	84.	115.	
23.	54.	85.	116.	
24.	55.	86.	117.	
25.	56.	87.	118.	
26.	57.	88.	119.	
27.	58.	89.	120.	
28.	59.	90.	121.	
29.	60.	91.	122.	
30.	61.	92.	123.	
31.	62.	93.	124.	

Critical Reasoning Answer Sheet

1.	32.	63.	94.
2.	33.	64.	95.
3.	34.	65.	96.
4.	35.	66.	97.
5.	36.	67.	98.
6.	37.	68.	99.
7.	38.	69.	100.
8.	39.	70.	101.
9.	40.	71.	102.
10.	41.	72.	103.
11.	42.	73.	104.
12.	43.	74.	105.
13.	44.	75.	106.
14.	45.	76.	107.
15.	46.	77.	108.
16.	47.	78.	109.
17.	48.	79.	110.
18.	49.	80.	111.
19.	50.	81.	112.
20.	51.	82.	113.
21.	52.	83.	114.
22.	53.	84.	115.
23.	54.	85.	116.
24.	55.	86.	117.
25.	56.	87.	118.
26.	57.	88.	119.
27.	58.	89.	120.
28.	59.	90.	121.
29.	60.	91.	122.
30.	61.	92.	123.
31.	62.	93.	124.

Sentence Correction Answer Sheet

1.	32.	63.	94.	125.
2.	33.	64.	95.	126.
3.	34.	65.	96.	127.
4.	35.	66.	97.	128.
5.	36.	67.	98.	129.
6.	37.	68.	99.	130.
7.	38.	69.	100.	131.
8.	39.	70.	101.	132.
9.	40.	71.	102.	133.
10.	41.	72.	103.	134.
11.	42.	73.	104.	135.
12.	43.	74.	105.	136.
13.	44.	75.	106.	137.
14.	45.	76.	107.	138.
15.	46.	77.	108.	139.
16.	47.	78.	109.	140.
17.	48.	79.	110.	
18.	49.	80.	111.	
19.	50.	81.	112.	
20.	51.	82.	113.	
21.	52.	83.	114.	
22.	53.	84.	115.	
23.	54.	85.	116.	
24.	55.	86.	117.	
25.	56.	87.	118.	
26.	57.	88.	119.	
27.	58.	89.	120.	
28.	59.	90.	121.	
29.	60.	91.	122.	
30.	61.	92.	123.	
31.	62.	93.	124.	